MW01102248

Contemporary Canadian Authors

Contemporary Canadian Authors

A Bio-Bibliographical Guide to
Current Canadian Writers in
Fiction, General Nonfiction, Poetry,
Journalism, Drama, Motion Pictures,
Television, and Other Fields

ROBERT LANG
Coordinating Editor

PAMELA WILLWERTH AUE
DAVID M. GALENS
Project Editors

volume 1

Gale Canada

An ITP Information/Reference Group Company

Changing the Way the World Learns

NEW YORK • LONDON • BONN • BOSTON • DETROIT
MADRID • MELBOURNE • MEXICO CITY • PARIS
SINGAPORE • TOKYO • TORONTO • WASHINGTON
ALBANY NY • BELMONT CA • CINCINNATI OH

STAFF

Robert Lang, *Coordinating Editor, Gale Canada*

John Sabljic, *Contributing Editor, Gale Canada*

Pamela Willwerth Aue, David M. Galens, *Project Editors*

Kathleen J. Edgar, Brandon Trenz, *Contributing Project Editors*

Christine M. Bichler, Jeff Chapman, Pamela S. Dear, Nancy G. Dziedzic, John D. Jorgenson, Thomas Ligotti, Scot Peacock, Terrie M. Rooney, Aarti Dhawan Stephens, Kathleen Wilson, *Contributing Editors*

Stacy A. McConnell, Daniel Jones, *Assistant Editors*

Mary Gillis, Lisa Harper, Susan Reicha, Pamela Shelton, Ken Shepherd, Les Stone Linda Tidrick, Elizabeth Wenning, Denise Wiloch, and Michaela Swart Wilson, *Sketchwriters*

Roger Matuz, *Managing Editor*

Victoria B. Cariappa, *Research Manager*

Andrew Guy Malonis and Barbara McNeil, *Research Specialists*

Maria Bryson, Mary Beth McElmeel, Tamara Nott, Tracie Richardson, and Norma Sawaya, *Editorial Associates*

Alicia Noel Biggers, Michelle Lee, Cheri Warnock, and Amy Wieczorek, *Editorial Assistants*

Cover Photos: Robertson Davies, Carol Shields, and Margaret Atwood (*Edward Regan*); Leonard Cohen (*John McNeil*); and Margaret Laurence (*William French*) all © *Globe and Mail.* Michel Tremblay, © *Les Paparazzi,* 1992.

Contemporary Canadian Authors: a bio-bibliographical guide to current writers in fiction, general nonfiction, poetry, journalism, drama, motion pictures, television, and other fields
Annual
1995-
ISSN 1203-2816
ISBN 1-896413-08-0
1. Canada--Bio-Bibliography. 2. Canadian Literature--Bio-Bibliography
3. Authors, Canadian--20th Century--Biography
Z1374.C65   C810.9'0054   C95-900865-9

I(T)P™ Gale Research Inc., an International Thomson Publishing Company.
ITP logo is a trademark under license.

Contents

Preface

Contemporary Canadian Authors (*CCA*) presents its information in a format similar to the *Contemporary Authors* (*CA*) series, offering information on authors working within a wide range of media, including:

- Current writers of fiction, nonfiction, poetry, and drama whose works have been issued by commercial publishers, risk publishers, or university presses (authors whose books have been published only by known vanity or author-subsidized firms are ordinarily not included)

- Prominent print and broadcast journalists, editors, photojournalists, syndicated cartoonists, screenwriters, television scriptwriters, and other media people

- Authors who write in languages other than English, provided their works have been published in Canada or the United States or translated into English or French

- Literary greats of the early twentieth century whose works are popular in today's high school and college curriculums and continue to elicit critical attention

A *CCA* listing entails no charge or obligation. Authors are included on the basis of the above criteria and their interest to *CCA* users. Sources of potential listees include trade periodicals, publisher's catalogs, librarians, and other users.

How Are Entries Compiled?

The editors make every effort to secure information directly from the authors; listees' responses to questionnaires and query letters provide a bulk of the information featured in *CCA*. Other reliable biographical sources, such as those indexed in Gale's *Biography and Genealogy Master Index,* and bibliographical sources, including *National Union Catalog, LC MARC,* and *British National Bibliography* are also consulted. Further details come from published interviews, feature stories, and book reviews, and often the authors' publishers supply material.

An asterisk (∗) at the end of a sketch indicates that the listing has been compiled from reliable secondary sources but has not been personally verified for this edition by the featured author.

What Kinds of Information Does an Entry Provide?

Sketches in *CCA* contain the following biographical and bibliographical information:

- **Entry heading:** the most complete form of author's name, plus any pseudonyms or name variations used for writing

- **Personal information:** author's date and place of birth, family data, educational background, political and religious affiliations, and hobbies and leisure interests

- **Addresses:** author's home, office, or agent's addresses as available

- **Career summary:** name of employer, position, and dates held for each career post; resume of other vocational achievements; military service

- **Membership information:** professional, civic, and other association memberships and any official posts held

- **Awards and honours:** military and civic citations, major prizes and nominations, fellowships, grants, and honourary degrees

- **Writings:** a comprehensive, chronological list of titles, publishers, dates of original publication and revised editions, and production information for plays, television scripts, and screenplays

- **Adaptations:** a list of films, plays, and other media which have been adapted from the author's work

- **Work in progress:** current or planned projects, with dates of completion and/or publication, and expected publisher, when known

- **Sidelights:** a biographical portrait of the author's development; information about the critical reception of the author's works; revealing comments, often by the author, on personal interests, aspirations, motivations, and thoughts on writing

- **Biographical and critical sources:** a list of books and periodicals in which additional information on an author's life and/or writings appears

Related Titles

Contemporary Authors Autobiography Series complements *CA* original and revised volumes with specially commissioned autobiographical essays by important current authors, illustrated with personal photographs they provide. Common topics include their motivations for writing, the people and experiences that shaped their careers, the rewards they derive from their work, and their impressions of the current literary scene.

Contemporary Authors Bibliographical Series surveys writings by and about important American authors since World War II. Each volume concentrates on a specific genre and features approximately ten writers; entries list works written by and about the author and contain a bibliographical essay discussing the merits and deficiencies of major critical and scholarly studies in detail.

Available in Electronic Formats

CD-ROM. Full-text bio-bibliographic entries from the entire *CA* series, covering approximately 100,000 writers, are available on CD-ROM through lease and purchase plans. The disc combines entries from the *CA, CANR,* and *Contemporary Authors Permanent Series* (*CAP*) print series, as well as many of the authors in *CCA,* to provide the most recent author listing. It can be searched by name, title, subject/genre, personal data, and by using boolean logic. The disc is updated every six months. For more information, call 1-800-877-GALE.

Online. The *Contemporary Authors* database is made available online to libraries and their patrons through online public access catalog (OPAC) vendors. Currently, *CA* is offered through Ameritech Library Services' Vista Online (formerly Dynix), and is expected to become available through CARL Systems, The Library Corporation, and Winnebago Software. More OPAC vendor offerings will soon follow.

Magnetic Tape. *CA* is available for licensing on magnetic tape in a fielded format. Either the complete database or a custom selection of entries may be ordered. The database is available for internal data processing and nonpublishing purposes only. For more information, call 1-800-877-GALE.

Suggestions Are Welcome

For comments and suggestions from users on any aspect of *CCA,* please contact: The Editors, *Contemporary Canadian Authors,* Gale Canada, 444 Front St. West, Toronto M5V 2S9, ON; fax at 416-585-5338.

A Sampling of Authors and Media People
Featured in This Book

Margaret Atwood
An award-winning poet and writer of fiction, Atwood enjoys critical and popular acclaim for her works including *The Handmaid's Tale* and *The Robber Bride.*

Leonard Cohen
Cohen has received critical accolades since the 1960s for his work as a songwriter, poet, and novelist. Among his best-known fiction is the 1966 novel, *Beautiful Losers.*

Douglas Coupland
Coupland is known for his 1991 novel, *Generation X: Tales for an Accelerated Culture,* which, in addition to coining a catch phrase, identified him as a generational spokesperson.

David Cronenberg
A preeminent screenwriter and director, Cronenberg is acclaimed for his work on contemporary films including *Scanners, The Fly, Naked Lunch,* and *M. Butterfly.*

Northrop Frye
One of the most respected literary critics of the twentieth century, Frye is perhaps best known for his volume *Anatomy of Criticism: Four Essays.*

John Kenneth Galbraith
Author of *The Affluent Society* and *The New Industrial State,* Galbraith is considered one of the twentieth century's foremost writers on economics.

Margaret Laurence
A lauded and sometimes controversial author, Laurence's fiction was often set in a fictional region known as Manawaka. She is best known for the novel *A Jest of God.*

Dorothy Livesay
Livesay, whose writings span more than four decades, has been called a major lyric poet whose work is personal and emotional as well as socially conscious.

Robert MacNeil
A broadcaster, commentator, and novelist, MacNeil is best known as co-anchor with Jim Lehrer of *The MacNeil/Lehrer NewsHour.* He is also known for his memoir, *Wordstruck.*

Antonine Maillet
Playwright/novelist Maillet has won numerous awards for her work. She is revered for her depictions of Acadian life and customs in such works as her lauded play *La Sagouine.*

Marshall McLuhan
Credited as a forerunner of media studies, McLuhan was a prolific author of texts such as the groundbreaking *The Medium Is the Massage.*

L. M. Montgomery
The creator of one of the most beloved characters in children's fiction, Anne of Green Gables, Montgomery penned over forty books during her career.

Alice Munro
A 1995 Lannan Literary Award-winner and recipient of several Governor General's Awards, Munro is acclaimed for such short story collections as *The Progress of Love.*

Carol Shields
In addition to the praise earned by her earlier works, Shields's widely acclaimed 1993 book, *The Stone Diaries,* garnered the Pulitzer Prize in 1995.

Mordecai Richler
Known for novels including *The Apprenticeship of Duddy Kravitz,* Richler is also a noted essayist on issues of religion and nationalism, including 1992's *Oh Canada! Oh Quebec!.*

Robin Skelton
A prolific author of poetry, fiction, and nonfiction, as well as an esteemed editor and translator, Skelton is also a founder/editor of the literary periodical the *Malahat Review.*

Michel Tremblay
Tremblay is an esteemed Quebecois playwright whose work is valued for its challenges to common perceptions regarding French-Canadian life.

A. E. Van Vogt
Science fiction author Van Vogt is considered a cornerstone of the genre during the 1940s. Among his numerous works are the novel *Slan* and the "Gosseyn" series.

Contemporary Canadian Authors

ACORN, Milton 1923-

PERSONAL: Born March 30, 1923, in Charlottetown, Prince Edward Island, Canada; son of Robert Fairclough (a customs officer) and Helen (a secretary; maiden name, Carbonelle) Acorn; divorced. *Education:* Educated in Charlottetown, Prince Edward Island, Canada. *Politics:* "For the working class." *Religion:* "My own religion."

ADDRESSES:Home—Waverley Hotel, 484 Spadina Ave., Toronto, Ontario, Canada, M5S 2H1.

CAREER: Poet, writer, and playwright. Worked as fireman, shipper, freight handler, longshoreman, and carpenter. *Military service:* Canadian Armoured Corps, 1939-43; served in England; received service medal.

*MEMBER:*Canadian Poets.

*AWARDS, HONOURS:*Canadian Poets award, 1970; Governor General's award, 1975.

WRITINGS:

POETRY, EXCEPT WHERE NOTED

In Love and Anger, privately printed, 1957.
The Brain's the Target, Ryerson, 1960.
Against a League of Liars, Hawkshead Press, 1960.
Jawbreakers, Contact Press, 1963.
I've Tasted My Blood: Poems 1956 to 1968, edited by Al Purdy, Ryerson, 1969.
I Shout Love and Shaving Off His Beard (poems and prose), Village Book Store Press, 1971.
More Poems for People, NC Press, 1972.
The Island Means Minago (poems and prose), NC Press, 1975.
(With Cedric Smith) *Road to Charlottetown* (two-act musical), first produced in Toronto, Ontario, 1976.
Jackpine Sonnets, Steel Rail, 1977.

Editor of *Moment* (magazine), 1960-62. Contributor to periodicals.

WORK IN PROGRESS: Poetry; newspaper and periodical articles.

SIDELIGHTS:

Milton Acorn was one of Canada's first "public poets." Dubbed by a *Toronto Quill and Quire* reporter as a "troubadour of the working class," Acorn sees himself as the spokesman of the laborer, whether he be a Nova Scotia seaman or an Ottawa farmer. He was a frequent poetry reader on the coffee house scene in the 1950's, appearing in such well-known coffee houses of that period as The Place, El Cortijo, The Bohemian Embassy, and l'Echourie. Acorn has often called himself a "revolutionary poet." He is probably the only poet in Canada to have had one of his readings disrupted by the police. Although once a member of the Communist party, the Trotskyites, and the Canadian Liberation Movement, Acorn disagreed with and resigned from all the leftist groups in which he participated. Acorn, however, is still strongly political and espouses a left-wing, nationalist stand. Al Purdy observed that Acorn is "a maverick" who "fits no aperture or easy definition."

CA INTERVIEW

Milton Acorn was interviewed in his Toronto apartment by Al Purdy on November 6, 1979.

CA: You grew up in Charlottetown, Prince Edward Island. Tell me something about your childhood.

ACORN: I learned to read at age three, but not well; I didn't learn to read well until I was ten. I was sick much of the time then and didn't get over it until I was in my teens. Just sickly, weak, without any particular reason. But it was strange: I got into a lot of fights anyway and always got beat up. But I learned to fight at fourteen and after that over the years, many of them, I came to avoid fights.

CA: When did you start writing?

ACORN: I was pretty young, maybe eight or ten years old. Me and another kid, name of "Silly"—his real name was Sylvanus—we both wrote poems and made drawings. I kept on writing.

CA: What were your mother and father like?

ACORN: My father was a working man. He'd been in the army in World War I, and got shell-shocked. He was a customs officer after the war. I guess you'd say we were middle class. My mother was boss of the household: when she said do something, you did it. No argument was possible. And I was writing so early; it was like playing games with words. Later, the urge to write was worse than needing a drink. I had to write. When I got to be a carpenter, I remember walking down the street swinging a lunch pail chanting to myself, "I've got to write. I've got to write."

CA: Did anybody encourage you?

ACORN: All my family were amateur writers. My grandfather was a correspondent for the *London Times*. My aunt was writing too. In fact there was no one who didn't write. My older brother taught me scansion in poems; they all taught me something.

CA: What books did you read?

ACORN: The first I can remember is *Dracula,* by Bram Stoker. Early science fiction. And H. G. Wells, Mark Twain, Rider Haggard. . . .

CA: That's some apprenticeship for a carpenter. When did you become one?

ACORN: I was always doing carpenter work, but my mother said, "Milt, you're no carpenter; you have no knack of the hands." So I went to carpenter school in 1946.

CA: You were in the army before that?

ACORN: The Black Watch regiment, but only briefly. I joined them when I was underage, sixteen. They discharged me. Then I went back to the Canadian Armoured Corps, still underage, but I got away with it that time. I was shipped to England in January, 1942, on the *Cameronian*. We were attacked by a submarine in the Atlantic, but there were no casualties except for me. My ears were blasted in by shellfire. After that my ears bled all the time; they called it *otitis media,* in the middle ear. I also remember being on pack drill in England, marching with a heavy pack on my shoulders. And an officer said, "He's enjoying it; take him out of there!" Of course you weren't

supposed to enjoy pack drill. Then the doctors decided my ear injuries were serious, and I got sent back to Canada. The war was over where I was concerned.

CA: All this time you were writing poems and reading?

ACORN: Yes, I was reading Dorothy Livesay, Joe Wallace, and when it came out in the sixties, *The New American Poetry, 1945-1960,* the book Donald Allen edited. And I read the classics, Shelley, Wordsworth, Coleridge, and many, many others.

CA: What were your politics in those years after the war?

ACORN: I was always a Red Tory, a red conservative, not a straight Communist. Anything the media attacked I was for. I don't mean the Nazis, of course, or Mussolini's fascists. It's just that anything the newspapers and television attack has a lot to be said for it.

CA: Apart from love poems, and many of yours are love poems, your largest subject is social injustice as you see it and wherever you see it. You wrote poems about Norman Bethune among the Chinese, about Ho Chi Minh, and Che Guevara.

ACORN: Sure, but I had to retract what I said about Guevara. He was a fine man but his tactics were absurd, though I agree with his goals.

CA: Should more writers be concerned with this kind of subject matter?

ACORN: Noble subjects and noble sentiments do not make noble poetry, not without noble work. I mean you have to have good syntax, scansion, rhyme if necessary.

CA: Should writers write from their own direct experience?

ACORN: Yes, the people-experience. One must write about people, the working class. But don't get too obsessed with it because poetry is a large area. The history of mankind is the history of poetry. And it's mankind that is the subject of all poetry.

CA: As it was with you in Jawbreakers?

ACORN:: Yes, it was—after I learned something from other writers.

CA: Who were they?

ACORN: Frank Scott, Wilson MacDonald, the Russians Vladimir Mayakovsky (he was great, but couldn't handle rhetoric) and Boris Pasternak. Also the Russian moderns, Andrei Voznesensky and Yevgeny Yevtushenko. The Americans, Robert Duncan and Charles Olson. I met Olson once and loved him. But I'm not like the Black Mountain people; my stress is in the syllable rather than metaphor. And Walt Whitman—he had some great lines, but too much rhetoric. And Robert Lowell, nice, nice—I admire him as a man, or did before his death, but then poets don't die, do they? And Pablo Neruda, but he should have had better translators. The Roy Campbell translations of Lorca, though, were excellent.

CA: You're not partial to the Black Mountain people, but you liked Charles Olson?

ACORN: Those rules of prosody Olson had in the *New American Poetry* were a put-on. Olson said as much in answer to a question by John Colombo in my presence about 1963. He cooked them up to refute people who criticized him, people who knew very little about writing anyway and couldn't tell whether he was talking horse—or not. And those rules were horse. His Black Mountain disciples give me the creeps.

CA: Do you see yourself as belonging to any tradition in poetry?

ACORN: I'm the start of one. But really, I'm the umpteenth revival of romanticism.

CA: Aren't you, therefore, in your own work, a guardian and protector of tradition?

ACORN: I don't protect, I threaten: if things don't change—and I mean social injustice and the few dominating the many—then I and others will make them change. You have to understand: my material is the world, the world as seen from Canada.

CA: What about Auden's line, "Poetry makes nothing happen"?

ACORN: Auden was wrong; things will change. To make it happen, I plan campaigns.

CA: What kind of campaigns?

ACORN: In the poems and prose I write, there is a concentration on particular subjects relating to social change. For instance, I wrote a column about abortion for the *Toronto Globe and Mail,* in their "Mermaid Inn" section on the editorial page. I'm against abortion: a poet must be pro-life. But Canadians are difficult to move about anything. They're a passive people. They have the ability to do anything, but they have to be told to do it. Just tell'em to take Vimy Ridge in World War I, and they did. But try to get them excited about any worthwhile cause and they sit on their asses. You have to light a fire under them. They're the most passive people in the world.

CA: Maybe that's because most of our directions come from the outside, such as in the case of multi-national companies from the United States. But not from across the sea, since we're not British any more.

ACORN: We're the other North Americans, Canadians are, and quite distinct from Americans. But they don't re-

alize this. Quite recently there was a stage play here; it was about Billy Bishop and had an American producer. Bishop was the great air hero of World War I, who shot down seventy-two German planes. It was a good play and did well at the box office. In fact, it did so well that the producer wanted to stage the play in the United States. And he wanted Billy Bishop to have guilt feelings about killing. He didn't realize that Canadian soldiers and airmen were mercenaries. Bishop did what he was paid to do, and any onus of guilt was on his employers.

CA: Do you see the United States, Canada, and Mexico as representing a break with European tradition?

ACORN: True enough. They weren't far out of feudalism when Europe settled North America, the days of barons and serfs not long past. We had a chance to be egalitarian with an equal chance for all. Of course it didn't work out that way.

CA: Didn't you break with European literary tradition when you wrote your Jackpine Sonnets *by making some of them thirteen lines long?*

ACORN: Others had been there first, as long ago as Shakespeare's time.

CA: Why thirteen lines and not eighteen or nineteen?

ACORN: Thirteen is a prime number. You can't make a regular poem of a prime number of lines.

CA: Why not?

ACORN: Nothing will divide a prime number equally—in formal form. Most of my sonnets are fourteen lines, the power of tradition being strong—although some are thirteen. But you can't make a formal traditional poem of thirteen lines, or one that you have started out to be possibly thirteen, because of that number. Shakespeare had one in his "Passionate Pilgrim" series of poems. But others wrote them too.

CA: I see what you mean about the formal poem, but then why not make it seventeen or nineteen lines? Nothing will divide into those numbers either. Anyway, from what you've said, you write poems in order to change the world socially?

ACORN: You pay your dues for being here. You owe the good people in the world, people of both past and present, for being alive, for helping you along the way.

CA: And you do it with poems. How do you feel about poetry in Canada now, generally speaking?

ACORN: It's a terrible mess. There are too many bad poets around. Since about ten years ago Canadian poetry has ignored questions of both form and content. And this aspect is even more noticeable now because there are thousands of poets writing now as compared to perhaps one hundred twenty years ago. Many of them just scribble anything that comes into their heads and don't bother at all about cadence. The majority of poetry published in Canada is not even good prose. There is no knowledge of the mode and method of writing poems. One reason for this is the importation of anarchistic ideas from the United States.

CA: Do you see any good younger poets writing now in Canada?

ACORN: Ted Plantos.

CA: Any others?

ACORN: Mary di Michele.

CA: And the known writers you think are good?

ACORN: Frank Scott, Margaret Atwood—Atwood is an awfully good novelist, but she writes cold poems, cold. Dorothy Livesay, too.

CA: Scott tried to change the country politically when he helped write the Regina Manifesto *for the Canadian Cooperative Federation in the 1930's, and also with his poems. You want to do that politically as well as socially?*

ACORN: You can't do one without doing the other. I've always been trying to change the world. The best poets have always been world-changers and prophets: Shelley, Blake, Whitman, Mayakovsky.

CA: Philosophy and politics: I remember George Bowering saying that you shouldn't mix politics into your poems, that they don't mix.

ACORN: I once saw a sign in an army officers' mess that said: "Conversation apropos sex, politics, and religion is unbecoming to an officer and gentleman." In other words, what do you talk about to replace them? Life is forbidden.

CA: There's a great deal of violence in some of your poems. Is that related to your general plan of changing the world?

ACORN: Well, it's a part of life. And some violence must be resisted with violence.

CA: Surely you're not advocating violence just because it exists in the world?

ACORN: Of course not. But violence is sometimes necessary, may even be a positive good.

CA: Your publisher is Steel Rail, which is a rather political organization despite being a publisher. What are its aims?

ACORN: Its politics are left of center and Canadian nationalistic. It's a strong force for Canadian independence.

CA: Apart from your brother and family who encouraged you years ago, who else has done that over the years?

ACORN: Everyone I meet encourages me. Even when I didn't want to be known as a poet, everyone said I was, even when I denied it. And I've learned from everyone, Mao Tsetung as a poet and leader, Norman Bethune as a man, and a great man. And Shelley, more for what he said than how.

CA: Do you have any kind of personal philosophy?

ACORN: I was born six billion years ago and I shall never die.

CA: Do you therefore live by your writing? I mean money.

ACORN: I live to write, I write to live. And money, it comes, it goes. I've rarely lacked, not lately anyhow.

CA: What are you writing now?

ACORN: Poems of course. Also newspaper and periodical writing, prose. I have a new prose book, *On Being Severe to Children*. My subject is Western arrogance, which thinks itself superior to all other societies. Eastern culture is much older, goes back milleniums, with dozens of different cultures, each with its own peculiar virtues. Western arrogance gives no credit to any other society but the one in which we live. And that is simply stupid.

CA: What other writing have you done lately?

ACORN: The "Road to Charlottetown." It's a play I wrote with Cedric Smith. It was pretty successful, a lot of people came to see it. In fact, some students here from China came down and asked to tape the play.

CA: What's it about?

ACORN: John Acorn and his struggles with authority. The odd thing is that I invented John Acorn for purposes of the play, made him up completely. But then my relatives searched the Prince Edward Island records in Charlottetown and found that he really did exist. Under the same name too. The play is a romp through island history.

CA: And the play will change the world?

ACORN: It'll help.

BIOGRAPHICAL/CRITICAL SOURCES:

BOOKS

Authors in the News, Volume 2, Gale, 1976.
Contemporary Literary Criticism, Volume 15, Gale, 1980.
ECW's Biographical Guide to Canadian Poets, ECW Press, 1993, pp. 176-81.

PERIODICALS

Antigonish Review, spring, 1988, p. 64.
Atlantic Insight, November, 1982, pp. 48-9.
Books in Canada, May, 1983, pp. 20, 22.
Canadian, December 18, 1976, pp. 16-17.

Canadian Forum, July, 1969, p. 88; March, 1974.
Canadian Literature, spring, 1969, pp. 33-42; autumn, 1969; winter, 1988, pp. 136-38; autumn, 1991, pp. 177-81.
Culture, June, 1964.
Fiddlehead, spring, 1988, pp. 99-101.
Quill & Quire, January, 1984, p. 29; May, 1987, p. 24.
University of Toronto Quarterly, July, 1961.

*   *   *

ALLAN, Andrew (Edward Fairbairn) 1907-1974

PERSONAL: Born August 11, 1907, in Arbroath, Scotland; immigrated to Australia; immigrated to the United States; immigrated to Canada, 1925; died January 15, 1974; son of William (a Presbyterian minister) and Agnes Hannah (Fairbairn) Allan; married Dianne Foster, 1951 (marriage ended, 1954); married Linda Trenholme Ballantyne, 1955. *Education:* Attended the University of Toronto, 1927-30.

CAREER: CFRB Radio, Toronto, Ontario, Canada, announcer, actor, scriptwriter, and producer, 1931-37; affiliated with advertising agencies in London, England, 1937-39; British Broadcasting Corporation (BBC), London, freelance writer and actor, 1937-39; Canadian Broadcasting Corporation (CBC), Vancouver, British Columbia, drama producer, 1939-43; CBC, Toronto, supervisor of drama, 1943-62, and television producer, 1955-62; Shaw Festival, Niagara-on-the-Lake, Ontario, artistic director, 1962-65; radio actor and commentator, 1965-74.

AWARDS, HONOURS: Christopher Award for outstanding achievement in television, 1952; John Drainie Award for distinguished service in broadcasting, 1969.

WRITINGS:

RADIO PLAYS; PRODUCED FOR THE CANADIAN BROADCASTING CORPORATION (CBC)

Mistress Nell, 1936.
Palatine Hill, 1937.
Mary Queen of Scots, 1939.
It Must Be Simple, 1940.
The Devil's Receipt, 1940.
Catherine the Great, 1940.
Dead Man's Business, 1940.
Sir Guy Proposes, 1940.
The Thing That Walked, 1940.
Proud Procession, 1941.
All the Bright Company, 1942.
(With John Bethune) *The Oracles Are Dumb,* 1942.
(With Bethune) *Peace in Our Time,* 1942.
(With Bethune) *Summer in Paradise,* 1943.
My Bonnie Boy, 1944.
Give Us Back Our Miracle, 1945.

There Are Very Few of Us Left, 1946.
Uncertain Glory, 1946.
The Lady Knows Too Much, 1950.
A Sense of Sin, 1953.
All the Bright Company: Radio Drama Produced by Andrew Allan (collection), edited by Howard Fink and John Jackson, Quarry (Kingston, Ontario)/CBC Enterprises (Toronto), 1987.

RADIO ADAPTATIONS; PRODUCED FOR CBC

The Mystery Play of the Nativity, 1940.
Henry V (from the William Shakespeare play), 1944.
The Snow Queen (from the Hans Christian Andersen story), 1946.
The Zeal of Thy House (from the Dorothy Sayers novel), 1948.
For the Time Being (from the W. H. Auden book of poems), 1948.
Heart of Darkness (from the Joseph Conrad novel), 1949.
The Way of the World (from the William Congreve play), 1949.
The Fifth Column (from the Ernest Hemingway play), 1949.
Salome (from the Oscar Wilde play), 1949.
Kidnapped (from the Robert Louis Stevenson novel), 1949.
Camille (from the Alexandre Dumas *fil* play *La Dame aux Camelias*), 1950.
The Liars (from the Henry Arthur Jones play), 1953.
The York Passion Play, 1954.
The Tempest (from the Shakespeare play), 1955.
Volpone (from the Ben Jonson play), 1955.
The Rivals (from the Richard Brinsley Sheridan play), 1956.
Becket (from the Alfred Tennyson play), 1956.
The Trojan Women (from the Euripides play), 1957.
Youth (from the Conrad story), 1957.
Venus Observed (from the Christopher Fry play), 1958.

OTHER

(Editor) William Allan, *Memories of a Blinkbonnie,* Nelson (Toronto), 1939.
Narrow Passage (stage play), produced at the Museum Theatre, Toronto, 1950.
Andrew Allan: A Self-Portrait (autobiography), introduction by Harry J. Boyle, Macmillan (Toronto), 1974.

Author of articles on broadcasting and the theater.

Most of Allan's signed scripts are housed at the CBC radio drama archives, Concordia University, Montreal.

SIDELIGHTS: Andrew Allan was the guiding force behind years of acclaimed radio productions during his tenure with the Canadian Broadcasting Corporation (CBC). As network supervisor of drama and producer of an award-winning series during the 1940s and '50s, Allan put together an ensemble of writers and actors that the *New York Times,* as noted in the *Dictionary of Literary Biography,* deemed "far and away the most exciting repertory group that can be heard" in 1946. Born in Scotland in 1907, Allan went on to attend college in Toronto but dropped out and took a job with a local radio station in 1931. There he became involved in several different facets of the broadcasting business and worked alternately as an announcer, actor, writer, and producer; for a time he was a writer for Canada's first radio soap opera, *The Family Doctor.* In 1937 he relocated to London, England, and gained further experience from a stint with the British Broadcasting Corporation (BBC). Allan returned to Canada in 1939 and joined the newly formed CBC; the work he did when affiliated with such dramatic series as *Baker's Dozen* earned him a promotion to supervisor of drama in 1943.

This new position gave Allan the control necessary to craft radio productions and drama series over the next two decades. One such weekly program, *Stage,* began in 1944 and utilized homegrown talent in its production and writing. As its producer and director, Allan sought out Canadian writers for the majority of *Stage*'s broadcasts. He wrote a number of the original works and many adaptations in collaboration with the stable of writers. Although sometimes characterized as difficult to work with, in retrospect Allan has been commended for allowing free artistic rein and even encouraging experimentation among the creative staff. Previously forbidden subjects and issues often surfaced in the CBC radio dramas, and "the result was a consistently bold, imaginative writers' theater of the air," asserted Jerry Wasserman in an essay on Allan for *Dictionary of Literary Biography* (*DLB*). Some of these radio plays were later assembled into the 1987 volume *All the Bright Company: Radio Drama Produced by Andrew Allan.*

Allan wrote one play for the stage, 1950's *Narrow Passage,* and later branched out into a new medium when CBC began television broadcasting in the 1950s. In 1962 he left the network to become the first artistic director of the Shaw Festival at Niagara-on-the-Lake, Ontario, but returned to radio a few years later. Just before his death in 1974 Allan completed his memoirs, *Andrew Allan: A Self-Portrait,* published posthumously; this final volume was comprised of Allan's reminiscences and essays culled from his radio commentaries. In summing up Allan's influential career, *DLB* contributor Wasserman contended: "The quality of his productions was unimpeachable, and they were without a doubt a major contribution to the development of Canadian culture in the postwar years."

BIOGRAPHICAL/CRITICAL SOURCES:

BOOKS

Allan, Andrew, *Andrew Allan: A Self-Portrait,* introduction by Harry J. Boyle, Macmillan (Toronto), 1974.
Dictionary of Literary Biography, Volume 88: *Canadian Writers 1920-1959,* Gale, 1989.
Drainie, Bronwyn, *Living the Part: John Drainie and the Dilemma of Canadian Stardom,* Macmillan, 1988.
Fink, Howard, and Brian Morrison, *Canadian National Theater on the Air, 1925-1961: CBC-CRBC-CNR Radio Drama in English; A Descriptive Bibliography and Union List,* University of Toronto Press, 1983.
Frick, N. Alice, *Image in the Mind: CBC Radio Drama, 1944-1954,* Canadian Stage and Arts Publications, 1987.

PERIODICALS

Canadian Forum, May, 1950, p. 35.
Maclean's, February 1, 1947, pp. 21-24.
Saturday Night, October 14, 1944, pp. 24-25.

*   *   *

ANDERSON, Patrick (John MacAllister) 1915-1979

PERSONAL: Born August 4, 1915 (one source cites 1917), in Ashted, Surrey, England; died in 1979, in Halstead, Essex, England; married Peggy Doernbach (divorced). *Education:* Earned B.A. and M.A. from Oxford University; earned M.A. from Columbia University.

CAREER: Poet and writer. Selwyn House School, Montreal, Quebec, teacher, 1940-46; McGill University, Montreal, assistant professor, 1948-50; Trent Park College, Barnet, Hertfordshire, England, member of faculty, 1957-79, principal lecturer and head of English department, 1968-79. Lecturer, University of Malaya, 1950-52, and Dudley Training College, 1954-57.

AWARDS, HONOURS: Commonwealth fellowship, 1938; Harriet Monroe Memorial Prize, 1946.

WRITINGS:

Poems, privately printed, 1929.
A Tent for April (poems), First Statement, 1945.
The White Centre (poems), Ryerson Press, 1946.
The Colour As Naked (poems), McLelland & Stewart, 1953.
Snake Wine: A Singapore Episode, Chatto & Windus, 1955.
First Steps in Greece, Chatto & Windus, 1958.
Search Me: Autobiography; The Black Country, Canada, and Spain, British Book Centre, 1958.

(Editor with Alistair Sutherland) *Eros: An Anthology of Friendship,* Blond, 1961, published as *Eros: An Anthology of Male Friendship,* Citadel Press, 1963.

Finding out about the Athenians, F. Muller, 1961.

The Character Ball: Chapters of Autobiography, Chatto & Windus, 1963.

Dolphin Days: A Writer's Notebook of Mediterranean Pleasures, V. Gollancz, 1963.

The Smile of Apollo: A Literary Companion to Greek Travel, Chatto & Windus, 1964.

Over the Alps: Reflections on Travel and Travel Writing with Special Reference on the Grand Tours of Boswell, Beckford, and Byron, Hart-Davis, 1969.

Foxed!; or, Life in the Country, Chatto & Windus, 1972.

A Visiting Distance (poems), Borealis Press, 1976.

Return to Canada: Selected Poems, McLelland & Stewart, 1977.

Member of editorial boards, including *Preview, En Masse,* and *Northern Review.* Cofounder of *Preview.*

SIDELIGHTS: Patrick Anderson is a significant figure in Canadian poetry. He was born in England in 1915, when Europe was in the throes of the first World War. Anderson's parents separated when he was only a child, whereupon he maintained a devotion to his mother—one that many have speculated bordered on unhealthy obsession. School, particularly for the sensitive Anderson, scarcely provided a suitable alternative to his somewhat troubled family life, though by early adolescence he was already impressing instructors with his flair for versification.

In the early 1930s Anderson studied at Oxford University, and in 1938—by which time he had privately printed two verse volumes—he received a fellowship that took him to the United States and Columbia University. While in the United States he met Peggy Doernbach, with whom he moved to Montreal in 1940. In Montreal, Anderson and Doernbach, who had become husband and wife, soon befriended various writers and intellectuals. With such individuals as F. R. Scott and Neufville Shaw, Anderson helped establish *Preview,* a literary journal intended, among other things, to support the Allied cause as World War II raged overseas.

Anderson continued to serve as an editor of *Preview* after the war ended and the journal was merged with the more overtly political *First Statement,* edited by the outspoken John Sutherland, to become *Northern Review.* Sutherland's modest publishing company, First Statement, had produced Anderson's first major poetry collection, *A Tent for April.* This volume readily marked Anderson as a sophisticated artist, one capable of exotic, mysterious imagery and Freudian perspectives. In addition, the book established Anderson as an essentially Canadian artist; that is, as an artist preoccupied with the Canadian landscape, its people, and their culture.

In 1946 Anderson—who had broken from Sutherland's press—completed *The White Centre,* a verse collection particularly memorable for Anderson's considerations of Canadian life. Such verses as "Poem on Canada" are considered among Anderson's most notable. Also prevalent, though, are Anderson's reflections on childhood. While the depictions relate a youth of innocence and enthusiasm, they are told from the perspective of a troubled adulthood.

During the late 1940s, as his marriage to Doernbach declined, Anderson traveled frequently from Montreal to England. He held a teaching position at Montreal's McGill University until 1950, when he assumed a post at the University of Malaya. In 1953 he published *The Colour As Naked,* a volume replete with autobiographical recollections and depictions of life in both Canada and Malaysia. In this work Anderson's celebrations of childhood and nature are increasingly tempered—sometimes with what has been perceived as excessive and confusing imagery—by acknowledgements of life's more somber aspects.

After completing *The Colour As Naked,* Anderson turned his attention from poetry to prose. In works such as *Snake Wine: A Singapore Episode, First Steps in Greece,* and *Over the Alps: Reflections on Travel and Travel Writing with Special Reference on the Grand Tours of Boswell, Beckford, and Byron,* he proved himself an engaging travel writer capable of capturing local color and conveying a sense of place to his readers. He also produced more autobiographical writings, notably *Search Me: Autobiography; The Black Country, Canada, and Spain,* which includes an account of his life among Montreal's artists and intellectuals during World War II.

By the late 1960s Anderson was again writing poetry, and in 1971—after being away for nearly twenty years—he returned to Canada, where he taught at the University of Ottawa. In 1976 Anderson published *A Visiting Distance,* which includes recent verse, revisions of previously published poems, and selections for earlier volumes. Anderson's perspective in these poems is considered somewhat aloof even though he is preoccupied with personal reflection and observation. As Susan Gingell noted in the *Dictionary of Literary Biography,* "His only intimacy is with himself." Anderson followed *A Visiting Distance* with *Return to Canada: Selected Poems,* a selection of his finest poems. Here Anderson again revised some of his earlier work although to a greater extent.

Anderson died in 1979. In the years since his death he has continued to be recognized as a formidable poet, one capable of both personal insight and reflection as well as broader evocations of Canada and its people.

BIOGRAPHICAL/CRITICAL SOURCES:

BOOKS

Anderson, Patrick *The Character Ball: Chapters of Autobiography,* Chatto & Windus, 1963.
Anderson, *Search Me: Autobiography; The Black Country, Canada, and Spain,* British Book Centre, 1958.
Dictionary of Literary Biography, Volume 68: *Canadian Writers, 1920-1959,* Gale, 1988.

PERIODICALS

Canadian Literature, autumn, 1962, pp. 21-34; winter, 1970, pp. 10-23; spring, 1973.
Canadian Poetry, spring/summer, 1979, pp. 93-119.
Northern Review, April/May, 1949, pp. 8-20, 25-34.
Observer, June 25, 1972.

OBITUARIES:

PERIODICALS

AB Bookman's Weekly, April 16, 1979.*

*   *   *

ARMSTRONG, Jeanette 1948-

PERSONAL: Born in 1948, on Okanagan Reserve, near Penticton, British Columbia, Canada. *Education:* Okanagan College, Diploma of Fine Arts; University of Victoria, B.F.A.

CAREER: En'Owkin Cultural Center, staff member, 1978—, director, 1985—. Penticton Band, member of council. University of Victoria, cofounder and director of En'Owkin School of International Writing, 1989—.

AWARDS, HONOURS: Mungo Martin Award, 1974; Helen Pitt Memorial Award, 1978; Vancouver Foundation Graduate Award, 1978.

WRITINGS:

Enwhisteetkwa: Walk on Water (juvenile fiction), Friesen Printers, 1982.
Neekna and Chemai (juvenile fiction), Theytus Books, 1984.
Slash (novel), Theytus Books, 1985; revised edition, 1988.
(Editor) *Looking at the Words of Our People: An Anthology of First Nation Literary Criticism,* Orca, 1993.

SIDELIGHTS: Jeanette Armstrong's novel *Slash* centers on the experiences of Thomas Kelasket, a young Okanagan man who becomes deeply involved in the American Indian Movement as he tries to come to terms with the racism of white society and his own identity as a Native Canadian. In his travels between the United States and Canada during the 1960s and 1970s, he comes in contact with many perspectives on Native affairs, ranging from assimilation to radical political action. While recovering from alcohol and drug addiction in a detoxification center, Thomas realizes that the key to his recovery and the future prosperity of the Native community is acceptance and understanding of the traditional ways of Native peoples. Variously identified as historical fiction, a fictional biography, and a young adult novel, *Slash* has been highly successful, though occasionally criticized for its overreliance on stream-of-consciousness narration and lack of information regarding specific historical events and figures. Critics have additionally faulted Armstrong's fiction for lacking in character development, but concur that her works succeed in documenting and exploring her people's past. Patty Lawlor has written of *Slash* that the novel "gives the readers insight into the implications of the assimilation policies practised in Canada and the United States, and it acknowledges the confusion, power struggles, and despair among the native peoples as they attempt to come to terms with the realities of the present and the likely realities of the future."

The first Native woman novelist in Canada, Armstrong was born on the Okanagan Reserve in British Columbia. A member of the Penticton band, she learned the traditions of the Okanagan people from her parents and elders and also attended local schools. During the sixties and seventies she participated to a limited extent in the American Indian Movement. Following the completion of her education in 1978, Armstrong received a Diploma of Fine Arts from Okanagan College and a Bachelor of Fine Arts from the University of Victoria. She worked as a researcher and writer at the En'Owkin Center, a cultural and educational organization operated by the Okanagan Nation, and since 1985 has served as the center's director. In 1989 she helped to found the En'Owkin School of International Writing. Affiliated with the University of Victoria, the En'Owkin School is the first credit-giving creative writing program in Canada to be managed and operated expressly by and for Native people.

A grandniece of Mourning Dove, the first Native American woman novelist, Armstrong has stated that one of her goals in writing is to educate young people about Native culture and history. In conjunction with the Okanagan Indian Curriculum Project, Armstrong has produced two works of juvenile fiction designed for use in the school system. *Enwhisteetkwa: Walk on Water* covers one year in the life of an Okanagan girl in the mid-1800s and provides a detailed account of daily and seasonal rituals and tasks; *Neekna and Chemai* likewise gives an account of traditional life from the perspective of two young girls.

BIOGRAPHICAL/CRITICAL SOURCES:

PERIODICALS

Books in Canada, December, 1982, p. 9.
Canadian Children's Literature, number 73, 1994, pp. 82-83.
Canadian Forum, January, 1988, p. 39-40.
Canadian Literature, spring-summer, 1990, pp. 138-52.
Quill & Quire, May, 1992, p. 35; June, 1992, p. 32.

*   *   *

ATWOOD, Margaret (Eleanor) 1939-

PERSONAL: Born November 18, 1939, in Ottawa, Ontario, Canada; daughter of Carl Edmund (an entomologist) and Margaret Dorothy (Killam) Atwood; married Graeme Gibson (a writer); children: Jess (daughter). *Education:* University of Toronto, B.A., 1961; Radcliffe College, A.M., 1962; Harvard University, graduate study, 1962-63 and 1965-67. *Politics:* "William Morrisite." *Religion:* "Immanent Transcendentalist."

ADDRESSES: Agent—Phoebe Larmore, 2814 Third St., Santa Monica, CA. 90405.

CAREER: Writer. University of British Columbia, Vancouver, Canada, lecturer in English literature, 1964-65; Sir George Williams University, Montreal, Quebec, Canada, lecturer in English literature, 1967-68; York University, Toronto, Ontario, Canada, assistant professor of English literature, 1971-72; House of Anansi Press, Toronto, editor and member of board of directors, 1971-73; University of Toronto, Toronto, writer-in-residence, 1972-73; University of Alabama, Tuscaloosa, writer-in-residence, 1985; New York University, New York City, Berg Visiting Professor of English, 1986; Macquarie University, North Ryde, Australia, writer-in-residence, 1987. Worked variously as camp counselor and waitress.

MEMBER: PEN International, Amnesty International, Writers' Union of Canada (vice-chairperson, 1980-81), Royal Society of Canada (fellow), Canadian Civil Liberties Association (member of board, 1973-75), Canadian Centre, American Academy of Arts and Sciences (honorary member), Anglophone (president, 1984-85).

AWARDS, HONOURS: E. J. Pratt Medal, 1961, for *Double Persephone;* President's Medal, University of Western Ontario, 1965; YWCA Women of Distinction Award, 1966 and 1968; Governor General's Award, 1966, for *The Circle Game,* and 1986, for *The Handmaid's Tale;* first prize in Canadian Centennial Commission Poetry Competition, 1967; Union Prize for poetry, 1969; Bess Hoskins Prize for poetry, 1969 and 1974; D.Litt., Trent University, 1973, Concordia University, 1980, Smith College, 1982,

University of Toronto, 1983, Mount Holyoke College, 1985, University of Waterloo, 1985, and University of Guelph, 1985; LL.D., Queen's University, 1974; City of Toronto Book Award, 1977; Canadian Booksellers' Association Award, 1977; Periodical Distributors of Canada Short Fiction Award, 1977; St. Lawrence Award for fiction, 1978; Radcliffe Medal, 1980; selection as a notable book of 1980, American Library Association for *Life before Man;* Molson Award, 1981; Guggenheim fellowship, 1981; named Companion of the Order of Canada, 1981; International Writer's Prize, Welsh Arts Council, 1982; Book of the Year Award, Periodical Distributors of Canada and the Foundation for the Advancement of Canadian Letters, 1983; Ida Nudel Humanitarian Award, 1986; Toronto Arts Award for writing and editing, 1986; *Los Angeles Times* Book Award, 1986, for *The Handmaid's Tale;* named Woman of the Year, *Ms.* magazine, 1986; Arthur C. Clarke Award, 1987; Commonwealth Literature Prize, 1987; Council for the Advancement and Support of Education silver medal, 1987; named *Chatelaine* magazine's Woman of the Year; City of Toronto Book Award, Coles Book of the Year Award, Canadian Booksellers' Association Author of the Year Award, Book of the Year Award Foundation for Advancement of Canadian Letters citation, Periodical Marketers of Canada Award, and Torgi Talking Book Award, all 1989, all for *Cat's Eye;* Harvard University Centennial Medal, 1990.

WRITINGS:

POEMS

Double Persephone, Hawkshead Press, 1961.
The Circle Game, Cranbrook Academy of Art (Bloomfield Hills, Michigan), 1964, revised edition, Contact Press, 1966.
Kaleidoscopes Baroque: A Poem, Cranbrook Academy of Art, 1965.
Talismans for Children, Cranbrook Academy of Art, 1965.
Speeches for Doctor Frankenstein, Cranbrook Academy of Art, 1966.
The Animals in That Country, Oxford University Press (Toronto), 1968, Atlantic-Little, Brown, 1969.
The Journals of Susanna Moodie, Oxford University Press, 1970.
Procedures for Underground, Atlantic-Little, Brown, 1970.
Power Politics, House of Anansi Press, 1971, Harper, 1973.
You Are Happy, Harper, 1974.
Selected Poems, 1965-1975, Oxford University Press, 1976, Simon & Schuster, 1978.
Marsh Hawk, Dreadnaught, 1977.
Two-Headed Poems, Oxford University Press, 1978, Simon & Schuster, 1981.

Notes Toward a Poem That Can Never Be Written, Salamander Press, 1981.

True Stories, Oxford University Press, 1981, Simon & Schuster, 1982.

Snake Poems, Salamander Press, 1983.

Interlunar, Oxford University Press, 1984.

Selected Poems II: Poems Selected and New, 1976-1986, Oxford University Press, 1986.

Morning in the Burned House (poems), McClelland & Stewart, 1995.

Also author of *Expeditions,* 1966, and *What Was in the Garden,* 1969.

NOVELS

The Edible Woman, McClelland & Stewart, 1969, Atlantic-Little, Brown, 1970.

Surfacing, McClelland & Stewart, 1972, Simon & Schuster 1973.

Lady Oracle, Simon & Schuster, 1976.

Life before Man, McClelland & Stewart, 1979, Simon & Schuster, 1980.

Bodily Harm, McClelland & Stewart, 1981, Simon & Schuster, 1982.

Encounters with the Element Man, Ewert, 1982.

Unearthing Suite, Grand Union Press, 1983.

The Handmaid's Tale, McClelland & Stewart, 1985, Houghton, 1986.

Cat's Eye, Doubleday, 1989.

The Robber Bride, McClelland & Stewart, 1993, Doubleday, 1993.

STORY COLLECTIONS

Dancing Girls and Other Stories, McClelland & Stewart, 1977, Simon & Schuster, 1982.

Bluebeard's Egg and Other Stories, McClelland & Stewart, 1983, Fawcett, 1987.

Murder in the Dark: Short Fictions and Prose Poems, Coach House Press, 1983.

Wilderness Tips and Other Stories, McClelland & Stewart, 1991.

Good Bones, Coach House, 1992, published as *Good Bones and Simple Murders,* Doubleday, 1994.

OTHER

The Trumpets of Summer (radio play), Canadian Broadcasting Corporation (CBC), 1964.

Survival: A Thematic Guide to Canadian Literature, House of Anansi Press, 1972.

The Servant Girl (teleplay), CBC-TV, 1974.

Days of the Rebels, 1815-1840, Natural Science Library, 1976.

The Poetry and Voice of Margaret Atwood (recording), Caedmon, 1977.

Up in the Tree (juvenile), McClelland & Stewart, 1978.

(Author of introduction) Catherine M. Young, *To See Our World,* GLC Publishers, 1979, Morrow, 1980.

(With Joyce Barkhouse) *Anna's Pet* (juvenile), James Lorimer, 1980.

Snowbird (teleplay), CBC-TV, 1981.

Second Words: Selected Critical Prose, House of Anansi Press, 1982.

(Editor) *The New Oxford Book of Canadian Verse in English,* Oxford University Press, 1982.

(Editor with Robert Weaver) *The Oxford Book of Canadian Short Stories in English,* Oxford University Press, 1986.

(With Peter Pearson) *Heaven on Earth* (teleplay), CBC-TV, 1986.

(Editor) *The Canlit Foodbook,* Totem, 1987.

(Editor with Shannon Ravenal) *The Best American Short Stories, 1989,* Houghton, 1989.

For the Birds, illustrated by John Bianchi, Firefly Books, 1991.

Contributor to anthologies, including *Five Modern Canadian Poets,* 1970, *The Canadian Imagination: Dimensions of a Literary Culture,* Harvard University Press, 1977, and *Women on Women,* 1978. Contributor to periodicals, including *Atlantic, Poetry, New Yorker, Harper's, New York Times Book Review, Saturday Night, Tamarack Review,* and *Canadian Forum.*

ADAPTATIONS: The Handmaid's Tale was filmed by Cinecom Entertainment Group, 1990.

SIDELIGHTS: As a poet, novelist, story writer, and essayist, Margaret Atwood holds a unique position in contemporary Canadian literature. Her books have received critical acclaim in the United States, Europe, and her native Canada, and she has been the recipient of numerous literary awards. Ann Marie Lipinski, writing in the *Chicago Tribune,* described Atwood as "one of the leading literary luminaries, a national heroine of the arts, the *rara avis* of Canadian letters." Atwood's critical popularity is matched by her popularity with readers. She is a frequent guest on Canadian television and radio, her books are best-sellers, and "people follow her on the streets and in stores," as Judy Klemesrud reported in the *New York Times.* Atwood, Roy MacGregor of *Maclean's* explained, "is to Canadian literature as Gordon Lightfoot is to Canadian music, more institution than individual." Atwood's popularity with both critics and the reading public has surprised her. "It's an accident that I'm a successful writer," she told MacGregor. "I think I'm kind of an odd phenomenon in that I'm a serious writer and I never expected to become a popular one, and I never did anything in order to become a popular one."

Atwood first came to public attention as a poet in the 1960s with her collections *Double Persephone,* winner of the E. J. Pratt Medal, and *The Circle Game,* winner of a Governor General's Award. These two books marked out the terrain which all of Atwood's later poetry would explore. *Double Persephone* concerns "the contrast between the flux of life or nature and the fixity of man's artificial creations," as Linda Hutcheon explained in the *Dictionary of Literary Biography. The Circle Game* takes this opposition further, setting such human constructs as games, literature, and love against the instability of nature. Human constructs are presented as both traps and shelters, the fluidity of nature as both dangerous and liberating. Sherrill Grace, writing in her *Violent Duality: A Study of Margaret Atwood,* identified the central tension in all of Atwood's work as "the pull towards art on one hand and towards life on the other." This tension is expressed in a series of "violent dualities," as Grace terms it. Atwood "is constantly aware of opposites—self/other, subject/object, male/female, nature/man—and of the need to accept and work within them," Grace explained. "To create, Atwood chooses violent dualities, and her art re-works, probes, and dramatizes the ability to see double."

Linda W. Wagner, writing in *The Art of Margaret Atwood: Essays in Criticism,* asserted that in Atwood's poetry "duality [is] presented as separation." This separation leads her characters to be isolated from one another and from the natural world, resulting in their inability to communicate, to break free of exploitative social relationships, or to understand their place in the natural order. "In her early poetry," Gloria Onley wrote in the *West Coast Review,* " . . . [Atwood] is acutely aware of the problem of alienation, the need for real human communication and the establishment of genuine human community—real as opposed to mechanical or manipulative; genuine as opposed to the counterfeit community of the body politic." Speaking of *The Circle Game,* Wagner wrote that "the personae of those poems never did make contact, never did anything but lament the human condition. . . . Relationships in these poems are sterile if not destructive."

Atwood's sense of desolation, especially evident in her early poems, and her use of frequently violent images, moved Helen Vendler of the *New York Times Book Review* to claim that Atwood has a "sense of life as mostly wounds given and received." About *The Circle Game* and *Procedures for Underground,* Peter Stevens noted in *Canadian Literature* that both collections contain "images of drowning, buried life, still life, dreams, journeys and returns." In a review of *True Stories* for *Canadian Forum,* Chaviva Hosek stated that the poems "range over such topics as murder, genocide, rape, dismemberment, instruments of torture, forms of torture, genital mutilation, abortion, and forcible hysterectomy," although Robert Sward of *Quill and Quire* explained that many reviewers of the book have exaggerated the violence and give "the false impression

that all 38 poems . . . are about torture." Yet, Scott Lauder of *Canadian Forum* spoke of "the painful world we have come to expect from Atwood."

Suffering is common for the female characters in Atwood's poems, although they are never passive victims. In more recent works they take active measures to improve their situations. Atwood's poems, the West Coast Revie's Onley maintained, concern "modern woman's anguish at finding herself isolated and exploited (although also exploiting) by the imposition of a sex role power structure." Atwood explained to Klemesurd in *The New York Times* that her suffering characters come from real life: "My women suffer because most of the women I talk to seem to have suffered." By the early 1970s, this stance had made Atwood into "a cult author to faithful feminist readers," as the *Chicago Tribune's* Lipinski commented. Atwood's popularity in the feminist community was unsought. "I began as a profoundly apolitical writer," she told Lindsy Van Gelder of *Ms.,* "but then I began to do what all novelists and some poets do: I began to describe the world around me."

Atwood's 1995 book of poetry, *Morning in the Burned House,* "reflects a period in Atwood's life when time seems to be running out," observed John Bemrose in *Maclean's.* Noting that many of the poems address grief and loss, particularly in relationship to her father's death and a realization of her own mortality, Bemrose added that the book "moves even more deeply into survival territory." Bemrose further suggested that in this book, Atwood allows the readers greater latitude in interpretation than in her earlier verse: "Atwood uses grief . . . to break away from that airless poetry and into a new freedom."

Atwood's feminist concerns also emerge clearly in her novels, particularly in *The Edible Woman, Surfacing, Life before Man, Bodily Harm,* and *The Handmaid's Tale.* These novels feature female characters who are, Klemesrud reported, "intelligent, self-absorbed modern women searching for identity . . . [They] hunt, split logs, make campfires and become successful in their careers, while men often cook and take care of their households." Like her poems, however, Atwood's novels "are populated by pained and confused people whose lives hold a mirror to both the front page fears—cancer, divorce, violence—and those that persist quietly, naggingly—solitude, loneliness, desperation," Lipinski wrote.

The Edible Woman tells the story of Marian McAlpin, a young woman engaged to be married, who rebels against her upcoming marriage. Her fiance seems too stable, too ordinary, and the role of wife too fixed and limiting. Her rejection of marriage is accompanied by her body's rejection of food; she cannot tolerate even a spare vegetarian diet. Eventually Marian bakes a sponge cake in the shape of a woman and feeds it to her fiance because, she explains, "You've been trying to assimilate me." After the engagement is broken, she is able to eat some of the cake herself.

Reaction to *The Edible Woman* was divided, with some reviewers pointing to the flaws commonly found in first novels. John Stedmond of *Canadian Forum,* for example, believed that "the characters, though cleverly sketched, do not quite jell, and the narrative techniques creak a little." Linda Rogers of *Canadian Literature* found that "one of the reasons *The Edible Woman* fails as a novel is the awkwardness of the dialogue." But other critics note Atwood's at least partial success. Tom Marshall, writing in his *Harsh and Lovely Land: The Major Canadian Poets and the Making of a Canadian Tradition,* called *The Edible Woman* "a largely successful comic novel, even if the mechanics are sometimes a little clumsy, the satirical accounts of consumerism a little drawn out." Millicent Bell of the *New York Times Book Review* termed it "a work of feminist black humor" and claimed that Atwood's "comic distortion veers at times into surreal meaningfulness." And Hutcheon described *The Edible Woman* as "very much a social novel about the possibilities for personal female identity in a capitalistic consumer society."

Surfacing, Atwood's second novel, is "a psychological ghost story," as Marshall described it, in which a young woman confronts and accepts her past during a visit to her rural home. She comes to realize that she has repressed disturbing events from her memory, including an abortion and her father's death. While swimming in a local lake, she has a vision of her drowned father which "drives her to a healing madness," Marshall stated. Hutcheon explained that "*Surfacing* tells of the coming to terms with the haunting, separated parts of the narrator's being . . . after surfacing from a dive, a symbolic as well as a real descent under water, where she has experienced a revealing and personally apocalyptic vision."

Many of the concerns found in Atwood's poetry reappear in *Surfacing.* The novel, Roberta Rubenstein wrote in *Modern Fiction Studies,* "synthesizes a number of motifs that have dominated [Atwood's] consciousness since her earliest poems: the elusiveness and variety of 'language' in its several senses; the continuum between human and animal, human being and nature; the significance of one's heritage . . . ; the search for a location (in both time and place); the brutalizations and victimizations of love; drowning and surviving." Margaret Wimsatt of *Commonweal* agreed with this assessment. "The novel," Wimsatt wrote, "picks up themes brooded over in the poetry, and knits them together coherently." Marshall asserted that both *The Edible Woman* and *Surfacing* "are enlargements upon the themes of [Atwood's] poems. In each of them a young woman is driven to rebellion against what seems to

be her fate in the modern technological 'Americanized' world and to psychic breakdown and breakthrough."

In *Life before Man,* Atwood dissects the relationships between three characters: Elizabeth, a married woman who mourns the recent suicide of her lover; Elizabeth's husband, Nate, who is unable to choose between his wife and his lover; and Lesje, Nate's lover, who works with Elizabeth at a museum of natural history. All three characters are isolated from one another and unable to experience their own emotions. The fossils and dinosaur bones on display at the museum are compared throughout the novel with the sterility of the characters' lives. As Laurie Stone noted in the *Village Voice, Life before Man* "is full of variations on the theme of extinction." Similarly, Rubenstein wrote in the *Chicago Tribune* that the novel is a "superb living exhibit in which the artifacts are unique (but representative) lives in progress."

Although *Life before Man* is what Rosellen Brown of *Saturday Review* called an "anatomy of melancholy," MacGregor pointed out a tempering humor in the novel as well. *Life before Man,* MacGregor wrote, "is not so much a story as it is the discarded negatives of a family album, the thoughts so dark they defy any flash short of Atwood's remarkable, and often very funny, insight." Comparing the novel's characters to museum pieces and commenting on the analytical examination to which Atwood subjects them, Peter S. Prescott of *Newsweek* wrote that "with chilly compassion and an even colder wit, Atwood exposes the interior lives of her specimens." Writing in the *New York Times Book Review,* Marilyn French made clear that in *Life before Man,* Atwood "combines several talents—powerful introspection, honesty, satire and a taut, limpid style—to create a splendid, fully integrated work."

The novel's title, French believes, relates to the characters' isolation from themselves, their history, and from one another. They have not yet achieved truly human stature. "This novel suggests," French wrote, "that we are still living life before man, before the human—as we like to define it—has evolved." Prescott raised the same point. The novel's characters, he wrote, "do not communicate; each, in the presence of another, is locked into his own thoughts and feelings. Is such isolation and indeterminacy what Atwood means when she calls her story 'Life before Man'?" This concern is also found in Atwood's previous novels, French argued, all of which depict "the search for identity . . . a search for a better way to be—for a way of life that both satisfies the passionate, needy self and yet is decent, humane and natural."

Atwood further explores this idea in *Bodily Harm.* In this novel Rennie Wilford is a Toronto journalist who specializes in light, trivial pieces for magazines. She is, Anne Tyler explained in the *Detroit News,* "a cataloguer of current fads and fancies." Isabel Raphael of the London *Times* called Rennie someone who "deals only in surfaces; her journalism is of the most trivial and transitory kind, her relationship with a live-in lover limited to sex, and most of her friends 'really just contacts.'" Following a partial mastectomy, which causes her lover to abandon her, Rennie begins to feel dissatisfied with her life. She takes on an assignment to the Caribbean island of St. Antoine in an effort to get away from things for a while. Her planned magazine story focusing on the island's beaches, tennis courts, and restaurants is distinctly facile in comparison to the political violence she finds on St. Antoine. When Rennie is arrested and jailed, the experience brings her to a self-realization about her life. "Death," Nancy Ramsey remarked in the *San Francisco Review of Books,* "rather than the modern sense of ennui, threatens Rennie and the people around her, and ultimately gives her life a meaning she hadn't known before."

Bodily Harm, Frank Davey of the *Canadian Forum* asserted, follows the same pattern set in Atwood's earlier novels: "Alienation from natural order . . ., followed by descent into a more primitive but healing reality . . ., and finally some reestablishment of order." Although Davey was "troubled" by the similarities between the novels and stated that "Atwood doesn't risk much with this book," he concluded that "these reservations aside, *Bodily Harm* is still a pleasure to read." Other critics have few such reservations about the book. Anatole Broyard of the *New York Times,* for example, claimed that "the only way to describe my response to [*Bodily Harm*] is to say that it knocked me out. Atwood seems to be able to do just about everything: people, places, problems, a perfect ear, an exactly-right voice and she tosses off terrific scenes with a casualness that leaves you utterly unprepared for the way these scenes seize you." Tyler called Atwood "an uncommonly skillful and perceptive writer," and went on to state that, because of its subject matter, *Bodily Harm* "is not always easy to read. There are times when it's downright unpleasant, but it's also intelligent, provocative, and in the end—against all expectations—uplifting."

In *The Handmaid's Tale* Atwood turns to speculative fiction, creating the dystopia of Gilead, a future America in which Fundamentalist Christians have killed the president and members of Congress and imposed their own dictatorial rule. In this future world, polluted by toxic chemicals and nuclear radiation, few women can bear children; the birthrate has dropped alarmingly. Those women who can bear children are forced to become Handmaids, the official breeders for society. All other women have been reduced to chattel under a repressive religious hierarchy run by men.

The Handmaid's Tale is a radical departure from Atwood's previous novels. Her strong feminism was evident in earlier books, but *The Handmaid's Tale* is dominated by the theme. As Barbara Holliday wrote in the *Detroit Free Press,* Atwood "has been concerned in her fiction with the painful psychic warfare between men and women. In 'The Handmaid's Tale,' a futuristic satire, she casts subtlety aside, exposing woman's primal fear of being used and helpless." Atwood's creation of an imaginary world is also new. As Mary Battiata noted in the *Washington Post, The Handmaid's Tale* is the first of Atwood's novels "not set in a worried corner of contemporary Canada."

Atwood was moved to write her story only after images and scenes from the book had been appearing to her for three years. She admitted to Mervyn Rothstein of the *New York Times,* "I delayed writing it . . . because I felt it was too crazy." But she eventually became convinced that her vision of Gilead was not far from reality. Some of the anti-female measures she had imagined for the novel actually exist. "There is a sect now, a Catholic charismatic spinoff sect, which calls the women handmaids," Atwood told Rothstein. "A law in Canada," Battiata reported, "[requires] a woman to have her husband's permission before obtaining an abortion." And Atwood, speaking to Battiata, pointed to repressive laws in the totalitarian state of Romania as well: "No abortion, no birth control, and compulsory pregnancy testing, once a month." *The Handmaid's Tale,* Elaine Kendall explained in the *Los Angeles Times Book Review,* depicts "a future firmly based upon actuality, beginning with events that have already taken place and extending them a bit beyond the inevitable conclusions. *The Handmaid's Tale* does not depend upon hypothetical scenarios, omens, or straws in the wind, but upon documented occurrences and public pronouncements; all matters of record." Stephen McCabe of the *Humanist* called the novel "a chilling vision of the future extrapolated from the present."

Yet, several critics voiced a disbelief in the basic assumptions of *The Handmaid's Tale.* Mary McCarthy, in her review for the *New York Times Book Review,* complained that "I just can't see the intolerance of the far right . . . as leading to a super-biblical puritanism." And although agreeing that "the author has carefully drawn her projections from current trends," McCarthy asserted that "perhaps that is the trouble: the projections are too neatly penciled in. The details . . . all raise their hands announcing themselves present. At the same time, the Republic of Gilead itself, whatever in it that is not a projection, is insufficiently imagined." Richard Grenier of *Insight* objected that the Fundamentalist-run Gilead does not seem Christian: "There seems to be no Father, no Son, no Holy Ghost, no apparent belief in redemption, resurrection, eternal life. No one in this excruciatingly hierarchized new clerical state . . . appears to believe in God." Grenier also

found it improbable that "while the United States has hur-
tled off into this morbid, feminist nightmare, the rest of
the democratic world has been blissfully unaffected."
Writing in the Toronto *Globe and Mail*, William French
stated that Atwood's "reach exceeds her grasp" in *The
Handmaid's Tale*, "and in the end we're not clear what
we're being warned against." Atwood seems to warn of
the dangers of religious fanaticism, of the effects of pollution on the birthrate, and of a possible backlash to militant
feminist demands. The novel, French stated, "is in fact a
cautionary tale about *all* these things . . . but in her scenario, they interact in an implausible way."

Despite this flaw, French saw *The Handmaid's Tale* as
being "in the honorable tradition of *Brave New World* and
other warnings of dystopia. It's imaginative, even audacious, and conveys a chilling sense of fear and menace."
Prescott also compared *The Handmaid's Tale* to other
dystopian novels. It belongs, he writes, "to that breed of
visionary fiction in which a metaphor is extended to elaborate a warning. . . . Wells, Huxley and Orwell popularized the tradition with books like 'The Time Machine,'
'Brave New World' and '1984'—yet Atwood is a better
novelist than they." Christopher Lehmann-Haupt identified *The Handmaid's Tale* as a book that goes far beyond
its feminist concerns. Writing in the *New York Times*,
Lehmann-Haupt explained that the novel "is a political
tract deploring nuclear energy, environmental waste, and
antifeminist attitudes. But it [is] so much more than
that—a taut thriller, a psychological study, a play on
words." Van Gelder agreed. The novel, she wrote, "ultimately succeeds on multiple levels: as a page-turning
thriller, as a powerful political statement, and as an exquisite piece of writing." Lehmann-Haupt concluded that
The Handmaid's Tale "is easily Margaret Atwood's best
novel to date." Again, in *The Robber Bride*, Atwood explores women's issues and feminist concerns, this time
concentrating on women's relationships, positive and negative, with each other. Based loosely on the Brothers
Grimm fairy tale "The Robber Bridegroom," the novel
chronicles the relationships of college friends Tony, Charis, and Roz with their backstabbing classmate Zenia.
Now middle-aged women, their paths and life choices
have diverged, yet Tony, Charis, and Roz have remained
friends. Throughout their adulthood, however, Zenia's
manipulations have nearly destroyed their lives and cost
them husbands and careers. Lorrie Moore opined in the
New York Times Book Review that the book "is Margaret
Atwood's funniest and most companionable book in
years," remarking that she "retains her gift for observing,
in poetry, the minutiae specific to the physical and emotional lives of her characters." About Zenia, Moore commented, "charming and gorgeous, Zenia is a misogynist's
grotesque: relentlessly seductive, brutal, pathologically
dishonest," postulating that "perhaps Ms. Atwood in-

tended Zenia, by the end, to be a symbol of all that is inex-
plicably evil: war, disease, global catastrophe." Judith
Timson commented in *Maclean's* that *The Robber Bride*
"has as its central theme an idea that feminism was supposed to have shoved under the rug: there are female pred-
ators out there, and they will get your man if you are not
careful," adding, "As a sort of grown-up sequel to Atwood's 1988 novel, *Cat's Eye,* the book seems to be saying
that if you think little girls can be mean to each other, you
should see what big ones can accomplish."

Atwood's 1992 collection *Good Bones*, published in 1994
as *Good Bones and Simple Murders*, "occup[ies] that
vague, peculiar country between poetry and prose," stated
John Bemrose in *Maclean's*. Describing Atwood as "storyteller, poet, fabulist and social commentator rolled into
one," Bemrose claimed that "the strongest pieces in *Good
Bones* combine a light touch with a hypnotic seriousness
of purpose." In the *New York Times Book Review*, Jennifer
Howard labeled *Good Bones and Simple Murders* a
"sprightly, whimsically feminist collection of miniatures
and musings, assembled from two volumes published in
Canada in 1983 and 1992." A *Publishers Weekly* reviewer,
who characterized the entries as "postmodern fairy tales,
caustic fables, inspired parodies, witty monologues," declared each piece to be "clever and sharply honed."

Survival: A Thematic Guide to Canadian Literature is Atwood's most direct presentation of her strong belief in Canadian nationalism. In the book Atwood discerns a
uniquely Canadian literature, distinct from its American
and British counterparts, and she discusses the dominant
themes to be found in it. Canadian literature, she argues,
is primarily concerned with victims and with the victim's
ability to survive. Atwood, Onley explained, "perceives a
strong sado-masochistic patterning in Canadian literature
as a whole. She believes that there is a national fictional
tendency to participate, usually at some level as Victim,
in a Victor/Victim basic pattern." But "despite its stress
on victimization," Hutcheon wrote "this study is not a
revelation of, or a reveling in, [masochism]." What Atwood argues, Onley asserted, is that "every country or culture has a single unifying and informing symbol at its core:
for America, the Frontier; for England, the Island; for
Canada, Survival."

Several critics find that Atwood's own work exemplifies
this primary theme of Canadian literature. Her examination of destructive sex roles and her nationalistic concern
over the subordinate role Canada plays to the United
States are variations on the victor/victim theme. As
Marge Piercy explained in the *American Poetry Review*,
Atwood believes that a writer must consciously work
within his or her nation's literary tradition. Atwood argues in *Survival*, Piercy wrote, "that discovery of a writer's
tradition may be of use, in that it makes available a con-

scious choice of how to deal with that body of themes. She suggested that exploring a given tradition consciously can lead to writing in new and more interesting ways." Because Atwood's own work closely parallels the themes she sees as common to the Canadian literary tradition, *Survival* "has served as the context in which critics have subsequently discussed [Atwood's] works," Hutcheon stated.

Atwood's prominent stature in Canadian letters rests as much on her published works as on her efforts to define and give value to her nation's literature. "Atwood," Susan Wood wrote in the *Washington Post Book World*, "has emerged as a champion of Canadian literature and of the peculiarly Canadian experience of isolation and survival." Hutcheon noted Atwood's "important impact on Canadian culture" and believes that her books, "internationally known through translations, stand as testimony to Atwood's significant position in a contemporary literature which must deal with defining its own identity and defending its value."

Although she has been labelled a Canadian nationalist, a feminist, and even a gothic writer, Atwood incorporates and transcends these categories. Writing in *Saturday Night* of Atwood's several perceived roles as a writer, Linda Sandler concluded that "Atwood is all things to all people . . . a nationalist . . . a feminist or a psychologist or a comedian . . . a maker and breaker of myths . . . a gothic writer. She's all these things, but finally she's unaccountably Other. Her writing has the discipline of a social purpose but it remains elusive, complex, passionate. It has all the intensity of an act of exorcism." Atwood's work finally succeeds because it speaks of universal concerns. Piercy wrote, "Atwood is a large and remarkable writer. Her concerns are nowhere petty. Her novels and poems move and engage me deeply, can matter to people who read them."

BIOGRAPHICAL/CRITICAL SOURCES:

BOOKS

Atwood, Margaret, *The Edible Woman*, McClelland & Stewart, 1969, Atlantic-Little, Brown, 1970.

Contemporary Literary Criticism, Gale, Volume 2, 1974, Volume 3, 1975, Volume 4, 1975, Volume 8, 1978, Volume 13, 1980, Volume 15, 1980, Volume 25, 1983, Volume 44, 1987.

Davidson, Arnold E., and Cathy N. Davidson, editors, *The Art of Margaret Atwood: Essays in Criticism*, House of Anansi Press, 1981.

Dictionary of Literary Biography, Volume 53: *Canadian Writers since 1960*, Gale, 1986.

Gibson, Graeme, *Eleven Canadian Novelists*, House of Anansi Press, 1973.

Grace, Sherrill, *Violent Duality: A Study of Margaret Atwood*, Vehicule Press, 1980.

Grace, Sherrill, and Lorraine Weir, editors, *Margaret Atwood: Language, Text and System*, University of British Columbia Press, 1983.

Lecker, Robert, and Jack David, editors, *The Annotated Bibliography of Canada's Major Authors*, ECW, 1980.

Marshall, Tom, *Harsh and Lovely Land: The Major Canadian Poets and the Making of a Canadian Tradition*, University of British Columbia Press, 1978.

Sandler, Linda, editor, *Margaret Atwood: A Symposium*, University of British Columbia, 1977.

Twigg, Alan, *For Openers: Conversations with Twenty-Four Canadian Writers*, Harbour, 1981.

Woodcock, George, *The Canadian Novel in the Twentieth Century*, McClelland & Stewart, 1975.

PERIODICALS

American Poetry Review, November/December, 1973, March/April, 1977, September/October, 1979.

Atlantic, April, 1973.

Book Forum, Volume 4, number 1, 1978.

Books in Canada, January, 1979, June/July, 1980, March, 1981.

Canadian Forum, February, 1970, January, 1973, November/December, 1974, December/January, 1977-78, June/July, 1981, December/January, 1981-82.

Canadian Literature, autumn, 1971, spring, 1972, winter, 1973, spring, 1974, spring, 1977.

Chicago Tribune, January 27, 1980, February 3, 1980, May 16, 1982, March 19, 1989.

Chicago Tribune Book World, January 26, 1986.

Christian Science Monitor, June 12, 1977.

Commonweal, July 9, 1973.

Communique, May, 1975.

Detroit Free Press, January 26, 1986.

Detroit News, April 4, 1982.

Essays on Canadian Writing, spring, 1977.

Globe and Mail (Toronto), July 7, 1984, October 5, 1985, October 19, 1985, February 15, 1986, November 15, 1986, November 29, 1986, November 14, 1987.

Hudson Review, autumn, 1973, spring, 1975.

Humanist, September/October, 1986.

Insight, March 24, 1986.

Journal of Canadian Fiction, Volume 1, number 4, 1972.

Los Angeles Times, March 2, 1982, April, 22, 1982, May 9, 1986, January 12, 1987.

Los Angeles Times Book Review, October 17, 1982, February 9, 1986, December 23, 1987.

Maclean's, January 15, 1979, October 15, 1979, March 30, 1981, October 5, 1992, October 4, 1993, February 6, 1995,

Malahat Review, January, 1977.

Manna, Number 2, 1972.

Meanjin, Volume 37, number 2, 1978.

Modern Fiction Studies, autumn, 1976.

Ms., January, 1987.

New Leader, September 3, 1973.

New Orleans Review, Volume 5, number 3, 1977.

Newsweek, February 18, 1980, February 17, 1986.

New York Times, December 23, 1976, January 10, 1980, February 8, 1980, March 6, 1982, March 28, 1982, September 15, 1982, January 27, 1986, February 17, 1986, November 5, 1986.

New York Times Book Review, October 18, 1970, March 4, 1973, April 6, 1975, September 26, 1976, May 21, 1978, February 3, 1980, October 11, 1981, February 9, 1986, October 31, 1993, December 11, 1994.

Observer, June 13, 1982.

Ontario Review, spring/summer, 1975.

Open Letter, summer, 1973.

Parnassus: Poetry in Review, spring/summer, 1974.

People, May 19, 1980.

Poetry, March, 1970, July, 1972, May, 1982.

Publishers Weekly, August 23, 1976, October 3, 1994.

Quill and Quire, April, 1981, September, 1984.

Room of One's Own, summer, 1975.

San Francisco Review of Books, January, 1982, summer, 1982.

Saturday Night, May, 1971, July/August, 1976, September, 1976, May, 1981.

Saturday Review, September 18, 1976, February 2, 1980.

Saturday Review of the Arts, April, 1973.

Shenandoah, Volume 37, number 2, 1987.

Studies in Canadian Literature, summer, 1977.

This Magazine Is about Schools, winter, 1973.

Time, October 11, 1976.

Times (London), March 13, 1986, June 4, 1987, June 10, 1987.

Times Literary Supplement, March 21, 1986, June 12, 1987.

University of Toronto Quarterly, summer, 1978.

Village Voice, January 7, 1980.

Vogue, January, 1986.

Washington Post, April 6, 1986.

Washington Post Book World, September 26, 1976, December 3, 1978, January 27, 1980, March 14, 1982, February 2, 1986.

Waves, autumn, 1975.

West Coast Review, January, 1973.*

B

BACLE, Claude
See GRIGNON, Claude-Henri

* * *

BAILLARGEON, Pierre   1916-1967
(Henri Brulard)

PERSONAL: Born September 10, 1916, in Montreal, Quebec; died while undergoing heart surgery, August 15, 1967, in Rochester, MN; son of Oliva (a political organizer) and Alphonsine (Mercier) Baillargeon; married Jacqueline Mabit (a writer), July (one source says August), 1939; children: Lise, Jeanne, Mireille, Claude. *Education:* Attended College Jean-de-Brebeuf, Montreal; studied medicine at Universite de Poitiers, France. *Religion:* Roman Catholic.

CAREER: Amerique francaise (a literary publication), founder and director, 1941-44; taught Latin and French in Vezelay and Normandy, France; journalist in France, *La patrie,* 1948-60, and *Le petit journal,* 1950-51; Editions Robert Laffont, translator, 1956; Canadian Embassy, Paris, secretary to ambassador, 1957-58; *Reader's Digest,* literary consultant, Paris, 1956-59; Bell Canada, editor, 1960-62; Canadien National, translator, 1962-66; writer. Past president of the Societe des Ecrivains Canadiens. *Military service:* Worked as a translator for the Royal Canadian Air Force during World War II.

MEMBER: Royal Society of Canada, elected fellow, c. 1962, PEN, Press Club.

AWARDS, HONOURS: Silver medal of the Academie francaise, arts et lettres, c. 1958; Canada Council Senior Arts Fellowship, 1959-60.

WRITINGS:

Hasard et moi (novel; title means "Chance and I"), Beauchemin (Montreal), 1940.

Eglogues (poetry; includes "Printemps," "Regards," and "Ombres"), illustrated by Jacques de Tonnancour, music composed by Jean Papineau-Couture, Amerique francaise (Montreal), 1943.

Les medisances de Claude Perrin (novel; title means "Claude Perrin's Slander"), Parizeau (Montreal), 1945.

Commerce (novel), Varietes (Montreal), 1947.

La Neige et le feu (title means "Snow and Fire"), Varietes (Montreal), 1948.

Le scandale est necessaire (nonfiction; title means "Scandal Is Necessary"), Jour (Montreal), 1962.

Madame Homere (play; produced at Ecole Normale Jacques-Cartier, Montreal, December 13, 1963), Lys (Monreal), 1964.

Le Choix: Essais (essays; title means "Choice"), edited by Robert Bernier, HMH (Montreal), 1969.

Contributor of poems and stories to periodicals, including *Amerique francaise, Cite libre, Le devoir,* and *La presse.* Author of works under the pseudomym Henri Brulard. Also author of an unpublished play, *Autour d'un gros bonhomme* (title means "About a Stout Fellow").

SIDELIGHTS: As a French-Canadian journalist, poet, and essayist, Pierre Baillargeon was an influential writer in the 1940s and 1950s, and was praised for the compactness of his writings, his polished use of language, and his concern for literary and social issues. Well-known for his outspoken manner, Baillargeon's criticisms often centered on education, the Roman Catholic Church, and literary critics in Quebec. Although at the time some reviewers seemed annoyed by Baillargeon's work, "he was later recognized as a 'prophet' and forerunner of the Quiet Revolution, though he did not take an active part in this movement," according to Jane Koustas in an entry for *Dictionary of Literary Biography.* The Quiet Revolution (the Revolution Tranquille), was a socio-political movement in Quebec during the mid-twentieth century, whose activists resolved to form an independent provincial government—separate from English-speaking Canada—advocating, among others, secularized French education free from the monopoly of the Roman Catholic Church, improved health care and social services, and regional industrial growth. Baillargeon became, according to a modern critic quoted by Koustas, "the guilty conscience of his era," for his numerous written scrutinies into current social issues, exposing the "total control" exercised over many institutions by the Roman Catholic clergy in Quebec.

Baillargeon was born in Montreal, Quebec, on September 10, 1916. As a boy he attended the Ecole Querbes d'Outremont and the College Jean-de-Brebeuf in Canada, then studied medicine at the Universite de Poitiers in France. While living in France he met and married Jacqueline Mabit in 1939. The couple remained in France until 1940 when they relocated to Canada. They eventually had four children; in December of 1940 the Baillargeons celebrated the birth of Lise, followed in 1943 by Jeanne, in 1945 by Mireille, and in 1949 by Claude. With the onset of World War II, Baillargeon served his country as a translator for the Royal Canadian Air Force.

In 1940 Baillargeon published his first book, *Hasard et moi,* translated "Chance and I." The narrative, part novel, part essay, and part diary, follows the internal dialogue of the main character, Pierre. Critics were pleased with the style, and compared the tome to the works of Maurice Blanchot, Claude Gauvreau, Francis Ponge, and Paul Valery. The following year saw Baillargeon's first journalistic endeavor with the founding of *Amerique francaise,* a publication for literary reviews which he organized and headed from 1941 until 1944. At various times he also contributed poems, stories, and essays to newspapers in Montreal, and to periodicals such as *Le Petit Journal, La Presse,* and *Cite libre.*

Eglogues, Baillargeon's 1943 volume of poetry, consists of three pieces: "Printemps," "Regards," and "Ombres." The work was accompanied by the efforts of two additional artists: Jacques de Tonnancour as illustrator, and Jean Papineau-Couture as composer of a musical score. Koustas wrote in the *Dictionary of Literary Biography* that "certain critics found the intellectual, conservative poetry written in measured verse too academic, claiming that Baillargeon did not explore images but concentrated on conveying a meaning." Nevertheless, the work was regarded as significant, and memorably brought together various notable talents of the day.

Baillargeon's next major work was published in 1945 as *Les medisances de Claude Perrin.* The title of the novel means "Claude Perrin's Slander." In this volume, Baillargeon introduces the semi-autobiographical Claude Perrin—a character who was to reappear in three later works as well. Often satiric in tone, the book emphasizes the urgent need for change. Perrin is a writer who, because of ill health, has withdrawn to a quiet village to complete his "spiritual testament." In the first part of the work, "Portrait," Perrin meditates on his family life and marriage, and concludes that his life is meaningless. Through Perrin's history the reader comprehends his present circumstances and his compulsion to put it all down on paper. Perrin's failures, moreover, may be seen as a microcosm of the failures of Quebec—Baillargeon's denunciation of Quebec's social ills in the novel is unmistakable. Other characters in the story include Perrin's daughter, his doctor (who could not cure Perrin's illness), and his priest (who does not understand Perrin). In the second part of the narrative, "Testament," Perrin offers advice to writers in Quebec in hopes of reforming society, and counsels them to avoid conformity. The public heralded the publication of *Les Medisances de Claude Perrin* as a literary event, and many reviewers lauded the effort.

Claude Perrin's adventures are continued in Baillargeon's 1947 novel *Commerce.* In this account, Perrin is the owner of a bookstore who enjoys opening the store for patrons to meet and share ideas—especially controversial opinions—on the Roman Catholic Church and the shortcomings of the educational system in Quebec. Narrated in a conversational manner by way of Baillargeon's trademark maxims, epigrams and morals, events in the story are related by a student who is a regular customer. The novel met with mixed reviews; some critics cited a repetition of Perrin's convictions from *Les Medisances de Claude Perrin*; other reviewers insisted that the negative comments only flowed from those who were not able to remain objective to the theme of Baillargeon's work.

After the war, Baillargeon lived in France for twelve years—from 1948 through 1960. During that time, he became a journalist for *La patrie,* publishing travel articles and interviews with various artists. His next principal work, 1948's *La Neige et le feu* (meaning "Snow and Fire"), has been called a "novel of manners." The character of Philippe Boureil (who resembles Claude Perrin in philosophy), flees Canada when his wife leaves him, and finds himself in France, admiring the freedoms of French literary society. Boureil becomes enamored of the intellectual Simone Audigny, but is compelled to return to Canada, his unsuccessful marriage, and his former—and stifling—job as a newspaperman in Quebec. Some clerical reviewers were quick to recognize Baillargeon's criticisms as directed toward the social climate of Quebec before the

Quiet Revolution, and were therefore uncomplimentary of Baillargeon's work; others, however, lauded the author's insights and bitter denunciation of clerical intolerance.

For the next fourteen years Baillargeon concentrated on his journalism in France and Canada, and did not produce another major work until 1962. Some have speculated that he was among many Quebecers whose artistic creativity was effectively stifled by the censorship enacted through the Law Concerning Publications and the Public Morale, sponsored by the government of Quebec and the Roman Catholic clergy in 1950. During this time, Baillargeon taught Latin and French in addition to his work as a journalist, and, in 1956, became a translator and a literary consultant for *Reader's Digest* in Paris. In 1957 he served as secretary to the ambassador at the Canadian Embassy in Paris for one year, and returned to Canada in 1959, having been awarded the silver medal of the Academie francaise in arts and letters in 1958. He accepted a position as an editor at Bell Canada by 1960. At this time he was active in the Societe des Ecrivains Canadiens, and was elected to the Royal Society of Canada.

The essay *Le scandale est necessaire,* released in 1962, is considered a literary classic. The title means "Scandal is Necessary." The essay was written with the intent of shocking readers into action during the Quiet Revolution. Compromising eight chapters, four are succinctly brief: in controversial maxims, Baillargeon cites the city's shortcomings targeting mediocrity and materialism; in a chapter of "Epigrammes," the author further reflects upon the real effects produced by the Quiet Revolution; in "Reflexions" the author's meditations become humorous moralisms; in "Litterature" Baillargeon addresses the reader as an intellectual. The next four chapters are longer—two attacking conformism, the repressive intellectual and social environment, and emphasizing the needed reforms in educational institutions of Quebec; the final two chapters contain vignettes of powerful people who influenced the author. Baillargeon's *Le Scandale est necessaire* was an immediate success both popularly and critically. The major social reforms of which Baillargeon championed had been gaining momentum in the 1960s through the Quiet Revolution, and the period was a pivotal point in the ultimate modernization of Quebec.

In addition to stories, poetry, and essays, Baillargeon wrote two plays: *Madame Homere,* featuring Agathe, the wife of classical poet Homer, produced at the Ecole Normale Jacques-Cartier in Montreal on December 13, 1963, and published in 1964; and *Autour d'un gros bonhomme,* an unpublished play featuring the character of Claude Perrin as "a stout fellow." *Madame Homere* was not well-received by critics upon its showing. Reviewers complained that "the play was completely out of touch with the social and cultural concerns of the Quiet Revolution,"

according to Koustas in the *Dictionary of Literary Biography.*

Baillargeon died at the Mayo Clinic in Rochester, Minnesota, where he was undergoing heart surgery. *Le Choix: Essais,* his volume of essays published two years after his 1967 death, was compiled and edited by Robert Bernier, a friend and former teacher at the College Jean-de-Brebeuf. Included in the collection are unpublished essays and a choice selection of works highlighting the author's trademark style of rigorous thought, from various stages of Baillargeon's literary career.

BIOGRAPHICAL/CRITICAL SOURCES:

BOOKS

Dictionary of Literary Biography, Volume 88: *Canadian Writers, 1920-1959,* Gale, 1989, pp. 6-10.

Toupin, Paul, *Au commencement etait le souvenir,* Fides, 1973, pp. 183-92.

PERIODICALS

L'Action nationale, January, 1975, pp. 339-51.
Livres et auteurs Quebecois, 1973, pp. 325-36.
Voix et images, September, 1975, pp. 57-71.
Voix et images du pays, volume 8, 1974, pp. 127-32.*

*   *   *

BAIRD, Irene (Todd) 1901-1981

PERSONAL: Born April 9, 1901, in Carlisle, Cumberland County, England; immigrated to Canada, 1919; died April 19, 1981, in Victoria, British Columbia, Canada; daughter of Robert and Eva Todd; married Robert Baird, c. 1920; children: Robert, June.

CAREER: Author of column for the *Vancouver Sun,* Vancouver, British Columbia, Canada, 1941; *Daily Province,* Vancouver, reporter, 1942; National Film Board of Canada, Ottawa, Ontario, Canada, touring lecturer, 1942-47, Canadian representative to the United States and Mexico, 1944; Federal Department of Mines and Resources, Ottawa, and the Department of Northern Affairs and National Resources (later the Department of Indian Affairs and Northern Development), Ottawa, senior information officer, 1947-62, chief of Information Services, 1962-67. United Nations consultant on information to Latin America, 1951.

WRITINGS:

John (novel), Lippincott (Philadelphia), 1937.
Waste Heritage (novel), Random House (New York), 1939.
He Rides the Sky (novel), Macmillan (Toronto), 1941.

The North American Tradition (collected radio addresses), Macmillan (Toronto), 1941.

The Climate of Power (novel; originally serialized in *Toronto Star Weekly,* 1971), Macmillan (Toronto), 1971.

Contributor to *The Canada Handbook,* Queen's Printer (Ottawa), 1967; also contributor of poems, short stories, and articles to *Saturday Night, Beaver, North, Canadian Geographical Journal,* and *UNESCO Courier.*

The manuscripts for Baird's final three novels are housed at the Macmillan collection, McMaster University, Toronto.

SIDELIGHTS: For over three decades Irene Baird enjoyed a diversified career as a novelist, journalist, and high-ranking Canadian civil servant. The subject matter of Baird's published efforts was often drawn from an extensive knowledge of Canada and its peoples, a familiarity gleaned in part from extensive travels in conjunction with her job as a government information officer. Born in England in 1901, Baird journeyed with her family to British Columbia as a teenager, married, and began raising a family before trying her hand at writing. In 1937, *John,* the first of her four novels, was published; it is the story of a Scottish immigrant to British Columbia who rejects the bourgeois expectations of his middle-class family and instead lives in isolation and peace on Vancouver Island.

Baird next penned perhaps her best-known work, one that has been compared to other novels of the Great Depression such as John Steinbeck's *Of Mice and Men* and *The Grapes of Wrath.* This 1939 novel, entitled *Waste Heritage,* is based on Baird's participation as an observer to an infamous incident in 1930s British Columbia. A thousand unemployed men trekked from Vancouver to Victoria in a labor march against hiring policies; Baird accompanied her physician when he went to look after the protesters. *Waste Heritage*'s protagonists are based on the strikers she met—unmarried men with nominal job skills and even less education. Such disadvantages gave them little hope of finding adequate work during the dismal years of the Depression. The novel impacted readers by making clear that even if the men did find sustaining employment, they could only look forward to a future of unending exploitation.

Waste Heritage was received to critical acclaim upon publication and struck a chord of empathy among Canadians for those on the lower economic rungs of their society. According to *Dictionary of Literary Biography,* a *Saturday Review* writer of the day termed it "a black novel—black and bitter and compassionate and intensely sincere. . . . Baird writes with both fists and an angry will to be heard." Catherine McLay also reflected in *Dictionary of Literary Biography* that *Waste Heritage* is "an effective vehicle of social protest as readers share in the daily humiliations and suffering of men whose only crime is to want employment. The dialogue is terse and realistic and Baird has handled her male characters convincingly."

Baird's third novel, 1941's *He Rides the Sky,* was based on her research into letters written home by young men serving in the Canadian air forces during World War II. The story's protagonist, Pete O'Halloran, grows up rapidly in the two short years of the novel, from a young and eager recruit into a mature officer, before he is tragically killed in action. The work received critical praise but was a commercial failure.

During this era Baird began writing for newspapers in British Columbia but then took a position with the National Film Board of Canada. This job required extensive travel across the provinces, and she eventually moved to a similar post with the Department of Northern Affairs and National Resources. Her work with this agency often involved treks to the more northerly regions of Canada near the Arctic Circle, a vast region unknown even to many Canadians; Baird wrote about her experiences in essays and poems published in Canadian magazines such as *Saturday Night* and *Canadian Geographical Journal.*

Upon her retirement in 1967 Baird relocated to London, England, where she penned her fourth and final novel, 1971's *The Climate of Power.* The story is set in the Department of National Projects and charts the final working days of a longtime government functionary. In the isolated outposts of northern Canada, he battles a nefarious colleague set to succeed him. Their showdown results in death for one and injury for the other. Baird returned to British Columbia in 1973, the same year that *Waste Heritage* was reprinted and hailed as an important contribution to Canadian literature.

BIOGRAPHICAL/CRITICAL SOURCES:

BOOKS

Dictionary of Literary Biography, Volume 68: *Canadian Writers, 1920-1959,* Gale, 1988.

PERIODICALS

Canadian Forum, October, 1974, pp. 36-38.*

*   *   *

BARBEAU, (Frederic Charles Joseph) Marius 1883-1969

PERSONAL: Born March 5, 1883, in Sainte-Marie-de-la-Beauce, Quebec, Canada; died February 27 (one source says March 27), 1969; son of Charles (a horse dealer) and Marie Virginie (Morency) Barbeau; children: Dalila, Helene. *Education:* College of Sainte-Anne-de-la Pocatiere, B.A., 1903; Laval University, LL.L., 1907; Oxford University, B.Sc., 1910; obtained Ph.D. from University of Montreal; attended the Sorbonne.

CAREER: Admitted to the bar in Canada, 1907; National Museum of Canada, ethnologist and folklorist, 1911-58; author of both nonfiction and fiction, 1915-69. Associate editor of *Journal of American Folklore,* 1916-50.

MEMBER: International Folk Music Council; Unesco (vice-president); Royal Society of Canada (elected fellow, 1950); L'Academie canadienne-francaise (cofounder); La Societe canadienne de musique folklorique (president).

AWARDS, HONOURS: Rhodes scholar, 1907; honorary fellow of Oriel College, Oxford; Lorne Pierce medal for literature, 1950; Canada Council grant for preparation of material on Canadian folk songs, 1957-58, for completion of *Repertoire de la chanson,* 1958-60, to prepare and continue work on a glossary and grammar of the Huron-Wyandot language, 1961-63; Canada Council medal, 1961-62; University of Alberta gold medal for music, 1965; Companion of the Order of Canada, 1966; Centennial medal, 1967; honorary doctorates from institutions including Laval University and Oxford University.

WRITINGS:

Huron and Wyandot Mythology, Government Printing Bureau (Ottawa), 1915.
Indian Days in the Canadian Rockies, Macmillan (Toronto), 1923.
The Downfall of Temlaham (novel) Macmillan, 1928.
(With Ramsay Traquair) *The Church of Saint Pierre, Island of Orleans, Quebec,* Bridgens (Toronto), 1929.
Totem Poles of the Gitksan, Upper Skeena River, British Columbia, F. A. Acland (Ottawa), 1929.
Au Coeur de Quebec, Zodiaque (Montreal), 1934.
Cornelius Krieghoff, Pioneer Painter of North America, Macmillan, 1934.
La Merveilleuse Aventure de Jacques Cartier, Levesque (Montreal), 1934.
Grand'mere raconte, Beauchemin (Montreal), 1935.
Il etait une fois, Beauchemin, 1935.
The Kingdom of Saguenay, Macmillan, 1936.
Quebec, Where Ancient France Lingers, Macmillan, 1936.
Romancero du Canada Macmillan, 1937.
Assomption Sash, National Museum (Ottawa), 1939.
Aux armes, Canadiens! Hutte Canadienne des Chevaliers de Colomb (Ottawa), 1941.
Henri Julien, Ryerson (Toronto), 1941.
Les Reves des chasseurs, Beauchemin, 1942.
Maitres artisans de chez-nous, Zodiaque, 1942.
Cote, the Wood Carver, Ryerson, 1943.
Les Enfants disent, Paysana (Montreal), 1943.
Mountain Cloud (novel), Macmillan, 1944.

Saintes Artisanes: I. Les Brodeuses, Fides (Montreal), 1944.
Allouette! Nouveau recueil de chansons populaires avec melodies, choisies dans le repertoire du Musee National du Canada, Lumen (Montreal), 1946.
Painters of Quebec, Ryerson, 1946.
Saintes Artisanes: II. Mille Petites Adresses, Fides, 1946.
Alaska Beckons, Macmillan, 1947.
L'Arbre des reves, Lumen, 1948; translated as *The Tree of Dreams,* Oxford (Toronto), 1955.
Le Reve de Kamalmouk (novel), Fides, 1948.
Totem Poles (two volumes), E. Cloutier (Ottawa), 1950-51.
Les Contes du Grand-Pere Sept-Heures (twelve volumes), Chantecler (Montreal), 1950-53.
(With V. E. Garfield and P. S. Wingert) *The Tsimshian, Their Arts and Music,* Augustin (New York), 1951.
Haida Myths Illustrated in Argillite Carvings, National Museum, 1953.
Haida Carvers in Argillite, National Museum, 1957.
I Have Seen Quebec, Macmillan, 1957.
Tresor des anciens Jesuites, National Museum, 1957.
Medicine-Men on the North Pacific Coast, National Museum, 1958.
Pathfinders in the North Pacific, Caxton (Caldwell, ID), 1958.
Roundelays; Folk Dances and Games Collected in Canada and New England, National Museum, 1958.
Huron-Wyandot Traditional Narratives, National Museum, 1960.
Tsimsyan Myths, National Museum, 1961.
Jongleur Songs of Old Quebec, Rutgers University Press (New Brunswick, NJ), 1962.
Le Rossignol y chante, National Museum, 1962.
Folklore, Academie Canadienne-Francaise (Montreal), 1965.
Indian Days on the Western Prairies, National Museum, 1965.
Peaux-Rouges d'Amerique: Leurs moeurs, leurs coutumes, Beauchemin, 1965.
Comment on decouvrit l'Amerique, Beauchemin, 1966.
Fameaux peaux-rouges d'Amerique du nord-est au nord-ouest, Beauchemin, 1966.
La Saguenay legendaire, Beauchemin, 1967.
Louis Jobin, statuaire, Beauchemin, 1968.
En Roulant ma boule, National Museum, 1982.
Art of the Totem, Hancock House (Surrey, BC), 1984.
Pantagruel in Canada, National Museum, 1984.
Le Roi Boit, National Museum, 1987.
Marius Barbeau's Photographic Collection: The Nass River, edited by Linda Riley, Canadian Museum of Civilization (Hull, Quebec), 1988.

EDITOR OR COMPILER

(Editor with Edward Sapir) *Folk Songs of French Canada,* Yale University Press (New Haven, CT), 1925.

(Compiler with Paul England) *Chansons canadiennes: French Canadian Folk Songs,* Boston Music (Boston), 1929.

(Editor) *Chansons populaires du Vieux Quebec,* National Museum, 1935; translated by Regina Lenore Shoolman as *Folk-Songs of Old Quebec.*

(Editor with Grace Melvin) *The Indian Speaks,* Macmillan, 1943.

(Editor with Arthur Lismer and Arthur Bourinot) *Come a Singing! Canadian Folk Songs,* Cloutier, 1947.

(Editor with Michael Hornyansky) *The Golden Phoenix, and Other French-Canadian Fairy Tales,* Oxford, 1958.

Also contributor of articles to periodicals, including *Journal of American Folklore* and *Archives de Folklore.*

SIDELIGHTS: Canadian anthropologist Marius Barbeau is best remembered for his expertise in the areas of French Canadian and Native Canadian culture, folklore, and folk music. Completely bilingual in French and English, he published many books in both languages on these and other subjects, as well as biographies of historical figures and artists. Barbeau also authored three novels—*The Downfall of Temlaham, Mountain Cloud,* and *Le Reve de Kamalmouk.* Some of his best-known nonfiction works include a volume he edited with Edward Sapir entitled *Folk Songs of French Canada;* his first publication *Huron and Wyandot Mythology; The Tsimshian, Their Arts and Music; Quebec, Where Ancient France Lingers;* and *Indian Days on the Western Prairies.* Barbeau's legacies as an anthropologist include his linking of modern cultural practices to more ancient cultures—for instance, he traced elements of Northeastern French Canadian culture back to medieval France, and elements of the culture of the Native Canadian Tsimshian tribe back to Asian ancestors. In addition to his numerous writings, Barbeau was a guest lecturer at many universities; according to Edith Fowke in *Dictionary of Literary Biography,* "he spared no effort to preserve and promote folklore in as many ways as he could." He is also responsible for the collection of thousands of traditional Canadian folk songs from several different ethnic backgrounds.

Barbeau was born in Sainte-Marie-de-la-Beauce, Quebec, in 1883. His father was a horse dealer. Barbeau himself thought to pursue a career in law and was admitted to the bar in 1907, but he accepted a Rhodes scholarship that same year and traveled to England to study anthropology, ethnology, and archaeology at Oxford University. He completed a degree in anthropology there, and lingered an extra semester investigating the ethnology of Native North American songs.

In 1911, Barbeau returned to Canada and took a position with the National Museum of Canada. Some of his first fieldwork explored the Huron Indian reserve at Notre-Dame-de-Lorette, not far from Quebec City. Limited by the technology of the times, he recorded songs and tales sung by an elderly Huron on wax cylinders developed by U.S. inventor Thomas Edison. Many such recordings of French Canadian and Native Canadian lore made by Barbeau still exist solely in the wax cylinder format. The research Barbeau did with this particular settlement of Hurons formed the basis for his first anthropological book, *Huron and Wyandot Mythology,* which saw print in 1915.

Barbeau subsequently studied the Salish tribes and other Native Canadians of the Northeast Woodlands region. Similarities he discovered between Native Canadian tales and legends popular among Canadians of French ancestry provoked his curiosity about French Canadian lore and custom. He was encouraged in this interest by famed anthropologist Franz Boas, whose acquaintance he had made before the publication of *Huron and Wyandot Mythology.* Barbeau traveled along the St. Lawrence River in 1916, recording French songs and folktales and discovering that there was much material to be added to that already found in Ernest Gagnon's landmark 1865 work, *Chansons populaires du Canada.*

Barbeau's investigations into anthropology and folklore informed his novels. The first of these, *The Downfall of Temlaham,* saw print in 1928. Based on historical events, the book tells, according to Fowke, "of a disturbance among the Indians of the Upper Skeena River in 1886 that shows the Indians' ambivalence toward the white man's civilization." Barbeau's second work of fiction, 1944's *Mountain Cloud,* reflected the anthropologist's interest in the blending of French and Native Canadian cultures, and concerned, in Fowke's words, "the custom of fur traders mating with Indian women, contrasting a Scotsman who deserts his Indian wife with a French-Canadian who shares his life with an Indian girl." Barbeau's third novel, *Le Reve de Kamalmouk,* was published in French in 1948.

Barbeau's contributions to Canadian anthropology were honored during his lifetime. In addition to several honorary doctorates, he received medals and awards and was named Companion of the Order of Canada in 1966. He continued to write on anthropological and folkloric matters until his death in 1969, and some of his works have been published posthumously, including *Art of the Totem* and *Pantagruel in Canada.*

BIOGRAPHICAL/CRITICAL SOURCES:

BOOKS

Dictionary of Literary Biography, Volume 92: *Canadian Writers, 1890-1920,* Gale, 1990.

PERIODICALS

Ethnomusicology, Volume 16, 1970, pp. 129-42.
Journal of American Folklore, Volume 74, 1961, pp. 374-78; Volume 82, 1969, pp. 264-66.*

—Sketch by Elizabeth Wenning

*   *   *

BEAUCHEMIN, Yves 1941-

PERSONAL: Born June 26, 1941, in Noranda, Quebec, Canada; son of Jean-Marie (a scaler) and Therese Maurice (a teacher) Beauchemin; married Viviane St.-Onge (a librarian), May 26, 1973; children: Alexis, Renaud. *Education:* College de Joliette, B.A., 1962; Universite de Montreal, licence es lettres, 1965. *Avocational interests:* Classical music, architecture and urban planning, politics, fine cooking, swimming, walking, travel.

ADDRESSES: Home—247 Saint-Jacques St., Longueuil, Quebec, Canada J4H 3B8. *Agent*—Jacques Fortun, 425 St. Jean Baptiste, Montreal, Canada H2Y 2Z7.

CAREER: Writer. College Universitaire Garneau (secondary school), Quebec City, Quebec, teacher of foreign literature, 1965-66; Universite Laval, Quebec City, Quebec, teacher of French literature, summer, 1966; Holt, Rinehart, and Winston, Montreal, Quebec, editor, 1966-69; Radio-Quebec, Montreal, researcher, 1969—. Associated with movements concerned with the preservation of historic architecture, including Sauvons Montreal, Les Amis de la montagne, 1985-87, and Association des residants du Vieux Longueuil, 1986—.

MEMBER: International PEN (French section), Association des ecrivains de langue francaise (France), Union des ecrivains quebecois (president, 1986-87), Amnesty International, Greenpeace, Societe Saint-Jean-Baptiste de Montreal, Parti quebecois, Heritage Montreal.

AWARDS, HONOURS: Prix France-Quebec from l'Association des ecrivains de langue francaise et l'Association France-Quebec, 1975, for *L'Enfirouape;* Prix des jeunes romanciers du *Journal de Montreal,* Prix de la communaute urbaine de Montreal, and Prix du roman de l'ete, Cannes, France, all 1982, all for *Le Matou;* selected as honorary member of Amnesty International.

WRITINGS:

L'Enfirouape (novel; title means "The Cheated One" or "The Sucker"), Editions La Presse (Montreal), 1974,

definitive edition published as *L'Entourloupe,* Editions Jean Picollec (Paris), 1985.
Le Matou (novel), Editions Quebec/Amerique (Montreal), 1981, translation by Sheila Fischman published as *The Alley Cat,* Holt, 1986.
Cybele (short story), Editions Art Global (Montreal), 1982.
Du sommet d'un arbre (autobiographical sketches; title means "Looking from a Treetop"), Editions Quebec/Amerique, 1986.
Juliette Pomerleau (novel), Editions Quebec/Amerique, 1989, translation by Fischman published as *Juliette,* McClelland & Stewart, 1993.
(With Andrae Ruffo) *Finalement!—les enfants,* Art Global, 1991.
Une histoire a faire japper, [Quebec], 1993.

Also author of *La Vache et d'autres animaux* (title means "The Cow and Other Animals"), a collection of poems for children, and "Sueurs" (title means "Sweat"), a short story published in the anthology *Fuites et poursuites,* both 1982. Author of radio scripts. Contributor of stories and articles to periodicals, including *Sept-jours, Dimensions, Liberte, L'Actualite, Le Devoir, Quebec/Amerique,* and *Dandelion.*

WORK IN PROGRESS: A fourth novel; a children's novel, publication expected in 1990.

ADAPTATIONS: International Cinema Corporation adapted *Le Matou* as a full-length feature film and a television miniseries, both directed by Jean Beaudin, both 1985.

SIDELIGHTS: Yves Beauchemin is one of French Canada's premier writers. Although relatively little known in English-speaking circuits, including those in his own country, Beauchemin has achieved literary fame in Quebec and France, where his 1981 novel *Le Matou* became a best-seller. Subsequently adapted as a feature film and a television miniseries, it is the only one of Beauchemin's books published in English translation, appearing as *The Alley Cat* in 1986. Acclaimed for its vibrancy, comedy, and political concerns, his writing is frequently compared to that of such celebrated nineteenth-century novelists as Charles Dickens and Honore de Balzac. Beauchemin, according to *Boston Globe* writer Robert Taylor, "is a gifted storyteller with a robust sense of humor and a capacity to create memorable characters."

A native of Quebec, Beauchemin is dedicated to preserving his province's French culture and heritage. "I still hope to see an independent Quebec one day," he announced in the *Amherst Daily News.* Beauchemin's strong nationalism is subsequently reflected in his writing. His first novel, the 1974 untranslated *L'Enfirouape,* is roughly based on an actual 1970 kidnapping in Quebec that was politically motivated. Depicting a young and abused hero victimized by a bureaucratic and unfair society, the novel won the Prix France-Quebec in 1975.

After the publication of *L'Enfirouape* Beauchemin spent the following seven years writing *The Alley Cat,* a novel many critics consider a masterful black comedy and political allegory. Set in Montreal, the story introduces Florent Boissonneault, a young and intelligent salesman with a strong desire to own his own restaurant. Florent meets an elderly and eccentric foreigner named Ratablavasky who acts as his benefactor, and he contracts a partnership with an Anglo friend named Slipskin to open a small eatery. As the restaurant succeeds, however, Florent becomes unaccountably weary and finds that he must sell out to Slipskin. He later discovers that he had been slowly poisoned by his partner, who conspired with Ratablavasky to defraud Florent of his life savings. Struggling to regain his restaurant and self-respect, Florent experiences a series of misadventures, encountering such colorful characters as a profane eight-year-old alcoholic, a hot-tempered French chef, and an absent-minded priest.

The Alley Cat garnered rave reviews. Deeming the work "a masterpiece that ought to put Beauchemin on the Canadian literary map," Toronto *Star*'s Judith Fitzgerald lauded: "Raucous, endearing and slightly mad, *The Alley Cat* stands as an imaginative testament to mordant wit and sardonic humor." Praising Beauchemin's characters who "leap off the page and rival the comic creations of Moliere," Fitzgerald added, "Beauchemin's genius lies in his ability to keep readers on the edge of the edge." William Johnson in the *Globe and Mail* agreed: "What impresses is the sheer profusion of everything, imagery, constantly refreshed, page after page. Humor, fantasy, observation, charm. Memorable characters." Writing in the *San Francisco Chronicle Review,* Richard Smoley proclaimed *The Alley Cat* "a very enjoyable book," finding it "rich, humorous and just a little bit creepy." And hailing the novel's "irrepressible metropolitan gusto" reminiscent of Dickens, Taylor labeled *The Alley Cat* "The Great Montreal Novel."

Though enjoyed by many reviewers as a picaresque adventure, *The Alley Cat* was also recognized as an allegory of French Canada's struggle for independence from Anglo domination. Some non-Quebecois critics were troubled by Beauchemin's political implications in the novel. Deciding that "a certain grumpiness has colored the French Canadian view of the non-French-speaking world" since New France was conquered by the British in 1759, Bob Coleman in the *New York Times Book Review* found "that grumpiness" to be "a fundamental flaw" in *The Alley Cat.* Coleman explained: "Beauchemin . . . displays prejudices and hostilities so deep his novel is more often bleak and portentous. . . . The French-speaking and the poor are so regularly virtuous, and Anglo-Canadians and

Americans are so regularly scum." Likewise, Judith Freeman in the *Los Angeles Times Book Review* observed, "There's a mean vein running down the center of this book, a subterranean streak of misanthropy."

Despite their criticism, detractors of *The Alley Cat* were greatly impressed with Beauchemin's talent. Coleman, for example, found the author's prose "energetic, inventive, and charmingly colloquial." He conceded: "Mr. Beauchemin is certainly gifted." And although Doug Beardsley in British Columbia's *Times-Colonist* remarked that a "disturbing irritation arises" from the novel's "anti-Anglo overtones," he nonetheless noted that the author's dynamism earns him the title of "the Balzac of Canadian fiction." The reviewer extolled *The Alley Cat* as a celebration of French-Canadian heritage: "[It] is a baroque novel filled with action. There is much joy, diversity, and pathos in Beauchemin's writing. It is often funny, satiric, complex, and always Quebec. . . . What we have here are the mazes of coincidences and red herrings of a life lived on the edge of the rich and savory oral tradition of Quebecois literature."

In addition to English, *The Alley Cat* has appeared in fifteen other languages, including Swedish, Norwegian, Danish, and Portuguese. Beauchemin is the author of various other titles, as yet untranslated from the French. His short stories have been published in numerous French-Canadian publications. *Du sommet d'un arbre,* a collection of autobiographical pieces Beauchemin wrote for CBC Radio, was published in 1986.

Beauchemin told *CA:* "I began to write around the age of seventeen. I learned very much about writing through reading Honore de Balzac, Charles Dickens, and John Steinbeck, and Russian authors such as Mikhail Bulgakov, Anton Chekhov, Leo Tolstoy, Ivan Turgenev, and Nikolai Gogol.

"I am guided by three firm beliefs in my work as a writer. First, the chief aim of literature is the enjoyment of the reader. A boring book has a sociological and historical existence, but it has no real literary existence because it has no readers (except possibly a few specialists). Second, pleasing at all cost is a trap because it forces the writer to rely only on tricks of the trade and, therefore, to shun any kind of originality. Without originality, of course, there is no genuine creation. Third, in literature as well as in science (as well as in anything), a person speaks well only of what he or she knows. Ernest Hemingway said something like that somewhere, I think. The aim (very ambitious, I readily admit) that I have determined for myself in writing fiction is to try to convey to my compatriots part of the world that I know well: Quebec. And if, while doing this, I am successful in remaining myself and in being just with my subject, I will perhaps have a chance to be understood by others, because I will have spoken of the human condition."

BIOGRAPHICAL/CRITICAL SOURCES:

BOOKS

Cagnon, Maurice, *The French Novel of Quebec,* Twayne, 1986.

Dictionary of Literary Biography, Volume 60: *Canadian Writers since 1960, Second Series,* Gale, 1987.

PERIODICALS

Amherst Daily News (Nova Scotia), May 13, 1986.
Boston Globe, December 24, 1986.
Globe and Mail (Toronto), June 19, 1981; March 22, 1986.
Los Angeles Times, May 24, 1990, section E, p. 12.
Los Angeles Times Book Review, November 9, 1986.
New York Times Book Review, January 11, 1987.
Philadelphia Inquirer, January 25, 1987.
San Francisco Chronicle Review, November 16, 1986.
Star (Toronto), April 27, 1986.
Times-Colonist (Victoria, British Columbia), May 11, 1986.
Winnipeg Free Press, May 9, 1986; May 10, 1986.

—*Sketch by Janice E. Drane*

*   *   *

BERNARD, Harry   1898-1979
(L'Illettre)

PERSONAL: Born May 9, 1898, in London, England; immigrated to Canada; died May 16, 1979, in Saint-Hyacinthe, Quebec, Canada; son of J. Horace and Alexandra (Boudreau) Bernard; married Louella Tobin (marriage ended); married Alice Sicotte; children: Louella, Marcelle. *Education:* Seminary de Saint-Hyacinthe, B.A., 1918; University of Montreal, Licence es Lettres, 1943, Litt.D., 1948. *Religion:* Roman Catholic. *Avocational interests:* Fishing, swimming, outdoor life.

CAREER: Le Droit, Ottawa, Ontario, Canada, assistant editor and parliamentary correspondent, 1919-23; *Le Courrier de Saint-Hyacinthe,* Saint-Hyacinthe, Quebec, 1923-70, became editor-in-chief. *L'Action Nationale,* director, 1933-34.

MEMBER: Union Nationale, Association des Hebdomadaires du Quebec.

AWARDS, HONOURS: Prix David for best novel of the year, 1924, for *L'Homme tombe,* and 1925, for *La Terre vivante;* Prix David for literature, 1931, for *Juana, mon aimee;* Pierre Chauveau Medal, Royal Society of Canada, 1959; Prix Oliver Asselin for journalism, Societe Saint-Jean-Baptiste de Montreal, 1961; awarded the Prix d'Action Intellectuelle six times.

WRITINGS:

L'Homme tombe (novel; title means "The Fallen Man"), Albert Levesque (Montreal), 1924.
La Terre vivante (novel; title means "The Living Earth", Bibliotheque de l'Action Francaise (Montreal), 1925.
La Maison vide (novel; title means "The Empty House"), Bibliotheque de l'Action Francaise, 1926.
La Dame blanche (short stories), Bibliotheque de l'Action Francaise, 1927.
Essais critiques (essays), Librairie d'Action Canadienne-Francais, 1929.
La Ferme des pins (title means "The Farm in the Pines"), Librairie d'Action Canadienne-Francais, 1930.
Juana, mon aimee, Albert Levesque, 1931.
Dolores, Albert Levesque, 1932.
Montcalm se fache (short stories), Albert Levesque, 1935.
Le Roman regionaliste aux Etats-Unis (1913-1940) (nonfiction; title means "The Regional Novel in the United States"), Fides (Montreal), 1949.
Les Jours sont longs (novel; title means "The Days Are Long"), Cercle du Livre de France (Montreal), 1951.
Portages et routes d'eau en Haute-Mauricie (travel and woodlore), Editions du Bien Public (Trois-Rivieres, Quebec), 1953.

Also author of *ABC du Petit naturaliste canadien* (nature studies), volume 1, 1936, volume 2, 1946; work represented in numerous periodicals, including *Enseignement Secondaire au Canada* and *Memoires de la Societe Royale du Canada;* contributor of articles and literary reviews to newspapers under the pseudonym L'Illettre.

SIDELIGHTS: Harry Bernard spent much of his life as a writer, journalist, and scholar in the Quebec community of Saint-Hyacinthe. The novelist settled there after immigrating from his native England as a young adult, receiving a degree from a seminary in the French-Canadian city in 1918 before joining the staff of *Le Courrier de Saint-Hyacinthe.* During his five decades as a journalist, however, Bernard also worked toward his doctorate degree from the University of Montreal and penned numerous novels distinguished by their depiction of French-Canadian life in the early twentieth century. The author was primarily interested in portraying the strong sense of nationalism among French-speaking Canadians in Quebec and the corrupting influence of modern life on their rural, farm-oriented way of life.

Bernard's first book, *L'Homme tombe* ("The Fallen Man") was published in 1924. It is the tale of a young doctor who marries a woman his family considers unworthy. Through the course of the novel, his conservative mother is proven correct as both the weak-willed wife and the hapless doctor fall prey to the glittering social whirl of city life. Rosanna Furgiuele, in an essay on Bernard for the

Dictionary of Literary Biography, observed that in *L'Homme tombe* Bernard's moralistic plot "illustrates how the illusory pleasures of city life, far from generating happiness, are instrumental in destroying family ties and in bringing about man's downfall."

This idea became a recurring theme throughout Bernard's body of work, especially in the trio of novels he wrote following *L'Homme tombe.* In 1925's *La Terre vivante* ("The Living Earth"), the patriarch of a farm family is heartbroken that all three of his children move to the city and are supremely disinterested in carrying on the agricultural traditions of their ancestors. The novel concludes happily, however, when a daughter jilted by her urban suitor returns and takes up with a neighboring lad. They eventually marry and settle on her family's land, thus insuring that the family's legacy is continued. *La Maison vide* ("The Empty House"), published in 1926, chronicles the decline of the Dumontiers, an affluent French-Canadian Catholic family residing in an Ottawa suburb. Seduced by the meaningless round of social activity that urban life offers, the offspring lose all sense of family and community; in the end, their moral deterioration is symbolized by a daughter's marriage to a Protestant English-speaking Canadian. Through these and other condemning actions in the plots of the novels, Bernard conveys a clear admonishment against the mixture of French and English cultures in Canada.

Assimilation through intermarriage again returns as a central theme in 1930's *La Ferme des pins* ("The Farm in the Pines"). Attempting to present another side of the French-English issue, the novel chronicles the adult years of James Robertson, an English-speaking Canadian who marries a French-Canadian woman. As the years progress he begins to consider his marriage a mistake in judgment and tries to prevent his children from straying down the same path. In the end, he purchases farmland in Ontario, among English-speaking Canadians, that will become a new homestead for future generations. "The themes presented in these three novels reiterate the agricultural ideology prevalent in French-Canadian regional literature of the time," wrote Furgiuele. "The characters lack depth and can be reduced to stereotypes whose primary function is to illustrate a moral."

Bernard's fifth novel, *Juana, mon aimee,* appeared in 1931 and is an attempt to break away from the formulaic style of the earlier works. A love story set in the Canadian prairies, it recounts the meeting of Raymond, an Ontario journalist, and a woman named Juana at a health spa in Saskatchewan. Interwoven throughout the romantic narrative are vivid descriptions of the beauty of the Saskatchewan landscape and the unique character of its pioneer settlers. In *Juana,* for the first time, Bernard attempts a more in-depth analysis of the characters' motiva-

tion. In his final novel, 1951's *Les Jours sont longs* ("The Days Are Long"), an aging narrator recounts his fulfilled life spent in the Canadian forest and the women he loved. Furgiuele described Bernard's sixth novel as "undoubtedly his most polished and convincing work . . . [showing] a marked improvement in literary technique and psychological analysis."

Over the course of Bernard's career his literary efforts were blessed with critical and commercial success and the writer was frequently bestowed with prestigious Canadian literary awards. Although already enjoying a dual career as a journalist and author, Bernard worked toward becoming a scholar of the genre of regional literature to which his own novels belonged. In 1948 he received his doctorate from the University of Montreal; his thesis, a survey of over three thousand examples of regional literature of the United States, was published in 1949 as *Le Roman regionaliste aux Etats-Unis (1913-1940)* ("The Regional Novel in the United States"). In addition to his earlier roster of novels, Bernard also penned a collection of short stories based on events in Canadian history (*La Dame blanche,* 1927) and a series of essays published in 1929 as *Essais critiques.* Furgiuele summarized his career and maintained that despite some shortcomings as a writer, Bernard "left his mark on the regional literature of French Canada and played a role in the development of the French-Canadian psychological novel."

BIOGRAPHICAL/CRITICAL SOURCES:

BOOKS

Dictionary of Literary Biography, Volume 92: *Canadian Writers, 1800-1920,* Gale, 1990.*

*   *   *

BERNE, Eric (Lennard) 1910-1970 (Lennard Gandalac, Ramsbottom Horsely, Peter Pinto, Cyprian St. Cyr)

PERSONAL: Born May 10, 1910, in Montreal, Quebec, Canada; became U.S. citizen, 1943; died July 15, 1970, in Monterey, CA; son of David Hillel (a physician) and Sara (Gordon) Berne; twice married (once to Dorothy DeMass, 1949), twice divorced; children: Ellen, Peter, Ricky, Terry; stepchildren: Robert Way, Janice Way (Mrs. Michael Farlinger). *Education:* McGill University, B.A., 1931, M.D. and C.M., 1935; attended Yale Psychiatric Clinic, 1936-38, New York Psychoanalytic Institute, 1941-43, and San Francisco Psychoanalytic Institute, 1947-56.

CAREER: U.S. Army, consultant to Surgeon General, 1951-54; Mount Zion Hospital, San Francisco, CA, adjunct psychiatrist, 1952-70; Langley Porter Neuropsychiatric Clinic, San Francisco, lecturer, 1960-70; McAuley Clinic, San Francisco, consultant in group therapy, 1962-70. Visiting lecturer, Stanford-Palo Alto Psychiatric Clinic, 1961-63. Diplomate of American Board of Psychiatry and Neurology. Conductor of free seminars for other therapists, San Francisco, 1958-70. *Military service:* U.S. Army, Medical Corps, 1943-46; became major.

MEMBER: American Psychiatric Association (fellow), American Medical Association, American Association for the Advancement of Science, International Transactional Analysis Association (founder; former chair of board), Indian Psychiatric Society.

WRITINGS:

The Mind in Action, Simon & Schuster, 1947, revised edition published as *Layman's Guide to Psychiatry and Psychoanalysis,* 1957, 3rd edition, 1968.
Transactional Analysis in Psychotherapy: A Systematic Individual and Social Psychiatry, Grove, 1961, reprinted, Ballantine, 1978.
The Structure and Dynamics of Organizations and Groups, Lippincott, 1963.
Games People Play: The Psychology of Human Relationships, Grove, 1964.
Principles of Group Treatment, Oxford University Press, 1966.
The Happy Valley (juvenile), Grove, 1968.
Sex in Human Loving, Simon & Schuster, 1970.
What Do You Say after You Say Hello?: The Psychology of Human Destiny, Grove, 1972.
Transactional Analysis Bulletin, Selected Articles from Volumes 1 through 9, edited by Paul McCormick, TA Press, 1976.
Intuition and Ego States: The Origins of Transactional Analysis, TA Press, 1977.
Hello Sigmund, This Is Eric, edited by L. H. Forman and J. S. Ramsburg, Sheed Andrews, 1978.
Beyond Games and Scripts, edited by Claude M. Steiner and Carmen Kerr, Ballantine, 1978.

Author of pieces under various pseudonyms, including Lennard Gandalac, Ramsbottom Horsely, Peter Pinto, and Cyprian St. Cyr. Contributor to psychiatric and other journals. Editor of *Transactional Analysis Bulletin,* 1962-70.

ADAPTATIONS: A musical comedy version of *Games People Play* was adapted for Broadway production by Cy Feuer and Ernest Martin.

SIDELIGHTS: "Life is really very simple," Eric Berne once said. "But if people have to face that fact they get very upset. So they invent religions and pastimes and games. These are the same people who then lament how awful it is that life is complicated. But all complications involve decisions, and a person must assess the probabilities and possibilities, make the best decision and then go down the street whistling."

After listening to his patients relating "games" for some thirty years, Berne decided to gather certain of these breezily-named games into a catalog. At first *Games People Play* was not a success. But three years after its publication, following much word-of-mouth praise, it set a record for remaining on the best-seller list longer than any other nonfictional work in the past ten years and sold over 2,500,000 copies.

Games People Play caused the more staid members of Berne's profession to wince at what they believed to be facile explanations of human interactions. A *Times Literary Supplement* reviewer called the book "little more than psychiatric gimmickry, a parlour game foisted upon the social exchanges common in daily life. . . . By no stretch of the imagination can the book be regarded as a contribution to psychological or psychiatric theory." Other reviewers, such as Ian Jeffries, found the book "fascinating and instructive." Jeffries added: "The question that arises is whether the author has made a real contribution to psychology: and the surprising answer, I think, is that he has. Not only does he offer a thesaurus of social transactions with their explanations and titles, but he does so in a way that makes social learning or training in group psychology quicker and less painful processes. The actual correctness of his scheme is more difficult to judge, but what he says is plausible." In 1967, Berne explained the book's success: "It's the recognition factor—some of us recognize ourselves, some recognize other people."

In many of his writings Berne advanced a theory which he called "transactional analysis," and which one young psychiatrist believes to be "an offshoot of psychoanalysis. It's a useful method of treatment, but it's thoroughly grounded in Freud." Transactions, according to Berne, are "the overt manifestations of social intercourse." Jack Langguth summarized Berne's method of analyzing these transactions: "Where Freud probed forces below the conscious level, Dr. Berne deals chiefly with the three 'different and inconsistent' selves—or ego states—that he believes alternate in speaking for each person. First there is the ego state which 'resembles that of parental figures.' The Parent, at its most benevolent, is the confident self that knows which fork to use, which temptations to resist. At worst, the Parent may crush all joyousness. . . . Second there is the ego state which 'is autonomously directed toward objective appraisal of reality.' This is the Adult. . . . Third, the ego state which 'was fixated in early childhood.' . . . The Child may be charming in its spontaneity or embarrassing in its willful folly." The objective of transactional analysis is to assist the patient in programming his personality in order to allow the proper ego state to function at the proper time. As Berne once put it: "We want to turn frogs into princes. We're not satisfied with making them braver frogs."

BIOGRAPHICAL/CRITICAL SOURCES:

PERIODICALS

American Journal of Public Health, November, 1963.
American Journal of Sociology, May, 1964.
Life, December 18, 1970.
Newsday, November 28, 1970.
New Statesman, April 29, 1966.
New York Times, July 16, 1970, July 17, 1972.
New York Times Book Review, April, 1967, October 8, 1967, May 11, 1969.
New York Times Magazine, July 17, 1966.
Times Literary Supplement, June 30, 1966.
Tulane Drama Review, summer, 1967.

*   *   *

BESSETTE, Gerard   1920-

PERSONAL: Born February 25, 1920, in Sainte-Anne-de-Sabrevois, Quebec, Canada; son of Jean-Baptiste and Victoria (Bertrand) Bessette; married Irene Bakowska (an attorney, law librarian, and professor), September 3, 1971. *Education:* University of Montreal, B.A., 1941, licence en lettres and M.A., 1946, D.Litt., 1950.

ADDRESSES: Home—270 Frontenac Street, Kingston, Ontario K7L 3S8. *Office*—Department of French, Queen's University, Kingston, Ontario K7L 3N6.

CAREER: University of Saskatchewan, Saskatoon, instructor, 1946-49, assistant professor of French, 1949-51; Duquesne University, Pittsburgh, PA, assistant professor of French, 1952-58; Royal Military College, Kingston, Ontario, associate professor of French, 1958-60; Queen's University, Kingston, professor of French, 1960—.

MEMBER: Royal Society of Canada, Societe des ecrivains canadiens, Union des ecrivains quebecois.

AWARDS, HONOURS: Olympic Games, 1948, bronze medal; Literary Prize of Quebec, 1965, for *L'incubation;* Governor General's Award, 1966, for *L'incubation,* and 1972, for *Le Cycle;* Prix David, 1980.

WRITINGS:

Poems temporels, Regain, 1954.
La Bagarre (novel), Cercle du Livre, 1958, translation by Marc Lebel and Ronald Sutherland published as *The Brawl,* Harvest House, 1976.

Le Libraire (novel), Rene Julliard, 1960, translation by Glen Shortliffe published as *Not for Every Eye,* Macmillan (Toronto), 1962.
Les Images en poesie canadienne-francaise (criticism), Beauchemin, 1960.
Les Pedagogues (novel), Cercle du Livre, 1960.
L'incubation (novel), Librarie Deom, 1965, translation by Shortliffe published as *Incubation,* Macmillan, 1967.
Une Litterature en ebullition (criticism), Editions du Jour, 1968.
Le Cycle (novel), Editions du Jour, 1971, translation by A. D. Martin-Sperry published as *The Cycle,* Exile Editions (Toronto), 1991.
Trois romanciers quebecois (criticism), Editions du Jour, 1973.
La Commensale (novel), Editions Quinze, 1975.
Les Anthropoides (novel), Editions La Presse, 1977.
Mes romans et moi, Editions Hurtubise, 1979.
Le Semestre, Editions Quebec-Amerique (Montreal), 1979.
La Garden-Party de Christophine, Editions Quebec/Amerique, 1980.
Les Dires d'Omer Marin: roman/journal, Editions Quebec/Amerique, 1985.

Also contributor to anthologies, including *Anthologie d'Albert Laberge,* 1962, and *De Quebec a Saint-Boniface,* 1968.

A collection of Bessette's papers is housed at the Bibliotheque nationale du Quebec, and Hubert Larocque has created a series of computerized concordances of Bessette's works.

SIDELIGHTS: Gerard Bessette's 1971 novel, *The Cycle,* translated into English twenty years later by A. D. Martin-Sperry, "continues the experimentation with stream-of-consciousness techniques that began with his 1965 novel *L'incubation (Incubation,* 1967)," commented Paul Stuewe in a review published in *Books in Canada.* The novel features seven narrators brought together by the death of their relative, Norbert Barre. Each narrator speaks in a distinctive voice, adding to the aggregate information imparted to the reader. The seemingly innocuous recollections and revelations of the speakers eventually reveal a tortured family life hidden behind an apparently ordinary and normal facade. Jo-Anne Elder remarked in *Canadian Literature* that Martin-Sperry successfully translates the seven disparate speakers, comparing this feat with listening to "seven melodies at a time." Elder added that, even in translation, all seven narrators "retain their distinctions of age, sex, [and] family relation," although the critic acknowledged that some subtleties "are more easily heard than others."

Throughout each speaker's voice in *The Cycle,* Bessette utilizes punctuation in distinctive ways to affect communication and comprehension. Stuewe notes that once readers adjust to Bessette's unusual use of hyphens and parentheses, *"The Cycle* offers a challenging and ultimately fascinating literary experience from an author who deserves to be better known among English-Canadian readers."

BIOGRAPHICAL/CRITICAL SOURCES:

BOOKS

Bessette, Gerard, *Mes romans et moi,* Editions Hurtubise, 1979.
Robidoux, Rejean, *La Creation de Gerard Bessette,* Editions Quebec/Amerique, 1987.
Robidoux, Rejean, *Livres et auteurs quebecois,* Editions Jumonville, 1971.
Smart, Patricia, editor, *Litterature canadienne-francaise,* University Press of Montreal, 1969.

PERIODICALS

Books in Canada, April, 1988, p. 34.
Canadian Literature, spring, 1991, pp. 159-61.
Queen's Quarterly, spring, 1989, pp. 183-84.*

*   *   *

BIRNEY, (Alfred) Earle   1904-1995

PERSONAL: Born May 13, 1904, in Calgary, Alberta; died September 3, 1995, in Toronto; son of William George and Martha (Robertson) Birney; married Esther Bull, April 7, 1937 (divorced, 1977); children: William. *Education:* University of British Columbia, B.A., 1926; University of Toronto, M.A., 1927, Ph.D., 1936; attended University of California, 1927-30, and University of London, 1934-35. *Avocational interests:* Travel and sports—formerly mountain climbing, now swimming.

ADDRESSES: Home—130 Carlton St., #1204, Toronto, Ontario, Canada M5A 4K3.

CAREER: University of British Columbia, Vancouver, lecturer during summer sessions, 1927-34, 1936-37; University of Utah, Salt Lake City, instructor in English, 1930-32, 1933-34; University of Toronto, Toronto, Ontario, Leonard fellow, 1932-33, lecturer, 1936-41, assistant professor of English, 1941-42; Canadian Broadcasting Corp. (CBC), Montreal, Quebec, supervisor of foreign language shortwave programs to Europe, 1945-46; University of British Columbia, professor of English literature, 1946-63, professor of creative writing and chair of department, 1963-65; University of Toronto, writer in residence, 1965- 67; University of Waterloo, Waterloo, Ontario, writer in residence, 1967-68; University of Western On-

tario, London, writer in residence, 1981-82. Visiting professor, University of Oregon, 1961, and University of California, 1968. Lectured in Japan and India, 1958, U.S. West Coast, 1960, and Latin America, 1962. Contributor of plays, talks, and readings to CBC "Transcanada" radio programs, 1945—; has made frequent appearances on CBC television panels, 1955—. *Military service:* Canadian Army, 1940-45; became major.

MEMBER: Royal Society of Canada (fellow).

AWARDS, HONOURS: Governor-General's medal for poetry, 1943, for *David and Other Poems,* and 1946, for *Now Is Time;* Stephen Leacock Medal for Humour, 1949, for *Turvey;* Borestone Mountain prize, 1951; Canadian government fellowship to France, 1953; Lorne Pierce Gold Medal, Royal Society of Canada, 1953; President's Medal for Poetry, University of Western Ontario, 1954; Nuffield fellowship, 1958-59; Canada Council traveling fellowships, 1962-63, 1968, 1970-71, 1973, and 1974-75; LL.D., University of Alberta, 1965; Canada Council Medal, 1968; Order of Canada, 1972; Canada Council senior arts fellowship, 1978-80; D.Litt., McGill University, 1979; named Officer of the Order of Canada, 1981; Litt.D., University of Western Ontario, 1981; honorary degree from University of British Columbia, 1987.

WRITINGS:

POEMS

David and Other Poems, Ryerson, 1942.
Now Is Time, Ryerson, 1945.
Strait of Anian, Ryerson, 1948.
Ice Cod Bell or Stone, McClelland & Stewart, 1962.
Near False Creek Mouth, McClelland & Stewart, 1964.
Selected Poems: 1940-1966, McClelland & Stewart, 1966.
Memory No Servant, New Books, 1968.
Poems, McClelland & Stewart, 1969.
Pnomes, Jukollages and Other Stunzas, Gronk Press, 1969.
Rag and Bone Shop, McClelland & Stewart, 1971.
The Bear on the Delhi Road, Chatto & Windus, 1973.
What's So Big about Green?, McClelland & Stewart, 1973.
Collected Poems, two volumes, McClelland & Stewart, 1975.
Alphabeings and Other Seasyours (visual poems), Pikadilly Press, 1976.
Ghost in the Wheels, McClelland & Stewart, 1977.
Fall by Fury, McClelland & Stewart, 1978.
Copernican Fix, ECW Press, 1985.
Last Makings, McClelland & Stewart, 1991.

Also author of *The Rugging and the Moving Times,* 1976, and *The Mammoth Corridors,* 1980.

Birney's poems have been translated and published in fifteen languages, including French, Spanish, Italian, Greek,

Romanian, Hungarian, Russian, Finnish, Dutch, Malayan, Chinese, Japanese and Swahili.

EDITOR

Twentieth Century Canadian Poetry (anthology), Ryerson, 1953.

Record of Service of the University of British Columbia in the Second World War, University of British Columbia Press, 1955.

(With Margerie Lowry) *Selected Poems of Malcolm Lowry,* City Lights, 1962.

(With Lowry) Malcolm Lowry, *Lunar Caustic* (novella), Grossman, 1962.

Also co-editor of *New Voices,* 1956.

OTHER

Turvey (novel), McClelland & Stewart, 1949, unexpurgated edition, 1976.

Trial of a City (verse play), Ryerson, 1952.

Down the Long Table (novel), McClelland & Stewart, 1955.

The Creative Writer (radio talks), Canadian Broadcasting Corp., 1966.

The Cow Jumped over the Moon: The Writing and Reading of Poetry (literary criticism), Holt, 1972.

The Damnation of Vancouver (verse play), McClelland & Stewart, 1977.

Big Bird in the Bush (short stories and sketches), Valley Editions, 1978.

Spreading Time: Remarks on Canadian Writing, 1926-1979 (autobiography), Vehicule Press, 1980.

(With Beryl Rowland) *Essays on Chaucerian Irony* (literary criticism), University of Toronto Press, 1985.

Words on Waves (radio plays), CBC Enterprises, 1985.

Also author, with J. Copithorne, B. Bissett, and A. Suknaski, of *Four Parts Sand,* 1972. Contributor to journals in Canada, the United States, Great Britain, Europe, New Zealand, and Australia. Literary editor, *Canadian Forum,* 1936-40; editor, *Canadian Poetry,* 1946-48; editor in chief, *Prism International,* 1964-65; advisory editor, *New American and Canadian Poetry,* 1966-70.

ADAPTATIONS: World Records recorded Birney reading sixty of his poems, set to music, in 1982.

SIDELIGHTS: Dubbed "a chronicler of Canada" by Desmond Pacey in his book *Ten Canadian Poets,* Earle Birney is regarded as one of the country's finest poets. Fred Cogswell of *Canadian Literature* writes: "Earle Birney, more than any other I poet know, is typical in thought and outlook of the average liberal-minded Canadian. . . . He is rare among our writers in his ability to use forms derived from the whole tradition of poetry to express brilliantly and freshly whatever insight he does have. Moreover, he has an intelligent dedication to his craft that only a professional can possess."

According to W. E. Fredeman of the *British Columbia Library Quarterly,* Birney's poetry can be divided into five major categories: satires, descriptions of war, nature, and love, and poems built on narrative or dramatic situations involving one or more of the other four categories. Due to Birney's extensive travels, his poems frequently become observations of life as seen through the eyes of a traveler (in a geographic as well as a spiritual sense); even his "Canadian" poems are the work of a man who obviously feels very much like a stranger in his own country. A common thread which runs through many of the poems is the theme of man's efforts as a microcosm to come to terms with the macrocosm (society, nature, and so on) within the brief space of a single lifetime. And all of them, claims Fredeman, are "autobiographical and extremely personal." In addition, Fredeman feels that "Birney's poetry is obviously didactic, but rarely in the pejorative sense, for it seldom preaches. [The philosophy it offers the reader is] a broad humanism positing individual involvement and responsibility combined with an insistence on the absolute autonomy of the human will." This will is "expressed with masculine forcefulness in both imagery and diction [which] protects Birney from the snare of sentimental didacticism."

Birney's skill as a satirist, according to most critics, is based on his natural instinct for identifying the ironic and ridiculous aspects of human behavior and, as Derek Stanford of *Books and Bookmen* puts it, on his "nose for the picaresque situation." Much of this satire appears in the form of clever sound and word play (often making use of the idiosyncracies of various dialects or of a particular professional jargon), a field in which Birney is considered an expert. George Woodcock writes in *Queen's Quarterly:* "Birney has always been ready to wear the mask and motley of the clown, in prose and in verse, but he has generally avoided the easy and empty facetiousness of the professional funny man; his comedy . . . is rather of the type— full of verbal quippery and social implication—that we once associated with the Marx Brothers. It is stringent, intelligent, irreverent, and a little irascible." William Walsh of the *Lugano Review,* referring to Birney's humor as "graven-faced and gravelled-voiced," claims that it nonetheless has a buoyancy and balance which sets it apart from ordinary humor. "It has to do with its having nothing abstractly or specifically comic about it. . . . The comic is simply a constituent of the vision and the poetry. It is because he evokes the actual with such presence and authenticity that what is comic in it—and the alert eye can always discern it—strikes one as just and irresistible."

An experimentalist by nature, Birney frequently relies on visual effects (such as a lack of punctuation, unusual spacing, two-tone print, and different type sizes) to add another dimension to his poetry (though his earlier work was written in a conventional manner Birney has since revised it to conform to his new style). These attempts, however, generally have not been well-received. Andy Wainwright of *Saturday Night* feels that in Birney's "concrete poems" (poems about buildings written in the shape of buildings, for example) "there is very little depth for the reader to draw on [they] contain the assumption that the linear aspect of poetry is not alive and to make it so one must make pictures with words. But they defeat their own purpose for, in giving his close attention to the word antics, the reader remains firmly rooted to the printed page. . . . Concrete poetry, in Birney's case, is a placing of style before content, and the content suffers as a result." George Bowering of *Canadian Literature* writes: "I still feel that all this is not really the avantgarde. Birney is usually, in these japes, doing something exciting and playful for his own amusement, and that is okay. But the reader is not similarly energized."

Hayden Carruth, commenting in the critical study *Earle Birney,* is somewhat more vehement in his criticism of the poet's visual experiments: "Mr. Birney is insensitive to the actual value of space in the typographical re-presentation of a poem. For what do his spaces accomplish? Exactly what his commas, semi-colons, and period accomplished [in the original versions], except that the spaces are harder to read and distractive. . . . The point is that space can be used to do something which cannot be done otherwise, and this is its appropriate use; Mr. Birney seems unaware of it. . . . What [he] has done . . . has no reasonable explanation whatever. It is prosodic fiddle-faddle."

Despite this criticism of Birney's long-standing interest in visual effects, most critics agree that in other respects he is a master of his craft. A reviewer for the *Times Literary Supplement* writes: "Earle Birney is not to be judged as a Canadian poet. In his best work Canada often provides the landscape for his fable or the referents of his argument, but never the limits of his language and imagination. . . . No poet draws upon a richer vocabulary—literary and colloquial, scientific and common. Few poets can handle so wide a range of rhythmic patterns so expressively. Even fewer have Birney's skill in dramatizing an action or anecdote. His ability to capture every level of variety of English speech is at least as rare. Only his ironic humour belongs to many modern poets." Walsh cites Birney's "gift for cut and graven detail, a flowing empathy and a natural rhythm in which the breathing meets the sense to produce an evolving, living line" as one of the poet's chief strengths. He continues his praise by pointing out that in Birney's poetry there is "a balance or proportion between subject and object, a wholeness and unity in the former recognizing the fullness and complexity of the latter. A

Birney poem is never—although it is that too—just the evocation of a scene. It always has an intellectual and moral structure. . . . Relaxed, casual and spontaneous [in appearance, it is, in fact,] very cunningly organized."

Commenting on *Selected Poems: 1940-1966,* a collection of poetry which virtually spans Birney's entire career, A. J. M. Smith offers this summation of his contributions to Canadian literature: "Earle Birney is one of our major poets, perhaps since the death of E. J. Pratt our leading poet. Certainly he is the only rival of Pratt as the creator of heroic narrative on a bold scale and, unlike Pratt, he has been consistently experimental. He has not always been successful, and he has sometimes aped styles and fashions that are unworthy of his real talents; but without a somewhat boyish spirit of adventure his successes would have been impossible too. The real triumph of *Selected Poems* is that it demonstrates so clearly and forcibly—as does indeed the whole of Birney's career—a unified personality of great charm, wit, strength, and generosity."

As Earle Birney himself comments at the end of his book *The Cow Jumped over the Moon: The Writing and Reading of Poetry,* "None of us wants merely to live but to affirm life. We all need the therapy of fancy and play, honest emotion, pity, laughter, joy. Especially the joy that comes when the words move someone else from mere living to being Alive, Alive-O!"

BIOGRAPHICAL/CRITICAL SOURCES:

BOOKS

Aichinger, Peter, *Earle Birney,* Twayne, 1979.
Contemporary Literary Criticism, Gale, Volume 1, 1973; Volume 4, 1975; Volume 6, 1976; Volume 11, 1979.
Nesbitt, Bruce, editor, *Earle Birney,* Ryerson, 1974.
Pacey, Desmond, *Ten Canadian Poets,* Ryerson, 1958.

PERIODICALS

Books and Bookmen, November, 1973.
British Columbia Library Quarterly, Number 23, 1960.
Canadian Forum, July, 1971.
Canadian Literature, Number 30, 1966; summer, 1971; summer, 1974.
Globe and Mail (Toronto), September 4, 1995, p. C4.
Lugano Review, Number 1, 1975.
Queen's Quarterly, Number 64, 1958.
Saturday Night, May, 1971.
Times Literary Supplement, October 26, 1973.

*   *   *

bissett, bill 1939-

PERSONAL: Born November 23, 1939, in Halifax, Nova Scotia, Canada; son of Frederick William and Katherine

Hamilton (Covert) Bissett; children: Ooljah. *Education:* Attended Dalhousie University, 1956-57, and University of British Columbia, 1963-65. *Politics:* "equality." *Religion:* "erth air fire n watr."

ADDRESSES: Home—Box 273, 1755 Robson St., Vancouver, British Columbia, Canada V6G 1C9. *Agent*—League of Canadian Poets, 24 Ryerson, Toronto, Ontario, Canada.

CAREER: Poet. Has worked as a record store clerk, library clerk, house painter, ditch digger, gas station attendant, bean picker, disc jockey, construction worker, sign painter, English tutor, fence builder, and hauler. Editor and printer, blewointmentpress, 1964—. Has had one-man art exhibitions at Vancouver Art Gallery, 1972, 1984, and Western Front Gallery, Vancouver, 1977, 1979.

MEMBER: League of Canadian Poets, Association of Canadian Publishers, Literary Press Group.

AWARDS, HONOURS: Canada Council grants, 1967, 1968, 1972, 1975, 1977, and travel grants, 1971, 1977.

WRITINGS:

POETRY

Th jinx ship nd othr trips; pomes-drawings-collage, Very Stone Press, 1966.
(Self-illustrated) *we sleep inside each other all,* Ganglia Press, 1966.
(Self-illustrated) *Fires in th Tempul,* Very Stone Press, 1967, new edition, Vancouver Art Gallery Publications, 1984.
Where is miss florence riddle, Luv Press, 1967.
Lebanon Voices, Weed/Flower Press, 1967.
Of th Land/Divine Service Poems, Weed/Flower Press, 1968.
Awake in th Red Desert!, Talonbooks, 1968.
Killer Whale, See Hear Productions, 1969.
Nobody Owns th Earth, House of Anansi, 1971.
Air 6, Air Press, 1971.
Tuff Shit Love Pomes, Bandit/Black Moss Press, 1971.
Dragon fly, Weed/Flower Press, 1971.
Drifting into war, Talonbooks, 1971.
(With Earle Birney, Judith Copithorne and Andy Suknaski) *Four Parts Sand: Concrete Poems,* Oberon Press, 1972.
Air 10-11-12, Air Press, 1972.
Pass the Food, Release th Spirit Book, Talonbooks, 1973.
Vancouver Mainland Ice & Cold Storage, Writers Forum, 1973.
Medicine my mouths on fire, Oberon Press, 1974.
Space travl, Air Press, 1974.
Living with the Vishyun, New Star Books, 1974.
Plutonium Missing, Intermedia, 1976.
An Allusyun to Macbeth, Black Moss Press, 1976.

Sailor, Talonbooks, 1978, 2nd edition, 1982.
Beyond Even Faithful Legends, Talonbooks, 1981.
Northern birds in color, Talonbooks, 1981.
Seagull on yonge street, Talonbooks, 1983.
Canada gees mate for life, Talonbooks, 1985.
Animal uproar, Talonbooks, 1987.
What we have, Talonbooks, 1988.
Inkorrect thots, Talonbooks, 1992.
The Last photo uv th human soul, Talonbooks, 1993.

POETRY; ALL PUBLISHED BY BLEWOINTMENTPRESS

What poetiks, 1967.
(Th) Gossamer Bed Pan, 1967, new edition, 1974.
Sunday Work?, 1969.
Liberating Skies, 1969.
The Lost Angel Mining Co., 1969.
A Marvellous Experience, 1969.
S th Story I to, 1970.
The Outlaw, 1970.
Blew trewz, 1970.
Rush what fukin thery, 1971.
Th Ice bag, 1972.
Pomes for yoshi, 1972.
Th first sufi line, 1973.
What, 1973.
Drawings, 1974.
You can eat it at th opening, 1974.
Th fifth sun, 1975.
Image being, 1975.
Stardust, 1975.
Venus, 1975.
Th wind up tongue, 1976.
Soul arrow, 1979.
Sa n th monkey, 1980.
S n his crystal ball, 1981.

Also author of *IBM.*

TELEVISION SCRIPTS

In search of innocence, 1963.
Strange grey day this, 1964.
Poets of the 60's, 1967.
Portrait (video), 1984.

ILLUSTRATOR

Jim Brown, *The Circus in the Boy's Eye,* Very Stone Press, 1966.

RECORDINGS

Awake in th Red Desert, See Hear Productions, 1968.
Medicine My Mouths on Fire, Oberon, 1976.
Northern Birds in Color, blewointmentpress, 1982.
Sonic Horses 1, Underwich Editions, 1984.

OTHER

(Editor) *The Last blewointment anthology: 1963-1983,* Nightwood Editions, 1986.

Rezoning: collage and assemblage, Vancouver Art Gallery, 1989.

SIDELIGHTS: Employing idiosyncratic spelling and grammar, bill bissett attempts in his poems to recreate the actual way in which language is spoken. His innovative use of typography and margins, and his use of lower-case letters in much of his work, reflects bissett's "idea that relationships such as hierarchy, cause-effect sequences, and linear writings are repressive," as Len Early explains in *Essays on Canadian Writing.*

Several reviewers see a naive quality in bissett's writing. Frank Davey of *Canadian Forum* argues that this naivety has its roots in bissett's basically religious sensibility. The poet's "vision," Davey writes, "is of a transcendent, static world, simple and hard in outline, paralleling our own complex and sordid one just beyond the usual limitations of human perception." The use of a simple, elemental vocabulary and idiosyncratic spelling are bissett's attempts to "write of an unqualified, pure, archetypical, visionary world. . . .[They are] simplifications, meant to indicate a consciousness more attuned to cosmic non-complexity than to earthly convention." Writing in *Canadian Literature,* Al Purdy believes "the very naivete of [bissett's] language and themes, the earnestnesss and complete personal belief he brings to poems—these make him oddly touching and, I think, worthwhile."

Commenting to *CA,* bissett writes that he is "continuing to xploor vizual n sound writing as well as conversahunal vois writing with accent on/tord picture in th word sound utterance—chants—nd what speech is for—wher it comes from—often without any correct grammar spelling syntax linear meening spelling mor 'phonetik' as sound."

BIOGRAPHICAL/CRITICAL SOURCES:

BOOKS

Contemporary Literary Criticism, Volume XVIII, Gale, 1981.

PERIODICALS

Canadian Forum, July-August, 1972.
Canadian Literature, autumn, 1972; spring, 1973; spring, 1974.
Essays on Canadian Writing, fall, 1976; spring, 1977.
Fiddlehead, spring, 1967.

BISSOONDATH, Neil (Devindra) 1955-

PERSONAL: Born April 19, 1955, in Trinidad, West Indies; immigrated to Canada, 1973; son of Crisen (in business) and Sati (a teacher; maiden name, Naipaul) Bissoondath. *Education:* York University, B.A., 1977.

ADDRESSES: Home—Quebec, Canada.*Agent*—c/o The Lucinda Vardey Agency, 297 Seaton St., Toronto, Ontario M5A 2T6

CAREER: Inlingua School of Languages, Toronto, Ontario, teacher of English and French, 1977-80; Language Workshop, Toronto, teacher of English and French, 1980-85; writer.

WRITINGS:

Digging up the Mountains (stories), Macmillan of Canada, 1985, Viking, 1986.
A Casual Brutality (novel), Macmillan of Canada, 1988, Clarkson N. Potter, 1989.
On the Eve of Uncertain Tomorrows (stories), Lester & Orpen Dennys, 1990, Clarkson N. Potter, 1991.

Contributor to periodicals, including *Idler* and *Saturday Night.*

SIDELIGHTS: Neil Bissoondath is a Trinidad-born Canadian writer who has won great acclaim for his fiction. His first book, *Digging up the Mountains,* is a short story collection marked by the author's frequent exploration of exile and domestic upheaval. John Gross noted as much when he wrote in the *New York Times* that "the vision of universal uprooting is one to which all [Bissoondath's] stories tend: they are stories of exile, estrangement, dislocations great and small." Such concerns are, perhaps, most explicit in the collection's title tale, where a Caribbean businessman longs to spend his final years quietly at home even as the tranquility of his surroundings is undone by political corruption and violence. Another tale, "Continental Drift," details the dismal plight of European migrant workers in France, while "Dancing" concerns a socially aspiring Trinidad woman's culture shock when she joins relatives in Canada. A more grueling perspective on immigrants in Canada is provided in "Veins Visible," in which a hapless hero endures an arduous winter even as his fellow immigrants expire or succumb to the despair of loneliness. Bob Shacochis, writing in the *Washington Post Book World,* found this tale "alarmingly prophetic."

Digging up the Mountains earned considerable praise upon its publication in the mid-1980s. Writing in the *New York Times Book Review,* Hanif Kureishi described the collection as "superb short stories . . . alive with movement and flight, leaving and returning, insecurity and impermanence." Kureishi was particularly impressed with Bissoondath's "gift for mood and detail" and "his ability to create character and drama." Similarly, John Gross wrote in the *New York Times* of Bissoondath's "remarkable sureness of touch," while Bob Shacochis, in his appraisal for the *Washington Post Book World,* noted Bissoondath's "psychological and historical insights" and his "fearless regard for complexity." *Digging up the Mountains,* Shacochis declared, is comprised of "powerfully compressed tales of distorted nationalism and cultural divorce."

Bissoondath followed *Digging up the Mountains* with *A Casual Brutality,* a novel about social upheaval in the Caribbean Islands. The novel's hero is Raj Ramsingh, a Caribbean native who has received his physician's education and training in Canada, then returned—with his Canadian wife—to a homeland increasingly undone by political corruption and violence. Eventually, Ramsingh's own family falls victim to mayhem, whereupon he uneasily considers a life in exile.

In reviewing *A Casual Brutality,* some critics objected to the novel's slow narrative and its dense, rich prose. Richard Eder, for example, complained in the *Los Angeles Times* that "the quality of the writing . . . makes the book hard to get through." Caryn James seemed to concede as much by writing in the *New York Times* that Bissoondath occasionally "strains for poetic effects." But to James such a defect ultimately proved inconsequential before the novel's "astute" perceptions. James asserted that "few first novels have the depth and reach of *A Casual Brutality,* and fewer have the honesty to leave the character's major conflict in an ambivalent state."

In *On the Eve of Uncertain Tomorrows,* Bissoondath's next book, he provides further exploration of cultural alienation and exile. Jim Shepard, writing about this short story collection in the *New York Times Book Review,* favorably compared it to its predecessors and added that "In this . . . book the focus on the plight of the exile seems more persistent." Notable among the tales in this volume are "Security," in which a middle-aged expatriate weighs the emotional—and, thus, spiritual—consequences of forsaking his violent homeland for a dire, gloomy existence; and the title work, in which a refugee anxiously awaits his acceptance into Canada. In still other tales Bissoondath explores the criminally unsavory aspects of political corruption. "Kira and Anya," for instance, features a former dictator who may have authorized his own wife's death, while in "Things Best Forgotten" an old man confides that he long ago assisted in the execution of a present guest's relative. In her review for the Toronto *Globe and Mail,* Beverley Daurio described this tale as "unflinching, and thought-provoking."

Bissoondath was lauded considerably for *On the Eve of Uncertain Tomorrows.* Jim Shepard, in his *New York Times Book Review* assessment, noted the book's "power,"

attributing it to "the reader's sense that these fictions will not let go of their subject until we have acknowledged a whole people's pain." Jasper Rees, writing in the London *Times,* found Bissoondath's collection "affecting," and Firdus Kanga expressed similar satisfaction in the *Times Literary Supplement.* With *On the Eve of Uncertain Tomorrows,* Kanga concluded, "Bissoondath has kept the amazing promise" made with his earlier work.

Bissoondath told *CA:* "I write mainly from my obsession about exile and restlessness. I attempt to tell people's stories, try to understand their fears and motivations, but avoiding easy sentimentalism. While some of my writing is 'Third World,' my interests extend beyond this to Canada and Europe, especially Spain."

BIOGRAPHICAL/CRITICAL SOURCES:

PERIODICALS

Books in Canada, February, 1993, pp. 43-44.
Callaloo, summer, 1990, p. 557.
Globe and Mail (Toronto), April 20, 1985; August 7, 1985; October 13, 1990.
London Review of Books, June 19, 1986, pp. 19-20.
Los Angeles Times, February 2, 1989.
Maclean's, November 23, 1992, p. 65.
New York Times, August 29, 1986, p. 19; February 4, 1989, p. 16.
New York Times Book Review, August 17, 1986, p. 10; February 22, 1989, pp. 14-15; May 26, 1991, pp. 3 and 14.
Publishers Weekly, January 6, 1989, pp. 79-80,
Quill & Quire, March, 1985, p. 71.
Saturday Night, October, 1994, pp. 11-22.
Spectator, December 1, 1990, pp. 48-49.
Times Literary Supplement, November 23-29, 1990, p. 1271.
Toronto Star, April 15, 1985; May 18, 1985.
Tribune Books (Chicago), February 26, 1989, p. 7.
Washington Post Book World, October 19, 1986, p. 6; January 22, 1989, p. 4.

*　　　*　　　*

BLAIS, Marie-Claire 1939-

PERSONAL: Born October 5, 1939, in Quebec, Canada; daughter of Fernando and Veronique (Nolin) Blais. *Education:* Attended Pensionnat St. Roch in Quebec; studied literature and philosophy at Laval University in Quebec. *Religion:* Catholic.

CAREER: Full-time writer.

MEMBER: PEN.

AWARDS, HONOURS: Prix de la Langue Francaise, L'Academie Francaise, 1961, for *La Belle bete;* Guggenheim fellowships, 1963 and 1964; Le Prix France-Quebec and Prix Medicis (Paris), both 1966, both for *Une Saison dans la vie d'Emmanuel;* Prix du Gouverneur General du Canada, 1969, for *Les Manuscrits de Pauline Archange,* and 1979, for *Le Sourd dans la ville;* elected member of Order of Canada, 1972; honorary doctorate from York University (Toronto), 1975; Prix Belgique, 1976; named honorary professor at Calgary University, 1978; Prix Athanase David, 1982; Prix de l'Academie Francaise, 1983.

WRITINGS:

La Belle Bete (novel), Institut Litteraire du Quebec, 1959, translation by Merloyd Lawrence published as *Mad Shadows,* Little, Brown, 1961.

Tete Blanche (novel), Institut Litteraire du Quebec, 1960, translation by Charles Fullman under same title, Little, Brown, 1961.

Le Jour est noir (novella; also see below), Editions du Jour (Montreal), 1962.

Pays voiles (poems), Garneau (Quebec), 1963.

Existences (poems), Garneau, 1964.

Une Saison dans la vie d'Emmanuel (novel), Editions du Jour, 1965, translation by Coltman published as *A Season in the Life of Emmanuel,* introduction by Edmund Wilson, Farrar, Straus, 1966.

Les Voyageurs sacres (novella), HMH, 1966.

L'Insoumise (novel), Editions du Jour, 1966, translation by David Lobdell published as *The Fugitive,* Oberon, 1978.

The Day Is Dark and *The Three Travelers* (contains Derek Coltman's translations of *Le Jour est noir* and *Les Voyageurs sacres*), Farrar, Straus, 1967.

David Sterne (novel), Editions du Jour, 1967, translation by Lobdell under same title, McClelland & Stewart, 1973.

Les Manuscrits de Pauline Archange (novel), Editions du Jour, 1968, translation by Coltman published with translation of *Vivre! Vivre!: La Suite des Manuscrits de Pauline Archange* as *The Manuscripts of Pauline Archange,* Farrar, Straus, 1970.

Vivre! Vivre!: La Suite des Manuscrits de Pauline Archange (novel), Editions du Jour, 1969.

Les Apparences (novel), Editions du Jour, 1970, translation by Lobdell published as *Durer's Angel,* McClelland & Stewart, 1974.

Le Loup (novel), Editions du Jour, 1972, translation by Sheila Fischman published as *The Wolf,* McClelland & Stewart, 1974.

Un Joualonais sa Joualonie (novel), Editions du Jour, 1973, reprinted as *A coeur joual,* Robert Laffont, 1977, translation by Ralph Manheim published as *St. Lawrence Blues,* Farrar, Straus, 1974.

Une Liaison parisienne (novel), Robert Laffont, 1976, translation by Fischman published as *A Literary Affair,* McClelland & Stewart, 1979.

Le Sourd dans la ville (novel), Stanke, 1979, translation by Carol Dunlop published as *Deaf to the City,* General Publishing, 1979.

(Editor with Richard Teleky) *The Oxford Book of French-Canadian Short Stories,* Oxford University Press, 1980.

Les Nuits de l'underground (novel), Stanke, 1982, translation by Ray Ellenwood published as *Nights in the Underground,* General Publishing, 1982.

Visions d'Anna (novel), Stanke, 1982, translation by Fischman published as *Anna's World,* Lester, Orpen & Dennys, 1985.

Pays voiles—Existences, Stanke, 1983, translation by Michael Harris published as *Veiled Countries in Veiled Countries* and *Lives,* Vehicule Press, 1984.

Pierre, la guerre du printemps 81, Primeur, 1984.

PLAYS

La Roulotte aux Poupees, produced in Quebec at Theatre de L'Estoc, 1960.

L'Execution (two-act; produced in Montreal at Theatre du Rideau Vert, 1967), Editions du Jour, 1968, translation by David Lobdell published as *The Execution,* Talon Books, 1976.

Fievre, Editions du Jour, 1974.

La Nef des sorcieres, Quinze Editeurs, 1976.

L'Ocean murmures, Quinze Editeurs, 1977.

Also author of *Eleanor,* produced in Quebec at Theatre de L'Estoc, and *Sommeil d'Hiver,* 1985, and *Fiere,* 1985.

TELEVISION SCRIPTS

L'Ocean, Radio-Canada, 1976.

Journal en images froides, Radio-Canada, 1978.

L'Exil, L'Escale, Radio-Canada, 1979.

RADIO SCRIPTS

Le Disparu, Radio-Canada, 1971.

L'Envahisseur, Radio-Canada, 1972.

Deux Destins, Radio-Canada, 1973.

Fievre, Radio-Canada, 1973.

Une Autre Vie, Radio-Canada, 1974.

Un Couple, Radio-Canada, 1975.

Une Femme et les autres, Radio-Canada, 1976.

L'Enfant Video, Radio-Canada, 1977.

Murmures, Radio-Canada, 1977.

Le Fantome d'une voix, Radio-Canada, 1980.

SIDELIGHTS: Marie-Claire Blais, according to Edmund Wilson in *O Canada: An American's Notes on Canadian*

Culture, is "a writer in a class by herself." Although each of her novels is written in a different style and mood, "we know immediately," writes Raymond Rosenthal, "that we are entering a fully imagined world when we start reading any of her books." Wilson wrote that Blais is a "true 'phenomenon'; she may possibly be a genius. At the age of twenty-four, she has produced four remarkable books of a passionate and poetic force that, as far as my reading goes, is not otherwise to be found in French Canadian fiction." That was in 1964; when Wilson read *A Season in the Life of Emmanuel* in 1965, he compared the novel to works by J. M. Synge and William Faulkner.

"*A Season in the Life of Emmanuel* is a particularly Canadian work of art," writes David Stouck, "for the sense of winter and of life's limitations (especially defined by poverty) are nowhere felt more strongly. Yet . . . these physical limitations serve to define the emotional deprivation that is being dramatized. That eroding sense of poverty is never externalized as a social issue, nor is the harshness of the Quebec landscape seen as an existentialist 'condition.' Rather, in the oblique and relentless manner of her writing Miss Blais remains faithful stylistically to the painful vision of her imagination and in so doing has created both a fully dramatic and genuinely Canadian work of art."

Writing in the *New York Times Book Review,* Robertson Davies claims that *The Day Is Dark* and *Three Travelers* are "less substantial than *A Season in the Life of Emmanuel,*" but, he adds, "all the writing of this extraordinary young woman is so individual, so unlike anything else being written on this continent, that admirers of her poetic vision of life may find them even more to their taste." Laurent LeSage, writing in *Saturday Review,* says of the two novellas: "Although the basic structures of fiction are still recognizable, they have been weakened and distorted to prevent any illusion of realistic dimension or true-to-life anecdote from distracting us from the author's intention. Without warning the narrative shifts from one character to another, chronology is jumbled, events are sometimes contradictory, and the fancied is never clearly separated from the real. By a series of interior monologues Mlle. Blais works along the lower levels of consciousness, and only rarely does she come to the surface. The world of her revery is the somber, shadowy one of primitive urges and responses. . . . Each [character] obeys a force that resembles a tragic predestination, leading [him] in a lonely quest through life to [his] final destruction." The novellas are actually prose poems, similar in some respects to works by Walter de la Mare. Rosenthal defines the genre as "a piece of prose that should be read more than once, preferably several times. If after reading it in the prescribed fashion," says Rosenthal, "the work assumes depth and color and value it did not have at the first reading, then the author

has written a successful prose poem. In a prose poem each word counts and Mlle. Blais generally doesn't waste a syllable."

Several critics comment on the pain found in Blais's works. In his study of Canadian literature, Wilson comments that "these novels of Marie-Claire Blais are the most unrelievedly painful that I remember ever to have read, and one questions . . . the inevitability of so much pain." L. Clark Keating, writing in *Romance Notes,* finds that Blais's "characters and situations, with but few exceptions, are hateful, perverse and repulsive. No crime, no meanness, no indecent thought, no deliberate breaking of the Ten Commandments are alien to her characters young or old, male or female." Keating concludes that Blais's writings are "as shocking as Zola's or the films used as evidence in the Nuremburg trials."

But Irving Wardle, although he admits that "harshness and squalor are there," sees that, at least in *A Season in the Life of Emmanuel,* these elements "are transformed in the writing into the material of adolescent fantasy. [Blais] has the myth-making faculty, and it is an exciting thing to watch." LeSage writes: "Marie-Claire Blais lets her words pour forth in a rhapsodic torrent. In *Three Travelers* they often form into verses, but everywhere they have the poetic qualities of image and cadence as they create laments and paeans, cries of love, lust, and hate for the wretched characters whose affliction is the sickness of life. The power of her writing is terrific." Wilson explains that "Blais has grown up in this cult, and the idea that man is born to sorrow, the agony of expiation, is at the base of her tragic consciousness. [Her work] is the refinement to a purer kind of poetry than that of the protesting patriots of the desperate cry that arises from the poverty, intellectual and material, the passionate self-punishing piety and the fierce defeated pride of Quebec."

Daniel M. Murtaugh observes that *A Season in the Life of Emmanuel* "has at its center an autobiographical sketch by a consumptive child whose writing is a cry of defiance against the misery of his life and the approach of his death. The manuscripts of a suffering child, a structural detail of that novel, are the sum and substance of its successor. *The Manuscripts of Pauline Archange* takes us through memories of almost unmitigated horror rendered bearable, redeemed even, for us as for the novel's heroine, by the fluid, re-creative medium of her prose. . . . What Pauline remembers does not fall into a conventional plot or lend itself easily to summary. Her life is lived out in the mental and physical squalor of a French Canadian slum, under the tyranny of repressed, frustrated adults who visit their failures in blows upon their consumptive, lamed offspring. To survive is to escape, to rebel, above all, to avoid pity. Pity 'stinks of death,' and only leads to torture and rape of the victims it cannot help. Pauline writes her manuscripts because, as her family tells her, she 'has no heart.' Only at such a cost does she live and speak to us."

Rosenthal emphasizes that Blais has done much to "put Canada on the literary map." He says of her work: "Mlle. Blais leaves out a great deal, almost all the familiar furniture of fiction, and yet her characters have a tenacious life and her themes, though often convoluted and as evanescent as the mist that dominates so much of her imagination, strike home with surprising force." "With *David Sterne,*" writes Brian Vintcent, "Mlle. Blais has placed herself firmly and uncompromisingly in the literary tradition of the French moralists leading back through Camus, Genet and Gide to Baudelaire. The book deals in one way or another with many of the themes explored by these writers, and this makes it somewhat derivative. It owes most, perhaps, to the more abstract and less sensational works of Jean Genet, in which the passionate existential wranglings, the rebellion, the life of crime and sensation are so prominent. The confessional and didactic style of the book will also strike echoes in the reader's mind. But *David Sterne* survives and transcends these comparisons. What allows it to do so is the immense compassion and tenderness Mlle. Blais displays for her characters in their whirlwind of struggle and suffering. The hard cold eye she casts on the cruel world of *Mad Shadows* has grown into one full of pity and profound sadness for the fate of men condemned to do battle with themselves."

In 1980, Blais published *Deaf to the City,* a novel told in one book-length paragraph. "Blais," Marjorie A. Fitzpatrick explains in the *French Review,* "brings to life—and then to death—the inhabitants of the gloomy little Montreal hotel that serves as the novel's setting. Like voices in a fugue or threads in a well-made tapestry, their lives weave in and out through each other to form a harmonious (though depressing) whole." Writing in the *Dictionary of Literary Biography,* Eva-Marie Kroeller states that *Deaf to the City* "fuses prose and poetry even more radically than Blais's earlier works." Fitzpatrick concludes that "If Blais can sustain in future works the combination of human authenticity and tight technical mastery that she found in [*A Season in the Life of Emmanuel*] and has achieved again in [*Deaf to the City*], she may well come to stand out as one of the most powerful fiction writers of French expression of this generation."

The *Virginia Quarterly Review* writer concludes that Blais's novels are "to be read slowly and carefully for the unusual insights they present in often difficult but provocative images and sometimes demanding but intriguing technical innovations. This is a serious, talented and deeply effective writer." Kroeller calls Blais "one of the most prolific and influential authors of Quebec's literary scene since the late 1950s." Blais, Kroeller believes, "has firmly established an international reputation as a writer who combines strong roots in the literary tradition of her province with an affinity to existentialist fiction of Western Europe and the United States."

BIOGRAPHICAL/CRITICAL SOURCES:

BOOKS

Contemporary Authors Autobiography Series, Volume 4, Gale, 1986.

Contemporary Literary Criticism, Gale, Volume 2, 1974, Volume 3, 1975, Volume 6, 1976, Volume 13, 1980, Volume 22, 1982.

Dictionary of Literary Biography, Volume 53: *Canadian Writers since 1960, First Series,* Gale, 1986.

Fabi, Therese, *Le Monde perturbe des jeunes dans l'oeuvre romanesque de Marie-Claire Blais: sa vie, son oeuvre, la critique,* Editions Agence d'Arc (Montreal), 1973.

Goldmann, Lucien, *Structures mentales et creation culturelle,* Editions Anthropos (Paris), 1970.

Marcotte, Gilles, *Notre roman a l'imparfait,* La Presse (Montreal), 1976.

Meigs, Mary, *Lily Briscoe: A Self-Portrait,* Talonbooks, 1981.

Meigs, *The Medusa Head,* Talonbooks, 1983.

Nadeau, Vincent, *Marie-Claire Blais: le noir et le tendre,* Presses de l'Universite de Montreal, 1974.

Stratford, Philip, *Marie-Claire Blais,* Forum House, 1971.

Wilson, Edmund, *O Canada: An American's Notes on Canadian Culture,* Farrar, Straus, 1965.

PERIODICALS

Books Abroad, winter, 1968.

Books in Canada, February, 1979.

Book Week, June 18, 1967.

Canadian Literature, spring, 1972.

Chatelaine, August, 1966.

Cite libre, July-August, 1966.

Coincidences, May-December, 1980.

Culture, March, 1968.

La Dryade, summer, 1967.

Etudes, February, 1967.

French Review, March, 1981.

Globe and Mail (Toronto), March 30, 1985.

Journal of Canadian Fiction, Number 25-26, 1979.

Lettres Quebecoises, winter, 1979-80.

Livres et Auteurs Quebecois, 1972.

Los Angeles Times, September 18, 1987.

New Statesman, March 31, 1967.

New York Times Book Review, April 30, 1967; September 20, 1987.

Nous, June, 1973.

Novel, autumn, 1972.

Observer, April 2, 1967.

Recherches Sociographiques, September-December, 1966.

Revue de l'Institut de Sociologie, Volume 42, number 3, 1969.
La Revue de Paris, February, 1967.
Romance Notes, autumn, 1973.
Saturday Review, April 29, 1967.
Times Literary Supplement, March 30, 1967.
Virginia Quarterly Review, autumn, 1967.
Voix et Images, winter, 1983.
Weekend Magazine, October 23, 1976.

* * *

BLUE CLOUD, Peter (Aroniawenrate) 1933-

PERSONAL: Born June 10, 1933, in Kahnawake, Quebec, Canada; son of Ahriron and Wahriah Williams; children: Meyokeeskow, Ariron, Kaherine. *Education:* Attended grammar school in Kahnawake, Quebec, Canada, and Buffalo, NY.

ADDRESSES: Home—P.O. Box 666, Kahnawake, Quebec, Canada J0L 1B0.

CAREER: Writer. Worked earlier as ironworker, logger, carpenter, and woodcutter; previously associated with newspapers *Akwesasne Notes* and *Indian Time.*

AWARDS, HONOURS: American Book Award, Before Columbus Foundation, 1981.

WRITINGS:

(Editor) *Alcatraz Is Not an Island* (nonfiction), Wingbow Press, 1972.
Coyote and Friends, Blackberry Press, 1976.
Turtle, Bear, and Wolf (poetry), Akwesasne Press, 1976.
Back Then Tomorrow (poetry/prose), Blackberry Press, 1978.
White Corn Sister (poetry/play), Strawberry Press, 1979.
Elderberry Flute Song (poetry/prose), Crossing Press, 1982.
(Editor with James Koller, Gogisgi Carroll Arnett, and Steve Nemirow) *Coyote's Journal* (poetry/prose), Bookpeople, 1983.
Sketches of Winter with Crows (poetry), Strawberry Press, 1984.
The Other Side of Nowhere (poetry/prose), White Pine, 1990.
Clans of Many Nations: Selected Poems, 1969-1992, White Pine, 1993.

WORK IN PROGRESS: Searching for Eagles: New Poems; short stories; a novel.

SIDELIGHTS: Noted for combining Native American myths with contemporary issues, Peter Blue Cloud often focuses on Native American history, the oral tradition, nature, and spiritual themes in his poetry and prose.

Blue Cloud, whose original name is Aroniawenrate, was raised on a Mohawk reservation in Kahnawake, Quebec. Although he was required by his family to speak only the Mohawk language during his childhood, his grandfather introduced him to books written in English, and he subsequently began writing poems and songs as a teenager. He first published in the journal *Akwesasne Notes,* for which he became poetry editor in 1975. In his critically acclaimed poetry collection *Turtle, Bear and Wolf,* which is comprised of three sections, Blue Cloud emphasizes Native Canadian spirituality and explores the interconnections between animals and humans. Each section of the book is devoted to one of the three animals mentioned in its title—these figures are prominent in Native Canadian legends and are considered by many Native cultures to be personality types. The coyote, another important character in Native Canadian myths, is the focus of *Elderberry Flute Song: Contemporary Coyote Tales.* This collection of free verse, prose poems, and short stories received praise for combining traditional coyote stories with contemporary images and a sense of the absurd. Coyote is also a prominent character in *The Other Side of Nowhere,* which depicts the legendary character's involvement in recent history in such poems as "The First Missiles" and "The 60s." James Ruppert commented: "Blue Cloud is deeply concerned with the spirit of that old world heralded in the stories and songs which tell of the days when man and animals lived together, talked to each other and understood each other."

BIOGRAPHICAL/CRITICAL SOURCES:

BOOKS

Native North American Literature, Gale, 1994.

* * *

BOWERING, Marilyn R(uthe) 1949-

PERSONAL: Born April 13, 1949, in Winnipeg, Manitoba, Canada; daughter of Herbert James (a carpenter) and Elnora (a purchasing agent; maiden name, Grist) Bowering. *Education:* Attended University of British Columbia, 1968-69; University of Victoria, B.A., 1971, M.A., 1973; also attended University of New Brunswick, 1975.

ADDRESSES: Home—3777 Jennifer Rd., Victoria, British Columbia, Canada V8P 3X1.

CAREER: Teacher in public schools at Masset, British Columbia, Canada, 1974-75; freelance writer and book reviewer, 1975-77; University of British Columbia, Vancouver, extension lecturer in poetry writing, 1977; Gregson/Graham (marketing and communications firm), Victoria, British Columbia, editor and writer, 1978-80; University of Victoria, British Columbia, visiting lecturer, 1978-82, lecturer in creative writing, 1982-86, 1989, visiting associate professor of creative writing, 1993-94; Noel Collins and Blackwells, Edinburgh, Scotland, freelance editor, 1980-82; freelance writer in Seville, Spain, 1990-92; Banff Centre, Banff, Alberta, member of faculty, 1992, writer-in-electronic-residence, 1993-94.

MEMBER: Writers Union of Canada, League of Canadian Poets.

AWARDS, HONOURS: Du Maurier Award for Poetry from Canada's National Magazine Awards, 1978, for "Rose Harbor Whaling Station"; National Magazine Award for Poetry, 1989; Long Poem prize, Malahat Review, 1994; recipient of various Canada Council Awards for poetry.

WRITINGS:

POETRY

The Liberation of Newfoundland, Fiddlehead Press (Retford, England), 1973.
One Who Became Lost, Fiddlehead Press, 1976.
The Killing Room, Sono Nis Press (Los Angeles), 1977.
Third/Child Zian, Sceptre Press (Bristol, England), 1978.
The Book of Glass, Sceptre Press, 1978.
Sleeping with Lambs, Press Porcepic, 1980.
Giving Back Diamonds, Press Porcepic, 1982.
The Sunday Before Winter, General Publishing, 1984.
Anyone Can See I Love You, Porcupine's Quill, 1987.
Grandfather Was a Soldier, Porcepic Books, 1987.
Calling All the World, Porcepic Books, 1989.
Love As It Is, Beach Holme, 1993.

NOVELS

The Visitors Have All Returned, Press Porcepic, 1979.
To All Appearances a Lady, Penguin Books (West Drayton, England), 1990.

OTHER

(Editor with David A. Day) *Many Voices: An Anthology of Contemporary Canadian Indian Poetry,* J. J. Douglas, 1977.
(Editor) *Guide to the Labor Code of British Columbia,* Government of British Columbia, 1980.

Work represented in anthologies, including *Whale Sound, North American Women Poets, New: West Coast, New Oxford Book of Canadian Verse, New Canadian Poets, Poets of the 80's,* and *Anything Is Possible.* Contributor to literary journals, including *Event, Toronto Life, Prism International, Malahat Review, Canadian Forum, New Poetry,* and *Signal Hill Broadsides.*

SIDELIGHTS: Marilyn R. Bowering's poems often have a surrealistic, dream-like quality. A Canadian poet and novelist, Bowering infuses her writings with mythological and symbolic imagery, and her work often depicts intense emotional experiences. In a review of her acclaimed collection *Giving Back Diamonds,* a contributor to *Canadian Literature* remarked that Bowering "writes with a kind of absolute pitch, her use of words spare, accurate, evocative. . . ."

In a review of an early work, *One Who Became Lost,* M. Travis Lane stated in *Fiddlehead* that "Bowering's poems are beautifully structured. . . . Poems that speak through dream imagery rather than through rationalized description and commentary are structurally nearer to painting or music than to prose, and we look for their structure in terms of themes and variations rather than terms of argument. Or again, we can understand them as we do a film by Bergman or Fellini, with the back of our mind, trusting our instincts—this *feels* right."

Doug Beardsly of the *Victoria Times* commented on another of Bowering's works, *The Visitors Have All Returned:* "As there are few stylists in our country, either in poetry or fiction, it's a real delight to come across Marilyn Bowering's first book of prose. . . . The author of several books of poems offers us a poetic prose, stripped bare, exposed, held up to the clear white light of the page. . . . Each paragraph seems chiselled, every important word chosen for its resonant qualities. What is left out is as significant as what's left in, and Michael Elcock's fine black-and-white photographs deepen the sense of mystery."

A later work, the novel *To All Appearances a Lady,* concerns Robert Lam, a half-Chinese, middle-aged bachelor who sets off to sea after the death of his 100-year-old stepmother, Lam Fan. The old woman's spirit joins him on board and begins revealing the details of Robert's mysterious ancestry, including the story of his mother, India Thackeray, an emigrant from Hong Kong who worked in a Vancouver opium factory and was marooned for several years in a leper colony. Robert's journey becomes one of self-realization and self-discovery.

To All Appearances a Lady garnered mixed critical reactions. Sybil Steinberg of *Publishers Weekly* described the book as a "strangely beautiful, haunting first novel," and *New York Times Book Review* contributor Edward Hower called the work "ambitious and often enjoyable." Other critics felt that the elaborate plot needlessly complicates the work. "[Bowering] must have spent months in the provincial archives," opined Sarah Harvey in the Toronto *Globe and Mail,* "savoring the delicious morsels of past lives and agonizing over which bits to use. It's a shame that she appears to have yielded to the temptation to use them all." Carolyn See of the *Los Angeles Times* concurred, writing, "The trouble is, with all this laudable research and history, the characters don't have room to breathe." "Marilyn Bowering does have a fascinating story to tell," Hower concluded, "If only she had told it more simply!" However, other critics thought the wealth of detail in Bowering's novel supported an impression of verisimilitude. Tom Adair of *Scotland on Sunday* commented: "Bowering writes at the edge of her talent: she is affirmative, clear, faithful to life's mysteries."

BIOGRAPHICAL/CRITICAL SOURCES:

BOOKS

Contemporary Literary Criticism, Volume 32, Gale, 1983.

PERIODICALS

Books in Canada, May, 1981, pp. 41-42; April, 1983, pp. 25-26.
Canadian Literature, winter, 1980, pp. 136-138; autumn, 1983, p. 96; autumn, 1989, p. 260.
Dalhousie Review, summer, 1977, p. 356; autumn, 1978, p. 567.
Fiddlehead, winter, 1977, pp. 156-160; summer, 1978, pp. 162-63.
Globe and Mail (Toronto), September 16, 1989.
Los Angeles Times, July 9, 1990.
New York Times Book Review, August 12, 1990, p.11.
Publishers Weekly, April 13, 1990, p. 55.
Scotland on Sunday, November 25, 1990.
Victoria Times, July 13, 1979.
Waves, volume 8, number 2, 1980; winter, 1983, pp. 88-92.
Windsor Star, November 12, 1977.

* * *

BREWSTER, Elizabeth (Winifred) 1922-

PERSONAL: Born August 26, 1922, in Chipman, New Brunswick, Canada; daughter of Frederick John and Ethel (Day) Brewster. *Education:* University of New Brunswick, Fredericton, B.A., 1946; Radcliff College, Cambridge, A.M., 1947; Kings College, London, 1949-50; University of Toronto, B.L.S., 1953; Indiana University, Ph.D., 1962.

ADDRESSES: Home—#206, 910 9th Street E., Saskatoon, Saskatchewan S7H 0N1. *Office*—Department of English, University of Saskatchewan, Saskatoon, Saskatchewan S7N 0W0 Canada.

CAREER: Cataloger, Carleton University Library, Ottawa, Ontario, 1953-57, and Indiana University Library, Bloomington, 1957-58; University of Victoria, Victoria, British Columbia, member of English department, 1960-61; Mount Allison University, Sackville, New Brunswick, reference librarian, 1961-65; New Brunswick Legislative Library, Fredericton, cataloger, 1965-68; Uni-

versity of Alberta, Edmonton, cataloger of rare books in university library, 1968-70, visiting assistant professor of English, 1970-71; University of Saskatchewan, Saskatoon, assistant professor, 1972-75, associate professor, 1975-80, professor of English, 1980-90, professor emeritus, 1990—.

AWARDS, HONOURS: Pratt Gold Medal and prize, Kings College, London, 1953; Senior Artists awards, Canada Council, 1971-72, 1976, 1978-79, and 1985-86; President's Medal, University of Western Ontario, 1979, for poetry; CBC award for poetry, 1990, for poem sequence "Wheel of Change." Litt.D., University of New Brunswick, 1982; Canadian Broadcasting Corporation award for poetry, 1991; Saskatchewan Arts Board, Lifetime Excellence in the Arts award, 1995.

WRITINGS:

POETRY

East Coast, Ryerson (Toronto), 1951.
Lillooet, Ryerson, 1954.
Roads and Other Poems, Ryerson, 1957.
(With others) *Five New Brunswick Poets,* edited by Fred Cogswell, Fiddlehead (Fredericton, New Brunswick), 1962.
Passage of Summer: Selected Poems, Ryerson, 1969.
Sunrise North, Clarke, Irwin (Toronto), 1972.
In Search of Eros, Clarke, Irwin (Toronto), 1974.
Sometimes I Think of Moving, Oberon (Ottawa), 1977.
The Way Home, Oberon, 1982.
Digging In, Oberon, 1982.
Selected Poems of Elizabeth Brewster, 1944-1984, two volumes, Oberon, 1985.
Entertaining Angels, Oberon, 1988.
Spring Again: Poems, Oberon, 1990.
Wheel of Change, Oberon, 1993.

PROSE

The Sisters: A Novel, Oberon, 1974.
It's Easy to Fall on the Ice: Ten Stories, Oberon, 1977.
Junction (novel), Black Moss (Windsor, Ontario), 1982.
A House Full of Women (short stories), Oberon, 1983.
Visitations (short stories), Oberon, 1987.
The Invention of Truth (memoir), Oberon, 1991.

Contributor to periodicals including, *Canadian Forum, Canadian Literature, Dalhousie Review,* and *Fiddlehead.*

SIDELIGHTS: Elizabeth Brewster has been described in *Benet's Readers Encyclopedia of American Literature, 1991* as "a poet of rural, nostalgic, everyday themes," and she herself is quoted in *Contemporary Poets* as saying that she writes " 'to come to a better understanding of myself, my world, and other people.' " Her "genius for understatement" is, according to *Contemporary Poets* contributor John Robert Colombo, among the qualities which make her poetry "like a wine which improves with age; its taste mellows in memory." Colombo suggested that Brewster's two volume *Selected Poems, 1944-84,* features some of her best work, and asserted that over the course of her career, "[Brewster] has found a way to turn fancies and musings into meaningful subjects for poems, and she has mastered the casual aside."

In *Spring Again Poems,* Brewster's work "allows the reader to overhear the inner conversations that produce her poems," according to Anne Rayner writing in *Canadian Literature.* Much of the volume is a personal response to Ezra Pounds' *Cantos,* and it has a distinctly journalistic, personal flavor. L. Maingon, writing in *CM,* describes the tension in the poems as Brewster's "playing [of] her feminine reality against the chaos of Pound's . . . masculine world." In this volume, Rayner notes, Brewster explores the relationship between "sources of myth" and "twentieth-century Canadian prairie reality": " 'I cannot make it new,' " Brewster exclaims, " 'but I can make it Canadian.' "

Wheel of Change, published in honour of Brewster's seventieth birthday, is a book of poems divided into sections in which each she meditates "on her life in [Canada] over the past fifty years," states Ian Dempsey in *CM.* While Dempsey notes that Brewster seeks "intellectual insight . . . in [her] mild, elegiac meditations" he also adds that "she never achieves ecstasy, only wonder." The title sequence of poems, "Wheels of Change," did win Brewster the CBC award for poetry in 1990.

In her memoir, *The Invention of Truth,* Brewster changes gears and offers her readers a text which is part-fact, part-imagination, part-poetry, and part-fiction. It is composed, according to Virginia Beaton's *Books in Canada* review, of "poems, some family photos, journal excerpts, and dreams," and it is largely "about memory, and the way truth changes over a lifetime." In Brewster's own words, reported by Barbara Pell in *Canadian Literature,* the book is a " 'sidelong autobiography' " which explores family, friends, and Brewster's belief "that art elevates 'deliberate ordinariness . . . to the level of myth.' "

Both Pell and Beaton, however, lament the many gaps in *The Invention of Truth.* Pell finds the book ultimately "has too many unacknowledged gaps . . . and depths . . . to be satisfying," while Beaton more generously allows that "the overall tone of *The Invention of Truth* . . . tantalizes the reader because of what is left unsaid."

In spite of the faint praise which these critics have for Brewster's single attempt at non-fiction, she remains well-known and well-respected for her poetry and her prose. According to Maingon, Elizabeth Brewster is not merely another talented writer, but in fact is "one of Canada's major poets."

BIOGRAPHICAL/CRITICAL SOURCES:

BOOKS

Benet's Readers Encyclopedia of American Literature, 1991.
Contemporary Poets, Gale, 1991.
Dictionary of Literary Biography, Volume 60: *Canadian Writers since 1960, Second Series,* Gale, 1987.

PERIODICALS

Ariel, July 1973.
Books in Canada, May, 1992, p. 50.
Canadian Literature, autumn, 1974; winter, 1992, pp. 137-39; spring, 1993, pp. 157-58.
CM, November 1990, pp. 291-92; March-April 1994, pp. 42-43.
Essays on Canadian Writing, summer-fall, 1980.

*   *   *

BROSSARD, Nicole   1943-

PERSONAL: Born November 27, 1943, in Montreal, Quebec, Canada; daughter of Guillaume (an accountant) and Marguerite (a homemaker; maiden name, Matte) Brossard; married Robert Soubliere, 1966 (divorced); children; Julie-Capucine Brossard-Soubliere. *Education:* Attended College Marguerite Bourgeoys, 1955-60; Universite de Montreal, B.A., 1965, Licencie en lettres, 1968, Scolarite de maitrise en lettres, 1972; Universite du Quebec a Montreal, baccalaureat, specialise en pedagogie, 1971. *Politics:* Radical feminist.

ADDRESSES: Home and office—34 avenue Robert, Outremont, Quebec, Canada H3S 2P2.

CAREER: Poet and novelist. *La Barre du jour* (literary magazine), Montreal, Quebec, co-founder and co-director, 1965-75; *Les Tetes de pioche* (feminist editorial collective), Montreal, co-founder, 1976-79; *La Nouvelle Barre du jour* (magazine), Montreal, co-founder, co-editor, and co-director, 1977-79; L'Integrale (publishing house), Montreal, founder and director, 1982—. Teacher in Montreal, 1969-70, 1971-72; visiting professor at Queen's University at Kingston, 1982-1984. Co-director and co-researcher of the film, "Some American Feminists," National Film Board, 1976. Queen's University, Kingston, Ontario, visiting professor of French, 1982-84; Princeton University, New Jersey, short term fellow, 1991.

Organizer of jazz and poetry events at the Pavillon de la jeunesse, Expo '67 in Montreal; co-organizer of "Celebrations," an event about women's texts; member of the organization committee for the "Recontre quebecoise internationale des ecrivains" on the subject of women and writing. Participant in colloquiums, conferences, and meetings, on Quebecois and feminist literary topics, including the Cultural Congress of Havana, 1968, "La Nuit de poesie," 1969, International Poetry Festival in Toronto, 1975, Festival international de poesie in Paris, 1978, "Production et affirmation de l'identite" in Toulouse, 1979, "Writers in Dialogue," with Adrienne Rich, in Toronto, 1981, Tournee europeenne de lectures et de conferences in Belgium, France, and Italy, 1981, Inter-American Conference of Women Writers in Mexico, 1981, National Writer's Conference in Nelson, British Columbia, 1982, "Emergence d'une culture au feminin" at the University of Montreal, 1982, Festival of Women's Writing in Victoria, British Columbia, 1983, Congres mondial des litteratures de langue francaise in Padua, Italy, 1983, "Ruptures et necessites" in Ste.-Adele, Quebec, 1983, Salon du livre in Paris, 1984, Holland Festival in Amsterdam, the Netherlands, 1985, International Poetry Festival in Oslo, Norway, 1985, Poetic Colloquium in Vancouver, 1985, Borderline Poetry Festival in Detroit, MI, 1985, festival national de poesie in Trois-Rivieres, Quebec, 1985, "Feminism and the Humanities" in Australia, 1986, and the Second International Fair of Feminist Books in Oslo, 1986.

MEMBER: L'Union des ecrivains quebecois (member of board of directors, 1977-79; vice-president, 1983-85); Conseil des Arts de la Communaute urbaine de Montreal, 1989—.

AWARDS, HONOURS: Governor General's Award for poetry from Canada Council, 1974, for *Mecanique jongleuse,* and 1984, for *Double Impression;* Grand Prize for poetry, Fondation des Forges, 1989, for *A tout regard* and *Installations;* Athanase-David Prize, 1991; Harbourfront Festival Prize, 1991.

WRITINGS:

POETRY

Aube a la saison (title means "Dawning Season"), published in *Trois,* A.G.E.U.M., 1965.
Mordre en sa chair (title means "Bite the Flesh"), Esterel (Montreal), 1966.
L'Echo bouge beau (title means "The Echo Moves Beautifully"), Esterel (Montreal), 1968.
Suite logique (title means "Logical Suite/Sequence"), Hexagone (Montreal), 1970.
Le Centre blanc, Orphee (Montreal), 1970 (also see below).
Mecanique jongleuse, Generation (Paris), 1973 (also see below), translation by Larry Shouldice published as *Daydream Mecanics,* Coach House Press (Toronto), 1980.

Mecanique jongleuse; Masculin grammaticale, Hexagone (Montreal), 1974.
La Partie pour le tout, L'Aurore (Montreal), 1975.
Le Centre blanc (collected poems; includes "Le centre blanc"), Hexagone (Montreal) 1978 (also see above).
D'Arcs de cycle la derive, etchings by Francine Simonin, Maison (St.-Jacques-le-Mineur), 1979.
Amantes, Quinze (Montreal), 1980, translation by Barbara Godard published as *Lovhers,* Guernica (Montreal), 1986.
Double Impression: Poemes et textes 1967-1984 (collected poems), Hexagone (Montreal) 1985.
L'Aviva, NBJ (Montreal), 1985.
(With Daphne Marlatt), *Mauve,* NJB (Montreal), 1985.
Domaine d'ecriture, NJB (Montreal) 1985.
(With Marlatt) *Character/Jeu de lettres,* NBJ (Montreal) 1986.
Sous la langue/Under the Tongue, translation by Susanne de Lotbimier-Harwood, L'Essentielle (Montreal), 1987.
(With Marlatt) *A tout regard,* BQ (Montreal) 1989.
Installations: avec et sans pronoms, Trois-Rivieres (Quebec, Forges), 1989.
Langues obscures: poesie, L'Hexagone (Montreal), 1992.
Typhon dru, Generation (Paris), 1990 (?).
Langues Obscures, Hexagone (Montreal), 1992.
La Nuit Verte du Parc Labyrinthe, Trois Rivieres (Laval, Quebec), 1992 (translation by Lou Nelson and Marina Fe published as *Green Night of Labyrinth Park).*

PROSE

Un Livre, Editions du jour (Montreal), 1970, translation by Larry Shouldice published as *A Book,* Coach House Press (Toronto), 1976.
Sold-out: Etreinte/illustration (novel), Jour (Montreal), 1973, translation by Patricia Claxton published as *Turn of a Pang,* Coach House Press (Toronto), 1976.
French Kiss: Etreinte/exploration (novel), Jour (Montreal), 1974, translation by Patricia Claxton published as *French Kiss; or, A Pang's Progress,* Coach House Press (Toronto), 1986.
L'Amer ou, Le Chapitre effrite: Fiction theorique, Quinze (Montreal), 1977, revised edition, Hexagone (Montreal), 1988, translation by Barbara Godard published as *These Our Mothers; or, The Disintegrating Chapter,* Coach House Press (Toronto), 1983.
Le Sens apparent (title means "Surfaces of Meaning"), Flammarion (Paris), 1980, translation, Coach House Press (Toronto), 1989.
Picture Theory (fiction), Nouvelle Optique (Montreal), 1982, translated by Barbara Godard and published by Roof (New York) and Guernica (Montreal), 1991.
Le Desert mauve, Hexagone (Montreal), 1987; as *Mauve Desert,* Coach House Press (Toronto), 1990.

La Lettre aerienne (essays), Editions Remue-Menage, 1985, translation by Marlene Wilderman published as *The Aerial Letter,* Women's Press, 1988.

OTHER

"Narrateur et personnages" (play), first aired by Radio Canada, 1971.
"L'Ecrivain" (monologue; first produced at Le Theatre du nouveau mode, Montreal, 1976), published in *La Nef des sorcieres,* Quinze, 1976, translation by Linda Gaborian published as *The Writer* in *A Clash of Symbols,* Coach House Press (Toronto), 1979.
"Une Impression de fiction dans le retroviseur," first aired by Radio Canada, 1978
(Editor) *The Story so Far: Les Strategies du reel* (anthology), Coach House Press (Toronto), 1979.
Journal intimes; ou, Voila donc un manuscrit (first aired by Radio Canada, 1983), Les Herbes rouges, 1984.
"La Falaise," first aired by Radio Canada, 1985.
(Contributor) *Emergence d'une culture au feminin,* Editions Saint-Martin, 1987.
(Editor with Lisette Girouard) *Anthologie de la poesie des femmes au Quebec,* Remue-Menage (Montreal), 1991.

Work represented in anthologies, including *La Poesie contemporaine de langue francaise,* St.-Germain-des-Pres, 1973; *Quebec mai francia kolteszete,* Europa, 1978; *The Poets of Canada,* Hurtig Publishers, 1978; *Antologia de la poesia francesa actual, 1960-1976,* Editora nacional, 1979; *Anthologie '80,* Editions le Castor astral, 1981; *La Poesie quebecoise: Des Origines a nos jours,* Editions Ripostes, 1981; *Poesia des Quebec,* Editions Ripostes, 1985; *Sp/elles,* Black Moss Press, 1986; and *Poesie du monde francophone,* Le Castor astral/Le Monde, 1986; *Deep Down,* 1988; *Cradle and All,* 1989. Work has been translated into English, German, Italian, and Spanish.

Also associated with *Reelles,* Quinze, 1980. Contributor to periodicals including *Opus International, Etudes francaises, La barre du Jour, La Nouvelle Barre du Jour, Liberte, Possibles, Protee, Cross Country, Contemporary Literature, Exile, Room of One's Own, Journal of Canadian Fiction, Essays on Canadian Writing, Fireweed, Prism International, Island Ethos, Resources for Feminist Research, Cistre, Journal des poetes, Masques, Actuels, Action poetique, Fem, Lisaon, Les Herbes rouges, Trois, La Vie en rose, Dalhousie French Studies, Tessera, How(ever), Writing, Between C and D, Notus, Estuaire, Die Horen Vlasta, Oracl, Jungle, Chemin de ronde, Les cahiers bleus,* and *Trivia.*

SIDELIGHTS: Nicole Brossard, one of the most famous figures of contemporary Quebecois literature, published her first volume of poetry, *Aube a la s aison,* which means "Dawning Season," when she was twenty-two. This early

work, along with Brossard's second book of poems, *Mordre en sa chair* ("Bite the Flesh"), followed in the path of the 1950's and 1960's Quebecois tradition of *appartenance.* Taken from the French word *appartenance,* meaning "to belong to," *appartenance* was adopted as a literary term referring to mapping out spatial territory; Quebecois writers believed that by describing their land's physical features they could define its essence. While Brossard's work in her first two volumes has been compared to that of poets Paul-Marie Lapointe, Gaston Miron, Fernand Ouellette, and Paul Chamberland, Brossard's "appartenance" is different. As Caroline Bayard observed in *Essays of Canadian Writing* about *Mordre en sa chair,* "what she sets out to map in 1966 is not Quebec's territory but the human body. . . . History or time takes on physiological features, it is made flesh, given corporeal pleasure, pain, veins, blood, hair and muscles." And Barbara Godard remarks in *Contemporary World Writers* that Brossard's focus on the female body "attempted to undermine the symbolic Woman to examine women's desires."

Unlike *Aube a la saison,* which adhered to conventional linguistic forms, *Mordre en sa chair* is more experimental. Beginning with *Mordre en sa chair* and increasing with each following set of poems, Brossard deviates from traditional syntax and semantics, challenging readers through experimentation with punctuation, spacing, and typography. Her work in the years between 1966 and 1975 was shaped by a literary view which condemns the idea of poetry or prose as a reflection of objective reality. Important from this critical perspective are, in Bayard's words, "the linguistic tensions among [the literary text's] visual, graphic, and sonic elements, and the way these are resolved." In Brossard's native Quebec, this way of looking at literature led to writing as a form of subversion. Confusing syntax and grammar became a way of overthrowing traditional logic, which seemed analogous to the desire of the Quebec separatists of the 1960's to rid themselves of English-speaking Canadian rule. Of Brossard's *Daydream Mechanics* and *La Partie pour le tout,* Bayard remarked, "[Brossard] stylistically remains on the offensive. Syntax, grammar, lay-out, punctuation, spelling, omissions, all concur, to different degrees, to upset the rules and give us a provocative text, lashed by blanks and typographical variations, ambiguous hyphens, brackets and parentheses."

Brossard uses similar techniques in her novels *A Book, The Turn of a Pang,* and *French Kiss; or, A Pang's Progress. French Kiss* is set in Montreal, but its landscape is not intended to reflect reality. The novel which focuses on the experiences of Marielle, also includes her brother Alexandre, his friend Georges, and two women named Lucy and Camomille. Brossard is more concerned with detailing the physical qualities of these characters—their movements, their smells, their textures—than with exploring their inner psychologies. In Bayard's words, "The novel's focus is upon objects, sensations, and the way they hit the eye or start chain reactions of varying orders and intensities in all five senses."

Beginning in the mid-1970's, Brossard's poetry collections and novels become concerned with making strong feminist and lesbian statements. *These Our Mothers* stemmed from Brossard's realization that patriarchal society had stifled women's voices and that she needed to break this imposed silence by giving voice to women's previously censored desires. If examined casually, this need to speak from a lesbian-feminist viewpoint might seem contradictory to the literary perspective she embraced earlier, which devalued the meaning of a text in favor of its stylistic features, leaving little room for social statements. Brossard resolves the apparent conflict with the argument that traditional syntax and punctuation were established by a patriarchal society. In this way, her continued subversion of textual expectation is also a subversion of male dominance. As Barbara Godard explained in *Profiles in Canadian Literature 6,* "women's writing, according to Brossard, must inevitably be fiction and Utopia, visionary, posturing, feigning. By remaining self-conscious, and [using] deliberate artifice, it avoids the trap of naturalization, of pretending to be reality, that has made traditional writing a weapon for the subjugation of women and reality." Thus Brossard explores feminist ideas with elusive syntax and meaning in *These Our Mothers:* "The figure is real like a political intent to subject her to the plural before our eyes, or, singularly to power. The realistic figure is thus the most submissive there is. Quite simply, she agrees. She can be reduced then to the general (to the house) by using the singular: woman or image of milk women, *lait figures.* "

Godard also notes in *Contemporary World Writers* that during the 1970s Brossard "entered a formalist phase stimulated by French post-structuralism, especially the work of Roland Barthes which, following Ferdinand de Saussure, stressed the non-referentiality of signs (words) articulated as a system of differences. Brossard realized that words could never capture the private life of her body: they could however, combine in an infinite number of ways to create multiple networks."

Brossard's involvement with literary and feminist magazines, such as *La Barre du jour* and *Les Tetes de pioche,* both of which she co-founded, provided a forum for discussing the theory behind her experimental writing. Between 1968 and 1970 Brossard published articles in *La Barre du jour* and *La Presse* about the meaning expressed by her writing style. Later, when her interest moved in the direction of feminism, she helped establish the feminist

newspaper *Les Tetes de pioche* and introduced feminist viewpoints into *La Barre du jour.*

Like other Quebecois writers of the 1970's and 1980's, Brossard, especially in *Amantes* and *Le Sens apparent,* often associates the writing and/or reading process with sexuality. She differs from many of her peers, however, by adding a lesbian, feminist perspective to the sexual imagery that she weaves into her textual stylistics. Speaking of this practice, Bayard suggested: "There is a complicity, but also an ironic sense of defiance, between the two movements, as if they were almost bent on similar ends and yet wanted to destroy each other at the same time. . . . Stylistic figures and sexual movements occasionally—but only occasionally—become one." Godard notes in *Contemporary World Writers* that the third phase of Brossard's career is concerned with taking "up [the] call to 'make the difference' and [in it she] develops a poetics and politics of sexual difference. Influenced by French by French feminist philosophers such as Luce Irigaray and Helene Cixous (*q.v.*), Brossard developed a mode of writing she calls 'fiction/theory,' fiction as a hypothesis forming potential worlds."

This new phase, and its focus on the connection between sexuality and textuality, is reflected in *Amantes* (translated and published in English as *Lovhers*), "a set of love poems written for another woman . . . richly erotic in language and theme," according to Louise H. Forsyth's review in *Canadian Literature.* Forsyth notes that in the book, the two lovers "have been brought into the world by their love, their awareness, their language and the exchange of their experience. The result is dazzling, with the poet's voice stating in the end that her 'body is enraptured.' "

According to Forsyth, *Picture Theory* "picked up in narrative form major images and expressions from *Amantes.* " Eileen Manion called the book "a relentlessly postmodern text" that departs from two classics of modernist literature: Djuna Barnes's *Nightwood* and James Joyce's *Ulysses.* Godard calls it Brossard's "major work to date. . . .[a] book of light" which "rewrites the great modernist books of the night, especially the works of James Joyce." While a *Publishers Weekly* review found the language of the book "flat and dull, and Brossard's interpretation of the relationship between language and desire . . .narcisstic," Manion finds that the female characters of the book "always interact intensely, exuberantly, ecstatically." Using the metaphor of the hologram, Brossard is able, for Manion, to "develop a new way of seeing, in order to explore a new way of being."

Surfaces of Sense further explores the French feminist philosophy of writing the body and the intersection of theory and fiction, as, in the words of Charlene Diehl-Jones review for *Books in Canada,* Brossard's work "finger[s] the surfaces of experience" and continues her experimentation with language, syntax, and narrative. *Mauve Desert,* however, is probably Brossard's most popular work according to Godard. While a *Publishers Weekly* review declares the book "functions well as a literary game" but is ultimately unable "to support the meta-literature" it aspires to, Godard notes that it is probably "her most accessible" work.

Mauve Desert is set in the Arizona desert and is structured in three parts: a journal written by a young girl, the story of another girl's (Laure Angstell) finding, reading, and gradually becoming enthralled with the journal, and Laure's translation of the journal, with minor changes. Elizabeth Anthony, writing for *Books in Canada* did find that the "philosophical abstractions" did sometimes "dematerialize the real," but concludes that the volume "glitters as one of these rarefied reals, condensed from the genetics of language recoded."

Forsyth compares *Mauve Desert* with *Amantes/Lovhers:* "Brossard writes with the assumption that both the both the personal and the poetic are political. *Lovhers* and *Le Desert mauve.* . . . both . . . contain characters who write, read and appreciate the texts of others: words have unlimited power to move the imagination." In other words, for Brossard, as Forsyth claims, "Love known is love expressed. The taste of lips is inseparable from the taste of words, however had the right ones are to find."

Installations also reflects Brossard's major preoccupations with writing, feminism, sexuality, and subjectivity. Neil B. Bishop calls it "excellent Brossard," "a joy," adding that "Feminism goes hand in hand with linguistic transgression" in one of the book's poems, "Chapitre." But what he finds "most interesting is the tone of euphoric contemplation . . . with which these themes are treated."

Green Night of Labyrinth Park is a prose poem which, according to Charlene Diehl-Jones in another review for *Books in Canada,* "tracks real and imagined landscapes." Like many of Brossard's other works, it is in part, writes Diehl-Jones, concerned with the "politics of subjectivity and representation" and has moments of "great loveliness."

Nicole Brossard once told *CA:* "I write to understand the process of writing, words, words traveling back and forth between reality and fiction. The mind is too fast for words. Fiction is a very old-fashioned word to express a holographic body spiralling into space."

This sense of movement or motion between poles is also reflected in her comments in an interview with *Books in Canada:* "In feminist writing. . . .You have to write two kinds of pages almost at the same time: one on which you try to understand and uncover the patriarchal lies; and an-

other on which you try to give your new values, your utopias, and everything you find positive about yourself and about women. You have to write an unedited version, something that is totally new, to shape it. You bring in thoughts that have never been thought, use words in ways they have never been used. You want to bring your anger but also your utopia and your connection and solidarity with other women."

BIOGRAPHICAL/CRITICAL SOURCES:

BOOKS

A Mazing Space: Writing Canadian Women Writing, edited by Shirley Neuman, Longspoon, 1986.
Brosard, Nicole, *These Our Mothers,* translated by Barbara Godard, Coach House Press, 1983.
Contemporary World Writers, Gale, 1993.
Dictionary of Literary Biography, Volume 53: *Canadian Writers Since 1960, First Series,* Gale, 1986.
Dupre, Louise, *Strategies du vertige: trois poetes, Nicole Brossard, Madeleine Gagnon, France Theoret,* Editions du Remue-menage, 1989.
Heath, Jeffery M., *Profiles in Canadian Literature 6,* Dundurn Press, 1986.
Royer, Jean, *Ecrivains contemporains, entretiens 2,* Hexagone (Montreal) 1983.
Traditionalism, Nationalism, and Feminism: Women Writers of Quebec, edited by Paul Gilbert Lewis, Westport, 1985.

PERIODICALS

Booklist, February 1, 1992, p. 1012.
Books in Canada, November, 1990, p. 47, June/July, 1990, p. 41-2, December, 1991, p. 49, March, 1991, pp. 19-21, summer, 1993, p. 38-40.
Brechs, fall, 1973.
Broadside, June, 1981.
Canadian Journal of Fiction, numbers 25 and 26, 1979.
Canadian Literature, autumn, 1989, pp. 190-93, winter, 1992, p. 158-60, spring, 1992, p. 177-79, fall, 1993, p. 166-67.
Essays of Canadian Writing, fall, 1977.
Etudes litteraires, April, 1981.
Globe and Mail (toronto), May 2, 1976.
Hobo-Quebec, January, 1974.
Incidences, January-April, 1979, May-December, 1980.
La Nouvelle Barre du jour, November/December, 1982.
La Presse, September 28, 1974.
Le Devoir, December 19, 1970, April 14, 1973, July 13, 1974, May 7, 1975, May 23, 1975, June 21, 9175, December 15, 1978, October 30, 1982.
Les Cahiers de la femme, spring, 1979.
Le Soleil, April 28, 1973, September 28, 1974.
Lettres quebecoises, November, 1976, winter, 1980.
Livres et auteurs quebecois, 1970, 1973, 1974, 1975, 1980.

Present, October, 1978.
Publishers Weekly, November 1, 1991, p. 77, April 12, 1992, p. 53.
Room of One's Own, volume 4, numbers 1 and 2, 1978.
Sortie, October, 1982.
Vlasta (Paris), spring, 1983.
Voix et images du pays, number 9, 1975, September, 1977, fall, 1979.
Unomi e libri (Milan), September/October, 1983.
—*Sketch by Elizabeth Thomas, revised by Lisa Harper*

*   *   *

BRUCE, Charles (Tory) 1906-1971

PERSONAL: Born May 11, 1906, in Port Shoreham, Nova Scotia, Canada; died December 19, 1971, in Toronto, Ontario, Canada; son of William Henry (a farmer-fisher) and Sarah Jane (a teacher; maiden name, Tory) Bruce; married Agnes King, December 13, 1929; children: Alan, Harry, Andrew, Harvey. *Education:* Attended Guysborough Academy, Nova Scotia; Mount Allison University, B.A., 1927. *Religion:* Protestant.

CAREER: Chronicle, Halifax, NS, reporter, 1927; *Canadian Press,* Halifax, editor, 1928-33; *Canadian Press,* Toronto, editor, became general superintendent, 1933-63; war correspondent, 1944-45; poet and author.

MEMBER: Canadian Authors' Association.

AWARDS, HONOURS: Governor General's award for poetry, 1951, for *the Mulgrave Road;* D. Litt. from Mount Allison University, 1952.

WRITINGS:

Wild Apples (poetry), Tribune Press, 1927.
Tomorrow's Tide (poetry), Macmillan (Toronto), 1932.
Personal Note (poetry), Ryerson (Toronto), 1941.
Grey Ship Moving (poetry), Ryerson, 1945.
The Flowing Summer (poetry), Ryerson, 1947.
The Mulgrave Road (poetry), Macmillan, 1951.
The Channel Shore (novel), Macmillan, 1954.
The Township of Time (short stories), Macmillan, 1959.
News and the Southams (nonfiction), Macmillan, 1968.
The Mulgrave Road: Selected Poems (poetry), Pottersfield Press (Porter's Field, Nova Scotia), 1985.

Also author of radio plays. Contributor of short stories and poems to periodicals, including the *Atlantic Advocate, Canadian Author and Bookman, Canadian Poetry, Dalhousie Review, Maclean's* and *Saturday Night.*

SIDELIGHTS: Charles Bruce was one of Canada's most respected journalists and is also distinguished for his regional poetry and prose—characterized by concrete imagery and direct language—which often centered on the fictional Channel Shore. Analogous to the Chedabucto Bay area of Nova Scotia where Bruce grew up, Channel Shore's weather and terrain feature prominently in Bruce's work, lending a sense of time and place which the author emphasizes throughout as important to an individual's personal development as well as to his kinship with the world. Bruce's poetry was influenced by William Bliss Carman, poet laureate of Canada in 1928, and by the Georgians, an early twentieth-century movement of English pastoral poets who celebrated nature and the rustic life.

Bruce's birth in Port Shoreham, Nova Scotia, occurred in 1906. His parents, William Henry and Sarah Tory Bruce, were descended from a long line of Nova Scotia residents as far back as the American Revolution in the late 1700s. Inspired by his heritage, Bruce explored themes of ancestry as a subject matter in many of his writings, and was encouraged by an older sister to submit his stories and poems to local newspapers such as the *Evening Echo* in nearby Halifax. Later, in his short story collection *The Township of Time: A Chronicle* (published in 1959), Bruce returned to the motif of family genealogy through linked stories following a fictional Nova Scotia family whose generations are traced back to 1786.

During his college years in Sackville, New Brunswick, Bruce was editor of the *Argosy,* a campus publication. Upon graduation in 1927 he privately published his first book of poems and sonnets, *Wild Apples.* That same year he joined the staff of a newspaper in Halifax, transferring soon thereafter to the Canadian Press news bureau where he would spend the remainder of his career. Bruce worked as a journalist in Halifax until 1933, then relocated to the Toronto office, where he served for the next thirty years as editor, war correspondent, and, ultimately, as general superintendent. He was married in 1929 to Agnes King; the couple had four children, one of whom, Harry, became a successful non-fiction writer.

Tomorrow's Tide, Bruce's second book of poetry, was released in 1932. According to J. A. Wainwright in an entry for *Dictionary of Literary Biography,* the finest poems in this collection draw on the author's "Nova Scotia experience," evocative of the characteristics of the region and its significance to the individual: "Although he wrote in a conventional manner, with fixed rhyme scheme and stress patterns, Bruce was more concerned with the physical landscape in which wind and water replace dream." Similarly *The Flowing Summer,* 1947's long narrative poem, centers on a region by the sea. Here were the beginnings of Bruce's trademark Channel Shore legend—a place where working the land enriches the life of an elderly couple, who pass along the secrets of farming and fishing to their grandchild visiting from the city.

The onset of World War II was to have a profound effect on Bruce's personal life, as well as on his subsequent poetry. Sent to the front as a war correspondent in 1944, Bruce survived a crash-landing in Belgium and was listed for twenty-four hours as missing in action. Both *Personal Note,* and *Grey Ship Moving* consist of poetic meditations on lives interrupted by war. In the title poem of *Grey Ship Moving,* the narration follows a discussion between four Canadian officers on their way from Halifax to England aboard the troopship *Sappho.* Wainright noted that the volume is also significant because "the essential aspect . . . is that in it Bruce includes those poems he began to write in the late 1930s, poems in which he broke away from his traditional manner of writing verse."

The Mulgrave Road, Bruce's 1951 tome, is an accumulation of lyrics (including some already published in the above-mentioned *Grey Ship Moving*) which was honored with the Governor General's award for poetry. Here Bruce again employs the Channel Shore to emphasize the heritage of land and sea, past and present, and people moving through " 'the skein of time,' " as Wainwright explained. A new edition of this volume featuring an introduction written by the poet's son Harry was released in 1985 as *The Mulgrave Road: Selected Poems of Charles Bruce.*

Although most often recognized for his poetry, Bruce also wrote a successful novel, 1954's *The Channel Shore.* Set in a farming-fishing town, the story follows events from 1919 through 1946 in a family linked to the land through time and change. The main character, Alan Marshall, discovers the secret of his birth, and thereby finds his loyalties challenged. Winding throughout the narrative is the everpresent Channel Shore—the region and the people— reflecting and inspiring Alan's devotion to both land and family. The exploration of relationships, is central to the story, as Wainwright observed in the *Dictionary of Literary Biography:* "The influence of individual experience is tempered by the heritage of community. . . . with the universal theme of human kinship."

Bruce's last book, *News and the Southams,* is an historical account of the *Southam Press,* written during the author's retirement from the Canadian Press. Bruce died in 1971 in Toronto, Ontario. Several of his works have been republished posthumously, including 1980s editions of *The Channel Shore* and *The Township of Time.*

BIOGRAPHICAL/CRITICAL SOURCES:

BOOKS

Dictionary of Literary Biography, Volume 68: *Canadian Writers, 1920-1959, First Series,* Gale, 1988, pp. 29-32.

Moss, John, *Patterns of Isolation,* McClelland & Stewart, 1974, pp. 166-88.
Wainwright, J. A., *World Enough and Time: Charles Bruce, A Literary Biography,* Formac, 1988.

PERIODICALS

Dalhousie Review, autumn, 1979, pp. 443-51.
Studies in Canadian Literature, Volume 8, 1983, pp. 238-47.*

*   *   *

BRULARD, Henri
See BAILLARGEON, Pierre

*   *   *

BRYAN, Michael
See MOORE, Brian

*   *   *

BUCKLER, Ernest   1908-1984

PERSONAL: Born July 19, 1908, in Dalhousie West, Nova Scotia, Canada; died after a long illness, March 4, 1984, in Bridgetown, Nova Scotia, Canada; son of Appleton (a farmer) and Mary (Swift) Buckler. *Education:* Dalhousie University, B.A., 1929; University of Toronto, M.A., 1930.

CAREER: Manufacturer's Life Insurance Co., Toronto, Ontario, actuarial work, 1931-36; farmer in Nova Scotia, beginning in 1936; free-lance writer, 1937-84.

AWARDS, HONOURS: $1,000 prize, *Maclean's,* 1948, for fiction; President's Medal, Governor-General Awards Board, 1957 and 1958, for best Canadian short story; Canada Council fellowships, 1960, 1963, and 1966; D.Litt., University of New Brunswick, 1969.

WRITINGS:

NOVELS

The Mountain and the Valley, Henry Holt, 1952.
The Cruelest Month, McClelland and Stewart, 1963.

OTHER

Oxbells and Fireflies: A Memoir, Knopf, 1968.

Also author of *Nova Scotia: Window on the Sea* (with photographs by Hans Weber), 1973; *The Rebellion of Young David and Other Stories,* 1975; and *Whirligig: Selected Prose and Verse,* 1977. Contributor of short stories to several collections, including *Atlantic Anthology*, McClelland and Stewart; *Maclean's Canada*, McClelland and Stewart; *Christmas in Canada*, Dent; and *Canadian Short Stories*, Ryerson. Writer of scripts for radio plays and talks. Contributor of stories and articles to *Coronet, Esquire, Atlantic Monthly, Country Gentlemen, Ladies' Home Journal, Chatelaine, Liberty, Star Weekly, Los Angeles Times,* and other magazines and newspapers. Former columnist, *Saturday Night.*

SIDELIGHTS: Ernest Buckler wrote lyrical, somber works about Nova Scotia. Buckler spent almost his entire life there, working as a writer and a farmer in the Annapolis Valley. His first and best-known novel, *The Mountain and the Valley,* follows the growth of a sensitive young Nova Scotian, David Canaan, toward adulthood. *The Cruelest Month,* Buckler's second novel, depicts a group of people who confront personal issues while on a retreat. In his memoir *Oxbells and Fireflies: A Memoir,* Buckler describes a rural life that was quickly passing into memory. Buckler's other writings, *Nova Scotia: Window on the Sea, The Rebellion of Young David and Other Stories,* and *Whirligig: Selected Prose and Verse,* feature his satires, essays, and poems.

BIOGRAPHICAL/CRITICAL SOURCES:

BOOKS

Canada Writes!, Writer's Union of Canada, 1977.
Contemporary Literary Criticism, Volume 13, Gale, 1980.

PERIODICALS

Maclean's, March 19, 1984.

*   *   *

**BUGNET, Georges (-Charles-Jules)   1879-1981
   (Henri Doutremont)**

PERSONAL: Born February 23, 1879, in Chalon-sur-Saone, France; immigrated to Canada, 1905; died January 11, 1981; son of Claude and Josephine (Sebut) Bugnet; married Julia Ley, c. 1904; children: nine. *Religion:* Catholic.

CAREER: Worked as the editor of a weekly journal in France, c. 1904; farmer and breeder of hybrid roses in Alberta, Canada; free-lance writer, beginning c. 1920.

WRITINGS:

UNDER PSEUDONYM HENRI DOUTREMONT

Le Lys de sang (novel; title means "The Blood Lily"), Garand (Montreal), 1923.
Nipsya (novel), Garand, 1924; translated by Constance Davies-Woodrow, Louis Carrier (New York), 1929.

UNDER NAME GEORGES BUGNET

Siraf (novel), Totem (Montreal), 1934.
La Foret (novel), Totem, 1935; translated by David Carpenter as *The Forest,* Harvest House (Montreal), 1976.
Voix de la Solitude (stories and poems; title means "Voices of Solitude"; includes "Le Pin du Maskeg"), Totem, 1938.
Poems, edited by Jean-Marcel Duciaume, Eglantier (Edmonton), 1978.
Journal, edited and annotated by Georges Durocher and Odette Tamer-Salloum, Institut de recherche de la Faculte Saint-Jean, University of Alberta (Edmonton), 1984.
Albertaines: Anthologie d'oeuvres courtes en prose, presented and annotated by Gamila Morcos, with preface by Guy Lecomte, Editions des Plaines (St. Boniface, Manitoba), 1990.

Also contributor of articles, plays, and short stories to periodicals, including *La Canada Francais.*

SIDELIGHTS: French-Canadian author Georges Bugnet is best remembered for his stories, novels, and poems in which nature is often one of the strongest characters. Critics differ on his importance relative to other Canadian writers, but E. D. Blodgett in the *Dictionary of Literary Biography* described Bugnet as "the one writer of French origin published in the twentieth century whose career was fundamentally Canadian." Blodgett explained the author's comparative obscurity in part by "the fact that his life was spent outside Quebec," noting that this "has prevented him from receiving the respect he is due as a major French-Canadian writer of the period between the two wars."

Bugnet was born in 1879 in Chalon-sur-Saone, France. Although his early career ambition was to enter the priesthood, he took a position as the editor of a weekly journal in 1904, the same year he married. By 1905, Bugnet and his wife had immigrated to Alberta. They bought a farm in the countryside near Edmonton. At first, he intended to return to France after making a profit, but he remained in Canada for the rest of his life. Among Bugnet's accomplishments as a farmer was the development of several hybrid species of roses.

By 1920 Bugnet had decided to supplement his farming income by writing fiction. That year he began his first novel, *Le Lys de sang,* which was published under the pseudonym "Henri Doutremont" in 1923. Set in the jungles of East Africa, *Le Lys de sang,* or "the blood lily," details the quest to find a legendary lily that finds its nourishment in human blood. Though later compared to the fictions of H. Rider Haggard and Jules Verne, *Le Lys de sang* went virtually unnoticed by readers and critics.

Bugnet achieved wider renown as a writer with his 1924 short story, "Le Pin du Maskeg," which was included in his collection *Voix de la solitude.* "Le Pin du Maskeg" centers on a pine tree that symbolizes the superiority of nature over humanity. It stands witness to the murder of a man by his wife's lover, and in its stillness, speaks to the indifference of the natural world to human schemes and machinations.

Nature also dominates Bugnet's 1924 novel, *Nipsya,* first published under the Doutremont pseudonym and translated into English in 1929. *Nipsya* considers the conflict faced by a young Metisse who must choose a husband from among three suitors. Bugnet followed *Nipsya* with a more abstractly philosophical novel, 1934's *Siraf.* Blodgett called *Siraf* "a scathing satire on the limitations of modernity, materialism, technology, and democracy," and noted that Bugnet's viewpoint was not typical of other French-Canadian authors, again contributing to his relative lack of position within that literary canon.

Bugnet's best-known work, *La Foret,* saw print in 1935 and was translated as *The Forest* in 1976. *The Forest* tells the story of a young couple who move from the city to the wilderness. Tragedy ensues because of their underestimation of nature and their false belief in its benevolence. Blodgett hailed the novel as "Bugnet's most accomplished work."

Bugnet's last book-length project was 1938's *Voix de la solitude,* or "voices of solitude," which comprises short stories and poetry. Some of the poems in this volume were published separately in 1978 under the title *Poems.* Since Bugnet's death in 1981, selections from his diaries have been published as *Journal,* and a collection of his short pieces entitled *Albertaines: Anthologie d'oeuvres courtes en prose* saw print in 1990.

BIOGRAPHICAL/CRITICAL SOURCES:

BOOKS

Bugnet, Georges, *Journal,* edited and annotated by Georges Durocher and Odette Tamer-Salloum, Institut de recherche de la Faculte Saint-Jean, University of Alberta, 1984.
Dictionary of Literary Biography, Volume 92: *Canadian Writers, 1890-1920,* Gale, 1990.
Papen, Jean, *Georges Bugnet, homme de lettres canadien,* Editions des Plaines (St. Boniface, Manitoba), 1985.

PERIODICALS

Journal of Canadian Fiction, fall, 1972; spring, 1973.*

—*Sketch by Elizabeth Wenning*

BURNFORD, Sheila (Philip Cochrane Every) 1918-1984

PERSONAL: Born May 11, 1918, in Scotland; died of cancer, April 20, 1984, in Bucklers Hard, Hampshire, England; daughter of Wilfred George Cochrane and Ida Philip (Macmillan) Every; married David Burnford, 1941; children: Peronelle Philip, Elizabeth Jonquil, Juliet Sheila. *Education:* Privately educated in England, France, and Germany. *Religion:* Anglican. *Avocational interests:* Hunting, mycology, astronomy.

CAREER: Writer, 1948-84.

MEMBER: Society of Authors (England), Canadian Authors Association, Authors Guild (United States).

AWARDS, HONOURS: Canadian Book of the Year for Children medal, 1963, Aurianne Award from American Library Association, 1963, Lewis Carroll Shelf Award, 1971, William Allen White Award, Dorothy Canfield Fisher Award, Young People's Choice Award from Pacific Northwestern Libraries Association, and honorable mention from Hans Christian Andersen Awards, all for *The Incredible Journey;* "Books for the Teen Age" citation from New York Public Library, 1980-82, for *Bel Ria.*

WRITINGS:

The Incredible Journey, illustrated by Carl Burger, Little, Brown, 1961, reprinted, Bantam, 1977.
The Fields of Noon (autobiographical essays), Little, Brown, 1964.
Without Reserve, Atlantic, 1969.
One Woman's Arctic, illustrated by Susan Ross, Little, Brown, 1973.
Mr. Noah and the Second Flood, illustrated by Michael Foreman, Praeger, 1973.
Bel Ria, Little, Brown, 1978, published in England as *Bel Ria: Dog of War,* McClelland and Stewart, 1977.

Contributor of essays to magazines and newspapers.

ADAPTATIONS: The Incredible Journey was twice adapted as a motion picture by the Walt Disney Studios.

SIDELIGHTS: A trio of personal pets inspired the late Sheila Burnford to write *The Incredible Journey,* a modern classic in children's literature. Set in the wilds of northern Ontario, *The Incredible Journey* recounts the efforts of an aging Bull Terrier, a Siamese cat, and a young Labrador Retriever as they try to find their way home through hundreds of miles of wilderness. First published in 1961, *The Incredible Journey* has been translated into more than twenty-five languages and has been the inspiration for two feature-length Disney films. It is one of several Burnford novels that have become favorites among younger teenaged readers.

Sheila Burnford was born in Scotland in 1918 and educated there and in England. In the midst of the Second World War she married Dr. David Burnford, then a surgeon in the Royal Navy. For long periods of time she was isolated in Sussex, subject to long nights without electric light as part of the government-mandated blackout. Her comfort during these trying times was an almond-eyed Bull Terrier named Bill. In a piece for *Profiles,* the author said: "I laugh when I look back upon it, for I used to read to [Bill] in the evenings—excerpts from the papers and a long session of Anthony Trollope. There was no one else to listen or to whom I could talk, as the two oldest children were only babies, so the terrier became my captive audience."

After the war, the Burnford family moved to Port Arthur, Ontario. There, as the children became school age, Bill acquired a new companion—a Siamese cat named Simon. Later, Burnford's husband bought a Labrador Retriever for hunting. The three animals showed uncanny perception and tolerance of one another, taking walks together and even sleeping in the same basket.

In the meantime, Burnford was honing her talents as a writer, producing scripts for the Port Arthur Puppetry Club and writing essays about Canada for British magazines. The death of the beloved Bull Terrier inspired her to begin work on *The Incredible Journey.*

In a style similar to Anna Sewell's *Black Beauty, The Incredible Journey* is a tale of hardship, friendship, and survival in the face of almost overwhelming odds. The three pets overcome attack by wild animals, hunger, fatigue, and bad weather to find their way back to the home and family they love. Through this simple animal story, Burnford illustrates the qualities that make friendships endure: devotion to a cause, courage, and bonds that are stronger than the individual will to survive. In *Children and Books,* May Hill Arbuthnot and Zena Sutherland write: "This beautifully written saga of three gallant animals is a superb story to read aloud either in the home or classroom."

In the wake of the success of *The Incredible Journey,* Burnford determined not to become merely an "animal novelist." Instead she devoted a great deal of time to her writing for adults, on such adult themes as the plight of the Arctic and the fate of Canada's Indian population. The author told *Publishers Weekly:* "I wanted to prove that I could *write* without using the crutch of animal popularity."

Nevertheless, Burnford's most widely read titles are those that include animals. *Mr. Noah and the Second Flood* is a cautionary tale about ecology and the survival of life on a polluted planet, and *Bel Ria* is a sentimental account of a small performing dog rescued during the Second World War by British soldiers and sent to live in England. Burn-

ford told *Publishers Weekly* that she always tried to create her animal characters with an eye towards realism. She conceded, however, that in our society—and our literature—pets provide an important function. "Animals remain unchanged, in character, by the winds of politics, greed, terrorism, oil spillage and all the daily horror with which the media bombard our minds," she said. "So I suppose they are a welcome turnoff."

Burnford died of cancer on April 20, 1984. She is one author who never enjoyed the process of writing as much as she did her numerous hobbies. "I'm happiest when I'm doing something creative with my hands—and it can be misery shut away with a typewriter and only one's mind for company," she admitted. "I'm a back-to-the-wall, deadline-looming, undisciplined-in-time writer whose mind starts functioning toward evening. . . . I write into the small hours for days and weeks at a time, growing ever more tired and miserable. And the more dejected I become, the more easily the words flow!"

BIOGRAPHICAL/CRITICAL SOURCES:

BOOKS

Arbuthnot, May Hill, and Zena Sutherland, *Children and Books,* Scott, Foresman, 1972, pp. 413-14.
Children's Literature Review, Volume 2, Gale, 1976.
Contemporary Authors New Revision Series, Volume 1, Gale, 1982.
Fourth Book of Junior Authors and Illustrators, Wilson, 1978.
McDonough, Irma, editor, *Profiles,* Canadian Library Association, 1975.
Something about the Author, Volume 3, Gale, 1972.

PERIODICALS

Canadian Children's Literature, number 12, 1978.
Christian Science Monitor, December, 1961.
Horn Book, June, 1961.
New York Times Book Review, December 16, 1973.
Publishers Weekly, March 27, 1978, pp. 6-7.

OBITUARIES:

PERIODICALS

Washington Post, May 1, 1984.*

*   *   *

BUTLER, Juan (Antonio)   1942-1981

PERSONAL: Born July 4, 1942, in London, England; immigrated to Canada, 1942; committed suicide, June 2, 1981; son of an insurance clerk; married in 1974 (marriage ended).

CAREER: Worked variously as a shoe salesperson, warehouse laborer, translator, insurance clerk, bartender, and cashier in a socialist bookstore.

AWARDS, HONOURS: Received grants from the Canada Council and the Ontario Arts Council, mid-1970s.

WRITINGS:

Cabbagetown Diary: A Documentary, PMA (Toronto), 1970.
The Garbageman, PMA, 1972.
Canadian Healing Oil, PMA, 1974.

"The Happy Gang Rides Again" appeared in *Northern Journey.*

SIDELIGHTS: The three novels of Juan Butler "are impassioned indictments of a squalid world that robs man of dignity," asserted *Oxford Companion to Canadian Literature* writer David Staines. Born in London, Butler immigrated to Toronto with his family shortly after his birth in 1942; he dropped out of school as a teenager and later alternated time in Europe with job stints that ranged from insurance firm clerk to warehouse laborer to shoe salesperson. In the late 1960s Butler lived in an infamous working-class neighborhood of Toronto known as Cabbagetown and began keeping a journal of his observations and impressions of the rough and poverty-stricken area. After three months of note-taking, he assembled his chronicle into the 1970 novel *Cabbagetown Diary: A Documentary.* Michael, its protagonist, shares certain traits with the author; an immigrant to Canada and a denizen of Cabbagetown eking out a living as a bartender, he manifests the effects of his life of privation. Explaining his rejection of a woman he has impregnated, he states simply, "Somebody had to show her how to make out in this world." Wayne Grady, in an essay on Butler for the *Dictionary of Literary Biography,* termed *Cabbagetown Diary* "a highly charged delineation of the mind-numbing effects of poverty" and "a powerful and compelling book." Grady also remarked, "It is not inappropriate that *Cabbagetown Diary* has been placed on reading lists for university sociology courses, for it is more social documentary than novel, an attempt to portray the effects of environment rather than to explore solutions to the poverty and violence."

Butler's second novel, *The Garbageman,* is similarly autobiographical. The 1972 work, completed in just six weeks, chronicles a period in the life of another troubled young male protagonist, Fred Miller. Miller rejects a budding career in his father's insurance business (as did Butler) to travel to Europe. He winds up in a psychiatric hospital back in Canada, however, and believes he may have committed two murders during the course of his travels. Much of the book is given over to recounting the gory particulars of each of the deeds. Butler sent *The Garbageman* to English writer Colin Wilson, who wrote back that he "found it very interesting although (as you probably expected) a bit revolting." Wilson urged Butler to move away from simple gratuitous violence in his writing and suggested that his opportunity to be heard might be better spent addressing the sociological issues that are the root of violence.

Butler's third novel, *Canadian Healing Oil,* appeared in 1974, after the writer had been awarded grants from Canadian arts agencies to travel to Puerto Rico and the Virgin Islands. He incorporated some of his experiences there into the surrealistic plot of this final literary effort. John, another confused male protagonist (employed in a bookstore, as Butler once was), becomes enamored of an exotic female customer; on her bed he dreams of a journey to the Caribbean, but then awakes and either dreams again of his sojourn or actually embarks upon it. When he arrives, somebody gives him a bottle of the "Canadian Healing Oil" that is to be applied "solely for the moment when you come face to face with your . . . destiny." Many elements in *Canadian Healing Oil* speak of Butler's own troubled introspection and identity crisis. John (Juan) wanders through both San Juan, Puerto Rico, and the island of St. John; St. John the Baptist also appears at various points in the narrative, as does Jean de Brebeuf, a Jesuit missionary killed by Iroquois in 1649. This "artist-as-martyr theme became a sad prophecy of Butler's final years," noted Staines in the *Oxford Companion to Canadian Literature,* "when his psychological suffering offered him no peace."

No further work of Butler's was published, and he was found dead in a psychiatric clinic in 1981, having hanged himself. In the *Dictionary of Literary Biography* essay, Grady praised the trio of books the writer left behind that "speak eloquently and convincingly of Butler's futile search for meaning in a universe he perceived as violent and illogical."

BIOGRAPHICAL/CRITICAL SOURCES:

BOOKS

Butler, Juan, *Cabbagetown Diary: A Documentary,* PMA (Toronto), 1970.
Butler, *Canadian Healing Oil,* PMA, 1974.
Dictionary of Literary Biography, Volume 53: *Canadian Writers since 1960,* Gale, 1986.
Oxford Companion to Canadian Literature, Oxford University Press, 1983.*

C

CALLAGHAN, Morley Edward 1903-1990

PERSONAL: Born September 22, 1903, in Toronto, Ontario, Canada; died August 25, 1990, in Toronto, Ontario, Canada; son of Thomas and Mary (Dewan) Callaghan; married Loretto Florence Dee, April 16, 1929; children: Michael, Barry. *Education:* St. Michael's College, University of Toronto, B.A., 1925; Osgoode Hall Law School, LL.B., 1928. *Religion:* Catholic. *Avocational interests:* Spectator sports.

CAREER: Novelist and short story writer, 1926-90. *Toronto Daily Star,* Ontario, reporter, beginning 1923. Called to the bar, 1928. Traveled across Canada for Canadian Broadcasting Company as chair of the radio program *Of Things to Come* (renamed *Citizen's Forum*), 1943-47. Panel member of radio quiz show *Beat the Champs,* beginning 1947, member of radio show *Now I Ask You,* and panelist on television show *Fighting Words,* beginning c. 1950. *Military service:* Worked during World War II with the Royal Canadian Navy on assignment for the National Film Board.

AWARDS, HONOURS: Governor General's Literary Award for fiction, 1952, for *The Loved and the Lost;* fiction prize, *Maclean's,* 1955, for *The Man with the Coat;* Lorne Pierce Medal for Literature, Royal Society of Canada, 1960, "for a body of work which will endure"; gold medal of Royal achievement of special significance in imaginative literature, 1960; medal of merit, City of Toronto, 1962; Honorary LL.D., University of Western Ontario, 1965; LL.D., University of Toronto, 1966; Canada Council Molson prize, 1970; Royal Bank of Canada award for distinguished work, 1970; Companion Order of Canada, 1983.

WRITINGS:

NOVELS

Strange Fugitive, Scribner, 1928.
It's Never Over, Scribner, 1930.
No Man's Meat (novella), Edward W. Titus, At the Sign of the Black Manikin (Paris), 1931.
A Broken Journey, Scribner, 1932.
Such Is My Beloved, Scribner, 1934, revised edition with an introduction by Malcolm Ross, McClelland & Stewart, 1957.
They Shall Inherit the Earth, Random House, 1935, revised edition with an introduction by F. W. Watt, McClelland & Stewart, 1962.
More Joy in Heaven, Random House, 1937, revised edition with an introduction by Hugo McPherson, McClelland & Stewart, 1960.
The Varsity Story, Macmillan (Toronto), 1948.
Luke Baldwin's Vow (juvenile), Winston, 1948.
The Loved and the Lost, Macmillan, 1951.
The Many Colored Coat, Coward, 1960, published as *The Man with the Coat,* Exile Editions, 1988.
A Passion in Rome, Coward, 1961.
A Fine and Private Place, Mason/Charter, 1975.
Close to the Sun Again, Macmillan, 1977.
No Man's Meat and The Enchanted Pimp, Macmillan (Toronto), 1978.
A Time for Judas, Macmillan (Toronto), 1983, St. Martin's, 1984.
Our Lady of the Snows (based on his novella *The Enchanted Pimp*), Macmillan (Toronto), 1985, St. Martin's, 1986.

OTHER

A Native Argosy (short stories), Scribner, 1929.
Now That April's Here, and Other Stories, Random House, 1937.

Turn Again Home (play; based on the novel *They Shall Inherit the Earth*), produced in New York City, 1940, produced under title *Going Home* in Toronto, 1950.

To Tell the Truth (play), produced in Toronto, 1949.

Morley Callaghan's Stories, Macmillan, 1959, two-volume edition, MacGibbon & Kee, 1962.

That Summer in Paris: Memories of Tangled Friendships with Hemingway, Fitzgerald, and Some Others, Coward, 1963.

Stories, Macmillan (Toronto), 1967.

An Autumn Penitent, Macmillan (Toronto), 1973.

Winter, photographs by John de Visser, New York Graphic Society, 1974.

The Lost and Found Stories of Morley Callaghan, Lester & Orpen Dennys/Exile Editions, 1985.

Also author of the play *Just Ask George,* 1940. Contributor to *Sixteen by Twelve: Short Stories by Canadian Writers,* edited by John Metcalf, Ryerson (Toronto), 1970. Also contributor of more than one hundred short stories to periodicals, including *Scribner's, New Yorker, Harper's Bazaar, Maclean's, Esquire, Cosmopolitan, Saturday Evening Post, Yale Review, New World, Performing Arts in Canada,* and *Twentieth Century Literature.*

ADAPTATIONS: Now That April's Here was adapted for film by Klenman-Davidson Productions, 1958.

SIDELIGHTS: Morley Edward Callaghan's fictional work, acclaimed for its cosmopolitan appeal and moral perspective, has been published not only in Canada, but also in the United States and France. Throughout his lifetime, Callaghan produced more than a dozen novels, hundreds of short stories, and several plays. Callaghan began his career as a reporter for the *Toronto Daily Star* while still in college, a job he received by offering to work free for the first week. He met Ernest Hemingway, the *Star*'s European correspondent, and they became friends. Hemingway encouraged and supported Callaghan's writing and provided connections for his short stories to be published in France and the United States.

By the time he graduated from law school, Callaghan already had many short stories and one book published; he then decided to become a writer. After the publication of his second book, Callaghan married and honeymooned in Paris, where he visited with Hemingway and became acquainted with F. Scott Fitzgerald. During this time Callaghan became renowned for besting Hemingway in a controversial 1929 fight. The contest, which ended when Callaghan knocked down the larger, more aggressive Hemingway, was marred by timekeeper F. Scott Fitzgerald's failure to end the first round at the agreed-upon time of one minute. Fitzgerald later claimed that he was so entranced by the contest that he completely forgot to end the round. In the fourth minute of nonstop action, Callaghan

grounded his opponent with a devastating blow to the jaw. Not only did the fight strain their relationship, Callaghan later contended that his pugilistic feat obscured his achievements as a writer.

Critics proposed other reasons why the prolific writer did not receive the recognition he deserved. Edmund Wilson writes in *O Canada:* "The Canadian Morley Callaghan, at one time well known in the United States, is today perhaps the most unjustly neglected novelist in the English-speaking world." Wilson notes that "when I talked about Callaghan [in the late 1950s], such people as remembered his existence were likely to think he was dead." Wilson offers several explanations for the fact that Callaghan is virtually unknown outside his native country, the most "striking" reason being "the partial isolation of that country [Canada] from the rest of the cultural world. . . . My further reading of Callaghan's novels has suggested another reason . . . for their relative unpopularity. Almost all of them end in annihilating violence or, more often, in blank unfulfillment. . . . All these endings have their moral point: recognition of personal guilt, loyalty in personal relationships, the nobility of some reckless devotion to a Christian ideal of love which is bound to come to grief in the world. But they are probably too bleak for the ordinary reader. . . . Only a very sober, self-disciplined and 'self-directed' writer could have persisted, from decade to decade, in submitting these parables to the public. They are almost invariably tragic, but their tragedy avoids convulsions and it allows itself no outbreak in tirades."

Callaghan's writings, including *Such Is My Beloved, They Shall Inherit the Earth, More Joy in Heaven,* and *A Time for Judas,* often focus on religious themes and imagery. *Such Is My Beloved,* his first major novel, tells the story of protagonist Father Dowling, a Christ-like figure who works to assist two reformed prostitutes, but is abandoned by the church and his parish. The church and parishoners are concerned about a scandal. Echoing the life of Christ, the action of the novel occurs between February and Easter. *Such Is My Beloved* generally met with good reviews. *Form and Century*'s Mary Colum finds Callaghan a sensitive writer, asserting that the Dowling character is "drawn with such subtlety and insight that it is powerfully convincing to readers."

Maintaining a religious theme in his novel *A Time for Judas,* Callaghan tells the story of a modern day archaeologist who uncovers a manuscript written by the scribe to Pontius Pilate. The scribe is also a friend and confidant of Judas Iscariot. Through this manuscript, biblical history during the last days of Christ's life is recreated explaining why Christ was betrayed, why Judas betrayed him, and why no one stopped Judas. "It makes clear the anti-establishment, populist roots of Christianity," states Margaret Atwood in her review for *Saturday Night.* She adds that the author "answers . . . questions that must have puzzled more people than Callaghan." The novel displays "Callaghan's continued mastery of narrative, his sweet inventiveness with plot. To put it bluntly, he remains one of the best story-tellers in Canada. . . . The twists and turns of *A Time for Judas* are rarely predictable. And this, in turn, pays tribute to Callaghan's subtlety at creating character," comments *Canadian Literature*'s Mark Abley. And Graham Carr concludes in his review of the book for *Essays on Canadian Writing* that "*A Time for Judas* is a delightful piece of writing . . . the text remains both vivid and comprehensible."

In addition to his acclaim as a twentieth-century novelist, Callaghan earned respect as a short story writer. A collection of his work was culled from magazines from 1930 to 1950 and put together by Callaghan's son Barry in 1985 as a tribute to his father. Titled simply *Morley Callaghan's Stories,* the book represents many of the author's best short stories. James C. MacDonald, describing the essence of the collection in a *Books in Canada* review, writes: "For Callaghan, the point of a story is the revelation of significant moment of self-awareness. The difficulty of its discovery lies in acknowledging the danger inherent in seemingly inconsequential events and having the courage and honesty to transcend them. These stories brilliantly show the variety of ways human beings can respond to the challenge." Praising Callaghan's skill and noting his place in contemporary literature, a *Canadian Forum* columnist reviewing *Morley Callaghan's Stories* summarizes this collection as "one of the few major achievements of Canadian prose, more powerful than any single Callaghan novel and more worthy of enduring than any single work of his better publicized peers: Anderson, Hemingway and Fitzgerald." While the columnist concedes that "Mr. Callaghan does have his limits: he plays no games with time and infinity. Literary innovations leave him cold, the corporational vulture which feeds us all never enters into his fiction." He/she also concludes, "there is one major unreality to which he returns time and time again: emotion. . . . But for his era, when the media, the false prophets, the corporations, did not place so much underbrush between the human being and life (underbrush which the modern writer must deal with), Callaghan created a method that worked extraordinarily well. Never has the urban low bourgeois been dealt with quite so humanely, quite so creatively."

BIOGRAPHICAL/CRITICAL SOURCES:

BOOKS

Cameron, Donald, *Conversations with Canadian Novelists, Part Two,* Macmillan (Toronto), 1973.
Conron, Brandon, *Morley Callaghan,* Twayne, 1966.

Contemporary Literary Criticism, Gale, Volume 3, 1975; Volume 14, 1980; Volume 41, 1987.
Dictionary of Literary Biography, Volume 68: *Canadian Writers, 1920-1959, First Series* Gale, 1988.
Hoar, Victor, *Morley Callaghan,* Copp, 1969.
Lecker, Robert and Jack David, editors, *The Annotated Bibliography of Canada's Major Authors 5,* ECW Press, 1984.
Morley, Patricia, *Morley Callaghan,* McClelland & Stewart, 1978.
Wilson, Edmund, *O Canada,* Farrar, Straus, 1965.

PERIODICALS

Books in Canada, April, 1986, pp. 32-33.
Canadian Forum, March, 1960, February, 1968.
Canadian Literature, summer, 1964; winter, 1984, pp. 66-69.
Dalhousie Review, autumn, 1959.
Essays on Canadian Writing, winter, 1984-85, pp. 309-15.
Form and Century, April, 1934.
New Republic, February 9, 1963.
New Yorker, November 26, 1960.
Queen's Quarterly, autumn, 1957.
Saturday Night, October, 1983, pp. 73-74.
Tamarack Review, winter, 1962.

OBITUARIES:

PERIODICALS

Chicago Tribune, August 29, 1990.
Los Angeles Times, August 29, 1990.
New York Times, August 27, 1990.
Times (London), August 28, 1990.
Washington Post, August 28, 1990.

*   *   *

CAMERON, Eleanor (Frances)   1912-

PERSONAL: Born March 23, 1912, in Winnipeg, Manitoba, Canada; daughter of Henry and Florence Lydia (Vaughan) Butler; married Ian Stuart Cameron (a printer and publisher), June 24, 1934; children: David Gordon. *Education:*Attended University of California, Los Angeles, 1931-33, and Art Center School, Los Angeles, one year.

ADDRESSES: Home—2865 Forest Lodge Rd., Pebble Beach, CA 93953.*Office*—E. P. Dutton, 2 Park Ave., New York, NY 10016.

CAREER: Public Library, Los Angeles, CA, clerk, 1930-36; Board of Education Library, Los Angeles, clerk, 1936-42; Foote, Cone & Belding (advertising agency), Los Angeles, research librarian, 1943-44; Honig, Cooper &

Harrington (advertising agency), Los Angeles, research librarian, 1956-58; Dan B. Miner Co., Los Angeles, librarian, 1958-59; writer. Member of advisory board, Center for the Study of Children's Literature, Simmons College (Boston), 1977—. Children's literature judge, National Book Awards, 1980. Gertrude Clarke Whittall Lecturer, Library of Congress, 1977.

MEMBER: PEN International, Authors Guild, Authors League of America, Audubon Society, Sierra Club, Wilderness Society, Save-the-Redwoods League.

AWARDS, HONOURS: Hawaiian Children's Choice Nene Award, 1960, for *The Wonderful Flight to the Mushroom Planet*; Mystery Writers of America Award, 1964, for *A Spell Is Cast*; California Literature Silver Medal Award from Common-wealth Club of California, 1965, for *A Spell Is Cast*, and 1970, for *The Green and Burning Tree: On the Writing and Enjoyment of Children's Books*; Southern California Council on Literature for Children and Young People Award, 1965, for distinguished contribution to the field of children's literature; *A Room Made of Windows, The Court of the Stone Children, To the Green Mountains, Julia and the Hand of God*, and *That Julia Redfern* are all American Library Association Notable Books; *Boston Globe-Horn Book* Award, 1971, for *A Room Made of Windows*; National Book Award for children's literature, 1974, for *The Court of the Stone Children*; National Book Award runner-up, 1976, for *To the Green Mountains*; Kerlan Award for a body of work, 1985.

WRITINGS:

The Unheard Music (adult novel), Little, Brown, 1950.
The Green and Burning Tree: On the Writing and Enjoyment of Children's Books (critical essays), Atlantic-Little, Brown, 1969.

"MUSHROOM PLANET" SERIES

The Wonderful Flight to the Mushroom Planet (Junior Literary Guild selection), illustrated by Robert Henneberger, Little, Brown, 1954.
Stowaway to the Mushroom Planet (Junior Literary Guild selection), illustrated by Henneberger, Little, Brown, 1956.
Mr. Bass's Planetoid (Junior Literary Guild selection), Little, Brown, 1958.
A Mystery for Mr. Bass, illustrated by Leonard Shortall, Little, Brown, 1960.
Time and Mr. Bass, illustrated by Fred Meise, Little, Brown, 1967.

"JULIA REDFERN" SERIES

A Room Made of Windows, illustrated by Trina Schart Hyman, Little, Brown, 1971.

Julia and the Hand of God (Junior Literary Guild selection), illustrated by Gail Owens, Dutton, 1977.
That Julia Redfern, illustrated by Owens, Dutton, 1982.
Julia's Magic, Dutton, 1984.
The Private Worlds of Julia Redfern, Dutton, 1988.

JUVENILE NOVELS

The Terrible Churnadryne (Junior Literary Guild selection), illustrated by Beth and Joe Krush, Little, Brown, 1959.
The Mysterious Christmas Shell (sequel to *The Terrible Churnadryne*; Junior Literary Guild selection), illustrated by B. and J. Krush, Little, Brown, 1961.
The Beast with Magical Horn, illustrated by B. and J. Krush, Little, Brown, 1963.
A Spell Is Cast (Junior Literary Guild selection), illustrated by B. and J. Krush, Little, Brown, 1964.
The Court of the Stone Children (Junior Literary Guild selection), Dutton, 1973.
To the Green Mountains, Dutton, 1975.
Beyond Silence, Dutton, 1980.

CONTRIBUTOR

Paul Heins, editor, *Crosscurrents of Criticism: "Horn Book" Essays, 1968-1969,* Horn Book, 1977.
Prelude: Mini-Seminars on Using Books Creatively, Series 4, Children's Book Council, 1979.
Virginia Haviland, editor, *The Openhearted Audience: Ten Authors Talk about Writing for Children,* Library of Congress, 1980.
Robert Bator, editor, *Signposts to Criticism of Children's Literature,* American Library Association, 1983.
Perry Nodelman and Jill P. May, editors, *Festschrift: A Ten Year Retrospective,* Children's Literature Association, 1983.
Compton Rees, editor, *Children's Literature,* Volume XII, Yale University Press, 1984.

Also contributor to *The First Steps: Best of the Early "Children's Literature Association Quarterly,"* edited by Patricia Dooley, 1984.

OTHER

Contributor to *Horn Book, Wilson Library Bulletin, Children's Literature Association Quarterly,* and other periodicals. Member of editorial board, *Cricket: The Magazine for Children,* 1973—, and *Children's Literature in Education,* 1982—.

The "Mushroom Planet" books have been translated into Spanish; the first book in the series, *The Wonderful Flight to the Mushroom Planet,* has been translated into Japanese and Iranian as well. *The Court of the Stone Children* also has been published in Spanish.

ADAPTATIONS: A Room Made of Windows was made into a sound recording by Crane Memorial Library in 1979. *The Court of the Stone Children* is being made into a play.

WORK IN PROGRESS: A second collection of critical essays on children's literature.

SIDELIGHTS: Ever since the appearance of Eleanor Cameron's *The Wonderful Flight to the Mushroom Planet* in 1954, critics, as well as the general public, have been almost unanimous in their praise of her children's books. One testament to Cameron's writing skill is the long-term popularity of her "Mushroom Planet" series; as recently as 1979 the series's second book, *Stowaway to the Mushroom Planet* (1956), was on the Scholastic Booklist of the one hundred best sellers. The five-book series, which evolved out of Cameron's son's request for a space story with magic in it, focuses on two young boys from earth, David and Tom, who travel to and from the Mushroom Planet Basidium, usually under the tutelage of Basidiumite scientist Mr. Bass. David and Tom perform several heroic feats to protect the Mushroom People and their planet from impinging modernism and various underhanded plots by the evil scientist Prewytt Brumblydge. According to Sue Garness and Grace Sulerud in the *Dictionary of Literary Biography,* "the series appeals to the child's desire to have a place of his own, unknown to adults, where he carries out momentous plans to save the world from destruction or to help others fulfill their destinies."

While Cameron herself admits in *Signposts to Criticism of Children's Literature* that "reviewers called [the 'Mushroom Planet'] stories alternately science fiction and space fantasy," she feels that the point is a moot one. She tends to agree with a friend's interpretation that her writings, in general, fall somewhere in the middle, "between the Red or S[cience] F[iction] end of the spectrum and the works with trolls that are likely to be over in the Violet or Fantasy end. . . . You are playing with and making gentle fun of all space gadgetry, but also you quite soberly present some of the marvelousness and splendor of the universe *as revealed by* physics and astronomy and their technologies."

For the most part, Cameron's stories for children involve fairly complex space or time fantasies that incorporate elements of humor, suspense, mystery, and the skillful fusion of fictive, historical, and scientific detail. Of Cameron's National Book Award-winning *The Court of the Stone Children,* Barbara Wersba writes in the *New York Times Book Review*: "In an age when writers are engulfing children with an almost gratuitous realism, it is exciting to read a story that glances back into the literary shadows of memory, fantasy, and dream." However, Cameron does

not create her fantasy worlds at the expense of reality. Regarding Cameron's *A Room Made of Windows,* Perry Nodelman writes in the *Children's Literature Association Quarterly* that "to read [the book] is to be convinced that one is reading an autobiography; the book simply *feels* real, like reminiscence rather than like storytelling. . . . Cameron has a double gift; her faith in the magic of self is balanced by a clearheaded knowledge of the world as it actually is. And despite her faith in the healing powers of fantasy, she never lets her characters get away with lies about the world as it actually is."

Unlike some juvenile authors, Cameron avoids "talking down" to her audience; in fact, several of Cameron's books, including *To the Green Mountains, A Room Made of Windows,* and *The Court of the Stone Children,* have been singled out as works which are so thoughtfully constructed that they easily bridge the gap between books written for children and those written for adults. Wersba considers *The Court of the Stone Children* to contain "the kind of writing that one associates with adult novels, and indeed the author has not made a single concession to the conventions of childhood. Her story is complex [and] multi-layered." Patience M. Canham concludes in the *Christian Science Monitor* that Cameron "has the knack of pointing out self-deceptions and other antics of growing up without making them appear either important or 'cute.' And all the while she is imparting ideas about integrity and consideration."

Cameron herself explained to *CA*: "I can't say what started me writing as a child, except that I had been a reading animal from the beginning. By the time I was eleven, the writing process already absorbed me and I knew I wanted to be a writer, an ambition confirmed when my writings were first accepted by the local Berkeley paper when I was twelve. I kept writing through my teens and into my twenties with nothing taken by any publisher until my first novel, *The Unheard Music,* was accepted by Atlantic when I sent it to them on request after the *Atlantic Monthly* rejected a short story. In that book I see now that I wanted to achieve the unfolding of a view of life. It had no plot; I was under the influence of Virginia Woolf, and so a life view, a feeling-tone, was what I had in mind and, to strongly evoke this, the creation of characters the reader could understand and identify with. I have always been much involved with character creation and am bored by novels in which characters have been indifferently felt and therefore indifferently portrayed. I am also drawn by the way a book is written, and therefore I myself have apparently been developing an individual style. I don't try for 'style' as something artificially created, but keep rewriting until I have said exactly what I want to say in just the way I want to say it.

"To begin with, of course, there is place. I have no novel if I have no place, because out of place rise my characters and they make the story move and give it life and meaning and reality. For me it would be hopeless to mechanically construct a plot, for there would be no way in which anything could come alive. Nor could I mechanically construct my characters by drawing up histories and lists of idiosyncrasies and things they must do. Everything grows very slowly over a period of from two to thirty years, during which time I am convinced the unconscious does much of the work.

"I write a book every other year, but I am always working, always thinking, making notes, getting illuminations for my novels from thinking and reading and remembering. When I'm writing a book, I can't always write every day, but write as long as I can when I'm in the midst of it. The book is *there*; it needs only to find the right tone and rhythm, and that is the difficult part. There is no struggle 'to make the characters come alive' or 'to make the plot work.' The characters present themselves and, through them, if I am convinced of the basic idea that seems to want to be expressed, the story grows naturally. It's up to me to find the fullness and extent of it through words that will reveal it most clearly and satisfyingly.

"Advice for aspiring writers: read the best in any field you want to write in—only the best. But you must have a point of view of your own. If you have no point of view, no convictions about life, no strong sense of self, you will have nothing to say, no base to write from, no ability to develop an individual style."

BIOGRAPHICAL/CRITICAL SOURCES:

BOOKS

Bator, Robert, editor, *Signposts to Criticism of Children's Literature,* American Library Association, 1983.
Children's Literature Review, Volume 1, Gale, 1976.
Dictionary of Literary Biography, Volume 52: *American Writers for Children since 1960: Fiction,* Gale, 1986.
Haviland, Virginia, editor, *The Openhearted Audience: Ten Authors Talk about Writing for Children,* Library of Congress, 1980.
Rees, Compton, editor, *Children's Literature,* Volume 12, Yale University Press, 1984.

PERIODICALS

Best Sellers, May 15, 1971.
Booklist, September 15, 1977.
Book World, May 9, 1971.
Children's Book News, November-December, 1969.
Children's Literature Association Quarterly, winter, 1980; winter, 1981; winter, 1982.
Christian Science Monitor, May 6, 1971.
New York Herald Tribune Book Review, May 14, 1950.

New York Times, November 14, 1954; September 23, 1956.
New York Times Book Review, November 1, 1959; April 25, 1971; May 2, 1971; November 4, 1973; November 9, 1975; March 6, 1983.
Saturday Review, November 13, 1954; September 22, 1956; April 17, 1971.
Saturday Review of Literature, June 25, 1950.

*　　*　　*

CAMERON, James 1954-

PERSONAL: Born August 16, 1954, in Kapuskasing, Ontario, Canada; immigrated to United States, 1971 (one source lists 1972); son of an electrical engineer (father); married second wife, Gale Anne Hurd (a motion picture producer), April, 1985 (divorced); married Kathryn Bigelow (a motion picture director; marriage ended); companion of Linda Hamilton (an actress); children: (with Hamilton) one. *Education:* Attended California State University at Fullerton. *Avocational interests:* Scuba diving.

ADDRESSES: Office—c/o Alexandra Drobac, Lightstorm Entertainment, 3100 Damon Way, Burbank, CA 91505. *Agent*—International Creative Management, 8899 Beverly Blvd., Los Angeles, CA 90048.

CAREER: Director, screenwriter, and producer, 1981—. Truck driver for two to three years during 1970s; New World Pictures, served various functions—including production assistant, second unit director, production designer, and miniature set builder—on several films, including *Battle beyond the Stars,* 1980, *Escape from New York* (1981), and *Android,* 1982; made debut as director with film *Piranha II: Flying Killers,* 1981, which was released on video as *Piranha II: The Spawning;* formed Lightstorm Entertainment, 1990; served as executive producer of 1991's *Point Break,* directed by then wife, Kathryn Bigelow; founder, with others, of Digital Domain, a special effects company specializing in computer-generated animation, c. 1993.

MEMBER: Directors Guild of America, Screenwriters Guild of America.

AWARDS, HONOURS: The Terminator was named one of the ten best films of 1984 by *Time* magazine; Academy Award for visual effects, Motion Picture Academy of Arts and Sciences, 1992, for *Terminator 2.*

WRITINGS:

(With William Wisher) *Terminator II: Judgment Day; The Book of the Film, an Illustrated Screenplay,* Applause Theatre Book Publishers, 1991.

SCREENPLAYS

(With Gale Ann Hurd; and director) *The Terminator*, Orion, 1984.

(With Sylvester Stallone) *Rambo: First Blood, Part II*, Tri-Star, 1985.

(And director) *Aliens* (based on story by Cameron, David Giler, and Walter Hill; based on characters created by Dan O'Bannon and Ronald Shusett), Twentieth Century-Fox, 1986.

(And director) *The Abyss*, Twentieth Century-Fox, 1989.

(With Wisher; and director and producer) *Terminator 2: Judgment Day* (also known as *T2*), Tri-Star, 1991.

(And director and coproducer) *True Lies* (based on the 1992 French comedy *La Totale!*), Twentieth Century-Fox, 1994.

Strange Days, Twentieth Century-Fox, 1995.

ADAPTATIONS: Characters from the *Terminator* movies, *The Abyss*, and *Aliens* have been adapted to comic book and graphic novel form by Marvel Comics and Dark Horse Publications.

WORK IN PROGRESS: A film version of the popular Marvel Comic *Spider-man*.

SIDELIGHTS: Screenwriter, director, and producer James Cameron is the creative force behind a body of film work that is often considered to have redefined contemporary action/science fiction cinema. Among the most popular of the genre, his films include such box-office smashes as *The Terminator, Aliens,* and *The Abyss.* Equally respected for his writing and directing talents, Cameron has become one of the most popular and sought-after filmmakers in Hollywood.

Born and raised in Ontario, Canada, Cameron moved to the United States with his family in the early seventies with hopes of becoming a marine biologist. "I thought I wanted to be the next Jacques Cousteau," he told Michael Singer in *Film Directors: A Complete Guide.* However, foreseeing a career "counting fish eggs," Cameron turned his attention to astronomy and physics at California State University. By the end of four semesters he had lost interest in academics and decided to learn about the world firsthand. He became a truck driver, spending his spare time polishing his writing. When he stopped trucking, Cameron decided to pursue a career in the field that had dazzled him since childhood—filmmaking.

Cameron had little experience in the realm of major motion picture production, so he sought training with Roger Corman. Corman's New World Pictures had a reputation as a kind of prep school for influential directors—Francis Ford Coppola (the *Godfather* trilogy, *Apocalypse Now*), Peter Bogdanovich (*The Last Picture Show, Mask*), and Martin Scorcese (*Taxi Driver, Raging Bull*) all started out

working for Corman. New World was also notorious for producing a large number of films on small budgets and short shooting schedules. People employed by Corman were usually overworked and pushed to perform at an extremely rapid pace, but the ones who survived the pressure often emerged as highly qualified professionals within the industry. Cameron started out as a member of the special effects team for a science fiction production called *Battle beyond the Stars.* When the film's art director was fired, Cameron was promoted to fill the vacancy—the first of several positions he held at New World. Working at Corman's frenetic pace, Cameron became a "jack-of-all-trades," receiving a crash course in virtually all aspects of filmmaking. He served as a production assistant and built miniature models for many of New World's science fiction films. Cameron soon realized that he desired a larger role in the creation of motion pictures. "I had a dawning awareness that directing was the only place where you got perfect confluence of the storytelling, visual and technical sides," Cameron told Singer. After working as a second unit director for the film *Galaxy of Terror,* Cameron was offered the job of directing *Piranha II: The Spawning*—he had graduated.

Cameron's experience as the director for *Piranha II* proved to be less than glorious. He was working with an unscrupulous producer and crew comprised entirely of Italians who did not speak English. The producer proclaimed himself a second unit director and set about filming topless women frolicking aboard yachts—footage that contributed nothing to the storyline of carnivorous fish terrorizing humans. The producer proved to be a thorn in Cameron's side in more ways than one. When production was completed, the producer quickly took the print back to Rome to edit—without Cameron even seeing the final footage that he had shot. Cameron followed him to Rome with hope of retaining some control over the final release. Although he was able to make a minor contribution to the film's postproduction, Cameron was unhappy with the finished version of *Piranha II.*

Cameron attempted to put the experience of *Piranha II* behind him. He began to devise a film story involving cyborgs and time travel. When he returned to Los Angeles he contacted Gale Anne Hurd, a fellow alumnus of New World and his romantic interest. With a third writer, William Wisher, Jr., Cameron and Hurd set about writing the script for the film that would come to be known as *The Terminator.* Cameron and Hurd struck a deal with Hemdale, a production company, so that Hurd would produce and Cameron direct the film.

The Terminator opens with dark shots of a ragged future world. A narration explains that this is the twenty-first century and that in the year 1997 a global nuclear holocaust will occur, an armageddon triggered by an automated defense system known as Skynet. In the wake of the war, the sentient Skynet computer controls the world. The surviving humans must now fight a second, more desperate war, the war with the machines. The film then cuts to the Los Angeles of 1984 and the arrival, on the city's outskirts, of a naked man amidst flashing light and electrical surges. The man, as played by bodybuilder-turned-actor Arnold Schwarzenegger, is large, muscular, and menacing. He dispassionately kills a gang of punks to get their clothes and makes his way into the city. He finds a phone book and looks up the name Sarah Connor—there are three people with that name. In a brutal and efficient manner, he tracks down the first two Sarah Connors and kills them. He arrives at the home of the third woman but mistakenly kills her roommate. Thinking his task completed, he turns to leave when the voice of the real Sarah comes on the answering machine, unwittingly giving her whereabouts to the murderer.

Meanwhile, another naked man has materialized in L.A. in the same fashion as the first. He too is seeking Sarah Connor. The second man locates the surviving Sarah and follows her into a nightclub. She notices him trailing her. By this time, news of a "phonebook killer" is well known throughout the city. Sarah mistakes this second man for the murderer, and in her terror does not notice the real killer approaching her with his gun drawn. As the large man aims the gun's laser sighting at Sarah's forehead, the second man opens fire on him, knocking him to the ground. Almost instantly—and seemingly uninjured—the large man is back on his feet and continuing his attack on Sarah. The second man pulls Sarah out of the bar and into a car, the attacker following close behind. As they make their escape, Sarah's rescuer introduces himself as Kyle Reese, a traveller from the future sent to protect her from the man now pursuing them. Reese explains that the other man is a Terminator, a machine covered in flesh, also from the future, sent to kill Sarah. He tells her that within the year, she will give birth to a son, John, who will survive the coming war and grow to be the leader of the human resistance against the machines. Skynet has sent the Terminator back in time to perform a "retro-active abortion" on Sarah and eliminate the threat of John Connor. The John Connor of the future has sent Reese back in time to protect Sarah and his unborn self. While fleeing the Terminator, Reese and Sarah fall in love. They manage to find some quiet moments but must soon resume their flight from the Terminator's ceaseless attack. The film climaxes with Reese and Sarah squaring off against the Terminator to decide the fate of mankind.

By combining elements of traditional action/adventure films with the punk aesthetic of science fiction literature by authors such as William Gibson and Bruce Sterling (purveyors of a science fiction sub-genre often referred to as "Cyperpunk"), Cameron created a film that is credited with reviving a flagging genre. Science fiction devotees and film studio executives alike praised Cameron for his unique cinematic style. Singer asked Cameron in *Film Directors* if he had consciously attempted to forge a new vision of science fiction cinema with the film. "I just came up with a way of juxtaposing futuristic elements with a kind of everyday reality," replied the director. This work ethic made *The Terminator* one of the most successful and popular films of the eighties. The film became ensconced in the popular culture, especially Schwarzenegger's memorable "I'll be back" line, which became a catchphrase used in commercials, in other films, and by millions of teenagers. The film's themes of paradoxical time travel and its relentless energy popularized it with a mass, worldwide audience. Film critics seemed to agree with the moviegoing public on the entertainment value of *The Terminator*. "This picture barrels with swank relentlessness through a giddily complicated premise and into an Armageddon face-off," declared Richard Corliss in *Time*. Reviewing the film in the *Nation*, Andrew Kopkind proclaimed: "They hardly make good 'B' movies like this anymore, but they should." *The Motion Picture Guide* (*MPG*) summarized: "*The Terminator* is a fresh, exciting and surprisingly witty science-fiction film that will thrill any adult audience."

While waiting for Schwarzenegger to complete his role in *Conan the Destroyer* so that filming could begin on *The Terminator*, Cameron decided to peddle himself as a screenwriter-for-hire. He was offered two major films to work on, both sequels to popular movies. The first project was *First Blood II: The Mission*, which would continue the story of Vietnam veteran John Rambo, a character who first appeared in the Sylvester Stallone picture *First Blood*. Cameron wrote two drafts of a script dealing with Rambo's haunted return to Vietnam and the psychological effects of facing his darkest fears. He submitted his screenplay to the producers, who in turn gave it to Stallone, the film's star, to further revise. The motion picture that was released, under the title *Rambo: First Blood, Part II*, was vastly different from the screenplay that Cameron wrote. According to Cameron in *Film Directors*, Stallone rewrote large portions of Cameron's script to fit his own politics and ideals, omitting much of the psychological drama and character development along the way. However, the next script that Cameron would work on would incorporate many of the themes of self-doubt, psychological damage, and the confrontation of fears that *Rambo*—or Stallone—neglected.

Alien II was Cameron's second sequel, building on characters and events from director Ridley Scott's 1979 film, *Alien*. In addition to writing the script, Cameron also convinced the production company that he and Hurd, now husband and wife, were the best choices to respectively direct and produce the film, which was now titled *Aliens.* "I had a lot of emotional investment in [the script]," he told Fred Schruers in *Rolling Stone,* "I didn't want to see it botched up by somebody else."

Aliens opens with an intergalactic exploration team's discovery of warrant officer Ripley, *Alien*'s sole human survivor, in deep space hibernation. Fifty-seven years have elapsed since she escaped on a small shuttle, and Ripley learns that much has changed in her absence. Back on Earth, she is brought to an inquest regarding the fate of her old ship, the Nostromo, destroyed in the final battle with the alien in the first film. During the proceedings it is revealed that the planet where the Nostromo last landed—where the ship's crew discovered the murderous alien's breeding ground—has been colonized by the quasi-bureaucratic business entity known only as the Company. Ripley is incredulous that the Company has put so many lives, including families, in dangerous proximity to scores of vicious aliens. The Company officials coolly reply that the colony has existed for several years and that Ripley really isn't qualified to judge the safety of its inhabitants.

Ripley returns to a vague semblance of ordinary life, scarred and frail. She is tormented by nightmares of her experience with the alien. When a panicked Company employee calls and informs her that contact with the colonized planet has been lost and her help is requested to assist a squad of marines in the sweep and rescue, Ripley sees it as a means to exorcise her personal demons. She volunteers for the mission.

Ripley and the marine team arrive at the colony to find it deserted, save for one small girl who is living in the heating ducts like a scavenger. When the marines ask the little girl where her family and the rest of the colony are, the child replies, "They're dead, okay? Can I go now?" Ripley is drawn to the girl, who, like herself, is the sole survivor of an alien attack. Ripley and the child, named Newt, quickly form a surrogate mother/daughter relationship. Meanwhile, the team has set off to survey the area. While exploring the dank subterranean levels of the colony, the marines come upon its missing inhabitants, encased in sticky, partial cocoons. As one of the colonists awakens, an alien creature bursts forth from her chest. The soldiers act quickly, using flamethrowers to destroy both the woman and the alien hatchling. The marines realize that the aliens have used the entire colony as incubators for their young creatures. Attempting to withdraw, the marines are beset by swarms of aliens in a bloody battle. Retreating to the upper levels, Ripley, Newt, and the surviving marines secure themselves in the infirmary against hordes of advancing aliens. The aliens break into the infirmary, sending the room's human occupants scrambling in different directions. Ripley loses Newt in the confusion

that ensues. In her desperate search for the little girl, Ripley discovers the egg chamber of the alien queen on the bottom level of the colony. There she finds Newt, encased as the other colonists were, about to be impregnated with an alien fetus. The two "mothers," Ripley and the queen, now face each other, each determined to protect her children.

"For sheer intensity, the final forty-five minutes of *Aliens* is not likely to be matched," proclaimed *Newsweek* critic David Ansen. "Cameron is a master at choreographing ever-more astonishing catastrophes." Audiences impressed with *The Terminator* seemed even more excited by Cameron's efforts in *Aliens.* His ability to utilize themes from Scott's original film while forging a vision of his own impressed critics as well as the filmgoers, who pushed *Aliens* far beyond its predecessor in ticket sales. Cameron told Singer in *Film Directors:* "For me, the opportunity to do *Aliens* was to take a lot of what I liked from the first film and weld it together with my own imagery. I was in equal parts intimidated and seduced by it." Cameron's reputation as a master of kinetic, thrill-a-minute filmmaking was intensifying. "*Aliens* is a mother of a thriller," declared David Edelstein in *Rolling Stone,* "a royal chamber of horrors. And, as he proved in *The Terminator,* Cameron knows How Things Work in a fun house: each plunge down a chute and pop-out demon moves you faster along to the next frightful spill, choking you somewhere between a giggle and a scream."

With *Aliens*'s success further solidifying his reputation, Cameron spent the next three years making his most ambitious film to date, *The Abyss.* Working with a budget that doubled the combined costs of *The Terminator* and *Aliens,* Cameron shot his underwater epic in abandoned nuclear cooling tanks. Rather than rely on miniatures, he built full-scale underwater sets within the massive tanks. As the film begins, an American nuclear submarine encounters an unidentified—and impossibly fleet—underwater object. The crew panics and crashes the sub onto a precipice, teetering on the brink of a deep abyss. A nearby underwater oil drilling colony, Deepcore, is enlisted to help a team of Navy SEALs (Sea-Air-Land specialists) ostensibly perform a rescue. The SEALs' real mission is to retrieve the sub's nuclear warheads before an enemy does. The undertaking becomes more intricate when the workers on Deepcore discover underwater aliens who appear to live down in the abyss. It was a craft belonging to these aliens that unintentionally caused the sub wreck. Most of the crew recognize that the aliens are intelligent and are in fact trying to make friendly contact. Trouble arises when the leader of the SEALs succumbs to pressure sickness from the water depth. He becomes paranoid and unpredictable—psychotic—viewing the aliens as a threat to national security. He sends an armed nuclear warhead down into the abyss to take care of the "enemy." Seeking to avert the possible destruction of an intelligent, undiscovered race, the oil rig's foreman suits up to follow the bomb down into the abyss and diffuse it. Using a special liquid form of oxygen that enables humans to withstand extreme depth pressure, the foreman plummets into the five mile abyss.

The Abyss met with mixed reviews. Some critics found it ambitious and thrilling, a competent reworking of several genre themes. As Ansen wrote in *Newsweek:* "There are variations on scenes you've seen a hundred times, . . . yet Cameron renders them with such white-knuckle conviction they regain their primal force." Other critics complained that the film tried to be too many things at once—an action/adventure tale, an account of bonding between humans and aliens, and a love story—and as a result did not address any of those subjects well. "*The Abyss* doesn't seem to go anywhere much except down," summarized *MPG*. Many fans of Cameron's action pictures were disappointed that his new film displayed a markedly different tone from his previous efforts. Rather than offer nonstop, breathtaking action, *The Abyss* spends more time on atmosphere and suspense, carefully charting out the story. Cameron wanted to produce a film that elicited a degree of thought from the audience, rather than one that incited the audience to shout during a screening. "*The Abyss* does not strike me as an audience participation picture like *Terminator* and *Aliens.* In a way that is good, really," Cameron explained to Ian Spelling in *Starlog*.

In terms of production scale and budgetary expenditure, *The Abyss* certainly ranked as one of the biggest and most expensive motion pictures ever made. In the light of *The Abyss*'s lukewarm showing at the box office (the film easily turned a respectable profit, but the studio, expecting a blockbuster, was disappointed), many industry observers felt that a film that matched or surpassed the cost and production scale of *The Abyss* would never be made. They were mistaken. Working with a budget that reportedly vacillated between eighty and one hundred million dollars, Cameron made *Terminator 2: Judgement Day,* then the biggest, most expensive film in history.

As *Terminator 2* begins, the audience learns that Sarah Connor has given birth to her savior son, John, who is now a young pre-teenager. The setting is ten years after the first movie and the nuclear war, judgement day, is approaching. Sarah has become near-crazy, obsessed with her knowledge of the impending war and the massive loss of human life it will entail. She has spent years training John in guerilla warfare, survival tactics, anything that will aid him in his future fight against the mechanized forces of the tyrannical Skynet computer. Unfortunately, Sarah's fanatical behavior has been detected by the authorities. As a result, she has lost custody of John. She is now locked away in a mental hospital, raving about the approaching apocalypse and the Terminator she encountered ten years before. Into these events come two separate men from the future. The first man resembles the Terminator in the original film, played by Arnold Schwarzenegger in both pictures. The second is a much smaller man, though no less imposing. Both are Terminators searching for John Connor. The smaller man, a new state-of-the-art Terminator model called the T-1000, has come to kill John. The Schwarzenegger character is an older Terminator, the same production model that caused all of the havoc in the original film. The Schwarzenegger Terminator has been sent by the adult John Connor, living in the future, to protect the present-day John Connor. The two Terminators find young John at the same time and attack each other in a vicious battle for John's life. John escapes on his motorcycle amid the chaos. Schwarzenegger manages to catch John after the T-1000 has pursued the boy in a perilous truck and motorcycle chase. He informs John that he has been sent to protect him. When John finds out that the Terminator is programmed to obey all of his commands, he orders the machine to help him break Sarah out of the mental hospital. With the T-1000 still pursuing John, and the freed Sarah now a fugitive, the trio escapes into the desert.

Sarah realizes that even if they survive this encounter with the T-1000, Skynet will continue its assaults from the future until John is finally killed. She contends that the only solution to save John and the human race is to prevent judgement day from occurring. To do this they must reach the man responsible for developing Skynet, Miles Dyson. Dyson works for Cyberdyne Systems, the company that will create and then sell the Skynet system to the Defense Department in the near future. Cyberdyne is also the company that will one day manufacture the Terminator line (Cameron also used "Cyberdyne" in *Aliens* as the manufacturer of an android character in that film). Dyson has been studying the secret remains of the Terminator that terrorized Sarah ten years ago. Examining the technology in the fragments of the machine has enabled him to make incredible advances on a computer chip that will eventually lead to the invention of the Skynet computer. Sarah, John, and the Terminator find Dyson and inform him of the results of his research. As Sarah explains in the voiceover narration: "It's not everyday that you find out you're responsible for three billion deaths." Dyson agrees to help them destroy his Skynet research and the remains of the first Terminator. The T-1000 pursues them to the Cyberdyne complex and another monstrous battle, also involving an army of police, ensues. Escaping the site of the battle, the three protagonists are again pursued by the relentless T-1000 to a steel forgery. At this site they must destroy the T-1000 or surrender their hope of averting the nuclear disaster of judgement day.

With its elephantine price tag and its ground-breaking special effects, *Terminator 2* gained a considerable amount of attention during its production and upon its release. Speculation was that most of the money was spent on the elaborate effects for the T-1000. Using computer animation and prosthetic applications, the special effects team was able to take the human form of T-1000 actor Robert Patrick and melt it into any variety of liquid metal shapes. Attention to the film was divided between the storyline and the special effects. *Washington Post* contributor Hal Hinson assessed: "Cameron manages to create a neat balance between the technical and the human." *New York Times* critic Janet Maslin enthused: "Mr. Cameron presents the T-1000 as a show-stopping molten metal creature capable of assuming or abandoning human form at will. Some of his tricks are cause for applause in their own right." Some critics lamented a lack of emotion in the film, though few doubted its ability to thrill an audience. "Cameron never relinquishes his grip on the audience, smoothly segueing from action sequence to action sequence and topping himself each time," praised Dave Kehr in *Chicago Tribune*.

Cameron's 1994 action film *True Lies*, starring Arnold Schwarzenegger, Tom Arnold, and Jamie Lee Curtis, "is a movie that goes out of its way *not* to be taken seriously," claims Joe Chidley in *Maclean's*. The protagonist, Harry Tasker (Schwarzenegger) has been working secretly as a CIA spy for fifteen years; his wife Helen (Curtis) believes him to be a somewhat boring and staid computer salesman. With his partner, Gib (played by Arnold), Tasker works to expose and defuse an Arab terrorist plot to take over world governments. While the CIA men are infiltrating the enemy, Helen, dissatisfied with her dull and monotonous life, does some investigating of her own with a potential lover who professes to be a government agent (but who in reality is a car salesman). Tasker eventually discovers his wife's supposed duplicity and turns his spy techniques on her to glean information about her liaison; he finally actually abducts her, in true "secret agent" form, concealing his identity, to interrogate her about her relationship with her so-called lover. Stanley Kauffmann remarks in the *New Republic*, "As the double-stranded plot slides forward, the picture takes on another dimension. It becomes a crystalline instance of postmodernism."

While Harry eventually resolves his personal relationship with Helen, he inadvertently involves her and their daughter in a scenario involving terrorists armed with nuclear weapons. Harry must confront the terrorists, save his family, and, in the process, save the world. After numerous special effects sequences involving big-budget pyrotechnics, the conclusion suggests that Helen, who now realizes the actual nature of her husband's job, and Harry may work together in future espionage endeavors. While the film earned critical kudos for its blockbuster effects, it also garnered criticism for what some reviewers consider its inappropriate treatment of women and Arabs. Chidley observes, "Director Cameron trundles out his grab bag of special-effects trickery to deliver a megaton blast of spectacle," concluding that "as broad comedy descends into action-movie stereotypes, it ends up a mishmash of banal witticisms and bad taste—a sort of James Bond meets Rambo meets the Three Stooges." Peter Travers notes in *Rolling Stone* that the film "is an excuse for Cameron, the digital cowboy of *Terminator 2*, to top himself with computer-enhanced stunts. He does so thrillingly. But that's no excuse for the film's gross stereotyping. Complaints are in about the depiction of Arabs as bumbling sadists. But how about the treatment of women . . . ?"

Mario Kassar, the chairman of Carolco, the company that financed *Terminator 2*, has called Cameron a "genius" at crafting high-tech entertainment. As Kassar explained to Kirk Honeycutt in *Los Angeles Times*, the secret to Cameron's success is that "he is a writer. Everything has to make sense to him. He's a very logical person." However, by the standards of major motion picture studios, Cameron has gone against the grain, against the industry's logic. Before *Aliens*, the idea of building a major action/adventure film around a female hero was, to say the least, uncommon. Yet by successfully casting Sigourney Weaver's character of Ripley as the centerpiece of that film, Cameron dispelled the misconception that a woman could not carry a major action/adventure release. To some extent, each of Cameron's films has featured strong female characters that are in direct contrast to the stereotyped female roles so prevalent in popular entertainment. "I like the Forties thing," Cameron told Schruers in *Rolling Stone*, "a strong, Howard Hawks-type woman. . . . Strong male characters have been done so many times. With strong females, there's still a lot of room for exploration." Attention to detail in character is as much a focus in Cameron's filmmaking as creating riveting action sequences or suspenseful moods. "Audiences have to relate to people that they're seeing within a film, or they have no emotional attachment," Cameron told Singer. "I think you get more out of a movie when the characters are accessible and you can feel for their problems."

Cameron's marketability and popular success have led to unusual financing promises for future films and other business opportunities. John Lippman of the *Los Angeles Times* reports that Cameron and Twentieth Century-Fox reached a "$500-million production and distribution agreement" in which the filmmaker and his production company, Lightstorm Entertainment, will either write, direct, or produce twelve pictures for Fox over a five-year period. In return, the studio will finance up to $15 million per picture. Lippman notes the advantages for Fox, commenting that "Cameron is considered on of the most 'bankable' filmmakers in Hollywood—trade parlance for a director whose work is almost guaranteed to earn big profits." In another arrangement, a 1993 joint venture with I.B.M. and two other of his Hollywood colleagues gives Cameron an ownership share of Digital Domain, a Los Angeles firm dedicated to developing and delivering state-of-the-art computer special effects through the use of sophisticated digital technologies.

Cameron has earned a great deal of respect from critics and moviegoers alike for his relatively small body of work. It is the favor of the latter group, the ticket-buying public, that appeals to major studios. In a time when no movie formula is "sure-fire," Cameron has had consistent success with his brand of movie making. He insists that he uses no formula in making his films—just common sense and good storytelling. "When I hear people shooting different endings for a movie I say 'God, how can you *do* that?'," he related in *Film Directors.* "For me, the ending comes first and then you write backwards, and all the threads converge on that. And when it happens, there's a rightness about it that resonates through the rest of the film."

BIOGRAPHICAL/CRITICAL SOURCES:

BOOKS

Cameron, James, Gale Anne Hurd, and William Wisher, Jr., *The Terminator* (screenplay), Orion, 1984.
Contemporary Theatre, Film, and Television, Volume 3, Gale, 1986, p. 84.
The Motion Picture Guide, Cinebooks, 1987, pp. 4111-12; *1986 Annual,* 1987, p. 159; *1987 Annual,* 1987, pp.7-8; *1990 Annual,* 1990, pp. 3-4.
Singer, Michael, "James Cameron," *Film Directors: A Complete Guide,* Lone Eagle Press, 1987, pp. 3-5, 8-9.

PERIODICALS

Chicago Tribune, July 3, 1991, pp. 1, 4.
Los Angeles Times, May 19, 1991, pp. 22, 42; July 2, 1991, pp. F1, F4; July 3, 1991, pp. F1, F6; April 23, 1992, pp. D1-2.
Maclean's, July 25, 1994, pp. 58-59.
Nation, January 26, 1985, p. 88.
New Republic, September 5, 1994, pp. 34, 36.
Newsweek, July 21, 1986, p. 64; August 14, 1989, p. 56.
New York, June 3, 1985, p. 72.
New York Times, July 3, 1991, pp. C11, C15, F1, F6; March 1, 1993, p. D3.
People, August 11, 1986, pp. 93-95.
Rolling Stone, May 22, 1986, pp. 49-50; August 28, 1986, pp. 41- 42; August 25, 1994, p. 96.
Starlog, January, 1990, pp. 29-32, 62.
Time, November 26, 1984, p. 105.
Washington Post, July 3, 1991, pp. B1-B2; July 5, 1991, p. 31.*

—*Sketch by David Galens*

*   *   *

CAMPBELL, Maria 1940-

PERSONAL: Born in April, 1940, in Park Valley, Saskatchewan, Canada; married; four children.

ADDRESSES: Home—Regina, Saskatchewan.*Office*—Coach House Press, 401 Huron St., Toronto, Ontario M5S 2G5.

CAREER: Writer. Cofounder of Edmonton Women's Halfway House and Women's Emergency Shelter. Writer-in-residence at University of Alberta, 1980, and University of Regina, 1982.

WRITINGS:

Halfbreed (autobiography), Saturday Review Press, 1973.
People of the Buffalo: How the Plains Indians Lived, Douglas & McIntyre, 1976.
Little Badger and the Fire Spirit, McClelland & Stewart, 1977.
The Red Dress (screenplay), National Film Board, 1977.
Riel's People (children's fiction), 1978.
(With Linda Griffiths and Paul Thompson) *Jessica* (drama), 1982.
(Editor) *Achimoona* (short fiction), 1985.
The Book of Jessica: A Theatrical Transformation (nonfiction), 1989.
Stories of the Road Allowance People, Orca, 1995.

Author of radio plays. Contributor to magazines, including *Maclean's,* and newspapers.

SIDELIGHTS: Maria Campbell is best known for her autobiography *Halfbreed* (1973), which relates her struggles as a Metis woman in Canadian society. A best-seller in her homeland, the book has been described by Hartmut Lutz as "the most important and seminal book authored by a Native person from Canada."

Of Scottish, Indian, and French descent, Campbell, the eldest daughter of seven children, was born in northern Saskatchewan. She was shunned by both whites and full-blooded Natives due to her Metis, or half-breed, heritage. When Campbell was twelve, her mother died. Forced to quit school and take care of her younger siblings, Campbell was then compelled to marry at age fifteen in order to prevent her brothers and sisters from being placed in an orphanage. Her attempt to keep her family united, however, was unsuccessful; her husband, an abusive, alcoholic white man, reported her to the welfare authorities, and her siblings were placed in foster care. After moving to Vancouver, where her husband deserted her, Campbell became a prostitute and drug addict. After two suicide attempts and a nervous breakdown, she was hospitalized and entered Alcoholics Anonymous. She began writing *Halfbreed* in an attempt to deal with her anger, frustration, loneliness, and the pressure to return to a life of drugs and prostitution. She commented: "I had no money, and I was on the verge of being kicked out of my house, had no food, and I decided to go back out in the street and work. I went out one night and sat in a bar. And I just couldn't, because I knew if I went back to that, I'd be back on drugs again. . . . I started writing a letter [to myself] because I had to have somebody to talk to, and there was nobody to talk to. And that was how I wrote *Halfbreed*." Campbell has since become an ardent supporter of the Native Rights movement and ran for president of the Metis community in the 1980s.

Relating the first thirty-three years of Campbell's life, *Halfbreed* recounts on a personal level the discrimination and racism to which the Metis have historically been subject from all sectors of Canadian society. Infused with a strong undercurrent of anger and bitterness, the book documents Campbell's search for self-identity, her attempts to overcome the poverty, prejudice, and harshness of Metis life, and finally, albeit briefly, her work as a political activist. The volume is also known for its humor, its documentation of Metis patois and rituals, and its tender portrait of Campbell's loving relationship with her grandmother, Cheechum. Campbell has noted that *Halfbreed* was intended to inform readers "what it is like to be a Halfbreed woman in our country. I want to tell you about the joys and sorrows, the oppressing poverty, the frustrations and the dreams." Campbell is additionally known for such children's works as *People of the Buffalo* (1976) and *Riel's People* (1978), which relate Metis traditions and history, and for *Jessica* (1982), the stage adaptation of *Halfbreed*. *The Book of Jessica* (1989) is a nonfiction account of Campbell's professional relationship with actress and playwright Linda Griffiths, with whom she collaborated on *Jessica*. The partnership was a source of consternation for both individuals, and *The Book of Jessica* is considered a testament to the aesthetic problems posed by collaboration, colonialism, and cross-cultural appropriation.

Campbell's reputation was established with and, for the most part, rests on *Halfbreed*. It has been both praised as a sociological tract of the Metis community and extolled as a moving historical account of the nationally sponsored and endorsed racism that has been inflicted upon the Metis people. Agnes Grant observes: "Though the book was written for non-Natives Maria keeps them at a distance. She writes of things she knows, which she believes her readers do not know. The humor and irony are very effective in pointing out to the readers that, indeed, Maria is right. There are things that we did not know. Until she wrote the book, 'halfbreed' was nothing but a common derogatory term; now it means a person living between two cultures. The ultimate irony is that her book has never been taken seriously as literature."

BIOGRAPHICAL/CRITICAL SOURCES:

BOOKS

Campbell, Maria, *Halfbreed*, Saturday Review Press, 1973.

PERIODICALS

Canadian Children's Literature, No. 31, 1983, p. 98, 105.
Canadian Journal of Native Studies, Vol. 12, no. 2, pp. 321-23.
Canadian Literature, Spring, 1990, p. 124; Spring, 1993, pp. 24-29.
Performing Arts in Canada, Spring, 1990, p. 36.
Quill & Quire, December, 1985, p. 24.

*   *   *

CAPE, Judith
   See PAGE, P(atricia) K(athleen)

*   *   *

CARMAN, (William) Bliss   1861-1929

PERSONAL: Born April 15, 1861, in Fredericton, New Brunswick, Canada; died of a brain hemorrhage, June 8, 1929, in New Canaan, Connecticut, United States; buried in Fredericton, New Brunswick; son of William (a barrister) and Sophia (Bliss) Carman. *Education:* Fredericton Collegiate School, 1872-78; University of New Brunswick, B.A., 1881, M.A. 1884; attended University of Edinburgh, 1882-83; Harvard University, 1886-88.

CAREER: Fredericton Collegiate School, teacher, 1883-84; studied law with the firm of James Douglas Hazen, Fredericton, 1884-86; private tutor, 1885; New York *Independent,* literary editor, 1890-92; *Current Literature,* staff member, 1892; *Cosmopolitan,* New York, staff member, 1894; *Atlantic Monthly,* Boston, staff member, 1895; Boston *Transcript,* columnist, 1895-1900; Small, Maynard and Company, Publishers, Boston, reader, 1897-1903; *Literary World,* Boston, editor, 1905; *Gentleman's Journal,* staff member, 1909; part-time advertising writer, 1909-19; made poetry reading tours of Canada from 1921.

MEMBER: Royal Society of Canada (corresponding member, 1925).

AWARDS, HONOURS: Lorne Pierce Medal, 1928, for contribution to Canadian writing; LL.D., University of

New Brunswick, 1906; Litt.D., Trinity College, Hartford, Connecticut; honorary degree, McGill University, Montreal, Canada.

WRITINGS:

Low Tide on Grand Pre: A Book of Lyrics, Webster, 1893.

(With Richard Hovey) *Songs from Vagabondia,* Copeland & Day, 1894.

Behind the Arras: A Book of the Unseen, Lamson, Wolffe, 1895.

(With Richard Hovey) *More Songs from Vagabondia,* Copeland & Day, 1895.

Ballads of Lost Haven: A Book of the Sea, Lamson, Wolffe, 1897.

By the Aurelian Wall, and Other Elegies, Lamson, Wolffe, 1898.

(With Richard Hovey) *Last Songs from Vagabondia,* Small, Maynard, 1900.

The Pipes of Pan, 5 volumes, Page, 1902-1905.

Ballads and Lyrics, Bullen, 1902.

The Kinship of Nature, Page, 1903.

The Friendship of Art, Page, 1904.

Poems, Scott-Thaw, 1904.

Sappho: One Hundred Lyrics, Page, 1904.

(Editor, with John Vance Cheney, Charles G. D. Roberts, Charles F. Richardson, and Francis H. Stoddard) *The World's Best Poetry,* Morris, 1904.

The Poetry of Life, Page, 1905.

The Making of Personality, Page, 1908.

The Rough Rider, and Other Poems, Kennerley, 1909.

Address to the Graduating Class MCMXI of the Unitrinian School of Personal Harmonizing, Tabard Press, 1911.

A Painter's Holiday, and Other Poems, F. F. Sherman, 1911.

Echoes from Vagabondia, Small, Maynard, 1912.

(With Mary Perry King) *Daughters of Dawn: A Lyrical Pageant or Series of Historic Scenes for Presentation with Music and Dancing,* Kennerley, 1913.

(With Mary Perry King) *Earth Deities, and Other Rhythmic Masques,* Kennerley, 1914.

April Airs: A Book of New England Lyrics, Small, Maynard, 1916.

James Whitcomb Riley: An Essay by Bliss Carman, and Some Letters to Him from James Whitcomb Riley (August 30, 1898-October 12, 1915), G. D. Smith, 1918.

Later Poems, McClelland & Stewart, 1921.

Far Horizons, Small, Maynard, 1925.

(Editor, with Lorne Pierce) *Our Canadian Literature: Representative Verse,* Ryerson, 1925.

Talks on Poetry and Life, edited by Blanche Hume, Ryerson, 1926.

(Editor) *The Oxford Book of American Verse,* Oxford University Press, 1927.

Sanctuary: Sunshine House Sonnets, McClelland & Stewart, 1929.

Wild Garden, McClelland & Stewart, 1929.

Bliss Carman's Poems, McClelland & Stewart, 1931.

The Music of Earth, edited by Lorne Pierce, Ryerson, 1931.

Selected Poems, edited by Lorne Pierce, McClelland & Stewart, 1954.

Letters of Bliss Carman, edited by H. Pearson Gundy, McGill-Queen's, 1981.

Many of Carman's papers are in the Hatheway Collection, Bonar Law-Bennett Library, Univeristy of New Brunswick. Some letters are housed in the Edith and Lorne Pierce Collection of Canadiana, Queen's University Library, Kingston, Ontario.

SIDELIGHTS: In his lifetime Carman was considered Canada's leading poet, the Canadian Parliament honoring him as the nation's poet laureate in 1928. His early collections especially gained admireres for their lyrical, moody depictions of nature and for a free-spirited bohemianism found particularly in the popular *Songs from Vagabondia.* Carman's poetic world revolves primarily around the beauty of things seen, the mystery of things unseen, and the music of language.

Carman, born in Fredericton, New Brunswick, was descended from American Loyalists who fled to Canada from New England during the Revolution. He was educated at Fredericton Academy and later attended the University of New Brunswick, the university of Oxford, Edinburgh, and Harvard. There he profited from contact with a brilliant generation of teachers and students, including Josiah Royce, William James, Bernard Berenson, and George Santayana. He also met Richard Hovey, with whom he composed the three collections of vagabond lyrics. Carman moved to New York in 1890, and for the next twenty years he worked for various American publications as editor and writer, while still returning frequently to Canada. In 1897 he met Mary Perry King, a proponent of the doctrine of unitrinianism, whose followers embraced a struggle for harmony of the mind, body, and soul. Always receptive to philosophical influences, Carman integrated this doctrine with the generally transcendentalist world view he maintained throughout his life.

Carman's first collection, *Low Tide on Grand Pre,* established what would become his most enduring artistic persona, that of a poet of delicate moods and mysterious landscapes. "Meditative," "melancholy," "haunted" are common epithets applied to these poems. Carman stated that he wanted to convey a unity to these poems. Carman stated that he wanted to convey a unity of tone in assembling the pieces in this collection. However, after a number of Carman's books had appeared, critics labeled this unity as monotony, though Odell Shepard has argued for the poet's range and variety. In *Behind the Arras,* Carman's predominately sad and somber voice strikes a note of deeper pessimism, while further developing a strain of visionary mysticism displaying the influence of Poe. Despite his frequently grave tone, Carman in recent decades has been criticized for his optimism. Commentators trace his hopefulness to the influence of Emerson's transcendentalist philosophy and the vague assurance Carman maintained that unseen powers are working for the good of the human spirit. In such essay collections as *The Kinship of Nature and The Friendship of Art* he outlines his optimistic and inspirational outlook.

In his elegiac poems to Shelley, Keats, and others Carman acknowledges some of his strongest influences, and critics point out many more, including Wordsworth, Whitman, Rossetti, Tennyson, Arnold, and Browning. The poems in the vagabond series are found by some critics to be the least derivative, though others view the boisterous bohemian tone as essentially affected. Carman's later poetry collections, such as *April Airs and Later Poems,* offer little artistic development and add nothing to his reputation. While he wrote in a number of traditional poetic forms, with ambitious attempts at lengthy narrative poems, Carman is chiefly remembered today as a lyric poet who, not often but conspicuously, excelled at conveying a personal, highly contemplative appreciation for the beauty and mystery he perceived in nature.

BIOGRAPHICAL/CRITICAL SOURCES:

BOOKS

Hathaway, R. H., *Later Poems by Bliss Carman,* Small, Maynard & Company, 1922.

Lynch, Gerald, *Bliss Carman: A Reappraisal,* University of Ottawa, 1991.

Morse, William Inglis, *Bliss Carman, Bibliography: Letters, Fugitive Verses and Other Data,* Hawthorne, 1941.

Pacey, Desmond, *Ten Canadian Poets,* ryerson, 1958.

Stephens, Donald, *Bliss Carman,* Twayne, 1966.

Twentieth-Century Literary Criticism, Volume 7, Gale, 1982.

PERIODICALS

Atlantic Provinces Book Review, September 15, 1986, p. 15; May 7, 1982.

Books in Canada, August, 1981, p. 6.

Canadian Literature, summer, 1991, pp. 130-33; winter, 1992, pp. 133-35.

Choice, July, 1982, p. 1556.

Essays on Canadian Writing, fall, 1993, pp. 247-55.

Northern Review, February-March, 1950, pp. 59-113.*

CARRIER, Roch 1937-

PERSONAL: Born May 13, 1937, in Sainte-Justine-de-Dorchester, Quebec, Canada; son of Georges (in sales) and Marie-Anna (Tanguay) Carrier; married Diane Gosselin, 1959; children: two daughters. *Education:* Attended College Saint-Louis; received B.A. from L'Universite de Montreal, M.A., 1961; further study at the Sorbonne, University of Paris, 1961-64.

ADDRESSES: Home—Montreal, Quebec, Canada.

CAREER: Novelist, poet, dramatist, screenwriter, and author of short fiction. Has held teaching positions at College Militaire Royal de Saint-Jean, Quebec, and at L'Universite de Montreal, Montreal, Quebec; lecturer. Theatre du Nouveau Monde, Quebec, secretary-general, 1970—; chairman, Salon du Livre, Montreal.

AWARDS, HONOURS: Prix Litteraire de la Province de Quebec, 1964, for *Jolis deuils: Petites tragedies pour adultes;* Grand Prix Litteraire de la Ville de Montreal, 1981.

WRITINGS:

TRANSLATED WORKS; NOVELS

La Guerre, Yes Sir!, Editions du Jour, 1968, translation by Sheila Fischman published under the same title, Anansi, 1970.

Floralie, ou es-tu?, Editions du Jour, 1969, translation by Fischman published as *Floralie, Where Are You?,* Anansi, 1971.

Il est par la, le soleil, Editions du Jour, 1970, translation by Fischman published as *Is It the Sun, Philibert?,* Anansi, 1972.

Le Deux-millieme etage, Editions du Jour, 1973, translation by Fischman published as *They Won't Demolish Me!,* Anansi, 1974.

Le Jardin des delices, Editions la Press, 1975, translation by Fischman published as *The Garden of Delights,* Anansi, 1978.

Il n'y a pas de pays sans grand-pere, Stanke, 1979, translation by Fischman published as *No Country without Grandfathers,* Anansi, 1981.

La Dame qui avait des chaines aux chevilles, Stanke, 1981, translation by Fischman published as *Lady with Chains,* Anansi, 1984.

De l'amour dans la ferraille, Stanke, 1984, translation by Fischman published as *Heartbreaks along the Road,* Anansi, 1987.

Prieres d'un enfant tres tres sage, Stanke, 1988, translation by Fischman published as *Prayers of a Very Wise Child,* Penguin, 1991.

TRANSLATED WORKS; FOR CHILDREN

Les Enfants du bonhomme dans la lune, Stanke, 1979, translation by Fischman published as *The Hockey Sweater, and Other Stories,* Anansi, 1979.

Un Champion, translation by Fischman published as *The Boxing Champion,* illustrated by Sheldon Cohen, Tundra Books, 1991.

A Happy New Year's Day, illustrated by Gilles Pelletier, Tundra Books, 1991.

Canada je t'aime—I Love You, illustrated by Miyuki Tanobe, Tundra Books, 1991.

Le Plus Long Circuit, Tundra Books, 1993, translation by Fischman published as *The Longest Home Run,* illustrated by Cohen, Tundra Books, 1993.

UNTRANSLATED WORKS

Les Jeux incompris (poems), Editions Nocturne, 1956.

Cherche tes mots, cherche tes pas, Editions Nocturne, 1958.

Jolis deuils: Petites tragedies pour adultes (stories), Editions du Jour, 1964.

L'Aube d'acier (poem), illustrated by Maurice Savoie, Les Auteurs Reunis, 1971.

Les Fleurs vivent-elles ailleurs que sur la terre, Stanke, 1980.

Les Voyageurs de l'arc-en-ciel, illustrations by Francois Olivier, Stanke, 1980.

Le Cirque noir, Stanke, 1982.

Ne faites pas mal a l'avenin (juvenile), Les Editions Paulinas, 1984.

L'Ours et le kangourou, Stanke, 1986.

Un Chameau en jordanie, Stanke, 1988.

Enfants de la planete, Paulines, 1989.

Un Bonne et heureuse annee (juvenile), Tundra Books, 1991.

L'Homme dans le placard (mystery), Stanke, 1991.

Contributor of short stories to periodicals, including *Etudes francaises* and *Ellipse.* Contributor of articles to periodicals, including *Ecrits du Canada francais.*

PLAYS

La Guerre, Yes Sir! (four-act; adapted from novel of the same title; produced in Montreal, 1970; English-language version produced in Stratford, Ontario, 1972), Editions du Jour, 1970, revised edition, 1973.

Floralie (adapted from Carrier's novel *Floralie, ou es-tu?;* produced in Montreal, 1974), Editions du Jour, 1974.

Il n'y a pas de pays sans grand-pere (adapted from novel of the same title), produced in Montreal, 1978.

La Celeste bicyclette (produced in Montreal, 1979; translation produced in Toronto as *The Celestial Bicycle,* 1982), Stanke, 1980.

SCREENPLAYS

Le Martien de Noel, National Film Board of Canada, 1970.

The Ungrateful Land, National Film Board of Canada, 1972.

The Hockey Sweater (short subject), animated by Cohen, National Film Board of Canada, 1980.

SIDELIGHTS: Quebec writer Roch Carrier is considered one of French Canada's most important novelists. With the translation of many of his works into English, he has also become one of the most widely read Quebecois writers in North America and England. Carrier first earned recognition with a trilogy of novels—*La Guerre, Yes Sir!; Floralie, Where Are You?;* and *Is It the Sun, Philibert?*—that together span about fifty years of Quebec's history. He has established a reputation for his sensitive portrayal of the often turbulent misunderstandings that exist between French-and English-speaking Canadians. Carrier incorporates dark humor, dense allegory, and political satire into the fictional confrontations his characters enact in small Quebec towns. Describing his style as "[combining] the classical poise of Voltaire with the burly gusto of Rabelais," Mark Abley writes in *Saturday Night* that Carrier "stylizes and heightens the speech of rural Quebec." Nancy Wigston agrees in the Toronto *Globe and Mail,* proclaiming Carrier "one of Quebec's . . . geniuses of the written word."

Carrier published several short stories and poems during the 1950s and 1960s. However, it was not until publication of *La Guerre, Yes Sir!* in 1968—and its translation into English two years later—that he began to earn substantial acclaim. Set in a small Quebec town during World War II, the novel focuses on the wake of a village boy whose coffin is carried into town by English soldiers. To the villagers, the dead boy becomes a challenge to the living; the wake is at first a rowdy, good-natured celebration. But the underlying bitterness the villagers feel at the return of so many dead from European battlefields—the result of an *anglais* war that they feel should not involve their largely French-speaking province—transforms their initial boisterousness to hostility toward the English soldiers who are present. The festivity turns violent; ultimately one of the soldiers is killed. "Despite [the villagers'] unanimous opposition to the war," summarizes Philip Stratford in *Dictionary of Literary Biography,* "it visits them one grotesque night characterized by absurdity and nightmare."

La Guerre was enthusiastically received. "[This] is a first novel of staggering sophistication and control, proving that there now exists in Montreal a major international writer," declares Robert J. Green in *Journal of Commonwealth Literature.* Commending Carrier for his "fine, demanding talent," Mark Levene in *Canadian Forum* praises the author's "brilliant sense of narrative pace" and his ability to move "between the comic and the grotesque, between the realistic and the nightmarish." In *Saturday Night,* Andy Wainwright calls *La Guerre* "a black comedy of devastating effect . . . strewn with humour [and] bitter irony."

Although published as the second novel of what would be Carrier's trilogy, the events in *Floralie, Where Are You?* precede those of *La Guerre;* the book centers on the wedding night of the parents of the dead boy of the first novel. After their wedding feast, Anthyme and Floralie Corriveau hastily drive towards home through thick woods. Unable to control his mounting passion, Anthyme stops in the forest to consummate the marriage, after which he suspects his wife of having had another lover. Floralie confesses that she is not a virgin, and, depressed, the couple separates from one another in the woods. They each encounter misadventures while wandering through the dark until they finally reunite. Exhausted, the couple falls asleep; awakened by the still-feasting wedding guests, Anthyme and Floralie wonder if they had merely dreamed their traumatic night.

Although critics were impressed with *Floralie, Where Are You?,* the book was generally deemed less successful than Carrier's first novel. "Despite the considerable power of the early sections," writes Levene, "*Floralie, Where Are You?* possesses little of the overall control and intensity which mark his other work." Ronald Sutherland in *Canadian Literature* agrees, but nonetheless finds *Floralie* "another impressive accomplishment . . . filled with boisterous, ribald humour and stylistic fireworks." Sutherland concludes that *Floralie, Where Are You?* "is rich in amusing dialogue and incident. It is entertainment of a high order. There can be no doubt that here is a major talent . . . capable of producing a great deal more and very likely to do so."

Is It the Sun, Philibert? is the concluding novel in Carrier's trilogy. Focusing on Philibert, the son of a grave digger who appeared in *La Guerre,* the novel records the young man's experiences after he leaves his rural village to travel to Montreal. Although demoralized while living in a city he finds ugly and hostile, Philibert remains optimistic, and his ability to love prevails—even at his death—over his bleak surroundings. Like Carrier's first two novels, *Is It the Sun, Philibert?* has been praised for its raucous humor, rich symbolism, and dark images. "It is not so much plot or character that are memorable in Carrier's trilogy," Stratford notes of Carrier's three novels, "as it is a series of original, kaleidoscopic images, made virtually indelible by their explosive violence, shot through with grim humor, and set against the little, down-trodden man's faith . . . that life should be beautiful."

Carrier has written several other novels which have been popular with his growing readership in both the original French version and in English translation. *They Won't Demolish Me!,* first published in French in 1973, captures what Brian Vintcent in *Saturday Night* labels "Roch Carrier's world" of the "bizarre, folkloric, [and] brawling." In the book, a comic cast of characters try unsuccessfully to save their rotting tenement building from being razed—a symbolic representation of the struggle between the disadvantaged and large and powerful capitalist concerns. *Garden of Delights* depicts an ex-convict who, while visiting a pub in a rural Quebec town, claims he wants to buy the rights to mine gold along a local river. When this news spreads, almost the entire town greedily tries to buy into the enterprise, resulting in a chaotic scene that ends in tragedy. More political in tone is Carrier's *No Country without Grandfathers,* possibly the author's most anti-English work. Centering on an elderly Quebecois man who muses about the injustices of the past from the confines of his rocking chair, the novel culminates in a final demonstration of freedom as the man takes action against his country's English rule.

Lady with Chains appeared in English translation in 1984. Set in the 1860s, the novel centers on a young pioneer couple, Victor and Virginie. When Victor's negligence causes the tragic death of their child, Virginie is unable to forgive him and falls mute, consumed with vengeful fantasies of murdering her husband. "When she finally decides to turn her fantasies into reality," explains Paul Stuewe in *Books in Canada,* "her actions set in motion a bizarre but believable chain of events that culminates in a cathartic revelation." *Lady with Chains* was widely praised as a powerful and compelling tale. Wigston deems the novel "a strange . . . exploration of a young woman's psyche," adding that "Carrier's tale unfolds in supple, incantatory rhythms that capture . . . loneliness and despair." Proclaiming the work "supremely moving literature," Stuewe declares that *Lady with Chains* "finds one of [Canada's] most talented authors writing at the top of his form."

Carrier's 1987 novel, *Heartbreaks along the Road,* is considered by critics to be his most ambitious work. A satire, it is based on the controversial regime, during the 1950s, of Maurice Duplessis, a corrupt premier of Quebec popularly known as "Le Chef." The work portrays Le Chef, hoping to earn votes, following through on a campaign promise to build roads in rural towns in an effort to bolster employment. The roads, however, lead to nowhere, and they are dismantled immediately following their construction, thus creating more jobs. Embracing a large cast of characters, the novel outlines how the people of Quebec fall prey to the unscrupulous politician. The novel elicited mixed reviews—although criticized for being digressive and overly long, the book earned acclaim for its robust humor and biting political satire. Brent Ledger in *Books in Canada,* for example, is "baffled by the endless parade of characters and the plethora of incident," but praises parts of the book as "powerful bits of writing" and "deeply impressive." Similarly, while *Canadian Forum* contributor Jeannette Urbas finds the novel uneven and repetitious, she adds that these weaknesses are "offset by the successful creation of a panoramic fresco of the Quebec rural scene." More enthusiastic about the book, Stratford thinks that *Heartbreaks along the Road* "displays Carrier's humor and compassion at their inventive best." And, in high praise of the work, Mark Abley of *Saturday Night* feels that in its ability to "transform and illuminate a fragment of the visible world with the grace and force of myth," *Heartbreaks along the Road* "is Carrier's best novel and one of the most important Canadian books of our time."

Carrier has written numerous books in his native French, as well as adapted several of his novels for the stage. In addition, he is the author of several works about and for children. Carrier's illustrated short story collection entitled *The Hockey Sweater,* exhibits his characteristic political overtones on such topics as French Canadian nationalism, fear of the English, and the English-French language barrier. Told mostly from the perspective of Roch, a young boy growing up in rural Quebec, the stories have been acclaimed for their poetic and allegorical nature. *The Hockey Sweater* is "a gem of a book," writes Michael Benazon in *Canadian Forum;* "it is Roch Carrier at his best, his most personal work of prose fiction thus far." As a companion to *The Hockey Sweater,* Carrier published *The Boxing Champion* featuring the same young protagonist as he leaves behind his passion for hockey in an attempt to become a champion in the boxing ring. Young Roch appeared in another book, *A Happy New Year's Day.* As with the two books before it, it is a memoir, viewing the events of childhood from the naivety of youth and the understanding that comes with age.

BIOGRAPHICAL/CRITICAL SOURCES:

BOOKS

Cameron, Donald, *Conversations with Canadian Novelists,* Macmillan of Canada, 1973, pp. 13-29.
Contemporary Literary Criticism, Gale (Detroit), Volume 13, 1980; Volume 78, 1994.
Dictionary of Literary Biography, Volume 53: *Canadian Writers since 1960, First Series,* Gale, 1986.
Northey, Margot, *The Haunted Wilderness: The Gothic and Grotesque in Canadian Fiction,* University of Toronto Press, 1976, pp. 79-87.
Sutherland, Ronald, *Second Image: Comparative Studies in Quebec/Canadian Literature,* New Press (Toronto), 1971.

PERIODICALS

Antigonish Review, autumn, 1981, pp. 91-94.
Books in Canada, November, 1979, p. 10; February, 1982, pp. 9-10; December, 1984; December, 1987; November, 1991, p. 48.
Canadian Forum, September, 1970, p. 220; June, 1971; July, 1971, p. 36; May-June, 1974; September, 1979, p. 30; March, 1980, pp. 36-37; December, 1987, pp. 41-42.
Canadian Literature, spring, 1967, pp. 86-87; spring, 1970; autumn, 1971, pp. 87-88; spring, 1979, pp. 120-31; spring, 1985, pp. 24-33; autumn-winter, 1989, pp. 209-11.
Essays on Canadian Writing, spring, 1990, pp. 32-39.
French Review, April, 1979, pp. 789-90.
Globe and Mail (Toronto), August 11, 1984; October 13, 1984; October 17, 1987.
Journal of Canadian Fiction, summer, 1972, pp. 43-47.
Journal of Commonwealth Literature, June, 1972.
Saturday Night, May, 1970, pp. 42-43; August, 1974; October, 1987, pp. 59-62.
Studies in Canadian Literature, Volume 17, number 2, 1992-93, pp. 92-108.
Studies in Twentieth Century Literature, fall, 1982, pp. 59-76.
Variety, August 23, 1972.
World Literature Today, winter, 1980, p. 67.

*   *   *

CHARBONNEAU, Jean (Joseph Baptiste)   1875-1960

PERSONAL: Born September 3, 1875, in Montreal, Quebec, Canada; died after a long illness, October 25, 1960, in the Hopital des deux Montagnes, Saint-Eustache, Quebec; son of Charles (a carpenter) and Emma (Laflamme) Charbonneau; married Marie-Anna Rheume, 1904. *Education:* Attended College Sainte Marie; Universite de Montreal, law degree, 1903.

CAREER: Poet, dramatist, literary critic, and historian. Actor with Soirees de Famille, under stage name Delagny, 1893-1901. Member, Groupe des Six Eponges, 1894-95. Cofounder, with Louvigny de Montigny, of Ecole Litteraire de Montreal, 1895, president, 1907-09. Translator for Legislative Assembly of Quebec.

MEMBER: Societe Royale du Canada.

AWARDS, HONOURS: Prix David, 1924, for *L'Ombre dans le miroir.*

WRITINGS:

Les Blessures (title means "The Wounds"), Lemerre (Paris), 1912.

Des influences francaises au Canada (title means "The Influence of French Literature on Canada"), 3 volumes, Beauchemin (Montreal), 1916-20.

L'Age de sang (title means "Age of Blood"), Lemerre (Paris), 1921.

Les Predestines, Beauchemin (Montreal), 1923.

L'Ombre dans le miroir (title means "The Shadow in the Mirror"), Beauchemin (Montreal), 1924.

La Flamme ardente, Beauchemin (Montreal), 1928.

L'Ecole litteraire de Montreal: Ses origines, ses animateurs, ses influences, Levesque (Montreal), 1935.

Tel qu'en sa solitude (title means "This Is Solitude"), Valiquette/A.C.F. (Montreal), 1940.

Sur la borne pensive: L'Ecrin de Pandore, Lemerre (Paris), 1952.

Contributor to collective volumes of the Ecole litteraire de Montreal, including *Les Soirees du chateau de Ramezay* and *Le terroir;* contributor of poetry to journals, including *Le Samedi* and *Le Monde Illustre.* Charbonneau's unpublished works and manuscripts, including his dramatic works, are held in the Center of Research in Canadian-French Civilization at the University of Ottawa.

SIDELIGHTS: A writer, literary critic, historian, and practicing attorney, Jean Charbonneau is best remembered for his poetry and his role in founding the literary school of Montreal, the Ecole litteraire de Montreal. One of Charbonneau's later works was a history of this literary movement entitled *L'Ecole litteraire de Montreal: Ses origines, ses animateurs, ses influences,* in which he analyzes the early 20th century rejection of romanticism, which had strongly influenced both both French and Quebecois literature. He also wrote about the role French literature played in forming the literature of Quebec in a multivolume work of criticism entitled *Des influences francaises au Canada.*

Charbonneau's poetry reflects his affinity for classical structure and formality in verse that often addresses the contrast between past and present. Works such as *Les Blessures* and *L'Age de sang* are based on moral principles, and decry the materialism and turpitude of humanity in the modern era. The poems in *L'Age de sang* also demonstrate his classical leanings: each one questions wise men of the ancient world, such as the Hebrew patriarchs, the Persian philosopher Zarathustra, and Jesus Christ, on matters of humanity and salvation. *Tel qu'en sa solitude* also reflects Charbonneau's classicism. Composed in alexandrines, an ancient verse form used by Greek poets, it mirrors the passion of human belief in, and hope for, the possibility of life beyond death. "Even within this context," Brien concludes, "Charbonneau remains true to his classical affiliations and shuns any poise of romanticism."

BIOGRAPHICAL/CRITICAL SOURCES:

BOOKS

Dictionary of Literary Biography, Volume 92: *Canadian Writers, 1890-1920,* Gale, 1990.

*   *   *

CHARBONNEAU, Robert   1911-1967

PERSONAL: Born February 3, 1911, in Montreal, Quebec, Canada; died of a heart attack, June 26, 1967; son of Joseph-Arthur and Alma (Robert) Charbonneau; married Madeleine Brisset; children: three. *Education:* Attended Ecole Saint-Stanislas, 1919-25, and College Sainte-Marie, 1925-33; University of Montreal, diploma in journalism, 1934.

CAREER: Journalist, novelist, editor, and broadcaster. Worked for newspaper *La Patrie,* Montreal, 1934-37, *Le Droit,* Ottawa, 1937-38, and *La Presse,* beginning 1949; *Le Canada,* Montreal, assistant news editor, 1938-42; founder, with Claude Hurtubise, of Les Editions de l'Arbre, 1940-48; editor and manager for Radio Canada, beginning 1950. Laborer for Canadian Pacific Railway, summers, 1925-33. Active in Jeune Canada (Young Canada) movement, beginning 1933. *Wartime service:* Advisor to Canadian government on matters of publication.

MEMBER: Academie Canadienne-Francaise (cofounder, 1944), Societe des editeurs canadiens (president, 1945-48), Societe des ecrivains (president, 1966-67).

AWARDS, HONOURS: Prix Duvernay, Saint-Jean-Baptiste Society, 1945, for *Fontile.*

WRITINGS:

Ils possederont la terre, Editions de l'Arbre (Montreal), 1941.

Connaissance du personnage, Editions de l'Arbre, 1944.

Fontile, Editions de l'Arbre, 1945.

Petit Poemes retrouves, Editions de l'Arbre, 1945.

La France et nous, Editions de l'Arbre, 1947.

Les Desirs et les jours, Editions de l'Arbre, 1948.

Aucune Creature, Beauchemin (Montreal), 1961.

Chronique de l'age amer, Editions du Sablier (Montreal), 1967.

Romanciers canadiens, Presses de l'Universite Laval (Quebec), 1972.

RADIO PLAYS

Precieuse Elisabeth, first broadcast on Radio-Canada, 1949.

Fontile, first broadcast on Radio-Canada, 1951.

Les Desirs et les jours, first broadcast on Radio-Canada, 1951.

OTHER

Contributor to *Cahiers de l'Academie Canadienne-Francaise,* Number 4, *Contes et Nouvelles,* 1959. Contributor to periodicals, including *Releve, Nouvelle Releve,* and *Ecrits du Canada Francais.* Founder, with Paul Beaulieu, of *La Releve,* 1934-40, and of *Nouvelle Releve.*

SIDELIGHTS: Robert Charbonneau was a major literary force in the province of Quebec for over three decades. From the time of his founding of the journal *La Releve* in 1934, through his presidency of the French-language Society of Writers which he held at the time of his death, Charbonneau promoted journalism, publishing, broadcasting, and the independence of the literature of his native province. His fervent Quebecois nationalism was evident in his writings. Through his novels, the writer "paved the way for subsequent novelists in Quebec," writes Valerie Raoul in the *Dictionary of Literary Biography,* "such as Andre Langevin and Andre Giroux, who have continued the tradition of psychological novels which he helped to instigate."

Charbonneau's early association with Quebec nationalism—he was a member of nationalist movement Jeune Quebec in his youth—helped him earn his early jobs at the newspaper *La Patrie,* His journalistic experience eventually led him to found his own publication, *La Releve,* "whose aim," according to Raoul, "was to provide a forum for the younger admirers of the French-Canadian nationalist Lionel Groulx." This in turn led to the founding of his own press and the publication of his first novels. During World War II, Charbonneau also published the works of writers in exile from Europe. When he tried to continue this practice after the war, however, he was critized by French publishers and writers, who accused Charbonneau of publishing the work of artists they considered to be German collaborators.

Ultimately, the end of the war, and the growing conflict over how much freedom Quebec culture should have from its French origins, marked the end of Charbonneau's independent press. The author and publisher moved into broadcasting, and most of his later work was for radio. His final novel, *Chronique de l'age amer,* was based in part on his own life and experiences. The protagonist of this book founds his own nationalistic magazine, and the story recreates the political and social life of Quebec in the mid 1930s. Nineteen years after his death, Charbonneau was featured in a special edition of the journal *Ecrits du Canada Francais*—"evidence," says Raoul, "that he is still considered important."

BIOGRAPHICAL/CRITICAL SOURCES:

BOOKS

Dictionary of Literary Biography, Volume 68: *Canadian Writers, 1920-1959, First Series,* Gale, 1988.
Ducrocq-Poirier, *Robert Charbonneau,* Fides (Montreal), 1973.
Ellis, Madeleine-Blanche, *Robert Charbonneau et la creation romanesque,* Editions du Levrier (Montreal), 1948.
Falardeau, Jean-Charles, *Notre Societe et son roman,* HMH (Montreal), 1967.
Marcotte, Gilles, *Une Litterature qui se fait,* HMH (Montreal), 1962.
Robidoux, Rejean, and Andre Renaud, *Le Roman canadien-francais du vingtieme siecle,* Ottawa University Press (Ottawa), 1966.

PERIODICALS

Ecrits du Canada Francais (special Robert Charbonneau issue), number 57, 1986.
L'Action Nationale, November, 1948, pp. 209-23; March, 1973, pp. 584-600.
Lettres Quebecoises, summer, 1983, pp. 55-56.
Mosaic, spring, 1981, pp. 145-63.
University of Toronto Quarterly, October, 1946, pp. 42-50.*

*   *   *

CHASE, Nicholas
See HYDE, Anthony

*   *   *

CHOQUETTE, Adrienne   1915-1973

PERSONAL: Born July 2, 1915, in Shawinigan Falls, Quebec, Canada; died October 13, 1973; daughter of Henri (a physician) and Rose-Albertine (Amyot) Choquette. *Education:* Attended Ursuline school, Trois-Rivieres, 1924-31. *Religion:* Roman Catholic.

CAREER: Animator, radio announcer, producer, and writer. *Le Bien public* (newspaper), Trois Rivieres, journalist, 1934; CHLN (radio station), Trois Rivieres, producer of *Varietes radiophoniques* and radio dramas, 1937-42; worked as an advertising editor, 1942-48; *Terre et foyer,* Department of Agriculture, Quebec, editor, publicist, 1948—. Guest lecturer on a variety of subjects, including literature.

AWARDS, HONOURS: Prix David, Quebec Ministry of Cultural Affairs, 1954, for *La Nuit ne dort pas: nouvelles;* Prix du Grand Jury des Lettres, Salon du Livre de Montreal, c. 1961, for *Laure Clouet.*

WRITINGS:

(Editor) *Confidences d'ecrivains canadiens-francais* (nonfiction), Bien Publique (Trois-Rovoeres, Quebec), 1939.

La Coupe vide (novel), Pilon (Montreal), 1948.

La Nuit ne dort pas (short stories), Institut litteraire du Quebec, 1954, enlarged edition (includes "Sortilege" and "Le Rendez-vous"), Presses Laurentiennes (Notre-Dame-des-Laurentides, Quebec), 1979.

Laure Clouet (novel), Institut litteraire du Quebec, 1961.

Je m'appelle Pax (for children), introduction by Robert Choquette, Presses Laurentiennes (Notre-Dame-des-Laurentides, Quebec), 1974.

Le Temps des villages (short stories), introduction by Suzanne Paradis, Presses Laurentiennes (Notre-Dame-des-Laurentides, Quebec), 1975.

Contributor of stories and articles to periodicals and journals, including *Amerique francaise, Les Cahiers de L'Academie canadienne-francaise, Carnets victoriens, Liaison, la Revue Dominicaine,* and *La Famille.*

SIDELIGHTS: Adrienne Choquette is an important literary figure and an acclaimed novelist for what many believe to be her finest work, the novel *Laure Clouet.* A multi-talented artist, Choquette was also a radio announcer and producer, a journalist, and the author of a book for children, *Je m'appelle Pax.* Her work is prized for its unique style, polished narration, and layers of meaning seemingly hidden just beneath the surface of the story. Romain Legare, in his 1975 introduction to a new combined publication of Choquette's *Laure Clouet* and *La Nuit ne dort pas,* wrote that Choquette has "a real literary talent, a deep sensibility, a solid gift for psychology, originality in style and inspiration."

Choquette was born on July 2, 1915 in Shawinigan Falls, Quebec, to Henri and Rose-Albertine Choquette. Orphaned as a young girl, Choquette grew up in Trois-Rivieres and attended the Ursuline school there. After graduation in 1931 she worked for a short time at a newspaper as a journalist, then transferred to radio station CHLN in Trois-Rivieres as an announcer and producer of radio drama. In 1939 Choquette edited a collection of interviews with French-Canadian authors, published as *Confidences d'ecrivains canadiens-francais.* She next turned to fiction with her ensuing book, 1948's *La Coupe vide,* the story of an erotic woman and her influence on four impressionable teenagers. Alexandre L. Amprimoz described critical reaction to the work in an entry for the *Dictionary of Literary Biography:* "A not-too-realistic first novel dealing with a daring subject, *La Coupe vide* was not a success. It found few enthusiastic readers in Church-dominated Quebec." The book was, however, Choquette's first to deal with female psychology, a theme which be-

came fully developed in 1961's award-winning *Laure Clouet.*

Choquette first found acclaim as a short story writer. Her *La Nuit ne dort pas,* a collection of short stories published in 1954, was widely successful; the work won the prestigious Prix David award from the Quebec Ministry of Cultural Affairs. Much later, in 1979, an enlarged edition of the book was published posthumously featuring two formerly unpublished stories, "Sortilege" and "Le Rendezvous." Also issued posthumously was a collection of short stories with an introduction by Quebecois author Suzanne Paradis in 1975, *Le Temps des villages.* This work, as described by Amprimoz, is "occasionally comic, [but] not at heart nostalgic. Violent acts occur in these stories," an effect which is contrasted and heightened by the serene setting of Quebec and Choquette's overall theme of solitude. Other short stories, written by Choquette and contributed to various periodicals and journals, have yet to be anthologized.

Laure Clouet, published in 1961, is believed by many to be Choquette's masterpiece. Described as an "urban" novel because the background is the city and traditions of Quebec, critics consider Choquette's efforts "rare," citing historically widespread use of the city of Montreal as a setting by other French Canadian authors. The main character, Laure Clouet, is an unmarried woman in her forties who begins to blossom socially as well as intellectually when she is confronted with making everyday decisions after her mother's death. Laure revels in the simple pleasures which this unaccustomed freedom affords. The novel depicts Laure's psychological awakenings through a mixture of form and structure; for example, the house which Laure inherits may symbolize the traditions which have shaped her life, and it is significant that she considers opening the house to a young couple, especially in view of contradictory advice given to her from friends and clergy. "What is really going on is happening between the message given and the message received," Amprimoz stated, "in the deceptively quiet silences of Laure's own choices."

Amprimoz wrote in the *Dictionary of Literary Biography* that *Laure Clouet* is "certainly one of the most refined attempts to represent the nostalgia of old French-Canadian traditions" yet the author transcends sentiment to invite the reader to see beyond the novel's "apparent simplicities" and recognize illusion. It is this veneer of reality, a layering of meaning perceptible beneath the surface of the story, which lends the book its unique charm. Modern critics have seen social implications in the novel, "a witness not so much to the particular life of a woman as to the more general, restricted character of life in the last years before the Quiet Revolution transformed ideology and politics as well as literature in modern Quebec," according to Amprimoz. *Laure Clouet* won the Prix du

Grand Jury des Lettres soon after the novel's 1961 publication.

One of Choquette's final works before her death in 1973 was written for children: *Je m'appelle Pax.* The book was published in 1974—only a short while after her demise—with an introduction by an older cousin of the author, the playwright and novelist Robert Choquette. The narrative follows the reflections of a contented pet dog named "Pax."

BIOGRAPHICAL/CRITICAL SOURCES:

BOOKS

Choquette, Adrienne, *Laure Clouet: La Nuit ne dort pas,* introduction by Romain Legare, Fides, 1975.
Dictionary of Literary Biography, Volume 68: *Canadian Writers, 1920-1959, First Series,* Gale, 1988, pp. 67-69.
De LaFontaine, *Contes et recits de la Mauricie,* Editions Cedoleq, 1982, pp. 11-30.
Marineau, Line, and De LaFontaine, *Adrienne Choquette: Nouvelliste de l'emancipation,* Presses Laurentiennes, 1984.
Menard, Jean, *La Vie litteraire au Canada francais,* Editions de l'Universite d'Ottawa, 1971, pp. 220-22.
Paradis, Suzanne, *Adrienne Choquette lue par Suzanne Paradis: Une Analyse de l'oeuvre litteraire de'Adrienne Choquette,* Presses Laurentiennes, 1978.
Poulin, Gabrielle, *Romans du pays,* Bellarmin, 1980, pp. 326-31.

PERIODICALS

Lectures, April, 1949, pp. 449-54.
Livres et Auteurs Quebecois, 1974, pp. 254-57.*

*　　*　　*

CLAMER, Adrien
　See LABERGE, Albert

*　　*　　*

CLARK, Catherine Anthony (Smith)　1892-1977

PERSONAL: Born May 5, 1892, in London, England; immigrated to Canada, 1914; died February 24, 1977, in Victoria, British Columbia, Canada; daughter of Edgar Francis (an antique expert) and Catherine Mary (Palmer) Smith; married Leonard Clark (a rancher), December 29, 1919; children: Leonard Hugh, Margaret. *Politics:* Conservative. *Religion:* Roman Catholic.

CAREER: Author.

MEMBER: Catholic Women's League, Royal Oak Women's Institute.

AWARDS, HONOURS: Canadian Library Association Book of the Year Medal, 1952, for *The Sun Horse.*

WRITINGS:

ALL PUBLISHED BY MACMILLAN (TORONTO), EXCEPT WHERE INDICATED

The Golden Pine Cone, 1950.
The Sun Horse, 1951.
The One-Winged Dragon, 1955.
The Silver Man, 1958, Macmillan (London), 1959.
The Diamond Feather; or, The Door in the Mountain: A Magic Tale for Children, 1962.
The Man with Yellow Eyes, 1963, St. Martin's (New York City), 1964.
The Hunter and the Medicine Man, 1966.

Columnist for the *Prospector,* in Nelson, British Columbia.

SIDELIGHTS: Catherine Anthony Clark was a distinguished writer of juvenile fantasy. She was born and educated in England, coming to Canada in her early twenties. In 1919 she married Leonard Clark and together they established a ranch in British Columbia. For the next three decades Clark occupied herself raising her two children and maintaining her home.

Clark became a published writer late in her life. Her first book, *The Golden Pine Cone,* appeared in 1950, when Clark was fifty-eight years old. *The Golden Pine Cone,* which appropriates Native Canadian folklore, readily established Clark as a skillful and engaging storyteller. The book concerns the experiences of two children, Bren and Lucy. Searching for their lost dog, the children stray from their cabin home and enter a fantastical land known as the Inner World. In this odd domain, they become involved in the search for a missing pine cone that possesses mystical powers. They eventually recover the artifact and return to its actual owner while also finding their missing pet.

Clark followed *The Golden Pine Cone* with what is generally considered to be her most acclaimed work, 1951's *The Sun Horse,* Like its predecessor, this book is a fantasy-based tale concerning the actions of two children. In *The Sun Horse* Mark and Giselle search for the latter's missing father, who has disappeared while seeking a dazzling stallion in a mysterious valley. The children's search leads them to the domain of the Thunderbird, an evil creature whose lofty perch affords it considerable protection and power over creatures below. The children overcome their fears and eventually undertake the dangerous climb to the Thunderbird's nest. They are thus able to rescue Giselle's father.

In 1955 Clark published her third book, *The One-Winged Dragon.* In this volume she follows a writing path similar to her first two books. Once again two children, Michael and Jenni, undergo an exciting adventure as they attempt to rescue of a young girl who is lost in the Inner World realm that Clark introduced in *The Golden Pine Cone.* During the course of their adventures, which ultimately compel them to confront the treacherous Flower-Witch, Michael and Jenni realize a greater understanding and mastery of their insecurities. The children's reunion with their respective parents also reinforces themes of family and love. Thus *The One-Winged Dragon,* like Clark's preceding stories, is as much an account of childhood maturation and values as it is a tale of thrills and magical experiences.

Clark's next book, 1958's *The Silver Man,* features a character many consider to be her most singularly memorable protagonist, the orphan Gilbert Steyne. In the book, Gilbert penetrates the enchanting Inner World while peering into a magical crystal, whereupon he befriends an Indian girl, Kawitha, who is determined to rescue her brother, the magical Silver Man. During the course of his adventures with Kawitha, Gilbert comes to understand the value of sacrifice and the importance of overcoming one's complacency and fears. In doing so, he realizes a measure of maturation.

In 1962 Clark published *The Diamond Feather; or The Door in the Mountain: A Magic Tale for Children,* in which two children, Jon and Firelei, enter the Inner World and encounter an obsessed miner whose lust for gold has already compelled him to abandon his family. In *The Diamond Feather,* Clark concentrates on the miner's maturation as much as she does that of her young protagonists, and the tale's central resolution involves the miner's understanding of the grief he has caused both himself and others.

Clark's final publication is *The Hunter and the Medicine Man,* a 1966 volume in which Clark again shifts emphasis away from her youthful characters, here named Richard and Anne, to concentrate on another character's conflict. The character of note in *The Hunter and the Medicine Man* is Hunter, who has grown unhappy with civilization and fled to the mountains. Richard and Anne search for Hunter and eventually convince him to return home and rescue his endangered brother.

Clark died in 1977 at the age of eighty-four. She is remembered as an accomplished storyteller, and her books are still prized as authentic Canadian myths that embody both native folklore and more generalized fairy-tale elements. As J. Keiran Kealy noted in the *Dictionary of Literary Biography,* Clark's contribution to Canadian literature "should not be underestimated. In a country with no real tradition of fantasy, she created six fantasies." Kealy went

on to characterize the author as "one of Canada's first and most successful children's fantasists."

BIOGRAPHICAL/CRITICAL SOURCES:

BOOKS

Dictionary of Literary Biography, Volume 68: *Canadian Writers, 1920-1959,* Gale, 1988.

PERIODICALS

British Columbia Library Quarterly, January, 1961, pp. 26-31.
Canadian Children's Literature, nos. 15-16, 1980, pp. 22-25.
Canadian Literature, winter, 1962, pp. 39-45; autumn, 1978, pp. 32-42.*

*   *   *

CLARKE, Austin C(hesterfield)   1934-

PERSONAL: Born July 26, 1934, in Barbados, West Indies; son of Kenneth Trothan (an artist) and Gladys Clarke; married Trinity Collego; children: Janice, Loretta, Jordan. *Education:* Harrison College, Barbados, West Indies, Oxford and Cambridge Higher certificate, 1950; additional study at University of Toronto.

ADDRESSES: Agent—Harold Ober Associates, 40 East 49th St., New York, NY 10017.

CAREER: Canadian Broadcasting Corp., Toronto, Ontario, producer and free-lance broadcaster, beginning 1963; Brandeis University, Waltham, MA, Jacob Ziskind Professor of Literature, 1968-69; Williams College, Williamstown, MA, Margaret Bundy Scott Professor of Literature, 1971-72; Barbados Embassy, Washington, DC, cultural and press attache, 1974-75; currently affiliated with Caribbean Braodcasting Corp., St. Michael, Barbados. Visiting professor of Afro-American literature and creative writing, Yale University, 1968-71. Member of Board of trustees, Rhode Island School of Design, Providence, 1970-75; member, Immigrations and Refugees Board of Canada, 1989.

MEMBER: Writers Guild, Writers' Union of Canada (founding member), Yale Club (New Haven).

AWARDS, HONOURS: Canada Council senior arts fellowships, 1968, 1970, 1974; University of Western Ontario President's medal for best story, 1965; Belmont Short Story Award, for "Four Stations in His Circle"; Casa de las Americas Literary Prize, 1980.

WRITINGS:

NOVELS

The Survivors of the Crossing, McClelland & Stewart, 1964.
Amongst Thistles and Thorns, McClelland & Stewart, 1965.
The Meeting Point, Macmillan, 1967.
Storm of Fortune, Little, Brown, 1973.
The Bigger Light, Little, Brown, 1975.
The Prime Minister, General Publishing, 1977.
Growing up Stupid under the Union Jack (autobiographical novel), McClelland & Stewart, 1980.
Proud Empires, Viking, 1986.
There Are No Elders, Exile, 1993.

SHORT STORIES

When He Was Free and Young and He Used to Wear Silks, Anansi, 1971, Little, Brown, 1974.
When Women Rule, McClelland and Stewart, 1985.
Nine Men Who Laughed, Penguin, 1986.

Author of *Short Stories of Austin Clark,* 1984.

OTHER

Also author of *myths and memories, African Literature,* and other filmscripts for Educational Television (ETV), Toronto, 1968—.

WORK IN PROGRESS: A study of the symbolism in Richard Wright's story, "The Man Who Lived Underground"; research concerning the position of black women in the Black American Revolution.

SIDELIGHTS: Austin C. Clarke's childhood in colonial Barbados and his experiences as a black immigrant to Canada have provided him with the background for most of his fiction. His writing is almost exclusively concerned with the cultural contradictions that arise when blacks struggle for success in a predominantly white society. Clarke's "one very great gift," in the words of a *New Yorker* critic, is the ability to see "unerringly into his characters' hearts," and this ability is what makes his stories memorable. Martin Levin writes in the *New York Times Book Review,* "Mr. Clarke is plugged into the fixations, hopes, loves and dreams of his characters. He converts them into stories that are charged with life."

Clarke's autobiographical novel, *Growing Up Stupid under the Union Jack,* is an example of the author's typical theme and style. The narrator, Tom, is a young man from a poor Barbadan village. Everyone in the village is proud that Tom is able to attend the Combermere School, for it is run by a "real, true-true Englishman"—an ex-British army officer who calls his students "boy" and "darky" and who flogs them publicly. The students eagerly imitate this headmaster's morals and manners, for to them, he represents "Mother England"; they are unaware that in England he would be looked down upon as a mere working-class soldier. The book is "a personal, captivating, provoking, and often humorous record of ignorance, inhumanity and lowly existence under colonial imperialism in World War II Barbados. . . . With its major emphasis on education and childhood, *Growing Up Stupid under the Union Jack* continues to draw attention to one of the chief preoccupations of the anti-colonial Anglo-Caribbean novel," writes Robert P. Smith in *World Literature Today.* The theme is well rendered in what Darryl Pinckney calls in the *New York Review of Books* Clarke's "tender, funny, unpolemical style."

Clarke's best known work is a trilogy detailing the lives of the Barbadan blacks who immigrate to Toronto hoping to better their lot. In these novels, *The Meeting Point, Storm of Fortune,* and *The Bigger Light,* "it is as if the flat characters of a Dickensian world have come into their own at last, playing their tragicomic roles in a manner which owes much to Clarke's extraordinary facility with the Barbadian dialect," writes Diane Bessai in *Canadian Literature.* Bessai also expresses eagerness for Clarke to "continue to create his Brueghel-like canvasses with their rich and contrasting detail and mood." "The sense of defeat among the poor islanders is enlivened by the humour of the characters and their glowing fantasies about the presumed wealth of relatives and friends who make it big in the fatlands of the United States or Canada," writes John Ayre in *Saturday Night.*

The first two novels dwell mostly on Bernice Leach, a live-in maid at a wealthy Toronto home, and her small circle of fellow immigrants. Martin Levin writes in the *New York Times Book Review:* "Mr. Clarke is masterful at delineating the oppressive insecurities of Bernice and her friends, and the claustrophobic atmosphere that envelops such a mini-minority" as the Caribbean blacks in Toronto. The third novel, *The Bigger Light,* explores the life of Boysie, the most successful of this immigrant group, and his wife, Dots. Boysie has at last realized the dream that compelled him to leave Barbados; he owns a prosperous business and his own home. However, in the process of realizing his goals, he has become alienated from his wife and his community. Now he searches for a greater meaning to his life—a "bigger light." "*The Bigger Light* is a painful book to read," writes David Rosenthal in the *Nation.* It is "a story of two people with many things to say and no one to say them to, who hate themselves and bitterly resent the society around them. . . . Certain African novelists have also dealt with the isolation of self-made blacks, but none with Clarke's bleak intensity." A *New Yorker* writer praises the book further, citing Clarke's strong writing skill as the element that lifts the book beyond social comment: "the universal longings or ordinary human beings are depicted with a simplicity and power that make us grateful for all three volumes of this long and honest record."

BIOGRAPHICAL/CRITICAL SOURCES:

BOOKS

Brown, Lloyd, *El Dorado and Paradise; A Critical Study of the Works of Austin Clarke,* Center for Social and Humanistic Studies, University of Western Ontario, 1989.
Contemporary Authors Autobiography Series, Volume 16, Gale, 1992.
Contemporary Literary Criticism, Volume 8, Gale, 1978; Volume 53, 1989.
Dictionary of Literary Biography, Volume 53: *Canadian Writers since 1960, First Series,* Gale, 1986; Volume 125: *Twentieth-Century Caribbean and Black African Writers,* 1993.
Gibson, Graeme, *Eleven Canadian Novelists,* Anansi, 1973, pp. 33-54.

PERIODICALS

Books in Canada, October, 1986, pp. 20-21.
Canadian Literature, summer, 1974; autumn, 1981, pp. 136-38; winter, 1982, pp. 181-85.
CLA Journal, September, 1985, pp. 9-32.
College Language Association Journal, December, 1992, pp. 123-33.
Listener, June 15, 1978.
Nation, November 1, 1975.
New Yorker, February 24, 1975.
New York Review of Books, May 27, 1982.
New York Times Book Review, April 9, 1972; December 9, 1973; February 16, 1975; August 23, 1987.
Saturday Night, October, 1971; June, 1975.
Times Literary Supplement, May 11, 1967, p. 404.
World Literature Today, winter, 1982.

* * *

CODERRE, Emile 1893-1970
(Jean Narrache, a pseudonym)

PERSONAL: Born June 10, 1893, in Montreal, Quebec, Canada; died April 6, 1970; son of Emile (a pharmacist) and Jeanne (Marchand) Coderre; adopted by M.-A. Ouimet; married Rose-Marie Delys Tasse, September 19, 1922. *Education:* University of Montreal, B.A., 1917, pharmaceutical license, 1921. *Religion:* Roman Catholic.

CAREER: Worked with Martin-Senours (paint company), beginning 1924; managed a pharmacy in Montreal; University of Quebec, assistant professor of pharmacy,

1954-64. Editor-in-chief of *Pharmacien,* 1939-42; secretary of the Quebec College of Pharmacists, 1943-61.

MEMBER: Ecole Litteraire de Montreal (1912-13); Quebec College of Pharmacists.

AWARDS, HONOURS: Silver medal and certificate from the Societe des Poetes canadiens-francais, 1933, for *Les Signes sur le sable.*

WRITINGS:

Les Signes sur le sable (poetry; title means "Signs on the Sand"), L'auteur (Montreal, Quebec), 1922.

UNDER PSEUDONYM JEAN NARRACHE

Quand j'parl' tout seul (poetry; title means "When I Talk All Alone"; includes "Les Deux Orphelines"), Levesque (Montreal, Quebec), 1932.
Histoires du Canada . . . vies ramanchees (nonfiction), L'Action Canadienne-Francaise (Montreal, Quebec), 1937.
J'parl' pour parler (poetry; title means "I Speak for the Sake of Speaking"; includes "Jasette a saint Francois d'Assise"), Valiquette (Montreal, Quebec), 1939.
Bonjour, les gars! Vers ramanches et pieces nouvelles (poetry; title means "Hello, Boys!"; includes "Meditation d'un gueux au pied de la croix"), Pilon (Montreal, Quebec), 1948.
J'parle tout seul quand Jean Narrache (poetry; title means "I Speak Alone When I Am Jean Narrache"), L'Homme (Montreal, Quebec), 1961.
Jean Narrache chez le diable (essays; title means "Jean Narrache at the Devil's House"), L'Homme, 1963.

Also the author *Reveries de Jean Narrache,* Pauvre Yabe (Montreal, Quebec). Author of several unpublished plays and sketches for stage and radio under the Narrache pseudonym.

Contributor of articles and poetry to periodicals, including *Revue Moderne* and *Grande Revue.*

ADAPTATIONS: Les Poemes de Jean Narrache avec Rene Caron (recording), Trans-Canada TC 782.

SIDELIGHTS: Emile Coderre, better known under his pseudonym Jean Narrache, was one of French-speaking Canada's most popular poets, particularly during the 1930s. His poetry is notable for its sharp wit and its sympathy for the working classes, often shown at the expense of the middle class. He produced several book-length collections of poetry, including the well-loved *Quand j'parl' tout seul* and *Bonjour, les gars! Vers ramanches et pieces nouvelles.* Narrache also penned works of prose, such as *Histoires du Canada . . . vies ramanchees* and *Jean Narrache chez le diable,* and created many unpublished plays for stage and radio. Though Narrache's oeuvre was widely read by the common people of Montreal and other parts of Quebec, it was somewhat overlooked by critics. Alexandre L. Amprimoz, however, discussing Narrache in the *Dictionary of Literary Biography,* observed that he "is one of the most underestimated Canadian poets and writers. His fundamental inspiration was the Depression, and he wrote about 'the little guy' from the East End of Montreal." Amprimoz further noted that "it was Narrache who introduced into French-Canadian literature the informal 'habitant' language that would later develop into 'joual,' the slang of Montreal's working classes."

Coderre was born in Montreal in 1893; his father was a pharmacist. The young Coderre was orphaned, however, at the age of four, and adopted by M.-A. Ouimet. His early education took place at the Seminaire de Nicolet, and there he began displaying his literary bent by publishing a student magazine called *Le Mercredi.* In pieces for this publication, according to Amprimoz, Coderre "gave the first signs of his propensity for humor."

Coderre became involved with the literary group Ecole Litteraire de Montreal as a young man, but he nevertheless decided, like his father, to pursue a career in pharmacology. He first completed a bachelor's degree at the University of Montreal, then obtained his pharmacist's license. He worked for a paint company for a while, then became the manager of a pharmacy in one of Montreal's poorest neighborhoods. By this time, the Great Depression had become a factor in Montreal's economy, and it was in watching the poor and working classes trying to cope with this era's poverty that Coderre was inspired to create his best-known work.

Before he had truly entered into his pharmaceutical career, Coderre had published a volume of verse under his own name. Though *Les Signes sur le sable* saw print in 1922, the poetry in it was primarily written almost a decade previously, during Coderre's association with the Ecole Litteraire de Montreal. As Amprimoz reported, *Les Signes sur le sable* met with unkind responses from most of the serious poetry critics of the time, who judged it "sentimental rubbish."

As Coderre began to think of publishing the poems inspired by the poor of Montreal, he decided to take on a pseudonym. The one he chose, Jean Narrache, is something of a pun in French; as Amprimoz explained, "Jean Narrache is the homonym for the phrase 'J'en arrache,' which means 'I'm tearing at it' or, less literally, 'People give me a hard time,' or 'It's a tough grind.' " The first collection of "Narrache's" poetry, then, was 1932's *Quand j'parl' tout seul.* This volume was greeted with a much better reception than that of *Les Signes sur le sable,* and Narrache was awarded the Silver Medal of the Societe des Poetes canadiens-francais after its publication. A typical

poem featured in *Quand j'parl' tout seul* is "Les Deux Orphelines," which tells in what Amprimoz hailed as "sharp, ironic observations" the tale of a comfortable bourgeois woman who goes to see a play about two orphans. Her emotions are touched to the point of copious sobs, but when she leaves the theater and encounters two real orphan girls who beg money from her, she attempts to drive them away and threatens to call the police. *Quand j'parl' tout seul* sold over six thousand copies in the year it was published, and it was the popularity of these poems which led to Narrache's creating plays and sketches for Montreal radio.

Narrache's next project was his prose book, *Histoires du Canada . . . vies ramanchees.* Though his purpose in this work was ostensibly to examine historical figures important in the development of Canada and of North America as a whole—such as explorers Christopher Columbus and Jacques Cartier—Narrache also managed to indict what he saw as corruption in the Canadian and Quebecois politics of his own day. "The reader can savor the humor directed at political life in the thirties," lauded Amprimoz, "the scandals related to road construction, tax evasion, and related fraud."

J'parl' pour parler, the next poetry collection by Narrache, featured a more bitter tone than *Quand j'parl' tout seul* in its quest to berate the middle-class establishment. The volume also featured a change in Narrache's poetic structure, from the regular stanzas of his previous work to a more free verse style. According to Amprimoz, the poems in *J'parl' pour parler,* particularly "Jasette a saint Francois d'Assise," "offer Narrache's vision of the role of the Christian artist." More specifically, this role is "a marginal position" taken "in order to criticize freely a society from which he does not ask anything for himself."

Narrache's poetry collections after *J'parl' pour parler* predominantly feature poems published previously with a sprinkling of new pieces. One notable example is his 1948 *Bonjour, les gars! Vers ramanches et pieces nouvelles.* Among its nine new poems is "Meditation d'un gueux au pied de la croix," which is two hundred and six lines long and is in the voice of a beggar witnessing the crucifixion of Jesus. The volume also contains a prose essay which, in Amprimoz's terms, explains "the principles of his populist poetics."

One of Narrache's later works is 1963's *Jean Narrache chez le diable.* The title means "Jean Narrache at the Devil's House," and the book is a series of dialogues with a demonic figure called Contradiction that allegedly take place after a descent to Hell. The dialogues examine topics of interest to Quebecois at the time, including art, journalism, politics, and separatism. In a departure from Narrache's usual style, the volume is written in standard

French rather than the slang that the author helped popularize. Amprimoz asserted that *Jean Narrache chez le diable* "deserves more attention" than it has previously received from reviewers. The critic linked it, through its portrayal of a devil who limps, with *La Nuit,* the work of Quebec separatist author Jacques Ferron.

In addition to his output as Jean Narrache, Coderre continued his work in pharmacology, eventually becoming an instructor in that field at the University of Quebec. He also served as editor of *Pharmacien* for a few years, as well as contributing articles on pharmacology to other professional journals. Coderre died in 1970.

BIOGRAPHICAL/CRITICAL SOURCES:

BOOKS

Dictionary of Literary Biography, Volume 92: *Canadian Writers, 1890-1920,* Gale, 1989.

PERIODICALS

Culture, June, 1952, pp. 164-67.
Le Canada Francais, October, 1922, pp. 133-43; February, 1933, pp. 569-73.
Le Devoir, April 18, 1967, p. 10.
L'Enseignement Secondaire au Canada, January, 1938, pp. 314-15.*

—Sketch by Elizabeth Wenning

*   *   *

COGSWELL, Fred(erick William) 1917-

PERSONAL: Born November 8, 1917, in East Centreville, New Brunswick, Canada; son of Walter Scott (a farmer) and Florence (White) Cogswell; married Margaret Hynes, July 3, 1944 (died May 2, 1985); married Gail Fox, November 8, 1985; children: Carmen Patricia, Kathleen Mary. *Education:* University of New Brunswick, B.A. (with honors), 1949, M.A., 1950; University of Edinburgh, Ph.D., 1952. *Politics:* New Democratic Party. *Religion:* Christian.

ADDRESSES: Home—Comp. AG, Site 6, R.R. 4, Fredericton, New Brunswick, Canada E3B 4X5.*Office*—University of New Brunswick, Fredericton, New Brunswick, Canada.

CAREER: University of New Brunswick, Fredericton, assistant professor, 1952-57, associate professor, 1957-61, professor of English, 1961-83, professor emeritus, 1983—. Editor and publisher, *Fiddlehead* magazine, 1952-66, and Fiddlehead Press, 1967-82. Scottish-Canadian exchange writer in residence, Edinburgh, Scotland, 1983-84. *Military service:* Canadian Army, 1940-45; became staff sergeant; was decorated.

MEMBER: Association of Canadian Publishers (honorary life member), League of Canadian Poets (honorary life member), Association of Canadian and Quebec Literatures (president, 1978-80), Atlantic Publishers Association (president, 1978-80; honorary life member).

AWARDS, HONOURS: I.O.D.E. Scholar for New Brunswick, 1950-52; Nuffield fellow, 1959-60; Gold Medal of Poets Laureate International presented by Republic of the Philippines, 1965; Canada Council Senior fellowship, 1967-68; Order of Canada, 1982; L.Ld., St. Francis Xavier University, 1983, and Mount Allison University, 1987; D.C.L., King's University, 1985; 125th Anniversary Medal, government of Canada, 1992.

WRITINGS:

The Stunted Strong, Fiddlehead, 1954.
The Haloed Tree, Ryerson, 1956.
(Translator) Robert Henryson, *The Testament of Cresseid,* Ryerson, 1957.
Descent from Eden, Ryerson, 1959.
Lost Dimension, Outposts Publication, 1960.
(Editor) *A Canadian Anthology,* Fiddlehead, 1960.
(Editor and contributor) *Five New Brunswick Poets,* Fiddlehead, 1962.
(Editor with Robert Tweedie and S. W. MacNutt) *The Arts in New Brunswick,* [Fredericton], 1966.
(Editor with T. R. Lower) *The Enchanted Land,* Gage, 1967.
Star-People, Fiddlehead, 1968.
Immortal Plowman, Fiddlehead, 1969.
In Praise of Chastity, New Brunswick Chapbooks, 1970.
(Editor and translator) *One Hundred Poems of Modern Quebec,* Fiddlehead, 1970.
(Editor and translator) *A Second Hundred Poems of Modern Quebec,* Fiddlehead, 1971.
The Chains of Liliput, Fiddlehead, 1971.
The House without a Door, Fiddlehead, 1973.
Light Bird of Life: Selected Poems, Fiddlehead, 1974.
(Editor) *The Poetry of Modern Quebec,* Harvest, 1976.
Against Perspective, Fiddlehead, 1977.
The Long Apprenticeship: The Collected Poems of Fred Cogswell, Fiddlehead, 1980.
Pearls, Ragweed, 1983.
(Editor and translator) *The Complete Poems of Emile Nelligan,* Harvest, 1983.
Charles G. D. Roberts and His Works, ECW Press, 1983.
Fred Cogswell: Selected Poems, edited by Antonio D'Alfonso, Guernica, 1983.
(Editor) *The Atlantic Anthology,* Ragweed, Volume 1 (prose), 1983, Volume 2 (poetry), 1985.
(Author of introduction) Graham Adams, editor, *The Collected Poems of Sir Charles G. D. Roberts,* Wombat Press, 1985.
Meditations: Fifty Sestinas, Ragweed, 1986.

An Edge to Life, Purple Wednesday Society, 1987.
Charles Mair, ECW Press, 1988.
The Best Notes Merge, Borealis, 1988.
Black and White Tapestry, Borealis, 1989.
(Editor with JoAnne Elder) *Revos inacheves: poesie contemporaine,* Presses de'Acadie, 1990.
(Editor with Elder) *Unfinished Dreams: Contemporary Poetry of Acadie,* Grosseland, 1990.
Watching an Eagle, Borealis, 1991.
When the Right Light Shines, Borealis, 1992.
In Praise of Old Music, Borealis, 1992.

Work represented in numerous anthologies, including *A Century of Canadian Literature,* edited by Henry Green and Guy Sylvestre, Ryerson, 1967; *Made in Canada: New Poems of the Seventies,* edited by Douglas Lochhead and Raymond Souster, Oberon, 1970; *The Oxford Anthology of Canadian Literature,* Oxford University Press, 1973; and *Introduction to Literature: British, American, Canadian,* edited by G. Thomas, R. Perkyns, K. MacKinnon, and W. Katz, Holt, 1981. Contributor of poems to over one hundred periodicals, as well as articles to *Dalhouse Review, Trace, Queen's, Canadian Forum,* and other periodicals. Editor, *Humanities Association Bulletin,* 1967-72.

SIDELIGHTS: Fred Cogswell is considered by many reviewers as one of Canada's notable literary figures. Gwendolyn Davies stated in *Dictionary of Literary Biography:* "Since World War II a major force in contributing to the vitality of Canadian literature has been the poet, publisher, translator, and critic Fred Cogswell. As the guiding power behind Fiddlehead Press, he was responsible for the publication of more than three hundred titles and gave unstinting support to promising young writers." Davies added that Cogswell "has written extensively on Canadian literature . . . and he has been effective in developing an overview of Atlantic Canada's literary-cultural life in the nineteenth century. . . . His own work as a poet has earned him a place in contemporary poetry circles, while his translations of French-Canadian verse have helped to bridge the gap between the two main language groups in the country."

Cogswell once told *CA:* "I have lived, counting my wartime experience, upwards of eight years in Europe (principally Scotland). I have a fluent reading knowledge of French. I am interested quite literally in everything in the universe and I am a monist. As a poet, anthologist, critic, editor, and biographer, I have been most concerned with sincerity, accuracy, imagination, and empathy. I also prefer the plain to the ornate and feel art ought to simplify—it is a training in grasping, expressing, and communicating essentials."

BIOGRAPHICAL/CRITICAL SOURCES:

BOOKS

Directory of Literary Biography, Volume 60: *Canadian Writers since 1960, Second Series,* Gale, 1987, pp. 33-41.

PERIODICALS

Quill and Quire, July, 1980.

*   *   *

COHEN, Leonard (Norman)   1934-

PERSONAL: Born September 21, 1934, in Montreal, Quebec, Canada; son of Nathan B. (a clothing business owner) and Marsha (a nurse; maiden name, Klinitsky) Cohen; companion of Rebecca De Mornay (an actress); children: Adam, Lorca. *Education:* McGill University, B.A., 1955; Columbia University, graduate study. *Religion:* Jewish.

ADDRESSES: Home—Montreal, Quebec, Canada; and Greece.

CAREER: Poet, novelist, singer, songwriter/composer, and recording artist. Formerly associated with Stranger Music, Inc., New York City. Gives concerts in the United States, Canada, and Europe; has also appeared on television in the documentary film *The Song of Leonard Cohen,* 1980, on the series *Miami Vice,* National Broadcasting Co., Inc. (NBC), and in music videos.

AWARDS, HONOURS: McGill University, Literary Award, 1956, honorary Doctor of Letters, 1992; Canada Council grant, 1960-61; Quebec Literary Award, 1964; LL.D., Dalhousie University, 1971; Literary Award for Poetry, Canadian Authors Association, 1985, for *Book of Mercy;* Crystal Globe Award, Columbia Records, for sales of five million albums; Officer of the Order of Canada; inductee into Juno Hall of Fame, Vancouver, 1991.

WRITINGS:

The Favorite Game (novel), Viking, 1963.
Beautiful Losers (novel), Viking, 1966.
Songs of Leonard Cohen, Macmillan, 1969.
The New Step (play), produced in London, 1972.
Sisters of Mercy: A Journey into the Words and Music of Leonard Cohen (play), produced at Niagara-on-the-Lake, Ontario, and in New York, 1973.

POETRY

Let Us Compare Mythologies, Contact Press, 1956.
The Spice Box of Earth, McClelland & Stewart (Toronto), 1961, Viking, 1965.
Flowers for Hitler, McClelland & Stewart, 1966.
Parasites of Heaven, McClelland & Stewart, 1966.

Selected Poems, 1956-1968, Viking, 1968.

The Energy of Slaves, McClelland & Stewart, 1972, Viking, 1973.

(With Jurgen Jaensch) *Credo,* Garuda Verlag, 1977.

Death of a Ladies' Man (includes journal entries), McClelland & Stewart, 1978, Viking, 1979.

Book of Mercy, Random House, 1984.

Stranger Music: Selected Poems and Songs, Pantheon, 1993.

Dance Me to the End of Love, Welcome Enterprises, 1995.

RECORDINGS

Songs of Leonard Cohen, Columbia, 1968.

Songs from a Room, Columbia, 1969.

Songs of Love and Hate, Columbia, 1971.

Live Songs, Columbia, 1972.

Leonard Cohen: Live Songs, Columbia, 1973.

New Skin for the Old Ceremony, Columbia, 1974.

The Best of Leonard Cohen, Columbia, 1975.

(With Phil Spector) *Death of a Ladies' Man,* Warner Brothers, 1977.

Recent Songs, Columbia, 1979.

Various Positions, Columbia, 1984.

I'm Your Man, Columbia, 1988.

The Future, Columbia, 1992.

OTHER

Also author of *Two Views* (poetry), 1980; also author of video production *I Am a Hotel.*

Contributor of poetry to anthologies, including *The Penguin Book of Canadian Verse,* edited by Ralph Gastafson, Penguin, 1967; *Five Canadian Poets,* edited by Eli Mandel, Holt-Rinehart (Toronto), 1970; and *The Norton Anthology of Poetry.*

Some of Cohen's work has been translated into Hebrew, Spanish, and French.

ADAPTATIONS: I'm Your Fan, a sound recording of some of Cohen's songs recorded by other artists, including REM, as a tribute to Cohen was released by Atlantic, 1991.

SIDELIGHTS: "It's hard to reconcile the different parts of Leonard Cohen: the lonely heart and the ladies' man, the ascetic and the tequila drinker, the depressed writer and the funny and warm person," comments Ian Pearson in *Saturday Night.* Pearson further states, "Leonard Cohen—the once gloomy poet, famous drinker, and legendary ladies' man—has transformed himself into a pop icon for the nineties, and also one of the best songwriters around." Cohen initially gained popularity as a coffeehouse singer with his songs of love and protest in the 1960s and 1970s. "His image is a touchstone . . . for an entire student generation. As poet, novelist and, above all, as a

composer/lyricist/singer, . . . he embodies the dreams of many young people," wrote a *Times Literary Supplement* reviewer in 1970. His work has continued to appeal to students, and today, state Pamela Andriotakis and Richard Bulahan in *People,* his followers "often are teenagers, the children of his early admirers."

Cohen began his career as a poet. His first collection, *Let Us Compare Mythologies,* won the 1956 McGill Literary Award. The prize was a plane ticket to the city of Cohen's choice. He elected to travel to Jerusalem but stopped in London, where friends encouraged him to discipline his writing. With their support, he remained in England and completed the first draft of a novel, *The Favorite Game,* in eight months. In 1960 Cohen moved to the Greek island of Hydra, which was his home for the next six years. During that time he published three books of poetry and two novels. He also wrote songs but made no attempt to sell them. Critics received his first books favorably. Samuel I. Bellman writes of *The Favorite Game* in *Congress Biweekly:* "[F. Scott] Fitzgerald is most strongly evoked here. . . . With the compassion of Philip Roth in *Letting Go* (1962), an intricate study of parent-child relationships, Cohen has given his itinerant, fatuous and self-alienated young poet a moment of greatness." Calvin Bedient in the *New York Times Book Review* credits Cohen's early poems as showing "a splashy imaginative energy that, combined with a hard attitude and frequent candor, [makes] them challenging." And a *Times Literary Supplement* reviewer writes of Cohen's second novel, *Beautiful Losers,* "like the early work of another all-embracing non-stylist, Thomas Wolfe, it has the fascination of its untamed energy." The books received critical acclaim, but, their author told Tom Chaffin in *Canadian Forum,* "I really couldn't meet any of my own bills." That situation was unexpectedly remedied in 1966 when, while visiting New York, Cohen was introduced to singer Judy Collins. She asked to hear his songs and was so impressed by them that she introduced several of them on her next album. They were hits, and soon other singers were eager to record Cohen's works. "Suzanne," "Sisters of Mercy," "The Story of Abraham and Isaac," and "Stories of the Street" were all successes for various recording artists. In 1968, Cohen decided to cut his own album, although he tells Chaffin: "Sometimes I think my voice is very bad. I can almost make myself cry with it very early in the morning." Chaffin writes, "While Cohen's fluid, opulently lyric guitar work is of studio musician calibre, his voice is deep, untrained, often off-pitch, sometimes unmercifully rasping—and somehow the perfect foil for his soft Debussy-like melodies." The public liked his first album, *Songs of Leonard Cohen,* and subsequent records also sold well. Concert tours were faithfully attended, and the Canadian poet had taken a major step toward becoming what Andriotakis and Bulahan call an "undisputed cult figure."

Cohen's fame caused some literary critics to examine his later poetry in relation to his popular songs. David Lehman in *Poetry,* for example, writes: "The real tension in Cohen's work is due . . . to a clash between poetry and the elements of songwriting which Cohen superimposes on it." "His poems have a randomness which betrays the lack of any sustained vision," writes a *Times Literary Supplement* reviewer. "They are, in short, the poems of a songwriter who is able to convince a semi-literate public that his talent goes deeper simply because his lyrics possess an apparent concern with deeper issues and avoid the more honest banalities of 'moon/June.'" James Healy's *Prairie Schooner* review also suggests that Cohen's real talent lies in songwriting, not poetry: "*The Energy of Slaves* (Viking Press) is a painful disappointment. . . . Cohen's music *is* his best weapon and maybe he will come to realize this." Leslie Fielder, however, states in *Running Man* that this sharp division between pop artist and literary artist is unrealistic and unnecessary. Today's poet works in "the new post-Modernist world in which the old distinctions between low and high art, mass culture and *belles-lettres* have lapsed completely." Reviewing *Death of a Lady's Man* in *Saturday Night,* Eli Mandel suggests that Cohen's work defies categorization and calls the book "wildly energetic, threatening to fly apart in any one of the thousand directions to which it is attracted, a witty, moving, despairing book, lyrical, dramatic, musical, endlessly entertaining, often boring, even terribly self-centered—further revelations of a mind and personality that will continue to baffle our best critics and to entrance and offend an audience he cultivates and seduces."

Cohen himself "reacts caustically to critics who have suggested that his recent celebrity has blunted his powers on the printed page," writes Chaffin. "He also rejects the notion of any tension between his roles as a solitary poet and public performer." Of his simple style, Cohen told Chaffin, "I like austerity. . . . I like it as a style." In Mandel's opinion, Cohen's work has a "magical luminosity" that accounts for his great success and popularity. "Cohen's method is without doubt surrealistic, what Robert Bly recently called 'leaping poetry,' the sudden alteration that occurs when something more than mere association develops in the poetic connection. It's enough to take you by the heart and shake you as if you were in a great windstorm or encountering for the first time one of those huge ships of imagination that Fellini or Rilke saw. Or, to use Bly's example, it's as if the poet suddenly leapt from one brain to another . . . Cohen is capable of those great leaps of imagination; that is why he remains one of [Canada's] best, most loved poets."

About his musical achievements, over a period of twenty-five years, Cohen has produced only nine studio albums; he explained the difficulty of his muse to Pearson in *Saturday Night:* "Composing hardly begins to describe what the process is. . . . It's something like scavenging, something like farming in sand, something like scraping the bottom of the barrel. The process doesn't have any dignity. It is work of extreme poverty." As he similarly mentions to DeCurtis in *Rolling Stone:* "'It's a serious enterprise. Some people write great songs in taxicabs, and some people write great songs in offices in the Brill Building. I wish I could work that way. For me, I've got to surrender to it, struggle with it and get creamed by it in the process.'" Yet, despite Cohen's early musical success, however difficult the composition process, his popularity gradually waned. Pearson comments, "After his astonishing transformation from a popular poet and novelist into a singer-songwriter in the sixties and seventies, his career had stalled by the early eighties." Remarks Nicholas Jennings in *Maclean's,* "Leonard Cohen, hailed twenty years ago as Canada's answer to Bob Dylan, had slipped into obscurity."

However, in 1986, Cohen's friend, singer Jennifer Warnes, recorded an album comprised mainly of his songs, and *Famous Blue Raincoat* launched a renaissance of interest in Cohen and his songs. Jennings declares that the songwriter's longevity in the music business has "helped to earn Leonard Cohen his role as rock's poet laureate," while Anthony DeCurtis remarks in *Rolling Stone* that "Cohen's willingness to go to the edge—and even, on occasion, to tumble headlong over it—is part of what has made him one of the rare Sixties icons whose appeal extends well into the twentysomething crowd." Known for, as *Saturday Night*'s Pearson describes, "the dessicated sack of gravel in his throat," Cohen received instant critical and popular success throughout Europe, Canada, and the United States with his 1988 album, *I'm Your Man.* The popularity of the album created recording opportunities with other musical artists, from rhythm and blues groups to funk rock bands. In 1991, eighteen popular young bands and performers contributed their own versions of some of Cohen's hits to an album in his honor, *I'm Your Fan.*

About *I'm Your Man,* Jennings observes in *Maclean's* that it "reaffirms Cohen's stature as one of pop's most literate voices." David Browne commends Cohen's efforts in *Rolling Stone,* observing, "What seemingly appeals to such a wide variety of musicians is Cohen's eye for poetic detail, his cutting barbs and his finely crafted melodies, . . . traits all in evidence on *I'm Your Man*" Pearson claims in *Saturday Night* that upon the publication of *I'm Your Man,* "He had become a rare phenomenon in a popular culture that worships youth: an artist who gets hipper as he gets older."

Cohen's next album, 1992's *The Future*—dedicated to actress Rebecca De Mornay, his companion, who helped him finalize two of his songs—extended his reign as "one of contemporary songwriting's most vital resources at the top of his high-altitude form," according to Jay Cocks in *Time*. Cocks further remarks that the album is "a typically eccentric mixture of Cohen tunes and moods—sensual, alarming, cautionary, caustic, devastating—that gives the music the eerie persistence of a half-heard spell." Brian D. Johnson writes in *Maclean's* that Cohen "is still the sardonic voluptuary, celebrating sex and freedom in the precious hours before an apocalyptic dawn." Comparing *The Future* to *I'm Your Man*, Johnson asserts, "The basic sound remains the same, with female choirs soaring over a cigarette-scarred voice that seems deeper and darker than ever. But the music is less regimented." About *The Future*, DeCurtis asserts in *Rolling Stone*: "He has a poet's instinctive sense of cadence. . . . His relationship with spoken language is at least as sensuous as it is intellectual—listening to his deep, grainy voice, you remember that speech is a physical act. The effect is hip and hypnotic."

Returning to the literary arena, Cohen's *Stranger Music: Selected Poems and Songs* provides Cohen aficionados with selections from his numerous varied output through the years. Douglas Fetherling notes in *Quill and Quire* that the book "celebrates his almost four decades of achievement in poetry and songwriting." While he labels the book's organization "confusing," Fetherling nevertheless describes Cohen as "like someone with the gifts of Cole Porter or a Noel Coward but who takes life (and politics) more seriously than they ever did," adding that "no one will miss its [the book's] message of change and growth." In *Library Journal*, Rochelle Ratner appreciates Cohen's accomplishments, "making over four hundred pages seem remarkably flimsy." While reading the "generous selection," a *Publishers Weekly* reviewer suggests that "one often hears the ghost of musical accompaniment, and sometimes its actual presence is missed."

BIOGRAPHICAL/CRITICAL SOURCES:

BOOKS

Contemporary Literary Criticism, Volume 3, Gale, 1975.
Gnarowski, Michael, *Leonard Cohen: The Artist and His Critics*, McGraw, 1976.
Nagel, Ira B., *Leonard Cohen: A Life in Art*, ECW, 1994.
Ondaatje, Michael, *Leonard Cohen*, McClelland & Stewart, 1970.
Sylvestre, Guy, and others, editors, *Canadian Writers*, revised edition, Ryerson, 1966.

PERIODICALS

Beloit Poetry Journal, winter, 1968-69.
Canadian Forum, July, 1967; September, 1970; August-September, 1983.
Canadian Literature, winter, 1965.
Congress Bi-Weekly, December 20, 1963.

Globe & Mail (Toronto), April 21, 1984.
Jewish Quarterly, autumn, 1972.
Library Journal, November 1, 1993, p. 97.
Life, June 28, 1968.
Maclean's, May 9, 1988, p. 69; December 7, 1992, pp.63-64, 66.
McCall's, January, 1969.
National Observer, September 9, 1968.
New Leader, May 23, 1966.
New York Review of Books, April 28, 1966.
New York Times, April 4, 1966.
New York Times Book Review, May 8, 1966; February 18, 1973.
People, January 14, 1980.
Poetry, December, 1973.
Prairie Schooner, summer, 1973.
Publishers Weekly, November 8, 1993, p. 61.
Quill and Quire, November, 1993, pp. 1, 31.
Rolling Stone, June 16, 1988, pp. 121-22; January 21, 1993, pp. 44-46, 56.
Running Man, July-August, 1969.
Saturday Night, February, 1968; November, 1978; March, 1993, pp. 44-49, 76-80.
Time, September 13, 1968; January 11, 1993, p. 51.
Times Literary Supplement, April 23, 1970; September 18, 1970; January 5, 1973.*

—*Sketch by Michaela Swart Wilson*

*   *   *

COHEN, Matt(hew) 1942-

PERSONAL: Born December 30, 1942, in Kingston, Ontario, Canada; son of Morris (a chemist) and Beatrice (Sohn) Cohen. *Education:* University of Toronto, B.A., 1964, M.A., 1965.

ADDRESSES: Home—P.O. Box 401, Verona, Ontario K0H 2W0, Canada.*Office*—Writers' Union of Canada, 24 Ryerson Ave., Toronto, Ontario M5T 2P3, Canada

CAREER: Writer, 1968—. McMaster University, Hamilton, Ontario, Canada, lecturer in religion, 1967-68; University of Alberta, Edmonton, Canada, writer-in-residence, 1975-76; University of Western Ontario, London, writer-in-residence, 1980-81. Visiting assistant professor of creative writing, University of Victoria, 1979; visiting professor, University of Bologna, 1984.

MEMBER: Writers Union of Canada (chair, 1985-86).

AWARDS, HONOURS: Senior Canadian Council Arts Award, 1977, 1984, and 1991; Canadian Fiction Award for best short story, 1982; Annual Contributor's Prize, *Canadian Fiction*, 1983, for "The Sins of Tomas Benares"; John Glasso Translation Prize, 1991.

WRITINGS:

ADULT FICTION

Korsoniloff (novella), House of Anansi, 1969.

Johnny Crackle Sings (novella), McClelland & Stewart, 1971.

Too Bad Galahad (short stories), illustrated by Margaret Hathaway, Coach House, 1972.

Columbus and the Fat Lady and Other Stories, House of Anansi, 1972.

The Disinherited (novel), McClelland & Stewart, 1974.

Wooden Hunters (novel), McClelland & Stewart, 1975.

The Colours of War (novel), McClelland & Stewart, 1977, Methuen, 1978.

Night Flights: Stories New and Selected, Doubleday, 1978.

The Sweet Second Summer of Kitty Malone (novel), McClelland & Stewart, 1979.

Flowers of Darkness (novel), McClelland & Stewart, 1981.

The Expatriate: Collected Short Stories, General Publishing, 1982, Beaufort Books, 1983.

Cafe Le Dog (short stories), McClelland & Stewart, 1983, published as *Life on This Planet and Other Stories,* Beaufort Books, 1985.

The Spanish Doctor (novel), McClelland & Stewart, 1984, Beaufort Books, 1985.

Nadine (novel), Viking, 1986, Crown, 1987.

Living on Water (short stories), Viking, 1988.

Emotional Arithmetic (novel), Lester & Orpen Dennys, 1990.

Freud: The Paris Notebooks (stories), Quarry Press, 1991.

OTHER

(Editor) *The Story So Far/2,* Coach House, 1973.

Peach Melba (poetry), Coach House, 1974.

The Leaves of Louise (children's book), illustrated by Rikki, McClelland & Stewart, 1978.

(Editor) *The Dream Class Anthology: Writings from Toronto High Schools,* Coach House, 1983.

(Editor with Wayne Grady) *Intimate Strangers: New Stories from Quebec* (translated from the French), Penguin, 1986.

In Search of Leonardo (poetry), illustrated by Tony Urquhart, Coach House, 1986.

Contributor of criticism and short stories to periodicals, including *Canadian Literature* and *Canadian Fiction.* Author's work has been translated into many languages, including Croatian, French, German, Italian, Portuguese, Russian, Dutch, Hungarian, and Spanish.

WORK IN PROGRESS: A novel.

SIDELIGHTS: Author Matt Cohen has gained a reputation as a prolific writer of experimental prose. Concerning himself with man's continuing quest for understanding and purpose in life, Cohen uses a variety of literary forms—short story, poetry, song, novella, and full-length novel—to illustrate his underlying theme: that summoning the energy needed to gain possession of oneself, to truly "get to be alive," creates the seeds of one's own destruction. "All values are violently subverted by the energy with which they are pursued," Jon Kertzer explains in *Essays on Canadian Writers.* "This central paradox explains the ferocity that prevails in Cohen's writing. The intense energy of life, which is the motive of passion, ambition, love, and conflict, is so powerful that it becomes destructive: life burns itself up."

Comprising what critics have hailed as some of his best work, Cohen's short story collections—including *Columbus and the Fat Lady, Too Bad Galahad, Night Flights, Cafe Le Dog,* and *Life on this Planet*—contain vignettes encapsulating his thematic search for self knowledge. *Night Flights,* published in 1978, received critical praise both for its perceptive insights into character and for the dreamlike quality of its prose. However, Cohen's initial story collections did not achieve a consensus of opinion among reviewers. Describing the array of protagonists in Cohen's early short works as "flat characters inhabiting vague landscapes and often involved in superficial relationships," J. M. Zezulka expresses criticism of Cohen's approach in *Dictionary of Literary Biography,* commenting that it is "as if the whole notion of personality stripped of accidentals were under scrutiny." By contrast, Zezulka notes, such later works as 1983's *Cafe Le Dog* manifest a shift by the author towards a more "joyful" style. And, commending Cohen for his ability to "catch the small moments, to notice the phrase or gesture or incident that lights up a major shift in the emotional alignment of the world," reviewer Douglas Hill goes on to praise Cohen for the understated humor and vivid narrative voice he employs throughout *Cafe Le Dog.* The shift away from the experimentation of Cohen's early writing towards a more traditional style is exemplified not only in his short stories but also in the author's longer fictional works.

In 1974 Cohen published the first of what would be a series of four novels taking as their setting the mythical Canadian town of Salem, Ontario. *The Disinherited,* a saga of the Thompsons, a farming family whose members have been wedded to the ancestral land for many years, is described by critic Eric Thompson as "an ambitious attempt to trace the disintegration of Ontario's myth of idyllic rural life over a span of four generations" in *Canadian Forum.* The three books that followed—*The Colours of War, The Sweet Summer of Kitty Malone,* and *Flowers of Darkness*—focus upon specific characters and situations in an examination of people's inner conflicts and outward responsibilities. Praising *Flowers of Darkness,* the last of Cohen's "Salem" novels, for its well-drawn characters and vivid portrayal of small-town life, Paul Stuewe comments in *Quill & Quire:* "There's a fine line between [telling] us more than we want to know and insufficient realism, which makes it difficult for us to feel a part of fictional creation, and I think that here Cohen has hit it just about right." The reviewer adds that Cohen "leaves no doubt . . . about the reality of Salem and its citizens, but we're also encouraged to use our imaginations in filling in some of the ambiguities which the author wisely refuses to resolve."

Distinguished from his later works by its relatively disjointed prose style, Cohen's early writing is full of "a lively sense of confusion and perversity . . . [shifting] deviously in time, tone, and point of view," according to Kertzer. The author's ability to shift from surrealism to realism within a single work has been compared by other critics to magic realist painting. In some instances, however, such shifts of time have generated confusion: "Lucid and descriptive moments are diluted by confusing transitions from . . . present to [past]," notes a reviewer in *West Coast Review of Books.* "Cohen's prose is crisp; his images, vivid; his characters believable; but his outlook is always guarded," adds Alan Cooper in *Library Journal.* And Linda Leith comments in *Essays on Canadian Writers* that Cohen's prose moves too deeply into the realm of experimentation. "He can write well when he relaxes and just writes," Leith states. "When he eschews the precious concern with technique and irritating cleverness that mar too many of his stories he achieves the very success that so eludes him when he strives for it."

Cohen's protagonists reflect his preoccupation with experimentation—his characters are typically social misfits: dropouts, nihilists, people discontented with their lives and with society. Many of the people that inhabit his fiction are burdened by life inside a physical shell that has been abused by alcohol or drugs, are infirm, or are in the process of physiological ageing. Others are engaged in a ceaseless internal dialogue with their pasts in an effort to distill a purpose through which to create a meaningful future. Still others border on the perverse: "Cohen leans toward a sort of Ontario Gothic—in which the physical deformities and impoverished lives of the inhabitants almost become too grotesque to be real," writes Michael Smith in *Books in Canada.* In his first novel, *Korsoniloff,* Cohen writes of the title character that he "cannot survive the consequences of his own existence." A schizophrenic assistant professor of philosophy, Andre Korsoniloff is engaged in a battle between, as Zezulka notes, "the roles he is expected to play, which will ensure some measure of acceptance, and his private urges, which alone can provide him with the sense of integrity and freedom he seeks." In the 1971 novella *Johnny Crackle Sings* the protagonist is a victim, not only of the drug-induced state into which he retreats, but also of the passage of time which results in

a future that is "a sideways mirror to the unforgotten past." Theodore Beam, a displaced and hesitant young man, is pulled in two directions on the time continuum when he embarks on a transcontinental train journey home to confront his alcoholic father in *The Colours of War;* in facing his father Beam himself is faced by both his past and his mortality. At the same juncture, Beam is drawn into another possible future when he becomes superficially involved with political insurrectionist activities aboard the train. Zezulka notes that though Cohen portrays his flawed characters in a sympathetic manner, hidden beneath this are "betrayals, raw sexuality, violence, and intrigue; against these forces his characters struggle to affirm whatever measure of human dignity they can manage."

Beyond Cohen's central theme of self-actualization, there are other elements unifying Cohen's prolific career as a writer. Throughout his works he juxtaposes the elements of Time and the concept of Family—the passing of one generation into the next in a continuum. Kertzer discusses the relationship integrating time and the family: "Cohen's characters find their struggle to unite the fragments of their lives both sustained and subverted by their families: sustained because the family confers identity, subverted because it obscures the individual within his lineage. On one hand, the family provides a continuity of kinship that triumphs over the dislocations of time. On the other, the family denies importance or uniqueness to the individual by subsuming his brief span of years within a larger process of regeneration and degeneration." Cohen's four "Salem" novels illustrate these themes through their concentration upon such subjects as inheritance, the diaries of ancestors that are read by an individual a map for his own future, the power that the "family land" has to dominate the individual. As Kertzer writes in a review for *Canadian Forum:* "[*Kitty Malone*] is suffused with time and morality. Image after image—clocks, lengthening shadows, family photos, heirlooms, layers of paint—signals the passing of time, reminding characters how they have forfeited their youth before they savoured it; how they are turning into copies of their parents; and worst of all, how they are losing hold of their very selves."

Cohen weaves a fiction that defines his native country as a Canada where, as Peter Gunn notes in the *Times Literary Supplement,* "vastness . . . is an illusion of the map." Cohen's protagonists age as he himself ages. 1969's *Korsoniloff* depicted a young man searching for meaning in his past in an effort to gain control over a future that stretched before him; twenty years later, in *Living on Water,* Gunn sees in Cohen's work a prescription for the predicament of the middle-aged: "a series of maintenance instructions for living in a place of confinement." Cohen's fictional characters view the rugged natural landscape of Canada from a distance, they are no longer participants in the struggle for autonomy, in the struggle to "get to be alive." "What is left, muffled by money and the urban clemencies for which Canadian cities are so justly renown, is the daily round," Gunn writes. Within his prolific outpouring of novels and short stories Cohen has outlined for his reader what he sees as life's central paradox: the struggle for self-possession without self-annihilation. As Nancy Wigston writes in the *Globe & Mail,* "he can balance the pathos and dark comedy of his reluctant hero's story, and let it speak for all the incongruities in our lives, the mysteries that make us what we are."

BIOGRAPHICAL/CRITICAL SOURCES:

BOOKS

Cohen, Matt, *Korsoniloff,* Anansi Press, 1969.
Cohen, Matt, *Johnny Crackle Sings,* McClelland & Stewart, 1971.
Contemporary Literary Criticism, Volume 19, Gale, 1981, pp. 111-16.
Gibson, Graeme, *Eleven Canadian Novelists,* Anansi Press, 1972, pp. 55-85.
Moss, John, *Sex and Violence in the Canadian Novel: The Ancestral Past,* McClelland & Stewart, 1977.
Twigg, Alan, *For Openers: Conversations with Twenty-Four Canadian Writers,* Harbour, 1981, pp. 175-84.
Woodcock, George, *The World of Canadian Writing: Critiques and Recollections,* University of Washington Press, 1980.
Zezulka, J. M., "Matt Cohen," *Dictionary of Literary Biography,* Volume 53: *Canadian Writers Since 1960,* Gale, 1986, pp. 135-41.

PERIODICALS

Books in Canada, April, 1979, p. 5; summer, 1993, p. 54; December, 1993, p. 49.
Canadian Children's Literature, Volume 21, 1987, pp. 80-82.
Canadian Forum, March, 1975, p. 39; December, 1977, p. 41; May, 1979.
Canadian Literature, autumn, 1980, pp. 122-23.
Essays on Canadian Writers, fall, 1978, pp. 56-59; spring, 1980, pp. 93-101; fall, 1992, p. 65; winter, 1992, p. 97.
Globe & Mail (Toronto), April 15, 1984; March 30, 1985; September 27, 1986; October 8, 1988; October 27, 1990.
Library Journal, April 15, 1978, p. 896.
Los Angeles Times Book Review, April 28, 1985, p. 4.
Maclean's, March 12, 1979, pp. 54, 175-184; May 21, 1991, p. 50.
New York Times Book Review, September 12, 1985, p. 18; February 16, 1986, p. 10; August 9, 1987, p. 20; May 1, 1988, p. 22.

Publishers Weekly, February 6, 1978, p. 90; February 13, 1978, p. 123.
Queen's Quarterly, autumn, 1989, pp. 717-19.
Quill & Quire, February, 1981, p. 45; August, 1990, p. 19; May 25, 1991, p. 25.
Saturday Night, November, 1969, pp. 61-63; September, 1977, pp. 73-75; March, 1981, pp. 50-51.
Times Literary Supplement, December 1, 1989, p. 1338.
Washington Post, April 21, 1987.
West Coast Review of Books, September, 1977, p. 34.

*   *   *

COLOMBO, John Robert   1936-

PERSONAL: Born March 24, 1936, in Kitchener, Ontario, Canada; son of John Anthony and Irene (Nicholson) Colombo; married Ruth Florence Brown (a professor), May 11, 1959; children: Jonathan, Catherine, Theodore. *Education:* Attended Waterloo College, Waterloo, Ontario, 1956-57; University of Toronto, B.A. (with honors), 1959, graduate study, 1959-60. *Avocational interests:* Reading.

ADDRESSES: Home—42 Dell Park Ave., Toronto, Ontario, Canada M6B 2T6.

CAREER: University of Toronto Press, Toronto, Ontario, editorial assistant, 1957-59; Ryerson Press, Toronto, assistant editor, 1960-63; York University, Toronto, occasional instructor, 1963-66; McClelland & Stewart, Toronto, advisory editor and editor-at-large, 1964-70; Mohawk College, Hamilton, Ontario, writer in residence, 1978; host, *Colombo's Quotes* (weekly television series), Canadian Broadcasting Corp. (CBC), 1978. Has given poetry readings throughout Canada and in New York and London. Representative for Canadian poetry, Commonwealth Arts Festival, Cardiff and London, 1965; advisor, Ontario Arts Council, 1965-69; member of advisory arts panel, Canada Council, 1968-70; honorary patron, North York Arts Council. Guest of the Writers' Unions of Russia, Romania, and Bulgaria.

MEMBER: PEN (Canada), Association of Canadian Television and Radio Artists (ACTRA).

AWARDS, HONOURS: Centennial Medal, 1967; Philips Information Systems Literary Prize, 1985; certificate of merit, Ontario Library Association; cited for best paperback of the year, Periodical Distributors of Canada; named Esteemed Knight of Mark Twain; recipient of Order of Cyril and Methodius (first class); Laureate, Order of Cyril and Methodius.

WRITINGS:

POEMS

Fragments, privately printed, 1957.

Variations, Hawkshead Press (Kitchener, Ontario), 1958.

This Citadel in Time, Hawkshead Press, 1958.

This Studied Self, Hawkshead Press, 1958.

In the Streets, Hawkshead Press, 1959.

Poem and Other Poems, Hawkshead Press, 1959.

Two Poems, Hawkshead Press, 1959.

This Is the Work Entitled Canada, Purple Partridge Press (Toronto), 1959.

Fire Escape, Fire Esc, Fire, Hawkshead Press, 1959.

The Impression of Beauty, Hawkshead Press, 1959.

Poems to Be Sold for Bread, Hawkshead Press, 1959.

Lines for the Last Day, Hawkshead Press, 1960.

The Mackenzie Poems, Swan Publishing (Toronto), 1965.

Miraculous Montages, Heinrich Heine Press (Don Mills, Ontario), 1966.

The Great Wall of China, Delta (Montreal), 1966.

Abracadabra, McClelland & Stewart (Toronto), 1967.

William Lyon Mackenzie Rides Again!, Guild of Hand Printers (Toronto), 1967.

John Toronto: New Poems by Dr. Strachan, Found by John Robert Colombo, Oberon Press (Ottawa), 1969.

Neo Poems, Sono Nis Press (Victoria, British Columbia), 1970.

The Great San Francisco Earthquake and Fire, Fiddlehead (Fredericton, New Brunswick), 1971.

Leonardo's Lists, Weed/Flower Press (Toronto), 1972.

Praise Poems, Weed/Flower Press, 1972.

The Great Collage, Oasis Books (Toronto), 1974.

Translations from the English: Found Poems, Peter Martin Associates (Toronto), 1974.

The Sad Truths, Peter Martin Associates, 1974.

Proverbial Play, Missing Link Press (Toronto), 1975.

Mostly Monsters, Hounslow (Toronto), 1977.

Variable Cloudiness, Hounslow, 1977.

Private Parts, Hounslow, 1978.

The Great Cities of Antiquity, Hounslow, 1979.

Recent Poems, League of Canadian Poets (Toronto), 1980.

Selected Poems, Black Moss Press (Windsor, Ontario), 1982.

Selected Translations, Black Moss Press, 1982.

Off Earth, Hounslow, 1987.

Luna Park: One Thousand Poems, Hounslow, 1994.

EDITOR

Rubato: New Poems by Young Canadian Poets, Purple Partridge Press, 1958.

The Varsity Chapbook, Ryerson, 1959.

(With Jacques Godbout) *Poesis 64/Poetry 64,* Ryerson and Editions du Jour, 1963.

(With Raymond Souster) *Shapes and Sounds: Poems of W. W. E. Ross,* Longman, Green (Canada), 1968.

How Do I Love Thee: Sixty Poets of Canada (and Quebec) Select and Discuss Their Favorite Poems from Their Own Work, Hurtig Publishers (Edmonton), 1970.

(With Roy Bentley) *Rhymes and Reasons: Nine Canadian Poets Discuss Their Work,* Holt, 1971.

New Direction in Canadian Poetry, Holt (Toronto), 1971.

An Alphabet of Annotations, Gheerbrant (Montreal), 1972.

Colombo's Canadian Quotations, Hurtig Publishers, 1974, published as *Concise Canadian Quotations,* 1976, published as *Colombo's New Canadian Quotations,* 1987.

Colombo's Little Book of Canadian Proverbs, Graffiti, Limericks & Other Vital Matters, Hurtig Publishers, 1975.

Colombo's Canadian References, Oxford University Press (New York), 1976.

Colombo's Book of Canada, Hurtig Publishers, 1978.

The Poets of Canada, Hurtig Publishers, 1978.

Other Canadas: An Anthology of Science Fiction and Fantasy, McGraw-Hill (Toronto), 1979.

CDN SF & F: A Bibliography of Canadian Science Fiction and Fantasy, Hounslow, 1979.

Colombo's Names and Nicknames, NC Press (Toronto), 1979.

Colombo's Book of Marvels, NC Press, 1979.

Waclaw Iwaniuk, *Dark Times: Selected Poems of Waclaw Iwaniuk,* Hounslow, 1979.

Colombo's Hollywood, Collins (Toronto), 1979, published as *Popcorn in Paradise,* Holt, 1980, published as *Wit and Wisdom of the Moviemakers,* Hamlyn, 1980.

The Canada Colouring Book, with drawings by Emma Hesse, Hounslow, 1980.

222 Canadian Jokes, with drawings by Peter Whalley, Highway Book Shop, 1981.

Blackwood's Books: A Bibliography Devoted to Algernon Blackwood, Hounslow, 1981.

(With Michael Richardson) *Not to Be Taken at Night: Classic Canadian Tales of Mystery and the Supernatural,* Lester, Orphen & Dennys (Toronto), 1981.

Friendly Aliens, Hounslow, 1981.

Poems of the Inuit, Oberon, 1981.

Blackwood's Books: A Bibliography, Hounslow, 1981.

Colombo's Laws, with drawings by Whalley, Highway Book Shop, 1982.

Colombo's Last Words, with drawings by Whalley, Highway Book Shop, 1982.

Years of Light: A Celebration of Leslie A. Crouch, Hounslow, 1982.

Windigo: An Anthology of Fact and Fantastic Fiction, Western Producer Prairie Books (Saskatoon), 1982.

George Faludy, *Learn This Poem of Mine by Heart,* Hounslow, 1983.

Colombo's 101 Canadian Places, with drawings by Whalley, Hounslow, 1983.

Colombo's Canadian Quiz Book, Western Producer Prairie Books, 1983.

Rene Levesque Buys Canada Savings Bonds and Other Great Canadian Graffiti, with drawings by David Shaw, Hurtig Publishers, 1983.

Songs of the Indians (two volumes), Oberon Press (Ottawa), 1983.

Great Moments in Canadian History, with drawings by Whalley, Hounslow, 1984.

The Toronto Puzzle Book, McClelland & Stewart, 1984.

Toronto's Fantastic Street Names, Bakka Books, 1984.

Canadian Literary Landmarks, Hounslow, 1984.

(With Michael Richardson) *We Stand on Guard: Poems and Songs of Canadians in Battle,* Doubleday (Canada) 1985.

1,001 Questions about Canada, Doubleday (Garden City, NY), 1986.

Off Earth, Hounslow, 1987.

Mysterious Canada: Strange Sights, Extraordinary Events, and Peculiar Places, Doubleday, 1988.

999 Questions about Canada, Doubleday, 1989.

Extraordinary Experiences: Personal Accounts of the Paranormal in Canada, Hounslow, 1989.

Songs of the Great Land, Oberon, 1989.

Quotations from Chairman Lamport, Pulp Press, 1990.

Mysterious Encounters: Personal Accounts of the Supernatural in Canada, Hounslow, 1990.

Voices of Ram, Oberon Press, 1990.

UFOs over Canada: Personal Accounts of Sightings and Close Encounters, Hounslow, 1991.

Dark Visions: Personal Accounts of the Mysterious in Canada, Hounslow, 1991.

Mackenzie King's Ghost: And Other Personal Accounts of Canadian Hauntings, Hounslow, 1991.

The Dictionary of Canadian Quotations, Stoddart, 1991.

Worlds in Small: An Anthology of Miniature Literary Compositions, Cacanadada, 1992.

Quotations on Sex and Love in Canada, Arsenal Pulp, 1992.

The Little Blue Book of Canadian UFOs, Arsenal Pulp, 1992.

(With Cyril Greenland) *Walt Whitman's Canada,* Hounslow, 1992.

The Mystery of the Shaking Tent, Hounslow, 1993.

Colombo's All-Time Great Canadian Quotations, Stoddart, 1994.

General editor, *The Canadian Global Almanac* (annual), Macmillan, 1991—.

TRANSLATOR

Robert Zend, *From Zero to One,* Sono Nis Press, 1973.

(With Irene Currie) Paul Eluard and Benjamin Peret, *152 Proverbs Adapted to the Taste of the Day,* Oasis Press, 1975.

(With Nikola Roussanoff) *Under the Eaves of a Forgotten Village: Sixty Poems from Contemporary Bulgaria,* Hounslow, 1975.

(With Roussanoff) *The Balkan Range: A Bulgarian Reader,* Hounslow, 1976.

(With Susana Wald) Ludwig Zeller, *When the Animal Rises from the Deep the Head Explodes,* Mosaic Press/Valley Editions, (poems), 1976.

(With Roussanoff) Lyubomir Levchev, *The Left-Handed One: Poems of Lyubomir Levchev,* Hounslow, 1977.

George Faludy, *East and West,* Hounslow, 1978.

(With Roussanoff) Andrei Germanov, *Remember Me Well: Poems of Andrei Germanov,* Hounslow, 1978.

(With Roussanoff) *Depths: Poems of Dora Gabe,* Hounslow, 1978.

(With Iwaniuk) Ewa Lipska, *Such Times,* Hounslow, 1981.

(With Ron D. K. Banerjee) Pavel Javor, *Far from You,* Hounslow, 1981.

(With Robert Zend) Robert Zend, *Beyond Labels,* Hounslow, 1982.

OTHER

Also author of plays and documentaries for CBC-TV. Contributor to *Open Poetry,* edited by Ronald Grose and George Quasha, Simon & Schuster (New York), 1973. Contributor of articles, art criticism, and reviews to many periodicals. Member of editorial board, *Tamarack Review,* 1960-82. Former editor, *Montrealer* and *Exchange.*

SIDELIGHTS: John Robert Colombo is known as an anthologist and editor whose books of Canadiana have been bestsellers and as an experimental writer of international reputation. Once called a Master Gatherer by Robin Skelton, Colombo is a devoted collector of information which he uses in his reference and trivia books. Colombo, who once took a speed-reading course, is a self-described "inveterate collector and a chronic listmaker." He told M. T. Kelly of *Toronto Life* magazine, "At any one time, I have a half dozen books in progress. I find relief and refreshment in going from project to project."

Colombo's earliest published works were poetry pamphlets. During his student days at the University of Toronto, he operated the Hawkshead Press to publish his own writings and those of other young poets; one of them was one "M. E. Atwood," today better known as novelist Margaret Atwood. Colombo's first real book was an outgrowth of his other efforts as a literary entrepreneur. He organized the first regular series of readings in a Canadian coffee house, and then edited a collection of the verse read there. *The Varsity Chapbook* appeared in 1959, the same year Colombo received his degree from the University of Toronto.

After a brief stint working as an editor with various Canadian book publishers, Colombo became a freelance writer and editor. He immersed himself in the Canadian literary community through his work as an advisor to the Canada Council, the powerful government arts funding body, and as a member of the editorial board of the now-defunct *Tamarack Review,* a small but influential Canadian literary journal. When not otherwise engaged, Colombo wrote newspaper and magazine articles, and continued to write and edit poetry.

While Colombo wrote some noteworthy original verse, what attracted far more attention were his experiments in "found poetry"—lines of other writers' prose which are cobbled together to form poems; Colombo himself terms the end result "redeemed prose." While the surrealist technique originated around the time of the First World War, it was a series of found poem books Colombo published in the mid-1960s which revived the art form and brought it to the attention of Canadian readers. In a review of *Abracadabra,* the first of Colombo's books of found poetry to be printed by a major publisher, Mungo James of *Saturday Night* calls Colombo "an interesting, inventive and original poet." James was more receptive to the concept of found poetry than were most other critics. As Douglas Fetherling notes in *Saturday Night,* "Some who were not disposed toward innovations, as well as others who found nothing wrong with tricks but thought Colombo's antics a substitute for creative talent, took harshly to the book." Undeterred, Colombo continued his experiments in the genre. As he explained in a "found introduction" to *Open Poetry,* found poetry is worthwhile in that it teaches the reader "to respond aesthetically to the universe around us, not just to those separate parts of the world called works of art. It is possible to act as if the universe itself were an immense piece of art, a collage perhaps."

In 1974 Colombo published *Translations from the English: Found Poems,* a collection which moved Douglas Barbour in the *Dictionary of Literary Biography* to call Colombo "a master of witty juxtapositions." *The Great Cities of Antiquity* is an innovative collection of poems taken from the *Encyclopaedia Britannica.* Beginning with the entries on ancient cities from the encyclopedia, Colombo "takes their words and shapes them into a variety of forms," Barbour explains. "He breaks the words down, he repeats phrases, he arranges them as visual designs or 'concrete poems,' he destroys original syntax to free the language of its referential quality and lend it poetic opaqueness."

Despite his love of poetry, in the early 1970s Colombo decided to change the direction of his work. As Barbour

points out, Colombo is "a shrewd market analyst and salesman [who] has recognized from the first that his major product is not this book or that book but rather John Robert Colombo, the maker of all kinds of books." In addition to publishing poetry he began to publish non-fiction books as well. *Colombo's Canadian Quotations,* a collection of six thousand quotations from 2,500 sources, was Colombo's first commercial success. Reviewer J. M. Bliss of the *Canadian Forum* comments, "This is an invaluable reference book. . . . [It] is worth more than it costs, which is the highest praise a reviewer can give these days."

Following on the success of *Colombo's Canadian Quotations,* Colombo continued to create reference books, commonplace books, and anthologies of quotations and unusual facts. Many of these books focus on Canada, its literature, history, geography and people. Among the most popular are *Colombo's Canadian References, Colombo's Book of Canada, Colombo's Book of Marvels* and *Colombo's Laws. Other Canadas* is the country's first anthology of its fantastic literature, and *Mysterious Canada* is its first, comprehensive study of supernatural and paranormal events and experiences. These books have an audience beyond Canada, however; that was the case with *1001 Questions about Canada,* which reviewer Don James of the *Los Angeles Times* praised as "a revelation about our next-door neighbor." James predicted that "browsers, researchers, teachers or trivia buffs will recognize it as a quality reference book."

Colombo once told *CA:* "My mission (in part at least) is to make inventories and make accessible previously snubbed materials from the tributaries and mainstreams, the highways and byways of the Canadian people. Such literary material reveals the human spirit and sheds some light on life in the northern half of the North American continent."

BIOGRAPHICAL/CRITICAL SOURCES:

BOOKS

Contemporary Poets, 5th Edition, St. James Press, 1991.
Dictionary of Literary Biography, Volume 53: *Canadian Writers since 1960,* Gale, 1986.
Grose, Ronald, and George Quasha, editors, *Open Poetry,* Simon & Schuster (New York), 1973, pp. 431-523.
Kostelanetz, Richard, editor, *Dictionary of the Avant Gardes,* A Capella Books, 1993.

PERIODICALS

Canadian Forum, June, 1975, pp. 44-45.
Canadian Literature, summer, 1966.
Essays on Canadian Writing, fall, 1976.

Globe and Mail (Toronto), June 4, 1966; March 18, 1967;
    January 28, 1984; November 7, 1987; January 9,
    1988; January 14, 1989; April 28, 1990.
Intrinsic, autumn, 1978, pp. 176-188.
Los Angeles Times, September 21, 1986.
Maclean's, August 1, 1994, p. 2.
Montreal Gazette, October 22, 1966.
Saturday Night, May, 1967, p. 44; May, 1974, pp. 31-34.
Times Literary Supplement, May 13, 1983.
Toronto Life, January, 1983, pp. 42-43.
Toronto Star, May 24, 1987.
University of Toronto Review, July, 1959; July, 1967; July,
    1968.

*   *   *

CONSTANTIN, Maurice
See CONSTANTIN-WEYER, Maurice

*   *   *

CONSTANTIN-WEYER, Maurice   1881-1964
(Maurice Constantin)

PERSONAL: Original name Maurice Constantin; name
changed after his second marriage; born April 24, 1881,
in Bourbonne-les-Bains (Haute-Marne), France; immigrated to Canada in 1904, naturalized citizen, 1908; died
October 22, 1964 in Vichy, France; son of Alphonse Marie
Louis Xavier (a cavalry officer and journalist) and Marie-
Amelie (Bompardt) Constantin; married Dina Proulx in
1910 (marriage ended); married Germaine Weyer; children: (first marriage) three children, (second marriage)
Francoise Constantin-Weyer. *Education:* Studied science
at the Sorbonne, 1898-1901.

CAREER: Novelist. Trapper, cowboy, farmer, lumberjack, and journalist between 1904 and 1914 in Canada.
Paris-Centre (newspaper), Nevers, France, editor,
1923-27; *Journal de l'Ouest et du Centre* (newspaper), Poitiers, France, editor, 1927-30. *Military service:* Served two
years in French Army; war-time service during World
War I.

MEMBER: Societe de Gens de Lettres de France.

AWARDS, HONOURS: Chevalier in the Legion
d'Honneur, 1920, for service during World War I, *officier,*
1932, for literary achievements; Prix Goncourt (literary
award), 1928, for *Un Homme se penche sur son passe.*

WRITINGS:

(Under name Maurice Constantin) *Les Images,* Librairie
    Leon Vanier (Paris), 1902.

Vers l'ouest, Renaissance du Livre (Paris), 1921, published
    in English as *Towards the West,* translation by Edwin
    Granberry, Macaulay (New York), 1931.
Manitoba, Reider (Paris), 1924.
La Bourrasque, Rieder, 1925, published in English as *A
    Martyr's Folly,* Macmillan (Toronto), 1930, published
    as *The Half-Breed,* translation by Marie M. G. Jolas,
    Macaulay, 1930.
Cavelier de La Salle, Rieder, 1927, published in English
    as *The French Adventurer: The Life and Exploits of
    LaSalle,* translation by Lyle Frederickson, Macaulay,
    1931.
Cinq Eclats de silex (title means "Five Flakes of Flint"),
    Rieder, 1927.
Un Homme se penche sur son passe, Rieder, 1928, pub-
    lished in English as *A Man Scans His Past,* translation
    by Slater Brown, Macaulay, 1929.
Morvan, Rieder, 1929.
Shakespeare, Rieder, 1929.
Clairiere: Recits du Canada, Stock/Delamain & Boutel-
    leau (Paris), 1929, published in English as *Forest
    Wild,* translation by Conrad Elphinstone, Routledge
    (London), 1932.
P. C. de compagnie, Rieder, 1930.
La Salamandre, Etincelles (Paris), 1930.
La Vie du General Yusuf, Gallimard (Paris), 1930.
Champlain, Plon (Paris), 1931.
Drapeau rouge, Editions des Portiques (Paris), 1931.
Du sang sur la neige, Cite des Livres (Paris), 1931.
Napoleon, Rieder, 1931.
L'Ame du vin, Rieder, 1932.
(With Germaine Constantin-Weyer) *Les Secrets d'une
    maitress de maison,* Rieder, 1932.
Source de joie, Rieder, 1932.
Une Corde sur l'abime (title means "A Rope over the
    Abyss"), Rieder, 1933.
Mon Gai Royaume de Provence, Rieder, 1933.
Vichy, ville du charme, Clermont-Ferrand (Quebec), 1933,
    republished as *Vichy, la vie d'eau eternelle,* Syndicat
    d'Initiatives (Vichy), 1946.
Un Sourire dans la tempete (title means "A Smile in the
    Storm"), Rieder, 1934.
Le Voyage de Leif L'Heureux, Le Masque (Paris), 1934.
La Croisiere du jour sans fin, Rieder, 1935.
Le Flaneur sous la tente, Stock/Delamain & Boutelleau
    (Paris), 1935.
Les Compagnons de la houle, Fayard (Paris), 1936.
La Demoiselle de la mort, Librairie des Champs-Elysees
    (Paris), 1936.
Telle qu'elle etait en son vivant (title means "As She Was
    in Her Lifetime"), Librairie des Champs-Elysees,
    1936, republished as *La Loi du nord; ou, Telle qu'elle
    etait en son vivant,* Librairie des Champs-Elysees,
    1947.

Aime une ombre, Librairie des Champs-Elysees, 1937.

La Marchande de mort, Librairie des Champs-Elysees, 1938.

Le Moulinet a tambour fixe: Peche tous les poissons avec toutes les esches, avec tous les leurres, Librairie des Champs-Elysees, 1938.

La Nuit de Magdalena, Librairie des Champs-Elysees, 1938.

Les Tombes-d'amour, Librairie des Champs-Elysees, 1938.

Autour de l'epopee canadienne, Floury (Paris), 1940.

L'Equipe sans nom, Librairie des Champs-Elysees, 1940.

La Chasse au brochet, Librairie des Champs-Elysees, 1941.

Le Cheval de prise, Aubanel (Avignon), 1941.

Le Maitre de la route, Milieu du Monde (Geneva), 1941.

La Verendrye, Didier (Toulouse), 1941.

(With Barbelay-Bertillot) *Canoes et kayaks,* Commissariat General a l'Education Generale et aux Sports (Vichy), 1942.

L'Aventure vecue de Dumas pere, Milieu du Monde, 1944.

L'Ame allemande, Grasset (Paris), 1945.

(With Clara Longworth-Chambrun) *Le Grand Will,* Editions de la Nouvelle France (Paris), 1945.

Le Bar de San Miguel, Simon (Paris), 1946.

La Chanson d'Ingrid, Grasset, 1946.

La Fille du soleil, Arts-France (Paris), 1946.

Sous le signe du vampire, L'Elan (Paris), 1947.

Vichy et son histoire (de ses origines a nos jours), Szabo (Vichy), 1947.

Pronunciamiento, L'Elan (Paris), 1948.

Dans les Pas du naturaliste, Stock, Delamain & Boutelleau, 1950.

Naundorff ou Louis XVII? SFELT (Paris), 1950.

La Vie privee des poissons, Stock, Delamain & Boutelleau, 1954, published in English as *The Private Life of Fishes,* translation by Ray Turrell, Bell (London), 1956.

Les Tragiques Amours de Bianca, Fayard (Paris), 1958.

Avec plus ou moins de rire, Editions des Plaines (Saint-Boniface, Manitoba), 1986.

Author of unpublished autobiographical works, "Journal," and "Propos d'un octogenaire."

Contributor to periodicals, including *L'Illustration* and *Les Oeuvres Libres.*

ADAPTATIONS: Un Sourire dans la tempete, Telle qu'elle etait en son vivant, and *A Man Scans His Past* were all adapted as films.

SIDELIGHTS: Maurice Constantin-Weyer drew upon a decade's adventures in early twentieth-century Canada as the raw material for his novels that romanticized western Canada's heroic past. A prolific writer and translator—his oeuvre extends to some sixty volumes—Constantin-Weyer's Canadian novels count as only a small part of the author's life-work but are among his best known and most popular. They also include what are considered his best written works, in particular *Un Homme se penche sur son passe* (1928, translated as *A Man Scans His Past,* 1929), which received the Prix Goncourt, France's highest literary award.

Born in France, Constantin-Weyer became interested in the classics early on, especially such novels of adventure as *Tom Jones, Don Quixote,* and *The Odyssey,* according to John J. O'Connor, writing in *Dictionary of Literary Biography* (*DLB*). After his studies at the Sorbonne were interrupted due to financial difficulties, and two years spent in military service to his native country, Constantin-Weyer emigrated to Canada, where he worked as a trapper, cowboy, farmer, lumberjack, and journalist before returning to France to fight in World War I. Quoting the author, O'Connor dubs this period "ces annees, ou je jouais au sauvage" ("those years when I played the savage"). Although the accuracy of Constantin-Weyer's depiction of these years was called into question by critic Donatien Fremont, they nonetheless form the basic experience for the author's best known works.

Constantin-Weyer reportedly married a Metis woman of sixteen, Dina Proulx, in 1910 and fathered three children before returning to France to fight in World War I. He was decorated several times for his efforts during the war, and while recuperating from a serious wound after the war met and married his second wife, Germaine Weyer, whose last name he added to his own. Constantin-Weyer was appointed editor of *Paris-Centre* in 1923 and began publishing fictionalized accounts of his adventures in western Canada in the 1920s.

Vers l'ouest (1921, translated as *Towards the West,* 1931) inaugurates a series promoted by Constantin-Weyer's publisher as an "Epopee canadienne," and, according to O'Connor, acts as a template for the other two Canadian works the author published during this period, *Manitoba* (1924) and *La Bourrasque* (1925, translated as *A Martyr's Folly* and as *The Half-Breed,* 1930). Beginning with a highly fictionalized account of celebrated Metis leader Louis Riel's life in *Towards the West* and ending with an account, marred by "blatant inaccuracies," according to O'Connor, of Louis Riel, Jr.'s rebellion in 1870, the three books were also criticized for bearing melodramatic plots, poor characterization, and false historical accounts. They did, however, reveal the author's "skill in describing prairie landscape and flora," and movingly warn of the destruction of prairie wildlife and native culture, wrote O'Connor. The author would take up these themes again in later, more successful, works.

Constantin-Weyer's subsequent novels drawing on his own experiences in Canada and on the nation's history include *Cavelier de La Salle* (1927, translated as *The French Adventurer: The Life and Exploits of LaSalle,* 1931), *Cinq Eclats de silex* (1927), *Clairiere* (1929, translated as *Forest Wild,* 1932), and *A Man Scans His Past.* The last title garnered Constantin-Weyer the prestigious Prix Goncourt and, though it resembles earlier works in theme and execution (and repeats verbatim, according to O'Connor, several pages from *Manitoba*), it is generally believed to succeed in areas where his other books fail. "Told with economy and energy," according to O'Connor, *A Man Scans His Past* recounts the story of Monge, a cowboy, fur trader, and farmer, his love for Hannah O'Molloy, his rivalry with a man named Archer, and his struggle to survive on Canada's harsh northern plains. Though the novel is marred "somewhat by unconvincing and unidiomatic English dialogue" and the repetition of passages from an earlier work, "Constantin-Weyer's handling of plot and setting is skillful and his treatment of character and theme is often original and compelling," O'Connor concluded.

Constantin-Weyer took the opportunity offered by the success of *A Man Scans His Past* to retire from the newspaper business in order to dedicate his time to writing, painting, and travelling in Europe in the 1930s. He published four subsequent novels set in Canada during this decade, including *Napoleon* (1931), "which borrows heavily from the themes and plot of *Un Homme se penche sur son passe* to demonstrate the victimization of prairie natives," O'Connor observed. *Une Corde sur l'abime* (1933), which centers on a Frenchman who sacrifices his life for the Indians, was published during this time, along with *Un Sourire dans la tempete* (1934), and *Telle qu'elle etait en son vivant* (1936), both of which recount the love of three men for one woman on the frontier of the Canadian northwest, and which, along with *A Man Scans His Past* were successfully made into films.

Constantin-Weyer continued to publish throughout World War II and the decades that followed, until his death in 1964, though none of these works are set in Canada. Often slighted in contemporary examinations of literature set in Canada, and nearly forgotten in his native France, Constantin-Weyer's novels brought the Canadian prairies and frontier characters to curious French audiences prior to World War II, an achievement that made him immensely popular during his lifetime. Fremont, an early critic whose expose *Sur le ranch de Constantin-Weyer* (1932) impelled Constantin-Weyer to distinguish between autobiography and fiction in his early works, was moved to reassess the author's work in 1959 in *Les Francais dans l'ouest canadien.* As quoted by O'Connor in *DLB:* "Quand il aborde l'histoire du pays, il la romance au point de la defiguer totalement; mais comme peintre de

la nature et de la vie de l'Ouest, on peut l'admirer sans reserve. . . . La faune et la flore de l'Ouest n'ont pas de secret pour lui. Il nous associe a la vie de la foret, de la prairie, du lac peuples de betes et de cris. Il est inimitable dans la notation realiste des minces evenements journaliers du monde des Metis et des colons" ("When he tackles the country's history, he fictionalizes it to the point of distorting it totally; but as a painter of the nature and of the life of the West, one can admire him without reservation. . . . The fauna and flora of the West have no secrets for him. He makes us a party to the life of the forest, of the prairie, of the lake inhabited by animals and cries. He is without equal in the realistic depiction of small daily events in the world of the Metis and the settlers"). Constantin-Weyer thus, in O'Connor's estimation, "merits attention in any contemporary investigation of western Canadian literature."

BIOGRAPHICAL/CRITICAL SOURCES:

BOOKS

Constantin-Fortin, Marguerite, *Une Femme se penche sur son passe,* Les Livres Nouveaux (Paris), 1940.
Dictionary of Literary Biography, Volume 92: *Canadian Writers, 1890-1920,* Gale, 1990, pp. 56-63.
Fremont, Donatien, *Les Francais dans l'ouest canadien,* Editions de la Liberte (Winnipeg), 1959.
Fremont, *Sur le ranch de Constantin-Weyer,* Editions de la Liberte, 1932.
Motut, Roger, *Maurice Constantin-Weyer: Ecrivain de l'Ouest et du Grand Nord,* Editions des Plaines (St. Boniface, Manitoba), 1982.
Valery Larbaud et ses contemporains bourbonnais Charles-Louis Philippe, Emile Guillaumin, Maurice Constantin-Weyer 31 mai-21 juin 1981, Bibliotheque municipale/Centre Culturel Valery Larbaud (Vichy, France), 1981.*

* * *

COULTER, John (William) 1888-1980

PERSONAL: Born February 12, 1888, in Belfast, North Ireland; immigrated to Canada, 1936; died December 1, 1980; son of Francis and Annie (Clements) Coulter; married Olive Clare Primrose (a writer), July 4, 1936; children: Primrose (Mrs. John T. Pemberton, Jr.), Clare Elizabeth Crieve. *Education:*Attended Municipal Technical Institute and School of Art, both in Belfast, Northern Ireland, and University of Manchester.

CAREER: Teacher of art and English at Coleraine Academical Institution, Coleraine, Ireland, 1913-14, Wesley College, Dublin, Ireland, 1914-19; writer.

MEMBER: Canadian Association for Theatre History (honorary member), Arts and Letters Club (Toronto).

AWARDS, HONOURS: The Family Portrait was named one of the BBC's finest twelve plays from the preceding fifteen years, 1935; awards from the Dominion Drama Festival, 1937, for *The House in the Quiet Glen;* D.Litt., York University, 1979.

WRITINGS:

RADIO PLAYS

Sally's Chance, British Broadcasting Company (BBC), 1925.

A Tale of Old Quebec, BBC, 1935, Canadian Broadcasting Company (CBC), 1935.

The Family Portrait (produced by the BBC, 1935, produced as *Stars of Brickfield,* CBC, 1938, also produced in Canada as *The Sponger*), Macmillan (Canada), 1937.

"Quebec in 1670," *The Living History Series,* CBS, 1940.

This Is My Country, CBC, 1941.

This Great Experiment, CBC, 1942.

The Trial of Joseph Howe, CBC, 1942.

Transit through Fire (opera libretto; music by Healy Willan; produced by the CBC, 1942, produced for television, CBC, 1955), Macmillan (Canada), 1942.

The Drums Are Out, first produced in Dublin, Ireland, at the Abbey Theatre, produced on *Wednesday Night,* CBC, 1950, *FM Theatre,* CBC, 1969, and at St. Paul University, 1971.

While I Live, CBC, 1951.

Riel (first produced in 1950; produced for *Wednesday Night,* CBC, 1951, produced for television on *GM Presents,* CBC, 1961), Ryerson, 1962.

God's Ulsterman CBC, 1974, originally produced for the stage as *The Red Hand of Ulster.*

PUBLISHED PLAYS; EXCEPT WHERE NOTED

The House in the Quiet Glen (adapted from his radio play *Sally's Chance*), Macmillan (Canada), 1937.

Radio Drama Is Not Theatre, Macmillan (Canada), 1937.

Deirdre of the Sorrows (opera libretto; music by Willan; produced as "Deirdre" for *Tuesday Night,* CBC, 1946), Macmillan (Canada), 1944, abridged version published as *Deirdre,* 1965.

The Trial of Louis Riel, Oberon Press, 1960.

The Crime of Louis Riel, Players Co-Op, 1966, produced for *Tuesday Night,* CBC, 1968.

Francois Bigot: A Rediscovery in Dramatic Form of the Fall of Quebec, Hounslow Press, 1978.

OTHER PRODUCED PLAYS

Father Brady's New Pig, produced at the Arts and Letters Club Theatre, Toronto, Ontario, Canada, 1937, pro-

duced as *Pigs,* CBC, 1940, produced as *Clogherbann Fair,* BBC, 1948.

Holy Manhattan, produced at the Arts and Letters Club Theatre, 1940.

Mr. Churchill of England, produced at the Arts and Letters Theatre, 1942, produced for radio, CBC, 1943.

Oblomov (stage adaptation of the work by Ivan Goncharov), produced at the Arts and Letters Club Theatre, 1946; broadcast on BBC, 1947; broadcast on *Wednesday Night,* CBC, 1961; as "Mr. Oblomov" on *Playdate,* CBC, 1962.

Sleep My Pretty One, produced in London at the St. James Theatre, 1954.

Come Back to Erin (television play), CBC, 1955.

Capful of Pennies, first produced in Toronto, Ontario, at Central Library Theatre, 1967, produced for radio, CBC, 1967, revised version entitled *Mr. Kean of Drury Lane,* 1980.

OTHER

Churchill (biography), Ryerson, 1944.

Turf Smoke (novel), Ryerson, 1945.

The Blossoming Thorn (verse), Ryerson, 1946.

Prelude to a Marriage: Letters and Diaries of John Coulter and Olive Clare Primrose, Oberon Press, 1979.

In My Day (autobiography), Hounslow Press, 1980.

The John Coulter Archive, compiled by K. Garay with Norma Smith, 2 vols., Hamilton (Ontario), 1982-83.

Also author of plays, unpublished and unproduced: *Highlights,* 1979; *Living Together,* 1979; and *The Fiddling Hind.* Editor, *Ulster Review,* 1926; assistant editor, *New Adelphi,* 1927-30. Contributor of plays, feature programs, criticism, and reviews to the BBC, CBC, and Radio Eireann. Contributor to journals and newspapers in England, Ireland, Canada, and United States.

SIDELIGHTS: John Coulter ranks as one of Canada's most celebrated playwrights. His works for radio, stage, and television are considered seminal in the development of modern Canadian drama. In addition to introducing Canadians to a refined approach in crafting plays, he also understood the need for financial backing of the arts. To that end he fostered arts and cultural support organizations, cofounding the Canadian Conference of the Arts and playing an instrumental role in the founding of the Canada Council and the renowned Stratford Shakespeare Festival. This combination of playwriting skill and devotion to artistic patronage led many to refer to Coulter as the "Dean of Canadian Playwrights."

Coulter was born in 1888 in Belfast, Northern Ireland, a land torn by the powerful religious antogonisms between Protestant and Catholic faiths. Although Coulter was himself a Protestant, the geographic location of his home between Protestant and Catholic neighborhoods assured that he regularly received thrashings from violent elements within both factions. Managing to avoid serious harm, he grew to engage scholarly pursuits. He studied at the Belfast School of Art and Technology and at the University of Manchester and, following his graduation, he taught at Wesley College in Dublin, Ireland. While in Dublin Coulter became a frequent patron of the Abbey Theatre, where the great poet and playwright William Butler Yeats was a prominent figure. Coulter eventually met Yeats and was sufficiently inspired to leave for Northern Ireland in 1919 and commence efforts to establish a theatre in Ulster. When unrest between Protestants and Catholics again exploded in his homeland, Coulter departed for England, where he found work writing plays for the radio service of the British Broadcasting Corporation (BBC). Prominent among Coulter's works from this period—the 1920s—is *The Family Portrait,* a drama about a family of self-absorbed Protestants in Ulster. The play, which was hailed as one of the BBC's finest twelve plays from the preceding fifteen years, was later produced on Canadian television under the titles *The Stars of Brickfield* and *The Sponger.*

In addition to writing plays while in England, Coulter supported himself by serving as managing editor of *New Adelphi,* a journal developed by J. Middleton Murray. Through Murray, Coulter met Clare Primrose, a young writer with whom he was soon romantically involved. When Primrose left England for Canada, Coulter followed. He married Primrose in 1936 and settled with her in Toronto.

Soon after establishing himself in Canada, Coulter scored on the stage with *The House in the Quiet Glen,* a somber, Ulster-set drama—derived from Coulter's earlier radio play *Sally's Chance*—which concerns a young woman who resists an arranged marriage to a rich widower and falls in love, instead, with the widower's son. The play nearly swept the awards when it played at the Dominion Drama Festival in 1937 (save one category, it won every award for which it qualified), and it served notice that Coulter would prove an imposing force in Canadian drama.

During the 1940s Coulter wrote for the stage and for radio and produced both fiction and opera librettos. In 1940 he triumphed again at the Dominion Drama Festival with *Father Brady's New Pig* and continued his series of plays for radio's *Living History Series.* In addition, he published both a novel, *Turf Smoke,* a Yeats-like poetry collection, *The Blossoming Thorn,* and he contributed librettos for composer Healey Willan's operas *Transit through Fire* and *Deirdre of the Sorrows,* both of which were broadcast on Canadian radio.

Coulter's best-known work from this decade, however, is probably *Oblomov,* his stage adaptation of Ivan Goncharov's masterpiece about a well-to-do idler who rarely strays from his bed. But whereas Goncharov concentrated on the title character's lethargy, Coulter chose to emphasize the efforts of Oblomov's friends to jar him into activity. *Oblomov* was staged in Canada in 1946, adapted for BBC radio in 1947, and produced for Canadian television in the early 1960s.

Towards the end of the 1940s and into the early 1950s, Coulter began writing plays on the Protestant-Catholic conflict in Northern Ireland. Prominent among these works are *The Drums Are Out,* about the emotional conflict endured by a Protestant officer who considers capturing his daughter's Catholic lover, a member of the outlawed Irish Republican Army (IRA); and *God's Ulsterman,* which depicts the IRA as a band of particularly dangerous individuals.

In the 1950s Coulter completed *Riel,* a historical drama about Louis Riel, the controversial Metis leader who headed the North-West Rebellion of 1885 and was later executed for treason. Coulter authority Geraldine Anthony, writing in the *Dictionary of Literary Biography,* noted that "*Riel* constituted the peak of Coulter's dramatic career in Canada." Coulter later expanded the work into a trilogy with the addition of the plays *The Crime of Louis Reil* and *The Trial of Louis Reil.*

When Coulter's wife died suddenly in 1971, he withdrew from playwriting and concentrated instead on preparing *Prelude to a Marriage,* a collection of his wife's journals, letters the couple exchanged, and autobiographical accounts. He followed that volume with another memoir, *In My Day.* By 1980 Coulter was again writing plays. Though many of these works remain unproduced, they have been collected and published in the two volume work *The John Coulter Archive.* By the time Coulter died in 1980, at the age of ninety-three, his contribution to Canadian drama had been widely recognized. Of his quest to develop Canada's artistic community through his own work and through the support of others, Anthony appraised in the *Dictionary of Literary Biography* that "John Coulter succeeded beyond his expectations."

BIOGRAPHICAL/CRITICAL SOURCES:

BOOKS

Anthony, Geraldine, *John Coulter,* Twayne, 1976.
Anthony, editor, *Stage Voices,* Doubleday, 1978, pp. 1-26.
Coulter, John, *Prelude to a Marriage,* Oberon Press, 1979.
Coulter, *In My Day,* Hounslow Press, 1980.
Dictionary of Literary Biography, Volume 68: *Canadian Writers, 1920-1959,* Gale, 1988.

PERIODICALS

Toronto Daily Star, November 24, 1966, p. 40.*

*   *   *

COUPLAND, Douglas 1961-

PERSONAL: Born December 30, 1961, on a Canadian military base in Baden-Sollingen, Germany; son of Douglas Charles Thomas (a doctor) and C. Janet (Campbell) Coupland. *Education:* Emily Carr College of Art and Design, Vancouver, Canada, c. 1984; completed a two-year course in Japanese business science, Hawaii, 1986.

ADDRESSES: Home—Vancouver, British Columbia, Canada. *Office*—c/o Pocket Books, 1230 Avenue of the Americas, New York, NY 10020.

CAREER: Author, sculptor, magazine writer, and editor.

WRITINGS:

Generation X: Tales for an Accelerated Culture (novel), St. Martin's (New York), 1991.
Shampoo Planet (novel), Pocket Books (New York), 1992.
Life after God (short story collection), Pocket Books, 1994.

Contributor of articles to periodicals, including *New Republic, New York Times, Wired,* and *Saturday Night.*

SIDELIGHTS: Douglas Coupland has become known as the voice of a generation, "the self-wrought oracle of our age," according to John Fraser in *Saturday Night,* who also called him "the Jack Kerouac of his generation." Coupland earned his reputation with his first novel, *Generation X: Tales for an Accelerated Culture,* which originated the term "Generation X" to refer to those Americans in their twenties and early thirties during the 1990s, defining their aggregate interests, concerns, and problems. About Coupland's status as mouthpiece for Generation X-ers, Fraser added that the author achieved it "with a distinctive style and up-market hustle that still leaves me breathless. Not once, so far as I can tell, did he do a sleazy thing to get where he is. He trudged all the way on his talent alone."

Generation X chronicles the story of three "twenty-something" friends living in Palm Springs, California, and mired in "McJobs"—a term coined by Coupland to indicate jobs with low pay, low dignity, and little future. The novel launched its twenty-nine-year-old author straight to the top of the bestseller lists. Coupland, German-born and Canadian-educated, is claimed by some to have written the defining document of his generation, "the new *Catcher in the Rye,*" a book about young people "with too many TVs and too few job opportunities," commented a *Newsweek* reviewer. In the novel, Andy, Claire, and Dag represent Generation X members—those born in the late baby boom period from the early 1960s to the early 1970s. This group foresees a drab future of "lessness" and an accompanying tedium as their fate in life. One of many neologisms, along with cartoons and slogans, which appear in the book, "lessness" implies the acceptance of lower expectations of material wealth than those of preceding generations. John Williams wrote in the *New Statesman and Society* that despite being "self-conscious as hell," *Generation X* is "charming" and "a surprisingly endearing read." Describing the novel as "funny, colourful and accessible," London *Times* contributor Michael Wright stated that Coupland's first novel possesses "dizzying sparkle and originality," further lauding it as "a blazing debut."

In *Shampoo Planet,* published a year after *Generation X,* Coupland turns his attention to "the Global Teens," the generation following the X-ers who were raised in the age of information and video stimulation. Tyler Johnson, the youthful narrator and younger brother of *Generation X*'s narrator, has what Sophronia Scott Gregory described in *Time* as "a Smithsonian-class collection of shampoos" (thus the book's title) plus a sister named Daisy, a waif-like, pseudo-hippie sporting blond dreadlocks, and a twice-divorced mother, Jasmine, a true 1960s hippie who seems to Tyler more in need of parenting than is he.

"Old people will always win," figures *Shampoo*'s narrator, but he remains hopeful about his future in a world experiencing "severe shopping withdrawal and severe goal withdrawal." Coupland is quoted in *Maclean's* as saying, "I'm not Pollyannaish, but I'm optimistic about the future. I think *Shampoo Planet* has an optimism about it that *Generation X* does not." *Time* contributor Gregory complained that Coupland's narrative lacks motivation, but she praised the author's quirky descriptive passages, noting that "the book thrives with the energetically bizarre." Gregory further observed, "Fascinating characters abound, but unfortunately they have little to do."

Other critics hail the book's fresh viewpoint and inventiveness. A *Publishers Weekly* reviewer called the novel "funny, sympathetic, and offhandedly brilliant." In *Maclean's,* Victor Dwyer assessed Coupland as "a maturing author artfully evoking the hopes and dreams of a generation that has good reason to have little of either."

Calling Coupland's 1994 collection, *Life after God,* "a series of short stories, constructed from snatches of highly personal narrative," John Lorinc of *Quill and Quire* added, "for readers in their late 20s and early 30s, [Coupland's] appeal clearly lies in his ability to dissect this generation's frustrations with the mire of consumer culture and the intellectual deficiencies of the hip, self-directed sarcasm of the 1980s." Joe Chidley asserted in *Maclean's* that the book "strips away the paraphernalia of an age-group to investigate the origins of its angst. Unfortunately, he also strips away much of its anger and wit. What remains in the ennui." Chidley further observed, "cumulatively, eight stories about the passing of things end up sounding like an extended whine." Brenda Peterson, writing in the *New York Times Book Review*, maintained that "though each of these very short tales has its own narrator, the voice never really varies: it drones where it might delve, it skims where it might seduce, it hoards where it might offer sustenance." Peterson concluded, "Mr. Coupland's vision is as perishable and trendy as the brand names that pass here for characters and story lines."

BIOGRAPHICAL/CRITICAL SOURCES:

PERIODICALS

Books in Canada, September, 1991, pp. 50-51; April, 1992, p. 13.
Maclean's, April 25, 1994, p. 62.
New Criterion, April, 1994, pp. 79-80.
New Statesman and Society, May 29, 1992, p. 40.
Newsweek, January 27, 1992, p. 58.
New York Times Book Review, May 8, 1994, p. 13; May 8, 1994, p. 13.
Paragraph, fall, 1994, pp. 32-33.
People Weekly, October 14, 1991, pp. 105-06; April 25, 1994, pp. 31-32.
Publishers Weekly, February 1, 1991, p. 77; June 15, 1992, p. 82.
Quill and Quire, February, 1994, p. 24; June, 1994, p. 38.
Saturday Night, March, 1994, pp. 8-9.
Time, October 19, 1992, p. 78.
Times (London), June 4, 1992, p. 6.
Times Literary Supplement, February 19, 1993, p. 23.
USA Today, March 7, 1994, p. D1-2.
Vanity Fair, March, 1994, pp. 92, 94.
Village Voice Literary Supplement, November, 1992, pp. 25-27.*

*   *   *

CRAVEN, Margaret   1901-1980

PERSONAL: Born March 13, 1901, in Helena, MT, United States; died July 19, 1980, in Sacramento, CA, United States; daughter of Arthur John (a judge) and Clara Emily (Kerr) Craven. *Education:* Stanford University, A.B. (with great distinction), 1924.

CAREER: San Jose Mercury, San Jose, CA, editorial writer and columnist, 1924-28; free-lance writer, 1928-80.

WRITINGS:

I Heard the Owl Call My Name (novel), Clark, Irwin Co., of Canada, 1967, Doubleday, 1973.

Walk Gently This Good Earth (novel), Putnam, 1977.
Again Calls the Owl (autobiography), Putnam, 1980.
The Home Front (short stories), Putnam, 1981.

Contributor of short stories to magazines, including *Ladies' Home Journal* and *Collier's,* 1928-41, and *Saturday Evening Post,* 1941-62.

SIDELIGHTS: Margaret Craven's first novel, *I Heard the Owl Call My Name,* explores the relationship between a dying Anglican priest and his parishioners, a tribe of British Columbian Indians. Set in a small fishing village in the Canadian wilderness, the novel depicts the Kwakiutl Indians of British Columbia struggling against assimilation into a modern civilization. Jennifer Farley Smith of the *Christian Science Monitor* called the novel a "shining parable about the reconciliation of two cultures and two faiths." The story demonstrates that "the Red Indian philosophy, firmly rooted in nature, is both a challenge to modern man and an undeniable comfort," noted *Times Literary Supplement* critic Elaine Moss. A best-selling novel, *I Heard the Owl Call My Name* was made into a movie for television in 1973. *Walk Gently This Good Earth,* Craven's second novel, also shows people responding to a changing world as it follows the Wescott family through the social upheavals of the Great Depression and World War II. Elizabeth Schmidt, writing in the *Christian Science Monitor,* found the book "comfortable and honest," saying also that "the characters are like old pieces of pewter, showing a faint stubborn luster." On the other hand, a *Kirkus Reviews* critic observed, "this brood . . . is noble and pure hearted beyond belief. Also cloying and a bit unreal." Craven's autobiography, *Again Calls the Owl,* is largely devoted to the research and travel that provided the foundation for much of her writing. Craven once spent several weeks with the Kwakiutl Indians, and she recalled those experiences in writing *I Heard the Owl Call My Name.*

BIOGRAPHICAL/CRITICAL SOURCES:

BOOKS

Contemporary Literary Criticism, Volume 17, Gale, 1981.
Craven, Margaret, *Again Calls the Owl,* Putnam, 1980.

PERIODICALS

Atlantic Monthly, April, 1980.
Booklist, May 1, 1980.
Christian Science Monitor, January 30, 1974; December 28, 1977.
Junior Bookshelf, December, 1974.
Kirkus Reviews, October 1, 1977.
Los Angeles Times, May 25, 1981.
New Statesman, August 2, 1974.
New York Times Book Review, February 3, 1974.
Times Literary Supplement, December 6, 1974.

Wilson Library Bulletin, February, 1978.

OBITUARIES:

PERIODICALS

Los Angeles Times, August 4, 1980.

[Sketch verified by niece, Elizabeth Craven]*

*   *   *

CRAWLEY, Alan 1887-1975

PERSONAL: Born August 23, 1887, in Cobourg, Ontario, Canada; died July 28, 1975, in Cordova Bay, British Columbia, Canada; son of Charles James (a banker) and Maude (Buck) Crawley; married Jean Horn, 1915; children: David, Michael.

CAREER: Affiliated with Machray, Sharpe (a law firm and later an investment banking concern), Winnipeg, Manitoba, Canada, as a clerk, 1905 (admitted to the bar, 1911), and as an attorney, 1911-18; founding member of Community Players of Winnipeg, a community theater group, 1915-25; founding partner in law firm, 1918-33; editor and author.

WRITINGS:

Editor of the poetry journal *Contemporary Verse: A Canadian Quarterly,* 1941-52.

Crawley's correspondence is housed at Queen's University, Kingston, Ontario, and at the University of Toronto.

SIDELIGHTS: Alan Crawley is credited with furthering the early careers of a number of Canadian poets during his twelve-year editorship of the influential journal *Contemporary Verse: A Canadian Quarterly.* Crawley, born in 1887, lived in several provinces across Canada over the course of his life, and a good part of his adult years were spent as a lawyer in Winnipeg. In 1933, then in his forties, Crawley retired from the profession when an infection robbed him of his eyesight. With his wife, Jean, and their two children he relocated to Victoria, British Columbia.

Crawley's newfound hours of enforced leisure became increasingly taken up with literary matters, long a passion of his. His wife often read aloud to him, and he learned Braille to further increase his knowledge of contemporary writers. At a lecture on American poetry, Crawley became acquainted with a number of writers then active in the burgeoning literary scene in British Columbia. He soon became a regular fixture among the group, lecturing and giving readings in the area, and known as an enthusiastic supporter of modernism. The poets and other writers associated with this literary direction were interested in break-ing away from some of the constraints and traditions that had kept Canadian poetry a few steps behind its British and American counterparts. When a group of like-minded western Canadian writers decided to start a literary journal, they invited Crawley to become its editor, and *Contemporary Verse: A Canadian Quarterly* was born.

The first issue appeared in 1941 and, from the start, Crawley tried to avoid the ideological infighting common to many forward-thinking artistic currents during this era. As editor he asserted in a manifesto statement that "the aims of CONTEMPORARY VERSE are simple and direct and seem worthy and worthwhile. These aims are to entice and stimulate the writing and reading of poetry and to provide means for its publication free from restraint of politics, prejudices and placations, and to keep open its pages to poetry that is sincere in theme and treatment and technique." Crawley, who tackled the business and editorial side of the publication with the help of the eyes of his wife and assistant editors, made the fourteen-page quarterly a respectable success early on. A section on *Contemporary Verse* in the *Oxford Companion to Canadian Literature* pointed out that the journal "played an important role at a time when there were few literary magazines in Canada. Crawley sought to maintain a high standard of writing, while keeping his pages open to poets of many inclinations."

Acclaimed Canadian writers such as Doris Ferne, Earle Birney, Dorothy Livesay, and P. K. Page were regular contributors to *Contemporary Verse.* Additionally—despite the difficulties his blindness sometimes presented—Crawley eagerly corresponded with less-established poets and offered encouragement and construction criticism. "A poem isn't a picture," he was quoted as saying in the *Dictionary of Literary Biography.* "It's a statement of an idea. . . . Make your language like your speech. Be brief, clear-cut." The initial work of many outstanding Canadian poets, including Phyllis Webb, Malcolm Lowry, and Raymond Souster, debuted in *Contemporary Verse.* A dozen exciting years had wrought numerous changes upon the Canadian literary scene, however, and newer journals, centered in Toronto and other eastern cities, eventually took away some of the import and influence of *Contemporary Verse.* In 1952, after thirty-nine issues, the journal ceased publication. Crawley's stewardship of the journal was the subject of Joan McCullagh's 1976 book *Alan Crawley and "Contemporary Verse,"* a tome that appeared a year after his death at the age of eighty-seven. In an essay for the *Dictionary of Literary Biography,* W. H. New described Crawley as "a champion of the Canadian voice, and of its relevance to literary modernism . . . [and] one of the leading forces that reshaped Canadian poetry in the 1940s."

BIOGRAPHICAL/CRITICAL SOURCES:

BOOKS

Dictionary of Literary Biography, Volume 68: *Canadian Writers, 1920-1959,* Gale, 1988.
McCullagh, Joan, *Alan Crawley and "Contemporary Verse,"* University of British Columbia, 1976.
Oxford Companion to Canadian Literature, Oxford University Press, 1983.

PERIODICALS

Canadian Literature, winter, 1964, p. 33; autumn, 1967, p. 63; summer, 1969, p. 89.
Tamarack Review, spring, 1957, p. 55.*

*   *   *

CRONENBERG, David   1943-

PERSONAL: Born May 15 (one source says March 15), 1943, in Toronto, Ontario, Canada; son of Milton (a writer and editor) and Esther (a pianist; maiden name, Sumberg) Cronenberg; married Margaret Hindson (divorced); remarried; wife's name, Carolyn (a homemaker); children: (first marriage) Cassandra; (second marriage) two children. *Education:* Attended University of Toronto, beginning in 1962. *Avocational interests:* Cars and auto racing.

ADDRESSES: Office—David Cronenberg Productions, 217 Avenue Rd., Toronto, Ontario M5R 2J3, Canada. *Agent*—Michael Marcus, Creative Artists Agency, 9830 Wilshire Blvd., Beverly Hills, CA 90212.

CAREER: Screenwriter, director, and actor. Producer, cameraman, and editor of *Stereo,* Emergent, 1969, *Crimes of the Future,* Emergent, 1970, and *Transfer;* director of film *The Dead Zone,* Paramount, 1983; actor in films, sometimes in cameo roles, including *Into the Night,* Universal, 1975, *The Fly,* Paramount, 1986, *Nightbreed,* Twentieth Century-Fox, 1990, and *Henry and Verlin,* 1995. Founding member of Film Canada in the 1970s; affiliated with the Canadian Broadcasting Corp. (CBC) in the 1970s.

AWARDS, HONOURS: Canada Council grant, 1975, to shoot *They Came from Within.*

WRITINGS:

SCREENPLAYS

(And director) *Stereo,* Emergent, 1969.
(And director) *Crimes of the Future,* Emergent, 1970.
(And director) *They Came from Within* (also known as *The Parasite Murders, Shivers,* and *Frissons*), Trans-American, 1975.

(And director) *Rabid* (also known as *Rage*), New World, 1976.
(And director) *Fast Company,* Topar, 1978.
(And director) *The Brood,* New World, 1978.
(And director) *Scanners,* AVCO-Embassy, 1979.
(And director) *Videodrome,* Universal, 1983.
(With Charles Edward Pogue; and director) *The Fly* (based on a story by George Langelaan), Paramount, 1986.
(With Norman Snider; and director) *Dead Ringers* (adapted from the novel *Twins* by Bari Wood and Jack Geasland), Twentieth Century-Fox, 1988.
(And director) *Naked Lunch* (adapted from the novel by William S. Burroughs), Twentieth Century-Fox, 1992.
(With David Henry Hwang; and director) *M. Butterfly* (based on the 1988 play by Hwang), Warner Brothers, 1993.

OTHER

Cronenberg on Cronenberg, edited by Chris Rodley, Knopf (Canada), 1992.

Also screenwriter and director of the short film *Transfer,* 1966; also director of the short film *From the Drain,* 1967.

SIDELIGHTS: "One of the reasons people like to see my movies," David Cronenberg was quoted as saying in *Saturday Night,* "is that they expect that I will go farther than they would. It's part of my relationship with my audience." Cronenberg takes that relationship seriously, having created a body of work that challenges his audience with graphic depictions of mental and physical degeneration. These films display a proclivity for psychic violence that is equally matched, if not overwhelmed, by grotesquerie and gore. This penchant for various bodily fluids has earned the filmmaker the sobriquet the Baron of Blood. The success of Cronenberg's films has won him both a following of dedicated fans and a place among the preeminent filmmakers of the 1980s and 90s, and his determination to transcend genre boundaries has solidified his reputation as an intellectual's horror director.

Born in Toronto, in 1943, Cronenberg grew up in an environment that nurtured creativity and intellectual growth. Although his formative years were spent during a period of conservative conformity in North America, Cronenberg's parents allowed him an unusual amount of freedom in his imaginative pursuits. Encouraged to engage in activities that would expand his perception of the world, he developed an interest in horror comics and science fiction novels as well as a fascination with insects. Along with the bugs and books, Cronenberg was also an avid fan of the cinema. Using money intended for guitar lessons, Cronenberg frequented local theaters, developing a voracious appetite for anything cinematic—even untranslated foreign films.

As Cronenberg began his coursework at the University of Toronto, he had every intention of becoming a research scientist who would also, like his idol Isaac Asimov, write novels in his spare time. However, a literary award won during his freshman year, in addition to a growing disassociation with fellow science majors, precipitated Cronenberg's switch from science to English. Fraternization with English majors opened his eyes to the rapidly expanding social trends of the 1960s. As he exposed himself to a culture of experimentation, Cronenberg encountered young people acting on their creative impulses, including a group of students making a film. "I was amazed to see a real movie that people could make themselves," Cronenberg enthused in *Saturday Night.* "It had *never* occurred to me that you could do that. Movies were something that came from somewhere else—a given, like a car. I said, 'That looks great! I gotta try that.' " After creating his first film, *Transfer,* Cronenberg devoted himself to a career in filmmaking.

Although only seven minutes long, *Transfer* began a flurry of cinematic activity for Cronenberg and set the thematic tone that would pervade much of his subsequent work. The film tells the story of a psychologist who becomes dependent on one of his patients, indicating Cronenberg's fascination with the mind. In 1969 he released *Stereo,* his first full-length film. *Stereo* deals with a sexual experiment within a community of telepaths. Central to the picture is a Cronenberg trademark; a sterile, obliquely sinister organization that manipulates—or somehow influences—the destiny of the major characters. A year later Cronenberg made *Crimes of the Future,* which envisions a North American society after a majority of the female population has died from a contaminant in cosmetics. The film suggests concepts of biological mutation, referring to "creative cancers" and "new organs." *Stereo* and *Crimes of the Future* earned Cronenberg little more than a cult following, but the films provided him with sufficient credentials to strike a deal with Cinepix, a production house in Montreal, Canada.

Cronenberg's first project for Cinepix was a script titled *Orgy of the Blood Parasites,* which eventually became the film *They Came from Within.* In the story, a deranged research scientist creates a sexual parasite that drives its host organism into a libidinous frenzy. Mayhem ensues when he unleashes the parasite on a self-contained apartment complex, a structure similar to the one at the center of J. G. Ballard's *High Rise.* The building's occupants are driven mad by their basest desires, stopping at nothing to attain their sexual pleasures. On the heels of *They Came from Within,* Cronenberg created another story of sexual feeding titled *Rabid.* In this film a young woman is sub-

jected to an experimental procedure that leaves her with a carnal desire for human blood. Fortunately for her, she has developed a mutation that allows her to quickly access a nearby artery via a phallus-like spike that emerges from her armpit. Unfortunately her victims transform into rabid, sex-crazed, monsters who inherit her lust for blood.

They Came from Within and *Rabid* widened Cronenberg's audience even though they were often dismissed by reviewers as exploitative horror; films that sacrifice narrative content to capitalize on gratuitous sex and/or violence. The *Motion Picture Guide* (*MPG*) complained that *They Came from Within* fails to provide involving characters and reduces the viewer's role to that of voyeur. *MPG* found *Rabid*'s premise interesting but found that the script "suffers from a lack of detail." In hindsight, however, many critics see these films as seminal to Cronenberg's later success. Cronenberg has stated that he seeks to confront his personal demons in his films. In the late seventies the director was facing a disintegrating marriage and the loss of his father to a long and ravaging illness. Some critics opined that these events had a profound effect on the director and his work. As Mark Czarnecki observed in *Maclean's,* Cronenberg's early films mirror his "tormented feelings at the time about women, sex, and disease."

Those elements—women, sex, and disease—play a prominent role in Cronenberg's next project, *The Brood.* Many perceive this film as the point at which Cronenberg's obsessions intersected with his artistic vision and gelled into a coherent piece of horror cinema. Czarnecki wrote in *Macleans* that the film "evokes a combination of horror and pathos that illuminates the darkest corners of the relationships between men and women." The story revolves around Frank and Nola, young parents who have just separated. Nola is unstable, susceptible to violent fits of rage. Seeking help with her problems, Nola checks into the Sommafree Institute of Psychoplasmics. In a radical therapy, her doctor encourages his patients to externalize their anger in physical form. Where other patients develop welts and boils, Nola's fury manifests womb-like sacs on the surface of her stomach. These sacs quickly grow into mutated children, murderous little beasts that carry out Nola's wrath. The film ends with Frank confronting his wife and her abominable "brood." John Colapinto, writing in *Saturday Night,* called *The Brood* "subtle and complex" and "a masterpiece of its genre."

Cronenberg broke through to the commercial mainstream with his next film, the literally mind-blowing *Scanners.* The premise involves an evil group of telepaths or "scanners" who are intent upon world power. While in utero, these scanners were exposed to a drug that bestowed potent telepathic powers upon them. Not only can scanners read minds, they can also blow them up. That is, they have control over the shape and motion of physical objects, including human bodies. A group of good scanners set out to stop the villains, resulting in a climactic meeting of the minds. *Scanners* attracted Cronenberg's largest audience to date; thrill seekers flocked to the film to experience the gruesome special effects, and intellectual horror buffs were drawn by the film's psychological underpinnings. As *Time* reviewer Richard Corliss appraised: "Cronenberg's movies are hip parables of contemporary moral malaise."

Scanners brought Cronenberg to the attention of the major Hollywood studios. Paramount, eager for fresh talent, hired him to direct their adaptation of Stephen King's novel *The Dead Zone*, which is the only Cronenberg film that he did not also script. Released in 1983, *The Dead Zone* was a critical and commercial success. Critics hailed it as one of the best adaptations of a King novel, and Cronenberg became, in the eyes of Hollywood, a bankable director. His new status meant access to the perks and luxuries of major studio filmmaking. He was able to command larger budgets for his films and cast well-known actors for his lead roles.

Industry observers speculated that Cronenberg would follow *The Dead Zone* with a bigger and bloodier variation on *Scanners.* Defying expectations, Cronenberg brought forth *Videodrome,* a dark and esoteric film that harrowingly depicts electronic media. *Videodrome* examines the seedy underbelly of cable and satellite television and the power the medium has over the mind. Max Renn is the owner of a small cable television station, Civic TV, that specializes in gauzy soft-core pornography. Max wants to give his viewers something they can't get from the competition, something stronger—programming with an edge. He finds it in Videodrome, a pirated satellite program with no plot or purpose, just sadomasochistic sex and murder. But Max soon discovers that Videodrome is not staged, it is "snuff " TV—real torture and murder proliferated for entertainment. Despite an associate's cryptic warning that Videodrome has a dangerous "philosophy," Max finds the program even more alluring, and he binges on tapes of Videodrome until he begins to hallucinate. In this confused state the walls of reality become translucent membranes. Alarmed by his distorted perception, Max seeks answers at the Cathode Ray Mission, a clinic run by the Reverend Brian O'Blivion. O'Blivion, who converses with people via videotapes and spouts cryptic predictions, is both a historian and mad prophet of the video age. Through O'Blivion Max learns that he has become a guinea pig for a mind control experiment conducted by Videodrome, which is run by a sinister multinational corporation. By weakening his mental defenses with images of sex and violence, Videodrome was able to send a signal to Max's brain, creating a tumor. Through this tumor Videodrome is able to manipulate Max, using him to as-

sassinate their enemies. With the help of O'Blivion's daughter, Max is able to break free from Videodrome's hold and join a mystical rebel force known as the "new flesh."

Videodrome displays Cronenberg's fascination with the effects of mass media on humankind. Like his character Reverend O'Blivion, Cronenberg sees television as a logical extension of the psyche, "the retina of the mind's eye." Cronenberg suggests in *Videodrome* that the human mind, the soul, can exist independent from the body—within the realm of microwaves and broadcast transmissions: a human television signal. This new state of being is the logical evolution of a society physically weakened by television consumption. While the mortal coil is weak, the "new flesh" is eternal. *Videodrome*'s intellectualization of mind and television precipitated opinions on the director's intentions. Some critics felt Cronenberg was hinting that sex and violence have come to be perceived as one and the same and that television has been a catalyst in this confluence. Lawrence O'Toole wrote in *Maclean's* that "a good deal is suggested . . . about the connections between sex, violence, and sensory stimulation." *Videodrome* did not yield a high return at the box office, but the film became popular on videotape and cable—mediums of television. While not all critics appreciated Cronenberg's film, a coterie of reviewers hailed the director for stretching the borders of the horror genre. "Cronenberg has a powerful imagination when it comes to conceptualizing his material," wrote O'Toole in *Maclean's,* "and his talents have become prodigal with *Videodrome.*" David Ansen summarized *Videodrome* in *Newsweek* as "a dark, disturbing (pop culturist Marshall) McLuhanesque nightmare, and it envelops you in its feverish pulse."

Cronenberg's follow-up to *Videodrome* proved to be his greatest success, a remake of the 1958 B-movie classic *The Fly.* The 1958 version of *The Fly* tells the story of a scientist who, via an experiment, accidentally switches heads with a common housefly. Rather than rework the original, Cronenberg remade the film, stripping it down to its most basic elements and building an entirely new narrative on top of them. Seth Brundle is a brilliant, though socially inept, young scientist. He meets Veronica Quaife, a reporter for a science magazine, at a convention. Seth clumsily tries to pick Veronica up, telling her he is working on a project "that will change the world" and inviting her to come and see it. What Seth is working on is teleportation, a process which disintegrates an object, transports the particles, and reintegrates them at another location. While he has been successful with inanimate objects, Seth's computer system has had considerable trouble reintegrating organic material—he has literally turned a baboon inside out. Working closely together the two fall in love, and Veronica is soon living with Seth in his lab. One evening Veronica gets an inflammatory call from her publisher and ex-lover, Stathis. She leaves to smooth things over. Seth, misinterpreting the situation, gets jealously drunk and, flushed with alcohol and envy, decides to transport himself. The teleportation succeeds, and, in a scene rife with images of new birth, Seth emerges from the receiving pod.

In the days that follow, Veronica notices changes in Seth. He is hyperactive, talking nonstop, and where he was once passive and calm, he is now pushy and edgy. Seth feels incredible and believes the teleportation has purified his system. Veronica is frightened by Seth, for not only is his behavior changing, his appearance is altering. His skin has become mottled and Veronica has discovered a coarse patch of hair on his back. When she takes these hairs to a lab to have them analyzed, she learns that they are not human hairs at all but insect follicles. Delving into his computer files, Seth learns that something else was in the pod when he teleported, something that the computer identifies as "not Brundle." Pressing for more information, Seth learns that the other object was a common housefly. In horror, Seth realizes that the computer has merged his molecules and those of the fly together, creating a being that is neither fly nor human.

As the genes of the fly compete with Seth's for dominance, he becomes ill. He loses his hair, his fingernails, his ears, and, eventually, his humanity. Mutated to an unrecognizable state, he tells Veronica: "I was an insect who dreamed he was a man and loved it. But now the dream is over . . . I'll hurt you if you stay." Veronica is devastated; she still loves Seth, and she is pregnant with his child. Not knowing whether the baby was conceived before or after Seth's teleportation, Veronica decides to be absolutely sure and abort the fetus. As she is about to have the abortion, a monstrous Seth crashes through the window and spirits Veronica away. He begs her not to wipe out the last shred of his humanity—the baby. He takes her back to his lab and proposes a scheme. He wants to teleport himself, Veronica, and the baby, fusing all three beings into a pure new organism. Veronica is moved by Seth's condition, but she is mortified by his proposition and refuses to participate. He forces her into a pod and begins the teleportation sequence. Just as the process is beginning, Stathis arrives in an attempt to rescue her.

Considered more than a horror movie, *The Fly* is hailed by many as Cronenberg's masterpiece, a film that effectively describes numerous themes. "*The Fly* has a stern purity," wrote David Denby in *New York*. "The arc through which it passes—from horror to satire to romantic tragedy—is clean, uncluttered, and powerful. Cronenberg never strains for an effect; he never goes, 'Boo!'" While the film's gruesome special effects repulsed some viewers (and delighted others), those who looked deeper found a horror story of unusual humanity. At one point

in Seth's metamorphosis, he is talking to Veronica when he reaches up to scratch behind his ear. As he does, his ear falls off. He picks the ear up in horror and grief. Although Seth is oozing slime and clearly repulsive, Veronica goes to him and hugs him—an act of tender comfort to his pain. The events that befall Seth and Veronica are science fiction, but Cronenberg roots their emotions and actions in a familiar reality. Denby praised Cronenberg's ability to make his characters real, stating that "in its weirdly self-confident way, *The Fly* goes right to the center of our lives." Richard Corliss, reviewing the film in *Time,* also admired Cronenberg's depiction of humanity facing extraordinary horror: "Director Cronenberg tells this story with no compromise but plenty of intelligent compassion." And David Ansen applauded Cronenberg's unique approach in *Newsweek,* stating: "This is the rare horror film (that most puritanical of genres) that dispenses with the notion of evil."

Cronenberg's next film, *Dead Ringers,* is the story of identical twins Elliot and Beverly Mantle, who are both doctors. Elliot is the public half of the brothers' successful gynecological practice. He is debonair—irresistible to both grant givers and women. Beverly is the inside man, the genius behind Elliot's high-flown medical boasts. The twins lead a symbiotic existence, sharing and feeding off one another's talents and experiences. Elliot will seduce a woman and then give her to Beverly, while the hapless woman thinks she has slept with only one man. Into this circle of two comes actress Claire Niveau, who is first a patient and then a lover to both Mantle brothers. When Claire discovers the brothers' game, she lashes out at them. Claire's brash confrontation affects the sensitive Beverly. Against his will he has fallen in love with Claire, and she is causing changes in his life, creating desires he is unwilling to permit in himself. He reacts violently, shunning Elliot's company. He becomes obsessive about "mutant women," ordering custom gynecological instruments made to correct the "imperfections" of the female reproductive system. Beverly's bizarre behavior is compounded by his growing dependence on drugs, which are slowly dragging him into a hazy madness. Elliot is also affected and soon joins his brother in a narcotic delirium.

The horror that Cronenberg presents in *Dead Ringers* is based in the mind and occurs in reality. There are no elements of super science or metaphysical powers. As Stuart Klawans wrote in the *Nation, Dead Ringers* "turns into a horror film only because the characters take that phrase literally." Corliss found the movie flat in places but had high praise for Cronenberg's ability to extract horror from a new context. Reviewing the film in *Time,* he stated: "Cronenberg can create tour-de-force tableaux with his effortless black magic."

"Exterminate all rational thought," says the protagonist in *Naked Lunch,* the follow-up to *Dead Ringers.* Cronenberg uses this decree to define his film. Based on William S. Burroughs's semiautobiographical novel of the same name, *Naked Lunch* is Cronenberg's perception of life on the fringe, across the border of reason. Bill Lee is a writer who no longer writes but rather works as an exterminator. Bill's wife, Joan, steals his bug powder and shoots it up. "It's a Kafka high," she tells him. "You feel like a bug." It's not long before Bill joins Joan in her entomological psychotropia. During one of their highs, Bill and his wife play out a "William Tell act" in which Bill, with a gun, attempts to shoot a glass that sits atop Joan's head. He misses and kills his wife. This act erases the line separating the real from the unreal for Bill. He is visited by a monstrous talking beetle who instructs him to go to Interzone and compile a report on the "assassination" of Joan Lee. It is unclear as to whether Interzone is a place on a map or a place in Bill's head.

Once in Interzone Bill encounters a vast array of oddities. He discovers a powder made from giant centipedes, a narcotic to which he quickly becomes addicted. His typewriter, actually a bizarre amalgam of beetle and typewriter, gives him instructions on his "mission" in Interzone. Amidst Interzone's hallucinatory night life of surreal other-worldly creatures and young male prostitutes, Bill meets Tom and Joan Frost, British writers working in Interzone. Joan Frost immediately grabs Bill's attention; not only does she share the first name of Bill's departed wife, she is nearly identical in physical appearance to the dead woman. Bill is drawn into the Frost's curious circle of friends, which includes Tom's own talking bug-typewriter and the couple's outlandish, dictatorial housekeeper. Bill is led on a wild chase to find the elusive Dr. Benway, a physician he met in New York who also happens to be the enigmatic force behind the centipede powder trade.

When Cronenberg set out to make *Naked Lunch,* a number of people, including the film's producer, Jeremy Thomas, felt that Burroughs's novel was unfilmable. The book is an example of Burroughs's "cut and paste" writing technique, a stream of consciousness rumination on a junkie's world that seeks to distill ordered meaning from its chaos. Adding to the book's "unfilmable" nature are passages of extreme violence and graphic depictions of homosexual intercourse. Rather than attempt a literal translation of the book, Cronenberg approached the film from an allegorical standpoint. He uses subtly modified episodes from Burroughs's own life to construct a narrative that, in spirit, touches on the general themes of the book. Friends of Burroughs's make disguised appearances throughout the film: Bill's friends Hank and Martin respectively represent Jack Kerouac and Allen Ginsberg,

and Joan and Tom Frost act as doubles for Paul and Jane Bowles. In this manner, Cronenberg fashions a film that metaphorically chronicles Bill/Burroughs's devastation from drug addiction and his arduous mental and physical resuscitation.

Numerous filmgoers and critics agreed with producer Thomas's opinion that *Naked Lunch* was unfilmable, complaining that the film was oblique and far too surreal to serve a proper narrative. Corliss wrote in Time that *Naked Lunch* does not "get inside the junkie's pocked skin. Burroughs lived and nearly died there; Cronenberg and the actors are only visiting." However, Corliss did credit the filmmaker with creating a nightmarish vision of the world of drug addiction: "Cronenberg takes us to the Hell pavilion at Walt Disney World." While she found the film as "impenetrable" as Burroughs's book, *New York Times* critic Janet Maslin praised Cronenberg's ability to evoke the novel while simultaneously forging a film that bears his distinct imprint: "The result, by turns bracing, brilliant, and vile, is a screen style as audacious as Mr. Burroughs's is on the page." As Maslin continued in her review of the film: "It's hard to imagine another filmmaker who could delve so deeply into the monstrousness of Mr. Burroughs's vision, in the end coming up with a bona fide monster movie of his own. Yet while Mr. Cronenberg's ingenious approach to his material matches Mr. Burroughs's flair for the grotesque, it also shares the author's perfect nonchalance and his ice-cold wit. Seldom has a filmmaker offered his audience a more debonair invitation to go to hell."

Cronenberg's next film, *M. Butterfly,* which cost $17 million to produce, is based on the Broadway play by David Henry Hwang (Cronenberg's co-author for the screenplay), which in turn is loosely based on an actual event. Beijing-based French diplomat Bernard Boursicot (Rene Gallimard in the film, played by actor Jeremy Irons), conducted a seventeen-year affair with an exotic female Chinese opera singer (Song LiLing in the film, played by Chinese American actor John Lone), who in reality was a male spy to whom Boursicot had revealed diplomatic secrets over the years. For nearly twenty years, Gallimard had been sexually active with Song and never realized "she" was a "he." Cronenberg told Robert Collison in *Saturday Night,* "*M. Butterfly* is about the transformation of a man's understanding of his own sexuality. It is about the degree to which individuals fuse fantasy and reality in their daily lives."

Somewhat of a departure from his earlier horror-genre films, *M. Butterfly* "marks another triumph in the time-lapse metamorphosis of a remarkable career: a film that refines his obsession with sexual mutation and takes it to a new level," asserted Brian D. Johnson in *Maclean's.* While *M. Butterfly* lacks the blood-and-guts special effects characteristic of *Shivers, Scanners,* and *The Fly,* Cronenberg suggested to Johnson that this film possesses its own "beast": "John [Lone] is the creature." As Collison wrote, "When he agreed to direct *M. Butterfly,* Cronenberg thought it would be his first film without elaborate special effects. 'But then I realized John was my one big special effect.' " The director acknowledged difficulties in transforming masculine features into a believable siren, citing problems disguising facial hair and John Lone's obvious Adam's apple. "It was agony shooting with him [John Lone]," Cronenberg explained to Johnson in *Maclean's,* "because we had to be so careful about the light, the hair, the throat." Some reviewers suggest that Cronenberg's efforts with actor Lone fall far short of convincing. Richard Corliss noted in *Time,* "Onscreen, the opera singer's gender is never in question: his five o'clock shadow gives him away to everyone but the diplomat." And Stanley Kauffmann commented in the *New Republic,* "John Lone always looks like a man in drag, which kills the ambiguities in the Frenchman's mind and makes some of the dialogue faintly risible." Yet, in *Saturday Night,* Collison applauded Cronenberg's interpretation of the transvestite character: "Acclaimed for his title role in Bernardo Bertolucci's epic, *The Last Emperor,* the New York-based Chinese actor John Lone undergoes a chilling, disturbing metamorphosis from a coquettish diva to a cynical double agent." And Johnson claimed in *Maclean's,* "As it turns out, Lone's female impersonation is more than convincing. It is a shrewd, seductive portrait of duplicity."

"The horror in the world of David Cronenberg is not the easy, external horror of the slasher, but the far creepier, insidious horror of the self, of self-consciousness," declared David Breskin in *Rolling Stone.* Cronenberg told Breskin: "I . . . believe . . . that the only meaning that there is in the universe comes from the human brain." Cronenberg sees the mind as the creator of the deepest horrors but also the key to understanding and facing one's terror. Each of his films has depicted the mental world impacting on the physical world—and vice versa. Nola's mental rage created physical abomination in *The Brood,* while Seth Brundle's physical degeneration in *The Fly* made a monster of his mind. As Corliss summarized the director's work ethic: "For Cronenberg the body is a haunted house whose rumblings trigger lust, mystery, and excruciating pain in the poor tenant."

Cronenberg's exploration of the human condition is his mode of operation. He presents films that take that theme to an extreme. Some of his harsher critics have complained that Cronenberg's films are merely expositions of grotesquerie and meaningless set pieces—potentially provoking ideas that are overshadowed by a desire to shock or show-off. However, Cronenberg has defended his work, stating that because something is repulsive does not mean

that it has no place in art or is completely without merit. As he told Mary Gaitskill in *Interview:* "Everything is permitted in art. It must be. It doesn't mean that everything is permitted in society. But there has to be an arena where everything is permitted and everything is discussed from every possible angle." Much as Cronenberg has used his filmmaking to confront those things that scare him—as a kind of catharsis—he also seeks to push his audience. It is a motivation to entertain his audience, but he also wants to "go farther," to push a film into the realm of art. He described his desired effect on an audience to Breskin in *Rolling Stone:* "I want to surprise them and confound them and intrigue them and jar them out of their expectations. . . . An entertainer wants to give you exactly what you want. . . . An artist wants to give you what you *don't know* you want. Something you might know you want the next time, but you never knew you wanted before."

Cronenberg's body of work has placed him in the preeminent ranks of Canadian filmmakers. He remains private about his personal life and family, yet his name is known throughout the world for his filmmaking achievements. *Maclean's* Johnson maintains that Cronenberg "incarnates a sublimely Canadian paradox: pathology lurking in the peaceable kingdom." Arguing that Cronenberg's work embodies a traditional definition of "Canadianness," despite its adherence to non-traditional Canadian themes, William Beard opined in *Mosaic:* "Cronenberg's cinema is most 'Canadian' in its bleakness of *Affekt,* its overriding sense of defeat and powerlessness, its alienated dualism of nature against consciousness, its fearful cautiousness in the face of a hostile universe, and its powerful feelings of isolation and exclusion. The fact that these characteristics exist within a narrative context also populated by excremental sex-parasites, exploding heads, horrific cancerous transformations of the body and obsessive representations of sexual pathology should not distract one from a recognition of their determining importance." Cronenberg has always been selective in his choice of films to direct, having turned down a number of movies which became runaway hits, including *Beverly Hills Cop, Top Gun, Interview with the Vampire,* and *The Firm.* Yet he makes no apologies for his careful and discriminating practice. As the filmmaker confessed to *Saturday Night's* Collison in 1993: " 'I want it all,' says Cronenberg, at fifty. 'I want to do exactly what I want to do; I want to do it the way I want to do it; and I want to be paid extremely well.' " About the body of Cronenberg's film work, Johnson concluded in *Maclean's:* "Cronenberg has made a career out of threatening the values of middle-class North America. Yet, in his own way, he has become a kind of Canadian institution. He has achieved a strange sort of respectability. He is a director who has dealt with the Hollywood devil without selling his soul."

BIOGRAPHICAL/CRITICAL SOURCES:

BOOKS

Cronenberg, David, and Charles Edward Pogue, *The Fly* (screenplay; based on a story by George Langelaan), Paramount, 1986.

Cronenberg, *Naked Lunch* (screenplay; adapted from the novel by William S. Burroughs), Twentieth Century-Fox, 1992.

Nash, Jay Robert, and Stanley Ralph Ross, editors, *The Motion Picture Guide,* Cinebooks, 1985, pp. 305, 518, 820, 2518, 3128, 3352.

Rodley, Chris, editor, *Cronenberg on Cronenberg,* Knopf (Canada), 1992.

PERIODICALS

Film Comment, March/April, 1980, pp. 36-39, 42; January/February, 1982, pp. 2-8.

Interview, January, 1992, pp. 80-82.

Maclean's, February 14, 1983, pp. 61-63; September 13, 1993, pp. 38-41; March 13, 1995, p. 66.

Mosaic, June, 1994, pp. 113-33.

Nation, October 31, 1988, pp. 431-32.

New Republic, November 1, 1993, pp. 26, 28.

Newsweek, February 14, 1983, pp. 85-86; August 18, 1986, p. 59.

New York, August 25, 1986, pp. 100-04.

New York Times, December 27, 1991, pp. C1, 14; March 25, 1994, p. D17.

Quill and Quire, April, 1992, p. 29.

Rolling Stone, February 6, 1992, pp. 68-70, 96.

Saturday Night, October, 1986, pp. 40-50; September, 1993, pp. 42-47.

Time, January 26, 1981, p. 60; August 18, 1986, p. 75; September 26, 1988, p. 84; December 30, 1991, p. 72; October 4, 1993, p. 85.

Times Literary Supplement, June 10, 1994, p. 35.*

—*Sketch by David M. Galens*

D

DAMORE, Leo 1929-

PERSONAL: Born October 20, 1929, in Port Colbourne, Ontario, Canada; came to United States in 1947, naturalized citizen, 1968; son of Nick (a barber) and Carmen (DeAngelo) Damore; married Dorothea Bush, October 15, 1955 (divorced, 1969); married June King Davison August 11, 1973; children: Leslie Joy, Charles Edward, Nicholas John. *Education:* Kent State University, B.A., 1952. *Politics:* Democrat. *Religion:* Roman Catholic.

ADDRESSES: Home—No. 1 Pickwick Ln., Old Saybrook, CT 06475.*Agent*—Luciann Goldberg, 255 West 84th St., New York, NY.

CAREER: Cape Cod News, Hyannis, MA, reporter, 1969-74, author of column "Current Events," 1976—; TRG Communications Consultants, North Branford, CT, communications consultant. Has also worked as bank clerk, menswear buyer, mason tender, and salesman.

AWARDS, HONOURS: Best editorial of the year award from New England Newspaper Alliance, 1974, for "Epitaph for Carrol Fonseca."

WRITINGS:

The Cape Cod Years of John Fitzgerald Kennedy, Prentice-Hall, 1967.
The "Crime" of Dorothy Sheridan, Arbor House, 1978.
Cache (novel), Arbor House, 1980.
In His Garden: The Anatomy of a Murderer (Literary Guild and Doubleday Book Club selections), Arbor House, 1981.
Senatorial Privilege: The Chappaquiddick Cover-Up (Literary Guild and Doubleday Book Club selections), Regnery Gateway, 1988.

Contributor of stories to *Cosmopolitan, Redbook,* and *Ellery Queen Mystery Magazine.*

WORK IN PROGRESS: Burden of Guilt: The Murder of Mary Pinchot Meyer.

SIDELIGHTS: Leo Damore learned his craft by serving as a reporter for the *Cape Cod News,* and most of his nonfiction concerns that community on the Atlantic seaboard. A longtime resident of Cape Cod, Damore has been able to develop and sustain contacts there who have provided him with a wealth of information on some of the region's most sensational events. A *Publishers Weekly* reviewer notes that Damore's "fine blend of research and on-the-spot witnessing" makes his work "as compelling as the most imaginative fiction."

Though presented from a local angle, Damore's books are case studies of moral and psychological issues—human dramas in which people are called upon to make hard choices and face the consequences of their actions. One such work is *The "Crime" of Dorothy Sheridan,* published in 1978. Mrs. Sheridan, a devout Christian Scientist, was convicted of manslaughter when her young daughter died of pneumonia. The distraught mother claimed that she was following her church's teachings when she consulted Christian Scientist practitioners rather than a medical doctor. Damore's account of the trial raises questions about freedom of religion and its relationship to state law, but it is also a personal tale of one family's agony. "Damore's account has the taut, spare tone of a mystery novel and maintains a detached and magisterial air throughout," writes Robert Kirsch in the *Los Angeles Times.* " . . . There are many complex questions raised in the course of the work and lucidly discussed. But it is the cast of characters and the human drama which compels reading."

Damore's 1988 book *Senatorial Privilege: The Chappaquiddick Cover-Up*—his first bestseller—offers a comprehensive investigation of Cape Cod's biggest scandal, the automobile accident that killed Mary Jo Kopechne and dashed the presidential hopes of Edward Kennedy. A painstakingly researched and detailed account of the crash and its aftermath, *Senatorial Privilege* spent nineteen weeks on the *New York Times* hardcover bestseller lists. Damore was particularly gratified by the book's success because his original publisher, Random House, not only refused to release the work but also sued the author for return of an advance payment. Damore's faith in the project enabled him to find another publisher, Regnery Gateway, and a large mainstream audience based more on word of mouth than on book reviews. The book was also a bestseller in paperback in 1989.

Senatorial Privilege offers a chilling appraisal of the Chappaquiddick incident based on candid interviews with some of Edward Kennedy's closest advisors. *Wall Street Journal* contributor David Brooks notes that Damore "is a disciplined and relentless writer who makes his case more devastating because he never steps back and editorializes. Each falsehood, blunder and evasion is in tight focus, and in the conglomeration of details the bigger issues emerge. One sees a group of prominent men who are blindly devoted to a Kennedy image that they themselves manufactured decades before. One also sees a group of lawyers and advisers who act as if they are too sophisticated for the truth." A *People* magazine reviewer calls the book "an achievement of reportorial diligence," adding: ". . . Random House may have thought the book too hot to handle; readers will find it hard to put down." Likewise, *National Review* correspondent Jeffrey Hart concludes: "At last we seem to have the whole truth about what happened at Chappaquiddick . . . and it's as ghastly as you always surmised. . . . [*Senatorial Privilege*] is one helluva book, exciting as the fastest-paced mystery novel, but at the same time utterly responsible, thorough, and convincing."

Damore told *CA:* "My career as a writer has been a very difficult one. From 1967 when I published *The Cape Cod Years of John Fitzgerald Kennedy* to 1978 when *The 'Crime' of Dorothy Sheridan* appeared, I published nothing, although I was agented and writing well. The singular accomplishment here is not finally publishing, but rather, persevering in the face of overwhelming discouragement to continue writing. I learned a valuable lesson from those years: every career is self-generating. One cannot depend on the encouragement of others to make a career viable. Once the commitment is made, the writing should be enough. To publish is, of course, the goal of every writer, but it cannot be the only goal."

"Robertson Davies, the Canadian man of letters, told me a strong moral backbone supports my work, that I write of the moral choices people must make in their lives and the consequences of these choices . . . made or not made . . . and on examination of my work I find his judgment

to be correct, although I do not consciously point to any moral, or seek to 'preach' in my work."

BIOGRAPHICAL/CRITICAL SOURCES:

BOOKS

Bestsellers 89, Issue 2, Gale, 1989.

PERIODICALS

American Spectator, August, 1988.
Los Angeles Times, November 13, 1978.
National Review, November 7, 1988.
New York Times, November 5, 1987; July 18, 1989.
New York Times Book Review, October 23, 1988.
People, October 3, 1988.
Publishers Weekly, June 5, 1978.
Wall Street Journal, August 16, 1989.
Washington Post Book World, July 23, 1989.

*   *   *

DANIELLS, Roy 1902-1979

PERSONAL: Born April 6, 1902, in London, England; emigrated to Canada in 1910; died April 13, 1979; son of James (a builder) and Constance Daniells; married Laurenda Francis, 1948; children: Susan, Sara. *Education:* University of British Columbia, B.A., 1930; University of Toronto, M.A., 1931, Ph.D., 1936.

CAREER: Victoria College, Toronto, Ontario, lecturer, 1934-37; University of Manitoba, Winnipeg, head of the department of English, 1937-46; University of British Columbia, Vancouver, head of the department of English, 1948-65, professor, 1965-74.

MEMBER: Royal Society of Canada (fellow; president, 1970-71).

AWARDS, HONOURS: LL.D., University of Toronto, 1964, Queen's University, Kingston, Ontario; Lorne Pierce medal, 1970; named Companion of the Order of Canada, 1972; also holds honorary degrees from McMaster University and the Universities of New Brunswick, Windsor, and British Columbia.

WRITINGS:

(Editor) Thomas Traherne, *A Serious and Pathetical Contemplation of the Mercies of God, in Several Most Devout and Sublime Thanksgivings for the Same . . .* (poetry), University of Toronto Press, 1941.
Deeper into the Forest (poetry), McClelland & Stewart, 1948.
(Contributor) J. Park, editor, *The Culture of Contemporary Canada,* Cornell University Press, 1957.
The Chequered Shade (poetry), McClelland & Stewart, 1963.

Milton, Mannerism, and Baroque, University of Toronto Press, 1963.

(Contributor and associate editor) S. F. Klinck, editor, *Literary History of Canada*, University of Toronto Press, 1965.

Alexander Mackenzie and the North West, Barnes & Noble, 1969.

(With others) *John Milton: Introductions,* edited by John Broadbeat, Cambridge University Press, 1973.

Represented in anthologies, including *Canadian Poetry in English*, edited by B. Carman and others, Ryerson Press, 1954; *Blasted Pine*, edited by F. R. Scott and A. J. M. Smith, Macmillan (Toronto), 1957; *Oxford Book of Canadian Verse in English and French*, selected and introduced by A. J. M. Smith, Oxford University Press, 1960; *Penguin Book of Canadian Verse*, compiled by Ralph Gustafson, Penguin (Harmondsworth), 1967. Contributor of poetry to periodicals, including *Fiddlehead, Canadian Literature, University of Toronto Quarterly, Dalhousie Review*; contributor of scholarly articles and reviews to learned journals in Canada and the United States.

SIDELIGHTS: Roy Daniells distinguished himself as both a poet and a literary critic. He was born in London, England, in 1902 and immigrated to Canada with his family in 1910. He graduated from the University of British Columbia in 1930 and earned a doctorate from the University of Toronto in 1936. In the ensuing decade Daniells taught at Victoria College and the University of Manitoba. While at Manitoba Daniells published his first book, editing a new edition of Thomas Traherne's *A Serious and Pathetical Contemplation of the Mercies of God, in Several Most Devout and Sublime Thanksgivings for the Same*. . . . The title of this work serves as an apt indication of Daniells's own religious interests, which he expresses in his verse.

In 1948 Daniells joined the faculty of the University of British Columbia, where he served as head of the English department until 1965. In 1948 Daniells also published his first poetry collection, *Deeper into the Forest*. The volume is comprised mainly of sonnets, Daniells's preferred poetic form, but it also contains "Farewell to Winnipeg," which is structured in quatrains. In this poem, as George Woodcock noted in the *Dictionary of Literary Biography*, "the folk hero Louis Riel becomes the center of a complex meditation on the threatened world in modern times."

When Daniells published *Deeper into the Forest* he was already forty-six years old. He followed that volume with only one more poetry collection, *The Chequered Shade*, which appeared in 1963. In this work Daniells again concentrated on the sonnet form. Many of the poems here are rooted in Biblical texts, notably the Psalms and the New Testament, and though they often focus on the inevitably

excruciating nature of human existence, they do so in a manner marked by sympathy and, moreover, humor.

In terms of technique, both *Deeper into the Forest* and *The Chequered Shade* bear the influence of earlier English masters, notably John Milton, and thus establish Daniells within the tradition of religious poets. A closer reading of both volumes, however, reveals a breadth of scope consistent with Daniells's other interests, including Canadian history and literature of both the nineteenth and twentieth centuries.

Although he is probably best known for his poetry, Daniells—befitting his career as an English professor—also proved himself adept in literary criticism. In 1963 he published *Milton, Mannerism, and Baroque,* in which he traced the great poet John Milton's interests in Italian art and culture. Several years later Daniells also collaborated with others on the volume *John Milton: Introductions,* which was edited by John Broadbeat.

Aside from his poetry collections and his Milton-related publications, Daniells wrote *Alexander Mackenzie and the North West,* a 1969 work that George Woodcock, in his *Dictionary of Literary Biography* entry on Daniells, described as "an excursion into Canadian history." Daniells also served as an associate editor of the 1965 publication *Literary History of Canada.*

In addition to his books, Daniells produced several essays, ranging in subject from Thomas Traherne—author of the aforementioned *Serious and Pathetic Contemplation of the Mercies of God*—to Canadian literature of the previous century.

Throughout his career in literature and academia, Daniells received substantial recognition for his various achievements. He was accorded honorary degrees from various Canadian institutions, including the Universities of Toronto and Windsor, and in 1970 he was given the Lorne Pierce Medal. Two years later Daniells was named a Companion of the Order of Canada.

BIOGRAPHICAL/CRITICAL SOURCES:

BOOKS

Dictionary of Literary Biography, Volume 68: *Canadian Writers, 1920-1959, First Series,* Gale, 1988.

PERIODICALS

British Columbia Library Quarterly, July, 1960.*

DAVIES, (William) Robertson 1913-
Samuel Marchbanks

PERSONAL: Born August 28, 1913, in Thamesville, Ontario, Canada; son of William Rupert (a publisher) and Florence Sheppard (McKay) Davies; married Brenda Matthews, February 2, 1940; children: Miranda, Jennifer (Mrs. C. T. Surridge), Rosamund (Mrs. John Cunnington). *Education:* Attended Upper Canada College, Toronto, and Queen's University at Kingston; Balliol College, Oxford, B.Litt., 1938.

ADDRESSES: Home—40 Oaklands Ave., Suite 303, Toronto, Ontario, Canada M4V 2Z3.*Office*—Massey College, University of Toronto, 4 Devonshire Pl., Toronto, Ontario, Canada M5S 2E1.*Agent*—Curtis Brown Ltd., 10 Astor Pl., New York, NY 10003.

CAREER: Old Vic Company, London, England, teacher and actor, 1938-40; *Saturday Night,* Toronto, Ontario, literary editor, 1940-42; *Examiner,* Peterborough, Ontario, editor and publisher, 1942-62; University of Toronto, Toronto, professor of English, 1960-81, master of Massey College, 1962-81, emeritus professor and master, 1981—. Also worked as a newspaperman for the Kingston Whig Standard (Ontario). Senator, Stratford Shakespeare Festival, Stratford, Ontario.

MEMBER: Royal Society of Canada (fellow), Playwrights Union of Canada, Royal Society of Literature (fellow), American Academy and Institute of Arts and Letters (honorary member), Authors Guild, Authors League of America, Dramatists Guild, Writers' Union (Canada), PEN International.

AWARDS, HONOURS: Louis Jouvet Prize for directing, Dominion Drama Festival, 1949; Stephen Leacock Medal for Humour, 1954, for *Leaven of Malice;* LL.D., University of Alberta, 1957, Queen's University, 1962, University of Manitoba, 1972, University of Calgary, 1975, and University of Toronto, 1981; D.Litt., McMaster University, 1959, University of Windsor, 1971, York University, 1973, Mount Allison University, 1973, Memorial University of Newfoundland, 1974, University of Western Ontario, 1974, McGill University, 1974, Trent University, 1974, University of Lethbridge, 1981, University of Waterloo, 1981, University of British Columbia, 1983, and University of Santa Clara, 1985; Lorne Pierce Medal, Royal Society of Canada, 1961; D.C.L., Bishop's University, 1967; Companion of the Order of Canada, 1972; Governor General's Award for fiction, 1973, for *The Manticore;* D.Hum. Litt., University of Rochester, 1983; honorary fellow of Balliol College, Oxford, 1986, and Trinity College, University of Toronto, 1987; City of Toronto Book Award, 1986; Canadian Authors Association Literary Award for Fiction, 1986, for *What's Bred in the Bone; What's Bred in the Bone* was shortlisted for Booker Prize,

1986; Banff Centre School of Fine Arts National Award, 1986; Lifetime Achievement Award from Toronto Arts Awards, 1986; Gold Medal of Honor for Literature from National Arts Club (New York), 1987; World Fantasy Convention Award for *High Spirits.*

WRITINGS:

THE "SALTERTON TRILOGY"; NOVELS

Tempest-Tost, Clarke, Irwin, 1951; Rinehart, 1952; reprinted, Penguin, 1980.
Leaven of Malice, Clarke, Irwin, 1954; Scribners, 1955; reprinted, Penguin, 1980.
A Mixture of Frailties, Scribners, 1958; reprinted, Penguin, 1980.
The Salterton Trilogy (contains *Tempest-Tost, Leaven of Malice,* and *A Mixture of Frailties*), Penguin, 1986.

THE "DEPTFORD TRILOGY"; NOVELS

Fifth Business, Viking, 1970.
The Manticore, Viking, 1972.
World of Wonders, Macmillan (Toronto), 1975; Viking, 1976.
The Deptford Trilogy (contains *Fifth Business, The Manticore,* and *World of Wonders*), Penguin, 1985.

THE "CORNISH TRILOGY"; NOVELS

The Rebel Angels, Viking, 1982.
What's Bred in the Bone, Viking, 1985.
The Lyre of Orpheus, Viking, 1988.

OTHER FICTION

High Spirits (stories), Viking, 1983.
Murther & Walking Spirits (novel), Viking, 1991.
The Cunning Man (novel), McClelland & Stewart, 1994.

NONFICTION

Shakespeare's Boy Actors, Dent, 1939, Russell, 1964.
Shakespeare for Young Players: A Junior Course, Clarke, Irwin, 1942.
The Diary of Samuel Marchbanks (collection of newspaper pieces originally published under pseudonym Samuel Marchbanks), Clarke, Irwin, 1947.
The Table Talk of Samuel Marchbanks (collection of newspaper pieces originally published under pseudonym Samuel Marchbanks), Clarke, Irwin, 1949.
(With Tyrone Guthrie and Grant Macdonald) *Renown at Stratford: A Record of the Shakespearean Festival in Canada,* Clarke, Irwin, 1953, new edition, 1971.
(With Guthrie and Macdonald) *Twice Have the Trumpets Sounded: A Record of the Stratford Shakespearean Festival in Canada,* Clarke, Irwin, 1954.
(With Guthrie, Boyd Neal, and Tanya Moiseiwitsch) *Thrice the Brinded Cat Hath Mew'd: A Record of the*

Stratford Shakespearean Festival in Canada, Clarke, Irwin, 1955.

A Voice from the Attic, Knopf, 1960 (published in England as *The Personal Art: Reading to Good Purpose,* Secker & Warburg, 1961, reprinted, Darby Books, 1983).

Le Jeu de centenaire, Comission du Centenaire, c. 1967.

Samuel Marchbanks' Almanack (collection of newspaper pieces originally published under pseudonym Samuel Marchbanks), McClelland & Stewart, 1967.

The Heart of a Merry Christmas, Macmillan (Toronto), 1970.

Stephen Leacock, McClelland & Stewart, 1970.

(Editor and author of introduction) *Feast of Stephen: An Anthology of Some of the Less Familiar Writings of Stephen Leacock,* McClelland & Stewart, 1970.

(With Michael R. Booth, Richard Southern, Frederick Marker, and Lise-Lone Marker) *The Revels History of Drama in English, Volume VI: 1750-1880,* Methuen, 1975.

One Half of Robertson Davies: Provocative Pronouncements on a Wide Range of Topics, Macmillan (Toronto), 1977, published as *One Half of Robertson Davies,* Viking, 1978.

The Enthusiasms of Robertson Davies, edited by Judith Skelton Grant, McClelland & Stewart, 1979.

(Contributor) Robert G. Lawrence and Samuel L. Macey, editors, *Studies in Robertson Davies' Deptford Trilogy,* English Literary Studies, University of Victoria, 1980.

The Well-Tempered Critic: One Man's View of Theatre and Letters in Canada, edited by Grant, McClelland & Stewart, 1981.

The Mirror of Nature (lectures), University of Toronto Press, 1983.

The Papers of Samuel Marchbanks (contains portions of *The Diary of Samuel Marchbanks, The Table Talk of Samuel Marchbanks,* and *Samuel Marchbanks' Almanack*), Irwin Publishing, 1985, Viking, 1986.

PLAYS

Fortune, My Foe (first produced in Kingston, Ontario, by the International Players, 1948), Clarke, Irwin, 1949.

Eros at Breakfast and Other Plays (contains "Eros at Breakfast" [first produced in Montreal, Quebec, at the Montreal Repertory Theatre, 1948], "Overlaid" [first produced in Peterborough, Ontario, at Peterborough Little Theatre, 1947], "The Voice of the People" [first produced in Montreal at the Montreal Repertory Theatre, 1948], "At the Gates of the Righteous" [first produced in Peterborough at the Peterborough Little Theatre, 1948], and "Hope Deferred" [first produced in Montreal at the Montreal Repertory Theatre, 1948]), with introduction by Tyrone Guthrie, Clarke, Irwin, 1949, revised edition published as *Four Favorite Plays,* 1968.

At My Heart's Core (first produced in Peterborough at the Peterborough Little Theatre, 1950), Clarke, Irwin, 1952.

A Masque of Aesop (first produced in Toronto, Ontario, at Upper Canada College, May, 1952), Clarke, Irwin, 1952.

A Jig for the Gypsy (first produced in Toronto at the Crest Theatre, 1954), Clarke, Irwin, 1955.

Love and Libel (based on *Leaven of Malice;* first produced in Toronto at the Royal Alexandra Theatre, November, 1960; first produced on Broadway at the Martin Beck Theatre, December, 1960), Studio Duplicating Service, 1960.

A Masque of Mr. Punch (first produced in Toronto at Upper Canada College, 1962), Oxford University Press, 1963.

The Voice of the People, Book Society of Canada, 1968.

Hunting Stuart and Other Plays (contains "Hunting Stuart" [first produced in Toronto at the Crest Theatre, 1955], "King Phoenix" [first produced in Peterborough, 1950], and "General Confession"), New Press, 1972.

"Brothers in the Black Art," first produced on Canadian Broadcasting Corporation, 1974.

Question Time (first produced in Toronto at the St. Lawrence Center, 1975), Macmillan, 1975.

"Pontiac and the Green Man," first produced in Toronto at the Macmillan Theatre, 1977.

OTHER

Columnist under pseudonym Samuel Marchbank.

SIDELIGHTS: The *Deptford Trilogy*—consisting of the novels *Fifth Business, The Manticore,* and *World of Wonders*—has brought Robertson Davies to international attention as one of Canada's leading men of letters. "These novels," Claude Bissell writes in *Canadian Literature,* "comprise the major piece of prose fiction in Canadian literature—in scope, in the constant interplay of wit and intelligence, in the persistent attempt to find a pattern in this[, as Davies states in the trilogy,] 'life of marvels, cruel circumstances, obscenities, and commonplaces.' "

The trilogy traces the lives of three Canadian men from the small town of Deptford, Ontario, who are bound together by a single tragic event from their childhood. At the age of ten, Dunstan Ramsay and Percy "Boy" Staunton are throwing snowballs at one another. Staunton throws a snowball at Ramsay which contains a rock. Ramsay ducks. The snowball strikes Mrs. Mary Dempster in the head, causing her to give birth prematurely to a son, Paul Dempster, and to have a mental breakdown that ends in her permanent hospitalization. Each novel of the trilogy revolves around this tragedy and deals primarily with one of the three men involved: *Fifth Business* with Dunstan

Ramsay, who becomes a teacher; *The Manticore* with Boy Staunton, a politician; and *World of Wonders* with Paul Dempster, a stage magician. "*Fifth Business* provides the brickwork," John Alwyne writes in the *New Statesman,* "the two later volumes, the lath and plaster. But what a magnificent building is the result. [The trilogy] bears comparison with any fiction of the last decade."

Davies did not intend to write a trilogy when he first began *Fifth Business.* His initial story idea prompted him to write the novel, he tells *Time* (Canada), "but found almost as soon as had finished it that wasn't all wanted to say." So Davies wrote *The Manticore* to tell more of his story. Reviewers then asked "to hear about the magician who appeared in the other two novels," Davies explains, "and I thought 'Well, I know a lot about magicians' and I wrote the third book."

Despite the unplanned development of the trilogy, it has garnered extensive critical praise and each volume has been an international bestseller. The first volume, *Fifth Business,* is, Sam Solecki maintains in *Canadian Forum,* "Davies' masterpiece and . . . among the handful of Canadian novels that count." In the form of an autobiographical letter written by Dunstan Ramsay upon his retirement, the novel delineates the course of Ramsay's life and how it was shaped by the pivotal snowball incident. Because he avoided being hit, and thereby caused Mrs. Dempster's injury, Ramsay has lived his life suffering under a tremendous guilt. This guilt inspired an interest in hagiology, the study of saints, and Ramsay becomes in later years the foremost Protestant authority on the lives of the saints. "All the lore on saints and myth," Judith Skelton Grant states in *Book Forum,* "is firmly connected to the central character, reflecting his interests, showing how he thinks, influencing his life, and playing a part in his interpretation of events." It is in terms of hagiology that Ramsay eventually comes to a realization about himself. His autobiographical letter finally "leads Ramsay to comprehension of his own nature—which is not saintly," John Skow reports in *Time.*

Much of this same story is reexamined in *The Manticore,* the second novel of the trilogy, which takes place after the mysterious death of prominent Canadian politician Boy Staunton. Staunton has been found drowned in his car at the bottom of Lake Ontario, a rock in his mouth. Investigation proves the rock to be the same one that Staunton threw at Mrs. Dempster some sixty years before. Ramsay, obsessed with the incident, had saved it. But how Staunton died, and why he had the rock in his mouth, is unknown. During a performance by the magician Magnus Eisengrim (Paul Dempster's stage name), a floating brass head is featured that answers questions from the audience. Staunton's son David asks the head an explosive question, "Who killed Boy Staunton?" In the tumult caused by his

outburst, David runs from the theater. His breakdown and subsequent Jungian psychoanalysis in Switzerland make up the rest of the novel. During his analysis, David comes to terms with his late father's career. "The blend of masterly characterization, cunning plot, shifting point of view, and uncommon detail, all fixed in the clearest, most literate prose, is superbly achieved," writes Pat Barclay in *Canadian Literature.*

The life story of Paul Dempster is told in *World of Wonders,* the final volume of the trilogy. As a young boy, Dempster is kidnapped by a homosexual stage magician while visiting a travelling carnival. Dempster stays with the carnival as it makes its way across Canada, intent on becoming a magician himself by learning the secrets of the man who abducted him. While learning the trade, Dempster works inside a mechanical fortune-telling gypsy, operating the gears that make it seem lifelike. When the carnival breaks up, Dempster heads for Europe where he finds work as a double for a popular stage actor. With his knowledge of magic and the stage manner he has acquired from the theater people he knows, Dempster strikes out on his own as a magician, becoming one of the most successful acts on the continent. *World of Wonders,* Michael Mewshaw states in the *New York Times Book Review,* is "a novel of stunning verbal energy and intelligence." L. J. Davis of *New Republic* believes the novel's "situation is shamelessly contrived, and the language fairly reeks of the footlights (to say nothing of, yes, brimstone)." Furthermore, Davis contends that *World of Wonders* "isn't so much a novel as it is a brilliant act whose strength lies in the complexity of its symbolism and the perfection of its artifice." It is, Davis judges, "a splendid conclusion" to the trilogy.

In each of these novels the lead character undergoes a psychological transformation. Dunstan Ramsay finds the key to himself in the study of saints and myth, using these archetypes for greater self-understanding. David Staunton relies on Jungian psychoanalysis to help him in discovering his true nature and in coming to terms with his father's disreputable life and mysterious death. Paul Dempster learns from his work as a magician and his life in the theater about reality and illusion, gaining insight into his own personality. The three novels are, Bissell explains, "essentially parts of a whole: three parallel pilgrimages." Grant, too, sees the essential search in which the three characters are engaged. She believes they explore different aspects of nature, however. "Dunstan moves toward God and Boy toward the Devil," Grant writes, "[while Dempster] experiences both." This experience of both good and evil, Grant believes, allows those dark aspects of the mind to be exposed and confronted. "Not everything that has been labeled Evil proves to be so," Grant states, "nor all that has been repressed ought to remain so. And the genuinely evil and justifiably banished are weaker if faced and understood." Grant believes that "together with the vigorous, lively and eccentric narrators of the [Deptford] trilogy, these moral, . . . mythic and psychological ideas have given these books a place among the dozen significant works of fiction published in Canada during the seventies." Peter S. Prescott, writing in *Newsweek,* sees the revelations of the three characters in similar terms. Davies, he writes, "means to recharge the world with a wonder it has lost, to re-create through the intervention of saints and miracles, psychoanalysts and sleight-of-hand a proper sense of awe at life's mystery and a recognition of the price that must be paid for initiation into that mystery."

Davies's 1994 novel *The Cunning Man* "is as substantial and as entertaining as any he has written," claims Isabel Colegate in the *New York Times Book Review.* According to Paul Gray in *Time,* "Canada's foremost living author . . . entertains with an old-fashioned fictional mixture that he seems to have invented anew: keen social observations delivered with wit, intelligence and free-floating philosophical curiosity." John Bemrose contends in *Maclean's* that "*The Cunning Man* takes the form of a memoir, but it reads more like an extended monologue by its narrator, Dr. Jonathan Hullah, a Toronto doctor nearing the end of his career." An aging physician who has assented to a series of interviews with a reporter writing a number of articles about "old Toronto," Hullah employs a notebook to separate his public reminiscences from his private reflections—those snippets of information and fact he agrees to reveal in print and those, some of which pertain to incidents in his own background, he prefers to reserve exclusively to himself. As the notebook containing his personal thoughts and musings grows, he realizes he is actually recording and defining his own character analysis, a true lifetime retrospective. Although as a physician Hullah relies on scientific observation and qualitative inquiry, he combines his diagnostic approach with consideration of other factors, including psychological and spiritual elements. In an interview with Mel Gussow in the *New York Times Book Review,* the reviewer notes, "Mr. Davies has said he is 'a moralist possessed by humor,' a description that would serve equally for Dr. Hullah, who, he says, 'is a moralist not because he dictates morals but because he observes what's wrong with his patients.' For both the author and the character, physical and emotional causes of disease are inseparable." As Stephen Smith describes in *Quill and Quire:* "Hullah makes his narration a guide through a landscape full of recognizable Davies landmarks. There is a suspicious death on a church altar, a miracle, a murder, a disappointment in love, and sundry asides into theatre, music, art and into the past of that most 'flat-footed, hard-breathing' of Canadian cities, Toronto, as seen from its upper crust." Colegate further comments that the novel "enlarges joyously on many of his

[the author's] familiar themes; the one that underlies all the others is his belief that religion and science, poetry and medicine, theater and psychoanalysis have a kind of meeting place where no one is quite sufficient without the others."

The recurring theme of self-discovery follows the pattern established by psychologist Carl Jung, although Davies does not adhere strictly to Jungian psychology. He has explored a number of models for "complete human identity," Patricia Monk writes in her *The Smaller Infinity: The Jungian Self in the Novels of Robertson Davies,* and though he has a "deep and long-lasting affinity with Jung, . . . Davies eventually moves beyond his affinity . . .to a more impartial assessment of Jungianism as simply one way of looking at the universe, one myth among a number of others." Still, in common with the Jungian belief in archetypal influence on the human mind, Davies presents in his fiction characters who "discover the meaning of their lives," Roger Sale writes in the *New York Review of Books,* "by discovering the ways those lives conform to ancient patterns." Peter Baltensperger, writing in *Canadian Literature,* sees this as a consistent theme in all of Davies's fiction, not only in the *Deptford Trilogy.* This theme Baltensperger defines as "the conquest of one's Self in the inner struggle and the knowledge of oneself as fully human."

Davies clarifies the primary concern in all of his work. "The theme which lies at the root of all my novels is the isolation of the human spirit," he explains. "I have not attempted to deal with it in a gloomy fashion but rather to demonstrate that what my characters do that might be called really significant is done on their own volition and usually contrary to what is expected of them. This theme is worked out in terms of characters who are trying to escape from early influences and find their own place in the world but who are reluctant to do so in a way that will bring pain and disappointment to others."

Many critics label Davies a traditionalist who is a bit old-fashioned in his approach to writing. I. M. Owen of *Saturday Night,* for example, places Davies "curiously apart from the main stream of contemporary fiction." A critic for the *Washington Post Book World* characterizes Davies as "a true novelist writing imagined stories, wonderful stories full of magic and incandescence, thought and literary art," something the critic does not find in other contemporary fiction. Davies is known as a moralist who believes in a tangible good and evil, a fine storyteller who consciously uses theatrical melodrama to enliven his plots, and a master of a wide variety of genres and styles.

Davies's strong moral sense is evident in the *Deptford Trilogy* where, Mewshaw finds, "no action is without consequences." This unflinching explication of his characters' behavior makes for "a constant, lively judging and damning of characters," as the writer for *Time* (Canada) reports. "The habit of stern judgment is missing from most modern discourse," he continues, "which tends charitably or fearfully to find excuses. But it is abundantly present in Davies's novels." These judgments are rooted in Davies's belief, Jean Strouse of *Newsweek* quotes him as saying, that "sin is the great unacknowledged element in modern life." It is sin which Davies explores in his novels, setting his characters to "grapple with magic, madness, mysticism, Gnosticism, miracles, freaks, saints, devils, Jung, Freud, God, mythic beasts, guilt, dominion and human nature."

Since he has written a number of plays, been a teacher and actor with the Old Vic Company, and served on the board of the Stratford Shakespeare Festival for many years, it is not surprising to find that Davies employs theatrical elements in his novels. He uses theatricality to move his story along at a quicker pace. In *World of Wonders,* a *Time* critic states, the characters "are brilliant talkers, but when they natter on too long, the highly theatrical author causes a grotesque face to appear at a window, drops someone through a trap door or stages a preposterous recognition scene." These melodramatic touches come naturally to Davies who, Davis remarks, "is a player in love with the play, and the kind of play he loves is melodrama." In his collection of lectures entitled *The Mirror of Nature,* Davies makes his case on behalf of melodrama and attempts, as Alberto Manguel writes in the Toronto *Globe & Mail,* "to save melodrama's lost honor." Davies argues in this book that "theatre is a coarse art. . . . It appeals immediately to primary, not secondary elements in human nature." Melodrama's emphasis on creating an emotional response in its audience, Davies continues, is true to theatre's fundamental purpose. Manguel concludes that Davies "succeeds" in justifying his own use of melodrama.

The range of Davies's abilities is reflected not only in the variety of genres in which he has written but in his ability to move "easily from the bawdiest humor to the loftiest abstraction, charging every character and idea with power and fascination," as Mewshaw states. Davies's work in the *Deptford Trilogy,* Strouse maintains, encompasses such divergent elements as "mystery, grotesquerie, desolation and psychological sagacity." Walter E. Swayze of *Canadian Forum* notes that although Davies has written in a "diversity of styles . . . direct expression and bold colour have been constant features." Admitting that Davies is a "fine writer—deft, resourceful, diverse and . . . very funny," John Kenneth Galbraith nonetheless writes in the *New York Times Book Review* that Davies's greatest strength is "his imagination."

Calling Davies "a compellingly inventive storyteller" who has garnered an "affectionate following," James Idema of the *Chicago Tribune Book World* explains the appeal of his fiction. It lies in "his way of placing ordinary humans in the midst of extraordinary events, of bringing innocent, resolutely straight characters into contact with bonafide exotics," Idema believes. "The 'real world' interests [Davies] only as a starting point. Enigma, myth, illusion and magic are the stuff of his elegant stories." Similarly, William Kennedy observes in the *New York Times Book Review* that Davies "conveys a sense of real life lived in a fully imagined if sometimes mythical and magical world." Comparing the role of the novelist with that of the magician, because both "mean us to believe in what never happened and to this end use many conjuror's tricks," Prescott defines Davies as one writer "who takes seriously his magician's role." In doing so, Davies has become "one of the most gifted and accomplished literary entertainers now writing in English," as a writer for *Time* remarks. In a speech given at the University of Windsor and quoted by *Time* (Canada), Davies observes that "though it is always an unwise thing to say too loudly—because you never know who may be listening—I am a happy man."

BIOGRAPHICAL/CRITICAL SOURCES:

BOOKS

Anthony, Geraldine, editor, *Stage Voices: 12 Canadian Playwrights Talk about Their Lives and Work,* Doubleday, 1978.
Bestsellers 89, Issue 2, Gale, 1989.
Buitenhuis, Elspeth, *Robertson Davies,* Forum House Publishing, 1972.
Cameron, Donald, *Conversations with Canadian Novelists,* Part 1, Macmillan, 1973.
Contemporary Dramatists, 4th edition, St. James, 1988.
Contemporary Literary Criticism, Gale, Volume 2, 1974; Volume 7, 1977; Volume 13, 1980; Volume 25, 1983; Volume 42, 1987; Volume 75, 1993.
Contemporary Novelists, 5th edition, St. James, 1991.
Davis, J. Madison, editor, *Conversations with Robertson Davies,* University Press of Mississippi, 1989.
Dictionary of Literary Biography, Volume 68: *Canadian Writers, 1920-1959, First Series,* Gale, 1988.
Dooley, D.J., *Moral Vision in the Canadian Novel,* Irwin, 1978.
Grant, Judith Skelton, *Robertson Davies,* McClelland & Stewart, 1978.
Grant, *Robertson Davies: Man of Myth,* Penguin, 1994.
Heath, Jeffrey M., editor, *Profiles in Canadian Literature #2,* Dundum Press, 1980.
Jones, Joseph and Johanna Jones, *Canadian Fiction,* Twayne, 1981.

King, Bruce, *The New English Literatures: Cultural Nationalism in a Changing World,* St. Martin's Press, 1980.

Klinck, Carl F., editor, *Literary History of Canada,* University of Toronto Press, 2nd edition, 1976.

Lawrence, Robert G. and Samuel L. Macey, editors, *Studies in Robertson Davies' Deptford Trilogy,* English Literary Studies, University of Victoria, 1980.

Lecker, Robert, and Jack David, editors, *The Annotated Bibliography of Canada's Major Authors,* Vol. 3, ECW Press, 1982.

Lecker, David, and Ellen Luigley, editors, *Canadian Writers and Their Works,* Vol. 6, ECW Press, 1985.

Monk, Patricia, *The Smaller Infinity: The Jungian Self in the Novels of Robertson Davies,* University of Toronto Press, 1982.

Moore, Mavor, *Four Canadian Playwrights,* Holt, 1973.

Morley, Patricia, *Robertson Davies,* Gage Educational Publishing, 1977.

Moss, John, *Sex and Violence in the Canadian Novel: The Ancestral Present,* McClelland and Stewart, 1977.

New, William H., editor, *Dramatists in Canada: Selected Essays,* University of British Columbia Press, 1972.

Peterman, Michael, *Robertson Davies,* Twayne, 1986.

Stone-Blackburn, Susan, *Robertson Davies: Playwright,* University of British Columbia Press, 1985.

Stouck, David, *Major Canadian Authors: A Critical Introduction,* University of Nebraska Press, 1984.

Sutherland, Ronald, *The New Hero: Essays in Comparative Quebec/Canadian Literature,* Macmillan, 1977.

Twigg, Alan, *For Openers: Conversations with 24 Canadian Writers,* Harbour Publishing, 1981.

Wyatt, David, *Prodigal Sons: A Study in Authorship and Authority,* Johns Hopkins University Press, 1980.

PERIODICALS

Acta Victoriana, 97, Number 2, 1973.
America, December 16, 1972.
American Spectator, May, 1989.
Ariel, July, 1979.
Atlantic, June, 1993.
Book Forum, Volume 4, Number 1, 1978.
Books in Canada, November, 1985; August, 1988.
Book World, December 13, 1970.
Canadian Drama, 7, No. 2, 1981 (special Davies issue).
Canadian Forum, June, 1950; December, 1975; October, 1977; December-January, 1981-82; February-March, 1989; November, 1991.
Canadian Literature, Spring, 1960; Winter, 1961; Winter, 1967; Spring, 1973; Winter, 1974; Winter, 1976; Spring, 1982; Winter, 1986.
Canadian Review, Fall, 1976.
Essays on Canadian Writing, Winter, 1984-1985.
Chicago Tribune, July 26, 1986.

Chicago Tribune Book World, January 31, 1982.
Christian Century, February 1, 1989; January 29, 1992.
Christian Science Monitor, July 14, 1986.
Commonweal, December 20, 1985.
Dalhousie Review, Autumn, 1981; Fall, 1986.
Design for Arts in Education, May-June, 1989
Detroit Free Press, January 22, 1989; February 6, 1989.
Economist, June 30, 1990.
English Studies in Canada, March, 1986; March, 1990.
Essays on Canadian Writing, Spring, 1977; Winter 1977-1978; Spring, 1987; Fall, 1989.
Financial Post, January 19, 1963.
Globe & Mail (Toronto), March 5, 1977; January 7, 1984; September 10, 1988; September 17, 1988.
Insight on the News, September 17, 1990.
Interview, March, 1989.
Journal of Canadian Fiction, Winter, 1972;3, no. 3, 1974; Winter, 1982.
Journal of Canadian Studies, November, 1974; February, 1977 (special Davies issue).
Journal of Commonwealth Literature, 22, Number 1, 1987.
Library Journal, January, 1989; January, 1990; October 1, 1991; April 1, 1992.
Library Quarterly, April, 1969.
Listener, April 15, 1971.
London Review of Books, November 10. 1988.
Los Angeles Times, January 29, 1982.
Los Angeles Times Book Review, December 1, 1985; January 29, 1989; January 30, 1989.
Maclean's, March 15, 1952; September, 1972; November 18, 1985; October 19, 1987; September 12, 1988; December 26, 1988; September 23, 1991.
Nation, April 24, 1982; October 24, 1994, p. 54.
New Republic, March 13, 1976; April 15, 1978; March 10, 1982; December 30, 1985; April, 24 1989.
New Statesman, April 20, 1973; April 4, 1980; October 14, 1988; November 22, 1991.
Newsweek, January 18, 1971; March 22, 1976; February 8, 1982.
New Yorker, January 27, 1986; February 10, 1992.
New York Review of Books, February 8, 1973; February 27, 1986; April 13, 1989.
New York Times, February 8, 1982; November 6, 1985; December 28, 1988; December 29, 1988.
New York Times Book Review, December 20, 1970; November 19, 1972; April 25, 1976; February 14, 1982; December 15, 1985; October 30, 1988; January 8, 1989; November 17, 1991; December 1, 1991; February 5, 1995, pp. 1, 23, 24.
Observer (London) May 31, 1987; October 2, 1988.
Performing Arts & Entertainment, Summer, 1992.
Publishers Weekly, October 14, 1988; February 2, 1990; September 6, 1991; January 25, 1993.

Queen's Quarterly, Spring, 1986.

Quill & Quire, August, 1988; September, 1994, pp. 1, 59, 62, 64.

Rolling Stone, December 1, 1977.

San Francisco Review of Books, Spring, 1987.

Saturday Night, April 26, 1947; December 13, 1947; February 14, 1953; November, 1967; October, 1985; December, 1987; August, 1988; October, 1988; November, 1990; October, 1991.

Saturday Review, December 26, 1970; April 3, 1976.

Spectator, August 21, 1982; October 8, 1988.

Studies in Canadian Literature, Winter, 1978; 7, No. 2, 1982; 12, No. 1, 1987.

Sunday Times, September 1991.

Tamarack Review, Autumn, 1958.

Time, January 11, 1971; May 17, 1976; December 26, 1988; March 13, 1995, pp. 100-01.

Time (Canada), November 3, 1975.

Times Literary Supplement, March 26, 1982; February 28, 1986; October 16, 1987; September 23, 1988.

Tribune Books, December 25, 1988.

University of Toronto Quarterly, Number 21, 1952.

U.S. News & World Report, January 16, 1989.

Wall Street Journal, July 15, 1986.

Washington Post, January 11, 1989.

Washington Post Book World, May 30, 1976; February 7, 1982; October 30, 1983; November 17, 1985; July 20, 1986; June 5, 1988; December 18, 1988.

World Press Review, November, 1988.*

*   *   *

DAVIS, Reuben
See SHIP, Reuben

*   *   *

DEACON, William Arthur   1890-1977

PERSONAL: Born April 6, 1890, in Pembroke, Ontario; died following a long illness, August 5, 1977; son of William Henry (a lawyer) and Sarah Annie (Davies) Deacon; married Gladys Coon, 1911 (divorced); married Sally Townsend Syme, c. 1923; children: (second marriage) William, Deirdre, Mary. *Education:* Attended Victoria College, University of Toronto; University of Manitoba, LL.B., 1918. *Religion:* Member of the Theosophical Society. *Avocational interests:* Letter writing, especially to aspiring authors.

CAREER: Pitblado Law Firm, Winnipeg, Manitoba, until 1922; *Manitoba Free Press,* Dauphin, Manitoba, assistant literary editor, 1921-22; *Saturday Night,* Toronto, On-

tario, literary editor, 1922-28; *Mail and Empire* (later the *Globe and Mail*), Toronto, began as editor, 1928-36, then literary editor, 1936-60, and news and gossip columnist, 1961-63. Canadian Authors' Association, charter member, 1921, Toronto Branch president, c. 1930, national president, 1946-48; Canadian Writers' Foundation, chair, 1944-49; Governor General's Awards, chair, 1944-49. Founder of Stephen Leacock Medal for Humour.

WRITINGS:

Pens and Pirates (essays), Ryerson (Toronto), 1923.

Peter McArthur, Ryerson (Toronto), 1923.

Poteen: A Pot-pourri of Canadian Essays, Graphic (Ottawa), 1926.

The Four Jameses, Graphic (Ottawa), 1927; revised edition, Ryerson (Toronto), 1953, republished, Macmillan (Toronto), 1974.

My Vision of Canada, Ontario Publishing (Toronto), 1933.

(Editor, with Wilfred Reeves) *Open House* (essays), Graphic (Ottawa), 1933.

Dear Bill: The Correspondence of William Arthur Deacon, edited by John Lennox and Michele Lacombe, University of Toronto Press (Toronto), c. 1988.

Author of the pamphlet *Sh-h-h . . . here comes the censor,* 1940. Also author of "Literature in Canada—in its Centenary Year," in *Yearbook of the Arts in Canada,* edited by Bertram Brooker, Macmillan, 1929; and "What a Canadian Has Done for Canada," in *Our Sense of Identity,* edited by Malcolm Ross, Ryerson, 1954; contributor of essays and critical reviews to numerous periodicals, including the *New York Times, New York Post, Manitoba Free Press, Canadian Magazine, Saturday Review of Literature,* and the *American Mercury.*

Deacon's manuscript collection is housed in the Thomas Fisher Rare Book Library of the University of Toronto. A computerized index of Deacon's papers, prepared by Michele Lacombe, John Lennox, and Clara Thomas, is available at the Scott Library, York University.

SIDELIGHTS: William Arthur Deacon was an influential essayist and journalist, and boasted the distinction of being Canada's first full-time literary journalist. Educated as a lawyer at the University of Manitoba, Deacon worked only briefly in law, choosing instead a vocation in journalism—for four decades he was the leading literary reviewer in Canada. Deacon gained a reputation for his clear, direct style as a critic, his activism in the development of promising authors through personal correspondence, and a lifelong alliance with the Canadian Authors' Association (CAA), a group dedicated to the development of Canadian literature.

Born on April 6, 1890 in Pembroke, Ontario, Canada, Deacon and his mother, Sarah, moved shortly thereafter to her parents' home in Quebec when Deacon's father died. Until 1907 the boy attended a Methodist boarding school, Stanstead College, where his uncle was principal. Deacon then enrolled at Victoria College in Toronto but quit two years later without completing degree requirements. Within the next few years, Deacon married Gladys Coon in 1911, began studying law at the University of Manitoba, and joined the Theosophical Society, a hybrid theological/philosophical organization. He practiced law for a time, but gave it up when he became convinced that writing was his true calling. Deacon was divorced, but in the early 1920s he remarried, settling down with Sally Townsend Syme; the couple eventually had three children.

Deacon's interest lay in literature from an early date; even as a member of the Pitblado law firm, Deacon had disciplined himself to write, contributing essays and articles to various periodicals both in Canada and the United States. In 1921 he was appointed assistant literary editor of the *Manitoba Free Press.* The following year found Deacon working for the prestigious weekly newspaper *Saturday Night.* His work there encompassed the years 1922 through 1928, during which Deacon originated the popular newspaper supplement "The Bookshelf." In 1928 Deacon left *Saturday Night* and began free-lancing, until—only months later—he was hired as literary editor of the *Mail and Empire.* There he also penned a news and gossip column, "The Fly Leaf," for many years. (In 1936 the *Mail and Empire* was bought by the *Globe,* and was thereafter known as the *Globe and Mail.*) Deacon continued as literary editor until his retirement in 1960, but continued to pen "The Fly Leaf" until 1963.

In 1923 Deacon published/penned the first of his books, *Pens and Pirates,* a collection of discussions on a wide range of subjects, including the well-known essay "Bogey of Annexation." *Pens and Pirates* was followed by *Peter McArthur,* a biographical memorial. The publication was part of a series in Lorne Pierce's Makers of Canadian Literature, and embraced both biographical information (Deacon had been personally acquainted with his subject) as well as a collection of McArthur's writings. Deacon's next work, *Poteen: A Pot-pourri of Canadian Essays,* turned to a discussion on Canadian national themes, often expressed in a humorous format. Clara Thomas, writing in the *Dictionary of Literary Biography,* declared that "the essays he wrote for *Poteen* on the current state of Canadian literature and criticism are important literary-historical documents."

The Four Jameses, first published in 1927, is Deacon's best-known and most often cited work. The narrative satirizes "pretentious literary criticism," according to Thomas, and ends as a witty tribute to four Canadian poets: James Gay, James Gillis, James McIntyre, and James MacRae. So popular is this classic that it was republished in 1953 and again in 1974. Deacon followed *The Four Jameses* with *My Vision of Canada,* his last book-length publication, written during the Great Depression of the 1930s. A pamphlet, *Sh-h-h . . . here comes the censor,* attacking censorship, was published in 1940.

Deacon's commitment to Canadian literature was also evident in his charter membership and subsequent leadership positions in the Canadian Author's Association, which began in 1921. As part of his work with the organization, he developed standardized book contracts and negotiated exclusive income tax considerations for Canadian writers. He was further instrumental in the formation of the Stephen Leacock Medal for Humour, the Canadian Writers' Foundation, and the CAA's Governor-General's Awards.

Besides his literary work in publishing and periodicals, Deacon's encouragement to other authors was legendary. He communicated with such Canadian writers as E. J. Pratt, Hugh MacLennan, Thomas Raddall, and June Callwood. A collection of this correspondence was published posthumously by biographer John Lennox and Michele Lacombe. When Deacon died in 1977 he had been working on his memoirs which remained unfinished due to his failing health.

BIOGRAPHICAL/CRITICAL SOURCES:

BOOKS

Beattie, Jessie Louise, *William Arthur Deacon: Memoirs of a Literary Friendship,* Fleming Press (Hamilton, Ontario), 1978.
Dictionary of Literary Biography, Volume 68: *Canadian Writers, 1920-1959, First Series* Gale, 1988, pp. 103-05.
Thomas, Clara, and John Lennox, *William Arthur Deacon: A Canadian Literary Life,* University of Toronto Press, 1982.

PERIODICALS

Essays on Canadian Writing, summer, 1978.
Globe and Mail, August 9, 1977.*

*   *   *

DELAHAYE, Guy
See LAHAISE, Francoise-Guillaume

*   *   *

de la ROCHE, Mazo   1879-1961

PERSONAL: Surname is pronounced day-lah-*rosh;* adopted de la Roche as surname as a child; born January

15, 1879, in Newmarket, Ontario, Canada; died July 12, 1961, in Toronto, Ontario, Canada; daughter of William Richmond (in sales and farming) and Alberta (a carpenter; maiden name, Lundy) Roche; children: (adopted) Rene (son), Esme (Mrs. David Rees). *Education:* Attended University of Toronto and School of Art, Toronto.

CAREER: Writer.

AWARDS, HONOURS: Two Daughters of the British Empire prizes, 1925, for plays; *Atlantic Monthly* prize, 1927, for *Jalna;* Lorne Pierce Medal, Royal Society of Canada, 1938, for distinguished contributions to Canadian literature; University of Alberta National Award in Letters, 1951.

WRITINGS:

"WHITEOAK CHRONICLES" SERIES; NOVELS

Jalna, Little, Brown, 1927.
Whiteoaks of Jalna, Little, Brown, 1929, published as *Whiteoaks,* Macmillan, 1929, reprinted, Fawcett, 1977.
Finch's Fortune, Little, Brown, 1931.
The Master of Jalna, Little, Brown, 1933, reprinted, Fawcett, 1975.
Young Renny, Little, Brown, 1935.
Whiteoak Harvest, Little, Brown, 1936.
Whiteoak Heritage, Little, Brown, 1940, reprinted, Fawcett, 1974.
Wakefield's Course, Little, Brown, 1941.
The Building of Jalna, Little, Brown, 1944.
Return to Jalna, Little, Brown, 1946, reprinted, Fawcett, 1977.
Mary Wakefield, Little, Brown, 1949, reprinted, 1977.
Renny's Daughter, Little, Brown, 1951, reprinted, Fawcett, 1975.
Whiteoak Brothers: Jalna 1923, Little, Brown, 1953.
Variable Winds at Jalna, Little, Brown, 1954, reprinted, Fawcett, 1975.
Centenary at Jalna, Little, Brown, 1958.
Morning at Jalna, Little, Brown, 1960.

OTHER

Explorers of the Dawn (collection of previously published sketches), Knopf, 1922.
Possession (novel), Macmillan, 1923, reprinted, C. Chivers, 1973.
Low Life: A Comedy in One Act (play; first produced as "Low Life" in Toronto, Ontario, at Trinity Memorial Hall, May 14, 1925), Macmillan, 1925.
Delight (novel), Macmillan, 1926, reprinted with introduction by Desmond Pacey, McClelland & Stewart, 1961.
Come True (play; first produced in Toronto at Trinity Memorial Hall, May 16, 1927), Macmillan, 1927.

"The Return of the Emigrant" (play), first produced in Toronto at Trinity Memorial Hall, March 12, 1928.
Low Life and Other Plays (contains "Low Life," "Come True," and "The Return of the Emigrant"), Little, Brown, 1929.
Portrait of a Dog (novel), Little, Brown, 1930.
Lark Ascending (novel), Little, Brown, 1932.
The Thunder of the New Wings, Little, Brown, 1932.
Beside a Norman Tower, Little, Brown, 1934.
(With Nancy Price) *Whiteoaks: A Play* (adapted from *Whiteoaks of Jalna;* first produced in London, England, at Little Theatre in the Adelphi, April 13, 1936; produced on Broadway, 1938), Macmillan, 1936.
The Very Little House (novel), Little, Brown, 1937.
Growth of a Man (novel), Little, Brown, 1938.
The Sacred Bullock and Other Stories of Animals, Little, Brown, 1939, reprinted, Books for Libraries Press, 1969.
The Two Saplings (novel), Macmillan, 1942.
Quebec: Historic Seaport (nonfiction), Doubleday, 1944.
"Mistress of Jalna," first produced in Bromley, Kent, England, at New Theatre, November 12, 1951.
A Boy in the House, and Other Stories, Little, Brown, 1952.
The Song of Lambert (juvenile), Macmillan, 1955, Little Brown, 1956.
Ringing the Changes: An Autobiography, Little, Brown, 1957.
Bill and Coo (juvenile), Macmillan, 1958, Little, Brown, 1959.
(Author of introduction) George F. Nelson, editor, *Northern Lights: A New Collection of Distinguished Writing by Canadian Authors,* Doubleday, 1960.
Selected Stories of Mazo de la Roche, edited and introduced by Douglas Daymond, University of Ottawa Press, 1979.

Contributor of short stories to U.S. and Canadian magazines.

SIDELIGHTS: Mazo de la Roche wrote a variety of novels, short stories, and plays, but her masterwork is the "Whiteoak Chronicles" series which during her lifetime sold more than eleven million copies in one hundred ninety-three English and ninety-two foreign editions. The series follows several generations of the Whiteoak family and evolves around a lakeside Ontario estate named "Jalna." The household is comprised of Adeline Whiteoak, Adeline's son, the pragmatic children from his first marriage who manage Jalna, and the artistic and temperamental children from his second marriage. Adeline's husband, an officer in the English-Indian Army, rarely appears in the narrative. The matriarch of the Whiteoak family lives to celebrate her one hundredth birthday, and, following her death, is succeeded by her equally spirited grandson, Renny.

The popular series was praised for its exceptional characterizations and, at the same time, criticized for focusing on what George Hendrick referred to in *Mazo de la Roche* as a "hermetically sealed world," far removed from reality. Noting the appeal of de la Roche's work to thousands of loyal readers, Hendrick observed that despite such criticism de la Roche's "audience was one that admired ornate style. Her readers were obviously entertained by [*Jalna*'s] appeal to snobbery, its romanticism, its erotic scenes, and its titillating incidents. All of these help to explain the popularity of *Jalna* and the novels which followed it."

Other critics, including Jo-Ann Fellows and Douglas M. Daymond, saw de la Roche's work as a significant part of Canadian culture and literature. In the *Dalhousie Review,* for example, Fellows commented: "The Jalna novels describe obliquely some very basic ideas of the Canadian national identity, at least of the English-speaking identity. Leaving aside consideration of the novels as literature, they provide a most interesting source for the student of social and intellectual history." *Dictionary of Literary Biography* contributor Daymond concluded: "Although Mazo de la Roche's work does not rank among the most important Canadian fiction, her achievement and her contribution to Canadian literature are considerable. At a time when Canadian writing was dominated by historical fiction and sentimental stories of village and rural life, she challenged prevailing fashions with novels such as *Possession* and *Delight,* and despite the many romantic elements in her work she added to the development of realism in the Canadian novel."

BIOGRAPHICAL/CRITICAL SOURCES:

BOOKS

de la Roche, Mazo, *Ringing the Changes: An Autobiography,* Little Brown, 1957.
Dictionary of Literary Biography, Volume 68: *Canadian Writers, 1920-1959, First Series,* Gale, 1988.
Hendrick, George, *Mazo de la Roche,* Twayne, 1970.

PERIODICALS

Dalhousie Review, summer, 1976.

OBITUARIES:

PERIODICALS

Newsweek, July 24, 1961.
New York Times, July 13, 1961.
Publishers Weekly, July 24, 1961.
Time, July 21, 1961.
Times (London), July 13, 1961.*

de LESTRES, Alonie
See GROULX, Lionel

*   *   *

DENISON, Merrill 1893-1975

PERSONAL: Born June 23, 1893, in Detroit, MI, United States; died June 13, 1975; son of Howard (a commercial traveler) and Flora (a dressmaker; maiden name, MacDonald) Denison; married Muriel Goggin (an author), 1926 (died, 1954); married Elizabeth Robert Andrews, 1957. *Education:* Attended University of Toronto, University of Pennsylvania, and the Ecole des Beaux-Arts, Bellevue-sur-Seine, France. *Avocational interests:* Conservation.

CAREER: Playwright, radio broadcaster, author, and historian. Hart House Theatre, Toronto, Ontario, art director, playwright, beginning in the early 1920s; owner and manager of a summer resort, Bon Echo, Ontario, 1921—; Canadian National Railways Trans-Continental Network (now known as the Canadian Broadcasting Corporation), Montreal, radio broadcaster and script writer, 1931-32; free-lance radio broadcaster and writer. British War Relief Society, chair of radio committee and publicity director, 1939. *Military service:* Served in an American ambulance unit and later in the United States Army during World War I.

WRITINGS:

The Unheroic North: Four Canadian Plays (contains *Brothers in Arms, From Their Own Place, The Weather Breeder,* and *Marsh Hay*), McClelland & Stewart (Toronto), 1923.
Boobs in the Woods: Sixteen Sketches by One of Them (essays), Graphic (Ottawa), 1927.
The Prizewinner (one-act play), Appleton (New York), 1928.
Henry Hudson and Other Plays: Six Plays for the Microphone from the "Romance of Canada" Series of Radio Broadcasts (contains *Henry Hudson, Pierre Radisson, Montcalm, Seven Oaks, Laura Secord,* and *Alexander MacKenzie*), Ryerson (Toronto), 1931.
On Christmas Night, French (New York), 1934.
The Educational Program, Radio Institute of the Audible Arts (New York), 1935.
Advancing America: The Drama of Transportation and Communication, Dodd, Mead (New York), 1936.
An American Father Talks to His Son, Council against Intolerance in America (New York), 1939.
Haven of the Spirit, Dramatists Play Service (New York), 1939.
The U.S. vs. Susan B. Anthony, Dramatists Play Service, 1941.

Klondike Mike: An Alaskan Odyssey (biography), Morrow (New York), 1943.

Canada, Our Dominion Neighbor, Foreign Policy Association (New York), 1944.

C.C.M.: The Story of the First Fifty Years, McLaren (Toronto), 1946.

Harvest Triumphant: The Story of Massey-Harris, a Footnote to Canadian History, McClelland & Stewart, 1948.

Bristles and Brushes, a Footnote to the Story of American War Production, Dodd, Mead, 1949.

The Barley and the Stream: The Molson Story, a Footnote to Canadian History, McClelland & Stewart, 1955.

The Power to Go: The Story of the Automotive Industry, Doubleday (Garden City, NY), 1956.

The People's Power: The History of Ontario Hydro, McClelland & Stewart, 1960.

Canada's First Bank: A History of the Bank of Montreal, two volumes, McClelland & Stewart, 1966-67.

STAGE PLAYS; ALL PRODUCED IN TORONTO AT HART
HOUSE THEATRE EXCEPT AS NOTED

Brothers in Arms, 1921.
From Their Own Place, 1922.
Balm, 1923.
The Weather Breeder, produced in Montreal at His Majesty's Theatre, 1923.
The Prizewinner, 1928.
The U.S. vs. Susan B. Anthony, 1929.
Haven of the Spirit, 1939.
Marsh Hay, 1974.

RADIO PLAYS

Great Moments from History (forty half-hour programs), J. Walter Thompson Company, 1932-33.
Pickwick Papers (series; dramatization of Charles Dickens's novel), NBC, 1933-34.
America's Hour (documentary), CBS, 1936-37.
Democracy in Action (series), CBS, 1938-39.
An American Father Talks to His Son, CBS, July 1, 1939.
Saint Joan (adaptation of George Bernard Shaw's play), CBS, February 9, 1941.
Measure of Achievement, Canadian Broadcasting Corporation, (CBC), October 17, 1943.
Somewhile before the Dawn (series), CBC, 1943-44.
Home Hour (commentaries), BBC, c. 1943-44.
The Forty-Four Months, CBC, August 15, 1945.
Brothers in Arms (adaptation of Denison's stage play), CBC, March 9, 1955.

ROMANCE OF CANADA SERIES; RADIO PLAYS; ALL
PRODUCED BY CANADIAN NATIONAL RAILWAYS TRANS-
CONTINENTAL NETWORK (CNRM)

Henry Hudson, Discoverer, 1931.
Madame La Tour, 1931.

The Plague of Mice, 1931.
The Land of Promise (two parts; adaptation of John Herries McCulloch's *The Land of Promise*), 1931.
Seven Oaks, 1931.
The Raid on Grand Pre (adaptation of Archibald McMechan's *Red Snow on Grand Pre*), 1931.
Marguerite de Roberval (adaptation of Thomas Guthrie Marquis's *Marguerite de Roberval*), 1931.
The Isle of Demons (dramatization of Marquis's work), 1931.
Laura Secord, 1931.
Drucour at Louisberg, 1931.
Pierre Radisson and the Founding of the Hudson's Bay Company, 1931.
Alexander MacKenzie, 1931.
David Thompson, 1931.
Montcalm, 1931.
Adam Dollard, 1931.
Nightpiece, 1931.
Kingston, 1932.
Pierre D'Iberville, 1932.
The Founding of Montreal, 1932.
Quebec, 1932.
The Great Race of Jean Baptiste Lagimodiere, 1932.
The Last Stand of Almighty Voice, 1932.
Valiant Hearts, 1932.
The Fathers of Confederation, 1932.

Also author of "Nationalism and Drama," in *Dramatists in Canada: Selected Essays,* edited by William H. New, University of British Columbia Press, 1972. Denison's works have been included in anthologies, including *Canadian Plays from Hart House Theatre,* Volume 1, edited by Vincent Massey, Macmillan, 1926, and *Canadian Short Stories,* edited by Raymond Knister, Macmillan, 1928. Contributor of articles to periodicals, including the *Toronto Star Weekly.*

Denison's collected papers and manuscripts are housed at the Douglas Library, Queen's University, in Kingston, Ontario. Several of his radio scripts are on file in the Broadcasting Archives at Concordia University, Montreal, and some *Romance of Canada* scripts are at the National Archives, in Ottawa.

SIDELIGHTS: A prolific writer in a variety of genres, Merrill Denison is often heralded as Canada's first distinguished English-language dramatist. The popularity of his stage comedies, performed at the Hart House Theatre in Toronto during the 1920s, encouraged the further development of native Canadian productions. Additionally, Denison was a pioneer in the development of plays targeted specifically for radio telecast, and he participated in broadcasts not only in Toronto and Montreal, but in New York City as well. Later, Denison turned to research and writing about Canadian commerce. Denison's career therefore embraced three definitive phases: playwriting, radio broadcasting, and writing historical publications relating to Canadian businesses, both industrial and corporate.

Denison was the son of an American father and a Canadian mother. His mother, a dressmaker and women's rights activist, traveled to the United States to give birth so that her child "would not be born in a monarchy," according to Chris Johnson in the *Dictionary of Literary Biography (DLB)*. Denison was consequently born in Detroit, Michigan, on June 23, 1893. As a young man, he attended the University of Toronto and the University of Pennsylvania, transferring to the Ecole des Beaux-Arts in Bellevue-sur-Seine, France, to study architecture. With the onset of World War I, Denison volunteered to work in an American ambulance unit, then later joined the United States army.

Following the war Denison returned to Canada and rose to the forefront of the Little Theatre movement in Toronto when he joined Hart House Theatre as an art director, designer, and playwright. An avid storyteller, he was encouraged to write down his tales of the people he had met through his family's summer resort at Bon Echo, Ontario. *Brothers in Arms* was the first such tale, produced in 1921, and joined thereafter by *From Their Own Place* in 1922, and *The Weather Breeder* in 1923; all were later published with an unproduced work, *Marsh Hay,* in *The Unheroic North: Four Canadian Plays.* The setting for all four plays is the backwoods area of Ontario north of Kingston, near Lake Mazinaw. The critically-praised *Brothers in Arms* concerns the misunderstanding and conflict that arises between a backwoodsman and a vacationing businessman. Bon Echo also provided the background for 1927's *Boobs in the Woods,* a series of short country comedy sketches, and 1928's *The Prizewinner,* a one-act play comparing the perspectives of country yokels versus city slickers. In addition to comic sketches, Hart House also produced several of Denison's social protest plays: *Balm,* produced in 1923, considers society's attitudes toward old age; *The U.S. vs. Susan B. Anthony,* produced in 1929, examines women's rights; and *Haven of the Spirit,* produced in 1939, explores religious prejudice.

Beginning in 1930, Denison began writing for the Canadian National Railways Trans-Continental Network (CNRM), which would evolve into the Canadian Broadcasting Corporation (CBC). He contributed scripts to the network's *Romance of Canada* radio series. Each sketch was a half-hour narration dramatizing Canadian history from the arrival of the English navigator and explorer Henry Hudson to Confederation. Similarly, Denison wrote scripts for *Great Moments from History,* an American program, and for *Democracy in Action,* a CBS series sponsored by the United States Office of Education. Dur-

ing World War II, Denison wrote *Somewhile before the Dawn,* a CBC production, and *Home Hour,* the British Broadcasting Corporation's vehicle for commentaries on the war effort.

Capitalizing on his many years of experience in drama and writing, Denison penned 1943's *Klondike Mike: An Alaskan Odyssey.* The fictionalized biography, focusing on the adventures of an 1890s gold prospector named Michael Ambrose Mahoney, became a best seller. In the next several years, Denison turned to corporate histories. His work was described by one critic as "engagingly written," and included *Harvest Triumphant: The Story of Massey-Harris, a Footnote to Canadian History,* 1948, *The Barley and the Stream: The Molson Story, a Footnote to Canadian History,* 1955, and *Canada's First Bank: A History of the Bank of Montreal,* in two volumes, published between 1966-67.

Denison died on June 13, 1975. His literary works have been compared to Eugene O'Neill and Sean O'Casey, and his contribution to the development of radio drama has long been acknowledged as influential. Further, Denison's corporate histories were, according to Johnson in *DLB,* "respected for an unusual objectivity and attention to detail, establishing himself as one of Canada's most significant nonacademic social historians."

BIOGRAPHICAL/CRITICAL SOURCES:

BOOKS

Dictionary of Literary Biography, Volume 92: *Canadian Writers, 1890-1920,* Gale, 1990, pp. 77-81.
Guthrie, Tyrone, *A Life in the Theatre,* Hamilton, 1961, pp. 64-68.
MacDonald, Dick, *Mugwump Canadian: The Merrill Denison Story,* Content, 1973.
Weir, E. Austin, *The Struggle for National Broadcasting in Canada,* McClelland & Stewart, 1965, pp. 51-63.

PERIODICALS

Canadian Drama/L'Art Dramatique Canadien, spring, 1977, pp. 9-19.
Theatre History in Canada/Histoire du Theatre au Canada, fall, 1980, pp. 135-148; spring, 1981, pp. 19-32.*

*   *   *

DesROCHERS, Alfred   1901-1978

PERSONAL: Born October 5, 1901, in Saint-Elie 'Orford, Quebec, Canada; died October 12, 1978; son of Honorius (a farmer) and Zephirine (Marcotte) DesRochers; married Rose-Alma Brault, in 1925; children: six.

CAREER: Poet, literary critic and theorist, journalist. Held a variety of odd jobs while a teenager, including delivery person, hardware store clerk, bushworker, and foundry apprentice. Affiliated with *La Tribune* (newspaper), Sherbrooke, Quebec, 1925-50; translator for Canadian Parliament in Ottawa; Canadian Press, translator, 1953-56; contributor of poems and articles to newspapers and journals throughout the 1940s and 1950s. *Military service:* Private in Canadian army during World War II.

MEMBER: Societe des Ecrivains de L'est (founder).

AWARDS, HONOURS: Prix David, 1932, for *A l'ombre de l'Orford;* Prix Duvernay, 1964; honorary doctorate, Universite de Sherbrooke, 1976; Companion of the Order of Canada, 1978.

WRITINGS:

L'Offrande aux vierges folles (poetry), privately printed (Sherbrooke, Quebec), 1928.
A l'ombre de l'Orford (poetry), privately printed (Sherbrooke, Quebec), 1929.
Paragraphes (criticism), Librairie d'Action Canadienne-Francaise (Montreal), 1931.
Le Retour de Titus (poetry), Editions de l'Universite d'Ottawa (Ottawa), 1963.
Elegies pour l'epouse en-allee (poetry), Parti Pris (Montreal), 1967.
Oeuvres poetiques (poetry), 2 volumes, edited by Romain Legare, Fides (Montreal), 1977.

Contributor to *La Poesie canadienne-francaise,* edited by Paul Wyczynski, Bernard Julien, Jean Menard, and Rejean Robidaux, Fides, 1969; articles have appeared in *Idees, Culture, Les Carnets Viatoriens,* and *Liberte.*

SIDELIGHTS: A cofounder of the Societe des Ecrivains de l'est, Alfred DesRochers rose to prominence as a leader of a literary movement in the 1920s and 1930s. A journalist, poet, and literary critic, he is considered to be among the most important Quebec authors during the inter-world-war period. DesRochers is noted for his poetry, which covered themes ranging from love, freedom, adventure, and the land, and he is acclaimed for his work as a literary critic which found him championing traditional modes of poetry and the voice of women.

The son of a farmer, DesRochers had to cut his schooling short when his father died and he was needed to work a variety of odd jobs to help support his family. In 1925, the year he married Rose-Alma Brault, with whom he eventually had six children, he entered the world of journalism. His association with the Sherbrooke, Quebec, newspaper *La Tribune* lasted until 1950, with time off in the 1940s to serve in the Canadian army during World War II. While working for *La Tribune* DesRochers met several like-minded writers, including Jovette-Alice Bernier and Eva Senecal, with whom he formed the Societe des Ecrivains de l'Est (Society of Writers of the East). It was

through the meetings of this group that DesRochers formed a lifelong friendship with Louis Dantin (Eugene Seers), a leading critic of French-Canadian literature.

DesRochers issued his first collection of poetry, *L'Offrande aux vierges folles,* in 1928, followed by *A l'ombre de l'Orford* in 1929. Although both books were self-published, they are considered his most important works. "These collections are the best organized and most balanced" of DesRochers's career, stated Richard Giguere in *Dictionary of Literary Biography.* "They also demonstrate DesRochers's versatility in handling a variety of themes," the critic continued, noting the presence of both romantic poems of love and realistic poems about farming and lumbering, the region's main industries. The poet experiments in these works with form, including the epic, as well as sonnets and rondeaux. "Good Parnassian that he was," Giguere observed, "he emphasized form, varied his tone, played with sound, and exploited the riches of vocabulary." *A l'ombre de l'Orford* was republished by a Montreal firm in 1930 and won three literary prizes, as well as critical acclaim.

In 1931, DesRochers published a collection of literary criticism, entitled *Paragraphes,* in the form of imaginary interviews with books, including several volumes by women. Giguere remarked of the poet's works of criticism as a whole, that "DesRochers showed himself to be a critic with a new and accurate assessment of Quebec writers both present and past, as well as a theorist, a keen defender of traditional poetry and versification." Apart from several critical articles, DesRochers's literary activity slowed down significantly in the 1940s and 1950s. His books of poetry from the 1960s are *Le Retour de Titus,* a tribute to the love of Roman emperor Titus for Berenice, and *Elegies pour l'epouse en-allee,* an elegaic homage to the poet's deceased wife.

The last decade of DesRochers's life marked his inclusion in the pantheon of celebrated Quebec writers. He received several prestigious awards, including being made a Companion of the Order of Canada, one of the highest honors the nation bestows on its citizens, in 1978, the year of his death. Along with his collections of poetry and literary criticism, DesRochers wrote numerous lectures, forewords, and prefaces, and corresponded with important writers of the 1930s and 1940s. Nonetheless, his reputation rests on his distinctive poetry, which handles both low subjects and high with a sure grasp of language, form, and theme.

BIOGRAPHICAL/CRITICAL SOURCES:

BOOKS

Bonenfant, Joseph, Janine Boynard-Frot, Richard Giguere, and Antoine Sirois, *A l'ombre de DesRo-*

chers: Le Mouvement litteraire des Cantons de l'Est,
La Tribune/Presses de l'Universite de Sherbrooke,
1985.
Dictionary of Literary Biography, Volume 68: *Canadian*
Writers, 1920-1959, Gale, 1988, pp. 113-16.

PERIODICALS

La Tribune, November, 1930.
Queen's Quarterly, winter, 1965, pp. 566-582.

*   *   *

DESROSIERS, Leo-Paul   1896-1967

PERSONAL: Born April 11, 1896, in Berthier-en Haut
(Berthierville), Quebec, Canada; died following a brief illness, April 20, 1967; son of Louis and Marie (Olivier) Desrosiers; married Marie-Antoinette Tardif (a writer; pen
name, Michelle Le Normand), June, 1922 (died, 1964);
children: Louis, Claude, Michelle. *Education:* Attended
Seminaire de Joliette; University of Montreal, LLL, 1919.
Religion: Roman Catholic.

CAREER: Novelist, short story writer, journalist, editor,
librarian. *Le Devoir,* Montreal, Quebec, Canada, journalist
covering Ottawa Parliament, 1920-28; *Proceeding and Or-*
ders of the House of Commons, Ottawa, Ontario, Canada,
French editor, 1928-41; Montreal Municipal Library,
Montreal, chief librarian, 1941-52. Also principal of
School of Library Science, Montreal.

MEMBER: Royal Society of Canada, Academie Canadienne-Francaise (co-founder, 1944), Societe des Dix, Societe historique de Montreal.

AWARDS, HONOURS: Prix d'Action Intellectuelle,
1922, for *Ames et paysages;* Vermeille medal, Academie
Francaise, 1931, for *Nord-Sud;* Prix de la Province de
Quebec, 1938, for *Les engages du Grand Portage;* Prix Duvernay, 1951, for *L'Ampoule d'or;* Lorne Pierce medal for
body of work, 1963.

WRITINGS:

Ames et paysages (short stories), Editions du Devoir
(Montreal), 1922.
Nord-Sud (novel), Editions du Devoir, 1931.
Le Livre des mysteres (short stories), Editions du Devoir,
1936.
L'Accalmie: Lord Durham au Canada (nonfiction), Editions du Devoir, 1937.
Les engages du Grand Portage (novel), Gallimard (Paris),
1938, Fides (Montreal), 1946; translated by Christina
van Oordt as *The Making of Nicolas Montour,* Harvest House (Montreal), 1978.
Commencements (nonfiction), Editions de l'Action Canadienne-Francaise (Montreal), 1939.

Les Opiniatres (novel), Imprimerie Populaire (Montreal),
1941, Brentano's (New York), 1941.
Sources (novel), Imprimerie Populaire, 1942.
Iroquoisie, 1534-1646 (nonfiction), Etudes de l'Institut
d'Histoire de l'Amerique Francaise (Montreal), 1947.
L'Ampoule d'or (novel), Gallimard, 1951, Fides (Mon-
treal), 1957.
Les Dialogues de Marthe et de Marie (biography), Fides,
1957.
Vous qui passez (novel), Fides, 1958.
Les angoisses et les tourments (novel), Fides, 1959.
Rafales sur les cimes (novel), Fides, 1960.
Dans le nid d'aiglons, la colombe: Vie de Jeanne Le Ber,
la recluse (biography), Fides, 1963.
Paul de Chomedey, Sieur de Maisonneuve (biography),
Fides, 1967.

Contributor of articles and stories to *La croix du chemin,*
edited by Societe Sainte-Jean-Baptiste de Montreal, 1916;
Ville o ma ville, edited by the Societe des Ecrivains Canadiens, 1941; and *Histoire veritable et naturelle des moeurs*
et productions du pays de la Nouvelle-France, edited by the
Societe Historique de Boucherville, 1964. Contributor to
journals, including *L'action francaise, Monde nouveau,*
Revue d'histoire de l'Amerique, Canada Francais, and *Au-*
jourd'hui Quebec.

SIDELIGHTS: The youngest son of a family of fourteen
children, Leo-Paul Desrosiers was the product of an established family of Quebec farmers. Characterized by Ivor A.
Arnold in *Dictionary of Literary Biography* as a man with
an "independent cast of mind" and a "retiring" personality, Desrosiers worked as a journalist, librarian, and editor
while writing his novels, biographies, and short stories celebrating rural Quebec and its heroes. As an author, Desrosiers is best remembered for his evocative descriptions of
the Quebec countryside, and for championing the strength
of spirit of its people.

After studying law at the University of Montreal, where
he was more intent on pursuing his own readings in literature than on his legal studies, Desrosiers became a journalist with the daily newspaper *Le Devoir* in 1920. During his
tenure with *Le Devoir* Desrosiers married Marie-
Antoinette Tardif, who wrote under the pen name of Michelle Le Normand. His first book was a collection of stories based, in part, on childhood memories. Published in
1922, the work was entitled *Ames et paysages* and shows,
according to critics, Desrosiers's early proficiency in language and storytelling techniques.

Finding journalism too time consuming and wanting to
dedicate himself more fully to writing fiction, Desrosiers
left *Le Devoir* to become the French editor of *Proceedings*
and Orders of the House of Commons in Ottawa in 1928.
His first full-length novel, *Nord-Sud,* published in 1931,

uses the economic depression of 1840s Quebec as background for the story of a young man's flight to California during the infamous Gold Rush. Describing rural life in the province during that era, the work follows Vincent Douaire as he sets out to improve his quality of life.

In 1936, Desrosiers saw publication of his second collection of short stories, *Le Livre des mysteres,* "in which he displayed a growing talent for accomplished psychological studies," according to Arnold in *Dictionary of Literary Biography.* Two nonfiction works followed: *L'Accalmie* (1937), which concerns Lord Durham, and *Commencements* (1939), which examines the role of the Iroquois Indians in French-Canadian history. During this time Desrosiers also issued a novel that critics consider to be his most accomplished, *Les engages du Grand Portage* (1938).

In *Les engages du Grand Portage* Desrosier tells the story of bitter rivalries between fur traders in frontier Canada working for the North West Company. Published in English as *The Making of Nicolas Montour,* the novel follows the character through various devious dealings as he gains prominence in the company in the early 1800s. In *Dictionary of Literary Biography* critic Arnold remarked that the author had succeeded in writing a novel with "a more tightly knit plot" than in his previous work. According to Arnold, Desrosiers demonstrated "a considerable skill in creating a sense of the epic grandeur of the rugged backdrop to the hardships of these early voyageurs."

Two subsequent novels also emphasize survival against overwhelming odds, although critics claim the result is less successful. *Les Opiniatres* (1941) describes the French colonists' struggle to exist in an era marked by constant hostilities with the area's native Canadian population. *Sources* (1942) pits a young woman in contemporary Canada against the land when she leaves a job in the city to live on a farm.

Derosiers's 1951 effort, *L'Ampoule d'or,* was also critically acclaimed. In the volume a young woman turns to the church and her faith after her father breaks up her affair with a married man. In *Dictionary of Literary Biography* Arnold characterized *L'Ampoule d'or* as "a psychological novel" and "a moving poetic study of the sufferings brought on to all appearances by the cruel fate of circumstance." This work, along with the earlier *Les Opiniatres* and *Sources,* according to Arnold in the same essay, "evoke in the reader a sense of Desrosiers's belief in the ordinary Quebecker's innate strength in the face of adversity, at times seemingly turning the latter into a near-mythic antagonist."

A less successful treatment of a similar theme runs through Desrosiers's last major work, the trilogy *Vous qui passez,* which includes *Vous qui passez* (1958), *Les angoisses et les tourments* (1959), and *Rafales sur les cimes*

(1960). Centering on an engineer and his wife, the novels pit the anti-materialist values of a traditional, Roman Catholic Quebec family against the degradations of modern society.

In 1941 Desrosiers left the House of Commons to become chief librarian for the Montreal Municipal Library. In 1947 he returned to the subject of the Indians' role in French-Canadian history with *Iroquoisie.* Toward the end of his career Desrosiers issued three biographies of important figures in Quebec history: *Les Dialogues de Marthe et de Marie* (1957) about Marguerite de Bourgeoys, *Dans le nid d'aiglons, la colombe* (1963) about Jeanne Le Ber, and *Paul de Chomedey, sieur de Maisonneuve* (1967).

Desrosiers pursued literary achievement throughout his life, despite the necessity of working jobs that consumed his time and energy. Desrosiers wrote about the Quebec countryside and people in works that celebrated both, bringing him national acclaim during his lifetime.

BIOGRAPHICAL/CRITICAL SOURCES:

BOOKS

Dictionary of Literary Biography, Volume 68: *Canadian Writers, 1920-1959,* Gale, 1988, pp. 117-19.
Gelinas, Michelle, *Leo-Paul Desroisers; ou le recit ambigu,* Presses de l'Universite de Montreal, 1973.
Oxford Companion to Canadian Literature, Oxford University Press, 1983, pp. 187-88.
Richer, Julia, *Leo-Paul Desrosiers,* Fides, 1966.*

*   *   *

DIXON, Franklin W.
    See McFARLANE, Leslie (Charles)

*   *   *

DOUTREMONT, Henri
    See BUGNET, Georges

*   *   *

DOWNES, G. V.
    See DOWNES, Gwladys (Violet)

*   *   *

DOWNES, Gwladys (Violet)   1915-
    (G. V. Downes)

PERSONAL: Born April 22, 1915, in Victoria, British Columbia, Canada; daughter of Gordon and Doris Gwendoline (Bywater-Jones) Downes. *Education:* Attended Victoria College (now University of Victoria); University of British Columbia, B.A., 1934, M.A., 1940; received teaching diplomas from the University of British Columbia and the Sorbonne; received doctoral degree from the University of Paris, 1953.

ADDRESSES: Home—2621 Lincoln Rd., Victoria, British Columbia V8R 6A5, Canada.

CAREER: Duncan High School, British Columbia, Canada, teacher, 1936-69; University of British Columbia, Vancouver, Canada, 1940-41, 1946-49; affiliated with University of Victoria, Victoria, British Columbia, beginning in 1951, professor of French, until 1978; Art Gallery of Greater Victoria, Victoria, archivist; translator, critic, and poet.

MEMBER: League of Canadian Poets, Association for Canadian and Quebec Literature, University Women's Club, Alliance francaise.

AWARDS, HONOURS: Senior Arts Award, Canada Council, 1969.

WRITINGS:

Lost Diver, Fiddlehead (Fredericton, New Brunswick), 1955.
When We Lie Together: Poems from Quebec and Poems by G. V. Downes, Klanak (Vancouver), 1973.
Out of the Violent Dark: Poems and Translations, Sono Nis (Victoria), 1978.

Essays and poems represented in numerous works, including *The World of W. B. Yeats: Essays in Perspective,* edited by Robin Skelton and Ann Saddlemeyer, University of Washington Press (Seattle), 1965; *40 Women Poets of Canada,* edited by Dorothy Livesay and Seymour Mayne, Ingluvin (Montreal), 1971; and *Poetry by Canadian Women,* edited by Rosemary Sullivan, Oxford University Press (Toronto), 1989. Contributor to periodicals, including *Malahat Review, Edge, Tamarack Review, Canadian Literature, Canadian Forum,* and *Prism International.*

SIDELIGHTS: The talents of educator, critic, poet, and translator Gwladys Downes have all contributed to contemporary Canadian literature. A native of British Columbia, Downes was born in 1915 and, after receiving advanced degrees from her province's university as well as the Sorbonne, she began an academic career that lasted for nearly three decades, primarily teaching French at the university level. The ease with which Downes switches between French and English led to a secondary career: she has often been invited to translate the work of luminary French-language poets such as Anne Hebert, Gustave Lamarche, and Rina Lasnier. This area of work combines Downes's linguistic skills with a passion for the written word, for she is a published poet in her own right. Her first volume of poetry, *Lost Diver,* appeared in 1955, presenting sixteen poems. Her verse is sometimes reminiscent of nineteenth-century French symbolist writers such as Charles Baudelaire, as well as that of twentieth-century English poet T. S. Eliot, noted Jeanette Lynes in an essay on Downes for the *Dictionary of Literary Biography.* These works, asserted Lynes, "primarily explore private, internalized landscapes and tend to be oriented toward mythic oppositions: innocence and experience, exile/underworld and garden." Submergence, especially under water, is symbolic thread common to many of the poems in *Lost Diver.*

Downes's subsequent pair of books contain both her translations of other poets' work as well as her own efforts. *When We Lie Together: Poems from Quebec and Poems by G. V. Downes,* published in 1973, contains English translations of poems by Lasnier, Paul-Marie Lapointe, and Yves Prefontaine, among others, followed by four of Downes's own selections. The diver/submerged person of her first book of poetry returns as a recurring theme. Lynes remarked that "the juxtaposition of her original poems and her translations is an interesting one because of the strong parallels that emerge between the two," such as the dying birds in Downes's "Mirror, Mirror" and the white birds in her translation of Lapointe's "Poem for Winter." *Out of the Violent Dark: Poems and Translations,* Downes's 1978 volume, contains twenty-seven translations of the poetry of Hebert, Lamarche, Hector de Saint-Denys Garneau and others, as well as seventy-one of Downes's own poems, although some had appeared in print previously. Regarding the newer selections, Lynes observed that while they are in some ways similar to the body of Downes's other work, "they also demonstrate a less rigid approach to form and make use of effective new images, such as the 'delicate networks / of waiting / neurones,' to convey the poet's inner experience." In summing up the achievements of Downes's multifaceted career, Lynes argued that the writer's "interest in language—both French and English—and her skills as poet and translator demonstrate an admirable range of abilities, and her bringing francophone poetry to anglophone readers represents a noteworthy contribution to Canadian letters."

BIOGRAPHICAL/CRITICAL SOURCES:

BOOKS

Dictionary of Literary Biography, Volume 88: *Canadian Writers, 1920-1959,* Gale, 1989.

DOYLE, Brian 1935-

PERSONAL: Born August 12, 1935, in Ottawa, Ontario, Canada; son of Hulbert and Charlotte (Duff) Doyle; married December 26, 1960; wife's name, Jacqueline; children: Megan, Ryan. *Education:* Carleton University, B.J. and B.A., 1957.

ADDRESSES: Home—539 Rowanwood, Ottawa, Ontario, Canada K2A 3C9.

CAREER: High school English teacher at Glebe Collegiate, Ottawa, Ontario, and Ottawa Technical High School, Ottawa; children's writer. Worked variously as a journalist, waiter, taxi driver, bricklayer, and jazz singer.

AWARDS, HONOURS: Book of the Year awards, Canadian Library Association, 1983, for *Up to Low,* and 1989, for *Easy Avenue;* Vicky Metcalf Body of Work Award, Canadian Authors Association; Mr. Christie Book of the Year Award; three time runner up, Governor General's Award, Canadian Authors Association.

WRITINGS:

Hey Dad!, Groundwood Books, 1978.
You Can Pick Me up at Peggy's Cove, Groundwood, 1979.
Up to Low, Groundwood Books, 1982.
(Editor with S. Scheiber) *The Impaired Physician,* Plenum, 1983.
Angel Square, Groundwood Books, 1984.
Easy Avenue, Groundwood Books, 1988.
English and Englishness (part of the "New Accents" series), Routledge, 1989.
Covered Bridge, Groundwood Books, 1990.
Spud Sweetgrass,, Groundwood Books, 1992.

Also author of children's plays.

ADAPTATIONS: A film directed by Ann Wheeler was based on *Angel Square.*

SIDELIGHTS: Brian Doyle is an award-winning writer for young adults whose respect for the clarity of children's insight radiates throughout his novels, inspiring him, according to many critics, to "write up" rather than to "write down" to his readers. Doyle's works turn on timeless coming-of-age themes and feature poetically crafted prose, hefty doses of tragedy and comedy, and realistic representations that acknowledge the imperfections of contemporary human life without overlooking its goodness. Some observers credit Doyle's success to his use of child narrators, who, through their naive wisdom, find balance and meaning in the most frantic of situations. "There's a pretty decent difference between depth of insight and sophisticated insight," Doyle commented. "Kids at ten know a lot—they're very wise, although they're not slippery, not good liars yet. A ten-year-old boy or girl is as smart as she'll ever get or he'll ever get. So it's

with that kind of belief I'm comfortable making the ten-year-old's insights as deep as I want."

Doyle's keen memories of childhood—the settings, the people, and the atmosphere—figure prominently in his novels. As Doyle grew up, his family lived in two locations, winters in an ethnically divided section of Ottawa, and summers in the Gatineau Hills north of town, in a log cabin where his great-grandfather had settled. Storytelling was one of the family's main pastimes. "I loved sitting around listening to my father and my grandfather and anyone else who was around," Doyle recalled. "Both of them were wonderful storytellers, and they didn't tell stories so much as they just talked. If in my work there is a kind of sound, that's where it comes from, rhythms inherited from sitting around listening to my father's family exchanging their world vision. Those people were verbally very poetic." Poetry ran on both sides of Doyle's family, but his mother provided a very different influence on his development as a writer. "My mother was a literary person. She was not a verbal person at all. She wrote well and wrote privately, but she'd show her poetry to me." Doyle's mother wrote the poem "Sea Savour" with which Doyle begins his second novel, *You Can Pick Me up at Peggy's Cove.*

Many critics have praised the knowledge of the inner workings of children's minds reflected in Doyle's novels. Although the author taught high school students for thirty-three years, it was his own children who originally instigated his fiction. His first two books, *Hey Dad!* and *You Can Pick Me Up at Peggy's Cove,* were each written for his children, Megan and Ryan. "I never could have gotten started without my own kids," Doyle commented. "I don't think I ever knew anybody as well as I did my daughter when she was that age. I felt like I was right inside her skin. So writing *Hey Dad!* and *You Can Pick Me Up at Peggy's Cove* was an attempt to capture that knowledge before it went away. I did the same thing for my son a couple years later, when he got to be that age." While the first two novels are contemporary, Doyle's next four novels go back in time to the mid-century, when Doyle himself was young. "My writing started with my daughter, then my son, and then I ran out of kids." So now, Doyle explained, "I find the kid inside of me, way back there."

Doyle's first novel, *Hey Dad!,* is, in its narrator Megan's words, "the story of how I hated my Dad for a while for some reason and how I loved him again for some reason and how I almost ruined a trip my family took to the Pacific Ocean and how all of a sudden I got independent for a while that summer when I was thirteen." After a thwarted attempt at running away from the family, watching her brother nearly fall off a mountain, and mistaking a dead man at the hot springs for her father, Megan grows beyond her childhood self-orientation and begins to worry about the instability of the world around her. She worries about strangers entering her life only to disappear forever, about the mysterious connection between love and death, and about ambiguities—even in the landscape. When Megan and her brother ask an Iroquois man they meet on the road how big the mountains are, he answers: "If they seem big to you from here, they won't seem as big when you get there. Everything is different than it looks to be."

Underneath Megan's strikingly familiar—and often very funny—teenage disgust at just about everything the family (but particularly her unconventional father) does, Doyle conveys a rather heroic struggle to grasp and cope with a confusing world. According to *In Review: Canadian Books for Children* contributor Irma McDonough, the family trip from Ottawa to Vancouver provides not only a "subliminally educational" rendering of Canada's geography, but also a vivid journey through some of the psychological pathways to maturity. The novel's two landscapes—internal and external—are related. In her *Canadian Children's Literature* review, Wendy R. Katz maintained that Doyle's child characters discover themselves through their relationships within the family, but also "in relation to people beyond the family, friends and strangers alike, to nature, and to the universe." Listening to the roar of the Athabaska River, Megan has a flash of comprehension illustrating the wonder and wisdom of an "unsophisticated" mind: "I was trying to stretch my mind so that I could think about how long an eon was. It was how long the Athabaska roared his deep roar. I stretched my mind. I grunted and held my breath and forced my mind to wrap around that long, long time. I thought of the summer and how long it was that I was in grade four and how long next year would be and then I thought of myself after Dad and Mum were dead and then after I was an old wrinkled lady and how *that* wouldn't be a century yet and then my mind kind of popped like a bubble gum bubble."

Before Canadian-based publishing house Groundwood Books saw *Hey Dad!*'s potential and agreed to publish it, several publishers had turned it down, suggesting that children would not be able to appreciate the poetic prose and the depth of the novel. Doyle believes, to the contrary, that children appreciate good writing. He commented: "They don't articulate why, but they do like stuff that's more than just plot. People who wouldn't publish my stuff were saying that kids won't know that so much is there, and I was saying it doesn't matter, they'll feel it. And we proved it. They don't know it, but they feel it. They laugh and they're sad, and they get it all. It's only the literary critics who go on and say why."

In *You Can Pick Me Up at Peggy's Cove,* the narrator Ryan is sent to stay with his aunt in the small, tourist-ridden Nova Scotia fishing town of Peggy's Cove when his father, who is suffering from the "C.O.L." (the change of life), runs away from home. "The C.O.L.," Ryan explains, "is when someone gets to be about forty-five years old and starts acting a little different because they start thinking about dying or getting old and all that. . . . The C.O.L. makes them do funny things. I guess the right word is unpredictable." Ryan thinks that if he gets into trouble, his father will have to return to save him. So, he becomes involved in stealing from tourists with the Drummer, the neglected son of a wealthy widow. Most mornings, however, Ryan goes out on a boat with the fisherman Eddie and his mute partner Wingding. With them he learns much about friendship, communication, heroism, and eventually, death. In the frenzy of events—some funny, some painfully sad—Ryan composes a letter to his father, hoping to hurt him or scare him into coming back.

The setting and the people in Peggy's Cove eventually orient Ryan to his own strange circumstances. While tourists frantically pursue perfect snapshots of the idyllic village life they expected to find in Peggy's Cove ("It would be a wonderful place to live," says one tourist. "It's so *realistic!*"), Ryan sees the town as it really is, a place where everyone has his or her own peculiarities and accepts the peculiarities of others. Thus after Ryan and the Drummer are arrested for stealing, Ryan's friends, Eddie and Wingding accept him back into the fold, as he will in turn accept and forgive his father's "unpredictable" behavior and apparent betrayal. *World of Children's Books* contributor Jon C. Stott commended the "social realism" with which Doyle "sensitively explores the strengths and weaknesses of his characters and understands well the need of everyone for love."

Doyle's realism is a layered blend of different stylistic approaches. Stott, who called Doyle a "superb stylist," asserted that in *You Can Pick Me Up at Peggy's Cove,* the shifts in style—from straightforward to slapstick—are well suited to the novel's great range of moods. Doyle commented: "The Peggy's Cove book is about friendship, and so what I try to do is treat that theme very realistically, as true as I can possibly make it. And then in the day to day—in the particulars—I'm dealing more in mythological kinds of views, the way I used to hear my father and grandfather depicting reality. The themes are very realistic, and the emotions in them are as close to 'reality' as I can possibly get. Whereas the novel may be comic and kind of caricaturish, at the same time it's rooted in true feeling."

With a notable change in tone and style, Doyle's third novel, *Up to Low,* takes place in the Gatineau Hills in mid-century, where the author spent his summers as a child. Its narrator, Tommy, travels up to Low with his father and his father's friend, Frank—an alcoholic with a new car that he crashes every third or fourth mile. On the way to Low, the travelers stop at many taverns, where Tommy is treated, often involuntarily, to cokes and tavern talk. Everyone, but particularly Tommy's father, a very able storyteller, is talking about a man called Mean Hughie up in Low and how he disappeared after he got sick from cancer. As the novel proceeds, Mean Hughie's history unfolds through the larger-than-life storytelling of the men of Low. Tommy's attention is particularly engaged when the story of Mean Hughie's daughter, Baby Bridgette, is told. Years before, the story goes, Baby Bridgette got in the way of the binding machine and got her arm cut off. Mean Hughie slapped her for getting in the way of the machine before he bound up the wound with binder twine so she wouldn't bleed to death. Tommy confides to the reader that, on his last visit to Low, he fell in love with Baby Bridgette and her trillium-shaped green eyes.

"This is a world ripe with story," commented Sarah Ellis in her *Horn Book* review, "with anecdote and rumor, scandal and tall tale, sentimental ballads that have passed down four generations, and a running gag we can see approaching from a mile away." The slapstick antics of the townspeople and Tommy's relatives are related in deadpan style. Tommy reports on the drunken antics of Frank, who drives into walls and falls in cow pies; on Frank's nemesis, the compulsive Aunt Dottie, who sprays disinfectant on raspberries before eating them and often wears a surgical mask to protect herself from germs; on the teeming throng of indistinguishable red-headed Hendricks (" 'Watch out you don't run down a Hendrick,' Dad was saying, 'you know it's unlucky.' "); and on the five indistinguishable chain-smoking uncles. Behind the comic portrayal of a static and somewhat nonsensical rural life, however, a steady lucidity emanates from Tommy. In creating Tommy, *Maclean's* reviewer Anne Collins commented, Doyle reverses the usual order of adult authority and teenage alienation, presenting "a sane and loving teenager who helps a slapstick and misfit world find its feet." While the townspeople, like the figures in their stories, remain largely the same, Tommy and Baby Bridgette move forward on a healing journey to find Mean Hughie. They become acquainted, according to Carol Munro in her *Canadian Children's Literature* review, "with the power of a real affection for another person, and with the range of those natural human foibles which are better tolerated with good humor than railed against." Ellis observed that *Up to Low,* with its elaborate plot and style, "takes a lot of risks." The reviewer added, however, that Doyle skillfully controls this "extravagant world" through the "voice of Tommy, whose quiet, observant, naive tone frames the whole rollicking crowded narrative in genuine human feeling."

Some critics have questioned the appropriateness of the humor in *Up to Low. Books in Canada* critic Mary Ainslie

Smith, who praised *Up to Low* as Doyle's finest work, described some of Doyle's humor as "black, to say the least, and sometimes heavy, of the out-house and open-coffin variety." Munro, while applauding the life-affirming power of the book, commented that "a reader might take issue with some of the models presented" by the book's adult characters. The bar-hopping and drunk driving, according to the Munro, "are perhaps examples not best set before the young reader." But Doyle believes that his place as an author is to set the world with all of its complexities before his readers. As a child, Doyle commented, "I recall sitting around listening to the adults in my life talking away. They never left me out, and they didn't explain or anything either. I think that's how I would like to treat kids that are around me, put it out there, let them figure it out." Katz, observing this tendency, commended Doyle for not segregating his children from the adult world, as many children's authors have done. Doyle's child characters, she remarked, "are in close and occasionally oppressive proximity to adults and adult concerns. In this sense the books are unique, as are their fully-rounded adult characters."

Tommy returns as narrator in *Angel Square,* Doyle's 1984 novel, this time back in his winter home in Ottawa's Lowertown. Every day Tommy must cross Angel Square, the site of three different schools, one attended by French Canadians, locally called Pea Soups, another attended by Irish Catholics, called Dogans, and Tommy's school, attended by Jewish kids, called Jews (although Tommy explains, "I'm not anything"). Hyperbolic descriptions of fighting among the factions in the square run intermittently throughout the novel, although no one seems to get hurt in the fights. Tommy reports on the furor nonchalantly, but in legendary proportions. "Over there, two Jews were tying a Dogan to a post. Over here, two Pea Soups were trying to tear off a Jew's arm. Over there, three Jews and a Dogan were torturing a Pea Soup with bats. In the centre some Pea Soups were burying alive a Dogan in a deep hole in the snow." But when anti-Semitism results in the beating and critical injury of the father of Tommy's best friend, Sammy Rosenberg, Tommy can no longer passively accept the irrational behavior of his community. He triumphs over bigotry by following in the footsteps of his radio hero, the Shadow, working through a network of Irish, Jewish, and French Canadian neighbors to find the culprit.

Bigotry is only one aspect of Tommy's life in the Lowertown community. Almost as concerned with buying Christmas presents as he is concerned with finding the assailant, Tommy's evocation of Lowertown at Christmastime achieves "special beauty," according to *Quill and Quire* contributor Paul Kropp. Whether invoking the sights, smells, and people at Woolworth's, conveying what a rubber duck means to his mentally handicapped sister, Pamela, "an angel who couldn't know anything," or showing the effects of a good teacher on his imagination, Tommy presents "a poignant message of tolerance and love," a *Children's Book News* reviewer remarked.

Doyle's fifth book, *Easy Avenue,* was published in 1988. It shifts to a new narrator, Hubbo O'Driscoll, an orphan in the care of a very kind distant relative, known only as Mrs. O'Driscoll. In a state of poverty, Hubbo and Mrs. O'Driscoll have moved from Ottawa's Lowertown to the Uplands Emergency Shelter. There, both of them enter Glebe Collegiate Institute—Hubbo as a student and his foster mother as the school's cleaning woman. They discover that in this part of town the division between rich and poor is pronounced—a division highlighted by Hubbo's descriptions of his daily bus ride. On the bus—an involuntary meeting place of the two classes—the rich people sit as far from the poor as they can, trying not to touch them and keeping "their noses pointed upwards so they wouldn't be breathing our air," Hubbo reports. Getting off the bus is a Doylesque frenzy. The poor people, who got on the bus first, have the window seats, and crawl over the rich people to get out. The rich people "couldn't get off first because there were piles of people, poor people, falling down the aisle and tumbling out the door and shoving and swearing and clawing their way out. . . . Everybody was touching the rich people now, putting their sticky hands on their nice coats, tromping all over their nice shiny shoes, breathing bad teeth right into their nice faces, bodies rubbing against their nice bodies, shoulders hitting shoulders, bony knees touching the backs of their nice fat legs."

Hubbo finds himself caught between factions. His real affections are with the people he knows at the shelter, especially Fleurette Featherstone Fitchell. Fleurette, Hubbo discovers, is the daughter of a prostitute. Back in Lowertown, Fleurette had a rather unsavory reputation, which she is intent on leaving behind. Hubbo likes her immediately. But, his aspirations to belong to an elite club at school lead him in another direction, causing him to pretend he doesn't know Mrs. O'Driscoll and to lie about his address. When Hubbo gets a job as a companion to a wealthy old woman and begins to receive money from a mysterious benefactor, he fabricates an identity for himself that is acceptable to the snobs in his school. The death of his employer and an estrangement from Fleurette, however, activate Hubbo's natural generosity, and the affection of his friends helps him to resist the pull of this social world.

Easy Avenue is often compared by critics to classic novels for young readers. Its plot and "eccentric characters" parallel nineteenth-century English writer Charles Dickens's *Great Expectations,* according to Pamela Young in her *Maclean's* review. *Canadian Children's Literature* contributor Lionel Adley, also noting the similarities to *Great Expectations,* added that "the hero's laid-back ridicule of fools in office" recalls American author J. D. Salinger's well-known novel, *The Catcher in the Rye.* And Eva Martin in her *Books for Young People* review compared Fleurette Featherstone Fitchell's transformation to the story of *Cinderella.* But reviewers agreed that although Doyle works with classic themes, his style is uniquely his own, and uniquely Canadian. Describing him as "regional yet universal," Martin commented that "Doyle's imagination is stimulated not by current social issues or middle-class fantasy worlds but by what the author has to say about himself and his community."

Doyle's next novel, *Covered Bridge,* continues Hubbo's story. The O'Driscolls have moved to a farm in the country, along with their newly-adopted dog, Nerves. For Hubbo, the well-deserved happiness that the makeshift family finds at the farm is represented by a nearby covered bridge—a symbol of the state of harmony that has existed for generations between nature and the human community. The bridge is also a memorial, to the romantic Hubbo, to the legend of two local lovers, Ophelia and Oscar. Years before, Ophelia, suffering gravely from a brain tumor, had jumped off the bridge to her death. Because of the suicide, Father Foley set her grave outside of the church cemetery. Her fiance Oscar makes daily visits to the site where she jumped, and Hubbo has seen her ghost there.

With its engaging mystery and good-natured satire, *Covered Bridge* depicts not only the effects of technological progress on the way of life in a rural Canadian town, but also the effects of the rural town upon progress. Hubbo plans to save the covered bridge, not in order to stop progress (a modern bridge is being built), but to keep the humanizing past alive in the rather intolerant and materialistic present. A petition, signed by the workers of the town, reads: "I, the undersigned, refuse to tear down the covered bridge. I would rather save it for Posterity. For, without a past, we have no future."

Covered Bridge, like so many of Doyle's novels, encompasses a large spectrum of contemporary problems within a framework of the old timeless questions yet manages to carry off a joke at the same time. Martin summarized that "Brian Doyle is one of the most daring and experimental writers of young-adult novels. He deals with the most sensitive of issues—racism, violence, anti-social activity of all sorts—with a tongue-in-cheek humor that never denigrates the human spirit."

BIOGRAPHICAL/CRITICAL SOURCES:

BOOKS

Children's Literature Review, Volume 22, Gale, 1991, pp. 27-34.
Doyle, Brian, *Hey Dad!,* Groundwood Books, 1978.
Doyle, *You Can Pick Me up at Peggy's Cove,* Groundwood Books, 1979.
Doyle, *Up to Low,* Groundwood Books, 1982.
Doyle, *Angel Square,* Groundwood Books, 1984.
Doyle, *Easy Avenue,* Groundwood Books, 1988.
Doyle, *Covered Bridge,* Groundwood Books, 1990.
Landsberg, Michele, *Reading for the Love of It: Best Books for Young Readers,* Prentice-Hall, 1987, pp. 77-98.

PERIODICALS

Books for Young People, October, 1988, pp. 12 and 18.
Books in Canada, February, 1983, pp. 32-33.
Canadian Children's Books, Authors, and Illustrators, 1985-86.
Canadian Children's Literature, Number 22, 1981, pp. 47-50; Number 37, 1985, pp. 67-70; Number 54, 1989, pp. 71-72.
Children's Book News, December, 1984, p. 3.
Horn Book, February, 1984, pp. 99-103.
In Review: Canadian Books for Children, autumn, 1978, p. 57; August, 1980, p. 45.
Maclean's, December 13, 1982, p. 56-58; December 26, 1988, p. 60.
Quill and Quire, August 1980, p. 30; November, 1982, p. 26; December, 1982, p. 27; November, 1984, p. 18.
World of Children's Books, 1981, pp. 27-33.

—Sketch by Sonia Benson

*   *   *

DUBE, Marcel 1930-

PERSONAL: Born January 3, 1930, in Montreal, Quebec, Canada; son of Eugene (an accountant) and Juliette (Belanger) Dube; married Nicole Fontaine, April, 1956. *Education:* College Sainte-Marie (Montreal), B.A., 1951; graduate study at University of Montreal during 1950s; attended theater schools in Paris, France, 1953-54.

CAREER: Writer. La Jeune Scene (theater group), in Quebec, founder and stage director, 1950-56; affiliated with National Film Board of Canada, 1956-57; affiliated with Office de la Langue Francaise au Quebec (Quebec Government agency for the French language), Quebec City, Quebec, beginning in 1977. Speechwriter for Quebec premier Jean Lesage, c. 1960. Executive vice-president of Theatre de l'Egregore. *Military service:* Canadian Army.

MEMBER: Federation des Auteurs et des Artistes du Canada (president, 1959), Societe des Auteurs et des Com-

positeurs (past president), Royal Society of Canada (fellow).

AWARDS, HONOURS: First prize from Western Quebec Drama Festival, 1952, for "De l'autre cote du mur"; grand prize from Dominion Drama Festival, 1953, for "Zone," and 1954, for "Chambres a louer"; grant from Canada Foundation, 1958; senior arts fellow of Canada Council, 1959-60; Prix Victor Morin from Societe Jean-Baptiste, 1966, for contributions to Quebec theater; grant from ministry of cultural affairs to prepare edition of collected plays, 1967; Prix David from province of Quebec, 1973, for complete body of work.

WRITINGS:

STAGE PLAYS

Le Bal triste (one-act), first produced by La Jeune Scene in 1950.
De l'autre cote du mur (one-act; first produced by La Jeune Scene in 1952), published in the collection *De l'autre cote du mur suivi de cinq courtes pieces,* Lemeac, 1973.
Zone (three-act; first produced by La Jeune Scene in 1952), Editions de la Cascade (Montreal), 1956, translation by Aviva Ravel, Playwrights Canada (Toronto), 1982.
Chambres a louer, first produced by La Jeune Scene in 1954, adapted for radio and television.
Le Barrage, first produced in Montreal by Theatre-Club at Theatre du Gesu, 1955.
Le Naufrage (first produced by Theatre-Club in 1955), revised, introduction by Jean Cleo Godin, Lemeac, 1971.
Les Temps des lilas (three-act; first produced in Montreal at Theatre du Nouveau Monde, February 25, 1958), published with *Un Simple Soldat,* Institut Litteraire du Quebec, 1958, adapted for television.
Un Simple Soldat (adapted from his television play of the same title; first produced in Montreal at Comedie-Canadienne, May 31, 1958), published as a five-act with *Les Temps de Lilas,* revised four-act version (first produced in Montreal at Comedie-Canadienne, 1967), Editions de l'Homme (Montreal), 1967.
Octobre (first produced in Montreal at Theatre de l'Essai de l'Ecole des Beaux-Arts, 1959), Lemeac, 1977.
Florence (two-act; adapted from his television play of the same title; first produced in Montreal at Comedie-Canadienne, October 20, 1960), Institut Litteraire du Quebec, 1960.
Les Beaux Dimanches (three-act; first produced in Montreal at Comedie-Canadienne, February, 1965), Lemeac, 1968.

(With Louis-Georges Carrier and Claude Leveillee) *L'Est un saison,* first produced in Montreal at Comedie-Canadienne, 1965.

Bilan (two-act; title means "Balance Sheet"; revised from his television play of the same title; first produced in Montreal at Comedie-Canadienne, 1965), Lemeac, 1968.

Au retour des oies blanches (two-act; first produced in Montreal at Comedie-Canadienne, October 21, 1966), Lemeac, 1969, translation by Jean Remple published as *The White Geese,* New Press (Toronto), 1972.

Equation a deux inconnus (adapted from his television play of the same title), first produced in Montreal at Theatre de l'Egregore, 1967.

Un Matin comme les autres (two-act; first produced in Montreal at Comedie-Canadienne, February 23, 1968), Lemeac, 1971.

La Vie quotidienne d'Antoine X (first produced in Montreal at Congres des Notaires), May 19, 1968.

Pauvre amour (first produced in Montreal at Comedie-Canadienne, 1968), Lemeac, 1969.

(With Louis-Georges Carrier) *Hold-up!* (first produced in Eastman, Quebec, at Theatre de la Marjolaine, 1969), published as *Hold-up! Photo-roman en dix chapitres,* Lemeac, 1969.

Le Coup de l'etrier [and] *Avant de t'en aller* (one-acts; first produced together in Montreal at Theatre du Rideau Vert, December 5, 1969), Lemeac, 1970.

Paradis perdu, published with the television play *L'Echeance du vendredi,* Lemeac, 1972.

Portes disparus, first produced in 1972.

De l'autre cote du mur suivi de cinq courtes pieces (collection; includes *De l'autre cote du mur* and the unproduced one-acts *L'Aiguillage, Le Visiteur, Les Freres ennemis, Le Pere ideal,* and *Rendez-vous du lendemain*), Lemeac, 1973.

Jeremie (ballet scenario; first produced in Montreal at Sir George Williams University, 1973), published with a translation by Jean Remple, Lemeac, 1974.

Virginie (four-act; first produced in Montreal at Compagnie Jean Duceppe, 1974), Lemeac, 1974.

L'Impromptu de Quebec; ou, Le Testament (first produced in Eastman, Quebec, at Theatre de la Marjolaine, 1974), Lemeac, 1974.

L'Ete s'appelle Julie, Lemeac, 1975.

(With Jean Barbeau) *Dites-le avec des fleurs,* Lemeac, 1976.

Le Reformiste; ou, L'Honneur des hommes (first produced in Montreal at Theatre du Nouveau Monde, 1977), Lemeac, 1977.

Also author of unproduced and unpublished plays, including *Port au Persil.* Translator of William Gibson's "Two for the Seesaw," first produced at Theatre de Perce, 1964.

TELEVISION PLAYS

L'Etranger, Radio Canada, (Canadian Broadcasting Corporation), 1953.

Chambres a louer (adapted from his stage play of the same title), Radio-Canada, 1954.

La Lettre, Radio-Canada, 1954.

La Bicyclette, Radio-Canada, 1954.

(With Louis-Georges Carrier) *Pour cinq sous d'amour,* Radio-Canada, 1955.

Florence, Radio-Canada, 1957.

Un Simple Soldat, Radio-Canada, 1957.

La Fin du reve, Radio-Canada, 1958, revised version broadcast as part of the series "Le Monde de Marcel Dube," 1969.

Meedee (first broadcast by Radio-Canada, 1958), Lemeac, 1973.

La Cellule (first broadcast by Radio-Canada, 1959, revised version broadcast as part of the series "Le Monde de Marcel Dube," 1969), Lemeac, 1973.

Equation a deux inconnus, Radio-Canada, 1959.

Bilan, Radio-Canada, 1960.

La Cote de Sable (series), Radio-Canada, 1960-62.

(With Georges Dor) *Aux voyageurs,* 1962.

Le Temps des lilas (adapted from his stage play of the same title), Radio-Canada, 1962.

L'Echeance du vendredi (first broadcast by Radio-Canada, 1962), revised version published with the stage play *Paradis Perdu,* Lemeac, 1972.

De 9 a 5 (series), Radio-Canada, 1963-65.

Le Monde de Marcel Dube (anthology series; includes the teleplays *La Fin du reve* and *La Cellule*), Radio-Canada, 1968-72, extracts published as *Entre midi et soir,* Lemeac, 1971.

Also author of *La Nuit se leve,* 1956. Translator of Arthur Miller's *Death of a Salesman,* Irwin Shaw's *Gentle People,* Ben Hecht's *The Front Page,* and Mac Shoub's *Ashes in the Wind.*

RADIO PLAYS

Pleure, pauvre Guillaume, Radio-Canada, 1951.

Cartes postales, Radio-Canada, 1951.

Pivart, le malin, Radio-Canada, 1951.

L'Anneau, Radio-Canada, 1952.

La Randonnee fantanstique, Radio-Canada, 1953.

Un Bord de la riviere, Radio-Canada, 1954.

Chambres a louer (adapted from his stage play of the same title), CKAC-Radio, 1955-56.

Un Bouquet d'immortelles, Radio-Canada, 1956.

(Translator) Mac Shoub, *Le Cage* (adapted from *Crack-Up*), Radio-Canada, 1959.

Manuel (first broadcast by CBFT-Radio, 1968), Lemeac, 1973.

OTHER

Le Train du nord: Le Roman de Francine, Editions du Jour (Montreal), 1961.
Textes et documents (poetry and prose), Lemeac, 1968.
La Tragedie est un acte de foi (writings about the theater), Lemeac, 1973.
Poemes de sable (poems), Lemeac, 1974.

Also author of poetry collections *Couleurs de jours meles* and *Ondes courtes.* Author of "Les Cloches de Notre-Dame" and "La Nuit perdue." Member of editorial board of *Ecrits du Canada Francais,* beginning in 1958. Contributor to periodicals, including *Actualites, Amerique francaise, Perspectives, Le Magazine Maclean,* and *Cite libre.*

SIDELIGHTS: Considered a pioneer of modern Quebec theater, Marcel Dube is one of the first playwrights to create a large body of work that examines the lives and concerns of French-speaking people in his province. His work often conveys a sense of imprisonment and frustration, inspired by the plight of the French-speaking minority in Canada, the strain that Quebec's conservative traditions place on the individual, or the human dilemma of living in an imperfect world. Dube's work reflects his appreciation for a wide variety of dramatists, including playwrights of ancient Greece, nineteenth-century realists such as Anton Chekhov (his personal favorite), and contemporaries such as Arthur Miller and Jean Anouilh. At the same time, however, Dube has noted the need for Quebec playwrights to distance themselves from the models of other cultures in order to create a distinct literary tradition for the province. In the late 1970s Dube extended his concerns for Quebec culture by joining a government office charged with nurturing the French language there.

Dube displayed his energy and talent early in his career. As a teenager he was strongly impressed by the debut of Gratien Gelinas's play *Tit-Coq,* a groundbreaking work that showed Quebecois characters in a realistic setting, and he saw the production five times. In 1950 he founded La Jeune Scene, a theater group that produced plays and sponsored lectures about drama. For the next few years, in addition to writing scripts for Societe Radio-Canada (the Canadian Broadcasting Corporation), he directed his own stage plays through La Jeune Scene. Dube soon gained recognition from the theater community, and he was determined to become a professional author after his second play, *Zone,* won national acclaim. Despite the artistic success of La Jeune Scene, financial problems drove it out of business in 1956, leaving Dube with the group's ten-thousand-dollar debt. He repaid the creditors as a prolific scriptwriter for radio and television. Some of Dube's audience came to know him principally for his television work, which included *De 9 a 5* and *La Cote de Sable,* two popular series that he wrote in the early 1960s. Several of

his best-known plays either began as television dramas or gained a wide audience by being adapted for the medium.

During the 1950s Dube often set his plays in the working-class neighborhoods of east Montreal, the scene of his own childhood. *Zone* shows a group of teenagers who resort to thrill-seeking and crime in an effort to transcend the reality of their Montreal slum (the "zone" of the title). Led by "Tarzan," a youth whose name evokes both bravery and pulp escapism, the gang prospers by smuggling cigarettes until their activities lead to the death of a customs officer. Then their world collapses amid betrayal and futile gestures of heroism. Though the police hunt down Tarzan and kill him, their own commander recognizes that the gangleader is not simply a criminal but a rebel against his oppressive surroundings. *Un Simple Soldat* opens as young Joseph Latour returns from military service in World War II. As he struggles with unemployment, the economic domination of anglophones, and an unhappy family life, Joseph regrets that the war ended before he could display his bravery in armed combat. Soon he volunteers for the Korean War, during which he is killed. The title character of *Florence* is a young secretary who has unthinkingly accepted the limited horizons imposed on her life by her repressed parents. Prepared to enter an uninspiring marriage to one of her co-workers, Florence reassesses her life after a sexual encounter with her free-living boss. She cancels her wedding plans, refuses the boss's offer for her to live with him, and moves out of her parents' home. As the play ends Florence has abjured Quebec entirely, deciding to pursue her new independence in New York City.

Reviewers suggest that the stunted lives of Dube's working-class characters are a metaphor for the larger paralysis of Quebec society. According to *Dictionary of Literary Biography* contributor Renate Usmiani, a speech by Florence's father summarizes Dube's criticism of Quebec's heritage of social repression. "I've been honest all my life, not out of honesty, but out of fear," the father says, translated by Usmiani. The father explains: "At school, in church on Sunday, at the electoral campaigns, in the factories, in the offices, everywhere we've been taught to be afraid." For leaders of French Quebec, social repression became, ironically, the means to preserve French culture in the face of hostility from the English-speaking majority in Canada. As the father concludes: "We've been taught that the best way to defend ourselves was to shut ourselves up in our houses and our parishes, away from danger. . . . No pleasures allowed, evil everywhere. . . . That's why we are nothing . . .!" Dube's sentiments coincided with the emergence of Quebec's Quiet Revolution in 1960, when political moderates came to power in the provincial government and began to curtail the longstanding control of Quebec society by political and religious conservatives. For a few years during this period, Dube wrote speeches for one of the movement's leaders, Quebec Liberal premier Jean Lesage.

But while Dube seemed fundamentally sympathetic to the new political and social dynamism that characterized Quebec in the 1960s and beyond, his plays continued to be marked by doubt about the human condition. He changed the setting of his work to Quebec's more affluent and sophisticated professional classes, showing the flaws of human nature that endure despite such prosperity. *Bilan* ("Balance Sheet") shows businessman Billy Larose as he undergoes massive personal disillusionment. His daughter walks out on her marriage; one son rejects him on philosophical grounds, then dies in a car crash; another son is revealed as an embezzler; Billy's wife turns out to be in love with his best friend. Prosperity has helped to destroy Billy's life, and at the end of the play he is bitter and isolated. In *Au retour des oies blanches* (published in translation as *The White Geese*), which some critics consider Dube's best work, the hypocritical lifestyle of an upper-class family has still more shattering consequences. A truth game takes place at the family dinner table, during which the father of the family is compelled to discuss his failed political career, including crimes that range from corruption to rape. Eventually the family's troubled daughter learns that her fun-loving "Uncle" Thomas, with whom she had an affair, is actually her biological father. After a burst of revulsion that recalls the ancient Greek tragedy of Oedipus, the daughter hangs herself. A later play, *Le Reformiste,* shows a well-educated Quebecois confronting the social realities of the province in the late 1970s. A strong-willed former Jesuit, he is dismayed by the changing values and numerous flaws he sees in Quebec society, and he finally commits suicide rather than compromise his ideals.

Despite the wrenching denouements of many of his plays, Dube has suggested that his determination to write is itself a sign of his faith in the future. As if to underscore this point, he titled his 1973 collection of writings about the theater *La Tragedie est un acte de foi*—"Tragedy Is an Act of Faith."

BIOGRAPHICAL/CRITICAL SOURCES:

BOOKS

Dictionary of Literary Biography, Volume 53: *Canadian Writers since 1960: First Series,* Gale, 1986.

Godin, Jean-Cleo and Laurent Mailhot, *Le Theatre quebecois,* HMQ (Montreal), 1970.

Hamblet, Edwin C., *Marcel Dube and French-Canadian Drama,* Exposition, 1970.

Laroche, Maximilien, *Marcel Dube,* Fides (Montreal), 1970.*

—Sketch by Thomas Kozikowski

E-F

ELIE, Robert 1915-1973

PERSONAL: Born April 5, 1915, in Montreal, Quebec, Canada; died January 19, 1973; son of Emile and Maria (Dubois) Elie; married Marie Marthe Huot, April 22, 1944; children: Jerome, Helene, Bernard, Suzanne. *Education:* College Sainte-Marie, B.A., 1935; attended University of Montreal; attended McGill University. *Religion:* Catholic.

CAREER: Cofounder of cultural magazine *La Releve,* 1934, contributor, 1935-40; *Le Canada,* Montreal, Quebec, translator, literary and music critic, 1940; *La Presse,* Montreal, reporter and art critic, c. 1941-43; Canadian Broadcasting Corporation (CBC), Montreal, journalist, 1943-47, director of press and information services, 1948-58; *Revue d'architecture,* founder, 1947; Ecole des Beaux-Arts, Montreal, director, 1958; Special Secretariat on Bilingualism, Ottawa, Ontario, assistant director, beginning 1966; Canada Council, associate director, 1970-73. President of the Conference Canadienne des Arts, 1959; cultural adviser to Paris, France, for the provincial government of Quebec, 1962.

MEMBER: Royal Society of Canada; Societe d'Art Contemporain (president, 1948).

AWARDS, HONOURS: Prix David for *La Fin des songes,* 1950; Canada Council grant, 1960.

WRITINGS:

Borduas (nonfiction), L'Arbre (Montreal), 1943.
(Editor with Jean Le Moyne; author of introduction) *Poesies completes: Regards et jeux dans l'espace; Les Solitudes,* by Hector de Saint-Denys Garneau, Fides (Montreal), 1949.
La Fin des songes (novel), Beauchemin (Montreal), 1950; translated by Irene Coffin as *Farewell My Dreams,*
Ryerson (Toronto), 1954, Bouregy & Curl (New York), 1955.
(Editor with Le Moyne) *Journal,* by Garneau, Beauchemin, 1954.
Il suffit d'un jour (novel; title means, "It Only Takes a Day"), Beauchemin, 1957.
(Editor with Le Moyne and Claude Hurtubise) *Lettres a ses amis,* by Garneau, HMH (Montreal), 1967.
Oeuvres (includes the novels *Elisabeth* and *Les Naufrages,* as well as short stories, essays, and plays), edited by Paul Beaulieu, Hurtubise/HMH (Cite de LaSalle, Quebec), 1979.

Also author of plays, including *L'Etrangere,* 1954, *Le Congres des illustres,* 1955, *Didi et Dada,* 1960, *La Place publique,* 1964, *Le Silence de la ville,* 1964, and *L'Inconnue,* 1964; contributor to periodicals, including *Ecrits du Canada francais, Liberte, Macleans,* and *Vie des arts.*

SIDELIGHTS: Best-known for his novels, French Canadian author Robert Elie also wrote poetry, drama, short fiction, and art criticism. His first novel, *La Fin des songes,* has been translated into English as *Farewell My Dreams* and garnered the prestigious Prix David award in 1950. Other honors presented to Elie during his career include a Canada Council grant awarded in 1960.

Elie was born in a working-class neighborhood of Montreal, Quebec, in 1915. As a young adult he befriended the poet Hector de Saint-Denys Garneau. Elie eventually helped edit three volumes of Garneau's work, and with Garneau and others founded the journal *La Releve* in 1934. A few years later, Elie made the acquaintance of painter Paul-Emile Borduas, whose aesthetic and social ideas he wrote about in his study *Borduas,* published in 1943. During his early career Elie also worked as a reporter and critic for such periodicals as *Le Canada* and *La*

Presse. He took a post with the Canadian Broadcasting Corporation (CBC) in 1943, first performing in a journalistic capacity, then becoming the director of the company's press and information services in 1948. The following year, Elie collaborated with Jean Le Moyne on editing their first collection of Garneau's pieces.

Farewell My Dreams was published in 1950. The book concerns the lives of two friends—Marcel Larocque and Bernard Guerin. When both are in their thirties, they begin to question the values they have been brought up with and have lived their lives pursuing. Marcel is deeply depressed by this crisis of being, and kills himself. Bernard, however, survives, and is even more determined to find meaning in his own life after the suicide of his friend. As Grazia Merler observed in the *Dictionary of Literary Biography,* "it has been suggested that Marcel's spiritual crisis resembles that experienced by the poet Garneau."

After helping to edit a volume of Garneau's private writings entitled *Journal* in 1954, Elie brought forth his own second novel. *Il suffit d'un jour,* or, "it only takes a day," reached readers in 1957. The action comprises one day in a small village in Quebec; an American canning company brings both business and temptation to the town. Though, as Merler pointed out, "the novel has been criticized for sketching in too short a time span too many characters and plots," most reviewers held up the novel's portrayal of the young girl Elisabeth for praise. She, and another character, Pierre, "live according to a standard of Christian charity, humanism, and free will," in Merler's words. Merler went on to conclude that "[the] moral themes Elie develops in *Il suffit d'un jour . . .* make it clear that this is a novel with a spiritual message."

For the rest of his life, Elie continued to promote the works of Garneau and wrote plays that were published in *Ecrits du Canada francais.* He also completed two novels, *Elisabeth* and *Les Naufrages,* that were posthumously published. In addition to his work as a writer, Elie spent his later years serving the cause of French Canadian culture. He became the director of Montreal's Ecole des Beaux-Arts in 1958 and officiated as president of the Conference Canadienne des Arts in 1959. Elie was a cultural adviser to Paris, France, for the government of Quebec in 1962; then he was appointed to the Special Secretariat on Bilingualism in 1966. When he died in 1973, he was serving as associate director of the Canada Council.

BIOGRAPHICAL/CRITICAL SOURCES:

BOOKS

Dictionary of Literary Biography, Volume 88: *Canadian Writers, 1920-1959, Second Series,* Gale, 1989.
Gagnon, Marc, *Robert Elie,* Fides, 1968.

Ouellet, France, and Michel Biron, *Inventaire sommaire du fonds Robert Elie,* Ministere des Affaires Culturelles, Bibliotheque Nationale du Quebec, 1988.

PERIODICALS

Revue de l'Universite d'Ottawa, October/December, 1973, pp. 573-586.*

—*Sketch by Elizabeth Wenning*

*   *   *

EPERNAY, Mark
   See GALBRAITH, John Kenneth

*   *   *

FERRIS, James Cody
   See McFARLANE, Leslie (Charles)

*   *   *

FERRON, Jacques   1921-1985

PERSONAL: Born January 20, 1921, in Louiseville, Quebec, Canada; died April 22, 1985; son of J. Alphonse and Adrienne (Caron) Ferron; married Madeleine Therien, 1943 (divorced); married Madelaine Lavallee, 1949 (some sources say 1952); children: (first marriage) Chaouac; (second marriage) Marie, Martine, Jean-Olivier. *Education:* Universite Laval, M.D., 1945.

CAREER: Practicing physician in Riviere Madeleine, Quebec, 1946-48, and Ville Jacques-Cartier, Quebec, 1949-85. President of Canadian Peace Congress, 1954; founder of the Rhinoceros Party, 1963. *Military service:* Canadian Army, Royal Canadian Medical Corps, 1945-46; became captain.

AWARDS, HONOURS: Governor General's Award in fiction, 1964, for *Contes d'un pays incertain;* named Chevalier of Merit of Longueuil.

WRITINGS:

Le Dodu; ou, Le Prix de bonheur (play; produced in Montreal, Quebec, at Theatre-Club, 1958), Orphee, 1956.
La Barbe de Francois Hertel (play), Orphee, 1956.
Tante Elise; ou, Le Prix de l'amour (play), Orphee, 1956.
Le Cheval de Don Juan (three-act play), Orphee, 1957.
Le Licou (play; produced in Montreal, Quebec, at Theatre-Club, 1958), Orphee, 1958.
Les Grands Soleils (play; produced in Montreal, Quebec, at Theatre du Nouveau Monde, January 27, 1968), Orphee, 1958.
Corolles (poems), Grassin, 1961.

Contes du pays incertain (stories), Orphee, 1962, translation by Betty Bednarski published as *Tales from the Uncertain Country,* House of Anansi Press, 1972.

Cotnoir (novella), Orphee, 1962, translation by Pierre Cloutier published as *Dr. Cotnoir,* Harvest House, 1973.

Cazou; ou, Le Prix de la virginite (three-act play), 1963.

Le Tete du roi (four-act play), Ageum, 1963.

Contes anglais et autres (stories), Orphee, 1964.

La Nuit (novel), Editions Parti Pris, 1965.

Papa Boss (novel), Editions Parti Pris, 1966.

Contes: Contes anglais, Contes du pays incertain, contes inedits, Editions HMH, 1968.

La Charrette (novel), Editions HMH, 1968.

Theatre (plays; includes Tante Elise, a revision of Les Grands Soleils, and Le Don Juan chretien, a revision of Le Cheval de Don Juan), Deom, 1968.

Le Ciel de Quebec (novel), Editions du Jour, 1969, translation by Ray Ellenwood published as *The Penniless Redeemer,* Exile Editions, 1984.

Historiettes (essays), Editions du Jour, 1969.

L'Amelanchier (novel), Editions du Jour, 1970, translation by Raymond Y. Chamberlain published as *The Juneberry Tree,* Harvest House, 1975.

Le Salut de l'Irlande (novel), Editions du Jour, 1970.

Les Roses sauvages: Petit roman suivi d'une lettre d'amour soigneusement presentee (novel), Editions du Jour, 1971, translation by Betty Bednarski published as *Wild Roses: A Story Followed by a Love Letter,* McClelland & Stewart, 1976.

Le Saint-Elias (novel), Editions du Jour, 1972, translation by Pierre Cloutier published as *The Saint Elias,* Harvest House, 1975.

La Chaise du marechal-ferrant (novel), Editions du Jour, 1972.

Les Confitures de coings et autres textes, Editions Parti Pris, 1972, translation by Ray Ellenwood published as *Quince Jam,* Coach House Press, 1977.

Du fond de mon arriere-cuisine, Editions du Jour, 1973.

Escarmouches: La Longue Passe, two volumes, Lemeac, 1975.

The Cart, Exile Editions, 1981.

Selected Tales of Jacques Ferron, House of Anansi Press, 1984.

Le Choix de Jacques Ferron dans l'oeuvre de Jacques Ferron, Laurentiennes, 1985.

Also author of the plays "L'Ogre," 1949, "La Sortie," 1965, and "Le Coeur d'une mere," 1969.

Contributor of articles, plays, and stories to French Canadian magazines. Also founder and editor of *Le Bicorne.*

SIDELIGHTS: Jacques Ferron was first known throughout Quebec as a medical doctor and a strong political voice for his country. Recognition of Ferron's literary talents did not come until he was in his forties, although he wrote essays, plays, and a novel early in his life. His work has become an important and much studied part of Canadian literary history.

Ferron was born on January 20, 1921, in Louisville, Quebec. He was the oldest child of Joseph-Alphonse and Adrienne (Caron) Ferron. Ferron received his early education at Trois-Rivieres and then attended the College Jean-de-Brebeuf in Montreal. It was here that Ferron first encountered the cultural heritage of Quebec. While studying medicine at Universite Laval in Quebec City, he married a communist woman named Madeleine Therien in 1943. Ferron received his M.D. in 1945 and then joined the Army. He served as a doctor in the camps in Quebec and New Brunswick until leaving the military. Ferron began his private medical practice in Quebec where he continued until his death in 1985. In 1947 he and his wife had a daughter, but they divorced soon after. Ferron then married Madelaine Lavallee, and they had three children. During the 1950s Ferron began contributing essays on a variety of topics to the L'Information Medicale et Paramedicale. He also wrote letters to the editor of several major newspapers and journals. Ferron's first play *L'Ogre* (1949) was published when he was 28 and was followed by a series of dramas. He became politically active in the 1950s. He is best known for acting as a government mediator during the October Crisis of 1970, for founding the satirical political organization the Rhinoceros Party in 1963, and for promoting the passage of the Quebec referendum. Ferron first gained recognition for his literary abilities with the publication of his first collection of short stories *Contes du pays incertain* (1962), which won the Governor General's Award for fiction in 1963. Ferron continued his literary career, writing several more short stories, novels, and essays, while practicing medicine and staying active in politics. He died on April 22, 1985, leaving behind a collection of short stories and an autobiographical essay published together as *La Conference inachevee* (1988).

Ferron's interest in medicine and politics pervades his literary work. While working as a doctor in Quebec, Ferron observed its people and culture, and this provided the background for his fiction. The image of Quebec as an exiled country that is portrayed in the title of his first short story collection Contes du pays incertain is used throughout his writing. Ferron often mixes and contrasts opposites, the imaginary and the real, madness and insanity. Madness and death are common themes explored in Ferron's work. His novel *Cotnoir* (1962) brings together his interest in medicine and his fascination with madness and death. The main character is a doctor who struggles with death and befriends a mental patient. The theme of a doctor struggling with death continues in *La Charrette* (1968). Ferron's novels *La Nuit* (1965) and *Papa Boss*

(1966) are explorations of spirituality and the soul and represent Ferron's political beliefs. The interaction between person and place is important to Ferron's fiction. Much of his work analyzes the effect of Quebec on its residents, such as *L'Amelanchier* (1975) and *Les Roses sauvages* (1971), and sometimes Ferron tackled the same issue in a different setting as in *Le Salut de l'Irlande* (1970).

Ferron's dramas written early in his career are commonly considered unremarkable. Critics did not begin to give Ferron's work attention until his collection *Contes du pays incertain* won the Governor General's Award. Then after several good translations of his work appeared, Ferron's work gained recognition beyond French-speaking Canada. His writing is still met with ambivalence by many English Canadians. Critics agree that Ferron has an affinity for the short story genre and many praise his mixture of fantasy and reality. Critics have found that Ferron had a preoccupation with death, and some point out that this probably resulted from his mother's death from tuberculosis in 1931. Ferron's first novel did not find an audience or praise from critics, but subsequent novels were praised for being interesting and effectively portraying important issues of Canadian culture and politics.

BIOGRAPHICAL/CRITICAL SOURCES:

BOOKS

Beaulieu, Victor-Levy, *La Tete de Monsieur Ferron; ou, Les Chians: Une Epopee drolatique tiree du Ciel de Quebec de Jacques Ferron*, VLB, 1979.

Boucher, Jean-Pierre, *Les 'Contes' de Jacques Ferron*, L'Aurore, 1974.

Boucher, *Jacques Ferron au pays des amelanchiers*, Presse de l'Universite de Montreal, 1973.

De Roussan, Jacques, *Jacques Ferron: Quatre Itineraires*, Presse de l'Universite du Quebec, 1971.

Dictionary of Literary Biography, Volume 60: *Canadian Writers since 1960, Second Series*, Gale, 1987.

Heath, Jeffrey M., editor, *Profiles in Canadian Literature, Volume 5*, Dundurn, 1986, pp. 121-28.

L'Herault, Jacques Ferron, *Cartographe de l'imaginaire*, Presses de l'Universite de Montreal, 1980.

Marcel, Jean, *Jacques Ferron malgre lui*, Editions du Jour, 1970; revised and enlarged, Parti Pris, 1978.

Potvin, Diane, editor, *La Nuit de Jacques Ferron*, Editions France-Quebec and Fernand Nathan, 1979, pp. 5-17.

Staines, David, editor, *The Callaghan Symposium*, University of Ottawa Press, 1981, pp. 37-46.

Taschereau, Yves, *Le Portuna: La Medecine dans l'oeuvre de Jacques Ferron*, L'Aurore, 1975.

Wyczynski, Paul, Bernard Julien, and Helene Beauchamp-Rank, editors, *Le Theatre Canadien-Francais: Evolution, temoignages, bibliographie*, Fides, 1976, pp. 581-96.

Ziroff, Mary, *A Study Guide to Jacques Ferron's "Tales from the Uncertain Country,"* Anansi, 1977.

PERIODICALS

Antigonish Review, Volume 61, spring, 1985, pp. 43-49.

Breches, Number 1, 1973, pp. 26-42.

Brick, Volume 16, fall, 1982; Volume 24, spring, 1985, pp. 6-9.

Canadian Fiction Magazine, Volume 13, summer, 1974, pp. 98-107.

Canadian Literature, Volume 88, spring, 1981, pp. 20-30; Volume 107, winter, 1985, pp. 193-95.

Culture Vivant, Volume 24, March, 1973, pp. 21-24.

Derives, Numbers 14-15, 1978, pp. 3-23.

Etudes Francais, Volume 4, February, 1968, pp. 208-15; Volume 5, February, 1969, pp. 185-93; Volume 12, October, 1976.

Fantasy Review, Volume 9, number, 5, May, 1986, p. 25.

Globe and Mail (Toronto), January 19, 1985; February 2, 1985.

Journal of Canadian Fiction, Volumes 25-26, 1979, pp. 175-85.

Modern Fiction Studies, Volume 22, winter, 1976, pp. 441-48.

Mosaic, Volume 14, summer, 1981, pp. 113-17.

Nord, Volume 7, 1977, pp. 165-79.

Presence Francophone, Volume 18, spring, 1979, pp. 127-33; Volume 22, spring, 1981, pp. 131-40; Volume 23, autumn, 1981, pp. 131-41.

Quebec, Volume 68, May, 1968, pp. 84-87.

Revue Frontenac, Volume 1, 1983, pp. 41-60.

Revue du Pacifique, Volume 4, spring, 1978, pp. 68-81.

Revue de l'Universite de Moncton, Volume 6, May, 1974, pp. 72-74.

Revue de l'Universite d'Ottawa, Volume 54, January/March, 1984, pp. 65-89.

Voix et Images, Volume 3, September, 1977, pp. 127-46; special issue on Ferron, Volume 8, spring, 1983.

Voix et Images du Pays, Volume 1, February, 1967, pp. 83-98; Volume 6, 1973, pp. 103-110, 111-21; Volume 9, 1975, pp. 163-80.*

*   *   *

FINDLEY, Timothy 1930-

PERSONAL: Born October 30, 1930, in Toronto, Ontario, Canada; son of Allan Gilmore and Margaret (Bull) Findley. *Education:* Self-educated beyond the ninth grade after illness interrupted formal education.

ADDRESSES: Agent—The Turnbull Agency, P.O. Box 757, Dorset, VT 05251.

CAREER: Actor for fifteen years; was a charter member of Stratford (Ontario) Shakespeare Festival, 1953; went from Canada to England as protege of Alec Guinness; contracted with H. M. Tennant Productions, London, England, 1954-55, to appear in *The Prisoner* (with Alec Guinness), 1954, and *The Matchmaker* (with Ruth Gordon), 1955; toured with *The Matchmaker* in the United States, 1956-57; wrote advertising copy at a small radio station in Canada; full-time professional writer. Playwright in residence, National Arts Centre, Ottawa, Canada, 1974-75; writer in residence, University of Toronto, 1978-79.

MEMBER: International PEN (president, English-Canadian Centre, 1986-87), Authors Guild, Authors League of America, Writers' Union of Canada (chair, 1977-78), Association of Canadian Television and Radio Artists.

AWARDS, HONOURS: Canada Council Junior Arts Award, 1968; Major Armstrong Award, 1970, for radio drama, "The Journey"; Association of Canadian Television and Radio Artists award, 1975, for "The National Dream"; Governor General's Award for fiction in English, and City of Toronto Book Award, both 1977, both for *The Wars;* Canada Council Senior Arts Award, 1978; ANIK Award, 1980, for television documentary, *Dieppe: 1942;* D.Litt., Trent University, 1982, University of Guelph, 1984, York University, 1989; Canadian Authors Association Literary Award, 1985, for *Not Wanted on the Voyage,* and 1991, for *Inside Memory: Pages from a Writer's Workbook;* Officer of the Order of Canada, 1986; Order of Ontario, 1991.

WRITINGS:

NOVELS

The Last of the Crazy People, Meredith, 1967.
The Butterfly Plague, Viking, 1969.
The Wars, Clarke, Irwin, 1977.
Famous Last Words, Clarke, Irwin, 1981.
Not Wanted on the Voyage, Penguin, 1984.
The Telling of Lies: A Mystery, Penguin, 1986.
Headhunter, HarperCollins, 1993.
The Piano Man's Daughter, HarperCollins, 1995.

SHORT STORIES

Dinner along the Amazon, Penguin, 1984.
Stones, Penguin, 1988.

Contributor of short stories to *Tamarack Review, New Orleans Review, Esquire, Cavalier,* and other periodicals.

PLAYS

Can You See Me Yet? (first produced in Ottawa at the National Arts Centre, 1976), Talonbooks, 1977.
John A.—Himself, first produced by Theatre London, London, Ontario, 1979.

The Stillborn Lover (first produced by the Grand Theatre, London, and the National Arts Centre, 1993), Blizzard Publishers, 1993.

SCREENPLAYS

The Paper People, Canadian Broadcasting Corp. (CBC-TV), 1967.
Don't Let the Angels Fall, National Film Board of Canada-Columbia, 1969.
The Whiteoaks of Jalna (based on the novels by Mazo de la Roche), CBC-TV, 1971-72.
(With William Whitehead) *The National Dream,* CBC-TV, 1974.
(With Whitehead) *Dieppe: 1942,* CBC-TV, 1979.
The Wars (based on his novel of the same title), Nielsen-Ferns, National Film Board of Canada, 1983.

OTHER

Inside Memory: Pages from a Writer's Workbook, Harper-Collins, 1994.

Also author of other television, radio, and film scripts, including *The Journey* (radio drama), 1970. Author of novellas, including *Hello Cheeverland, Goodbye,* 1978, and *Lemonade,* 1981. Contributor of critical reviews and essays to magazines and newspapers, including Toronto *Globe and Mail, Toronto Life,* and *Saturday Night.*

WORK IN PROGRESS: Pilgrim, a novel; *Other People's Children,* a play.

SIDELIGHTS: Timothy Findley is a Canadian actor-turned-novelist who started writing when he was in his teens. "At that time I had glandular fever," he told *Books.* "I was in bed for the whole of one winter and did little more than sleep, wake up, eat, and go back to sleep." When he wasn't sleeping, Findley wrote what he calls "a kind of modern day romance." His serious writing began almost a decade later when he wrote a story entitled "About Effie" to prove a point to actress Ruth Gordon with whom he was performing at the time.

"We had been to an exhibition of paintings in Manchester, all done by people under thirty years of age," he explained in an interview with Alison Summers in *Canadian Literature.* "I was in my twenties then. When we came out, Ruth asked me 'Why are you people so damned negative about everything? All those pictures were black, depressing, ugly. Can't you say *yes* to anything?' Aloud I said to her, 'I don't think we're negative, Ruth.' I had an argument, or rather a pleasant conversation, with her. Secretly I decided, 'I'll prove that we're not.' I went back to my digs and I wrote a story." As Findley told *Books,* it was " a very sad and negative story. But she loved it." Gordon lent him an old typewriter, showed his story to Thornton Wilder, and suggested to Findley that perhaps literature, not theatre, was his natural milieu.

Since that time, Findley has written seven novels and three novellas, as well as numerous short stories, plays, and films. An actor no longer, he still infuses his writing with the pageantry of the stage. "The importance of sound, spectacle, and style to a full appreciation of Findley's fictions, whether they be scripts intended to be *listened to* on the radio, scripts intended to be *seen* on television, the movie screen, or the theatre-stage, or whether they be the texts of short-stories and novels, cannot be overemphasized," John F. Hulcoop writes in *Canadian Literature.* "His work compels the critic to recover his senses (*see* more, *hear* more) by making direct appeals to the viewer-listener-reader through sight, sound and style: these are what force us to pay attention—to look and listen and mark his words."

In addition to stylistic similarities, Findley's fictions share some common themes. Fraught with violence, laced with images of fire, his books abound in symbolic details that reveal man's basic fears. "Everyone is so afraid of life itself that they would prefer to be locked up in an insane asylum," Findley commented in a 1981 CBC-TV interview. In several of his novels, including *The Last of the Crazy People* and *The Butterfly Plague,* Findley examines individuals who do insane things in order to clarify what, in his words, is "bright and good."

Peter Klovan believes that this idea receives its most powerful treatment in Findley's 1977 novel, *The Wars.* "Here," Klovan writes in *Canadian Literature,* "the device of a story-within-a-story is used to illustrate how a personality transcends elemental forces even while being destroyed by them. . . . As Findley's narrator realizes, 'People can only be found in what they do.' His problem in *The Wars* is to understand the actions of Robert Ross, a young Canadian officer, who when caught up in a German offensive during the Great War, tries and fails to save one hundred and thirty horses from being killed. Robert's failure leaves him horribly burned, and in many ways is simply the inevitable outcome of the pattern of futility which characterized his brief life. . . . But, in the process, Robert's struggle is raised to mythological proportions as a metaphor of fate and man's place in the universe, so that an apparent defeat is turned into a triumph. Indeed, 'tragic' is not too strong a term to describe *The Wars.*"

In a later work, a curious mix of fantasy and Old Testament legend entitled *Not Wanted on the Voyage,* Findley retells the story of Noah and the Great Flood, portraying the ark's builder as a "sinister" individual, "given to brutal sacrifices and experiments," according to a *Publishers Weekly* reviewer. Findley's Noah sees God's plan to flood the earth as "the perfect opportunity to exclude, to con-

demn, to sacrifice the unwanted masses," writes Isabel Raphael of the London *Times,* and indeed, Noah dooms the Faeries by refusing to allow them on the ark, then sentences females and undesirable species to live below deck. Lucifer also appears—disguised as a mysterious geisha named Lucy—and schemes his way aboard, thus ensuring the presence of evil after the flood.

Not Wanted on the Voyage is enlivened with Findley's whimsical touches: he creates a talking cat and a shy unicorn, and describes how God's visit to Noah is heralded by a chorus of singing lambs. But the tone of the novel is pessimistic. To Raphael's thinking, *Not Wanted on the Voyage* "is a very angry book, indeed. It deals with exploitation and devastation on a mighty scale, all in the name of God that man has created in his own flawed image." William French, writing in the Toronto *Globe and Mail,* declared, "Timothy Findley clearly believes that . . . the world would have been a better place if its post-flood history hadn't owed its origin to a drastic act of vengeance."

Critical response to *Not Wanted on the Voyage* was positive. Douglas Hill of the *Globe and Mail* calls the work "an imaginative reinvention of the Biblical account of Noah and the Flood," and French states: "Findley's ark is freighted with a heavy cargo of symbolism, baggage that Noah didn't have to contend with. But he uses it effectively to get several messages across that have contemporary significance—equality for women, the need for conservation . . . the threat posed by fundamentalists and anti-evolutionists, the danger of obsessive beliefs and blind, unquestioning faith."

Findley's body of work has brought him both critical and popular acclaim. In the words of *Globe and Mail* reviewer Margaret Cannon, Findley is "one of [Canadian literature's] shiniest stars. His literary honors include the highest awards Canada offers. His literary concerns—memory, the burden of the past—are the hautest of concerns. His pages drip with symbolism . . . and his prose is supremely refined." And Neil Bissoondath, also writing in the *Globe and Mail,* opines, "[Findley] is a writer of prodigious talents who, through an uncalculated modesty, maintains the illusion that he is a simple spinner of tales. And yet it is through this modesty that he achieves a quiet grandeur."

BIOGRAPHICAL/CRITICAL SOURCES:

BOOKS

Atwood, Margaret, *Second Words,* Anansi Press, 1982.
Contemporary Literary Criticism, Volume 27, Gale, 1984.
Dictionary of Literary Biography, Volume 53: *Canadian Writers since 1960, First Series,* Gale, 1986.

PERIODICALS

Books, June, 1967.
Canadian Forum, June, 1968.
Canadian Literature, winter, 1981; autumn, 1982.
Chicago Tribune Book World, August 1, 1982.
Fiddlehead, summer, 1968.
Globe and Mail (Toronto), July 14, 1984; November 24, 1984; November 2, 1985; October 25, 1986; November 15, 1986; November 19, 1988.
Los Angeles Times, February 8, 1990.
Los Angeles Times Book Review, August 29, 1982.
Newsweek, July 19, 1982.
New Yorker, August 21, 1978; August 9, 1982.
New York Times, June 22, 1982.
New York Times Book Review, June 16, 1967; July 9, 1978; August 15, 1982; November 10, 1985, p. 14; October 9, 1988, p. 34; April 29, 1990, p. 38.
Profiles in Canadian Literature, number 51, 1982.
Publishers Weekly, June 28, 1985, pp. 62-63.
Time, August 2, 1982.
Times (London), October 31, 1985; March 19, 1987.
Times Literary Supplement, March 5, 1970; April 15, 1988, p. 421.
Saturday Night, May, 1967.
Washington Post Book World, July 18, 1982.

* * *

FORD, R(obert) A(rthur) D(ouglass) 1915-
(Robert A. D. Ford)

PERSONAL: Born January 8, 1915, in Ottawa, Ontario, Canada; son of Arthur Rutherford (a journalist) and May Lavinia (Scott) Ford; married Maria Thereza Gomes, June 27, 1946 (deceased). *Education:* University of Western Ontario, B.A., 1938; Cornell University, M.A., 1939.

ADDRESSES: Home—La Poivriere, Randan 63310, France.

CAREER: Gazette, Montreal, Quebec, reporter, 1938; Cornell University, Ithaca, NY, instructor in history, 1938-40; Canadian Department of External Affairs, Ottawa, Ontario, third secretary, 1940-41; Canadian Embassy, Rio de Janeiro, Brazil, third secretary, 1941-45; Canada House, London, England, second secretary, 1945-46, first secretary, 1947-49; Canadian Embassy, Moscow, Soviet Union, second secretary, 1946-47; Canadian Department of External Affairs, Ottawa, first secretary for United Nations Affairs, 1949-51; Canadian Embassy, Moscow, charge d'affaires, 1951-54; Canadian Department of External Affairs, Ottawa, head of European division, 1954-57; ambassador to Columbia, 1957-58, ambassador to Yugoslavia, 1959-61, ambassador to United

Arab Republic (now Arab Republic of Egypt) and the Sudan, 1961-63, ambassador to the Soviet Union in Moscow, 1964-80, dean of diplomatic corps in Moscow, 1971-80, and ambassador to Mongolia, 1974-80. Special advisor to the Canadian Government on East-West relations, 1980-84; member of the Independent Commission on Disarmament and Security Issues (Palme Commission), 1980; board member, International Institute of Geopolitics; advisor, Canadian Institute for Global Security.

MEMBER: League of Canadian Poets, France-Canada Association, Cercle des Ecrivains Bourbonnais.

AWARDS, HONOURS: Governor General's Award, 1957, for *A Window on the North;* D.Litt. from University of Western Ontario, 1965; Companion of Order of Canada, 1971; gold medal from Professional Institute of Public Service of Canada, 1971; LL.D. from University of Toronto, 1987.

WRITINGS:

POETRY

A Window on the North, Ryerson, 1956.
The Solitary City: Poems and Translations, McClelland & Stewart, 1969.
Holes in Space, Hounslow Press, 1979.
Needle in the Eye: Poems New and Selected, Mosaic, 1983.
Doors, Words and Silence, Mosaic, 1985.
Dostoyevsky and Other Poems, Mosaic, 1989.
Coming from Afar: Selected Poems, McClelland & Stewart, 1990.

CONTRIBUTOR TO ANTHOLOGIES

Canadian Poetry in English, Ryerson, 1954.
Penguin Book of Canadian Verse, Penguin (London), 1958.

Also contributor to *The Oxford Book of Canadian Verse in English and French, Twentieth-Century Canadian Poetry,* and *Modern Canadian Verse.*

UNDER NAME ROBERT A. D. FORD

Our Man in Moscow: A Diplomat's Reflections on the Soviet Union, University of Toronto Press, 1989.
Diplomate et Poete a Moscow, Editions Collignon, 1990.

Contributor to *Encounter, Malahat Review, Maryland Quarterly, Canadian Forum, Montreal Gazette, Financial Post,* and *Foreign Affairs.* Works have been translated into Russian, French, Spanish, and Portuguese.

OTHER

(Translator) *Russian Poetry: A Personal Anthology,* Mosaic, 1986.

WORK IN PROGRESS: A Moscow literary notebook.

SIDELIGHTS: R. A. D. Ford considers himself a diplomat first and a poet second. Having spent much of his life outside the borders of his Canadian homeland, he is not easily grouped with other contemporary Canadian poets. He told *CA:* "A very active diplomatic career limited the amount of time I had for poetry, but it also extended my horizons, exposing me to the misery of the world— Columbia, Yugoslavia, Egypt, Sudan, what was then the USSR. This had the effect of creating a pessimistic view of the world and mankind, and is reflected in my verse." Also reflected in his poetry is Ford's lifelong battle with "a form of muscular atrophy which has helped to shape a rather somber view of the world," according to Ford. This sadness permeates Ford's poems, which are often set in the arctic wastes of Canada and Russia.

In addition to his original verse, Ford has also published a number of translated poems, many of which are included in his volume *Russian Poetry: A Personal Anthology.* "I was completely bilingual in French and had learned Latin, German, and Russian at school," he told *CA.* "I subsequently added Serbo-Croation, Portuguese, Spanish, and Italian." In the author's note included in his book *A Window on the North,* he explains that his goal in translating poetry is "to make of each adaptation as fine or even finer a poem in his (the translator's) own language," a goal which often requires the taking of "considerable liberties with the verse form and rhyme in order to transmit the spirit of the original."

Russian verse, in particular, has often been the subject of Ford's interpretation. He once told *CA:* "The richness of Russian literature, and above all Russian poetry . . . is so little appreciated because of the difficulty of the language." He later told *CA:* "The 20th century poets who have most influenced me are Eliot, Auden, William Carlos Williams, Garcia Lorca, Rilke, Eluard, and the great Russians—Pasternak, Akhmatova, Tsvetaeva, and Esenin."

BIOGRAPHICAL/CRITICAL SOURCES:

BOOKS

Dictionary of Literary Biography, Gale, Volume 88: *Canadian Writers, 1920-1959,* Second Series, 1989.
Ford, R. A. D., *A Window on the North,* Ryerson, 1956.
Ford, *Needle in the Eye,* Mosaic, 1983.

PERIODICALS

Globe and Mail (Toronto), October 13, 1984.

*   *   *

FORD, Robert A. D.
   See FORD, R(obert) A(rthur) D(ouglass)

FOWLER, Marian (Elizabeth)   1929-

PERSONAL: Born October 15, 1929, in Newmarket, Ontario, Canada; daughter of Robert Daniel (a car dealer) and Dorothy Gertrude (a school teacher; maiden name, Maconachie) Little; married Rodney Fowler, September 19, 1953 (divorced, 1978); children: Timothy Evan, Caroline Jane. *Education:* University of Toronto, B.A. (with honors), 1951, M.A., 1965, Ph.D., 1970. *Religion:* Protestant. *Avocational interests:* Travel, bird-watching, antique collecting.

ADDRESSES: Home—Kilmara, Box 20, R.R.2, Lisle, Ontario, Canada L0M 1M0.

CAREER: Clarke, Irwin & Co. (publisher), Toronto, Ontario, Canada, promotion writer, 1951-53; T. Eaton Co. (department store), Toronto, advertising copywriter, 1953-54; homemaker, 1954-71; York University, Downsview, Ontario, course director and lecturer in English and Canadian studies at Atkinson College, 1971-82; full-time writer, 1982—.

MEMBER: International P.E.N., Writers Union of Canada, Association for Canadian Studies, Association of Canadian University Teachers of English.

AWARDS, HONOURS: Governor-General's Gold Medal, 1951; Canadian Biography Award, Association for Canadian Studies, 1979, for a proposed biography of Sara Jeannette Duncan (*Redney: A Life of Sara Jeannette Duncan*).

WRITINGS:

The Embroidered Tent: Five Gentlewomen in Early Canada, House of Anansi Press, 1982.
Redney: A Life of Sara Jeannette Duncan, House of Anansi Press, 1983.
Below the Peacock Fan: First Ladies of the Raj, Viking/Penguin, 1987.
Blenheim: Biography of a Palace, Viking/Penguin, 1989.

WORK IN PROGRESS: A nonfiction book on five American heiresses who married British dukes.

SIDELIGHTS: Best known as a biographer, Marian Fowler has written absorbing accounts of the lives of several interesting people. Her best-known book is titled *Below the Peacock Fan: First Ladies of the Raj.* In this work, Fowler profiles the consorts—one sister and three wives—of four of India's Governor-Generals or Viceroys during British Colonial rule. Joanna Motion of the *Times Literary Supplement* notes, "The idea of writing the story of these eminent Victorian women was an excellent one. . . . Fowler moves easily and readably through the vignettes and social set-pieces of this high domesticity." Despite the fact that Fowler focused on these four women because they resided in India during Queen Victoria's reign, some critics have objected to her choice of only four "first ladies" when the British presence in India lasted nearly two hundred years. Audrey C. Foote observes in the *Washington Post Book World,* "It seems a shame Fowler did not complete the story with a fifth chapter on the last vicereine, Edwina, who helped Lord Mountbatten to dismantle the Raj and finally liberate India."

William French claims in the Toronto *Globe & Mail* that the book exceeds mere historical recounting: "One of the virtues of Below the Peacock Fan is that it's more than four mini-biographies. Fowler examines the experience of the four women in the context of the whole history of the British in India, and her book, intended or not, becomes a scathing indictment of imperialism." French, who describes Fowler as "perceptive and tough-minded," admires the author's achievement, remarking that her "prose is as colorful as her subject, and her narrative is thoroughly documented."

In 1989 Fowler issued another biography, this time detailing the life of Blenheim Palace, one of the oldest and largest castles in England. Commissioned by the first Duke of Marlborough, John Churchill, after he was awarded a thousand acres of land by Queen Anne in reward for his 1704 military victory against the French at Blenheim, the palace was designed by architect John Vanbrugh. It has become the ancestral home of the Spencer-Churchill family since then. *Blenheim: Biography of a Palace* "is an unusual book that is partly the history of a famous family, partly a chronicle of changing domestic attitudes and manners among the English aristocracy during the past 250 years, and partly, and the subtitle suggests, the biography of a building," comments Witold Rybczynski in the Toronto *Globe & Mail.* The reviewer adds, "The result is a vivid historical account which . . . provides compelling and illuminates a neglected subject—the way that the genius of a place forms the fortunes of its inhabitants." Marian Fowler once told *CA:* "My writing career began late in life, and I divide my time between Canada and England. I work long hours at my desk partly because I am very ambitious to make my name as a writer, but mainly because for me writing is a joyous and rewarding activity.

"I am interested in the kinds of social and psychological accommodations women have had to make to conform to accepted female roles. I began with a doctoral dissertation on Jane Austen, in which I looked closely at women's roles and behavior in early nineteenth-century England. I began to wonder how such upper-middle-class women, taught to be decorative and docile, adapted and developed when suddenly transplanted to a rough, Canadian frontier society.

"This interest sparked my first book, *The Embroidered Tent: Five Gentlewomen in Early Canada,* in which I ex-amined the remarkable effects a Canadian wilderness setting had on five genteel women raised in Britain. Next, I wrote a biography of a nineteenth-century Canadian woman who was an intrepid and daring journalist, feminist, and novelist. She, too, experienced sudden cultural displacement, having spent her married life in India trying desperately to adapt and to write novels. While working on that book, *Redney: A Life of Sara Jeannette Duncan,* I became intrigued by the whole era of the British Raj in India and decided to write a book on five of the viceroys' wives and the ways in which India changed them, titled *Below the Peacock Fan.* The effect of a house on its inhabitants was my next project, resulting in *Blenheim: Biography of a Palace.*"

BIOGRAPHICAL/CRITICAL SOURCES:

PERIODICALS

Globe & Mail (Toronto), August 29, 1987; August 20, 1988; December 16, 1989.
Los Angeles Times Book Review, September 1, 1991, p. 10.
Quill and Quire, January, 1984; June, 1987, p. 33.
Times Literary Supplement, March 16, 1984; October 23, 1987, p. 1160.
Washington Post Book World, December 27, 1987, p. 7; January 1, 1989, p. 12.*

*   *   *

FRASER, Sylvia 1935-

PERSONAL: Born March 8, 1935, in Hamilton, Ontario, Canada; daughter of George Nicholas (a steel inspector) and Gladys (Wilson) Meyers; married Russell James Fraser (a lawyer), May 30, 1959 (divorced, 1977). *Education:* University of Western Ontario, B.A. (with honors), 1957.

ADDRESSES: Home—382 Brunswick Ave., Toronto, Ontario, Canada M5R 2Y9.

CAREER: Toronto Star Weekly, Toronto, Ontario, journalist, 1957-68; full-time novelist, 1968—. Guest lecturer, Banff School of Fine Arts, 1973-79, 1985, 1987, and 1988; writer-in-residence, University of Western Ontario, 1980; director of Maritime Writers Workshop, University of New Brunswick, 1985. Member of arts advisory panel to Canada Council, 1978-81; member of Canadian Cultural Delegation to China, 1985.

AWARDS, HONOURS: Canadian Womens Press Club Awards, 1967 and 1968; President's Medal for Canadian Journalism from University of Western Ontario, 1969; Canadian Authors Association Non-Fiction Book Award, 1987, for *My Father's House: A Memoir of Incest and of Healing.*

WRITINGS:

NOVELS

Pandora, McClelland & Stewart, 1972, Little, Brown, 1973.

The Candy Factory, Little, Brown, 1975.

A Casual Affair, McClelland & Stewart, 1978, Macmillan, 1979.

The Emperor's Virgin, Doubleday, 1980.

Berlin Solstice, McClelland & Stewart, 1985.

My Father's House: A Memoir of Incest and of Healing, Doubleday (Toronto), 1987, Ticknor & Fields (New York City), 1988.

The Book of Strange: A Spiritual Journey, Doubleday, 1992.

The Quest for the Fourth Monkey: A Thinking Person's Guide to Psychic and Spiritual Phenomena, Key Porter, 1994.

OTHER

Contributor to *Saturday Night.*

SIDELIGHTS: Sylvia Fraser's novels graphically depict antagonistic and exploitive relationships between men and women, often containing scenes of sexual violence, incest, and perversion. With the publication of the nonfiction account *My Father's House: A Memoir of Incest and of Healing,* Fraser revealed that she had suffered childhood sexual abuse, abuse she only recalled at the age of 48 after engaging in self-hypnosis. Since remembering this period in her life, Fraser has turned from writing novels to the chronicling of spiritual matters.

Fraser began her writing career as a journalist with the *Toronto Star Weekly* before turning to fiction. Her first novel, *Pandora,* is the story of a Canadian girl growing up during the Second World War. While young Pandora Gothic tells her own story, Fraser as narrator of the novel gives the broader picture of the world around Pandora that the child can not see. "This multiple viewpoint," Rae McCarthy writes in the *Dalhousie Review,* "results in several layers of matter and meaning." As Lorna Irvine explains it in *Mosaic: A Journal for the Interdisciplinary Study of Literature, Pandora* "presents the family as the ground in which certain sexual tensions first blossom, the place where civilization establishes and develops its discontents." Irvine finds that in the novel, "much of society reflects a perverted masculinity." "Although at first glance [*Pandora*] appears to be little more than a brilliantly-written description of a war-time Ontario childhood," notes Pat Barclay in *Canadian Literature,* "in reality it is as packed with abstractions as the mythical Pandora's Box. In fact, the book is really an allegory, making it closer akin to *Lord of the Flies* than to *Anne of Green Gables.*"

In her next novel, *The Candy Factory,* Fraser again uses allegory to look at "materialism, superficiality, cynicism, and hypocrisy" as represented in the workings of a large candy manufacturer, according to Rae McCarthy MacDonald in the *Dalhousie Review.* Francis Mansbridge, writing in *Canadian Literature,* finds that "the candy factory becomes a suitable metaphor for our contemporary society." As Michael Taylor notes in the *Fiddlehead,* in this novel Fraser exhibits a "determination to be original, clever and witty using language in a forceful and often startling manner." But he also notes that Fraser introduces "rather revolting acts of sex, excretion and violence" into the story.

These disturbing acts reappear in Fraser's *The Emperor's Virgin,* set in imperial Rome, the book contains "a series of anatomically detailed copulation scenes of various kinds," as I. M. Owen writes in *Books in Canada,* as well as "crass historical errors." In *A Casual Affair* Fraser spoofs old fairy tale versions of perfect romance to argue that in the contemporary world, male-female relationships are hopeless. As Lois Gottlieb explains in the *Journal of Canadian Fiction* "the novel stacks the deck against fairy tales, against love and happiness emerging from any new style of coupling; it also stacks the deck against the old style of coupling by making conventional marriage—portrayed at one point as a gigantic, voracious snake—a symbol of emotional abuse and social oppression."

At the age of 48, Fraser came to the realization that she had been sexually abused by her father when she was a child. She had suppressed these memories by creating two separate personalities: one personality suffering abuse, the other oblivious to it. The abuse nonetheless had its effects on her later life. As an adult she experienced fits similar to epilepsy whenever she became physically intimate with a man. Her compulsive affair with an older man led to the destruction of her marriage. "When . . . Fraser recovered these buried memories through hypnosis," Jane O'Grady explains in the London *Times,* "she felt she at last understood her self-sabotage, and why her novels always turned out to be full of sexual violence."

Fraser tells of her years of abuse in *My Father's House: A Memoir of Incest and Healing,* using the techniques of a novelist to present her story. "As with her novels," writes Janet Hamilton in *Quill & Quire,* "the energy of the prose and an eye for telling detail propel the reader along; her signature descriptions of places and people deftly suggest a child's felt world." But O'Grady feels that "however insistently Fraser brandishes incest as the missing link both in her past and present writings, it remains artistically unassimilated. . . . Even her terrible experiences with her father . . . are wrapped in layers of literary allusion and processed through melodrama." Hamilton concludes that "the unconvincing application of the terms of analysis . . . undermine the reader's confidence" in the account.

Since writing *My Father's House* Fraser has turned her attention to writing of spiritual matters. *The Book of Strange: A Spiritual Journey* "is an idiosyncratic and highly personal look at psychic and paranormal phenomena," as Jerry Horton writes in *Quill & Quire.* Exploring haunted houses, faith healing, and related topics, Fraser presents her own experiences with these phenomena and explains how her initial skepticism led to belief. In this work Fraser creates "a fantastic, sometimes astonishing tale expertly told," Horton concludes.

In *The Quest for the Fourth Monkey: A Thinking Person's Guide to Psychic and Spiritual Phenomena,* Fraser presents her view that psychic phenomena have been suppressed in Western culture by an Aristotelian materialism. She argues that the Western world is now moving beyond strict logic to a spiritual awakening in which many psychic phenomena will become understandable. Ilene Cooper, writing in *Booklist,* finds that "although there are plenty of books about psychic phenomena out there, few provide a philosophical framework with which to consider these ideas. Fraser does that and much more."

BIOGRAPHICAL/CRITICAL SOURCES:

BOOKS

Contemporary Literary Criticism, Volume 64, Gale, 1991.

PERIODICALS

Booklist, October 1, 1994, p. 212.
Books in Canada, April, 1980, p. 16; December, 1992, p. 51.
Boston Globe, June 27, 1988, p. 20.
Broadside, December-January, 1988, pp. 8-9.
Canadian Literature, spring, 1974, pp. 109-10; winter, 1976, pp. 104-05; summer, 1981, pp. 45-55; winter, 1985, pp. 134-36.
Canadian Materials, January, 1989, pp. 12-13; March, 1990, p. 78.
Canadian Medical Association Journal, April 15, 1989, p. 938.
Chicago Tribune, September 4, 1988, Sec. 6, p. 3.
Dalhousie Review, winter, 1972-73, pp. 701, 703-04; autumn, 1975, pp. 558-60; summer, 1978, pp. 370-72.
Essays on Canadian Writing, summer, 1978, pp. 130-34.
Fiddlehead, winter, 1976, pp. 112-13.
Globe and Mail (Toronto), November 19, 1984.
Journal of Canadian Fiction, Numbers 31-32, 1981, pp. 261-63.
London Review of Books, February 2, 1989, p. 23.
Los Angeles Times Book Review, July 23, 1989, p. 14.
Mosaic: A Journal for the Interdisciplinary Study of Literature, spring, 1984, pp. 223-33.
New York Times, October 2, 1988, p. 24.
New York Times Book Review, June 5, 1988, p. 41.
Quill & Quire, August, 1987, p. 33; August, 1992, pp. 21-22.
Times (London), February 26, 1989, p. G13.
Women's Review of Books, October, 1988, p. 16.

*   *   *

FREDERICKS, Frohm
  See KERNER, Fred

*   *   *

FRYE, (Herman) Northrop   1912-1991

PERSONAL: Born July 14, 1912, in Sherbrooke, Quebec, Canada; died of a heart attack, January 22, 1991, in Toronto, Ontario, Canada; son of Herman Edward (a hardware merchant) and Catherine Maud (Howard) Frye; married Helen Kemp, August 24, 1937 (died, 1986); married Elizabeth Brown, 1988. *Education:* University of Toronto, B.A. (philosophy and English; with honors), 1933; Emmanuel College, ordained, 1936; Merton College, Oxford, M.A., 1940. *Religion:* United Church of Canada.

CAREER: Worked as a pastor of a congregation near Shaunavon, Saskatchewan, 1934; University of Toronto, Victoria College, Toronto, Ontario, lecturer in English, 1939-41, assistant professor, 1942-46, associate professor, 1947, professor of English, 1948-91, chair of department, 1952-59, principal, 1959-67, University Professor, 1967-91. Chancellor, Victoria University, Toronto, 1978-91. Visiting professor at Harvard University, Princeton University, Columbia University, Indiana University, University of Washington, University of British Columbia, Cornell University, University of California, Berkeley, and Oxford University. Andrew D. White Professor-at-Large, Cornell University, 1970-75; Charles Eliot Norton Poetry Professor, Harvard University, 1974-75. Member of board of governors, Ontario Curriculum Institute, 1960-63; chair of Governor-General's Literary Awards Committee, 1962. Canadian Radio Television and Telecommunications Commission, advisory member, 1968-77.

MEMBER: Modern Language Association of America (executive council member, 1958-62; president, 1976), English Institute (former chair), Royal Society of Canada (fellow), American Academy of Arts and Sciences (foreign honorary member), British Academy (corresponding fellow), American Philosophical Society (foreign member), American Academy and Institute of Arts and Letters (honorary member).

AWARDS, HONOURS: Guggenheim fellow, 1950-51; Lorne Pierce Medal of the Royal Society of Canada, 1958;

Canada Council Medal, 1967; Pierre Chauveau Medal of the Royal Society of Canada, 1970; Canada Council Molson Prize, 1971; Companion of the Order of Canada, 1972; honorary fellow, Merton College, Oxford, 1974; Civic Honour, City of Toronto, 1974; Royal Bank Award, 1978; Governor General's Award, 1987. Thirty-six honorary degrees from colleges and universities in Canada and the United States, including Dartmouth College, Harvard University, Princeton University, and University of Manitoba.

WRITINGS:

Fearful Symmetry: A Study of William Blake, Princeton University Press, 1947.

Anatomy of Criticism: Four Essays, Princeton University Press, 1957.

(With others) *The English and Romantic Poets and Essayists: A Review of Research and Criticism,* Modern Language Association of America, 1957.

Culture and the National Will, Carleton University, for Institute of Canadian Studies, 1957.

(With Kluckhohn and Wigglesworth) *Three Lectures,* University of Toronto, 1958.

By Liberal Things, Clarke, Irwin, 1959.

(Editor) William Shakespeare, *The Tempest,* Penguin, 1959.

(Editor) *Design for Learning,* University of Toronto Press, 1962.

(With L. C. Knights and others) *Myth and Symbol: Critical Approaches and Applications,* edited by Bernice Slote, University of Nebraska Press, 1963.

The Developing Imagination (published together with an essay by A. R. MacKinnon), Harvard University Press, 1963.

The Changing Pace of Canadian Education, Sir George Williams University (Montreal), 1963.

The Well-Tempered Critic, Indiana University Press, 1963.

T. S. Eliot: An Introduction, Grove, 1963.

Fables of Identity: Studies in Poetic Mythology, Harcourt, 1963.

(Editor) *Romanticism Reconsidered: Selected Papers from the English Institute,* Columbia University Press, 1963.

The Educated Imagination, Indiana University Press, 1964.

A Natural Perspective: The Development of Shakespearean Comedy and Romance, Columbia University Press, 1965.

The Return of Eden: Five Essays on Milton's Epics, University of Toronto Press, 1965.

(Editor) *Selected Poetry and Prose,* McGraw, 1966.

(Editor) *Blake: A Collection of Critical Essays,* Prentice-Hall, 1966.

Fools of Time: Studies in Shakespearean Tragedy, University of Toronto Press, 1967.

The Modern Century (Whidden Lectures), Oxford University Press, 1967.

A Study of English Romanticism, Random House, 1968.

Silence in the Sea, Memorial University of Newfoundland, 1969.

The Stubborn Structure: Essays on Criticism and Society, Methuen, 1970.

The Bush Garden: Essays on the Canadian Imagination, House of Anansi Press, 1971.

The Critical Path: An Essay on the Social Context of Literary Criticism, Indiana University Press, 1971.

On Teaching Literature, Harcourt, 1972.

The Secular Scripture: A Study of the Structure of Romance, Harvard University Press, 1976.

Spiritus Mundi: Essays on Literature, Myth and Society, Indiana University Press, 1976.

Northrop Frye on Culture and Literature: A Collection of Review Essays, edited by Robert Denham, Chicago University Press, 1978.

Creation and Recreation, University of Toronto Press, 1980.

Criticism As Education, School of Library Service, Columbia University, 1980.

The Great Code: The Bible and Literature, Harcourt, 1982.

Divisions on a Ground: Essays on Canadian Culture, House of Anansi Press, 1982.

The Myth of Deliverance: Reflections on Shakespeare's Problem Comedies, University of Toronto Press, 1982.

(Editor with Sheridan Baker and George W. Perkins) *The Harper Handbook to Literature,* Harper, 1985.

Northrop Frye on Shakespeare, edited by Robert Sandler, Yale University Press, 1986.

(With others) *The Practical Imagination,* Harper, 1987.

On Education, University of Michigan Press, 1988.

Northrop Frye—Myth and Metaphor: Selected Essays, University Press of Virginia, 1990.

Reading the World: Selected Writings, Peter Lang, 1990.

Words with Power: Being a Second Study of "The Bible and Literature," Harcourt, 1990.

Has written educational radio and television programs for the Canadian Broadcasting Co. Work represented in anthologies. Contributor to professional journals. *Canadian Forum,* literary editor, 1947-49, editor, 1949-52.

SIDELIGHTS: Because of the influential theories on literary criticism that he presented in *Anatomy of Criticism: Four Essays* and other books, Northrop Frye was regarded as one of the most important literary critics of his generation. Although Frye made no effort during his life to form a school of criticism based on his ideas, his ability to categorize the different approaches used to analyze literature put the field of criticism as a whole into new perspective. The critic and educator was also once a pastor for the United Church of Canada, and even though he abandoned this career for that of a university professor his religious background led to an interest in the relationship between the Bible and Western literature. Influenced by the poet William Blake, Frye saw the Bible not as something holy in itself, but rather as a text that could lead one to higher spirituality through contact with the Holy Spirit dwelling within each human being. According to Harold Bloom in the *New York Times,* Frye's "true greatness" was his advocacy "of a Protestant and Romantic tradition that has dominated much of British and American literature, the tradition of the Inner Light, by which each person reads Scripture for himself or herself without yielding to a premature authority imposed by Church or State or School." But for others familiar with Frye's work, like *New York Times Book Review* contributor Robert M. Adams, the critic will be remembered primarily as "one of the bold, inventive—and unhappily rare—schematizers of our literature."

Many of Frye's ideas about literature came from Blake, the eighteenth-century English poet, artist, and critic about whom Frye wrote *Fearful Symmetry: A Study of William Blake.* Before the publication of this book, critics approached Blake's poetry as being "private, mystical, or deranged," according to *Dictionary of Literary Biography* contributor Robert D. Denham. But Frye showed " . . . that Blake's poetry is typical, that he belongs squarely in the tradition of English literature, and that he should be read in imaginative, rather than simply historical, terms." Although Blake's use of symbolism was unique, Frye argued that the basis of this symbolism was universal and could be compared to writings by "Edmund Spenser and John Milton, and especially the Bible." By studying the unity of imagination in Blake's work, Frye extrapolated in *Fearful Symmetry* "that all symbolism in all art and religion is mutually intelligible among all men, and that there is such a thing as the iconography of the imagination."

Frye elaborated upon this theory in *Anatomy of Criticism,* a book that "forced itself" on him when he was trying to write about another subject. After writing *Fearful Symmetry,* Frye was determined at first to apply Blake's principles of literary symbolism and Biblical analysis to the poet Edmund Spenser. But "the introduction to Spenser became an introduction to the theory of allegory, and that theory obstinately adhered to a much larger theoretical structure," Frye explained in *Anatomy*'s preface. "The basis of argument became more and more discursive, and less and less historical and Spenserian. I soon found myself entangled in those parts of criticism that have to do with

such words as 'myth,' 'symbol,' 'ritual,' and 'archetype'. . . . Eventually, the theoretical and the practical aspects of the task I had begun completely separated." But rather than abandon the project, Frye simply shifted his focus, writing not about Spenser in particular, but about literature in general. When he finished, he had produced four essays of what he calls "pure critical theory." Published together in 1957, these essays comprise *Anatomy of Criticism,* a schematic, non-judgmental theory of literature and the first, according to David Schiller in *Commentary,* "which enables a student to tell where, in the totality of his literary experiences, an individual experience belongs."

Frye believed that the field of literary criticism was an art that was not only misunderstood, but also in disarray, and that setting down a general framework would help to organize all the different theories of criticism. "It is all very well for Blake to say that to generalize is to be an idiot," Frye wrote in his study, "but when we find ourselves in the cultural situation of savages who have words for ash and willow and no word for tree, we wonder if there is not such a thing as being too deficient in the capacity to generalize." To remedy the problem, Frye set out to develop "a coordinating principle, a central hypothesis which, like the theory of evolution in biology, will see the phenomena it deals with as parts of a whole."

His idea was to approach poetry (and by poetry Frye means all literature) the way Aristotle did—"as a biologist [approaching] a system of organisms, picking out its genera and species, formulating the broad laws of literary experience and, in short, writing as though . . . there is a totally intelligible structure of knowledge attainable about poetry which is not poetry itself, or the experience of it, but poetics." To figure out what these "poetics" were, Frye surveyed the whole phenomena of literary experience, isolating each genre, myth and archetypal literary symbol and then relating it to literature as a whole. He organized his findings into categories and came up with the four critical approaches that would eventually form the basis of his essays. They are: historical criticism (theory of modes), ethical criticism (theory of symbols), archetypal criticism (theory of myths), and rhetorical criticism (theory of genres). Although Frye allotted each of these approaches a place in his hypothetical structure, his own particular emphasis was on literary archetypes and how they relate to myths.

When Frye wrote about archetypes, he was referring not to the Jungian concept of a racial consciousness, but to certain "typical" images that recur in poetry. In literature, the repetition of such common images of physical nature as the sea or the forest cannot be explained away as "coincidence," Frye argued. Instead, he asserted that each is an "archetype" or "symbol which connects one poem with another and thereby helps to unify and integrate our literary experience." When we study a masterpiece, Frye explained in his study, the work "draws us to a point at which we seem to see an enormous number of converging patterns of significance. We begin to wonder if we cannot see literature, not only as complicating itself in time, but as spread out in conceptual space from some kind of center that criticism could locate." That center represents the primitive myths from which archetypes spring.

Frye contended that archetypal criticism provides an effective means of deriving the structural principles of literature because it assumes a larger context of literature as a whole. Employing an analogy, Frye compared literature to painting, showing that just as the structural principles of painting are related to plane geometry, so too are the structural principles of literature related to religion and mythology. The Biblical archetypes of the "city" the "garden," and the "sheepfold" are as pervasive in religious writing as gods and demons are in myths, Frye maintained. Thus Frye turned to the symbolism of the Bible and to classical mythology employing both "as a grammar of literary archetypes" to use his words.

Although post-classical literature rarely seems mythic, Frye argued that the myth has simply been "displaced" or covered over with a veneer of realism, making the new work "credible, logically motivated, or morally acceptable" to its audience. In Nathaniel Hawthorne's *The Marble Faun,* for example, there is a girl of singular purity and gentleness who lives in a tower surrounded by doves. Wrote Frye: "The doves are very fond of her; another character calls her his 'dove,' and remarks indicating some special affinity with doves are made about her by both author and characters. If we were to say that [she] is a dove-goddess like Venus . . . we should not be reading the story quite accurately in its own mode; we should be translating it into straight myth." But, Frye claimed, to recognize that Hawthorne employs an archetypal pattern is not irrelevant, or unfair. In fact, he postulated that a person "can get a whole liberal education simply by picking up one conventional poem and following its archetypes as they stretch out into the rest of literature."

One of the most controversial features of Frye's schema is the role it assigns critics. The historical function of criticism, from the time of Samuel Johnson to T. S. Eliot, has been to provide a means of discriminating good writing from bad. But Frye's interest was in what makes works of literature similar to one another, not what makes them different, and he adamantly rejected the notion of critic as judge. It is not, he asserted, the critic's responsibility to evaluate poetry or to say that one poem is better than another because his judgment, while informed, is really nothing more than a reflection of taste. And, "the history of taste is no more a part of the structure of criticism than

the Huxley-Wilberforce debate is part of the structure of biological science," Frye wrote. Matters of judgment are best left to book reviewers, not critics, in Frye's point of view.

But W. K. Wimsatt, in an essay in *Northrop Frye in Modern Criticism,* charged Frye with inconsistency: "He can and is willing to distinguish 'ephemeral rubbish,' mediocre works, random and peripheral experience, from the greatest classics, the profound masterpieces in which may be discerned the converging patterns of the primitive formulas. At other moments, however, he says that criticism has nothing whatever to do with either the experience or the judging of literature. The direct experience of literature is central to criticism, yet somehow this center is excluded from it." The effect, Wimsatt concluded, is that the reader remains unsure whether Frye "wishes to discredit all critical valuing whatever, or only the wrong kinds of valuing."

Another important feature of Frye's schema is his view in general and poetry in particular. According to A. Walton Litz, writing in the *Harvard Guide to Contemporary American Writing,* Frye "share[d] with his modern predecessors a poet-Romantic view of the poem as an autonomous organism, which exists independently from the intentions of its creator." And in his study, Frye employed a metaphor that bears out Litz's supposition. "The poet who writes creatively rather than deliberately," Frye said, "is not the father of his poem; he is at best a midwife, or, more accurately still, the womb of Mother Nature herself. . . . The fact that revision is possible, that a poet can make changes in a poem not because he likes them better, but because they are better, shows clearly that the poet has to give birth to the poem as it passes through his mind. He is responsible for delivering it in as uninjured a state as possible, and if the poem is alive, it is equally anxious to be rid of him, and screams to be cut loose from all the navel-strings and feeding-tubes of his ego."

If the poet is the "midwife" of the poem, the critic, according to Frye, may be conceived of as the nurse who presents the creation to the world. And in this role as a describer and classifier of literature, the critic assumes a position that is not subservient, but equal to that of the artist, as Litz explained: "If *Anatomy of Criticism* is a major work of enduring importance, as I believe it to be, then it is the first great work of English or American literary criticism not produced by a practicing artist, and signals a decisive turn toward the continental model. The critic is no longer the servant of the artist but a colleague, with his own special knowledge and powers. . . . [Frye provided] a system which tempts the critic to interpose himself between the artist and the audience as an independent creative force." Despite his admiration for *Anatomy,* Litz said that Frye's system "when manipulated by less subtle minds—tend[s] to homogenize literature and give the critic a spurious authority."

Nor was this the only objection raised against Frye's theory. Some critics charged that Frye's preoccupation with myth and convention isolates literature from its social context, while others accused him of ignoring history and imprisoning literature in a timeless vacuum of archetypal myths. Wimsatt articulated this objection this way: "The Ur-Myth, the Quest Myth, with all its complications, its cycles, acts, scenes, characters, and special symbols, is not a historical fact. And this is so not only in the obvious sense that the stories are not true, but in another sense, which I think we tend to forget and which mythopoeic writing does much to obscure: that such a coherent, cyclic, and encyclopedic system, such a monomyth, cannot be shown ever to have evolved actually either from ritual, anywhere in the world, or ever anywhere to have been entertained in whole or even in any considerable part. We are talking about the myth of myth. As Frye himself, in his moments of cautionary vision, observe[d], the 'derivation' of the literary genres from the quest myth is 'logical,' not historical. [But,] if we take Frye at his word and attempt to deduce his system 'logically,' we will reject it, for the structure which he shows us is . . . divided between truism and *ad libitum* fantasy."

As a way of countering these charges, Frye, in his subsequent writings, frequently employed subtitles that insist upon the social reference of his criticism, according to Scott Sanders in *Cambridge Review*. Frye's publications, *The Stubborn Structure: Essays on Criticism and Society* and *The Critical Path: An Essay on the Social Context of Literary Criticism* are two such examples. Sanders said that in such publications, however, Frye was "less concerned with the communal sources of literature than he is with the potential role of the humanities, informed by literature, in directing social change." In addition to addressing issues raised by his adversaries, Frye's later writing also elucidates his original theory, and offers some of the practical criticism that was absent in his masterwork. In *A Natural Perspective: The Development of Shakespearean Comedy and Romance,* for instance, Frye turned to Shakespeare to demonstrate his belief that art does not imitate life directly, but instead art imitates art.

With *The Great Code: The Bible and Literature* and its companion study, *Words with Power: Being a Second Study of "The Bible and Literature,"* Frye attempted "his most ambitious literary ascent: a two-volume assault on the central and highest massif in Western civilization," according to John B. Breslin in *Washington Post Book World.* The Bible was for Frye the single most important book upon which the overall structure and mythology behind literature could be based. Indeed, he asserted in *The Great Code* that a "student of English literature who does

not know the Bible does not understand a good deal of what is going on in what he reads." Viewing the New and Old Testaments with the eye of a critic rather than a theologian or historian, Frye professed that the Bible could only be fully understood when subjected to systematic literary study.

The Great Code, as the title implies, analyzes the words of the Bible. Frye examined the text typologically, that is, as words representing things, people, and events in the Old Testament that foreshadow those in the New Testament. According to *New York Review of Books* contributor J. M. Cameron, this approach was necessary in Frye's view, "not because this is an interesting pattern after we have given the kaleidoscope a shake, but because this is how the Biblical authors, in the main, wrote." Viewing the Bible this way, the reader can see the relationship between the Old and New Testaments, such as how the twelve tribes of Israel are reflected in the twelve apostles, how Moses receiving the Ten Commandments is reflected by Jesus's "Sermon on the Mount," and how Israel's defeat of its enemies in Canaan is reflected by the victory of the Resurrection, to give only a few examples.

If the Testaments were written as literary reflections of each other, their historicity might then be brought into question, since this would imply that they are artistic rather than historical works. But Frye was not concerned with proving the historical verity of the Bible in *The Great Code.* Instead, as Rachel Trickett noted in the *Times Literary Supplement,* he "define[d] the linguistic idiom of the Bible as '*kerygma,* proclamation,'" meaning that the Bible was written for the primary purpose of proclaiming a message. Frye also asserted that "myth is the linguistic vehicle of *kerygma,* and to . . . 'demythologize' any part of the Bible would be the same thing as to obliterate it." The Bible, in other words, uses myth as a device to proclaim its message of salvation, the importance of which far outweighs any of the specifics behind the stories it relates. As Frye put it, "It is the words themselves that have the authority, not the events they describe." "[The] Bible deliberately blocks off the sense of the referential from itself," Frye later concluded; "it is not a book pointing to a historical presence outside itself, but a book that identifies itself with that presence. At the end the reader, also, is invited to identify himself with the book." By eliminating any preoccupations with the events in the Bible (and thus the necessity for interpretations, either from outside authorities or from any of the reader's preconceived ideas), only the message of salvation remains. Cameron explained that to Frye the Bible's "function is not to point beyond itself, and to summon us to faith, with its conjoined virtues of humility and obedience, but to elevate us beyond faith to the higher life of vision."

The Great Code thus illustrates the imaginative unity of the Bible, and how its use of myths and symbols combine to convey a message (or "theme") of salvation. In Frye's terms, according to W. J. Keith in the *Globe and Mail, The Great Code* is therefore a study of the " 'centripetal' coherence" of the Bible. The companion book to *The Great Code,* on the other hand, "moves outward in a 'centrifugal' manner to demonstrate 'the extent to which the canonical unity of the Bible indicates or symbolizes a much wider imaginative unity in secular European literature.' " *New York Times* critic Michiko Kakutani summarized that *Words with Power* "helps the reader recognize some of the recurring myths that connect religious and secular literature, and [Frye] shows how ideological and social changes can cause changes in the interpretation and emphasis of those myths."

Frye published *Words with Power* just before his death early in 1991, thus completing the last part of "the big book about the Bible" that he had "set out to write as long ago as 1957," but which was set aside for what was to become *Anatomy of Criticism,* according to *New York Times Book Review* contributor Hugh Kenner. As with his other books, Frye set out to study his subject as systematically and scientifically as possible. But a few critics felt that some of Frye's personal beliefs still linger behind his attempted objective analysis. "Frye's career has been devoted unswervingly to the delicate task of placing the Christian religion on a scientific footing," declared Paul H. Fry in the *Yale Review.* "This he has attempted by claiming, first, that his method is indeed scientific, . . . and second, somewhat less candidly, I think, that the object of his discipline is not the Christian revelation, but mythopoetic thinking wherever it appears. It seems to me that Frye is caught in a bind that he cannot acknowledge, one that is perforce more apparent in *The Great Code* than hitherto: he cannot admit the religious basis of his undertaking without admitting that his analytic point of departure . . . is not quite dispassionately chosen." But a number of reviewers have praised Frye's studies of the Bible and its influence in literature. This "is a magnificent book," averred Cameron in his review of *The Great Code,* "a necessary recall to some fundamental principles of Biblical interpretation, and a collection of problems and questions of the first importance for critics, Biblical scholars, and the educated public in general." And *Washington Post Book World* critic Alfred Corn judged *Words with Power* to be "one of the most intelligent and passionate surveys of mythology-and-literature ever written, with Frye's earlier books as its only real competitors."

While Frye's ideas on structuralism have given way to other schools of criticism since the publication of *Anatomy of Criticism,* the critic and his work are still widely admired. "[Frye's] was a hard mind with an intricate and

completely assured gift for the patterning of concepts and attitudes," wrote Adams. "[His] wit was concise and dry, his erudition compendious. The first two books [he wrote] expressed exactly the nature of his interests: one was an anatomy, the other laid bare a symmetry. He was always getting down to the bare bones of things while demonstrating the way they could be articulated into larger and larger structures." Nevertheless, Frye's "[d]etractors termed some of his writing turgid and pedantic reworkings of his earlier theories in efforts to rebut critics," according to a *New York Times* obituary by Peter B. Flint. *Sewanee Review* critic Douglas Paschall countered, however, that "Frye has unquestionably earned his right to continuity in his principles, even to his numerous reiterations of them, but less because they have provided a complete universal system than because . . . they have enabled him at best to enliven and inform his readers as few other living critics have done." Novelist Margaret Atwood, who once studied with Frye, praised him in the *Globe and Mail* for making the field of literary criticism available to a nonprofessional audience. As one of only a handful of critics to be read by the general public, Frye "did not lock literature into an ivory tower; instead he emphasized its centrality to the development of a civilized and humane society."

BIOGRAPHICAL/CRITICAL SOURCES:

BOOKS

Ayre, John, *Northrop Frye: A Critical Biography,* General Publishing (Don Mills, Canada), 1988.
Contemporary Literary Criticism, Volume 24, Gale, 1983.
Denham, Robert, *Northrop Frye and Critical Method,* Pennsylvania State University Press, 1978.
Denham, Robert, *Northrop Frye: An Annotated Bibliography of Primary and Secondary Sources,* University of Toronto Press, 1988.
Dictionary of Literary Biography, Gale, Volume 67: *Modern American Critics since 1955,* 1988, Volume 68: *Canadian Writers, 1920-1959, First Series,* 1988.
Frye, Northrop, *Anatomy of Criticism: Four Essays,* Princeton University Press, 1957.
Frye, Northrop, *The Great Code: The Bible and Literature,* Harcourt, 1982.
Hoffman, Daniel, editor, *Harvard Guide to Contemporary American Writing,* Belknap Press, 1979.
Krieger, Murray, editor, *Northrop Frye in Modern Criticism: Selected Papers from the English Institute,* Columbia University Press, 1966.

PERIODICALS

Book Week, July 19, 1964.
Cambridge Review, May 7, 1971.
Chicago Tribune Book World, May 16, 1982.
Commentary, September, 1968.
Commonweal, September 20, 1957.

Criticism, summer, 1967.
Fiddlehead, summer, 1967.
Globe and Mail (Toronto), October 4, 1986; December 1, 1990.
Nation, February 19, 1968.
New York Review of Books, April 14, 1977; April 15, 1982.
New York Times, April 18, 1976; December 4, 1990.
New York Times Book Review, April 18, 1976; April 11, 1982; November 30, 1986; March 31, 1991.
Partisan Review, winter, 1969.
Sewanee Review, January, 1980.
South Atlantic Quarterly, spring, 1967.
Times Literary Supplement, August 12, 1965; July 2, 1982; February 17, 1984; April 26, 1985.

Washington Post Book World, May 16, 1982.
Yale Review, autumn, 1957; spring, 1964; spring, 1967; March, 1971; summer, 1983.

OBITUARIES:

PERIODICALS

Chicago Tribune, January 24, 1991; January 27, 1991.
Globe and Mail (Toronto), January 24, 1991.
New York Times, January 25, 1991.
Times (London), January 26, 1991.*

—Sketch by Kevin S. Hile

G

GALBRAITH, John Kenneth 1908-
(Mark Epernay, Herschel McLandress)

PERSONAL: Born October 15, 1908, in Iona Station, Ontario, Canada; naturalized United States citizen, 1937; son of William Archibald (a politician and farmer) and Catherine (Kendall) Galbraith; married Catherine Atwater, September 17, 1937; children: John Alan, Peter, James, Douglas (deceased). *Education:* University of Toronto, B.S. (agriculture), 1931; University of California, Berkeley, M.S., 1933, Ph.D. (economics), 1934; attended Cambridge University, 1937-38. *Politics:* Democrat.

ADDRESSES: Home—30 Francis Ave., Cambridge, MA 02138; Newfane, VT (summer); Gstaad, e Switzerland (winter). *Office*—207 Littauer Center, Harvard University, Cambridge, MA 02138.

CAREER: Harvard University, Cambridge, MA, instructor and tutor, 1934-39; Princeton University, Princeton, NJ, assistant professor of economics, 1939-42; U.S. Office of Price Administration, Washington, D.C., administrator in charge of price division, 1941-42, department administrator, 1942-43; *Fortune* magazine, member of board of editors, 1943-48; Harvard University, lecturer, 1948-49, professor, 1949-59, Paul M. Warburg Professor of Economics, 1959-75; Paul M. Warburg Professor emeritus, 1975—; U.S. Ambassador to India, 1961-63. Reith Lecturer, 1966; Trinity College, visiting fellow, Cambridge, 1970-71. Director of U.S. Strategic Bombing Survey, 1945, and Office of Economic Security Policy, U.S. Department of State, 1946. Presidential adviser to John F. Kennedy and Lyndon B. Johnson. Affiliated with television series *The Age of Uncertainty,* on the British Broadcasting Corporation (BBC), 1977.

MEMBER: American Academy and Institute of Arts and Letters (president, 1984-87), American Academy of Arts and Sciences (fellow), American Economic Association (president, 1972), Americans for Democratic Action (chairman, 1967-69), American Agricultural Economics Association, Twentieth Century Fund (trustee), Century Club (New York), Federal City Club (Washington DC), Harvard Club (New York), Saturday Club (Boston).

AWARDS, HONOURS: Research fellowship, University of California, 1931-34; Social Science Research Council fellowship, 1937-38; Medal of Freedom, 1946; Sarah Josepha Hale Award, Friends of the Richards Free Library, 1967; President's Certificate of Merit. LL.D., Bard College, 1958, Miami University (Ohio), 1959, University of Toronto, 1961, Brandeis University, 1963, University of Massachusetts, 1963, University of Guelph, 1965, University of Saskatchewan, 1965, Rhode Island College, 1966, Boston College, 1967, Hobart and William Smith Colleges, 1967, University of Paris, 1975, Harvard University, 1988, Moscow State University, 1988, Smith College, 1989, Oxford University, 1990.

WRITINGS:

(With Henry Sturgis Dennison) *Modern Competition and Business Policy,* Oxford University Press, 1938.

A Theory of Price Control, Harvard University Press, 1952, reprinted with new introduction by Galbraith, 1980.

American Capitalism: The Concept of Countervailing Power, Houghton, 1952, reprinted with new introduction by Galbraith, M. E. Sharpe, 1980, revised edition, Transaction Publishers, 1993.

Economics and the Art of Controversy, Rutgers University Press, 1955.

The Great Crash, 1929, Houghton, 1955, reprinted with new introduction by Galbraith, 1988.

(With Richard H. Holton and others) *Marketing Efficiency in Puerto Rico,* Harvard University Press, 1955.

Journey to Poland and Yugoslavia, Harvard University Press, 1958.

The Affluent Society, Houghton, 1958, 4th edition, 1984.

The Liberal Hour, Houghton, 1960.

Economic Development in Perspective, Harvard University Press, 1962, revised edition published as *Economic Development,* 1964.

(Under pseudonym Mark Epernay) *The McLandress Dimension* (satire), Houghton, 1963, revised edition, New American Library, 1968.

The Scotch (memoir), Houghton, 1964, 2nd edition, 1985 (published in England as *Made to Last,* Hamish Hamilton, 1964, and as *The Non-potable Scotch: A Memoir on the Clansmen in Canada,* Penguin, 1964).

The Underdeveloped Country (text of five radio broadcasts), Canadian Broadcasting Corp., 1965.

The New Industrial State, Houghton, 1967, 4th edition, 1985.

How to Get Out of Vietnam: A Workable Solution to the Worst Problem of Our Time, New American Library, 1967.

The Triumph: A Novel of Modern Diplomacy, Houghton, 1968.

(With Mohinder Singh Randhawa) *Indian Painting: The Scene, Themes and Legends,* Houghton, 1968.

How to Control the Military, Doubleday, 1969.

Ambassador's Journal: A Personal Account of the Kennedy Years, Houghton, 1969.

(Author of introduction) David Levine, *No Known Survivors: David Levine's Political Prank,* Gambit, 1970.

Who Needs the Democrats, and What It Takes to Be Needed, Doubleday, 1970.

A Contemporary Guide to Economics, Peace, and Laughter (essays), edited by Andrea D. Williams, Houghton, 1971.

Economics and the Public Purpose, Houghton, 1973.

A China Passage, Houghton, 1973.

(Author of introduction) Frank Moraes and Edward Howe, editors, *India,* McGraw-Hill, 1974.

Money: Whence It Came, Where It Went, 1975, revised edition, Houghton, 1995.

The Age of Uncertainty (based on the 1977 BBC television series), Houghton, 1977.

The Galbraith Reader: From the Works of John Kenneth Galbraith, selected and with commentary by the editors of *Gambit,* Gambit, 1977.

(With Nicole Salinger) *Almost Everyone's Guide to Economics,* Houghton, 1978.

Annals of an Abiding Liberal, edited by Williams, Houghton, 1979.

The Nature of Mass Poverty, Harvard University Press, 1979.

A Life in Our Times: Memoirs, Houghton, 1981.

The Anatomy of Power, Houghton, 1983.

The Voice of the Poor: Essays in Economic and Political Persuasion, Harvard University Press, 1983.

A View from the Stands: Of People, Politics, Military Power, and the Arts, edited by Williams, Houghton, 1986.

Economics in Perspective: A Critical History, Houghton, 1987, published as *A History of Economics,* 1987.

(With Stanislav Menshikov) *Capitalism, Communism and Coexistence: From the Bitter Past to a Better Present,* Houghton, 1988.

A Tenured Professor (novel), Houghton, 1990.

The Culture of Contentment, Houghton, 1992.

(Editor and author of introduction) Thomas H. Eliot, *Recollections of the New Deal: When the People Mattered,* Northeastern University Press, 1992.

A Short History of Financial Euphoria: A Hymn of Caution, Whittle Books/Viking, 1993.

The Triumph: A Novel of Modern Diplomacy, Houghton, 1993.

A Journey through Economic Time: A Firsthand View, Houghton, 1994.

The World Economy since the Wars: An Eyewitness Account, Houghton, 1994.

Contributor to books, including *Can Europe Unite?,* Foreign Policy Association (New York City), 1950, and *The Past Speaks to the Present,* by Yigael Yadin, Granada TV Network Limited, 1962. Author of drafts of speeches for political leaders, including Franklin D. Roosevelt, Adlai Stevenson, John F. Kennedy, Lyndon B. Johnson, and Robert Kennedy. Editor of "Harvard Economic Studies" series, Harvard University Press. Contributor to scholarly journals. Reviewer, under pseudonym Herschel McLandress, of *Report from Iron Mountain.*

Galbraith's works have been translated into numerous foreign languages.

SIDELIGHTS: John Kenneth Galbraith is considered one of the twentieth century's foremost writers on economics and among its most influential economists. A prolific and diverse writer, whose more than thirty books range over a variety of topics, Galbraith is the author of such classic texts as *The Affluent Society* and *The New Industrial State.* In addition to his writings, he has also held positions as a government economist, presidential adviser, foreign ambassador, and for over twenty years was the Paul M. Warburg Professor of Economics at Harvard University. Galbraith's blend of skills make him a rarity among economists. "As a raconteur and a literary stylist, he stands with the best," states James Fallows in the *New York Times Book Review,* while "as a thinker," notes Lowell Ponte in the *Los Angeles Times Book Review,* "Galbraith has made major contributions to the economic arguments of our time." In addition to originating several terms that are part of the vernacular of economists and laymen alike—

such as "affluent society," "conventional wisdom," and "countervailing power"—Galbraith is famous as a witty guide to twentieth-century economics. A *New Yorker* reviewer calls him "a wizard at packing immense amounts of information into a style so entertaining that the reader does not realize he is being taught." Eugene D. Genovese writes in the *New York Times Book Review* that Galbraith "has admirably demonstrated that respect for the English language provides everything necessary to demystify economics and render its complexities intelligible."

Galbraith's writing abilities, including his accessibility to non-economist audiences, have at times overshadowed his achievements as an economist. "Galbraith's irreverent wit and lucid style lead many to underestimate his importance in the history of economic thought," Walter Russell Mead notes in the *Los Angeles Times Book Review.* "Like Adam Smith . . . Galbraith has spent a career attacking the entrenched errors of conventional wisdom." Galbraith is well-known as a formidable critic of modern economic policies and economists. Richard Eder in the *Los Angeles Times* depicts him as "liberal, witty, polemical and a man who tends to charm his antagonists because the dunce caps he fits on them are so finely made that they almost flatter." As a critic, Galbraith has made significant contributions to economics by highlighting its shortcomings. According to Genovese, Galbraith's "services" include: "his early warnings that Keynesians were paying inadequate attention to the danger of inflation; his thoughtful if not always convincing discussions of the political and economic relationship of the free market sector to the managed sector; his bold exploration of the possibilities and actualities of socialism; and his humane concern for the problems of women, the poor, the blacks and others conveniently forgotten by most academic economists." Godfrey Hodgson, in the *Washington Post Book World,* compares Galbraith to eighteenth-century French satirist Voltaire, "a man whose sardonic wit and careful urbanity are worn like masks to hide both the anger he feels for sham and complacent greed, and the pity he feels for their victims."

The son of a Canadian politician and farmer, Galbraith became interested in the study of economics during the Depression. In the 1930s and early 1940s, he taught at both Harvard University and Princeton University, and became influenced by economist John Maynard Keynes. In 1941, at the age of 33, he was appointed administrator of the price operations of the U.S. Office of Price Administration, and was responsible for setting prices in the United States. His 1952 book, *A Theory of Price Control,* outlines many of Galbraith's fundamental economic principles, as does another early book, *American Capitalism: The Concept of Countervailing Power,* which explores postwar American economy and the role of labor as a

countervailing force in a market economy. Samuel Lubell in the *New York Herald Tribune Book World* called *American Capitalism* "one of the most provocative economic essays since the writings of the late John Maynard Keynes," adding that "even where one disagrees, [Galbraith's] ideas stimulate a spring cleaning of old beliefs and outworn, if cherished, notions—which is perhaps all that can be asked of any new theory." Galbraith commented to Victor Navasky in the *New York Times Book Review* on his decision to write about economics: "I made up my mind I would never again place myself at the mercy of the technical economists who had the enormous power to ignore what I had written. I set out to involve a large community. I would involve economists by having the larger public say to them 'Where do you stand on Galbraith's idea of price control?' They would *have* to confront what I said."

Galbraith broadened his readership with his 1955 book, *The Great Crash, 1929,* which recounts the harried days leading up to the stock market crash and Great Depression. Written at the suggestion of historian Arthur Schlesinger, Jr., who queried Galbraith as to why no one had ever written an economic account of the depression, *The Great Crash, 1929* was praised for being both illuminating and readable. "Economic writings are seldom notable for their entertainment value, but this book is," C. J. Rolo commented in *Atlantic,* adding, "Mr. Galbraith's prose has grace and wit, and he distills a good deal of sardonic fun from the whopping errors of the nation's oracles and the wondrous antics of the financial community." R. L. Heilbroner wrote in the *New York Herald Tribune Book Review:* "Mr. Galbraith has told the tale of the great bust with all the verve, pace, and suspense, of a detective story. . . . For any one who is interested in understanding the recent past or attempting to achieve a perspective on the future of American economic history, . . . this book will be of great interest."

Following these books, Galbraith wrote the bestselling *The Affluent Society.* A major assessment of the U.S. economy, *The Affluent Society* questions priorities of production and how wealth is to be divided. As Galbraith states in the book: "The final problem of the productive society is what it produces. This manifests itself in an implacable tendency to provide an opulent supply of some things and a niggardly yield of others. This disparity carries to the point where it is a cause of social discomfort and social unhealth." According to Heilbroner, Galbraith raises three important issues: "One of these is the moral problem of how an Affluent Society may be prevented from becoming merely a Rich one. A second is the efficacy of Mr. Galbraith's reforms to offset the inertia and the vested interests of a powerful social structure. A third is what form of social cohesion can replace our troublesome but useful absorption in Production." Heilbroner called *The Affluent*

Society "as disturbing as it is brilliant. . . . with which it is easy to cavil or to disagree, but which it is impossible to dismiss."

Galbraith's 1967 bestseller *The New Industrial State,* a sequel to *The Affluent Society,* examines the diminishing role of individual choice in the market enterprise. "I reached the conclusion that in 'The Affluent Society' I had only written half the book I should have," Galbraith commented to the *New York Times Book Review.* " 'The Affluent Society' says the more you have the more you want. And for obvious reasons, as people become richer it is easier to persuade them as to their wants. But I hadn't really examined the role of the great corporations, the industrial system, in the persuasion process." Arthur Selwyn Miller commented in the *New Republic:* "If Galbraith is correct—and I am inclined to agree in large part with him—then we . . . are ruled by nameless and faceless managers in the technostructures of the private governments of the supercorporations and their counterparts in the public bureaucracy. That's an event of considerable significance." Raymond J. Saulnier in the *New York Times Book Review* called *The New Industrial State* "a tightly organized, closely reasoned book, notable for what it says about the dynamics of institutional change and for certain qualities of its author: a sardonic wit, exercised liberally at the expense of conservatives, and unusual perception."

In his 1973 book, *Economics and the Public Purpose,* Galbraith, according to Leonard Silk in the *New York Times,* goes "beyond his earlier books to describe the whole modern capitalist economy, which he sees as split roughly in twain between 'the planning system' and what he calls 'the market system'—a collection of imperfect competitors and partial monopolists that includes such producers as farmers, television repairmen, retailers, small manufacturers, medical practitioners, photographers and pornographers. He regards the market system as the exploited and relatively feeble half of the economy—although it obviously includes some not particularly exploited people. . . . Yet, although some members of the market system make out quite nicely, it is the planning system of the great corporations, he says, that dominates the state, unbalances social and economic development, exacerbates inequality, corrupts foreign policy and befouls the atmosphere."

The *New Yorker*'s Naomi Bliven commented that Galbraith "offers his account of the American economic system and his ideas of how to correct—a word he uses frequently—its irrationality." She added that although "his intensity sometimes makes his wit painfully abrasive. . . . because his work is intelligent, stimulating, and comprehensive—Galbraith knows (in fact, insists) that an economic theory implies an ethical system, a political pur-

pose, and a psychological hypothesis—one forgives this unrelenting critic."

In addition to over twenty-five other books on economics, the prolific Galbraith is also the author of three novels and of acclaimed volumes of memoirs. As in his other books, these writings display Galbraith's characteristic wit and insight. His 1968 novel *The Triumph,* set amidst a revolution in a fictional Latin American nation, depicts the bungled efforts of U.S. foreign policy officials to put an acceptable leader in power. Robert Brown in the *New Republic,* while expressing reservations about the novel's tone which he described as "loftily condescending and relentlessly witty," called the book "quite devastating" and acknowledged Galbraith's "detailed knowledge of the scene." Galbraith's 1990 novel, *A Tenured Professor,* is the tale of a professor who, with his wife, develops a successful stock forecasting mechanism that makes them very wealthy. With their new money, the couple begins supporting various liberal causes, such as identifying companies that do not employ women in top executive positions. "Lurking in the background of his story is enough economics to satisfy Wall Street game players and enough of a cheerful fairy tale for grown-ups to please the most liberal dreamers . . . ," notes Herbert Mitgang in the *New York Times.* "A whimsical fellow is John Kenneth Galbraith, who knows that money makes people and institutions jump through hoops and over their own cherished principles." He added: "Readers who know and admire the author as an acerbic political voice are not shortchanged in his biting new novel. . . . Satirical one-liners and paragraphs fall lightly from the pen of the author and from the lips of his characters all through the story."

Galbraith's memoirs give insights into his diverse career as economist, writer, and participant in the political scene. Regarding *A Life in Our Times,* Ward Just commented in the *Chicago Tribune Book World:* "[Galbraith] has rarely been at the center of events, though he has been on the fringes of most everything, so this is not a memoir of the and-then-I-told-the-President variety. . . . The charm and consequence of this book is not the career as such, but the manner in which the author has chosen to describe it, with singular range, style, and wit, and a sure grasp of absurdity and pomposity, particularly as they apply to government and politics." Regarding the essays in *A View from the Stands: Of People, Politics, Military Power, and the Arts,* Richard Eder wrote in the *Los Angeles Times* that Galbraith "has a priceless sense of the absurd. . . . [Yet,] for someone who makes an art out of polite irreverence, Galbraith manages to be equally artistic in his strong admirations. . . . His portraits of, among others, Ambassador Chester Bowles, President Lyndon B. Johnson and First Lady Eleanor Roosevelt are both warm and strikingly perceptive." *A View from the Stands* reveals a man, according to John Freeman in the *Times Literary Supplement,* who is "substantial, interesting, frequently perverse, occasionally silly, almost always stimulating—at least hardly ever a bore—opinionated, funny, fastidious, loyal, on the whole generous and magnificently infallible even when he is wrong."

In *The Culture of Contentment,* Galbraith "scathingly denounces a society in which the affluent have come to dominate the political arena, guaranteeing their continued comfort while refusing to address the needs of the less fortunate," claims Victor Dwyer in *Maclean's.* Galbraith asserts that satisfied citizens—the top twenty percent regarding annual earnings who live a moneyed lifestyle—tend to, by their very prosperity, guarantee their eventual downfall by ignoring the fundamental requirements of the underclasses. Their blindness to social reform has historically led to inflation and the need for greater government intervention, thereby causing a resulting eventual decline in economic security even for the elite, maintains the author. Galbraith warns that the upper-class ignores economic, political, and social necessities of the lower classes at their own peril. Galbraith told Dwyer that *The Culture of Contentment* exceeds the scope of his other books: " 'What I am attempting is to formulate the political consequences of self-satisfied well-being,' said Galbraith. 'In the wake of Mr. Reagan and Mr. Bush,' he added, 'it seemed that the time was right.' " Robert N. Bellah observes in the *New York Times Book Review,* " 'The Culture of Contentment' is certainly no savage jeremiad. It is a very amusing volume, but by the end one's laughter has turned hollow and one wants to weep. For all its gentle appearances, it is a bombshell of a book, and the story it tells is one of devastation." Aidan Rankin comments in the *Times Literary Supplement:* "The reassuring, old-fashioned elegance of John Kenneth Galbraith's prose is at once the most striking and the most disturbing feature of *The Culture of Contentment.* Striking, because it contrasts so markedly with the jargon and euphemism of modern economics, disturbing in the force and clarity of its critique of contemporary democracy."

About *A Short History of Financial Euphoria,* Robert Krulwich explains in the *New York Times Book Review* that it "is John Kenneth Galbraith's quick tour through four centuries of financial bubbles, panics and crashes, with an eye toward instructing today's investors on how to see cautionary signs before it is too late." Galbraith describes, through myriad examples, a historic pattern of financial ebb and flow creating highs and lows in the economic climate. He denounces the oblivious attitude engendered by successful investments, blinding individuals to warning signs and potential disasters. As Krulwich simplifies, "How people become blockheads is the real subject of his treatise," concluding that Galbraith reminds readers that "rich people aren't smart. They're just lucky."

A Journey through Economic Time traces economic development from the time of World War I (or the "Great War") through the highlights of the twentieth century, including other wars and military conflicts, the philosophies of influential pundits, and the practices and ideologies of various presidential administrations. "Somehow, with an astonishing and no doubt deceptive ease, Mr. Galbraith is able to compress eras, reducing their unwieldy bulk to graspable essence and extracting coherence from their thematic tangle," remarks Alan Abelson in the *New York Times Book Review.* Abelson admired the readability of the book, asserting, "He's opinionated, incorrigibly sardonic and murder on fools. . . . In a profession in which statistical surfeit, abused syntax and impenetrable prose are prerequisites to standing, Mr. Galbraith's lucidity and grace of articulation are excommunicable offenses." Donald McCloskey hails Galbraith's tome in the Chicago *Tribune Books,* summarizing, "What makes it good is the Old Economist showing you page after page how to think like one," ultimately urging readers to "buy it or borrow it. You'll be a better citizen and will not believe so easily the latest economic idiocy from Washington or the Sierra Club or the other fonts of conventional wisdom."

William Keegan notes in *New Statesman and Society* that *The World Economy since the Wars* "can be thoroughly recommended to those interested in the economic debate, but [who are] not quite sure where to start." Galbraith's efforts involve "sifting and reducing a lifetime's observations to an essential core," describes Keegan. While the reviewer suggests that much of this volume has already appeared in other forms in earlier books, he nevertheless maintains, "This is a highly engaging memoir, which holds the attention even of people, such as myself, who are thoroughly familiar with most of Galbraith's work."

For more than half a century, Galbraith has proven himself a brilliant writer, critical thinker, perspicacious social analyst, and astute economic observer/commentator. Rankin opined in the *Times Literary Supplement* that "Galbraith has contributed substantially to the liberal tradition in the United States and the social democratic tradition in Western Europe." About the author's multiple interests and abilities, McCloskey comments in the Chicago *Tribune Books,* "As much as he would rather be a writer, converting people to his government-loving faith, he [is] an economist down to his shoes." Dwyer describes Galbraith in *Maclean's* as "America's foremost liberal thinker," adding that he "is most passionate about the state of American society." McCloskey concluded, "We need more of him because he's an economist who can speak to non-economists. . . . Galbraith is one of a handful of professors who can make the Dismal Science sing."

CA INTERVIEW

CA interviewed John Kenneth Galbraith by telephone on May 2, 1988, at his home in Cambridge, Massachusetts.

CA: Studying animal husbandry just out of high school at what you've called the "worst college in the English-speaking world," Ontario Agricultural College, did you have any notion of becoming an economist and a writer?

GALBRAITH: I must be kinder and say that it wasn't the worst college—I'm sorry for that—but one of the least good. No, I certainly didn't have any notion of becoming an economist. My father was a livestock breeder, and Ontario Agricultural College was exceptionally inexpensive in those days. It was only when I was in my junior year that it occurred to me that making agricultural products more efficiently was not the problem; the problem was that they couldn't be sold for a remunerative price. That was what led me over to economics—a not surprising reaction, for this was in the early years of the Great Depression.

CA: Your career has included what seems a fine mix of academia, government service, and writing, the last of which has brought you a tremendous popular readership and perhaps at times more visibility than you might have liked. How easily have these aspects of your work meshed?

GALBRAITH: Very easily. Life is too short to confine yourself to one career. I regard with both surprise and sympathy those who waste their entire lives, for example, making money.

CA: One of your best-known books is The Affluent Society, *published in 1958 and republished in later editions. The title became a part of our language. Are we just as intent on the overproduction of consumer goods now as we were then, in your view?*

GALBRAITH: I never really regarded it as the overproduction of consumers' goods. What I argue in that book is that wants are no longer inherent in the individual psyche, that they are extensively created by the institutions that then sought to supply them. This, of course, is one of the great roles of modern advertising. So I rather resist the word *overproduction;* what I was describing was a process. And I would say that what I identified then is much more in evidence now.

CA: Should we be learning something from the very successful Japanese about business and finance?

GALBRAITH: Unquestionably, yes—several things. First, we should learn from the fact that they've put a very large part of their energy these last thirty years into the production of civilian goods and services, whereas we've committed a very large part of ours to the relatively sterile production of military goods and services. They also have

seen the modern enterprise in a much more modern form, as a cooperative arrangement between all the participants. They have tended to give greater tenure to their workers. They have even gone to the point, which we would regard as subversive, of reducing executive salaries when it's necessary to keep their products at a competitive price.

All of these are things we can learn from the Japanese, and doubtless there are others. One of the most important things is that the Japanese do not regard government and industry as naturally hostile entities. The result has been a great deal closer cooperation between the government and the Japanese corporations, for the benefit of both.

CA: Most women now are working outside the home, with varying degrees of success and income. What changes in consumer spending is this causing, and what are the long-term implications?

GALBRAITH: I've talked about this at some length in one of my books, *Economics and the Public Purpose.* In the consumer society you have not only the problem of getting the consumers goods but the problem of administering their use. This, in the past, has been one of the functions of women: to manage the household, the automobile, the entertainment. That is a much larger task than economists have commonly recognized.

Now, as wives increasingly seek employment, one has a greater reliance on the services that are a substitute for the household economy. That includes, of course, restaurants, entertainments, social activities. One aspect of this change is some return from suburban to urban residence.

CA: There seems to be a trend now, among young women with small children, to try staying at home with them, even if it means giving up quite good jobs.

GALBRAITH: We have a way, on occasion, of identifying trends before they develop. It is my impression that the movement is still very much in the opposite direction. One manifestation is the increasing agitation over the whole question of child care.

CA: In American Capitalism, *published in 1952, and later in* Economics and the Public Purpose, *1973, you set forth the concept of "countervailing power," a balance by which government would keep big business and unions in control. How well do you think the principle of countervailing power is working in the economy today?*

GALBRAITH: I never regarded it as a solution for the problem of power, and on reflection I think I exaggerated its role in American capitalism. But having said that, I feel no doubt that when one is subject to an unwelcome exercise of power, the answer is not to destroy that source of power but to organize in opposition. This is spectacularly true in the field of labor relations; but commonly, through all life, the answer to power is to create an opposing position. I continue to regard this as one of the basic facts of life.

CA: How do you feel more than forty years later about the Keynesian ideas incorporated in the Employment Act of 1946?

GALBRAITH: These are still central to our thinking. I can't help speculating on how Keynes, from wherever he is watching, must view the Reagan Administration and its deficit financing. A great discovery that we have made in these last fifty years is that inflation yields much less easily to Keynesian action than do unemployment and depression. Unemployment and depression call for government expenditure, reduced taxes, reduced interest rates, all of which are politically pleasant. Inflation, as we saw it in the last seventies, calls for higher taxes, higher interest rates, perhaps lower social expenditure, and some special design for controlling the wage-price spiral. All of that is politically very difficult. So, as I've often said, there is a political asymmetry in the Keynesian system which those of us who had something to do with carrying it into public practice did not foresee.

CA: In an article in the Atlantic Monthly, *you drew some parallels between that time and the time of the stock market crash of 1929. Would you comment on the subsequent stock market plunge on October 19, 1987, and what it might have been telling us about our economy?*

GALBRAITH: I don't think it was telling us so much about our economy; it was telling us a great deal about the securities markets. In both the months and year preceding 1929, and similarly the months and years before October, 1987, there was a speculative boom. People and institutions were in the market, either in the expectation that it would go up forever or the equally innocent belief that their particular genius would allow them to ride it up and get out before the fall. These speculative episodes never end gradually; they always end with a crash. When one saw this happening in 1986 and 1987, one could only assume that a crash was in the offing. That was the point I made in the *Atlantic Monthly* article, which, sadly, had its principal influence and readership after the crash.

CA: Economists have been out of favor with the Reagan administration, as they were earlier during the Nixon administration. How much of a voice do you feel they will have in government in the upcoming decade?

GALBRAITH: I don't think they were out of favor in the Nixon Administration. I think, on the whole, Nixon made good use of his economists. Arthur Burns, for example, who was very close to Nixon, was very influential, and also George Schultz. I think the resistance of the Reagan Administration to economists is a reflection of Reagan's

difficulty in finding economists who support his aberrant economic policy. And I think economists will certainly continue to be a voice in public affairs.

CA: Your friend Arthur M. Schlesinger, Jr., has written about the cyclical view, which originated with his father, that there is a predictable and inevitable thirty-year swing between liberal and conservative political climates. Do you feel any sort of economic parallel can be made?

GALBRAITH: I am persuaded that there are such movements in the public mood as regards politics and political concerns. I'm less persuaded as regards economic cycles. These are much more subject to the influence of external events: war, aberrant economic policy such as that of President Reagan, and other episodic influences that I don't think have a cyclical form.

CA: Do you feel liberalism and conservatism have lost their intellectual and philosophical underpinnings?

GALBRAITH: No, but I do have the feeling that there has been some substantial movement away from ideological commitment, that conservatives have discovered that government is still a necessary instrument of modern life, and indeed necessary on occasion for the bailing out of business enterprises themselves; and that American liberals have moved to accept pragmatically the operation of the market, as, in increasing measure, have socialists. I think this is very much an age of declining ideological commitment on all sides.

CA: You were early opposed to the war in Vietnam. How do you think the Vietnam experience applies to the current relationship between the United States and Central America?

GALBRAITH: I think the war in Vietnam was a very useful lesson on the limits of our power and the limits of needed intervention. The experience has certainly been a restraining influence as regards Central America. We have had the impulse in these last years to show that we have a certain amount of muscle. That has led us to ridiculous concern for what might be happening in those small countries in Central America. We seem to want small enemies, and Grenada wasn't quite sufficient.

CA: In your book, Capitalism, Communism and Coexistence, *you and the Russian economist Stanislav Menshikov have a dialogue about the similarities of our systems, the differences, and some ways in which we might cooperate more effectively and indeed are beginning to do so in some instances. How hopeful are you about future cooperation between the United States and Russia?*

GALBRAITH: I have never thought, for example, that there was a great trading opportunity. They need our wheat and feed grains, and there are some things that we buy from them besides caviar; but the Socialist countries are not great trading communities. I hope to see cooperation in reducing world tension and tension between the two countries. I certainly support the promotion of trade, but I don't see a great possibility of the expansion of trade. Let us remember always that we sit on the same side of the table knowing that both capitalism and communism would be destroyed equally in a nuclear war.

CA: As a teacher yourself for many years at Harvard and also in other universities, how do you feel about the teaching of economics? What's done well and what would you like to see done better or not done at all?

GALBRAITH: I have no great complaints. I have always been on the side of some shift from rigorous theory to a greater political and social concern. But a mix between the two doesn't bother me. I've always had the feeling that if all economists concerned themselves all the time with public-policy issues, the competition for those of us who do so concern ourselves would be too great. I'm very glad to have some of my colleagues bury themselves in purely theoretical matters.

CA: Writing fiction seems to give you as much pleasure as doing the other books, and you've said recently that you're working on another novel.

GALBRAITH: Yes. With fiction, you move into a world of your own creation and live in that world. You have the pleasure of feeling for a few months, or the year or so that you spend on a novel, that you are socially and politically irrelevant, and that's a very pleasant relief from the sense of heavy responsibility. I look back especially on the time I spent writing *The Triumph,* which was a bestseller in its day, as among the happiest months of my life. I wrote part of it in Switzerland, part of it in Venice, part of it in Majorca, and part of it in Vermont; but all of that time I was really living in the fictional community of Puerto Santos, the locale of most the novel. I came to love that country.

CA: I've read in the past that you especially liked to write in Switzerland. Do you take the writing along wherever you travel?

GALBRAITH: I always do some writing wherever I am. I'm subject to the Somerset Maugham syndrome: he said something to the effect that, until you're fifty, writing is hard work; then it becomes just another bad habit.

CA: You said at the end of A Life in Our Times, *"I've noticed that those who write their memoirs have difficulty in knowing when, on public matters, they should stop. The obvious stopping point is when the view is from the stands."* It's very hard to accept any picture of you in the stands. How much are you involved politically now, and what involvement do you plan for the future?*

GALBRAITH: That statement at the end of my memoirs was for public effect rather than an exact expression of truth. On the other hand, where I would have felt obliged in past elections to involve myself with one or another of the candidates, I haven't done so this time. Michael Dukakis is a friend of mine of many years' standing, but I've been content to believe that he has more advice than he can use.

CA: Would you like to be more in the public eye in the future, possibly? Are you tempted at all?

GALBRAITH: I'm very content with the present situation.

BIOGRAPHICAL/CRITICAL SOURCES:

BOOKS

Contemporary Issues Criticism, Volume 1, Gale, 1982.
Galbraith, John Kenneth, *The Affluent Society,* Houghton, 1958.
Galbraith, *A Journey through Economic Time: A Firsthand View,* Houghton, 1994.
Galbraith, *A Life in Our Times: Memoirs,* Houghton, 1981.
Galbraith *The Scotch,* Houghton, 1964.
Galbraith, *A View from the Stands: Of People, Politics, Military Power, and the Arts,* Houghton, 1986.
Galbraith, *The World Economy since the Wars: An Eyewitness Account,* Houghton, 1994.
Reisman, D. A., *Galbraith and Market Capitalism,* New York University Press, 1980.
Reisman, D. A., *Tawney, Galbraith, and Adam Smith,* St. Martin's, 1982.

PERIODICALS

American Economic Review, December, 1952.
Atlantic Monthly, June, 1955; January, 1987.
Chicago Tribune, June 1, 1958.
Chicago Tribune Book World, April 19, 1981.
Library Journal, May 15, 1993, pp. 78-79.
Look, March 27, 1970.
Los Angeles Times, December 3, 1986.
Los Angeles Times Book Review, May 24, 1981; November 11, 1987; March 4, 1990; June 19, 1994, pp. 4, 11.
Maclean's, May 25, 1992, pp. 61-62.
Nation, July 30, 1955.
New Republic, June 9, 1958; July 8, 1967; May 4, 1968.
New Statesman and Society, July 22, 1994, p. 47.
Newsweek, June 26, 1967; July 3, 1967.
New Yorker, January 6, 1968; December 31, 1973; May 2, 1977.
New York Herald Tribune Book Review, June 29, 1952; April 24, 1955; June 9, 1958.
New York Times, June 1, 1958; September 18, 1973; February 24, 1990.

New York Times Book Review, June 25, 1967; September 7, 1975; May 3, 1981; February 11, 1990; April 5, 1992, p. 10; July 18, 1993, p. 8; July 19, 1994, p. 9.
Playboy (interview), June, 1968.
Publishers Weekly, May 17, 1993, p. 58.
Spectator, November 10, 1967.
Time, February 16, 1968.
Times Literary Supplement, March 13, 1987; May 29, 1992, p. 26.
Tribune Books (Chicago), February 18, 1990; September 25, 1994, p. 4.
Washington Post Book World, October 21, 1979; February 11, 1990.

—Sketch by Michael E. Mueller

—Interview by Jean W. Ross and Hugh S. Norton

*   *   *

GALLANT, Mavis 1922-

PERSONAL: Born Mavis Young, August 11, 1922, in Montreal, Quebec, Canada. *Education:* Educated at schools in Montreal and New York City.

ADDRESSES: Home—14 rue Jean Ferrandi, Paris 6, France. *Agent*—Georges Borchardt, 136 East 57th St., New York, NY 10022.

CAREER: Worked at National Film Board of Canada, Montreal, early 1940s; *The Standard,* Montreal, Quebec, feature writer and critic, 1944-50; freelance writer, 1950—. Writer in residence at University of Toronto, 1983-84.

MEMBER: PEN, Authors Guild, Authors League of America, American Academy and Institute of Arts and Letters (foreign honorary member), Royal Society of Literature (fellow).

AWARDS, HONOURS: Canadian Fiction Prize, 1978; named Officer of the Order of Canada, 1981; Governor General's Award, 1981, for *Home Truths: Selected Canadian Stories;* honorary doctorates from University of St. Anne, Nova Scotia, and York University, Ontario, both 1984, and University of Western Ontario, 1990; Canada-Australia Literary Prize, 1985.

WRITINGS:

FICTION

The Other Paris (short stories), Houghton, 1956.
Green Water, Green Sky (novel), Houghton, 1959.
My Heart Is Broken: Eight Stories and a Short Novel, Random House, 1964, published in England as *An Unmarried Man's Summer,* Heinemann, 1965).
A Fairly Good Time (novel), Random House, 1970.

The Pegnitz Junction: A Novella and Five Short Stories, Random House, 1973.
The End of the World and Other Stories, McClelland & Stewart, 1974.
From the Fifteenth District: A Novella and Eight Short Stories, Random House, 1979.
Home Truths: Selected Canadian Stories, Macmillan, 1981.
Overhead in a Balloon: Stories of Paris, Macmillan, 1985.
In Transit: Twenty Stories, Random House, 1989.
Across the Bridge: Nine Short Stories, Random House, 1993.
The Moslem Wife and Other Stories, McClelland & Stewart, 1993.

OTHER

(Author of introduction) Gabrielle Russier, *The Affair of Gabrielle Russier,* Knopf, 1971.
(Author of introduction) J. Hibbert, *The War Brides,* PMA (Toronto), 1978.
What Is To Be Done? (play; first produced in Toronto at Tarragon Theatre, November 11, 1982), Quadrant, 1983.
Paris Notebooks: Essays and Reviews, Macmillan (Toronto), 1986.

Contributor of essays, short stories, and reviews to numerous periodicals, including *New Yorker, New York Times Book Review, New Republic, New York Review of Books,* and *Times Literary Supplement.*

WORK IN PROGRESS: A novel.

SIDELIGHTS: Canadian-born Mavis Gallant is widely considered one of the finest crafters of short stories in the English language. Her works, most of which appear initially in the *New Yorker* magazine, are praised for sensitive evocation of setting and penetrating delineation of character. In the words of *Maclean's* magazine contributor Mark Abley, Gallant "is virtually unrivalled at the art of short fiction," an exacting artist whose pieces reveal "an ability to press a lifetime into a few resonant pages as well as a desire to show the dark side of comedy and the humor that lurks behind despair." *Time* magazine correspondent Timothy Foote calls Gallant "one of the prose masters of the age," and adds that no modern writer "casts a colder eye on life, on death and all the angst and eccentricity in between." Since 1950 Gallant has lived primarily in Paris, but she has also spent extended periods of time in the United States, Canada, and other parts of Europe. Not surprisingly, her stories and novellas show a wide range of place and period; many feature refugees and expatriates forced into self- discernment by rootlessness. As Anne Tyler notes in the *New York Times Book Review,* each Gallant fiction "is densely-woven, . . . rich in people and plots—a miniature world, more satisfying than many full-scale novels. . . . There is a sense of limitlessness: each story is like a peephole opening out into a very wide landscape."

Dictionary of Literary Biography essayist Ronald B. Hatch observes that the subject of children, "alone, frightened, or unloved," recurs often in Gallant's work. This, he notes, reflects Gallant's own difficult youth. The author underwent a solitary and transient childhood, attending seventeen different schools in the United States and Canada. Her father died while she was in grade school, and her mother, soon remarried, moved to the United States, leaving the child with strangers. Speaking to how her formative years influenced her writing, Gallant told the *New York Times:* "I think it's true that in many, many of the things I write, someone has vanished. And it's often the father. And there is often a sense that nothing is very safe, and you're often walking on a very thin crust." One advantage of Gallant's far-flung education has endured, however. As a primary schooler in her native Montreal, she learned French, and she remained bilingual into adulthood.

Gallant matured into a resourceful young woman determined to be a writer. At the age of twenty-one she became a reporter with the Montreal *Standard,* a position that honed her writing talents while it widened her variety of experiences. Journalism, she told the *New York Times,* "turned out to be so valuable, because I saw the interiors of houses I wouldn't have seen otherwise. And a great many of the things, particularly in . . . [fiction] about Montreal, that I was able to describe later, it was because I had seen them, I had gone into them as a journalist." She added: "If I got on with the people, I had no hesitation about seeing them again. . . . I went right back and took them to lunch. I could see some of those rooms, and see the wallpaper, and what they ate, and what they wore, and how they spoke, . . . and the way they treated their children. I drew it all in like blotting paper." From these encounters Gallant began to write stories. In 1950 she decided to leave Montreal and begin a new life as a serious fiction writer in Paris. At the same time she began to send stories to the *New Yorker* for publication. Her second submission, a piece called "Madeline's Birthday," was accepted, beginning a four-decade relationship with the prestigious periodical. Gallant used the six- hundred-dollar check for her story to finance her move abroad. Paris has been her permanent home ever since.

Expatriation provided Gallant with new challenges and insights that have formed central themes in her fiction. In *The Other Paris* and subsequent story collections, her characters are "the refugee, the rootless, the emotionally disinherited," to quote a *Times Literary Supplement* reviewer, who adds: "It is a world of displacement where journeys are allegorical and love is inadequate." Gallant portrays postwar people locked into archaic cultural presuppositions; often dispossessed of their homes by haphazard circumstances, they are bewildered and insecure, seeking refuge in etiquette and other shallow symbols of tradition. *Time* correspondent Patricia Blake maintains that Gallant's "natural subject is the varieties of spiritual exile. . . . All [her characters] are bearers of a metaphorical 'true passport' that transcends nationality and signifies internal freedom. For some this serves as a safe-conduct to independence. For others it is a guarantee of loneliness and despair." Gallant also presents the corollary theme of the past's inexorable grip on its survivors. In her stories, *New York Review of Books* essayist V. S. Pritchett contends, "we are among the victims of the wars in Europe which have left behind pockets of feckless exiles. . . . History has got its teeth into them and has regurgitated them and left them bizarre and perplexed." Whether immersed in the past or on the run from it, vainly trying to "turn over a new leaf," Gallant's characters "convey with remarkable success a sense of the amorphousness, the mess of life," to quote *Books and Bookmen* contributor James Brockway. Spiritually and physically marginal, they yearn paradoxically for safety, order, and freedom. "Hearts are not broken in Mavis Gallant's stories . . . ," concludes Eve Auchincloss in the *New York Review of Books.* "Roots are cut, and her subject is the nature of the life that is led when the roots are not fed."

Most critics applaud Gallant's ability to inhabit the minds of her characters without resorting to condescension or sentimentality. Abley claims that the author "can write with curiosity and perceptiveness about the kind of people who would never read a word of her work—a rarer achievement than it might sound. She is famous for not forgiving and not forgetting; her unkindness is usually focused on women and men who have grown complacent, never reflecting on their experience, no longer caring about their world. With such people she is merciless, yet with others, especially children bruised by neglect, she is patient and even kind. In the end, perhaps, understanding can be a means of forgiveness. One hopes so, because Mavis Gallant understands us terribly well." In the *Chicago Tribune Book World* Civia Tamarkin suggests that Gallant's works "impose a haunting vision of man trapped in an existential world. Each of the stories is a sensitive, though admirably understated, treatment of isolation, loneliness, and despair. Together they build an accumulating sense of the frustrating indifference of the cosmos to human hopes."

Gallant is best known for her short stories and novellas, but she has also written two novels, *Green Water, Green Sky* and *A Fairly Good Time.* Hatch contends that these works continue the author's "exploration of the interaction between an individual's thoughts and his external world." In *Green Water, Green Sky,* according to Constance Pendergast in the *Saturday Review,* Gallant "writes of the disaster that results from a relationship founded on the mutual need and antagonism of a woman and her daughter, where love turns inward and festers, bringing about inevitably the disintegration of both characters." Lighter in tone, *A Fairly Good Time* follows the blundering adventures of a Canadian, Shirley Perrigny, who lives in France. Hatch notes that the novel "may well be the funniest of all her works. . . . As a satire on the self-satisfied habits of the French, *A Fairly Good Time* proves enormously high-spirited. Yet the novel offers more than satire. As the reader becomes intimately acquainted with Shirley, her attempts to defeat the rigidity of French logic by living in the moment come to seem zany but commendable."

Home Truths: Selected Canadian Stories, first published in 1981, has proven to be one of Gallant's most popular collections. In Abley's view, the volume "bears repeated witness to the efforts made by this solitary, distant writer to come to terms with her own past and her own country." The stories focus on footloose Canadians who are alienated from their families or cultures; the characters try "to puzzle out the ground rules of their situations, which are often senseless, joyless and contradictory," to quote *Nation* reviewer Barbara Fisher Williamson. *New York Times Book Review* contributor Maureen Howard observes that in *Home Truths,* Canada "is not a setting, a backdrop; it is an adversary, a constraint, a comfort, the home that is almost understandable, if not understanding. It is at once deadly real and haunting, phantasmagoric." Phyllis Grosskurth elaborates in *Saturday Night:* "Clearly [Gallant] is still fighting a battle with the Canada she left many years ago. Whether or not that country has long since vanished is irrelevant, for it has continued to furnish the world of her imagination. . . . She knows that whatever she writes will be in the language that shaped her sensibility, though the Canada of her youth imposed restraints from which she could free herself only by geographic separation. Wherever she is, she writes out of her roots. . . . Her Montreal is a state of mind, an emotion recalled, an apprenticeship for life." *Home Truths* won the 1981 Governor General's Award, Canada's highest literary honor. *Books in Canada* correspondent Wayne Grady concludes that it is not a vision of Gallant's native country that emerges in the book, but rather "a vision of the world, of life: it is in that nameless country of the mind inhabited by all real writers, regardless of nativity, that Mavis Gallant lives. We are here privileged intruders."

The *New Yorker* has been the initial forum for almost all of Gallant's short fiction—and much of her nonfiction, too—since 1950. Critics, among them *Los Angeles Times* reviewer Elaine Kendall, feel that Gallant's work meets the periodical's high literary standards; in Kendall's words, Gallant's stories "seem the epitome of the magazine's traditional style." Readers of the *New Yorker* expect to find challenging stories, and according to Hatch, Gallant offers such challenges. "The reader finds that he cannot comprehend the fictional world as something given, but must engage with the text to bring its meanings into being," Hatch writes. "As in life, so in a Gallant story, no handy editor exists ready to point the moral." Foote expresses a similar opinion. "Gallant rarely leaves helpful signs and messages that readers tend to expect of 'literature': This way to the Meaning or This story is about the Folly of Love . . . ," the critic concludes. "In the end the stories are simply there—haunting, enigmatic, printed with images as sharp and durable as the edge of a new coin, relentlessly specific."

The critical reception for Gallant's work has been very positive. *Washington Post Book World* reviewer Elizabeth Spencer suggests that there is "no writer in English anywhere able to set Mavis Gallant in second place. Her style alone places her in the first rank. Gallant's firmly drafted prose neglects nothing, leaves no dangling ends for the reader to tack up. . . . She is hospitable to the metaphysics of experience as well as to the homeliest social detail." Grosskurth writes: "Gallant's particular power as a writer is the sureness with which she catches the ephemeral; it is a wry vision, a blend of the sad and the tragi-comic. She is a born writer who happens to have been born in Canada, and her gift has been able to develop as it has only because she could look back in anger, love, and nostalgia." *New York Times Book Review* contributor Phyllis Rose praises Gallant for her "wicked humor that misses nothing, combined with sophistication so great it amounts to forgiveness." The critic concludes: "To take up residence in the mind of Mavis Gallant, as one does in reading her stories, is a privilege and delight."

BIOGRAPHICAL/CRITICAL SOURCES:

BOOKS

Contemporary Literary Criticism, Gale, Volume 7, 1977; Volume 18, 1981; Volume 38, 1986.

Dictionary of Literary Biography, Volume 53: *Canadian Writers since 1960, First Series,* Gale, 1986.

Lecker, Robert and Jack David, editors, *The Annotated Bibliography of Canada's Major Authors,* Volume 5, ECW (Ontario), 1984.

Merler, Grazia, *Mavis Gallant: Narrative Patterns and Devices,* Tecumseh, 1978.

Moss, John, editor, *Present Tense,* NC Press (Toronto), 1985.

Reference Guide to Short Fiction, St. James Press, 1993.

Short Story Criticism, Volume 5, Gale, 1990.

PERIODICALS

Atlantis, autumn, 1978.
Books and Bookmen, July, 1974.
Books in Canada, October, 1979; October, 1981; April, 1984; October, 1985.
Canadian Fiction, number 28, 1978; number 43, 1982.
Canadian Forum, February, 1982; November, 1985.
Canadian Literature, spring, 1973; spring, 1985.
Chicago Tribune Book World, November 11, 1979.
Christian Science Monitor, June 4, 1970.
Globe and Mail (Toronto), October 11, 1986; October 15, 1988.
Los Angeles Times, April 15, 1985.
Los Angeles Times Book Review, November 4, 1979; May 24, 1987.
Maclean's, September 5, 1964; November 9, 1981; November 22, 1982.
Nation, June 15, 1985.
New Republic, August 25, 1979; May 13, 1985.
New York Review of Books, June 25, 1964; January 24, 1980.
New York Times, June 5, 1970; October 2, 1979; April 20, 1985; July 9, 1985; March 4, 1987.
New York Times Book Review, February 26, 1956; September 16, 1979; May 5, 1985; March 15, 1987.
Quill and Quire, October, 1981; June, 1984.
Rubicon, winter, 1984-85.
Saturday Night, September, 1973; November, 1981.
Saturday Review, October 17, 1959; August 25, 1979; October 13, 1979.
Spectator, August 29, 1987; February 20, 1988.
Time, November 26, 1979; May 27, 1985.
Times (London), February 28, 1980.
Times Literary Supplement, March 14, 1980; February 28, 1986; January 22-28, 1988; September 25-October 1, 1987.
Virginia Quarterly Review, spring, 1980.
Washington Post Book World, April 14, 1985; March 29, 1987.

*   *   *

GANDALAC, Lennard
See BERNE, Eric (Lennard)

*   *   *

GARNER, Hugh 1913-1979
(Jarvis Warwick)

PERSONAL: Born February 22, 1913, in Batley, Yorkshire, England; brought to Canada in 1919; died June 30, 1979; son of Matthew and Annie (Fozard) Garner; married Marie Alice Gallant, July 5, 1941; children: Barbara Ann, Hugh, Jr. *Education:* Attended technical high school in Toronto, Ontario, Canada.

CAREER: Novelist, short story writer, and journalist. Public relations director for J. K. Cooke Enterprises, 1951. *Military service:* Machine gunner in International Brigade, 1937; served in Spain. Canadian Army, 1939-40. Royal Canadian Navy, 1940-45; served in Africa and Atlantic theater.

MEMBER: Association of Canadian Television and Radio Artists, Saint George Society.

AWARDS, HONOURS: Shared *Northern Review* prize, 1951, for "The Conversion of Willie Heaps," which was included in *Best American Short Stories* for 1952; Canadian Governor General's Award for Fiction, 1963, for *Hugh Garner's Best Stories;* the Hugh Garner Cooperative, a housing development in Toronto's Cabbagetown was dedicated in his honor, 1982; recipient of three Canada Council senior arts fellowships.

WRITINGS:

Storm Below (novel), Collins, 1949, Simon & Schuster, 1970.
Cabbagetown, Collins, 1950, revised edition, Ryerson, 1968.
(Under pseudonym Jarvis Warwick) *Waste No Tears,* Export, 1950.
Present Reckoning, Collins, 1951.
The Yellow Sweater, and Other Stories, Collins, 1952.
The Silence on the Shore, McClelland and Stewart, 1962.
Best Stories, Ryerson, 1963, published as *Hugh Garner's Best Stories,* Ryerson, 1968, reprinted, 1987.
Author, Author! (humorous essays), Ryerson, 1964.
Men and Women: Stories, Ryerson, 1966.
A Trip for Mrs. Taylor (one-act play), first produced in Brockville, Ontario, at the Brockville Theatre Guild, November 4, 1966.
(Author of foreword) Alice Munro, *Dance of the Happy Shades,* Ryerson, 1968.
The Sin Sniper (detective novel), Simon & Schuster of Canada, 1970, published as *Stone Cold Dead,* Paperjacks, 1978.
A Nice Place to Visit (detective novel), Ryerson, 1971.
Violation of the Virgins, and Other Stories, McGraw-Hill Ryerson, 1971.
Three Women: A Trilogy of One-Act Plays (contains *Some Are So Lucky, The Magnet,* and *A Trip for Mrs. Taylor*), Simon and Pierre, 1973.
One Damn Thing after Another (memoirs), McGraw-Hill Ryerson, 1973.
Death in Don Mills: A Murder Mystery, McGraw-Hill Ryerson, 1975.

The Intruders (novel), McGraw-Hill Ryerson, 1976.
The Legs of the Lame, and Other Stories, Borealis Press, 1976.
Murder Has Your Number: An Inspector DuMont Mystery, McGraw-Hill Ryerson, 1978.
A Hugh Garner Omnibus, McGraw-Hill Ryerson, 1978.

Also author of television dramas aired in Canada, England, and Australia. Writer of daily column in *Toronto Telegram,* 1966. Contributor of about five hundred articles and stories to magazines. Associate editor of *Saturday Night,* 1952-54; editor of *Liberty,* 1963. Garner's work has been translated into several languages, including Afrikaans and Rumanian, and is represented in more than seventy anthologies. His papers are collected at the Douglas Library at Queen's University.

SIDELIGHTS: In a career that spanned thirty years, novelist, short story writer, and journalist Hugh Garner authored seventeen books, more than four hundred pieces of journalism, numerous short stories, and several radio and television scripts. Born in England and brought to Toronto, Ontario, Canada, at the age of six by his parents, Garner developed an early empathy with the working-class poor after his mother was deserted by his father. During the Depression, he road the rails throughout the United States and Canada prior to volunteering in the Mackenzie-Papineau brigade of the Loyalist cause in the Spanish civil war. After a brief stint in the army, Garner enlisted in the navy, to which he ascribed the origins of his lifelong battle with liquor dependency. Referring to Garner's heavy-smoking, hard-drinking lifestyle, Barbara Amiel remarked in *Maclean's* that "it was a moot point whether it was the alcohol or coal tar that had finally stopped him," for at the time of his death, Garner "had already passed into literary legend." Describing him as a "maverick in his life and in his fiction," J. M. Zezulka noted in a *Dictionary of Literary Biography* essay: "His vision, in his novels and in the short stories which are his most memorable work, was formed by his multifarious experiences during the Depression, the Spanish civil war, North Atlantic convoy duty, and by his sympathy for what he called the bottom half of humanity."

In a *Canadian Literature* review of Garner's memoirs, *One Damn Thing after Another,* George Woodcock described the author as "dedicated and obsessed." And although in *Saturday Night,* Doug Fetherling referred to Garner as "just an intellectual misanthrope," he felt that this also made him "fresh and rather appealing." Characterizing Garner as a "comfortable writer," Sandra Martin stated in a *Books in Canada* review of his last collection of stories, *The Legs of the Lame:* "Invariably he tells a story that has both a beginning and an end and he uses a style that, while colourful, is devoid of artifice and pretentiousness." Pointing out that "Garner avoided pretension

as assiduously as he shunned literary coteries or fashions," Zezulka added that Garner "loved telling stories, and he had tremendous respect for his craft."

Drawing upon his experiences in the navy, Garner's first novel, *Storm Below,* focuses on the death of a sailor at sea; however, "the novel's real interest lies in Garner's handling of the crew's superstitious reactions to the presence of a dead body aboard ship and in his exploration of their private thoughts and lives," wrote Zezulka. And Claude T. Bissell found "many shining virtues" in what he described in the *University of Toronto Quarterly* in 1950 as "the best Canadian novel based upon war experience" thus far. While his fiction is described by Desmond Pacey in a *Contemporary Novelists* essay as "honest and workmanlike," he is especially praised for his skillful characterizations. Garner created characters "who live in all dimensions," said Nancy Kavanaugh, adding in a *Canadian Author and Bookman* review of *Men and Women,* a collection of short stories, that although his characters are "uncomfortable to read about," his stories are "fascinating, perhaps because we recognize some aspects of our own lives or personalities here portrayed." Describing Garner's general fictional world as "filled with little people," Martin elaborated, however, that "whether bartenders, clerks, mechanics, prostitutes, drunks, or murders, the characters are diminished by the sordid pettiness of their lives; they respond physically, often brutally."

It was Garner's second novel, however, that provided the author with a bestseller and critical plaudits as well; and according to Fetherling in *Saturday Night,* the novel has "dominated his reputation." *Cabbagetown,* named after the Toronto slum of Garner's own youth, chronicles the struggles of several families to survive the Depression. Garner returned to Cabbagetown in other volumes, including *Waste No Tears,* a story about the poor and what they must do to survive slum life, *The Silence on the Shore,* about the complex interrelationships among tenants in a run-down boarding house, and finally *The Intruders,* a novel in which he focused "on the disillusioned suburbanites who have infiltrated Cabbagetown in search of community involvement," wrote Zezulka. "What these middle-class professional families discover, however, is that consciousness is difficult to overcome. In the end they relinquish the neighborhood to those who have always been there, the punks and the drunks and the working poor."

In the opinion of Val Clery, in *Books in Canada,* Garner is "unique amongst Canadian writers in being able to catch authentically the North American furies that haunt the lonely and the rootless and the poor." Noting that "Garner has often been praised for his good heart when it is really his good ear and sharp eye that deserve our admiration," Miriam Waddington added in *Canadian Literature* that the author's "concern with truth places his work in the realm of social realism." Suggesting, however, that Garner comes very close "to the ideals of American naturalism," J. R. MacGillivray explained in the *University of Toronto Quarterly* that "he concentrates on the plight of the little man in an industrialized and war-minded society; he accumulates details that render the ugliness and monotony of the urban background."

While some critics have responded negatively to what they detect as a certain repetitive and cliched quality to Garner's work, other critics find this sentiment irrelevant. For instance, in a *Tamarack Review* piece about *Silence on the Shore,* Michael Hornyanski indicated that despite the fact that "Garner's writing is often bad—repetitious, cliched, ponderous, insistent on labouring the obvious," the author effectively re-created "just the basic bedrock reality which we all start from." And according to John Moss in *Patterns of Isolation,* "Garner has successfully wedded document and melodramatic sentiment into a steadfastly singular and ironic vision of reality."

Although a writer of realism who championed the cause of the down-and-out, he had no "doctrinaire political or social remedies to preach," wrote Pacey. Garner's deep novelistic insight represents "the depth of experience, of actuality, rather than of philosophy or moral vision," suggested Moss. And according to Amiel, "He was something of a cracker-barrel philosopher and it was his populist message that made his novels more than just a good read." In Pacey's estimation, "Garner has earned a special niche in Canadian literary history by the way in which he has persevered in the realistic treatment of urban life," adding in a *Contemporary Novelists* essay that Garner "remained consistently true to social realism and . . . eschewed experiments with symbolism, surrealism, or stream of consciousness." Calling him the "true journeyman of Canadian writing," Clery maintained that Garner "deserves (and is too infrequently given) the attention and the respect of the writers in his wake."

BIOGRAPHICAL/CRITICAL SOURCES:

BOOKS

Contemporary Literary Criticism, Volume 13, Gale, 1980.
Contemporary Novelists, St. James/St. Martin's, 1976.
Dictionary of Literary Biography, Volume 68: *Canadian Writers, 1920-1959, First Series,* Gale, 1988.
Fetherling, Doug, *Hugh Garner,* Forum House, 1972.
Garner, Hugh, *One Damn Thing after Another* (memoirs), McGraw-Hill Ryerson, 1973.
Moss, John, *Patterns of Isolation,* McClelland and Stewart, 1974.
Stuewe, Paul, *Hugh Garner and His Works,* ECW, 1984.

PERIODICALS

Books in Canada, November, 1971, March, 1977.

Canadian Author and Bookman, autumn, 1966.
Canadian Literature, autumn, 1971, winter, 1974.
Journal of Canadian Fiction, spring, 1972.
Maclean's, July 16, 1979.
Saturday Night, November, 1968, November, 1973, July-August, 1976.
Tamarack Review, winter, 1963, fall, 1969.
University of Toronto Quarterly, April, 1950, April, 1952.*

—*Sketch by Sharon Malinowski*

*   *   *

GEDDES, Gary   1940-

PERSONAL: Born June 9, 1940, in Vancouver, British Columbia, Canada; son of Laurie James (a carpenter and shipwright) and Irene (Turner) Geddes; married Norma Joan Fugler (a nurse), 1963 (divorced, 1969); married Jan Macht (a publisher), May 2, 1973; children: (first marriage) Jennifer, (second marriage) Charlotte, Bronwen Claire. *Education:* University of British Columbia, B.A., 1962; University of Reading, diploma in education, 1964; University of Toronto, M.A., 1966, Ph.D., 1975.

ADDRESSES: Home—RR1, Dunvegan, Ontario, Canada K0C 1J0. *Office*—Department of English, Concordia University, 1455 de Maisonneuve Blvd W., Montreal, Quebec H3G 1M8, Canada.

CAREER: Affiliated with University of Toronto, Toronto, Ontario, Canada, 1965-70; York University, North York, Ontario, instructor in English, 1966-67; Ryerson Polytechnical Institute, Toronto, instructor in English, 1966-69; Trent University, Peterborough, Ontario, visiting lecturer in English, 1969; Carleton University, Ottawa, Ontario, visiting assistant professor in English, 1971-72; University of Victoria, Victoria, British Columbia, Canada, lecturer in English, 1972-74; British Columbia Institute of Technology, Vancouver, lecturer in English, 1974-76; University of Alberta, Edmonton, Canada, writer-in-residence, 1976, visiting assistant professor in English, 1977; Concordia University, Montreal, Quebec, Canada, associate professor of English, 1978-87, writer-in-residence, 1979, professor of English, 1987—; poet. Founded three literary presses, including Quadrant Editions, 1981, and Cormorant Books, 1984; gives numerous worldwide poetry readings and public lectures.

MEMBER: League of Canadian Poets, Writers' Union of Canada, International PEN.

AWARDS, HONOURS: Province of Ontario graduate fellowship, 1965-66; Imperial Oil graduate fellowship, 1968-70; Canada Council doctoral fellowship, 1968-70; Canada Council arts grants, 1971, 1974, 1977, 1979, 1981, 1987, and 1988; E. J. Pratt medal and prize, University of

Toronto, 1970, for *Letter of the Master of Horse;* Ontario Arts Council Writers Reserve Grant, 1984-88; National Poetry Prize, Canadian Authors' Association, 1982, for *The Acid Test;* first prize in Americas division, British Airways Commonwealth Poetry Competition, 1985, for *The Terracotta Army;* National Magazine Gold Award, 1987, and Writers' Choice Award, 1988, both for play *Hong Kong;* Archibald Lampman Poetry Prize, 1990, for *No Easy Exit/Salida dificil;* runner-up silver medal from Milton Acorn Poetry Competition, 1991.

WRITINGS:

POETRY

Poems, Waterloo Lutheran Press, 1971.
Rivers Inlet, Talon Books, 1973.
Letter of the Master of Horse, Oberon Press, 1973.
Snakeroot, Talon Books, 1973.
War and Other Measures, House of Anansi, 1976.
The Acid Test, Turnstone Press, 1981.
The Terracotta Army, Oberon Press, 1984.
Changes of State, Coteau Books, 1986.
Hong Kong Poems, Oberon Press, 1987.
No Easy Exit/Salida dificil, Oolichan Books, 1989.
Light of Burning Towers: New and Selected Poems, Vehicule Press, 1990.
The Girl by the Water, Turnstone Press, 1994.

EDITOR

Twentieth-Century Poetry & Poetics, Oxford University Press, 1969.
Heart of Darkness and Other Stories by Joseph Conrad, Nelson, 1971.
Fifteen Canadian Poets, Oxford University Press, 1971.
Skookum Wawa: Writings of the Canadian Northwest, Oxford University Press, 1975.
Divided We Stand, Peter Martin Associates, 1977.
Chinada: Memoirs of the Gang of Seven, Quadrant Editions, 1983.
The Inner Ear, Quadrant Editions, 1983.
Vancouver: Soul of a City, Douglas & McIntyre, 1986.
(With Hugh Hazelton) *Companeros: An Anthology of Writings about Latin America,* Cormorant Books, 1990.
The Art of Short Fiction: An International Anthology, HarperCollins, 1992.

OTHER

(Cofounder with Hugo McPherson) *Studies in Canadian Literature,* fifteen volumes, Copp Clark Publishing, 1969-75, McGill-Queen's Press, 1975-79, Douglas & McIntyre, 1979-85.
Conrad's Later Novels, McGill-Queen's University Press, 1980.

Les Maudits Anglais (full-length play; produced in Montreal and Toronto by Theatre Passe Muraille, 1978), Playwrights Cooperative, 1984.
(Translator with George Liang) *I Didn't Notice the Mountain Growing Dark* (poems of Li Bai and Du Fu), Cormorant Books, 1986.
The Unsettling of the West (short stories), Oberon Press, 1986.
Hong Kong, (full-length play adaptation of Geddes's book *Hong Kong Poems*), produced in Winnipeg, 1986.
Letters from Managua: Meditations on Politics and Art, Quarry Press, 1990.

Contributor to periodicals, including *Edmonton Journal, Saturday Night, Globe and Mail, Ellipse, Fiddlehead, Ecrits du Canada Francais, Moosehead Review, Canadian Forum, Capilano Review, Best Canadian Stories, Canadian Literature, Books in Canada, Oxford Companion to Canadian Literature, Open Letter,* and *Lyric Paragraph.*

Geddes's work has been translated into French, Spanish, Dutch, and Chinese.

WORK IN PROGRESS: A new collection of poems tentatively titled *Afterbirth;* publication of a *Selected Poems* edition; two long-poem projects.

SIDELIGHTS: Gary Geddes—considered "Canada's best political poet" by *WQ Reviews* contributor George Woodcock—is distinguished for his political poetry that explores human relations. Describing the poet's work in a review of the 1990 collection *Light of Burning Towers, Vancouver Sun* reviewer John Moore stated: "His rigorous blend of instinct, insight and eloquence are the timeless qualities of greatness." In his verse Geddes stresses one's responsibility for other people and the need for compassion, and he displays his ethics through his dedicated promotion of Canadian writing. Geddes's poetry focuses on subjects, such as the relationship between art and politics, rather than language usage. In an interview with Alan Twigg in *Strong Voices: Conversations with Fifty Canadian Authors,* Geddes declared: "I am preoccupied with injured figures, figures caught in the machinery of society or politics or religion," which he said is possibly a result of harboring "a degree of violence that desperately needs capping." Geddes also revealed that he writes long poems because this type of presentation is the "most exciting form in my view" and that writing is "a way of getting in touch with my deepest feelings."

Geddes depicts an injured figure plagued by dreams and memories of war in his 1976 long poem *War and Other Measures.* Examining the agony and futility of war, the book focuses on a character similar to Paul Joseph Chartier, a man who died in May 1966 when a bomb he brought into the House of Commons detonated. When journalists wrote that Chartier had bungled a terrorist attack, Geddes instead wondered if the man intended to kill himself solely to make a political statement without injuring other people. Such a death, according to Geddes, would have been an even more powerful statement. Geddes told Twigg that he found Chartier's suicide to be "a symbol for something tragic and deadly in our culture," which is how he portrays war in *War and Other Measures.* Geddes also maintains that Chartier, and subsequently the figure in his poem, had "no means of redressing injustices." Laurie Ricou, writing in *Dictionary of Literary Biography,* described Chartier as "an outcast quebecois who must live life in a language other than his own," which is a prominent theme, Ricou proclaimed, in Geddes's works.

In 1984, some eight years after publishing *War and Other Measures,* Geddes produced another poem about war, politics, and art, called *The Terracotta Army.* Including twenty-five dramatic monologues, the book characterizes a select group of soldiers that potter Lao Bi sculpted for the first emperor of China, Ch'in Shi Huang, in the third century B.C. The emperor had the clay soldiers made in order to protect him in his afterlife. Geddes claims he was inspired to humanize the figures when he saw those that had been excavated from the emperor's grave in China between 1974 and 1980. His depictions of the soldiers interconnect art and politics; as Geddes explains, the politics of the soldiers are made immortal through his poetry. Revolving around Bi's sculpting, the monologues reveal political views, the soldiers' vain and selfish personalities, and the degradation of the State at the hands of the conceited, tyrannical emperor. The soldiers fear and respect Bi; he, in turn, is aware of his power and uses it to their mutual advantage. Instead of having a monologue of his own, the potter is described by the soldiers, who make contradictory observations about his character. John Cook, writing in *Queen's Quarterly,* observed that with *The Terracotta Army,* Geddes has "matured into an uncommonly good poet."

Geddes continued to delve into the subject of war and politics in his 1987 *Hong Kong Poems.* The volume takes the reader on a poetic journey into Canada's involvement in China during World War II. In 1941 Geddes's countrymen were sent ill-prepared into the British colony of Hong Kong to establish a Canadian presence there even though Canadian military leaders knew Japan could take over the island. Defeated by overwhelming odds, the surviving Canadian soldiers were incarcerated for three-and-a-half years, then returned from China only to find themselves denied their rights as veterans. In *Hong Kong Poems* Geddes calls for compassion from the Canadian people by writing about the soldiers' traumatic experiences in China and attempts to motivate his nation's citizens and government to take responsibility for their troops. A *Fiddlehead*

review, called Geddes's interpretation of this emotionally volatile subject "masterfully restrained and controlled."

In 1989, Geddes went to Nicaragua and recorded his experiences with the country's politics and art in the form of letters. He made his journey during the tenth anniversary of the Sandinista revolution named for insurrectionist Augusto Cesar Sandino, which resulted in the Sandinistas seizing power in 1979 from the Somoza dictatorship. In his 1990 book, *Letters from Managua: Meditations on Politics and Art,* Geddes laments poetry's diminishing popularity in North American society, and rejoices over finding poets and poetry to be an important part of Nicaraguan society and politics. Ken McGoogan, writing in the *Calgary Herald,* commented that the author's work is a "call to action rarely seen in Canadian poetry," and added that "perhaps we would be better off if we ignored our empty-headed politicians and listened to poets like Gary Geddes." In *Canadian Literature,* Donald Stephens described Geddes as "not only a poet to watch but also a poet who will continually surprise and please."

Geddes told *CA:* "I have a sustained interest in poetics in general and the long poem in particular. The contemporary poem-sequence, at its best, includes the intensity of the lyric and the inclusiveness of the epic. I don't share the contemporary unease with narrative. Our lives are organized and enriched by narrative; we could not live without our capacity to explore, shape, and render meaningful our human experience. I also believe that writers have to take control of the promotion, distribution, and critical understanding of their own work, rather than leave it to chance and to commercial interests. In addition to doing my own writing, I review books widely, I have started three literary presses, and I have edited some forty books through publication. I continue to believe in art as a sign of the collective health of a society."

BIOGRAPHICAL/CRITICAL SOURCES:

BOOKS

Dictionary of Literary Biography, Volume 60: *Canadian Writers since 1960, Second Series,* Gale, 1987.
Twigg, Alan, editor, *Strong Voices: Conversations with Fifty Canadian Authors,* Harbour, 1988.

PERIODICALS

Calgary Herald, August 4, 1990.
Canadian Forum, December, 1985, p. 24.
Canadian Literature, no. 95 winter 1982, p. 150.
Globe and Mail (Toronto), August 18, 1990.
Journal of Canadian Poetry, Volume 6, 1991, pp. 60-62.
Queen's Quarterly, Volume 93, 1986, p. 2.
Vancouver Sun, September 20, 1990, p. D20.
WQ Reviews, Winter, 1982, p. 14.

—Sketch by Jane M. Kelly

GIBSON, Graeme 1934-

PERSONAL: Born August 9, 1934, in London, Ontario, Canada; son of Thomas Graeme (a military officer) and Mary (Cameron) Gibson; married Shirley Mann (divorced); partner of Margaret Atwood (a poet and novelist); children: (with Shirley Mann) Matthew, Graeme; (with Margaret Atwood) Jess Atwood (daughter). *Education:* Attended University of Edinburgh, 1955-56; University of Western Ontario, B.A. (with honours), 1957, graduate study, 1957-58.

ADDRESSES: Agent—Charlotte Sheedy, Charlotte Sheedy Literary Agency, Inc., 145 West 86th St., New York, NY 10024.

CAREER: Ryerson Polytechnic Institute, Toronto, Ontario, teacher of English, 1961-68; writer, 1968—. Writer in residence at University of Waterloo, 1982-83; conducts creative writing workshops; gives readings. Book and Periodical Development Council, founding member, 1975, chair, 1976, executive director, 1977.

MEMBER: Writers Union of Canada (founding member; chair, 1974-75), Writers' Development Trust (founding member, 1977; chair, 1978), Amnesty International, Federation of Ontario Naturalists.

AWARDS, HONOURS: Scottish Canadian Exchange fellow, 1978-79.

WRITINGS:

NOVELS

Five Legs, House of Anansi (Toronto), 1969.
Communion, House of Anansi, 1971.
Perpetual Motion, McClelland & Stewart (Toronto), 1982, St. Martin's, 1983.
Gentleman Death, McClelland & Stewart, 1993.

OTHER

Eleven Canadian Novelists Interviewed by Graeme Gibson, House of Anansi, 1973.

Also author of screenplay *As for Me and My House* and of radio and television scripts. Contributor to periodicals.

SIDELIGHTS: Graeme Gibson is a novelist whose works have explored new territory in Canadian fiction. As Stan Dragland explains in the *Dictionary of Literary Biography,* "Gibson's first two novels each create their own category of Canadian fiction, and the third novel extends a mainstream tradition in Canadian letters, the pioneering story." Gibson's first two novels, *Five Legs* and *Communion,* feature the character Felix Oswald, a graduate student in Ontario. In *Five Legs* Oswald and Lucan Crackell, his professor, travel to the funeral of a student friend who has died in a hit-and-run accident. "Black comedy,"

writes Dragland, "attends the single day on which all the events take place, and the mental excursions into the past." The reviewer for the *Calgary Herald* finds that "Gibson pares away at [his two characters'] respective consciousnesses, revealing a stifling sanctimoniousness which has warped the experiences of both men."

Oswald reappears in *Communion,* a novel set after the events related in *Five Legs,* as a worker in a pet store. When a dog suffering from fits is marked for destruction, Oswald pities the animal and releases him from the store. The decision costs him his job. Traveling to Detroit, Oswald is set afire by a youth gang when he attempts to rescue an old man from their attacks. As Dragland summarizes the novel, because of the many hallucinatory scenes and possible fantasy sequences, "it is very difficult to locate a stable, simple present in the novel."

In *Perpetual Motion* Gibson writes a panoramic novel of 19th century expansion into western Canada. Telling the story of Robert Fraser, a farmer who dreams of inventing a perpetual motion machine financed by the fees he charges for viewing a prehistoric skeleton found on his property, the novel "succeeds in implying an analogy between the folly of Fraser's project and contemporary environmental decimation through land speculation and development," according to a critic for *Publishers Weekly.* Written with "thickly textured sensual detail," the novel becomes, Dragland writes, "an elegy for lost abundance and promise."

After a break of eleven years Gibson published *Gentleman Death,* the story of another man named Robert Fraser, a middle-aged Toronto writer. Attempting to write a new novel, Fraser begins with the story of a Canadian traveling to Scotland to keep a mysterious rendezvous. When this story falters, a new story begins, telling of Dunbar, a Canadian in Germany who has an affair with a German woman. Ultimately the novel turns to Fraser himself and his troubled relations with his wife and children. Fraser is, writes Valerie Compton in *Quill & Quire,* "a lovingly drawn, anachronistic character who believes in living honourably and writing honestly."

"Death," writes Don McGreger in *Canadian Forum,* "is an ever-present character [in *Gentleman Death*], informing each word and event of the tale. Gibson stares this common adversary in the eye, while exploring the life he knows, to reveal what is satisfying and redeeming in the human experience." Carole Giangrande in *Books in Canada* agrees. "Concern with death," she writes, "abounds in this well-titled novel: the need to come to terms with mortality, the grief and loss it entails, and the long shadow it casts over the dying of ecosystems, whole societies, and the earth itself." Joe Chidley of *Maclean's* concludes that *Gentleman Death* is "an engaging exploration of memory and death. Complex yet accessible, it is an illuminating guide through the rich territory that W. B. Yeats called the 'rag-and-bone shop of the heart.' "

BIOGRAPHICAL/CRITICAL SOURCES:

BOOKS

Davey, Frank, *From There to Here: A Guide to English-Canadian Literature since 1960,* Press Porcepic (Erin, Ontario), 1974, pp. 116-18.
Dictionary of Literary Biography, Volume 53: *Canadian Writers since 1960, First Series,* Gale, 1986.
Moss, John, *Sex and Violence in the Canadian Novel: The Ancestral Present,* McClelland & Stewart, 1977, pp. 160-67.

PERIODICALS

Books in Canada, summer, 1993, p. 50.
Canadian Forum, May, 1993, pp. 36-38; December, 1993, pp. 39-40.
Financial Post, June 12, 1993, p. S8.
Maclean's, May 31, 1993, p. 47.
New York Times, September 15, 1983.
New York Times Book Review, September 25, 1983.
Paragraph Magazine, winter, 1993, p. 54.
Publishers Weekly, March 25, 1988, p. 60.
Quill & Quire, May, 1993, p. 23; January, 1994, p. 7.*

*   *   *

GIBSON, William (Ford)   1948-

PERSONAL: Born March 17, 1948, in Conway, South Carolina, United States; immigrated to Canada; son of William Ford (a contractor) and Otey (a homemaker; maiden name, Williams) Gibson; married Deborah Thompson (a language instructor), June, 1972; children: Graeme Ford Gibson, Claire Thompson Gibson. *Education:* University of British Columbia, B.A., 1977.

ADDRESSES: Home—Vancouver, British Columbia, Canada. *Agent*—Martha Millard Literary Agency, 204 Park Ave., Madison, NJ 07940; (for film and television) Martin S. Shapiro, Shapiro-Lichtman Talent, 8827 Beverly Blvd., Los Angeles, CA 90048.

CAREER: Writer.

AWARDS, HONOURS: Nebula Award nomination from Science Fiction Writers of America, c. 1983, for short story "Burning Chrome"; Hugo Award for best novel of 1984 from World Science Fiction Society, Philip K. Dick Award for best U.S. original paperback of 1984 from Philadelphia Science Fiction Society, Nebula Award for best novel of 1984 from Science Fiction Writers of America, and Porgie Award for best paperback original novel in sci-

ence fiction from *West Coast Review of Books,* all 1985, and Ditmar Award from Australian National Science Fiction Convention, all for *Neuromancer.*

WRITINGS:

Neuromancer (novel; first in "Cyberspace" trilogy), Ace, 1984.
Count Zero (novel; second in "Cyberspace" trilogy), Arbor House, 1986.
(With John Shirley, Bruce Sterling, and Michael Swanwick) *Burning Chrome* (short stories; includes "Burning Chrome," "Johnny Mnemonic," "New Rose Hotel," and one story with each coauthor), introduction by Sterling, Arbor House, 1986.
Mona Lisa Overdrive (novel; third in "Cyberspace" trilogy), Bantam, 1988.
Dream Jumbo (text to accompany performance art by Robert Longo), produced in Los Angeles, California, at UCLA Center for the Performing Arts, 1989.
(With Sterling) *The Difference Engine* (novel), Gollancz, 1990, Bantam, 1991.
Virtual Light, Viking, 1993.
Johnny Mnemonic (screenplay; based on Gibson's short story of the same name), TriStar, 1995.

Work represented in anthologies, including *Shadows 4,* Doubleday, 1981; *Nebula Award Stories 17,* Holt, 1983; and *Mirrorshades: The Cyberpunk Anthology,* edited with an introduction by Sterling, Arbor House, 1986. Contributor of short stories, articles, and book reviews to periodicals, including *Omni, Rolling Stone,* and *Science Fiction Review.*

SIDELIGHTS: Science-fiction author William Gibson had published only a handful of short stories when he stunned readers with his debut novel, *Neuromancer.* Published in 1984, *Neuromancer* became the first work ever to sweep the major honors of science fiction—the Hugo, Nebula, and Philip K. Dick awards. Combining the hip cynicism of the rock music underground and the dizzying powers of high technology, the novel was hailed as the prototype of a new style of writing, promptly dubbed "cyberpunk." Gibson, who was also earning praise as a skillful prose stylist, disliked the trendy label but admitted that he was challenging science fiction traditions. "I'm not even sure what cyberpunk means," he told the *Philadelphia Inquirer,* "but I suppose it's useful as a tip-off to people that what they're going to read is a little wilder."

The surface features of Gibson's allegedly cyberpunk style—tough characters facing a tough world, frantic pacing, bizarre high-tech slang—alienated some reviewers. "Like punk rock . . . Cyberpunk caters to the wish-fulfillment requirements of male teenagers," complained science-fiction novelist Thomas M. Disch in the *New York Times Book Review,* "and there is currently no more accomplished caterer than William Gibson." In *Science Fiction Review,* Andrew Andrews blasted the "style and execution" of *Count Zero,* a novel typical of Gibson's work during the 1980s. "It is hodgepodge; spastic; incomprehensible in spots, somehow just *too much,*" the reviewer declared. "I prefer a novel that is concise, with fleshy, human characters." Beneath the flash, however, admirers detected a serious purpose. Writers like Gibson, suggested J. R. Wytenbroeck in *Canadian Literature,* are really describing the world "in which we live today, with all its problems taken to their logical extreme." In particular, the advance of technology is shown to cause as many problems as it solves. "Technology has *already* changed us, and now we have to figure out a way to stay sane," Gibson observed in *Rolling Stone.* "If you were to put this in terms of mainstream fiction and present readers with a conventional book about modern postindustrial anxiety, many of them would just push it aside. But if you put it in the context of science fiction, maybe you can get them to sit still for what you have to say." Along with "adrenalin verve and random pyrotechnics," wrote Colin Greenland in the *Times Literary Supplement,* Gibson's work is "intellectually substantial." "His style," Greenland wrote, "is deadpan and precise, with the tone of the classic crime thriller: canny, cool and undeceived, yet ultimately the very opposite of the callousness it imitates, because motivated by a desire for justice."

Gibson grew up in a small town in southwest Virginia, on the edge of the Appalachian Mountains. "It was a boring, culturally deprived environment," he recalled in the *Sacramento Union.* "The library burned down in 1910, and nobody bothered to rebuild it." In such a place, he told *Interview,* "science-fiction books were the only source I had for subversive information." By his late teens Gibson had left behind the conventional authors who filled the genre with shining cities and benevolent scientists. Instead he began to prefer iconoclasts, such as J. G. Ballard and Philip K. Dick, who described a grim and frightening future. Some of his favorites might not qualify with purists as science-fiction writers at all: both William S. Burroughs and Thomas Pynchon were intricate stylists whose core following was among literary intellectuals. Such writers used the fantastic element of science fiction as a device to explore the ugly potentials of the human heart. Science fiction, Gibson realized, was a way to comment on the reality of the present day.

The 1960s youth culture also drew Gibson's attention. (A long-term rock fan, he counts the hard-edged music of Lou Reed as a major influence.) In 1967 he dropped out of high school and journeyed to Canada, ending up in Toronto, which had a thriving hippie scene. "We had our own version of the Summer of Love there," he said in the *Sacramento Union.* "If I'd gone to New York or San Fran-

cisco, I can't imagine what would have happened to me." Uneager to be drafted into the Vietnam War, he remained in Canada and eventually married. The couple settled in Vancouver, where their lives soon centered around the University of British Columbia (UBC)—Gibson's wife was a teacher and he was a "permanent pseudo-grad student" who earned his bachelor's degree shortly before he turned thirty. After graduating "I was clueless," he recalled in the *Chicago Tribune.* "A lot of my friends were becoming lawyers and librarians, things that filled me with horror." So he became a science-fiction writer, even though at the time "it seemed like such a goofy, unhip thing to do," as he told *Rolling Stone.* Gibson began his career almost in spite of himself, after he enrolled in a science-fiction course at UBC in hope of an easy credit. Unwilling to submit a term paper, he accepted the teacher's challenge to compose a short story—an ordeal that lasted three months. As Gibson settled into life as a househusband, however, he realized that writing more stories was the best way he could earn money while watching over his children.

His writing blossomed with amazing speed. By the early 1980s he was a favorite of fiction editor Ellen Datlow, who helped make *Omni* magazine a showcase of rising science-fiction talent. In *Omni* stories such as "Johnny Mnemonic" (1981) and "Burning Chrome" (1982) Gibson began to sketch his own grim version of the future, peopled with what *Rolling Stone* called "high-tech lowlifes." The title character of "Johnny Mnemonic," for instance, stashes stolen computer data on a microchip in his brain. He is marked for murder by the Yakuza, a Japanese syndicate that has moved into high-tech crime, but he is saved by Molly Millions, a bionic hitwoman with razors implanted under her fingernails. "I thought I was on this literary kamikaze mission," Gibson informed *Rolling Stone.* "I thought my work was so disturbing it would be dismissed and ignored by all but a few people." Instead, on the basis of a few short stories, he began to gain a powerful reputation: "Burning Chrome" was nominated for a Nebula Award, and Ace Books editor Terry Carr encouraged him to expand his vision into a novel. Meanwhile, "cyberpunk" was becoming a trend throughout the science-fiction world. After writing a third of his novel, Gibson went to see the 1982 film *Blade Runner,* director Ridley Scott's stylish, punked-out interpretation of a book by Philip K. Dick. "It looked so much like the inside of my head," reported Gibson in *Saturday Night,* "that I fled the theatre after about thirty minutes and have never seen the rest of it."

Neuromancer, together with its sequels *Count Zero* and *Mona Lisa Overdrive,* fleshes out the future society of Gibson's short stories. Here technology is the main source of power over others, and the multinational corporations that develop and control technology are more important than governments. The world is a bewildering splatter of cultures and subcultures; Gibson skirts the issue of whether the United States or Canada are still viable countries, but his multinationals are generally based in Europe or Japan. While shadowy figures run the world for their own benefit, a large underclass—the focus of Gibson's interest—endures amid pollution, overcrowding, and pointlessness. People commonly drug themselves with chemicals or with "simstims," a form of electronic drug that allows users to experience vicariously the life of another, more glamorous, human being.

Though such a future seems hopeless, Gibson remains in some sense a romantic, observers note, for he chronicles the efforts of individuals to carve out a life for themselves in spite of hostile surroundings. His misfit heroes often exist on the crime-infested fringes of society, thus lending his works some of the atmosphere of a traditional crime thriller. Along with the expected cast of smugglers, prostitutes, murderers, and thieves, Gibson celebrates a distinctly modern freebooter, the computer hacker. Computers of the future, Gibson posits, will be linked worldwide through "cyberspace"—an electronically generated alternate reality in which all data, and the security programs that protect it, will appear as a palpable three-dimensional universe. Computer operators will access cyberspace by plugging into it with their brains, and hackers—known as "cowboys"—will sneak in to steal data, fill their bank accounts with electronic money, or suffer death when a security program uses feedback to destroy their minds. "The Street," wrote Gibson in *Rolling Stone,* "finds its own uses for things—uses the manufacturers never imagined."

Gibson's wandering youth did not hinder—and may have helped—his ability to create such a world. "I didn't invent most of what's strange in the [books'] dialogue," Gibson told the *Mississippi Review,* as quoted in *Whole Earth Review.* "There are so many cultures and subcultures around today that if you're willing to listen, you start picking up different phrases, inflections, metaphors everywhere you go. A lot of stuff in *Neuromancer* and *Count Zero* that people think is so futuristic is probably just 1969 Toronto dope-dealers' slang, or bikers' slang." Gibson lacked an education in computers, but he knew about computer people. "They have this whole style of language . . . which attracted me simply for the intensity with which they talked about their machines," he said in *Rolling Stone.* "I immediately heard in that a real echo of the teenagers I grew up with talking about cars." Cyberspace came from watching a new generation of youth in video arcades. "I could see in . . . their postures how *rapt* these kids were," Gibson informed *Mississippi Review,* adding: "Everyone who works with computers seems to develop an intuitive

faith that there's some kind of actual *space* behind the screen."

The plots of Gibson's works, some reviewers suggest, are less important than the way of life he describes: even admirers find the narratives rather complicated and difficult to summarize. As Gibson told *Interview,* he "do[es]n't really start with stories" but prefers to assemble images, "like making a ball out of rubber bands." *Neuromancer* centers on Henry Case, a skilled computer "cowboy" who has been punished for his exploits by being given a powerful nerve poison that leaves him unable to plug into cyberspace. As the book opens he is scrounging a living on the seamy side of Japan's Chiba City when a mysterious patron offers him restorative surgery in exchange for more computer hacking. Case assents, and in the company of Molly Millions (one of Gibson's many recurring characters) he travels from one bizarre setting to the next in pursuit of a goal he cannot even understand. Finally Case arrives on a space station controlled by the wealthy Tessier-Ashpool clan, a family of genetic clones that owns two Artificial Intelligences—powerful computers which, like humans, have self-awareness and free will. Case realizes that one of the computers, named Wintermute, has hired him to help it take control of the other, named Neuromancer; the combined Artificial Intelligence that would result could break free of its human masters.

"*Neuromancer* was a bit hypermanic—simply from my terror at losing the reader's attention," Gibson recalled in *Rolling Stone.* For the sequel, *Count Zero,* "I aimed for a more deliberate pace. I also tried to draw the characters in considerable detail. People have children and dead parents in *Count Zero,* and that makes for different emotional territory." Thus instead of taking one main character on a manic ride throughout human society, *Count Zero* tells the stories of three more fleshed-out individuals whose lives gradually intertwine. The "Count Zero" of the title is really Bobby Newmark, a poor teenage computer "cowboy" with dreams of greatness. On his first illicit run into cyberspace, he finds it much more colorful than Case did a few years earlier: the Artificial Intelligences of *Neuromancer* seem to have broken apart into many cyberspace entities, some of whom manifest themselves as voodoo gods. The "gods" have human worshippers who take custody of Bobby after he apparently has a religious experience while he is hacking. Meanwhile, art dealer Marly Krushkova tries to find an artist with mysterious powers, only to encounter an old "cowboy" who also believes that God lives in cyberspace. And Turner, a mercenary who rounds up scientists for multinationals, finds himself the protector of a strange young woman named Angie Mitchell. Angie has a unique gift: her scientist father placed microchips in her brain that give her direct access to cyberspace and sometimes make her the mouthpiece for its ghostly inhabitants. "The resolution [of the plot] is figuratively left in the hands of the Haitian Computer Gods," wrote Dorothy Allison of the *Village Voice*. "They are particularly marvelous, considering that the traditional science-fiction model of an intelligent computer has been an emotionless logician."

Gibson's third novel, *Mona Lisa Overdrive,* "brilliantly pyramids the successes of its predecessors," wrote Edward Bryant in *Bloomsbury Review*. The book is set several years after *Count Zero,* using a similar structure of plotlines that slowly interconnect. When *Mona Lisa* opens, Bobby Newmark has grown up into an accomplished cowboy. Now he leaves his body in a coma so that he can explore the electronically generated universe inside a unique and costly microchip that he stole from the Tessier-Ashpool clan. Angie Mitchell, Bobby's sometime girlfriend, has become a simstim star, struggling against drug abuse and unsure of her future. In *Mona Lisa Overdrive,* wrote Richard Mathews of the *St. Petersburg Times,* "Gibson employs the metaphor of addiction as the central fact of existence. Addictions to drugs, information, and sensuality permeate society and form the basis of all economic transactions." The drug-abusing Angie, for example, is herself a "mere fix . . . piped to millions of simstim addicts to enrich [her producers]." Bobby is also a junkie—"a metaphor for society, increasingly techno-dependent, and hopelessly addicted to the excitement of high-tech power trips and head games."

As *Mona Lisa* unfolds amid complex intrigues, the power of technology looms so large as to challenge the meaning of human identity itself. Characters seek friendship and advice from the personalities recorded on microchips; Angie comes face-to-face with "Mona Lisa," a confused teenage junkie who has been surgically altered to resemble Angie herself as part of a bizarre abduction plot. In the violent climax of the novel, during which Angie dies of a brain hemorrhage, the simstim producers stumble upon Mona and gladly recruit her as a new star. Then, in an astonishing burst of fantasy, Gibson shows Angie reunited with Bobby in his microchip universe—a computer-generated heaven. By then, Mathews observed, "Gibson has us re-evaluating our concepts of 'life,' 'death' and 'reality,' all of which have been redefined by the impact of the information matrix. What makes Gibson so exceptional a writer is that you haven't just seen or thought about this future; you've been there."

Increasingly Gibson was hailed as a master of observant, evocative, economical prose. "If the pace [of *Mona Lisa Overdrive*] is rather less frantic than in the earlier books," observed Paul Kincaid of the *Times Literary Supplement,* "it is because Gibson's writing has improved, and the space given to more vividly presenting mood, place and character slows the action." Even the skeptical Thomas

Disch quoted a passage from *Mona Lisa* and, as other reviewers have done, observed how deftly Gibson could suggest a whole society with a handful of words. "Gibson is writing brilliant prose," declared Ellen Datlow in the *Philadelphia Inquirer,* "work that can be compared to anything being written inside or outside the science-fiction field."

Gibson seemed bemused by his new life as a best-selling novelist. At book signings he was greeted by disparate groups of hackers and punks whom he termed "M & M's" (for "modems and Mohawks"). As a soft-spoken, conservatively dressed father of two, Gibson realized that his wilder fans were sometimes disappointed to see him in person. "There was a classic case in San Francisco when two huge motorcyclists came screeching up," he continued in the *Chicago Tribune*. "One of them looked at me, picked up a book and shook his head and said, 'You can sign it anyway.'" To Gibson's surprise he quickly attracted the attention of the Hollywood film industry, and two years after *Neuromancer* was published he sold the rights for $100,000. Soon he was recruited as screenwriter for the projected third film in the highly profitable *Aliens* series. But after he wrote several drafts, the film studio had a management shuffle and he lost his job—a common fate in Hollywood. Paradoxically, the very fact that he was involved with such a high-profile effort made it easy for him to find more film work. Though Gibson stresses that *Mona Lisa Overdrive* is not autobiographical, he admits that the simstim subplot was inspired by his introduction to America's film capital. As he told the *Philadelphia Inquirer:* "Sitting in the Polo Lounge talking to 20-year-old movie producers with money coming out of their ears— *that's* science fiction, boy."

By the time *Mona Lisa Overdrive* was published in 1988, Gibson and many reviewers were glad to say farewell to the cyberpunk era. "It's becoming fashionable now to write 'cyberpunk is dead' articles," he noted in the *Bloomsbury Review*. The author teamed with fellow novelist Bruce Sterling to write *The Difference Engine,* a sort of retroactive science-fiction novel set in Victorian England. The book is named for one of several mechanical computers that were designed during the nineteenth century by mathematician Charles Babbage. Babbage failed to build his most sophisticated machines, for their manufacture was beyond his budget and he was unable to secure public funding. Gibson and Sterling, however, imagine the consequences if he had succeeded. With the help of mechanical computers, the Victorians develop airplanes, cybernauts, and a huge steam-powered television. *The Difference Engine,* Gibson warned, "sounds cuter than it is. It's really a very, very chilly semi-dystopia." In this novel, as in most of Gibson's work, technology proves corrupting, and society is painfully divided between the haves and have-nots. Gibson knows that a Victorian fantasy may baffle his old fans; at last, however, he might free himself of labels. "One of the reasons we cooked this up was so people wouldn't be able to say it was more cyberpunk writing," Gibson told the *Chicago Tribune.* "There won't be one guy with a silver Mohawk in the whole book."

After the short vacation from Cyberpunk that *The Difference Engine* afforded him, Gibson returned to a familiar dystopian future with his next novel, *Virtual Light.* Set in the geographic conglomerate known as the Sprawl (which is most likely a fusion of most of North America), the novel centers on the adventures of an unlikely pair of allies who are thrown together by circumstance. While Gibson's trademarks are still present: biotechnology, evil corporate empires, and ghosts in the machines, *Virtual Light* was perceived by critics as more character-driven than the author's previous Cyberpunk work. The technology serves the advancement of the plot rather than existing as the locus of the narrative.

In addition to his return to Cyberpunk writing, Gibson also revisited the arena of Hollywood scriptwriting. Although his efforts for *Alien 3* were fruitless, he returned with a produced screenplay in 1995. Adapting his short story "Johnny Mnemonic," Gibson worked closely with director and artist Robert Longo (who had previously collaborated with the author on a performance art piece titled *Dream Jumbo*) to bring his vision of the near future to the screen. With slight alterations to the original story—the remorselessly fierce Molly Millions character was turned into a softer, more accessible female mercenary—the film was released to mixed reviews. While many credited the work with faithfully creating the "look" of the Gibson universe, there were numerous complaints regarding the film's pacing and the acting of Keanu Reeves, who essayed Johnny.

As Gibson extends his narrative vision to realms beyond the printed page—his work is often exchanged and discussed on the Internet and other computer systems—his ideas will reach newer and larger audiences. Much as he envisioned back in 1984, information and communication has become the fastest growth industry of the late twentieth century. The geometric growth of online computer services can be construed as one possible avenue that could have led to the world he first depicted in "Johnny Mnemonic" and "Burning Chrome." Despite the prophetic aura one can bestow upon Gibson's ideas, it is his storytelling ability that continues to hold his readers' interests.

BIOGRAPHICAL/CRITICAL SOURCES:

BOOKS

Contemporary Literary Criticism, Volume 39, Gale, 1986.

McCaffery, Larry, editor, *Across the Wounded Galaxies: Interviews with Contemporary American Science Fiction Writers,* University of Illinois Press, 1990.
Sterling, Bruce, editor, *Mirrorshades: The Cyberpunk Anthology,* Arbor House, 1986.

PERIODICALS

Analog, November, 1984; December, 1986; January, 1987; April, 1989; October, 1989.
Austin American-Statesman, November 27, 1988.
Best Sellers, July, 1986.
Bloomsbury Review, September, 1988.
Canadian Literature, summer, 1989.
Chicago Tribune, November 18, 1988; November 23, 1988.
Entertainment Weekly, August 13, 1993, p. 66.
Fantasy Review, July, 1984; April, 1986.
Film Comment, January, 1990.
Fortune, November 1, 1993.
Heavy Metal, May, 1985.
Impulse, winter, 1989.
Interview, January, 1989.
Isaac Asimov's Science Fiction Magazine, August, 1986.
Listener, October 11, 1990.
Locus, August, 1988.
Los Angeles Times Book Review, January 29, 1989.
Maclean's, April 29, 1991, p. 63.
Magazine of Fantasy and Science Fiction, August, 1985; August, 1986.
Mississippi Review, Volume 16, numbers 2 and 3, 1988.
Nation, May 8, 1989.
New Statesman, June 20, 1986; September 26, 1986.
New York Times Book Review, November 24, 1985; December 11, 1988; March 10, 1991, p. 5.
Oregonian (Portland), November 24, 1988.
People Weekly, October 25, 1993, p. 45.
Philadelphia Inquirer, April 15, 1986; October 30, 1988.
Pittsburgh Press, October 19, 1986.
Playboy, August, 1993, p. 32.
Publishers Weekly, July 12, 1993, p. 72.
Punch, February 6, 1985.
Reason, November, 1991, p. 61.
Rolling Stone, December 4, 1986; June 15, 1989.
Sacramento Union, October 26, 1988.
St. Petersburg Times, December 18, 1988.
San Francisco Chronicle, January 1, 1987.
Saturday Night, March, 1989.
Science Fiction Review, fall, 1985; summer, 1986; winter, 1986.
Seattle Times, October 24, 1988.
Spin, December, 1988.
Times Literary Supplement, December 7, 1984; June 20, 1986; August 12, 1988.
Utne Reader, July, 1989.

Village Voice, July 3, 1984; July 16, 1985; May 6, 1986; January 17, 1989.
Washington Post Book World, July 29, 1984; March 23, 1986; October 25, 1987; November 27, 1988.
West Coast Review of Books, September, 1985.
Whole Earth Review, summer, 1989.*

*　　*　　*

GODBOUT, Jacques   1933-

PERSONAL: Born November 27, 1933, in Montreal, Quebec, Canada; son of Fernand and Mariette (Daoust) Godbout; married Ghislaine Reiher, July 31, 1954; children: Alain, Sylvie. *Education:* University of Montreal, Canada, B.A., 1953, M.A., 1954.

ADDRESSES: Home—815 Pratt, Montreal, Quebec H2V 2T7, Canada. *Office*—C.P. 6100, Outremont, Montreal, Quebec H4N 2N4, Canada.

CAREER: University of Addis Ababa, Ethiopia, assistant professor of French, 1954-57; National Film Board of Canada, filmmaker, 1957—. *Liberte,* cofounder, 1959; University of Montreal, lecturer, 1969; University of California, Berkeley, lecturer, 1985.

MEMBER: Union des Ecrivains Quebecois, Composers, Authors, and Publishers Association of Canada (CAPAC), Societe des Auteurs, Recherchistes, Documentalistes, et Compositeurs (SARDEC).

AWARDS, HONOURS: Prix France-Quebec, 1962, for *L'Aquarium;* Prix de L'Academie Francais, 1965, for *Le Couteau sur la table;* Governor General's Award, Conseil des Arts du Canada, 1968, for *Salut Galarneau!;* various awards for film work.

WRITINGS:

Carton-pate (poetry), Seghers, 1956.
Les Paves secs, Beauchemin, 1958.
C'est la chaude loi des hommes (poetry), Editions de l'Hexagone, 1960.
L'Aquarium (novel), Seuil, 1962.
(Editor, with John Robert Colombo) *Poesie/Poetry 64,* Editions du Jour, 1963.
(Editor with Claude Jasmin) *Textes inedits de Gilles Carle, Jacques Godbout, et Claude Jasmin sur le long metrage canadian Cain,* Cooperatio, 1965.
Le Couteau sur la table (novel), Seuil, 1965, translation by Penny Williams, with introduction by Gillian Davies, published as *Knife on the Table,* McClelland & Stewart, 1968.
Salut Galarneau! (novel), Seuil, 1967, translation by Alan Brown published as *Hail Galarneau!,* Longman, 1970.

(With Colombo) *Le Grande Muraille de Chine* (poem; title means "The Great Wall of China"), Editions du Jour, 1969.
D'Amour, P.Q. (novel), Seuil, 1972.
(With Pierre Turgeon) *L'Interview: texteradiophonique,* Lemeac, 1973.
Le Reformiste: textes tranquilles (title means "The Reformer"), Quinze, 1975.
L'Isle au dragon, Seuil, 1976, translation by David Ellis published as *Dragon Island,* Musson, 1978.
Les Tetes a Papineau, Seuil, 1981.
Le Murmure marchand (essay), Boreal Express, 1984.
Souvenirs Shop: Poemes et prose 1956-1960, Editions de l'Hexagone, 1984.
Une Histoire Americaine (novel), Seuil, 1986, translation by Yves Saint-Pierre published as *An American Story,* University of Minnesota Press, 1988.
(With Luc Plamondon) *Un Coeur de Rockeur* (song lyrics; title means "Rocker's Heart"), introduction by Godbout, Editions de l'Homme, 1988.
L'ecrivain de province (diary; title means "Writer from the Province"), Seuil, 1991.

Also author of essay *L'Ecran de bonheur,* 1990. Contributor to numerous anthologies, reviews, magazines. Author of written material for numerous films.

SIDELIGHTS: A native of French-speaking Quebec, Jacques Godbout is recognized as one of the province's most well-known literary figures. In addition to his mainstay of filmmaking for the National Film Board, Godbout has produced prose and verse at a steady pace. His imaginative novels, which have been published in France, are stylistically innovative and rife with social commentary. Of them, *Le Couteau sur la table (Knife on the Table), Salut Galarneau! (Hail Galarneau!), L'Isle au dragon (Dragon Island),* and *Une Histoire Americaine (An American Story)* have attracted a following in anglophone Canada as well. "Godbout belongs to a generation of novelists who have radically changed the direction which the Quebec novel has taken during the past twenty years. In helping to create a 'new' novel for Quebec, Godbout has experimented with various techniques borrowed from other literatures, but in the process has succeeded in producing a type of novel which is truly 'quebecois,' both in form and content," wrote Richard G. Hodgson in *Dictionary of Literary Biography (DLB).*

Godbout uses nontraditional techniques of point of view, time shifts, and language, particularly the *joual* dialect of Quebec. In his best-known work, *Hail Galarneau!,* a first-person account of an introspective hot-dog vendor, Godbout combines *joual,* word games, and English language phrases. The theme of revolution is a common thread in most of Godbout's novels, beginning with *L'Aquarium,* which won the Prix France-Quebec in 1962. The comedy

Les Tetes a Papineau, about a couple in Quebec who are the parents of a two-headed infant, is the vehicle through which Godbout satirizes the bilingualism of the province. The anti-hero of *An American Story* is forced by blackmail to abandon his revolutionary aspirations. In *Knife on the Table* Godbout focuses on the cultural differences of a French-Canadian soldier and a rich English-Canadian girl, which he portrays through the couple's ill-fated romance. "There is always a sense of deja vu, and there is a sense of rhythm of poetic image rather than the usual episode or plot. Yet, the techniques are not imposed upon the subject matter," remarked Kent Thompson in *Fiddlehead.* "Partly because of its technique, the novel avoids pat, intellectual allegory" and focuses instead on human circumstances.

S. R. Schulman in *Choice* characterized Godbout's novels as "meditations," declaring that, "rather than flow into the actual," the works "stop within the relm of the virtual." This quality, combined with Godbout's imaginative storytelling, produces a characteristically surrealistic style which has become popular. "In contrast to the works of many other new novelists, both in Quebec and elsewhere," summarized Hodgson in *DLB,* "Godbout's novels have found a wide circle of readers, from those interested in his stylistic innovations to those who see in his work a manifestation of the attitudes and ideas of the new Quebec, a society transformed by the Quiet Revolution of the 1960s and early 1970s. The themes of Godbout's novels are those of much of contemporary Quebec literature—social satire, alienation, total liberation from social and political, as well as literary, traditions, in other words, revolution in the fullest sense of the word."

BIOGRAPHICAL/CRITICAL SOURCES:

BOOKS

Bellemare, Yvon, *Jacques Godbout romancier,* Parti Pris, 1984.
Dictionary of Literary Biography, Volume 53: *Canadian Writers Since 1960, First Series,* Gale, 1986, pp. 214-19.
Smith, Andre, *L'Univers romanesque de Jacques Godbout,* Aquila, 1979.

PERIODICALS

Canadian Forum, July, 1968.
Choice, November, 1988, p. 497.
Fiddlehead, summer, 1968, p. 90.

*   *   *

GOVIER, Katherine   1948-

PERSONAL: Surname is pronounced "Go-*vee*-ay"; born July 4, 1948, in Edmonton, Alberta, Canada; daughter of George Wheeler (an engineer) and Doris (a teacher; maiden name, Kemp) Govier; married John A. Honderich (a newspaper editor); children: Robin (son), Emily. *Education:* University of Alberta, B.A. (with first class honors), 1970; York University, M.A., 1972.

ADDRESSES: Agent—Lucinda Vardey Agency, 297 Seaton St., Toronto, Ontario, Canada, M5A 2T6.

CAREER: Ryerson Polytechnical Institute, Toronto, Ontario, instructor in English, 1973-75; free-lance writer, 1975—. Visiting lecturer in creative writing, York University, 1982-86; writer in residence, Parry Sound Public Library, 1988; writer-in-electronic-residence, 1988-91, coordinator of Writers-in-Electronic-Residence Program, Toronto, 1991—. Toronto Arts Awards literature jury, member, 1986, chair, 1991; chair of Writers' Development Trust, 1989-92; representative to board of governors of Canadian Conference of the Arts, 1989-90. Writer for Canadian Broadcasting Corp. (CBC) Radio and Television. Participated in TV-Ontario's *Academy on the Short Story;* speaks and reads work at schools, universities, and public libraries.

MEMBER: PEN International, Writers' Union of Canada (Ontario representative, 1987-88).

AWARDS, HONOURS: Authors' Award, Periodical Distributors of Canada, and National Magazine Awards, both 1979, for article "Radical Sheik" in *Canadian Business; Books in Canada* First Novel Shortlist, 1979, and second place Author's Award for best paperback of the year, Periodical Distributors of Canada, 1980, both for *Random Descent;* third prize, CBC Literary Contest, 1989, for short story "The Immaculate Conception Photo Gallery"; honorable mention for Talking Book of the Year, Canadian Institute for the Blind, 1991, for *Between Men;* Book Award, City of Toronto, 1992, for *Hearts of Flame.*

WRITINGS:

NOVELS

Random Descent, Macmillan (Canada), 1979, New American Library, 1980.
Going through the Motions, McClelland & Stewart, 1982, St. Martin's, 1983.
Between Men, Viking, 1987.
Hearts of Flame, Viking, 1991.

SHORT STORIES

Fables of Brunswick Avenue, Penguin Books, 1985.
Before and After, Viking, 1989.
The Immaculate Conception Photography Gallery and Other Stories, Little, Brown, 1994.

OTHER

(Editor) *Without a Guide: Contemporary Women's Travel Adventures,* Macfarlane, Walter & Ross, 1994.

Also author of scripts of three stories from *Before and After* for radio dramatization for CBC program *Morningside,* 1989. Contributor to *To See Ourselves,* Secretary of State (Canada), 1975.

Contributor to anthologies, including *Canadian Short Stories: Fourth Series,* edited by Robert Weaver, Oxford University Press, 1985; *Celebrating Canadian Women,* edited by Greta Hofmann Nemiroff, Fitzhenry & Whiteside, 1989; and *Slow Hand,* edited by Michelle Slung, Harper-Collins, 1992.

Author of "Relationships," a monthly column in *Toronto Life,* 1975-77. Contributor to periodicals, including *Maclean's, Canadian Business, New Society, Canadian Forum, Chatelaine, Cosmopolitan, Toronto Globe and Mail, Quest,* and *Saturday Night.* Associate editor, *Weekend,* 1978.

WORK IN PROGRESS: A novel; short stories; a television script.

SIDELIGHTS: Katherine Govier told *CA:* "Each of my six books thus far has been rooted in a strongly recognizable place—whether it is Toronto's Brunswick Avenue, or, in *Between Men,* Calgary in the oil boom of the nineteen eighties with the historical murder of a Cree woman one hundred years earlier playing as a ghost-plot. But this isn't travel writing. My interest is entirely in character. The question is how the character is created and what events flow from a human personality. Now I'm writing a fictional biography; the main character has lived through most of this century and in many places."

One of the books that aligns with Govier's concern with place is *Hearts of Flame. Books in Canada* contributor Merna Summers notes that it "is a novel about fashion and friendship and life in the fast track—and the possibility of dropping out." In particular, *Hearts of Flame* tracks the lives of four friends, one-time folk-group singers, and the disappearance of one of them. Yet, as Summers reports, "the main character of the novel . . . is the city of Toronto itself." Thus, Summers concludes that although "Govier is good at writing bizarre people" and the novel sustains some "wonderful vignettes," she believes that the novel might be most relished by someone who can truly "appreciate the aptness of Govier's observation" about the city—in other words, someone who is from Toronto.

Bizarre characters and situations resurface in Govier's short story collection, *The Immaculate Conception Photography Gallery and Other Stories.* In addition to containing the title story, which won an award in a Canadian

Broadcasting Corporation (CBC) literary contest, the book features a wide-ranging array of narratives. In one story, a woman takes an ape for a lover, in another, a woman has a close encounter with a UFO, and in yet another, a young man's newly transplanted heart (donated by the female victim of a fatal car crash) begins to communicate with him. For Gary Draper writing in *Books in Canada,* these stories are about "people who cope," and they often describe "rebirths" and "fresh starts" for these characters, who Draper describes as the victims of a "capricious" fate. Lynne van Luven, writing in *Quill and Quire,* describes some of these stories as "slight," and feels that Govier often "delivers a jocular caricature rather than illuminating exploration," but she concedes that some of the selections are "excellent tales."

Books in Canada's Draper, however, remarks that Govier's stories work "simultaneously in two modes." For him, the collection presents both "naturalistic fiction" and "fables," and the best stories move between the two modes so that the border between the real and the fantastic is shown to be "more apparent than real." Thus he pronounces the stories "vivid and arresting" and supports his assertion that, over the course of her career, Govier has "chart[ed] a territory that is by now distinctly her own." Govier's entry in the *Feminist Companion to Literature in English,* further delineates this territory, as it claims that her novels portray women discovering the various modes through which, in the words of one Govier's characters " 'Lives can come together without warning—and fragments make sense.' "

Govier's fascination with place also has connections to her work as the editor of *Without a Guide,* a collection of essays that focus on the traveling adventures of various women. The book earned high praise from Nancy Wigston, writing in *Quill and Quire,* and Libby Scheier, writing in *Books in Canada.* Both reviewers point out the diversity of the collection in which Govier pulls together essays about North American and non-North American women travelling both in and out of their native lands. The result, for Wigston is a "beguiling collection" which has "a series of stunning moments." Often, Wigston notes, the essays "read more like narratives than mere descriptions," and she asserts that the collection proves that "It's obvious that women don't travel in the same way men do—gender determines quite a lot about being on the road." For Scheier, the book "provide[s] rich insights into the crisscrossing subjects of gender, culture, and spirit."

About her position as coordinator of Toronto's writers-in-electronic-residence program, Govier explained to *CA* that it "involves teaching students in creative writing in thirty high schools across Canada via telecommunications and modem."

BIOGRAPHICAL/CRITICAL SOURCES:

BOOKS

Contemporary Literary Criticism, Volume 51, Gale, 1989.
Blain, Virginia, Patricia Clements, and Isobel Grundy, *Feminist Companion to Literature in English,* Yale University Press (New Haven, CT), 1990, p. 447-48.

PERIODICALS

Books in Canada, November, 1991, pp. 40-41; December, 1994, pp. 41-43; February, 1995, pp. 37-38.
Quill and Quire, September, 1994, p. 58; December, 1994, p. 23.*

* * *

GRAHAM, Gwethalyn   1913-1965

PERSONAL: Born Gwethalyn Graham Erichsen-Brown, January 18, 1913, in Toronto, Ontario, Canada; died of cancer, November 25, 1965, in Montreal, Canada; daughter of Frank Erichsen (a lawyer) and Isabel Russell (MacCurdy) Brown (a feminist); married John McNaught, September 24, 1932 (divorced); married David C. Yalden-Thomson (a professor), 1947; children: (first marriage) Francis Anthony Graham. *Education:* Attended Havergal College; Pensionnat Les Allieres, Lausanne, Switzerland, 1929-30; and Smith College, 1931-32.

CAREER: Novelist. Worked as a book seller for Jonathan Cape publishers in the 1930s.

AWARDS, HONOURS: Governor General's Awards for fiction, 1938, for *Swiss Sonata,* and 1944 for *Earth and High Heaven;* Anisfield-Wolf Award for fiction, 1945, for *Earth and High Heaven.*

WRITINGS:

NOVELS

Swiss Sonata, Scribners (New York City), and Cape (London), 1938.
Earth and High Heaven, introduction by Eli Mandel, Lippincott (New York City), and Cape, 1944.

NONFICTION

(With Solange Chaput-Rolland) *Dear Enemies: A Dialogue on French and English Canada,* Macmillan (Toronto), 1963, French translation published as *Chers ennemis,* Editions du Jour (Montreal), 1963.

Contributor to numerous publications, including *Canadian Author & Bookman, Canadian Forum, Chatelaine, Chicago Daily News, Maclean's, Saturday Night,* and *Wings.*

TELEVISION PLAYS

Two Terrible Women (adaptation of play *Deux Femmes terribles,* by Andre Laurendeau), Canadian Broadcast Company (CBC), 1965.

SIDELIGHTS: Although her literary oeuvre spanned only two novels, author Gwethalyn Graham gained international renown for her second, and final, work in the genre, *Earth and High Heaven.* Published in 1944 and translated into nine languages, the book is Graham's depiction of life in Montreal during World War II and focuses on the racial tensions between Jews and Gentiles. *Earth and High Heaven* received the Anisfield-Wolf Award for its contribution to improving race relations as well as earning Graham her second Governor General's Award. Active in humanitarian efforts throughout her life, Graham's two novels and the numerous articles she wrote for periodicals—though slight in quantity—have been praised by critics as a significant contribution to the human rights causes she so deeply espoused.

Both the war-torn era in which she was raised and her family background inspired Graham's lifelong interest in civil rights and politics. Her parents were each active in human rights and the promotion of civil liberties: Her father was a lawyer and painter, her mother a leader in the Canadian women's suffrage movement. Graham's maternal grandfather, professor James F. MacCurdy, also inspired her commitment to the quest for racial justice through his battle against nationalist and racially motivated slang and other prejudicial behaviours that had become facets of everyday life. Graham thrived in the intellectually stimulating environment of her parents' home. Although she was a motivated student who would later go on to excel academically, her school years would also be marked by adolescent traumas and ultimately end in an ill-conceived elopement. The friendships she made, as well as the unhappiness she experienced during those first years away from home, would inspire her first novel, *Swiss Sonata.*

During her sophomore year at Smith College, Graham eloped with the son of a wealthy financier. Her college education was cut short; the marriage was fleeting, lasting through the birth of her son. Graham moved to Montreal and began to write, living on a fixed allowance from her soon-to-be ex-husband and a part-time job selling books for British publishing firm Jonathan Cape, who would release *Swiss Sonata* in 1938.

Set in a Swiss finishing school similar to one that Graham had attended as a girl, *Swiss Sonata* takes place in 1935. The Jew-baiting and racial and national factionalism evident among the novel's fictional student body reflected the racial tensions existing throughout Europe during this pre-war period. Barbara Opala noted in the *Dictionary of*

Literary Biography that *Swiss Sonata* was overambitiously plotted, with too many characters, to effectively make its philosophical point. "But its notable achievements more than offset these failings," noted Opala, "for the witty and often humorous dialogues ring true, and most of the characterizations are vivid and powerful." Graham won her first Governor General's Award for the work in 1938.

That same year, Graham spent six months in Europe, where she witnessed the plight of the Jewish families displaced from their homes after Hitler's occupation of Austria. She returned to Toronto and wrote several articles for *Saturday Night,* alerting her fellow Canadians to the need to harbour these refugees. Her serious romantic involvement with a Jewish lawyer—with whom her father refused to speak—during this period provided Graham with the inspiration for what would become her best-selling novel.

Earth and High Heaven, which takes place during World War II, examines a rift between a father and daughter based on conflicting emotions and latent anti-Semitism. Erica Drake, a young woman from a prominent WASP family, falls in love with a first-generation Jew who has moved to Erica's small Ontario town. Although the young man is a lawyer and an army captain waiting to be sent overseas to join the front lines, Erica's supposedly liberal father will not acknowledge the couple's relationship until a family tragedy causes him to re-evaluate his prejudice. *Earth and High Heaven* was praised by critics; it won several awards, including a second Governor General's Award for Graham, and topped best seller lists after its publication in 1944. "[The novel] remains a perceptive and powerful examination of anti-Semitism," noted Opala, "and a classic of its kind in Canadian literature."

BIOGRAPHICAL/CRITICAL SOURCES:

BOOKS

Dictionary of Literary Biography, Volume 88: *Canadian Writers, 1920-1959, Second Series,* Gale (Detroit), 1989, pp. 88-91.*

*   *   *

GRANDBOIS, Alain   1900-1975

PERSONAL: Born May 25, 1900, at Saint-Casimir de Port-neuf, Quebec, Canada; died March 18, 1975; son of Henri (a physician) and Bernadette (Rousseau) Grandbois. *Education:* Attended College de Montreal, and Seminaire de Quebec; St. Dunstan's University, B.A.; enrolled in Faculty of Law, University Laval.

CAREER: Poet, lecturer, and lawyer. Called to the bar, 1925. World traveller, 1918-38; radio lecturer for Canadian Broadcasting Corporation (CBC), beginning 1939;

bibliographer at Bibliotheque Saint-Sulpice. Cofounder, with Victor Barbeau, of L'Academie canadienne-francaise, 1944.

AWARDS, HONOURS: Prix David, 1941, for *Les Voyages de Marco Polo;* Canada Council fellowship, 1960-61; honorary doctorate from Universite Laval, 1967; Academie Francaise award for body of work, 1968; Prix David, 1970; received Prix Duvernay, the Lorne Pierce Medal, and was awarded Prix David once more.

WRITINGS:

Ne a Quebec: Louis Jolliet, Messein (Paris), 1933, translation by Evelyn M. Brown published as *Born in Quebec: A Tale of Louis Jolliet,* Palm (Montreal), 1964.

Les Voyages de Marco Polo, Valiquette (Montreal), 1941.

Les Iles de la nuit, Parizeau (Montreal), 1944, critical edition, Fides (Montreal), 1972.

Avant le chaos, Editions Moderne (Montreal), 1945, translation by Larry Shouldice published as *Champagne and Opium,* Quadrant (Dunvegan, ON), 1984.

Rivages de l'homme (title means "Shores of Man"), Charrier (Quebec), 1948.

L'Etoile pourpre (title means "The Purple Star"), Hexagone (Montreal), 1957.

Alain Grandbois: Textes choisis et presentes par Jacques Brault, Fides (Montreal and Paris), 1958, revised and enlarged edition, Seghers (Paris), 1968.

Poemes: Les Iles de la nuit, Rivages de l'homme, L'Etoile pourpre, Hexagone (Montreal), 1963, revised and enlarged edition, 1979.

Selected Poems, translation by Peter Miller, Contact (Toronto), 1964.

(With Alain Bosquet, Simone Routier, Francois Hertel, and Saint-Denys Garneau) *La poesie canadienne,* Seghers (Paris), 1962, published as *Poesie du Quebec,* 1968.

Visages du monde: Images et souvenirs de l'entre-deux-guerres, HMH (Montreal), 1971.

Presence d'Alain Grandbois avec quatorze poemes parus de 1956 a 1969, Presses de l'Universite Laval (Quebec), 1974.

(Contributor) Rene Pageau, *Rencontres avec Simone Routier, suivies des lettres d'Alain Grandbois,* Parabole (Joliette, Quebec), 1978.

Deliverance du jour et autres inedits, Sentier (Montreal), 1980.

Dossier de presse 1944-1980, Seminaire de Sherbrooke (Sherbrooke, Quebec), 1981.

Poemes inedits, edited by Ghislaine Legendre, Marielle Saint-Amour, and Jo-Ann Stanton, Presses de l'Universite de Montreal (Montreal), 1985.

Lettres a Lucienne et deux poemes inedits, Hexagone (Montreal), 1987.

Poesie (critical edition), edited by Legendre, Saint-Amour and Stanton, Presses de l'Universite de Montreal (Montreal), 1990.

Also author of booklet *Poemes d'Hankeou* (title means "Hankow Poems"), 1934. A catalogue of Grandbois's manuscripts, entitled *Fonds Alain Grandbois*, was published by the Bibliotheque nationale du Quebec in 1977.

SIDELIGHTS: Alain Grandbois is descended from a French explorer who arrived in the New World in the early seventeenth century. Grandbois replayed his ancestor's wanderlust in his own life; he spent about fourteen years, between 1925 and 1939, living, writing, and travelling in Europe, North Africa, and the Far East. It was while living in Europe just before the outbreak of World War II that Grandbois published his first two works of fiction: *Ne a Quebec: Louis Jolliet,* and *Les Voyages de Marco Polo,* both about other men with the same uprootedness and restlessness as the author. "The primary interest of the work[s]," writes David F. Rogers in the *Dictionary of Literary Biography,* "is that of allowing the reader to get a glimpse of the motivations behind Grandbois the traveler; the book is a witness to the strength of Grandbois's imagination, to the real world attaining the dimension of a dream."

However, "beginning in the early 1940s," Rogers continues, "it became increasingly clear that Grandbois's real voice was that of a poet." The works that the author published, including *Avant le chaos, Les Iles de la nuit,* and *Rivages de l'homme,* also look at themes of love, death, and fate. *Avant le chaos,* like Grandbois's prose works, has characters who are "people without roots, exiled from the Paris of the interwar period," Rogers explains. *Les Iles de la nuit* received a review in the literary magazine *Revue populaire,* calling its publication the most important event in the history of Quebecois literature. *Rivages de l'homme,* states Rogers, "is written under the sign of life. The poet reaches here a new order where truth, fraternity, action, and the present reign." Grandbois's work, the reviewer concludes, "reflects the constants of his creation: the search for truth and for a fullness of life in this world."

BIOGRAPHICAL/CRITICAL SOURCES:

BOOKS

Ballard, Sylvie, *L'Univers poetique d'Alain Grandbois,* Editions Cosmos (Sherbrooke, ON), 1975.
Blais, Jacques, *Presence d'Alain Grandbois,* Presses de l'Universite Laval (Quebec), 1974.
Brault, Jacques, *Alain Grandbois,* Hexagone/Seghers (Montreal/Paris), 1968.
Bolduc, Yves, *Alain Grandbois: Le douloureux destin,* Presses de l'Universite de Montreal (Montreal), 1982.

de Grandpre, Pierre, *Dix ans de vie litteraire au Canada francais,* Beauchemin (Montreal), 1966.
Dictionary of Literary Biography, Volume 92: *Canadian Writers, 1890-1920,* Gale, 1990, 127-31.
Grandbois vivant: Communications du colloque, Hexagone (Montreal), 1990.
Greffard, Madeleine, *Alain Grandbois,* Fides (Montreal), 1975.
Parizeua, Lucien, *Periples autour d'un langage: L'oeuvre poetique d'Alain Grandbois,* Hexagone (Montreal), 1988.

PERIODICALS

Amerique francaise, December, 1954, pp. 473-76.
Liberte 60 (special double issue on Grandbois), number 9-10, May-August, 1960, pp. 145-228.
Revue populaire, August, 1944.*

*   *   *

GREVE, Felix Paul (Berthold Friedrich) 1879-1948
(Frederick Philip Grove)

PERSONAL: Born February 14, 1879, in Radomno, Prussia (now Poland); immigrated to Canada, c. 1909, naturalized Canadian citizen, 1921; died August 19, 1948, in Simcoe, Ontario, Canada; son of Karl Eduard (an estate manager and city transit official) and Bertha (Reichentrog) Greve; married Else Hildegard Ploetz, c. 1904 (separated); married Catherine Wiens in 1914; children: (second marriage) one daughter and one son. *Education:* Attended University of Bonn, 1898-1900, and Maximiliens University, Munich, 1901-02; University of Manitoba, B.A., 1921.

CAREER: Writer and translator in Germany, 1902-09; school teacher in various towns in Manitoba, Canada, including Haskett in 1913, Winkler, 1913-15, Virdin, 1915-16, Gladstone, 1916-17, Ferguson, 1918, Eden, 1919-22, and Rapid City, 1922-24; Graphic Press, Ottawa, Ontario, Canada, editor, 1929-31; *Canadian Nation,* associate editor, 1929; farm manager in Simcoe, Ontario, 1931-38.

AWARDS, HONOURS: Pierce Gold Medal, 1934; Royal Society of Canada fellow, 1941; D.Litt from University of Manitoba, 1945; Governor General's Award for nonfiction, 1947.

WRITINGS:

POETRY

Wanderungen, Littauer (Munich, Germany), 1902.
Helena und Damon: Ein Spiel in Versen, Littauer, 1902.

TRANSLATIONS

Oscar Wilde, *Das Bildnis Dorian Grays,* Bruns (Minden, Germany), 1902.

Ernest Dowson, *Dilemmas,* Insel (Leipzig, Germany), 1903.

Wilde, *Fingerzeige,* Bruns, 1903.

H. G. Wells, *Die Riesen kommen!,* Bruns, 1904.

Wells, *Die Zeitmaschine,* Bruns, 1904.

Wilde, *Die Sphinx,* Bruns, 1904.

Wilde, *Das Granatapfelhaus,* Insel, 1904.

Robert Browning, *Paracelsus: Dramatische Dichtung,* Insel, 1904.

Browning, *Briefe von Robert Browning and Elizabeth Barrett-Browning,* Fischer (Berlin), 1905.

Andre Gide, *Der Immoralist,* Bruns, 1905.

Gide, *Paludes (Die Suempfe),* Bruns, 1905.

George Meredith, *Richard Feverals Pruefung,* Bruns, 1905.

Wilde, *Eine Frau ohne Bedeutung,* Wiener (Leipzig and Wien, Germany), 1906.

Henri Murger, *Die Boheme: Szenen aus dem Pariser Kuenstlerleben,* Insel, 1906.

Gustave Flaubert, *Gesammelte Werke,* Volume 4: *Die Versuchung des heiligen Antonius,* Volume 7: *Briefe ueber meine Werke,* Volume 8: *Reiseblaetter,* Volume 9: *Briefe an Zeit-und Zunftgenossen,* Insel, 1906-08.

Walter Pater, *Marius der Epikureer,* two volumes, Insel, 1908.

Honore de Balzac, *Menschliche Komoedie,* Volume 1: *Ein Junggesellenheim,* Volume 2: *Erzaehlungen aus der napoleonischen Sphaere,* Volumes 6 and 7: *Glanz und Elend der Kurtisanen,* Volume 11: *Das Meisterwerk,* Insel, 1908-1911.

Alexandre Dumas, *Der Graf von Monte Cristo,* Reiss (Berlin), 1909.

Gide, *Die enge Pforte,* Reiss, 1909.

Wilde, *Werke,* Volume 10: *Bunbury* (translation of *The Importance of Being Earnest*), Globus (Berlin), 1918.

Also produced German translations of books by Miguel de Cervantes and Alain-Rene Lesage.

NOVELS; UNDER NAME FELIX PAUL GREVE

Fanny Essler, Juncker (Stuttgart), 1905, translation by Christine Helmers, A. W. Riley, and Douglas O. Spettigue, edited with an introduction by Riley and Spettigue, Oberon Press, 1984.

Maurermeister Ihles Haus, Schnabel (Berlin), 1906, translation by Paul P. Gubbins published as *The Master Mason's House,* edited with an introduction by Riley and Spettigue, Oberon Press, 1976.

OTHER

Oskar Wilde, Gose and Tetzlaff (Berlin), 1903, translation by Barry Asker published by Hoffer (Vancouver), 1984.

Randarabesken zu Oskar Wilde, Bruns, 1903.

Work represented in books, including *Portraets,* edited by Adalbert Luntowski, Nues Leben (Berlin); Volume 7 of *Oskar Wildes saemtliche Werke in deutscher Sprache,* Wiener, 1908.

NOVELS; UNDER NAME FREDERICK PHILIP GROVE

Settlers of the Marsh, Ryerson Press (Toronto), Doran (New York), 1925.

A Search for America, Graphic (Ottawa), 1927, Carrier (New York), 1928.

Our Daily Bread, Macmillan, 1928.

The Yoke of Life, Macmillan (Toronto), R. R. Smith (New York), 1930.

Fruits of the Earth, Dent, 1933.

The Master of the Mill, Macmillan, 1944.

Consider Her Ways, Macmillan, 1947.

Also author of the juvenile novel *The Adventure of Leon Broadus, Canadian Boy,* published in *Canadian Children's Literature,* Volume 40, April 7-June 23, 1940, and republished in Volume 27-28, 1982; the text of the novel is also included in *The Genesis of Grove's "The Adventure of Leon Broadus": A Text and Commentary,* edited with commentary and notes by Mary Rubio, Canadian Children's Press, 1983.

SHORT STORIES; UNDER NAME FREDERICK PHILIP GROVE

Tales from the Margin: The Selected Short Stories of Frederick Philip Grove, edited by Desmond Pacey, Ryerson Press/McGraw Hill, 1971.

SKETCHES; UNDER NAME FREDERICK PHILIP GROVE

Over Prairie Trails, McClelland & Stewart, 1922.

The Turn of the Year, McClelland & Stewart, 1923.

OTHER; UNDER NAME FREDERICK PHILIP GROVE

(Translator) Gustav Amann, *The Legacy of Sun Yatsen: A History of the Chinese Revolution,* Carrier, 1929.

It Needs to be Said, Macmillan, 1929.

Two Generations: A Story of Present-Day Ontario, Ryerson Press, 1939.

In Search of Myself (autobiography), Macmillan, 1946.

The Letters of Frederick Philip Grove, edited by Pacey, University of Toronto Press, 1976.

An Edition of Selected Unpublished Essays and Lectures by Frederick Philip Grove Bearing on His Theory of Art, edited by Henry Makow, National Library of Canada, 1984.

Work represented in books, including *A Stranger to My Time: Essays By and about Frederick Philip Grove,* edited by Paul Hjartarson, NeWest, c. 1986. Contributor to journals and periodicals, including *Neue Revue, 3, Canadian Forum,* and *University of Toronto Quarterly.*

Most of the author's papers are housed in the Grove Collection at the Elizabeth Dafoe Library, University of Manitoba.

SIDELIGHTS: Felix Paul Greve's body of work is comprised of a complex subject encircled by the author's own fascinating dual life. Greve originally worked as a writer in his native Germany in the early years of the twentieth century, but is better known as the author Frederick Philip Grove, a pioneer of modern Canadian literature. He was at the forefront of a distinct "prairie" realism that made him an elder statesman of Canadian letters by the time of his death. Greve never disclosed the truth about his European origins and fictionalized his own persona and background in both official documents and autobiographical works. His ruse went undiscovered until the early 1970s, when a Canadian literary scholar established that the early German author Felix Paul Greve—who had simply vanished one day in 1909 Europe—was the same man that appeared four years later as Frederick Philip Grove, a rural Canadian schoolteacher who went on to achieve wide recognition as a writer. Modern critics have attempted to reconcile the European literary traditions the exiled writer had earlier explored with his subsequent distinct and innovative New-World realism.

Greve was born in the Prussian village of Radomno in 1879, an area that is in present-day Poland. His family moved to Hamburg, Germany, when he was very young, where his father was a railway conductor. He later studied philosophy at the University of Bonn, but quit the university at the age of nineteen. He then traveled extensively and became acquainted with eminent personalities such as the French writer Andre Gide, German poet Stefan George, and Otto Julius Bierbaum, editor of the avant-garde literary journal *Die Insel.* During this time, Greve attempted to earn a living as a writer and translator. His German publications appeared under a variety of names, including Felix Paul Greve, Friedrich Carl Gerden, Felix Grafe, Elsa Greve, Konrad Thorer, and Edouard Thorne. Although he published two volumes of poetry and translated numerous books into German, including works by British novelists Oscar Wilde and H.G. Wells, he was only moderately successful and incurred large debts. In 1903 he was jailed for fraud, and upon his release the following year, married his first wife, Else Hildegard Ploetz. Greve continued to translate the works of other writers such as the English poet Robert Browning and French novelist Gustave Flaubert while also completing two novels of his own, *Fanny Essler* and *Maurermeister Ihles Haus,* or "The Master Mason's House."

In both works the issues of sexual freedom and money are explored through the development of female characters, and Greve attempts to set a specific mood through minutely-detailed accounts of persons and places. The first of these novels, *Fanny Essler,* was a five-hundred page story of a young woman from the country and her quest for emancipation within the rigid patriarchal German society of the late-nineteenth century. In this, Greve's first major work, he reflected his ties with the bohemian literary milieu of Munich and Berlin at the time of the novel's publication in 1905. The protagonist of the title leaves her impoverished rural background in a search for financial and personal independence by becoming an actress. She ultimately fails and loses her respectability by indulging in relationships with several men. Greve followed this work with 1906's *Maurermeister Ihles Haus,* a novel whose themes of female emancipation closely parallel *Fanny Essler.* The three main characters of Ihles, his wife, and daughter, are part of a dysfunctional family rocked by rampant materialism and a deep repression that envelopes the two women. Reviews praised Greve's character development of the daughter, Suse. Critic Anthony W. Riley, commenting on the two novels in *Reappraisals: Canadian Writers. The Grove Symposium,* proclaimed that "Greve's skill—and daring—in conjuring up the emotional life of a woman of the 1890s is great." Despite the attention these novels received from later critics, the books attained little commercial or critical success at the time of their publication. Plagued by numerous debts and disappointed by his lack of literary acclaim, it is believed that sometime around 1909 Greve took drastic measures to change the course of his life.

In the early 1970s, the Canadian critic Douglas O. Spettigue unraveled the mystery surrounding the untimely death of one Felix Paul Greve in 1909 and the appearance of the teacher and later author Frederick Philip Grove on the Canadian literary scene a few years later. Apparently Greve left clues leading to the supposition that he had committed suicide aboard a ship bound for Sweden, but in reality had left Germany with his wife for North America. It is believed that the couple spent time in the United States, but then separated. In 1912 he applied for a teaching position in Manitoba and was employed for the next decade as both a teacher and principal in various communities there. In 1914 he married his second wife, Catherine Wiens and devoted himself to his teaching and writing.

Though this version of Greve/Grove's life was later documented by Spettigue, the author's public comments and autobiographical writings presented a different picture of himself. In these Grove claimed that he was born in Moscow, Russia, the son of wealthy Swedish-Russian landowners. After growing up in Southern Sweden, he supposedly took on the life of an well-to-do intellectual, attending universities in numerous European cities. Grove never mentioned his years of struggle and hardship in Germany and instead emphasized his elaborate tours of Europe, Asia, Australia, and finally, North America. It was while he was traveling through the United States and Canada in 1892, Grove alleged, that he learned that his father had gone bankrupt in Europe. He then turned to working and after years of steady effort, established himself as a teacher and author. This false persona that Grove created played a role in his literary success, according to Walter Pache in *Dictionary of Literary Biography,* because it appealed to the self-identity of many Canadians. "Uniting in one person the adventurous pioneer and the distinguished intellectual," Pache wrote, "Grove seemed to provide a literary tradition, a specifically Canadian synthesis of . . . European culture and the wilderness of the north."

Grove's first work to be published in Canada, *Over Prairie Trails,* appeared in 1922, followed by 1923's *The Turn of the Year.* They are first-person accounts of Grove's encounters with and reflections on the harsh locale of the Canadian plains. Critics praised his descriptive talents and found the works reminiscent both of his earlier highly detailed novels and of the essays of other writers, such as Henry David Thoreau, on the relationship between man and his environment. Lorne Pierce, reflecting on the sum of these two works in his essay on Grove for *Proceedings and Transactions of the Royal Society of Canada,* noted that in these books the author "achieves some of his most memorable descriptions. . . . His sincerity and sanity, his integrity as both artist and man, the hard clean core of his fine intelligence, are here revealed for all to see." These volumes finally brought Grove the success he had so craved in Germany, and he gave up teaching in 1924 to write full-time.

Settlers of the Marsh, Grove's first attempt in English at the novel form, received attention mostly for its racy depiction of love and lust on the prairie although the book was quite serious in tone. The plot concerns a Swedish immigrant's unhappy marriage, the murder of his wife in a fit of jealousy, the man's incarceration, and eventual redemption. Although commercially unsuccessful due to a general wave of conservatism, critics hailed Grove's fusion of personal tragedy with the bleak leitmotif of the prairie. Writing in the *Saturday Review of Literature,* Arthur L. Phelps praised *Settlers of the Marsh*'s "vivid, compelling intensity" and concluded that the novel translates its Manitoba setting into a "spiritual territory of the soul."

Though critics were appreciative of Grove's early Canadian efforts, his next publication signaled the start of a period of even greater literary success for the author. *A Search for America,* written earlier but published in 1927, is the account of a young man's emigration from his European homeland and his adjustment to his new life and country, a subject that was quite familiar to many Canadians. Part autobiographical, part allegorical, the work was well received and led to a series of speaking tours that heralded Grove as a Canadian literary sage. Fueled by prosperous times and a developing sense of a distinct Canadian nationalism, the writer's persona as both a European-trained intellectual and pragmatic pioneer of the plains appealed to readers and critics alike.

Many of Grove's lectures and essays from this period were collectively published in a 1929 volume with the title of *It Needs to Be Said.* The writer, who had earlier moved his family to Ottawa, held various editorial positions over the next few years while continuing to write. Two of his novels from this period—*Our Daily Bread* and *The Yoke of Life*—continued in the same vein as *Settlers of the Marsh,* but were less successful and not well received. The Groves left the city in 1931 for a rural Ontario town where the author added the occupation of farmer to his varied careers. Grove continued to write and publish, including *Fruits of the Earth* and *Two Generations: A Story of Present-Day Ontario,* works that appeared respectively in 1933 and 1939.

During the 1940s Grove completed two more novels and an autobiography, but he failed to achieve the same popular success that had followed the publication of *A Search for America.* He did gain further his status as an important Canadian author, however; he was awarded a monthly stipend from the Canadian Writer's Fund and was elected a fellow of the Royal Society of Canada. The 1944 novel *The Master of the Mill* was an epic that chronicled three generations of an Ontario mill-owning family. The work again explores Canada's pioneer legacy, this time contrasting the early development of the mill with the modern technology employed in the 1900s.

Grove's 1946 autobiography, entitled *In Search of Myself,* received a Governor General's Award for nonfiction, although, ironically, it was partly fictional. The book chronicled the author's false persona as a European aristocrat and intellectual who befriended some of the greater luminaries of his age. The second part of *In Search of Myself* relates his life in Canada and is closer to the actual truth.

Grove's final novel, *Consider Her Ways,* is a departure from Grove's previous works. The book—which was begun over two decades earlier—is the allegorical tale of a female ant who ventures from South America to New York City, leading an expedition that hopes to catalog all forms of life. Grove's strong female protagonist meets with severe adversity on her journey, while ruminating on observed human follies, including self-absorption and a lack of respect for the environment. Ronald Sutherland, in his book *Frederick Philip Grove,* asserted that *Consider Her Ways* "abounds with fascinating incidents skillfully presented," hailing the volume as "Grove's best book."

A series of strokes in the 1940s crippled the writer and brought ill health until his death in 1948. Grove's body of work continued to receive critical attention for its contribution to modern Canadian literature. Yet his invention of an alternate persona, undiscovered until twenty-five years after his death, also revealed much about Canadian culture and identity. Critics have noted that Grove's invented past was readily accepted by his peers among the Canadian intelligentsia because of a need to find a distinct voice, separate from what they perceived as American mediocrity. Pache, in *Dictionary of Literary Biography,* summarized the duality of the author's life in noting that "by inventing a new self, Grove turned his life into art, casting off all restrictions that his own past, the historical background, and contemporary literature might have placed on his existence."

BIOGRAPHICAL/CRITICAL SOURCES:

BOOKS

Bader, Rudolf, in *Gaining Ground: European Critics on Canadian Literature,* edited by R. Kroetsch and R. M. Nischik, NeWest, 1985, pp. 222-23.

Bierbaum, Otto Julius, in *Die Insel, 3,* 1901-02, pp. 195-96.

Blodgett, E. D., *Configuration: Essays on the Canadian Literatures,* ECW, 1982, pp. 112-53.

Bonheim, Helmut, in *Encounters and Explorations: Canadian Writers and European Critics,* edited by F. K. Stanzel and W. Zacharasiewicz, Koenigshausen (Wuerzburg), 1986, pp. 58-72.

Dooley, D. J., *Moral Vision in the Canadian Novel,* Clarke, Irwin, 1979, pp. 13-23.

Dudek, Louis, in *Reappraisals: Canadian Writers. The Grove Symposium,* edited by John Nause, Ottawa University Press, 1974, pp. 89-99.

Eggleston, Wilfrid, in *Reappraisals: Canadian Writers. The Grove Symposium,* edited by Nause, Ottawa University Press, 1974, pp. 101-10.

Eggleston, Wilfrid, in *Our Living Tradition,* edited by Claude T. Bissell, University of Toronto Press, 1957, pp. 105-27.

Frederick Philip Grove, Department of Cultural Affairs and Historical Resources (Winnipeg, Manitoba), 1981.

Gide, Andre, *Oeuvres Completes d'Andre Gide,* edited by Louis Martin-Chauffier, Volume 9, NRF (Paris), 1932-39, pp. 133-43.

Hjartarson, Paul, *A Stranger to My Time: Essays by and about Frederick Philip Grove,* NeWest, 1986.

Kreisel, Henry, in *Contexts of Canadian Criticism,* edited by Eli Mandel, University of Chicago Press, 1971, pp. 254-66.

McCourt, Edward, *The Canadian West in Fiction,* Ryerson Press, 1970, pp. 56-69.

McMullen, Lorraine, in *Reappraisals: Canadian Writers. The Grove Symposium,* edited by Nause, Ottawa University Press, 1974, pp. 67-76.

The Oxford Companion to Canadian Literature and History, Oxford University Press, 1967.

Pacey, Desmond, *Frederick Philip Grove,* Ryerson Press, 1945.

Pacey, Desmond, introduction to *Tales from the Margin: The Selected Short Stories of Frederick Philip Grove,* Ryerson Press/McGraw-Hill, 1971, pp. 1-19.

Pache, Walter, in *Deutsch Canadisches Jahrbud,* Volume 5, edited by Hartmut Froeschle, Historical Society of Mecklenburg, Upper Canada, 1979, pp. 121-36.

Pache, Walter, in *Dictionary of Literary Biography,* Volume 92: *Canadian Writers, 1890-1920,* Gale, 1990, pp. 143-56.

Phelps, Arthur L., *Canadian Writers,* McClelland & Stewart, 1951, pp. 36-42.

Ricou, Laurence, *Vertical Man/Horizontal World: Man and Landscape in Canadian Prairie Fiction,* University of British Columbia Press, 1973, pp. 38-64.

Riley, Anthony W., in *The Old World and the New: Literary Perspectives of German-speaking Canadians,* edited by Walter E. Riedel, University of Toronto Press, 1984, pp. 37-58.

Riley, Anthony W., in *Reappraisals: Canadian Writers. The Grove Symposium,* edited by Nause, Ottawa University Press, 1974, pp. 55-66.

Riley, Anthony W., and Spettigue, Douglas O., introduction to *The Master Mason's House* by Frederick Philip Grove, Oberon Press, 1976, pp. 5-10.

Ross, Malcolm, introduction to *Over Prairie Trails* by Grove, McClelland & Stewart, 1957, pp. v-x.

Spettigue, Douglas O., *Frederick Philip Grove,* Copp Clark, 1969.

Spettigue, Douglas O., *FPG: The European Years,* Oberon Press, 1973.

Stobie, Margaret R., *Frederick Philip Grove,* Twayne, 1973.

Sutherland, Ronald, *Frederick Philip Grove,* McClelland & Stewart, 1969.

Sutherland, Ronald, in *The New Hero: Essays in Comparative Quebec/Canadian Literature,* Macmillan, 1977, pp. 39-50.

Twentieth-Century Literary Criticism, Volume 4, Gale, 1981.

Twentieth-Century Western Writers, Gale, 1991.

Williams, David, in *Canada and the Nordic Countries,* edited by Jorn Carlsen and Berge Steuyffert, Lund University Press (Lund, Sweden), 1988, pp. 365-75.

Woodcock, George, in *The Canadian Imagination: Dimensions of a Literary Culture,* edited by David Staines, Harvard University Press, 1977.

PERIODICALS

ARIEL, April, 1973, pp. 34-48.

Canadian Forum, September, 1948, pp. 121-22.

Canadian Literature, winter, 1960, pp. 17-22; winter, 1962, pp. 28-38; winter, 1970, pp, 67-76; summer, 1971, pp. 10-27; spring, 1979, pp. 63-70; autumn, 1981, pp. 73-90, 111-23.

Dalhousie Review, Volume 19, 1939, pp. 147-63; Volume 43, No. 2, summer, 1963, pp. 235-41; Volume 58, autumn, 1978, pp. 418-33, 528-40.

Gants du Ciel, Volume 4, winter, 1946, pp. 15-40.

Humanities Association Review, Volume 25, summer, 1974, pp. 225-31.

Journal of Canadian Fiction, Volume 3, No. 3, 1974, pp. 65-73.

Journal of Commonwealth Literature, August, 1979, pp. 9-17.

Journal of Modern Literature, March, 1983, pp. 71-90.

Mosaic, April, 1970, pp. 19-33; winter, 1974, pp. 89-100.

Ontario Library Review, Volume 13, No. 3, 1928, pp. 60-62.

Proceedings and Transactions of the Royal Society of Canada, June, 1949, pp. 113-19.

Queen's Quarterly, spring, 1972, pp. 1-2.

Saturday Review of Literature, January 30, 1926, p. 529.

Seminar, June, 1973, pp. 148-55.

Studies in Canadian Literature, Volume 7, No. 2, 1982, pp. 241-57.

University of Toronto Quarterly, January, 1947, pp. 202-06; spring, 1978, pp. 189-99.

World Literature Written in English, spring, 1985, pp. 104-11.*

—*Sketch by Carol A. Brennan*

*   *   *

GRIGNON, Claude-Henri 1894-1976
(Valdombre; Claude Bacle)

PERSONAL: Original name Eugene-Henry Grignon; born July 8, 1894, in Sainte-Adele, Quebec, Canada; died, 1976; son of Wilfrid (a doctor and veterinarian) and Eugenie (Baker) Grignon; married Therese Lambert, 1916; children: Claire (adopted). *Education:* Attended College Saint-Laurent, 1909-10, and Institut Agricole d'Oka; also privately tutored. *Religion:* Roman Catholic.

CAREER: Novelist, journalist, short story writer, literary critic, pamphleteer, radio and television scriptwriter, politician. Worked variously as a journalist, customs official, civil servant, and publicist. As a journalist, worked for *L'Avenir du Nord* under pseudonym of Claude Bacle, as well as for *La Minerve,* 1920, *Le Nationaliste,* 1921-22, and *Le Matin,* 1923-24, also contributed to *La Revue populaire,* 1931-34, *Le Canada,* 1931, *L'Ordre,* 1934-35, *La Renaissance,* 1935, and *Bulletin des Agriculteurs,* 1941-70, under a variety of pseudonyms. *En Avant,* literary editor, 1937-39. Writer, printer, financer, and distributor of the monthly *Les Pamphlets de Valdombre,* 1936-43. Secretary to Irene Vautrin, member of the National Assembly, and minister in charge of Departement de la Colonisation, in the early 1930s. Mayor of Sainte-Adele, 1941-51, and prefect of Terrebonne county.

MEMBER: Ecole Litteraire de Montreal, Royal Society of Canada (elected fellow, 1961).

AWARDS, HONOURS: Prix David, 1935, for *Un Homme et son peche.*

WRITINGS:

Le Secret de Lindbergh (novel), Editions de la Porte d'Or (Montreal), 1928.

Ombres et clameurs: Regards sur la litterature canadienne (essays), Albert Levesque (Montreal), 1933.

Un Homme et son peche (novel), Editions du Totem (Montreal), 1933, appeared in English as *The Woman and the Miser,* translation by Yves Brunelle, Harvest House (Montreal), 1978, adapted for film by Grignon under the original French title, Quebec Productions Corporation, 1948, again adapted for film by Grignon as *Seraphin Poudrier,* Quebec Productions Corporation, 1949.

Le Deserteur et autres recits de la terre (short stories), Editions du Vieux Chene (Montreal), 1934.

Precisions sur "Un Homme et son peche" (nonfiction), Editions du Vieux Chene, 1936.

Also author of *Le restaurant d'en face* and "Rhumba des radio-romans." Grignon also produced scripts for the *Les belles histoires des pays d'en haut* series on radio (1939-62) and television (1956-70) based on his novel *Un Homme et son peche.* Also author of political pamphlet series under pseudonym Valdombre, 1936-43. Contributor to periodicals, including *Photo-journal, Bulletin des agriculteurs,* and *La Revue populaire. Un Homme et son peche* was also translated by Frances Ebbs-Canavan as "A Man and His Sin: Romance," but was not published.

ADAPTATIONS: Un Homme et son peche was adapted twice for film in 1948 and 1949, for a television (1956-70) and a radio (1939-62) series under the title *Les belles histoires des pays d'en haut,* and for radio CKVL, 1963. *Le*

Deserteur et autres recits de la terre was produced for radio, as was *Le restaurant d'en face* and "Rhumba des radio-romans" (a series).

SIDELIGHTS: As reported by Kenneth Landry in *Dictionary of Literary Biography,* Claude-Henri Grignon once described himself in the following way: "I am thin-skinned and passionate, a peasant, self-taught, a man of the earth earthy, a dreamer, a romantic, an indomitable individualist, a poet, a devout Catholic. . . . I have chosen to become a writer in order to be free and to assert myself." Most famously the author of long-running television and radio series based on one of his novels, and as publisher of an outspoken political pamphlet series under the pseudonym Valdombre, Grignon celebrated and defended rural life and values as a writer and as a politician in Quebec.

Grignon was born in a small community in the Laurentian mountain region of Quebec, north of Montreal. The youngest son of a doctor, he was educated at home and briefly in schools. Grignon worked a variety of jobs in Montreal after his father's death in 1915, including posts in the two areas that would be his mainstay as an adult, journalism and civil service. In 1916 he married Therese Lambert and, under a variety of pseudonyms, including Claude Bacle, penned articles in political newspapers of a liberal and nationalist bent, a career that would continue alongside his work as politician, fiction writer, and scriptwriter throughout his life.

As a journalist, Grignon defended traditional values and French-Canadian nationalism, as well as critiquing the region's literature in reviews and articles. Some of his essays on literature are collected in *Ombres et clameurs: Regards sur la litterature canadienne* (1933). His political commentary culminated in the publication of a series of pamphlets written and published by the author from 1936 until 1943, entitled *Les Pamphlets de Valdombre.* The "two main targets" of Grignon's stringent satires in *Les Pamphlets de Valdombre,* Landry remarked, "provincial politics . . . and literature (both French and French-Canadian), afforded him an ideal opportunity to vindicate his staunchly traditional beliefs as a Roman Catholic and as a defender of the rights of rural Quebeckers, whom he called 'la paysannerie.' "

Grignon's fiction took on many of the same subjects as his political diatribes. *Un Homme et son peche* (1933), the author's best known work, dramatizes the effects of the Great Depression of the 1930s through the marriage of a cruel miser and his cowering wife. "Its strength lies in its realistic style and in the portrayal of the sado-masochistic relationship of the lustful husband and the submissive wife," commented Lucie Robert in the *Oxford Companion to Canadian Literature.* Adapted by the author into two

films, and a radio and television series, *Un Homme et son peche* was an immensely popular and successful representation of rural Quebec life. In response to contemporary critics who found the novel sordid, Grignon wrote *Precisions sur "Un Homme et son peche,"* noting that the work depicts real-life characters and events that were fictionalized in his novel.

In *Le Deserteur et autres recits de la terre* (1934), a collection of short stories, Grignon praised the superiority of rural over urban lifestyles once again. Although critic Robert faulted this aspect of the work, she also noted that the book "reveals Grignon's knack for creating interesting characters and for depicting popular customs." Grignon is also the author of *Le Secret de Lindbergh,* a fictionalized account of Charles Lindbergh's flight over the Atlantic that celebrates the subject's heroism.

As both a provincial politician and as a writer, Grignon championed rural life in Quebec. As a journalist and pamphleteer, the author gave vent to his strong conservative opinions in ways that infuriated his opponents and made him infamous in his own day. Although Grignon's attempts at fiction were sometimes marred by an overly moralistic strain, his novel *Un Homme et son peche* and its serialization on radio and television as *Les Belles Histoires des pays d'en haut* is considered a classic of rural Quebec life and one of the few attempts to portray this culture that avoids sentimentality and idealization.

BIOGRAPHICAL/CRITICAL SOURCES:

BOOKS

Dictionary of Literary Biography, Volume 68: *Canadian Writers, 1920-1959,* Gale, 1988, pp. 149-52.
Oxford Companion to Canadian Literature, Oxford University Press, 1983, p. 322.

PERIODICALS

Journal of Canadian Fiction, Number 19, 1977.
La Presse, April 10, 1976.
Modern Language Studies, Fall, 1976.

*   *   *

GROULX, Lionel (Adolphe) 1878-1967
(Alonie de Lestres, Lionel Montal)

PERSONAL: Born January 13, 1878, in Vaudreuil, Quebec; died May 23, 1967; son of Leon and Philomene Salomee (Pilon) Groulx. *Education:* Attended Seminaire de Ste.-Therese-de-Blainville (now renamed for Groulx), 1884-99; attended the Grand Seminaire de Montreal; studied in Rome, Paris, and Fribourg, 1906-1909. *Religion:* Roman Catholic.

CAREER: Ordained as a Roman Catholic priest, 1903; Seminaire de Valleyfield, teacher, 1901-1915; Universite Laval de Montreal (now Universite de Montreal), 1915-49; free-lance writer, 1906-67. Editor of *L'Action francaise* (now *L'Action nationale*), 1921-28; founder of the Institut d'Histoire de l'Amerique Francaise and its *Revue,* 1946; visiting lecturer throughout Quebec, and on radio and television.

MEMBER: Ligue des Droits du Francais.

AWARDS, HONOURS: Tyrrel Medal of the Royal Society of Canada; special recognition from the Canadian Historical Association; numerous awards from nationalist, historical, and literary groups in Quebec and France; honorary degrees from universities, including Universite de Montreal, Universite d'Ottawa, and Memorial University.

WRITINGS:

L'Education de la volonte en vue du devoir social, A.C.J.C. (Montreal), 1906.

Une Croisade d'adolescents, L'Action Sociale (Quebec City), 1912.

Les Rapaillages (vieilles choses, vieilles gens) (short stories), Le Devoir (Montreal), 1916.

La Confederation canadienne, Le Devoir, 1918.

La Naissance d'une race, Bibliotheque de l'Action Francaise (Montreal), 1919.

Chez nos ancetres, Bibliotheque de l'Action Francaise, 1920.

Lendemains de conquete, Bibliotheque de l'Action Francaise, 1920.

Vers l'emancipation, Bibliotheque de l'Action Francaise, 1921.

Notre maitre, le passe, first series, Bibliotheque de l'Action Francaise, 1924, second and third series, Granger (Montreal), 1936, 1944.

Dix ans d'Action francaise, Bibliotheque de l'Action Francaise, 1926.

L'Enseignement francais au Canada (two volumes), Volume 1, Albert Levesque (Montreal), 1931, Volume 2, Granger, 1933.

Le Francais au Canada, Libraire Delagrave (Paris), 1932.

Orientations, Editions du Zodiaque (Montreal), 1935.

Directives, Editions du Zodiaque, 1937.

Histoire du Canada francais depuis la decouverte (four volumes), L'Action Nationale (Montreal), 1950-52.

Pour batir, L'Action Nationale, 1953.

Rencontres avec Dieu, Fides (Montreal), 1956.

Une Femme de genie au Canada: La Bienheureuse Mere d'Youville, Comite des Fondateurs de l'Eglise Canadienne (Montreal), 1957.

Notre Grande Aventure: L'Empire francais en Amerique du Nord (1535-1760), Fides, 1958.

Dollard est-il un mythe? Fides, 1960.

Le Canada francais missionaire, Fides, 1962.

Chemins de l'avenir, Fides, 1964.

La Decouverte du Canada: Jacques Cartier, Fides, 1966.

Constantes de vie, Fides, 1967.

Roland-Michel Barrin de La Galissoniere, 1693-1756, Presses de l'Universite Laval (Quebec City), 1970; translated by John Flinn, University of Toronto Press (Toronto), 1970.

Mes Memoires (four volumes; autobiography), Fides, 1970-74.

Abbe Groulx: Variations on a Nationalist Theme, translations by Joanne L'Heureux and Susan Mann Trofimenkoff, edited by Trofimenkoff, Copp Clark (Vancouver), 1973.

Lionel Groulx, Journal 1895-1911, Presses de l'Universite de Montreal (Montreal), 1984.

NOVELS; UNDER PSEUDONYM ALONIE DE LESTRES

L'Appel de la race, Bibliotheque de l'Action Francaise, 1922; translated by J. S. Wood as *The Iron Wedge,* Carleton Library (Ottawa), 1986.

Au Cap Blomidon, Le Devoir, 1932.

OTHER

Contributor of poems to periodicals, including *Le Semeur,* under the pseudonym Lionel Montal.

SIDELIGHTS: A Catholic priest and strong advocate of Quebec nationalism, Groulx was the author of many historical and political works. He primarily labored in the genres of nonfiction, but his volume of short stories, *Les Rapaillages (vieilles choses, vieilles gens),* proved very popular in his home province. He also authored two novels with French-Canadian nationalist themes, the first of which was translated into English as *The Iron Wedge.* Though Groulx is little known to English-speaking Canadians, Phyllis M. Senese reported in the *Dictionary of Literary Biography* that "[anyone] who attempts to understand Quebec and the Quebecois in the years before 1967 must come to terms with Groulx and the body of his writing."

Groulx was born in Quebec in 1878. A month after Groulx's birth, his father died of smallpox, and two of his three siblings died during an outbreak of diphtheria. Following these tragedies, his mother remarried. His new family was apparently a happy one, and from childhood Groulx showed evidence of a strong religious faith. While studying for the priesthood, he began writing poetry. Some of this verse was eventually published in periodicals under the pseudonym Lionel Montal, but Groulx seems to have abandoned poetry later in his literary career. Ordained in 1903, Groulx continued his studies in Paris, Rome, and Fribourg. He taught at the seminary of Valleyfield and in 1915 started his long tenure at the Universite de Montreal.

Though Groulx's first book was published in 1906, the best known of his early volumes is his 1916 collection of autobiographical short stories, *Les Rapaillages.* Throughout his career he wrote in support of French Canadian nationalism, and some of the best known of these include *La Naissance d'une race, Notre maitre, le passe,* and *Chemins de l'avenir.* In these and other works, including a four-volume history of French-speaking Canada, Groulx advocated a deep commitment to Catholicism as a key element in preserving Quebec's cultural independence and in winning its political freedom. Senese explained that according to Groulx, "Catholicism was the paramount national characteristic. In a truly French Quebec, Catholic social values, not secular materialism, would inspire a society that was economically and politically modern and progressive." Groulx saw increasing secularization as a threat to Quebec's independence. But, in Senese's analysis, "Groulx never understood, or admitted, the extent to which nationalism exhibited a tendency to become a religion in its own right, destroying in its wake the spiritual values Groulx so keenly professed." Though Groulx's importance in and inspiration to the movement for Quebec's independence cannot be overestimated, and though, in Senese's words, "he had made separatism, as a political option, respectable," he was not entirely pleased by the direction that movement took. According to Senese "Groulx was distressed by much of what occurred. The impressive gains in nationalist terms were offset by the steady decline of Catholicism as the system of values guiding society."

Groulx also expressed his sentiments about French Canadian nationalism in novel form. Published in 1922 under the pen name Alonie de Lestres, his first novel, *The Iron Wedge,* concerns Jules de Lantagnac, a French Canadian who sacrifices his heritage to achieve financial and social success. He weds an Anglican wife, who, though she converts to Catholicism, is intensely proud of her own English heritage. When Jules, at mid-life, suffers a crisis of faith and attempts to return to his French-speaking roots, his wife separates from him. Jules also risks his position in parliament by fighting against the elimination of French education in Ontario. Thus Groulx demonstrates both the cultural and the political odds against French-speaking Canadians, and, according to Senese, symbolically portrays "the disastrous 'mixed marriage' of French and English in the Canadian Confederation."

Groulx's only other novel, 1932's *Au Cap Blomidon,* "was far less didactic and controversial" than *The Iron Wedge,* "but no less popular," reported Senese. This book relates the story of Jean Berube, a young man of Acadian descent, whose ancestors had fled Nova Scotia for Quebec during the Acadian deportations of 1755. To fulfill a condition of his inheritance, Jean travels to Nova Scotia to reclaim the family homestead. Senese called *Au Cap Blomidon* "a platform on which Groulx could display his concerns about national survival, pride, and integrity. It also allowed him to expound at length on the virtue of struggle to achieve national strength and self-reliance."

In addition to his many writings, Groulx supported the Quebec nationalist movement in many other ways. He joined the *Ligue des Droits du Francais,* the political group which founded the magazine *L'Action francaise.* Groulx himself founded the *Institut d'Histoire de l'Amerique Francaise* in 1946, and edited its periodical, the *Revue.* He also lectured on French Canadian nationalism at universities and on radio and television. Groulx remained active until his death in 1967 at the age of eighty-nine; after his death he was honored by Quebec with a state funeral and an official day of mourning. Many streets, the seminary school at which he studied, and a subway station in Montreal now bear his name as a tribute to him.

BIOGRAPHICAL/CRITICAL SOURCES:

BOOKS

Dictionary of Literary Biography, Volume 68: *Canadian Writers, 1920-1959, First Series,* Gale, 1988.
Giguere, Georges-Emile, *Lionel Groulx: Biographie,* Bellarmin, 1978.
Groulx, Lionel, *Mes Memoires* (four volumes), Fides, 1970-74.

PERIODICALS

L'Action Nationale, June, 1968.
Revue d'Histoire de l'Amerique Francaise, December, 1978.*

—*Sketch by Elizabeth Wenning*

*   *   *

GROVE, Frederick Philip
  See GREVE, Felix Paul (Berthold Friedrich)

*   *   *

GUEVREMONT, (Marianne) Germaine   1893-1968

PERSONAL: Born April 16, 1893, in Saint-Jerome, Quebec, Canada; died August 21, 1968; daughter of Joseph-Jerome (a lawyer) and Valentine (a painter; maiden name, Labelle) Grignon; married Hyacinthe Guevremont, May 24, 1916; children: Louise, Marthe, Jean, Lucile, Marcelle. *Education:* Attended convent schools and Loretto Abbey, Toronto. *Religion:* Catholic.

CAREER: Novelist and scriptwriter. *Le Courrier de Sorel,* Quebec, associate editor, 1928-35; *Gazette,* Montreal, correspondent from 1935; *L'oeil,* Montreal, columnist, 1940-42; *Paysana,* Montreal, member of editorial staff, 1942; *Le nouveau journal,* Montreal, columnist, 1961-62. Lectured throughout Quebec.

MEMBER: Academie Canadienne-Francaise, PEN, Societe des Ecrivains Canadiens (head of secretariat, 1938-47), Centre du Canada Francaise (former president), Royal Society of Canada (fellow, 1961).

AWARDS, HONOURS: Prix Duvernay, 1945, and Prix Sully-Olivier de Serres, Paris, and Prix David, Quebec, both 1947, all for *Le Survenant;* medal from Academie Canadienne-Francaise, 1947, for *Marie-Didace;* Governor General's Award for literature, 1951, for *The Outlander;* D.L., University of Laval, 1952; Canada Council arts fellowship, 1965-66; Centennial medal.

WRITINGS:

FICTION

En pleine terre (short stories), Editions Paysana (Montreal), 1942, enlarged edition, 1946.
Le Survenant (novel), Beauchemin (Montreal), 1945, translation by Eric Sutton published in *The Outlander,* Whittlesey House (New York City), 1950.
Marie-Didace (novel), Beauchemin, 1947, revised, 1948, translation by Sutton published in *The Outlander.*
The Outlander (collection of Guevremont's two novels), translation by Sutton, introduction by Anthony Mollica, Whittlesey House, and McGraw Hill (Toronto), 1950, published in England as *Monk's Reach,* Evans (London), 1950.

PLAYS

Une Grosse nouvelle, Montreal Repertory Theatre, 1938, adapted for television, Radio-Canada, 1954.
Le Survenant, au chenal du moine [and] *Marie-Didace* (radio play; based on her novels of the same names), Radio-Canada, 1951, adapted for television, Radio-Canada, 1954-1960.
L'adieu aux illes, Radio-Canada, 1968.

Contributor to periodicals, including *Amerique francaise, Bulletin des agriculteurs, Cahiers de l'Academie Canadienne-Francaise, Chatelaine, Le Devoir, Liaison, Le mond Francaise, Le petit journal, La revue moderne, La revue populaire, Nouveau Journal,* and *Samedi.*

SIDELIGHTS: Novelist Germaine Guevremont was a popular writer who focused on life in rural Canada. Her portraits of the *habitants* living within the region of islands

and inlets near Quebec's St. Lawrence River marked her as one of the last of a generation of writers idealizing rural existence. Guevremont received several awards for her novels *Le Suvremont* and *Marie-Didace,* both of which gained an additional following after she adapted them for radio and television broadcast in the 1950s.

Guevremont was born in Saint-Jerome, Quebec, into a creative middle-class household. Both her father, an attorney who wrote articles and poetry as a hobby, and her mother, a painter, inspired their young daughter. In addition, her cousin, Claude-Henri Grignon, was a successful novelist who provided encouragement to her budding literary efforts. After attending convent schools as a child, Guevremont was sent to study at Loretto Abbey in Toronto at the age of 18; when she returned to Quebec in 1912, she took a job as a secretary, meanwhile publishing her first article.

Four years later, Guevremont married and accompanied her husband to his rural hometown village of Sorel, where he worked in a family-run business. The couple lived there for fifteen years before moving to Montreal. There Guevremont resumed working as a secretary, while also contributing numerous articles about her experiences in Sorel to the Canadian magazine *Paysana.* These articles would form the basis for her first book, *En pleine terre.*

In her short story collection *En pleine terre,* Guevremont creates an idealized, fictional world based on her experiences on the Sorel Islands. While praised for her use of colorful native speech and charming descriptions of place, the work contained little of the social significance increasingly of interest to the modern reader. While reviews were generally favorable, Guevremont's book received scant attention from critics when it was first published in 1942.

However, with the publication of her first novel, *Le Survenant,* in 1945, Guevremont soon achieved international popularity among French-language readers, both in her native Canada and in Paris. The first part of an intended trilogy, *Le Survenant* introduces readers to the Beauchemins, a tightly woven, rural family that faces extinction while confronting an increasingly modernizing world. The novel's setting is the period directly preceding World War I; when a stranger breaks into the family's isolated world, the Beauchemins—as well as the rest of the community—are thrown into a state of disruption and confusion that mirrors that of the Western world at the dawn of the industrial age. Guevremont's use of a subtle irony throughout the novel helps to suggest the inevitable demise of the life she so lovingly portrayed.

Marie-Didace followed *Le Survenant* in 1947. The second novel in Guevremont's planned trilogy, it would ultimately be followed only by the single chapter, "Le plomb dans l'aile," which appeared in *Cahiers de l'Academie*

Canadienne-Francaise in 1959. *Marie-Didace* describes the extinction of the Beauchemin family's male line with the birth of Marie-Didace, and the community's ability to rally into the modern era despite hardships. The novel received praise from critics, prompting the English translation of both novels. Published together as *The Outlander,* Guevremont's translated work received additional awards. While her works gained repeated recognition after she adapted both novels for broadcast on CBC radio and television, they gradually fell out of favor in the wake of the trend towards novels incorporating a more urban-based realism into a dramatic plot, characteristics absent from Guevremont's gentle portrayals of country life.

BIOGRAPHICAL/CRITICAL SOURCES:

BOOKS

Dictionary of Literary Biography, Volume 68: *Canadian Writers, 1920-1959, First Series,* Gale, 1988, pp. 160-63.
Duquette, Jean Pierre, *Germaine Guevremont: une route, une maison,* University Press of Montreal, 1973.
Leclerc, Rita, *Germaine Guevremont,* Fides (Montreal and Paris), 1963.
Roy, Paul-Emile, *Etudes litteraires: Germaine Guevremont,* Meridian (Montreal), 1989.
Urbas, Jeanett, *From "Thirty Acres" to Modern Times,* McGraw-Hill Ryerson (Toronto), 1976, pp. 25-31.

PERIODICALS

Cahiers de l'Academie Canadienne-Francais, Volume 14, 1972, pp. 33-43.
Chantelaine, April, 1967, pp. 31-33, 84, 86, 88.
Critere, January 1974, pp. 11-18.
Globe & Mail, April 13, 1946, p. 9.
La Presse, February 3, 1968, pp. 12-15.*

* * *

GUNNARS, Kristjana 1948-

PERSONAL: Born March 19, 1948, in Reykjavik, Iceland; emigrated to Canada; daughter of Gunnar (a scientist) and Tove (an artist; maiden name, Christensen) Bodvarsson; married Charles Kang 1967, (separated, 1980); children: Eyvindur Kang. *Education:* Oregon State University, B.A., 1973; University of Saskatchewan, M.A., 1978; doctoral study at University of Manitoba.

ADDRESSES: Office—Turnstone Press, 607-100 Arthur St., Winnipeg, Manitoba R3B 1H3.

CAREER: High School Teacher in Althyduskolinn, Eidum, Iceland, 1974-75; University of Regina, Regina, Saskatchewan, instructor in twentieth-century literature,

1979; *Iceland Reviews,* Reykjavik, editorial assistant, 1980-81; free-lance writer, editor, and translator, 1981—. Juror of Manitoba Arts Council, 1983-84.

MEMBER: PEN, Writers' Union of Canada, Manitoba Writers Guild, Association of Canadian Television and Radio Artists, Composers Authors and Publishers Association of Canada.

AWARDS, HONOURS: Ontario Arts Council Awards, 1981, 1984; Manitoba Arts Council Awards, 1983, 1985; Alberta Foundation for the Literary Arts Award, 1986, 1987; runner-up, CBC Literary Prize for poetry, 1988; McNally Robinson Prize and Manitoba Book of the Year, both 1989, for *The Prowler.*

WRITINGS:

POETRY

Settlement Poems I, Turnstone Press (Winnipeg), 1980.
Settlement Poems II, Turnstone Press, 1980.
One-Eyed Moon Maps (poems), Press Porcepic, 1981.
Wake-Pick Poems, House of Anansi (Toronto), 1982.
The Night Workers of Ragnarok, Press Porcepic, 1985.
Carnival of Longing, Turnstone, 1989.

FICTION

The Axe's Edge (stories), Press Porcepic, 1983.
The Prowler (novel), Red Deer College Press (Red Deer, Alberta), 1989.
The Guest House and Other Stories, House of Anansi, 1992.
The Substance of Forgetting, Red Deer College Press, 1992.

EDITOR

The Whale and Other Icelandic Folktales, translation by Helga Miller and George Hauser, Queenston House, 1984.
Crossing the River: Essays in Honour of Margaret Laurence, Turnstone, 1988.
Unexpected Fictions: New Icelandic Canadian Writing, Turnstone, 1989.

OTHER

(Translator) Finnbogi Gudmundsson, *Stephan G. Stephansson: In Retrospect, Seven Essays,* Menningarsjodur, 1982.
Zero Hour (nonfiction), Red Deer College Press, 1991.

Work represented in anthologies, including *Sundogs,* edited by Robert Kroetsch, Coteau Books, 1981; *The Icelanders,* edited by D. Arnason and M. Olito, Turnstone Press, 1981; *Draft,* edited by Dennis Cooley, Turnstone Press, 1981; *The New Oxford Book of Canadian Verse,* edited by Margaret Atwood, Oxford University Press, 1982;

Canadian Poetry Now, edited by Ken Norris, House of Anansi, 1984.

Contributor to magazines in the United States, Canada, and Iceland.

Member of editorial board of *Icelandic Canadian.* Cofounder Gunnars and Campbell, a publishing house devoted to translation.

WORK IN PROGRESS: Spitcrag, a novel, for House of Anansi; a biography of Stephan G. Stephansson; translating *Af Manna Voeldum* (a novel by Alfrun Gunnlaugsdottir), *Bref til Laru* (a novel by Thorbergur Thordarson), and *Snaran* (a novel by Jakobina Sigurdardottir).

SIDELIGHTS: Kristjana Gunnars once told *CA:* "Although I have been writing poems and short stories for as far back as I can remember, I did not think of publication and writing as a career until the late 1970's in Saskatchewan. The Saskatchewan Writers' Guild influenced me to take the first steps in the direction of professionalism. One of the main motivations for my work has been a sense of dislocation and an attempt to bridge the cultural gap between North America and Scandinavia. Perhaps I felt divided and wanted to become whole through writing about the people I had left. The circumstance of the immigrant in North American society also interested me. Often people who have migrated to this continent from other countries are accused of being other than what they are. The problem of stereotypes and prejudices hinders the cultural exchange that should be occurring here, and I wanted to destroy some of the images I found current in Canada about Scandinavians in general and Icelanders in particular. Aside from all this I am really mostly working out of a delight in narrative poetry and a love for Scandinavian cultures—in particular the Danish and Icelandic peoples to whom I feel closely bound—and the joy of language.

"For me, writing is a constant attempt to counteract the deadening forces of twentieth-century life. The sterile destructiveness of the modern age has led me to seek out possible alternative meaning in my Scandinavian roots. The old Icelandic rhythms and lore I know from my childhood strike at the heart of northern and western European cultures we have inherited in the New World and tell us something new about why the modern age is as it is. Much of my work deals with the migrations of the Icelanders into the New World because this provides me with a historical context for my own thoughts. I also believe much of the Scandinavian mentality today is a healthy one, and I mean to incorporate what I can of it into North American literature. The Nordic cultures of the past provide a powerful fascination with life when we seem continually pulled in the direction of non-life by contemporary events."

In *Settlement Poems I* and its counterpart, *Settlement Poems II,* Gunnars recreates the lives of a group of Icelandic pioneers who settled in Manitoba, in the last quarter of the nineteenth century. Based on journals and documents, the poems portray a people tough, resourceful, and superstitious. John S. Matthiasson, writing in the *Icelandic Canadian,* noted that "it is striking how Gunnars has been able to take such material and weave from it a fabric of flowing poetry that captures the dignity and pride which kept the spirit alive in bitterly trying times."

Employing Old Germanic meters and language spare in the use of adjectives and adverbs, Gunnar's volumes read like diaries written by the pioneers themselves. In a *CRNLE Reviews Journal* critique, Uma Parameswaran called the author's style "compelling, almost epic," George Johnston, writing in *Canadian Literature,* concurred, applying the term "heroic" to Gunnar's treatment. And *Icelandic Review* critic W. D. Valgardsson found *Settlement Poems* "mythic." "Many people write verse," he said, "but seldom, perhaps only once or twice in a generation, does a poet arise who has the power, like a magician, to create illusions which demand our attention. Kristjana Gunnars is one of those magicians. . . . She has reached back into the past and recreated, as art, the lives of the early Icelandic immigrants. In doing this she has both made the settlers human and understandable while also raising their lives to a mythic level."

Gunnars's 1989 collection, *Carnival of Longing,* is, according to Martin Ware in *Canadian Literature,* "a major departure" for Gunnars. As Bruce Whitman describes in *Books in Canada,* it takes as its subject "the poet's state of heart and mind during the absence of a lover." While Whitman finds the book "touching at times," he concludes that "one finally has the sense that the sequence is too protracted," and he complains that it is often repetitious and flat. Ware, however, has high praise for Gunnars's "haunting and elegant muse and love poems." For him, Gunnars "belongs to the number of those select poets in the record who have written about love and absence with finely honed poetic skills, emotional conviction, as well as a sophisticated awareness of the constraints that language throws in their way." In one poem, Gunnars explains what she writes about, namely "What cannot be said of desire/with desire."

Gunnars's award-winning first novel, *The Prowler,* is "an exemplar of feminist critical theory and of post-modern narrative convention, yet it is neither cerebral nor pedantic," according to John Moss's review in *Canadian Forum.* The novel tells the story of an Icelandic girl, but is really, as Gardar Baldvinsson explains in *Canadian Literature,* "the story of stories, a metastory." As Baldvinsson reports, the unnamed, homeless protagonist is a voracious reader, and the reader of Gunnars's novel discovers that "prowling in the field of literature is prowling within one's self." The complexity of the novel, however, arises from its subversion of conventional narrative forms. For in telling "the story of fragmentation in an Icelandic girl's experience of growing up," John Moss asserts that the book's form mirrors its content. As Moss notes, the book has no page numbers and the story is told "in a succession of 167 sections . . . Gunnars prowls among the random pieces of her narrator's life; her narrator is a prowler in her own recollected life, and you, as reader, prowl the text as well, among discrete passages which seem to slide elliptically across the narrative plane." Yet the book remains "down to earth" for Moss: Gunnars "accedes to the function of art as an expression not of the intellect but of intuition . . . of the body itself."

Gunnars's second novel, *The Substance of Forgetting,* is also metafictional—a story about how we tell stories. It "explores the ways language, writing, and desire both define and confuse the meaning of individual existence and one's sense of self," claims Daniel Jones in *Books in Canada.* Jones writes that *The Substance of Forgetting* is "a philosophical novel" about a brief love affair "in which the action is mediated through contemporary theories of psychoanalysis, linguistics, and discursive practice." Moreover, he points out that the affair, between an English speaking Canadian and a Quebecoise separatist, is also "a metaphor for Canadian unity." While Jones finds that the stories in Gunnars second story collection, *The Guest House and Other Stories,*—which was reviewed in the same article—"fail in comparison" to the novel, the writing talent evident in both volumes is praiseworthy and leads him to call her "one of the finest prose stylists writing in Canada."

Like her two novels, Gunnars's nonfiction account of her father's struggle with cancer can be classified as a postmodern text. Keith Garebian, writing in *Quill and Quire,* claims that "Like her novel *The Prowler, Zero Hour* consists of only a thin skin of a story stretched across a metaphor." The metaphor, as Stephan Scobie explains in his uniquely structured review of Gunnars's book in *Canadian Literature,* is "Zero," and Gunnars makes use of mathematical, literary, and theoretical models of "zero" in order to explore and come to terms with the death of her father. The text, too, is densely allusive, as Scobie notes references to Roland Barthes, Ernest Hemingway, Andrew Marvell, and Gibbons. Scobie also claims that Gunnars "is on her guard against any sentimentality" and "searches for a style so clean, so pure, so ascetic that it will exclude any hint of sweetness. An emotion so utterly personal can only be expressed in a style of blank impersonality." He adds her style aspires "towards innocence. Towards zero" and everything in the book moves towards an "emptiness," towards an absence, which is ultimately "im-

possible to maintain." There is, then, says Scobie, "no pure loss. Thus writing, always, moves us away from zero."

Gunnars has also edited a volume of Icelandic folktales, *The Whale and Other Icelandic Folktales,* a volume of short stories by Icelandic Canadian writers, *Unexpected Fictions,* and a critical volume of essays about Canadian writer, Margaret Laurence, *Crossing the River.* A reviewer in *Books in Canada* found that a number of the eight stories in *Unexpected Fictions* were "simply good stories" that would be suitable for inclusion in any number of short fiction collections and each, as Gunnars notes in her introduction, "share a mainstream Canadian sensibility." The essays Gunnars has collected in *Crossing the River,* focus long overdue attention on a little studied—but major—Canadian author, according to Heather Murray's review of the volume in *Canadian Literature.* Murray reports that the essays present a range of approaches to Laurence's work—feminist, semantic, narrative, genre criticism, postcolonial—and as such hint "of work to come" and are a "fitting tributary to Margaret Laurence's double-flowing river."

BIOGRAPHICAL/CRITICAL SOURCES:

BOOKS

Feminist Companion to Literature in English, Yale University Press (New Haven, CT), 1990, p. 468.

PERIODICALS

Arts Manitoba, fall, 1982.
Books in Canada, March, 1984; January, 1990, p. 20; June-July, 1990, pp. 42-43; February, 1993, p. 45.
Canadian Forum, September, 1990, p. 30-31.
Canadian Literature, spring, 1982; summer, 1991, pp. 207-08; autumn, 1991, pp. 173-75; winter, 1992, pp. 157-57, 194-96.
Connections Two: Writers and the Land, Manitoba School Library Audio Visual Association, 1983.
CRNLE Reviews Journal, December, 1982.
Icelandic Canadian, summer, 1981, autumn, 1982.
Iceland Review, April, 1980.
Manitoba Heritage Review, spring, 1984.
Morgunbladid, August 16, 1981.
Newert Review, September, 1981.
Poetry Canada Review, summer, 1982.
Prairie Fire, winter, 1984.
Quill and Quire, April, 1991, p. 33; December, 1992, p. 20.
Winnipeg Free Press, February 11, 1984.
Writers News Manitoba, Volume 3, number 2, 1981.

GUSTAFSON, Ralph (Barker) 1909-

PERSONAL: Surname is pronounced "Gus-*taf*-son"; born August 16, 1909, in Lime Ridge, Quebec, Canada; son of Carl Otto (a photographer) and Gertrude (Barker) Gustafson; married Elisabeth Renninger, October 3, 1958. *Education:* Oxford University, B.A. (with honors), 1933, M.A., 1963. *Avocational interests:* Music, including a collection of piano records dating from the inception of the gramophone; travel.

ADDRESSES: Home—P.O. Box 172, North Hatley, Quebec, Canada J0B 2CO.

CAREER: St. Alban's School, Brockville, Ontario, master, 1934; lived in London, England, 1934-38; British Information Service, 1942-46; writer in New York City, 1965-66; Bishop's University, Lennoxville, Quebec, lecturer, 1963-64, assistant professor, 1965-66, associate professor, 1967-71, professor of English, 1971-77, poet-in-residence. Poetry delegate to United Kingdom, 1972, 1985, to U.S.S.R., 1976, to Washington, DC, 1977, and to Italy, 1981-82. Music critic, Canadian Broadcasting Corp. (CBC), 1960—.

MEMBER: Keble Association, Oxford (life member), League of Canadian Poets (charter member), Writers Union of Canada, Quebec Society for the Promotion of English Language & Literature, Federation English Writers of Quebec.

AWARDS, HONOURS: Prix David, Quebec government, 1935, for *The Golden Chalice;* Canada Council senior fellowship, 1959-60, 1971-72; Borestone Mountain Poetry Award, 1961, for *Rocky Mountain Poems;* D.Litt., Mount Allison University, 1973; Governor General's Award for Poetry, 1974, and A.J.M. Smith Award, Michigan State University, 1974, both for *Fire on Stone;* D.C.L., Bishop's University, 1977; Queen's Silver Jubilee Medal, 1978.

WRITINGS:

POETRY

The Golden Chalice, Nicholson & Watson, 1935.
Alfred the Great, M. Joseph, 1937.
Epithalamium in Time of War, privately printed, 1941.
Lyrics Unromantic, privately printed, 1942.
Flight into Darkness, Pantheon, 1944.
Rocky Mountain Poems (also see below), Klanak Press, 1960.
Rivers among Rocks, McClelland & Stewart, 1960.
Sift in an Hourglass, McClelland & Stewart, 1966.
Ixion's Wheel, McClelland & Stewart, 1969.
Theme and Variations for Sounding Brass (also see below), privately printed, 1972.
Selected Poems, McClelland & Stewart, 1972.
Fire on Stone, McClelland & Stewart, 1974.

Corners in the Glass, McClelland & Stewart, 1977.
Soviet Poems (also see below), Turnstone Press, 1978.
Sequences (includes *Rocky Mountain Poems, Theme and Variations for Sounding Brass, Soviet Poems,* and portions of other books), Black Moss Press, 1979.
Landscape with Rain, McClelland & Stewart, 1980.
Conflicts of Spring, McClelland & Stewart, 1980.
Nine Poems, League of Canadian Poets, 1980.
Dentelle/Indented, The Press at Colorado College, 1982.
Gradations of Grandeur, Sono Nis Press, 1982.
The Moment Is All: Selected Poems 1944-1983, McClelland & Stewart, 1983.
Solidarnosc: Prelude, Progressive Publications, 1983.
Impromptus, Oolichan Books, 1984.
Directives of Autumn, McClelland & Stewart, 1984.
At the Ocean's Verge, Black Swan Books, 1984.
Twelve Landscapes, Shaw Street Press, 1985.
Manipulations on Greek Themes, Roger Ascham Press, 1986.
Collected Poems, Sono Nis Press, 1987.
Winter Prophecies, McClelland & Stewart, 1987.
The Celestial Corkscrew and Other Strategies, Mosaic Press, 1989.
Shadows in the Grass, McClelland & Stewart, 1991.
Configurations at Midnight, ECW Press, 1992.
Tracks in the Snow, Oolichan Books, 1994.
Collected Poems Vol. 3, Sono Nis Press, 1994.

Poetry is also included in numerous anthologies. Contributor of poetry to literary magazines in Canada and abroad. Has recorded his poetry for the Library of Congress in Washington, DC, and for the League of Canadian Poets with music by Richard Arnell.

EDITOR

Anthology of Canadian Poetry, Penguin, 1942.
A Little Anthology of Canadian Poets, New Directions, 1943.
Canadian Accent, Penguin, 1944.
The Penguin Book of Canadian Verse, Penguin, 1958, 4th edition, 1984.

Also editor of Canadian poetry issue of *Voices,* 1943.

OTHER

Poetry and Canada: A Guide to Reading, Canadian Legion Educational Services, 1945.
The Brazen Tower (short stories), Roger Ascham Press, 1975.
The Vivid Air (short stories), Sono Nis Press, 1980.
A Literary Friendship: The Correspondence of Ralph Gustafson and W. W. E. Ross, edited by Bruce Whiteman, ECW Press, 1984.
Plummets and Other Partialities (essays), Sono Nis Press, 1987.

Short stories included in *The Best American Short Stories,* 1948, 1950, *Canadian Short Stories,* 1960, and *A Book of Canadian Stories,* 1962. Contributor to *Oxford Quarterly of Music* and of short stories and critical articles to literary periodicals and journals in Canada, the United States, and abroad.

SIDELIGHTS: Ralph Gustafson, according to David McFarlane in a *Books in Canada* article, "can be ranked among the very best of our poets." Gustafson is often praised for the beauty of the imagery in his poems and for his skillful and musical use of the English language. In a review of *Flight into Darkness,* Gustafson's 1944 collection of poetry, Darrel Abel of *Poetry* wrote: "[Gustafson's] poems about the war are the excellently pointed and finely sympathetic observations of an imaginative bystander. He has a poignant and well controlled elegiac note." In a *Springfield Republican* article, C. M. Sauer said that *Flight into Darkness* "contains a sensitive Canadian's reactions to this present day world—reactions passionately, ironically and realistically expressed. This is a volume for readers who delight in discovering modern poetry with singing strength, original phrasing, excellent technique, and fullness of vocabulary."

Commenting in *Quill & Quire* on a lengthy poem included in *Sequences,* Rosemary Aubert says that "the rich imagery (especially images of taste and smell), and the sustained tone make this a poem of beauty reminiscent of some of Pound's cantos." Similarly, Barry Dempster, also writing in *Quill & Quire,* states that in *Landscape with Rain* Gustafson "is in fine form, probing beyond history and mythology to the present imbued with all the magic of the past. . . . Gustafson is a cultured man, a complete poet." As a *Contemporary Literary Criticism* contributor notes, the poet may not have the wide reading he deserves, possibly because of his "use of unorthodox syntax, archaic words and phrases, and elaborate metaphors," but he is nonetheless "regarded by many scholars as a witty, passionate, and erudite poet who has made a significant contribution to Canadian literature."

Gustafson has also been a music critic for the Canadian Broadcasting Corporation, and his interest in music is evident in his collection *At the Ocean's Verge,* which is laced with musical allusions and influences. Fraser Sutherland notes in the Toronto *Globe and Mail* that Gustafson sometimes gives musical titles such as "Rondo in Triads" and "Gothic Fugue" to his poems, in which he plays "possibly piccolo in the short lines, bassoon in the long ones," producing in some cases "mellifluous and contrapuntal charms."

Critics agree that Gustafson's most significant poetry is that which he has written since 1960. Louis Dudek of the *Globe and Mail* finds that the poet's essays—"the intellec-

tual counterpart of [his] poetry"—follow and reflect this same pattern. Writing in *Dictionary of Literary Biography,* Wendy Robbins comments that *Flight into Darkness,* a collection of poems written from 1936 to 1943, mirrors "a period of dislocation and change in Gustafson's life. His faith in the goodness of nature and the harmony of the human, natural, and divine was eroded by exposure to the Depression and the war," as well as his mother's long, losing struggle with cancer.

Robbins points out in closing that "Gustafson's development as a poet provides a miniature history of Canadian literature, moving from outdated imitation of romantic nature poets, through a transitional phase of dependency on the early modernists, to a more fully independent yet still richly eclectic style, his late work riveted unselfconsciously on Canadian experience and on the universal cycles of life and death which Canada's four sharply defined seasons seem to magnify. . . . His unified but constantly evolving vision, articulated with impeccable artistry, has staked for him a valid and enduring claim among the foremost ranks of contemporary Canadian poets."

BIOGRAPHICAL/CRITICAL SOURCES:

BOOKS

Contemporary Literary Criticism, Volume 36, Gale, 1986.
Dictionary of Literary Biography, Volume 88: *Canadian Writers: 1920-1959,* Gale, 1989.
Keitner, Wendy Roberts, *Ralph Gustafson,* Hall, 1979.
Klink, C., editor, *Literary History of Canada,* University of Toronto Press, 1965.
McCarthy, Dermot, *Ralph Gustafson,* E.C.W. Press, 1987.

PERIODICALS

Books in Canada, April, 1980.
Globe and Mail (Toronto), January 5, 1985; March 5, 1988.
New York Times, February 25, 1945.
Poetry, May, 1945.
Quill & Quire, January, 1980; May, 1980.
Springfield Republican, February 19, 1945.

*   *   *

GUY, Ray 1939-

PERSONAL: Born April 22, 1939, in Come-by-Chance, Newfoundland, Canada; son of George Hynes and Alice Louise Guy; married Katherine Housser, 1975; children: Anne, Rachel. *Education:* Attended Memorial University, St. John's, Newfoundland, Canada, 1957; Ryerson Polytechnic Institute, received degree in journalism, 1963.

ADDRESSES: Office—c/o Breakwater Books, 277 Duckworth St., P.O. Box 2188, St. John's, Newfoundland, Canada A1C 6E6.

CAREER: Freelance journalist, short story writer, playwright, and actor. *Evening Telegraph,* St. John's, Newfoundland, Canada, began as general reporter, became writer of commentary, 1963-75; *Sunday Express,* St. John's, reporter.

AWARDS, HONOURS: Canadian National Newspaper Award for Feature Writing, 1967, for article "No more 'round the mountain We'll be riding' CN busses," published in *Evening Telegraph;* Stephen Leacock Medal for Humour, 1977, for *That Far Greater Bay;* inducted into Canadian News Hall of Fame; Canadian National Magazine Awards for humorous writing, 1980 and 1984; Newfoundland Arts Council Award, 1985.

WRITINGS:

You May Know Them As Sea Urchins, Ma'am (columns), edited by Eric Norman, Breakwater Books (Portugal Cove, Newfoundland), 1975, revised edition, 1985.

That Far Greater Bay (columns), edited by Norman, Breakwater Books, 1976, revised edition, 1985.

Outhouses of the East (local history), photographs by Sherman Hines, West House (Halifax, Nova Scotia), 1978.

Beneficial Vapours (columns), edited by Norman, Jesperson Press (St. John's, Newfoundland), 1981.

An Heroine for Our Time (fiction), Harry Cuff Publications (St. John's), 1983.

Newfoundland/Labrador, with photographs by Hines, Nimbus Publishing (Halifax), 1984.

This Dear and Fine Country, Breakwater Books (St. John's), 1985.

Young Triffie's Been Made Away With (play), Resource Centre for the Arts (St. John's), 1985.

Author of plays for radio and television, including "Old Skipper's" monologues for CBC-TV program *All around the Circle* and episodes of CBC-TV's *Up at Ours* series. Contributor to magazines and newspapers, including *Atlantic Insight, Newfoundland Quarterly,* and *This Week.* Work represented in several anthologies, including *Baffles of Wind and Tide: An Anthology of Newfoundland Poetry, Prose, and Drama,* edited by Clyde Rose, Breakwater Books (Portugal Cove), 1973; *The Blasty Bough,* edited by Rose, Breakwater Books (Portugal Cove), 1976; and *Landings: A Newfoundland and Labrador Literature Anthology,* edited by Norman and others, Breakwater Books (St. John's), 1984.

SIDELIGHTS: Journalist and author Ray Guy enjoyed a long association with the *Evening Telegraph* in St. John's, Newfoundland, where he produced dozens of columns espousing his views on a variety of topics, from politics and social concerns to observances of events in everyday life. Guy's columns, often punctuated with his satirical sense of humor, earned him several important awards for humorous writing, including the Stephen Leacock Medal for Humour and induction into the Canadian News Hall of Fame. *Dictionary of Literary Biography* contributor W. H. New described Guy as a "people-watcher and eavesdropper" who has a "keen eye and a good ear. Some of his essays deal with the meanings of words, the origins of phrases, the strength that Newfoundlanders have in their use of strong language."

Guy's first two books, *You May Know Them As Sea Urchins, Ma'am* and *That Far Greater Bay,* and another publication, *Beneficial Vapours,* are collections of his *Evening Telegraph* columns and other writings contributed elsewhere, all edited by Eric Norman. These columns represent what is considered the best of Guy's writings and showcase his cynical commentary targeted, primarily, on Newfoundland politics. Quoting the columnist in a Toronto *Globe and Mail* article, Joan Marie Sullivan related one of Guy's typical comments on the economy: " 'The Newfoundland economy took an unexpected upswing this week,' Guy wrote in an Express column earlier this year, 'when the Minister of Finance found a $20 bill in an old pants pocket.' "

Guy's local government, however, is only one of the victims of his pen, as he frequently lambastes fashion and food trends, tourists, religious groups, and others in his own fashion. *Globe and Mail*'s Douglas Hill commented on the "rough, scratchy texture" of Guy's style, adding that "polish is unevenly applied or lacking altogether." Nevertheless, Hill opined, "the stuff has power, even eloquence, a wealth of homely charm, and sometimes beauty and tears. . . . Guy is a curious uneven mix of hopeless idealism, amused anger and sharp cynicism. He's a bit of an acquired taste, but addictive."

A multi-talented writer, Guy has also issued a book of fiction, *An Heroine for Our Time,* a fable about a giant child who is exploited for commercial purposes. In addition, Guy's credits list several plays, including *Young Triffie's Been Made Away With,* a black comedy murder mystery he was asked to write by the Resource Centre for the Arts in St. John's, Newfoundland. Guy told Sullivan in her *Globe and Mail* interview: "For Triffie, the money was in place, and they approached me about writing something. My wife reads 10 or 12 trashy novels a week, and I thought I could plagiarize a plot, so I blurted out that I would do a murder mystery! I knew nothing about how things work on stage." Despite Guy's inexperience, *Triffie* enjoyed a provincial tour and subsequent production in Toronto. He has since been commissioned by the Centre to write another play. Guy told Sullivan he would be "more intimidated" by writing plays if he were "more serious about it, but I just want people to get their ticket price out of it, and whatever they paid the babysitter."

Although he joined the staff of St. John's *Sunday Express* for a short time after leaving the *Evening Telegram,* Guy finds freelancing better suits his creative style, telling Sullivan he now has "the freedom to attempt almost anything." Freedom seems to suit both the writer and his critics, as his writing has been widely praised for its skill and breadth. As New summarized in the *Dictionary of Literary Biography:* "The range of Guy's topics is immense. . . . Seemingly any subject can provide him the core of one of his columns. What makes his writing stand out is his ver-

bal dexterity. He creates moods and situations and draws miniature character sketches with economy and skill. Above all Guy is a very funny man."

BIOGRAPHICAL/CRITICAL SOURCES:

BOOKS

Dictionary of Literary Biography, Volume 60: *Canadian Writers since 1960, Second Series,* Gale, 1987. pp. 106-09.

PERIODICALS

Globe and Mail (Toronto), November 3, 1985; April 23, 1988.*

H

HAIG-BROWN, Roderick (Langmere) 1908-1976

PERSONAL: Born February 21, 1908, in Lancing, Sussex, England; died October 9, 1976, in Campbell River, British Columbia, Canada; son of Alan Roderick (an Army officer) and Violet M. (Pope) Haig-Brown; married Anne Elmore (a high school librarian), January 20, 1934; children: Valerie Joan, Mary Charlotte, Alan Roderick, Evelyn Celia. *Education:* Attended Charterhouse School, Godalming, England.

ADDRESSES: Home—2250 Campbell River Rd., Campbell River, British Columbia V9W 4N7, Canada. *Agent*—Harold Ober Associates, Inc., 40 East 49th St., New York, NY 10017.

CAREER: Naturalist and author. Logger, guide, fisherman, and trapper in Washington State and British Columbia, 1926-30, and 1931-34; Family and Children's Court, Campbell River, judge, 1941-75. University of Victoria (British Columbia), chancellor, 1971-73. Federal Electoral Boundary Commission, commissioner, 1965-66, member, 1972-73, and 1975; International Salmon Commission, member, 1970—. Member, Federal Saltwater Sports Advisory Committee. Consultant, National Film Board, Canadian Broadcasting Company, and Vancouver Public Aquarium. *Military service:* Canadian Army, 1939-45; served overseas; became major; assigned to Royal Canadian Mounted Police, 1944.

MEMBER: Authors Guild, Canadian Writers Association, Society of Authors.

AWARDS, HONOURS: Canadian Library Association medals, 1947, for *Starbuck Valley Winter,* and 1963, for *The Whale People;* Governor General's Award, 1948, for *Saltwater Summer;* LL.D., University of British Columbia, 1952; Crandall Conservation Trophy, 1955; National Award in Letters, University of Alberta, 1956; Barien Library Award, 1964, for *Fisherman's Fall;* Vicky Metcalf Award (juvenile writing), 1965; Conservation Award, Trout Unlimited, 1965; J. B. Harkin Award, 1977.

WRITINGS:

Silver: The Life Story of an Atlantic Salmon, A. & C. Black, 1931.
Pool and Rapid, J. Cape, 1932.
Ki-Yu: A Story of Panthers, Houghton, 1934, revised edition published as *Panther: The Story of a North American Mountain Lion,* Collins, 1967.
The Western Angler: An Account of Pacific Salmon and Western Trout in British Columbia, Derrydale, 1939.
Return to the River: The Story of the Chinook Run, Morrow, 1941.
Timber: A Novel of Pacific Coast Loggers, Morrow, 1942.
Starbuck Valley Winter, Morrow, 1943.
A River Never Sleeps (autobiography), Morrow, 1946.
Saltwater Summer, Morrow, 1948.
On the Highest Hill, Morrow, 1949.
Measure of the Year, Morrow, 1950.
Fisherman's Spring, Morrow, 1951.
Mounted Police Patrol, Morrow, 1954.
Fisherman's Winter, Morrow, 1954.
Captain of the Discovery: The Story of Captain George Vancouver, Macmillan, 1956.
Fabulous Fishing in Latin America: Your Guide to the 60 Best Fishing Areas in Mexico, the Caribbean, Central and South America, Pan American World Airways, 1956.
Fisherman's Summer, Morrow, 1959.
(Contributor) *The Face of Canada,* Clarke, Irwin, 1959.
The Farthest Shores, Longmans, Green, 1960.
The Living Land: An Account of the Natural Resources of British Columbia, Macmillan, 1961.
Fur and Gold, Longmans, Green, 1962.

The Whale People, Collins, 1962.
(Contributor) Anthony Netboy, editor, *The Pacific Northwest,* Doubleday, 1963.
A Primer of Fly-Fishing, Morrow, 1964.
Fisherman's Fall, Morrow, 1964.
(Contributor) J. M. S. Careless and R. Craig Brown, editors, *The Canadians,* Macmillan, 1967.
(With Ralph Wahl) *Come Wade the River,* Superior Publishing, 1971.
The Salmon, Fisheries Marine Service, 1974.
The Master and His Fish: From the World of Roderick Haig-Brown, University of Washington Press, 1981.
Writings and Reflections: From the World of Roderick Haig-Brown, University of Washington Press, 1982.

Also contributor to numerous periodicals, including *Atlantic Monthly, Sports Illustrated,* and *Life.*

SIDELIGHTS: Roderick Haig-Brown was well known for his numerous writings about the Canadian wilderness. In books such as *Fisherman's Spring* and *The Living Land,* he mixed scientific facts with almost poetic descriptions of his adopted country; in novels such as *Saltwater Summer* and *On the Highest Hill,* Haig-Brown explored the complex, and sometimes unhealthy, relationship between man and nature. All of Haig-Brown's work stressed the need for conservation of natural resources, whether these resources be wildlife or the land itself. In an article for *Canadian Children's Literature,* Heather Kirk noted that the author "challenged children to think hard about life and to feel profoundly by presenting them with a complete view of the world to which they could relate which was exciting yet sobering."

BIOGRAPHICAL/CRITICAL SOURCES:

BOOKS

Dictionary of Literary Biography, Volume 88: *Canadian Writers, 1920-1959, Second Series,* Gale, 1989, pp. 104-08.

PERIODICALS

British Columbia Library Quarterly, July, 1958.
Canadian Children's Literature, Number 51, 1988, pp. 25-42.
Globe and Mail (Toronto), June 22, 1991.

*　　*　　*

HAILEY, Arthur 1920-

PERSONAL: Born April 5, 1920, in Luton, England; immigrated to Canada, 1947, naturalized citizen (retaining British citizenship), 1952; son of George Wellington (a factory worker) and Elsie Mary (Wright) Hailey; married Joan Fishwick, 1944 (divorced, 1950); married Sheila Dunlop, July 28, 1951; children: (first marriage) Roger, John, Mark; (second marriage) Jane, Steven, Diane. *Education:* Attended elementary school in England. *Avocational interests:* Travel, reading, music, boat handling, fishing.

ADDRESSES: Home—Lyford Cay, P.O. Box N-7776, Nassau, Bahamas. *Office*—Seaway Authors Ltd., First Canadian Place-6000, P.O. Box 130, Toronto, Ontario, Canada M5X 1A4.

CAREER: Office boy in London, England, 1934-39; clerk in London, 1939; Maclean-Hunter Publishing Co., Toronto, Ontario, assistant editor of *Bus and Truck Transport,* 1947-49, editor, 1949-53; Trailmobile Canada Ltd., Toronto, sales promotion manager, 1953-56; full-time writer, 1956—. *Military service:* Royal Air Force, fighter pilot, 1939-47; served in Europe, the Middle East, and the Far East; became flight lieutenant.

MEMBER: Writers Guild of America, Authors League of America, Association of Canadian Television and Radio Artists (honorary life member), Lyford Cay Club (Bahamas).

AWARDS, HONOURS: Gold medal of Canadian Council of Authors and Artists, 1956; Best Canadian Playwright Award, 1957 and 1958; Emmy Award, c. 1957, for *No Deadly Medicine;* Doubleday Canadian Prize Novel Award, 1962, for *In High Places;* gold medal of Commonwealth Club of California, 1968, for *Airport.*

WRITINGS:

NOVELS

(With John Castle) *Flight into Danger* (based on *Zero Hour!,* film version of Hailey's television play *Flight into Danger*), Souvenir Press (London), 1958, published as *Runway Zero Eight,* Doubleday, 1959.
The Final Diagnosis (based on his television play *No Deadly Medicine*), Doubleday, 1959.
In High Places, Doubleday, 1962.
Hotel, Doubleday, 1965.
Airport, Doubleday, 1968.
Wheels, Doubleday, 1971.
The Moneychangers, Doubleday, 1975.
Overload, Doubleday, 1979.
Strong Medicine, Doubleday, 1984.
The Evening News, Doubleday, 1990.

OTHER

Flight into Danger (television play), CBC, 1956.
(With Hall Bartlett and John Champion) *Zero Hour!* (screenplay based on his television play *Flight into Danger*), Paramount, 1957.

Close-up on Writing for Television (collection of television plays), Doubleday, 1960.

Author of over twenty television plays, including *No Deadly Medicine*, 1957, and *Course for Collision*, 1962; performed on numerous programs, including *Westinghouse Studio One, Playhouse 90*, and *Kraft Theatre*.

All of Hailey's novels have appeared in foreign editions, and most have been published in as many as thirty-one languages.

ADAPTATIONS: Films based on Hailey's novels include *The Young Doctors*, based on *The Final Diagnosis*, United Artists, 1961; *Hotel*, Warner Brothers, 1967; *Airport*, Universal, 1969; *Wheels*, Universal, 1977; *The Moneychangers*, Paramount, 1977; and *Overload*. In addition, the films *Airport 1975, Airport 1977*, and *Concorde—Airport 1979*, although not based on Hailey's work, were produced as sequels to the original *Airport*.

SIDELIGHTS: Arthur Hailey's career as a professional writer began in 1955 when, on a business flight across Canada, he began to fantasize about what might happen if both the pilot and copilot suddenly became incapacitated—leaving him, a rather rusty World War II fighter pilot, the only person able to land the plane. It took Hailey just six evenings and two weekends to turn the daydream into his first television play, *Flight into Danger*. Being unfamiliar with the conventions of television writing, he wrote the play in standard theatrical form without camera directions; and not knowing anyone in the TV industry, he simply mailed it to "Script Department, Canadian Broadcasting Corp." The play reached Nathan Cohen, script editor of CBC's *General Motors Theatre*, who ironically noticed it amidst countless other unsolicited scripts precisely because of the peculiar style in which it was written. The initial broadcast on April 7, 1956, drew rave reviews and extraordinary viewer response; it was subsequently presented on networks in the United States and Great Britain where it was equally well received. Since then, Hailey's success as a writer for television and especially as a novelist has been phenomenal. He has had six consecutive best sellers, and several major motion pictures have been based on his books.

Strangely it is Hailey's success that has caused the most discourse among critics. In an attempt to explain the author's ability to turn out consistent best-sellers, some reviewers accuse him of writing "formula" or "programmed" novels, and others say that he sets out to write books that will make good films. Joseph McLellan outlines the supposed Hailey formula: "Start with something large and complicated, a business or institution that touches the lives of large numbers of people and is not fully understood by the public. Ideally, the subject should have a touch of glamour and some element of risk in its

routine activities. The writer takes the reader inside this subject, letting him see it from various points of view and tossing in an occasional little sermon on public responsibilities. Numerous characters are formed out of available material (cardboard will do nicely) and they are set in motion by a series of crises, small, medium, and large, which illustrate the nature and particularly the weaknesses of the activity that is the real subject (in a sense the real hero) of the book." And yet, if there is a formula that Hailey follows, it seems to have little effect on his readers who flock to the bookstores at the mere hint of a press release from his publisher. As Peter Andrews puts it: "Hailey's novels are such genuine publishing events that to criticize them is like putting the slug on the Rockettes. It's not going to change anything. No sooner is his contract inked than mighty lumberjacks start to make their axes ring. Paperback houses and book clubs fairly whimper to give him money while the work is still in progress, and Ross Hunter calls up the old actors' home to begin casting his next blockbuster. At the publication party itself the last deviled egg is still to be consumed when his book busts through on the best-seller list."

Most criticism Hailey takes philosophically; he admits that he prefers good reviews to bad, but concedes that the critics have made a few good points. He does, however, take offense at the charge that he writes programmed fiction. In an interview with Ned Smith, Hailey says: "The word formula is used frequently in reviews and commentaries. And I react to it. Maybe over-sensitively. But I feel that if the books I write are formulas, then why doesn't someone else take the same formula, if it's that evident? Well, it isn't a formula. As I see it, what I write is a cut, a profile of a section of the life and times in which we live. And just as some writers use a profile of an individual— one person— so I take a profile that involves the technology, the dilemmas, the shortcomings, the science of our time, and write about that." He is also quick to respond to those who accuse him of writing with the best-seller list in mind. He told Smith: "People say 'Hailey sets out to write, (a) a best seller, (b) something that book clubs will want, (c) to sell to the movies.' But I really don't think of these things. I pick a subject that interests me, one that I think will interest readers. I try to find something with a fairly basic common denominator, but there has to be some chemistry in me that arouses interest and enthusiasm, because if I haven't that myself, I can't translate it to the reader over the three years that I'm working on a book. But I don't try to outguess the best-seller lists or book clubs or movies. Because you can't outguess them all, and if I tried it, I'd fall flat on my face."

No doubt the formula accusations stem from certain characteristics that are evident in all of Hailey's writing: the meticulous attention to detail, the multiple plots and sub-plots, and his penchant for choosing as subjects monolithic structures (a hotel, an airport, the automobile industry) about which most people know little, but with which they are unquestionably fascinated. Hailey's ability to research a subject with unusual vigor and tenacity has resulted in a group of books that truly take the reader into the hearts of these otherwise unapproachable institutions. Patricia MacManus, in a review of *Hotel,* says that the book "undoubtedly covers every department in the curriculum of Cornell's School of Hotel Administration." And she feels that there are "enough intersecting story-lines to keep even the most plot-addicted readers scurrying to stay abreast of the multi-layered goings-on at the St. Gregory, the fictitious New Orleans hostelry of *Hotel.*" Robert Cromie writes that Hailey covers his subject in *Airport* with such great detail that the book is likely "to upset airline executives, managers of non-mythical airports, and perhaps the Federal agencies." Some of the sensitive areas include "the dangers inherent in too-short runways, the curtailing of power during the vital early stages of takeoff as a sop to nearby homeowners, the possibility that the easy availability of insurance at every major field may encourage bomb-for-profit schemes, the frantic efficiency which *usually* prevails in the radar room as traffic is supervised, and even the airlines' pregnancy plan for unwed stewardesses." And Kenneth R. Clark of the *Chicago Tribune* finds Hailey's *Evening News,* a thriller about the inner workings of a network news bureau, to be a "breakneck tale" that is "right on the mark, right down to the tiniest nuances of office politics, internecine squabbling, journalistic scorn of authority, and the mechanics of covering late-breaking news."

If there can be said to be a formula or pattern to Hailey's work, it is the now-famous system he has developed in order to garner the vast quantity of detail and technical information with which he packs his books. He spends about a year researching his subject, six months reviewing notes and planning, and eighteen months writing. While researching *Hotel,* he read twenty-seven books about hotels and twelve on New Orleans. At the same time he collected numerous clippings from hotel trade publications as well as those sent to him by his agent and friends. He studied five large hotels in depth (including a six-week stay as a paying guest at an old hotel in New Orleans), and twenty-eight smaller ones. During his research for *Airport,* Hailey spent hours in the airports of New York, Los Angeles, Chicago, Washington, D.C., Tampa, Toronto, Montreal, London, Paris, and Brussels, interviewing airport and airline employees and absorbing the atmosphere. Hailey's interviews with people inside an industry are noted for their relaxed nature; he carries no tape recorder and takes no notes. Instead he waits until after the session to record his impressions into a dictation machine for later transcription by his secretary. One especially noteworthy

conversation yielded eight pages of single-spaced notes; he is, as he says, a bit precise. His writing technique is equally exacting. He is known to write six hundred words, more or less, per day, a rather small amount in comparison to many authors. Hailey's six hundred words, however, are ready for publication; he does his rewriting as he goes along, sometimes revising a paragraph as many as twenty times. Reports of his researching and writing methods have appeared in print so often that Hailey has begun to tire of having them presented as a set of unbreakable rules. He insists that he does not feel bound by this or any other system. Yet he is undeniably a careful planner and it is with this type of structured method that he works most effectively.

One facet of Hailey's craft that induces some agreement among the critics is his ability to weave an interesting tale. Frank Cameron, in an explanation of the author's rise to success, writes: "For one thing, no one has yet devised a satisfactory substitute for innate talent and Hailey is a born story teller. In this sense he is reminiscent of Somerset Maugham although without Maugham's urbanity of style. Hailey is Hailey. He has his own crisp style which has the twin virtues of economy and sustained suspense. A Hailey novel or a Hailey television play is meant to entertain. There is no emphasis on the introspective agonizing of any character. An obscure reference or bit of *avant-garde* rhetoric does not exist in his works. Moralizing he leaves to other writers unless he can weave it into his own story in ways that do not interrupt the plot and pace." Hailey told Patricia Farrell: "It is very obvious that people like reading facts as a background to fiction and this I try to do. It just seems that I happen to have the ability to do it, but I don't strive to be a proselytizer, a crusader, an educator, a consumer advocate; I'm none of those things. I'm a story teller and anything else is incidental."

BIOGRAPHICAL/CRITICAL SOURCES:

BOOKS

Bestsellers 90, Issue 3, Gale, 1990.
Contemporary Literary Criticism, Volume 5, Gale, 1976.
Dictionary of Literary Biography, Volume 88: *Canadian Writers, 1920-1959, Second Series,* Gale, 1989.
Dictionary of Literary Biography Yearbook, 1982, Gale, 1983.
Hailey, Sheila, *I Married a Bestseller,* Doubleday, 1978.

PERIODICALS

America, May 8, 1965, November 20, 1971.
American Way, July, 1975.
Best Sellers, February 15, 1965; April 1, 1968; October 15, 1971; April, 1975.
Booklist, March 1, 1965; April 15, 1968; November 15, 1971; April 15, 1975.

Books and Bookmen, May, 1965; September, 1975.
Book Week, January 24, 1965.
Book World, January 24, 1965; April 14, 1968.
Chicago Sunday Tribune, December 13, 1959.
Chicago Tribune, April 23, 1990.
Flying, May, 1968.
Kirkus Reviews, January 15, 1959; November 1, 1978.
Library Journal, March 1, 1962; March 1, 1968.
Miami Herald, June 1, 1975.
National Observer, April 1, 1968; November 6, 1971; May 3, 1975.
National Review, June 20, 1975.
New Republic, October 23, 1971.
New Statesman, July 4, 1975.
New Yorker, October 3, 1959; January 27, 1962.
New York Herald Tribune, October 18, 1959.
New York Times, April 5, 1959; April 20, 1968; July 28, 1975; December 18, 1978.
New York Times Book Review, September 20, 1959; February 21, 1965; April 7, 1968; September 19, 1971; May 18, 1975; February 11, 1979.
Observer, May 2, 1965.
Publishers Weekly, October 30, 1975.
San Francisco Chronicle, April 19, 1959; December 13, 1959; February 4, 1962.
Saturday Evening Post, November, 1975.
Time, March 26, 1965; March 22, 1968; October 11, 1971; April 14, 1975.
Wall Street Journal, September 21, 1971; March 20, 1975.
Washington Post, July 25, 1969; March 23, 1975.
Washington Post Book World, March 23, 1975; January 15, 1979.
Writer's Digest, August, 1972.
Writer's Yearbook, Number 39, 1967.

*   *   *

HARLOW, Robert   1923-

PERSONAL: Born November 19, 1923, in Prince Rupert, British Columbia, Canada; son of Roland Alden (a roadmaster for Canadian National Railways) and Kathleen Isobel (Grant) Harlow; married Sally Ireland, 1986; children: Gretchen, Roseanne, Genevieve, Kathleen, and two others. *Education:* University of British Columbia, B.A., 1948; University of Iowa, M.F.A., 1950.

ADDRESSES: Home—Mayne Island, British Columbia, Canada.

CAREER: Canadian Broadcasting Corporation (CBC), talks producer, 1951-53, station manager of CBU-Radio, Vancouver, British Columbia, 1954, director of radio for British Columbia region, 1955-64; University of British Columbia, Vancouver, instructor, 1952-53 and 1963-64,

visiting lecturer, 1964-65, associate professor, 1965-70, professor of creative writing, 1970-89, professor emeritus, 1989—, head of department, 1965-77, associate dean of arts, 1968-69. Member of board of Gordon House, 1952-64, Vancouver Little Theatre, 1957, New Play Centre, 1970-81, and Koerner Foundation, 1975-88; associated with Theatre under the Stars, 1959, and Vancouver International Festival, 1959-61. *Military service:* Royal Canadian Air Force, bomber pilot, 1941-45; became flying officer; received Distinguished Flying Cross.

MEMBER: Writers Union of Canada, Humanities Association (Vancouver branch; vice president, 1958, president, 1959).

AWARDS, HONOURS: Canada Council, special award, 1970-71, senior fellowship, 1976-77.

WRITINGS:

Portraits of Three Towns (radio documentary), Canadian Broadcasting Corporation (CBC), 1953.
The Sound of a Horn, Klanak Press, 1959.
Royal Murdoch (novel), Macmillan (Toronto), 1962.
The Eye (radio play), CBC, 1963.
A Gift of Echoes (novel), Macmillan, 1965, St. Martin's (New York City), 1966.
Anti-Semitism in the Christian Church (television documentary), CBC, 1967.
(Author of introduction) *Man in the Glass Octopus,* Sono Nis Press (Delta, British Columbia), 1968.
Scann (novel), Sono Nis Press, 1972.
Making Arrangements (novel), McClelland & Stewart (Toronto), 1978.
(Author of introduction) *British Columbia,* Oxford University Press (Toronto), 1979.
Paul Nolan (novel), McClelland & Stewart, 1983.
Felice: A Travelogue (novel), Dolichan Books (Lantzville, British Columbia), 1986.
The Saxophone Winter (novel), Douglas & MacIntyre, 1988.

Also author of the film *When Tomorrow Dies,* 1966. Work represented in anthologies, including *Ernest Buckler: Critical Views on a Canadian Writer,* 1972; *Matinees Daily,* Quadrant Editions, 1981; and *The Rocket, the Flower, the Hammer, and Me,* Pole Star Press, 1988. Contributor of stories, articles, and reviews to periodicals, including *Books in Canada, Canadian Fiction, Canadian Literature,* and *Canadian Weekend.*

SIDELIGHTS: Robert Harlow has, according to Jill Williams in *Canadian Author & Bookman,* "given Canada some of its finest literary work." In seven novels, Harlow has written of his native western Canada, describing its customs and people in an honest and realistic style. In the novel *Scann,* Harlow tells the story of a middle-aged man who explores the past of his small British Columbian town. In *The Saxophone Winter,* Harlow recreates his early years as a budding musician in a small British Columbian town during the 1930s.

Harlow began writing just after leaving the Canadian military where he served as a bomber pilot in the Second World War. After attending the University of British Columbia, where he studied under poet Earle Birney, Harlow was invited to join the University of Iowa's Writer's Workshop, "the first Canadian author to receive such an invitation," as Williams explains. After three years at Iowa, Harlow joined the Canadian Broadcasting Corporation's fledgling radio network in 1950. Beginning as a producer, he eventually became director of radio for the British Columbian region. In 1965 he began teaching creative writing at the University of British Columbia. He also served as head of the university's creative writing department, the first such department in Canada.

In *Scann* Harlow presents Amory Scann, the editor of a local newspaper in the British Columbian town of Linden, who, for the newspaper's fiftieth anniversary, decides to write a history of Linden. Writing the history involves Scann in a saga spanning four generations and a host of characters and incidents. His historical account has, according to Peter Buitenhuis in the *Dictionary of Literary Biography,* "a ramshackle air that sometimes baffles the reader. It is held together by the unlovely character of Scann, who is a coward, voyeur, fool, clown, adulterer, adventurer, and truth seeker." While the novel is filled with colorful scandal, violence, and sexual adventures, it is also a study of the nature of history and of the problems a writer faces in recording the truth.

Harlow's novel *The Saxophone Winter* is set in Long River, British Columbia, in the winter of 1938-39 and tells the coming-of-age story of Christopher Waterton. Writing in *Books in Canada,* Louis K. MacKendrick states that "Harlow's teen-agers . . . are not fumbling, inarticulate, embarrassing gawks; they are sensible, intelligent individuals, with range, depth, and substance. . . . Perhaps the first real ones in the Canadian novel." Patricia Bradbury in *Quill & Quire* finds Harlow's prose style to be "unobtrusively fluid," moving "like jazz riffs beyond the self-consciousness of writing into pure storytelling."

"I grew up in a time," Harlow tells Williams, "when this country had no culture. What culture it did have was either from Britain or America." Because of this belief, Harlow decided that "if I end up writing, I've got to give it back somehow. Because if we don't have a culture of our own, we're just going to be part of the States. And I don't want to be that."

Harlow told *CA:* "In the beginning I was lucky. I was invited to the Writers' Workshop at Iowa in 1948 and arrived from Vancouver ignorant. I've never minded ignorance; it's curable, and knowing very little at the start of something important can be an advantage. I'd written the requisite trunkload of short fiction that showed neither much talent nor a great deal of flair, but I know now that my writing was full of energy—a kind that is made up of eager anger, eager wonder, and eager ambition. I remember people being amused, sometimes embarrassed, often puzzled by my gaucheries, but mostly they were good friends.

"What I learned from them—or perhaps taught myself with their helpful permission—was that I had enough content to last me a lifetime and so what was important was craft. I learned to read for it, and then I learned to write for it. What's best said now is that an art that uses objects that have pliable meanings which combine to say Yes, Right, like chessmen to be played, horses to be handicapped, blue notes to be found, or words to be strung, needs a craft that fosters—absolutely brings—revelation. Gustave Flaubert using up a morning inserting a comma and an afternoon taking it out is one measure of the craft needed to fuel an art that gives up (surrenders) *Madame Bovary.* I aspire to the full spirit of that morning and afternoon."

BIOGRAPHICAL/CRITICAL SOURCES:

BOOKS

Dictionary of Literary Biography, Volume 60: *Canadian Writers since 1960, Second Series,* Gale, 1987.
MacKendrick, L., *Robert Harlow and His Works,* ECW Press, 1990.
Moss, John, *Sex and Violence in the Canadian Novel: The Ancestral Present,* McClelland & Stewart, 1977, pp. 232-54.

PERIODICALS

Alberta Report, October 24, 1988, p. 43.
Books in Canada, August-September, 1988, p. 28.
Canadian Author & Bookman, summer, 1992, pp. 9-10.
Canadian Fiction Magazine, autumn, 1975.
Globe and Mail (Toronto), February 8, 1986.
Journal of Canadian Fiction, Numbers 31-32, 1981, pp. 248-51.
Quill & Quire, May, 1988, p. 22.

*　　*　　*

HARRIS, Christie (Lucy) Irwin 1907-

PERSONAL: Born November 21, 1907, in Newark, NJ; emigrated to Canada in 1908; daughter of Edward (a farmer) and Matilda (Christie) Irwin; married Thomas Arthur Harris (a Canadian immigration officer), February

13, 1932; children: Michael, Moira (Mrs. Donald Johnston), Sheilagh (Mrs. Jack Simpson), Brian, Gerald. *Education:* Attended University of British Columbia, 1925. *Religion:* Church of England.

ADDRESSES: Home—302-975 Chilco St., Vancouver, British Columbia, Canada V6G 2R5.

CAREER: Novelist, author of historical fiction, short stories, and plays especially for young people. Teacher in British Columbia, 1926-32; free-lance writer for Canadian Broadcasting Corp. Radio, beginning 1936.

MEMBER: Writers' Union of Canada.

AWARDS, HONOURS: First award in educational radio and television competitions in Columbus, Ohio, for school radio series, "Laws for Liberty"; Book of the Year for Children Medal from Canadian Association of Children's Librarians, 1967 and 1977; Children's Literature Prize from Canada Council, 1981; member of the Order of Canada, 1981; Vickie Metcalf Award, 1982.

WRITINGS:

PUBLISHED BY ATHENEUM, EXCEPT AS INDICATED

Cariboo Trail, Longmans, Green, 1957.
Once upon a Totem, 1963.
You Have to Draw the Line Somewhere, illustrations by daughter, Moira Johnston, 1964.
West with the White Chiefs, 1965.
Raven's Cry, illustrations by Bill Reid, foreword by Robert Davidson and Margaret B. Blackman, 1966.
Confessions of a Toe Hanger, 1967.
Forbidden Frontier, 1968.
Let X Be Excitement, 1969.
(With Johnston) *Figleafing through History: The Dynamics of Dress,* 1971.
Secret in the Stlalakum Wild, 1972.
(With husband, Thomas Arthur Harris) *Mule Lib,* McClelland & Stewart, 1972.
Once More upon a Totem, 1973.
Sky Man on the Totem Pole?, 1975.
Mystery at the Edge of Two Worlds, 1979.
The Trouble with Princesses, 1980.
The Trouble with Adventures, illustrations by Douglas Tait, 1982.
Something Weird Is Going On, Orca, 1994.

"MOUSE WOMAN" SERIES; PUBLISHED BY ATHENEUM

Mouse Woman and the Vanished Princesses, 1976.
Mouse Woman and the Mischief-Makers, 1977.
Mouse Woman and the Muddleheads, 1979.

OTHER

Also author of twelve adult plays, juvenile stories, and radio scripts, including several hundred school programs. Women's editor, *A S & M News.*

SIDELIGHTS: Although a diversified writer with over nineteen books to her credit, Christie Irwin Harris is noted and respected most for her works depicting Indian legends and the Canadian West. As a child, Harris grew up in a log cabin in British Columbia, and this region of western Canada is the chief source of Harris's material.

Kenneth Radu explains in *Canadian Children's Literature: A Journal of Criticism and Review*: "Indian folk-lore and mythology have quite clearly made their imprint upon Mrs. Harris's imagination. Her finest work is directly concerned with the Indian life and legends of the Northwest. *Raven's Cry* . . . remains a singularly moving paean to the now extinct Haida civilization of the Queen Charlotte Islands. Fully and accurately researched, *Raven's Cry* portrays the complexities and uniqueness of the Haida culture with insight, wonder, and compassion. Mrs. Harris's view is neither sentimental, romantic, nor patronizing. She reports Haida life as it was lived on the islands with the clear eye and honesty of the sympathetic chronicler."

The Republic of Childhood: A Critical Guide to Canadian Children's Literature in English author Sheila Egoff also recognizes Harris's talent for interpreting Indian legends. "The potential for children's literature inherent in the Indian legends is most fully realized by Christie Harris in *Once upon a Totem*," Egoff writes. "Other collections may have more charm, or a more fluid style, but the legends chosen by Harris and her interpretation of them are outstanding in that they seek quietly to illuminate universal values. The stories are very much a part of early Indian life and very much a part of today."

Priscilla L. Moulton notes in *Horn Book Magazine* that Harris has "rediscovered and reproduced a dignified and inspiring picture of [Haida] culture in a work of epic proportions [*Raven's Cry*]. Painstaking research and intense absorption in anthropological details have enabled the author to write with rare commitment and involvement from the Haida point of view. . . . Dealing as it does in a highly artistic and complicated manner with the whole range of human emotion and character, it makes demands of the reader but rewards him with new understanding of the forces that shape civilizations. . . . This distinguished work, probably classified as fiction, will occupy a respected position in historical, anthropological, and story collections."

Critics often cite Harris's sensitivity in portraying Indian tales as one reason for her large and loyal readership. It has been said that she makes the myths or legends come alive, and many of the young readers, in turn, better understand the ways of their Indian brothers. For example, S. Yvonne MacDonald of *In Review* believes that *Raven's Cry* and *Forbidden Frontier* "combine the author's knowledge of Indian folklore and custom with historical fact to describe the collision between European white man's civilization and Indian culture. Harris writes with sympathy for the Indians, apparently determined to tell their side of the story. . . . This knowledge of legend and folklore seems to me to be the author's main strength, whether in her collections of myths or in her novels."

While it has been written that Harris writes all her books with sensitivity, realism, and a strong respect for history, it also has been suggested that it is her sense of humor that makes her books an enjoyable learning experience for her readers. Kenneth Radu contends that "the hallmark of [Harris's] style is good-humored briskness which carries the story along in an uncomplicated, well-placed narrative." Critic Priscilla L. Moulton writes in another review published in *Horn Book Magazine* that she feels that Harris usually writes with "an abundance of humor—a rare quality in exploration accounts." And in her *Washington Post* review of *You Have to Draw the Line Somewhere*, Margaret Sherwood Libby notes that "Harris has achieved a minor miracle, a romance-career story that is sparkling and well written, filled with humor that springs naturally from character and situation."

Readers and critics alike have also delighted in Harris's books for the sometimes unusual, often comical, and almost always life-like characters she creates. A perfect example of her use of a strong, dominant character to carry her message is offered by S. Yvonne MacDonald. She writes that *Mouse Woman and the Vanished Princesses,* a "collection of legends from the mythology of the Northwest Coast Indians of Canada, is uniquely linked through the character of Mouse Woman, a Narnauk or Supernatural Being. . . . The stories are clearly and lyrically told, with perhaps the most distinctive quality being the characterizations of the Narnauks. Harris manages to evoke the magical and essentially alien World of the Supernaturals and also its familiarity to the Indians, for these spirits were a daily part of their lives."

New York Times Book Review critic Benjamin Capps explains in a review of *West with the White Chiefs* that "the journal of two Englishmen . . . who crossed western Canada in 1863 is the basis for this fictionalized account of a perilous trip through little-known, difficult land. . . . Comic relief is supplied by a roguish Irishman, a ridiculous, helpless freeloader who intrudes into the party and makes the journey with the explorers. He quotes Latin aphorisms, is generally unavailable for any work, always makes outrageous demands on the others. He is a wonderful creation, a delightful contrast to the hard-working, se-

rious Indians and Englishmen." And Sriani Fernando of *In Review* writes in an article about *The Trouble with Princesses* that "within each story, the characters are distinctive and adequately developed. The difference in impetus—depending on whether the protagonists resort to wit, cunning or magic to achieve their ends—lends variety to the stories."

Besides tales of Indian lore and adventures in western Canada, Harris is also the author of other books for young people. Several of her books are based on the experiences of her own family. For example, *Let X Be Excitement* is based on the life of her oldest son, Michael (Ralph to Harris's readers). Julie Losinski writes that in *Let X Be Excitement* "for Ralph, discovering his life's occupation meant finding a job that offered intellectual challenge and satisfied his love of excitement and the outdoors. . . . Ralph's satisfaction in doing what comes naturally, combined with a sense of humor, results in a appealing zest for living. Readers (boys particularly) facing career decisions will empathize with Ralph, and enjoy, even though they may not be able to equal, his adventures." In *Confessions of a Tow Hanger,* comments Shirley Ellison of *Profile,* "Mrs. Harris ventured once more into family collaboration to tell the story of her younger daughter, Sheilagh. . . . The humorous but poignant account of the 'ordinary' middle child in a talented family is now the favourite reading of Sheilagh's own daughters." Ellison continues to explain that Harris's *You Have to Draw the Line Somewhere* "recreates the story of her older daughter, Moira, a fashion artist. It was undertaken at Moira's suggestion." Helen M. Kovar of *School Library Journal* notes that *You Have to Draw the Line Somewhere* "is the story of a young Canadian girl who aspires to become a *Vogue* fashion artist. The British Columbia setting is refreshing and the style is humorous. . . . It is a frank picture of the non-glamorous side of fashion art and modeling and the amount of work necessary to become first-rate in either profession. With a light touch the story offers depth and mature values. . . . This has much more to offer than most girls' fiction."

BIOGRAPHICAL/CRITICAL SOURCES:

BOOKS

Contemporary Literary Criticism, Volume 12, Gale, 1980.
Egoff, Sheila, *The Republic of Childhood: A Critical Guide to Canadian Children's Literature in English,* 2nd edition, Oxford University Press, 1975.

PERIODICALS

American Museum of Natural History, November, 1967.
Canadian Children's Literature: A Journal of Criticism and Review, Number 2, 1975; Number 5, 1976; Num-

ber 6, 1976; Number 51, 1988, pp. 6-24; summer, 1994, pp. 5-15.

Horn Book Magazine, April, 1963; June, 1964; June, 1965; October, 1966; April, 1968; April, 1975.

In Review, autumn, 1975; autumn, 1976; August, 1980.

Kirkus Review, March 1, 1973; March 15, 1975; April 15, 1976.

New York Times Book Review, May 12, 1963; April 4, 1965.

Profile, 1971.

Quill & Quire, December, 1994, p. 33.

School Library Journal, April, 1964; September, 1969.

Scientific American, December, 1966.

VOYA, August, 1993, p. 152.

Washington Post, May 17, 1964.

—*Sketch by Margaret Mazurkiewicz*

* * *

HEARNE, John (Edgar Caulwell) 1926-
(John Morris, a joint pseudonym)

PERSONAL: Born February 4, 1926, in Montreal, Quebec, Canada; son of Maurice Vincent and Doris (May) Hearne; married Joyce Veitch, September 3, 1947 (divorced); married Leeta Mary Hopkinson (a teacher), April 12, 1955; children: two. *Education:* Attended Jamaica College; Edinburgh University, M.A., 1950; University of London, teaching diploma, 1950. *Religion:* Christian.

ADDRESSES: Home—P.O. Box 335, Kingston 8, Jamaica.*Office*—Creative Arts Centre, University of the West Indies, Kingston 7, Jamaica.*Agent*—Claire Smith, Harold Ober Associates, Inc., 40 East 49th St., New York, NY 10017.

CAREER: Teacher at schools in London, England, and in Jamaica, 1950-59; information officer, Government of Jamaica, 1962; University of the West Indies, Kingston, Jamaica, resident tutor in extramural studies, 1962-67, head of Creative Arts Centre, 1968—. Visiting Gregory Fellow in Common-wealth Literature at University of Leeds, England, 1967; Colgate University, New York, visiting O'Conner Professor in Literature, 1969-70, and visiting professor in literature, 1973. *Military service:* Royal Air Force, air gunner, 1943-46.

MEMBER: International PEN.

AWARDS, HONOURS: John Llewelyn Rhys Memorial Prize, 1956, for *Voices under the Window;* Silver Musgrave Medal from Institute of Jamaica, 1964.

WRITINGS:

NOVELS

Voices under the Window, Faber, 1955, reprinted, 1985.

Stranger at the Gate, Faber, 1956.

The Faces of Love, Faber, 1957, published as *The Eye of the Storm,* Little, Brown, 1958.

The Autumn Equinox, Faber, 1959, Vanguard Press, 1961.

Land of the Living, Faber, 1961, Harper, 1962.

(With Morris Cargill, under joint pseudonym John Morris) *Fever Grass,* Putnam, 1969.

(With Cargill, under joint pseudonym John Morris) *The Candywine Development,* Collins, 1970, Lyle Stuart, 1971.

The Sure Salvation, Faber, 1981, St. Martin's, 1982.

SHORT STORIES

Contributor of short stories to anthologies, including *West Indian Stories,* edited by Andrew Salkey, Faber, 1960, and *Stories from the Caribbean,* edited by Salkey, Elek, 1965, published as *Island Voices: Stories from the West Indies,* Liveright, 1970. Contributor of short stories and articles to periodicals, including *Atlantic Monthly, New Statesman,* and the *Trinidad Guardian.*

OTHER

(With Rex Nettleford) *Our Heritage,* University of the West Indies, 1963.

(Editor and author of introduction) *Carifesta Forum: An Anthology of Twenty Caribbean Voices,* Carifesta 76 (Kingston, Jamaica), 1976.

(Editor and author of introduction) *The Search for Solutions: Selections from the Speeches and Writings of Michael Manley,* Maple House Publishing Co., 1976.

(With Lawrence Coote and Lynden Facey) *Testing Democracy through Elections: A Tale of Five Elections,* edited by Marie Gregory, Bustamante Institute of Public and International Affairs (Kingston, Jamaica), 1985.

Also author of teleplays, including *Soldiers in the Snow,* with James Mitchell, 1960, and *A World Inside,* 1962; author of stage play *The Golden Savage,* 1965. Work represented in anthologies, including O. R. Dathorne's *Caribbean Narrative: An Anthology of West Indian Writing,* Heinemann, 1966, and Barbara Howes's *From the Green Antilles: Writings of the Caribbean,* Macmillan, 1966.

SIDELIGHTS: A West Indian writer who sometimes collaborates with Morris Cargill as the pseudonymous John Morris, John Hearne is known for his vivid depictions of life among the West Indies and their people. In particular, several of his writings focus on Jamaica—the native land of his parents—and address complex social and moral issues affecting both individual relationships and, to a lesser extent, the cultural and political aspects of the island. Much of Hearne's fiction—including the novels *Stranger at the Gate, The Faces of Love, The Autumn Equinox,* and *Land of the Living*—also takes place on Cayuna, a mythical counterpart of Jamaica. More generally, his work relates a broad, first-hand account of the Caribbean experience and features elements of racial and social inequities as well as recurrent themes of betrayal and disenchantment. Especially noteworthy are Hearne's acclaimed narrative skill and descriptive style, which distinguish his fiction as characteristically evocative and lifelike.

Hearne's 1981 novel, *The Sure Salvation,* takes place in the southern Atlantic Ocean aboard a sailing ship of the same name. Set in the year 1860, the story chronicles the illegal buying and selling of negroes more than fifty years after England first enacted laws prohibiting the practice commonly known as slave trade. Through a "series of deft flashbacks," observed *Times Literary Supplement* critic T. O. Treadwell, Hearne recounts individual circumstances that led to his characters' unlawful fraternity on board the *Sure Salvation.* Risking constant danger and the death penalty if they are caught, the captain and crew hope to amend their ill-fated lives with monies paid for the vessel's charge of five hundred Africans. While the "beastliness isn't played down," Treadwell noted, we come "to understand, and even sympathize with" these men and their despicable dealings due to Hearne's successful literary craftsmanship and execution. Treadwell further announced that the "author's gift for irony . . . that the slavers are no freer than" their shackled cargo, provides this "absorbing" tale with its utmost pleasures, and he concluded that *The Sure Salvation* proves the "power of the sea story . . . as potent as ever."

Hearne commented that his writing is influenced by his growing up in an island society large enough to be interesting but small enough for "characters" to be known intimately. He added: "I have been much concerned with politics (as a commentator) as Jamaica has tried to fashion itself into a newly independent society since the early 1960s."

BIOGRAPHICAL/CRITICAL SOURCES:

BOOKS

James, Louis, editor, *The Islands In Between: Essays on West Indian Literature,* Oxford University Press, 1968.
Ramchand, Kenneth, *The West Indian Novel and Its Background,* Barnes & Noble, 1970.

PERIODICALS

Times Literary Supplement, June 19, 1981.

HEBERT, Anne 1916-

PERSONAL: Born August 1, 1916, in Sainte-Catherine-de-Fossambault, Quebec, Canada; daughter of Maurice-Lang (a literary critic) and Marguerite Marie (Tache) Hebert. *Education:* Privately educated; attended College Saint-Coeur de Marie, Merici, Quebec, and College Notre Dame, Bellevue, Quebec.

ADDRESSES: Home—24 rue de Pontoise, 75005 Paris, France.

CAREER: Poet and novelist. Worked for Radio Canada, 1950-53, and for National Film Board, 1953-54, 1959-60.

MEMBER: Royal Society of Canada.

AWARDS, HONOURS: Grants from the Canadian government, 1954, Canadian Council of Arts, 1960 and 1961, Guggenheim Foundation, 1963, and the province of Quebec, 1965; Prix de la Province de Quebec, France Canada prize, and Duvernay prize, all 1958, all for *Les Chambres de bois;* Molson prize, 1967; French booksellers prize, 1971; Governor General award, 1975; grand priz de Monaco, 1975; award from the French Academy, 1975; Prix David of the province of Quebec, 1978; Prix Femina, 1982, for *Les Fous de Bassan;* D.Litt., University of Toronto, 1967, University of Quebec, 1979, McGill University, 1980, University of Laval, and University of Laurentienne.

WRITINGS:

POETRY

Les Songes en equilibre (title means Dreams in Equilibrium), Les Editions de l'Arbre, 1942.
Le Tombeau des rois, Institut Litteraire du Quebec, 1953, translation by Peter Miller published as *The Tomb of the Kings,* Contact Press (Toronto), 1967, augmented French edition published as *Poemes* (includes *Mystere de la parole*), Editions du Seuil, 1960, translation by Alan Brown published as *Poems,* Musson, 1975.
Saint-Denys Garneau and Anne Hebert (selected poetry), translation by F. R. Scott, Klanak Press (Vancouver, British Columbia), 1962, revised edition, 1978.
Eve: Poems, translation by A. Poulin, Jr., Quarterly Review of Literature, 1980.
Anne Hebert: Selected Poems, translation by Poulin, Boa Editions, 1987.
Day Has No Equal but Night, translation by Poulin, Boa Editions, 1994.

Contributor of poems to literary journals.

NOVELS

Le Torrent: Nouvelles, Beauchemin, 1950, new edition published as *Le Torrent, suivi de deux nouvelles inedites,* Editions HMH (Montreal), 1963, translation by

Gwendolyn Moore published as *The Torrent: Novellas and Short Stories,* Harvest House (Montreal), 1973.

Les Chambres de bois, Editions du Seuil, 1958, translation by Kathy Mezei published as *The Silent Rooms,* Musson, 1974.

Kamouraska, Editions du Seuil, 1970, translation by Norman Shapiro, Crown, 1973.

Les Enfants du Sabbat, Editions du Seuil, 1975, translation by Carol Dunlop-Hebert published as *Children of the Black Sabbath,* Crown, 1977.

Heloise, Editions du Seuil, 1980, translation by Sheila Fischman, Stoddart (Toronto), 1982.

Les Fous de Bassan, Editions du Seuil, 1982, translation by Fischman published as *In the Shadow of the Wind,* Stoddart, 1982.

Le Premier Jardin, Editions du Seuil, 1988, translation published as *The First Garden,* Anansi, 1990.

L'Enfant charge de songes (title means "The Child Filled with Dreams"), Editions du Seuil, 1992.

Le Jour n'a d'egal que la nuit, Boreal, 1992.

OTHER

Les Invites au proces, Le Theatre du grand prix (radio play), Radio-Canada, 1952.

(With others) *Trois de Quebec* (radio play), Radio-Canada, 1953.

Les Indes parmi nous (screenplay), National Film Board, 1954.

La Canne a peche (screenplay), National Film Board, 1959.

Saint-Denys Garneau (screenplay), National Film Board, 1960.

Le Temps sauvage, La Merciere assassinee, Les Invites au proces: Theatre (plays; *Le Temps sauvage* first produced in Quebec, Canada, at the Theatre du Nouveau Monde at the Palais Montcalm, October 8, 1966), Editions HMH, 1967.

(With F. R. Scott) *Dialogue sur la traduction,* edited by Jeanne Lapointe, Editions HMH, 1970.

La Cage: L'Ile de la demoiselle (play), Boreal, 1990.

Also author of *Drole de mic-mac* and *Le Medecin du nord,* both 1954, and *Le Deficient mental,* 1960.

SIDELIGHTS: Anne Hebert was born into an intellectually stimulating environment. Her father, Maurice-Lang Hebert, was a distinguished literary critic, and among his friends were some of the finest minds in Quebec. Due to a childhood illness Hebert was educated privately and spent most of her time at the family's country home in Sainte-Catherine-de-Fossambault.

She began writing poetry in her adolescence with the advice and guidance of her father and her cousin, the poet Hector de Saint-Denys Garneau. Unlike Saint-Denys

Garneau, who remained in self-isolation until his death, Hebert emerged from the spiritual struggle described in her first two books of poetry. *Les Songes en equilibre,* Hebert's first book of poetry, chronicled the experiences of a young woman who traveled from the easiness of childhood fun to the renunciation of pleasure and the acceptance of a lonely life of spiritual and poetic duty. Hebert received a strict Roman Catholic training as a child, and believed the poet to be a spiritual force in man's salvation.

In her second book of poetry, Hebert revealed that the austere life she had chosen for herself was stifling her work. It is in this volume of her poetry that Hebert emerged from a dark and deep spiritual struggle. Samuel Moon observed: "[*The Tomb of the Kings*] is a book closely unified by its constant introspection, by its atmosphere of profound melancholy, by its recurrent themes of a dead childhood, a living death cut off from love and beauty, suicide, the theme of introspection itself. Such a book would seem to be of more interest clinically than poetically, but the miracle occurs and these materials are transmuted by the remarkable force of Mlle. Hebert's imagery, the simplicity and directness of her diction, and the restrained lyric sound of her *vers libre.*"

Although known primarily as a poet, Hebert has also written for the stage and television, and is the author of several published novels. Characteristic of Hebert's novels is the theme of the inhibiting burden of the past, which binds any freedom for future actions. Many critics have noted that this theme is a French-Canadian phenomenon.

Kamouraska is Hebert's second novel and it has drawn praise from both Canadian and American critics. A *Choice* reviewer noted: "[This novel] conveys the same sense of mounting and almost unendurable excitement that one felt on first reading a Bronte novel—except that *Kamouraska* is modern in style and explicitness. The events are a stream-of-consciousness re-creation of a murder of passion that actually occurred in 1840. Hebert's poetic vision draws the thoughtful reader to be one with each of the frenzied characters." A *Canadian Forum* critic compared Hebert's "highly complex style and imagery" with that of Proust, Kafka, and Joyce, and stated that "the greatness of this work resides in the happy mixture of particularity and universality, unity and complexity, vitality and artistic originality, and, above all, in the way the author makes simplistic moral judgment of the characters impossible."

Mel Watkins of the *New York Times* called Hebert a "stylist of the first rank" in his review of *Children of the Black Sabbath,* a novel that deals with a young novice who is possessed by the devil. Watkins observed that Hebert "both complements and heightens this eerie, aphotic atmosphere with the verity and density of her minor characters and with the restrained elegance of her prose. The result is an impressionistic tale that moves smoothly. . . . The vitality of the prose, of itself, makes it one of the best of its kind." Suspense and atmosphere are keys to Hebert's later works, as well. *Heloise* recounts the tale of a Paris vampire, and *Le Fous de Bassan* concerns the reactions of several people to a savage crime. For the latter work, Hebert received the Prix Femina, an award which honors a novel written by a woman.

BIOGRAPHICAL/CRITICAL SOURCES:

BOOKS

Contemporary Literary Criticism, Gale, Volume 4, 1975; Volume 13, 1980; Volume 29, 1984.
Contemporary World Writers, St. James Press, 1993.
Dictionary of Literary Biography, Volume 68: *Canadian Writers, 1920-1959, First Series,* Gale, 1988.
Lewis, Paula Gilbert, editor, *Traditionalism, Nationalism, and Feminism: Women Writers of Quebec,* Greenwood, 1985.
Russell, Delbert W., *Anne Hebert,* Twayne, 1983.

PERIODICALS

American Review of Canadian Studies, fall, 1987.
Booklist, March 15, 1994, p. 1323.
Canadian Forum, November/December, 1973.
Canadian Literature, Volume 58, 1973; spring, 1981; summer, 1985.
Choice, September, 1973.
Essays on Canadian Writing, Volume 12, 1978; summer, 1983.
French Review, May, 1986.
Journal of Canadian Fiction, Volume 2, number 1, 1972.
Library Journal, March 15, 1994, p. 74.
Modern Fiction Studies, summer, 1981.
New York Times, September 7, 1977.
New York Times Book Review, July 22, 1984.
Poetry, June, 1968.
Publishers Weekly, March 28, 1994, p. 91.
Quebec Studies, Volume 3, 1985; Volume 4, 1986; Volume 5, 1987; Volume 6, 1988; Volume 8, 1989.
Studies in Canadian Literature, Volume 14, number 1, 1989.
Waves, spring, 1982.
World Literature Today, autumn, 1994, p. 781.
Yale French Studies, Volume 65, 1983.

* * *

HELWIG, David (Gordon) 1938-

PERSONAL: Born April 5, 1938, in Toronto, Ontario, Canada; son of William Gordon (a cabinetmaker) and Ivy (Abbott) Helwig; married Nancy Keeling, September 19, 1959; children: Sarah Magdalen, Kathleen Rebecca. *Education:* University of Toronto, B.A., 1960; University of Liverpool, M.A., 1962. *Avocational interests:* Singing.

ADDRESSES: 4380 avenue de Chateaubriand, Montreal, Quebec, Canada, H2J 2T8.

CAREER: Queen's University, Kingston, Ontario, assistant professor of English, 1962-74, member of English faculty, 1976-80; Canadian Broadcasting Corp., television drama department, literary manager and story editor for crime series *Sidestreet,* 1974-76.

AWARDS, HONOURS: Centennial Award, for *A Time of Winter;* first prize in an annual Canadian Broadcasting Corporation poetry competition, 1983, for *Catchpenny Poems.*

WRITINGS:

NOVELS

The Day before Tomorrow, Oberon, 1971, published as *Message from a Spy,* Paperjacks, 1975.
The Glass Knight (first volume in Kingston tetralogy), Oberon, 1976.
Jennifer (second volume in Kingston tetralogy) Oberon, 1979, Beaufort, 1983.
The King's Evil, Oberon, 1981, Beaufort, 1984.
It Is Always Summer (fourth volume of Kingston tetralogy), Stoddart, 1982, Beaufort, 1982.
A Sound Like Laughter (third volume in Kingston tetralogy), Stoddart,1983, Beaufort, 1983.
The Only Son, Stoddart, 1984, Beaufort, 1984.
The Bishop, Viking, 1986, Penguin, 1986.
A Postcard from Rome, Penguin, 1988.
Old Wars, Penguin, 1990.
Of Desire, Viking, 1990.

POETRY

The Sign of the Gunman, Oberon, 1969.
The Best Name of Silence, Oberon, 1972.
Atlantic Crossings, Oberon, 1974.
A Book of the Hours, Oberon, 1979.
The Rain Falls Like Rain, Oberon, 1982.
Catchpenny Poems, Oberon, 1983.
The Hundred Old Names, Oberon, 1988.
The Beloved, Oberon, 1992.

EDITOR

(With Tom Marshall) *Fourteen Stories High: Best Canadian Stories of 71,* Oberon, 1971.
(With Joan Harcourt) *New Canadian Stories,* annual volumes, Oberon, 1972-75.
The Human Elements (critical essays), Oberon, 1978.
Love and Money: The Politics of Culture, Oberon, 1980.

The Human Elements, Second Series, Oberon, 1981.
(With Sandra Martin) *Coming Attractions* (short stories), annual volumes, 1983-1985.
(With Martin) *Best Canadian Stories,* annual series, Oberon, 1983-1986.
(With daughter, Maggie Helwig) *Coming Attractions 5,* Oberon, 1987.
(With M. Helwig) *Best Canadian Stories,* annual series, Oberon, 1988-1990.

OTHER

Figures in a Landscape (poems and three plays: *A Time of Winter,* produced in Kingston, Ontario, by Domino Theatre, 1967, *The Dreambook,* and *The Dancers of Kolbek*), Oberon, 1968.
The Streets of Summer (short stories), Oberon, 1969.
(By Billie Miller as told to Helwig) *A Book about Billie* (documentary), Oberon, 1972.

Work represented in numerous anthologies, including *Canadian Short Stories,* edited by Robert Weaver, Oxford University Press, 1968, and *Canadian Poetry: The Modern Era,* edited by Newlove, McClelland & Stewart, 1977. Co-editor of *Quarry,* 1962-74; editor-at-large, Oberon Press, 1973-74.

SIDELIGHTS: Versatile and prolific, David Helwig has produced realistic and dreamlike novels, spy fiction, short stories, plays, radio and television scripts, and poetry collections, and has edited numerous books. His career has placed him among the more prominent Canadian men of letters of the generation that includes former classmate Margaret Atwood and former colleague Michael Ondaatje.

Helwig's "most substantial achievement in fiction," according to Tom Marshall in the *Dictionary of Literary Biography,* is his tetralogy of novels set in Kingston, Ontario, which "provide[s] an impressive panorama of contemporary life in this unique eastern Ontario city." The first, *The Glass Knight,* says Gary Draper in *Books in Canada,* "tells the story of Robert Mallen's not-very-successful affair with the exotic Elizabeth Ross." Robert's ex-wife is the title character of the second volume, *Jennifer.* Both these novels, Draper says, "are novels of character. Robert and Jennifer are ordinary people, caught in the ordinary confusions of growing older and falling in and out of love."

It Is Always Summer, the third in the tetralogy to be published, is fourth in its fictive chronological sequence. "It has the virtues of its predecessors and more," declares Draper. Taking place ten years after *The Glass Knight,* the work is more ambitious than the first two books, with a larger cast of characters. "Helwig shows the different faces (or facets) that each character reveals in different social contexts," Draper writes. "In addition, . . . the six

central characters reveal their private, inner spaces. . . . Some of the most successful passages in the book are those in which Helwig orchestrates a conversation of many voices. There are some real virtuoso pieces here, drawing power from a sub-surface of sexuality." *Publishers Weekly* reviewer Barbara A. Bannon calls the book "a sophisticated novel of manners."

A Sound Like Laughter, which completes the tetralogy, is Helwig's first comic novel. The laughter is dark, however; Jim Moore, writing in the *Los Angeles Times Book Review,* draws from the novel this moral: "Better let the gods do the laughing." This book, says I. M. Owen in *Books in Canada,* "is about the disastrous messes we can get ourselves into in the pursuit of what seem to us reasonable goals." Marianne, a middle-aged mental health center administrator, is having an affair with Ernest, a hapless college voice coach. In the course of a novel, she makes love to a drug dealer who burglarizes her home; Ernest makes love to the babysitter who has helped the burglar. "Helwig writes in a laconic, limpid style," Moore comments, "he keeps lines of action sublimely straight." Describing the novel as "exuberant comedy" as well as "very sad," Owen praises Helwig's "beautiful prose."

Helwig's first novel after completing the tetralogy, *The Only Son,* is a study of Canadian society. The main character, Walter, is a young Torontonian whose British parents are servants in a wealthy household; the plot follows Walter's successful attempt to escape from the servant class and attain social respectability by becoming a philosophy professor. Reviewing the book for the Toronto *Globe and Mail,* William French calls it "compelling" and "a rare example of Canadian fiction that deals with our class structure."

An earlier novel that shows Helwig's versatility, the 1981 *The King's Evil,* stands out for its poetic, fairy-tale atmosphere. The novel is a narrative within a narrative. The frame device shows us a CBC radio producer who has suffered a nervous breakdown and who, during his convalescence, does research into Canadian Loyalist history. The dreamlike tale within the tale postulates that King Charles I of England was not beheaded, but was taken to Virginia. Praising Helwig's handling of archetypal symbols, Hilda Kirkwood in claims in *Canadian Forum,* "It is a strange and very beautiful dream, the work of a poet casting his spell upon us." D. W. Nichol, in *Books in Canada,* finds the novel as a whole "diffuse," but commends "its exploration of fakes within fakes."

The 1986 novel *The Bishop* is a character study of an Anglican bishop who, after suffering a paralytic stroke, lies in bed remembering his life. Stating that the novel contains "passages of great beauty," *Globe and Mail* contributor Douglas Hill adds, "Helwig has gifts of making much out of the ordinary and unspectacular." In his 1989 novel, *Old Wars,* Helwig switches both genre and locale. A spy novel set partly in Greece, *Old Wars* is "moody, suspenseful, and very well written," comments Newgate Callendar in the *New York Times Book Review.*

If *The King's Evil* is poetry in prose, Helwig has produced a large amount of poetry in verse as well. From Helwig's early work, Tom Marshall singles out the long poem *Atlantic Crossings* as the finest. The four-part poem concerns the New World explorations of St. Brendan, Columbus, the Norsemen, and a slave trader. *The Rain Falls Like Rain,* published in 1982, is an omnibus volume containing poems from Helwig's five previous collections as well as newer work. In *Books in Canada,* reviewer Peter O'Brien comments: "There is a marvelously complex simplicity in Helwig's finest work. . . . Helwig's poems are not only understated, they are poems of breath, with all the mystery and strength that breathing implies." Helwig's *Catchpenny Poems* of 1983 won first prize in an annual competition sponsored by the Canadian Broadcasting Corporation.

BIOGRAPHICAL/CRITICAL SOURCES:

BOOKS

Dictionary of Literary Biography, Volume 60: *Canadian Writers since 1960,* Second Series, Gale, 1987, pp. 114-117.
Marshall, Tom, *Harsh and Lovely Land,* University of British Columbia Press, 1979, pp. 162-170.
Moss, John, editor, *Present Tense,* NC Press, 1985, pp. 112-121.
Pearce, John, editor, *Twelve Voices: Interviews with Canadian Poets,* Borealis, 1981, pp. 25-41.

PERIODICALS

Books in Canada, November, 1979, p. 8; October, 1981, pp. 13, 15; May, 1982, p. 12; June, 1982, p. 30; March, 1983, pp. 22-3; April, 1983, pp. 20-1; March, 1984, p. 14; August, 1986, p. 18; March, 1987, p. 29; April, 1988, p. 25; August, 1989, p. 6; October, 1990, p. 46.
Canadian Forum, January, 1969; March, 1970; February, 1982, p. 44; June-July, 1982, p. 38.
Fiddlehead, January-February, 1969.
Globe & Mail (Toronto), March 10, 1984; May 26, 1984; September 29, 1984; December 14, 1985; November 29, 1986; September 12, 1987, November 14, 1987; December 17, 1988; October 21, 1989.
Los Angeles Times Book Review, October 30, 1983, p. 9; January 13, 1985, p. 7.
Maclean's, October 22, 1979, p. 58; March 1, 1982, p. 56; April 25, 1983, p. 56.
New York Times Book Review, July 8, 1984, p. 20; January 11, 1987, p. 23; October 22, 1989, p. 37.
Poetry, August, 1984, p. 307.
Publishers Weekly, June 18, 1982, p. 59; May 27, 1983, p. 60; November 30, 1990, p. 56.
Queen's Quarterly, Volume 81, number 2, 1974, pp. 202-214.
Quill and Quire, March, 1982.
Saturday Night, December, 1971, pp. 38-9, 43.
Times Literary Supplement, May 14, 1976; May, 1983, p. 64.

*　　*　　*

HEMON, Louis 1880-1913

PERSONAL: Born October 12, 1880, in Brest, Brittany, France; died after being hit by a train, July 8, 1913, in Chapleau, Ontario, Canada; son of Felix (Inspector General of Public Education) and Louise (Le Breton) Hemon; lived with (some sources say married) Lydia O'Kelley; children: Lydia Kathleen. *Education:* Lycee Louis-le-Grand, 1896-97; Sorbonne, bachelor's degree in law, maritime law, and a certificate of specialization in Annamese, 1901.

CAREER: Freelance journalist, sportswriter, and novelist. Worked as a salesman and translator; Le Velo, correspondent, 1904. *Military service:* French army, 1901-1902, served at Chartres.

WRITINGS:

Maria Chapdelaine: Recit du Canada francais, Le Febvre, 1916, Grasset, 1921, Macmillan, 1921, translation by W. H. Blake published as *Maria Chapdelaine: A Tale of the Lake St. John Country,* Macmillan, 1921, translation by Andrew Macphail published as *Maria Chapdelaine: A Romance of French Canada,* Chapman, 1921, Lane, 1921.
La Belle que voila, Grasset, 1923, Nelson, 1925, translation by William Aspenwall Bradley published as *My Fair Lady,* Macmillan, 1923.
Colin-Maillard, Grasset, 1924, translation by Arthur Richmond published as *Blind Man's Bluff,* Macmillan, 1924, Macmillan, 1925.
The Journal of Louis Hemon, translation by Bradley, Macmillan, 1924.
Battling Malone, pugiliste, Grasset, 1925, translation by Bradley published as *Battling Malone and Other Stories,* Butterworth, 1925.
Monsieur Ripois and Nemesis, translation by Bradley, Macmillan, 1925, published in original French as *Monsieur Ripois et la Nemesis,* Grasset, 1950.
Louis Hemon: Lettres a sa famille, edited by Nicole Deschamps, Presses de l'Universite de Montreal, 1968.
Recits sportifs, edited by Aurelien Boivin and Jean-Marc Bourgeois, Royaume, 1982.

Itineraire de Liverpool a Quebec, Calligrammes, 1985.

Also author of *Nouvelles londoniennes,* published by Le Castor Astral.

SIDELIGHTS: Though a Frenchman, Louis Hemon is best known for his novel on French Canadian life, *Maria Chapdelaine,* which was first published in 1916. The work has been a subject of controversy in French Canadian literature since its first appearance, and its popularity has risen and fallen several times throughout the years.

Hemon was born on October 12, 1880, in Brest, Brittany, France, to Felix and Louise (Le Breton) Hemon. His father was a teacher and was appointed to various educational posts throughout Hemon's childhood and eventually was appointed the Inspector General of Public Education. In 1897 Hemon graduated from the Lycee Louis-le-Grand, after which he entered the Faculty of Law at the Sorbonne, where he received a bachelor's degree in law and maritime law and a certificate of specialization in Annamese in 1901. He spent the next two years in the French military at Chartres from 1901 to 1903. After completing his military service, Hemon left for London where he had a daughter, Lydia Kathleen, with Lydia O'Kelley in 1909. There is no record of a marriage between Lydia O'Kelley and Hemon, but some sources do cite her as his wife. In 1911, after O'Kelley was institutionalized, Hemon abandoned her and his daughter to immigrate to Canada. After traveling through Montreal and Quebec City, Hemon settled in Lac Saint-Jean where he worked as a hired hand. His experiences in Lac Saint-Jean led him to write his novel *Maria Chapdelaine.* The novel was published posthumously; in 1913 Hemon died when he was hit by a train while walking down the wrong side of the tracks.

Maria Chapdelaine is set in the traditional French Canadian farming community of Lac Saint-Jean and centers on the life choices of the title character. Maria has three suitors from whom she must choose her husband. When the one she truly loves dies, she is left with a choice between an exciting urban life in America and the traditional agricultural life of the community in which she was raised. Hemon also wrote a journal of his travels published as *Itineraire de Liverpool a Quebec* (1985); many of the same themes from *Maria Chapdelaine* are present in this account of his experiences in Canada.

Critical reception to Hemon's work has been mixed. While many assert that *Maria Chapdelaine* is an accurate portrayal of the French Canadian culture, certain Quebec nationalists have complained that the work is written by an outsider for outsiders. They also complain that Hemon portrayed French Canadians as uneducated farmers. Despite these nationalist concerns, many critics praise the novel for its structure and contribution to the genre of the French Canadian novel. Critics have asserted that

Hemon's other writing, such as his journal, *Intineraire de Liverpool a Quebec,* and his collected letters to his family, *Louise Hemon: Lettres a sa famille,* (1968) shed light on the themes and importance of *Maria Chapdelaine,* but some critics maintain that these writings exhibit little literary value.

BIOGRAPHICAL/CRITICAL SOURCES:

BOOKS

Ayotte, Alfred, and Victor Tremblay, *L'aventure Louis Hemon,* Fides, 1974.
Nicole Deschamps, Raymonde Heroux, and Normand Villeneuve, *Le Mythe de Maria Chapdelaine,* University Press of Montreal, 1980.

PERIODICALS

Canadian Ethnic Studies, Volume 23, 1991, pp. 159-61.
Canadian Literature, autumn, 1990, p. 180; winter, 1992, p. 184; fall-winter, 1994, pp. 63-74.
Canadian Materials, October, 1992, p. 275.
Modern Language Review, April, 1971, p. 415.

*   *   *

HERTEL, Francois   1905-1985

PERSONAL: Born Rodolphe Dube, May 31, 1905, in Riviere-Ouelle, Quebec, Canada; died October 4, 1985; son of Joseph and Alice (Levesque) Dube. *Education:* Attended College de Sainte-Anne-de-la-Pocatiere and Seminaire de Trois-Rivieres; received *licence* in philosophy and theology and Ph.D. from Scolasticat de l'Immaculee Conception.

CAREER: Priest, poet, novelist, essayist, short story writer, playwright, philosopher, teacher, literary critic, and publisher. Ordained a Roman Catholic priest, 1938, taught at Jean-de-Brebeuf, Sainte-Marie, and Andre Grasset colleges in Montreal and College des Jesuites in Sudbury, Ontario, Canada. Founder of *L'Ami du Peuple* (a newspaper) in Sudbury; director of *Amerique Francaise* (a literary and cultural review), 1946-47; director of *Rythmes et Couleurs* (an art review) in Paris, France; director of La Diaspora Francaise (a publishing house) in Paris. Wrote, published, taught, and lectured throughout France, from the 1950s through the 1970s.

WRITINGS:

Les Voix de mon reve, Albert Levesque (Montreal), 1934.
Leur Inquietude, Albert Levesque, 1936.
L'Enseignement des Belles-Lettres, Aux Ateliers de l'Entr'aide (Montreal), 1939.
Le Beau Risque, Bernard Valiquette/Editions de l'Action Canadienne-Francaise (Montreal), 1939.

Mondes chimeriques, Bernard Valiquette (Montreal), 1940.

Axe et parallaxes, Editions Varietes (Montreal), 1941.

Pour un ordre personnaliste, Editions de l'Arbre (Montreal), 1942.

Strophes et catastrophes, Editions de l'Arbre, 1943.

Anatole Laplante, curieux homme, Editions de l'Arbre, 1944.

Nous ferons l'avenir, Fides (Montreal), 1945.

Cosmos: Poemes, Serge Brousseau (Montreal), 1945.

Journal d'Anatole Laplante, Serge Brousseau, 1947.

Quatorze, Rene Debresse (Paris), 1948.

Six Femmes, un homme, Editions de l'Ermite (Paris), 1949.

Jeux de mer et de soleil, Editions de l'Ermitage, 1951.

Mes Naufrages, Editions de l'Ermite, 1951.

Un Canadien errant, Editions de l'Ermite, 1953.

Claudine et les ecueils, suivi de La Folle, Editions de l'Ermite, 1954.

Afrique, Nouvelles Editions de l'Ermite (Paris), 1955.

Jeremie et Barabbas, Editions de la Diaspora Francaise (Paris), 1959.

O Canada, mon pays, mes amours, Editions de la Diaspora Francaise, 1959.

Journal philosophique et litteraire, Editions de la Diaspora Francaise, 1961.

Poemes europeens, Editions de la Diaspora Francaise, 1962.

Du separatisme quebecois, Editions de la Diaspora Francaise, 1963.

Meditations philosophiques, 1952-1962, Editions de la Diaspora Francaise, 1964.

Anthologie 1934-1964, Editions de la Diaspora Francaise, 1964.

La Morte, Editions de la Diaspora Francaise, 1965.

Poemes perdus et retrouves, anciens et nouveaux, Editions de la Diaspora Francaise, 1966.

Vers une sagesse, Editions de la Diaspora Francaise, 1966.

Louis Prefontaine apostat: Autobiographie approximative, Editions du Jour (Montreal), 1967.

Cent Ans d'injustice? Un Beau Reve: Le Canada, Editions du Jour, 1967.

Poemes d'hier et d'aujourd'hui, 1927-1967, Editions de la Diaspora Francaise, 1967.

Du metalangage, Editions de la Diaspora Francaise, 1968.

Divagations sur le langage, suivies de quelques discours aux sourds, Editions de la Diaspora Francaise, 1969.

Tout en faisant le tour du monde, Editions de la Diaspora Francaise, 1971.

Souvenirs, historiettes, reflexions, Editions de la Diaspora Francaise, 1972.

Noveaux Souvenirs, nouvelles reflexions, Editions de la Diaspora Francaise, 1973.

Mystere cosmique et condition humaine, La Presse (Montreal), 1975.

Souvenirs et impressions du premier age, du deuxieme du troisieme age: memoires humoristiques et litteraires, Stanke (Montreal), 1976.

Contributor to periodicals, including *Action Nationale, Action Universitaire, Cite libre,* and *Cahiers de l'Academie Canadienne-Francaise.*

SIDELIGHTS: Born Rodolphe Dube, Francois Hertel took the name of a French-Canadian soldier and hero who lived from 1642 until 1722 as his nom de plume for all of his numerous publications. A philosopher, theologian, priest, and teacher as well as a writer of fiction and poetry, Hertel was an iconoclastic figure in French-Canadian society of the mid-twentieth century. He was considered "a raiser of consciousness, a humanist in the broad sense of the term, a writer full of spirit and often of rancor," according to Richard Giguere, writing in *Dictionary of Literary Biography.* Hertel was both lauded by students and colleagues and derided by his equally passionate detractors.

Born in 1905, Hertel entered the priesthood in 1938. While teaching literature and history at various colleges in Quebec and Ontario, Hertel decided to leave Canada and the priesthood in 1947 following a religious crisis in his life. Subsequently, he established a permanent residence in Paris in 1949. Hertel wrote on a variety of subjects throughout his life, though most of his works are underpinned by the concept of God according to critics. Hertel published, wrote, taught and lectured for three decades in France, making occasional return visits to his native Quebec.

As a philosopher and essayist, Hertel confronted various trends of the middle twentieth century, including atheistic and Christian existentialism, and personalism. Critics claim that his dedication to the search for answers and his rejection of dogmatism of any kind, however, kept him from formulating an organized philosophical response to these questions. After 1947, Hertel's works were devoid of references to God, yet still included the concept of a higher power.

Hertel also wrote on social and political questions of his day, taking on capitalism in *Pour un ordre personnaliste* (1942) and commenting on the generation that came of age in the 1930s in *Leur Inquietude* (1936). In such works as *Nous ferons l'avenir* (1945), *Du separatisme quebecois* (1963), and *Cent Ans d'injustice?* (1967), Hertel vehemently critiqued Quebec society. Three works published in the 1970s, *Souvenirs, historiettes, reflexions* (1972), *Nouveaux Souvenirs, nouvelles reflexions* (1973), and *Souvenirs et impressions du premier age, du deuxieme age du troisieme age* (1976), collect the author's impressions and memories of Quebec society of the 1930s and 1940s. Hertel also produced volumes on his theories on language. The works included *Du metalangage* (1968) and *Divagations sur le langage, suivies de quelques discours aux sourds* (1969). Giguere remarked: "Hertel never freed himself of a spiritualistic vision of the world and of an essentially humanistic culture as represented by the Bible, the Greek and Roman traditions, the French classics, and the works of world-renowned poets."

Hertel is best remembered as a poet, according to Giguere, who noted that the author's poems "are bittersweet, lyrical, ironic, vindictive, and at times choleric; sometimes they are descriptive, sometimes philosophical, but always speculative." The author has been compared to French poet Paul Claudel for the style and tone in his verse. Like other Quebec poets during World War II, Hertel penned verse of a spiritual nature during that era. Following the war, Hertel's poetry became overly philosophical, religious, and metaphysical. His verse of the 1950s and 1960s, returned to the more personal voice and classical forms of his work of the 1930s.

Hertel also wrote the novels *Le Beau Risque* (1939), *Anatole Laplante, curieux homme* (1944), and *Journal d'Anatole Laplante* (1947) that satirize Quebec society. These works became the subject of heated debates in the public sphere, earning their author both fans and enemies. Hertel also penned short story collections, including *Six Femmes, un homme* (1949) and *Jeremie et Barabbas* (1959).

Despite his numerous polemical writings on important social, political, religious, and philosophical questions of his day, Hertel occupies a small place in the history of Quebec literature. As a person of "unpredictable and unmethodical temperament," in the words of critic Giguere, Hertel was more successful at disrupting the status quo with his iconoclastic pronouncements and controversial satires of French-Canadian society, than he was at formulating a consistent response to his world. Giguere concludes that, undeniably brilliant and influential in his own lifetime, Hertel is all but forgotten even by those university students most affected by his life's work.

BIOGRAPHICAL/CRITICAL SOURCES:

BOOKS

Blais, Jacques, *De l'Ordre et de l'Aventure, La Poesie au Quebec, 1934-1944,* Presses de l'Universite Laval, 1975.
Dictionary of Literary Biography, Volume 68: *Canadian Writers, 1920-1959,* Gale, 1988, pp. 175-79.

PERIODICALS

Action Nationale, March, 1947, pp. 332-46.

Voix et Images, September, 1976, pp. 47-59.

*   *   *

HIGHWAY, Tomson 1951-

PERSONAL: Born December 6, 1951 (some sources say 1952), in northwest Manitoba, Canada. *Education:* Attended Guy Hill Indian Residential School, The Pas, Manitoba, 1957-66; Churchill High School, Winnipeg, Manitoba, graduated 1970; University of Manitoba, Faculty of Music; University of Western Ontario, B. Mus. (with honors), 1975, and B.A. in English, 1977.

ADDRESSES: Office— Playwrights Canada, 54 Wolseley St., 2nd Floor, Toronto, Ontario M5C 1A5.

CAREER: Worked with Canadian writer James Reaney on the plays *The Canadian Brothers* and *Wacousta;* associated with numerous Native support groups; De-ba-jehmu-jig Theatre Group, then located in West Bay, Ontario; Native Earth Performing Arts, Inc., Toronto, Ontario, artistic director, until 1992.

MEMBER: Playwrights Union of Canada.

AWARDS, HONOURS: Chalmers Award, 1986, Dora Mavor Moore Award, 1987-88, both for *The Rez Sisters;* four Dora Mavor Moore Awards, including one for best play, for *Dry Lips Oughta Move to Kapuskasing; The Rez Sisters* was selected to represent Canada at Edinburgh Festival, 1988; Wang Festival Award, 1989.

WRITINGS:

The Rez Sisters (two-act play), first produced at National Canadian Centre, Toronto, Ontario, 1986; published by Fifth House, 1988.
Aria (monologues), produced at Makka Kleist Annex Theatre, Toronto, Ontario, 1987.
Dry Lips Oughta Move to Kapuskasing (play; also known as *The Red Brothers*), first produced at Theatre Passe Muraille, Toronto, Ontario, 1989; published by Fifth House, 1989.
(With Rene Highway and Bill Merasty) *The Sage, the Dancer, and the Fool* (play), first produced at National Canadian Centre, Toronto, Ontario, 1989.

Also collaborated with Rene Highway on the multimedia dance production *New Song . . . New Dance,* 1987-88.

SIDELIGHTS: Thomson Highway has won Canadian awards for his plays, several of which have been performed in New York City. As artistic director of Native Earth Performing Arts, the only professional Native American theater company in Toronto, he has served as producer, actor, stage manager, and playwright. His Native Earth Performing Arts company is one of the few places in North America dedicated to the development of Native dramatic art and has won major awards for its productions and has provided a training ground for talented indigenous people of Canada. An annual festival of new Native playwrights is staged at the Native Canadian Centre of Toronto during the summer season. Highway's work has been recognized by the Dora Mavor Moore Award during the 1988-1989 season, and the prestigious Wang Festival Award in 1989.

Born in 1951 to a family of Cree trappers and fishermen on the Brochet Reserve in Manitoba, Highway was the eleventh of twelve children. He studied music and literature at the University of Western Ontario, later continuing his academic work in England.

When Thomas King published an excerpt from Highway's 1986 play *The Rez Sisters* in his anthology *All My Relations: An Anthology of Contemporary Canadian Native Fiction,* he stated that it celebrated the value of community, defining community as "the intricate webs of kinship that radiate from a Native sense of family." The characters in Highway's plays have inhabited the same place for many generations, have become intimately familiar with the local plants and animals, have been imbued by the weathers, the winds, the waters with a shared sensibility, and know each other so well that they can communicate in a kind of private code like members of a family. Highway's characters, wrote King, in his introduction, "are related to one another through blood, marriage, adoption, or acceptance." This sense of a continuous communal identity constitutes the major defining trait of Native literature, since non-Native writers "prefer to imagine their Indians as solitary figures poised on the brink of extinction." Therefore, the presentation of such inter-related survivors of all the genocidal assaults that have been endured is the most important theme, and the raucous good humor with which they celebrate their endurance is the significant tone of this drama.

The Rez Sisters takes place on Manitoulin Island. Seven women fantasize about winning the million-dollar jackpot in a bingo game, feverishly imagining how it will change their lives on the island in Lake Huron. The dramatist set his play in a Manitoulin reservation that he called the Wasayshigan Hill Indian Reserve. Involved in the excursion are Marie-Adele Starblanket, mother of fourteen; Emily Dictionary, whose lover has just been killed in a motorcycle accident; Veronique St. Pierre, who has adopted a mentally-impaired daughter; Annie Cook who aspires to be a country-rock singer; Philomena Moosetail who hopes to purchase a real toilet with her winnings; Pelagia Rosella Patchnose who is trying to reshingle her little welfare house and dreams of sailing away somewhere; and Zhaboonigan Peterson. Their farcical dialogue compensates for their bleak existence, which has forced their men off-

shore to attempt to make a living in far-flung places. Fragments of their traditional culture surface in references to "the old stories, the old language. Almost all gone." There are references to the mythical cannibal giant, Windigo, to the tribal trickster, Nanabush, and off-handed uses of Anishinabe phrases such as "Aw-ni-ginaw-ee-dick" ["Oh, go on"]. *The Rez Sisters* was given a two-week run at the New York Theatre Workshop in December of 1993. It was presented in collaboration with the American Indian Community House where it previewed beginning on December 3, 1993.

The Red Brothers, which Highway later changed to *Dry Lips Oughta Move to Kapuskasing,* won the Dora Mavor Moore Award for best new play and received its Canadian staging at the Theatre Passe Muraille in Toronto from April 25 to May 21, 1989. Earlier that same year, another play of Thomson's, *The Sage, the Dancer, and the Fool,* was performed at the Native Canadian Centre of Toronto. Reviewers were struck by the gusto and courage of Highway's people. The *New York Times* singled out his "colorful creation of community" among those who "are proud of their Indian heritage but also caught by the promises of an alien culture." The spare sets and sparse stagings—a circle of birch trees and some wooden chairs—serve as metaphors for the magic of the oral tradition. An entire world is recreated in this meager setting simply by means of talk.

BIOGRAPHICAL/CRITICAL SOURCES:

BOOKS

King, Thomas, editor *All My Relations: An Anthology of Contemporary Canadian Native Fiction,* McClelland and Stewart, 1990.

Lutz, Hartmut, *Contemporary Challenges: Conversations with Canadian Native Authors,* Fifth House Publishers, 1991, pp. 89-95.

Native North American Literature, Gale, 1994.

Petrone, Penny, *Native Literature in Canada: From the Oral Tradition to the Present,* Oxford University Press, Canada, 1990, pp. 138-81.

PERIODICALS

Advocate, June 18, 1991, p. 76.

Canadian Literature, autumn, 1991, pp. 169-70.

Maclean's, May 8, 1989, p. 62; April 29, 1991, pp. 60-61.

The New York Times, January 5, 1994, pp. C15, C21.

Quill and Quire, March, 1989, pp. 76-77.

Theater, winter, 1992, pp. 88-92.

Theatre Research International, autumn, 1992, pp. 217-25.

HINE, (William) Daryl 1936-

PERSONAL: Born February 24, 1936, in New Westminster (some sources say Burnaby), British Columbia, Canada; son of Robert Fraser and Elsie (James) Hine. *Education:* Attended McGill University, 1954-57; University of Chicago, M.A., 1965, Ph.D., 1967.

ADDRESSES: Home—2740 Ridge Ave., Evanston, IL 60201.

CAREER: Poet, novelist, translator, playwright. Assistant professor of English, University of Chicago, 1967-69, visiting professor, 1978.

AWARDS, HONOURS: Canada Foundation-Rockefeller fellowship, 1958; Canada Council grant, 1959; Ingram Merrill Award, 1962, 1963, 1983; Canada Council senior arts grant, 1979; Guggenheim fellowship, 1980; American Academy and Institution of Arts and Letters award, 1982; MacArthur Foundation fellowship, 1986.

WRITINGS:

POETRY

Five Poems, Emblem Books, 1955.
The Carnal and the Crane, Contact Press, 1957.
The Devil's Picture Book, Abelard, 1960.
Heroics: Five Poems, Grosswiller (France), 1961.
The Wooden Horse, Atheneum, 1965.
Minutes, Atheneum, 1968.
Resident Alien, Atheneum, 1975.
In and Out, privately printed, 1975, revised edition, 1989.
Daylight Saving, Atheneum, 1978.
Selected Poems, Oxford University Press (Toronto), 1980, Atheneum, 1981.
Academic Festival Overtures, Atheneum, 1985.
In and Out: A Confessional Poem, Knopf, 1989.
Postscripts, Random House, 1990, Knopf (New York), 1991.

Also author of the poetry collection *Arrondissements,* 1988.

PLAYS

A Mutual Flame (radio play), BBC, 1961.
The Death of Seneca, produced in Chicago, 1968.
Alcestis (radio play), BBC, 1972.

TRANSLATOR

The Homeric Hymns and the Battle of the Frogs and Mice, Atheneum, 1972.
(And author of commentary) *Theocritus: Idylls and Epigrams,* Atheneum, 1982.
Ovid's Heroines: A Verse Translation of the Heroides, Yale University Press, 1991.

OTHER

The Prince of Darkness & Co. (novel), Abelard-Schuman, 1961.
Polish Subtitles: Impressions from a Journey (nonfiction), Abelard-Schuman, 1962.
(Editor with Joseph Parisi) *The "Poetry" Anthology, 1912-1977,* Houghton, 1978.

Contributor of poems to the *New Yorker* and other magazines.

Editor, *Poetry,* 1968-78.

WORK IN PROGRESS: More poems and translations.

SIDELIGHTS: Formerly the editor of *Poetry* magazine, Daryl Hine is an accomplished Canadian poet whose classical education permeates his original writing as well as his translations of Homeric verse. Considered a poet's poet with an affinity for structured rhyme and meter, Hine has experimented with villanelles, sestinas, alexandrines, and what Louis Dudek in his *Selected Essays and Criticism,* calls a variety of "other formal metrical rhyme schemes that he can send spinning into the heights of philosophical outerspace." Though his early verse addresses abstract subjects like history, art, and literature, Hine's more recent poems have become personal in content, exploring such sensitive issues as his unhappy childhood and his emerging homosexuality. Whatever his subject, Hine's poems "have the authority of the maker in firm control of his craft," according to *New York Times Book Review* contributor Daniel Hoffman.

Technically flawless in the minds of many, Hine's poems nonetheless strike some critics as bloodless and detached. "In Daryl Hine," writes Dudek, "we have an amazingly capable poet for whom poetry is not a mimetic art, whose eye is not in a fine frenzy rolling, who does not overflow with powerful emotion, who does not feed and water the passions, who is not an original, or a legislator, or a man speaking to me . . . but a poet from whom poetry is a series of extremely recherche, abstract, contrived word forms, containing oblique and ambiguous philosophical essays and meditations." In his *Alone with America: Essays on the Art of Poetry in the United States since 1950,* Richard Howard acknowledges that Hine's approach to verse is controlled, but points out that ideally the ordered form should release rather than suppress emotion. Using that criterion, Howard believes Hine's early books fall short: "We are not aware, in Daryl Hine's first poems, of the nagging presence of anything so extraneous or so impure as 'the real world'—the poet never appeals to it as a means of settling or solving the difficulties of art; for him, the poem is always the statement of itself, a piece of language with which no more can be done and which, if it fails in its own terms, cannot be ransomed or relieved."

Not until the publication of *The Wooden Horse,* Hine's sixth book of verse, do the poems begin to break out of what *New York Review of Books* contributor Marius Bewley describes as "their armorial cocoons of meter and syntax." Howard notes that a relaxation of tone "characterizes most of *The Wooden Horse,* which is to say that it is in closer contact with the disorder of life than the earlier, the younger decorum of wit allowed. . . . The world, in Hine's first poems, came to a stop but also lit up. Now it is no longer incandescent, but it moves." In his later poems, Hine continues his exploration of the personal, prompting Phoebe Pettingell to suggest in the *New Leader* that "what has changed is the depth of suffering and vulnerability resonating through much of his output."

Academic Festival Overtures, Hine's 1985 publication, demonstrates his investigation of painful personal themes. Written in alternating rhymed lines of twelve and thirteen syllables, the poem is "autobiography in classical disguise," according to *New York Times book Review* contributor Harold Beaver, who describes it as a "virtuoso achievement" and "a remarkable record of a yearning, bookish and inhibited boyhood. Beyond the metrical screen Mr. Hine imposes on his memoirs, he paces to and from—as if watching from behind the self-imposed bars of his caged existence. . . . [*Academic Festival Overtures*] merges memory and desire, bookishness and smut, with the most dexterous and expert touch."

In and Out, the poet's 1989 work, is a long, narrative poem about Hine's brief flirtation with the Catholic church following the failure of a college love affair (the young man left Hine for a woman). While he eventually realizes that his sexuality cannot be subsumed or avoided by committing himself to the church, the work provides the occasion for a series of meditations on sexuality and spirituality. Writing in *Chicago Tribune,* Larry Kart calls it a "very readable book . . . at once supple and prickly, bitchy and cute," and Richard Ryan calls it "stylish but flawed" in *Washington Post,* in part because Hine fails to account for or fully explore the reason for his conversion. Written entirely in anapestic meter—which Hine points out "looks like free verse but isn't"—the poem's "prosody offers genuine pleasure" for Ryan, but doesn't dispel his sense that "the elegance dresses up banality." *New Republic* contributor D. J. Enright, however, finds that "In these confessions, spiritual and sexual, the ebullience and even comicality of the erotic element help to preserve a decency rarely found in literary dealings with the subject, whatever their bias." Enright calls *In and Out* a "lightly epic poem" and notes that there are moments in which "we enjoy fascinating conversations" between the narrator and the Abbe of a monastery he visits. Genevieve Stuttaford, writing in *Publishers Weekly,* simply calls the poem "remark-

able" and, noting its "narrative pleasures," appraised that work has "the breadth of a novel."

First published in 1990, *Postscripts* represented Hine's first collection of lyric poems in 13 years. The book received mixed reviews from both Louis McKee in *Library Journal* and Jim Elledge in *Booklist.* While Elledge calls Hine's work "urbane, witty, even scholarly," he finds that it often seems too emotionally distanced from its subject matter. Elledge complained that the poems often serve as "a showplace for Hine's intellect" as opposed to conveying any kind of emotional attachment or incident. McKee's *Booklist* review notes that while at times the poems flow "majestically," they also intimate far too much attention to detail and the mechanics of form. McKee concludes that Hine's fixation with the technical side of his writing reduces these poems to "mere wordplay."

Despite intermittent complaints regarding his dedication to form—such as McKee's—many critics consider Hine a forerunner in contemporary poetry. His work is praised for both perpetuating conventional styles and exploring new territory. Commenting on Hine's development as a poet, the *New Leader*'s Pettingell concludes, "Daryl Hine made a strong beginning as a poet, but . . . he has traveled far. Today he is one of the most powerful voices addressing the human condition."

BIOGRAPHICAL/CRITICAL SOURCES:

BOOKS

Contemporary Literary Criticism, Volume 15, Gale, 1980.
Dudek, Louis, *Selected Essays and Criticism,* Tecumseh, 1978.
Howard, Richard, *Alone with America: Essays on the Art of Poetry in the United States since 1950,* Atheneum, 1969.

PERIODICALS

Booklist, January, 1991, p. 108; February 15, 1991, p. 1174.
Canadian Literature, summer, 1988, pp. 173-74.
Chicago Tribune, March 5, 1989, section 14, p. 3.
Chicago Tribune Book World, September 13, 1981.
Library Journal, January, 1991, p. 108.
New Leader, September 7, 1981; March 6, 1989, p. 15.
New Republic, May 15, 1989, p. 46-48.
New York Review of Books, March 31, 1966.
New York Times Book Review, September 4, 1966; November 24, 1968; March 2, 1986.
Publishers Weekly, December 2, 1988, p. 40-41.
Saturday Night, February, 1981.
Saturday Review, March 15, 1969.
Time, September 25, 1978.
Times Literary Supplement, August 15, 1975; October 20, 1978.

Washington Post, July 9, 1989, p. 3.
Washington Post Book World, October 22, 1978; August 2, 1981.

*   *   *

HORSELY, Ramsbottom
See BERNE, Eric (Lennard)

*   *   *

HOUSTON, James A(rchibald) 1921-

PERSONAL: Born June 12, 1921, in Toronto, Ontario, Canada; came to the United States in 1962; son of James Donald (a clothing importer) and Gladys Maud (Barbour) Houston; married Alma G. Bardon, 1950 (divorced, 1966); married Alice Daggett Watson, December 9, 1967; children: John James, Samuel Douglas. *Education:* Attended Ontario College of Art, 1938-40, Ecole Grand Chaumiere, Paris, 1947-48, Unichi-Hiratsuka, Tokyo, 1958-59, and Atelier 17, Paris, 1961. *Religion:* Church of England. *Avocational interests:* Fishing, sketching, sculpting.

ADDRESSES: Home—24 Main Street, Stonington, CT 06378 (winter); P.O. Box 43, Tlell, Queen Charlotte Islands, British Columbia, V0T 1Y0, Canada (summer).*Office*—Steuben, 717 Fifth Ave., New York, NY 10022.

CAREER: Author, illustrator, designer, educator, and filmmaker. Canadian Guild of Crafts, Arctic adviser, 1949-52; Federal Government of Canada, northern service officer, Northwest Territories, 1952-57, officer in charge of East Arctic Patrol, 1953-55, first civil administrator for West Baffin Island, Northwest Territories, 1958-62; Steuben Glass, New York City, associate director of design, 1962-72, consultative director of design, 1972—; master designer, 1988—. Visiting lecturer at Wye Institute, Rhode Island School of Design, and Northern Illinois University. Film work includes associate producer and techical adviser of *The White Dawn,* Paramount, 1974; producer, director, and screenwriter of documentaries for the Devonian Foundation, including *So Sings the Wolf,* 1976, *Kalvak's Arctic Visions,* 1976, *Legends of the Salmon People,* 1977, and *Art of the Arctic Whaleman,* 1978; screenwriter and technical adviser for *Kenojuak,* National Film Board of Canada, 1961. Chair of board of directors of Canadian Arctic Producers, 1976-77, and American Indian Art Center; member of board of directors of Alaskan Indian Arts, Canadian Eskimo Arts Council, and Arctic Society of Canada; member of board of governors of Anthropology Museum of Brown Univer-

sity; president of Indian and Eskimo Art of the Americas; vice-president of West Baffin Eskimo Cooperative and Eskimo Art, Inc.; member of primitive art committee of Metropolitan Museum of Art. Art has appeared in exhibitions with Canadian Guild of Crafts, 1953, 1955, and 1957; Robertson Galleries, Ottawa, 1953; Calgary Galleries, 1966; Canadiana Galleries, Edmonton, 1977; Yaneff Gallery, Toronto, 1983 and 1986; Steuben Glass, 1987 and 1991; Century Association, 1991. Art represented in collections of National Museum of Canada, Winnipeg Art Gallery, Glenbow-Alberta Museum of Art, Montreal Museum of Fine Arts, National Gallery of Art, Ottawa. *Military service:* Canadian Army, Toronto Scottish Regiment, 1940-45; became warrant officer.

MEMBER: Producers Guild of America, Writers' Union of Canada, Indian and Eskimo Art of the Americas, Explorers Club, Century Association, World Wildlife Fund, Escoheag School Historical Society (president, 1976—).

AWARDS, HONOURS: American Indian and Eskimo Cultural Foundation award, 1966; Canadian Library Association Book of the Year awards, 1966, for *Tikta'liktak: An Eskimo Legend,* 1968, for *The White Archer: An Eskimo Legend,* 1980, for *River Runners: A Tale of Hardship and Bravery,* and runner-up, 1982, for *Long Claws: An Arctic Adventure;* American Library Association Notable Books awards, 1967, for *The White Archer,* 1968, for *Akavak: An Eskimo Journey,* and 1971, for *The White Dawn: An Eskimo Saga;* decorated officer of Order of Canada, 1972; Amelia Frances Howard-Gibbon award runner-up, 1973, for *Ghost Paddle: A Northwest Coast Indian Tale;* Canadian Authors Association Metcalf award, 1977; Queen Elizabeth Silver Anniversary Medal, 1977; Inuit Kuavati Award of Merit, 1979; Metcalf Short Story award, 1980, for "Long Claws" in *The Winter Fun Book;* Canada Council's Children's Literature Prize, special mention for illustrations, 1986; British Columbia Book Prize, 1987, for *The Falcon Bow: An Arctic Legend;* Canadian nominee, Hans Christian Andersen Award, 1987 and 1991; Citation of Merit Award, Royal Canadian Academy of Arts, 1987; Max and Greta Ebel Award, Canadian Society of Children's Authors, Illustrators, and Performers, 1989, for *Whiteout;* Canadian Authors Association literature award for fiction, 1990, for *Running West;* corecipient of film awards, National Film Board of Canada, for *The Living Stone, Legend of the Raven,* and *Kenojuak;* D.Litt., Carleton University, 1972; D.H.L., Rhode Island College, 1975; D.F.A., Rhode Island School of Design, 1979; D.D.L., Dalhousie University, 1987; honorary fellow, Ontario College of Art, and fellow, Royal Society of Art, London, 1981.

WRITINGS:

FOR CHILDREN; SELF-ILLUSTRATED

Tikta'liktak: An Eskimo Legend, Harcourt, 1965.
Eagle Mask: A West Coast Indian Tale, Harcourt, 1966.
The White Archer: An Eskimo Legend, Harcourt, 1967.
Akavak: An Eskimo Journey, Harcourt, 1967.
Wolf Run: A Caribou Eskimo Tale, Harcourt, 1971.
Ghost Paddle: A Northwest Coast Indian Tale, Harcourt, 1972.
Kiviok's Magic Journey: An Eskimo Legend, Atheneum, 1973.
Frozen Fire: A Tale of Courage, Atheneum, 1977.
River Runners: A Tale of Hardship and Bravery, Atheneum, 1979.
Long Claws: An Arctic Adventure, Atheneum, 1981.
Black Diamonds: A Search for Arctic Treasure, Atheneum, 1982.
Ice Swords: An Undersea Adventure, Atheneum, 1985.
The Falcon Bow: An Arctic Legend, Macmillan, 1986.
Whiteout, Key Porter, 1988.
Drifting Snow: An Arctic Search, Macmillan, 1992.

ILLUSTRATOR

Shoot to Live, Queen's Printer, 1944.
Alma Houston, *Nuki,* Lippincott, 1955.
Raymond de Coccola and Paul King, *Ayorama,* Oxford University Press, 1956, revised edition published as *The Incredible Eskimo,* Hancock House, 1986.
Tuktut/Caribou, Queen's Printer, 1957.
Elizabeth Pool, *The Unicorn Was There,* Bauhan, 1966.
(And author of introduction) George Francis Lyon, *The Private Journal of Captain G. F. Lyon of H.M.S. Hecla, During the Recent Voyage of Discovery under Captain Parry, 1921-23,* Imprint Society, 1970.
Mary Jo Wheeler-Smith, *First Came the Indians,* Atheneum, 1983.
J. Kenneth Keatley, *Place Names of the Eastern Shore of Maryland,* Queen Anne Press, 1987.

SCREENPLAYS

(And technical adviser) *Legend of the Raven* (animated), Crawley Films of Canada, 1954.
(Written with John Feeney; and technical adviser) *The Living Stone,* National Film Board of Canada, 1956.
(Coauthor) *Kenojuak,* National Film Board of Canada, 1961.
Shingibus (animated), National Broadcasting Company (NBC), 1963.
Legend of the Eagle (animated), NBC, 1964.
Tikta-liktak (animated), Canadian Broadcasting Corporation (CBC), 1966.
The White Archer (animated), CBC, 1967.
Akavak (animated), CBC, 1969.

The White Dawn, Paramount, 1974.
The Mask and the Drum, Swannsway Productions, 1975.
So Sings the Wolf, Devonian Group, 1976.
Kalvak's Arctic Visions, Devonian Group, 1976.
Legends of the Salmon People, Devonian Group, 1977.
Art of the Arctic Whaleman, Devonian Group, 1978.
Ghost Fox, Sefel Pictures, 1979.
Whiteout, Owl-TV Productions, 1987.

OTHER

Canadian Eskimo Art, Queen's Printer, 1955.
Eskimo Graphic Art, Queen's Printer, 1960.
Eskimo Prints, Barre Publishing, 1967, 2nd edition, 1971.
The White Dawn: An Eskimo Saga (novel; Book-of-the-Month Club main selection), Harcourt, 1971.
(Editor and illustrator) *Songs of the Dream People: Chants and Images from the Indians and Eskimos of North America,* Atheneum, 1972.
Ojibwa Summer, photographs by B. A. King, Barre Publishing, 1972.
Ghost Fox (novel), Harcourt, 1977.
Spirit Wrestler (novel), Harcourt, 1980.
Eagle Song (novel), Harcourt, 1983.
Running West (novel), Crown, 1989.

Ghost Fox has been recorded on eight cassettes by Crane Memorial Library, 1978. Contributor of short stories to periodicals. Houston's manuscripts are collected at the National Library of Canada, Ottawa.

SIDELIGHTS: An author popular with both children and adults, Houston has received numerous awards for his tales of Canada's indigenous peoples, including the Canadian Library Association's Book of the Year award in 1966, 1968, and 1980. While Houston often portrays Native Canadian communities before European settlement, he also delineates the native peoples' attempts to adapt to European influences. Houston's narratives frequently focus on a young male's struggle to survive and to attain spiritual and emotional maturity in a hostile environment. Although Houston's works are largely marketed toward children, the author has stated: "There are no children's stories [in native communities], only adult myths and legends and truths about life. My stories are not really children's stories. They are simply northern stories that are suitable for both children and adults."

Houston's first book, *Tikta'liktak: An Eskimo Legend* (1965), chronicles a young Inuit boy's struggle for survival and triumph over adversity as he finds himself isolated on an ice floe and later on a desolate island. Houston also focuses on Inuit tradition in *Wolf Run: A Caribou Eskimo Tale* (1971), in which a boy searching for food in the hostile wilderness suffers numerous hardships before being saved by two wolves inhabited by the spirits of his grandparents. Although some commentators faulted *Wolf Run* for unsound logic and graphic scenes thought unsuitable for children, other reviewers lauded the work as "a moving and memorable story of human determination and courage." *Long Claws: An Arctic Adventure* (1981) depicts the efforts of a boy named Pitohok and his sister, Upik, to locate food for their starving family. The two children must contend with inclement weather, famine, and a bear attack before they are guided to food and safety by a friendly owl.

In *The White Archer: An Eskimo Legend* (1967), Kungo, an Inuit boy, seeks revenge against the Indian attackers who killed his parents and kidnapped his sister. Throughout the course of the story Kungo learns that the Indians he seeks assaulted his family to avenge the murder of one of their own people by an Inuit man. This knowledge, coupled with Kungo's newly-discovered capacity for mercy and forgiveness, results in Kungo's reunion with his sister and an alliance with his former adversaries. Critics lauded *The White Archer* for its dramatic intensity and described the work as an epic, comparing Kungo to the legendary King Arthur. In *The Falcon Bow: An Arctic Legend* (1986), the sequel to *The White Archer,* Kungo mediates a dispute between Inuit and Indian peoples and prevents a possible war. Although the plot of *The Falcon Bow* has been characterized as simplistic and contrived, critics recognize the value of the book's explanations of such Inuit and Indian practices as building an igloo, starting a fire with a bow drill, and building and piloting a kayak. The title character of *Akavak: An Eskimo Journey* (1968) satisfies his grandfather's dying wish by aiding the old man in his attempt to traverse a treacherous mountain range to visit his brother. Akavak demonstrates his strength and courage on the journey, and although his grandfather dies before completing his trip, Akavak benefits from his elder's wisdom and experience. Critics commended Houston's emotional expression and characterization in *Akavak,* noting the harmony between the characters and their environment.

Unlike his earlier tales of Inuit life, in which his protagonists are at the mercy of nature, Houston's native Canadian stories portray man as the primary antagonist. *Eagle Mask: A West Coast Indian Tale* (1966) depicts the coming-of-age of Skemshan, grandson of Hooits, leader of the Eagle clan. In proving his maturity, Skemshan encounters a group of hostile marauders, defends himself in a bear attack, becomes involved in a whaling expedition, and receives a spiritual message from an eagle. While *Eagle Mask* was faulted by some critics for a lack of unity and weak structure, others praised Houston's ability to convey interesting details of Indian life and write exciting adventure passages. Although it was published in 1972, *Ghost Paddle: A Northwest Coast Indian Tale,* is a "prequel" to *Eagle Mask* and delineates Hooits's own coming-of-age

when he joins his father and a group of young people on a peacemaking mission to land of the Inland River People. Hooits wins a battle reminiscent of David and Goliath with a massive Inland River slave and proves his maturity by successfully wielding a ghost paddle fashioned after his father's dream vision. While some critics observed that *Ghost Paddle* lacked the dramatic intensity of Houston's Inuit tales, others echoed Zena Sutherland, who commented: "[*Ghost Paddle*] is so deftly imbued with the spirit and the cultural details of Hooits' people that the incorporation seems effortless and the theme has a pertinence for today."

River Runners: A Tale of Hardship and Bravery (1979), follows Andrew Stewart, a 15-year-old white boy, and Pashak, a Naskapi Indian teen, as they attempt to build a winter fur trading depot in northern Canada. The two successfully complete the depot, but are faced with starvation when the caribou herds that would provide them with food throughout the winter do not arrive. Due to Pashak's background and knowledge, the teens are able to travel south with a Naskapi family to an area rich with caribou. In the spring they return to their original post, but because of Andrew's superior attitude and naivete, lose much of the fur they had managed to trap. Andrew learns respect for native skills and culture and vows to remain in the Arctic to complete the project he began. Critics praised Houston's attention to authentic details, but faulted the work's loosely constructed plot and weak character development.

In the late 1970s Houston began depicting more contemporary situations involving white and native teenagers. *Frozen Fire: A Tale of Courage* (1977), the first book in a trilogy, traces the escapades of Matthew Morgan, a white teenager, and Kayak, his Inuit friend, as the two attempt to rescue Matthew's father, a prospector whose helicopter crashed in an Arctic storm. The teens are faced with numerous obstacles along the way, including running out of fuel for their snowmobile, losing their equipment, and becoming lost in a blizzard. They are finally saved by an Inuit "wildman" who gives them shelter in his underground home. While underground, Matt discovers the gold for which his father had been searching, and the two are rescued after they combine their survival skills to signal a passing plane. Matt is eventually reunited with his father, who had been rescued by an Inuit man. Critics applauded Houston's ability to fairly represent and illustrate the merits of both white and Inuit culture in *Frozen Fire.*

In the second book of the trilogy, *Black Diamonds: A Search for Arctic Treasure* (1982), the characters from *Frozen Fire* return to the Arctic to locate the gold Matthew discovered on the previous expedition. In *Ice Swords: An Undersea Adventure* (1985), the last book in the trilogy, Matthew and Kayak embark upon an underwater excursion in search of the narwhal, a type of whale. The two become involved in various predicaments, but finally emerge unscathed. *Black Diamonds* and *Ice Swords* were considered by critics to be disappointing sequels to *Frozen Fire,* largely because in these works Matthew and Kayak learn very little from their adventures. Many commentators agreed with Ray Jones, who remarked, "At the end [of *Black Diamonds*], we have no sense that the journey has been other than a mechanical device for creating melodramatic adventures."

In *Whiteout* (1988) Houston introduces teenager Jon Aird, who has been convicted of drug possession and sent to live with a strict uncle in Nanuvik, an Arctic settlement. While in the Arctic, Jon must complete a year of community service teaching at a government school. The majority of the book's action takes place while Jon, his girlfriend Panee, and her brother Pudlo, are on an ice-fishing expedition. A storm ensues, and Jon learns to respect and value Inuit survival skills in the harsh Arctic climate. *Whiteout* has been widely commended for its treatment of cultural conflict and integration, young love, and the strength and nobility of Canada's Arctic peoples.

BIOGRAPHICAL/CRITICAL SOURCES:

BOOKS

Children's Literature Review, Volume 3, Gale, 1978, pp. 83-88.
Egoff, Sheila, *The Republic of Childhood: A Critical Guide to Canadian Children's Literature in English,* Oxford University Press, 1975.
Something about the Author Autobiography Series, Volume 17, Gale, 1994.
Taylor, Charles, *Six Journeys: A Canadian Pattern,* House of Anansi, 1977, pp. 73-104.
Twentieth-Century Children's Writers, 3rd edition, St. James Press, 1989, pp. 468-470.

PERIODICALS

American Library Journal, summer, 1987, pp. 391-402.
Booklist, October 15, 1992, p. 430.
Christianity Today, May 14, 1990, p. 60.
Canadian Children's Literature, Volume 31/32, 1983.
Connecticut Magazine, January, 1993, pp. 34-39.
Globe and Mail (Toronto), November 30, 1985; November 12, 1988.
In Review: Canadian Books for Children, winter, 1969, pp. 26-27.
New Yorker, August 29, 1988, pp. 33-47.
New York Times Book Review, October 8, 1967; December 13, 1981, p. 39; February 14, 1988, p. 23.
Washington Post, April 15, 1983.

HUGHES, Monica (Ince) 1925-

PERSONAL: Born November 3, 1925, in Liverpool, England; naturalized Canadian citizen, 1957; daughter of Edward Lindsay (a mathematician) and Phyllis (Fry) Ince; married Glen Hughes (in city government), April 22, 1957; children: Elizabeth, Adrienne, Russell, Thomas. *Education:* Attended Edinburgh University, 1942-43. *Avocational interests:* Swimming, walking, beachcombing ("very difficult on the prairies"), gardening.

ADDRESSES: Home—13816 110-A Ave., Edmonton, Alberta, Canada T5M 2M9. *Agent*—M.G.A. Agency, 10 St. Mary St., Suite 510, Toronto, Ontario, Canada M4Y 1P9.

CAREER: Dress designer in London, England, 1948-49, and Bulawayo, Rhodesia (now Zimbabwe), 1950; bank clerk in Umtali, Rhodesia, 1951; National Research Council, Ottawa, Ontario, laboratory technician, 1952-57; full-time writer, 1975—. Writer in residence at several universities, including University of Alberta, 1984-85. *Military service:* Women's Royal Naval Service, 1943-46.

MEMBER: International PEN, Writers Union of Canada, Canadian Society of Children's Authors, Illustrators, and Performers, SF Canada, Writers Guild of Alberta.

AWARDS, HONOURS: Vicky Metcalf Award, Canadian Authors Association, 1981, for body of work, and 1983, for short story; Alberta Culture Juvenile Novel Award and Bay's Beaver Award, both 1981, Canada Council prize for children's literature, 1982, American Library Association (ALA) Best Book for Young Adults citation, and Young Adult Canadian Book Award, both 1983, all for *Hunter in the Dark;* Canada Council prize for children's literature, 1981, for *The Guardian of Isis;* ALA Best Book for Young Adults citation, 1981, and International Board on Books for Young People's honor list citation, 1982, both for *The Keeper of the Isis Light;* Guardian Award runner-up, 1983, for *Ring-Rise, Ring-Set;* Alberta R. Ross Annett Award, Writers Guild of Alberta, 1983, 1984, 1986; Hans Christian Andersen Award nomination, 1984.

WRITINGS:

NOVELS FOR JUVENILES

Gold-Fever Trail: A Klondike Adventure, illustrated by Patricia Peacock, John LeBel, 1974.
Crisis on Conshelf Ten, Copp, 1975.
Earthdark, Hamish Hamilton, 1977.
The Ghost Dance Caper, Hamish Hamilton, 1978.
The Tomorrow City, Hamish Hamilton, 1978.
Beyond the Dark River, Atheneum, 1979.
Hunter in the Dark, Atheneum, 1982.
Ring-Rise, Ring-Set, F. Watts, 1982.

The Beckoning Lights, illustrated by Richard A. Conroy, F. Watts, 1982.

The Treasure of the Long Sault, illustrated by Conroy, John LeBel, 1982.

Space Trap, MacRae, 1983, F. Watts, 1984.

My Name Is Paula Popowich, Lorimer, 1983.

Devil on My Back, MacRae, 1984.

Sandwriter, MacRae, 1984.

The Dream Catcher, MacRae, 1986.

Blaine's Way, Irwin, 1986.

Log Jam, Irwin, 1987, published in England as *Spirit River,* Methuen, 1988.

Little Fingerling: A Japanese Folktale, illustrated by Brenda Clark, Kids Can Press, 1989.

The Promise, Methuen, 1990.

Invitation to the Game, Simon & Schuster, 1990.

The Refuge, Doubleday, 1990.

The Crystal Drop, Methuen, 1992.

Sandwriter, Simon & Schuster, 1993.

"ISIS" TRILOGY

The Keeper of the Isis Light, Atheneum, 1980.

The Guardian of Isis, Atheneum, 1981.

The Isis Pedlar, Atheneum, 1982.

OTHER

A Handful of Seeds, illustrated by Luis Garay, Lester, 1993.

Contributor to numerous books including, *Magook,* McClelland & Stewart, 1977; *Dragons and Dreams,* Harper, 1985; *Take Your Knee Off My Heart,* Methuen, 1990; and *Mother's Day,* Methuen, 1992.

Hughes's papers are housed in a permanent collection at the University of Calgary, Alberta.

WORK IN PROGRESS: The Golden Aquarians, a science fiction novel; *The Castle Tourmandyne,* a modern novel.

SIDELIGHTS: Monica Hughes is generally considered to be one of Canada's finest writers for children and young adults—"a writer of rare integrity and great narrative powers," according to Marcus Crouch in *Junior Bookshelf.* Prolific in many genres, she is best known for her science fiction. Like her other work, it is often praised for its lively plotting, well-grounded characterizations, and sensitive exploration of moral issues. Sarah Ellis adds in *Horn Book* that "a documentary flair is also a factor in one of Monica Hughes's great strengths as a science fiction writer—her technical neatness. She always manages to give the essential scientific background economically, without becoming bogged down in hardware."

Hughes travelled the world for many years before settling in Canada and beginning to write seriously. Most of her novels are set in Canada or in an alien world very similar to it. Her first published work was a Canadian historical adventure entitled *Gold-Fever Trail: A Klondike Adventure.* Thanks to Hughes's extensive research, the setting is made vividly real, and "the reader becomes completely engrossed" in the author's evocation of Canada's Gold Rush, writes Marion Pape in the *World of Children's Books.* Marion Brown notes in *In Review: Canadian Books for Children* that "Ms. Hughes's prose style is straightforward, lucid and extremely readable, and her characters are believable flesh and blood people. . . . I only wish that the author had spent twice as much time and effort to make the book twice as long." *Gold-Fever Trail* was used as a supplemental history text in the schools of Alberta, Canada.

Hughes moved into science fiction with her second novel, *Crisis on Conshelf Ten.* Like much of her work in this genre, it is set in the near future and involves a logical projection of present-day events on Earth. In *Crisis on Conshelf Ten,* the exploitation of Third World countries has been extended to lunar and undersea colonies. Outlaw bands of settlers strike back against the greedy corporations that oppress them by sabotaging oil and fishery plants. While some reviewers find Hughes's political message somewhat overstated, most praise her for a fast-moving story and a fascinating portrayal of undersea living.

Themes of ecological and cultural harmony also dominate *Beyond the Dark River.* The story takes place some time after a Canadian nuclear holocaust. City dwellers have become savage mutants; only the inhabitants of certain isolated communities have survived unharmed. Groups who have always been self-sufficient, such as the Cree Indians and the German Hutterites, have suffered little from the collapse of the great urban centers, but when a mysterious plague begins to claim the small children of these communities, two young people—an Indian girl and a Hutterite boy, aged fifteen and sixteen—join forces to brave the urban mutants in their search for effective medicine. Once again Hughes was praised for her enlightening portrait of both the Cree and Hutterite cultures, as well as her "vividly realized post-apocalypse Canada," as Neil Philip describes it in the *Times Educational Supplement.* The author's message about the importance of living in harmony with the earth never overpowers her story, believes Patrick Verrour; he writes in *In Review: Canadian Books for Children* that *Beyond the Dark River* proves "that [Hughes] can write fast-moving narrative without neglecting to touch on some deep concerns she has about technology's threat to individual freedom."

Hughes's most acclaimed work is her "Isis" trilogy; *The Keeper of the Isis Light, The Guardian of Isis,* and *The Isis Pedlar.* The trilogy embraces many of its author's favorite themes, including moral growth through struggle, survival in alien environments, and the integration of cultures. Deep in space and far in the future, the planet Isis has been settled only by a scientist couple from Earth and their child, born on Isis. At the opening of *The Keeper of ι. . Isis Light,* however, the planet is inhabited only by an extraordinarily intelligent robot, The Guardian, and Olwen Pendennis, a sixteen-year-old girl. Olwen has no memory of her life before the age of five, when her parents were killed. The Guardian saved Olwen and surgically altered her body to ensure her survival in Isis's atmosphere. When a new party of settlers arrives, Olwen cannot understand why they are repulsed by her leathery green-gold skin and huge nostrils. They offer to take her in if she will submit to more surgical alterations—alterations which would make her physically acceptable to the colonists, but also dependent on their life-support systems. Olwen eventually decides to remain free, although that means she must accept her aloneness as well. Thoughtful and absorbing, *The Keeper of the Isis Light* "reverberates in the reader's mind long after . . . the last world," declares *In Review: Canadian Books for Children* contributor Irma McDonough.

The Guardian of Isis and *The Isis Pedlar* follow the descendants of the planet's second settlers as they quickly regress to a primitive superstitious state. The Guardian has come to be worshipped as a god; the unnaturally long-lived Olwen is regarded as a witch. Together they manage to set the budding society of Isis on the right course. "It is a long time since I was so impressed by a book about the future," writes Crouch in a *Junior Bookshelf* review of *The Guardian of Isis.* "Monica Hughes tells a grand story; she is also a serious anthropologist and philosopher and she knows how the human mind works. . . . [She] brings before us the strange world of Isis in all its beauty and integrates setting and action and character in exemplary fashion. Her book is an excellent 'read,' a tract on society and relevant commentary on the history of our own times."

This trilogy has been called "superior science fiction" by Ann A. Flowers in *Horn Book.* "Because of one writer—Monica Hughes—Canada shines in the field of science fiction," pronounces Kit Pearson in the *Christian Science Monitor.* "Perhaps her country's most distinguished writer for children, she is also one of its most prolific, writing realistic fiction as well. Her trilogy, *The Keeper of the Isis Light, The Guardian of Isis,* and *The Isis Pedlar . . . ,* although set in the future, is truly Canadian in its theme—immigrants to a new land dealing with the accompanying pressures of prejudice and culture clash."

Sarah Ellis describes her feelings on Hughes's talents as a science fiction writer in *Horn Book:* "Canada's finest writer of science fiction for children is the English-born Monica Hughes. . . . There is a gentleness to her books that is rare in science fiction. The hairsbreadth escapes,

the exotic flora and fauna, the humanoids, the vast intergalactic reaches, the villains and the heroes—all are enclosed in one overriding concern, subtle but ever-present: the value of kindness. . . . Hers is a major contribution to the fields of Canadian writing for children and of juvenile science fiction."

Hughes shares her philosophy of writing for children in her essay in *Canadian Children's Literature: A Journal of Criticism and Review:* "I think one of the functions of a good writer for children (besides, obviously, being entertaining) is to help them explore the world and the future. And to find acceptable answers to the Big Questions: 'What's life about?' 'What is it to be human?' As I said before, those are the questions that demand truthful answers, not part ones. So I think my chief criterion for a story for children—it should be for all fiction in fact, of course, but very especially that written for the young—is that one should write as truthfully as possible, even if it isn't easy or painless. One faces oneself in the darkest inside places of one's memory and one's subconscious, and out of that comes both joy and sorrow. But always—and I think again this is perhaps the second crucial thing for children—always there must come hope.

"And then one writes and one scribbles out and then one writes again, and then maybe after half a dozen drafts (as one of my favourite writers, Alan Garner says) maybe—then—a book will emerge. And if it is good enough, it will probably be for children."

BIOGRAPHICAL/CRITICAL SOURCES:

BOOKS

Children's Literature Review, Volume 9, Gale, 1985, pp. 61-79.
Meet the Authors and Illustrators, Scholastic, 1991.
Presenting Children's Authors, Illustrators, and Performers, Pembroke, 1990.
Signal Review I: A Selective Guide to Children's Books, Thimble Press, 1983.
Sixth Book of Junior Authors and Illustrators, edited by Sally Holmes Holtze, H. W. Wilson, 1989.

PERIODICALS

Booklist, April 15, 1977; June 1, 1985.
Books in Canada, December, 1982; December, 1983; March, 1984.
Canadian Children's Literature: A Journal of Criticism and Review, Number 13, 1979, pp. 20-26; Number 17, 1980; Number 26, 1982, pp. 4-27; Number 33, 1984, pp. 40-45; Number 37, 1985, pp. 18-28; Number 44, 1986, p. 618; Number 48, 1987, pp. 15-28.
Christian Science Monitor, October 5, 1984, pp. B8-B9.
Globe and Mail (Toronto), May 2, 1987.

Growing Point, March, 1976, pp. 2820-2821; November, 1978; November, 1979, p. 3615; September, 1982; January, 1984; September, 1984, p. 4309.

Horn Book, June, 1982, pp. 298-299; September/October, 1984, pp. 661-664; May/June, 1985.

In Review: Canadian Books for Children, summer, 1976; June, 1979; August, 1979; April, 1980; February, 1981, pp. 11-13; April, 1982; Number 33, 1984.

Junior Bookshelf, June, 1977; October, 1978; December, 1978; June, 1980, p. 144; October, 1981, p. 212; August, 1982; December, 1983; October, 1984.

Language Arts, May, 1982; January, 1984, p. 74.

Maclean's, June 28, 1982.

Quill and Quire, April, 1982, p. 32.

School Librarian, September, 1980; December, 1983; September, 1984, pp. 259-60.

Science Fiction and Fantasy Book Review, March, 1982, p. 21; July/August, 1982.

Times Educational Supplement, August 18, 1978; February 15, 1980; June 5, 1981; November 19, 1982, p. 34; June 8, 1984, p. 16.

Times Literary Supplement, March 28, 1980; September 18, 1981; July 23, 1982.

World of Children's Books, spring, 1988.

*   *   *

HYDE, Anthony 1946-
(Nicholas Chase, a joint pseudonym)

PERSONAL: Born January 1, 1946, in Ottawa, Ontario, Canada; son of Lawrence Evelyn (an artist) and Betty Marguerite (a teacher; maiden name, Bambriege) Hyde; married Kathleen Moses (a public servant), January 21, 1966. *Education:* Attended Carleton University, 1963-65. *Politics:* "Various; usually on left." *Avocational interests:* "Photography, Leica cameras, sailing, psychoanalysis, and, currently, the poetry of Ezra Pound."

ADDRESSES: Home—Ottawa, Ontario, Canada.*Agent*—Lucinda Vardey Agency, 297 Seaton St., Toronto, Ontario, Canada M5A 2T6.

CAREER: Free-lance writer, 1968—.

WRITINGS:

(With brother, Christopher Hyde, under joint pseudonym Nicholas Chase) *Locksley* (novel), St, Martin's, 1983.

The Red Fox (thriller), Knopf, 1985.

China Lake (thriller), Knopf, 1992.

Formosa Straits, Knopf, 1995.

Author of short stories. Contributor to periodicals, including *Our Generation* and *Quill & Quire.*

SIDELIGHTS: Anthony Hyde is best known as the author of *The Red Fox,* a highly-regarded thriller about a free-lance writer who finds himself embroiled in international intrigue. The writer, Robert Thorne, is visiting his late father's home in rural Pennsylvania when he receives a call for help from May Brightman, a former lover. Thorne learns that the woman's father, Harry Brightman, has disappeared. The missing Brightman, it is soon disclosed, has had a long and murky involvement with the Soviet Union. Brightman's apparent Soviet ties—both romantic and financial—have also drawn the interest of various thugs and shadowy figures. Despite the sizeable risk, Thorne continues his investigation even after Brightman's corpse is uncovered in Detroit. Trekking across the United States and Canada, then to Europe and, eventually, the Soviet Union, Thorne finally learns the truth of Brightman's disappearance and death. The novel ends with considerable action and a shattering revelation.

The Red Fox won widespread attention upon publication in 1985. Anthony Olcott, in his review for the *Washington Post Book World,* described *The Red Fox* as an "unusually human and civilized novel." *Maclean's* reviewer Gillian Mackay also provided a favorable assessment, praising the book as "absorbing" and "suspenseful." And *New York Times* critic John Gross noted the novel's "excitement" and added that *The Red Fox* "really is a superior and unusually intelligent example of its genre, and . . . a remarkably assured performance."

Hyde followed *The Red Fox* with *China Lake,* another foray into international intrigue. The novel's two protagonists are a retired intelligence officer and a physicist whose respectable career was scuttled amid accusations of spying for the Soviet Union. The novel takes the two men through various countries and into their own pasts, eventually arriving at the story's centerpiece, a top-secret naval weapons facility known as China Lake.

Hyde and his brother Christopher, jointly writing under the pseudonym Nicholas Chase, also wrote the novel *Locksley.* The book is a retelling of the Robin Hood legend, with the Hyde brothers making slight alterations in the original story to accomodate character motivation and historical fact. Writing in the *Washington Post,* Barbara Mertz noted that *Locksley* is "a merry romp in every sense of the word, and a pleasant treat for lovers of adventure-historical novels . . . ."

Hyde told *CA:* "One of my publishers once said to me that the goal of my artistry was to recover bits of forgotten history. Fair enough."

BIOGRAPHICAL/CRITICAL SOURCES:

BOOKS

Contemporary Literary Criticism, Volume 42, Gale, 1987, pp. 225-28.

PERIODICALS

Chatelaine, June, 1992, p. 10.

Globe and Mail (Toronto), September 14, 1985.

Los Angeles Times Book Review, September 29, 1985, p. 8.

Maclean's, September 23, 1985, p. 64; June 29, 1992, p. 54.

Newsweek, September 23, 1985, p. 72.

New York Times, August 23, 1985, p. C24.

New York Times Book Review, September 1, 1985, p. 8.

Time, June 1, 1992, p. 87.

Washington Post, October 31, 1983; April 27, 1992, section D, p. 4.

Washington Post Book World, September 22, 1985, p. 7.

I-J

IRWIN, P. K.
  See PAGE, P(atricia) K(athleen)

*   *   *

JACOBSEN, Josephine   1908-

PERSONAL: Born August 19, 1908, in Cobourg, Ontario, Canada; daughter of Joseph Edward (a doctor) and Octavia (Winder) Boylan; married Eric Jacobsen, March 17, 1932; children: Erlend Ericsen. *Education:* Educated by private tutors and at Roland Park Country School, 1915-18. *Politics:* Democrat. *Religion:* Roman Catholic.

ADDRESSES: Home—220 Stony Ford Rd., Baltimore, MD 21210. *Agent*—McIntosh & Otis Inc., 475 Fifth Ave., New York, NY 10017.*Office*—Poetry Office, Library of Congress, Washington, DC 20540.

CAREER: Library of Congress, Washington, DC, poetry consultant, 1971-73, honorary consultant in American letters, 1973-79. Lecturer for the American Writers Program annual meeting, Savannah, GA, 1984. Member of the literature panel, National Endowment for the Arts, 1979-83, and of the poetry committee of Folger Library.

MEMBER: Poetry Society of America (vice president, 1978-79), PEN, Corporation of Yaddo, Baltimore Citizens' Planning and Housing Association, Baltimore Center Stage Association, Baltimore Museum of Art, Walters Art Gallery, Hamilton Street Club.

AWARDS, HONOURS: The Shade-Seller: New and Selected Poems was nominated for a National Book Award; *A Walk with Raschid and Other Stories* was selected one of the Fifty Distinguished Books of the Year by *Library Journal;* recipient of award from the American Academy and Institute of Arts and Letters for Service to Literature;

received fellowships from Yaddo, the Millay Colony for the Arts, and the MacDowell Colony; Doctor of Humane Letters from Towson State University, Goucher College, College of Notre Dame of Maryland, and Johns Hopkins University; Literary Lion, New York Public Library, 1985; Shelley Memorial Award for lifetime service to literature, Poetry Society of America, 1992; inducted into the American Academy of Arts and Letters, 1994.

WRITINGS:

POETRY

For the Unlost, Contemporary Poetry, 1946.
The Human Climate, Contemporary Poetry, 1953.
The Animal Inside, Ohio University Press (Athens, OH), 1966.
(Editor) *From Anne to Marianne: Some American Women Poets,* Library of Congress (Washington, DC), 1972.
The Instant of Knowing, Library of Congress, 1974.
The Shade-Seller: New and Selected Poems, Doubleday (New York City), 1974.
One Poet's Poetry, Agnes Scott College, 1975.
The Chinese Insomniacs: New Poems, University of Pennsylvania Press (Philadelphia), 1981.
The Sisters: New and Selected Poems, Bench Press (Oakland, CA), 1987.
Distances, Bucknell University Press (Cranbury, NJ), 1992.
Collected Poems, Johns Hopkins University Press (Baltimore), 1995.

SHORT STORIES

A Walk with Raschid and Other Stories, Jackpine (Winston-Salem, NC), 1978.
Adios, Mr. Moxley, Jackpine, 1986.
On the Island, Ontario Review Press, 1989.

OTHER

(With William R. Mueller) *The Testament of Samuel Beckett* (dramatic criticism), Hill & Wang (New York City), 1964.
(With Mueller) *Ionesco and Genet: Playwrights of Silence* (dramatic criticism), Hill & Wang, 1968.
Substance of Things Hoped For, Doubleday, 1987.

Also contributor to books and anthologies, including *The Way We Live Now,* Ontario Press, 1986; *Best American Short Stories,* 1966; *O. Henry Prize Stories,* 1967, 1971, 1973, 1976, 1985, and 1993; *Fifty Years of the American Short Story,* 1970; *A Geography of Poets,* edited by William Field; *A Treasury of American Poetry,* edited by Nancy Sullivan; *Night Walks: Short Stories,* edited by Joyce Carol Oates; *A Treasury of American Short Stories,* edited by Sullivan; *Pushcart Prizes Six; Belles Lettres,* 1986; *Best American Poetry,* 1991 and 1993; *Scarecrow Poetry; Diamonds Are a Girl's Best Friend; No More Masks;* and *A Formal Feeling Comes,* 1993 and 1994.

ADAPTATIONS: Three poems from *The Chinese Insomniacs: New Poems* were set to Jean Eigelberger Ivey's composition "Notes toward Time," March, 1984; the poem "The Monosyllable" from *The Chinese Insomniacs* was performed at the Baltimore Museum of Art, Baltimore, MD, 1987.

SIDELIGHTS: Josephine Jacobsen is "extremely interested" in the theatre, and has acted with the Vagabond Players in Baltimore. Equally interested in travel, she has visited Mexico, Guatemala, Venezuela, the Caribbean Islands, France, Italy, Greece, Morocco, Kenya, Tanzania, Portugal, Madeira, Spain, and Canada.

BIOGRAPHICAL/CRITICAL SOURCES:

PERIODICALS

New York Times Book Review, April 4, 1982.
Poetry, March, 1983.

*   *   *

JASMIN, Claude   1930-

PERSONAL: Born November 10, 1930, in Montreal, Quebec, Canada; son of Edouard (a ceramist) and Germaine (Lefevre) Jasmin; married Raymonde Boucher; children: Eliane, Daniel. *Education:* Attended College Grasset; Ecole des Arts Appliques, diploma, 1951. *Politics:* "Disciple of Henry David Thoreau." *Religion:* "I believe in God."

ADDRESSES: Home—Box 24, Route 1, Ste.-Adele, Quebec, Canada J0R 1L0.

CAREER: Writer. Affiliated with Canadian Broadcasting Corporation, beginning in 1956; television designer for Radio Canada; theatrical instructor for the Montreal Parks Department. Director of literary and art pages for *La Presse* and *Journal de Montreal.* Has been a ceramist, a painter, and an art teacher.

MEMBER: International PEN, Canadian Society of Authors, Composers, Searchers, and Publishers, Writers Union of Quebec, Amnesty International, Le Groupe des Sept.

AWARDS, HONOURS: Prix Cercle du Livre de France, from Tisseyre Editor, 1960, for *La Corde au cou;* Prize from Dominion Drama Festival, 1963, for "Le Veau dort"; Prix France Quebec from government of France—Ministry of Cultural Affairs of Quebec, 1964, for *Ethel et le terroriste;* Prix Wilderness Anik from the Canadian Broadcasting Corporation, 1971, for "Un Chemin de croix dans le metro"; Prix France-Canada from government of Quebec—Ministry of Cultural Affairs jointly with Cultural Affairs Ministry of France, for *La Sabliere;* Prix Duvernay from Society of Saint John the Baptist of Montreal, 1981.

WRITINGS:

La Corde au cou (novel), Le Cercle du livre de France, 1960.
Deliverez-nous du mal (novel), Editions a la page, 1961.
Blues pour un homme averti (play), Editions parti pris, 1964.
Ethel et le terroriste (novel), Librairie Deom, 1964, translation by David S. Walker published as *Ethel and the Terrorist,* Harvest House, 1965.
Pleure pas, Germaine (novel), Editions parti pris, 1965.
(Editor) Robert Roussil, *Manifeste,* Editions du jour, 1965.
Et puis tout est silence (novel), Les Editions de l'homme, 1965, translation by David Lobdell published as *The Rest Is Silence,* Oberon Press, 1981.
(Editor with Jacques Godbout) *Textes inedits de Gilles Carle, Jacques Godbout, et Claude Jasmin sur le long metrage canadian Cain,* Cooperatio, 1965.
Les Artisans creatures, Lidec, 1966.
Les Coeurs empailles (short stories), Editions parti-pris, 1967, Guerin (Montreal), 1988.
Rimbaud, mon beau salaud! Editions du jour, 1969.
Jasmin: Dossier sur moi-meme, C. Langevin, 1970.
Tuez le veau grass (play), Editions Lemeac, 1970.
L'Outaragasipi (historical novel), L'Actuelle, 1971.
C'est toujours la meme histoire (play), Editions Lemeac, 1972.
La Petite Patrie, La Presse, 1972.
Pointe-Calumet boogie-woogie, La Presse, 1973.
Sainte-Adele-la vaisselle, La Presse, 1974.

Danielle, ca va marcher! (biography), A. Stanke, 1975.
Le Loup de Brunswick City (novel), Editions Lemeac, 1976.
Revoir Ethel (novel), A. Stanke, 1976.
Feu a volonte (nonfiction), Editions Lemeac, 1976.
Feu sur la television (nonfiction), Editions Lemeac, 1977.
La Sabliere (novel), Editions Lemeac, 1979, translation by Lobdell published as *Mario,* Oberon Press, 1985.
L'Armoire de Pantagruel (novel), Editions Lemeac, 1982.
Maman-Paris, Maman-la-France (novel), Editions Lemeac, 1982.
(With father, Edouard Jasmin) *Deux Mats, une galere,* Editions Lemeac, 1983.
Le Crucifie du Sommet-Bleu (novel), Editions Lemeac, 1984.
L'Etat-maquereau, l'etat-maffia (manifesto), Editions Lemeac, 1984.
Une Duchesse a Ogunquit (novel), Editions Lemeac, 1985.
Des Cons qui s'adorent (novel), Editions Lemeac, 1986.
Alice vous fait oire bon soir (novel), Editions Lemeac, 1987.
The Dragon and Other Laurentian Tales, translation by Patricia Sillers, Oxford University Press, 1987.
Paul et Virginia, Editions Lemeac, 1987.
Pour tout vous dire, Guerin, 1988.
Comme un fou: recit, Hexagone (Montreal), 1992.
La vie suspendue: roman, Editions Lemeac, 1994.

Also author of *Un Chemin de croix dans le metro, Le Veau dort,* and *Une Saison en studio.* Author of radio plays and television dramas, including *Rue de la liberte, Ses Mains vides, La Mort dans l'ame, Process devant juge seul,* and *Nous sommes tous des orphelins.* Contributor of scripts for numerous television series.

ADAPTATIONS: A film version of *Mario* for English Speaking Canada, 1984; a television series based on *La Petite Patrie,* beginning in 1974.

WORK IN PROGRESS: Writing for theatre and television.

SIDELIGHTS: Claude Jasmin is one of Quebec's most acclaimed writers of fiction. His first published novel, *La Corde au cou,* the story of a schizophrenic who commits murder to find relief from his feelings of cultural and economic disconnectedness, won the Prix Cercle du Livre de France in 1960, but his *Ethel and the Terrorist* is better known to English speaking readers. *Ethel,* which is based on real events of Quebec's political separatist movement of the 1960s, won Jasmin the Prix France-Quebec in 1964. In addition to many novels, Jasmin has published plays, critical pieces, and interviews.

Much of Jasmin's earlier fiction explores violent themes. His *Deliverez-nous du mal,* published in 1961, centers on a homosexual relationship in which one man's jealousy leads him to commit murder. *Ethel and the Terrorist* is based on an incident involving the Front de Liberation du Quebec (FLQ), a terrorist separatist organization. The story is told through the reflections of a man held by the FLQ who, despite his unsuccessful attempts at escape, is eventually forced to kill. Most of the protagonists of the stories in Jasmin's 1967 collection *Les Coeurs empailles* are women whose hopes for love, happiness, and social appreciation are ruthlessly dashed. The surprise endings are often the result of violence or suicide.

Jasmin's work is also concerned with the realities of his native Montreal. In addition to often featuring the working-class melting pot neighborhood of northeast Montreal where he grew up, Jasmin frequently puts the flavor of Montreal's language into his fiction. Particularly in *Pleure pas, Germaine,* which depicts a family's attempt to trace their roots during a car trip to Gaspe, Quebec, Jasmin experiments with *joual. Joual* is a term for "corrupted" language taken from a rural Quebec dialect pronunciation of *Cheval,* meaning "horse." In Quebecois literary circles, *joual* novels use the uneducated speech of the lower class in Montreal as the main medium of expression instead of standard French, which then sometimes intrudes in marginal ways, usually with comic effect. The use of *joual* in literature is frequently accompanied by themes of violence and alienation; thus many of Jasmin's novels are typical of the *joual* movement. Jasmin's variety of *joual* includes the use of many anglicisms, and other themes which recur in his fiction are hatred for the wealthy, disgust for intellectualism and pretension, and revulsion for weak father figures.

After Jasmin went through a period of nine years producing no fiction, he published three volumes in three years. The 1976 *Revoir Ethel* was a kind of sequel to *Ethel and the Terrorist* in which a former terrorist who now rejects violence is unwillingly induced to join in a bomb plot on Montreal's Olympic Stadium. Jasmin also wrote *Le Loup de Brunswick City* in 1976, a novel based on the supposedly true story of a boy lost at the age of two and recovered at thirteen after living with wolves. Most successful of the three novels, however, was the 1979 *Mario.* Complimented as "exotic" by Bronwyn Drainie of the Toronto *Globe and Mail, Mario* is the story of a mildly retarded ten-year-old boy whose brain is deteriorating from meningitis, and his teenage brother, Clovis. The novel details their last summer together at the family's vacation cottage—Clovis must find a job in Montreal the next summer. He wants to make this vacation a special one for Mario, and, in Drainie's words, "he wraps him in a fantasy web of battles from bygone days," recreating with his little brother the eighth-century Arab holy war conquest of Europe. The boys plan to reenact the seizure of Paris and then to imagine traveling to the New World to convert the Indians to Islam. But even fantasy is beset with problems.

The seventh volume of Clovis's mailorder encyclopedia has not yet arrived, so they do not know that the Arabs will be defeated by Charles at Poitiers before they reach Paris.

That is the least of boy's problems. Reality harshly interrupts their make-believe—their parents decide that Mario's mental deterioration is such that he must be institutionalized. When Mario is put into the hospital, Clovis helps him escape, and the brothers return to the cottage as winter is about to set in. They despair of help until a Cistercian monk offers to let Mario live and work on his order's communal farm. Drainie concluded that *Mario* "explores a special relationship in a fresh and exhilarating way," and Anne Verrier-Skutt, reviewing *Mario* in *Books in Canada,* agreed that it is "a thoroughly worthwhile novel."

In 1982 Jasmin published *Maman-Paris, Maman-la-France,* the journal of a Quebec man's first trip to France, and the more widely reviewed *L'Armoire de Pantagruel.* Loosely based on the life of Richard Blass, a notorious Quebec criminal, *L'Armoire* takes its name from the various *Armoires* in the protagonist's life. The balcony cupboard he was confined in for punishment as a child, the container of his church's sacred vessels, the beer refrigerator of a neighborhood bar, his jail cell—all may be summed up by the French word "Armoire." Labeled an "economically presented tale" by Stephen Smith in *French Review,* *L'Armoire* harks back to Jasmin's earlier novels in that it details a vengeful killing spree by its protagonist, Richard Mars. Mars bribes the guard stationed in front of the hospital room after getting out of prison by feigning illness. Three hours later, he has machine-gunned, among others, his parents, the psychiatrist who condemned him as dangerous, the judge who tried him, and his former lover, Carole Malbeuf—based on the delator Carole Deveau—who corroborated what the police had put together on Mars. The murders, except for Carole's, are presented in "a tone of ritual inevitability," Smith claimed. Carole stands out from the rest because Jasmin uses her perspective for the narrative at certain points in the novel, and she speaks a long monologue before her death. In the words of Smith, "she emerges as a mediocre but understandable person," with whom Mars could have been happy if he had been able to forget the pain she caused him. At the end of the book, Mars is on his way to lock up his old friends in the beer refrigerator of Pantagruel's bar and set the establishment on fire. This act would rid him of any witnesses to his presence in the area where his killings have taken place and give him revenge against those who were hesitant to tell him of Carole's whereabouts. But as Smith points out, locking his friends in the *armoire* "is destined also to make his solitude . . . total."

BIOGRAPHICAL/CRITICAL SOURCES:

PERIODICALS

Books in Canada, December, 1981, January/February, 1986.
Canadian Literature, summer, 1988, pp. 151-54.
French Review, February, 1984.
Globe and Mail (Toronto), April 5, 1986.

—*Sketch by Elizabeth Thomas*

*   *   *

JOHNSON, Pauline   1861-1913
(Tekahionwake)

PERSONAL: Full name Emily Pauline Johnson; also known as Tekahionwake; born in 1861, at Six Nations Reserve, near Brantford, Ontario, Canada; died of cancer in 1913, in Vancouver, British Columbia, Canada; daughter of George Martin Henry (Chief Teyonnhehkewea) and Emily Susanna (Howells) Johnson. *Education:* Educated at home until 1875; attended Brantford Collegiate, Brantford, Ontario, 1875-77.

CAREER: Poet, short story writer, essayist, and lecturer. Began publishing poetry in late 1870s; presented poems at public readings during the 1880s; toured Canada, the United States, and England, 1892-1909; contributed articles and stories to magazines, 1907-12; collaborated with Joseph Capilano, a Squamish chief, to recreate Chinook stories in *The Legends of Vancouver,* 1911.

AWARDS, HONOURS: Prize for fiction by *Dominion Magazine* for "A Red Girl's Reasoning," 1892.

WRITINGS:

The White Wampum (poems), Lane, 1895.
Canadian Born (poems), Morang, 1903.
The Legends of Vancouver (stories), Saturday Sunset, 1911.
Flint and Feather (poems), Mussen, 1912; revised and enlarged 1913; revised and enlarged as *Flint and Feather: The Complete Poems of E. Pauline Johnson,* 1917.
The Mocassin Maker (stories and essays), Briggs, 1913.
The Shagganappi (stories), Briggs, 1913.

Work represented in anthologies, including *Songs of the Great Dominion,* edited by W. P. Lighthall, 1889; and *Spider Woman's Granddaughters,* edited by Paula Gunn Allen, 1989. Contributor to magazines and newspapers, including *Gems of Poetry, Mother's Magazine,* and *Boy's World.*

SIDELIGHTS: Emily Pauline Johnson was the first Native Canadian (and the first author) to have her likeness and name commemorated on a postage stamp. She is remembered for her contributions to First Nations literature (as work by indigenous Canadians is called) and to the acceptance of Native women of letters. Johnson was descended from the well-known Brant and Johnson families of the Mohawk Nation. Her distant relative Joseph Brant (also known as Thayendanegea ["He Who Places Two Bets"]) had been a steadfast ally of the British during the French and Indian War and the American Revolution. Joseph's sister, Molly Brant (also known as Degonwadonti) had married William Johnson, British trader and Superintendent of Indian Affairs for the Crown. She became something of a diplomat and liaison for her people and the English-Canadians.

Often called "Pauline Johnson" by Canadian writers, Emily was born March 10, 1861, in Chiefswood, Ontario, not far from Brantford and next to the Six Nations (Iroquois) Indian Reserve. Her father, Henry Martin Johnson (Onwanonsyshon) was a Mohawk chief whose full name is sometimes reported as George Martin Henry Johnson. Her mother was Emily S. Howells, an Englishwoman and an aunt of American writer William Dean Howells. Some contemporary accounts erroneously list Brant's parents as George Mansion and Lydia Bestman. This may be the result of the sheer size and prominence of the Brant and Johnson families, and their frequent use of first names such as "Emily" and "Molly."

As a youngster, Johnson loved to read. She particularly enjoyed the classics of British literature, and as was the custom for Victorian ladies of her day, she paid close attention to the Romantic writers as well as Shakespeare. She tried her hand at writing early on, but doubted her own talent. Coupled with her shyness, this lack of confidence kept her from sharing much of her early pieces. Taught at home until she was ready to enter Brantford College in her mid-teens, she also lacked an audience in front of which to gain recitation experience.

Still in her teens and attending college, Johnson began winning accolades from teachers for her poetry. She took drama classes and branched out into theatrical performance, appearing in plays and learning to develop a charisma that held her listeners. In the mid-1870s, Johnson sent a manuscript of a single poem to the Brantford newspaper, hoping it might be published. Although she aspired to a professional writing career, she had not as yet had any of her efforts reviewed for publication. With modest dreams, Emily mailed off the poem and was delighted to receive a very favorable critique from the newspaper's editor. However, he suggested she set her sights higher, even for a first effort. He advised her to send it to poetry journals or a large-scale magazine.

When magazines such as *Harper's Weekly* and the *Athenaeum* published her poems, Johnson was elated. Her confidence growing, she was determined to begin public readings in order to interpret her work in front of an audience. Her local readings led to an invitation to present her poetry at a Canadian literature forum in Toronto. The 1892 event was sponsored by the Young Liberals Club of Toronto, and the highlight of the evening was Johnson's reading of her poem entitled "A Cry from an Indian Wife." The story of the Northwest Rebellion, Johnson's tome was enhanced by the visual impact of the author dressed in traditional clothing. The coupling of Johnson's message—that Canada was still Indian land wrested unfairly from indigenous hands—with the stunning drama of her recitation literally stole the show. Soon, Johnson was a national sensation. As word spread, eager audiences queued up for her full evening performances, and she tailored several new works for dramatic reading, the most popular of which was "The Song My Paddle Sings." Her performances centered clearly on indigenous themes and Native rights, but which were presented in the Romantic lilt of Victorian-style cadences. Johnson's familiar form arose out of her love of British literature and the popular style of the day, making it understandable to most audiences. In 1885, however, just as her professional career blossomed, Johnson's beloved father died. To be closer to her newly-famous daughter, Emily Howells Johnson moved into Brantford, and the two supported each other in their shared grief.

Songs of the Great Dominion, Johnson's first book-length collection, appeared in 1889. Soon, she was on a poetry recital tour of Canada, and word of her talent spread to the United States and England. She was invited to London in 1894, and she fulfilled a girlhood dream of being introduced to famous British authors. Wherever she went, Johnson's readings were well-attended and her public praises grew. John Lane Publishers of London contracted with Johnson to print her next poetry collection. *White Wampum* was released in 1895, again to critical success. On the strength of the new volume, she returned to Canada for a triumphal tour, including several U.S. cities.

Throughout the 1890s, Emily Pauline Johnson traveled and read her poems, donning her now famous Mohawk clothing. A popular place for dramatic readings in those days in Canada was saloons, and through such venues, Johnson was able to bring her poetry to working-class Canadians and rural residents in the northern and western reaches of the country. That she did not confine her tours to large halls in major cities or to places where only cultured intellectuals would venture endeared her to the common folk of Canada. Her 1903 edition, *Canadian Born,* was a reflection of this growing interest; Johnson stressed the shared heritage of Canadians, while still keeping the integrity of Native cultures and history central to her themes. Although she still loved interacting with her audiences, Johnson tired of the continual travel, and her health began to suffer.

Johnson subsequently scaled back her touring to focus more on writing. She committed to paper the traditional stories she had collected from many First Nations in her years of travel. Settling far from her Mohawk homeland, she now made her home in Vancouver and the traditional tales of British Columbia Natives captured her heart. In 1911, she offered *Legends of Vancouver,* recounting and interpreting tribal stories she had learned from Chief Joe Capilano. Although the collection of tribal stories was already a mainstay of academically oriented writing on Native people, her articulate commentary aimed at a general reading audience and was innovative. It has since become a commonly held belief that the authorship of fiction and nonfiction alike by Native women is "preservative"—that Native women writers preserve traditional stories and customs by weaving them into their narratives, creating a "printed museum."

Meanwhile, Johnson's fiction was developing new themes. She continued to write about Native characters, usually women, but now she included the experiences of white pioneer women (especially from the prairie provinces of Alberta, Saskatchewan, and Manitoba) and their commonality with Native women in their struggles to survive. She also began to focus more keenly on the difficult position of the "metis," the large mixed-blood segment of Canada's population. Metis were often interpreters for both Indian and non-Indian interests, and Johnson saw her work as an author and performer as the natural outgrowth of this role. She dramatically explored the alienation many metis felt in trying to find their identity in Canadian society. In this, she anticipated a common genre of modern Native writing.

While 1912's *Flint and Feather* carried on the now-familiar format of collections of Johnson's Indian-themed poetry, her 1913 work, *The Moccasin Maker,* introduced her new interests in pioneer women and metis. Critically acclaimed and widely popular, the work put Johnson squarely in a ground-breaking position. Women were then generally believed to be incapable of writing long works of prose. That a Native woman could accomplish this feat was almost unthinkable. In fact, prior to Johnson's *The Moccasin Maker,* the only widely read fiction written by a Native woman had been the works of Sarah Callahan (a Cree author). Johnson's contemporary, Okanagan writer Humishuma (also known as Chrystal Quintasket), wrote a short novel, *Coqewea, the Half-Blood,* which eclipsed Johnson's in sales. However, Johnson is considered the more influential Native woman author due to her breadth

of writing styles and to the success of her poetic performances.

For some time, Johnson had been suffering from cancer, a battle she lost on March 7, 1913, just three days before her fifty-third birthday. She died in her home in Vancouver and was honored by her adopted hometown when she was interred in Stanley Park. Johnson's last work, *The Shagganappi,* was published posthumously, and her work continued to sell briskly for several years after her death. *Legends of Vancouver* was reprinted in 1922, and a revised *Flint and Feather: The Complete Poems of Pauline Johnson* appeared in 1972.

Johnson has often been called the unofficial poet laureate of Canada. The country issued a commemorative five-cent postage stamp 1961, coinciding with the hundredth anniversary of her birth. Its design shows Johnson in profile in Victorian apparel in the foreground, with a traditionally-clad figure appearing in the background, arms spread skyward in a dramatic gesture reminiscent of her public performances. In 1974, she was the subject of a biographical study of her life and times, *Pauline Johnson and Her Friends,* authored by Walter McRaye and published by Toronto's Ryerson Press.

BIOGRAPHICAL/CRITICAL SOURCES:

BOOKS

Gridley, Marion E., *American Indian Women,* Hawthorn Books, 1974, pp. 67-73.
Loosley, Elizabeth, *The Clear Spirit: Twenty Canadian Women and Their Times,* edited by Mary Quayle Innis, University of Toronto Press, 1966, pp. 74-90.
McRaye, Walter, *Pauline Johnson and Her Friends,* Ryerson Press, 1947, 182 p.
Petrone, Penny, *Native Literature in Canada: From the Oral Tradition to the Present,* Oxford University Press, Canada, 1990, pp. 71-94.

*   *   *

JOHNSTON, Basil H. 1929-

PERSONAL: Born July 13, 1929, in Parry Island, Ontario, Canada; son of Rufus Francis and Mary (Lafreniere) Johnston; married Lucie Bella Desroches, July 29, 1959; children: Miriam Gladys, Elizabeth Louise, Geoffrey Lawrence. *Education:* Loyola College, Montreal, Quebec, graduated (cum laude), 1954; Ontario College of Education, secondary school teaching certificate, 1962. *Politics:* "Apolitical."

ADDRESSES: Home—253 Ashlar Rd., Richmond Hill, Ontario, Canada.*Office*—Royal Ontario Museum, 100 Queens Park, Toronto, Ontario, Canada.

CAREER: History teacher in secondary school, Toronto, Ontario, 1962-69; Royal Ontario Museum, Toronto, lecturer in North, Central, and South American history, 1969-72, member of ethnology department, 1972—. Night school teacher of English, 1965-70; lecturer in Indian culture. Vice-president of Canadian Indian Centre of Toronto, 1963-69; secretary of Indian consultations with Canadian Government, 1968; committee member of Indian Hall of Fame, 1968-70.

MEMBER: Union of Ontario Indians; Toronto Indian Club (president, 1957); Indian Eskimo Association, member of executive committee, 1965-68.

AWARDS, HONOURS: Member of Indian Hall of Fame, 1968-70; Samuel S. Fels literary award from Coordinating Council of Literary Magazines, 1976, for *Zhowmin and Mandamin*; member of Order of Ontario, 1989.

WRITINGS:

(Contributor) *The Only Good Indian,* New Press, 1970.
(Contributor) *Travel Ontario,* New Press, 1971.
(Contributor) *Teacher's Manual for History,* Ginn, 1972.
(Contributor) *Starting Points in Reading,* Ginn, 1974.
Ojibway Heritage (nonfiction), Columbia University Press, 1976.
How the Birds Got Their Colors (juvenile), Kids Can Press, 1978.
Moose Meat & Wild Rice (stories), McClelland & Stewart, 1978; published as *Ojibway Tales,* University of Nebraska Press, 1993.
Ojibway Language Course Outline (nonfiction), Ministry of Indian Affairs and Northern Development (Ottawa), 1979.
Ojibway Language Lexicon for Beginners and Others (nonfiction), Ministry of Indian Affairs and Northern Development, 1979.
Tales the Elders Told: Ojibway Legends (legends), Royal Ontario Museum, 1981.
Ojibway Ceremonies (nonfiction), McClelland & Stewart, 1983; University of Nebraska Press, 1990.
By Canoe and Moccasin (juvenile), Waapone Publishing, 1987.
Indian School Days (autobiography), Key Porter, 1988; University of Oklahoma Press, 1989.
Tales of the Anishinaubaek: Ojibway Legends (legends), University of Toronto Press, 1994.

Also contributor of stories, essays, articles, and poems to educational readers, literary magazines, and newspapers. Translator of brochures and travel guides into Ojibway. Guest editor of *Tawow,* publication of Indian Affairs Branch of Department of Indian Affairs and Northern Development.

Also author of *Zhowmin and Mandamin.* Work represented in anthologies, including *Flowers of the Wild,* edited by Ziles Zichman and James Hodgins, Oxford University Press (Toronto), 1982; *First People, First Voices,* edited by Penny Petrone, University of Toronto Press, 1983; and *Contexts: Anthology Three,* edited by Clayton Graves, Thomas Nelson, 1984. Contributor to periodicals, including *Toronto Native Times, Ontario Indian, Whetstone, Sweetgrass, Canadian Fiction,* and *Native American Prose and Poetry.*

WORK IN PROGRESS: Book tentatively called *The Manitous: The Spiritual World of the Ojibway,* scheduled for publication in the United States by HarperCollins and Key Porter in Canada, 1995.

SIDELIGHTS: Basil H. Johnston is the author of numerous stories, articles, poems, essays, and books, including several guides for teaching and learning the Ojibway language. His writings describe the diversity of the Ojibway culture and the changes it has undergone in the past century. His essays strive to preserve aspects of his heritage, such as his native language and people's accomplishments, before they are lost or integrated into mainstream society. For his work on behalf of the Native community, he received the Centennial Medal in 1967. In 1976 he received the Samuel S. Fels Literary Award for *Zhowmin and Mandamin* and in April 1989 he received the Order of Ontario for his many contributions to society in Ontario and elsewhere; on June 8, 1994, the University of Toronto awarded him an honorary doctorate.

Johnston was born on July 13, 1929, to Rufus and Mary Lafreniere Johnston on the Parry Island Indian Reserve in Ontario. He attended elementary school at the Cape Croker Indian Reserve school until the age of 10. By this time his parents had separated and Johnston, his mother, and four sisters were living with his grandmother. Johnston and one sister were "selected" by an Indian agent and the local priest to attend residential school in Spanish, Ontario. He attended St. Peter Claver's Indian Residential School, commonly referred to as "Spanish" after the town where it was located. The school, run by Jesuit priests, offered discipline, education, and taught the boys trades that they could pursue once they were released at the age of 16. Subsidized by the government, the boys generally performed every task necessary to keep the institution running. Under the guidance of the Jesuits, they grew their own vegetables, helped to bake and prepare food, made their clothes and shoes, maintained the buildings and grounds, and raised and sold cattle, chickens, and hogs.

Johnston was released from St. Peter Claver's in 1944 to enter secondary school. Three months short of completing the ninth grade, he dropped out of Regiopolis College in Kingston at the end of March 1945. After spending the following months at miscellaneous jobs, including fishing, farming, and trapping, Johnston found it difficult to support himself. He describes his decision to return to school in *Indian School Days*: "Maybe it would be better to go back to school. I had heard vague rumors that Spanish was offering a high-school program. If it were true, I would return. It was my only chance to escape a life of cutting wood."

During Johnston's absence, many changes had taken place at St. Peter Claver's. The trades that the boys were being taught had become obsolete. Jobs for chicken farmers, cobblers, and tailors were scarce due to machines and equipment that had replaced human labor. The new Father Superior, R. J. Oliver, S.J., appointed in 1945, believed that the boys needed a solid secondary school program if they were to have any advantage in life. He began to institute changes to prepare for a high school curriculum and interscholastic sporting events. Johnston wrote to the Father Superior, requesting to return to the institution. He re-enrolled in what was now called the Garnier Residential School for Indian Boys in 1947.

In 1950 Johnston graduated valedictorian from Garnier and then attended Loyola College in Montreal. Again graduating with honors, he earned a B.A. from Loyola in 1954. From 1955 through 1961 he was employed by the Toronto Board of Trade. After receiving a Secondary School Teaching Certificate from the Ontario College of Education in 1962, he took a position teaching history at the Earl Haig Secondary School in North York until 1969. He then joined the Ethnology Department of the Royal Ontario Museum where he served as lecturer. He has presented academic lectures at universities and conferences across Canada and the United States.

Johnston's writings began appearing in print in 1970. His first essay, "Bread Before Books or Books Before Bread," which appeared in *The Only Good Indian: Essays by Cana-dian Indians,* recounts events contributing to the deterioration of the Native American heritage. The essay concludes with a summary stressing the accomplishments of the Native people from the Incas through the North American Indians. Johnston writes, "Men like to be judged not only by the great men and great works they have fostered, but also for standards of courage, perseverance, and endurance. Indian people in addition to these attributes like to be known for magnanimity, fortitude and resourcefulness."

For the Ministry of Indian and Northern Affairs Johnston wrote the *Ojibway Language Course Outline* and the *Ojibway Language Lexicon for Beginners* in 1978. He is often sought as a translator, perhaps because his translations display a sensitivity to both the Ojibway and English languages. A respected author, many of his books have been credited with presenting his tribal mythology in a way that both renews and reveals the Ojibway attitudes and insights toward life.

BIOGRAPHICAL/CRITICAL SOURCES:

BOOKS

Dictionary of Literary Biography, Volume 60: *Canadian Writers since 1960, Second Series,* Gale, 1987.
Lutz, Hartmut, ed., *Contemporary Challenges: Conversations with Canadian Native Authors,* Fifth House Publishers, 1991, pp. 229-39.

PERIODICALS

Books in Canada, August-September, 1988, p. 31.
Globe and Mail, April 16, 1988.
Quill & Quire, May, 1988, p. 27.
West Coast Review of Books, March-April, 1990, pp. 40-41.
The Western Historical Quarterly, May, 1991, pp. 219-20.
World Literature Today, Autumn, 1977, p. 665.

K

KEEBLE, John 1944-

PERSONAL: Born November 24, 1944, in Winnipeg, Manitoba, Canada; naturalized U.S. citizen; son of Raymond Charles William and Olivia (Wallace) Keeble; married Claire Sheldon (a violinist), September 4, 1964; children: Jonathan Sheldon, Ezekiel Jerome, Carson R.C. *Education:* University of Redlands, B.A. (magna cum laude), 1966; University of Iowa, M.F.A., 1969. *Politics:* "No comment." *Religion:* "No comment."

ADDRESSES: Home—R.R. 2, Box 147-2, Medical Lake, WA 99022. *Agent*—Georges Borchardt, Georges Borchardt, Inc., 136 East 57th St., New York, NY 10022.

CAREER: Grinnell College, Grinnell, Iowa, member of staff, 1979-72, writer-in-residence, 1971-72; Eastern Washington University, Cheney, assistant professor, 1973-77, associate professor of English, 1977—, director of creative writing program, 1982-83; author.

AWARDS, HONOURS: Trustee's Medal, Eastern Washington University, 1980; Guggenheim fellowship, 1982-83.

WRITINGS:

Crab Canyon (novel), Grossman, 1971.
(With Ransom Jeffrey) *Mine* (novel), Grossman, 1974.
Salt (play), first produced by The Shade Co., New York, 1975.
Yellowfish (novel), HarperCollins, 1981.
Broken Ground (novel) HarperCollins, 1987.
Out of the Channel: The Exxon Valdez Oil Spill in Prince William Sound (nonfiction), HarperCollins, 1991.

Also contributor to *Works in Progress, No. 1,* Literary Guild of America, 1970; *American Review, No. 25* edited by Ted Solataroff Bantam, 1976; *Dialogues with Northwest Writers: Interview with Nine Writers, Including Tom Rob-bins, Mary Barnard, and Richard Hugo,* edited by John Witte, Northwest Review Books, 1982.

WORK IN PROGRESS: Ghost Versions, a novel, for HarperCollins.

SIDELIGHTS: John Keeble's *Yellowfish* "is a novel of self-discovery disguised as a thriller," wrote Rick De-Marinis in the *Chicago Tribune Book World.* "This is not to say that it fails on either level. On the contrary, John Keeble has managed to convince us that the act of self-discovery is a thrilling, dangerous adventure." The story of a smuggler, Wesley Erks, and his attempt to transport four illegal aliens from British Columbia to San Francisco, *Yellowfish* has been praised for its evocative portrait of the landscape and history of the Pacific Northwest. "The smuggler's route from Vancouver to San Francisco," says Jay Tolson in the *Washington Post,* "provides the occasion for an elaborate discourse on the land—the forests and glaciers, the orchard country, the high desert stretching from Washington to Nevada, the great rivers and mountains—as well as its people and history. An amateur historian, Erks possesses a wealth of information, and his musings, whether they concern the folkways and lore of Native Americans, the travel narratives of early explorers and settlers, or the elaborate patterns of human migrations, provide a kind of historical analogue to the central action deepening the significance of the journey."

Los Angeles Times critic Ralph B. Sipper finds the combination of landscape and plot in *Yellowfish* unsatisfactory, and feels that what he describes as "a serious attempt to reflect on huge chunks of Pacific Northwest History," detracts from the novel. "What might have a been a competent, fully realized thriller," he continues, "caves in under the ponderous weight of its intentions." DeMarinis, however, insists that Keeble's use of setting and history is essential to his story. "In the adventure stories that last, the ones we come back to again and again," he argues, "the lure is this: The exterior odyssey is ultimately interior, and the demons we encounter are the ones that live within us, dictating our lives." John Keeble, he concludes, "has gone after this oldest of themes and has come back with the gold."

Keeble's fourth novel, 1987's *Broken Ground,* again uses the land as a metaphor for the spiritual struggles of its protagonist, Hank Lafleur. Lafleur is a troubled Vietnam veteran who has separated from his wife after the drowning death of their daughter. After his father suffers a severe stroke, Lafleur agrees to take over the construction of a secretive penal institute in a remote part of Oregon. But the project turns out to be more than he bargained for as he comes up against the head of the multinational corporation behind the construction. The very nature of the building itself is a force that raises perplexing moral questions for Lafleur: there is a section of the planned structure that he is convinced (by its physical design) will be used as a torture chamber. Why the chamber is needed and on who it will be used provides the novel's narrative thrust.

Although Sybil Steinberg's review of *Broken Ground* in *Publishers Weekly* found the details of the novel sometimes "excessive," she also asserts that there are numerous points that will hold a reader's interest, especially "the wider resonance of [Lafleur's] story." Likewise, Tom Nolan, writing in the *New York Times Book Review,* calls the novel "engrossing," and even though he found the book's attempts to deal with its philosophical themes—among them the relationship between perception and the environment, and "the mechanisms of personal guilt"—"disappointing," Nolan asserts that Keeble's book succeeds in "skillfully blending elements from" a variety of sources, including thrillers and magical realism. In his review of the novel, *Los Angeles Times Book Review* writer Don G. Campbell calls Keeble a "lyrical writer," and states that "mood fares better than plot." He claims, however, that "if the motivations" of some of the characters, "including many of the protagonist's—remain maddeningly fuzzy," the book still "does an excellent job of painting corporate and personal greeds in conflict against the brooding background of a harsh land."

Keeble's 1991 foray into nonfiction, *Out of the Channel: The Exxon Valdez Oil Spill in Prince William Sound,* is "a hard-hitting, gripping account," of the repercussions and political and corporate handling of the environmental disaster which occurred when an Exxon oil tanker spilled 11 million gallons of oil into the Prince William Sound in Alaska, according to Genevieve Stuttaford in *Publishers Weekly.* It was the "nation's largest oil spill" to date, reports Timothy Egan in the *New York Times Book Review,* and, according to Egan, Keeble's work succeeds in showing "the spill was all the more dramatic because it was a clash of two extremes: the industrial world . . . versus primordial nature." Dennis Drabelle, reviewing the book for the *Washington Post Book World,* notes that Keeble's work fully shows how "the disaster's ramifications extend throughout American Culture." For Egan, Keeble's book "tells the story of the great spill in a style and tone that is more impressionistic that it could have been," and the result is "engaging," if unstructured. Keeble's greatest talent concludes Egan, is "to find ironies in catastrophes"—like the fact that more oil was used in the clean-up effort than was actually spilled.

BIOGRAPHICAL/CRITICAL SOURCES:

PERIODICALS

Chicago Tribune Book World, February 17, 1980.
Los Angeles Times, February 14, 1980.
Los Angeles Times Book Review, December 20, 1987, p. 7.
Newsweek, February 11, 1980.
New Yorker, April 28, 1980.
New York Times Book Review, February 10, 1980; March 6, 1988, p. 20; April 28, 1991, p. 23.
Publishers Weekly, September 25, 1987, p. 92; February 22, 1991, p. 206. *Time,* February 2, 1980.
Washington Post, March 24, 1980; April 26, 1991, p. B3.
Washington Post Book World, October 4, 1987, p. 12.*

*   *   *

KEENE, Carolyn
    See McFARLANE, Leslie (Charles)

*   *   *

KEITH, Marian,
    See MacGREGOR, Mary Esther

*   *   *

KENNER, (William) Hugh   1923-

PERSONAL: Born January 7, 1923, in Peterborough, Ontario, Canada; son of Henry Rowe Hocking (a high school principal) and Mary Isabel (Williams) Kenner; married Mary Josephine Waite, August 30, 1947 (died, 1964); married Mary Anne Bittner, August 13, 1965; children: (first marriage) Catherine, Julia, Margaret, John, Michael; (second marriage) Robert, Elizabeth. *Education:* University of Toronto, B.A., 1945, M.A., 1946; Yale University, Ph.D., 1950. *Religion:* Roman Catholic.

ADDRESSES: Home—203 Plum Nelly Rd., Athens GA 30606.

CAREER: Assumption College (now University of Windsor), Windsor, Ontario, assistant professor, 1946-48; University of California, Santa Barbara, instructor, 1950-51, assistant professor, 1951-56, associate professor, 1956-58, professor of English, 1958-73, department chairman, 1956-62; Johns Hopkins University, Baltimore, MD, professor of English, 1973-75, Andrew W. Mellon Professor of Humanities, 1975-91, department chairman, 1980-84; University of Georgia, Athens, Franklin Professor and Callaway Professor, College of Arts and Sciences, 1991—. Visiting professor, University of Michigan, 1956, University of Chicago, 1962, and University of Virginia, 1963. Alexander Lecturer, University of Toronto, 1973; T.S. Eliot Memorial Lecturer, University of Kent, 1975; Christian Gauss Lecturer, Princeton University, 1975; F.W. Bateson Memorial Lecturer, Oxford University, 1987. Northrop Frye Chair, University of Toronto, 1985; Ames Professor, University of Washington, 1988.

MEMBER: Royal Society of Literature (fellow), American Academy of Arts and Sciences (fellow).

AWARDS, HONOURS: American Council of Learned Societies fellow, 1949; Porter Prize, 1950; American Philosophical Society fellow, 1956; Guggenheim fellow, 1957-58, 1964; National Institute of Arts and Letters/ American Academy of Arts and Letters prize, 1969; Christian Gauss Award, 1972, for *The Pound Era.* D.H.L. University of Chicago, 1976, Trent University 1977, Marlboro College, 1978, and University of Windsor, 1983. LL.D., University of Notre Dame, 1984.

WRITINGS:

Paradox in Chesterton, introduction by Marshall McLuhan, Sheed & Ward, 1947.
The Poetry of Ezra Pound, New Directions, 1951, reprinted, University of Nebraska Press, 1985.
Wyndham Lewis, New Directions, 1954.
Dublin's Joyce, Chatto & Windus, 1955, Indiana University Press, 1956, reprinted, Columbia University Press, 1987.
Gnomon: Essays in Contemporary Literature, McDowell, Obolensky, 1958.
The Invisible Poet: T.S. Eliot, McDowell, Obolensky, 1959.
Samuel Beckett, Grove, 1962, revised edition published as *Samuel Beckett: A Critical Study,* University of California Press, 1968.
Flaubert, Joyce and Beckett: The Stoic Comedians, Beacon Press, 1962, published as *The Stoic Comedians: Flaubert, Joyce and Beckett,* University of California Press, 1974.
The Counterfeiters: An Historical Comedy, Indiana University Press, 1968, reprinted, University of California Press, 1987.
The Pound Era, University of California Press, 1971.

A Reader's Guide to Samuel Beckett, Farrar, Strauss, 1973.
Bucky: A Guided Tour of Buckminster Fuller, Morrow, 1973.
A Homemade World: The American Modernist Writers, Knopf, 1975.
Geodesic Math and How to Use It, University of California Press, 1976.
Joyce's Voices, University of California Press, 1978.
Ulysses, Allen & Unwin, 1980, revised edition, Johns Hopkins University Press, 1987.
A Colder Eye: The Modern Irish Writers, Knopf, 1983.
Heath-Zenith Z-100 User's Guide, Brady, 1984.
The Mechanic Muse, Oxford University Press, 1987.
A Sinking Island: The Modern English Writers, Knopf, 1988.
Magic and Spells (chapbook), Bennington, 1988.
Mazes (essays), University of Georgia Press, 1989.
Historical Fictions: Essays, North Point Press (San Francisco), 1990.
Chuck Jones: A Flurry of Drawings, University of California Press, 1994.
(With Charles O. Hartman) *Sentences,* Sun & Moon Press (Los Angeles), 1995.

EDITOR

The Art of Poetry, Rinehart, 1959.
T.S. Eliot: A Collection of Critical Essays, Prentice-Hall, 1962.
Seventeenth Century Poetry: The Schools of Donne and Jonson, Holt, 1964.
Studies in Change: A Book of the Short Story, Prentice-Hall, 1965.
(And author of introduction) *The Translations of Ezra Pound,* Faber, 1970.
(With Seamus Cooney, Bradford Morrow, and Bernard Larourcade) *Blast 3,* Black Sparrow Press, 1985.
Desmond Egan: The Poet & His Work, Northern Lights, 1990.
(And author of introduction) *Desmond Egan, Selected Poems,* Creighton University Press, Kavanagh Press, 1992.

Contributor to essay collections, including *Essays by Divers Hands,* London, 1958, *Eliot in His Time,* A. Walton Litz, editor, Princeton University Press, 1973, *Literary Theory and Structure: Essays Presented to William K. Wimsatt,* Yale University Press, 1973, *Sylvia Plath: New Views on the Poetry,* Johns Hopkins University Press, 1979, and *The State of the Language,* Leonard Michaels and Christopher Ricks, editors, University of California Press, 1980. Contributor of reviews and articles to journals and periodicals.

SIDELIGHTS: Hugh Kenner is one of the nation's leading literary critics, particularly known for his works on this century's modernist writers. As Michiko Kakutani states in the *New York Times,* "Kenner has earned a well-deserved reputation as our pre-eminent expert on modernism in English." His books on Ezra Pound, T. S. Eliot, Wyndham Lewis, Samuel Beckett, and James Joyce have been received as important contributions to modern literary criticism. Joann Gardner, in an article for the *Dictionary of Literary Biography,* explains that Kenner "has put his hand to most of the major modern writers, defining their positions historically and offering unique perspectives on difficult and essential works."

In analyzing the works of modernist writers, Kenner often relies on the methods proposed by the writers themselves. He takes their literary criteria as the standard by which to judge their work. As Gardner notes, "Kenner invests the artist with an authority and stature often disallowed by modern criticism." This approach has been well received. Douglas Baiz of the *Chicago Tribune* maintains that "Kenner gives literary criticism a good name. His writing is muscular: clean, direct, free of jargon and obscurities. He wears his considerable learning lightly, even wittily . . . , and he displays an obvious sympathy for the writers he is examining. He flays no dead horses, scatters no red herrings, demolishes no straw men, and when he enters a lecture hall, he comes to praise Caesar, not to bury him."

Kenner's works on Ezra Pound in particular have been pivotal in establishing the author's reputation. A poet, critic, editor, and translator, Pound was the catalytic force behind much of modern literature. In addition to publishing books of poetry, criticism, and translation, he also edited the works of many other writers who later achieved prominence, such as T. S. Eliot, and worked to get the talents of promising writers appreciated by the literary community. But during the Second World War, Pound lost what respect and position he had in the literary world. Convinced that the government of Italian strongman Benito Mussolini was successfully overcoming the economic problems caused by the depression, and in the process circumventing the dire influences of bureaucracy and the banking community, Pound broadcast a series of radio messages on behalf of the Italian government during the war. At war's end, Pound was charged with treason. Found to be unfit for trial, he was hospitalized for some fourteen years in a mental asylum.

In 1951, Kenner's *The Poetry of Ezra Pound* was the first book to be published in the United States to decry Pound's political beliefs and yet argue persuasively on behalf of his literary achievement. Bonamy Dobree of the *Spectator* believes that in this book "Kenner has gone far to achieve what he set out to do, make the reader see Mr. Pound as

a poet possibly great, and certainly important to our time." Kenner's argument for taking Pound's literary work seriously proved to be influential. Writing in the *Saturday Review,* C. David Heymann noted that since the publication of Kenner's study, "the first published in this country, . . . the traffic of detailed and far-reaching investigations of and about Pound in the way of exegetical studies and explications, theses and dissertations, memoirs and biographies, has been practically non-stop." Gardner believes that Kenner's studies of Pound and British writer Wyndham Lewis have "done much to establish these figures as central to the modern tradition."

In *The Pound Era,* published in 1971, Kenner examines the course of twentieth-century literary history, tracing how the modernist writers created an aesthetic divorced from the artistic values of the nineteenth century. He sees Pound as an essential part of this development. "He sets out," Gardner explains, "to discover how the twentieth century had extricated itself from the influence of fin-de-siecle literature, and he places Ezra Pound at the vortex of the cultural movement." As Heymann notes, this movement "produced the likes of Eliot, Joyce, Wyndham Lewis, and their contemporaries, and . . . Pound was unquestionably the central and moving force."

Although some observers questioned the centrality of Pound's influence and felt that Kenner had exaggerated his importance, *The Pound Era* won praise for its depiction of Pound's role in twentieth century literature. Charles Molesworth, reviewing the book for the *Nation,* calls it "clearly the capstone of [Kenner's] illustrious career" and maintains that it "clarifies our reading of Pound and his era better than any single book of criticism. Kenner's book is, quite simply, a work of art." Writing in the *New York Review of Books,* Michael Wood calls *The Pound Era* "a brilliant, fascinating, and otherwise altogether satisfactory book," while the reviewer for the *New Republic* describes Kenner himself as "our most knowing and enthusiastic Pound scholar, a true disciple who partakes of the Pound conciseness, lives the Pound vision of art and language."

Kenner's analysis of the works of James Joyce has also proven to be influential. He has written two books about the author, *Dublin's Joyce* and *Joyce's Voices,* and a study of Joyce's most famous book, *Ulysses.* Kenner has also written of Joyce in several critical surveys. In all of these works, he has succeeded in rendering comprehensible Joyce's often difficult prose. A. Walton Litz of the *Times Literary Supplement* claims that "for over thirty years [Kenner] has been our finest reader of *Ulysses.*" In his study of *Ulysses,* also entitled *Ulysses,* Kenner "shows the reader how to read [the novel] — and shows him how exciting the experience can be," as the reviewer for the *South Atlantic Quarterly* remarks. Kenner has also turned his critical attention to other experimental writers, like Samuel Beckett, and presented their ideas and concerns in clear, understandable prose. Gardner maintains that Kenner's "analyses of Joyce, Beckett, and others have made the literary avant-garde accessible to a generation of scholars and students."

When writing of the major authors of the twentieth century, Kenner employs a witty and accessible prose that shows a great concern for the proper use of language. Thomas R. Edwards comments on Kenner's style in the *New York Times Book Review*. "It's always an unexpected pleasure," he states, "to find serious literary criticism written as if the English language still mattered, as Hugh Kenner's writing insists that it does. In book after book . . . strong and supple thought finds its proper medium in a style of uncommon wit and pungency, writing whose powers of intellectual entertainment brazenly violate the first law of academic criticism: Be Thou Dull." Kenner's work also possesses an enthusiasm that several observers appreciate for its energy and willingness to take chances. As Richard Eder writes in the *Los Angeles Times Book Review,* "Kenner doesn't write about literature; he jumps in, armed and thrashing. He crashes it, like a partygoer who refuses to hover near the door but goes right up to the guest of honor, plumps himself down, sniffs at the guest's dinner, eats some, and begins a one-to-one discussion. You could not say whether his talking or his listening is done with greater intensity."

Following the example of Pound, Kenner often unites disparate elements of information in a single work in order to show connections between events and ideas that a more conventional approach may not reveal. Speaking in particular of Kenner's method in his critical surveys of British, Irish, and American modernists, John W. Aldridge of the *New York Times Book Review* calls it a "curious but on the whole effective amalgam of anecdotes, character portraits, textual analysis, intellectual history and what Gore Vidal likes spenetically to call 'book chat'." Wood finds that Kenner "combs the world like a critical Sherlock Holmes, isolating details, making distinctions, collecting verbal and technological specimens." "Like Pound," Thomas Flanagan observes in the *Washington Post Book World,* "[Kenner] knows how to argue by juxtaposition and surprise, how to use wit as a form of logic. He knows the value of the exact image and the resonant anecdote. And like Pound, he is a skilled swordsman; reading Kenner is a lively and illuminating experience but it is best to keep one's guard up."

Kenner's collection *Mazes* brings together an eclectic variety of essays, reviews, and columns. In it he discusses subjects as diverse as the literary canon, dictionaries, the movie *King Kong,* Charlie Chaplin, Georgia O'Keefe, and Einstein's theory of time. Suggesting that *Mazes* is charac-

teristic of Kenner's "playfully associative method," *Publishers Weekly* contributor Genevieve Stuttaford claimed that the collection is "occasionally brilliant in its . . . interconnections." Sonja Bolle stated in a *Los Angeles Times* review that although "the essays sometimes give the impression of grand contrivance rather than thoughtful expression . . . much of the information . . . is vastly entertaining" Writing in the *New York Times Book Review,* Lois E. Nesbitt described Kenner's style as "verbal lacework," and noted that "Mr. Kenner is fascinated by how the human mind selects and organizes data," no matter what the object of contemplation is. Such engagement makes the essays "a pleasure to read," wrote Nesbitt.

The author's diverse interests and critical abilities also emerge in *Chuck Jones: A Flurry of Drawings,* a profile of the Warner Brothers' master animator, creator of Road Runner and Wile E. Coyote. A departure from Kenner's more serious work as a literary critic, *Chuck Jones* is "an entertaining profile" according to John Canemaker in *New York Times Book Review.* Canemaker noted that "throughout the book Mr. Kenner connects literature to the master animator," and cited Kenner's remark that " 'The stuff of animation is metamorphosis, and its theoretician ought to have been Ovid.' " "A more graceful and amusing appreciation of studio animation's history, art and craft," declared Canemaker, "would be hard to find."

The collection of essays following *Mazes,* entitled *Historical Fictions,* again demonstrates Kenner's formidable depth and breadth of knowledge. "The man knows too much," opined Joseph Coates in the *Chicago Tribune,* and Judith Shulevitz asserted in the *New York Times Book Review* that "his giant wings prevent him from walking." Shulevitz's claim is that Kenner's ideas simply are too large for the forms presented in these essays. In spite of this observation—and although, as Shulevitz points out, Kenner "blithely ignores the past two decades of critical theory (as well as much of anything having to do with minorities and women)"—*Historical Fictions,* is deemed a pleasurable, informative book by both critics. Its project, as articulated by Coates, is "to protect from loss or manhandling . . . 'writers—a few of them per century— who make a permanent difference.' "

C. K. Stead, writing in the *Times Literary Supplement,* is more critical of Kenner's work. Stead claims that it is hard to ignore or dismiss Kenner's own dismissal of Pound's problematic political views: "Sometimes one has had the feeling that Kenner's confidence has become complacency." Yet in the end, Stead, too, acknowledges Kenner's achievement, concluding "Kenner's writing has a personal voice. He has the civility to be himself—not to pretend to be nobody; or God. His criticism is demanding, yet it is also open and available, without needless and pretentious obscurity . . . spiked with small pertinent narratives and with off-beat facts. He is the most readable of living critics, the one I should least like to be without."

For some four decades, Kenner's literary criticism has illuminated many of the major works and authors of twentieth century literature. "He is both the scholar and the celebrant of the Modernist movement, and has written well and instructively about its masters," Flanagan observes. Jane Larkin Crain of the *Saturday Review* ranks Kenner "among the most distinguished of contemporary literary critics, justly celebrated for the felicity and the accessibility of his prose." Michael Rosenthal, writing in the *New York Times Book Review,* claims that "Kenner bestrides modern literature if not like a colossus then at least a presence of formidable proportions." Aldridge notes that for "over 40 years, he has written authoritatively and at length about most of the major 20th-century writers . . . and has established himself as one of the most distinguished critics now at work in the field."

BIOGRAPHICAL/CRITICAL SOURCES:

BOOKS

Dictionary of Literary Biography, Volume 67: *Modern American Critics since 1955,* Gale, 1988.
Goodwin, Will, *Kenner on Joyce: A Bibliography,* E.A. Kopper, 1991.

PERIODICALS

Booklist, August, 1994, pp. 2012, 2032.
Bookworld, August 4, 1968, May 28, 1989, p. 12.
Chicago Tribune, March 3, 1987, January 29, 1988, July 20, 1989, p. 3, September 30, 1990, p. 9, January 15, 1995, p. 6.
Denver Quarterly, spring, 1977.
Kirkus Reviews, July 1, 1994, p. 926.
Los Angeles Times Book Review, January 31, 1988, June 25, 1989, p. 6.
Nation, March 20, 1972.
New Republic, March 25, 1972, November 29, 1975.
New York Review of Books, February 13, 9169, February 8, 1973, April 17, 1975, May 12, 1983.
New York Times, Mach 28, 1972, February 4, 1975, November 29, 1986, December 28, 1990, p. 36.
New York Times Book Review, March 26, 1972, November 25, 1973, February 9, 1975, July 31, 1983, February 21, 1988, July 9, 1989, p. 19, September 30, 1990, p. 28, October 30, 1994, p. 38.
Publishers Weekly, February 10, 1989, p. 60.
Saturday Review, May 13, 1972, April 5, 1975.
South Atlantic Quarterly, winter, 1983.
Spectator, November 16, 1951, September 9, 1978.
Times Literary Supplement, May 5, 1978, December 12, 1980, January 25, 1991, p. 7.
Tribune Books, September 30, 1990, p. 9.

Village Voice, May 24, 1983.
Voice Literary Supplement, December, 1983.
Washington Post, July 9, 1989, p. 4, October 2, 1994, p. 13.
Washington Post Book World, May 8, 1983, April 3, 1988.

—*Sketch by Thomas Wiloch*

* * *

KERN, E. R.
See KERNER, Fred

* * *

KERNER, Fred 1921-
(Frohm Fredericks, E. R. Kern, Frederick Kerr, M. N. Thaler)

PERSONAL: Born February 15, 1921, in Montreal, Quebec, Canada; son of Sam and Vera (Goldman) Kerner; married second wife, Sally Dee Stouten, May 18, 1959; children: (first marriage) Jon; (second marriage) David, Diane. *Education:* Sir George Williams University (now Concordia University), B.A., 1942.

ADDRESSES: Home—1555 Finch Ave., Apt. 1405, Willowdale, Ontario, Canada M2J 4X9. *Office*—Publishing Projects, Inc., 55014 Fairview Mall, Willowdale, Ontario, Canada M2J 5B9.

CAREER: Saskatoon Star-Phoenix, editorial writer, 1942; *Montreal Gazette,* Montreal, Quebec, assistant sports editor, 1942-44; worked variously as newsperson, editor, and news executive for the Canadian Press in Montreal, Toronto, and New York City, 1944-50; Associated Press, New York City, assistant night city editor, 1950-56; Hawthorn Books, Inc., New York City, editor, 1957-58, president and editor-in-chief, 1964-68; Fawcett Publications, Inc., New York City, editor-in-chief of Crest and Premier Books, 1958-64; Hall House, Inc., Greenwich, CT, editor, 1963-64; Centaur House Publishers, Inc., New York City, president and editor-in-chief, 1964-75; Publishing Projects, Inc., New York City and Toronto, president, 1968—; Communications Unlimited, Toronto, president, 1969—; Book and Educational Division, Reader's Digest Association (Canada), publishing director, 1968-75; Harlequin Books Ltd., Don Mills, Ontario, vice president and publishing director, 1975-83, editor emeritus and senior consulting editor, 1983—. Lecturer at Long Island University, 1968; editor-in-residence at several writers' conferences in the United States and Canada. Judge, Cobalt National Poetry Contest; trustee, Canadian Authors Association Literary Awards, Benson & Hedges Awards, Gibson Awards, Sir George Williams University journalism awards, and Rothman Literary Award of Merit; director, Publitex International Corp., Peter Kent, Inc., Pennorama Crafts, Inc., Disque Design, Inc., National Mint, Inc., and Personalized Services, Inc.; member of board of governors, Concordia University, Montreal, 1973-77, Canadian Writers' Foundation, and Academy of Canadian Writers; vice-chair, Federal Public Lending Right Commission and Canadian Copyright Institute; member of local school boards in New York City and Westmount, Quebec, Canada.

MEMBER: International Platform Association, Canadian Authors Association (president of Montreal branch, 1972-75; vice president, 1973-80; national president, 1982-83), Organization of Canadian Authors and Publishers (founding member; member of board of governors, 1977-83), Canadian Book Publishers' Council (honorary life member), CAA Fund to Develop Canadian Writers (founding president, 1983), Canadian Association for the Restoration of Lost Positives (president, 1969—), Mystery Writers of America (editor of *The Third Degree*), Overseas Press Club (chair of election committee, 1960-64; chair of library and book-night committee, 1961), Word on the Street (founding member), Canadian Society of Professional Journalists, Writer's Union of Canada, Periodical Writers' Association of Canada, Authors Guild, Authors League of America, American Academy of Political and Social Science, European Academy of Arts, Sciences and Humanities, American Management Association, Edward R. Murrow Fund (chair of publisher's committee), Advertising Club of New York, Association of Alumni of Sir George Williams University (president of New York branch, 1959-64; president, 1973-75), Authors' Club (London, England), Toronto Men's Press Club (founding director), Canadian Society (New York), Dutch Treat Club (New York), Deadline Club (New York), Sigma Delta Chi.

AWARDS, HONOURS: Montreal YMCA Literature Award, 1938, 1939, and 1940; Crusade for Freedom Award, American Heritage Foundation, 1954; Queen's Silver Jubilee Medal, 1979, for contributions to international publishing; Air Canada Literary Award, 1979, for contributions to Canadian writing; Allan Sangster Award, Canadian Authors Association, 1982; Apex Award, 1992, for newsletter editing; *Toronto Star* short fiction award, 1988; Lyn Harrington Diamond Jubilee Award, 1989; Mercury Award, 1990, for outstanding achievement in professional communications.

WRITINGS:

(With Leonid Kotkin) *Eat, Think, and Be Slender,* Hawthorn, 1954, new edition, Wilshire, 1960.
(With Walter Germain) *The Magic Power of Your Mind,* Hawthorn, 1956.

(With Joyce Brothers) *Ten Days to a Successful Memory,* Prentice-Hall, 1957.
Stress and Your Heart, Hawthorn, 1961.
(Under pseudonym Frederick Kerr) *Watch Your Weight Go Down,* Pyramid Publications, 1963.
(With Germain) *Secrets of Your Supraconscious,* Hawthorn, 1965.
(With David Goodman) *What's Best for Your Child—and You,* Hawthorn, 1966.
(With Jesse Reid) *Buy High, Sell Higher!,* Hawthorn, 1966.
(Under pseudonym M. N. Thaler) *It's Fun to Fondue,* Centaur Press, 1968.
(With Ion Grumeza) *Nadia,* Hawthorn, 1977.
Mad About Fondue, Irwin, 1986.
Careers in Writing, CAA, 1986.
(With Andrew Willman) *Prospering Through the Coming Depression,* Fitzhenry & Whiteside, 1988.
Home Emergency Handbook, McClelland & Stewart, 1990.

Contributor to books, including *Successful Writers and How They Work,* edited by Larston Farrar, Hawthorn, 1958; *Words on Paper,* edited by Roy Copperud, Hawthorn, 1960; *The Overseas Press Club Cookbook,* edited by Sigrid Schultz, Doubleday, 1962; *The Seniors' Guide to Life in the Slow Lane,* Eden Press, 1986; *The Writer's Essential Desk Reference,* edited by Glenda Tennant Neff, Writer's Digest Books, 1991; *Lifetime: A Treasury of Uncommon Wisdoms,* Macmillan Canada, 1992. Author of several columns, including "A Word to the Wise" in *Canadian Author & Bookman.* Contributor to periodicals, including *American Weekly, Maclean's, Science Digest, Reader's Digest, Best Years, Weight Watchers,* and *True.* Editor, *Third Degree* and *National Newsline.* Also scriptwriter for Joyce Brothers's television program for two years. Ghostwriter for columns by actress Anita Colby and publisher Enid Haupt of *Seventeen* magazine; sometimes writes under pseudonyms Frohm Fredericks and E. R. Kern.

Many of Fred Kerner's books have been translated into French, Spanish, German, Portuguese, Italian, and Japanese.

EDITOR

Love Is a Man's Affair, Fell, 1958.
A Treasury of Lincoln Quotations, Doubleday, 1965.
The Canadian Writer's Guide, Fitzhenry & Whiteside, 11th edition, 1992.

WORK IN PROGRESS: Canadian English usage; *1001 Ways to Have Good Luck; Public Speaking for Fun and Profit;* children's books on word-play.

SIDELIGHTS: Fred Kerner gave *CA* his advice to aspiring writers: "If you wish to develop your style, you must first learn to love the basic tools of the writer's craft: *words.* Learn to love them for their color, their texture, their weight, their sound—even their visual impact. Learn to fully appreciate them as your tools. English is the most flexible language and its use—properly and appropriately—is the most important aspect of being a competent and capable writer."

* * *

KERR, Frederick
See KERNER, Fred

* * *

KING, Thomas 1943-

PERSONAL: Born April 24, 1943, in Sacramento, California, United States; son of Robert Hunt and Kathryn K. King; married Kristine Adams, 1970 (marriage ended, 1981); partner of Helen Hoy; children: Christian, Benjamin Hoy, Elizabeth. *Education:* California State University, Chico, B.A., 1970, M.A., 1972; University of Utah, Ph.D., 1986. *Avocational interests:* Photography.

ADDRESSES: Agent—Denise Bukowski, Bukowski Agency, 182 Avenue Rd., Suite 3, Toronto M5R 2J1, Ontario.

CAREER: Photojournalist in Australia and New Zealand; Boeing Aircraft, tool designer; University of Utah, Salt Lake City, director of Native studies, 1971-73; California State University, Humboldt, associate dean for student services, 1973-77; University of Utah, coordinator of History of the Indians of the Americas Program, 1977-79; University of Lethbridge, Lethbridge, Alberta, assistant professor of Native studies, 1979-89; University of Minnesota-Twin Cities, Minneapolis, associate professor of American and Native studies, 1989, chairperson of Native studies.

AWARDS, HONOURS: Canadian Governor General's Award, 1992, for *A Coyote Columbus Story;* PEN/Josephine Miles Award for *Medicine River,* also nominated for the Commonwealth Writer's Prize.

WRITINGS:

(Editor with Cheryl Dawnan Calver and Helen Hoy) *The Native in Literature: Canadian and Comparative Perspectives,* illustrated by Jay Belmore, ECW Press, 1987.
(Editor) *All My Relations: An Anthology of Contemporary Canadian Native Fiction,* McClelland and Stewart, 1990.

Medicine River (fiction), Viking, 1990.
A Coyote Columbus Story (children's book), illustrated by William K. Monkman, Groundwood, 1992.
Green Grass, Running Water (fiction), Houghton Mifflin, 1993.
One Good Story, That One (short stories), Harper, 1993.

Also author of the screenplay *Medicine River,* broadcast by CBC-TV, 1993, and the radio drama *Medicine River,* CBC-Radio, 1993. Contributor of poems to periodicals, including *Canadian Literature, Soundings, Whetstone,* and *Tonyon Review.* Editor of *Canadian Fiction,* 1988.

SIDELIGHTS: Typically classified as a writer of Canadian Native fiction, Thomas King is known for works in which he addresses the marginalization of Amerindians, delineates "pan-Indian" concerns and histories, and attempts to abolish common stereotypes about Native Americans.

Born in Sacramento, California, King is of Greek, German, and Native American descent. His father, of Cherokee origins, abandoned the family when King was only a child. Although King visited his Cherokee relatives in Oklahoma as a youth, he was primarily raised white and the Natives in his works are typically of Blackfoot descent. After graduating from high school, King traveled abroad, eventually working as a photojournalist in New Zealand and Australia. During this time he began writing, but he describes these early attempts as "real pukey stuff." Returning to the United States, King entered college, earning a B.A. and M.A. in English from California State University in the early 1970s and a Ph.D. in American Studies and English in 1986 from the University of Utah. He resumed writing while doing doctoral work and teaching at the University of Lethbridge in Alberta. A citizen of Canada, the setting for most of his works, and the United States, King has since taught in both countries and acknowledges that Natives are his primary audience. Nevertheless, he questions attempts to define him solely as a Canadian Native writer: "There's only a problem in the sense that I am not originally from Canada, and the Cherokee aren't a Canadian tribe. Now that becomes a problem only if you recognize the particular political line which runs between Canada and the U.S., and if you agree with the assumptions that that line makes."

The exclusion of Native Americans from white society, history, and culture is prevalent in much of King's writings. For example, *Medicine River* (1990) focuses on Will, a mixed blood of Blackfoot descent. Returning to his hometown of Medicine River, Alberta, where he works as a photographer, Will must come to terms with the alienation he feels within his circle of family and friends as well as the stereotypes projected on—and at times perpetuated by—Native Americans. A cycle of vignettes and an intimate portrait of small-town life, *Medicine River* tries to subvert misperceptions about Natives while including such traditional Native characters as the coyote trickster figure. The coyote persona, which has the power to create and destroy, is also prominently featured in *A Coyote Columbus Story* (1992), a children's book that relates the creation of the world and the "discovery" of the Americas by Christopher Columbus from a Native perspective, and in King's 1993 novel, *Green Grass, Running Water.* Incorporating shifting viewpoints and a convoluted, circular storyline, *Green Grass, Running Water* follows, in part, the actions of four ancient Indian spirits. Perceived by whites as insane and aged, these spirits have been confined to a mental institution from which they periodically escape in order to "fix" the world; in this instance, they hope to prevent an environmental catastrophe from occurring in the small Canadian town of Blossom. The novel also concerns several members of the Blackfoot nation who reside in Blossom, their interpersonal relationships, their attempts to make a living in the white world, and their ongoing debate over a proposal to build a hydroelectric dam in the region.

King's skill as a humorist and satirist is evident in this work: one character runs a highly profitable restaurant by claiming to sell "hound burgers" to white tourists. In another instance, the Indian spirits rewrite Hollywood history by colorizing old black-and-white Westerns and allowing the Indian "savages" to triumph over John Wayne and the United States Calvary. Irony, colonization, assimilation, and the oral tradition are also central to King's 1993 short story collection, *One Good Story, That One,* which has been praised for its use of Indian dialect. The critically acclaimed title story, for instance, relates an elderly Native's attempts to hoodwink anthropologists by trying to pass off a comic version of the Judeo-Christian creation myth as authentically Native. Juxtaposing Christian and Native religious imagery with references to popular culture, the narrator recalls the actions and motivations of the practical woman Evening, the dimwitted Ahdamn, and their angry, selfish god. King has additionally edited anthologies of critical and creative works dealing with Canadians, indigenous peoples, and their literatures.

King's work has been well received by critics. He won a Governor General's award for *A Coyote Columbus Story* and a PEN/Josephine Miles Award for *Medicine River,* which was also nominated for the Commonwealth Writer's Prize. His novels and short stories are known for their humor and irony, evocation of place, focus on Native society and culture, and for their inventive manipulation of plot and attempts at historical revisionism.

BIOGRAPHICAL/CRITICAL SOURCES:

PERIODICALS

Books in Canada, April, 1993, pp. 40-1.
Canadian Literature, spring-summer, 1990, pp. 243-50, 307-08; Winter, 1991, pp. 212-13.
Chicago Tribune, March 28, 1993, pp. 1, 9.
Choice, November, 1988, p. 500.
The Christian Science Monitor, October 3, 1990, p. 13; March 31, 1993, p. 13.
English Journal, January, 1994, p. 84.
Globe and Mail, February 3, 1990.
The Horn Book Magazine, September-October, 1993, pp. 636-38.
Los Angeles Times Book Review, October 4, 1992, p. 12; March 25, 1993, p. E2.
Maclean's, October 18, 1993, p. 65.
Newsweek, April 12, 1993, p. 60.
New York Times Book Review, September 23, 1990, p. 29.
Publishers Weekly, March 8, 1993, pp. 56-57.
Quill and Quire, April, 1990, p. 26; March, 1993, p. 46; September, 1993, p. 61.
The Sewanee Review, spring, 1992, pp. 323-30.
The Washington Post, April 16, 1993, p. B2.
World Literature Today, autumn, 1989, pp. 723-34.
World Literature Written in English, autumn, 1990, pp. 62-84.*

*   *   *

KINSELLA, W(illiam) P(atrick) 1935-

PERSONAL: Born May 25, 1935, in Edmonton, Alberta, Canada; son of John Matthew (a contractor) and Olive Mary (a printer; maiden name, Elliot) Kinsella; married Myrna Salls, December 28, 1957 (divorced, 1963); married Mildred Irene Clay, September 10, 1965 (divorced, 1978); married Ann Ilene Knight (a writer), December 30, 1978; children: (first marriage) Shannon, Lyndsey, Erin. *Education:* University of Victoria, B.A., 1974; University of Iowa, M.F.A., 1978; Laurentian University, D.Litt., 1990. *Religion:* Atheist.

ADDRESSES: Home—15325 19-A Ave., White Rock, British Columbia, Canada V4A 8S4; Box 2162, Blaine, WA 98230-2162.*Agent*—Nancy Colbert, 55 Avenue Rd., Toronto, Ontario, Canada M5R 3L2.

CAREER: Government of Alberta, Edmonton, clerk, 1954-56; Retail Credit Co., Edmonton, Alberta, manager, 1956-61; City of Edmonton, Edmonton, account executive, 1961-67; Caesar's Italian Village (restaurant), Victoria, British Columbia, owner, 1967-72; student and taxicab driver in Victoria, 1974-76; University of Iowa, Iowa City, instructor, 1976-78; University of Calgary, Calgary,

Alberta, assistant professor of English and creative writing, 1978-83; author, 1983—.

MEMBER: American Amateur Press Association, Society of American Baseball Researchers, American Atheists, Enoch Emery Society.

AWARDS, HONOURS: Award from Canadian Fiction, 1976, for story "Illianna Comes Home"; honorable mention in *Best American Short Stories 1980,* for "Fiona the First"; Houghton Mifflin Literary fellowship, 1982, Books in Canada First Novel Award, 1983, and Canadian Authors Association prize, 1983, all for *Shoeless Joe;* Writers Guild of Alberta O'Hagan novel medal, 1984, for *The Moccasin Telegraph;* Alberta Achievement Award for Excellence in Literature; Stephen Leacock Medal for Humor, 1987, for *The Fencepost Chronicles;* Author of the Year Award, Canadian Booksellers Association, 1987; University of Victoria, D.Let, 1991.

WRITINGS:

Dance Me Outside (stories), Oberon Press, 1977, published as *Dance Me Outside: More Tales from the Ermineskin Reserve,* David Godine, 1986.
Scars (stories), Oberon Press, 1978.
Shoeless Joe Jackson Comes to Iowa (stories), Oberon Press, 1980, Southern Methodist University Press, 1993.
Born Indian, Oberon Press, 1981.
Shoeless Joe (novel; based on title story in *Shoeless Joe Jackson Comes to Iowa*), Houghton, 1982.
The Ballad of the Public Trustee (chapbook), William Hoffer Standard Editions, 1982.
The Moccasin Telegraph (stories), Penguin Canada, 1983, published as *The Moccasin Telegraph and Other Tales,* David Godine, 1984, published as *The Moccasin Telegraph and Other Stories,* Penguin, 1985.
The Thrill of the Grass (chapbook), William Hoffer Standard Editions, 1984.
The Thrill of the Grass (story collection; contains "The Thrill of the Grass"), Penguin Books, 1984.
The Alligator Report (stories), Coffee House Press, 1985.
The Iowa Baseball Confederacy (novel), Houghton, 1986.
Five Stories (chapbook), William Hoffer Standard Editions, 1986.
The Fencepost Chronicles (stories), Collins, 1986, Houghton, 1987.
Red Wolf, Red Wolf (stories), Collins, 1987.
The Further Adventures of Slugger McBatt: Baseball Stories by W. P. Kinsella, Collins, 1987, Houghton, 1988.
(With wife Ann Knight) *The Rainbow Warehouse* (poetry), Pottersfield, 1989.
Two Spirits Soar: The Art of Allen Sapp (art book), Stoddard, 1990.
The Miss Hobbema Pageant, HarperCollins, 1990.

The First and Last Annual Six Towns Area Old Timers' Baseball Game, Coffee House Press, 1991.
Box Socials (novel), HarperCollins, 1992.
A Series for the World, Woodford, 1992.
The Dixon Cornbelt League (stories), HarperCollins, 1993.
Brother Frank's Gospel Hour (stories), HarperCollins, 1994.

Contributor to *Ergo!: The Bumbershoot Literary Magazine,* edited by Judith Roche, Bumbershoot, 1991. Also author of foreword to *Hummers, Knucklers, and Slow Curves: Contemporary Baseball Poems,* edited by Don Johnson, University of Illinois Press, 1991.

Contributor to numerous anthologies, including *Best Canadian Stories: 1977, 1981, 1985, Aurora: New Canadian Writing 1979, Best American Short Stories 1980, More Stories from Western Canada, Oxford Anthology of Canadian Literature, Pushcart Prize Anthology 5, The Spirit That Moves Us Reader, Introduction to Fiction, The Temple of Baseball, Penguin Book of Modern Canadian Short Stories, The Armchair Book of Baseball, Small Wonders, Illusion Two, West of Fiction, Anthology of Canadian Literature in English, Volume II,* and *Here's the Story.*

Also contributor of more than 200 stories to American and Canadian magazines, including *Sports Illustrated, Arete: Journal of Sports Literature, Story Quarterly, Matrix,* and *Canadian Fiction Magazine.*

WORK IN PROGRESS: If Wishes Were Horses, The Ladies Are Dancing Alone, Butterfly Winter, The Winter Helen Dropped By, and *Conflicting Statements,* all novels; *Bull,* a story collection.

ADAPTATIONS: Shoeless Joe was adapted and produced as the motion picture *Field of Dreams,* released in 1989 by Universal; *Dance Me Outside* was produced as a motion picture by Norman Jewison in 1995.

SIDELIGHTS: W. P. Kinsella, a Canadian author of novels and stories, has attracted an international readership with his imaginative fictions. Many of Kinsella's short stories follow the daily escapades of characters living on a Cree Indian reservation, while his longer works, *Shoeless Joe* and *The Iowa Baseball Confederacy,* mix magic and the mundane in epic baseball encounters. A determined writer who published his first story collection at the age of forty-two, Kinsella has won numerous awards, among them the prestigious Houghton Mifflin Literary fellowship. He commented: "I am an old-fashioned storyteller. I try to make people laugh and cry. A fiction writer's duty is to entertain. If you can then sneak in something profound or symbolic, so much the better."

"Fiction writing," Kinsella told the Toronto *Globe and Mail,* " . . . consists of ability, imagination, passion and stamina." He suggested that stamina is the most important ingredient of success, and he defined the quality as "keeping your buns on the chair and writing even when you don't feel like it" and "getting up at 5 a.m., running hot water over your fingers so they will make the typewriter keys work for an hour or two before you go off to your hateful job." He admitted: "I did that for 20 years while I beat my head against the walls of North American literature." Indeed, Kinsella calculates that he wrote more than fifty unpublishable stories while perfecting his craft. He also worked at numerous jobs in Edmonton, Alberta, and Victoria, British Columbia, including managing a credit company, running his own pizza restaurant, and driving a taxicab. "No matter what I did, I always thought of myself as a writer," he remembered in *Publishers Weekly.* "You're born with a compulsion to write." Kinsella was in his thirties when he began attending college at the University of Victoria and in his forties when his fiction began to sell regularly. Reflecting on his own experiences, he told the *Globe and Mail:* "I know it's a cliche, but though inspiration is nice, 98 per cent of writing is accomplished by perspiration."

A Cree Indian named Silas Ermineskin brought Kinsella literary recognition beginning in 1974. Kinsella experienced his first sustained success writing about a fictional cast of reservation-dwellers from Silas's point of view, and since then he has published nearly one hundred short stories about the Cree, many of which are collected in *Dance Me Outside, Scars, Born Indian* and *The Moccasin Telegraph.* Both Canadian and American critics express admiration for Kinsella's accomplishment. *Prairie Schooner* contributor Frances W. Kaye notes: "W. P. Kinsella is not an Indian, a fact that would not be extraordinary were it not for the stories Kinsella writes about . . . a Cree World. Kinsella's Indians are counterculture figures in the sense that their lives counter the predominant culture of North America, but there is none of the worshipfully inaccurate portrayal of 'the Indian' that has appeared from Fenimore Cooper through Gary Snyder." In *Wascana Review,* George Woodcock likewise cites Kinsella for an approach that "restores proportion and brings an artistic authenticity to the portrayal of contemporary Indian life which we have encountered rarely in recent years." Anthony Brennan offers a similar assessment in *Fiddlehead,* writing that *Dance Me Outside* "is all the more refreshing because it quite consciously eschews ersatz heroics and any kind of nostalgic, mythopoeic reflections on a technicolor golden age."

Critics also praise Kinsella's Indian stories for their insight into human nature. *Village Voice* contributor Stanley Crouch commends Kinsella for his "ability to make what superficially seems only Indian problems come off as the universal struggle with insipid laws and bureaucrats."

Kaye feels that what makes the stories work is Kinsella's "eye for detail and his sense of how a few remembered images come together to create a place and a people that compel belief." Brennan calls the fiction "low-key, deliberately unspectacular, full of rueful mirth and a carefully accumulated wisdom," concluding, "It is pleasant to find a man who can mock the pathetic attempts of the 'apples'—those with red skin desperate to be white inside—and who would surely be able to nail those white writers who desperately try to invent a new identity as red warriors."

In 1980 Kinsella published *Shoeless Joe Jackson Comes to Iowa,* a collection of short pieces set in Iowa, urban Canada and San Francisco. The title story also was selected to appear in an anthology entitled *Aurora: New Canadian Writing 1979.* An editor at Houghton Mifflin saw Kinsella's contribution to *Aurora* and contacted the author about expanding the story into a novel. "It was something that hadn't occurred to me at all," Kinsella recalled in *Publishers Weekly.* "I told [the editor], 'I've never written anything longer than 25 pages, but if you want to work with me, I'll try it.' " Much to Kinsella's surprise, the editor agreed. Kinsella set to work expanding "Shoeless Joe Jackson Comes to Iowa," but he decided instead to leave the story intact as the first chapter and build on the plot with a variety of other material. "I enjoyed doing it very much," he said. "They were such wonderful characters I'd created, and I liked being audacious in another way. I put in no sex, no violence, no obscenity, none of that stuff that sells. I wanted to write a book for imaginative readers, an affirmative statement about life."

Shoeless Joe, a novel-length baseball fable set on an Iowa farm, won Kinsella the Houghton Mifflin Literary fellowship in 1982. The story follows a character named Ray Kinsella in his attempts to summon the spirits of the tarnished 1919 Chicago White Sox by building a ballpark in his cornfield. Among the ghostly players lured to Kinsella's perfectly mowed grass is Shoeless Joe Jackson, the White Sox star player who fell in scandal when it was revealed that his team threw the World Series. As the story progresses, the same mysterious loudspeaker voice that suggested construction of the ballpark says, "Ease his pain," and Ray Kinsella sets off to kidnap author J. D. Salinger for a visit to Fenway Park. The novel blends baseball lore with legend and historical figures with fictional characters. "I've mixed in so much, I'm not sure what's real and what's not," Kinsella told *Publishers Weekly,* "but as long as you can convince people you know what you're talking about, it doesn't matter. If you're convincing, they'll believe it."

Kinsella does seem to have convinced most critics with the novel *Shoeless Joe.* According to Alan Cheuse in the *Los Angeles Times,* the work "stands as fictional homage to our national pastime, with resonances so American that the book may be grounds for abolishing our northern border." *Detroit News* writer Ben Brown claims: "What we have here is a gentle, unselfconscious fantasy balanced perilously in the air above an Iowa cornfield. It's a balancing act sustained by the absolutely fearless, sentimentality-risking honesty of the author. And it doesn't hurt a bit that he's a master of the language. . . . This is an utterly beautiful piece of work." A dissenting opinion is offered by Jonathan Yardley in the *Washington Post,* who suggests that *Shoeless Joe* "is a book of quite unbelievable self-indulgence, a rambling exercise the only discernible point of which seems to be to demonstrate, ad infinitum and ad nauseum, what a wonderful fellow is its narrator/author." Conversely, *Christian Science Monitor* contributor Maggie Lewis praises the work, concluding: "The descriptions of landscape are poetic, and the baseball details will warm fans' hearts and not get in the way of mere fantasy lovers. This book would make great reading on a summer vacation. In fact, this book *is* a summer vacation." Cheuse concludes that *Shoeless Joe* "in its ritual celebration of the game of baseball proves its author to be a writer worth further conjuring. A baseball book for this season, and perhaps many more to come, it takes its time to create a world of compelling whimsy."

Kinsella continues his fascination with baseball in his 1986 novel *The Iowa Baseball Confederacy.* Jonathan Webb describes the work in *Quill and Quire:* "*The Iowa Baseball Confederacy* contains bigger magic, larger and more spectacular effects, than anything attempted in *Shoeless Joe.* Kinsella is striving for grander meaning: the reconciliation of immovable forces—love and darker emotions—on conflicting courses." Time travel and a ballgame that lasts in excess of 2,600 innings are two of the supernatural events in the story; characters as diverse as Teddy Roosevelt and Leonardo da Vinci make cameo appearances. *Chicago Tribune Book World* contributor Gerald Nemanic writes: "Freighted with mythical machinery, *The Iowa Baseball Confederacy* requires the leavening of some sprightly prose. Kinsella is equal to it. His love for baseball is evident in the lyrical descriptions of the game."

In the *Globe and Mail,* William French suggests that Kinsella lifts baseball to a higher plane in his novels. The author, French notes, is "attracted as much to the metaphysical aspects as the physical, intrigued by how baseball transcends time and place and runs like a subterranean stream-of-consciousness through the past century or so of American history. . . . His baseball novels are animated by a light-hearted wit and bubbling imagination, a respect for mystery and magic." "To be obsessed with baseball is to be touched by grace in Kinsella's universe," writes Webb, "and a state of grace gives access to magic." Webb feels that in *The Iowa Baseball Confederacy,* Kinsella fails

to persuade the reader to go along with his magic. French likewise states: "In the end [of the novel], Kinsella's various themes don't quite connect. But it hardly matters; we're able to admire the audacity of Kinsella's vision and the sheen of his prose without worrying too much about his ultimate meaning." *Los Angeles Times Book Review* contributor Roger Kahn calls *The Iowa Baseball Confederacy* "fun and lyric and poignant." Kahn adds: "We are reading a writer here, a real writer, Muses be praised. But we are also adrift in a delicate world of fantasy, weird deaths and, I suppose, symbolism. Sometimes the work is confusing, as Kinsella adds a fantasy on top of an illusion beyond a mirage. But I never lost my wonder at how the ballgame would turn out; any author who can hold you for 2,614 innings deserves considerable praise."

Although baseball surfaces as a theme in Kinsella's 1991 novel *Box Socials,* the author revolves his work primarily around the young narrator, Jamie O'Day, and the quirky characters who live in and around 1940s Fark—a small town near Edmonton, Alberta, Canada. Filled with "crackpots bizarre enough to put [American humorist] Garrison Keillor to shame," ventures Joyce R. Slater in *Chicago Tribune Book World, Box Socials* features such individuals as Little Wasyl Podolanchuk, one of the only Ukrainian dwarfs in the province; teenaged Truckbox Al McClintock, who once batted against Hall of Fame pitcher Bob Feller; and bachelor Earl J. Rasmussen, who lives in the hills with six hundred sheep and delights in belting out "Casey at the Bat" at whim. Many reviewers note that *Box Socials* is essentially a coming-of-age tale about the curious and wide-eyed Jamie, who learns about sex by listening in on the women who gab with his mother, and who attends his first box social and bids on poor, downtrodden Bertha Sigurdson's lunch, even though Velvet Bozniak paid him to bid on hers. "The 'little box social' turns out to be a humdinger," Fannie Flagg maintains in the *New York Times Book Review,* "if you've never been to a box social, go to this one. Along with a lot of laughs, we are given a touching and sensitive portrayal of the love, sometimes happy, sometimes heartbreaking, between young men and young women, and experience the pangs of first love through Jamie's eyes." Other reviewers commend Kinsella's leisurely narrative style. Patrick Goldstein in the *Los Angeles Times Book Review* asserts that *Box Socials* is "a delightful comic ramble, written in a quirky, digressive style that reads like a cross between [American avant-garde writer] Gertrude Stein and [American cartoonist] Al Capp." "If long-winded, seemingly pointless stories make you anxious," points out Slater, "Kinsella's not your man. If you're patient enough to stay for the payoff, if you're an admirer of the perfect wry phrase buried in verbiage, he will give you more than your money's worth."

The success of his baseball books notwithstanding, Kinsella continues to produce short fiction on a variety of themes. *The Alligator Report,* also published in 1986, contains stories that pay homage to surrealist Richard Brautigan, one of Kinsella's favorite authors. In a *Village Voice* review, Jodi Daynard claims: "Kinsella's new stories replace humor with wit, regional dialect with high prose. . . . He uses surrealism most effectively to highlight the delicate balance between solitude and alienation, not to achieve a comic effect. . . . These are images that resonate—not comic ones, alas, but stirring, not woolly-wild, but urban gothic." *New York Times Book Review* contributor Harry Marten contends that in *The Alligator Report* Kinsella continues "to define a world in which magic and reality combine to make us laugh and think about the perceptions we take for granted."

Once again Kinsella mixes magic and baseball in his 1993 work, *The Dixon Cornbelt League.* In this collection of nine stories Kinsella uses mysticism and conflict to explore human nature. Supernatural events permeate many of the stories: "The Baseball Wolf," shows what happens when a shortstop transforms into a wolf in order to revive his fading career; in "The Fadeaway," even death cannot stop pitcher Christy Mathewson from relaying pitching tips to the Cleveland Indians through a dugout phone. Stephen Smith of *Quill and Quire* notices the lack of "baseball activity" in *The Dixon Cornbelt League* and instructs the reader to "choose your own baseball imagery" when judging the stories. The story "Eggs" takes on a more realistic and serious topic. "Eggs" is an account of a pitcher's premature retirement due to the loss of his ability to throw a fastball. The pitcher's aspiration to return to baseball is unsupported by his wife and his unhappiness grows. *Publisher's Weekly* critic Sybil S. Steinberg appreciates Kinsella's stories because they "read like lightening" and present "fascinating scenarios," yet she feels Kinsella does not fully satisfy his readers, does not offer enough substance and depth in the characters and their stories.

In his 1994 book of short stories, *Brother Frank's Gospel Hour,* Kinsella revisits the inhabitants of Hobbema, Alberta. Two familiar inhabitants include Silas Ermineskin, a Cree writer, and his comical partner Frank Fencepost. The humorous pair return in the short story "Bull," a light-hearted rendering of an artificial insemination case in the Alberta Supreme Court. The other stories in *Brother Frank* cover a range of topics. "Rain Birds," looks at the results of corporate farming on nature; the reality of child abuse is explored in "Dream Catcher;" a boy ascertains the parallels between the sexes in "Ice Man;" and in "Brother Frank's Gospel Hour" comedy turns a staid gospel show upside down. Criticism of *Brother Frank* has been predominantly positive. Scott Anderson of *Quill and Quire* credits Kinsella for his "understanding of human

foibles" and his revelry in "the inventiveness of the human spirit in adversity."

Kinsella received his master's degree from the University of Iowa in 1978 and subsequently taught English and creative writing at the University of Calgary until 1983. Since then he has supported himself by writing and has indulged a favorite whim by traveling across the United States and Canada to see major league baseball games. "I'm not a fanatic," he told *Publishers Weekly.* "It may appear so, but I'm not. My feeling for baseball is a little like Cordelia's statement to King Lear. She said she loved him as a daughter loves a father. No more and no less." He went on to admit that his enthusiasm for the game is purely that of a spectator. "I don't play baseball," he said. "I throw like a girl." Kinsella has expressed stronger opinions about what he feels are the necessary components of good fiction. "The secret of a fiction writer," he told the *Globe and Mail,* "is to make the dull interesting by imagination and embellishment, and to tone down the bizarre until it is believable. . . . Stories or novels are not about events, but about the people that events happen to. The fact that the Titanic is sinking or a skyscraper toppling—or even that the world is ending—is not important unless you have created an appealing character who is going to suffer if the dreaded event happens." The author who has been called "a fabulist of great skill" and "a gifted Canadian writer" once commented: "There are no gods, there is no magic; I may be a wizard though, for it takes a wizard to know there are none. My favorite quotation is by Donald Barthelme: 'The aim of literature is to create a strange object covered with fur which breaks your heart.'"

BIOGRAPHICAL/CRITICAL SOURCES:

BOOKS

Contemporary Authors Autobiography Series, Volume 7, Gale, 1988.
Contemporary Literary Criticism, Gale, Volume 27, 1984, Volume 43, 1987.

PERIODICALS

Books in Canada, October, 1981; February, 1984; November, 1984.
Canadian Forum, August-September, 1985, pp.29-30.
Canadian Literature, summer, 1982.
Chicago Tribune Book World, April 25, 1982; March 30, 1986; May 3, 1992, p. 6.
Christian Science Monitor, July 9, 1982.
Detroit Free Press, May 4, 1986.
Detroit News, May 2, 1982; May 16, 1982.
Fiddlehead, fall, 1977; spring, 1981.
Globe and Mail (Toronto), November 17, 1984; April 27, 1985; April 12, 1986.
Library Journal, February 1, 1982.

Los Angeles Times, August 26, 1982.

Los Angeles Times Book Review, May 23, 1982; July 6, 1986; March 29, 1992, p. 6.

Maclean's, May 11, 1981; April 19, 1982; July 23, 1984; May 1, 1989, p.66; November 11, 1991, p.90; July 12, 1993, pp. 60-61.

Newsweek, August 23, 1982.

New York Review of Books, November 5, 1992, pp. 41-45.

New York Times Book Review, July 25, 1982; September 2, 1984; January 5, 1986; April 20, 1986; July 12, 1992, p. 33; December 19, 1993, p. 14.

Prairie Schooner, spring, 1979.

Publishers Weekly, April 16, 1982; December 5, 1994, pp. 65-66.

Quill and Quire, June, 1982; September, 1984; April, 1986; December, 1991, p. 17; June, 1993, p. 27; July, 1994, p. 94.

Saturday Night, August, 1986, pp. 45-47.

Village Voice, December 4, 1984; April 1, 1986.

Wascana Review, fall, 1976.

Washington Post, March 31, 1982.

Western American Literature, February, 1978.

*   *   *

KLEIN, A(braham) M(oses)   1909-1972

PERSONAL: Born February 14, 1909, in Ratno, Ukraine; immigrated to Canada, 1910; died August 21, 1972, in Montreal, Quebec, Canada; son of Colman and Yetta (Morantz) Klein; married Bessie Kozlov, February 14, 1935; children: Colman, Sandor, Sharon. *Education:* McGill University, B.A., 1930; University of Montreal, B.C.L., 1933. *Religion:* Jewish.

CAREER: Writer. *Judaea* (Zionist youth periodical), editor, 1928; Young Judaea, educational director, 1928-32; called to the Bar of Quebec, 1933; practiced law in Montreal, Quebec, 1933-36 and beginning in 1938, and in Rouyn, Quebec, 1937-38; Zionist Organization of Canada, associate director, 1936; in public relations for Samuel Bronfman in Montreal beginning in 1939; McGill University, Montreal, lecturer in poetry, 1945-46; Co-operative Commonwealth Federation candidate for Parliament from Montreal Cartier riding, 1949; member of public relations staff of Seagram Co. Ltd.

AWARDS, HONOURS: Edward Bland fellowship, 1947; Governor General's Award, 1948, for *The Rocking Chair, and Other Poems;* Quebec literary prize, 1952; Kovner memorial award, 1952; Lorne Pierce Gold Medal, Royal Society of Canada, 1957, for outstanding contribution to Canadian literature.

WRITINGS:

POEMS

Hath Not a Jew . . . , Behrman's Jewish Book House, 1940.

The Hitleriad, New Directions, 1944.

Poems, Jewish Publication Society of America (Philadelphia), 1944.

Poems of French Canada, Canadian Jewish Congress, 1947.

Seven Poems, Canadian Jewish Congress, 1947.

The Rocking Chair, and Other Poems, Ryerson Press, 1948.

The Collected Poems of A. M. Klein, edited with an introduction by Miriam Waddington, McGraw-Hill Ryerson, 1974.

A. M. Klein: Complete Poems, edited by Zailig Pollock, Volume 1: *Original Poems, 1926-1934,* Volume 2: *Original Poems, 1937-1955, and Poetry Translations,* University of Toronto, 1990.

Also author of *Huit Poemes canadiens (en anglais),* 1948. Contributor of poetry to periodicals, including *Canadian Forum, Judean, McGill Daily, Poetry,* and *Nation.*

OTHER

Hershel of Ostropol (play), published in *Canadian Jewish Chronicle* 26 and 27, 1939.

The Second Scroll (novel), Knopf, 1951.

(Translator) Israel Rabinovich, *Of Jewish Music, Ancient and Modern,* Montreal Book Centre, 1952.

(Adaptor) *Conscience* (from the play *The Hands of Euridice* by Pedro Bloch), translation by Claude Vincent, produced in New York City, 1952.

Beyond Sambation: Selected Essays and Editorials, 1928-1955, edited by M. W. Steinberg and Usher Caplan, University of Toronto Press, 1983.

A. M. Klein: Short Stories, edited by Steinberg, University of Toronto Press, 1983.

A. M. Klein: Literary Essays and Reviews, edited by Steinberg and Caplan, University of Toronto Press, 1987.

Translator of Moishe Dickstein's *From Palestine to Israel,* 1951. Editor of *Canadian Zionist,* 1936-37, and *Canadian Jewish Chronicle,* 1939-55.

Klein's papers are housed at the Public Archives of Canada, Ottawa.

SIDELIGHTS: The poetry of A. M. Klein reflects the Jewish experience—the cultural heritage of his people as well as the wealth of Jewish legend, tradition, and folklore to which the late poet turned for inspiration. Klein believed the function of his writing to be educational; as M. W. Steinberg noted in the *Dictionary of Literary Biography,* Klein sought "to inform the non-Jewish world of the

Jewish condition—its achievements and its plight—but even more important, to convey to the young Jewish North American-born generation some knowledge of their cultural heritage."

Klein's first volume of poetry, *Hath Not a Jew,* contains poems that reflect the Judaic culture throughout history, and which focus on the anti-Semitism so politically and socially pervasive at the time the volume was published in 1940. While Leon Edel was somewhat critical of the work in his review in *Poetry,* and noted that "the collection does Klein a distinct disservice in that it is not sufficiently representative of his remarkable gifts, the gift above all of eloquent rebellion," he went on to note that "despite their flaws, these poems are a poetic key to an ancient, deep-rooted, emotional and intellectual tradition. As such, they can lay claim to vitality and importance." *The Hitleriad,* in which Klein more specifically addressed the Nazi threat to European Jewry, is a satirical poem on the crimes of the German government. While the poem is a sound satire of the Nazi leader, the work was not successful with the general public: as Steinberg noted, "the horror of the Holocaust and the evil of its perpetrators cannot be conveyed through the conventions of satire, no matter how great nor how sincere the poet's indignation and rage."

Klein's only published novel, *The Second Scroll,* was inspired by a trip he made to European and North African refugee camps at the close of World War II under the sponsorship of the Canadian Jewish Congress. It is a symbolic tale of a modern-day search for a Messiah who would lead the Jews to the Promised Land; the title's significance lies in the fact that the Jewish faith is based on the Old Testament of the Bible, also referred to as the First Scroll. Harvey Swados praised the work in the *Nation,* calling it "the most profoundly creative summation of the Jewish condition by a Jewish man of letters since the European catastrophe." *The Second Scroll* proved to be Klein's final work—during the period he was at work on the novel, he became severely depressed and suicidal. Klein soon ceased writing altogether, leaving several collections of poems and essays to be published after his death.

Throughout the body of Klein's work—his essays, his fiction, and his many works of poetry—is an eloquent plea for understanding of the Jewish people and the cause other oppressed minorities as well. Although critics have found fault with his tendency to use archaic terminology, foreign words, and unconventional cadence, Klein's ability— gained through his years spent as a practicing lawyer—to construct a sound, reasonable argument and defend his position with a quick wit, has given readers a stimulating chronicle of the period in which he wrote. Steinberg's summation of Klein's work contains high praise for his "passionate convictions, his humor and wit," which give

Klein's work "a depth and sophistication which, together with the broad appeal of a sentimental yearning for the past, for the childlike and fanciful, and for the simple virtues, ensure him an eminent place on the Canadian literary roster."

BIOGRAPHICAL/CRITICAL SOURCES:

BOOKS

Contemporary Literary Criticism, Volume 19, Gale, 1981.
Dictionary of Literary Biography, Volume 68: *Canadian Writers, 1920-1959,* Gale, 1988, pp. 194-205.
Fischer, G. K., *In Search of Jerusalem: Religion and Ethics in the Writings of A. M. Klein,* McGill-Queen's University Press, 1975.
Reference Guide to English Literature, 2nd edition, St. James Press, 1991.

PERIODICALS

Canadian Forum, February, 1941; January, 1942; November, 1974, p. 18; November, 1982, p. 21.
Dalhousie Review, fall, 1986, p. 368.
Journal of Canadian Studies, summer, 1984.
Nation, November 3, 1951.
New York Herald Tribune Book Review, December 2, 1951.
New York Times, November 25, 1951.
New York Times Book Review, October 6, 1985, p. 46.
Poetry, April, 1941.

OBITUARIES:

PERIODICALS

Detroit News, August 22, 1972.
New York Times, August 23, 1972.

*   *   *

KOGAWA, Joy Nozomi   1935-

PERSONAL: Born June 6, 1935, in Vancouver, British Columbia, Canada; daughter of Gordon Goichi (a minister) and Lois (a kindergarten teacher; maiden name, Yao) Nakayama; married David Kogawa, May 2, 1957 (divorced, 1968); children: Gordon, Deidre. *Education:* Attended University of Alberta, 1954, Anglican Women's Training College, 1956, Conservatory of Music, 1956, and University of Saskatchewan, 1968.

ADDRESSES: Home—P.O. Box 2950, Station D, Ottawa, Ontario, Canada.

CAREER: Office of the Prime Minister, Ottawa, Ontario, staff writer, 1974-76; free-lance writer, 1976-78; University of Ottawa, Ottawa, writer in residence, 1978; free-lance writer, 1978—.

MEMBER: League of Canadian Poets, Writers Union of Canada.

AWARDS, HONOURS: Books in Canada first novel award, Canadian Authors Association book of the year award, Before Columbus Foundation American book award, Periodical Distributors best paperback award, and American Library Association notable book citation, all for *Obasan.*

WRITINGS:

Obasan (novel), Lester and Orpen Dennys, 1981, David Godine, 1982.
Naomi's Road (juvenile fiction), Oxford University Press, 1986.

POETRY

The Splintered Moon, Fiddlehead Poetry Books, 1967.
A Choice of Dreams, McClelland & Stewart, 1974.
Jericho Road, McClelland & Stewart, 1977.
Woman in the Woods, Mosaic, 1985.

Contributor of poems to magazines in the United States and Canada, including *Canadian Forum, West Coast Review, Queen's Quarterly, Quarry, Prism International,* and *Chicago Review.*

SIDELIGHTS: Joy Nozomi Kogawa's *Obasan* is a fictionalization of her own experiences as a Japanese-Canadian during World War II. Like *Obasan*'s narrator, Naomi Nakane, Kogawa was torn from her family by government officials and exiled into the Canadian wilderness. Critics praise her novel as subtle and multileveled. "A history of what appears at first only a minor persecution . . . grows into a quietly appalling statement about how much hatred can cost when it is turned into a bureaucratic principle," writes Edith Milton in the *New York Times Book Review. Los Angeles Times Book Review* contributor Edward M. White notes that in spite of *Obasan*'s bleak subject matter—racism and persecution—the novel has "a magical ability to convey suffering and privation, inhumanity and racial prejudice, without losing in any way joy in life and in the poetic imagination." Milton concludes: "It is a tour de force, a deeply felt novel, brilliantly poetic in its sensibility."

BIOGRAPHICAL/CRITICAL SOURCES:

PERIODICALS

Los Angeles Times Book Review, July 11, 1982.
New York Times Book Review, September 5, 1982.

KORMAN, Gordon 1963-

PERSONAL: Full name, Gordon Richard Korman; born October 23, 1963, in Montreal, Quebec, Canada; son of C. I. (an accountant) and Bernice (a journalist; maiden name, Silverman) Korman. *Education:* New York University, B.F.A., 1985. *Avocational interests:* Music, travel, sports.

ADDRESSES: Home—20 Dersingham Cres., Thornhill, Ontario, Canada L3T 4E7.*Office*—c/o Scholastic Inc., 730 Broadway, New York, NY 10003.*Agent*—Curtis Brown Ltd., 10 Astor Place, New York, NY 10003.

CAREER: Writer, 1975—.

MEMBER: Writers Union of Canada, Canadian Society of Children's Authors, Illustrators, and Performers (CANSCAIP), Canadian Authors' Association, ACTRA, Society of Children's Book Writers.

AWARDS, HONOURS: Air Canada Award, Canadian Authors' Association, 1981, for "Most Promising Writer under Thirty-five"; Ontario Youth Award, International Year of the Youth Committee of the Ontario Government, 1985, for contributions to children's literature; Children's Choice Award, International Reading Association, 1986, for *I Want to Go Home!,* and 1987, for *Our Man Weston;* Markham Civic Award for the Arts, 1987; IRA Children's Choice Award for *Our Man Weston,* 1987; American Library Association (ALA) Editors' Choice and ALA Best Book List for *A Semester in the Life of a Garbage Bag,* 1988; ALA Best Book List for *Losing Joe's Place,* 1991; Manitoba Young Readers' Choice Award for *The Zucchini Warriors,* 1992; *The Twinkie Squad* was a Junior Library Guild selection, and was named an "Our Choice" book by the Canadian Children's Book Center, both 1992.

WRITINGS:

FOR CHILDREN AND YOUNG ADULTS

This Can't Be Happening at Macdonald Hall!, illustrated by Affie Mohammed, Scholastic, 1977.
Go Jump in the Pool!, illustrated by Lea Daniel, Scholastic, 1979.
Beware the Fish!, illustrated by Daniel, Scholastic, 1980.
Who Is Bugs Potter?, Scholastic, 1980.
I Want to Go Home!, Scholastic, 1981.
Our Man Weston, Scholastic, 1982.
The War with Mr. Wizzle, Scholastic, 1982.
Bugs Potter: Live at Nickaninny, Scholastic, 1983.
No Coins, Please, Scholastic, 1984.
Don't Care High, Scholastic, 1985.
Son of Interflux, Scholastic, 1986.
A Semester in the Life of a Garbage Bag, Scholastic, 1987.
The Zucchini Warriors, Scholastic, 1988.
Radio Fifth Grade, Scholastic, 1989.

Losing Joe's Place, Scholastic, 1990.

Macdonald Hall Goes Hollywood, Scholastic, 1991.

(With Bernice Korman) *The D-minus Poems of Jeremy Bloom,* Scholastic, 1992.

The Twinkie Squad, Scholastic, 1992.

The Toilet Paper Tigers, Scholastic, 1993.

The Three Zs, Scholastic, 1994, also published as *Why Did the Underwear Cross the Road?,* Scholastic, 1994.

Something Fishy at Macdonald Hall, Ingram, 1995.

Korman's books have been translated into French, Swedish, Danish, Norwegian, and Chinese.

SIDELIGHTS: Since publishing his first book when he was only fourteen years old, author Gordon Korman has written many best-selling novels for children and young adults. Korman's trademark storylines—featuring slapstick humor, madcap adventures, and high-spirited, rebellious characters—have helped make his books popular favorites with school-age readers across Canada and the United States. "Many of Mr. Korman's plots revolve around the frustrations of rambunctious boys forced to submit to stuffy academic authorities," noted Leslie Bennetts in the *New York Times.* Korman, whose books have sold over four million copies, strives to write stories that provide a healthy dose of humor for his young readers. "My books are the kind of stories I wanted to read and couldn't find when I was ten, eleven, and twelve," he was quoted as saying in *Something about the Author.* "I think that, no matter what the subject matter, kids' concerns are important, and being a kid isn't just waiting out the time between birth and the age of majority."

Korman was born in 1963 in Montreal, Quebec, where his father worked as an accountant and his mother wrote an "Erma Bombeck-type column" for a local newspaper, as he told Bennetts. In elementary and junior high school, Korman was always fond of writing—especially his own brand of zany stories and scenarios. "I wasn't a big reader for some reason," he remarked to Chris Ferns in *Canadian Children's Literature.* "But I always tried to put in creativity where I could: if we had a sentence with all the spelling words for that week, I would try to come up with the stupidest sentences, or the funniest sentences, or the craziest sentences I could think of."

Korman's professional writing career began at the age of twelve with a story assignment for his seventh-grade English class. "The big movies at the time were 'Jaws' and 'Airplane,' and everyone decided they were going to write action stories," he told Bennetts. "It was my mother who brought me down to earth. She told me to write about something a little closer to home." In response, Korman created the characters of Boots and Bruno, roommates in a private boarding school who are, according to Bennetts "best friends and incorrigible troublemakers." After such

antics as replacing the Canadian flag at a school hockey game with a flag from their imaginary country of Malbonia, Boots and Bruno are separated by the headmaster. The two boys are forced to move in with new roommates and forbidden to see each other. In the boisterous tale that follows, Korman unfolds the boys' adventures as they reunite and stir up even more trouble together.

"I got kind of carried away . . . and I accidentally wrote the first book," Korman told Ferns. "The characters sort of became real people to me, and they more or less wrote the book for me. The class had to read all the assignments at the end of the whole business, and a lot of people were coming to me and saying how they really liked it. I suppose anyone who writes 120 pages for class is going to attract a certain amount of attention anyway—and I just got the idea of seeing if I could get the book published." Korman sent his manuscript to the publisher Scholastic, Inc., and two years later at the age of fourteen experienced the publication of both his first book and first best-seller, *This Can't Be Happening at Macdonald Hall.*

After his initial success, Korman published books at the rate of one per year, writing them during summers when he was on vacation from school. At the age of eighteen he was voted the "Most Promising Writer under Thirty-five" by the Canadian Author's Association, and was a popular author on school and reading tours across Canada and the United States. In addition to such Boots and Bruno novels as *Beware the Fish, The War with Mr. Wizzle,* and *Go Jump in the Pool,* his other best-selling books feature characters that similarly test boundaries of authority. Bugs Potter, in the 1980 novel *Who Is Bugs Potter?* and the 1983 novel *Bugs Potter Live at Nickaninny,* is a rock-and-roll drummer who lives for his music. Simon Irving in Korman's 1986 novel, *Son of Interflux,* organizes a high school campaign to save school land from being purchased by his father's corporation. Artie in the 1984 publication, *No Coins, Please,* to the frustration of his counselors, pulls off scams for money whenever his summer-camp group visits the city. The stories' far-fetched plots have in common the fact that their young characters succeed in areas that are usually considered adult domains. Korman commented to Ferns: "How many books have you read—and good books—about a kid who makes money: oh boy, isn't he cute, he raised sixty bucks, a hundred bucks, something like that? I mean, why can't an eleven-year-old make $150,000? If Bugs Potter is a good drummer, why can't he be the best drummer in the world?"

Korman acknowledges that his characters are something like he was as a child, but more active in their rebelliousness. He told Bennetts: "I was a gutless troublemaker; I probably did a lot more with my mouth than anything else. I talked back a lot; I was a pain in the neck. I'd be the type of guy who, if I caught a teacher in a mistake, would make a federal case out of it. I never really was a favorite with my teachers." But, while Korman's characters display a healthy disrespect for authority, part of their wider appeal is that they draw the line between disrespect and anarchy. "I think the books are very respectful of people," Korman told Ferns. "I was writing at the time of [the 1978 *National Lampoon* film] *Animal House. . . .* I think one of the things which makes the books fairly strong, so that they defy being compared to things like that, is that they don't cross that line. Considering how crazy the books are, I keep a firm foot in reality."

Not surprisingly for someone who began a writing career at the age of twelve, Korman's works changed in perspective and tone as he matured. His earlier children's books, relying more heavily on slapstick and farce, were known for their caricaturizations and their chaotic, high-paced plots. Korman described the approach he used in the 1982 *Our Man Weston* and the 1983 *Bugs Potter Live at Nickaninny* to Ferns: "What I was dealing with at the time was a lot of contrivance of events. So-and-so does this, and it just happens that at the same time this happens, and it happens at exactly the right moment. Those books tended to have an incredible number of contrived circumstances; they also had a large number of adult characters, many of whom were crazy and wild."

As Korman moved into adolescence, so did his characters, and he began to more fully develop their personalities and relationships with each other. His slapstick humor, although remaining a significant part of the action in his stories, began to share the stage with some realistic depictions of adolescent life. In his 1987 novel, *A Semester in the Life of a Garbage Bag,* Korman introduces Raymond Jardine, whose desire to win a school contest (and therefore spend the summer in Greece rather than at his uncle's New Jersey fish-gutting plant) stimulates a chain of events in the life of his English class partner, Sean Delancey. There is no shortage of absurdity in this novel. Among the characters who become involved in the plot are Sean's grandfather, a yo-yo prodigy, his younger sister (whom he calls "Genghis Khan in training"), and his rival in romance, the muscular but not-too-bright Steve "Cementhead" Semenski. The plot also includes a thirty-three million dollar experimental power plant that doesn't work. But along with the caricatures and absurdity there are real teenage emotions and interrelations. Ferns commented in his review of *A Semester in the Life of a Garbage Bag* that Korman's "lunatic comic inventiveness . . . is accompanied by a perceptive eye for the quirks of adolescent behaviour." Ferns added that "the comedy and the observation almost seem to be pulling in different directions," and summarized that, although in this novel he is stretching into new, not yet mastered territory, "Gordon Korman's comic imagination is as fertile as ever."

Radio Fifth Grade, Korman's 1989 novel about a student-run radio show, contains Korman's customary zany elements—a stubborn parrot, a school bully who insists on radio air time to read his short stories about kittens, and an adviser who is too busy reading pulp science fiction to help the students with the show. The book was praised by Todd Morning in *School Library Journal* for its comic value. "This story works well on the level of sheer farce," Morning stated. "Korman is good at creating chaotic, if not always believable, situations." A *Publishers Weekly* critic, however, who found value beyond the book's humor, stated that *Radio Fifth Grade* is "feelingly written, and earns a place with the best middle-grade fiction; more than a romp, it has genuine charm."

Korman's 1990 book, *Losing Joe's Place,* is the story of Jason Cardone and two friends who, at the age of sixteen, sublet Jason's brother Joe's Toronto apartment while he is away in Europe. Everything that can go wrong does go wrong for the three boys while they strive to pay their rent each month, and the story is filled with the farcical characters and chaotic situations that Korman is known for. Again, the book offers more than its comic strain. Several critics noted the depth of characterization of Jason, who narrates the tale. Shirley Carmony commented in *Voice of Youth Advocates* that Jason "is a lovable adolescent whose hopes and fears are rather typical ones for a 16 year old boy. His humorous viewpoint is a pleasure." Jack Forman summarized in his *School Library Journal* review of *Losing Joe's Place:* "Surprisingly, it's not the quick twists and turns of the farcical plot that keep this very funny story moving. It's Jason's spirited narrative, his self-effacing sense of humor, and his finely tuned ear for the ridiculous that make these unbelievable antics work and create characters from these caricatures."

Korman attributes the popularity of his books to his portrayal of young characters that achieve power and success in an adult world—something a popular writer who began his career at the age of twelve knows about firsthand. "Whatever an adult can do, somewhere in the world there's one sixteen-year-old who can do it as well," he commented to Ferns. "The problem is with the age level where kids are starting to be able to do things, but it still seems unnatural. And I think that's one of the reasons why the books do well in that age bracket . . . because they address that situation of kids being able to triumph over the adults, and in many cases with the adults coming to terms with it."

In 1985 Korman received a B.F.A. degree in dramatic and visual writing from New York University. His later books have been geared more towards young adult readers, and he has hopes to one day write an adult novel. "I'm torn between doing something totally different, and going back," he once told Ferns, "I'd like—and I don't know whether it's a romantic notion or not—I'd like to write, not necessarily the great Novel that's going to reshape the world, but a book that makes the sort of splash that [Joseph Heller's] *Catch-22* made. . . . What I see happening is that one day I'll set out to write about a seventeen-year-old character, and it'll just turn out that this guy isn't seventeen—he's twenty-three or so, and he's an adult. That's how I think the transition will come."

BIOGRAPHICAL/CRITICAL SOURCES:

BOOKS

Something about the Author, Volume 49, Gale, 1987, pp. 146-50.

PERIODICALS

Bulletin of the Center for Children's Books, November, 1985; December, 1985; November, 1986.
Canadian Children's Literature, Number 38, 1985; Number 52, 1988.
Canadian Statesman, January 23, 1980.
Globe and Mail (Toronto), June 28, 1980; November 18, 1980; October 19, 1985; December 2, 1989.
Horn Book, March/April, 1986; November/December, 1987.
Jam, spring, 1981.
Journal of Commonwealth Literature, February, 1982.
New York Times Biographical Service, July, 1985, pp. 862-63.
Publishers Weekly, July 24, 1987; June 30, 1989.
School Library Journal, October, 1987; September, 1988; September, 1989, p. 252; May, 1990, p. 124.
Toronto Star, July 29, 1978; December 14, 1982.
Voice of Youth Advocates, December, 1986; August-September, 1987; October, 1988, pp. 182-183; June, 1990, p. 106.

*   *   *

KREISEL, Henry   1922-1991

PERSONAL: Born June 5, 1922, in Vienna, Austria; naturalized Canadian citizen; died April 22, 1991; son of David Leo (in sales) and Helen (Schreier) Kreisel; married Esther Lazerson (an archivist), June 22, 1947; children: Philip. *Education:* University of Toronto, B.A., 1946, M.A., 1947; University of London, Ph.D., 1954. *Religion:* Jewish. *Avocational interests:* Art collecting, music, travel.

CAREER: University of Alberta, Edmonton, lecturer, 1947-50, assistant professor, 1950-55, associate professor, 1955-59, professor of English, 1959-87, professor emeritus, 1987-91, head of department, 1961-67, member of board of governors, 1966-69, senior associate dean of graduate studies, 1967-69, acting dean of graduate studies,

1969-70, academic vice-president, 1970-75, University Professor, 1975-91. Visiting professor of English, University of British Columbia, 1951; visiting fellow, Wolfson College, Cambridge University, 1975-76. Member, Advisory Committee on Fine Arts, Canadian Department of Transportation, 1959; chair of English panel, postgraduate scholarship committee of Canada Council, 1963-65; member, Governor-General's Awards Jury for Literature, 1966-69, 1990; member of council, Edmonton Art Gallery, 1967-70; chair, Canadian Studies Program, 1979-82; president, Edmonton Chamber Music Society, 1980-83. Advisor to Canadian Secretary of State (Multiculturalism), 1987.

MEMBER: Philosophical Society of University of Alberta (president, 1955-56), Association of Canadian University Teachers of English (president, 1962-63), Royal Society of Arts (fellow), International Institute of Arts and Letters (fellow), Association of Academic Staff of University of Alberta (vice-president, 1959-60; president, 1960-61), Humanities Association of Canada (national executive, 1964-66).

AWARDS, HONOURS: President's medal for short story writing from University of Western Ontario, 1959, for "The Travelling Nude"; J. I. Segal Foundation Award for Literature, 1983; Rutherford Award for excellence in teaching, 1986; Sir Frederick Haultain Prize for Fine Arts, 1986; appointed Officer of the Order of Canada, 1987.

WRITINGS:

PLAYS

He Who Sells His Shadow: A Fable for Radio (radio play), broadcast on *Wednesday Night,* Canadian Broadcasting Corp. (CBC), 1956.
The Betrayal (teleplay), broadcast on television on *Bob Hope Theatre,* CBC, 1965.
The Broken Globe (adapted from a short story; first produced in Edmonton), CBC-TV, 1976.

Author of stage play adaptation of *The Rich Man,* 1987. Also author of radio and television plays in the 1950s for CBC, for programs including *Anthology* and *Stage.*

OTHER

The Rich Man (novel), McClelland & Stewart, 1948.
(Editor and author of introduction) John Heath, *Aphrodite, and Other Poems,* Ryerson, 1959.
The Betrayal (novel), McClelland & Stewart, 1964.
The Almost Meeting, and Other Stories (includes "The Travelling Nude"), NeWest (Edmonton), 1981.
Another Country: Writings by and about Henry Kreisel, edited by Shirley Neuman, NeWest, 1985.

Work represented in anthologies, including *Modern Canadian Stories,* edited by Roberto Ruberto and Glose Rimanelli, Ryerson, 1962; *The Best American Short Stories,* edited by Martha Foley and David Burnett, Houghton, 1966; *A Book of Canadian Stories,* edited by Desmond Pacey, Ryerson, 1966; *Stories from Western Canada,* edited by Ruby Weibe, Macmillan, 1972. Contributor of articles and stories to literary journals, including *Literary Review, Canadian Forum, Canadian Literature, Tamarack Review, Queen's Quarterly, University of Toronto Quarterly,* and *Prism.*

Kreisel's papers are housed in the archives and special collections of the University of Manitoba Libraries.

SIDELIGHTS: Henry Kreisel, a noted Canadian author and academic, was perhaps best known for his portrayal of the immigrant experience in his novels and many of his short stories. Kreisel's works "document what he calls the 'double experience' of the immigrant struggling to bridge (or widen) the temporal, spiritual, and psychological gulfs between European background and Canadian foreground," describes Neil Besner in the *Dictionary of Literary Biography.* "To dissociate himself from either world, or to misperceive it, diminishes his humanity."

Kreisel based his writing on personal experience as an immigrant. Born in Vienna, Austria, on June 5, 1922, Kreisel fled the Nazis in 1938 with his family, seeking shelter in England. He and his father, however, were interned as "enemy aliens" by the British government from May of 1940 to late in 1941. Sent to camps in Canada, Kreisel kept a journal recording his immediate, day-to-day impressions. Upon his release, he decided to remain in Canada and pursue his dream of becoming a writer.

Kreisel's first novel, *The Rich Man,* focuses on Jacob Grossman, an immigrant returning to his European roots. Creating a wealthy image to impress his family, Jacob poses as a successful clothes designer when he is actually a lowly clothes presser in a Toronto factory. On the eve of World War II and Hitler's invasion, he arrives to find a struggling city, anti-Semitism on the increase, and widespread unemployment. His own family is also in the midst of difficult times. It is only when he is asked for financial help that his deception is revealed. "The strength of the novel lies in Kreisel's sensitive and carefully controlled exploration of Jacob's failings," Besner comments. "With understated compassion he shows how Jacob, an immigrant Everyman, remolds his experience in the New World to fit his family's dreams, returning to present himself as a fifty-two-year-old prodigal, the incarnation of their hopes."

In *The Betrayal,* Kreisel brings a European to Canada to show the war experience from a different viewpoint. Mark Lerner, the narrator, is a young college professor lecturing students about the French Revolution. Through one of his students, Katherine Held, he meets Theodore Stappler, "the lone survivor of a group of Austrian refugees betrayed twelve years earlier by Joseph Held, Katherine's father," describes Besner. Held had been forced by the Nazis to choose between the safety of his own family or that of the refugees. Stappler is in Canada seeking revenge on Held, but he is hampered by feelings that he, too, may have betrayed the group through his own actions. Stappler confides in Lerner, and the professor is then forced to judge the two men's actions, looking at history in a personal, rather than detached, way. Finally, Stappler departs without his revenge, leaving Lerner to contemplate the meaning of Stappler's story. "The Betrayal *is more ambitious, more complex, more technically accomplished, and more explicitly a literary novel than* The Rich Man," judges Besner.

Kreisel was also the author of several short stories, some of which have been collected in *The Almost Meeting, and Other Stories.* Within his short fiction, Besner explains, "Kreisel continues to explore the ruptures, discontinuities, and 'almost meetings' between Old and New World characters and visions." Of himself, Kreisel once commented: "I came to this country from Austria, via England, having escaped the Nazis in 1938. In my writings I have used the European as well as Canadian experience. This double experience, and its reflection in novels and stories, has been my major contribution to the literature of this country."

BIOGRAPHICAL/CRITICAL SOURCES:

BOOKS

Dictionary of Literary Biography, Volume 88: *Canadian Writers, 1920-1959, Second Series,* Gale, 1989.

PERIODICALS

Canadian Fiction, May, 1965, p. 45.
Quill & Quire, January, 1982, p. 31.

*   *   *

KROETSCH, Robert 1927-

PERSONAL: Born June 26, 1927, in Heisler, Alberta, Canada; son of Paul (a farmer) and Hilda (Weller) Kroetsch; married Mary Jane Lewis, January 13, 1956 (divorced, 1979); married Smaro Kamboureli, July 17, 1982; children: (first marriage) Laura Caroline, Margaret Ann. *Education:* University of Alberta, B.A., 1948; McGill University, graduate study, 1954-55; Middlebury College, M.A., 1956; University of Iowa, Ph.D., 1961.

ADDRESSES: Home—4081 Cedar Hill Rd., Victoria, British Columbia, Canada. *Office*—Department of English, University of Manitoba, Winnipeg, Manitoba, Canada R3T 2N2.*Agent*—MGA Agency, 10 St. Mary St., Suite 510, Toronto, Ontario, M4Y 1P9, Canada.

CAREER: Yellowknife Transportation Co. (riverboats), Northwest Territories, Canada, laborer and purser, 1948-50; U.S. Air Force, Goose Bay, Labrador, civilian information and education specialist, 1951-54; State University of New York at Binghamton, assistant professor, 1961- 65, associate professor, 1965-68, professor of English, 1968-78; University of Manitoba, Winnipeg, professor of English, 1978-85, Distinguished Professor, 1985—.

MEMBER: Modern Language Association of America, American Association of University Professors.

AWARDS, HONOURS: Fellowship to Bread Loaf Writers' Conference, 1966; Governor General's Award for fiction, 1969, for *The Studhorse Man;* Royal Society of Canada fellow.

WRITINGS:

NOVELS

But We Are Exiles, St. Martin's, 1966.
The Words of My Roaring, St. Martin's, 1966.
The Studhorse Man, Simon & Schuster, 1970.
Gone Indian, New Press, 1973.
Badlands, New Press, 1975.
What the Crow Said, General Publishing, 1978.
Alibi, Beaufort Books, 1983.

Also author of the novel *The Puppeteer,* 1992.

POEMS

The Stone Hammer Poems, 1960-1975, Oolichan Books, 1975.
Seed Catalogue: Poems, Turnstone Press, 1978.
The Ledger, Brick/Nairn, 1979.
The Sad Phoenician, Coach House Press, 1979.
The Criminal Intensities of Love As Paradise, Oolichan Books, 1981.
Field Notes, General Publishing, 1981.
Advice to My Friends: A Continuing Poem, Stoddart, 1985.
Excerpts from the Real World: A Prose Poem in Ten Parts, Oolichan Books, 1986.
The Complete Field Notes: The Long Poems of Robert Kroetsch, McClelland, 1989.

OTHER

Alberta: Description and Travel, St. Martin's, 1959.
(With James Bacque and Pierre Gravel) *Creation,* New Press, 1970.
(Author of introduction) Glen Sorestad, *Prairie Pub Poems,* Thistledown, 1976.
(Editor) *Sundog: Stories from Saskatchewan,* Coteau Books, 1980.

The Crow Journals, NeWest Press, 1980.
(Author of preface) Eli Mandel, *Dreaming Backwards,* General Publishing, 1981.
(Editor) Daphne Marlatt, *How Hug a Stone,* Turnstone, 1983.
Letters to Salonika, Grand Union Press, 1983.
(Editor with Smaro Kamboureli) Douglas Barbour, *Visible Visions: The Selected Poetry of Douglas Barbour,* NeWest Press, 1984.
(Editor with Reingard M. Nischik) *Gaining Ground: European Critics on Canadian Literature,* NeWest Press, 1985.
The Lovely Treachery of Words: Essays Selected and New, Oxford University Press, 1989.
(Author of foreword) Simone Vauthier, *Reverberations: Explorations in the Canadian Short Story,* General Distribution Services, Inc., 1993.

Also contributor to *Montrealer, Maclean's, Globe and Mail, Books in Canada, Essays on Canadian Writing, Journal of Canadian Fiction, Canadian Review of American Studies, Canadian Literature,* and other publications.

ADAPTATIONS: The Words of My Roaring was adapted for the stage and first produced in Calgary at Theatre Calgary in 1980; *The Studhorse Man* was adapted for the stage and first produced in Toronto at Theatre Passe Muraille in 1981.

SIDELIGHTS: Robert Kroetsch is considered one of Canada's foremost practitioners and theoreticians of postmodern literature. Like many experimental writers, Kroetsch subverts such literary conventions as plot and character development and writes in a playful, self-reflexive style that embraces multiple, often contradictory meanings. Central to Kroetsch's fiction is the impact of place on the individual psyche; his work often reflects tensions from his childhood in the prairieland of Alberta.

Kroetsch's childhood on a farm in Heisler, Alberta, where much of his work is set, informs both his fiction and his poetry. His family's penchant for storytelling imbued Kroetsch with a deep appreciation of oral narrative, which often emerges in his writing in the form of tall tales and ribald humor. After graduating from the University of Alberta in 1948 with a bachelor's degree in philosophy and English literature, Kroetsch worked for six years on riverboats in northern Canada. He subsequently received his master's degree from Middlebury College, Vermont, in 1956, and his doctorate from the University of Iowa in 1961, before he began teaching at the State University of New York at Binghamton from 1961 to 1978. He later moved to Canada.

Kroetsch's first and most conventional novel, *But We Are Exiles* (1965), is based on the myth of Narcissus, who fell in love with his own reflection in a pool of water, believing it to be another person. In this novel, as in many of his other works, Kroetsch employs the theme of the *doppelganger,* the ghostly counterpart of a living person, to relate the story of his protagonist. *But We Are Exiles* centers on Peter Guy, who pilots a boat down the Mackenzie River in search of the corpse of Michael Hornyak, his boss, ex-friend, and sexual rival, whom he discovers has died aboard ship in an explosion that was possibly Guy's fault. Although Kroetsch leaves the novel's ending ambiguous, Guy joins his counterpart at the novel's end after the crew decides to place Hornyak's body in a cast-off barge, suggesting that the two men represent the combative yet complementary aspects of narcissistic self-obsession.

Kroetsch's next three novels, *The Words of My Roaring* (1966), *The Studhorse Man* (1969), and *Gone Indian* (1973), comprise what he calls his *Out West* "triptych." In these works, Kroetsch blends folklore related to the Canadian prairies of his homeland with Greek and Roman myths while recording momentous social changes in Alberta from the 1930s to the 1970s. *The Words of My Roaring* chronicles political upheavals in Depression-era Alberta, centering on a charismatic undertaker who wins a seat in the Legislative Assembly by promising to bring rain to drought-stricken farmers. *The Studhorse Man,* for which Kroetsch received the Governor General's Award, is a contemporary retelling of Homer's *Odyssey* narrated by Demeter Proudfoot, a disturbed Native American writing from inside an insane asylum. The novel takes the form of a biography of Hazard LePage, the last "studhorse man," who seeks the ideal mare to mate with his prize stallion, Poseidon, the last of a breed of horses nearing extinction because of increasing mechanization in rural Alberta. The novel ends ironically as LePage impregnates his fiancee just before being trampled to death by Poseidon, and the horse is sacrificed to create a birth control ingredient for human use. Several critics have interpreted *The Studhorse Man* as a parable about the North American West. *Gone Indian,* the final volume of the *Out West* trilogy, deals with several themes common to Kroetsch's work: differences between spoken and written language, distinctions between Canadians and other North Americans, and contrasts between rigid forms of civilization and primitive types of existence. In *Gone Indian,* an English professor urges a student suffering from writer's block and sexual impotence to leave his New York college and apply for a post at the University of Alberta. The student discovers the benefits of the northern wilderness and conquers his problems by modeling himself after Grey Owl, an Englishman who adopted a Native American lifestyle.

Kroetsch's novel *Badlands* (1975) revolves around a 1916 paleontological expedition led by William Dawe, a scientist who was obsessed with achieving world renown by finding dinosaur fossils in Alberta. Writing more than fifty years after the event, Dawe's daughter Anna comments on her father's sparse field notes, denouncing the absurdity of the project and of male ambitions in general. *Alibi* (1983), cited by many critics as Kroetsch's most self-conscious novel, relates the dilemma of a man who comes to question humanity's arbitrary systematization of the universe while attempting to locate the "perfect spa" for a mysterious oilman and collector of objects. Through his quest, the protagonist comes to understand the basic dichotomies between body and soul, sex and art, and death and life, which define all human attempts to assign meaning to the world. *The Puppeteer* (1992) makes similar use of concepts drawn from literary theory and philosophy.

Several themes in Kroetsch's fiction are echoed in his poetry. In his early verse collected in *The Stone Hammer Poems: 1960-1975* (1975), Kroetsch defines prairie life through particularized imagery. Much of his subsequent poetry displays an irreverence toward language designed to thwart its inherent limitations. Since 1975 Kroetsch has composed an extended poem-in-progress collected as *Complete Field Notes: The Long Poems of Robert Kroetsch.* A collage of memories, anecdotes, documents, and tall tales that reflect his preoccupation with the difficulties of literary expression, authorial persona, and the exhaustion of traditional poetic forms, *Field Notes* has been published in partial form in such volumes as *The Ledger* (1975), *Seed Catalogue* (1977), *The Sad Phoenician* (1979), and *Advice to My Friends* (1985). Some critics place *Field Notes* in the tradition of such epic poems as Ezra Pound's *Cantos* and William Carlos Williams's *Paterson;* like his fiction, Kroetsch's poetry strives, in his words, to "demystify the written word."

Kroetsch is also highly regarded as a literary critic. His essays, many of which are collected in *The Lovely Treachery of Words: Essays Selected and New* (1989), evidence his background and interest in such diverse disciplines as phenomenology, structuralism, poststructuralism, and linguistics. Kroetsch cofounded and served briefly as editor of *Boundary 2,* a journal devoted to postmodern literature.

BIOGRAPHICAL/CRITICAL SOURCES:

BOOKS

Bessai, Diane, and David Jackel, editors, *Figures in a Ground: Canadian Essays on Modern Literature Collected in Honour of Sheila Watson,* Western Producer Prairie Books, 1978.
Contemporary Literary Criticism, Gale, Volume 5, 1976, Volume 23, 1983, Volume 57, 1990.
Dictionary of Literary Biography, Volume 53: *Canadian Writers since 1960,* Gale, 1986.
Keith, W. J., editor, *A Voice in the Land: Essays by and about Rudy Wiebe,* NeWest Press, 1982.
Lecker, Robert, *Robert Kroetsch,* Twayne, 1986.

Neuman, Shirley, and Robert R. Wilson, *Labyrinths of Voice: Conversations with Robert Kroetsch,* NeWest Press, 1982.

Stephens, Donald G., editor, *Writers of the Prairies,* University of British Columbia Press, 1973.

Thomas, Peter, *Robert Kroetsch,* Douglas & McIntyre, 1980.

Twigg, Alan, *For Openers,* Harbour, 1981.

PERIODICALS

Arts Manitoba, January/February, 1977.

Books in Canada, October, 1983.

Canadian Fiction Magazine, spring/summer, 1977.

Canadian Forum, October-November, 1978; June-July, 1981.

Canadian Literature, summer, 1974; summer, 1978.

Canadian Studies, fall, 1982.

Compass, spring, 1979.

Dandelion, Volume 10, number 2, 1983.

Essays on Canadian Writing, fall, 1977; summer, 1978; summer/fall, 1980.

Grain, May, 1982.

Island, Number 7, 1980.

Journal of Canadian Fiction, summer, 1972.

Kunapipi, Number 2, 1979.

Mosaic, spring, 1981.

New Quarterly, spring, 1985.

New York Times Book Review, April 26, 1970.

Open Letter, spring, 1978; spring, 1983; summer/fall, 1984.

Red Cedar Review, spring, 1985.

Studies in Canadian Literature, winter, 1976; summer, 1977.

University of Windsor Review, spring, 1972.

*   *   *

KURELEK, William   1927-1977

PERSONAL: Surname is pronounced "Coo-*reh*-lehk"; born March 3, 1927, in Whitford, Alberta, Canada; died November, 1977, in Toronto, Ontario, Canada; son of Metro and Mary (Hululak) Kurelek; married Jean Andrews, October 8, 1962; children: Catherine, Stephen, Barbara, Thomas. *Education:* University of Manitoba, B.A., 1949. *Religion:* Roman Catholic.

CAREER: Picture framer in Toronto, Ontario, 1959-71; artist in Toronto, 1960-77. *Exhibitions:* Work has appeared in more than fifty one-man and group exhibitions in galleries throughout Canada, Great Britain, and the United States, including the Isaacs Gallery, Toronto, 1960, 1962-64, 1966, 1968, 1970, 1972-74, 1976, 1978, and 1980, J. B. Speed Art Museum, Louisville, KY, 1962, Ban-

fer Gallery, New York, 1963, Montreal Museum of Fine Arts, 1963, Rochester Memorial Art Gallery, New York, 1963, National Gallery of Canada, Ottawa, 1963, 1965, and 1968, Commonwealth Gallery, London, England, 1963, Edmonton Art Gallery, 1965 and 1970, Winnipeg Art Gallery, 1965, Yellowstone Art Center, Montana, 1967, Cornell University, 1971, Burnaby Art Gallery, British Columbia, 1973, and Canada House Gallery, London, 1978; paintings are also represented in various permanent collections, including Museum of Modern Art, New York, and National Gallery of Canada.

MEMBER: Royal Canadian Academy of Art.

AWARDS, HONOURS: Canada Council senior arts grant, 1969; *New York Times* Best Illustrated Children's Book Award, 1973, for *A Prairie Boy's Winter,* and 1974, for *Lumberjack; Horn Book* Honor Book for Illustration, 1974, for *A Prairie Boy's Winter;* Canadian Association of Children's Librarians Illustrators Award, for *A Prairie Boy's Summer;* honorary Doctor of Law, University of Windsor, 1976; Christian Culture Award, 1977; Order of Canada, 1977.

WRITINGS:

SELF-ILLUSTRATED

A Prairie Boy's Winter (juvenile), Houghton, 1973.

O Toronto, New Press, 1973.

Some One with Me (autobiography), Center for Improvement of Undergraduate Education, Cornell University, 1973, revised edition, McClelland & Stewart, 1980.

Lumberjack (juvenile), Houghton, 1974.

The Passion of Christ According to St. Matthew, Niagara Falls Art Gallery and Museum, 1975.

Kurelek Country, Houghton, 1975, published as *Kurelek's Canada,* Pagurian Press (Scarborough, Ontario), 1975.

Fields, Tundra Books (Plattsburgh, NY), 1975.

A Prairie Boy's Summer (juvenile), Houghton, 1975.

(With Abraham Arnold) *Jewish Life in Canada,* Hurtig, 1976.

The Last of the Arctic, Pagurian Press, 1976.

A Northern Nativity: Christmas Dreams of a Prairie Boy (juvenile), Tundra Books (Montreal), 1976.

The Ukrainian Pioneer, Niagara, 1980.

Illustrator of *Look Who's Coming,* by Mary Paximadas, Press, 1976, *Who Has Seen the Wind,* by W. O. Mitchell, 1976, and *Fox Mykyta,* by Ivan Franko, 1978.

ADAPTATIONS: The following three films have been made of the artist's life and work: *Kurelek,* documentary film, National Film Board of Canada, 1967; *Pacem in Terris,* film of his drawings and paintings, 1971; and *The*

Maze, psychological film study of his struggle with depression, Cornell University, 1971.

SIDELIGHTS: Canadian William Kurelek was a self-taught painter and illustrator. The artist was best known for the books he made for boys and girls that showed his pioneer childhood in Canada's Ukrainian farming communities of the 1930s. His deep religious faith was also reflected in his many works for both adults as well as children. An award-winning artist whose work was rich in color and lifelike, Kurelek portrayed historical events and landscapes in a realistic manner. A critic in Saturday Night related that William Kurelek was "one of the most distinctive Canadian painters of the century," while Queen Elizabeth II of England included some of the artist's paintings in her collection.

Born in Whitford, Alberta, Canada, on March 3, 1927, William Kurelek was raised on farms by his parents Metro and Mary Kurelek. They operated a grain farm in Alberta when Kurelek was born and later a dairy farm in Manitoba. Kurelek's father was a Ukrainian immigrant, and many people from his homeland lived nearby in the rural communities along the prairie of western Canada. Kurelek was later to remember the features of country life during the years of the Depression, illustrating many of the events of his youth when he created children's stories.

Kurelek's boyhood summers began with the closing of the one-room schoolhouse in June. He had many chores during the hot months which followed, including milking cows and operating machinery. He drove the tractor that pulled the heavy mowing machine. The artist also learned how to bundle grain with his hands when tractors could not be used after heavy rains. For entertainment, Kurelek went swimming and played softball. He also enjoyed watching the huge thunderstorms which rolled across the prairie. When the artist wrote his award-winning prairie boy books as an adult, including A Prairie Boy's Winter and A Prairie Boy's Summer, he pictured his boyhood vividly for boys and girls.

When Kurelek was twelve years old, he had a series of unusual dreams. In these dreams, he saw the Nativity in a special way. The Holy Family was not in Bethlehem, but in diverse places which Kurelek knew. The artist never forgot these dreams. When he grew up, he painted the story of Mary, Joseph, and the Baby Jesus in twenty dream sequences in his book, A Northern Nativity; Christmas Dreams of a Prairie Boy. The Christmas story was depicted happening among cowboys and lumberjacks rather than shepherds. A country mission, fishing boat, abandoned grain elevator, and garage took the place of the traditional stable in the Christmas story.

Kurelek asked boys and girls to ponder what would happen if the Nativity were enacted in new settings with his illustrations. A reviewer in Canadian Children's Literature wrote, "Teachers of art and writing could have some challenging lessons using those paintings; children could write and/or illustrate their own 'What if' dreams. The universal meaning of Christmas has a uniquely Canadian interpretation as the result of the spiritual integrity and the creative talents of this well-recognized Canadian artist."

When Kurelek was sixteen years old, he attended high school in Winnipeg. After graduation, Kurelek entered the University of Manitoba. During the summer of 1946, the artist earned money for college working in Ontario as a lumberjack. He received his B.A. degree in 1949. In 1951, Kurelek also worked as a lumberjack to make enough money to go to Britain and study painting overseas. While he was in Britain, Kurelek was treated in a psychiatric hospital for depression. His melancholy lasted four years, until the artist rediscovered his religious faith, a faith that kept him mentally healthy for the remainder of his life. He then returned to Canada and worked as a picture framer in Toronto from 1959 until 1971. In March, 1960, his paintings were launched successfully in a one-man exhibition at the Isaacs Gallery in Toronto. Two years later, Kurelek married Jean Andrews, with whom he would have four children.

During the years which followed, Kurelek maintained an active career while he and his wife raised their children Catherine, Stephen, Barbara, and Thomas. The artist recreated scenes from his years working in the Canadian forest in his book Lumberjack. Boys and girls were shown the way wood was cut to make into paper pulp during the times before modern machinery. Kurelek illustrated camp life through winter and summer in twenty five paintings. The artist inserted realistic details, including cots, clothes, food, and mosquitoes, in his award-winning illustrations. Robert Newton Peck related in the New York Times Book Review, "It's a good book, good chow, good bunkside reading. Lumberjacks, like flapjacks, are plain and yet filling."

Although the artist was best known for his children's books, Kurelek exhibited work in fifty one-man shows during his career. His paintings were placed in collections of prominent museums, including the Museum of Modern Art in New York and the National Gallery of Canada. Most critics noted the influence of the sixteenth century artist Pieter Bruegel, who also painted everyday scenes of adults and children at work or play, on the artist's style. His Catholic faith inspired the painting entitled The Maze as well as the series of paintings entitled The Passion of Saint Matthew. Books of paintings which the artist published for adults included Kurelek's Country and The Passion of Christ According to Saint Matthew. His life and work were documented in three films, including one made by the National Film Board of Canada entitled *Kurelek*. William Kurelek died in Toronto on November 3, 1977. He revealed in a diary excerpt cited in *Something about the Author* the importance of "a good long day of painting" to the artist when he wrote, "This is my earthly happiness—my work and good music together."

BIOGRAPHICAL/CRITICAL SOURCES:

BOOKS

Children's Literature Review, Volume 2, Gale, 1976.
Kurelek, William, *Some One with Me,* McClelland & Stewart, 1980.
Something about the Author, Volume 8, Gale, 1976, pp. 106-108.

PERIODICALS

Canadian Children's Literature, Number 14, 1979.
Horn Book, December, 1974; August, 1975.
New York Times Book Review, December 9, 1973; November 3, 1974, p. 29.
Saturday Night, May, 1980.
Time, December 23, 1974.

OBITUARIES:

PERIODICALS

New York Times, November 5, 1977.*

L

LABERGE, Albert 1871-1960
(Adrien Clamer)

PERSONAL: Born February 18, 1871, in Beauharnois, Quebec, Canada; died April 4, 1960; son of Pierre (a farmer) and Josephine (a farmer; maiden name, Boursier) Laberge. *Education:* Attended College Sainte-Marie; studied law.

CAREER: La Presse, Montreal, Quebec, sports reporter and art critic, 1896-1932, free-lance writer, c. 1895-1960.

MEMBER: Ecole Litteraire de Montreal.

AWARDS, HONOURS: Prize for a realistic story from the newspaper *Le Samedi,* 1895.

WRITINGS:

PRIVATELY PRINTED IN MONTREAL, QUEBEC; EXCEPT AS NOTED

La Scouine (novel), 1918; translated by Conrad Dion as *Bitter Bread,* Harvest House (Montreal), 1977.
Quand chantait la cigale (short stories), 1936.
Visages de la vie et la mort (short stories), 1936.
Peintres et ecrivains d'hier et d'aujourd'hui (nonfiction), 1938.
La Fin du voyage (short stories), 1942.
Scenes de chaque jour (short stories), 1942.
Journalistes, ecrivains et artistes (nonfiction), 1945.
Charles de Belle, peintre-poete (biography), 1949.
Le Destin des hommes (short stories), 1950.
Fin de roman (short stories), 1951.
Images de la vie (short stories), 1952.
Le Dernier Souper (short stories), 1953.
Propos sur nos ecrivains (nonfiction), 1954.
Hymnes a la terre (short stories), 1955.

Anthologie d'Albert Laberge (short stories), edited by Gerard Bessette, Cercle du Livre de France (Montreal), 1963.

Also contributor of articles and short stories, some under the pseudonym Adrien Clamer, to periodicals, including *Le Samedi, La Presse,* and *La Semaine.*

ADAPTATIONS: La Scouine was adapted as a ballet with the same title choreographed by Fernard Nault and performed by Les Grands Ballets Canadiens in Montreal, in 1977.

SIDELIGHTS: Albert Laberge is the author of *La Scouine,* the first realistic novel in Canadian literature. Following the controversy surrounding that work, however, Laberge withheld his subsequent books from publication until his retirement in 1932 from his position as a journalist with the newspaper *La Presse.* As B.-Z. Shek declared in the *Dictionary of Literary Biography,* "Laberge was a pioneer of naturalism and realism in French-Canadian fiction, modes that developed late in Quebec because of the powerful conservative influences of clerical and lay ideologues." Laberge's work experienced a resurgence in popularity during the 1960s, and *La Scouine* was translated into English as *Bitter Bread* in 1977.

Laberge was born into a family of Quebecois farmers who had occupied the same land since the mid-seventeenth century. He began pursuing a career in the Church, entering the College Sainte-Marie in Montreal in 1888. He was expelled, however, when he admitted reading unapproved works of fiction, probably those by such French authors as Honore de Balzac and Emile Zola. Having been kicked out of the program leading to the priesthood, Laberge turned first to studying law. In 1895 he won a prize from the newspaper *Le Samedi,* which had advertised for realistic fiction, and in the following year he joined the staff of *La Presse.*

Laberge began working on *Bitter Bread* in 1895. During his early career he was sometimes associated with the literary group Ecole de Montreal. He read chapters of his novel in progress before them and published excerpts of the work in various French Canadian periodicals. One chapter, which included a sex scene between the heroine's brother and a drunken Irishwoman, reached readers through *La Semaine* in 1909 and provoked the archbishop of Montreal to condemn it as pornographic. Intimidated by the influence of the Church and fearing loss of employment, Laberge did not publish any further chapters for seven years; when the entire novel saw print in 1918, it was released in a private edition of only sixty copies. In publishing excerpts of his next novel, which he never finished, Laberge adopted the pseudonym "Adrien Clamer."

Set in the nineteenth century, *Bitter Bread* presents the story of the Deschamps family, who live in the same Quebec countryside where Laberge was born. Shek discussed *Bitter Bread*'s "basic pessimism and fatalism and shabby portrait of human behavior," noting that "a key naturalist trait of the work is its general assimilation of humans and animals, with stress on man's lower, purely biological behavior." While pointing out other critics' belief that the novel is "bereft of any ideological insights or explanations," Shek observed Laberge's "clear sympathy for the francophones who are prevented from voting and beaten and humiliated by anglophone Tories."

Laberge waited until after his retirement from *La Presse* before publishing his short stories as well as his works of art and literary criticism and biography. After the 1960s, when the Quebecois intellectual climate became more sympathetic to Laberge's style, subject matter, and viewpoint, there were several reprints of *Bitter Bread* in its original French, and of course, its English translation. In 1963, three years after the author's death, Gerard Bessette edited a collection of Laberge's short fiction gathered from many of the privately printed volumes, and made them available to a wider audience of French-Canadian readers. The year 1977 saw a ballet adaptation of *Bitter Bread,* under the original French title of *La Scouine,* reach the Montreal stage. As Shek concluded, Laberge's work has been "given its rightful place" among Quebec letters, "in spite of its inadequacies and rough-hewn character."

BIOGRAPHICAL/CRITICAL SOURCES:

BOOKS

Brunet, Jacques, *Albert Laberge, sa vie et son oeuvre,* Editions de l'Universite d'Ottawa, 1969.
Dictionary of Literary Biography, Volume 68: *Canadian Writers, 1920-1959, First Series,* Gale, 1988.

PERIODICALS

Voix et Images, September, 1977, pp. 116-26.*

—Sketch by Elizabeth Wenning

*   *   *

LAHAISE, Francoise-Guillaume   1888-1969 (Guy Delahaye)

PERSONAL: Born March 18, 1888, in Saint-Hilaire-sur-Richelieu, Quebec, Canada; died October 2, 1969; son of Pierre-Adelard (co-owner with his wife of a general store) and Evangeline (Cheval) Lahaise; married Marie Saint-Georges (a nurse), February 21, 1927. *Education:* Attended Seminaire de Saint-Hyacinthe and College Sainte-Marie; Universite de Montreal, B.A., 1910; graduate study at Institut Pasteur, Paris, France.

CAREER: Poet, physician, and psychiatrist. Traveled and studied in France, Cuba, and the United States, 1912-24; Hopital Saint-Jean de Dieu, Montreal, Quebec, physician and psychiatrist, until 1959. Member of faculty of medicine, Universite de Montreal.

WRITINGS:

UNDER PSEUDONYM GUY DELAHAYE

Les Phases: Tryptiques, Deom (Montreal), 1910.
Mignonne, allons voir si la rose . . . Portrait (title means "Lovely One, Let's Go See if the Rose . . . Portrait"), Deom (Montreal), 1912.
Chemin de la Croix d'un ancien retraitant: L'Unique Voie a l'unique but, Imprimerie le Messager (Montreal), 1934.
Guy Delahaye: Oeuvres parues et inedites, edited by Robert Lahaise, HMH (Quebec), 1988.

SIDELIGHTS: "At the turn of the century," writes Alexandre L. Amprimoz in the *Dictionary of Literary Biography,* "Guy Delahaye could have been the Guillaume Apollinaire of Quebec." However, Delahaye—a pseudonym for the physician-poet Francoise-Guillaume Lahaise—faced different social and political circumstances than did the symbolist Apollinaire in France. Delahaye lived in Quebec where, according to Amprimoz, "a traditional Catholic church and a conservative state controlled all cultural activity to the point of censorship." Delahaye's innovative writings were not welcome in early twentieth century Quebec. Apollinaire found a way in France to blend his native Catholic faith and his progressive ideas. Delahaye, in a more restrictive society, did not. The Quebecois published only two small collections and published no more poetry for the remaining fifty years of his life.

Delahaye's poetry has received little critical attention. His first collection, *Les Phases*—a study of the clash between constancy and change—was a work full of promise, highly personal in nature and very self-revealing. However, says Amprimoz, critics, led by a churchman, the Abbe Camille Roy, "accused Delahaye of being a symbolist, of imitating the French decadent movement, and of being intentionally obscure."

According to Amprimoz, Delahaye's second volume of verse, *Mignonne, allons voir si la rose . . . Portrait,* is "a book of jokes and plays on words—verbal acrobatics," in which the poet continued to push the boundaries established by his conservative critics. Wrote Amprimoz, this work foreshadowed a new—and in Delahaye's society, generally unappreciated—theory of literature characterized by "technical experimentation and attention to psychology." Considered by contemporary scholars to have been ahead of his time, Delahaye turned from writing poetry and pursued a professional life in medicine and psychiatry. His literary works, neglected for many years, have only recently come again to critical notice and appreciation.

BIOGRAPHICAL/CRITICAL SOURCES:

BOOKS

Dictionary of Literary Biography, Volume 92: *Canadian Writers, 1890-1920,* Gale, 1990.
Lahaise, Robert, *Guy Delahaye et la modernite litteraire,* HMH (Quebec), 1987.

*   *   *

LAPOINTE, (Joseph-) Gatien (-Fernand) 1931-1983

PERSONAL: Born December 18, 1931, in Sainte-Justine-de-Dorchester, Quebec, Canada; died September c. 15, 1983, in Trois-Rivieres, Quebec, Canada; son of Evangeliste (a farmer) and Elisa (a farmer; maiden name, Lessard) Lapointe. *Education:* Attended the Petit Seminaire in Quebec City, 1944-50; attended Ecole des Arts Graphiques in Montreal, 1950-52; Universite de Montreal, B.A., 1955, M.A., 1956; doctoral studies at the Sorbonne.

CAREER: College Militaire de Saint-Jean, Quebec City, Quebec, instructor in French and French-Canadian literature, 1962-69; Universite du Quebec a Trois-Rivieres, Trois-Rivieres, instructor in creative writing, 1969-83; founder and director of Ecrits des Forges (a publishing house), c. 1971-83. Visiting professor at McGill University, 1963-64, and Carleton University, 1965.

AWARDS, HONOURS: Fellowship from the Royal Society of Canada, 1956-58; Prix du Club des Poetes, Prix Du Maurier, and a Governor General's Award, all 1963, all

for *Ode au Saint-Laurent, precede de J'appartiens a la terre;* Prix de la Province de Quebec, 1967, for *Le Premier Mot, precede de Le Pari de ne pas mourir.*

WRITINGS:

POETRY

Jour malaise (title means "Difficult Day"), [Montreal, Quebec], 1953.
Otages de la joie (title means "Hostages of Joy"), Editions du Muy (Montreal, Quebec), 1955.
Le Temps premier, Grassin (Paris, France), 1962.
Ode au Saint-Laurent, precede de J'appartiens a la terre, Editions du Jour (Montreal, Quebec), 1963.
Le Premier Mot, precede de Le Pari de ne pas mourir, Editions du Jour, 1967, "Face a Face" (poem), translated by Fred Cogswell as *Confrontation,* Fiddlehead (Fredericton, New Brunswick), 1973.
Arbre-radar, Editions de l'Hexagone (Montreal, Quebec), 1980.
Barbare inoui, Ecrits des Forges (Trois-Rivieres, Quebec), 1981.
(With Mia and Klaus Matthes) *Quebec,* Libre Expression (Montreal, Quebec), 1981.
Corps et graphie, Editions du Sextant (Trois-Rivieres, Quebec), 1981.
Corps transistor (title means "Transistor-Body"), Editions du Sextant, 1981.
Le Premier Passage (title means "First Passage"), drawings by Christine Lemire, Ecrits des Forges, 1983.

Contributor of poems to periodicals, including *Le Soleil, Le Devoir, L'Action, Liberte, Hobo-Quebec,* and *Estuaire.*

SIDELIGHTS: French-Canadian poet Gatien Lapointe is perhaps best remembered for his 1963 work, *Ode au Saint-Laurent, precede de J'appartiens a la terre.* A lengthy poetic piece, it is, as the title reveals, a tribute to the St. Lawrence River. For its composition, Lapointe received three prestigious Canadian awards—the Prix du Club des Poetes, the Prix Du Maurier, and the Governor General's Award. Gatien garnered prizes and fellowships for other poems as well, and further served the arts in his country and province by teaching classes in French-Canadian literature and creative writing. His career was cut short when he died in 1983.

Lapointe was born on a Quebec farm near the border with the United States in 1931. The surrounding farmland of his childhood, according to Alexandre L. Amprimoz in the *Dictionary of Literary Biography,* "provided the raw material of his poetry." Lapointe's father died when he was about twelve years old—another event which affected his later writing. Amprimoz holds this tragedy responsible for what he terms "the courageous pessimism" of Lapointe's work.

Lapointe began writing poetry at the age of seventeen, and had his first collection published when he was still completing his studies at the Universite de Montreal. This was the acclaimed *Jour malaise*. In Amprimoz's view, the volume "concerns the pain of growing up, both on an individual level and for the whole of a Quebec society striving for cultural maturity." Other critics felt that *Jour malaise* was in tune with Quebec's emotional mood during the period that saw the book's publication. Surely *Jour malaise*, and Lapointe's 1955 follow-up effort, *Otages de la joie*, were a large part of the reason the Royal Society of Canada gave the poet a fellowship during the years between 1956 and 1958. With this award, Lapointe continued his studies in Paris.

In Paris, Lapointe continued to explore his long fascination with the work of French surrealist poet Paul Eluard, to whom he had dedicated the last poem in *Otages de la joie*. But it was also while in Paris that Lapointe created his masterwork, *Ode au Saint-Laurent*. Amprimoz termed the fact that Lapointe penned this poem away from the land that informs it "a detail that recalls [Irish novelist] James Joyce's notion of the necessity of exile for a powerful insight into the life of one's native land." In the 493-line *Ode au Saint-Laurent*, Lapointe equates the mighty river that runs through Quebec with the French language that unites its people. Explained Amprimoz: "The paramount theme is one of belonging to Quebec. . . . Its effectiveness stems from the recurrent declaration of the image of the river in Quebec culture."

Another notable volume of Lapointe's poetry is the 1967 effort, *Le Premier Mot, precede de Le Pari de ne pas mourir*. For this the poet received the Prix de la Province de Quebec. *Le Premier Mot* includes a prose introductory section entitled "Le Pari de ne pas mourir," in which, according to Amprimoz, "the author outlines his poetics: poetry is the negation of death; human dignity is the only possible response to fate." After *Le Premier Mot*, Lapointe turned towards more experimental modes in his poetry. As Amprimoz observed, Lapointe's later poems "rely upon typographical effects, artwork, and musical scores." Among his last collections are *Corps et graphie, Corps transistor*, and *Le Premier Passage*.

BIOGRAPHICAL/CRITICAL SOURCES:

BOOKS

Dictionary of Literary Biography, Volume 88: *Canadian Writers, 1920-1959, Second Series*, Gale (Detroit, MI), 1989.
Pozier, Bernard, *Gatien Lapointe: L'Homme en marche*, Ecrits des Forges (Trois-Rivieres, Quebec), 1987.

PERIODICALS

Cahiers de Sainte-Marie, Vol. 4, 1967, pp. 103-124.

Etudes francaises, November, 1967.
Etudes litteraires, April, 1975.
Les lettres quebecoises, winter, 1981-82.
Voix et Images du Pays, Vol. 2, 1969, pp. 90-106; Vol. 7, 1973, pp. 167-182.*

*   *   *

La ROCQUE, Gilbert   1943-1984

PERSONAL: Born April 29, 1943, in Rosemont, Quebec (some sources say Montreal), Canada; died of a cerebral hemorrhage, November 26, 1984; son of Charles-Edouard (a tinsmith) and Lucie (Savard) La Rocque; married Murielle Ross, July 10, 1965; children: Sebastien, Catherine.

CAREER: Worked as a tinsmith, a construction worker, bank employee, and city clerk prior to 1970; entered the field of publishing, c. 1970; Editions de l'Homme, Montreal, Quebec, chief editor, 1972-74; Editions de l'Aurore, Montreal, literary director, 1974-75; VLB Editeur, founding member, 1975; Editions Quebec/Amerique, Montreal, literary director, 1978-84.

MEMBER: Union des Ecrivains Quebecois.

AWARDS, HONOURS: Prix Litteraire Canada-Suisse, and the Grand Prix du *Journal de Montreal*, both 1981, both for *Les Masques; Les Masques* also short-listed for the Governor General's Award and for the Prix France-Quebec; elected Grand Montrealais de l'Avenir for contributions to Quebec literature, 1982.

WRITINGS:

NOVELS; EXCEPT AS NOTED

Le Nombril, Editions du Jour (Montreal, Quebec), 1970.
Corridors, Editions du Jour, 1971.
Apres la boue, Editions du Jour, 1972.
Serge d'entre les morts, VLB (Montreal, Quebec), 1976.
(With Claude Jodoin) *Le voleur: Une confession bouleversante* (biography), Editions de l'Homme (Montreal, Quebec), 1976.
(With Paul Provencher) *Provencher, le dernier des coureurs de bois* (biography), translated by A. D. Martin-Sperry as *Provencher: Last of the coureurs de bois*, Burns & MacEachern (Don Mills, Ontario), 1976.
(With Andre Steinmann) *La petite barbe: J'ai vecu 40 ans dans le Grand Nord* (biography), Editions de l'homme, c. 1977.
Le Refuge: Theatre (play), VLB, 1979; aired on Radio-Canada's *Scenario* program in four installments, November 4, 11, 18, and 25, 1977.
Les Masques, Quebec/Amerique (Montreal, Quebec), 1980, translated by Leonard W. Sugden as *The Masks*, Montreal Press (Montreal, Quebec), 1990.

Le Passager, Quebec/Amerique, 1984.

Contributor to periodicals, including *Quebec/Amerique;* author of several unpublished works.

SIDELIGHTS: French-Canadian author and editor Gilbert La Rocque is perhaps best remembered for his 1980 novel *Les Masques,* which was translated into English as *The Masks* in 1990. *The Masks* either won or was nominated for several of Canada's most prestigious literary prizes. La Rocque penned several other novels, collaborated on biographies, and wrote a play, but he has also been praised for his contribution to French-Canadian literature as an editor who encouraged young authors. Two years after being elected Grand Montrealais de l'Avenir for these and other literary efforts in 1982, he died suddenly of a cerebral hemorrhage. La Rocque has been compared to French author Marcel Proust, American Southern author William Faulkner, as well as French author Louis-Ferdinand Celine.

La Rocque was born in Rosemont, Quebec, in 1943. His father worked as a tinsmith, and the family moved to the northern part of Montreal when the young La Rocque was eleven years old. The future author and editor did not attend college, and worked in tin for a time as his father had, as well as in construction and clerical work before getting his first publishing job in 1970. La Rocque learned enough in his first two years in the field to become chief editor of the Montreal company Editions de l'Homme. He served quite a few different Montreal publishing firms, but ended his career as the literary director of Editions Quebec/Amerique.

La Rocque saw all of his novels as part of one great work; perhaps accordingly, they are all very similar in theme. As Patricia Merivale reported in the *Dictionary of Literary Biography,* in five out of six "a hero tries to fight free of his obsession with a series of childhood traumas, among which the (accidental?) drowning of a young child is frequent." In *The Masks,* which Merivale asserted contains "some of the best Quebec prose ever written," the drowning involved is that of the protagonist's young son. During the course of the novel, this man must endure a huge family party taking place next to the river where his son died.

The Masks is La Rocque's fifth novel; his first, *Le Nombril,* saw print in 1970, and was eventually adapted by the author as a play which aired on Radio Canada, *Le Refuge.* His third, *Apres la boue,* is worthy of mention because it differs from the rest of La Rocque's books in that it has a female protagonist, Gaby. She, too, suffers from past psychological injury, though the horrors that have touched her did not all take place during her childhood. *Apres la boue* also differs from most of La Rocque's oeuvre in that, like *The Masks,* it holds out hope of recovery and eventual happiness. Merivale hailed La Rocque's use of a heroine rather than a hero as "surprisingly successful," and further noted that "Gaby's three adult traumas, a connubial rape, a self-inflicted abortion, and an attack upon her blind old father . . . [lead] to a moderately successful therapy, an acceptance of herself, and some prospect of a new life."

La Rocque's fourth novel, *Serge d'entre les morts,* has the rare distinction of having portions of it featured in yet another novel by another author. In Gerard Bessette's *Le Semestre,* the characters study *Serge d'entre les morts* in a literature class and find that their lives become entwined with the novel's text. La Rocque's sixth novel, *Le Passager,* is a fictionalization of the author's real life literary feud with critic Reginald Martel. In Merivale's opinion, this long-standing rivalry was "occasioned at least in part by La Rocque's sensitivity to the supposed critical neglect or undervaluing of his own work."

In addition to his creations of the imagination, La Rocque collaborated on some biographical adventures with the people who lived them. One of them, which he penned with Paul Provencher, was translated into English and bears the title *Provencher: Last of the Coureurs de Bois.* At the time of his death, La Rocque left a number of unpublished or uncompleted works; these may well see print in the future.

BIOGRAPHICAL/CRITICAL SOURCES:

BOOKS

Dictionary of Literary Biography, Volume 60: *Canadian Writers since 1960, Second Series,* Gale (Detroit, MI), 1987.
Smith, Donald, and others, *Gilbert La Rocque: L'Ecriture du reve,* Quebec/Amerique (Montreal, Quebec), 1985.

PERIODICALS

Canadian Literature, spring, 1983, pp. 147-149; winter, 1985, pp. 182-184; spring, 1987, p. 124-126.
Le Devoir, December 1, 1984, p. 25.
Quebec/Amerique, February, 1985.*

*   *   *

LAURENCE, (Jean) Margaret (Wemyss) 1926-1987

PERSONAL: Born July 18, 1926, in Neepawa, Manitoba, Canada; died of cancer, January 5 (some sources say January 6), 1987, in Lakefield, Ontario, Canada; buried in Lakefield, Ontario, Canada; daughter of Robert Harrison (a lawyer) and Verna Jean (Simpson) Wemyss; married John Fergus Laurence (a civil engineer), 1947 (divorced,

1969); children: Jocelyn, David. *Education:* University of Manitoba, B.A., 1947.

ADDRESSES: Home—Lakefield, Ontario, Canada. *Agent*—Cushman Associates, 24 East 38th St., New York, NY 10016.

CAREER: Writer. Worked as a reporter with the *Winnipeg Citizen;* writer in residence at University of Toronto, 1969-70, and University of Western Ontario, 1973; Trent University, Peterborough, Ontario, writer in residence, 1974, chancellor, 1981-83.

MEMBER: Royal Society of Canada (fellow).

AWARDS, HONOURS: First Novel Award, Beta Sigma Phi, 1961; President's Medal, University of Western Ontario, 1961, 1962, and 1964, for best Canadian short stories; Governor General's Literary Award in fiction ($2,500), 1967, for *A Jest of God,* and 1975; senior fellowships from Canada Council, 1967 and 1971; honorary fellow of United College, University of Winnipeg, 1967; Companion of Order of Canada, 1971; Molson Prize, 1975; B'nai B'rith award, 1976; Periodical Distributors award, 1977; City of Toronto award, 1978; writer of the year award from Canadian Booksellers Association, 1981; Banff Centre award, 1983; numerous honorary degrees from institutions including Trent, Carleton, Brandon, Mount Allison, Simon Fraser, Queen's, McMaster, and Dalhousie universities and universities of Winnipeg, Toronto, and Western Ontario.

WRITINGS:

(Editor) *A Tree for Poverty* (Somali poetry and prose), Eagle Press (Nairobi), 1954.
This Side Jordan (novel), St. Martin's, 1960.
The Prophet's Camel Bell, Macmillan (London), 1963, published as *New Wind in a Dry Land,* Knopf, 1964.
The Tomorrow-Tamer, and Other Stories (short stories), Knopf, 1964.
The Stone Angel (novel), Knopf, 1964.
A Jest of God (novel), Knopf, 1966, published as *Rachel, Rachel,* Popular Library, 1968, published as *Now I Lay Me Down,* Panther, 1968.
Long Drums and Cannons: Nigerian Dramatists and Novelists 1952-1966, Macmillan, 1968.
The Fire-Dwellers (novel), Knopf, 1969.
A Bird in the House (short stories), Knopf, 1970.
Jason's Quest (for children), Knopf, 1970.
The Diviners (novel), Knopf, 1974.
Heart of a Stranger (essays), McClelland & Stewart, 1976, Lippincott, 1977.
Six Darn Cows (for children), Lorimer, 1979.
The Olden Days Coat (for children), McClelland & Stewart, 1979.
The Christmas Birthday Story (for children), Knopf, 1980.

Dance on the Earth: A Memoir, McClelland & Stewart, 1989.

Contributor of short stories to *Story, Prism, Queen's Quarterly, Saturday Evening Post,* and *Post Stories: 1962.*

ADAPTATIONS: The Jest of God was adapted as the film "Rachel, Rachel," starring Joanne Woodward and directed by Paul Newman, Warner Bros., 1968.

SIDELIGHTS: Though she was not prolific, Margaret Laurence's fiction made her "more profoundly admired than any other Canadian novelist of her generation," according to Toronto *Globe and Mail* critic William French. Often set in the fictional Canadian small town of Manawaka, her novels and short stories earned praise for their compassion and realism and the skill with which they were told. They also aroused controversy—religious fundamentalists attempted to have one novel, *The Diviners,* banned from schools because it contained explicit descriptions of an abortion and a sexual affair. Laurence frequently explored the predicaments of women in society, and some of her characters are recognized as early feminists. Reviewers judge her work a powerful influence on Canadian writing; in an *Atlantic* review of *The Fire-Dwellers* one writer deemed her "the best fiction writer in the Dominion and one of the best in the hemisphere."

Non-Canadian subjects also appeared in Laurence's works. *The Prophet's Camel Bell* is an account of her experiences while living for two years in the Haud desert of Somaliland (now Somalia), with her husband, sharing the hardships and privations of desert life with their Somali workers. West Africa serves as the setting for the stories in *The Tomorrow-Tamer* and the source of the literature Laurence discussed in *Long Drums and Cannons: Nigerian Novelists and Dramatists 1952-1966.* In addition Laurence wrote short stories, some of which were published in periodicals such as *Queen's Quarterly* and the *Saturday Evening Post.* She also edited and translated *A Tree for Poverty: Somali Poetry and Prose* and wrote books for children. In collaboration with her daughter Laurence completed *Dance on Earth: A Memoir* shortly before her death.

BIOGRAPHICAL/CRITICAL SOURCES:

BOOKS

Contemporary Literary Criticism, Gale, Volume 3, 1975, Volume 6, 1976, Volume 13, 1980, Volume 50, 1988.
Dictionary of Literary Biography, Volume 53: *Canadian Writers since 1960, First Series,* Gale, 1986.
Hind-Smith, Joan, *Three Voices: The Lives of Margaret Laurence, Gabrielle Roy, and Frederick Philip Grove,* Clarke Irwin, 1975.
Laurence, Margaret, *Dance on the Earth: A Memoir,* McClelland & Stewart, 1989.
Morley, Patricia, *Margaret Laurence,* Twayne, 1981.

New, W. H., editor, *Margaret Laurence: The Writer and Her Critics,* McGraw Hill Ryerson, 1977.

Thomas, Clara, *Margaret Laurence,* McClelland & Stewart, 1969.

Thomas, *The Manawaka World of Margaret Laurence,* McClelland & Stewart, 1975.

Verduyn, Christi, editor, *Margaret Laurence: An Appreciation,* Broadview Press, 1988.

Woodcock, George, editor, *A Place to Stand On: Essays by and about Margaret Laurence,* NeWest Press, 1983.

PERIODICALS

Atlantic, June, 1969, March, 1970.
Canadian Forum, February, 1969, September, 1970.
Chicago Tribune Book World, December 7, 1980.
Christian Science Monitor, June 12, 1969, March 26, 1970.
Fiddlehead, Number 80, 1969.
Globe and Mail (Toronto), December 14, 1985, January 10, 1987, March 5, 1988, November 4, 1989.
Maclean's, May 14, 1979.
New York Times Book Review, April 19, 1970.
Saturday Night, May, 1969.
World Literature Today, winter, 1982.

OBITUARIES:

PERIODICALS

Globe and Mail (Toronto), January 10, 1987.
Los Angeles Times, January 17, 1987.
Maclean's, January 19, 1987.
New York Times, January 7, 1987.
Publishers Weekly, February 20, 1987.
Times (London), January 7, 1987.
Washington Post, January 7, 1987.*

*   *   *

LAYTON, Irving (Peter) 1912-

PERSONAL: Original surname, Lazarovitch; name legally changed; born March 12, 1912, in Neamtz, Romania; immigrated to Canada, 1913; son of Moses and Keine (Moscovitch) Lazarovitch; married Faye Lynch, September 13, 1938 (marriage ended); married Frances Sutherland, September 13, 1946 (marriage ended); married Aviva Cantor (a writer of children's stories), September 13, 1961 (marriage ended); married Harriet Bernstein (a publicist; divorced, March 19, 1984); married Anna Pottier, November 8, 1984; children: (with Sutherland) Max Rubin, Naomi Parker; (with Cantor) David Herschel; (with Bernstein) Samantha Clara. *Education:* Macdonald College, B.S., 1939; McGill University, M.A., 1946.

ADDRESSES: Home—6879 Monkland Ave., Montreal, Quebec, Canada H4B 1J5. *Agent*—Lucinda Vardey Agency, 297 Seaton St., Toronto, Canada M5A 2T6.

CAREER: Jewish Public Library, Montreal, Quebec, lecturer, 1943-58; high school teacher in Montreal, 1945-60; Sir George Williams University (now Sir George Williams Campus of Concordia University), Montreal, lecturer, 1949-65, poet in residence, 1965-69; University of Guelph, Guelph, Ontario, poet in residence, 1969-70; York University, Toronto, Ontario, professor of English literature, 1970-78; University of Ottawa, poet in residence, 1978; Concordia University, Sir George Williams Campus, Montreal poet in residence 1978; University of Toronto, writer in residence, 1981; Concordia University, adjunct professor, 1988; Concordia University, writer in residence, 1989. Co-founding editor, *First Statement,* later *Northern Review,* Montreal, 1941-43; associate editor, *Contact* magazine and Contact Press, Toronto, 1952-54 and *Black Mountain Review,* North Carolina. *Military service:* Canadian Army, Artillery, 1942-43; became lieutenant.

MEMBER: PEN, Canadian Civil Liberties Union, Honorary Member Istituto Pertini (Florence, Italy).

AWARDS, HONOURS: Canada Foundation fellow, 1957; Governor-General's Award, 1959, for *A Red Carpet for the Sun;* Canada Council awards, 1959 and 1960; President's Medal, University of Western Ontario, 1961, for poem "Keine Lazarovitch 1870-1959"; Prix Litteraire de Quebec, 1963, for *Balls for a One-Armed Juggler;* Canada Council Special Arts Award, 1963 and 1968; Centennial Medal, 1967; D.C.L., Bishops University, 1970, and Concordia University, 1976; Canada Council Senior Arts Fellowship and travel grant, 1973 and 1979; Order of Canada, 1976; Encyclopedia Brittanica Life Achievement Award, 1978; Canada Council long term arts award, 1979-81; nominated for Nobel Prize by Italy and S. Korea, 1982, again by Italy, 1983.

WRITINGS:

POETRY, EXCEPT AS INDICATED

Here and Now, First Statement, 1945.
Now Is the Place (poems and stories), First Statement, 1948.
The Black Huntsmen, privately printed, 1951.
Love the Conqueror Worm, Contact, 1951.
(With Louis Dudek and Raymond Souster) *Cerberus,* Contact, 1952.
In the Midst of My Fever, Divers, 1954.
The Long Peashooter, Laocoon, 1954.
The Cold Green Element, Contact, 1955.
The Blue Propeller, Contact, 1955.
The Bull Calf, Contact, 1956.

Music on a Kazoo, Contact, 1956.

The Improved Binoculars (selected poems), introduction by William Carlos Williams, Jargon, 1956.

A Laughter in the Mind, Jargon, 1958.

A Red Carpet for the Sun (collected poems), McClelland & Stewart, 1959.

The Swinging Flesh (poems and short stories), McClelland & Stewart, 1961.

Balls for a One-Armed Juggler, McClelland & Stewart, 1963.

The Laughing Rooster, McClelland & Stewart, 1964.

Collected Poems, McClelland & Stewart, 1965.

Periods of the Moon, McClelland & Stewart, 1967.

The Shattered Plinths, McClelland & Stewart, 1968.

Selected Poems, McClelland & Stewart, 1969.

The Whole Bloody Bird: Obs, Aphs, and Pomes, McClelland & Stewart, 1969.

Nail Polish, McClelland & Stewart, 1971.

The Collected Poems of Irving Layton, McClelland & Stewart, 1971.

Lovers and Lesser Men, McClelland & Stewart, 1973.

The Pole-Vaulter, McClelland & Stewart, 1974.

Seventy-five Greek Poems, McClelland & Stewart, 1974.

The Darkening Fire: Selected Poems, 1945-1968, McClelland & Stewart, 1975.

The Unwavering Eye: Selected Poems, 1969-1975, McClelland & Stewart, 1975.

For My Brother Jesus, McClelland & Stewart, 1976.

The Covenant, McClelland & Stewart, 1977.

The Collected Poems of Irving Layton, McClelland & Stewart, 1977.

The Uncollected Poems of Irving Layton, 1936-1959, Mosaic Press, 1977.

The Selected Poems of Irving Layton, New Directions, 1977.

The Tightrope Dancer, McClelland & Stewart, 1978.

The Love Poems of Irving Layton, McClelland & Stewart, 1979, (deluxe edition); also published by McClelland & Stewart, 1980.

Droppings from Heaven, McClelland & Stewart, 1979.

(With Carlo Mattioli) *Irving Layton, Carlo Mattioli,* Edizioni (Milan, Italy), 1978.

For My Neighbors in Hell, Mosaic Press, 1980.

Europe and Other Bad News, McClelland & Stewart, 1981.

A Wild Peculiar Joy, McClelland & Stewart, 1982.

Shadows on the Ground, (portfolio) Mosaic/Valley Editions, 1982.

The Gucci Bag, Mosaic Press, 1983; also published by McClelland & Stewart, 1983.

The Love Poems of Irving Layton, with Reverence & Delight, Mosaic/Valley Editions, 1984.

A Spider Danced a Cosy Jig, Stoddart, 1984.

Dance with Desire: Love Poems, McClelland & Stewart, 1986.

Final Reckoning: Poems 1982-1986, Mosaic/Valley Editions, 1987.

Fortunate Exile, McClelland & Stewart, 1987.

A Wild Peculiar Joy: Selected Poems 1945-1989, McClelland & Stewart, 1989.

Fornalutx: Selected Poems, 1928-1990, McGill-Queen's University, 1992.

Also author of *Il Freddo Verde Elemente,* Einaudi, 1974; *In un'eta di ghiaccio* (title means "In an Ice Age"; bilingual selected poems), 1981; (with Salvatore Fiume) *A Tall Man Executes a Jig* (portfolio), 1985; *Selected Poems,* [Seoul, South Korea], 1985; *Where Burning Sappho Loved,* [Athens, Greece], 1985; *Tutto Sommato Poesie 1945-88* (a bilingual Italian-English edition of selected poems), 1989; *Il Cacciatore Sconcertato* (a bilingual Italian-English edition of selected poems), Longo, Ravenna, 1993; *Danza di Desiderio* (a bilingual Italian-English edition of *Dance with Desire*), Piovan, 1993.

Work represented in numerous anthologies, including, *Book of Canadian Poetry,* edited by A. J. M. Smith, Gage, 1948; *Book of Canadian Stories,* edited by D. Pacey, Ryerson, 1950; *Canadian Short Stories,* edited by R. Weaver and H. James, Oxford University Press, 1952; *Oxford Book of Canadian Verse,* edited by Smith, Oxford University Press, 1960; *How Do I Love Thee: Sixty Poets of Canada (and Quebec) Select and Introduce Their Favourite Poems from Their Own Work,* edited by John Robert Colombo, M. G. Hurtig, 1970; *Irving Layton/Aligi Sassu Portfolio,* 1978. Contributor of poetry and stories to various periodicals, including *Poetry, Canadian Forum,* and *Sail.*

EDITOR

(With Louis Dudek) *Canadian Poems, 1850-1952,* Contact, 1952, 2nd edition, 1953.

Pan-ic: A Selection of Contemporary Canadian Poems, Alan Brilliant, 1958.

Love Where the Nights Are Long: Canadian Love Poems, McClelland & Stewart, 1962.

Rawprint (Concordia University Workshop Anthology), The Workshop, 1989.

Also editor and author of introduction, *Poems for Twenty-seven Cents,* [Montreal], 1961; *Anvil Blood: A Selection of Workshop Poems,* [Toronto], 1973; editor of *Anvil: A Selection of Workshop Poems,* [Montreal], 1966; *Shark Tank,* [Toronto], 1977. Cofounder and editor, *First Statement* and *Northern Review,* 1941-43; former associate editor, *Contact, Black Mountain Review,* and several other magazines.

OTHER

(Author of introduction) *Poems to Colour: A Selection of Workshop Poems,* York University, 1970.

Engagements: The Prose of Irving Layton, edited by Seymour Mayne, McClelland & Stewart, 1972.

Taking Sides (prose), McClelland & Stewart, 1977.

(With Dorothy Rath) *An Unlikely Affair: The Irving Layton-Dorothy Rath Correspondence,* Mosaic/Valley Editions, 1980.

(With David O'Rourke) *Waiting for the Messiah: A Memoir* McClelland & Stewart, 1985.

Wild Gooseberries: Selected Letters of Irving Layton, 1939-89, edited by Francis Mansbridge, Macmillan, 1989.

(With Robert Creeley) *Irving Layton & Robert Creeley: The Complete Correspondence,* University of Toronto Press, 1990.

Layton's writings have been translated into more than ten languages, including Italian and Spanish. His papers are housed at the library of Concordia University.

ADAPTATIONS: Layton's poetry has been released on several audio recordings. Layton has also been the subject of two National Film Board documentaries on video cassette: *Poet: Irving Layton Observed,* directed by Donald Winkler (available in 1 hour format or abridged 1/2 hour format), 1986; *A Tall Man Executes a Jig,* directed by Donald Winkler (1/2 hour), 1986.

SIDELIGHTS: A controversial and outspoken literary figure, Irving Layton is known for writing energetic, passionate, and often angry verse. In an attempt to "disturb the accumulated complacencies of people," Layton confronts what he views as sources of evil in the twentieth century, suggesting that these "malignant forces" have contributed to moral and cultural decay in the modern world. A prolific writer, Layton has published nearly fifty volumes of poetry in as many years, with verse ranging, as noted Canadian critic George Woodcock wrote in his book *Odysseus Ever Returning,* "from the atrocious to the excellent."

Layton was born in Romania to Jewish parents and immigrated to Canada with his family at age one. His father Moses was a religious man whom Layton has described as "a visionary, a scholar"; his mother Keine supported the family by running a small grocery store. In 1939 Layton received a bachelor of science degree from McDonald College and in 1946 he earned a master's degree in economics and political science from McGill University. While living in Montreal in the early 1940s, Layton, along with Louis Dudek and John Sutherland, began editing *First Statement;* some of his earliest poems were published in this literary journal which highlighted the work of young Canadian writers and emphasized the social and political aspects of Canadian life. Layton published his first volume of poetry, *Here and Now* in 1945. His earliest volumes met with minimal success, but in the 1950s, ac-

cording to Ira Bruce Nadel in the *Dictionary of Literary Biography,* "Layton discovered a voice that could unite his skeptical vision and energetic, provocative language." *A Red Carpet for the Sun,* which included some of his best-known poems from previous volumes, proved to be his first major success, earning him popular praise as well as the Governor General's Award for Poetry in 1959. At this time he became what Tom Marshall called in *Harsh and Lovely Land* an "unusual phenomenon—a genuinely popular poet." Layton went on to write several more collections of verse over the next thirty years, maintaining a consistent thematic approach as well as exhibiting a forthright and contentious public personality.

Many critics discuss Layton as a romantic poet in the tradition of William Blake and Walt Whitman; he explores elemental passions, exalts the individual—particularly the poet—and examines the relationship between the physical and the spiritual. In his works he rails against social injustice, identifying keenly with the helpless and innocent; as a result many of his poems feature images of trapped and wounded animals. Constituting a significant portion of his oeuvre, his love lyrics—sensual, erotic, and explicitly sexual—are intended to shock a Puritanical society, and their effectiveness is due in part to the juxtaposition of images of love and beauty with those of violence and death. Thus, in his poetry of liberation, Layton challenges what he views as the unhealthy gentility and complacency of Canadian society. A number of Layton's poems deal with his approach to religion. He addresses cultural, historical, and philosophical aspects of Judaism, avoiding, as Howard Baker points out, the purely religious elements. Baker has explained that Layton "is devoted to the secular aspects of Judaism . . . , and to the question of Jewish survival in a hostile world." Layton's view of organized religion as a source of evil and corruption dating from ancient times to the present day has aroused controversy among his readers. Particularly inciteful are some of the poems in *For My Brother Jesus* (1976) in which he suggests that, "by publicizing a stereotype of the Jew for nearly two thousand years," Christendom "prepared the soil on which the death camps and the crematoria could spring-up and flourish." Layton explores the horrors of the Holocaust in a number of works, including "For Anne Frank" and "The Final Solution." Commentators note that, beginning with *Balls for a One-Armed Juggler* (1963), Layton became increasingly concerned with addressing what he has described as "the exceptionally heinous nature of twentieth-century evil," citing the Holocaust as a primary example. He offers poetry as a means of salvation, however, and asserts that the poet has an obligation to address social ills in an attempt to counteract corruption, greed, and complacency.

A number of critics have commented on Layton's poetic mission. David Stouck has described the sense of two different writers at work in Layton's poetry: "the noisy social rebel" and "the serious literary craftsman." Stouck suggests that Layton's self-appointed role as prophet and social outcast has resulted in some "second-rate" poetry. Several commentators, however, praise Layton's vitality, power, and range. While many critics acknowledge Layton's role in broadening Canadian literary standards to include sexually explicit imagery, his erotic love poetry—and his views on women in general—have aroused considerable indignation. Some scholars assert that his love poems do not, as Layton has asserted, celebrate sexual love; Joann Lewis has suggested that "the language of Layton's poetry does more than break the puritan embargo on writing about sexuality in sexually explicit terms; it degrades both women and human sexuality." Layton stated in a 1978 interview with Kenneth Sherman that he believes women have merely "a biological creativity" and that "the women artists that have achieved fame and greatness have done so in a very limited way." Stouck has acknowledged that "the poet's public personality, his egotism and arrogance, obtrude on the reader's appreciation of his work. . . . Yet Layton has an ear for the rhetoric and rhythms of great poetry and has produced several pieces that will surely live on."

Layton commented: "One of my sisters thought I should be a plumber or an electrician; another saw in me the ability to become a peddlar; my third and oldest sister was sure I was devious and slippery enough to make a fine lawyer or politician. My mother, presiding over these three witches, pointed to the fly-spotted ceiling, indicating God by that gesture, and said, 'He will be what the Almighty wants him to be.'

"My devout mother turned out to be right. From earliest childhood I longed to match sounds with sense; and when I was older, to make music out of words. Everywhere I went, mystery dogged my steps. The skinny dead rat in the lane, the fire that broke out in our house on Sabbath eve, the energy that went with cruelty and the power that went with hate. The empty sky had no answers for my queries and the stars at night only winked and said nothing.

"I wrote my first poem for a teacher who was astonishingly beautiful. For weeks I mentally drooled over the white cleavage she had carelessly exposed to a precocious eleven-year-old. So there it was: the two grand mysteries of sexuality and death. I write because I'm driven to say something about them, to celebrate what my limited brain cannot comprehend. To rejoice in my more arrogant moods to think the Creator Himself doesn't comprehend His handiwork. I write because the only solace He has in His immense and eternal solitude are the poems and stories that tell Him—like all creators, He too is hungry for praise—how exciting and beautiful, how majestic and terrible are His works and to give Him an honest, up-to-date report on His most baffling creation, Man. I know whenever I put in a good word for the strange biped He made, God's despair is lessened. Ultimately, I write because I am less cruel than He is."

BIOGRAPHICAL/CRITICAL SOURCES:

BOOKS

Bennet, Joy, and James Polson, *Irving Layton: A Bibliography, 1934-1977,* Concordia University Libraries, 1979.

Burgess, G C. Ian, *Irving Layton's Poetry: A Catalogue and Chronology,* McGill University, 1974.

Cameron, Elspeth, *Irving Layton: A Portrait,* Stoddart, 1985.

Contemporary Literary Criticism, Gale, Volume 2, 1974, Volume 15, 1980.

Dictionary of Literary Biography, Volume 88: *Canadian Writers, 1920-1959, Second Series,* Gale, 1989.

Dudek, Louis, *Selected Essays and Criticism,* Tecumseh Press, 1978.

Francis, Wynne, *Irving Layton and His Works,* ECW, 1984.

Layton, Irving, *For My Brother Jesus,* McClelland & Stewart, 1976.

Mandel, Eli, *Irving Layton,* Forum House, 1969, revised edition published as *The Poetry of Layton,* 1981.

Marshall, Tom, *Harsh and Lovely Land,* University of British Columbia Press, 1979, pp. 67-75.

Mayne, Seymour, editor, *Irving Layton: The Poet and His Critics,* McGraw Hill/Ryerson Press, 1978.

Meyer, Bruce, and Brian O'Riordan, *In Their Words: Interviews with Fourteen Canadian Writers,* Anasi, 1984, pp. 10-25.

Rizzardi, Alfredo, editor, *Italian Critics on Irving Layton,* Editore Piovan (Albano, Italy), 1988.

Woodcock, George, *Odysseus Ever Returning: Essays on Canadian Writers and Writing,* McClelland & Stewart, 1970, pp. 76-92.

PERIODICALS

Canadian Forum, June, 1969; February-March, 1989, p. 28.

Canadian Literature, autumn, 1962, pp. 21-34; spring, 1972, pp. 102-04; autumn, 1972, pp. 70-83; winter, 1973, pp. 12-13, 18; winter, 1980, pp. 52-65.

Fiddlehead, spring, 1967, summer, 1967.

Maclean's, November 19, 1990, p. 45.

Mosaic, January, 1968, pp. 103-11.

New Republic, July 2, 1977.

New York Times Book Review, October 9, 1977.

Queen's Quarterly, winter 1955-1956, pp. 587-591.

The Record (Sherbrooke, Quebec), November 2, 1984.

Saturday Night, April, 1988, p. 59.
Village Voice, March 31, 1966.
Waves, winter, 1987, pp. 4-13.

*   *   *

LEACOCK, Stephen (Butler) 1869-1944

PERSONAL: Born December 30, 1869, in Swanmoor, Hampshire, England; immigrated to Canada, 1876; died of throat cancer, March 28, 1944, in Canada; married Beatrix Hamilton in 1900. *Education:* Attended Upper Canada College, 1882-87, and Strathroy Collegiate Institute; University of Toronto, B.A., 1891; University of Chicago, Ph.D., 1903.

CAREER: Taught at Uxbridge, late 1880s; Upper Canada College, master in modern languages, 1889-99; McGill University, Montreal, Quebec, lecturer in economics and political science, 1903-36, chair of department beginning in 1908; writer and public speaker.

AWARDS, HONOURS: Received Mark Twain Medal, Lorne Pierce Medal from Royal Society of Canada, Governor General's Award, and honorary degrees from institutions including Dartmouth College, Brown University, Bishop's University, and McGill University; Stephen Leacock Medal for Humour established in his honor, 1947.

WRITINGS:

Elements of Political Science, Houghton, 1906, new and enlarged edition, 1921.
Baldwin, Lafontaine, Hincks: Responsible Government, Morang, 1907, enlarged edition, edited by W. P. M. Kennedy, published as *MacKenzie, Baldwin, La Fontaine, Hincks,* Oxford University Press, 1926.
Greater Canada, an Appeal: Let Us No Longer Be a Colony, Montreal News Company, 1907.
Literary Lapses: A Book of Sketches (includes "My Financial Career," "The Conjurer's Revenge," "Hoodoo McFiggin's Christmas," "A Lesson in Fiction," "The New Food," "Saloonio: A Study in Shakespearean Criticism," "The Awful Fate of Melpomenus Jones," "A, B, and C: The Human Element in Mathematics," "A New Pathology," and "Boarding-House Geometry"), Lane, 1910, with introduction by Robertson Davies, McClelland & Stewart, 1957.
Nonsense Novels (includes "Q: A Psychic Pstory of the Psuper Natural," "Caroline's Christmas," "Hoodoo McFiggin's Christmas," "Guido the Gimlet of Ghent: A Romance of Chivalry," and "Gertrude the Governess; or, Simple Seventeen"), Lane, 1911, with introduction by S. Ross Beharriell, McClelland & Stewart, 1963.
Sunshine Sketches of a Little Town (includes "The Hostelry of Mr. Smith," "The Speculations of Jefferson

Thorpe," "The Marine Excursion of the Knights of Pythias," "The Ministrations of the Rev. Mr. Drone," "Extraordinary Entanglement," "The Great Election in Missinaba County," "The Candidacy of Mr. Smith," and "L'Envoi: The Train to Mariposa"), Lane, 1912, with preface by Malcolm Ross, McClelland & Stewart, 1960.
"Behind the Beyond," and Other Contributions to Human Knowledge (contains "Familiar Incidents," "Parisian Pastimes," "The Retroactive Existence of Mr. Juggins," "Making a Magazine," "Homer and Humbug," and three-act play *Behind the Beyond,* first produced in Cambridge, England, 1922), illustrations by A. H. Fish, Lane, 1913, with introduction by Donald Cameron, McClelland & Stewart, 1969.
Adventurers of the Far North: A Chronicle of the Frozen Seas, Brook, 1914.
Arcadian Adventures with the Idle Rich (includes "A Little Dinner with Mr. Lucullus Fyshe" and "The Rival Churches of St. Asaph and St. Osoph"), Lane, 1914, with introduction by Ralph L. Curry, McClelland & Stewart, 1969.
The Dawn of Canadian History: A Chronicle of Aboriginal Canada and the Coming of the White Man, Brook, 1914.
The Mariner of St. Malo: A Chronicle of the Voyages of Jacques Cartier, Brook, 1914.
The Methods of Mr. Sellyer: A Book Store Study, Lane, 1914.
Moonbeams from the Larger Lunacy (contains "Spoof: A Thousand-Guinea Novel," "The Reading Public," "Afternoon Adventures at My Club," "Ram Spudd: The New-World Singer," "Aristocratic Anecdotes," "Education Made Agreeable," "An Every-day Experience," "Truthful Oratory," "Our Literary Bureau," "Speeding up Business," "Who Is Also Who," "Passionate Paragraphs," "Weejee the Pet Dog," "Sidelights on the Supermen," "The Survival of the Fittest," "The First Newspaper: A Sort of Allegory," and "In the Good Time after the War"), Lane, 1915, with introduction by Robertson Davies, McClelland & Stewart, 1964.
(With Basil Macdonald Hastings) *Q: A Farce in One Act* (adapted from story "Q: Psychic Pstory of the Psuper Natural"; produced in the West End, 1915), S. French, 1915.
Further Foolishness: Sketches and Satires on the Follies of the Day (includes "Peace, War and Politics," "Movies and Motors, Men and Women," "Follies in Fiction," "Timid Thoughts on Timely Topics," "Humour as I See It," "The Snoopopaths; or, Fifty Stories in One," and "Are the Rich Happy?"), Lane, 1916.
Essays and Literary Studies (contains "The Apology of a Professor," "The Devil and the Deep Sea," "Litera-

ture and Education in America," "American Humour," "The Woman Question," "The Lot of the Schoolmaster," "Fiction and Reality," "The Amazing Genius of O. Henry," and "A Rehabilitation of Charles II"), Lane, 1916.

(Editor) *The Greatest Pages of American Humor,* Sun Dial Press, 1916.

Frenzied Fiction (contains "My Revelations As a Spy," "Father Knickerbocker—A Fantasy," "The Prophet in Our Midst," "Personal Adventures in the Spirit World," "The Sorrows of a Summer Guest," "To Nature and Back Again," "The Cave Man As He Is," "Ideal Interviews," "The New Education," "The Errors of Santa Claus," "Lost in New York," "This Strenuous Age," "The Old, Old Story of How Five Men Went Fishing," "Back from the Land," "The Perplexity Column," "Simple Stories of Success; or, How to Succeed in Life," "In Dry Toronto," and "Merry Christmas"), Lane, 1918, with introduction by David Dooley, McClelland & Stewart, 1965.

The Hohenzollerns in America; with the Bolsheviks in Berlin and Other Impossibilities (includes "Echoes of the War," "The Lost Illusions of Mr. Sims," "Heroes and Heroines," and "The Discovery of America"), Lane, 1919.

The Unsolved Riddle of Social Justice, Lane, 1920.

Winsome Winnie, and Other New Nonsense Novels (contains "Winsome Winnie; or, Trial and Temptation," "John and I; or, How I Nearly Lost My Husband," "The Split in the Cabinet; or, The Fate of England," "Who Do You Think Did It?; or, The Mixed-up Murder Mystery," "Broken Barriers; or, Red Love on a Blue Island," "The Kidnapped Plumber: A Tale of the New Time," "The Blue and the Grey: A Pre-War War Story," and "Buggam Grange: A Good Old Ghost Story"), Lane, 1920, published as *Winsome Winnie and Other Nonsense Novels,* Books for Libraries Press, 1970.

My Discovery of England (includes "The Balance of Trade in Impressions," "I Am Interviewed by the Press," "Impressions of London," "A Clear View of the Government and Politics of England," "Is Prohibition Coming to England?," " 'We Have with Us To-night,' " "Oxford as I See It," and "Have the English Any Sense of Humour?"), Dodd, 1922, with introduction by George Whalley, McClelland & Stewart, 1961.

College Days, Dodd, 1923.

Over the Footlights (includes "Nature Men," "Personal Experiments with the Black Bass," and "Abolishing the Heroine"), Dodd, 1923, published in England as *Over the Footlights, and Other Fancies,* Lane, 1923.

The Garden of Folly (contains "Concerning Humour and Humourists," "The Secrets of Success," "The Human

Mind up to Date," "The Human Body: Its Care and Prevention," "The Perfect Salesman" [also see below], "Romances of Business," "The Perfect Lover's Guide," "The Progress of Human Knowledge," "Glimpses of the Future in America," "My Unposted Correspondence," and "Letters to the New Rulers of the World"), Dodd, 1924.

The Raft (play), produced in Toronto, Ontario, 1924.

Winnowed Wisdom: A New Book of Humour (contains "The Outlines of Everything," "Brotherly Love among the Nations," "Studies in the Newer Culture," "In the Good Old Summer Time," "Travel and Movement," "Great National Problems," "Round Our City," and "The Christmas Ghost"), Dodd, 1926.

Short Circuits (contains "Short Circuits in the Social Current," "Short Circuits in the Open Air," "Save Me from My Friends," "People We Know," "Short Circuits in Education," "Short Circuits by Radio and Cinema," "Short Circuits in International Relations," "Bygone Currents," "Short Circuits in Current Literature," "The Cash and Carry of the Light Brigade," "The Old Men's Page," "The Great Detective," "The Epilogue of This Book," and "An Elegy near a City Freight Yard"), Dodd, 1928, with introduction by D. J. Dooley, McClelland & Stewart, 1967.

The Iron Man and the Tin Woman, with Other Such Futurities: A Book of Little Sketches of To-day and To-morrow (includes "Pictures of the Bright Time to Come," "Great Lives in Our Midst," "The Intimate Disclosures of a Wronged Woman," and "Conversations I Can Do Without"), Dodd, 1929.

Economic Prosperity in the British Empire, Houghton, 1930.

Laugh with Leacock: An Anthology of the Best Works of Stephen Leacock, Dodd, 1930.

Wet Wit and Dry Humour, Distilled from the Pages of Stephen Leacock, Dodd, 1931.

Back to Prosperity: The Great Opportunity of the Empire Conference, Macmillan, 1932.

Afternoons in Utopia: Tales of the New Times (includes "Utopia Old and New," "Grandfather Goes to War," "The Doctor and the Contraption," "Rah! Rah! College; or, Tom Buncom at Shucksford," "The Band of Brothers," and "A Fragment from Utopia"), Dodd, 1932.

The Dry Pickwick and Other Incongruities, Lane, 1932.

Mark Twain, Davies, 1932, Appleton, 1933.

Charles Dickens: His Life and Work, Davies, 1933, Doubleday, Doran, 1934.

Lincoln Frees the Slaves, Putnam, 1934.

The Perfect Salesman (contains "The Split in the Cabinet," "Broken Barriers," "Back from the Land,"

"The Sorrows of a Summer Guest," "The Perfect Salesman: A Complete Guide to Business," "Oroastus: A Greek Tragedy," "Caroline's Christmas," and "Buggam Grange"), edited by E. V. Knox, McBride, 1934.

The Pursuit of Knowledge: A Discussion of Freedom and Compulsion in Education, Liveright, 1934.

Stephen Leacock, Methuen, 1934.

(Editor) *The Greatest Pages of Charles Dickens,* Doubleday, Doran, 1934.

Humor: Its Theory and Technique, with Examples and Samples; a Book of Discovery, Dodd, 1935.

Funny Pieces: A Book of Random Sketches, Dodd, 1936.

The Gathering Financial Crisis in Canada: A Survey of the Present Critical Situation (first published in *London Morning Post,* 1936), Macmillan, 1936.

Hellements of Hickonomics, in Hiccoughs of Verse Done in Our Social Planning Mill, Dodd, 1936.

Here Are My Lectures and Stories (includes "How Soon Can We Start the Next War?," "What I Don't Know about Drama," and "My Fishing Pond"), Dodd, 1937.

My Discovery of the West: A Discussion of East and West in Canada, Hale, Cushman & Flint, 1937.

Humour and Humanity: An Introduction to the Study of Humour, Butterworth, 1937, Holt, 1938.

Model Memoirs and Other Sketches from Simple to Serious (includes "The Anatomy of Gloom"), Dodd, 1938.

Too Much College; or, Education Eating up Life, with Kindred Essays in Education and Humour, Dodd, 1939.

The British Empire: Its Structure, Its Unity, Its Strength, Dodd, 1940, published in England as *Our British Empire: Its Structure, Its Unity, Its Strength,* Lane, 1940.

Stephen Leacock's Laugh Parade, Dodd, 1940.

Canada: The Foundations of Its Future, Gazette, 1941.

Montreal: Seaport and City, Doubleday, Doran, 1942, revised edition, edited by John Culliton, McClelland & Stewart, 1963.

My Remarkable Uncle, and Other Sketches, Dodd, 1942, with introduction by John Stevens, McClelland & Stewart, 1965.

Our Heritage of Liberty, Its Origin, Its Achievement, Its Crisis: A Book for War Time, Dodd, 1942.

How to Write, Dodd, 1943.

Happy Stories, Just to Laugh At (includes "Boom Times" and "Mariposa Moves On"), Dodd, 1943.

Last Leaves (includes "Living with Murder"), Dodd, 1945, with introduction by J. M. Robinson, McClelland & Stewart, 1970.

While There Is Time: The Case against Social Catastrophe, McClelland & Stewart, 1945.

The Leacock Roundabout: A Treasury of the Best Works of Stephen Leacock (contains "Humor as I See It," "Personal Experiences and Recollections," "Nonsense Novels and Model Memoirs," "Detective Stories," "Fishing and Other Madness," "Friends and Relatives," "Drama," "Homer and Humbug," "Lectures," and "Foibles and Follies"), Dodd, 1945.

The Boy I Left behind Me (memoir), Doubleday, 1946.

The Bodley Head Leacock, edited by J. B. Priestley, Bodley Head, 1957, published as *The Best of Leacock,* McClelland & Stewart, 1957.

The Unicorn Leacock, edited by James Reeves, illustrations by Franciska Themerson, Hutchinson, 1960.

Selected Writings of Stephen Leacock: Education and Living, Tyrex, 1960.

Other People's Money: An Outside View of Trusts and Investments, Royal Trust, 1963.

My Victorian Girlhood: Memoires d'une jeune fille victorienne, French translation by Jean Gattegno, M. J. Minard, 1964.

Caroline's Christmas, Cooper & Beatty, 1969.

Hoodoo McFiggin's Christmas, Cooper & Beatty, 1970.

Feast of Stephen: An Anthology of Some of the Less Familiar Writings of Stephen Leacock, edited by Robertson Davies, McClelland & Stewart, 1970.

The Social Criticism of Stephen Leacock (contains "Greater Canada: An Appeal," "Literature and Education in America," "The Apology of a Professor: An Essay on Modern Learning," "The Devil and the Deep Sea: A Discussion of Modern Morality," "The Woman Question," "The Tyranny of Prohibition," and "The Unsolved Riddle of Social Justice"), edited by Alan Bowker, University of Toronto Press, 1973.

The Penguin Stephen Leacock, Penguin, 1981.

Christmas with Stephen Leacock: Reflections on the Yuletide Season, Natural Heritage/Natural History, 1988.

Also author of full-length and one-act plays, including a four-act adaptation of his *Sunshine Sketches* titled *Sunshine in Mariposa* and one-acts *Damned Souls* and *The Sub-Contractor,* both 1923; author of pamphlets, including *All Right, Mr. Roosevelt (Canada and the United States),* Farrar & Rinehart, 1939.

Some of Leacock's works have been produced as sound recordings, including *Gertrude the Governess and Other Works,* read by Christopher Plummer, Caedmon, 1977.

Leacock's papers are housed in MacLennan Library at McGill University and Leacock Memorial Home, Orillia, Ontario.

ADAPTATIONS: Material from *Sunshine Sketches* was adapted by Michael Morton as the four-act play *Jeff,* produced in 1916, and by Mavor Moore as the musical comedy *Sunshine Town,* produced in Toronto, Ontario, and Montreal, Quebec, 1955; some Leacock works were adapted for the stage by V. C. Clinton-Baddeley.

SIDELIGHTS: Stephen Leacock was an economist by profession, but his greatest renown came from his avocation as a humorist; as J. B. Priestley wrote in his introduction to *The Bodley Head Leacock,* "He lives by what he did in his spare time for fun." Through his many volumes of short sketches, which included *Literary Lapses* and *Sunshine Sketches of a Little Town,* Leacock poked fun at popular literature and culture, small-town foibles, and all kinds of hypocrisy, incongruity, and pretense. His work was frequently described as uniquely Canadian. British nonsense humor and use of anticlimax mingled with American exaggeration and cutting wit, all of it shaped by his own down-to-earth manner. Though often somewhat satirical, his sketches were noted for their humanity and generosity of spirit; he believed humor should never wound or offend. According to Priestley, Leacock's work was that of "a very shrewd but essentially good-natured and eupeptic man, anything but an angry reformer." Louis K. MacKendrick, writing in a *Dictionary of Literary Biography* essay, called Leacock "the first immortal in the ranks of Canadian humorists."

Literary Lapses, Leacock's first collection of humorous sketches, "clearly shows that Leacock was already master of the comic craft," asserted S. Ross Beharriell in *Literary History of Canada: Canadian Literature in English.* Favorite Leacockian devices of humor that first surfaced in this volume included "careful malapropism" and "the resolutely literal reading of metaphor or cliche," noted MacKendrick. One of the most anthologized stories in this collection, "My Financial Career," demonstrates his sensitivity to the plight of a "little man" dealing with an imposing institution; a fellow establishes a bank account and then accidentally withdraws his deposit. "The collection is buoyant and vivacious, rife with imaginative merriment, and its human constants remain unfailingly fresh," MacKendrick wrote.

Leacock followed *Literary Lapses* with *Nonsense Novels,* in which he parodied the popular fiction of his day. Melodramas, feud sagas, and sea stories all became targets of his wit and showcases for his own nonsense. As MacKendrick related, "Leacock manipulates metaphors and types with enthusiastic assurance" throughout this book. "His travesties are consistently treasures of verbal acrobatics." Peter McArthur, in his book *Stephen Leacock,* commented that the success of *Nonsense Novels* "established Stephen Leacock's fame."

If *Literary Lapses* introduced him and *Nonsense Novels* popularized him, *Sunshine Sketches of a Little Town* immortalized Leacock. A collection of related tales, it "has long been acknowledged as Leacock's creative masterpiece," mused MacKendrick, "and is deservedly his most critically celebrated book." In these sketches Leacock nostalgically pokes fun at the pettiness, provinciality, and pre-tensions rampant in a fictional small town, Mariposa, that was based on his own home town of Orillia, Ontario. Although, as some writers noted, the tales' occasionally sharp satire mingles with sympathy, pathos, and regret for the passing of simpler times, Orillia's residents were among the few not amused by their humor. Canadian novelist Robertson Davies, writing in *Our Living Tradition: Seven Canadians,* suggested that the townsfolk were offended because Leacock revealed their home as "merely human" in a way that was "not only extremely funny, but also ferocious and mordant." Orillians' opinions notwithstanding, Davies surmised that "of all his books it is the one most likely to live."

"Leacock's other major critical success," according to MacKendrick, was *Arcadian Adventures with the Idle Rich.* Deemed similar to but darker in tone than *Sunshine Sketches,* the book contained pieces attacking greed, self-deception, and corruption in an increasingly capitalist society. In it MacKendrick perceived "Leacock's lament for the dearth of simplicity—along with a controlled irony directed at all forms of ego inflation." Although expressing sympathy for simpler folk, Leacock repeatedly showed innocent characters falling victim to corrupt ones. For Priestley, Leacock's work in *Arcadian Adventures* was "very good indeed."

In addition to crafting humorous sketches, Leacock wrote about humor in books such as *Humour and Humanity.* In this volume he discussed different kinds of humor and the various expressions of it in narrative and verse, word and situation. According to MacKendrick, Leacock defined humor as "the kindly contemplation of the incongruities of life, and the artistic expression thereof." Some critics considered Leacock's emphasis on kindly humor his book's most distinctive feature. G. G. Sedgewick, writing in the *University of Toronto Quarterly,* said that "what is significant in his views is not their matter but his emphasis. . . . He finds that [humor] has been tending more and more in the direction of sympathy and kindliness." MacKendrick, in turn, found this emphasis linked to the genial slant of Leacock's own work. Praising the humorist's use of "apt illustrations and humane grace" in the book, MacKendrick added that "both his conviction and the broad categories he suggests are his virtues here."

Whatever his insights into his craft, Leacock remained most important to his field as a humorist who, "at the top of his form," had "a range and brilliance not often equalled," as Davies asserted. Some writers suggested that he reached his peak early in his career and later was driven by his popularity to produce volumes in a mechanical fashion. Acknowledging this failing, MacKenzie nonetheless noted that "his substantial corpus of humor is still seen to possess a verve and comic imagination that are remarkable, and whose subjects appeal across international boundaries." George Mikes, in his book *Eight Humorists,* also observed a certain pattern to Leacock's work, but in his opinion the humorist "found a formula because he never looked for one." For Mikes, Leacock's formula was that "life was confused, illogical and silly but very amusing and worth living."

Priestley summarized Leacock as "a unique national humorist with a manner and style all his own," an assessment that many have since echoed. Drawing on disparate traditions, Leacock added personal insights and a homey approach to create a distinctive, lasting humor of his own. "Against the background of his own time," McArthur wrote, "the mass of his productions has a scope and richness that will enable it to bear comparison with the work of master artists working in other times and in other circumstances." But because he chose to express his views through humor and not fiction or philosophy, some lamented, Leacock failed to receive the degree of recognition he deserved. As Davies ruefully remarked, despite his wide and eager audience, "he lived at a time—a time which is still not completely past—when Canada was ready to acknowledge that a poet or a novelist might be an artist, worthy of the somewhat suspicious and controlled regard which our country accords to artists, but when a humorist was obviously a clown."

BIOGRAPHICAL/CRITICAL SOURCES:

BOOKS

Bissell, Claude T., editor, *Our Living Tradition: Seven Canadians,* University of Toronto Press, 1957, pp. 128-49.
Cameron, Donald, *Faces of Leacock: An Appreciation,* Ryerson, 1967.
Curry, Ralph L., *Stephen Leacock: Humorist and Humanist,* Doubleday, 1959.
Curry, *Stephen Leacock and His Works,* ECW, 1988.
Davies, Robertson, *Stephen Leacock,* McClelland & Stewart, 1970.
Dictionary of Literary Biography, Volume 92: *Canadian Writers, 1890-1920,* Gale, 1989, pp. 184-95.
Kimball, Elizabeth, *The Man in the Panama Hat,* McClelland & Stewart, 1970.
Klinck, Carl F., editor, *Literary History of Canada: Canadian Literature in English,* revised edition, University of Toronto Press, 1966, pp. 327-53.
Legate, David M., *Stephen Leacock: A Biography,* Doubleday, 1970.
Lynch, Gerald, *Stephen Leacock: Humour and Humanity,* McGill-Queen's University Press, 1988.
McArthur, Peter, *Stephen Leacock,* Ryerson, 1923.
Mikes, George, *Eight Humorists,* Allan Wingate, 1954, pp. 45-65.

Moritz, Albert, and Theresa Moritz, *Leacock: A Biography,* Stoddart, 1985.
Priestley, J. B., editor, *The Bodley Head Leacock,* Bodley Head, 1957.
Staines, David, editor, *Stephen Leacock: A Reappraisal,* University of Ottawa Press, 1986.
Twentieth-Century Literary Criticism, Volume 2, Gale, 1979, pp. 377-83.

PERIODICALS

Canadian Literature, summer, 1960, pp. 21-42; winter, 1969, pp. 5-19 and 34-42; winter, 1973, pp. 23-40.
Dalhousie Review, summer, 1976, pp. 268-82; autumn, 1976, pp. 493-509.
Journal of Canadian Fiction, Volume 19, 1977, pp. 95-105.
Journal of Canadian Studies, summer, 1982, pp. 128-36.
Mosaic, spring, 1981, pp. 76-92.
Queen's Quarterly, summer, 1951, pp. 208-19.
Studies in Canadian Literature, winter, 1979, pp. 167-76; volume 7, number 2, 1982, pp. 227-40.
University of Toronto Quarterly, October, 1945, pp. 17-26.

*   *   *

LEE, Dennis (Beynon) 1939-

PERSONAL: Born August 31, 1939, in Toronto, Ontario, Canada; son of Walter and Louise (Garbutt) Lee; married Donna Youngblut, June 24, 1962 (divorced); married Susan Perly, October 7, 1985; children: (first marriage) two daughters, one son. *Education:* University of Toronto, B.A., 1962, M.A., 1964.

ADDRESSES: Agent—MGA, 10 St. Mary's St., Suite 510, Toronto, Ontario, Canada M4Y 1P9.

CAREER: Writer. University of Toronto, Victoria College, Toronto, Ontario, lecturer in English, 1964-67; Rochdale College (experimental institution), Toronto, self-described "research person," 1967-69; House of Anansi Press, Toronto, cofounder and editor, 1967-72. Editorial consultant, Macmillan of Canada, 1973-78; poetry editor, McClelland & Stewart, 1981-84. Lyricist for television series, *Fraggle Rock,* 1982-86.

AWARDS, HONOURS: Governor-General's Award for Poetry, 1972, for *Civil Elegies;* Independent Order of Daughters of the Empire award, 1974; Canadian Association of Children's Librarians, Best Book Medals, 1974 and 1977, and English Medal, 1975, for *Alligator Pie;* named to Hans Christian Andersen Honour List and recipient of Canadian Library Association award, both 1976, both for *Alligator Pie;* Philips Information Systems Literary Award, 1984; Vicky Metcalf Award, Canadian Authors' Association, 1986, for body of work for children.

WRITINGS:

POETRY

Kingdom of Absence, House of Anansi, 1967.
Civil Elegies, House of Anansi, 1968, revised edition published as *Civil Elegies and Other Poems,* 1972.
Wiggle to the Laundromat (juvenile), New Press, 1970.
Alligator Pie (juvenile), Macmillan (Toronto), 1974, Houghton, 1975.
Nicholas Knock and Other People (juvenile), Macmillan, 1974, Houghton, 1975.
The Death of Harold Ladoo, Kanchenjunga Press, 1976.
Garbage Delight (juvenile), Macmillan, 1977, Houghton, 1978.
The Gods, McClelland & Stewart, 1979.
Jelly Belly (juvenile), Macmillan, 1983.
The Dennis Lee Big Book (anthology), Macmillan, 1985.
The Difficulty of Living on Other Planets (some poems previously published in *Nicholas Knock and Other People* and *The Gods*), Macmillan, 1987.
The Ice Cream Store (juvenile), HarperCollins, 1991.

OTHER

(Co-editor) *The University Game* (essays), House of Anansi, 1968.
(Editor) *T.O. Now: The Young Toronto Poets* (poetry anthology), House of Anansi, 1968.
Savage Fields: An Essay in Cosmology and Literature, House of Anansi, 1977.
The Ordinary Bath (juvenile), McClelland & Stewart, 1977.
Lizzy's Lion (juvenile), Stoddart, 1984.
(Editor and author of introduction) *New Canadian Poets, 1970-1985* (poetry anthology), McClelland & Stewart, 1985.

Also co-editor of two high school poetry anthologies.

WORK IN PROGRESS: Nightwatch, for McClelland & Stewart.

ADAPTATIONS: Coauthor, with Jim Henson, of story adapted by Terry Jones for the screenplay of the Henson Associates Inc./Lucasfilm Ltd. production, *Labyrinth,* 1985.

SIDELIGHTS: In a speech delivered at the 1975 Loughborough Conference in Toronto and reprinted in *Canadian Children's Literature,* Canadian author Dennis Lee examines the way his attitude toward children's verse evolved. As an adult and parent, he contemplates Mother Goose and discovers: "The nursery rhymes I love . . . are necessarily exotic. . . . But they were in no way exotic to the people who first devised them and chanted them. . . . The air of far-off charm and simpler pastoral life which now hangs over Mother Goose was in no way a part of those rhymes' initial existence. . . . The people who told nursery rhymes for centuries would be totally boggled if they could suddenly experience them the way children do here and now, as a collection of references to things they never see or do, to places they have never heard of and may never visit, told in words they will sometimes meet only in those verses."

Out of concern that his own children were learning that "the imagination leads always and only to the holy city of elsewhere," Lee decided to build his imaginary "city" from the language of familiar objects—elements of contemporary life made extraordinary by their unique use and sound in verse. Maintaining that "you are poorer if you never find your own time and place speaking words of their own," he believes the "fire hydrants and hockey sticks" of today can be the stuff of nursery rhymes, just as the curds and whey were for children of a previous time. Thus, he says, "to look for living nursery rhymes in the hockey-sticks and high-rises that [children know] first-hand [is not] to go on a chauvinistic trip, nor to wallow in a fad of trendy relevance. It [is] nothing but a rediscovery of what Mother Goose [has been] about for centuries."

Lee's poetic narratives, tongue-twisters, and riddles have been compared to the nonsense verse of Lewis Carroll and A. A. Milne. Lee, however, emphasizes the here-and-now objects of daily life in his work—things children may or may not recognize. Canadian places, history, politics, and colloquial diction, as well as purely invented words, all play a part in his pieces. Many critics feel the readability and repeatability of the poems—rather than references to far-away places—are what fascinates young children. As Betsy English writes in *In Review: Canadian Books for Children,* the strong rhythms, rhymes, and other sound devices in Lee's work produce "a sense of gaiety, an appeal that shouts for reading aloud."

BIOGRAPHICAL/CRITICAL SOURCES:

PERIODICALS

Books in Canada, February, 1980, p. 21; December, 1984, p. 12; December, 1993, p. 37.
Canadian Children's Literature, number 4, 1976; number 33, 1984, p. 15; number 42, 1986, p. 103; number 52, 1988, p. 56; number 63, 1991, p. 61-71; number 67, 1992, p. 102.
Canadian Forum, February, 1986, p. 38.
Canadian Literature, autumn, 1989, p. 228.
Canadian Materials, March, 1992, p. 86; March-April, 1994, p. 46.
Christian Science Monitor, October 5, 1984, p. 88.
Essays on Canadian Writing, Spring, 1988, p. 110-22; spring, 1994, p. 126-31.
In Review: Canadian Books for Children, spring, 1971, winter, 1975.

New Yorker, December 1, 1975, p. 184.
New York Times Book Review, November, 1977, p. 47.
Poetry, February, 1970, p. 353.
Quill & Quire, November, 1983, p. 25; November, 1984, p. 11; August, 1985, p. 44; fall, 1991, p. 35; October, 1993, p. 28.
Saturday Night, January, 1978, p. 74; November, 1979, p. 61.

* * *

Le ROSSIGNOL, James Edward 1866-1969

PERSONAL: Born October 24, 1866, in Quebec, Canada; died December 4, 1969; son of Peter (a merchant) and Mary (Gillespie) Le Rossignol; married Jessie Katherine (one source says Catherine) Ross, September 2, 1898; children: Edward Ross, Helen, Marian Henderson. *Education:* McGill College, A.B., 1888; Leipzig University, A.M., Ph.D., 1892. *Avocational interests:* Trout and salmon fishing, bridge, chess, college football, reading.

CAREER: University professor, fiction and nonfiction writer. Public school teacher, Montreal, Quebec, Canada, 1888-89; Clark University, Worcester, MA, fellow in psychology, 1892; University of Ohio, professor and department chair of psychology and ethnics, 1892-94; University of Denver, Colorado, professor of economics, 1894-1911, also served stint as chair of history and economics department and chair of economics department; University of Nebraska, professor of political economy, 1908-09 (on leave from University of Denver), professor of economics, 1911-44, director of School of Commerce, 1913-19, dean of School of Commerce, and founder and head of College of Business Administration, 1919-41. McGill University, special lecturer in economics, 1900; University of Wisconsin, lecturer in political science, summer, 1903; Stanford University, acting professor of economics, summer, 1923, and University of California at Los Angeles, summer, 1926. Lancaster County Fuel Committee, chair, 1917-19; University of Nebraska Council on Postwar Reconstruction, chair, 1943-45; Lincoln Committee of British War Relief Society, chair.

MEMBER: American Academy of Political and Social Science, American Economic Association, American Association of Collegiate Schools of Business (president 1925-26), Canadian Authors' Association, Nebraska Writers Guild (president 1930-31), Denver Philosophical Society (president 1902-03), Colorado Schoolmasters' Club, Rotary Club, The Club, Round Table (Lincoln, NE), Chi Phi, Beta Gamma Sigma, Alpha Kappa Psi, Phi Beta Kappa.

WRITINGS:

The Ethical Philosophy of Samuel Clarke, [Leipzig], 1892.

Monopolies Past and Present, Crowell (New York), 1901.
Taxation in Colorado, Bishop (Denver), 1902.
History of Higher Education in Colorado, Government Printing Office (Washington, D.C.), 1903.
Orthodox Socialism: A Criticism, Crowell, 1907.
Little Stories of Old Quebec (short stories), Eaton & Mains (New York), 1908.
(With William Downie Stewart) *State Socialism in New Zealand,* Crowell, 1910.
Jean Baptiste: A Story of French Canada (novel), Dent (Toronto), 1915.
What Is Socialism?: An Explanation and Criticism of the Doctrines and Proposals of "Scientific Socialism," Crowell, 1921.
Economics for Everyman: An Introduction to Social Economics, Holt (New York), 1923.
First Economics, Shaw (Chicago and New York), 1926.
The Beauport Road (Tales of Old Quebec) (short stories), McClelland & Stewart (Toronto), 1928.
The Flying Canoe (La Chasse-galerie) (short stories), McClelland & Stewart, 1929.
The Habitant-Merchant (short stories), Macmillan (Toronto), 1939.
From Marx to Stalin: A Critique of Communism, Crowell, 1940.
Backgrounds to Communist Thought, Crowell, 1968.

Also author of *Inflation and How to Scotch It,* 1943.

SIDELIGHTS: James Edward Le Rossignol, a university professor of wide-ranging interests, often wrote moralistic fiction set in an idealized rural Quebec of the past. Born and educated in Quebec, Le Rossignol worked as a schoolteacher briefly before travelling to Germany to complete his education at Leipzig University. He then began his lifelong career as a university professor in the United States. In addition to teaching in the fields of psychology, economics, and political science, he also headed the University of Nebraska's School of Commerce and helped found its College of Business Administration. His numerous publications reflect his expertise in these disciplines, though he most often published in the field of economics, in particular on the economic theory of socialism.

Le Rossignol's five volumes of fiction, published between 1908 and 1939, combine concepts from his various academic interests with simple, folkloric characters and settings, according to John Stockdale in *Dictionary of Literary Biography.* Stockdale remarked: "[Le Rossignol's] detailed grasp of all these fields informs his primarily rural fiction, making for a stimulating blend of simple settings and complex issues." Drawing on folktales and his memory of life in rural Quebec in the nineteenth century, Le Rossignol composed *Little Stories of Old Quebec, The Beauport Road (Tales of Old Quebec), The Flying Canoe (La Chasse-galerie),* and *The Habitant-Merchant,* four collections of short stories. The most accomplished of these, *The Habitant-Merchant,* contains stories that juxtapose a paradoxically naive commercial salesperson with the wise but rustic local merchant.

Le Rossignol's novel, *Jean Baptiste: A Story of French Canada,* concerns a young man who embodies the conflict between Roman Catholic Quebec's traditional values and the secular ambitions of a more modern generation. According to critics, the novel depicts an idealized rural past that was destroyed by industrialization and the commercial values of the modern world. Like other French-Canadian novels written during the first half of the twentieth century, *Jean Baptiste* evokes "the idea that the heart of the nation rests in the people, in the old habits of the farm communities, and in their sturdy support of the Roman Catholic religion," Stockdale observed.

Like other writers of his generation and background, Le Rossignol lamented the passing of a more simple life in the Canadian countryside in stories that drew on folktales and stock characters to draw attention to the value of tradition. While he was best known during his lifetime as a university professor and administrator, and as the author of several well-written books on economics, Le Rossignol's five volumes of fiction provide a revealing look at rural life in Quebec in the late nineteenth century.

BIOGRAPHICAL/CRITICAL SOURCES:

BOOKS

Dictionary of Literary Biography, Volume 92: *Canadian Writers, 1890-1920,* Gale, 1990, pp. 196-97.

*   *   *

L'ILLETTRE
  See BERNARD, Harry

*   *   *

LITTLE, (Flora) Jean   1932-

PERSONAL: Born January 2, 1932, in T'ai-nan, Formosa (now Taiwan); daughter of John Llewellyn (a physician and surgeon) and Flora (a physician; maiden name, Gauld) Little. *Education:* University of Toronto, B.A., 1955; attended Institute of Special Education; received teaching certificate from University of Utah. *Religion:* Christian. *Avocational interests:* Designing and hooking rugs.

ADDRESSES: Home—198 Glasgow St. N., Guelph, Ontario, Canada N1H 4X2.

CAREER: Teacher of children with motor handicaps, Canada; specialist teacher at Beechwood School for Crip-

pled Children, Guelph, Ontario; writer. Visiting instructor at Institute of Special Education and Florida University; summer camp director and leader of church youth groups.

MEMBER: Canadian Authors Association, Writers' Union of Canada, Authors League of America, Council for Exceptional Children, United Church Women.

AWARDS, HONOURS: Canadian Children's Book Award, joint award of American and Canadian branches of Little, Brown, 1961, for *Mine for Keeps;* Vicky Metcalf Award, Canadian Authors Association, 1974, for body of work inspirational to Canadian boys and girls; Governor General's Literary Award for Children's Literature, Canada Council, 1977, for *Listen for the Singing;* Children's Book Award, Canada Council, 1979; Children's Book of the Year Award, Canadian Library Association, and Ruth Schwartz Award, both 1985, for *Mama's Going to Buy You a Mockingbird;* Boston Globe-Horn Book Honor Award, 1988, for *Little by Little: A Writer's Education;* numerous Junior Literary Guild awards.

WRITINGS:

It's a Wonderful World (poems), privately printed, 1947.
Mine for Keeps, illustrated by Lewis Parker, Little, Brown, 1962.
Home from Far, illustrated by Jerry Lazare, Little, Brown, 1965.
Spring Begins in March, illustrated by Parker, Little, Brown, 1966.
When the Pie Was Opened (poems), Little, Brown, 1968.
Take Wing, illustrated by Lazare, Little, Brown, 1968.
One to Grow On, illustrated by Lazare, Little, Brown, 1969.
Look through My Window, illustrated by Joan Sandin, Harper, 1970.
Kate, Harper, 1971.
From Anna, illustrated by Sandin, Harper, 1972.
Stand in the Wind, illustrated by Emily Arnold McCully, Harper, 1975.
Listen for the Singing, Dutton, 1977.
Mama's Going to Buy You a Mockingbird, Viking, 1984.
Lost and Found, illustrated by Leoung O'Young, Viking, 1985.
Different Dragons, Viking, 1986.
Hey World, Here I Am!, illustrated by Barbara DiLella, Kids Can Press, 1986, illustrated by Sue Truesdell, Harper, 1989.
Little by Little: A Writer's Education (autobiography), Viking, 1987.
Stars Come out Within (autobiography), Penguin, 1990.
(With Maggie de Vries) *Once upon a Golden Apple,* illustrated by Phoebe Gilman, Viking, 1991.

Jess Was the Brave One, illustrated by Janet Wilson, Viking, 1992.

Revenge of the Small Small, illustrated by Wilson, Viking Children's Books, 1993.

Bats about Baseball, illustrated by Kim LaFave, Viking Children's Books, 1995.

Also author of novel *Let Me Be Gentle.* Contributor to periodicals, including *Horn Book, Canadian Library Journal,* and *Canadian Author and Bookman.*

Little's works have been translated into Dutch, German, Danish, Japanese, and Russian.

ADAPTATIONS: Hey World, Here I Am and *Little by Little: A Writer's Education* are available on audiocassette; *Mama's Going to Buy You a Mockingbird* was adapted as a television movie.

SIDELIGHTS: Jean Little is recognized throughout Canada and the United States for her candid and unsentimental portrayals of adolescent life. A teacher of handicapped children, Little herself is only partially sighted, and she uses much of her real-life experience as the basis for her books. Her characters often deal with physical disabilities, including cerebral palsy or blindness, or confront psychological difficulties involving fear or grief. However, none of her characters find magical cures for their problems. Instead they learn to cope with and survive the challenges they face, and thus they are led to greater self-understanding. "Ultimately," explained Meguido Zola in *Language Arts,* "that is the real thrust of Jean Little's novels—recognizing and mastering the enemy within rather than tilting at the one without." For her writings, Little has won numerous awards, including the Canadian Children's Book Award and the Vicky Metcalf Award.

Little was born in 1932 in Formosa (which later became Taiwan). Soon afterward, doctors detected scars over both her corneas, the "windows" that cover the eyes. Though she could see—she responded to light as an infant—her eyesight was significantly impaired, and she was diagnosed as legally blind. Her pupils were also off-center, so she had trouble focusing on one object for more than a brief moment. Later, schoolchildren would taunt her by calling her "cross-eyed."

Fortunately, Little's family was very supportive. Her parents read to her frequently, and as she gained limited vision, they taught her to read on her own. "Reading became my greatest joy," she wrote in her first autobiography, *Little by Little: A Writer's Education.* By 1939 Little's family had moved to Toronto. There she first attended a class for students with vision problems. By fourth grade, however, she transferred into a regular class and no longer received specialized treatment—large-print books, for example, or oversized lettering on the chalkboard. As a re-

sult, she struggled with many everyday tasks. "If I wanted to read what was written on the board," she recalled in *Little by Little,* "I would have to stand up so that my face was only inches away from the writing. Then I would have to walk back and forth, following the words not only with my eyes but with my entire body."

As Little progressed through school, she discovered that she enjoyed writing. Seeing her obvious talent, her father encouraged her and often edited her work. "From the first my Dad was my greatest critic and supporter," she told *Something about the Author* (*SATA*). "He plagued me to rewrite." When Little was fifteen, her father collected and printed her first booklet of poems, *It's a Wonderful World.* And a few years later, when the magazine *Saturday Night* published two of her verses, her father proudly read them aloud. "I listened," she remembered in *Little by Little,* "and [when] his voice broke, I knew why I wanted to be a writer."

Deciding to pursue a degree in English, Little entered Victoria College's English language and literature program. Just before classes began, though, her father suffered a severe heart attack. Throughout the following weeks and months his health improved just slightly, yet his enthusiasm for his daughter's schoolwork never diminished. "When I got to college [my father] did research on every essay topic I had," she recalled in *SATA,* "and insisted on tearing apart everything I wrote. He drove me crazy. Not until he died did I come to appreciate his unflagging zeal on my behalf."

Following her freshman year Little completed her first novel, *Let Me Be Gentle,* about a large family with a mentally retarded six-year-old girl. "When I carefully typed 'The End,' " she wrote in *Little by Little,* "I gazed at that stack of typed pages with intense satisfaction. . . . I was convinced that the entire world would be as fond of my characters as I was. After all, I had written a practically perfect book." Nevertheless, her manuscript was soon returned by publisher Jack McClelland, who pointed out its choppiness and lack of focus. Little was hardly discouraged, though—McClelland also told her she had talent.

In 1955 Little graduated with her bachelor's degree in English, and although she primarily wanted to write, she applied for a position teaching handicapped children. With her experience—she had spent three summers working with children with motor handicaps—and with additional training, she was hired. For the next six years she worked with handicapped children in camps, at special schools, and in their homes. She also taught at the Institute of Special Education in Salt Lake City, Utah, and at Florida University. These years helped inspire her to write for children. "Remembering how I had never found a cross-eyed heroine in a book," she remarked in *Little by Little,*

"I decided to search for books about children with motor handicaps. I did not for one moment intend to limit my students to reading about crippled kids. I knew that . . . they actually became [fictional animal characters] Bambi, Piglet and Wilbur. I did not think they needed a book to help them adjust. I did believe, however, that crippled children had a right to find themselves represented in fiction."

As Little explained to Zola in *Language Arts,* the few books of the late 1950s and early 1960s that did portray handicapped children presented inaccurate views of them. Full of self-pity, the children were usually shown brooding over their limitations while dreaming of becoming more like their "normal" friends. And typically, by each story's end, they would undergo miraculous recoveries. "How my [students] laughed at all this silliness," Little told Zola. "And yet how cheated they felt. And so my first book—for them."

Mine for Keeps turns on Sally Copeland, a young girl with cerebral palsy, a disability frequently resulting from brain damage during birth. In the novel, Sally returns home after years of seclusion in a residential treatment center, then she learns to adjust to classes at a regular school. Her family and friends, too, must adapt to her special needs. *Mine for Keeps* "was different from *Let Me Be Gentle,*" Little recalled in *Little by Little,* "because I had intended the first for my family and friends and only afterwards wondered if it were publishable. This one I had written purposely for strangers to read. I had worked much harder and longer on it." Not knowing exactly how to proceed after her manuscript was finished, Little took the advice of a librarian and submitted the story to the Little, Brown Canadian Children's Book Award committee. And in May of 1961—in a letter signed by the same Jack McClelland who had rejected *Let Me Be Gentle* years earlier—she found out her book had won.

Little dedicated *Mine for Keeps* to her father, and since its publication in 1962 she has gone on to write almost twenty additional books. Among these are *Look through My Window* and *Kate,* a pair of stories that revolve around both Emily, a withdrawn, only child, and Kate, a young girl of both Jewish and Protestant descent. In *Look through My Window* Emily deals with her family's sudden move to the country and with the prolonged visit of her four boisterous cousins. She also begins to recognize the value of her newfound friendship with Kate. In *Kate* the title character struggles to understand not only her religion but also herself and her family's roots. She too learns to treasure her friendship with Emily. "*Kate* is a beautiful tribute to the power of love," concluded John W. Conner in the *English Journal.*

Little addresses the subject of blindness in *From Anna* and *Listen for the Singing,* which won the Governor General's Literary Award for Children's Literature in 1977. In the first story, Anna, a shy and awkward young girl, moves with her family from Germany to Canada just before the start of World War II. The move is painful for her since she not only dreads living in a strange land, she also fears her new teachers—who will undoubtedly criticize her inability to read. When Anna is found to have impaired vision, however, she is placed in a special class, and there she begins to overcome her insecurities. *Listen for the Singing,* which opens the day England declared war on Germany, follows Anna as she begins her first year in a public high school. Because of her nationality, she faces hostility and prejudice, yet she also finds friends who are willing to defend her. In addition she comes to accept her disability and is then able to help her brother survive the shock of a tragic accident. "This is a story of courage, then, in one of its more unspectacular guises," declared Susan Jackel in the *World of Children's Books:* "the courage of a young person who anticipates almost certain humiliation and nonetheless wins through to a number of small victories."

In 1985 Little won the Canadian Children's Book of the Year Award for *Mama's Going to Buy You a Mockingbird.* As the narrative unfolds, twelve-year-old Jeremy learns that his father, Adrian, is dying of cancer. To ease Jeremy's sorrow, Adrian introduces him to Tess, a strong, compassionate young girl who has withstood several tragedies of her own. Through Tess Jeremy discovers the strength to survive his father's death, and he also finds the courage to comfort his grieving mother and sister. "The story has depth and insight," noted a reviewer for the *Bulletin of the Center for Children's Books,* "and it ends on a convincingly positive note."

In 1987, Little chronicled her childhood in an autobiography entitled *Little by Little: A Writer's Education,* which concludes with the announcement that *Mine for Keeps* had been accepted for publication. Three years later, in 1990, Little completed her second autobiographical installment, *Stars Come out Within.* Beginning each chapter with a fitting quote from American poet Emily Dickinson—in whose writings Little finds solace and encouragement—the author details in the work her depression over the subsequent loss of her left eye from glaucoma, and her frustration in dealing with the deteriorating vision in her remaining eye. She also recounts her experiences learning to work with Zephyr, her guide dog, and her struggles to compose her books by using a talking computer invented for blind writers. Eliciting praise from reviewers, *Stars Come out Within* was deemed an uplifting memoir. Phyllis G. Sidorsky in *School Library Journal* decided that "Little's refusal to let her disability dominate her life . . . makes this a memorable account," while a *Horn Book* commentator found that in *Stars Come out Within* "one not only marches with [Little] through the marshes of despair but ultimately ascends with her the mount of triumph."

When not writing Little keeps abreast of her audience by working with young people in the church, schools, and community. She also closely monitors the field of children's literature. "Children's books are chiefly what she reads," observed Zola in *Language Arts*. "She reads them because, for the most part, they are among the few books that still rejoice in life, still pulse with awe and wonder at its miracle, and still communicate a sense of growth and hope and love. It is in this spirit that she writes, to celebrate life."

BIOGRAPHICAL/CRITICAL SOURCES:

BOOKS

Children's Literature Review, Volume 4, Gale, 1982.
Little, Jean, *Little by Little: A Writer's Education,* Viking, 1987.
Little, *Stars Come out Within,* Penguin, 1990.
The Republic of Childhood: A Critical Guide to Canadian Children's Literature in English, Oxford University Press, 1975.
Something about the Author, Volume 68, Gale, 1992.
Something about the Author Autobiography Series, Volume 17, Gale, 1994.

PERIODICALS

Books for Young People, April, 1987; December, 1987; autumn/winter, 1991, p. 24.
Bulletin of the Center for Children's Books, September, 1962; January, 1973; June, 1985, p. 189; October, 1986.
Canadian Children's Literature: A Journal of Criticism and Review, Numbers 5 and 6, 1976; Number 12, 1978.
CM, January, 1986.
English Journal, March, 1972, pp. 434-35.
Horn Book, September, 1988; September, 1989; January/February, 1992, p. 93.
In Review: Canadian Books for Children, autumn, 1970.
Kirkus Reviews, May 1, 1992, p. 613.
Language Arts, January, 1981, pp. 86-92.
Lion and the Unicorn, fall, 1977.
Publishers Weekly, April 6, 1992, p. 63; March 8, 1993, p. 76.
Quill and Quire, November, 1990.
Reader's Digest (Canadian), May, 1990, p. 73.
School Library Journal, October, 1985; October, 1986; June, 1988; July, 1989; January, 1992, p. 129; July, 1992, p. 60.
Times Literary Supplement, June 7, 1985.

World of Children's Books, spring, 1978, pp. 81-83.

*   *   *

LIVESAY, Dorothy (Kathleen) 1909-

PERSONAL: Born October 12, 1909, in Winnipeg, Manitoba, Canada; daughter of John F. B. (general manager of Canadian Press) and Florence (a writer; maiden name, Randal) Livesay; married Duncan Cameron Macnair, August 14, 1937 (deceased); children: Peter, Marcia. *Education:* University of Toronto, Trinity College, B.A., 1931, attended School of Social Work, 1933-34; Sorbonne, University of Paris, Diplome d'Etudes Superieures, 1932; University of British Columbia, M.Ed., 1966. *Politics:* No affiliation. *Religion:* Unitarian Universalist.

ADDRESSES: Home and office—1151 Oxford St., Victoria, British Columbia, Canada V0N 1P0.

CAREER: Poet. Memorial House, Englewood, NJ, social worker, 1935-36; British Columbia Department of Social Welfare, Vancouver, social worker, 1936-39; Toronto Daily Star, Toronto, Ontario, correspondent, 1946-49; documentary scriptwriter, Canadian Broadcasting Corporation (CBC), 1950-55; Young Women's Christian Association (YWCA), Vancouver, British Columbia, young adult director, 1953-55; University of British Columbia, Vancouver, lecturer in English, 1955-56; Vancouver (British Columbia) School Board, high school teacher, 1956-58; UNESCO English Specialist, program specialist in Paris, France, 1958-60, specialist in English-teacher training in Northern Rhodesia (now Zambia), 1960-63; University of British Columbia, lecturer in poetry, department of creative writing, 1965-66; University of New Brunswick, Fredericton, writer-in-residence, 1966-68; University of Alberta, Edmonton, associate professor of English, 1968-71; University of Victoria, Victoria, British Columbia, visiting lecturer in English, 1972-74; University of Manitoba, St. John's College, Winnipeg, writer-in-residence, 1974-75; University of Ottawa, Ottawa, Ontario, writer-in-residence, 1977; Simon Fraser University, Burnaby, British Columbia, writer-in-residence, 1980, associated with creative writing seminar, 1981; University of Toronto, New College, Toronto, writer-in-residence, 1983. Reader of poetry at universities and high schools throughout Canada, 1971-91.

MEMBER: League of Canadian Poets (founding member).

AWARDS, HONOURS: Jardine Memorial prize, 1927, for poetry; Governor General's Literary Award in poetry, 1944, for *Day and Night,* and 1947, for *Poems for People;* Lorne Pierce Medal of Royal Society of Canada, 1947, for *Poems for People;* President's Medal of University of

Western Ontario, 1954, for a single poem, "Lament"; Canada Council grants, 1958, 1975, and 1982; D.Litt., University of Waterloo, 1973, Magill University, 1984, University of Toronto, 1984, University of British Columbia, 1990, University of Victoria, 1990; honorary fellow, St. John's College, University of Manitoba, 1976, and Trinity College, University of Toronto, 1983; Person's Case Award, 1984; Officer, Order of Canada, 1987.

WRITINGS:

POETRY EXCEPT AS INDICATED

Green Pitcher (chapbook), Macmillan (Toronto), 1928.
Signpost, Macmillan, 1932.
Day and Night, Ryerson, 1944.
Poems for People, Ryerson, 1947.
(Editor) *The Collected Poems of Raymond Knister,* Ryerson, 1949.
Call My People Home (chapbook), Ryerson, 1951.
New Poems (chapbook), Emblem Press, 1955.
Selected Poems of Dorothy Livesay, 1926-1956, Ryerson, 1957.
The Colour of God's Face (chapbook), Vancouver Unitarian Service Committee, 1964.
The Unquiet Bed, Ryerson, 1967.
The Documentaries: Selected Longer Poems (poems and reminiscences), Ryerson, 1968.
Plainsongs (chapbook), Fiddlehead Press, 1969.
(Contributor) *How Do I Love Thee: Sixty Poets of Canada (and Quebec) Select and Introduce Their Favourite Poems from Their Own Work* (anthology), edited by John Robert Colombo, M. G. Hurtig (Edmonton), 1970.
(Contributor) *Contexts of Canadian Criticism,* edited by Eli Mandel, University of Chicago Press, 1971.
(Editor with Seymour Mayne) *Forty Women Poets of Canada* (anthology), Ingluvin (Montreal), 1971.
Collected Poems: The Two Seasons, McGraw (Toronto), 1972.
A Winnipeg Childhood (short stories), Peguis Press, 1973.
(Editor) *Woman's Eye: Twelve British Columbian Women Poets* (anthology), Air Publications, 1975.
Ice Age, Press Porcepic, 1975.
Right Hand Left Hand (autobiography), Press Porcepic, 1977.
The Woman I Am, Press Porcepic, 1978.
The Raw Edges, Turnstone Press, 1981.
The Phases of Love, Coach House Press, 1983.
Feeling the Worlds, Fiddlehead Press, 1984.
Beyond War: The Poetry, [Vancouver], 1985.
Selected Poems: The Self-Completing Tree, Press Porcepic, 1986.
Les Ages de l'Amour Guernica Press, 1989.
The Husband (novella), Ragweed Press, 1990.
Journey with Myselves, Douglas & McIntyre, 1991.

Also author of monographs and of "Call My People Home," a documentary drama about Japanese-Canadians, produced by the CBC, 1950.

Contributor to anthologies, including *Book of Canadian Poetry,* Oxford University Press; *Oxford Book of Canadian Verse, Penguin Anthology of Canadian Poetry, Canadian Anthology,* W. J. Gage; *Anthology of Commonwealth Poetry,* 1966; *Poets between the Wars,* edited by Milton T. Wilson, McClelland & Stewart, 1967; *Fifteen Canadian Poets Plus Five,* edited by Gary Geddes, Oxford University Press, 1981; *Canadian Poetry,* Volume 1, edited by John David and Robert Lecker, ECW Press, 1982; and *New Oxford Book of Canadian Verse,* Oxford University Press, 1982.

Contributor to periodicals, including *Canadian Literature, Canadian Forum, Fiddlehead, Quarry, Tamarack Review, Queen's Quarterly, Dalhousie Review, Prison International, Canadian Dimension,* and *Journal of Canadian Fiction.* Editor-in-chief, *CV/II* (a quarterly of poetry criticism), 1975—.

SIDELIGHTS: D. V. Smith writes that Dorothy Livesay "is a poet remarkable for her strong, pioneering personality. For me she is the spirit of Pound—steeped in literature, rugged, artistically and socially conscious. . . . She is probably a major poet of the English language of the 20th century. She is prolific as well as she is brilliant. At any rate, she is just that for me—a major poet."

"Dorothy Livesay believes in the human value of writing poetry, which is to say that she urges people—everyone—to write poems," writes Kent Thompson in discussing *The Unquiet Bed.* She "cannot be tied to any school of poets. . . . Miss Livesay's poems use what is necessary to their success. She is not afraid of rich metaphor, nor even of literary allusions. . . . Miss Livesay seems to have allowed the poems to make their own demands, and she has not imposed patterns on either her poetic craft or her eyesight, which is why, I think, the poems are so successful."

Mary Novik of the Vancouver Sun writes of *Ice Age:* "This volume reaffirms Livesay's presence as the most lyric of our older generation of modern poets. The personal voice runs through her work, always emotional, always immediate. Her love poems are the most frankly sensual of those written in Canada today. In fact, the title seems at first to be ironic, for old age is no ice age to Livesay, but a time of passion and fury." Zoe Huggins of the *Ottawa Citizen* surmises: "For more than 40 years, Dorothy Livesay's poetry has displayed her lively interests. She has an acute social conscience and a vibrant awareness of the changing world outside—and she explores the self honestly and with passion. *Ice Age,* her new collection, is a characteristic blend of intensely personal poems and unabashedly public ones, linked by a concern with aging. Sometimes funny and often pathetic, the public poems describe the plight of the old in a society geared for the young. . . . Livesay dedicates this slim volume 'to my younger' because she has set out to introduce a young world to the perceptions and concerns of those not so young." Livesay commented: "My work has been the evocation of the Canadian scene through the writing of lyrical and documentary poetry from 1928 to 1968. My range of interest as exemplified in the poetry is personal, sexual, social, educational and political. My chief passion is to encourage young poets in self-knowledge and self-expression."

Livesay has traveled in the British Isles, Europe, and Central and East Africa. There is a manuscript collection of her work at the University of Alberta, Edmonton.

BIOGRAPHICAL/CRITICAL SOURCES:

BOOKS

Contemporary Literary Criticism, Gale, Volume 4, 1975, Volume 15, 1980.
Dictionary of Literary Biography, Volume 68: *Canadian Writers, 1920-1959, First Series,* Gale, 1988.
Mandel, Eli, editor, *Contexts of Canadian Literature,* University of Chicago Press, 1974.

PERIODICALS

Canadian Forum, April, 1969.
Canadian Literature, winter, 1971, autumn, 1973, spring, 1974.
Fiddlehead, summer, 1967, March-April, 1969.
Globe and Mail (Toronto), January 26, 1985, April 21, 1990.
The Human Voice, winter, 1967-68.
Queen's Quarterly 4, winter, 1969.

*   *   *

LOWTHER, Pat(ricia Louise) 1935-1975

PERSONAL: Born July 29, 1935, in Vancouver, British Columbia, Canada; murdered, c. September 24, 1975, near Squamish, British Columbia, Canada; daughter of Arthur (a caretaker) and Virginia (a dancer) Tinmuth; married Bill Domphousse, 1953 (divorced, c. 1957); married Roy Armstrong Lowther (a teacher and activist), 1963; children: (first marriage) Alan, Catherine, (second marriage) two daughters. *Education:* Took creative writing classes during the 1950s and early 1960s. *Politics:* Socialist.

CAREER: Worked in many clerical positions in Vancouver, British Columbia, during the 1950s and 1960s; secretary for one year for the New Democratic Party's Little Mountain Constituency, Vancouver, British Columbia, c.

1972; University of British Columbia, Vancouver, creative writing instructor, 1975.

MEMBER: League of Canadian Poets (co-chair, 1975).

AWARDS, HONOURS: Two Canadian Council Grants; a memorial prize given in her name annually.

WRITINGS:

This Difficult Flowering, illustrated by S. Slutsky, Very Stone House (Vancouver, British Columbia), 1968.
(Contributor) *Forty Women Poets of Canada,* edited by Dorothy Livesay, Ingluvin (Montreal, Quebec), 1971.
The Age of the Bird (limited edition unbound portfolio), Blackfish Press, 1972.
Milk Stone (includes "In the Continent Behind My Eyes" and "Moonwalk Summer"), Borealis (Ottawa, Ontario), 1974.
A Stone Diary, Oxford University Press (Toronto, Ontario), 1977.
Final Instructions: Early Uncollected Poems, edited by Dona Sturmanis and Fred Candelaria, *West Coast Review*/Orca Sound Publications (Vancouver, British Columbia), 1980.

Also contributor of poems to periodicals.

SIDELIGHTS: Poet Pat Lowther only lived for forty years, and her literary output was somewhat slender, but "her place in Canadian literature is assured," according to Hilda L. Thomas in the *Dictionary of Literary Biography.* Her first collection, *This Difficult Flowering,* saw print in 1968; posthumous volumes of Lowther's poems were published in 1977 and 1980. Perhaps the most widely read and reviewed of her works is 1977's *A Stone Diary.* Of the poems therein, considered by critics to be Lowther's most mature work, Thomas declared "the tone . . . is unfaltering, the voice austere, calm, yet insistent. There is what fellow poet Milton Acorn has called 'the unmistakable note of truth' in this volume."

Lowther was born Patricia Louise Tinmuth in Vancouver, in 1935. Her parents were of the working class, and, though she was bright and demonstrated a love of writing at an early age, Lowther left school at the age of sixteen to take a clerical job. She married her first husband, Bill Domphousse, when she was only eighteen. Lowther had a son and daughter with Domphousse; when they divorced in 1957, she got custody of the daughter while he kept the son.

Following her divorce, Lowther began taking creative writing classes, which she continued to do through the early 1960s. There she made contacts with Canadian West Coast poets such as Dorothy Livesay and Pat Lane. By 1963 she had married her second husband, Roy Armstrong Lowther, a public school teacher who shared her socialist-leaning political views. Mr. Armstrong's views, in fact, were so radical that eventually he was fired from his teaching position. After that, the couple periodically lived on welfare. Lowther had two more daughters with her second husband.

Lowther's friend Lane—and another acquaintance, Seymour Mayne—owned a small press called the Very Stone House. They encouraged Lowther in her efforts to write poetry, and they eventually published her first volume of poetry, *This Difficult Flowering.* In *This Difficult Flowering,* Thomas judged, "already . . . there is the mark of an original voice, and evidence of Lowther's ability to develop and sustain a complex theme." The critic went on to explain that "the poems seek through a minute and particular observation of the natural world to achieve a dialectical understanding of the tensions and contradictions in human experience."

Lowther's next published collection was a limited edition unbound portfolio entitled *The Age of the Bird.* The poems in *The Age of the Bird* speak of revolution in South American countries; one of them is a eulogy for Chilean poet Pablo Neruda, whose work greatly touched and influenced Lowther. Only one hundred and fifty copies of *The Age of the Bird* were printed.

More well-known is Lowther's third collection, *Milk Stone,* which came off the press in 1974. This volume includes the long poem "In the Continent Behind My Eyes," which, according to Thomas, "creates a mythic, prehistoric world . . . as a vision of evolving human consciousness." The other poems in *Milk Stone* concern themselves primarily with the experiences of women, including relationships and pregnancy. One poem, "Moonwalk Summer," particularly exemplifies these themes.

In the year following the publication of *Milk Stone,* Lowther had had another volume of poetry accepted by Oxford University Press. She had begun teaching creative writing classes at the University of British Columbia, and had become a force within the League of Canadian Poets. Lowther's literary career was on the brink of a major expansion, but she disappeared in 1975, during the month of September. Her body was found three weeks later in a creek near Squamish, British Columbia; nearly two years later, her second husband was convicted of Lowther's murder.

Lowther's last volume, *A Stone Diary,* was published by Oxford University Press in 1977. As she had in *The Age of the Bird,* the poet discusses upheaval in the country of Chile, and offers tribute once more to Neruda in a set of five letter-poems. There are many evocations of violence and pain in *A Stone Diary,* and a number of reviewers found them ironic foreshadowing of the poet's death. In 1980, some unpublished and uncollected poems of Low-

ther's were gathered and edited by Dona Sturmanis and Fred Candelaria under the title *Final Instructions: Early Uncollected Poems.* Since Lowther's murder, a memorial prize has been given every year in her name.

BIOGRAPHICAL/CRITICAL SOURCES:

BOOKS

Dictionary of Literary Biography, Volume 53: *Canadian Writers Since 1960, First Series,* Gale, 1986.

PERIODICALS

Canadian, June 5, 1976, pp. 13-19.
Canadian Literature, autumn, 1977, pp. 21-29.*

—*Sketch by Elizabeth Wenning*

*　　*　　*

LUNN, Janet (Louise Swoboda) 1928-

PERSONAL: Born December 28, 1928, in Dallas, TX; naturalized Canadian citizen, 1963; daughter of Herman Alfred (a mechanical engineer) and Margaret (Alexander) Swoboda; married Richard Lunn (a teacher), 1950 (died, 1987); children: Eric, Jeffrey, Alexander, Katherine, John. *Education:* Attended Queen's University of Kingston, 1947-50. *Politics:* New Democratic Party. *Hobbies and other interests:* Art, archeology, history, sketching, gardening, and compulsive reading.

ADDRESSES: Home—R.R. 2, Hillier, Ontario KK 2J, Canada.

CAREER: Free-lance editor and writer, editorial consultant, and lecturer. Clarke Irwin & Co., Toronto, Ontario, children's editor, 1972-75; writer in residence, Regina Public Library, Regina, Saskatchewan, 1982-83; writer in residence, Kitchener Public Library, Ontario, 1988—.

MEMBER: Writers Union of Canada (chair, 1984-85), Canadian Society of Children's Authors, Illustrators, and Performers, PEN.

AWARDS, HONOURS: Canada Council grant, 1978; Ontario Arts grants, 1978, 1980, and 1983; *The Twelve Dancing Princesses* was named one of the ten best children's books of 1979 by the Canadian Library Association, and was awarded the children's book award from Toronto branch of International Order of Daughters of the Empire, 1980; Vicki Metcalf Award for body of work from Canadian Authors Association, 1981; *The Root Cellar* was awarded the Book of the Year for Children Medal by the Canadian Library Association in 1981, received first honorable mention by the Canada Council of Children's Literature Prize, 1982, named a notable book by the American Library Association in 1983, named an outstanding science trade book for children by a joint committee of the National Science Teachers Association and the Children's Book Council, and was named to the honor list of the International Board of Books for Young People in 1984; *Shadow in Hawthorn Bay* was awarded the Book of the Year for Children Medal by the Canadian Library Association in 1986, and was named to the *Horn Book* honor list of books for older readers in 1989.

WRITINGS:

CHILDREN'S BOOKS

(Adapter) Jakob Ludwig Karl and Wilhelm Karl Grimm, *The Twelve Dancing Princesses,* illustrations by Laszlo Gal, Methuen, 1979.

Amos's Sweater (picture book), illustrations by K. LaFave, Groundwood, 1988, Camden House, 1991.

A Hundred Shining Candles, illustrations by Lindsay Grater, Lester & Orpen Dennys, 1989, Scribner, 1991.

Duck Cakes for Sale (picture book), illustrations by Kim LaFave, Groundwood (Toronto), 1989.

YOUNG ADULT FICTION

Double Spell (mystery), illustrations by Emily Arnold McCully, Peter Martin, 1968, published with illustrations by A. M. Calder, Heinemann, 1985, also published as *Twin Spell,* Harper, 1969.

The Root Cellar, Lester & Orpen Dennys, 1981, Scribner, 1983.

Shadow in Hawthorn Bay, illustrations by Emma Chichester-Clark, Lester & Orpen Dennys, 1986, Scribner, 1987.

One Proud Summer, Penguin, 1988.

OTHER

(With husband, Richard Lunn) *The County* (history of Prince Edward County, Ontario), County of Prince Edward, 1967.

Larger Than Life (Canadian historical profiles), illustrations by Emma Hesse, Press Procepic, 1979.

(With Christopher Moore) *The Story of Canada* (history), illustrations by Alan Daniel, Lester & Orpen Dennys, 1990.

(Editor) *The Unseen: Scary Stories,* Lester, 1994.

Also author of scripts for Canadian Broadcasting Corporation. Contributor of articles and short stories to periodicals, including *Starting Points in Language Arts.*

WORK IN PROGRESS: The Rowan Tree, a historical novel for young people; a picture book.

SIDELIGHTS: American-born Canadian author, editor, and reviewer, Janet Lunn has crafted award-winning fiction that melds fantasy and mystery with historical accu-

racy. Valuing the past and close family relationships, Lunn draws upon her own national duality as well as her keen interest in history in books that frequently explore the search for identity, whether national or individual. In addition to her novels for young adults, Lunn has written nonfiction about Canadian heroes and history, has adapted a fairy tale, and has contributed text to a couple of children's picture books.

Born in Dallas, Texas, in 1928, Lunn was raised in Vermont, New York, and New Jersey, before journeying to Canada to complete her education at Queen's University in Ontario. She became a Canadian citizen after her marriage and the birth of her children. She started writing in her early twenties, articles, stories, and reviews of children's books, but was nearly forty when she published her first book, *The County,* a history of Prince Edward County in Ontario that she co-authored with her husband.

Most of Lunn's work is fictional, though. And in an autobiographical essay in *Twentieth-Century Children's Writers,* she explains that she likes to set her stories in different historical periods: "I like how events in one time are connected to events in other times and I sometimes wonder if time mightn't flow in more than one direction—like a reversing falls." In her first published novel, *Double Spell,* which was issued in the United States under the title *Twin Spell,* Lunn writes about twin sisters who become involved in a mystery when they discover an old doll in an antique shop. Lunn superimposes nineteenth-century Toronto on the present as the twins are controlled by memories of events that occurred in the early 1800s. The sisters search for information about the doll's origins and almost duplicate a tragedy that struck their own ancestors, says Margaret A. Dorsey in *School Library Journal,* referring to the book as a "mildly chilling story of ghostly possession."

Lunn believes in ghosts; she believes she shares her Hillier home with a friendly female ghost. And in her award-winning *The Root Cellar,* Lunn writes about this house. Rosa, an orphan from New York, is sent to Canada to live with relatives after her grandmother dies. She discovers she can travel through time by going back and forth through the root cellar. She goes back to the 1860s where she meets Susan and Will; and when Will does not return home from the Civil War, she and Susan travel to Virginia to look for him. Writing in the *Times Literary Supplement,* Stephanie Nettell finds the book "a marvellously warm, slightly old-fashioned, piece of storytelling." And according to Kathleen Leverich in the *Christian Science Monitor,* the book "brings to life an historical period and its formative events, as it deftly depicts one contemporary adolescent's struggle to discover who she is and where she belongs." In her acceptance speech for the Canadian Library Association Book of the Year Award, reprinted in *Canadian Library Journal,* Lunn says that the book is about "duality and reconciliation," adding that "it's a story of friendship across and through time, of growing up and belonging. It's a story of opposites—of civil war, of here and there, of then and now and young and old, of one reality and another—and it's a story of where those opposites touch and are sometimes reconciled, that precarious, elusive place where writers live, in and out and at the edge of two worlds." Calling Rosa "a ghost of the future," Jean M. Mercier writes in *Publishers Weekly* that "Lunn melds past and present neatly" in a ghost story that is "quietly humorous rather than terrifying."

In another story about ghosts, *Shadow in Hawthorn Bay*, Lunn writes about fifteen-year-old Mary, a Scottish Highlander who, in 1815, psychically intuits that her Canadian cousin is in trouble and needs her. She journeys across the ocean to discover that he has committed suicide; however, Mary adjusts to a different culture, makes connections with the community, and marries a neighbor. She also comes to terms with her gift of seeing both the past and the future. In *School Library Journal*, Michael Cart praises Lunn's ability to "integrate these psychic elements into her plot without compromising the credibility of its ample historical detail." Lauding Lunn's style and "her strong storytelling ability," Sarah Ellis writes in *Horn Book* that "this idea, that Mary and indeed all young people are the old ones of the future, reveals a respect for the young adult both as audience and as subject that is rare and welcome."

"There are many riches to savour in Janet Lunn's novels—not the least of which is the engrossing narrative drive—but the quality I appreciate most is their completeness," writes Sandra Martin in *Books for Young People*. "The facts are accurate, the settings authentic, and the characters so plausible that one slides effortlessly into her world." A sense of place and identity are vital to Lunn's stories, which frequently involve ghosts or other misfits. "The message that people must often return to what they are running away from in order to be able to accept themselves is an important one," states James Harrison in *Canadian Children's Literature*. "But so is the message that

they can move on, can find new aspects to themselves by adjusting to a new and initially daunting environment."

BIOGRAPHICAL/CRITICAL SOURCES:

BOOKS

Canada Writes!, Writers' Union of Canada, 1977.
Children's Literature Review, Volume 18, Gale, 1989.
Lunn, Janet, Autobiographical essay in *Twentieth-Century Children's Writers*, 3rd edition, St. James, 1989.
Profiles, revised edition, Canadian Library Association, 1975.
Sixth Book of Junior Authors & Illustrators, edited by Sally Holmes Holtze, Wilson, 1989.

PERIODICALS

Booklist, November 15, 1990.
Books for Young People, February, 1987, p. 5.
Bulletin of the Center for Children's Books, June, 1987.
Canadian Children's Literature, Volume 46, 1987, pp. 60-63; Volume 57, 1990.
Canadian Library Journal, October, 1982, pp. 329-30.
Christian Science Monitor, November 4, 1983.
Globe and Mail (Toronto), November 29, 1986.
Horn Book, December, 1969; October, 1983; September/October, 1987, pp. 619, 640-43.
In Review, April, 1980.
Kirkus Reviews, March 1, 1980; June 15, 1983; May 15, 1987.
Maclean's, December 15, 1986; December 26, 1988.
New York Times Book Review, May 11, 1980.
Observer, August 7, 1983; April 3, 1988.
Publishers Weekly, May 13, 1983, p. 56; May 8, 1987.
Quill and Quire, March, 1980; October, 1994, p. 38.
School Librarian, June, 1986.
School Library Journal, October 15, 1969, pp. 3821-22; March, 1980; September, 1983; September, 1987, p. 197.
Times Literary Supplement, March 29, 1985, p. 354.
Voice of Youth Advocates, August/September, 1987.

M

MacEWEN, Gwendolyn (Margaret) 1941-1987

PERSONAL: Born September 1, 1941, in Toronto, Ontario, Canada; died November 30, 1987, in Toronto; daughter of Alick James and Elsie Doris (Mitchell) MacEwen.

CAREER: Writer. Left school at eighteen to concentrate on writing poetry and fiction. Writer in residence, University of Western Ontario, 1984-85, and University of Toronto, 1986-87. Has given numerous poetry readings across Canada.

MEMBER: PEN, Writers' Union of Canada, League of Canadian Poets, Playwrights Union of Canada, Association of Canadian Television and Radio Artists.

AWARDS, HONOURS: Several Canada Council grants; Governor General's Award for poetry, 1970, for *The Shadow-Maker*; A. J. M. Smith Poetry Award, 1973, for *The Armies of the Moon*.

WRITINGS:

POETRY

Selah, Aleph, 1961.
The Drunken Clock, Aleph, 1961.
The Rising Sun, Contact Press, 1963, published as *The Rising Fire,* 1964.
A Breakfast for Barbarians, Ryerson, 1966.
The Shadow-Maker, Macmillan, 1969.
The Armies of the Moon, Macmillan, 1972.
Magic Animals: Selected Poems Old and New, Macmillan, 1974, published as *Magic Animals: Selected Poetry of Gwendolyn MacEwen,* Stoddart Publishing, 1984.
The Fire-Eaters, Oberon, 1976.
The T. E. Lawrence Poems, Mosaic, 1982.
Earthlight: Selected Poetry of Gwendolyn MacEwen, 1963-1982, General Publishing, 1982.

Afterworlds, McClelland & Stewart, 1987.

OTHER

Julian the Magician: A Novel, Corinth Books, 1963.
King of Egypt, King of Dreams: A Novel, Macmillan, 1971.
Norman (stories), Oberon, 1972.
Mermaids and Ikons: A Greek Summer (travel), Anansi, 1978.
The Trojan Women: A Play (first produced as *The Trojan Women: a new version* in Toronto at St. Lawrence Centre, November, 1978), Playwrights Co-Op, 1979.
(Translator with Nikos Tsingos) *Trojan Women: "The Trojan Women" by Euripedes and "Helen and Orestes" by Ritsos,* Exile Editions, 1981.
The Chocolate Moose (juvenile), illustrated by Barry Zaid, NC Press, 1981.
(Translator) *The Honey Drum: Seven Tales from Arab Lands* (juvenile), Mosaic, 1983.
Noman's Land: Stories, Coach House Press, 1985.
Dragon Sandwiches (juvenile), Black Moss Press, 1987.

Also author of several documentaries, verse dramas, and of radio plays, including "Terror and Erebus," "Tesla," and "The World of Neshiah." Translator of some of Greek poet Yannis Ritsos's writings. Work represented in numerous anthologies and literary magazines. Much of her poetry has been translated into Swedish, Italian, Portuguese, French, and Spanish for anthologies.

SIDELIGHTS: Gwendolyn MacEwen once told *CA*: "I write in order to make sense of the chaotic nature of experience, of reality—and also to create a bridge between the inner world of the *psyche* and the 'outer' world of things. For me, language has enormous, almost magical power, and I tend to regard poetry in much the same way as the ancients regarded the chants or hymns used in holy festivals: as a means of invoking the mysterious forces which move the world and shape our destinies. "I write to communicate joy, mystery, passion—not the joy that naively exists without knowledge of pain, but that joy which arises out of and conquers pain. I want to construct a myth." MacEwen "has indeed constructed one," according to Margaret Atwood in *Second Words: Selected Critical Prose.* "MacEwen is not a poet interested in turning her life into myth; rather, she is concerned with translating her myth into life, and into the poetry which is a part of it. The informing myth, developed gradually but with increasing clarity in her poetry, is that of the Muse, author and inspirer of language and therefore of the ordered verbal cosmos, the poet's universe." Critics have praised MacEwen's poetry for its sounds and imagery. Douglas Barbour, for example, writes in *Dalhousie Review* that MacEwen "has a powerful command of tone, an ability to create mesmerizing patterns of sound and rhythm which make her best poems truly enchanting." And D. G. Jones explains in *Butterfly on Rock: A Study of Themes and Images in Canadian Literature* that "MacEwen is another who cannot resist the appeal of old visions, and her language becomes hieratic, incantatory. Yet she does not abandon her immediate world or the intonations, the accent of contemporary speech. She too would suggest that the concern to be inclusive, to take an inventory, to make a dumb wilderness vocal, and in a speech that is true to its time and its place, cuts across the division frequently drawn between myth-makers and realists. All eloquence need not be lies, all myths academic."

BIOGRAPHICAL/CRITICAL SOURCES:

BOOKS

Atwood, Margaret, *Second Words: Selected Critical Prose,* Anansi, 1982.
Bartley, Jan, *Invocations: The Poetry and Prose of Gwendolyn MacEwen,* University of British Columbia Press, 1983.
Contemporary Literary Criticism, Volume 13, Gale, 1980.
Dictionary of Literary Biography, Volume 53: *Canadian Writers since 1960, First Series,* Gale, 1986.
Jones, D. G., *Butterfly on Rock: A Study of Themes and Images in Canadian Literature,* University of Toronto Press, 1970.

PERIODICALS

Canadian Literature, summer, 1964, summer, 1970, summer, 1977.
Dalhousie Review, winter, 1975-76.
Globe and Mail (Toronto), February 22, 1986.
Saturday Night, January, 1972.

OBITUARIES:

PERIODICALS

Times (London), December 3, 1987.*

MacGREGOR, Mary Esther 1874(?)-1961 (Marian Keith)

PERSONAL: Born c. August 27, 1874, in Rugby, Oro, Ontario, Canada; died February 10, 1961, in Toronto, Ontario, Canada; daughter of John (a schoolteacher) and Mary (McIan) Miller; married Donald Campbell MacGregor (a missionary), 1909. *Education:* Attended Collegiate Institute, Orilla; graduated from the Toronto Normal School, 1896. *Religion:* Presbyterian.

CAREER: Central Public School, Orilla, Ontario, teacher, 1899-1906; author.

AWARDS, HONOURS: Honored by Toronto Women's Press Club, 1911.

WRITINGS:

UNDER PSEUDONYM MARIAN KEITH

Duncan Polite, the Watchman of Glenoro (published serially in *Westminster* magazine, 1904-05), Westminster (Toronto), and Revell (New York City), 1905, Hodder & Stoughton (London), 1906.
The Silver Maple (published serially in *Westminster*), Westminster, Revell, and Hodder & Stoughton, 1906.
Treasure Valley (published serially in *Westminster*), Westminster, Hodder & Stoughton, and Doran (New York City), 1908.
'Lizbeth of the Dale, Westminster, and Hodder & Stoughton (New York City and London), 1910.
The Black Bearded Barbarian: The Life of George Leslie Mackay of Formosa, Foreign Missions Committee, Presbyterian Church of Canada (Toronto), and Missionary Education Movement (New York City), 1912.
The End of the Rainbow, Westminster and Hodder & Stoughton/Doran (New York City), 1913, as *The Pot o' Gold: At the End of the Rainbow,* Hodder & Stoughton, 1914.
In Orchard Glen, McClelland, Goodchild & Stewart (Toronto), and Doran, 1918.
Little Miss Melody, McClelland & Stewart and Doran, 1921.
The Bells of St. Stephen's, McClelland & Stewart and Doran, 1922, Hodder & Stoughton, 1923.
A Gentleman Adventurer: A Story of the Hudson's Bay Company, McClelland & Stewart and Doran, 1924, Hodder & Stoughton, 1925.
Under the Grey Olives, McClelland & Stewart and Doran, 1927.
The Forest Barrier, McClelland & Stewart, 1930.
(With Mabel Burns and L. M. Montgomery) *Courageous Women,* McClelland & Stewart, 1934.
Glad Days in Galilee: A Story of the Boyhood of Jesus, McClelland & Stewart (New York City), 1935, as *Boy of*

Nazareth, Abingdon-Cokesbury (New York City), 1950.
As a Watered Garden, McClelland & Stewart, 1947.
Yonder Shining Light, McClelland & Stewart, 1948.
Lilacs in the Dooryard, McClelland & Stewart, 1952.
The Grand Lady, McClelland & Stewart, 1960.

Contributor to periodicals, including *Westminster.*

SIDELIGHTS: Under the pseudonym Marian Keith, author Mary Esther MacGregor wrote several novels about small-town life in rural Ontario. Along with fellow Canadians L. M. Montgomery and Nellie McClung, MacGregor was considered part of a revival of writing by women that occurred during the early decades of the twentieth century. Her rural upbringing, Scottish heritage, and strong religious sentiments played a strong part in novels rife with humorous characters, Scots dialect, and the interrelationship between young and old, Presbyterian and Methodist, and Scots and their English and Irish neighbors.

Several of MacGregor's novels were drawn from Canadian history: *The Silver Maple* recounts the 1885 expedition of lumbermen up the Nile River to rescue a fellow-Canadian, General Charles Gordon, at Khartoum; *The Forest Barrier* describes the early-nineteenth-century roots of Scottish-Canadian history; and in *A Gentleman Adventurer; A Story of the Hudson's Bay Company,* she recounts the events surrounding the Red River Rebellion of 1869-70, as Louis Riel fought for self-rule in what is now the province of Manitoba. She also collaborated on *Courageous Women,* a collection of biographical portraits of famous Canadian women written with authors Montgomery and Mabel Burns McKinley.

MacGregor's religious faith proved to be another inspiration for her writing. *Glad Days in Galilee: A Story of the Boyhood of Jesus,* published in 1935, is a fictional rendering of Jesus Christ's childhood written for church school readers. And in *Little Miss Melody,* a pastor provides a young girl with the inspiration to do good works.

In the early 1940s, MacGregor and her husband moved to Owen Sound, which would become the setting for three of her last four novels. 1947's *As a Watered Garden* illustrates the strength of living in a small, tightly linked community of caring neighbors through its telling depiction of the everyday lives of farm women; *Yonder Shining Light,* published a year later, and MacGregor's 1952 novel, *Lilacs in the Dooryard,* completed her trilogy revolving around a traditional, rural, Christian community. While popular with contemporary readers in the early 1900s, the simplistic, rural subject matter and overt religious sentiment underlying MacGregor's novels has, over time, made them more suitable for younger readers.

BIOGRAPHICAL/CRITICAL SOURCES:

BOOKS

Dictionary of Literary Biography, Volume 92, *Canadian Writers, 1890-1920,* Gale, 1990, pp. 169-71.

PERIODICALS

Saturday Night, July 22, 1910.*

*   *   *

MacLENNAN, (John) Hugh   1907-1990

PERSONAL: Born March 20, 1907, in Glace Bay, Nova Scotia, Canada; died November 7, 1990, in Montreal, Quebec, Canada; son of Samuel John (a doctor) and Katherine (MacQuarrie) MacLennan; married Dorothy Duncan (a writer), June 22, 1936 (died, 1957); married Frances Walker, May 15, 1959. *Education:* Dalhousie University, B.A. (honors), 1929; Oriel College, Oxford (Rhodes Scholar), B.S., 1932; Princeton University, M.A., Ph.D., 1935. *Avocational interests:* Tennis and gardening.

CAREER: Writer and teacher, 1935-62; McGill University, Montreal, Quebec, teacher, 1951-67, professor of English literature, 1967-85.

MEMBER: Royal Society of Literature (United Kingdom), Royal Society of Canada (fellow), McGill Faculty Club, Montreal Indoor Tennis Club.

AWARDS, HONOURS: Guggenheim fellowship, 1943; Governor General's Award in fiction for *Two Solitudes,* 1946, *The Precipice,* 1949, and *The Watch That Ends the Night,* 1959; Governor General's Literary Award in nonfiction for *Cross Country,* 1950, and *Thirty and Three,* 1955; Lorne Pierce Medal, 1952, for contributions to Canadian literature; Molson Award for services to literature and the nation, 1967; Canadian Authors Association Literary Award for fiction, 1982, for *Voices in Time.* Honorary degrees from many institutions of higher learning, including D.Litt. from University of Western Ontario, University of Manitoba, Waterloo Lutheran University, McMaster University, and Laurentian University; LL.D. from Dalhousie University, University of Saskatchewan, and University of Toronto; D.C.L. from Bishop's University.

WRITINGS:

Oxyrhynchus: An Economic and Social Study, Princeton University Press, 1935.
Barometer Rising (novel), Duell, Sloan & Pearce, 1941.
Two Solitudes (novel), Duell, Sloan & Pearce, 1945.
The Precipice (novel), Duell, Sloan & Pearce, 1948.
Cross Country (nonfiction), Collins, 1949.
Each Man's Son (novel), Little, 1951.

The Present World As Seen in Its Literature (speech), University of New Brunswick, 1952.

Thirty and Three (essays), edited by Dorothy Duncan, Macmillan, 1954.

The Future of the Novel As an Art Form (lecture), University of Toronto Press, 1959.

The Watch That Ends the Night (novel), Scribner, 1959.

Scotchman's Return and Other Essays, Scribner, 1960, published in England as *Scotman's Return and Other Essays,* Heinemann, 1960.

(Editor) *McGill: The Story of a University,* Allen & Unwin, 1960.

Seven Rivers of Canada, Macmillan (Toronto), 1961, published as *The Rivers of Canada,* Scribner, 1962.

The History of Canadian-American Relations (lecture), Goddard College, 1963.

Return of the Sphinx (novel), Scribner, 1967.

The Colour of Canada, McClelland, 1967, Little, 1968, revised edition, 1978.

The Other Side of Hugh MacLennan: Selected Essays Old and New, edited by Elspeth Cameron, Macmillan (Toronto), 1978.

Voices in Time (novel), Macmillan (Toronto), 1980, St. Martin's, 1981.

Quebec, photographs by Mia and Klaus, McClelland & Stewart, 1981.

On Being a Maritime Writer, Mount Allison University, 1984.

Wrote monthly essay for *Montrealer,* 1951-57, and weekly column for Toronto Star syndicate, 1962-63; contributor to *Holiday, Saturday Review, Maclean's Magazine* and other periodicals.

ADAPTATIONS: Two Solitudes was filmed in 1978.

SIDELIGHTS: To anyone who wants to understand Canada, Edmund Wilson, writing in *O Canada,* recommended a reading of the novels and essays of Hugh MacLennan. MacLennan, he wrote, was "so special a figure that he requires some explanation. I should describe him as a Highlander first; a patriotic Nova Scotian second . . . ; a spokesman for Canada third; and—but simultaneously with all of these—a scholar of international culture and a man of the great world." *Dictionary of Literary Biography* contributor Elspeth Cameron explained that MacLennan "was the first Canadian novelist to attempt to set the local stage on which the nation's dramas might be played before an international audience." His essays and novels, especially *Barometer Rising* and *Two Solitudes,* she added, earned him a reputation as "the Grand Old Man of Canadian Letters."

Wilson remembered that he first became interested in MacLennan's work when he read the essays in *Scotchman's Return.* He found therein "a point of view surpris-

ingly and agreeably different from anything else I knew in English. MacLennan writes . . . with much humor and shrewd intelligence about Canada, Scotland, England, the Soviet Union and the United States. I came to recognize that there did now exist a Canadian way of looking at things which had little in common with either the 'American' or the British colonial one and which has achieved a self-confident detachment in regard to the rest of the world."

Barometer Rising, MacLennan's first published novel, drew its story from the author's past. It climaxes with the cataclysmic collision between two ships—one of them carrying a load of TNT—in the harbor of Halifax, Nova Scotia, in 1917, an event that nearly leveled the town and one that MacLennan had witnessed himself. "To Canadian readers," Cameron declared, "*Barometer Rising* seemed to express, as no Canadian novel had yet done, the nationalism that had blossomed gradually over the past two decades." When the novel first appeared in 1941, J. S. Southron wrote in the *New York Times:* "Unless you had been told you could not have known this to be a first novel. . . . Both in conception and workmanship it is first class." Wilson, writing more than twenty years later, said that *Barometer Rising* was the most sustained example of "how excellent Mr. MacLennan's writing can be when he is carried along by the sweep of one of his large descriptions or impassioned actions that are solidly realistic and yet never without their poetry. . . . It seems to me that *Barometer Rising* should not merely be accepted, as it is, as a landmark in Canadian writing but also, as an artistic success, be regarded as one of its authentic classics."

Two Solitudes, MacLennan's second novel, was also enthusiastically reviewed. It examines what Oakland Ross termed in the Toronto *Globe and Mail* "the troubled psychic borderland between Canada's two cultures," the conflict between the Catholic, French-speaking heritage and the Protestant, English-speaking one. It was published (in New York, ironically) to great critical and popular acclaim. "This volume," L. L. Marchland wrote in the *Boston Globe,* "is definitely your passport to two evenings of rare literary delight." Its themes, said Ross, "continue to resonate for Canadians as insistently as they did when the book was first published." *Two Solitudes,* the reviewer concluded, marked "the beginning of something quite new, a Canadian novel that was essentially about Canada." MacLennan reexamined the problem—still a volatile subject in Canada—in *Return of the Sphinx.*

MacLennan's gift for eliciting understanding and appreciation of Canada and its people was in fact one of his most conspicuous talents. But his novels did not meet with unqualified acclaim; Wilson wrote: "In an essay called 'The Story of a Novel,' in which he describes the writing of *The Watch That Ends the Night,* he explains that after putting down 'millions of words' and tearing up 'again and again . . . I refined my style and discovered new techniques I had previously known nothing about.' But when one comes to the novel, it is hard to see what he means by 'new techniques,' except that the story is told partly, by now a pretty familiar device, in a series of flashbacks that alternate with the narrative of the later happenings. The one feature of MacLennan's novels that does seem to me new and interesting is his use of the geographical and the meteorological setting. He always shows us how the characters are situated—as they pursue their intrigues, undergo their ordeals or are driven by their desperate loves—in a vast expanse of land and water, the hardly inhabited spaces of the waste upper margins of a continent."

Therefore, even though his later novels were reviewed with some disappointment, MacLennan had already secured his place in contemporary letters. As Dick Adler said in his *Book World* review of *Return of the Sphinx,* although this was "not so warm and richly woven a novel as *The Watch That Ends the Night,* . . . MacLennan's talent and the personality behind that talent are more than enough to recommend the book most highly." Similarly, Peter Buitenhuis observed in the *New York Times Book Review* that the novel "seems disconnected"; but, he added, "the parts themselves are written with great perception and grace and a rare command of social, professional and political milieux." This ability was in evidence throughout MacLennan's career.

BIOGRAPHICAL/CRITICAL SOURCES:

BOOKS

Buitenhuis, Peter, *Hugh MacLennan,* Forum House, 1969.
Cameron, Elspeth, *Hugh MacLennan: A Writer's Life,* University of Toronto Press, 1981.
Cameron, editor, *Hugh MacLennan 1982: Proceedings of the MacLennan Conference at University College,* University College Canada Studies Program, 1982.
Cockburn, Robert H., *The Novels of Hugh MacLennan,* Harvest House, 1971.
Contemporary Literary Criticism, Gale, Volume 2, 1974; Volume 14, 1980.
Dictionary of Literary Biography, Volume 68: *Canadian Writers, 1920-1959,* Gale, 1988.
Goetsch, Paul, editor, *Hugh MacLennan,* McGraw Hill Ryerson, 1973.
Lucas, Alex, *Hugh MacLennan,* McClelland & Stewart, 1970.
MacLulich, T. D., *Hugh MacLennan,* Twayne, 1983.
Morley, Patricia, *The Immoral Moralists: Hugh MacLennan and Leonard Cohen,* Clarke Irwin, 1972.
Wilson, Edmund, *O Canada,* Farrar, Straus, 1964.

Woodcock, George, *Hugh MacLennan,* Copp Clark, 1969.

PERIODICALS

Books, October 12, 1941.
Book World, November 5, 1967.
Boston Globe, January 17, 1945.
Canadian Forum, January, 1959.
Commonweal, October 1, 1948; April 20, 1951.
Globe and Mail (Toronto), May 18, 1985; April 18, 1987.
New York Times, October 5, 1941.
New York Times Book Review, August 20, 1967.

OBITUARIES:

PERIODICALS

New York Times, November 10, 1990, p. 29.*

*   *   *

MacLEOD, Alistair   1936-

PERSONAL: Born July 20, 1936, in North Battleford, Saskatchewan, Canada; son of Alexander Duncan and Christene (a teacher; maiden name, MacLellan) Mac-Leod; married Anita MacLellan (a homemaker), September 4, 1971; children: Alexander, Lewis, Kenneth, Marion, Daniel, Andrew. *Education:* Nova Scotia Teachers College, teaching certificate, 1956; St. Francis Xavier University, B.A., B.Ed., 1960; University of New Brunswick, M.A., 1961; University of Notre Dame, Ph.D., 1968. *Religion:* Roman Catholic.

ADDRESSES: Home—231 Curry Ave., Windsor, Ontario, Canada N9B 2B4. *Office*—Department of English, Sunset Ave., University of Windsor, Windsor, Ontario, Canada N9B 3P4.

CAREER: Worked variously as miner, logger, and farmhand. Schoolteacher on Port Hood Island, 1956-57; Nova Scotia Teachers College, Truro, lecturer in English, 1961-63; University of Notre Dame, South Bend, IN, lecturer in English, 1964-66; associated with English faculty, Indiana University (now Indiana University-Purdue University) at Fort Wayne, 1966-69; University of Windsor, Windsor, Ontario, professor of English, 1969—; associated with faculty, Banff School of Fine Arts, summer program, 1981-86.

MEMBER: Writers Union of Canada, Writers Federation of Nova Scotia.

AWARDS, HONOURS: Selected as the Canadian participant in a Canada-Scotland writers-in-residence exchange program, 1984-85.

WRITINGS:

SHORT STORIES

The Lost Salt Gift of Blood (short stories; includes "The Boat"), McClelland & Stewart, 1976, published as *The Lost Salt Gift of Blood: New and Selected Stories,* Ontario Review Press, 1988.

As Birds Bring Forth the Sun and Other Stories, McClelland & Stewart, 1986.

Work represented in anthologies, including *Best American Short Stories,* 1969, 1975; *Best Canadian Short Stories; Best Modern Canadian Short Stories,* Hurtig, 1978.

PLAYS

The Lost Salt Gift of Blood, Mulgrave Road Co-Op Theatre Company, tour of twenty Maritime communities, 1982.

The Boat (based on short story), Mulgrave Road Co-Op Theatre Company, tour of Maritimes, spring, 1983, Canadian National Tour, summer-fall, 1983, and tour of England and Scotland, spring, 1984.

OTHER

Author of *A Textual Study of Thomas Hardy's "A Group of Noble Dames,"* 1968. Contributor to periodicals, including *Tamarack Review, Antigonish Review, Canadian Forum, Dalhousie Review, Quarry, Fiddlehead,* and *Amethyst.* Fiction editor of *University of Windsor Review,* 1973—.

WORK IN PROGRESS: A novel; a collection of short stories.

SIDELIGHTS: Short story writer and educator Alistair MacLeod is one of the "most important chronicler[s] in fiction of the landscape and folkways of Cape Breton to appear on the Canadian literary scene in recent years," declares James Doyle in the *Dictionary of Literary Biography.* Known for his concise style and "historic present" narration, MacLeod has published work in periodicals, including several pieces of poetry, and collected many of his stories into two books. As Doyle explains, "Although his creative output is small, . . . [MacLeod] has earned the respect of critics and editors in both Canada and the United States, especially for his mastery of the short-story form."

Born in Saskatchewan in 1936 to natives of Cape Breton Island, MacLeod moved with his family back to Nova Scotia while he was still quite young. He grew up in the small, close-knit Maritime communities which later became central to his writing. MacLeod's work recreates "the scenery and human drama of his native region," describes Doyle. "Virtually all his stories are devoted to the exposition and dramatization of the folkways, socioeco-

nomic realities, and relationships of family and community in Cape Breton." MacLeod also uses a form of narration in which the past is described and remembered in terms of the present in many of his tales. His "repeated use of [this technique] indicates that he values its aura of the old-fashioned, its suggestion of stories being swapped around a hot stove. And even the stories which don't use the technique share a tone of thoughtful nostalgia," notes Laurence Ricou in *Canadian Literature.*

MacLeod's first collection, *The Lost Salt Gift of Blood,* contains seven stories. "Initiation into adulthood, separation from family, return to the place of origin from an adult life faraway, become occasions and themes for the narrators reflections," writes Richard Lemm in *Atlantic Provinces Book Review.* Titles such as "The Return" and "The Road to Rankin's Point" deal with a homecoming; "In the Fall" with a family facing emotional and economic stress; while mining life is the focus of "The Vastness of the Dark." "The Boat," which was adapted for stage, concerns a father and son relationship. The narrator, a college professor, remembers his childhood, especially his deceased father who spent his life as a fisherman. For MacLeod's characters, "a literary education is very much a two-edged sword, serving to alienate characters from their origins even as it releases them from the more gruelling demands of necessary labor," comments *Canadian Literature* contributor Colin Nicholson.

"MacLeod's writing strikes home with immediacy, intensity and poetic beauty," declares Lemm. "MacLeod's stories grow from their roots in a particular place and people to a universality of human experience and insight." Nicholson also praises the "immediacy and intensity" of MacLeod's tales in *The Lost Salt Gift of Blood,* noting: "It is in the sculpting of the emotional infrastructure of any given situation that MacLeod's talent shines." Jon Kertzer, writing in *Canadian Forum,* judges that "The great merit of these stories [in *The Lost Salt Gift of Blood*] is their power and authenticity of detail. . . . The weakness of the book is a tendency to excess," citing that "one tale ceases to dramatize and lapses into moralizing; another indulges in a poolroom melodrama; another allows its tone to become remorselessly elegiac." Kertzer concludes: "But at his best, MacLeod weds his characters to their locales so that each is enriched by the other."

MacLeod published a second collection, *As Birds Bring Forth the Sun and Other Stories,* ten years after *The Lost Salt Gift of Blood.* The stories in *As Birds Bring Forth the Sun* "recall and at the same time transcend the heart of this earlier collection," representing "a mature and complex acceptance of the problematic and ultimately tragic nature of experience," comments Janice Kulyk Keefer in *Antigonish Review.* Stories are played against the backdrop of Atlantic Canada, and include "The Tuning of Perfection" in which a seventy-eight-year-old man watches traditions die or get twisted beyond recognition. Tales of fishermen and miners are also a part of *As Birds Bring Forth the Sun,* as in "Vision," which presents a slice of life in a fishing town, and "The Closing Down of Summer," where the mining group leader justifies his choice of mining over a college education. In "Winter Dog" a man remembers, while waiting for news of a dying relative, the childhood pet that once saved his life. Thomas P. Sullivan praises "Winter Dog" in *Quill & Quire,* writing: "This is memory as private myth (another of MacLeod's recurring themes). The effect is hypnotic; the imagery is burned into the brain and lingers."

"Death, sexual love, and the power of the past: these are the themes that run through all the stories and unify" *As Birds Bring Forth the Sun,* notes David Helwig in *Queen's Quarterly,* judging that the collection has "a powerful poetic unity." "While very much aware of the hardness of life for the people he writes about, MacLeod's wise heart perceives their secret longings, admires their patient strengths, and records with great authority the small triumphs in their struggle for dignity, pride, and love," comments Jack Hodgins in *Books in Canada. American Book Review* contributor Russell Brown declares that "MacLeod is one of the best literary craftsmen in Canada, capable of conveying intense emotions in a prose that never strains for effect."

"MacLeod—ex-miner, ex-logger, ex-farmboy, professor of English and creative writing—blends a country man's clear-eyed and unselfconscious awareness with a sometimes stunning ability to write, to succeed in virtually everything he tries," judges Sullivan. Doyle writes in his conclusion: "The folkloric elements, as well as discursive narrative and interior rumination, are the vital means of exploring and preserving an image of life that relatively few people may have experienced in its specific detail but that is universal in its implications. . . . MacLeod is a subtle, economical, forceful writer, whose small but important output must not be overlooked."

BIOGRAPHICAL/CRITICAL SOURCES:

BOOKS

Contemporary Literary Criticism, Volume 56, Gale, 1989.
Dictionary of Literary Biography, Volume 60: *Canadian Writers since 1960,* Gale, 1987.
Reference Guide to Short Fiction, St. James Press, 1993.

PERIODICALS

American Book Review, May-June, 1988, pp. 10, 21.
Antigonish Review, summer-autumn, 1986, pp. 113-16.
Atlantic Provinces Book Review, December, 1982, p. 9.
Books in Canada, August-September, 1986, pp. 12-13.
Canadian Forum, June-July, 1976, p. 51.

Canadian Literature, spring, 1978, pp. 116-18; winter, 1985, pp. 90-101.
Queen's Quarterly, winter, 1987, pp. 1022-24.
Quill & Quire, May, 1986, p. 25.

*   *   *

MacNEIL, Robert (Breckenridge Ware) 1931-

PERSONAL: Born January 19, 1931, in Montreal, Quebec, Canada; son of Robert A. S. (in Canadian foreign service) and Margaret Virginia (Oxner) MacNeil; married Rosemarie Anne Copland, 1956 (divorced, 1964); married Jane J. Doherty, May 29, 1965 (divorced, 1983); children: (first marriage) Catherine Anne, Ian B.; (second marriage) Alison N., William H. *Education:*Attended Dalhousie University, 1949-51; Carleton University, B.A., 1955.

ADDRESSES: Home—Manhattan, NY; Connecticut; and Jordan Bay, Nova Scotia, Canada. *Agent*—Bill Adler, 551 Fifth Ave., Suite 923, New York, NY 10017.*Office*—c/o WNET/13, 356 West 58th St., New York, NY 10019.

CAREER: Canadian Broadcasting Corp. (CBC), Halifax, Nova Scotia, radio actor, 1950-52; Station CJCH, Halifax, all-night disc jockey, 1951-52; Station CFRA, Ottawa, Ontario, announcer and newswriter, 1952-54; CBC, Ottawa, radio and television host, 1954-55; Rueters News Agency (wire service), London, England, subeditor to filing editor, 1955-60; National Broadcasting Co. (NBC), New York City, foreign news correspondent in London, 1960-63, news correspondent at Washington, DC, bureau, 1963-65, nightly news anchor for WNBC-TV in New York City and co-anchor of *The Scherer-MacNeil Report,* 1965-67; British Broadcasting Corp. (BBC), London, reporter for *Panorama,* 1967-72; Public Broadcasting Service (PBS), Washington, DC, senior correspondent for National Public Affairs Center for Television (NPACT) and co-moderator of *Washington Week in Review,* 1972-73; BBC, reporter for *Panorama,* 1973-75; PBS, executive editor and co-anchor of *The Robert MacNeil Report* (later became *The MacNeil/Lehrer Report;* became *The MacNeil/Lehrer News Hour,* September, 1983) for WNET/WETA-TV, 1975-95.

Stringer for CBC, 1955-60; newscaster for NBC-Radio, 1965-67; co-anchor of *A Public-Affair/Election '72, America '73,* and Senate Watergate hearings, 1973, all for PBS. The MacDowell Colony, fellow and chairperson, 1993—; fellow, American Association for the Advancement of Science.

MEMBER: American Federation of Television and Radio Artists, Association of Radio and Television News Analysts, Writers Guild of America, Century Association, American Yacht Club.

AWARDS, HONOURS: Emmy Award from Academy of Television Arts and Sciences, 1974, for coverage of Senate Watergate hearings; George Foster Peabody Award from University of Georgia, 1977; Alfred I. DuPont Award from Columbia School of Journalism, 1977; honor award from University of Missouri, 1980; William Allen White Award from University of Kansas, 1982. L.H.D. from William Patterson College, 1977, Beaver College and Bates College, both 1979, Lawrence University, 1981, Bucknell University, 1982, George Washington University, Trinity College (Hartford), and University of Maine, all 1983, Brown University, 1984, Colby College, Carleton College, and University of South Carolina, all 1985, Franklin and Marshall College, 1987, Nazareth College and Washington College, both 1988, Kenyon College, 1990, and University of Western Ontario, 1992; Medal of Honor, University of Missouri School of Journalism, 1980; William Allen White Award, University of Kansas, 1982; *Wordstruck: A Memoir* was on the *New York Times* bestseller list for six weeks, 1985; Paul White Award, RTNDA, 1990; Broadcaster of the Year Award, IRTS, 1991 .

WRITINGS:

The People Machine: The Influence of Television on American Politics, Harper, 1968.
The Right Place at the Right Time, Little, Brown, 1982.
(With Robert McCrum and William Cran) *The Story of English* (narrative to accompany nine-part public television series), Viking, 1986, revised edition, Penguin Books, 1993.
(Editor) *The Way We Were: 1963, the Year Kennedy Was Shot* (Book of the Month Club selection), Carroll & Graf (New York), 1988.
Wordstruck: A Memoir, Viking, 1989.
Eudora Welty: Seeing Black and White, University Press of Mississippi, 1990.
Burden of Desire (novel), Doubleday, 1992.
The Voyage (novel), Doubleday, 1995.

Correspondent for television documentaries, including *The Big Ear,* NBC; *The Right to Bear Arms,* NBC; *The Whole World Is Watching,* Public Broadcasting Laboratories; and *The Impeachment of Andrew Johnson,* BBC, 1974; host of videocassette series *The Story of English* (nine-part series broadcast on PBS-TV; has accompanying book of the same title), Part 1: "An English Speaking World," Part 2: "Mother Tongue," Part 3: "A Muse of Fire," Part 4: "The Grid Scots Tongue," Part 5: "Black on White," Part 6: "Pioneers, O Pioneers!," Part 7: "The Muvver Tongue," Part 8: "The Loaded Weapon," Part 9: "Next Year's Words: A Look into the Future," Films Inc. (Chicago), 1986; narrator of motion picture (also released as video recording and videocassette under same title), *Slow Fires: On the Preservation of the Human Record,*

American Film Foundation, 1987; author of sound cassette recording of *Wordstruck* (audio adaptation of his book of the same title), Simon & Schuster Audioworks, 1989; host with Jim Lehrer of anniversary special videocassette *Fifteen Years of MacNeil/Lehrer,* WNET-TV (New York) and WETA-TV (Washington), 1990.

Contributor of chapters to books. Contributor of articles to periodicals, including *Harper's Magazine, Nation, Listener, TV Guide,* and *Travel and Leisure.*

WORK IN PROGRESS: Looking for My Country, about his personal search for a Canadian identity.

SIDELIGHTS: Robert MacNeil began his broadcasting career in 1950 as a radio actor for the Canadian Broadcasting Corporation. This led to stints as radio announcer and disc jockey; by 1954 he was appearing on television as the host of CBC's *Let's Go to the Museum,* a weekly visit to Ottawa's National Museum of Canada. In 1955 MacNeil moved to England, hoping to become a playwright, but lack of success made him turn to journalism. For the next five years he learned that trade at the Rueters News Service bureau in London.

In 1960 MacNeil was hired by NBC-TV as a London-based roving foreign correspondent, covering major news events around the world. (He was in Havana at the onset of the Cuban missile crisis.) By 1963 he had been reassigned to Washington, D.C., where he covered the White House beat; he was riding in President John F. Kennedy's motorcade in Dallas on November 22, 1963, and reported on the president's assassination. In 1965 MacNeil was again moved—this time to New York City. There he anchored a sixty-minute nightly newscast for WNBC-TV, prepared television documentaries, and co-hosted the *Scherer-MacNeil Report.*

Growing disillusionment with network television and news anchoring prompted MacNeil to leave WNBC and join the British Broadcasting Corporation's television documentary series *Panorama* in 1966. For the next four years he covered such news stories as the resignation of French President Charles de Gaulle and the 1968 Democratic National Convention in Chicago. MacNeil returned to the United States in 1971, when he took a new job as senior correspondent for the National Public Affairs Center for Television (NPACT), the news and public affairs division of the Public Broadcasting Service. There he moderated *Washington Week in Review* and covered the 1972 presidential election campaign and the 1973 Senate Watergate hearings. He soon resigned from that post, however, because of the Nixon administration's attempts to control public broadcasting. According to MacNeil—and later corroborated by documents from the White House Office of Telecommunications Policy—the Nixon administration was trying to turn public television into a "domestic Voice of America" which would broadcast "nothing but the Administration line."

For the next two years MacNeil returned to work for *Panorama.* He then signed with WNET-TV in New York City, hosting his own news analysis program, the *Robert MacNeil Report.* The show intermixed background material, panel discussions, interviews with experts, and filmed segments to examine a single news story in depth. "[The] *Robert MacNeil Report* is for my money this year's most exhilarating innovation on public television," wrote Karl E. Meyer in a *Saturday Review* critique. "It is an exercise in point counterpoint, throwing off particles of light." The program was co-anchored by James Lehrer in Washington, D.C., at WETA-TV, and proved highly successful. By 1976 it was renamed the *MacNeil/Lehrer Report* and became nationally distributed, seen by an average of four million people on more than 230 PBS stations.

Exploring such diverse subjects as nuclear reactor safety, whitecollar crime, Iranian militancy, and the deteriorating taste of tomatoes, the *MacNeil/Lehrer Report* enlisted public figures and those whom MacNeil called "people who really know—the staff assistant, and not necessarily the senator" in an hour of questioning and discussion. MacNeil believes that the show's popularity springs from the need of television viewers to have more than "confetti thrown at them for a half-hour every night." "Our feeling is that perhaps people are becoming bored by these rushed recitals," he told Dennis Duggan in *Newsday.* MacNeil commented again in *New York*: "Network people who contend that you have sixty seconds to make a point before viewers begin to lose interest, said it couldn't and shouldn't be done in television. Now, 1,000 shows later, while we aren't giving them any sleepless nights over our ratings, we have proved, at least, that in-depth journalism has its place on TV."

MacNeil wrote about the television news medium in his 1968 work, *The People Machine: The Influence of Television on American Politics.* The book examines the frailties of television news organizations, which "are dependent and often at the mercy of a corporate body whose prime motive is profit," Laurence Goldstein noted in the *Nation.* MacNeil then examines the more serious problem of the interplay between television and politics: the politician's use of television, the television industry's strong influence in Washington, and the control exerted by the White House on television networks. "[MacNeil] has written a wide-ranging and frequently disconcerting account of how television news operates *vis-a-vis* politicians, special interest groups, and the entertainment side of TV," noted *New Leader* critic Herbert Dorfman.

The People Machine was praised as valuable reading by other critics as well. In the *New York Times,* Elliot Fre-

mont-Smith called it an "acute, detailed and quite damning book. . . . It should make someone who counts in television to more than wince off-screen." *A Saturday Review* critic remarked that the book "offers a full, fair, critical, informed, and fascinating look into the techniques of the business and how they influence the public." Joseph O. Dougherty, writing in *Best Sellers,* described *The People Machine* as "a provocative book, to say the least, and should be a 'must' for every person who wants to be known as 'well-read.'" And Goldstein concluded: "The value of MacNeil's book is its overwhelming concern for the integrity of television, his excellent research into its problems, and his ability to point out many of the hidden defects within its present structure."

In 1982 MacNeil wrote *The Right Place at the Right Time,* a volume of memoirs that recounts his journalism career in England and America. The title reflects the author's ready acknowledgment that few journalists have had the consistent good fortune that he has enjoyed over the past twenty-five years; according to Betty Lukas in the *Los Angeles Times Book Review,* MacNeil has had "access" throughout his career, and he has known how to use it. "His short book of memoirs contains roughly what one would expect from a liberal Canadian with a brow in the upper middle," reflected Christopher Hitchens in the *Times Literary Supplement.* "It is a humane and worthy story, quite deftly told, and it derives most of its interest from the scenes (Katanga, Cuba, Teheran, Washington) in which the action takes place."

Some critics expressed disappointment that this book of recollections shared so little of the man himself. Lukas noted that "aside from being lucky . . . and aside from certain political and professional positions, there is little here about Robert MacNeil the person." *Washington Post Book World* reviewer Christopher Lydon concurred, writing that "as an autobiography the book has grave flaws. . . . MacNeil is shy about himself." The critic also expressed disappointment in the "slight" and "tentative" treatment the author gives the subject of the *MacNeil/Lehrer Report,* to Lydon's mind "the model for the best there is in modern television news." "One doesn't get much feel for the way this remarkable program—a TV show run by journalists and editors, not producers—gets on the air night after night," the reviewer contended.

Still, Lydon did find MacNeil's discussion of his medium's handling of the Vietnam War "frank and . . . redeeming." Similarly, Neil Hickey pointed out in a *Columbia Journalism Review* critique that the author's chapter on the Kennedy assassination "has a fine narrative drive that makes it worth the scrutiny of both aspiring and working journalists" and that his meditations on the nature of television news early in the book are so apt "that I hereby recommend they be committed to a parchment scroll and copies sent to all television newsrooms and schools of journalism." "[*The Right Place at the Right Time* is] a richly detailed and rollicking good job of picaresque storytelling," Hickey concluded.

About the book written to accompany the nine-part PBS series *The Story of English,* co-authored with Robert Mc-Crum and William Cran, Douglas Balz of the *Chicago Tribune* labelled it "an admirable undertaking: explaining our language to the people who use it every day." Examining the historic development of the English language, " 'The Story of English' is handsomely illustrated, lavishly displayed and competently, occasionally eloquently, written," according to Balz. He also deemed both the television series and the book "an honorable project, well worth a reader's or viewer's attention."

MacNeil's 1988 book, *The Way We Were: 1963, the Year Kennedy Was Shot,* "is a fine old-fashioned picture story," asserted Genevieve Stuttaford in *Publishers Weekly.* A compilation of photographs, interviews, and narrative, the book is "part newsreel, part Kennedy family album, part pop culture scrapbook," commented Robert F. Nardini in the *Library Journal.* A *Publishers Weekly* reviewer considered the book an "excellent synthesis" of information available from 1963 and capsulized in this book.

Although born in Montreal, MacNeil grew up in Halifax, and it is this locale he remembers so fondly in *Wordstruck: A Memoir.* A *Time* critic declared that at its best, the book evokes "the salty tang of fog descending on proud, poky Halifax as winter comes." Acclaimed by Gillian MacKay in *Maclean's* as "a thoughtful, charming chronicle of a lifelong romance with words," the book examines the newsman's "abiding passion for the English language." MacNeil describes vivid memories of his mother's voice telling him stories and reading aloud children's classics, including *Winnie the Pooh, Peter Pan, A Child's Garden of Verses,* and *Treasure Island.* Helen Benedict remarked in the *New York Times Book Review* that MacNeil "reexplores these works with care, turning their words over as sensuously as if they were rare Oriental delicacies and recapturing their power." MacKay added, "In his own prose, MacNeil employs the straightforward, soothing style of the broadcaster effectively, rising to more poetic heights in his evocation of a happy childhood. He is most touching when he describes his parents. . . ." Benedict concluded in the *New York Times Book Review,* "Mostly the book draws us into an appreciation of language that seems rare in this crass and overbearing age."

Halifax also serves as the setting for MacNeil's first novel, *Burden of Proof.* John DeMont stated in *Maclean's* that the book explores "the lives of two men and a woman buffeted by the winds of change blowing through Halifax in the years during the First World War." DeMont explained further: "The novel touches on weighty matters: sexual morality, religious faith, the psychiatric theories of Freud and Carl Jung, and the emergence of a Canadian identity during the carnage of the First World War." Constructed around an actual event—the 1917 collision and subsequent explosion of two freighters in the Halifax harbor, resulting in massive death and property destruction— the book focuses on Julia Robertson, who keeps a diary of her private sexual thoughts while her husband is overseas fighting in the war. After the harbor explosion, her diary disappears, transported accidentally in the pocket of a jacket donated to needy survivors of the devastation. It ends up in the hands of a cleric, who falls in love with the woman revealed on the pages. In attempting to trace the owner of the diary, he shares it with his psychologist friend, who reads it and also learns to love her. Together, they discover Julia's identity, and Julia eventually becomes involved with one of the men after her husband is killed.

Susan Fromberg Schaeffer observed in the *New York Times Book Review* that the novel "is at once an intricate, satisfying romance and an exploration of how difficult it is for a society to give up its well-loved ideas. . . . It is a novel filled with riches and alight with understanding of the small events that lead to the huge upheavals in life." She additionally opined that *Burden of Desire* "is at once a wonderful romance involving one of the more appealing triangles in recent fiction and a thoughtful dissection of the glacial pace of social change."

As his successful career as a writer blossoms, MacNeil announced in 1994 his plans to retire from the *MacNeil/ Lehrer NewsHour* in October, 1995. Citing problems with PBS financing, particularly with Station WNET-TV in New York, he added that Jim Lehrer would become sole anchor of the news show to be based exclusively in Washington, D.C., Lehrer's domain. Jane Hall reported in the *Los Angeles Times:* " 'My colleagues know that I've been thinking about when to retire, and the twentieth anniversary provides a nice symmetry,' MacNeil said in an interview, 'but what confirmed me was the coincidence of our need to save money. We were faced with a budget shortfall in our funding. . . .' " About MacNeil's future career plans, Hall recounted, "MacNeil, who has written several novels, said he hopes to write more fiction and nonfiction after he departs 'NewsHour.' " According to DeMont in *Maclean's,* "MacNeil says that he has always had literary ambitions. 'I set out to be a writer, not a journalist,' he said."

CA INTERVIEW

CA interviewed Robert MacNeil by phone on August 3, 1982, at his office in New York City.

CA: As the title of your new book suggests, more often than not you've been in the right place at the right time—certainly in establishing The MacNeil/Lehrer Report *on PBS. Is it as exciting now as it was five years ago?*

MacNEIL: Oh, yes. I think that's because of the reaction to it and the reception of it. It has grown well beyond anything we expected, and the kind of resonance that it has in the country and in the journalistic community is much larger and deeper than we could even have dreamed.

CA: The MacNeil/Lehrer Report *grew out of a need for the kind of in-depth analysis of issues that the regular network newscasts weren't providing. Did you have any initial concern about attracting a large enough audience to sustain the show?*

MacNEIL: I don't think we were worried about that. Maybe we had foolish confidence, but I think we assumed that if enough people could hear that we were around doing something like this, they would want to watch it.

CA: It was interesting to learn from The Right Place at the Right Time *that you hire young journalists, some of them just beginners, to cover the issues that you want to deal with. Do you and Mr. Lehrer decide on the issues in advance, or do they sometimes grow out of the work of your helpers?*

MacNEIL: Both. We're organized really like a small newspaper or a magazine, and ideas bubble up from the reporters who are covering beats. They may say to us, "Hey, it's time to do a report on the budget—it's coming up next week," that type of thing, as all reporters do. We also make suggestions to them as we see things in the news that we think we should be covering. And then some things are just obvious.

CA: Are you able to work much in advance on your shows?

MacNEIL: Some programs, sure. For instance, we recently did one on a women's prison in Kentucky, and the reporter and producer were working on that on and off for about two and a half months. They had been talking to us about it, doing more research, going to the prison, and then eventually getting permission and filming—altogether it took about two and a half months. Some programs can be very long-term while others just come on in a few hours in reaction to some big news development.

CA: One of the important differences in your show is that it airs both sides of an issue without editorial slant or summing up. Is it ever hard to be an objective moderator when you have very strong feelings about an issue?

MacNEIL: I don't find it hard and neither does Jim Lehrer. A lot of people ask the question that you have because they assume it must be. They wonder, when we're talking to somebody whose ideas seem outrageous to the viewer, why the interviewer isn't just as outraged. But in a way you just detach yourself. When you have a conversation at a party with somebody whose politics you don't agree with, you don't explode and say, "You're stupid! How could you believe such a thing!" You probably listen politely because you have good manners and you want to give him a chance to explain his point of view. You may argue with him gently or test his beliefs, but you don't want to get in a fight with him because it isn't good manners to do so. I think that is the way most people operate in social life, and it really isn't much different in professional life. Doctors, lawyers, psychiatrists, judges, teachers, all kinds of people sometimes have to keep their personal reactions to themselves, and it is not that hard or different in journalism.

CA: Critical response to the show has been great, as the awards attest. What kind of response do you get routinely from viewers? Do you get a lot of mail?

MacNEIL: We get quite a lot of mail asking for transcripts, and the rest falls into two categories. One kind is from people saying they really like the show, and why don't we do a program on such and such? Usually we write back and say we'll refer that idea to one of our reporters and see what comes up. The other letters say, we really loved the show until you disappointed us last night because you missed this point or you had the wrong guest. Those are the two kinds of letters that we get—many more of the first than of the second.

CA: Do you respond to all the mail?

MacNEIL: Somebody responds. When people write just to tell us what a nice program it was and ask for a transcript, they get a transcript back with a card that has a printed response on it. If they have a complaint or a suggestion, then either Jim or I, depending on who received the letter, will write back personally. Sending the printed response in cases where there isn't a complaint or a suggestion weeds it down to a few. There's always a little stack on my desk, but it's not overwhelming.

CA: Have any shows been particularly controversial?

MacNEIL: The only ones that have been were a few where we, as we occasionally do, put one newsmaker on for a full half hour and interviewed him. We did that with Tip O'Neill, the Speaker of the House, about a year and a half ago. People misunderstand, and they write saying, "You're normally a well-balanced program. Why did you give a full half hour to this man?" And we've had it the other way around when we had Alexander Haig on for half an hour or Caspar Weinberger for half an hour. People don't seem to see that we're just using a different form, that we are testing the person with our questions. I've had complaints about those, but I think they are the only ones that have really brought a lot of angry mail.

CA: With your schedule, how did you manage to write The Right Place at the Right Time?

MacNEIL: The schedule isn't that rough, really. I get in about 10:30 in the morning, and I'm here until 7:30 in the evening. I like to get up early, so most of the writing was done in the early morning. You know, if you can do a couple of hours a day, you can get quite a lot done. And then some of it was done on weekends and some on a couple of holidays, working in the mornings.

CA: Starting out, you were interested in an acting career, and then you wanted to be a playwright or a fiction writer. Has television satisfied those urges?

MacNEIL: Not quite, no. It hasn't satisfied the urge to write fiction. I keep dabbling with that. I'd love to do a novel.

CA: Your first book, The People Machine *(1968), presented a detailed analysis of the use of television for marketing political candidates. Do you think the situation is any better now?*

MacNEIL: No. I think it has gone much further. The only way I could say there has been any improvement is to the degree that the amount spent on political campaigns has been restricted by the election laws. But it has't been restricted very much, and I think the problem only goes further and gets worse. There is more resorting to the sort of manipulative devices of Madison Avenue in selling candidates now than there ever was.

CA: Do you think the television audiences are any more alert to it?

MacNEIL: I don't know; I don't have any data for that. I only have my own feelings, and they are that it's dreadful. You know, we haven't had a president since Eisenhower who completed two full terms. And it makes me wonder whether we haven't developed a consumer philosophy toward our politicians. I wrote about this in an article a few years ago, speculating that it could be part of the reason politicians are jettisoned so quickly now, particularly presidents. You buy a tube of toothpaste, and if you don't like it you throw it away. If a car begins to rattle after two and a half years you trade it in. And I wonder whether people aren't getting—on top of all the other reasons for doubting government, such as Vietnam and Watergate—something of a consumer philosophy about political figures, whether the marketing of candidates doesn't reduce the political decision of a voter to the level of a consumer decision.

CA: You and Jim Lehrer anchored the Senate Watergate hearings for PBS. Do you think Watergate has had lasting effects?

MacNEIL: Yes. I think Watergate, coming right on top of Vietnam, provided people with two profound reasons to be much more skeptical of their elected political leaders and the people around them. It certainly had a lot of interesting effects on the press. It resulted in a period of a sort of aggressive negativism in Washington and that gradually becomes programmed into the career-thinking of younger reporters who realize that the way to make their mark is to be very, very negative about government. That is wearing off a little bit now, but I think it is going to be a lasting effect.

CA: Because of political attempts to manipulate public broadcasting you resigned from NPACT in 1973 and returned fulltime to BBC. Are you aware of any similar political harassment now in the background?

MacNEIL: No, I'm not. And I think we would probably feel it more than anybody because we do the nightly news program; that is a sensitive area. There is the cutting of federal funds for public television. But food stamps and a lot of other things are also being cut, and in fact some of the cuts proposed for public broadcasting have been restored in the Senate. But as far as political interference of the kind that the Nixon people were up to, no, absolutely no hint of it.

CA: You worked at BBC from 1967 to 1971, then from 1973 until you returned to PBS to start The MacNeil/Lehrer Report. *Do you think American television can learn something from British television?*

MacNEIL: It *has* learned quite a lot, actually; so much British television has been shown on public television and other channels here. For instance, I think American television owes the BBC its inspiration for the miniseries, for which public television provided a kind of shop window here. It has become a popular institution. There have been subtler effects, but the most important thing I think British television could teach American television—and it's probably too late for this—is that there can be a really healthy competition and creative tension between public broadcasting and commercial broadcasting. In Britain the public-interest broadcasting, the BBC, was the established reality for years and years because the government gave it a monopoly in radio and television, and it wasn't until 1955 that it allowed commercial television to come in and compete with the BBC. I think it's a healthy relationship because, as somebody said, commercial television keeps the BBC from getting too stuffy and highbrow and the BBC keeps commercial television from putting all four feet into the through at the same time.

CA: Do you think cable is going to bring improvement in television here or just proliferate the existing problems?

MacNEIL: I don't think anyone quite knows at the moment, but my fear is the latter. I have just finished writing a chapter of a book on what they're calling the third age of television. My contribution is on the American experience with this new kind of multichannel availability. My conclusion is that the jury is really out on whether cable is going to make that much difference or not. I think it's an open question whether cable is going to be profitable, whether it's going to be superseded by direct satellite delivery within ten years, and whether it's going to mean just more mass-appeal programming available on more channels.

CA: What other news shows do you watch?

MacNEIL: Almost none. I can't watch the evening news on the networks because that's when we're actually on in New York. Occasionally I watch the CBS morning news, but mainly I listen to the radio for up-to-the-minute news, mostly CBS radio news and national public radio's "Morning Edition" program, which I find very good. The rest I get from the newspapers.

CA: What magazines and papers do you read?

MacNEIL: Normally I read—and that means "look at"—the *Wall Street Journal,* the *New York Times,* the *Washington Post,* and the *Christian Science Monitor.* Those are the ones I happen to get. Our staff looks at a great many others from around the country.

CA: Do you watch any television for entertainment?

MacNEIL: Sure. I watch an occasional movie and sometimes a baseball game. Last night I watched an episode from the Canadian series *The Music of Man.* Yehudi Menuhin is the host of it, and this episode was about the rise of the large symphony orchestra in the nineteenth century. It took us through a musical history of the period from Paganini to Wagner. It was fascinating. I happen to be very interested in music.

CA: I know you enjoy reading too. The article in Current Biography Yearbook *(1980) says that you especially like* Proust.

MacNEIL: Yes. When that article was being written I was going into *A la recherche du temps perdu* again. There's a new reworking of the Scott Moncrieff translation out, and it seems to me very much more readable—or else I am more susceptible to the material than I was.

CA: Do you get to travel much now?

MacNEIL: I don't much anymore, no. I go to Washington now and then; other trips are quite rare. The traveling I did to promote *The Right Place at the Right Time* early this summer was about as much as I've done in a long time.

CA: How do you relax when you're away from work?

MacNEIL: I sail. I'm a sailor and I have a boat. I usually go from New York up to Maine in it once a year and cruise around in the waters of Maine and then bring it back again.

CA: Are there future writing plans you'd like to talk about?

MacNEIL: Writing plans are more in the stage of yearnings at the moment rather than specific projects. I am looking for another nonfiction book to write and am considering a number of different subjects with the publisher. And I am still toying, as I always seem to be doing, with the idea of some fiction. It takes various forms. None of it has been very successful yet, but I still have hopes.

CA: Since you were so interested in acting before, would you consider taking part in a play or a production of some kind?

MacNEIL: I have a fantasy that someone will come along and offer me the part of the chorus in *Henry the Fifth.* I really love Shakespeare; I know the lines already, and that's one of my favorite bits. It's kind of like a reporter, you see. If I'm ever offered that I might do it, provided I can get to the theatre from the studio here by eight o'clock.

BIOGRAPHICAL/CRITICAL SOURCES:

BOOKS

MacNeil, Robert, *Robert MacNeil, Journalist* (sound cassette recording), National Public Radio (Washington, D.C.), 1986.
MacNeil, *The Right Place at the Right Time,* Little, Brown, 1982.
MacNeil, *Wordstruck: A Memoir,* Viking, 1989.

PERIODICALS

Best Sellers, December 1, 1968.
Chicago Tribune, September 29, 1986, section 5, p. 3.
Columbia Journalism Review, July/August, 1982.
Detroit News, June 8, 1982.
Library Journal, November 1, 1988, p. 95.
Los Angeles Times, October 11, 1994, pp. F2, 9.
Los Angeles Times Book Review, September 19, 1982.
Maclean's, April 10, 1989, p. 79; March 16, 1992, p. 53.
Nation, April 14, 1969.
New York Times, October 7, 1968.
New York Times Book Review, March 26, 1989, p. 6; March 8, 1992, pp. 10-11.
New Leader, November 18, 1968.
Newsday, May 10, 1976.
New York, August 27, 1979.
New Yorker, September 6, 1982.
Observer Review, June 7, 1970.
Publishers Weekly, September 30, 1988, p. 54.

Saturday Review, December 14, 1968; May 15, 1976.
Time, April 24, 1989, p. 87.
Times Literary Supplement, October 7, 1983.
Virginia Quarterly Review, spring, 1969.
Washington Post Book World, June 20, 1982.

—*Sketch by Nancy Pear*

—*Interview by Jean W. Ross*

*   *   *

MAILLET, Antonine 1929-

PERSONAL: Born May 10, 1929, in Bouctouche, New Brunswick, Canada; daughter of Leonide (a teacher) and Virginie (a teacher; maiden name, Cormier) Maillet. *Education:* College Notre-Dame d'Acadie, Moncton, B.A., 1950; University of Moncton, M.A., 1959; University of Montreal, LL.D., 1962; Laval University, Ph.D., 1970.

ADDRESSES: Home—735 Antonine Maillet Ave., Montreal, Quebec, Canada H2V 2Y4; Bouctouche, New Brunswick, Canada E0A 1G0. *Office*—355 Gilford St., Montreal, Quebec, Canada H2T 1M6. *Agent*—Mercedes Palomino, 355 Gilford St., Montreal, Quebec, Canada H2T 1M6.

CAREER: Writer. Taught at College Notre-Dame d'Acadie, Moncton, New Brunswick, 1954-60, University of Moncton, Moncton, New Brunswick, 1965-67, College des Jesuites, Quebec, Quebec, 1968-69, Laval University, Quebec, Quebec, 1971-74, University of Montreal, Montreal, Quebec, 1974-75, National Drama School, Montreal, Quebec, 1989-91, University of Moncton, associate professor of French Studies, chancelor, 1989.

MEMBER: PEN, Association des Ecrivains de Langue Francaise, Royal Society of Canada, Academie Canadienne-Francaise, Societe des Auteurs et Compositeurs Dramatiques de France, Societe des Gens de Lettres de France, Ordre des francophones d'Amerique.

AWARDS, HONOURS: Prize for best Canadian play, Dominion Drama Festival, 1958, for *Poire-Acre;* Prix Litteraire Champlain from Le Conseil de la Vie Francaise, 1960, for the novel *Pointe-aux-Coques;* Canada Council Prize, 1960, for the play *Les Jeux d'enfants sont faits;* grants from the Canada Council, 1962-63, 1963-64, 1974-75, and 1977, and from Quebec Department of Cultural Affairs, 1972-73; Governor General's Literary Award from the Canada Council, 1972, for the novel *Don l'Orignal;* grand prize of the Ville de Montreal, 1973, Prix des Volcans from L'Auvergne, 1975, and France-Canada Prize from the Association France-Quebec, 1975, all for the novel *Mariaagelas;* named Officer of the Order of Canada, 1976; Prix Litteraire de la Presse from La Presse,

1976, for *La Sagouine;* Four Juries Prize, 1978, for the novel *Les Cordes-de-Bois;* Prix Goncourt from the Goncourt Academy, 1979, for the novel *Pelagie-la-Charrette;* Chalmers Canadian Play Award from the Ontario Arts Council, 1980, for *La Sagouine.*

Officer des Palmes Academiques francaises, 1980; Chevalier de l'Ordre de la Pleiade (A.I.F.L.F.), Fredericton, New Brunswick, 1981; Companion of the Order of Canada, 1982; Officer of Arts and Letters of France, 1985; Officer of l'Ordre national du Quebec, 1990; member of the Queen's Privy Council for Canada, 1992; translation prize from the Association quebecoise des critiques de theatre, 1992-93, for *La Nuit des Rois;* Commandeur de l'Ordre du merite culturel de Monaco, 1993.

Has received honorary degrees from many universities, including University of Moncton, 1972, Carleton University, 1978, University of Alberta, 1979, Mount Allison University, 1979, St. Mary's University (Halifax, Nova Scotia), 1980, University of Windsor, 1980, Acadia University, 1980, Laurentian University of Sudbury, 1981, Dalhousie University, 1981, McGill University, 1982, University of Toronto, 1982, Queen's University (Kingston, Ontario), 1982, Francis Xavier University (Antigonish, Nova Scotia) 1984, St. Thomas University (Fredericton, New Brunswick) 1986, Mount St. Vincent University, 1987, Universite Ste. Anne, 1987, Bowling Green State University, 1988, Universite Laval, 1988, Universite de Lyon, (Lyon, France), 1989, Simon Fraser University, 1989, Concordia University (Montreal, Quebec), 1990, and University of Maine, 1990, British Columbia University, 1991, and Royal Military College of Canada, 1992.

WRITINGS:

NOVELS

Pointe-aux-Coques, Fides, 1958, Lemeac (Montreal), 1972.
On a mange la dune, Beauchemin, 1962, Lemeac, 1977.
Don l'Orignal, Lemeac, 1972, translation by Barbara Goddard published as *The Tale of Don l'Orignal,* Clark & Irwin, 1978.
Mariaagelas, Lemeac, 1973, Grasset, 1975, translation published as *Mariaagelas, Daughter of Gelas,* Simon & Pierre (Toronto), 1986.
Emmanuel a Joseph a Davit, Lemeac, 1975.
Les Cordes-de-Bois, Grasset, 1977.
Pelagie-la-Charrette, Lemeac, 1979, Grasset, 1979, translation by Philip Stratford published as *Pelagie: The Return to a Homeland,* Doubleday (New York), 1982.
Cent Ans dans les bois, Lemeac, 1981.
La Gribouille, Grasset, 1982.
Crache-a-Pic, Lemeac, 1984, Grasset, 1984, translation published as *The Devil Is Loose,* Lester, Orpan & Dennys, 1986.

Le Huitieme Jour, Lemeac, 1986.

L'Oursiade, Lemeac, 1990, Grasset, 1993.

Les Confessions de Jeanne de Valois, Lemeac, 1992, Grasset, 1993.

PUBLISHED PLAYS

Les Crasseux (one act), Holt (New York), 1968, revised edition, 1974.

La Sagouine (monologues; first broadcast by Radio Canada, 1970; first performed on stage in Moncton, New Brunswick, 1971; adapted for television and broadcast by Canadian Broadcasting Corporation [CBC], 1975; first English television adaptation broadcast by CBC, 1979), Lemeac, 1971-74, Grasset, 1976; translation by Luis de Cespedes, Simon & Pierre, 1979.

Gapi et Sullivan, Lemeac, 1973.

Evangeline Deusse, Lemeac, 1975.

Gapi, Lemeac, 1975.

La Veuve enragee, Lemeac, 1977.

Le Bourgeois Gentleman, Lemeac, 1978.

La Contrebandiere, Lemeac, 1981.

Les Drolatiques, Horrifiques, et Epouvantables Aventures de Panurge, ami de Pantagruel, Lemeac, 1983.

Garroches en Paradis (first produced in Montreal, Quebec, 1986), Lemeac, 1986.

Margot la Folle (first produced in Ottawa, Ontario, 1987), Lemeac, 1987.

(Translator into French) William Shakespeare, *Richard III* (first produced in Ottawa, Ontario, 1989), Lemeac, 1989.

William S. (first produced in Ottawa, Ontario, 1991), Lemeac, 1991.

UNPUBLISHED PLAYS

Entr'acte (two acts), first produced with College Notre Dame d'Acadie in Bathurst, New Brunswick, at Dominion Drama Festival, 1957.

Poire-Acre (two acts), first produced with College Notre Dame d'Acadie in Sackville, New Brunswick, at Dominion Drama Festival, 1958.

Bulles de savon (one act), first produced with College Notre Dame d'Acadie in Moncton, New Brunswick, 1959.

Les Jeux d'enfants sont faits (two acts), first produced in Halifax, Nova Scotia, at Dominion Drama Festival, 1960.

Mariaagelas, first produced in Montreal at Theatre du Rideau Vert, 1973.

Emmanuel a Joseph a Davit (based on the novel of the same name) first produced in Montreal, Quebec, 1978.

La Joyeuse Criee (two acts), first produced in Montreal, Quebec, at Theatre du Rideau Vert, 1982.

OTHER

Par derriere chez mon pere, Lemeac, 1972.

L'Acadie pour quasiment rien, Lemeac, 1973.

Christophe Cartier de la Noisette dit Nounours (children's story), Hachette/Lemeac, 1981.

(Translator into French) William Shakespeare, *La Nuit des Rois* (first produced in Ottawa, Ontario, 1993), Lemeac, 1993.

Also author of television script *Echec au destin,* 1983, and contributor to periodicals, including *En Route, Modes et travaux, Le Monde,* and *Les Nouvelles Litteraires.*

ADAPTATIONS: Gapi was adapted into a film released by the CBC in 1982.

SIDELIGHTS: The first author to write in her local French-Canadian vernacular about the French-descendent Canadians known as Acadians, Antonine Maillet has earned recognition through her writings as a spokesperson for Acadia and a preserver of its cultural and linguistic traditions and identity.

Acadia is the area around Canada's Bay of Fundy which was colonized by the French in the early seventeenth century. By the mid-eighteenth century Acadia had gained such strength as a unified French-speaking community that the British government, which controlled Canada at the time, viewed it as a threat to British rule. So in 1755, in what is known as *La Dispersion*—variously translated as the "Great Deportation" and the "Great Disruption"—the British burned down Acadia's capital city, Grand Pre, killed the Acadians' livestock, and forced as many Acadians as they could find into ships, which deposited them at various spots along the Atlantic coast from Maine to Georgia. Many eventually settled in Louisiana.

Acadia today exists mostly as a subculture in parts of Nova Scotia and New Brunswick and is comprised of descendents of Acadians who either avoided *La Dispersion* or returned afterward. Today the colony is not recognized as a viable, cohesive political force; nor can its identity be defined in terms of territory or community. Acadians, however, have retained a shared heritage, passed on largely through storytellers, and a language derived from seventeenth- and eighteenth-century French that is different in many ways from both the French spoken in Quebec and that spoken in modern France.

Maillet has taken this language, which has been passed down primarily through oral tradition, and attempted to transcribe it in order to tell her tales in the words of her Acadian heritage, imitating and thus preserving the storytelling style of her culture. She also writes about Acadians, both how they live today and how they might have lived two hundred years ago. In doing so, she hopes to salvage what little Acadian history has survived by word of mouth and to promote an awareness of Acadian culture among her readers.

In 1971 Maillet captured public attention with the theatrical premiere of *La Sagouine*. Considered by some critics to be Maillet's masterpiece, *La Sagouine* is a monologue of an old Acadian cleaning woman as she washes the floor, considers the history of her "beaten and forgotten people," and puzzles over what remains of her Acadian heritage. Maillet once told *CA* about the evolution of the *La Sagouine* character: "I didn't invent the word *sagouine,* but I practically put it into common language. Before, you had the masculine *le sagouin,* but *la sagouine* didn't exist that much in French. It's hardly in the dictionary. In spoken Acadian we would use it, though not very often. We would use the diminutive more, *la sargailloune,* which was a little pejorative, and for that reason I didn't want to give that name to my heroine. So I called her La Sagouine, which was a little better. Now everybody who works as a cleaning woman is a *sagouine,* since I wrote the book."

The novel's influence has been felt beyond the world of literature. "The village of Bouctouche," Maillet told *CA,* "is officially called the town of La Sagouine. We have the *Jeux d'Acadie,* which means more or less the Olympics of Acadia, which we have every year; they're called the Jeux d'Acadie au Pays de La Sagouine, the Acadian Games at La Sagouine's Country. So the people identify themselves now as coming from the country of Sagouine, which means to be Acadian."

Maillet's novels have also earned critical acclaim. Her 1973 novel, *Mariaagelas,* which concerns a young Acadian woman who smuggles alcohol during the period of Prohibition in the United States, became in 1975 the first of Maillet's novels to be published in France and one of twenty-five books considered for France's most prestigious literary award, the Prix Goncourt.

Maillet came even closer to winning the Prix Goncourt in 1977 with her novel *Les Cordes-de-Bois,* missing the prize by only one vote. The latter novel concerns a hilltop settlement on the New Brunswick coast. This settlement, called Les Cordes-de-Bois, is populated by a group of disreputable people known as the Mercenaires. Led by courageous, determined women, the Mercenaires are comprised of social outcasts, including orphans, criminals, vagabonds, idiots, and the infirm, and they are beleaguered by the "respectable" population at the foot of the hill. "The feud between the two groups," remarked Emile J. Talbot in *World Literature Today,* "takes on the dimensions of a moral struggle which . . . justifies the humanity of the poor and lowly." In relating this struggle, the narrator, ostensibly drawing from several Acadian storytellers' accounts of the past while incorporating their techniques and styles of delivery, presents a few different versions of

the "facts," thus allowing Les Cordes-de-Bois to gain what Talbot described as "a legendary dimension." Moreover, Talbot concluded, "The use of Acadian French, earthy and colorful, the humor of many of the situations, the fascinating array of unusual characters, all contribute to a delightful evocation of a culture little known outside its region."

With the publication of her next novel, *Pelagie-la-Charrette,* Maillet won the 1979 Prix Goncourt, becoming the first non-European to do so. In the novel, Maillet relates the story of a group of displaced Acadians who, fifteen years after *La Dispersion* scattered them throughout the American colonies, begin a return trek by oxcart to their homeland. The main character of the story is the group's leader, Pelagie, a widow whose strength, patience, and determination to take her family and other fellow exiles back to Acadia results in her being called, in English translation, Pelagie-the-Cart. The novel's other characters include Pelagie's lover, an exiled Acadian named Beausoleil who lives aboard his hijacked British schooner, the *Grand'Goule,* and periodically assists Pelagie and her company in times of trouble; Pelagie's four children; the crippled medicine woman Celina; and the ninety-year-old storyteller Belonie.

During the grueling ten-year journey through the American colonies to Acadia, Pelagie and her original companions are joined by other displaced Acadians, some of whom complete the trip, others of whom turn back or head for the French subculture of colonial Louisiana. The oxcart caravan endures the American Revolution, Indian warfare, "famine, drought, rains, epidemics, quarrels, defections" before arriving in the much-dreamed-about homeland. Pelagie, however, does not finish the journey. Just before reaching Acadia, she dies, but not before hearing that her homeland is still inaccessible; the British still rule Acadia, and Acadians must live undercover if they live in Acadia at all.

But the survivors of Pelagie's trek and their descendents do settle in Acadia, albeit secretly, and one hundred years later narrate *Pelagie-la-Charrette,* passing on Pelagie's story in the oral tradition by which they learned it themselves. The narrators at times disagree with each other and offer varying accounts of their ancestors' ten-year journey. But together, as an *Atlantic Monthly* reviewer explained, they "gradually weave a tale with the quality of legend— everything is larger than life but blurred around the edges." This legendary or mythic quality of Maillet's work was also noted by David Plante in his *New York Times Book Review* critique of *Pelagie-la-Charrette.* Remarked Plante, "The novel is narrated . . . by 'descendents of the carts,' . . . and in the recounting Pelagie and Beausoleil take on the aura of mythological figures[;] . . . in the end they become people of legend."

The character of Pelagie has also become what Henry Giniger of the *New York Times* described as "a symbol and champion of the [Canadian] French-speaking minority's determination to survive on an English-speaking continent." In her stoic strength and patient persistence she represents the stubborn will of the Acadians to retain their heritage despite the discriminatory treatment by English-speaking Canadians that exists to this day. Moreover, in winning the Prix Goncourt for *Pelagie-la-Charrette,* Maillet has gained for the Acadian language recognized legitimacy in the literary world and hope for Acadians that their linguistic and cultural traditions will be preserved and respected. The story of Pelagie, as Mark Abley explained in his *Times Literary Supplement* review of *Pelagie-la-Charrette,* "is written from a proud sense of community and Maillet's individual voice seems all the stronger for it."

Maillet told *CA* that the Prix Goncourt legitimized the Acadian language and validated her work and heritage: "According to the rules of the Goncourt, the prize could be given only to a work written in French. So if I had won the prize, that meant that my work was French. The Acadian language was therefore officially recognized as being a French language. That's why I was so proud. I knew that it meant a lot more to me than it could have meant to a Frenchman getting the prize. It was more than a person getting it; it was a whole country and a whole culture." She also spoke of the logistics involved in committing to paper a language formulated in the seventeenth century that existed solely through oral tradition. "When I wrote *Pelagie* and *La Sagouine,* I had to create a written language that had never been written in my country. That language that was Rabelais's or Moliere's was written by those authors, but it's not quite the same language that we have, because it had evolved in a different country. We have an American French language. I had to figure out how I could handle that as a written language. I had to invent some kind of a syntax, a style. That was my originality, in a sense. . . . I had to invent a grammar, almost, and to find a way of spelling words that had never been spelled before. I wanted to capture the flavor of the spoken language, and I had to get the pronunciation right, which meant inventing an accent." Furthermore, Maillet told *CA* that although the character of Pelagie is fictional, "she's a symbol really of the kind of women who figured in the stories that were told to me. I created the character, but what happened to her is history."

Maillet believes that although it is becoming more difficult to preserve Acadian traditions due to the ambivalence of many members of its younger generation, enough care will be taken to prevent a total loss of its uniqueness. "Acadians are discovering their identity more and more," she told *CA,* "and they feel that it's not just by keeping the tra-

ditions that they're going to get that culture; it's by reliving it and putting it into a new frame. The young people want to be modern. They want to live a life of today—they want television and all that, and they have it; but they feel that can be done in an Acadian way."

BIOGRAPHICAL/CRITICAL SOURCES:

BOOKS

Contemporary Literary Criticism, Gale, Volume 54, 1989.
Godin, Jean-Cleo, and Laurent Mailhot, editors, *Theatre Quebecois,* HMH, 1980, pp. 147-64.
Le Blanc, Rene, editor, *Derriere la Charrette de Pelagie: lecture analytique du roman d'Antonine Maillet, "Pelagie-la-Charrette,"* Presses de l'Universite Sainte-Anne, 1984.
Smith, Donald, *Voices of Deliverance: Interviews with Quebec & Acadian Writers,* Anansi, 1986, pp. 243-68.

PERIODICALS

Acadiensis, spring, 1983, pp. 171-80.
American Review of Canadian Studies, summer, 1988, pp. 239-48.
Atlantic Monthly, April, 1982.
Atlantic Provinces Book Review, May, 1982.
Books in Canada, May, 1982.
Canadian Forum, October, 1986, pp. 36-8.
Canadian Children's Literature, No. 41, 1986, p. 63.
Canadian Literature, spring, 1981, pp. 157-61; spring, 1988, pp. 43-56; winter, 1988, pp. 143-49; spring, 1989, pp. 193-96; winter, 1992, pp. 192-94.
Canadian Theatre Review, No. 46, 1986, pp. 58-64 and 65-71.
Chicago Tribune, January 2, 1983.
Ecrits du Canada Francais, No. 36, 1973, pp. 9-26.
En Route, August, 1983.
Figaro, September 14, 1979; September 23, 1979; November 20, 1979.
France-Soir, November 20, 1979.
French Review, May, 1985, p. 919.
Le Monde, September 14, 1979; November 20, 1979.
Les Nouvelles Litteraires, September 29, 1977.
L'Express, September 8, 1979; December 8, 1979.
Maclean's, May 5, 1980.
New Statesman, July 2, 1982.
New York Times, November 20, 1979; December 5, 1979.
New York Times Book Review, March 7, 1982.
Philadelphia Inquirer, October 16, 1983.
Quebec Studies, No. 4, 1986, pp. 220-336.
Queen's Quarterly, fall, 1992, pp. 642-52.
Quill & Quire, February, 1985, p. 14; June, 1986, p. 37; August, 1986, p. 43.
Revue d'Histoire Litteraire du quebec et du Canada Francais, summer-fall, 1986, pp. 17-33 and 35-49.
Studies in Canadian Literature, No. 2, 1981, pp. 211-20.

Times Literary Supplement, December 3, 1982.
Toronto Star, February 13, 1982.
Washington Post Book World, March 28, 1982.
World Literature Today, summer, 1978, pp. 429-30; autumn, 1982, p. 646.

*   *   *

MAJOR, Kevin (Gerald) 1949-

PERSONAL: Born September 12, 1949, in Stephenville, Newfoundland, Canada; son of Edward (a fisherman and boiler-room worker) and Jessie (Headge) Major; married Anne Crawford (a librarian), July 3, 1982; children: Luke, Duncan. *Education:* Memorial University of Newfoundland, B.Sc., 1973. *Religion:* Anglican.

ADDRESSES: Home—Box 85, Eastport, Newfoundland, Canada A0G 1Z0. *Office*—Writers' Union of Canada, 24 Ryerson Ave., Toronto, Ontario, M5T 2P3. *Agent*—c/o Nancy Colbert, The Colbert Agency, 303 Davenport Rd., Toronto, Ontario, Canada M5R 1K5.

CAREER: Teacher, Roberts Arm, Newfoundland, 1971-72, and Carbonear, Newfoundland, 1973; Eastport Central High School, Eastport, Newfoundland, teacher of special education and biology, 1974-76; writer, 1976—. Substitute teacher, 1976—. Guest on television and radio programs.

MEMBER: Writers Union of Canada.

AWARDS, HONOURS: Children's Literature Prize from Canada Council, Book-of-the-Year Award from Canadian Association of Children's Librarians, and Ruth Schwartz Children's Book Award from Ruth Schwartz Charitable Foundation and Ontario Arts Council, all 1979, all for *Hold Fast; Hold Fast* was also named to the Hans Christian Andersen Honor List by the International Board on Books for Young People, and to the *School Library Journal* list of Best Books of the Year, both 1980; *Far from Shore* received the Canadian Young Adult Book Award from the Young Adult Caucus of the Saskatchewan Library Association, and was named to the *School Library Journal* list of Best Books of the Year, both 1981.

WRITINGS:

YOUNG ADULT NOVELS

Hold Fast, Clarke, Irwin, 1978, Delacorte, 1980.
Far from Shore, Clarke, Irwin, 1980, Delacorte, 1981.
Thirty-six Exposures, Delacorte, 1984.
Dear Bruce Springsteen, Doubleday/Delacorte, 1987.
Blood Red Ochre, Doubleday/Delacorte, 1989.
Eating between the Lines, Doubleday, 1991.
Diana: My Autobiography, 1993.

OTHER

(Editor and contributor of illustrations) *Doryloads: Newfoundland Writings and Art,* Breawater Books, 1974.
(With James A. Tuck) *Terra Nova National Park: Human History Study,* Parks Canada, 1983.

Hold Fast has been translated into French, German, and Danish.

SIDELIGHTS: Kevin Major has been recognized as one of the most important figures in Canadian young adult literature. Often dealing with problems encountered by youth in the author's native province of Newfoundland, Major's novels are known for their frank treatment of profane language and sexuality—for which they have sometimes been banned from school libraries and curricula. "Sex and strong language play no greater or no lesser a part in my work than they do in real life," Major stated in *School Libraries in Canada.* "The truth is both are preoccupations of adolescents as is their family life, school, their relationships with their friends. So why the great fear?"

In an interview with Sherie Posesorski for *Books in Canada,* Major related his start in writing: "As a substitute teacher, I saw that young people were voraciously reading the new genre of American realistic young adult fiction by Judy Blume, Robert Cormier, and S. E. Hinton. . . . I saw that there were no comparable stories for a similar age group situated in Newfoundland, so I decided to write a story about young people growing up in the outports, dramatizing situations that would be relevant to their lives." Major's first novel, *Hold Fast,* won three of Canada's major awards for books for young people and was also named a Hans Christian Andersen honor book. The author once commented, "In *Hold Fast* I wanted to capture the Newfoundland way of life, its way of speaking and manner of dealing with people, and I wanted to convey some of my pride in our traditions—fishing, hunting, and the general closeness to nature."

However, such traditions are challenged by modern trends. Major told Posesorski that "Newfoundland society is in the midst of tremendous changes. The young are caught between the old traditional values of Newfoundland outport society and the onslaught of American popular culture." More generally commenting on situations encountered by youth, Major stated in *School Libraries in Canada* that "Adolescence is often a worrisome period of pressures—pressure to do well in school, to gain acceptance from friends, to cope with problems without the fund of experience that adults often take for granted."

After writing *Hold Fast,* Major produced several books that experimented with writing style. Major once commented: "One of the things I am interested in doing is trying to tell stories in different ways. I think a lot of books for young people are very similar in that they are told through the first person. There are not many chances taken in narrative form." *Far from Shore* uses five characters' points of view in depicting a family's disintegration and reunification. *Thirty-six Exposures,* a story about a high school student with interests in poetry and photography, employs a more radical narrative structure. "The story is episodic, at times to a fault (perhaps an attempt to unfold it like frames from a roll of film)," asserted *Booklist* reviewer Sally Estes. *Dear Bruce Springsteen* is an epistolary novel about a Newfoundland boy whose letters to the rock star of the title are a substitute for communication with his own absent father.

Major deals with the European settlers' destruction of Native American tribes in *Blood Red Ochre,* in which narratives of a modern high school student and a nineteenth-century young man of the Beothuk tribe alternate until, mysteriously, the protagonists meet at a Beothuk burial ground. Major "continues to be one of our strongest and most technically innovative writers for young adults," asserts Sarah Ellis in an article for *Horn Book.*

Although the protagonists of Major's novels are young adults, the author commented that he is often dissatisfied with the way his works are categorized: "I've never really been content with the term 'young adult book,' which is usually how they're labeled, because it tends to place a limit on the readership, on the kind of audience the labelers think the books would appeal to. I'd like to think of them as being good novels to begin with, to be enjoyed by readers of any age; and it does seem that a fair number of adults are reading the books and enjoying them."

BIOGRAPHICAL/CRITICAL SOURCES:

BOOKS

Children's Literature Review, Volume 11, Gale, 1986, pp. 123-33.
Contemporary Literary Criticism, Volume 26, Gale, 1983.
Dictionary of Literary Biography, Volume 60: *Canadian Writers since 1960, Second Series,* Gale, 1987.
Gallo, Donald R., editor and compiler, *Speaking for Ourselves,* National Council of Teachers of English, 1990, pp. 133-34.
Moss, John, *A Reader's Guide to the Canadian Novel,* McClelland & Stewart, 1981.
Twentieth-Century Children's Writers, 3rd edition, St. James Press, 1989, pp. 629-31.

PERIODICALS

Atlantic Books Today, summer, 1993, p. 14.
Atlantic Insight, November, 1984.
Best Sellers, January, 1982.
Booklist, November 1, 1984, p. 361.

Books in Canada, December, 1980; December, 1984, pp. 24-25; June, 1989, p. 34; October, 1993, p. 58.
Canadian Children's Literature: A Journal of Criticism and Review, Number 14, 1979, pp. 81-83.
Children's Literature Association Quarterly, Fall, 1985, pp. 140-41.
Globe and Mail (Toronto), March 26, 1988; March 11, 1989.
Horn Book, September/October 1989, pp. 659-661; September/October, 1989, p. 659.
In Review: Canadian Books for Children, summer, 1978; February, 1981.
Maclean's, December 17, 1979; December 15, 1980.
Ottawa Journal, June 19, 1979.
Quill and Quire, November, 1980; November, 1984; September, 1991, p. 57-58; April, 1993, p. 31.
Saturday Night, October, 1978.
School Libraries in Canada, spring, 1984, pp. 15-16.
Toronto Sun, June 29, 1978.
World of Children's Books, fall, 1978, pp. 56-59.*

*   *   *

MARCHBANKS, Samuel
   See DAVIES, (William) Robertson

*   *   *

MARROW, Bernard
   See MOORE, Brian

*   *   *

MAYNE, Seymour   1944-

PERSONAL: Born May 18, 1944, in Montreal, Quebec, Canada. *Education:* McGill University, B.A. (with honors), 1965; University of British Columbia, M.A., 1966, Ph.D., 1972.

ADDRESSES: Office—University of Ottawa, Department of English, 175 Waller, Ottawa, Ontario, Canada K1N 6N5.

CAREER: Poet. Jewish Institute, Montreal, Quebec, lecturer in Jewish Canadian literature, 1964; Very Stone House, Vancouver, British Columbia, cofounder and managing editor, 1966-69; Ingluvin Publications, Montreal, cofounder and literary editor, 1970-73; University of British Columbia, Vancouver, lecturer in English, 1972; University of Ottawa, Ottawa, Ontario, assistant professor, 1973-78, associate professor, 1978-85, professor of English, 1985—; Mosaic Press/Valley Editions, Oakville,

Ontario, cofounder and editor, 1974-83. Visiting professor, Hebrew University of Jerusalem, 1979-80, 1983-84, and Concordia University, 1982-83. Writer in residence, Hebrew University, 1987-88.

AWARDS, HONOURS: Canada Council arts grants, 1969, 1973, 1977, 1979, and 1984; Ontario Arts Council grants, 1974, 1976, 1983, 1985, 1987, and 1992; J. I. Segal Prize in English-French Literature, 1974, and York Poetry Workshop Award, 1975, both for *Name;* Canada Council senior arts grant, 1984; American Literary Translators Association (ALTA) Poetry Translation Award, 1990; Multiculturalism and Citizenship Canada Award, 1991.

WRITINGS:

POETRY

That Monocycle the Moon, Catapult, 1964.
Tiptoeing on the Mount, McGill Poetry Series, 1965, 2nd revised edition, Catapult, 1965.
From the Portals of Mouseholes, Very Stone House, 1966.
Touches, University of British Columbia, 1966.
I Am Still the Boy (broadside), Western Press, 1967.
Anewd, Very Stone House, 1969.
earseed (broadside), Very Stone House, 1969.
the gigolo teaspoon (broadside), Very Stone House, 1969.
Manimals (poetry and prose), Very Stone House, 1969.
Mutetations, Very Stone House, 1969.
ticklish ticlicorice (broadside), Very Stone House, 1969.
Mouth, Quarry Press, 1970.
Face, Blackfish, 1971.
For Stems of Light, Very Stone House, 1971, revised edition, Mosaic Press/Valley Editions, 1974.
Name, Press Porcepic, 1975, 2nd edition, Mosaic Press/Valley Editions, 1976.
Begging (broadside), Valley Editions, 1977.
Diasporas, Mosaic Press/Valley Editions, 1977.
Racoon (broadside), Valley Editions, 1979.
Abel and Cain (broadside), Sifrei HaEmek (Jerusalem), 1980.
The Impossible Promised Land: Poems Selected and New, Mosaic Press/Valley Editions, 1981.
Seven Poems, League of Canadian Poets, 1983.
Neighbour Praying (broadside), Sifrei HaEmek, 1984.
Vanguard of Dreams: New and Selected Poems, Sifriat Poalim (Tel Aviv), 1984.
Crazy Leonithas (broadside), Valley Editions, 1985.
Children of Abel, Mosaic Press, 1986.
Diversions, Noovo Masheen (Ottawa), 1987.
Down Here (broadside), Tree, 1990.
Simple Ceremony, Hakibbutz Hameuchad, 1990.
Ha'arava Le'sinai (broadside), Sifrei Hamek, 1992.
Killing Time, Mosaic Press, 1992.
Arbeh Ha'dmamah, Iton 77 Editions, 1993.

EDITOR

(With Patrick Lane) *Collected Poems of Red Lane,* Very Stone House, 1968.
(With Victor Coleman) *Poetry of Canada,* Intrepid Press, 1969.
(With Dorothy Livesay) *Forty Women Poets of Canada,* Ingluvin Publications, 1971.
Engagements: The Prose of Irving Layton, McClelland & Stewart, 1972.
Cutting the Keys, Writing Workshop of the University of Ottawa, 1974.
(And author of introduction) *The A. M. Klein Symposium,* University of Ottawa Press, 1975.
Splices, Writing Workshop of the University of Ottawa, 1975.
(And author of introduction) *Choice Parts,* Writing Workshop of the University of Ottawa, 1976.
(And author of introduction) *Irving Layton: The Poet and His Critics,* McGraw, 1978.
(And cotranslator) Rachel Korn, *Generations: Selected Poems,* Mosaic Press, 1982.
(And author of introduction) *Essential Words: An Anthology of Jewish Canadian Poetry,* Oberon Press, 1985.
(And cotranslator) Moshe Dor, *Crossing the River: Selected Poems,* Mosaic Press, 1989.
(And contributor) *Six Ottawa Poets,* Mosaic Press, 1990.

TRANSLATOR

(With Catherine Leach) Jerzy Harasymowicz, *Genealogy of Instruments,* Valley Editions, 1974.
Burnt Pearls: Ghetto Poems of Abraham Sutzkever, Mosaic Press, 1981.
(With Laya Firestone-Seghi and Howard Schwartz) Dan Jaffe, editor, *Jerusalem as She Is: New and Selected Poems of Shlomo Vinner,* BkMk Press, 1991.
Melech Ravitch, *Night Prayer and Other Poems* (contains both Yiddish and English), Mosaic Press, 1993.

OTHER

Contributor to various anthologies, including *The Penguin Book of Canadian Verse,* edited by Ralph Gustafson, Penguin, 1975; *Aurora: New Canadian Writing 1979,* edited by Morris Wolfe, Doubleday, 1979; *Voices within the Ark: Modern Jewish Poets,* edited by Anthony Rudolf and Howard Schwartz, Avon, 1980; *The New Oxford Book of Canadian Verse,* edited by Margaret Atwood, Oxford University Press, 1982; *The Lyric Paragraph: Canadian Prose Poems,* edited by R. Allen, Quadrant Editions, 1986; *Relations,* edited by Kenneth Sherman, Mosaic Press, 1986; *Ghosts of the Holocaust,* edited by S. Florsheim, Wayne State University Press, 1989; *The Other Language: English Poetry of Montreal,* edited by E. Farkas, Muses' Co., 1989.

Also contributor of poetry and prose to journals, including *Canadian Forum, Fiddlehead, Jewish Dialog, Prism International,* and *West Review.* Coeditor of *Cataract,* 1961-62; poetry editor of *Forge,* 1961-62, and *Viewpoints,* 1990—; editor of *The Page,* 1962-63, *Catapult,* 1964, *Jewish Dialog,* 1974-81, *Stoney Monday,* 1978, and *Parchment,* 1991—; contributing editor at *Viewpoints,* 1982-90, and *Tel Aviv Review,* 1989—; consulting editor of *Bywords,* 1990—, and *Poet Lore,* 1992—. Some of Mayne's poetry has been translated into French, Hebrew, Polish, and Spanish.

ADAPTATIONS: Mayne's poetry and criticism have been broadcast on Canadian Broadcasting Corp. (CBC-Radio) programs, including *New Canadian Writing, Anthology, Critics on Air,* and *The Arts in Review.*

WORK IN PROGRESS: Translations of Yiddish and Hebrew poetry.

SIDELIGHTS: The predominant theme of Seymour Mayne's poetry is death, a point illustrated by Kenneth Sherman's description of Mayne in *Canadian Literature* as a "poet of lamentations" with an "uncanny ability to capture the essential, singular qualities of the departed and to render that humanness in vivid and sympathetic terms, making the reader forcefully aware of the loss." However, Mayne's works offer more than sadness and pain. In the *Dictionary of Literary Biography* David Staines wrote that although "a bleak, even pessimistic, vision of life permeates his powerful verse, . . . Mayne finds hope in his steadfast commitment to his Jewish traditions and in man's awareness and acceptance of the cyclic pattern of life."

Even though Staines called Mayne's early works *That Monocycle the Moon* and *Tiptoeing on the Mount* "lighthearted explorations of human passion and sensuality," he acknowledged that in *Mouth,* which *Contemporary Poets* contributor John Robert Colombo called Mayne's "central publication," the poet "begins to examine the body in mystical rather than merely sensual terminology." Writing in *Canadian Literature,* Joseph Pivato remarked that even Mayne's earlier poems had "the added perspective of painful separations, sickness and death, and [were] thus saved . . . from being simply titillating juvenilia." Staines asserted that Mayne was influenced early on by professor Louis Dudek and poetry instructor Irving Layton, but also acknowledged that "Mayne is the direct literary descendant of A. M. Klein, the disciplined control of his verse reminiscent of Klein's poetry and the increasing emphasis on Jewish characters, idiom, and traditions reminiscent of Klein's early writings."

Some of Mayne's works focus on the Holocaust, including those in the collection *The Impossible Promised Land: Poems Selected and New,* which emphasize "remember-ing, bringing back to life for a moment the many who have been erased by the Holocaust and its fallout," observed John Oughton in *Books in Canada.* Oughton also commented that while "death negated the being of many, . . . Mayne is determined to replace that negation with some affirmation of their continuation in the collective memory of culture or the individual recall of the poet."

BIOGRAPHICAL/CRITICAL SOURCES:

BOOKS

Contemporary Poets, 5th edition, St. James, 1991.
Dictionary of Literary Biography, Volume 60: *Canadian Writers since 1960, Second Series,* Gale, 1987.

PERIODICALS

Books in Canada, March, 1982, p. 15; April, 1982, p. 34; November, 1985, p. 26; March, 1987, p. 27.
Canadian Forum, October, 1965, p. 164; March, 1968, p. 282; November, 1970, p. 310.
Canadian Literature, spring, 1964; winter, 1968; spring, 1972; summer, 1975; spring, 1979; winter, 1982.
Choice, July, 1979, p. 667; July, 1982, p. 1560; March, 1986, p. 1060.
Quill & Quire, December, 1978.

*   *   *

McDOUGALL, Colin (Malcolm)   1917-1984

PERSONAL: Born July 13, 1917, in Montreal, Quebec, Canada; died June 3, 1984; son of Errol (a judge) and Mary Wynifred (Rankin) McDougall; married Diana Ekers, January 4, 1941; children: one son, three daughters. *Education:* Attended Lower Canada College, 1929-36; McGill University, B.A., 1940. *Religion:* Anglican.

CAREER: McGill University, Montreal, Quebec, student counsellor, 1946-47, director of placement service, 1947-57, registrar, 1957-73, secretary general, 1973-84. First president of the Service for Admission to Colleges and Universities, 1966-68; member of the College Entrance Exam Board and the Committee on International Education. *Military service:* Served in Italy in World War II as part of Princess Patricia's Canadian Light Infantry; attained rank of major.

AWARDS, HONOURS: First prize in *Maclean's* fiction contest, and President's Medal from the University of Western Ontario for best Canadian short story, both c. 1953, both for "The Firing Squad"; Governor General's Award, and Quebec Literary Prize, both for *Execution,* both c. 1959.

WRITINGS:

Execution (novel), St. Martin's (New York, NY), 1958.

Contributor of short stories, including "Cardboard Soldiers," "The Firing Squad," and "Love is for the Birds," to *Maclean's* during the early 1950s.

SIDELIGHTS: Canadian author Colin McDougall spent most of his career in education, holding various positions throughout nearly four decades of service at Montreal's McGill University. He published only one novel and a few short stories, but the critical acclaim and literary prizes awarded his output have guaranteed him a place in Canadian literature. *Execution,* McDougall's 1958 novel set in World War II, has drawn comparisons to the works of American novelists Ernest Hemingway, Stephen Crane, Norman Mailer, and Joseph Heller. It garnered the prestigious Governor General's Award in 1959, as well as the Quebec Literary Prize the same year.

McDougall was born in Montreal, Quebec, in 1917. His father was a noted Canadian judge. McDougall began his secondary-level education at Lower Canada College, completing his bachelor's degree at McGill in 1940. He served in World War II after his graduation, reaching the rank of major within Princess Patricia's Canadian Light Infantry. McDougall became a company commander while he and his unit were stationed in Italy; it is this experience that informs the bulk of his fiction.

Following the war, McDougall began his long career at McGill, where he worked in student counselling and placement services, followed by seventeen years as registrar and more than a decade as secretary general, a post he held at the time of his death. As Hallvard Dahlie observed in the *Dictionary of Literary Biography,* "it is possible to see [the author's] writing career merely as one of many activities he pursued throughout a balanced, orderly, and fruitful life." He began submitting short stories to *Maclean's* in the early 1950s; the first to see print in that periodical was 1951's "Cardboard Soldiers." Much better known, however, was 1953's "The Firing Squad." This tale won both the *Maclean's* fiction contest and a President's Medal from the University of Western Ontario for best Canadian short story.

"The Firing Squad" also became the basis for the novel *Execution,* ostensibly a war story whose "fundamental substance," according to Dahlie, "is philosophical and moral rather than military." The novel is, at one level, about two executions: the first of some Italian deserters whom Dahlie described as "harmless"; the second of "innocent" young Rifleman Jones, whose death is demanded by both Canadian and American officials. In Dahlie's analysis, McDougall uses the literal examples of the two executions to frame an examination of the moral, ethical, and "metaphysical implications" of the relationships between and among those responsible for ordering and carrying out the executions and those sentenced to the pun-

ishment. Wrote Dahlie, the characters of "[Major] Bazin, [Gunner] Adam, and [Rifleman] Jones are all personally implicated in the initial execution . . . . Throughout the subsequent action Bazin and Adam attempt to exorcise their own personal guilt and to rationalize the guilt of mass man, as represented by their company." Jones, a simpler man who feels no guilt, continues as usual until his accidental involvement in the death of an American soldier requires his execution. Among the characters in *Execution* is a soldier named Krasnick, originally from Manitoba, who has no trouble killing German soldiers, but refuses to shoot horses. Dahlie concluded that "McDougall's novel avoids sentimentality and didacticism, and in its blend of objective realism and carefully controlled symbolism it allows for both a credibility and an expansible interpretation that have confirmed its continuing relevance and significance."

BIOGRAPHICAL/CRITICAL SOURCES:

BOOKS

Dictionary of Literary Biography, Volume 68: *Canadian Writers, 1920-1959, First Series,* Gale, 1988.

PERIODICALS

Canadian Literature, winter, 1966, pp. 20-31.*

*   *   *

McFARLANE, Leslie (Charles)   1902-1977 (Franklin W. Dixon, James Cody Ferris, Carolyn Keene, Roy Rockwood, house pseudonyms)

PERSONAL: Born October 25, 1902, in Carleton Place, Ontario, Canada; died September 6, 1977, in Whitby, Ontario, Canada; son of John Henry (an elementary school principal) and Rebecca (Barnett) McFarlane; married Amy Ashmore (died, 1955); married Beatrice Greenaway Kenney, 1957; children: (first marriage) Patricia, Brian, Norah. *Education:* Attended schools in Haileybury, Ontario, Canada.

CAREER: Author, screenwriter, producer, and director. Newspaper reporter during the 1910s and 1920s, working for the *Haileyburian,* Haileybury, Ontario, *Cobalt Daily Nugget,* Cobalt, Ontario, *Sudbury Star,* Sudbury, Ontario, *Ottawa Journal,* and *Montreal Herald; Springfield Republican,* Springfield, MA, reporter, 1926; Stratemeyer Syndicate, East Orange, NJ, ghost writer of books for children, 1926-46; National Film Board of Canada, Montreal, Ontario, documentary film producer and director, 1943-57; head of television drama script department for Canadian Broadcasting Corp. (CBC), 1958-60.

AWARDS, HONOURS: British Film Academy Award, 1951, for *Royal Journey;* nomination for Academy Award for best one-reel short subject from Academy of Motion Picture Arts and Sciences, 1953, for *Herring Hunt; Liberty* magazine award, 1960's, for best television playwright of the year; award from "Canada Day" festival of Canadian literature, Mohawk College, Hamilton, Ontario, 1977.

WRITINGS:

UNDER PSEUDONYM FRANKLIN W. DIXON; BOOKS IN THE "HARDY BOYS" SERIES

The Tower Treasure, illustrations by Walter S. Rogers, Grosset, 1927, facsimile of original edition, Applewood Books, 1991.

The House on the Cliff, illustrations by Rogers, Grosset, 1927, facsimile of original edition, Applewood Books, 1991.

The Secret of the Old Mill, illustrations by Rogers, Grosset, 1927, facsimile of original edition, Applewood Books, 1991.

The Missing Chums, illustrations by Rogers, Grosset, 1928.

Hunting for Hidden Gold, illustrations by Rogers, Grosset, 1928.

The Shore Road Mystery, illustrations by Rogers, Grosset, 1928.

The Secret of the Caves, illustrations by Rogers, Grosset, 1929.

The Mystery of Cabin Island, illustrations by Rogers, Grosset, 1929.

The Great Airport Mystery, illustrations by Rogers, Grosset, 1930.

What Happened at Midnight, illustrations by Rogers, Grosset, 1932.

While the Clock Ticked, illustrations by J. Clemens Gretter, Grosset, 1932.

The Sinister Sign Post, illustrations by Gretter, Grosset, 1936.

A Figure in Hiding, illustrations by Paul Laune, Grosset, 1937.

The Secret Warning, illustrations by Laune, Grosset, 1938.

The Flickering Torch Mystery, illustrations by Laune, Grosset, 1943.

The Short-Wave Mystery, illustrations by Russell H. Tandy, Grosset, 1945.

The Secret Panel, illustrations by Tandy, Grosset, 1946.

The Phantom Freighter, illustrations by Tandy, Grosset, 1947.

UNDER PSEUDONYM CAROLYN KEENE; BOOKS IN THE "DANA GIRLS" SERIES

By the Light of the Study Lamp, illustrations by Ferdinand E. Warren, Grosset, 1934.

The Secret at Lone Tree Cottage, illustrations by Warren, Grosset, 1934.

In the Shadow of the Tower, illustrations by Warren, Grosset, 1934.

A Three-Cornered Mystery, illustrations by Warren, Grosset, 1935.

UNDER PSEUDONYM ROY ROCKWOOD; BOOKS IN THE "DAVE FEARLESS" SERIES

Dave Fearless under the Ocean; or, The Treasure of the Lost Submarine, Garden City Publishing Co., 1926.

Dave Fearless in the Black Jungle; or, Lost Among the Cannibals, Garden City Publishing Co., 1926.

Dave Fearless Near the South Pole; or, The Giant Whales of Snow Island, Garden City Publishing Co., 1926.

Dave Fearless Caught by Malay Pirates; or, The Secret of Bamboo Island, Garden City Publishing Co., 1926.

Dave Fearless on the Ship of Mystery; or, The Strange Hermit of Shark Cove, Garden City Publishing Co., 1927.

Dave Fearless on the Lost Brig; or, Abandoned in the Big Hurricane, Garden City Publishing Co., 1927.

Dave Fearless at Whirlpool Point; or, The Mystery of the Water Cave, Garden City Publishing Co., 1927.

BOOKS IN THE "CHECKMATE" SERIES

Agent of the Falcon, Methuen, 1975.

The Dynamite Flynns, Methuen, 1975.

The Mystery of Spider Lake, Methuen, 1975.

Squeeze Play, Methuen, 1975.

Breakaway, Methuen, 1976.

The Snow Hawk, Methuen, 1976.

OTHER

Streets of Shadow (adult novel), Dutton, 1930.

The Murder Tree (adult novel), Dutton, 1931.

(And director) *The Boy Who Stopped Niagara* (film), J. Arthur Rank, 1947.

Royal Journey (documentary film), United Artists, 1951.

Herring Hunt (documentary film), RKO, 1953.

The Last of the Great Picnics (juvenile), illustrations by Lewis Parker, McClelland & Stewart, 1965.

McGonigle Scores!, McClelland & Stewart, 1966.

Fire in the North: A Play Commemorating the Fiftieth Anniversary of the Haileybury Fire (first broadcast on CBC radio as part of the series *The Bush and the Salon,* 1972), Highway Book Shop (Cobalt, Ontario), 1972.

A Kid in Haileybury (autobiography), Highway Book Shop, 1975.

Ghost of the Hardy Boys (autobiography), Methuen/Two Continents Publications, 1976.

Also author, under pseudonym James Cody Ferris, of *The X Bar X Boys with the Border Patrol,* Grosset. Also author, producer, or director of more than fifty films, including

A Friend at the Door, 1950. Also author of dozens of unpublished radio plays, including *Something to Remember.* Also author of more than seventy plays for television, including *The Eye-Opener Man* and *Pilgrim, Why Do You Come?* Contributor of one hundred novelettes, two hundred short stories, and numerous serials to magazines, including *Maclean's Magazine, Toronto Star Weekly, Argosy, Liberty, Vanity Fair, Canadian Home Journal, Country Gentleman, Adventure, West, Red-Blooded Stories, Mystery Stories, Top Notch, Real Detective, Detective Fiction Weekly, All-Star Detective, Thrilling Sport, Sport Story,* and *Knockout.*

SIDELIGHTS: A writer whose career spanned five decades and whose work included plays, books for adults and children, and film, radio, and television scripts, Leslie McFarlane is best remembered for the books he wrote in the "Hardy Boys" series, the popular mystery/adventure series for boys. McFarlane wrote twenty-one of the early Hardy Boys adventures, including the first eleven volumes, and helped set the tone for the enduring series. Estimated sales of the Hardy Boys books still run at over 2 million copies a year, with a total of over 60 million copies sold throughout the world. The first volume in the series, *The Tower Treasure,* written by McFarlane, has sold over 1.5 million copies alone. The Hardy Boys books have been translated into French, Italian, Dutch, Norwegian, Swedish, Danish, and other languages, and the characters have been adapted for television, comic books, and a host of toys and game products. Jonathan Cott, writing in *Esquire,* called the Hardy Boys' series "the most popular boys' books of all time."

In 1926, while working as a reporter for the *Springfield Republican,* McFarlane answered an ad for fiction writers in a journalism trade magazine. The ad was placed by the Stratemeyer Syndicate, a packager of such popular children's series as Nancy Drew, the Bobbsey Twins, and Tom Swift. McFarlane was offered an opportunity to write for the Dave Fearless series—an ongoing saga about a young deep-sea diver and underwater explorer—working from chapter-by-chapter outlines provided by Edward Stratemeyer himself, head of the syndicate. Pay was a straight one hundred dollars per book, no royalties. The books would be published under the Stratemeyer house pseudonym of Roy Rockwood. McFarlane considered the offer. "By working full time for the Stratemeyer Syndicate I could easily whack out four books a month, double my income and get some sleep at night," he explained in his autobiography *Ghost of the Hardy Boys.* McFarlane accepted the offer. His first assignment, *Dave Fearless Under the Ocean,* was written quickly: "I heaved a gusty sigh as the typewriter clattered 'The End' and I pulled the final page from the typewriter. The manuscript, unread, unrevised and uncorrected, went into a large,

brown envelope which, in turn, went into the outgoing mail basket. There wasn't even a carbon copy."

McFarlane was soon a regular contributor to Stratemeyer, writing a total of seven books in the Dave Fearless series. McFarlane claimed in *Ghost of the Hardy Boys:* "In the forty-seven years since then, . . . I have never encountered anyone who has ever heard of Dave Fearless. I have never seen a Dave Fearless book in a bookstore, on a paperback rack, on a library shelf or even in any of the dusty caves in obscure shops where old books go when they die. I have never come across any reference to Dave in any book or article. On a shelf in my small library the yellowing volumes I hammered out for Edward Stratemeyer stand as the solid evidence that there actually was a Dave Fearless series. Otherwise I might begin to doubt."

Edward Stratemeyer's next project for McFarlane proved to be more durable than the Dave Fearless books. Inspired by the popularity of mystery novels for adults, particularly the mysteries of S. S. Van Dine, Stratemeyer reasoned that a boys' mystery series featuring two young detectives might do very well. He approached McFarlane with the idea for the Hardy Boys, two brothers named Frank and Joe Hardy who solve mysteries in their hometown of Bayport. The Hardy Boys books would be published under the Stratemeyer house pseudonym of Franklin W. Dixon. McFarlane recalled in *Ghost of the Hardy Boys:* "Stratemeyer noted that the books would be clothbound and therefore priced a little higher than paperbacks. This in turn would justify a little higher payment for the manuscript—$125 to be exact. He had attached an information sheet for guidance and the plot outline of the initial volume."

McFarlane accepted the assignment. "It seemed to me," he wrote in his autobiography, "that the Hardy Boys deserved something better than the slapdash treatment Dave Fearless had been getting. It was still hack work, no doubt, but did the new series have to be all that hack? There was, after all, the chance to contribute a little style, occasional words of more than two syllables, maybe a little sensory stimuli."

To make the Hardy Boys a cut above the usual Stratemeyer series, McFarlane made sure the books were full of humor, reasoning that young readers would appreciate some laughs. Where the Stratemeyer outline called for an ordinary scene, McFarlane often turned it into a comic scene as well. Characters introduced merely to further one book's plot became in McFarlane's hands enduring favorites whose comic idiosyncracies were appreciated in many subsequent Hardy Boys adventures. The character Aunt Gertrude, for instance, was introduced as a helper to Mrs. Hardy. But she immediately became a comic foil whose constant badgering of the boys was a running joke in many later books. "A school teacher told me a while back," McFarlane recounted in *Ghost of the Hardy Boys,* "that when she asked her class to name their favorite characters in fiction she found Aunt Gertrude right up there with Huckleberry Finn. This caused her no little embarrassment. She had never heard of Aunt Gertrude and didn't care to lose face by asking."

In every book, McFarlane also included scenes of the boys eating food, remembering that when he was a young boy he appreciated food. "Boys are always hungry," as he explained in his autobiography. Whenever the boys were about to go out on a case, Mrs. Hardy got busy making sandwiches for them. And often, in addition to a handsome cash reward, the boys were paid for their crime-solving efforts with a hefty meal as well. In every Hardy Boys adventure Joe and Frank had at least one big feast, each bite of which was lovingly described by McFarlane.

Speaking to David Palmer in *Canadian Children's Literature,* McFarlane commented: "I did take trouble with the writing of [the Hardy Boys books], you know. Many of the writers of boys' books of that time wrote very hastily, and some of them weren't very good writers anyway. Some man who was interviewed said that Stratemeyer hired hacks, drunks and broken-down newspaper men and so on to write them. Well, I think that's a bit of slander, but we weren't all that good, let's say."

Writing in his autobiography, McFarlane explained that he developed a professional attitude towards his work. "The professional attitude was difficult to define," he stated. "If one is willing to accept money for writing a certain kind of material, he should do his best. The young, the uncultured or unsophisticated reader is not to blame for his condition and should not be despised—certainly not by the writer who lives by that reader's nickels and dimes.

"The Dave Fearless outlines had been outrageous fantasies, bordering on burlesque. Viewed in one light, they were comic works. 'The Hardy Boys' were likewise contrived for wish fulfillment but I had learned not to despise them. They had their lowly place in the world of commercial publishing, with its variety of reading matter as infinite as the mind of man. They were written swiftly, but not carelessly. I gave thought to grammar, sentence structure, choice of words, pace, the techniques of suspense, all within the limits of the medium which was in this case mass-produced, assembly-line fiction for boys."

McFarlane went on to write twenty-one volumes of the Hardy Boys mysteries. He told Palmer: "The stories were almost ridiculously easy to write. You hardly seemed to be working at all, you could do them very quickly." In time, however, McFarlane grew tired of the series. "It was drudgery, real drudgery, after a while," he told Palmer.

He explained in *Ghost of the Hardy Boys:* "There was no quarrel, no dramatic break with the Syndicate for which I had toiled over a period of twenty years and ground out more than two million words. I merely sent in the manuscript with a note to the effect that I was too busy to take on any further assignments. The Syndicate didn't plead with me to continue. In fact, the Syndicate didn't seem to care much one way or the other. Other spooks were always available." The Hardy Boys have since been written by a score of other writers, all of whom have published under the Stratemeyer house pseudonym Franklin W. Dixon.

McFarlane claimed that he paid no attention to the Hardy Boys' books after he was through writing them. "I never read them," he wrote in his autobiography. "Whenever a new one arrived I might skim through a few pages and then the volume would join its predecessors on a bookcase shelf. Under glass, like a row of embalmed owls, so the dust wouldn't get at them." He had no idea that the Hardy Boys were popular with young readers until his son approached him in the mid-1940s and asked about the books on the shelf. "Did you read them when you were a kid?" his son asked. "Read them? I wrote them," McFarlane replied. His son's astonished awe puzzled him until it was explained that all his son's friends read the Hardy Boys. "You can buy them in Simpson's," his son said. "Next day I went to the department store," McFarlane recalled in his autobiography, "and damned if the lad wasn't right! They *did* have shelves of them. . . . I began to see the Hardy Boys books wherever I went, in small bookstores and large, even in railway depots and corner stores. There seemed to be an epidemic."

Despite the phenomenal success of the Hardy Boys McFarlane received relatively little money for his work. As he explained in his autobiography, however, the low pay did not upset him: "I was not swindled. I accepted the terms of Edward Stratemeyer and the importance of the money was related to my needs. I was free to reject any of the assignments. Writing is not a profession on which one embarks under duress. No one forces anyone to become a writer. No one even asks him. He writes because he enjoys writing, and if he doesn't enjoy it he should get out of the profession. It follows, then, that if he is doing something he enjoys he should not complain if the financial rewards are less than he expected or thinks he deserves."

After leaving the Stratemeyer Syndicate, McFarlane worked for the National Film Board of Canada. During his twelve years with the board, he wrote, directed or produced over fifty documentary films. Later he moved to the Canadian Broadcasting Corp., writing numerous radio scripts and over seventy plays for television. In the 1970s several of his pulp magazine serials from the 1930s—

wilderness adventure tales and sports stories—were re-vamped and issued in book form as part of Methuen's Checkmate series.

Palmer summed up McFarlane as "one of the world's most popular children's authors and a prolific contributor to Canadian popular culture." Writing in the *Dictionary of Literary Biography,* J. Kieran Kealy claimed that the title of McFarlane's autobiography, *Ghost of the Hardy Boys,* "suggests that McFarlane fully realized that, despite a lifetime of writing under his own name, he would be best remembered for the books he ghosted. But he also suggests that one should not underestimate his contributions to these formulaic texts. Moreover, when one compares the rather bland, humorless boys' adventures being published today by a more 'modern' stable of ghostwriters with the original Hardy Boys adventures, one is inclined to agree with McFarlane's own appraisal of the boys' first exploits: 'I thought that I had written a hell of a good book—of its kind. . . .' "

BIOGRAPHICAL/CRITICAL SOURCES:

BOOKS

Billman, Carol, *The Secret of the Stratemeyer Syndicate: Nancy Drew, the Hardy Boys, and the Million Dollar Fiction Factory,* Ungar, 1986.

Dictionary of Literary Biography, Volume 88: *Canadian Writers, 1920-1959, Second Series,* Gale, 1989, pp. 213-215.

Johnson, Deidre, editor and compiler, *Stratemeyer Pseudonyms and Series Books: An Annotated Checklist of Stratemeyer and Stratemeyer Syndicate Publications,* Greenwood Press, 1982.

McFarlane, Leslie, *Ghost of the Hardy Boys,* Methuen/Two Continents Publications, 1976.

Prager, Arthur, *Rascals at Large; or, The Clue in the Old Nostalgia,* Doubleday, 1971.

PERIODICALS

Canadian Children's Literature, Number 11, 1978, pp. 5-19.

Esquire, June, 1986, pp. 225-226.

Rolling Stone, September 9, 1976, pp. 36-40; October 21, 1976, p. 10.

Weekend Magazine, December 15, 1973, pp. 12-15.*

*   *   *

McLANDRESS, Herschel
See GALBRAITH, John Kenneth

McLAREN, Floris (Marion) Clark   1904-1978

PERSONAL: Born December 18, 1904, in Skagway, AK; immigrated to Canada, 1925; died April 15, 1978, in Victoria, British Columbia, Canada; daughter of Henry (a farmer and horticulturist) and Marion (a farmer; maiden name, Granger) Clark; married John Angus McLaren, 1925; children: John Angus, Jr., Bruce Allen. *Education:* Attended Western Washington University.

CAREER: Taught school in Skagway, AK, 1923-25; co-founder and business manager of *Contemporary Verse,* 1941-52.

WRITINGS:

Frozen Fire (poetry), Macmillan (Toronto, Ontario), 1937.

Also contributor of poems and articles to periodicals, including *Contemporary Verse* and *Tamarack Review.*

SIDELIGHTS: Floris Clark McLaren only published one volume of poetry, *Frozen Fire,* during the course of her literary career. Part of her importance to the genre in Canada, however, is her role in the founding of *Contemporary Verse,* a quarterly magazine devoted to showcasing the best in Canadian poetry regardless of its motivating ideology. In addition to helping found the publication and serving as its business manager from 1941 to 1952—the span of its existence—McLaren was a frequent poetic contributor to *Contemporary Verse.* As Donald A. Precosky explained in the *Dictionary of Literary Biography,* "Canadian poetry felt its way into modernism hesitantly over a prolonged transition period which stretched from the 1920s to the 1940s. These two decades produced a number of poets who, though not great talents, contributed to the change. One was Floris Clark McLaren."

The poet was born Floris Marion Clark in Skagway, Alaska. She attended Western Washington University, and then returned to Skagway to teach for two years; she did not move to Canada until she married her husband, John Angus McLaren, in 1925. While raising two sons, McLaren also penned poetry; her only collection, *Frozen Fire,* was published by Macmillan in 1937. In Precosky's view, it was unimpressive. He called it "a melange of nineteenth- and twentieth-century techniques and attitudes," and noted that despite the poems' varying line lengths of free verse, "the iambic meter and the rhymes make them sound old-fashioned."

In the spring of 1941, McLaren got together with such Canadian poetic notables as Dorothy Livesay, Doris Ferne, and Anne Marriott to plan a new quarterly poetry showcase for Canadian writers. McLaren later recalled the birth of *Contemporary Verse* in an article for the *Tamarack Review,* observing that the group felt the magazine necessary because "the chances of publication in Canada for an unknown writer, or a writer experimenting with new verse forms, or concerned with social or political themes, were almost nonexistent." Under the editorship of Alan Crawley, according to Precosky, *Contemporary Verse* "reflected . . . tolerant and eclectic tastes."

Much of McLaren's own work found a home in the pages of *Contemporary Verse.* During the first half of the quarterly's run, McLaren's contributions, in Precosky's opinion, were primarily reflective. Though they often concerned the poet's "alienation," Precosky assessed, "they lack the ring of anger or commitment." In the last few years of McLaren's poetic output, however, she achieved more passionate verse, and seemed, in Precosky's judgment, to be rewriting *Frozen Fire,* "but with a surer control over her free verse and less obvious sentimentality." After *Contemporary Verse* ceased publication in 1952, McLaren contributed poetry only rarely to other periodicals. She died in 1978.

BIOGRAPHICAL/CRITICAL SOURCES:

BOOKS

Dictionary of Literary Biography, Volume 68: *Canadian Writers, 1920-1959, First Series,* Gale, 1988, pp. 251-52.
McCullagh, Joan, *Alan Crawley and "Contemporary Verse,"* University of British Columbia Press (Vancouver, British Columbia), 1976.

PERIODICALS

Tamarack Review, spring, 1957, pp. 55-63.*

*   *   *

McLUHAN, (Herbert) Marshall   1911-1980

PERSONAL: Born July 21, 1911, in Edmonton, Alberta, Canada; died after a long illness, December 31, 1980, in Toronto, Ontario, Canada; son of Herbert Ernest (a real estate and insurance salesman) and Elsie Naomi (an actress and monologuist; maiden name, Hall) McLuhan; married Corinne Keller Lewis, August 4, 1939; children: Eric, Mary McLuhan Colton, Teresa, Stephanie, Elizabeth, Michael. *Education:* University of Manitoba, B.A., 1932, M.A., 1934; Cambridge University, B.A., 1936, M.A., 1939, Ph.D., 1942. *Religion:* Roman Catholic.

CAREER: University of Wisconsin—Madison, instructor, 1936-37; St. Louis University, St. Louis, Mo., instructor in English, 1937-44; Assumption University, Windsor, Ontario, associate professor of English, 1944-46; University of Toronto, St. Michael's College, Toronto, Ontario, associate professor, 1946-52, professor of English, 1952-80, creator (by appointment) and director of Center

for Culture and Technology, 1963-80. Lecturer at numerous universities, congresses, and symposia in the United States and Canada; Albert Schweitzer Professor of Humanities at Fordham University, 1967-68. Chairman of Ford Foundation seminar on culture and communications, 1953-55; director of media project for U.S. Office of Education and National Association of Educational Broadcasters, 1959-60. Appointed by Vatican as consultor of Pontifical Commission for Social Communications, 1973. Consultant to Johnson, McCormick & Johnson Ltd. (public relations agency), Toronto, 1966-80, and to Responsive Environments Corp., New York City, 1968-80.

MEMBER: Royal Society of Canada (fellow), Modern Language Association of America, American Association of University Professors.

AWARDS, HONOURS: Governor General's Literary Award for critical prose, 1963, for *The Gutenberg Galaxy: The Making of Typographic Man;* Fordham University Communications Award, 1964; D.Litt. from University of Windsor, 1965, Assumption University, 1966, Grinnell College, 1967, Simon Fraser University, 1967, St. John Fisher College, 1969, University of Edmonton, 1972, and University of Western Ontario, 1972; Litt.D. from University of Manitoba, 1967; Molson Prize of Canada Council for outstanding achievement in the social sciences, 1967; Carl-Einstein-Preis, German Critics Association, 1967; Companion of the Order of Canada, 1970; Institute of Public Relations President's Award (Great Britain), 1970; LL.D. from University of Alberta, 1971; Christian Culture Award, Assumption University, 1971; Gold Medal Award, President of the Italian Republic, 1971, for original work as philosopher of the mass media; President's Cabinet Award, University of Detroit, 1972.

WRITINGS:

"Henry IV": A Mirror for Magistrates (originally published in *University of Toronto Quarterly*), [Toronto], 1948.
The Mechanical Bride: Folklore of Industrial Man, Vanguard, 1951, reprinted, Beacon Press, 1967.
Counterblast, privately printed, 1954, revised and enlarged edition, designed by Harley Parker, Harcourt, 1969.
(Editor and author of introduction) Alfred Lord Tennyson, *Selected Poetry,* Rinehart, 1956.
(Editor with Edmund Carpenter) *Explorations in Communication* (anthology), Beacon Press, 1960.
The Gutenberg Galaxy: The Making of Typographic Man, University of Toronto Press, 1962, New American Library, 1969.
Understanding Media: The Extensions of Man (originally written as a report to U.S. Office of Education, 1960), McGraw, 1964.

(Compiler and author of notes and commentary with Richard J. Schoeck) *Voices of Literature* (anthology), two volumes, Holt (Toronto), 1964-65, Volume 1 published as *Voices of Literature: Sounds, Masks, Roles,* 1969.

(With Quentin Fiore) *The Medium Is the Massage: An Inventory of Effects* (advance excerpt published in *Publishers Weekly,* April 3, 1967), designed by Jerome P. Agel, Random House, 1967.

(With V. J. Papanek and others) *Verbi-Voco-Visual Explorations* (originally published as Number 8 of *Explorations*), Something Else Press, 1967.

(With Fiore) *War and Peace in the Global Village: An Inventory of Some of the Current Spastic Situations That Could Be Eliminated by More Feedforward* (excerpt entitled "Fashion: A Bore War?" published in *Saturday Evening Post,* July 27, 1968), McGraw, 1968.

(With Parker) *Through the Vanishing Point: Space in Poetry and Painting,* Harper, 1968.

The Interior Landscape: The Literary Criticism of Marshall McLuhan, 1943-1962, edited and compiled by Eugene McNamara, McGraw, 1969.

Culture Is Our Business, McGraw, 1970.

(With Wilfred Watson) *From Cliche to Archetype,* Viking, 1970.

(With Barrington Nevitt) *Executives—Die-Hards and Dropouts: Management Lore in the Global Village,* Harcourt, 1971.

(With Nevitt) *Take Today: The Executive as Dropout,* Harcourt, 1972.

(Author of introduction) Harold Adams Innis and Mary Quale, editors, *Empire and Communications,* University of Toronto Press, 1972.

(Author of foreword) Willy Blok Hanson, *The Pelvic Tilt: Master Your Body in Seven Days,* McClelland & Stewart, 1973.

(With Sorel Etrog) *Spiral,* Fitzhenry & Whiteside, 1976.

(With Robert Logan) *Libraries without Shelves,* Bowker, 1977.

(With son, Eric McLuhan, and Kathy Hutchon) *City as Classroom: Understanding Language and Media,* Book Society of Canada, 1977.

(With Pierre Babin) *Autre homme, autre chretien a l'age electronique,* Chalet, 1978.

(With E. McLuhan and Hutchon) *Media, Messages, and Language: The World as Your Classroom,* preface and introduction by David A. Sohn, National Textbook Co., 1980.

Letters of Marshall McLuhan, edited by Matie Molinaro, Corinne McLuhan, and William Toye, Oxford University Press, 1988.

(With E. McLuhan) *Laws of Media: The New Science,* University of Toronto Press, 1989.

Contributor of chapters to books, including *Mass Culture,* edited by Bernard Rosenberg and David Manning White, Free Press of Glencoe, 1957; *The Compleat "Neurotica," 1948-1951,* edited by G. Legman, Hacker Art Books, 1963; *The Electronic Revolution* (published as a special issue of *American Scholar,* spring, 1966), United Chapters of Phi Beta Kappa, 1966; *McLuhan—Hot and Cool: A Primer for the Understanding of and a Critical Symposium with a Rebuttal by McLuhan,* edited by Gerald Emanuel Stearn, Dial, 1967; *The Meaning of Commercial Television,* (University of Texas-Stanford University seminar held in Asilomar, Calif., 1966), University of Texas Press, 1967; *Beyond Left and Right: Radical Thoughts for Our Times,* edited by Richard Kostelanetz, Morrow, 1968; *Innovations,* edited by Bernard Bergonzi, Macmillan, 1968; *Exploration of the Ways, Means, and Values of Museum Communication with the Viewing Public* (seminar held at the Museum of the City of New York, October 9-10, 1967), Museum of the City of New York, 1969; and *Mutacoes em educacao Segundo McLuhan,* Editora Vozes, 1971.

Author of a multimedia bulletin, *The Marshall McLuhan Dew-Line Newsletter,* published monthly by Human Development Corp., beginning 1968. General editor, with Ernest Sirluck and Schoeck, of "Patterns of Literary Criticism" series, seven volumes, University of Chicago Press and University of Toronto Press, 1965-69. Contributor of articles and essays to numerous periodicals, including *Times Literary Supplement, Vogue, American Scholar, Kenyon Review, Sewanee Review, Family Circle, Encounter,* and *Daedalus. Explorations,* co-editor with Carpenter, 1954-59, editor, beginning 1964; member of editorial board, *Media and Methods,* beginning 1967.

SIDELIGHTS: "The medium is the message," quipped Marshall McLuhan, and the world took notice. Summarized in this aphorism, McLuhan's novel insights into the functions of mass media and their implications for the future of our technological culture earned him both international acclaim and vitriolic criticism. He was variously called a prophet, a promoter, a poet, a prankster, an intellectual mad-hatter, a guru of the boob tube, a communicator who could not communicate, and a genius on a level with Newton, Darwin, Freud, Einstein, and Pavlov. Considered the oracle of the electronic age by advertising, television, and business executives who often admitted not understanding much of what he said, McLuhan made pronouncements on a vast range of contemporary issues, including education, religion, science, the environment, politics, minority groups, war, violence, love, sex, clothing, jobs, music, computers, drugs, television, and automobiles; all these pronouncements, however, were based on his belief that human societies have always been shaped more by the nature of the media used to communicate than by the content of the communication. Though he expressed his ideas in an abstruse style that reflected a predilection for puns, in books that declared the book obsolete, his influence was, and is, unmistakable. "One must admit regardless of whether he agrees with McLuhanism," observes Richard Kostelanetz in *Master Minds,* that McLuhan was "among the great creative minds—'artists'—of our time."

Contrary to his public image, McLuhan was by training a man of letters. At the University of Manitoba, he first studied engineering because of an avowed "interest in structure and design," notes Kostelanetz, but later changed his major to English literature and philosophy. After earning his first M.A. in 1934 with a thesis on "George Meredith as a Poet and Dramatic Parodist," McLuhan pursued medieval and Renaissance literature abroad at Cambridge University, ultimately producing a doctoral thesis on the rhetoric of Elizabethan writer Thomas Nashe. His writing career began with a critical study of Shakespeare's "Henry IV," and his contributions to professional journals included essays on T. S. Eliot, Gerard Manley Hopkins, John Dos Passos, and Alfred Lord Tennyson. Kostelanetz points out that even after McLuhan became known as a communications theorist, "academic circles regard[ed] him as 'one of the finest Tennyson critics.' "

A combination of circumstances, however, gradually led McLuhan to transcend his literary upbringing. The lectures of I. A. Richards and F. R. Leavis at Cambridge initiated an interest in popular culture that blossomed when McLuhan, a Canadian whose first two teaching jobs were in the United States, found himself "confronted with young Americans I was incapable of understanding," he said in *Newsweek.* "I felt an urgent need to study their popular culture in order to get through."

McLuhan's first published exploration of the effects of mass culture on those engulfed in it was *The Mechanical Bride: Folklore of Industrial Man.* The book deals with "the pop creations of advertising and other word-and-picture promotions as ingredients of a magic potion, 'composed of sex and technology,' that [is] populating America with creatures half woman, half machine," writes Harold Rosenberg in the *New Yorker.* Exposing the effects of advertising on the unconscious, the book describes the "mechanical bride" herself as that peculiar mixture of sex and technology exemplified in attitudes toward the automobile.

Kostelanetz believes that although the book was "sparsely reviewed [in 1951] and quickly remaindered, *The Mechanical Bride* has come to seem in retrospect, a radical venture in the study of American mass culture. Previous to McLuhan, most American critics of integrity were disdainfully

horrified at the growing proliferation of mass culture—the slick magazines, the comic books, the Hollywood movies, radio, television. . . . McLuhan, in contrast, was probably the first North American critic to inspect carefully the forms the stuff in the mass media took and then wonder precisely how these forms influenced people; and while he was still more scornful than not, one of his more spectacular insights identified formal similarities, rather than differences, between mass culture and elite art."

Specifically, McLuhan noticed the abrupt apposition of images, sounds, rhythms, and facts in modern poems, symphony, dance, and newspapers. Discontinuity, he concluded in *The Mechanical Bride,* is a central characteristic of the modern sensibility: "[It] is in different ways a basic concept of both quantum and relativity physics. It is the way in which a Toynbee looks at civilization, or a Margaret Mead at human cultures. Notoriously, it is the visual technique of a Picasso, the literary technique of James Joyce."

Following *The Mechanical Bride* and his promotion to full professor at St. Michael's College of the University of Toronto, McLuhan expanded his study of the relationship between culture and communication. From 1953 to 1955 he directed a Ford Foundation seminar on the subject and, with anthropologist Edmund Carpenter, founded a periodical called *Explorations* to give seminar members an additional forum for their ideas. By the late 1950s, his reputation as a communications specialist extended into the United States, earning him an appointment as director of a media project for the U.S. Office of Education and the National Association of Educational Broadcasters. The University of Toronto acknowledged his growing importance by naming him the first director of its Center for Culture and Technology, founded in 1963 to study the psychic and social consequences of technology and the media.

McLuhan's work during this period culminated in what many regard as his two major books, *The Gutenberg Galaxy: The Making of Typographic Man*—which in 1963 won Canada's highest literary honor, the Governor General's Award—and *Understanding Media: The Extensions of Man,* which eventually brought him worldwide renown. Drawing on his own impressive erudition, the analytical techniques of modern art criticism, and the theories of, among others, political economist Harold Adams Innis, McLuhan presented in these books his view of the history of mass media as central to the history of civilization in general. Borrowing Buckminster Fuller's metaphor that a tool of man's is essentially an extension of man, McLuhan claimed that the media not only represent extensions of the human senses but that they, by their very nature as determinants of knowledge, dictate "the character of perception and through perception the structure of mind," summarizes James P. Carey in *McLuhan: Pro and Con.* "The medium"—more than the content—"is the message" because it shapes human perception, human knowledge, human society.

Thus, according to McLuhan in *The Gutenberg Galaxy,* the rise of the printing press revolutionized Western civilization. By placing an overemphasis on the eye, rather than the ear of oral cultures, print reshaped the sensibility of Western man. Human beings came to see life as they saw print—as linear, often with causal relationships. Print accounted for such phenomena as linear development in music, serial thinking in mathematics, the liberal tradition, nationalism, individualism, and Protestantism (the printed book encouraged thinking in isolation; hence, individual revelation). By giving man the power to separate thought from feeling, it enabled Western man to specialize and to mechanize, but it also led to alienation from the other senses and, thus, from other men and from nature itself.

The theme of alienation was "central to the argument of Innis," notes Carey, "[but McLuhan went] beyond this critique and argue[d] that the reunification of man, the end of his alienation, the restoration of the 'whole' man will result from autonomous developments in communications technology." The electronic media of the modern era—telegraph, radio, television, movies, telephones, computers—according to McLuhan in *Understanding Media,* are reshaping civilization by "moving us out of the age of the visual into the age of the aural and tactile." Because electronic media create a mosaic of information reaching us simultaneously through several senses, our sensibility is being radically transformed as evidenced, for example, by the revolution in modern art. This redistribution and heightening of sensory awareness signifies a return to our tribal roots, where communication was multisensory and immediate. United by electronic media, the world is rapidly becoming a "global village," where all ends of the earth are in immediate touch with one another.

From this view of history branded "informational technological determinism" by Kostelanetz, McLuhan extrapolated numerous ideas in *The Gutenberg Galaxy, Understanding Media,* and subsequent books about the effects of education (the book is passe; one needs to be "literate" in many media), the concept of childhood, the landscape of social organization, the problem of personal privacy, war and propaganda, moral relativism, "hot" and "cool" media (a "cool" medium requires more sensory and mental participation than a "hot" one), the generation gap, television (those who worry about the programs on TV—a "cool" medium—are missing its true significance), modern art, and other topics. "McLuhan's performance was breathtaking," writes John Leonard in the *New York Times.* "He ranged from physics to Cezanne, from Africa

to advertising, from the Moebius strip to Milman Parry's treatise on the oral character of Yugoslav epic poetry. Euclidean space, chronological narrative, artistic perspective, Newtonian mechanics, and capitalist economics were all called into question. They were lies of the dislocating eye."

McLuhan's ideas, however, were not as neatly nor as modestly presented as this brief summary might suggest, for he considered his books "probes"—invitations to explore—rather than carefully articulated arguments. McLuhan, notes Kostelanetz, believed "more in probing and exaggerating—'making discoveries'—than in offering final definitions, as well as raising . . . critical discourse to a higher level of insight and subtlety. For this reason, he [would] in public conversation rarely defend any of his statements as absolute truths, although he [would] explain how he developed them. 'I don't agree or disagree with anything I say myself' [was] his characteristic rationale."

To further dramatize his "probes," McLuhan eschewed the traditional, print-age, linear, expository structure of introduction, development, elaboration, and conclusion, attempting instead "to imitate in his writing the form of the TV image, which he describe[d] as 'mosaic,' " says Rosenberg. A typical McLuhan book or paragraph, according to Kostelanetz, "tends to make a series of analytic statements, none of which become an explicitly encompassing thesis, though all of them approach the same body of phenomena from different angles or examples. These become a succession of exegetical glosses on a mysterious scriptural text, which is how McLuhan analogously regard[ed] the new electronic world. . . . This means that one should not necessarily read his books from start to finish—the archaic habit of print-man. True, the preface and first chapter of *The Mechanical Bride* . . . really do *introduce* the themes and methods of the book; but beyond that, the chapters can be read in any order. The real introduction to *The Gutenberg Galaxy* is the final chapter, called 'The Galaxy Reconfigured'; even McLuhan advise[d] readers to start there; and the book itself is all but a galaxy of extensive printed quotations."

In addition to these stylistic features, McLuhan had a "predilection for positively blood-curdling puns," says a *New Republic* contributor, as well as a penchant for aphorisms. Deliberately punning on his famous dictum "The medium is the message," for example, McLuhan titled his 1967 photo-montage *The Medium Is the Massage: An Inventory of Effects* to convey his belief that instead of neutrally presenting content, "all media work us over completely. They are so pervasive in their personal, political, esthetic, psychological, moral, ethical, and social consequences that they leave no part of us untouched, unaffected, unaltered. The medium is the massage." He said the 1967 book was designed to clarify the ideas in *Under-*

standing Media by depicting "a collide-oscope of inter-faced situations."

McLuhan's habitual, mosaic mixture of fact and theory, pun and picture, came to be characterized as "McLuhanese," which George P. Elliott describes in *McLuhan—Hot and Cool* as "deliberately antilogical: circular, repetitious, unqualified, gnomic, outrageous." The late Dwight Macdonald refers to "McLuhanese" in *Book Week* as "impure nonsense, nonsense adulterated by sense," and in another *Book Week* article Arthur M. Schlesinger, Jr., calls it "a chaotic combination of bland assertion, astute guesswork, fake analogy, dazzling insight, hopeless nonsense, shockmanship, showmanship, wisecracks, and oracular mystification, all mingling cockily and indiscriminately in an endless and random monologue . . . , [which] contains a deeply serious argument."

The novelty of McLuhan's ideas coupled with their unconventional presentation gave rise by the late 1960s "to an ideology . . . and a mass movement producing seminars, clubs, art exhibits, and conferences in his name," reports James P. Carey. One of the most frequently quoted intellectuals of his time, McLuhan became, in Carey's words, "a prophet, a phenomenon, a happening, a social movement." Advertising and television executives hailed him as the oracle of the electronic age, although as Alden Whitman states in the *New York Times*, "he did not think highly of the advertising business. 'The hullabaloo Madison Avenue creates couldn't condition a mouse,' he said." In 1965, avant-garde composer John Cage visited him in Toronto to discuss his insights. Publisher William Jovanovich later invited him to collaborate on a study of the future of the book. McLuhanisms soon appeared everywhere, including the popular American television show "Rowan and Martin's Laugh-In." And in 1977, Woody Allen persuaded him to make a cameo appearance in the Oscar-winning film "Annie Hall" to defend his theories.

Despite winning a great deal of admiration, McLuhan was also feared and rejected, "especially . . . by journalists and television personalities who saw themselves threatened by his analyses because they did not understand either him or his equally important sources," says E. C. Wheeldon in the London *Times*. He was often denounced as a fakir, a charlatan, and—because he considered TV the most influential medium of the electronic age—a guru of the boob tube. Critics charged him with oversimplification, faulty reasoning, inconsistency, confusion of myth and reality, as well as undermining the entire humanist tradition, and these charges continue to be leveled.

John Simon, writing in *McLuhan: Pro and Con*, considers McLuhan's "worst failing" to be "the wholesale reinterpretation of texts to prove his preconceived argument,"

and others scoff at McLuhan's attempt to explain virtually every social and cultural phenomenon in terms of the media. "For McLuhan," writes Harold Rosenberg, "beliefs, moral qualities, social action, even material progress play a secondary role (if that) in determining the human condition. The drama of history is a crude pageant whose inner meaning is man's metamorphosis through the media. As a philosophy of cultural development, *Understanding Media* is on a par with theories that trace the invention of the submarine to conflicts in the libido."

In the *New York Review of Books,* D. W. Harding praises McLuhan's "probes" as maneuvers that try "to break free from self-inhibition and sterile dispute," yet he believes they are ultimately self-defeating: "How in the face of independent common sense could McLuhan get away with, for example, his claim that primitive cultures are oral and auditory and ours is visual? Questionable even in the limited context of the psychiatrist's article he bases it on, the notion as a generalization is wildly implausible. The American Indians' skill in tracking, the bedouins' astonishing capacity for reading camel spoor, these are ordinary instances of the familiar fact that in many habitats the survival of a primitive people depended on constant visual alertness, acute discrimination, and highly trained inference from visual data. . . . One is left with the truism that we read a lot and preliterates don't. The implications of that fact are well worth exploring, but we get no help from stories of alteration in some physiologically and psychologically undefined 'sensory ratio.' "

"McLuhan is a monomaniac who happens to be hooked on something extremely important," concludes Tom Nairn in the *New Statesman,* "but the colossal evasiveness, the slipshod reasoning, and weak-kneed glibness accompanying the mania make him dangerous going. . . . Capable of the most brilliant and stimulating insight into relationships other historians and social theorists have ignored, he systematically fails to develop this insight critically. Consequently, his view of the connection between media and society is an unbelievable shambles: his dream-logic turns necessary conditions into sufficient conditions, half-truths into sure things, the possible into a *fait accompli.*"

The overriding source of irritation for many readers is McLuhan's intricate style. John Fowles, for example, finds *From Cliche to Archetype* "as elegant and as lucid as a barrel of tar." The book, according to Fowles in *Saturday Review,* "makes one wonder whether Marshall McLuhan's celebrated doubts over the print medium don't largely stem from a personal incapacity to handle it. Perhaps the graceless style, the barbarously obscuring jargon, the incoherent hopping from one unfinished argument into the middle of the next are all meant to be subtly humorous. But the general effect is about as subtle and humorous as a Nazi storm trooper hectoring the latest train-load of Jews. It is all barked fiat: off with your head if you dare to disagree."

David Myers suggests in *Book World* that, ultimately, it is "as a poet and only as a poet that McLuhan can be read without exasperation," and others seem to agree. Kenneth Burke maintains in the *New Republic* that McLuhan "transcends the distinction . . . between 'prove' and 'probe,' both from the Latin *probare.* 'Proof' requires a considerable sense of continuity; 'probing' can be done at random, with hit-and-run slogans or titles taking the place of sustained exposition. And in the medium of books, McLuhan with his 'probing' has 'perfected' a manner in which the non sequitur never had it so good." "Even at his worst," insists Tom Wolfe in *Book World,* "McLuhan inspires you to try to see and understand in a new way, and in the long run this may prove to be his great contribution."

The aim of McLuhan's "poetry," however, remains a matter of dispute. James P. Carey, who considers McLuhan "a poet of technology," claims his work "represents a secular prayer to technology, a magical incantation of the gods, designed to quell one's fears that, after all, the machines may be taking over. . . . McLuhan himself is a medium and that is his message." But McLuhan maintained that rather than predicting the future of our technological age, he was merely extrapolating current processes to their logical conclusions. "I don't approve of the global village," he once told a *Playboy* interviewer, "I say we live in it." Writing in *McLuhan: Pro and Con,* John Culkin supports the detachment of McLuhan's viewpoint: "Too many people are eager to write off Marshall McLuhan or to reduce him to the nearest and handiest platitude which explains him to them. He deserves better. . . . He didn't invent electricity or put kids in front of TV sets; he . . . merely [tried] to describe what's happening out there so that it can be dealt with intelligently. When someone warns you of an oncoming truck, it's frightfully impolite to accuse him of driving the thing."

Richard Kostelanetz, moreover, believes that McLuhan was "trenchantly a humanist." He quotes McLuhan as saying, "By knowing how technology shapes our environment, we can transcend its absolutely determining power. . . . My entire concern is to overcome the determination that results from people trying to ignore what is going on. Far from regarding technological change as inevitable, I insist that if we understand its components we can turn it off any time we choose. Short of turning it off, there are lots of moderate controls conceivable."

Whether McLuhan was a poet of technology, a detached observer, or a trenchant humanist, "what remain paramount are his global standpoint and his zest for the new,"

concludes Harold Rosenberg. "As an artist working in a mixed medium of direct experience and historical analogy, he [gave] a needed twist to the great debate on what is happening to man in this age of technological speedup. [Whereas] other observers . . . [repeated] criticisms of industrial society that were formulated a century ago, . . . McLuhan, for all his abstractness, . . . found positive, humanistic meaning and the color of life in supermarkets, stratospheric flight, the lights blinking on broadcasting towers. In respect to the maladies of de-individuation, he . . . dared to seek the cure in the disease, and his vision of going forward into primitive wholeness is a good enough reply to those who would go back to it."

A happening entitled "McLuhan Megillah," based on *Understanding Media* and *The Gutenberg Galaxy* and combining dance, film, painting, poetry, sculpture, and other art forms, was produced at Al Hansen's Third Rail Time/Space Theatre in Greenwich Village in January of 1966. A McLuhan television special based on *The Medium Is the Massage* was produced on NBC-TV, March 19, 1967. In September of 1967, Columbia Records released a four-track LP based on *The Medium Is the Massage* and produced by Jerome P. Agel.

BIOGRAPHICAL/CRITICAL SOURCES:

BOOKS

Contemporary Literary Criticism, Volume 37, Gale, 1986.
Crosby, Harry H. and George R. Bond, compilers, *The McLuhan Explosion* (casebook on McLuhan and *Understanding Media*), American Book Co., 1968.
Duffy, Dennis, *Marshall McLuhan,* McClelland & Stewart, 1969.
Fekete, John, *The Critical Twilight: Explorations in the Ideology of Anglo-American Literary Theory from Eliot to McLuhan,* Routledge & Kegan Paul, 1978.
Finkelstein, Sidney Walter, *Sense and Nonsense of McLuhan,* International Publishers, 1968.
Fiore, Quentin and Marshall McLuhan, *The Medium Is the Massage: An Inventory of Effects,* Bantam, 1967.
Gross, Theodore L., *Representative Men,* Free Press, 1970.
Kostelanetz, Richard, *Master Minds: Portraits of Contemporary American Artists and Intellectuals,* Macmillan, 1969.
McLuhan, *The Mechanical Bride: Folklore of Industrial Man,* Vanguard, 1951.
McLuhan, *Understanding Media: The Extensions of Man,* McGraw, 1964.
McLuhan, *The Gutenberg Galaxy: The Making of Typographic Man,* University of Toronto Press, 1962.
Miller, Jonathan, *Marshall McLuhan,* Viking, 1971.
Rosenthal, Raymond, editor, *McLuhan: Pro and Con,* Funk, 1968.

Stearn, Gerald Emanuel, editor, *McLuhan—Hot and Cool: A Primer for the Understanding of and a Critical Symposium with a Rebuttal by McLuhan,* Dial, 1967.
Theall, Donald F., *The Medium Is the Rear View Mirror: Understanding McLuhan,* McGill-Queens University Press, 1971.

PERIODICALS

American Dialog, autumn, 1967.
Antioch Review, spring, 1967.
Books, September, 1965, January, 1967.
Books and Bookmen, March 1971.
Book Week, June 7, 1964, March 19, 1967.
Book World, October 29, 1967, September 15, 1968, July 27, 1969, November 30, 1969, December 6, 1970.
Canadian Forum, February, 1969.
Chicago Tribune, January 1, 1981.
Christian Science Monitor, May 17, 1972.
Commentary, January, 1965.
Commonweal, January 20, 1967, June 23, 1967.
Critic, August, 1967.
Esquire, August, 1966.
Globe and Mail (Toronto), December 24, 1988.
Harper's, November, 1965, June, 1967.
Kenyon Review, March, 1967.
L'Express, February 14-20, 1972.
Life, February 25, 1966.
Listener, September 28, 1967, October 19, 1967.
Maclean's Magazine, January 7, 1980, March 17, 1980.
Nation, October 5, 1964, May 15, 1967, December 4, 1967, December 8, 1969.
National Review, November 19, 1968.
New Republic, February 7, 1970, June 10, 1972.
New Statesman, December 11, 1964, September 22, 1967.
Newsweek, February 28, 1966, March 6, 1967, September 23, 1968, January 12, 1981.
New Yorker, February 27, 1965.
New York Review of Books, August 20, 1964, November 23, 1967, January 2, 1969.
New York Times, October 21, 1951, February 27, 1967, September 7, 1967, January 1, 1981.
New York Times Book Review, May 1, 1966, March 26, 1967, September 8, 1968, December 21, 1969, July 12, 1970, December 13, 1970, February 26, 1989.
New York Times Magazine, January 29, 1967.
Partisan Review, summer, 1968.
Playboy, March, 1969.
Publishers Weekly, January 23, 1981.
Saturday Night, February, 1967.
Saturday Review, November 26, 1966, March 11, 1967, May 9, 1970, November 21, 1970.
Sewanee Review, spring, 1969.
Time, July 3, 1964, March 3, 1967, January 12, 1981.
Times (London), January 2, 1981.

Times Literary Supplement, August 6, 1964, September 28, 1967, May 6, 1988, August 25, 1989.
Twentieth-Century Literature, July, 1970.
Village Voice, May 12, 1966, December 26, 1970.
Vogue, July, 1966.
Western Humanities Review, autumn, 1967.

OBITUARIES:

PERIODICALS

AB Bookman's Weekly, January 19, 1981.
Chicago Tribune, January 1, 1981.
Newsweek, January 12, 1981.
New York Times, January 1, 1981.
Publishers Weekly, January 23, 1981.
Time, January 12, 1981.
Times (London), January 2, 1981.

* * *

McNEIL, Florence 1940-

PERSONAL: Born May 8, 1940, in Vancouver, British Columbia, Canada; daughter of John (a contractor and carpenter) and Jean (Gillies) McNeil; married David Mc-Neal (a professor), January 4, 1973. *Education:* University of British Columbia, B.A., 1961, M.A., 1965.

ADDRESSES: Home and office—20 Georgia Wynd, Delta, British Columbia, Canada V4M 1A5.

CAREER: Western Washington State College (now University), Bellingham, instructor in English, 1965-68; University of Calgary, Calgary, Alberta, assistant professor of English, 1968-73; University of British Columbia, Vancouver, assistant professor of education and English, 1973-76; writer, 1976—.

MEMBER: League of Canadian Poets, Writers Union of Canada, Canadian Society of Children's Authors, Illustrators, and Publishers.

AWARDS, HONOURS: Macmillan of Canada Prize for Poetry, 1965; awards from Canada Council, 1976, 1978, 1980, 1982; Canadian National Magazine Award for Poetry, 1980, for a selection of poems from *Barkerville.*

WRITINGS:

POEMS

A Silent Green Sky, Klanak, 1965.
Walhachin, Fiddlehead, 1972.
Rim of the Park, Sono Nis, 1972.
Ghost Towns, McClelland & Stewart, 1975.
Emily, Clarke, Irwin, 1975.
A Balancing Act, McClelland & Stewart, 1979.
The Overlanders, Thistledown, 1982.
Barkerville, Thistledown, 1984.

Swimming out of History: New and Selected Poems, Oolichan, 1992.

PLAYS

Barkerville: A Play for Voices (one-act), first broadcast by CBC-Radio, December 13, 1980.

Also author of *Pictures from a Cardboard Stage* (one-act).

OTHER

When Is a Poem (criticism), League of Canadian Poets, 1980.
Miss P. and Me (young adult novel), Clarke, Irwin, 1982, Harper, 1984.
(Editor) *Here Is a Poem* (anthology), League of Canadian Poets, 1983.
All Kinds of Magic (young adult novel), Douglas & McIntyre, 1984.
Catriona's Island (young adult novel), Douglas & McIntyre, 1988.
(Editor) *Do Whales Jump at Night? and Other Poems,* Groundwood, 1990.
Breathing Each Other's Air (novel), Polestar, 1994.

Work represented in anthologies, including *Skookum Wawa: An Anthology of the Northwest,* edited by G. Geddes, Oxford University Press, 1975; *The Poets of Canada,* Hurtig Press, 1980; *Forty Women Poets of Canada; D'Sonoqua.* Contributor of poems to magazines, including *Queen's Quarterly, Fiddlehead,* and *Canadian Forum.*

SIDELIGHTS: Florence McNeil is a poet whose work uses strong visual imagery. McNeil, writes Rita Donovan in *Books in Canada,* "is well established as a visual poet." In addition to her books of poetry, McNeil has also published several novels for young adults.

Speaking of her poetry, McNeil told *CA:* "I'm interested in visual interests and in contrasts. Therefore my work is often about art and visual media, and my imagery is mainly visual." This interest is evident in her *Swimming out of History: New and Selected Poems,* a collection of poems taken from seven earlier books along with more recent, uncollected works. Many of these poems are based on photographs, paintings or other visual images which McNeil uses as inspiration to write of isolated or elderly characters. Although Donovan finds that a major limitation of using visual images as a basis for poetry is that the poems possess "a vaguely disturbing silence," she nonetheless concludes that "McNeil has written many strikingly beautiful poems."

McNeil also told *CA:* "I like to write about the family, an important historical link or connection to me. I come from Hebridean Scots, newly emigrated in the 1920's, who brought with them the Gaelic language and a romantic, ironic, self-effacing world view. They have crept into many of my poems—in the sense of continuity with the past, the ties of an extended family, and with a culture in many ways at odds with the North American culture. These things provide much of my material. The family is important in two of my novels for young people. *"Miss P. and Me* and *All Kinds of Magic* deal in very different ways with family situations. In one, a girl's busy, contemporary family ignores her and she then sets her sights on a talent which is alien to her, and thus lands in many difficulties. In the other book a child in a single-parent family has a fierce rivalry with and jealousy for a new step-brother she meets in the summer, and only through a series of magical events is she able to come to terms with tenderness."

McNeil's novel *Catriona's Island* concerns a young girl, newly arrived in Canada from her native Scotland, whose family moves to Heron Island when her grandfather becomes a lighthouse keeper. Essentially a coming-of-age story, the novel also provides a look at the life of immigrants to Canada in the 1930s and the problems they faced. Writing in *Books in Canada,* Linda Granfield finds that "Catriona's recollections of her first year in Canada are evocatively written."

McNeil's one novel for adults, *Breathing Each Other's Air,* tells the story of Elizabeth, a historian investigating the mysterious sinking years before of the *Anabelle* off the coast of western Canada. The actress Ursula La Fontaine had drowned in the accident and Elizabeth is intent on discovering the facts behind her death. McNeil presents the two women's stories in a stream-of-consciousness style. "As Ursula's reconstructed life becomes a tangle of conjecture and jeopardizes the biography Elizabeth is writing," Julie Adam states in *Quill & Quire,* "Elizabeth is forced to examine her own life from a new perspective."

BIOGRAPHICAL/CRITICAL SOURCES:

PERIODICALS

Books in Canada, December, 1984, p. 11; April, 1989, p. 37; summer, 1992, p. 60-61; September, 1994, p. 55.
Books for Young People, April, 1989, p. 12.
Canadian Children's Literature, Volume 54, 1989, pp. 81-82.
Canadian Literature, autumn, 1977.
Canadian Materials, May, 1992, p. 175.
CVII, autumn, 1982.
Quill & Quire, November, 1984, p. 11; July, 1990, pp. 36-37; August, 1994, pp. 26-27.

*   *   *

MERRITT, E. B.
See WADDINGTON, Miriam

MICHAELS, Lorne 1944-

PERSONAL: Born Lorne David Lipowitz, November 17, 1944, in Forest Hill, Toronto, Canada; emigrated to the United States; naturalized U.S. citizen, April 1, 1987; son of Abraham (a furrier) and Florence (Becker) Lipowitz; married Rosie Schuster (a comedy writer), November, 1967 (divorced, 1980); married Susan Forristal (an actress and art gallery owner), September 13, 1981 (divorced); married Alice Barry, April, 1991; children: One. *Education:* Graduated from University of Toronto, 1966.

ADDRESSES: Office—Broadway Video, 1619 Broadway, New York, NY 10019; National Broadcasting Company, 30 Rockefeller Plaza, 9th Floor, New York, NY 10020.

CAREER: Worked for Film Canada, c. 1967; writer and performer, with Hart Pomerantz, for Canadian television, until 1968; producer and performer, with Pomerantz, of comedy specials for Canadian Broadcasting Corporation (CBC), 1969-73; producer of television specials, various networks, 1973—; creator and producer of *Saturday Night Live,* National Broadcasting Company (NBC), 1975-80, executive producer, 1985—; chair of Broadway Video, 1979—; producer of motion pictures, including *Mr. Mike's Mondo Video, Wayne's World, The Coneheads,* and *Tommy Boy,* 1979—; creator and producer of *The New Show,* NBC, 1984; creator and executive producer of *Michelob Presents Sunday Night,* NBC, 1987-89; executive producer of *The Kids in the Hall,* CBC and Home Box Office (HBO), 1988-92; executive producer of *Late Night with Conan O'Brien,* NBC, 1993—; executive producer of *Exit 57,* Comedy Central, 1994—.

MEMBER: American Federation of Television and Radio Artists, Writers Guild of America (board member), Astoria Foundation.

AWARDS, HONOURS: Emmy Award, best writing in comedy-variety special, 1973, for *Lily;* Writers Guild of America award, best variety, 1975, and Emmy Award, best writing in a comedy-variety special, 1976, both for *The Lily Tomlin Special;* Emmy Awards, outstanding producer of a comedy-variety series, 1976, outstanding writing in a comedy-variety series, 1977 and 1989, all for *Saturday Night Live;* San Francisco Film Award, 1976; Emmy Award, outstanding writing in a comedy-variety special, 1978, for *The Paul Simon Special;* The Charlie Local and National Comedy Awards, named best in the comedy business, 1988; received Peabody Award for *Saturday Night Live;* numerous other awards.

WRITINGS:

TELEVISION SERIES

(With Hart Pomerantz and others) *The Beautiful Phyllis Diller Show,* NBC, 1968.

(With Pomerantz and others) *Rowan and Martin's Laugh-In,* NBC, 1968.
(With others; and producer) *The Burns and Schreiber Comedy Hour,* ABC, 1973.
(With others) *Saturday Night Live,* NBC, 1975-81, 1985—.
(With others) *The New Show,* NBC, 1984.

TELEVISION SPECIALS

(With others) *Lily,* CBS, 1973.
(With Bob Wells and Johnny Bradford) *The Perry Como Winter Show,* CBS, 1973.
(With others; and producer) *Flip Wilson . . . Of Course,* NBC, 1974.
(With others; and producer, with Jane Wagner) *Lily,* ABC, 1975.
(With others; and producer, with Wagner) *The Lily Tomlin Special,* ABC, 1975.
(With Alan Zweibel, Dan Ackroyd, and John Belushi; and producer) *The Beach Boys Special,* NBC, 1976.
(With others; and producer) *The Paul Simon Special,* NBC, 1977.

Also producer and writer, with Pomerantz, of triannual comedy specials for the Canadian Broadcasting Corporation, including *The Hart and Lorne Terrific Hour* and *Today Makes Me Nervous,* 1969-71.

OTHER

(With others; and producer and director) *Gilda Live from New York* (stage performance), produced at the Winter Garden Theatre, New York City, 1979, released as a motion picture, Warner Brothers, 1980.
(With Steve Martin and Randy Newman; and producer) *The Three Amigos* (motion picture), Orion, 1987.

Joke writer for Woody Allen, New York City, 1968.

WORK IN PROGRESS: Working on plans for more movie spin-offs featuring characters from *Saturday Night Live.*

SIDELIGHTS: Playboy contributor David Rensin described film and television producer Lorne Michaels as "the unofficial godfather of modern comedy." Known primarily for creating, producing, and writing the late night program *Saturday Night Live* (or as it is commonly referred to, *SNL*), Michaels is credited with pioneering a style of television comedy that was revolutionary when the show debuted in 1975. With its political, social, and often confrontational content, *SNL* took viewers by surprise and established a loyal audience for more than eighteen years. As the show grew in popularity, Michaels branched out and began work on other projects, including writing and producing numerous television programs and acting as producer for a variety of films, including the immensely popular *Wayne's World.* In 1993, Michaels was chosen by the National Broadcasting Company (NBC) to create and produce a new late night show to replace the celebrated *Late Night with David Letterman.* His work has permeated popular culture to the point where lines of dialogue from his shows and films are used by millions of people worldwide as catch-phrases in regular conversation. David Marc appraised Michaels's career in the *Voice,* stating that "his mastery of television history and gesture, and his willingness to take chances with both pen and camera put late-night TV satire on the cultural map."

Lorne David Michaels entered the world on November 17, 1944, in Toronto, Canada. Growing up in the affluent Forest Hill area, Michaels was raised in the burgeoning age of visual media. "I watched everything," he told Michael Winship in *Television.* "I remember television sort of being a miracle." As Michaels matured, so too did television, evolving from the sparse staging of live shows like *The Honeymooners* (a favorite of Michaels's that would greatly influence his career) to more sophisticated, prerecorded material. Initially, however, Michaels did not consider television as his future career. As the son of a successful furrier, he was expected to follow the traditional path of college and career. As a result, Michaels found himself enrolled in the English program at the University of Toronto, heading toward a profession in law or teaching.

While attending college, Michaels became involved with a theatre group and began acting, writing, and directing. Most of the projects he was involved with were satirical revues, shows that featured sketch comedy and humorous musical numbers. Those productions increased his interest in show business, and their popularity proved to Michaels that his brand of humor was appealing to others. Despite this, a career in television was not the foremost thing in his mind. As Michaels told Winship, "I think I was headed more toward theater or to film. I was from the what-I-really-want-to-do-is-direct generation." He paired with Hart Pomerantz, whom he had met while producing a revue, and the duo began writing and performing a comedy act. In the course of presenting their material, Michaels and Pomerantz attracted the attention of some influential people. "Through a series of happy accidents," Michaels told Winship, "we got to write for some good comedians, and that material got shown to other people. We were sent out to California to do a television series, and that led to another television series."

The "good comedians" that Michaels mentioned to Winship included Woody Allen, who would later go on to make such films as *Sleeper* and *Annie Hall.* The television series that he and Pomerantz wrote for were *The Beautiful Phyllis Diller Show* and *Rowan and Martin's Laugh-In.* While Diller's show lasted only one season, when the team

began work on *Laugh-In* in 1968 the show was one of television comedy's most popular. Michaels and Pomerantz were contracted to write opening monologues for the show's hosts, Dan Rowan and Dick Martin. As junior writers on the program, however, the duo was subjected to the whims and tastes of the senior writing staff. As a result, much of the material they wrote was extensively rewritten—sometimes to an unrecognizable degree. Disillusioned with the process of television writing, the pair returned to Canada. They eventually came to the conclusion that if they were to continue working in television, they would have to produce their own shows. As Michaels told Timothy White in *Rolling Stone:* "I became a producer to protect my writing, which was being [ruined] by producers."

Michaels and Pomerantz made an agreement with the Canadian Broadcasting Corporation (CBC) to write, produce, and star in a series of specials. Over the course of three years, beginning in 1969, they created three specials a year with titles such as *The Hart and Lorne Terrific Hour* and *Today Makes Me Nervous.* The format of these specials, which would later provide loose blueprints for *SNL,* had Hart and Lorne hosting a program of sketch comedy with musical guests like Cat Stevens and James Taylor. While the shows were moderately popular and made Michaels and Pomerantz well-known among younger viewers, they also served in an instructional capacity for Michaels. He related in Winship's *Television:* "I learned how to do television mostly because the CBC was this tremendous training ground. If you were prepared to work from midnight to eight, you could edit all you wanted. I began to feel very comfortable in a television studio. . . . I was able to learn an enormous amount in a very short time." Michaels became so interested in the processes behind the cameras that he eventually lost interest in performing. He and Pomerantz severed their partnership on these grounds, with Hart continuing to perform and Michaels going on to produce several programs for the CBC. While Michaels was indebted to Canadian television for his technical knowledge, he realized that the real media opportunities—the real test of his talent—lay in the much larger American market. So in 1971, confident of his ability, he returned to California and American network television.

Upon his return to America, Michaels landed a job producing and writing a show built around the comedy team of Burns and Schreiber. The show was unsuccessful and Michaels moved on to other projects. In 1973 he was introduced to comedian Lily Tomlin, who was enjoying a wave of success following her role as a regular performer on *Laugh-In.* In their first meeting, Tomlin and Michaels talked for nearly seven hours. After that first impression, Tomlin hired Michaels as a writer on her second television special for the Columbia Broadcasting System (CBS), which she was just starting to produce. Titled *Lily,* the show proved a turning point for Michaels. While he and Tomlin clashed over certain issues, neither could deny that their work together created great comedy. When Tomlin signed on with the American Broadcasting Company (ABC) for two more specials, she named Michaels as a chief writer and coproducer. "Tomlin's specials were daring," wrote Doug Hill and Jeff Weingrad in their book *Saturday Night: A Backstage History of Saturday Night Live,* "they seemed to have *experimental* written all over them." The shows contained pieces that were surreal for the television standards of the 1970s, and they often dealt strongly with such taboo topics as drugs and politics— issues that had plagued and later scuttled the popular *Smothers Brothers Show.* While her material found a significant audience with young urban viewers, Tomlin and her creative team's renegade approach incensed executives at both CBS and ABC. Her specials were not expanded into series form, as she and Michaels had hoped. As Tomlin went on to star in such films as Robert Altman's *Nashville,* Michaels halfheartedly worked on several TV specials for entertainers such as Perry Como and Flip Wilson. He quit after producing one of four specials for Wilson, once again disillusioned with television.

When Michaels first returned to the United States, his agent arranged a meeting with executives at NBC. The purpose of the meeting was for Michaels to pitch his idea for a new show to the network. Having long been a fan of the television series produced by the comedy troupe Monty Python, Michaels wanted to do a show in America that reflected the off-kilter, anarchic spirit of the English group. Armed with videotape of choice Python bits and excerpts from the Hart and Lorne shows, he pitched his idea to the men in charge of America's viewing habits. They laughed heartily at the material they were shown, but at the end of the meeting the executives told Michaels that no one in America would appreciate that type of humor. By 1975, about the time that Michaels was contemplating a permanent separation from television work, executives at NBC were trying to develop a new show that would air at 11:30 on Saturday nights, replacing the reruns of the *Tonight Show* that the network had been airing. The problem was that they couldn't find a producer with a concept that appealed to them. Michaels was approached by an NBC vice president, Dick Ebersol, with the prospect of pitching a show. He was told to meet two of NBC's top decision-makers in the Polo Lounge of the Beverly Hill Hotel. That meeting would change late night television history.

The show that Michaels pitched to the NBC executives that morning in the Polo Lounge was a radical departure from current television standards—and yet its foundation

lay in practices from TV's early years. Michaels described the show as such: as its backbone, it would have a regular, troupe-style cast performing in various sketch pieces; it would be hosted by a different celebrity each week; a different musical guest would also be featured each week; it would highlight the work of unique artists such as filmmaker Albert Brooks and puppeteer Jim Henson; and, to the discomfort of the executives, the show would be produced live. Despite their reservations, the NBC executives liked Michaels's ideas enough to give him a chance at producing the show.

They decided to call the show *Saturday Night* (it would not be until 1977 that the word "live" was officially added to the title). The fact that live television had given way to prerecording and that live telecasts were basically limited to sporting events and news programs did little to faze Michaels. To the contrary, the prospect of a show in which mistakes could not be corrected and anything could happen excited the producer. As he told Lillian Ross in *Interview,* "I wanted to be able to combine television technique with theater technique. . . . The [television] technology meshing with the live comedy is a miracle." Further addressing his reasons for producing the show live, Michaels later told Rensin, "I believe *The Tonight Show* lost its soul when it moved out of New York and stopped being live. I liked it, when I was a kid, that they *were up* at eleven-thirty. People are different when they're up at eleven-thirty."

Saturday Night would be produced in New York City and broadcast from studio 8H in the network's facility at 30 Rockefeller Plaza. Once it was committed to a debut, Michaels set about building the team that would create the show. He assembled a group of writers and production staff based on people whose work he knew—or was at least familiar with. Among this group were the writing and performing team of Al Franken and Tom Davis, dark comedy specialist Michael O'Donoghue, and Michaels's wife at the time, Rosie Schuster. To make the show really work, however, the producer needed to put together a cast that could write as well as perform, that had little or no preconceptions regarding the limits of television, and, most importantly, that reflected his own comic sensibilities. In preparing the first show, Michaels explained to Winship, "I just did a show that I would watch if I were the audience. Everyone else I assembled in the first year really had just sprung from the audience. With one or two exceptions, they weren't people with very long resumes." For his seven cast members, to be dubbed the Not Ready for Prime Time Players (the name was later dropped in the early 1980s), Michaels chose a varied group of performers. Dan Ackroyd was a writer and comedian with whom Michaels had worked when he and Pomerantz were producing their specials for the CBC. Ackroyd had previously worked with the Canadian version of the comedy troupe Second City. From a similar source, the National Lampoon comedy group, Michaels chose John Belushi, Chevy Chase, and Gilda Radner. To round the cast out he selected Laraine Newman, Jane Curtin, and Garrett Morris. The key players were in place, Michaels had the production staff he needed, now all that was required was getting America's late night television audiences to watch.

Saturday Night's first show aired on October 11, 1975, with popular comedian George Carlin hosting. In homes across North America, people tuned into a program that took chances, spoke frankly, and was a fresh departure from the usual television crop of sitcoms, police dramas, and variety shows hosted by egotistical celebrities. As *Playboy,* described it, "The humor was hip, the music contemporary, and young urban adults responded enthusiastically." The second show featured a reunion of the legendary music duo (Paul) Simon and (Art) Garfunkel, who had disbanded in the early 1970s. Michaels's creation was up and running. As the first season progressed, several of the performers distinguished themselves with energetic and inspired performances, establishing several popular and recurring characters. A noteworthy performer on *SNL*'s maiden voyage was Chase, who captured viewers' attention with his dry, off-the-cuff delivery and his slapstick pratfalls, which he often performed in the show's prologue segment. It was these prologues, a traditional sequence preceding the show's theme music and opening credits, that ended with the now legendary line "Live, from New York, it's Saturday Night!," a signal to the audience that the show's festivities were under way.

As *SNL* grew in popularity, so too did the attention lavished on Chase. At the end of the first season, Chase announced that he would be leaving the show to pursue a career in the movies. The performer's departure was a harbinger of things to come for Michaels, as future years would see the defection of other cast members, lured by the stardom and financial rewards that Hollywood offered. To replace Chase, Michaels chose Bill Murray, a young comedian who had distinguished himself in his work with the Chicago chapter of Second City as well as the National Lampoon troupe. With the addition of Murray, the Not Ready for Prime Time Players recovered from Chase's absence and began producing the shows that are considered definitive of *SNL*'s heyday.

Throughout the latter half of the 1970s, *Saturday Night Live* became the event of Saturday night television, with each of the Not Ready for Prime Time Players proving themselves key comedic players. Curtin assumed the reins of Chase's mock news segment, "Weekend Update" (which has, throughout the show's history, been a staple), and also created the role of Prymaat in the popular "Coneheads" skits. Newman specialized in parodies of the more

outrageous personalities found in 1970s society, including spaced-out hippies, bubble-headed talk show hostesses, and jaded partygoers. And Morris not only proved himself a capable comedian but a gifted singer. Despite the strong work of these three performers, many critics consider the work done by Ackroyd, Belushi, Murray, and Radner during this time to be among the best ever presented on *SNL*. Ackroyd not only distinguished himself with a host of characters, including Beldar Conehead, sleazy cable-TV host E. Buzz Miller, and ex-presidents Richard Nixon and Jimmy Carter, but as a linchpin on the show's writing staff. Belushi's kinetic energy was translated into such lasting performances as the Samurai warrior, a satiric Captain James T. Kirk (in a sketch spoof of the popular show *Star Trek*), and the proprietor of a Greek diner that offered a limited menu of cheeseburgers and cola ("No Coke . . . Pepsi!"). Radner created such beloved characters as prissy "Weekend Update" commentator Emily Littella, crass "Update" commentator Rosanne Rosanna Danna, and the nerdish, runny-nosed Lisa Lupner. Playing a spastic Romeo to Lisa Lupner's bespectacled Juliet was the equally nerdy, sexually and scatologically obsessed Todd DeLamucca, created by Murray. Murray also came forth with a greasy, no-talent lounge singer and a variety of shallow egomaniacal game show hosts.

With the establishment of the Not Ready for Prime Time Players as recognizable stars, *SNL* reached its greatest popularity. The show was a top-rated success that audiences repeatedly watched. Michaels related to White in *Rolling Stone* that he felt the show's success boiled down to the audience identifying with what *SNL* presented. As Michaels stated, "I always felt that the show at its best was a record of what had gone on that week in the country, the world, and in the lives of the people doing the show." Writing in *Interview,* Ross commented that the show was able to both challenge and entertain its audience using intellect and irreverence: "From the start, *Saturday Night Live* under Michaels, has been pitched . . . to a higher level of sophistication than any other comedy on American network television. It was obvious that Michaels did not worry about whether his show was too sophisticated or not." Michaels responded in the same *Interview* article, "What we did, and what I was incredibly serious about doing, was to establish that in comedy it was and still is perfectly proper to question the official version of everything. We have always played to a *movie* and a *book* audience and not to the audience of television."

The combination of *SNL*'s success and the youth of the writers and cast fostered an era of camaraderie and fertile creativity; from the years 1975 to 1978, the show flourished. Michaels described these early years to Winship as a "state of grace." As time progressed, however, the environment of *SNL* began to change. Michaels told Winship:

"I don't know how long groups can stay together in a kind of innocence. I think there's a point at which the age of experience takes over, and people view each other and themselves differently. They become conscious of 'Is this the best sketch for me to be doing?' The *work* ceases to be the guiding thing and this other word—*career*—begins to take over." Several of the cast members had embarked on outside projects during *SNL*'s summer vacations. Radner had parlayed many of her *SNL* characters into a hit stage show, *Gilda Live*—which Michaels cowrote, produced, and directed—and Radner, Curtin, and Newman had starred in a special, *Bob and Ray, Jane, Laraine, and Gilda,* with legendary radio comedians Bob Elliot and Ray Goulding. Following Chase's lead into movies, John Belushi took a role in the college fraternity comedy *National Lampoon's Animal House.* The movie became a large commercial success and Belushi became a viable movie star. Belushi and Ackroyd then teamed to make a movie adaption of their popular *SNL* characters the Blues Brothers. The taste of Hollywood success proved too alluring for Ackroyd and Belushi, and they announced that they would be leaving *SNL* at the end of the 1978 season.

The remainder of the cast, Curtin, Morris, Murray, Newman, and Radner returned for the 1979 season, joined by supporting players Harry Shearer, Don Novello (known primarily for his Father Guido Sarducci character), and the team of Franken and Davis. To many critics and viewers, however, it was clear that the *SNL* spark was fading. Michaels was upset by the departure of Belushi and Ackroyd, and he was also distressed by the current perception of the show. As he told Rensin in *Playboy,* "Everything we did was now popular. If we could do an old thing, we did. Worse, *Saturday Night Live* began to be perceived as a step, not an end. It changed the attitude of the people who worked there. I was trying to hold the show together. . . . It gave me all I needed, used all my talent, all my energy. But for others, it was time to move on." With the remaining cast members growing restless and his own attitude toward the show becoming jaded, Michaels announced his departure in 1980, at the end of the *SNL*'s fifth season. The entire cast and crew of the show also left at the end of that season, marking the end of *SNL*'s first chapter.

With the old cast now pursuing careers in films, Michaels decided to distance himself from television for a while. As a result he lent his talents to producing occasional television specials and concert events, including Simon and Garfunkel's reunion concert in New York City's Central Park. He also built up his production company, Broadway Video, and produced a film, *Nothing Lasts Forever,* that was written and directed by former *SNL* writer Tom Schiller. By 1984, however, he was ready to commit himself to regular television work once again. NBC asked him

to develop a new comedy show that would air at ten o'clock on Friday nights.

Assembling many of the writers from *SNL,* Michaels created a show that bore a format similar to his old show. Unlike *SNL,* however, Michaels's new show, titled *The New Show,* would not have a guest host. Rather, it would feature three guests—usually actors or comedians—per week who would join the regular cast in sketches. The show would also feature a special musical guest. Michaels assembled a small regular cast to work with each week's guests: well-known comedy writer and performer Buck Henry, *SCTV* (a Canadian comedy show similar to *SNL*) alumnus Dave Thomas, and comedian Valri Bromfield, whom Michaels had unsuccessfully recruited for the original cast of *SNL.* The show debuted in January of 1984 to a less than enthusiastic response from the network. Despite the fact that virtually the same creative team that had driven *SNL* to its zenith was working on it, *The New Show* could not quickly establish the viewer loyalty that its predecessor had enjoyed, and NBC was unwilling to give the show a lengthy chance to build an audience. *The New Show* was cancelled in March, three months after its debut.

While *The New Show* failed, its quick demise could not be compared to the troubles plaguing *Saturday Night Live* in the years after Michaels left the show. The season following Michaels's departure, NBC hired Jean Doumanian as the producer and charged her with putting together a new creative staff. Doumanian's new *Saturday Night Live* was greeted with brutal reviews, receiving negative publicity from a majority of the critics and viewers who watched it. Amid several behind the scenes conflicts, Doumanian, her entire production staff, and all but two of the cast members were fired. Dick Ebersol, the man who was instrumental in securing Michaels's position as creator and producer of *SNL* in 1975, assumed the role of producer in 1981. Ebersol produced one show before a writer's strike shut down production. After the strike, Ebersol managed to somewhat revitalize the show and simultaneously launch the careers of cast members Joe Piscopo and Eddie Murphy. But the show's budget had gone up and its ratings were not justifying the money. By the end of the 1985 season, Ebersol had left the show over a budget dispute and NBC began looking for a new producer.

NBC contacted Michaels about returning to *SNL* in the spring of 1985. He accepted the network's offer and agreed to put together a new staff, work with a reduced budget, and deliver the first new show by November of that year. "When I was asked to return," Michaels told Susan Orlean in *Rolling Stone,* "everyone advised me against doing it. But it's what I do, so I decided to come back." Rather than resume his role as active producer, Michaels decided to let the Franken and Davis team handle that job. He would act as executive producer, contributing writing and advice and overseeing the entire production. Despite putting together a cast that featured some promising newcomers, Michaels's return season was plagued by a number of troubles. Foremost was the short amount of time that he had to put his first show together. Cast members and writers were hired in a rush and many of them had no experience working in television. Several well-known actors, Anthony Michael Hall, Randy Quaid, and Robert Downey, Jr., were hired to improve the appeal of the all new cast. As the season got underway, however, many critics complained that these film actors were out of place in SNL's live comedy arena and were actually a detriment to the show. It also didn't help the show that, after ten seasons, it was no longer seen as a novel concept. By the end of the season, NBC laid out plans to cancel Saturday Night Live.

Michaels managed to save SNL from cancellation by appealing to NBC entertainment president Brandon Tartikoff. He promised Tartikoff a significant change in the cast and writing staff and also guaranteed the executive better ratings. Retaining only two performers, Nora Dunn and Dennis Miller, from the 1985 season, Michaels set about recruiting a new cast. This time he used the ethic that had guided him in selecting the first SNL cast in 1975. He went for virtual unknowns, people who were hungry and were fighting for territory in the comedy landscape. Joining Dunn and Miller for the 1986 season were Jon Lovitz, Victoria Jackson, Phil Hartman, Dana Carvey, Jan Hooks, and supporting player Kevin Nealon. Reviews for the new ensemble were enthusiastic and viewers once again began watching. Bolstered by the cast and a revitalized staff of writers, Michaels's SNL once again bloomed into a popular show.

As they had in the show's first incarnation, recurring characters began appearing on SNL and gaining popularity among viewers. There was Lovitz's Tommy Flanagan, a pathological liar whose catch-phrase was "Yeah, that's the ticket!" Hooks and Dunn created the Sweeney Sisters, a terrible singing duo whose roots could be traced back to Bill Murray's lounge singer. And Carvey brought forth a host of characters and impersonations, including Andy Rooney, Jimmy Stewart, and U.S. president George Bush. Carvey also contributed the Church Lady, a holier-than-thou TV evangelist who is fond of sarcastically proclaiming "Isn't that special?!?" when guests on her show display prideful behavior. As SNL progressed through the late 1980s, its popularity grew. In an interview with Bob Guccione, Jr. in Spin, Michaels attributed the show's rebirth to some troubleshooting he did at the end of the 1985 season: "By the end of '85, I was able to see: Wait a minute, we need . . . we don't have enough of this. So I tried bringing in two or three key performers who could balance what

I already had, a couple of writers who were better writers for them." Michaels also began featuring players who would earn their stripes in supporting roles and eventually become full cast members. Nealon was added the cast in this manner, as was Mike Myers, Chris Rock, and Chris Farley. By maintaining a steady influx of new talent, Michaels was able to weather the defections of key cast members like Miller, Hooks, and Carvey without having the whole show fall apart in the process. His formula worked so well that by the early 1990s, SNL was enjoying its highest ratings ever—this despite personnel changes.

As Michaels made his return to SNL in 1985, he was also expanding his influence in other areas. During his years away from the show he had developed his company Broadway Video, which, in addition to creating new programs, administered the syndication of SNL reruns. He also returned to the business of making movies, a venture he had unsuccessfully attempted in the late 1970s with Nothing Lasts Forever and SNL writer O'Donoghue's Mr. Mike's Mondo Video. This time teaming with comedian and frequent SNL host Steve Martin and singer/songwriter Randy Newman, Michaels wrote the script for a film called The Three Amigos, which he also produced. The film stars Martin along with former SNL cast members Chevy Chase and Martin Short, who appeared on the show during Dick Ebersol's reign as producer.

Chase, Martin, and Short star as Dusty Bottoms, Lucky Day, and Ned Nederlander, silent movie stars who are known collectively as the Three Amigos. Dressed in sombreros and Mexican-style costumes, the Amigos are a colorful crime-fighting team patrolling the western frontier in Hollywood films. Bottoms, Day, and Nederlander feel that their Amigo characters are popular American icons who deserve more respect—in the form of money. So the three confront the head of the studio that produces the Three Amigo films and demand more money. The studio boss laughs in their faces and throws them out on their collective behinds.

Things appear dark for the Amigos until a telegram arrives from Mexico. A young woman named Carmen has requested a performance by the Three Amigos in her village, and she has promised to pay the actors handsomely for their services. The three immediately agree to appear. Unknown to the Amigos, however, Carmen's communique was poorly translated. Having seen newsreel footage of the Amigos rescuing a town and then refusing reward money, Carmen believes that the three men are real heros carrying out egalitarian crusades against evil. She has asked them to come—free of charge—and rescue her poor village from the terrors of the outlaw El Guapo. The Amigos arrive in town with the belief that they will be playacting a gun battle, but instead come face-to-face with the deadly serious El Guapo. In the climax, the three actors must live up to their screen personas and actually rescue the town.

Critical reaction to *The Three Amigos* was mixed, with most reviewers agreeing upon the film's lightheartedness. *Washington Post* contributor Rita Kempley had the least patience for the film, calling it "the cinematic equivalent of Montezuma's revenge [diarrhea]." Writing in the *New York Times,* Janet Maslin complained of the film's excessive indulgence in sets and bad jokes, but she did praise the film as "likable" with "a strain of subtle wit," proclaiming that *The Three Amigo*'s "best gags reflect an enjoyable sophistication." Finding the film very entertaining, Patrick Goldstein wrote in the *Los Angeles Times:* "There's hardly a moment in 'Three Amigos' that isn't silly—make that incredibly, outrageously and breathtakingly silly. Maybe that's why this tale . . . is such a goofy delight." Goldstein went on to praise the film as "one of the daffiest comedies of the year."

In addition to making *The Three Amigos,* Michaels also became involved in a number of other television projects. He served as executive producer for the program *Michelob Presents Sunday Night,* which was hosted by jazz musician David Sanborn and featured musicians from a variety of backgrounds getting together and jamming. When he was faced with the possibility of NBC cancelling *SNL,* Michaels went in search of new talent. While in Toronto, he came across a comedy troupe called The Kids in the Hall (the moniker is taken from the nickname comedian Jack Benny bestowed upon his writing staff). Michaels was interested in recruiting fresh talent for the beleaguered *SNL,* but as he told Guccione in *Spin,* "I've always had a sort of taboo in my mind about breaking up comedy groups. I just know how hard it is for an ensemble to get together." Despite seeing potential *SNL* cast members among the Kids, Michaels admired their comedy too much to risk breaking up the group. Instead, he became the troupe's executive producer and arranged a deal for them with the Home Box Office (HBO) cable channel. The Kids in the Hall proved so popular on HBO that CBS offered them a late night network spot. The group amicably separated with Michaels when they signed with CBS in 1992. Despite the comparisons made between *The Kids in the Hall* and *SNL,* Michaels told Guccione that he doesn't view the show as a rival: "I think they do something different than what we do here and I think that they're brilliant."

With the re-emergence of *Saturday Night Live* as a powerful comedic voice, Michaels's talents as a creator became an in-demand commodity. In the early 1990s, he signed a production deal with Paramount Pictures, agreeing to create and produce a series of motion picture comedies for the studio. For his first film Michaels went to familiar territory. Approached by *SNL* cast member Mike Myers about making a film, Michaels suggested expanding the popular "Wayne's World" sketch into a feature. Like the sketch, the resulting movie is titled *Wayne's World* and, in a loose narrative, follows the exploits of teenagers Wayne Campbell, played by Myers, and his faithful sidekick Garth Algar, played by *SNL* regular Dana Carvey.

While *Wayne's World* has a loose plot, most of the attention the film received focused on the characters of Wayne and Garth; the storyline is a backdrop for Myers and Carvey to display their comedic talents. The film went on to tremendous success, becoming the number one moneymaker of 1992. *Wayne's World* appealed to young adults, who incorporated such Wayne and Garth phrases as "Yeah, and monkeys might fly out my butt" (a dismissal of a patently absurd statement), "Schwing!" (a proclamation of sexual arousal), and the immensely popular "Not!" (which is a sarcastic tag that follows a falsely sincere statement) into their everyday speech. While many adults (mostly parents of the kids mimicking Wayne and Garth) found the film ridiculous beyond compare, several critics were quick to notice *Wayne's World*'s lightheaded appeal. As Anne Billson wrote in the *New Statesman and Society,* "the jokes come thick and fast. Some *are* just thick, but the best are howlingly clever." *New York* contributor David Denby stated that the film "is funny in a nagging sort of way." "*Wayne's World* is a goofy, good-natured comedy," affirmed Brian D. Johnson in *Maclean's,* "a movie so wilfully sophomoric that no matter how inane it gets, it never loses its charm."

"In a world of recycled entertainment in which movies end up being pilots for television shows . . . and old television shows turn out to be previews for movies . . . it makes perfect sense to take . . . characters whose natural comedic life span is about five minutes and extend it by a factor of twenty." This sentiment stated by Emily Yoffe in *Rolling Stone* regarding the justification of making a movie out of the "Wayne's World" skit was echoed by Michaels. The success of the *Wayne's World* film proved to him that, done properly, characters from short pieces could be sustained throughout longer formats. So, in 1993, Michaels again parlayed an *SNL* sketch into a full-length motion picture. Going back to the show's "golden" era, Michaels met with former cast member Ackroyd to formulate a movie idea based on one of *SNL*'s most popular and enduring sketches, "The Coneheads." The movie that Michaels ended up producing is titled simply *The Coneheads* and was released in the summer of 1993. It tells the story of the familiar Conehead family, Beldar, his wife Prymaat (played, respectively, by Ackroyd and Curtin in a reprisal of the roles they originated on *SNL*), and their daughter Connie, natives of the planet Remulak.

Despite his success with movies, however, Michaels is still most often associated with his television work. "Michaels revolutionized late-night television with a live show that defied network censors," Johnson wrote of the series in another *Maclean's* article. *Saturday Night Live* and Lorne Michaels are often mentioned in the same breath, and to many he is the personification of the show. Critics such as Johnson have pointed to Michaels's work on the show as defining modern comedy on television. As Elizabeth Kolbert wrote in the *Detroit Free Press*, "By now *SNL* has been on the air so long it has shaped the comic sensibilities of an entire generation."

For all of the praise directed toward *SNL* and its creator, Michaels is modest about the work that he and his numerous cohorts have produced since 1975. In his discussion with Rensin, Michaels explained his *SNL* career by way of Stanley Myron Handelman's variation on the monkey/typewriter theory: if a group of monkeys are placed in a room with typewriters, they will eventually write the entire works of Shakespeare. As Michaels related to Rensin: "He [Handelman] left the monkeys in the room, and a couple of weeks later, he looked in on them, and he said, 'You know something? They were just fooling around.' " Michaels continued, "I always loved that joke because for me it represented what we were doing at the show: We were just fooling around." When Rensin later asked him if he agreed that *SNL* was his life's work, Michaels responded: "To a large extent. Being with the show has been like meeting somebody and falling in love when you're young, and it ends up that it's the person you're with for your entire life—and you think you must have made some mistake."

Although Michaels jokes about his role as a comedy innovator, others are quick to appraise his worth and the reasons for his successes. Ross wrote in *Interview* that "Michaels is attracted to talented people, and talented people are attracted to him." This holds true in Michaels's friendships as well as his business relationships. He has many close friends in the artistic community, a few of whom summarized Michaels for Ross. Singer/songwriter Paul Simon said of Michaels: "His intelligence is exhibited in the context of his wit. People are attracted to Lorne because they feel safe with his comedic sensibility. All this makes him the perfect producer." Writer/director Mike Nichols (*Catch-22, Silkwood*) also described his friend to Ross: "The main thing about Lorne is his generosity. He sees people in the most positive way, and then they become their best selves. As an artist and as a friend, Lorne demonstrates more loyalty and love through his acts than anyone else I know. As his humor is unsentimental in the extreme, I think it is the tension and the contradiction between his heartless humor and the great heart with which he lives that distinguishes him from others in his field. He's also very cute, and that's why the girls like him."

BIOGRAPHICAL/CRITICAL SOURCES:

BOOKS

Hill, Doug, and Jeff Weingrad, *Saturday Night: A Backstage History of Saturday Night Live,* Morrow, 1987, pp. 32-41, 480-505.
Winship, Michael, *Television,* Random House, 1988, pp. 196-203.

PERIODICALS

Details, March, 1993, pp. 103-08.
Detroit Free Press, March 22, 1993, p. 7D.
Films in Review, February, 1987, pp. 97-98.
Interview, June, 1988, pp. 53-61, 113-15.
Los Angeles Times, December 12, 1986.
Maclean's, June 9, 1986, pp. 38-41; February 24, 1992, p. 58.
Metro Times (Detroit), July 28/August 3, 1993, p. 29.
New Statesman and Society, May 22, 1992, p. 36.
Newsweek, December 18, 1986, p. 83; April 13, 1987, p. 70.
New York, January 9, 1984, pp. 41-43; February 24, 1992, p. 118.
New York Times, December 12, 1986; October 1, 1989, pp. 31, 40.
Playboy, March, 1992, pp. 51-64.
Rolling Stone, December 27, 1979; June 19, 1986, pp. 33-34, 96; November 20, 1986, pp. 45-46; March 19, 1992, pp. 34-40.
Spin, February, 1993, pp. 65-69, 90-93.
Time, December 29, 1986, p. 71.
Voice, November 19, 1985, p. 33.
Washington Post, December 12, 1986.

—Sketch by David M. Galens

*   *   *

MISTRY, Rohinton 1952-

PERSONAL: Born in 1952, in Bombay, India; immigrated to Canada, 1975; naturalized Canadian citizen; son of Behram (in advertising) and Freny (a homemaker; maiden name, Jhaveri) Mistry; married Freny Elavia (a teacher). *Education:* University of Bombay, B.Sc., 1975; University of Toronto, B.A., 1984.

ADDRESSES: Home—Toronto, Ontario, Canada.*Agent*—Lucina Vardey Agency, 297 Seaton St., Toronto, Ontario, Canada M5A 2T6.

CAREER: Worked in a bank in Toronto, Ontario, Canada; full-time writer, 1985—.

AWARDS, HONOURS: First Prize, Hart House Literary Contest, 1983 and 1984; Annual Contributor's Award,

Canadian Fiction, 1985; *Tales from Firozsha Baag* was shortlisted for the Governor General's Award for best fiction, 1987; *Such a Long Journey* received the Governor General's Award for best fiction and was shortlisted for the Booker Prize, both 1991, and received the Commonwealth Writers Prize, 1992.

WRITINGS:

Tales from Firozsha Baag (stories), Penguin (Toronto), 1987, published as *Swimming Lessons, and Other Stories from Firozsha Baag,* Houghton, 1989.
Such a Long Journey (novel), Knopf, 1991.

Work represented in anthologies, including *Black Water: The Book of Fantastic Literature,* edited by Alberto Manguel, 1984; *Coming Attractions,* edited by David Helwig, Oberon Press, 1986; *From Ink Lake: Canadian Stories,* edited by Michael Ondaatje, 1992. Contributor to periodicals, including *Antigonish Review, Canadian Fiction, Canadian Forum, Fiddlehead, Malahat Review, Quarry,* and *Toronto South Asian Review.*

WORK IN PROGRESS: A novel.

SIDELIGHTS: Rohinton Mistry is a prominent storyteller who has, as Val Ross noted in the Toronto *Globe and Mail,* won comparisons with writers ranging from Charles Dickens (*Great Expectations, A Tale of Two Cities*) to Salman Rushdie (*The Satanic Verses*). Mistry was born in Bombay, India, in 1952 and was raised, according to Ross, "in the classical British Empire traditions." In 1974 he completed studies for a degree in mathematics from the University of Bombay. The following year Mistry and his wife immigrated to Canada and settled in Toronto. He eventually entered the university there as well, and in 1984 he obtained his second degree, a baccalaureate in literature and philosophy. He then determined to become a writer.

In 1987 Mistry published *Tales from Firozsha Baag* in Canada. This collection of stories, as Nancy Wigston reported in her Toronto *Globe and Mail* review, "is a series of episodes all taking place in a semi-decrepit apartment complex in Bombay." The inhabitants of the Firozsha Baag housing complex are predominantly Parsi, an Indian subculture, and their lives are significantly intertwined. As a result, the story of one tenant may overlap another's tale and vice versa, with key incidents reiterated by various characters as time passes. Among the stories are "Auspicious Occasion," about a middle-aged couple, in which old world Parsi values come up against the tide of change on a high holy day, forcing the husband to reassess his self-image; "Condolence Visit," in which a widow violates decorum and bestows one of her late husband's artifacts upon a young man in need; and "Paying Guests," where perplexing, mentally unbalanced tenants defy their

meek landlord's efforts to displace them. In the volume's final episode, "Swimming Lessons," one of the children mentioned early in the book has grown to adulthood and emigrated to Canada. Now an author, the young man intermittently reminisces on his childhood while also imagining his parents, still in Bombay, reading a book he has written. In these recollections, the characters and stories from Firozsha Baag are tied together and revealed as not only individual episodes but as parts of a larger story of a Parsi community.

Upon publication *Tales from Firozsha Baag* earned Mistry significant attention from reviewers. Wigston, for instance, hailed him in her *Globe and Mail* assessment as an "extraordinarily talented young writer," and *Maclean's* reviewer Alberto Manguel affirmed that "every story in the collection is finely crafted." Further acclaim came for Mistry in 1989 when the book was published in the United States as *Swimming Lessons, and Other Stories from Firozsha Baag.* Janette Turner Hospital, in her *Los Angeles Times Book Review* appraisal, declared that Mistry writes "with intelligence, compassion, wit, and memorable flair," and the *New York Times*'s Michiko Kakutani, who proclaimed *Swimming Lessons* a "fine new collection," acknowledged the author's skill in creating "a world and a time," and she compared the volume to both R. K. Narayan's Malgudi books and James Joyce's *Dubliners.* Another critic, Hope Cooke, noted in the *New York Times Book Review* that Mistry's "ability through antic humor and compassion to make the repellent—or, at the very least, sad—story material . . . life-affirming, even ebullient, is astonishing given the horrifyingly stunted lives he depicts."

In 1991 Mistry published his first novel, *Such a Long Journey.* In the story, a humble bank clerk realizes tragic consequences when he becomes involved in political intrigue. The novel's hero is Gustad Noble, a Bombay patriarch whose average life is irrevocably changed when he grants a favor to a friend. He is drawn into a covert operation of the Indian intelligence agency that involves the diversion of government funds. Gustad believes that he is aiding insurgents in East Pakistan who eventually secede from that country to form the independent state of Bangladesh. The more involved he becomes, however, the more Gustad learns that he has been a pawn in a game that he does not understand. By the novel's end, the protagonist's life is far from enriched by his experiences. He has learned that his government—more specifically prime minister Indira Gandhi—is manipulative and duplicitous. As shattering as this information is to Gustad, the realization that he has no control over his fate, that his life is an element controlled by other forces, is his greatest source of devastation.

With *Such a Long Journey* Mistry won the Governor General's Award for fiction, the Commonwealth Writers Prize, and further praise from critics. David Ray stated in the *New York Times Book Review* that "Mistry's is a strong voice, and a welcome one," while Richard Eder, writing in the *Los Angeles Times Book Review,* proclaimed *Such a Long Journey* "authentically Dickensian" and affirmed that the novel's "major characters and some of its minor ones are unforgettable and deeply and broadly moving." Clark Blaise, in a Toronto *Globe and Mail* review, while questioning some of the novel's politics, conceded that *Such a Long Journey* proves "a complex and rather alien narrative, eventually rewarding and occasionally moving." And Lucasta Miller, writing in *New Statesman and Society,* observed that *Such a Long Journey* is "fluent, pithy and unclogged by artifice" and characterized the novel as "both utterly unpretentious and brilliantly perceptive."

BIOGRAPHICAL/CRITICAL SOURCES:

BOOKS

Contemporary Literary Criticism, Volume 71, Gale, 1992, pp. 265-76.
Leckie, Barbara, *Rohinton Mistry,* ECW Press, 1995.

PERIODICALS

Atlantic Monthly, May, 1991, p. 124.
Books in Canada, August-September, 1987, pp. 25-6; April, 1992, pp. 11-15.
Canadian Forum, April, 1989.
Canadian Literature, spring, 1992, pp. 4-5.
Fiddlehead, winter, 1989, pp. 109-12.
Globe and Mail (Toronto), May 2, 1987; September 4, 1991, p. E1; November 30, 1991, p. E2.
London Review of Books, April 4, 1991, p. 19.
Los Angeles Times Book Review, March 5, 1989, pp. 2, 11; April 21, 1991, p. 3.
Maclean's, September 21, 1987, pp. 53-54; May 27, 1991, p. 67.
New Statesman and Society, March 22, 1991, p. 46.
New York Times, February 3, 1989, p. C32.
New York Times Book Review, March 5, 1989, p. 26; July 7, 1991, p. 13.
Quill & Quire, June, 1987, p. 32; March, 1991, p. 62.
Time, April 8, 1991, pp. 76-77.
Times Literary Supplement, March 3, 1991, p. 20.
Village Voice, October 18, 1988, pp. 52-3, 101.
Washington Post, June 27, 1991, p. D3.

MITCHELL, Joni   1943-

PERSONAL: Born Roberta Joan Anderson, November 7, 1943, in Fort Macleod, Alberta, Canada; daughter of William (a grocery store manager) and Myrtle (a teacher; maiden name, McKee) Anderson; married Chuck Mitchell (a musician), June, 1965 (divorced); married Larry Klein (a musician and producer), November 21, 1982 (divorced, c. 1993). *Education:* Attended Alberta College of Art.

ADDRESSES: Home—New York City; Vancouver, British Columbia, Canada; Malibu, CA. *Agent*—c/o Elliot Roberts, Lookout Management, 9120 Sunset Blvd., Los Angeles, CA 90069.

CAREER: Painter, singer, songwriter, and recording artist. Exhibitions of Mitchell's paintings have toured the United States and Europe.

AWARDS, HONOURS: Grammy award for best folk artist from the National Academy of Recording Arts and Sciences, 1969, for *Clouds*; Playboy award for best female artist, 1974; Rocky award for best female vocalist, 1975.

WRITINGS:

Joni Mitchell Complete, Knopf, 1977.
Both Sides Now (children's songbook), illustrated by Allan Baker, Scholastic, 1992.
The Circle Game, illustrated by Mark Graham, Scholastic, 1993.

Also author of *Joni Mitchell Songbook: Complete Volume Number 1* and *Complete Volume Number 2.*

RECORDINGS; AUTHOR OF LYRICS AND MUSIC, EXCEPT WHERE NOTED

Song to a Seagull, Reprise, 1968.
Clouds, Reprise, 1969.
Ladies of the Canyon, Reprise, 1970.
Blue, Reprise, 1971.
For the Roses, Asylum, 1972.
Court and Spark, Asylum, 1974.
Miles of Aisles (concert recording), Asylum, 1974.
The Hissing of Summer Lawns, Asylum, 1975.
Hejira, Asylum, 1976.
Don Juan's Reckless Daughter, Asylum, 1977.
(Some music by Mitchell and Charles Mingus) *Mingus* Asylum, 1979.
Shadows and Light, Asylum, 1980.
(Some music by Mitchell and Larry Klein) *Wild Things Run Fast,* Geffen, 1982.
(Some music by Mitchell and Klein) *Dog Eat Dog,* Geffen, 1985.
(Some music by Mitchell and Klein) *Chalk Mark in a Rainstorm,* Geffen, 1988.

(Some music by Mitchell and Klein) *Night Ride Home*, Geffen, 1991.

(Some music by Mitchell and Klein) *Turbulent Indigo,*, Geffen, 1994.

SIDELIGHTS: Joni Mitchell, one of pop music's most versatile and enduring performers, was nine years old when she first performed before an audience. Hospitalized over the Christmas holidays after having contracted polio, she sang Christmas carols from her hospital bed. "I used to sing them real loud," Mitchell told Cameron Crowe of *Rolling Stone.* "When the nurse came into the room I would sing *louder.* . . . And I discovered I was a ham."

When she was in high school, Mitchell bought a ukelele. She later taught herself to play guitar with the help of a Pete Seeger instruction record. She sang for friends at parties, but at the time, her interest in performing was "no more ambitious than that," she commented to Crowe. "I was planning all the time to go to art school." Of her early singing career, Mitchell said, "It was a hobby that mushroomed," explaining: "I wrote poetry and I painted all my life. I always wanted to play music and dabbled with it, but I never thought of putting them all together. . . . It wasn't until Dylan began to write poetic songs that it occurred to me that you could actually *sing* those poems."

Following her graduation from high school, Mitchell attended the Alberta College of Art, but left after a brief period to pursue a career as a folk musician. She began by performing in coffee-houses, first in Toronto, then in Detroit, and finally in New York City. Her impressions of her early years in New York are contained in her first album, *Song to a Seagull.*

Mitchell's popularity grew as her songs were recorded by such established folk artists as Tom Rush, Buffy Sainte-Marie, and Judy Collins. Another factor that contributed to the artist's growing fame was her song "Woodstock," in which she described the famous 1969 rock music festival of the same name. By 1970 Mitchell had received a Grammy award for her second album, *Clouds.* Like the albums that would follow, *Clouds* explored "the joys and travails of being loved and unloved, of looking at the world through the eyes of a female," observed Ellen Sander in *Saturday Review.* In *Melody Maker,* Jacoba Atlas noted that Mitchell's songs were "reflections of a very feminine way of looking at life. All too seldom in music, and indeed in any art form, is the female view of the world set down. Joni does just that."

By the time her third album, *Ladies of the Canyon,* was released, Mitchell was living in California's Laurel Canyon, near Los Angeles. Although she was becoming increasingly successful, she was not entirely comfortable with that success. "The adoration seemed out of line," she later told Crowe. "I thought, 'You don't even know who

I am. You want to *worship* me?' That's why I became a confessional poet. I thought, 'You better know who you're applauding up here.' It was a compulsion to be honest with my audience."

According to *Rolling Stone*'s Steve Pond, Mitchell's desire to be truthful with her audience compelled her to write about herself as "a woman uneasily navigating the new-found sexual freedom of the times." And as she "struggled to grow up in public . . . she sealed her bond with an audience that had come to hang on her every word," Pond noted. "For many members of a generation recoiling from a disorienting string of social changes and retreating into uneasy introspection and doubt, turning to an articulate, probing, admittedly confused ex-flowerchild was a natural."

The early seventies saw the release of Mitchell's albums *Blue, For the Roses,* and *Court and Spark,* each one a critical and popular success. *Court and Spark,* which critic Janet Maslin called "exquisitely snug, passionate, and yet perfectly controlled," featured the sound of the L.A. Express, a group of jazz musicians. In her next album, *The Hissing of Summer Lawns,* Mitchell continued her experimentation with jazz. "She introduced jazz overtones, veered away from confessional songwriting, and received a nearly unanimous critical drubbing," wrote Crowe. Mitchell was stunned by the negative reception that greeted *The Hissing of Summer Lawns.* Because the album contained social description rather than the personal confession that people had come to expect from her, it "met with a tremendous amount of resentment," she explained. "People thought suddenly that I was secure in my success, that I was being a snot and was attacking *them.*"

Nonetheless, Mitchell continued to experiment. In *Hejira,* her next album, she "eschewed the security of pop melodicism, opting instead for free-form verse shoved up against the beat," wrote Vic Gabarini in *Musician.* Described by Pond as "an evocative, guitar-based set of reveries on flight and escape," *Hejira* "is as sophisticated and arresting as anything she's done," commented Ariel Swartley in *Rolling Stone.* "Her new songs take a long, sometimes painful look at a problem of particular concern to ambitious women: how to reconcile the demands of one's chosen work with the demands of love and family." With the release of *Don Juan's Reckless Daughter,* the double album that followed *Hejira,* Mitchell's continuing departure from the pop mainstream again met with a largely negative critical response. But as Don Heckman noted in his review of the album for *High Fidelity:* "A record with the size, scope, and ambitiousness of 'Reckless Daughter' obviously can't be written off with . . . the damnation of an easy expletive. Much of what Mitchell has tried here doesn't work at all. A lot more works very well indeed. Credit her, at least, with aiming for the sun, even if she only has managed to wind up in an eccentric solar orbit. That's still higher than most of us will ever get."

In a discussion of Mitchell's musical experimentation, Garbarini observed that the artist "garnered little credit for introducing . . . fresh elements and innovations into popular music. In fact, she was often roundly castigated for even trying." Reflecting on the critics' response to *Don Juan's Reckless Daughter*, Mitchell told Crowe: "If I experience any frustration, it's the frustration of being misunderstood. . . . All the way along, I *know* that some of these projects are eccentric. I *know* that there are parts that are experimental. . . . But they lay the groundwork for further developments. Sooner or later, some of those experiments will come to fruition. So I have to lay out a certain amount of my growing pains in public." If Mitchell's experimenting succeeded in alienating some listeners, it impressed others. One who was impressed by her risk-taking work was the legendary black bassist-composer Charles Mingus. In 1978 Mingus, who was suffering from a terminal illness, sent word to Mitchell that he was interested in working with her. He wanted her to write lyrics for his latest compositions. The album that resulted from the Mingus-Mitchell collaboration was entitled *Mingus* and was released in 1979, just months after Mingus's death. In an article about the album that appeared in *Rolling Stone* shortly before Mingus died, Ben Sidran wrote: "The ironies of this unique student/teacher collaboration will undoubtedly be more apparent to Charles Mingus' fans than to Joni Mitchell's. Mingus' reputation in the music world is based not only on his musical virtuosity but also on his unrelenting criticism of whites. . . . To think that now, so late in Mingus' life, his music will be heard in hundreds of thousands of homes interpreted by a leading white female pop singer is perhaps the ultimate twist to an extremely stormy career."

Describing the process by which she wrote the lyrics to Mingus's songs, Mitchell told Sidran: "Initially, [Mingus] just gave me the melodies . . . and it was my job to set words to them. I asked what each of the moods suggested to him. The first one, he said, was 'the things I'm going to miss'. . . . He looked at me, and in that look I knew that no matter how much you've done in a life, when you're confronted with the possible finality of it, there are a million things you've left undone. So I simply became him in my imagination and wrote what he would miss. . . . I cut myself off from everything and meditated on it."

After *Mingus*, Mitchell released *Shadows and Light*, a live album, and, in 1982, *Wild Things Run Fast*, which, according to Pond, "contains the most commercial music she's made since 1974's *Court and Spark*." With *Wild Things Run Fast*, Mitchell returned to the confessional style of her earlier work. Uncharacteristically, however,

she confessed more joyful feelings than she had in past lyrics. "It made me nervous as a cat to write like that," she admitted in her discussion of the album with Pond. "Because, y'know, I've always had a hard time tapping into my joy. It was always, 'This is nice now, *but*. . . . ' Always a *but*. Now I sing, 'Yes I do. I love you.' . . . .You never heard a comment like that out of *me* before."

Wild Things Run Fast heralded Mitchell's "reentry into the pop mainstream," Garbarini observed. "You could call it the Concorde version of *Court and Spark*: supersonic production values, razor-edged guitars, streamlined hooks and melodies—all the nuances of vocal phrasing and rhythmic sophistication she picked up on her jazz pilgrimage applied to good ol' rock 'n' roll. In short, rock strategy enhanced by jazz tactics."

Wild Things Run Fast heralded the beginning of Mitchell's personal and professional collaboration with bassist and producer Larry Klein, whom she wed the year that album was released. She would work with Klein throughout the 1980s and into the 1990s. The albums produced during this period brought Mitchell a renewed respect among both critics and her listeners. 1985's *Dog Eat Dog* found the artist augmenting her traditional acoustic sounds with experimental electronic ones. *Chalk Mark in a Rain Storm* (released in 1988) further honed the melding of electronic and acoustic instruments and yielded Mitchell's most acclaimed recording of the 1980s. The first half of the 1990s saw Mitchell and Klein continuing in the path set forth by their previous two albums with 1992's *Night Ride Home* and the 1994 release *Turbulent Indigo*, which many critics, Guy Garcia of *Time* included, viewed as the dark half of the coin first presented twenty-three years before with *Blue*. The difference being Mitchell's maturation as an arranger and performer and her shift away from the confessional lyric style epitomized by *Blue*. The newer albums are, in fact, so outwardly focused that Mitchell and Klein's divorce prior to *Indigo* is nowhere in evidence within that album's lyrics.

In the years since Joni Mitchell began her musical pilgrimage in Toronto cofeehouses, her ever-evolving style has earned her numerous labels: she has been called a folk artist, a rock star, and a jazz musician. But as she confessed to Leonard Feather in *down beat*: "Pigeonholes all seem funny to me. I feel like one of those lifer-educational types that just keeps going for letters after their name—I want the full hyphen: folkrock-country-jazz-classical . . . so finally when you get all the hyphens in, maybe they'll drop them all, and get down to just some American music."

BIOGRAPHICAL/CRITICAL SOURCES:

BOOKS

Contemporary Literary Criticism, Volume 12, Gale, 1980.

Miller, Jim, editor, *The Rolling Stone Illustrated History of Rock and Roll*, Random House, 1976.

PERIODICALS

Bulletin (Philadelphia), January 27, 1974.
Crawdaddy, February, 1978.
down beat, September 6, 1979.
High Fidelity, March, 1978; January, 1983.
Melody Maker, June 20, 1970.
Musician, January, 1983.
People, November 10, 1980.
Rolling Stone, February 10, 1977; March 9, 1978; December 28, 1978; July 26, 1979; November 25, 1982; December 23, 1982.
Saturday Review, July 26, 1969.
Time, December 16, 1974.*

—Sketch by Mary Sullivan

*   *   *

MITCHELL, W(illiam) O(rmond) 1914-

PERSONAL: Born March 13, 1914, in Weyburn, Saskatchewan, Canada; son of Ormond S. and Margaret Letitia (MacMurray) Mitchell; married Merna Lynne Hirtle, August 15, 1942; children: Ormond Skinner, Hugh Hirtle, Willa Lynne. *Education:* Attended University of Manitoba, 1932-34; University of Alberta, B.A., 1942. *Politics:* Liberal. *Religion:* Presbyterian. *Avocational interests:* Angling, orchid culture, dramatics.

ADDRESSES: Home—Calgary, Alberta, Canada.

CAREER: Author. High school principal in Castor, Alberta, and in New Dayton, Alberta, 1942-44; *Maclean's,* Toronto, Ontario, fiction editor, 1948-51; writer-in-residence at University of Calgary, 1968-71, University of Windsor, 1979-87, University of Alberta, York University, and University of Toronto. Instructor in creative writing at the Banff Centre. Actor, appearing in *Anne of Green Gables Sequel: Road to Avonlea.*

MEMBER: Delta Kappa Epsilon.

AWARDS, HONOURS: Eugene Field Award, 1947, for *Who Has Seen the Wind;* President's medal from University of Western Ontario, 1953; *Maclean's* Novel Award, 1953; Stephen Leacock Memorial Medal, 1962, for *Jake and the Kid;* received the Order of Canada, 1972; Chambers Award, 1975, for "Back to Beulah"; Drama Award from Canadian Authors Association, 1984, for "Back to Beulah"; Sir Frederic Haltaine Award, 1989; Stephen Leacock Memorial Medal, 1990.

WRITINGS:

Who Has Seen the Wind, Little, Brown, 1947.
Jake and the Kid (story collection), Macmillan, 1961.

The Kite, Macmillan, 1962.
The Black Bonspiel of Wullie MacCrimmon (novella), Frontiers Unlimited, 1965, with illustrations, McClelland & Stewart, 1994.
The Vanishing Point, Macmillan, 1973.
How I Spent My Summer Holidays, Macmillan, 1982.
Since Daisy Creek (novel), Macmillan, 1984.
Ladybug, Ladybug (novel), McClelland & Stewart, 1988.
According to Jake and the Kid (short stories), McClelland & Stewart, 1989.
Roses Are Difficult Here (novel), McClelland & Stewart, 1990.
For Art's Sake (novel), McClelland & Stewart, 1992.

PLAYS

The Devil's Instrument (first produced in Ottawa at the National Arts Centre, 1972), Simon & Pierre, 1973.
Back to Beulah, first produced in Calgary, 1974.
Sacrament (film script), produced by the Canadian Broadcasting Co. (CBC), 1978.
The Day Jake Made 'er Rain, first produced in Winnipeg, 1979.
The Dramatic W. O. Mitchell (includes *The Devil's Instrument, The Kite,* and *The Black Bonspiel of Wullie MacCrimmon* [first produced in Calgary, 1979]), Macmillan, 1982.

OTHER

Work appears in anthologies, including *The Best American Short Stories: 1946,* edited by Martha Foley, Houghton, 1946; *Book of Canadian Stories,* edited by Desmond Pacey, Ryerson Press, 1950; *Calvacade of the North,* edited by G. E. Nelson, Doubleday, 1958; *Three Worlds of Drama,* edited by J. P. Livesley, Macmillan, 1966; *Wild Rose Country: Stories from Alberta,* edited by David Carpenter, Oberon Press, 1977. Work also appears in *Canadian Short Stories,* 1960.

Also author of weekly radio series "Jake and the Kid," for CBC, 1950-58. Contributor to *Maclean's, Atlantic, Queen's Quarterly, Liberty, Canadian Forum, Ladies' Home Journal,* and *Imperial Oil Review.*

ADAPTATIONS: Who Has Seen the Wind and *According to Jake and the Kid* have been adapted into audiocassettes, McClelland & Stewart, 1990.

WORK IN PROGRESS: Brotherhood True or False, The Black Bonspiel, and *The Devil's Instrument,* all novels; *Wild Rose,* a feature film, for Meadow Lark Films.

SIDELIGHTS: One of Canada's most well-respected writers, W. O. Mitchell is known for his humor and nostalgic re-creation of small town Canadian life as well as for his love for the people and places of his native Saskatchewan. In addition to "Jake and the Kid," a popular radio series aired by the Canadian Broadcasting Corporation (CBC), Mitchell has also penned novels, short stories, and plays. In all of these genres, Michael Peterman writes in *Profiles in Canadian Literature,* Mitchell "has developed his talents with admirable agility and energy."

"Jake and the Kid" was first broadcast on June 27, 1950, and ran until 1958. Set in the imaginary small town of Crocus, Saskatchewan, the series concerned a young boy, "the Kid," and his friendship with Jake, the hired man on his mother's farm. Told from the Kid's perspective, Mitchell's gentle satire of small town life and his skillfully created characters were extremely popular with Canadian radio listeners. "We experience again," Catherine McLay writes in the *Journal of Popular Culture,* "our own childhood and our own pastoral roots." Part of the reason for the show's popularity was the character of Jake, who seems to embody something of the Canadian pioneering past. "Jake's appeal," McLay believes, "is that of the original frontier hero: he is physically strong, self-reliant, practical, free, unburdened by wife and child, illiterate and uncultured but optimistic in his outlook on life." Mitchell uses the same characters in a series of short stories first published in *Maclean's* and later collected as *Jake and the Kid.* Winner of the Stephen Leacock Memorial Medal, the collection contains stories that "were among the first," Margaret Laurence states in *Canadian Literature,* "that many of us who lived on the prairies had ever read concerning our own people, our own place and our time."

A young boy in the Canadian west is also the focus for Mitchell's first novel, *Who Has Seen the Wind.* Described by Richard Sullivan of the *New York Times Book Review* as "a piece of brilliantly sustained prose, a very beautiful, keen, perceptive rendering of human beings engaged in the ordinary yet profoundly—almost mysteriously—meaningful drama of every day," *Who Has Seen the Wind* enjoys a reputation as a Canadian classic. Peterman calls the work "a remarkable novel," while S. Gingell of *Canadian Studies in Literature* notes that "in studies of Canadian Prairie literature and in surveys of the development and outstanding achievements of Canadian fiction, W. O. Mitchell's novel *Who Has Seen the Wind* has been uniformly praised for its evocative style."

The novel is, William H. New explains in *Articulating West: Essays on Purpose and Form in Modern Canadian Literature,* "a study of Brian O'Connal's transition from the perfection of sensitive childhood, through conflict, to a balance that is achieved in early maturity." Along the way, the boy is influenced by many adult characters who live in his small Saskatchewan town. Although these other characters are carefully developed and the events they share with O'Connal are vividly presented, "Brian's growth to responsibility always remains central," New writes. The novel achieves, Peterman judges, "an extraor-

dinary power and charm. Its success, I would argue, lies in its focussing so precisely upon Brian's growth; all the events . . . serve that purpose."

In contrast to *Who Has Seen the Wind,* Mitchell's novel *The Kite* focuses on adult characters, although it again depicts a learning relationship between a younger and an older male. David Lang is a middle-aged reporter who comes to interview Daddy Sherry, reputed to be the world's oldest living man. The relationship that develops between the two men becomes the central focus of the novel, echoing the earlier relationships between Jake and the Kid and between Brian O'Connal and the adult characters he meets. However, "the educative relationship," Peterman writes, "between a boy and his older guide is less effective when the boy becomes a middle-aged man." Nonetheless, the passive Lang is transformed by the example of Daddy Sherry's wisecracking vitality. As New believes, both Lang and O'Connal "undergo a process of growth and development that results in their increased awareness of realities beyond the physical."

A similar concern is central to *The Vanishing Point,* Mitchell's next novel. First published as a serial in *Maclean's* under the title "The Alien," it concerns Carlyle Sinclair, a white man on a Canadian Indian reservation who serves as school teacher and Indian agent. The vanishing point is the point in artistic perspective where "parallel lines" meet to give the illusion of three-dimensional depth. The relationship between illusion and reality is constantly examined as Sinclair, according to New in a review of the book for *Canadian Forum,* discovers "the extent to which illusion confuses the real world in which he must live." Herbert Rosengarten makes the same point in *Canadian Literature.* The vanishing point of the title, he notes, is a metaphor for "the lines men draw for themselves and for others in their desire to impose order, purpose, direction, on human life." The results of this recurring discrepancy between reality and illusion are, New states, "often very funny."

Mitchell experiments in *The Vanishing Point* with stream-of-consciousness techniques and a nonchronological structure. Peterman judges this to be adventurous, but Rosengarten does not believe the approach works. Mitchell's oblique creation of his characters, Rosengarten argues, "takes a long time, and in Carlyle's case doesn't seem complete—he remains flat and featureless."

The familiar Saskatchewan small town setting is returned to in *How I Spent My Summer Holidays,* the reminiscences of the narrator about his boyhood. Although similar to Mitchell's earlier treatments of such material, *Summer Holidays* differs "in the discordant note set at the beginning—bizarre, darkly sexual," Paul Roberts writes in *Saturday Night.* The worst characters in previous Mitchell novels are, if not entirely honorable, at least harmless. But in *Summer Holidays,* one character, King Motherwell, is an alcoholic and bootlegger who murders his wife and lands in an insane asylum. Mark Abley of *Maclean's* notes that "these pages are liberally sprinkled with madmen, whores, religious fanatics, prigs, bigots, and drunkards." Arguing that Mitchell has consistently dealt with the theme of innocence, Guy Hamel sees Motherwell as "a tragic catalyst who brings about for Hugh [the young boy of the novel] the end of his childhood." Thus, *Summer Holidays,* although less gentle than previous works, presents Mitchell's familiar themes of transition into manhood. Hamel, writing in *Fiddlehead,* describes the book as Mitchell's "most sophisticated novel formally."

With *Summer Holidays,* Candas Jane Dorsey ventures in a review of *Roses Are Difficult Here* in the Toronto *Globe and Mail,* Mitchell "tunnelled, not for the first time but for the first sustained journey, down below that calm, deceptively flat surface to the great depths and layers beneath the strata of human frailty and complexity and astonishing variety. And since then his books have never completely returned to the sunny summer." *Since Daisy Creek,* Mitchell's first novel after *Summer Holidays,* looks at the regeneration of Colin Dobbs, a middle-aged creative writing instructor who for the past decade has been unable to write successfully. To offset his problem, he undertakes a new avocation as a grizzly-bear hunter, until an adult female bear nearly batters him to death. His ensuing, painful recovery—both physical and emotional—is eased by the aid of his daughter, who has returned after running away years earlier. At least one commentator, Patrick O'Flaherty of *Canadian Forum,* claims that *Since Daisy Creek* contains excessive profanities and that the work becomes mawkish, especially toward its conclusion: "Whatever is the root cause of all the cusswords," the critic writes, "it has not quite driven sentimentality out of the picture." Conversely, Jamie Conklin of *Quill and Quire* applauds Mitchell's effort, calling *Since Daisy Creek* "a wonderful novel, packed with action, emotion, and insight." The reviewer concludes that the author has "dodged the dangers of cliche and imitation, and in doing so has once again achieved the high standard of storytelling for which he is known."

A retired English professor figures as the protagonist in Mitchell's 1988 thriller *Ladybug, Ladybug,* a novel that combines both comedy and tragedy. Aging and widowed Kenneth Lyon, divested of his status as emeritus professor—and consequently ousted from his office—places a newspaper ad for domestic help, so he can write his biography of Mark Twain from his home. Nadya, a twenty-seven-year-old aspiring actress and single mother, answers his ad, bringing into Lyon's life not only her young daughter, Rosemary, but her spurned former lover, a psychotic

who is bent on revenge. Although Toronto *Globe and Mail* reviewer William French believes that *Ladybug, Ladybug* is overly sentimental—"Mitchell builds the doom-laden tension to the breaking point, and shamelessly manipulates our emotions"—the commentator acknowledges that Mitchell's characteristic humor surfaces as well. In one scene, French points out, the author chronicles an argument over which academic candidate should receive an honorary degree. Among the nominees is a pioneering psychologist who has overseen an investigation entitled "Phallometric Study of Erotic Preferences of Deviate and Non-Deviate Males through Measurement of Changes in Penis Volume."

A multitude of offbeat characters populate Mitchell's 1990 *Roses Are Difficult Here,* a novel that explores the structure of a small prairie town through the eyes of a university scholar. Set in the 1950s in the fictional community of Shelby, the work turns on June Melquist, an attractive sociologist who arrives from a neighboring institute to conduct an intense study of Shelby's social makeup. For assistance, she enlists the aid of Matt Stanley, editor of the *Shelby Chinook,* who introduces her to colorful town locals ranging from Mame Napoleon, wife of Shelby's septic-tank cleaner, to Nettie Fitzgerald, arrogant wife of the town doctor who snubs June in the fear "that the sociologist will trumpet the cultural backwardness of Shelby to a world that is just waiting for an excuse to ridicule the town," maintains Victor Dwyer in *Maclean's.*

Although Mitchell is sometimes classified as a regional humorist, Dick Harrison sees him as a writer who uses humor to explores serious issues. Writing in *Unnamed Country: The Struggle for a Canadian Prairie Fiction,* Harrison notes that Mitchell's "sensibility enlivens fairly traditional comic forms to a breadth and depth of human comedy never approached by [other Western Canadian writers]. . . . He faces seriously the questions of man's relationship to the prairie [and] is the only major writer in the period of 'prairie realism' to present a reconciliation of the human spirit with the prairie." Mitchell himself might not agree with such an academic analysis of his literary technique: "It's a very uncerebral process," he told H. J. Kirchhoff in the Toronto *Globe and Mail.* "If the reader is giggling or moved to tears, that's the criticism that counts."

Mitchell commented: "The use of humor by a fiction writer is dangerous. Critically so. I say this because if laughter is an ingredient in his fiction recipe, the writer will get no respect from the either-or people, and there are a lot of those folks out there, the sturm und drangers, who have never noticed that life does not sound only the low notes of storm and stress, but chords of both high and low. So too must the fiction illusions of actuality. Geoffrey Chaucer knew that. So did Charles Dickens and John

Steinbeck and Mark Twain. Henry James did not, nor did Thomas Mann. William Shakespeare did though. He called it comic relief, which causes the emotional pendulum to swing higher and lower, through contrast between tears and laughter.

"I take humor to be a very serious matter. Its main quality has to be logical surprise, unpredictable as life itself. Its use must be responsible. If not, then satire becomes simply invective, directed against undeserving targets. Comedy turns into one-liner slapstick. No space given to irony."

BIOGRAPHICAL/CRITICAL SOURCES:

BOOKS

Cameron, Donald, *Conversations with Canadian Novelists,* Part 2, Macmillan (Toronto), 1973.
Contemporary Literary Criticism, Volume 25, Gale, 1983.
Harrison, Dick, *Unnamed Country: The Struggle for a Canadian Prairie Fiction,* University of Alberta Press, 1977.
Heath, Jeffrey M., editor, *Profiles in Canadian Literature,* Volume 2, Dundurn Press, 1980.
McCourt, Edward A., *The Canadian West in Fiction,* Ryerson Press, 1970.
New, William H., *Articulating West: Essays on Purpose and Form in Modern Canadian Literature,* New Press, 1972.
Vertical Man/Horizontal World: Man and Landscape in Canadian Prairie Fiction, University of British Columbia Press, 1973.

PERIODICALS

Booklist, March 15, 1947.
Books in Canada, November, 1981; April, 1983.
Canadian Forum, April, 1947; May/June, 1974; November, 1984, p. 36.
Canadian Literature, autumn, 1962; winter, 1962; summer, 1963; winter, 1963; summer, 1974; summer, 1978.
Canadian Studies in Literature, Volume 6, number 2, 1981.
Chicago Sun Book Week, August 17, 1947.
Fiddlehead, July, 1982.
Globe and Mail (Toronto), October 27, 1984; October 29, 1988; October 21, 1989; November 25, 1989; October 13, 1990.
Journal of Canadian Fiction, spring, 1973; spring, 1974.
Journal of Canadian Studies, November, 1970; November, 1975.
Journal of Popular Culture, fall, 1980.
Maclean's, November 2, 1981; November 5, 1990, p. 82.
New York Herald Tribune Weekly Book Review, March 2, 1947.
New York Times Book Review, February 23, 1947.

Publishers Weekly, October 18, 1985, p. 48.
Quill and Quire, November, 1984, p. 35; February, 1989, p. 24.
San Francisco Chronicle, March 13, 1947.
Saturday Night, October, 1981; November, 1981.
Tamarack Review, winter, 1963.

*   *   *

MONTAL, Lionel
See GROULX, Lionel

*   *   *

MONTGOMERY, L(ucy) M(aud)   1874-1942

PERSONAL: Born November 30, 1874, in Clifton (now New London), Prince Edward Island, Canada; died April 24, 1942, in Toronto, Ontario, Canada; buried in Cavendish Cemetery, Cavendish, Prince Edward Island; daughter of Hugh John (a merchant) and Clara Woolner (Macneill) Montgomery; married Ewan Macdonald (a Presbyterian minister), July 5, 1911; children: Chester Cameron, Hugh Alexander, Ewan Stuart. *Education:* Prince of Wales College, Charlottetown, Prince Edward Island, second-class teacher's certificate, 1894, first-class teacher's license, 1895; attended Dalhousie College (now Dalhousie University), Halifax, Nova Scotia, 1895-96. *Avocational interests:* Knitting, crocheting, astronomy, sewing, designing needlepoint lace, books, photography, the outdoors.

CAREER: Schoolteacher in Bideford, Prince Edward Island, 1894-95 and 1896-97, and Belmont Lot 16 and Lower Bedeque, Prince Edward Island, 1897-98; assistant postmistress, Cavendish, Prince Edward Island, 1898-1911; staff member, *Halifax Daily Echo,* 1901-02; novelist and author for children.

MEMBER: Royal Society of Arts and Letters, Canadian Authors Association, Canadian Women's Press Association, Toronto Woman's Press.

AWARDS, HONOURS: Fellow, Royal Society of Arts, 1923; Officer, Order of the British Empire, 1935; a Canadian stamp has been issued commemorating Montgomery and *Anne of Green Gables;* various museums on Prince Edward Island have been dedicated to Montgomery; *Anne of Green Gables* has appeared on several children's "favorites" lists in North America and Eastern Europe.

WRITINGS:

"ANNE" SERIES

Anne of Green Gables, illustrated by M. A. and W. A. J. Claus, Page, 1908.
Anne of Avonlea, illustrated by George Gibbs, Page, 1909.

Chronicles of Avonlea, in Which Anne Shirley of Green Gables and Avonlea Plays Some Part (short stories), illustrated by Gibbs, Page, 1912.

Anne of the Island, illustrated by H. Weston Taylor, Page, 1915.

Anne's House of Dreams, Stokes, 1917.

Rainbow Valley, Stokes, 1919.

Further Chronicles of Avonlea: Which Have to Do with Many Personalities and Events in and about Avonlea (short stories), illustrated by John Goss, Page, 1920.

Rilla of Ingleside, Stokes, 1921.

Anne of Windy Poplars, Stokes, 1936, published as *Anne of Windy Willows,* McClelland & Stewart, 1936.

Anne of Ingleside, Stokes, 1939.

Anne of Green Gables has appeared in several editions with different illustrators and has been translated into sixty languages; the "Anne" series has been translated into more than thirty-five languages.

OTHER NOVELS

Kilmeny of the Orchard, illustrated by George Gibbs, Page, 1910.

The Story Girl, illustrated by Gibbs, Page, 1911.

The Golden Road, illustrated by Gibbs, Page, 1913.

Emily of New Moon, Stokes, 1923.

Emily Climbs, McClelland & Stewart, 1924, Stokes, 1925.

The Blue Castle, Stokes, 1926.

Emily's Quest, Stokes, 1927.

Magic for Marigold, McClelland & Stewart, 1927, Stokes, 1929.

A Tangled Web, Stokes, 1931, published as *Aunt Becky Began It,* Hodder & Stoughton, c. 1931.

Pat of Silver Bush, Stokes, 1933.

Mistress Pat: A Novel of Silver Bush, Stokes, 1935.

Jane of Lantern Hill, Stokes, 1937.

POSTHUMOUSLY PUBLISHED COLLECTIONS

The Green Gables Letters, from L. M. Montgomery to Ephraim Weber, 1905-1909, edited by Wilfrid Eggleston, Ryerson, 1960.

The Alpine Path: The Story of My Career (autobiographical articles originally published in the Toronto magazine *Everywoman's World,* 1917), Fitzhenry & Whiteside, 1974.

The Road to Yesterday (short stories), McGraw/Ryerson, 1974.

The Doctor's Sweetheart and Other Stories, selected and introduced by Catherine McLay, McGraw/Ryerson, 1979.

My Dear Mr. M.: Letters to G. B. MacMillan from L. M. Montgomery, edited by Francis W. P. Bolger and Elizabeth R. Epperly, McGraw/Ryerson, 1980.

Spirit of Place: Lucy Maud Montgomery and Prince Edward Island, selected and edited by Francis W. P. Bol-

ger, photography by Wayne Barrett and Anne MacKay, Oxford University Press, 1982.

The Selected Journals of L. M. Montgomery, Volume 1: *1889-1910,* Volume 2: *1910-1921,* edited by Mary Rubio and Elizabeth Waterston, Oxford University Press, 1985-87.

The Poetry of Lucy Maud Montgomery, selected and introduced by John Ferns and Kevin McCabe, Fitzhenry & Whiteside, 1987.

Akin to Anne: Tales of Other Orphans (short stories), edited by Rea Wilmhurst, McClelland, 1988.

Along the Shore: Tales by the Sea, edited by Wilmhurst, McClelland, 1989.

Among the Shadows: Tales from the Darker Side, edited by Wilmhurst, McClelland, 1990.

Days of Dreams and Laughter: The Story Girl and Other Tales (includes *The Story Girl, The Golden Road,* and *Kilmeny of the Orchard*), Avenel, 1990.

OTHER

The Watchman, and Other Poems, McClelland & Stewart, 1916, Stokes, 1917.

(With Marian Keith and Mabel Burns McKinley) *Courageous Women* (biography), McClelland & Stewart, 1934.

Excerpts from Montgomery's writings appear in *The Years before "Anne": The Early Career of Lucy Maud Montgomery,* by Francis W. P. Bolger, Prince Edward Island Heritage Foundation, 1974. Contributor of articles, verses, and short stories to magazines and newspapers.

ADAPTATIONS: Anne of Green Gables has been adapted into motion pictures released by Realart Pictures, 1919, and RKO Radio Pictures, 1934; a stage production, by Wilbur Braun, published by Samuel French, 1937; a musical, by Donald Harron and Norman Campbell, presented yearly at the Charlottetown Summer Festival, Prince Edward Island, 1965—, published by Samuel French, 1972; a filmstrip, released by the National Film Board of Canada, 1953; a television play, by Julia Jones, BBC-1, 1972, and a televised sequel based on *Anne of Avonlea* and *Anne of the Island,* 1975; a television play, by Kevin Sullivan and Joe Wiesenfeld, *WonderWorks,* PBS, c. 1986, and a sequel, *Anne of Avonlea: The Continuing Story of Anne of Green Gables,* by Sullivan, The Disney Channel, 1987; other television productions based on *Green Gables* have aired on CBC. *Green Gables* has also been adapted into several children's editions.

Anne of Windy Poplars has been adapted into a motion picture, released by RKO Radio Pictures, 1940; and *Jane of Lantern Hill* has been adapted into an audiocassette, narrated by Mairon Bennett, released by Bantam Audio, 1989, and a television play, cowritten by Sullivan, The Disney Channel, 1990.

A television feature, based in part on Montgomery's diaries, aired on CBC, 1974.

SIDELIGHTS: L. M. Montgomery is recognized worldwide as the creator of "Anne," the sprightly, imaginative orphan first introduced in the author's classic tale *Anne of Green Gables.* Published in 1908, *Green Gables* became an immediate popular success and propelled its author to wealth and fame. Sequels followed, including *Anne of Avonlea* and *Anne of the Island,* as well as other memorable books featuring young, self-directed heroines; but it is primarily for the character of Anne that Montgomery's reputation has endured. Throughout the years critical reaction to Montgomery's entire body of work has been mixed—many feel that the quality of her books after *Green Gables* steadily declines. However, most agree that her abiding popularity stems from her storytelling ability and her sensitive understanding of children. Montgomery "remembered exactly how it was to be a child," explained Jean Little in *L. M. Montgomery: An Assessment.* "More than that, she was able to record the experience of being a child so faithfully and vividly that reading children, years later, find themselves in her stories."

Montgomery's own childhood was a rather lonely one. She was born in 1874 in Clifton, Prince Edward Island, a beautiful landscape that was to provide the setting for many of her books. When the young Montgomery was two, her mother died of tuberculosis, and a few years later her father moved to Prince Albert to remarry and begin a new family. The youngster was sent to live with her stern, devout grandparents in Cavendish, P.E.I. There she met with verbal abuse, constant references to her father's "abandonment," and punishments for youthful infractions for which she was made to kneel for long periods of time. Humiliated and lonesome, the sensitive youngster retreated inward into a dreamy, fanciful world filled with princesses, fairies, and haunted woods. "Life never held for me a dull moment," she later wrote, as quoted by Jon C. Stott in *Writers for Children.* "I had, in my vivid imagination, a passport to the geography of Fairyland." She indulged her active imagination in the books of such well-known nineteenth-century writers as Charles Dickens, Lord Byron, and Henry Wadsworth Longfellow, and from an early age, she recognized what she most wanted to do: become a writer.

"I cannot remember the time when I was not writing, or when I did not mean to be an author," she remembered in her autobiography, *The Alpine Path.* "To write has always been my central purpose around which every effort and hope and ambition of my life has grouped itself." Her early childhood scribblings took the form of anecdotes, verses, descriptive passages, and tragic romances. By the time she was nearly sixteen, a local paper had published one of her poems, and from then on many of her short works were published in various periodicals. In hopes of furthering her literary career, she worked industriously, grinding out story upon story, but she soon realized she needed a more secure career plan. So she obtained her teacher's certificate in 1894 and worked variously as a schoolteacher, a staff person at the *Halifax Daily Echo,* and the caretaker of her widowed grandmother. Then in 1904, while searching for an idea for another serial, she found scratched in an old notebook: " 'Elderly couple apply to orphan asylum for a boy. By mistake a girl is sent them.' . . . I began to block out the chapters," she recalled in her autobiography, "and 'brood up' my heroine. Anne . . . soon seemed very real to me and took possession of me to an unusual extent. She appealed to me, and I thought it rather a shame to waste her on an ephemeral little serial. Then the thought came, 'Write a book. You have the central idea. All you need do is to spread it out over enough chapters to amount to a book.' "

Completed in October of 1905, the book became *Anne of Green Gables,* and three years later, after enduring a handful of rejections from publishers, Montgomery held the published copy in her hands. "There . . . lay material realization of all the dreams and hopes and ambitions of my whole conscious existence—my first book," she recalled in her autobiography, as quoted in *Writers for Children.* "Not a great book, but mine, mine, mine, something which I had created." *Green Gables* literally became an overnight success. Six editions were printed in six months, and by 1910 Montgomery had earned more than seven thousand dollars in royalties (at a time when working women's yearly salaries averaged less than three hundred dollars). In response to her publisher's request for a sequel, Montgomery produced *Anne of Avonlea,* but her enthusiasm for the project had already begun to wane. "If I'm to be dragged at Anne's chariot wheels the rest of my life," she remarked, as quoted by Mollie Gillen in *The Wheel of Things,* "I'll bitterly repent having 'created' her." The pattern of writing a book first for her own interest, then producing sequels at the demand of publishers and readers was to characterize Montgomery's entire literary career.

Montgomery completed *Kilmeny of the Orchard* and *The Story Girl* (her favorite), before her marriage in 1911 to Reverend Ewan Macdonald; the couple then moved to Leaskdale, Ontario. Outwardly, Montgomery seemed comfortable with her life. Her roles as wife and mother hardly encumbered her writing output, for she produced nine more books before 1925, including four additional "Anne" novels as well as the first two stories in her "Emily" series. Inwardly, though, she struggled with intense pain. News about World War I saddened her; she mourned the loss of her second son (he was stillborn); she suffered through her husband's extreme onslaughts of depression; and she endured nine years of disputes with her publisher, L. C. Page, who had printed copies of old manuscripts without her permission. In the 1930s Montgomery satisfied popular demand by completing two more "Anne" books, as well as writing her "Pat" series and *Jane of Lantern Hill.* But in the last decade of her life, she became increasingly despondent. In the late 1930s she suffered a mental and physical collapse, and by December of 1941 she had plummeted even further into despair. "You do not know the blows that have fallen on my life for years," she disclosed to a friend, as cited in *The Wheel of Things.* "I feel my mind is going. . . . My husband is very miserable. I have tried to keep the secret of his melancholic attacks for twenty years . . . but the burden broke me at last, as well as other things. And now the war [World War II]. I do not think I will ever be well again." Nearly five months later, Montgomery died.

Throughout her career Montgomery struggled with an inner conflict: to satisfy public taste by writing the light romances that sustained her career, or fulfill her own desire to produce a serious literary work. She never realized, though, that with *Anne of Green Gables* she *had* produced a classic. With P.E.I. as its backdrop, the story centers on the title character, a sensitive, creative youngster who is adopted by Matthew, a shy, retiring bachelor, and Marilla, his spinster sister. Feisty and overimaginative, Anne desperately craves love and security, and the narrative recounts how through a series of often comical episodes she realizes her dream of becoming "Anne of Green Gables" and even wins the hearts of her elderly custodians and local neighbors. Critics note that the book's popularity stems in part from its picturesque setting, viewed through the appreciative eyes of a lonely orphan, and its fairy tale theme, in which a bereft child finds acceptance and love. Yet most importantly, its lasting fame springs from the well-rounded character of Anne. She is trouble-prone—she inadvertently colors her hair green, for example, and must cut it off—yet she good-naturedly accepts her mishaps as learning experiences. Sometimes she indulges in mischief, such as the time she hopes to awe her friends and instead falls from a roof and breaks her ankle. But she develops an admirable sense of responsibility: she gives up a college scholarship to remain with Marilla after Matthew's death. Anne is "the dearest, and most lovable child in fiction since the immortal Alice," Mark Twain told Montgomery in a note, as quoted in *The Wheel of Things.* The book not only continues to captivate a multitude of followers, but has also inspired motion pictures, stage productions, and an Emmy Award-winning television film.

In all, Montgomery wrote seven books in the "Anne" series, from *Anne of Avonlea,* in which the title character becomes a teacher, to *Anne of Ingleside,* by which time Anne has married and is raising a family. However, most critics agree—as did Montgomery herself—that as the series progresses, the plots become more and more contrived, and as Anne settles into her socially accepted roles of wife and mother, she loses her vitality and free-spiritedness. "I have gone completely 'stale' on Anne and must get a new heroine," the author complained after completing *Rilla of Ingleside,* as quoted in *Writers for Children.* Although public demand forced a revival of the "Anne" series almost fifteen years after *Rilla,* Montgomery did succeed in creating three other major heroines during her career: the title characters of *Emily of New Moon, Pat of Silver Bush,* and *Jane of Lantern Hill.* Emily is the best known of these and considered among reviewers as the most autobiographical of Montgomery's characters. An orphan and an aspiring writer, Emily faces disapproval from her relatives, yet she achieves literary success through her determination, incorporating the P.E.I. countryside and its natives into her stories. Pat and Jane also face adversity— Pat loses her cherished home in a fire, and Jane meets with dominant, interfering relatives—but each finds comfort in her natural surroundings. Pat anticipates a better life after she marries and moves to Canada's west coast, and Jane succeeds in reuniting her parents in the family home on P.E.I.

Around 1900, Montgomery wrote, "I know that I can never be a really great writer," as cited *The Wheel of Things.* "My aspiration is limited to this—I want to be a good *workman* in my chosen profession. I cannot be one of the masters but I hope to attain to a recognized position among the everyday workers of my time." Montgomery certainly has attained that distinction. Although some reviewers dispute her literary status, her work has received increasing scholarly attention since her death. And the popularity of her stories has never diminished among lay readers, many of whom frequent the P.E.I. museums devoted to her and attend the musical production of *Green Gables* that has played on the Island since 1965. "Montgomery remained a child at heart," wrote Frances Frazer in the *Dictionary of Literary Biography,* "with an exhaustive, unforgiving memory of what a thin-skinned, imaginative child can suffer and an unquenchable delight in children's pleasures." She depicted the fears, confusion, joys, and triumphs of youth, and in doing so captured the attention of readers around the world. "Youth is not a vanished thing," she once wrote, as quoted in a Charlottetown Summer Festival publicity release, "but something that dwells forever in the heart."

BIOGRAPHICAL/CRITICAL SOURCES:

BOOKS

Authors and Artists for Young Adults, Volume 12, Gale, 1994, pp. 147-59.

Children's Literature Review, Volume 8, Gale, 1985, pp. 107-40.

Dictionary of Literary Biography, Volume 92, *Canadian Writers, 1890-1920,* Gale, 1990, pp. 246-53.

Egoff, Sheila, *The Republic of Childhood: A Critical Guide to Canadian Children's Literature in English,* 2nd edition, Oxford University Press, 1975, pp. 292-309.

Fisher, Margery, *Who's Who in Children's Books: A Treasury of the Familiar Characters of Childhood,* Holt, 1975, p. 23.

Gillen, Mollie, *The Wheel of Things: A Biography of L. M. Montgomery, Author of "Anne of Green Gables,"* Fitzhenry & Whiteside, 1975.

L. M. Montgomery: An Assessment, edited by John Robert Sorfleet, Canadian Children's Press, 1976.

Montgomery, L. M., *The Alpine Path: The Story of My Career* (autobiographical articles originally published in the Toronto magazine *Everywoman's World,* 1917), Fitzhenry & Whiteside, 1974.

Phelphs, Arthur L., *Canadian Writers,* McClelland & Stewart, 1951, pp. 85-93.

Reimer, Mavis, editor, *Such a Simple Little Tale: Critical Responses to L. M. Montgomery's "Anne of Green Gables,"* Scarecrow, 1992.

Ridley, Hilda M., *The Story of L. M. Montgomery,* Ryerson, 1956.

Twentieth-Century Children's Writers, 3rd edition, St. James Press, 1989, pp. 690-91.

Twentieth-Century Literary Criticism, Volume 51, Gale, 1994.

Twentieth-Century Romance and Historical Writers, 2nd edition, St. James Press, 1990, pp. 469-70.

Waterston, Elizabeth, *The Clear Spirit: Twenty Canadian Women and Their Times,* edited by Mary Quayle Innis, University of Toronto Press, 1966, pp. 198-220.

Writers for Children, edited by Jane M. Bingham, Charles Scribner's Sons, 1988, pp. 415-22.

Yesterday's Authors of Books for Children, Volume 1, Gale, 1977, pp. 182-92.

PERIODICALS

Bookman, October, 1909, p. 152.

Canadian Children's Literature, autumn, 1975; Number 30, 1983, pp. 5-20; Number 37, 1985, pp. 5-16, 40-46, and 47-52; Number 38, 1985, pp. 68-80; Number 42, 1986, pp. 29-40; Number 52, 1988, pp. 67-68; Number 53, 1989, pp. 46-47; Number 55, 1989, pp. 8-17.

Children's Literature in Education, Volume 20, number 3, 1989, pp. 165-73.

Dalhousie Review, April, 1944, pp. 64-73; summer, 1976, pp. 247-51.

Growing Point, January, 1978, pp. 3244-45; January, 1980.

Horn Book, March/April, 1986, pp. 174-75; September/October, 1988, pp. 663-66.

In Review: Canadian Books for Children, summer, 1977, pp. 42-43.

Maclean's, December 7, 1987, p. 50.

Nation, September 2, 1909, p. 212; August 10, 1911, p. 122.

Nature Canada, winter, 1987, pp. 30-35.

New York Times, April 25, 1942, p. 13.

New York Times Book Review, July 18, 1908, p. 404; September 21, 1919, p. 484; September 11, 1921, p. 23; August 26, 1923, pp. 24, 26; July 30, 1939, p. 7.

Publishers Weekly, September 18, 1915, p. 790; August 16, 1919, pp. 484-85.

Saturday Night, November, 1987, pp. 52-58.

School Library Journal, May, 1990, p. 73.

Times Literary Supplement, September 13, 1923, p. 105.

Publicity release from Charlottetown Summer Festival, Confederation Centre of the Arts, Charlottetown, Prince Edward Island.*

*   *   *

MOORE, Brian 1921-
(Michael Bryan, Bernard Marrow)

PERSONAL: Born August 25, 1921, in Belfast, Northern Ireland; immigrated to Canada, 1948; Canadian citizen; son of James Brian (a surgeon) and Eileen (McFadden) Moore; married Jean Denney, October, 1967; children: Michael. *Education:* Graduated from St. Malachy's College, 1939.

ADDRESSES: Home—33958 Pacific Coast Hwy., Malibu, CA 90265. *Agent*—Perry Knowlton, Curtis Brown Ltd., 10 Astor Place, New York, N.Y. 10003.

CAREER: Montreal Gazette, Montreal, Quebec, proofreader, reporter, and rewrite man, 1948-52; writer, 1952—. *Wartime service:* Served with British Ministry of War Transport in North Africa, Italy, and France during World War II.

AWARDS, HONOURS: Author's Club first novel award, 1956; Quebec Literary Prize, 1958; Guggenheim fellowship, 1959; Governor General's Award for Fiction, 1960, for *The Luck of Ginger Coffey,* and 1975, for *The Great Victorian Collection;* U.S. National Institute of Arts and Letters fiction grant, 1961; Canada Council fellowship for travel in Europe, 1962 and 1976; W. H. Smith Prize, 1972, for *Catholics;* James Tait Black Memorial Award, 1975, for *The Great Victorian Collection;* Booker shortlist for *The Doctor's Wife,* 1976; Booker shortlist for *Lies of Silence,* 1990; Neill Gunn International Fellowship from the Scottish Arts Council, 1983; "ten best books of 1983" citation from *Newsweek,* 1983, for *Cold Heaven;* Heinemann Award from the Royal Society of Literature, 1986, for

Black Robe; Booker Prize shortlist citation, 1987, and *Sunday Express* Book of the Year Prize, 1988, both for *The Color of Blood;* honorary literature degree, Queens University, Belfast, Ireland, 1989; honorary literature degree, National University of Ireland, Dublin, Ireland, 1991; Fellow of the Royal Society of Literature.

WRITINGS:

NOVELS

Judith Hearne, A. Deutsch, 1955, published as *The Lonely Passion of Judith Hearne,* Little, Brown, 1956.
The Feast of Lupercal, Little, Brown, 1957.
The Luck of Ginger Coffey, Little, Brown, 1960.
An Answer from Limbo, Little, Brown, 1962.
The Emperor of Ice-Cream, Viking, 1965.
I Am Mary Dunne, Viking, 1968.
Fergus, Holt, 1970.
The Revolution Script, Holt, 1971.
Catholics, J. Cape, 1972, Harcourt, 1973.
The Great Victorian Collection, Farrar, Straus, 1975.
The Doctor's Wife, Farrar, Straus, 1976.
The Mangan Inheritance, Farrar, Straus, 1979.
Two Stories, Santa Susana Press, 1979.
The Temptation of Eileen Hughes, Farrar, Straus, 1981.
Cold Heaven, Holt, 1983.
Black Robe, Dutton, 1985.
The Color of Blood, Dutton, 1987.
Lies of Silence, Doubleday, 1990.
No Other Life, Doubleday, 1993.

OTHER

(With others) *Canada* (travel book), Time-Life, 1963.
The Luck of Ginger Coffey (screenplay; based on his novel of same title), Continental, 1964.
Torn Curtain (screenplay), Universal, 1966.
Catholics (television script; based on his novel of same title), Columbia Broadcasting System, 1973.
Black Robe (screenplay; based on his novel of the same title), Alliance Communications, 1987.

Also author of screenplays *The Slave* (based on his novel *An Answer from Limbo*), 1967, *The Blood of Others,* 1984, *Brainwash,* 1985, and *Gabrielle Chanel,* 1988. Contributor of articles and short stories to *Spectator, Holiday, Atlantic,* and other periodicals. *The Lonely Passion of Judith Hearne, Lies of Silence, The Color of Blood,* and *Cold Heaven* have been recorded on audiocassette.

ADAPTATIONS: The Lonely Passion of Judith Hearne was produced as a feature film by Island Pictures in 1988; *The Temptation of Eileen Hughes* was produced for television by the British Broadcasting Corporation in 1988; *Cold Heaven* was produced as a feature film, 1991.

SIDELIGHTS: Brian Moore is a Canadian citizen of Irish origin. He is also a novelist who "has gradually won the recognition his stubborn artistry deserves," to quote Walter Clemons in *Newsweek.* For more than thirty years Moore has been publishing fiction that reflects his multinational wanderings, his fascination with Catholicism's influence on modern life, and his insight into strained interpersonal relationships. "Book by book," writes Bruce Cook in *New Republic,* "Brian Moore has been building a body of work that is, in its quietly impressive way, about as good as that of any novelist writing today in English." Cook adds: "If Moore lacks the fame he deserves, he nevertheless has an excellent reputation. He is a writer's writer. His special virtues—his deft presentation of his characters, whether they be Irish, Canadian, or American, and the limpid simplicity of his style—are those that other writers most admire."

Many of Moore's plots are conventional in their inception, but typically the author brings additional depth of characterization to his stories so that they transcend genre classifications. As Joyce Carol Oates observes in the *New York Times Book Review,* Moore has written "a number of novels prized for their storytelling qualities and for a wonderfully graceful synthesis of the funny, the sardonic, and the near tragic; his reputation as a supremely entertaining 'serious' writer is secure." In *Saturday Night,* Christina Newman notes that Moore has a growing readership which has come to expect "what he unfailingly delivers: lucidity, great craftsmanship, and perceptions that evoke our fears, dreams, and shameful absurdities." *New York Times Book Review* contributor Julian Moynahan calls Moore "one of the most intelligent and accessible novelists now working. . . . He seems to have no crochets to hook or axes to grind and is adept at reworking his personal experience for the fiction public on both sides of the Atlantic." Oates feels that the author's works "succeed most compellingly on an immediate level: rich with convincing detail, communicating the admixture of drollery and sorrow that characterizes 'real' life, populated with individuals who speak and act and dream and breathe as if altogether innocent of the fact that they are mere fictitious characters."

In the *Spectator,* Francis King explains how Moore constructs his stories: "His sentences are unelaborate and his vocabulary narrow. . . . But, mysteriously, beneath this surface flatness, strange creatures thresh, slither and collide with each other. Many sentences may seem bare, some may even seem banal; but the cumulative impression left by a sequence of them is one of complexity and originality." *Village Voice* reviewer Alan Hislop similarly contends that Moore's prose "is disarming and seductive: you are led, nay drawn, into alarming stories . . . so polite that you never suspect there might be a trap door in the scrupulously polished floor." Beneath that "trap door" is a view of the dark side of human events; temptation, guilt, disillusionment, and dissatisfaction often play primary roles in Moore's characters' lives. In the *Washington Post Book World,* Alan Ryan states that it is this skillful exploration of human failings that makes Moore's work such thoughtful entertainment. "In most of Brian Moore's writing," the critic concludes, "one is always aware of larger, and darker, worlds lurking just out of view."

"Brian Moore comes from the middle-class sector of the submerged and currently beleaguered Catholic minority of Belfast in Ulster," writes Moynahan. "Like many Irish writers before him, he has followed the path of voluntary exile in managing a successful career as a novelist and is the only writer I know of who has lived and worked, and collected a number of impressive literary prizes, in no less than four English- speaking countries—Ireland, England, Canada and the United States." Moore left his native land and rejected his Catholic upbringing at an early age. Shortly after completing war-time service he emigrated to Canada, and from there he began to write about the Belfast he knew as a youth. According to Christopher Hawtree in the *Spectator,* this transatlantic stance "has yielded some sharp views both of his native Ireland and of Canada and America." *Time* contributor Patricia Blake feels that Moore's expatriation has produced "a special talent for pungent portraiture of those Irish men and women who are, as James Joyce put it, 'outcast from life's feast': desperate spinsters, failed priests, drunken poets." Other critics note that the very process of moving from place to place fuels Moore's fiction. In *Critique: Studies in Modern Fiction,* John Wilson Foster contends that Moore's novels as a group "trace the growing fortunes in a new continent of one hypothetical immigrant who has escaped Belfast's lower middle-class tedium." London *Times* correspondent Chris Petit also concludes that absence is important to Moore's writing. "The stories have an air of cosmopolitan restlessness, often cross borders, and can be summarized as a series of departures," Petit states.

Eventually Moore moved to the United States—first to New York and then to Malibu, California. As Kerry McSweeney notes in *Critical Quarterly,* while the author retains Canadian citizenship, and Canada "was the halfway house which mediated his passage from the old world to the new, it has not stimulated his imagination in the way that America has done." Paul Binding elaborates in *Books and Bookmen:* "It is America, with its vigorous non-realistic, especially Gothic literary tradition, which would seem to have supplied Brian Moore with the fictional forms that he needed, that can express—with their violent epiphanies and their distortions and eruptions of the irrational—the anguishes of the uprooted and spiritually

homeless, and the baffling diversities of Western society which can contain both puritan, taboo- ridden, pleasure-fearing Belfast and hedonistic, lost, restless California." In *Nation,* Jack Ludwig writes: "Moore is, like Joyce, essentially a city writer and, again like Joyce, someone who reacts to the city with lyric double awareness—the ugliness is there, but also the vigor. . . . The paralysis, hopelessness, colorlessness of Moore's first two novels is, I think, a dramatic equivalent of his Belfast. And it is not Europe which stands opposed to Belfast. It is New York."

Moore's early novels, *Judith Hearne, The Feast of Lupercal, The Luck of Ginger Coffey,* and *The Emperor of Ice-Cream,* are character studies in which the protagonists rebel— sometimes unsuccessfully—against the essentially closed society of Northern Ireland. McSweeney suggests that the works "are studies of losers, whose fates are determined by the claustrophobic gentility of Belfast and the suffocating weight of Irish Catholicism. [They] illustrate one of the quintessential *donnees* of Moore's fiction: that (in his own words) 'failure is a more interesting condition than success. Success changes people: it makes them something they were not and dehumanizes them in a way, whereas failure leaves you with a more intense distillation of that self you are.' " In *Critique,* Hallvard Dahlie examines Moore's predilection for characters mired in hopelessness: "Moore [chooses] for his central figures people in their late thirties or early forties who [are] failures of one sort or another, and [have] been failures for some time. In his first four novels, Moore exploited the constituents of failure so skillfully and sensitively that the characters achieve much more stature than many triumphant heroes of less gifted writers. But with none of these earlier characters do we sense the likelihood of any lasting triumph over their limitations or obstacles." *Chicago Tribune Book World* reviewer Eugene Kennedy finds these novels "a look beneath the aspects of Irish culture that, with a terrible mixture of repression and misuse of its religious heritage, can create pitiable monsters fated to groan eternally beneath the facades of their hypocritical adjustments."

Judith Hearne, Moore's first and best-known novel, is, to quote *Los Angeles Times* reviewer Leonard Klady, "an acclaimed work about an aging woman's struggle to find her identity as the secure elements in her life start to disintegrate." Set in Belfast, the story—which has never been out of print since 1955—revolves around Judith Hearne's desperate and futile attempts to gain the affection of a paunchy and unscrupulous suitor. *New York Times Book Review* contributor Frances Taliaferro notes that the Irish setting gives "a special poignancy to this portrait of a sad middle class spinster resolutely slipping into emotional destitution." In *Commonweal,* William Clancy observes that in the novel, Moore "has taken an Irish city and laid bare its most secret soul through characters who could not have been born elsewhere. . . . In its relentless pursuit of this woman's sorrow, in its refusal to sentimentalize or easily alleviate her plight, the book achieves a kind of vision, and it is a tragic vision. As she accepts, finally, the end of all her hopes, Judith Hearne attains . . . a certain grandeur." *Saturday Review* essayist Granville Hicks is among the critics who have praised *Judith Hearne.* "As a book by a young man about a middle-aged woman," Hicks writes, "it [is] a remarkable tour de force, but it [is] more than that, for in it one [feels] the terrible pathos of life as it is often led."

A fascination with Catholicism is central to much of Moore's work. He told the *Los Angeles Times:* "I am not a religious person, but I come from a very religious background. Always in the back of my mind, I've wondered what if all this stuff was true and you didn't want it to be true and it was happening in the worst possible way?" According to Paul Gray in *Time,* a refrain common to all of Moore's novels is this: "When beliefs can no longer comfort, they turn destructive." Such is the case in a variety of Moore's works, from *Judith Hearne* to the more recent *Cold Heaven, Black Robe, Catholics,* and *The Color of Blood.* Craig writes: "Someone who is heading for the moment of apostasy . . . is almost statutory in a Moore novel. . . . A frightening emptiness takes the place of whatever ideology had kept the character going." The opposite may also apply in some of Moore's tales; occasionally non-believing characters are forced to pay heed to the deity through extreme means. "Mr. Moore's later novels show the vestigial religious conscience straining to give depth to North American life," observes a *Times Literary Supplement* reviewer. "Faith itself is unacceptable, making unreasonable demands on the behaviour of anyone who is sporadically forced to be honest with himself. Yet bourbon, bedrooms and success do not content the soul: in this, at least, the priests were always right." Craig concludes that Moore is "an author who in the past has used the emblems of Catholicism with conspicuous success. . . . No one has examined with greater acuity the moral deficiencies inherent in a Belfast Catholic upbringing."

Several of Moore's novels—*Fergus, The Great Victorian Collection,* and *Cold Heaven*—make use of miracles and the supernatural to advance the stories. In *The Great Victorian Collection,* for instance, a college professor finds his vivid dream about an exhibit of Victorian memorabilia transformed into reality in a hotel parking lot. Binding suggests that in these works Moore "has tried to explore the complexities of American/Californian life while coming to further terms with the ghosts of his Irish past." These miracles and ghostly visitations do not comfort or sustain; Moore's vision of the supernatural "is terrifying:

a brutal energy that mocks our pretensions and transcends our ideas of good and evil," to quote Mark Abley in *Books in Canada.* Peter S. Prescott likewise notes in *Newsweek* that Moore is "concerned with a secular sensibility confronting the more alien aspects of Roman Catholic tradition. . . . He warns us of the ambiguities of miracles in a world that is darker, more dangerous and above all more portentous than we think." Such plot devices can strain verisimilitude, but according to David MacFarlane in *Maclean's,* the author's strength "is his ability to make tangible the unbelievable and the miraculous." MacFarlane adds: "His consistently fine prose and the precision of his narrative create a reality in which characters and readers alike are forced to believe the improbable. Moore inhabits a world which is partly that of a religious visionary and partly that of a thriller writer."

"Mr. Moore is not only the laureate of Irish drabness but also a psychological writer with some interest in the quirkier aspects of profane love," writes Taliaferro. "Throughout his career, one has been able to rely on Mr. Moore for narrative competence and psychological interest." Through novels such as *I Am Mary Dunne, The Doctor's Wife,* and *The Temptation of Eileen Hughes,* Moore has attained a reputation for uncovering the pitfalls in modern emotional entanglements, especially from the female point of view. In *Nation,* Richard B. Sale comments that the author "has never avoided the silliness, selfishness and sexuality that constitute most people's waking and dreaming thoughts. . . . He can extend the embarrassing scene beyond the point where the ordinary naturalistic novelist would lower the curtain." *Times Literary Supplement* reviewer Paul Bailey notes that it is "typical of Brian Moore's honesty that he should acknowledge that, superficially at least, there are certain liaisons which bear a shocking resemblance to those described in the pages of women's magazines: life, unfortunately, has a nasty habit of imitating pulp fiction." However, *Spectator* correspondent Paul Ableman points out that Moore's characters "are not formula figures, whose responses to any situation are predictable, but rather fictional beings that behave like people in the world, generally consistent or revealing a thread of continuity, but always quirky, volatile and sometimes irrational." Bailey also admits that it is "a hallmark of Brian Moore's art that it respects and acknowledges a state of unhappiness as raw and as ugly as an open wound."

Prescott characterizes Moore as a novelist who "enjoys playing with his readers' expectations. Aha, he seems to say, you thought I was writing about this; now don't you feel a little foolish to discover that I was really up to something else—something more innocent and yet more terrible—all along?" Moore himself echoes this sentiment in the *Los Angeles Times:* "I find it interesting to lull the reader into a sense that he's reading a certain kind of book and then jolt the reader about halfway through to make him realize that it's a different kind of book. That is not a recipe for best sellerdom; it's the opposite." Even the thriller format in such works as *Black Robe* and *The Color of Blood* becomes "a vehicle to explore serious political and theological issues," to quote Anne-Marie Conway in the *Times Literary Supplement*. It is this willingness to explore and experiment that contributes to Moore's novelistic originality, according to critics. McSweeney writes: "One of the most impressive features of Moore's canon has been his ability to keep from repeating himself. Over and over again he has found fresh inventions which have developed his novelistic skills and enabled him to explore his obsessive themes and preoccupations in ways that have made for an increasingly complex continuity between old and new." Moreover, while the author's critical reputation is high, he is not particularly well-known to American readers—a state of affairs he welcomes. "I have never had to deal with the problem of a public persona becoming more important than the fiction," he said in the *Los Angeles Times*. "I've had a life where I've been able to write without having had some enormous success that I have to live up to."

Moore's success may not be enormous, but it is substantial in Canada and Great Britain. Cook claims that the author's retiring personality affects the tenor of his work for the better. "In a way," Cook concludes in *Commonweal*, "the sort of writer [Moore] is—private, devoted to writing as an end in itself—is the only sort who could write the intensely felt, personal, and close novels he has. The style, once again, is the man." Bailey writes: "It isn't fashionable to praise novelists for their tact, but it is that very quality in Brian Moore's writing that deserves to be saluted. It is a measure of his intelligence and his humanity that he refuses to sit in judgment on his characters. It is, as far as I am concerned, an honourable and a considerable measure." Perhaps the best summation of Moore's authorial talents comes from *Washington Post Book World* reviewer Jack Beatty, who says of the writer: "Pick him up expecting high talent in the service of a small design, go to him anticipating economy of style, characterization and description, as well as the pleasure of a plot that keeps you reading until the last page, and I can assure that your expectations will get along splendidly with his abilities."

BIOGRAPHICAL/CRITICAL SOURCES:

BOOKS

Contemporary Literary Criticism, Gale, Volume 1, 1973, Volume 3, 1975, Volume 5, 1976, Volume 7, 1977, Volume 8, 1978, Volume 19, 1981, Volume 32, 1985.
Dahlie, Hallvard, *Brian Moore*, Copp, 1969.
Flood, Jeanne, *Brian Moore*, Bucknell University Press, 1974.
McSweeny, Kerry, *Four Contemporary Novelists: Angus Wilson, Brian Moore, John Fowles, V.S. Naipaul*, University of Toronto Press, 1983.
Raban, Jonathan, *The Techniques of Modern Fiction*, Edward Arnold, 1968.
O'Donoghue, Jo, *Brian Moore: A Critical Study*, McGill, Queens, 1991.

PERIODICALS

Books & Bookmen, December, 1968; February, 1980.
Books in Canada, October, 1979; November, 1983.
Chicago Tribune, November 2, 1987.
Canadian Literature, fall, 1986, pp. 150-2; spring, 1989, pp. 147-50.
Chicago Tribune Book World, July 12, 1981; October 30, 1983; May 19, 1985.
Commonweal, August 3, 1956; July 12, 1957; September 27, 1968; August 23, 1974.
Critical Quarterly, summer, 1976.
Critique: Studies in Modern Fiction, Volume 9, number 1, 1966; Volume 13, number 1, 1971.
Detroit News, October 14, 1979; May 19, 1985.
Globe & Mail (Toronto), March 30, 1985; September 5, 1987.
Harper's, October, 1965.
Life, June 18, 1968; December 3, 1972.
London Review of Books, April 8, 1993, p. 15.
Los Angeles Times, September 14, 1983; July 2, 1987; September 15, 1987; December 23, 1987; January 1, 1988; April 10, 1988.
Los Angeles Times Book Review, September 11, 1983; April 7, 1985; September 3, 1990, pp. 3, 9.
Maclean's, September 17, 1979; September 5, 1983.
Nation, March 15, 1965; June 24, 1968; October 12, 1970.
New Republic, August 17, 1968; June 9, 1973; October 24, 1983; November 2, 1987, p. 47.
New Statesman, February 18, 1966; October 17, 1975; November 25, 1983.
Newsweek, June 2, 1975; September 20, 1976; October 15, 1979; July 20, 1981; September 5, 1983; March 18, 1985.
New York Review of Books, December 6, 1990, p. 22; October 21, 1993, p. 3.
New Yorker, May 11, 1957; August 4, 1975; October 3, 1983; July 8, 1985.
New York Times, October 1, 1976; September 12, 1979; July 3, 1981; September 14, 1983; January 15, 1984; March 25, 1985; September 1, 1987; December 23, 1987; December 25, 1987.
New York Times Book Review, October 24, 1965; December 5, 1965; June 23, 1968; September 27, 1970; November 28, 1971; March 18, 1973; June 29, 1975; Sep-

tember 26, 1976; September 9, 1979; August 2, 1981; September 18, 1983; March 31, 1985; September 27, 1987; November 6, 1988, p. 34; September 2, 1990, p. 1; September 12, 1993, p. 1.

People, October 12, 1987.

Saturday Night, September, 1968; November, 1970; July-August, 1975; October, 1976.

Saturday Review, October 13, 1962; September 18, 1965; June 15, 1968; February 12, 1972; July 26, 1975; September 18, 1976.

Spectator, November 1, 1975; November 10, 1979; October 10, 1981; November 12, 1983; July 13, 1985.

Time, June 18, 1956; June 21, 1968; October 12, 1970; July 14, 1975; September 6, 1976; September 19, 1983; March 18, 1985.

Times (London), October 1, 1981; November 3, 1983; June 13, 1985; September 24, 1987.

Times Literary Supplement, February 3, 1966; October 24, 1966; April 9, 1971; January 21, 1972; November 10, 1972; October 17, 1975; November 23, 1979; October 9, 1981; October 28, 1983; June 7, 1985; October 2, 1987; April 20, 1990, p. 430; February 19, 1993, p. 22.

Village Voice, June 30, 1957; October 22, 1979.

Washington Post, January 22, 1988.

Washington Post Book World, April 8, 1973; June 1, 1975; October 17, 1976; September 23, 1979; December 9, 1979; June 21, 1981; September 11, 1983; March 31, 1985; September 6, 1987; February 14, 1988.

*   *   *

MOORE, (James) Mavor   1919-

PERSONAL: Born March 8, 1919, in Toronto, Ontario, Canada; son of Francis John (a clergyman) and Dora (an actress; maiden name, Mavor) Moore; married Darwina Faessler, October 14, 1943 (divorced, 1969); married Phyllis Langstaff Grosskurth (a writer), October, 1969 (marriage ended, 1978); married Alexandra Browning (a singer and teacher), August 15, 1980; children: (first marriage) Dorothea, Rosalind, Marili, Charlotte; (third marriage) Jessica. *Education:* University of Toronto, B.A. (with first class honors), 1941.

*ADDRESSES: Home—*3815 West 27th Ave., Vancouver, British Columbia, Canada V6S 1R4.

CAREER: Professional actor on stage, radio, television, and screen, 1933-41; Canadian Broadcasting Corp. (CBC), Toronto, Ontario, radio feature producer, 1941-43, chief producer of CBC International, Montreal, Quebec, 1945-46, radio producer for Pacific region, Vancouver, British Columbia, 1946; New Play Society, Toronto, manager, 1946-50; CBC-TV, chief producer for English Network, 1950-53, assistant program director, 1954;

New Play Society, manager, 1955-58; Mavor Moore Productions Ltd., Toronto, president, 1956-74; York University, Downsview, Ontario, professor of fine arts, theater, and English, 1974-84, professor emeritus, 1984—, chair of university board of governors, 1974-75, chair of Faculty of Fine Arts Council, 1978-79; University of Victoria, Victoria, British Columbia, adjunct professor, beginning in 1984; playwright. Teacher at Academy of Radio Arts, Toronto, 1946-49; guest lecturer at University of Toronto, University of Guelph, University of Lethbridge, University of Calgary, Simon Fraser University, University of British Columbia, Western University, McMaster University, Laurentian University, Memorial University of Newfoundland, Queen's University (Kingston, Ontario), Mount Allison University, Brock University, Cornell University, Oregon State University, University of North Carolina, Raleigh, State University of New York College at Plattsburgh, New School for Social Research, and Washington State University. Executive producer, Information Division of the United Nations, New York City, 1946-50 and 1955-60; producer and director for Crest Theatre, Vancouver Festival, Vancouver Playhouse, and Neptune Theatre (Halifax, Nova Scotia), beginning in 1946; Stratford Ontario Festival, member of board of directors, 1953-54, member of senate, 1955-74; founding president, Canadian Theatre Centre, 1955-56; producer for Canadian Players, 1957-58; stage director, Canadian Opera Company, 1959-61; governor, National Theatre School of Canada, 1960-73; general director, Confederation Centre, Charlottetown, Prince Edward Island, 1963-65; president, Legendrama (Sound and Light) Ltd., 1964-67; founding artistic director, Charlottetown Festival, 1964-68; founding general director, St. Lawrence Centre for the Arts, Toronto, 1965-70. Host of *Performance* on CBC-TV, 1981-84; screen actor, with roles in *Thresholds,* 1982, *The Killing Fields,* 1983, and *Shell Game,* 1985. Chair, UNESCO Conference on Education, 1949; member of executive committee, Canadian Conference of the Arts, 1962-70; co-chair, National Centennial Conference, 1965-67; member of board of directors, Fathers of Confederation Foundation, 1968-74; Canada Council, member, 1974-79, chair, 1979-83; member of advisory board, Center for Inter-American Studies (New York City), 1982-84, and Cultural Council of the Americas Society, 1983-84; member of executive committee, Canadian Music Centre, beginning in 1984; honorary chair, Canada-Israel Cultural Foundation, beginning in 1984; national president, Youth and Music Canada (Jeunesses Musicales), beginning in 1985. Lecturer. *Military service:* Canadian Army Intelligence Corps, Psychological Warfare, 1943-45; served abroad; became captain.

MEMBER: Guild of Canadian Playwrights (founding chair, 1977-78), Canadian Association for Adult Education (member of executive committee, 1949-52), United

Nations Association of Canada (member of executive committee, 1947-50), Dramatists Guild (United States).

AWARDS, HONOURS: Peabody Awards, 1947, 1949, and 1957; Television Award from Canadian Association of Authors and Artists, 1955; Canadian Centennial Medal, 1967; D.Litt. from York University, 1969; Officer, Order of Canada, 1973; Queen's Medal, 1977; LL.D. from Mount Allison University, 1982; John Drainie Award from Association of Canadian Television and Radio Artists, 1982; LL.D. from Memorial University of Newfoundland, 1984; D.Litt. from University of Guelph, 1985; Diplome d'Honneur from Canadian Conference of the Arts, 1985; Companion, Order of Canada, 1988.

WRITINGS:

PLAYS

I Know You, produced in Toronto at Toronto Arts and Letters Club, Ontario, 1944.

Spring Thaw (revue), produced in Toronto, 1947.

Who's Who, produced in Toronto at New Play Society, 1949.

The Optimist (musical adaptation of Voltaire's *Candide),* broadcast by CBC-Radio, 1952; produced in Toronto at New Play Society, 1955; broadcast by CBC-TV as *The Best of All Possible Worlds,* 1968.

Sunshine Town (musical adaptation of *Sunshine Sketches of a Little Town* by Stephen Leacock), broadcast on television as *The Hero of Mariposa,* 1954; produced in Toronto at New Play Society, 1956; broadcast by CBC-TV, 1957.

The Ottawa Man (adaptation of Nikolai Gogol's *The Inspector General),* broadcast by CBC-TV, 1959; produced in Toronto at Crest Theatre, 1961.

(With Jacques Languirand) *Louis Riel* (opera, with libretto; performed in Toronto by Canadian Opera Company, 1967; produced in Washington, DC, at Kennedy Center, 1975), Canadian Music Centre (Toronto), 1967.

(Translator) Gratien Gelinas, *Yesterday the Children Were Dancing* (produced in Charlottetown, Prince Edward Island, at Charlottetown Festival, 1967; broadcast by CBC-TV, 1969), Clarke, Irwin, 1968.

(Translator) *Tit-coq,* Clarke, Irwin, 1967.

(Translator) Marie-Claire Blais, *The Puppet Caravan,* broadcast by CBC-TV, 1968.

(Translator) Jacques Languirand, *Man, Inc.,* produced in Toronto at St. Lawrence Centre for the Arts, 1969.

Johnny Belinda (musical), produced at Charlottetown Festival, 1969; broadcast by CBC-TV, 1976.

Getting In (broadcast on television, 1970), Samuel French, 1973.

The Pile (broadcast on radio, 1970), published in *A Collection of Canadian Plays,* Volume II, edited by Rolf Kalman, Simon & Pierre, 1973.

Inside Out (broadcast on television, 1971), published in *A Collection of Canadian Plays,* Volume II, edited by Rolf Kalman, Simon & Pierre, 1973.

The Store (broadcast on television, 1972), published in *A Collection of Canadian Plays,* Volume II, edited by Rolf Kalman, Simon & Pierre, 1973.

Come Away, Come Away (broadcast on television, 1972), published in *Encounter,* Methuen, 1969.

The Argument, published in *Performing Arts,* winter, 1973.

(With Frank R. Scott) *The Roncarelli Affair* (broadcast on television, 1974), published in *The Play's the Thing: Four Original Television Dramas,* edited by Tony Gifford, Macmillan of Canada, 1975.

La Roulotte aux poupees, published in *Joie de Vivre,* Copp Clark, 1976.

Customs, published in *Cues and Entrances,* Gage Publishing, 1977.

Abracadabra (opera), performed in British Columbia, at Courtenay Music Festival, 1979.

Love and Politics (adapted from the play *The Fair Grit* by Nicholas Flood Davin), produced in St. Catherines, Ontario, at Press Theatre, 1979.

Fauntleroy (musical; adapted from the novel *Little Lord Fauntleroy* by Frances Hodgson Burnett), produced at Charlottetown Festival, 1980.

(Translator) Moliere, *The Imaginary Invalid,* produced in Vancouver at University of British Columbia, 1984.

Ghost Dance (opera), performed in Toronto at Comus Music Theatre, 1985.

A Christmas Carol (musical adaptation of Charles Dickens's novel of the same title), produced in Vancouver at Carousel Theatre, 1988.

PLAY COLLECTIONS

The Pile, Inside Out, The Store, Simon & Pierre (Toronto), 1973.

Six Plays by Mavor Moore (contains *The Apology, The Store, The Pile, Getting In, The Argument,* and *Come Away, Come Away*), Talonbooks (Vancouver), 1989.

TELEVISION SCRIPTS

The Inspector General (adapted from Gogol's play), Canadian Broadcasting Corporation (CBC), 1952.

To Tell the Truth (adapted from play of same title by Morley Callaghan), CBC, 1952.

The Coventry Miracle Play, CBC, 1952.

The Black Eye (adapted from play of same title by James Bridie), CBC, 1954.

Catch a Falling Star, CBC, 1955.

The Man Who Caught Bullets, First Performance, CBC, 1958.

The Master of Santiago (adapted from the play *Le Maitre de Santiago* by Henry de Montherlant), CBC, 1959.

The Crucible (adapted from play of same title by Arthur Miller), CBC, 1959.

The Well, CBC, 1960.

Wise Guy (adapted from story of same title by Christopher Isherwood), CBC, 1961.

The Man Born to Be King (adapted from radio play of same title by Dorothy L. Sayers), CBC, 1961.

Mary of Scotland (adapted from play *Festival* by Maxwell Anderson), CBC, 1966.

The Puppet Caravan (adapted from the play *La Roulotte aux poupees* by Marie Claire Blais), CBC, 1967.

Enoch Soames (adapted from a story by Max Beerbohm), CBC, 1967.

Yesterday the Children Were Dancing (translated and adapted from the play *hier, les enfants dansaient* by Gratien Gelinas), CBC, 1967.

The Lyons Mail (adapted from the play of same title by Charles Reade), CBC, 1973.

(With F. R. Scott) *The Roncarelli Affair,* CBC, 1974.

RADIO SCRIPTS

Christmas Carol—1941 (adapted from *A Christmas Carol* by Charles Dickens), CBC Radio, 1941.

The Great Flood, CBC Radio, 1948.

William Tell (adapted from play of same title by Friedrich von Schiller), CBC Radio, 1949.

To Tell the Truth (adapted from play of same title by Morley Callaghan), CBC Radio, 1949.

Call It a Day (adapted from play of same title by Dodie Smith), CBC Radio, 1950.

The First Mrs. Fraser (adapted from play of same title by St. John Ervine), CBC Radio, 1951.

The Drums Are Out (adapted from play of same title by John Coulter), CBC Radio, 1951.

The Son, CBC Radio, 1958.

(With others) *Old Moore's Almanac,* CBC Radio, 1958.

Don Juan in Hell (adapted from play *Man and Supreman* by Bernard Shaw), CBC Radio, 1959.

Our Emblem Dear, CBC Radio, 1959.

Catch My Death, CBC Radio, 1959.

Gulliver's Travels (adapted from the novel of same title by Jonathan Swift), CBC Radio, 1959.

Brave New World (adapted from novel of same title by Aldous Huxley), CBC Radio, 1960.

Fact or Fancy (adapted from story by Oscar Wilde), CBC Radio, 1961.

The Rise and Fall of Witchcraft, CBC Radio, 1961.

The Cachalot (adapted from poem of same title by Edwin John Pratt), CBC Radio, 1961.

Fast Forward, CBC Radio, 1968.

A Matter of Timing, CBC Radio, 1971.

Freak, CBC Radio, 1975.

RECORDINGS

The Store, Earplay, 1975.

Customs, Earplay, 1975.

Inside out and Other Stories by Mavor Moore (includes *A Matter of Timing, Come Away, Come Away, The Pile, Inside Out,* and *Getting In*), CBC International, 1979.

(With Jacques Languirand) *Louis Riel,* Centrediscs, 1985.

OTHER

And What Do YOU Do?: A Short Guide to the Trades and Professions (poems), Dent (Toronto), 1960.

(Editor) *The Awkward Stage: The Ontario Theatre Report,* Methuen (Toronto), 1969.

(Author of introduction) Murray Edwards, *A Stage in Our Past,* Methuen, 1970.

(Editor with Roy Bentley) *Four Canadian Playwrights: Robertson Davies, Gratien Gelinas, James Reaney, George Ryga,* Holt (Toronto), 1973.

(Editor) *An Anthology of Canadian Plays,* New Press (Toronto), 1973.

(Author of introduction) *Two Plays by George Ryga,* Turnstone Press, 1982.

Slipping on the Verge: The Performing Arts in Canada with Theatre as a Case Study, Canadian Embassy (Washington, DC), 1983.

(Author of introduction) Arthur L. Murphy, *Three Bluenose Plays,* Lancelot Press, 1984.

Contributor to books, including *Cultures and Writers,* Multi-Heritage Alliance of Toronto, 1983, *Organizational Culture,* Sage Publications, 1985, and *Two Hundred Years,* Queen's Printer, 1985. Work represented in anthologies, including *Twentieth Century Canadian Poetry,* Ryerson, 1953; and *The Arts in Canada,* Macmillan of Canada, 1958. Theater critic for *Canadian Commentator,* 1956-57, and Toronto *Telegram,* 1958-60. Author of column on art and society for Toronto *Globe and Mail* in the 1980s; contributor of poems, articles, and reviews to journals, including *Canadian Drama, Maclean's, Canadian Forum, Saturday Night, Connoisseur,* and *Canadian Poetry.* Member of editorial board, *Canadian Theatre Review,* 1974-78, and *On-Stage Studies,* beginning in 1982. Moore's papers are collected at the library of York University, Toronto.

SIDELIGHTS: Mavor Moore is, according to Paula Sperdakos in the *Canadian Theatre Review,* an " 'artistic polymath,' actor, director, producer, critic, teacher, composer and playwright . . . [Moore] has been involved in virtually all aspects of the development of theatre in this country since the late 1930s." Moore's long and varied career includes stints as a radio and television writer, cofounder of the Stratford Festival as well as of several other theatre companies, serving as chief producer for the fledgling Canadian Broadcasting Corporation television network, and working as an actor and director in many theatrical productions. His efforts have earned him three Peabody Awards, a Centennial Medal and the Queen's Medal; he has also been made an Officer of the Order of Canada and Companion of the Order of Canada.

Moore comes from a distinguished family. His mother, Dora Mavor Moore, was a well-known actress (the annual awards of the Toronto theatre community are named in her honor), while his grandfather, James Mavor, was a prominent economist. Moore came to theatre early in life, beginning as a writer and actor for the Canadian Broadcasting Corporation (CBC) while still in college. He made his professional stage debut in 1941 and joined the staff of the CBC that same year as a producer. In 1943 Moore joined the Canadian military, working in the Army Intelligence Corps. during World War II.

Following the war, Moore cofounded with his mother the New Play Society. "The company," writes Chris Johnson in the *Dictionary of Literary Biography,* "represented a milestone in the evolution of Canadian theater: it trained a generation of actors." Moore served as general manager of the company from 1946 until 1958, and also acted in many of their productions. The New Play Society was to produce many of Moore's own plays, beginning in 1947 with *Spring Thaw,* a revue that became an annual event and "launched the careers of many Canadian singers and comedians," as Johnson notes.

During his career Moore has written prolifically in a variety of styles, ranging from adaptations of other writers' works to historical dramas and from innovative experiments to popular musicals. Among his most successful works has been *The Ottawa Man,* in which he transposes Nikolai Gogol's story *The Government Inspector* to 19th century Manitoba. Moore's accurate depictions of the respective speech of his French, Irish, German and English characters is especially noted, as is his pointed satire of Canadian racism. His adaptation of the comic works of Stephen Leacock about the fictional town of Mariposa resulted in *Sunshine Town,* a work that has seen productions on radio and television as well as on the stage.

Six Plays by Mavor Moore gathers together some of Moore's shorter and more experimental works. Included are "The Pile," in which a businessman and an engineer discuss ways to get rid of a pile of some unspecified substance, which may be the audience itself, "The Argument," in which a man and a woman, named M and W respectively, debate in highly illogical terms, and "The Store," concerning a store manager confronted by an angry customer who blames him for every ill in her life.

Sperdakos calls these plays "the kinds of richly subtextual dramatic exercises that an actor would find challenging, that a director would take pleasure in . . . , and that would amuse and intrigue an audience."

In 1994 Moore published *Reinventing Myself,* an autobiographical account of his first fifty years. It is, according to Brian Fawcett in *Books in Canada,* "a fascinating book." Covering such topics as Moore's early involvement with radio and television, his work as an actor, director, and producer, and his role as organizer of theatrical festivals, the book also presents many of the interesting people Moore has met and worked with during his career. Writing in *Quill & Quire,* Douglas Fetherling complains that the memoir reveals "precious little about the private Mavor Moore," although he does admit that it contains much about "the remarkable generation that built most of today's Canadian cultural infrastructure." Fawcett, reacting to Moore's announcement in the book of a life-long battle with manic depression, sees *Reinventing Myself* as "an epic tale of courage and resourcefulness."

BIOGRAPHICAL/CRITICAL SOURCES:

BOOKS

Bryden, Ronald, editor, *Whittaker's Theatre: A Critic Looks at Stages in Canada and Thereabouts,* Whittaker Project (Greenbank, ON), 1985, pp. 45-51.
Dictionary of Literary Biography, Volume 88: *Canadian Writers, 1920-1959,* Second Series, Gale, 1989.
Edmonstone, Wayne, *Nathan Cohen: The Making of a Critic,* Lester & Orpen (Toronto), 1977, pp. 153-182.

PERIODICALS

Books in Canada, March, 1990, pp. 34-35; summer, 1994, pp. 44-45.
Canadian Drama/L'Art Dramatique Canadien, Volume 8, 1982, pp. 129-44; Volume 9, 1983, pp. 254-67, 343-51.
Canadian Theatre Review, winter, 1978, pp. 94-98; fall, 1980, pp. 18-33; summer, 1991, pp. 111-13.
Quill & Quire, June, 1994, p. 6.
Theatre History in Canada, spring, 1991, pp. 97-104.
Theatrum, June-August, 1990, p. 33.
Variety, November 2, 1992, p. 32.

*   *   *

MORRIS, John
See HEARNE, John (Edgar Caulwell)

MOWAT, Farley (McGill) 1921-

PERSONAL: Born May 12, 1921, in Belleville, Ontario, Canada; son of Angus McGill (a librarian) and Helen Elizabeth (Thomson) Mowat; married Frances Thornhill, December 21, 1947 (marriage ended, 1959); married Claire Angel Wheeler (a writer), March, 1964; children: (first marriage) Robert Alexander, David Peter. *Education:* University of Toronto, B.A., 1949.

ADDRESSES: Home—Port Hope, Ontario, and Cape Breton, Nova Scotia. *Office*—c/o Key Porter Books Ltd., 70 The Esplanade, Toronto, Ontario M5E 1R2, Canada.

CAREER: Author. *Military service:* Canadian Army Infantry, 1939-45; became captain.

AWARDS, HONOURS: President's Medal for best short story, University of Western Ontario, 1952, for "Eskimo Spring"; Anisfield-Wolfe Award for contribution to interracial relations, 1954, for *People of the Deer;* Governor General's Medal, 1957, and Book of the Year Award, Canadian Association of Children's Librarians, both for *Lost in the Barrens;* Canadian Women's Clubs Award, 1958, for *The Dog Who Wouldn't Be;* Hans Christian Andersen International Award, 1958; Boys' Clubs of America Junior Book Award, 1962, for *Owls in the Family;* National Association of Independent Schools Award, 1963, for juvenile books; Hans Christian Andersen Honours List, 1965, for juvenile books; Canadian Centennial Medal, 1967; Stephen Leacock Medal for humor, 1970, and L'Etoile de la Mer Honours List, 1972, both for *The Boat Who Wouldn't Float;* D.Lit., Laurentian University, 1970; Vicky Metcalf Award, 1970; Mark Twain Award, 1971; Doctor of Law from Lethbridge University, 1973, University of Toronto, 1973, and University of Prince Edward Island, 1979; Curran Award, 1977, for "contributions to understanding wolves"; Queen Elizabeth II Jubilee Medal, 1978; Knight of Mark Twain, 1980; Officer, Order of Canada, 1981; Doctor of Literature, University of Victoria, 1982, and Lakehead University, 1986; Author's Award, Foundation for the Advancement of Canadian Letters, 1985, for *Sea of Slaughter;* Book of the Year designation, Foundation for the Advancement of Canadian Letters, and named Author of the Year, Canadian Booksellers Association, both 1988, both for *Virunga;* Gemini Award for best documentary script, 1989, for *The New North;* Take Back the Nation Award, Council of Canadians, 1991.

WRITINGS:

NONFICTION

People of the Deer, Little, Brown, 1952, revised edition, McClelland & Stewart, 1975.

The Regiment, McClelland & Stewart, 1955, revised edition, 1973.

The Dog Who Wouldn't Be, Little, Brown, 1957.

(Editor) Samuel Hearne, *Coppermine Journey: An Account of a Great Adventure,* Little, Brown, 1958.

The Grey Seas Under, Little, Brown, 1958.

The Desperate People, Little, Brown, 1959, revised, McClelland & Stewart, 1976.

(Editor) *Ordeal by Ice* (first part of "The Top of the World" series), McClelland & Stewart, 1960, Little, Brown, 1961.

The Serpent's Coil, McClelland & Stewart, 1961, Little, Brown, 1962.

Never Cry Wolf, Little, Brown, 1963, revised edition, McClelland & Stewart, 1973.

Westviking: The Ancient Norse in Greenland and North America, Little, Brown, 1965.

(Editor) *The Polar Passion: The Quest for the North Pole, with Selections from Arctic Journals* (second part of "The Top of the World" series), McClelland & Stewart, 1967, Little, Brown, 1968, revised edition, 1973.

Canada North, Little, Brown, 1967.

This Rock within the Sea: A Heritage Lost, photographs by John de Visser, Little, Brown, 1969, new edition, McClelland & Stewart, 1976.

The Boat Who Wouldn't Float, McClelland & Stewart, 1969, Little, Brown, 1970.

Sibir: My Discovery of Siberia, McClelland & Stewart, 1970, revised edition, 1973, published as *The Siberians,* Little, Brown, 1971.

A Whale for the Killing, Little, Brown, 1972.

Wake of the Great Sealers, illustrated by David Blackwood, Little, Brown, 1973.

(Editor) *Tundra: Selections from the Great Accounts of Arctic Land Voyages* (third part of "The Top of the World" series), McClelland & Stewart, 1973, Peregrine Smith, 1990.

(Editor) *Top of the World Trilogy* (includes *Ordeal by Ice, The Polar Passion,* and *Tundra*), McClelland & Stewart, 1976.

The Great Betrayal: Arctic Canada Now, Little, Brown, 1976, published as *Canada North Now: The Great Betrayal,* McClelland & Stewart, 1976.

And No Birds Sang (memoir), McClelland & Stewart, 1979, Little, Brown, 1980.

The World of Farley Mowat: A Selection from His Works, edited by Peter Davison, Little, Brown, 1980.

Sea of Slaughter, Atlantic Monthly Press, 1984.

My Discovery of America, Little, Brown, 1985.

Woman in the Mists: The Story of Dian Fossey and the Mountain Gorillas of Africa, Warner Books, 1987, published as *Virunga: The Passion of Dian Fossey,* McClelland & Stewart, 1987.

The New Founde Land: A Personal Voyage of Discovery, McClelland & Stewart, 1989.

Rescue the Earth, McClelland & Stewart, 1990.

My Father's Son: Memories of War and Peace, Houghton, 1993.

Born Naked: The Early Adventures of the Author of "Never Cry Wolf," Key Porter, 1993, Houghton, 1994.

FOR YOUNG ADULTS

Lost in the Barrens (novel), illustrated by Charles Geer, Little, Brown, 1956, published as *Two against the North,* illustrated by Alan Daniel, Scholastic-TAB, 1977.

Owls in the Family, illustrated by Robert Frankenberg, Little, Brown, 1961.

The Black Joke (novel), illustrated by D. Johnson, McClelland & Stewart, 1962, illustrated by Victory Mays, Little, Brown, 1963.

The Curse of the Viking Grave (novel), illustrated by Geer, Little, Brown, 1966.

OTHER

The Snow Walker (short stories), McClelland & Stewart, 1975, Little, Brown, 1976.

Also author of television screenplays *Sea Fare* and *Diary of a Boy on Vacation,* both 1964. Contributor to *Cricket's Choice,* Open Court, 1974; contributor to periodicals, including *Argosy, Maclean's,* and *Saturday Evening Post.*

Mowat's books have been translated into more than thirty languages and anthologized in more than two hundred works.

A collection of Mowat's manuscripts is housed at McMaster University, Hamilton, Ontario.

ADAPTATIONS: A Whale for the Killing (television movie), American Broadcasting Companies, Inc. (ABC-TV), 1980; *Never Cry Wolf* (feature film), Buena Vista, 1983; *The New North* (documentary), Norwolf/Noralpha/CTV, 1989; *Sea of Slaughter* (award-winning documentary; part of "The Nature of Things" series), Canadian Broadcasting Corporation (CBC-TV), 1990; *Lost in the Barrens* (television movie), Atlantis Films, 1990; *Curse of the Viking Grave* (television movie), Atlantis Films, 1992. Several of Mowat's books have been recorded onto cassette, including *Grey Seas Under, Lost in the Barrens, People of the Deer, The Snow Walker,* and *And No Birds Sang.*

WORK IN PROGRESS: Two feature films; an autobiography.

SIDELIGHTS: Farley Mowat is one of Canada's most internationally acclaimed writers. His many books for both young-adult and adult readers offer a reflective glimpse at the ill-fated future of wild species at the hand of mankind, and he presents a clear warning as to the consequences of our continued drain on the earth's limited natural resources. Although often categorized as a nature writer, Mowat considers himself a storyteller or "saga man" whose works derive from his concern about the preservation of all forms of life. An outspoken advocate for the Canadian North with an irreverent attitude toward bureaucracy, Mowat has repeatedly aroused the ire of Canadian officials through his harsh indictments of government policies concerning the treatment of endangered races of people as well as endangered animal species. With characteristic bluntness, Mowat once remarked in *Newsweek:* "Modern man is such an arrogant cement head to believe that he can take without paying."

Mowat first became aware of humanity's outrages against nature in the late 1940s when he accepted a position as a government biologist in the barren lands of northern Canada. He took the assignment in part because it offered him a respite from civilization—Mowat had recently returned from the battlefields of World War II where he served in the Canadian Army and witnessed brutal combat during the invasion of Italy. "I came back from the war rejecting my species," he told Cheryl McCall in *People* magazine. "I hated what had been done to me and what I had done and what man did to man."

Mowat's assignment in the Barrens was to study the area's wolf population and their behavior. The federal government suspected that the wolves were responsible for the dwindling caribou population and enlisted Mowat to get evidence to corroborate their suspicions. However, after months of observing a male wolf and his mate—whom he named George and Angeline—Mowat discovered wolves to be intelligent creatures who ate only what they needed for survival. Subsisting primarily on a diet of field mice, the wolves would only eat an occasional sickly caribou—by killing the weakest of the species, the wolves actually helped strengthen the caribou herd.

Although the results of his study were quickly dismissed by the government, as were any expectations he may have had of further employment, Mowat eventually fashioned his findings into a fictional work, *Never Cry Wolf,* which was published in 1963. A *Chicago Tribune Book World* critic calls Mowat's experience "a perfect example of the bureaucrats getting more than they bargained for." Much to Mowat's dismany, according to a reviewer for *Atlantic,* "the Canadian government . . . has never paid any discernible attention to the information it hired Mr. Mowat to assemble." Fortunately, through his book Mowat's message was heeded by both the reading public and the governments of other countries. Shortly after a translation of *Never Cry Wolf* appeared in Russia, officials in that country banned the slaughter of wolves, whom they had previously thought to be arbitrary killers. Noting the long-range repercussions of the book, David Graber comments in the *Los Angeles Time Book Review* that "by writing

Never Cry Wolf [Mowat] almost single-handedly reversed the public's image of the wolf, from feared vermin to romantic symbol of the wilderness."

Although not popular with officials of the federal government, *Never Cry Wolf* was welcomed by both readers and critics. Harry C. Kenney notes that the book "delightfully and instructively lifts one into a captivating animal kingdom" in his review for the *Christian Science Monitor.* "This is a fascinating and captivating book, and a tragic one, too," writes Gavin Maxwell in *Book Week,* "for it carries a bleak, dead-pan obituary of the wolf family that Mr. Mowat had learned to love and respect. It is an epilogue that will not endear the Canadian Wildlife Service to readers. . . . Once more it is man who displays the qualities with which he has tried to damn the wolf."

During the months spent studying wolves in the Barrens, Mowat also befriended an Inuit tribe called the Ihalmiut, or "People of the Deer," because they depend almost solely on caribou for food, clothing, and shelter. After learning a simplified form of their native language, Mowat was able to learn that the Ihalmiut people had been dwindling in numbers for several years due to the decreasing availability of caribou. Mowat, enraged at the government's apathy toward preserving the tribe, immediately began to compose scathing letters that he distributed to government officials. When such letters only resulted in the loss of his job, he turned his pen to a more productive enterprise. In the book *People of the Deer,* published in 1952, Mowat put the plight of the Ihalmiut squarely before the Canadian people. As *Saturday Review* contributor Ivan T. Sanderson observes: "What [Mowat] learned by living with the pathetic remnants of this wonderful little race of Nature's most perfected gentlemen, learning their language and their history, and fighting the terrifying northern elements at their side, so enraged him that when he came to set down the record, he contrived the most damning indictment of his own government and country, the so-called white race and its Anglo-Saxon branch in particular, the Christian religion, and civilization as a whole, that had ever been written."

Other reviewers have expressed admiration for *People of the Deer.* A *Times Literary Supplement* reviewer writes: "The author traces with a beautiful clarity the material and spiritual bonds between land, deer and people, and the precarious ecological balance which had been struck between the forefathers of this handful of men and the antlered multitude." Albert Hubbell agrees: "It is not often that a writer finds himself the sole chronicler of a whole human society, even of a microcosmic one like the Ihalmiut, and Mowat has done marvelously well at the job, despite a stylistic looseness and a tendency to formlessness," he observes in the *New Yorker.* "Also, his justifiable anger at the government's neglect of the Ihalmiut, who are its

wards, intrudes in places where it doesn't belong, but then, as I said, Mowat is something of a fanatic on this subject. His book, just the same, is a fine one." T. Morris Longstreth concludes in *Christian Science Monitor:* "Mr. Mowat says of his book, 'This is a labor of love, and a small repayment to a race that gave me renewed faith in myself and in all men.' It will widen the horizons of many who are at the same time thankful that this explorer did the widening for them."

Mowat has written several other books about man's mistreatment of wildlife. *A Whale for the Killing,* published in 1972, recounts the slow torture of a marooned whale in a pond in Newfoundland. But his most bitter account of man's abuse of nonhuman life has been *Sea of Slaughter,* published in 1984. "Built of the accumulated fury of a lifetime," according to Graber, *Sea of Slaughter* has been counted by critics as among the author's most important works. Tracy Kidder notes in the *Washington Post Book World* that compared to *Never Cry Wolf,* this book "is an out and out tirade." The book's title refers to the extinction and near-extinction of sea and land animals along the North Atlantic seaboard in the area extending from Cape Cod north to Labrador. Mowat traces the area's history back to the sixteenth century when the waters teemed with fish, whales, walruses, and seals, and the shores abounded with bison, white bears (now known as polar bears because of their gradual trek northward), and other fur-bearing mammals. Currently, many of these species have been either greatly diminished or extinguished because of "pollution, gross overhunting . . . , loss of habitat, destruction of food supplies, poachings and officially sanctioned 'cullings,' " writes Kidder.

Mowat depicts the stark contrast between past and present in a manner that is tremendously affecting, reviewers note. Although admitting that the book contains some inaccuracies and a lack of footnotes, *Detroit News* contributor Lewis Regenstein claims that these "shortcomings pale in comparison to the importance of its message: We are not only destroying our wildlife but also the earth's ability to support a variety of life forms, including humans. As Mowat bluntly puts it, 'The living world is dying in our time.' " Graber believes that "the grandest anguish comes from Mowat's unrelenting historical accounts of the sheer *numbers* of whales, bears, salmon, lynx, wolves, bison, sea birds; numbers that sear because they proclaim what we have lost, what we have thrown away." And Ian Darragh writes in *Quill & Quire:* "Mowat's description of the slaughter of millions of shorebirds for sport, for example, is appalling for what it implies about the aggression and violence apparently programmed into man's genetic code. There is little room for humour or Mowat's personal anecdotes in this epitaph for Atlantic Canada's once bountiful fish and wildlife." Concludes *Commonweal* critic Tom

O'Brien: "*Sea of Slaughter* provides some heavier reading [than Mowat's other books]; the weight in the progression of chapters starts to build through the book like a dirge. Nevertheless, it may help to focus the burgeoning animal rights movement in this country and abroad. The cause has no more eloquent spokesperson."

Sea of Slaughter received some unintended but nevertheless welcome publicity in 1984 when Mowat was refused entrance into the United States, where he was planning to publicize the book. While boarding a plane at a Toronto airport, Mowat was detained by officials from the United States Immigration and Naturalization Service (INS) who acted on the information that Mowat's name appeared in the *Lookout Book,* a government document that lists the names of those individuals who represent a danger to the security of the United States. Mowat later speculated in the *Chicago Tribune* about some possible reasons for his exclusion: "At first, . . . the assumption was that I was excluded because of the two trips I made to the Soviet Union [in the late 1960s]. . . . Then some guy at the INS supposedly said I was being kept out because I'd threatened the U.S. Armed Forces by threatening to shoot down American aircraft with a .22 caliber rifle. The fact is the Ottawa Citizen [where the story supposedly appeared in 1968] can't find any record of it, but that doesn't matter. I admit it, happily." Mowat added that the suggestion was later put forth that the "gun lobby and anti-environmentalists" might have wanted to prevent efforts to promote *Sea of Slaughter.*

Mowat's works for children contain a gentler, more light-hearted echo of his message to adult readers—his nature books for young people have given him a reputation as one of the best known Canadian writers for children outside his homeland. *Lost in the Barrens* is a novel about a pair of teenaged boys who become lost and must face the winter alone in the tundra. *The Dog Who Wouldn't Be* and *Owls in the Family* are memoirs of eccentric family pets. "[Mowat] knows children and what they like and can open doors to adventures both credible and entertaining to his young readers," notes Joseph E. Carver in his essay in the *British Columbia Library Quarterly.* "His stories are credible because Mowat wanted to write them to give permanence to the places, loyalties and experiences of his youth, entertaining because the author enjoys the telling of them." Mowat continues to take his role as a children's author seriously, viewing it as "of vital importance if basic changes for the good are ever to be initiated in any human culture," he noted in *Canadian Library Journal.*

Mowat departs from his usual focus—the Canadian wilderness—in *And No Birds Sang,* a memoir describing his experiences in the Canadian Army Infantry during World War II. Written in 1979, thirty years after his return from the war, Mowat wrote the memoir in response to the

growing popularity of the notion that there is honor in dying in the service of one's country. The book chronicles Mowat's initial enthusiasm and determination to fight, the gradual surrender to despair, and its culmination in a horrifying fear of warfare that Mowat calls "The Worm That Never Dies." Reviewers have expressed reservations about the familiar nature of Mowat's theme, but add that Mowat nevertheless manages to bring a fresh perspective to the adage, "War is hell." David Weinberger remarks in *Macleans:* "Everybody knows that war is hell; it is the author's task to transform that knowledge into understanding." While noting that the book occasionally "bogs down in adjectives and ellipsis," Weinberger praises the work: "It takes a writer of stature—both as an author and as a moral, sensitive person—to make the attempt as valiantly as Mowat has." A similar opinion is expressed by Jean Strouse in *Newsweek:* "That war is hell is not news, but a story told this well serves, particularly in these precarious, saber-rattling days, as a vivid reminder." *And No Birds Sang* has been called by some reviewers a valuable addition to the literature of World War II. *Washington Post Book World* contributor Robert W. Smith calls the book "a powerful chunk of autobiography and a valuable contribution to war literature." *Time* critic R. Z. Sheppard writes: "*And No Birds Sang* needs no rhetoric. It can fall in with the best memoirs of World War II, a classic example of how unexploded emotions can be artfully defused."

In 1985, shortly after the death of noted primatologist Dian Fossey, Mowat was approached by Warner Books to write her biography. Although he initially refused—because he had never written a commissioned book—after reading one of Fossey's *National Geographic* articles, he reconsidered. Mowat told Beverly Slopen of *Publishers Weekly* that while reading Fossey's letters and journals he "began to realize that the importance of the book was her message, not my message. . . . I really became her collaborator. It was the journals that did it. They weren't long, discursive accounts. They were short, raw cries from the heart."

Mowat's biography *Woman in the Mists: The Story of Dian Fossey and the Mountain Gorillas of Africa* was published in 1987. The work relies heavily on Fossey's journal entries and letters to tell the story of her life: Her invitation by anthropologist Louis Leakey to study primates in the African Congo in 1967, an invitation that culminated in an escape to Uganda in the wake of political uprisings, and ultimately in her establishment of a research center on the Rwandan side of the Virunga Mountains where Fossey remained until her death. Fossey's murder has not been solved, but the book "goes a long way toward revealing what it was about her that made a violent death seem inevitable," notes Eugene Linden in the *New York Times*

Book Review. Fossey was known to stalk gorilla poachers and she lived by the biblical motto, "An eye for an eye." She also angered government officials by opposing "gorilla tourism" and the development of park land for agrarian purposes. But Mowat's biography also reveals a side of Fossey that was generous, kind, witty, and romantic. She had a succession of affairs throughout her lifetime, including one with Leakey, and longed for a stable, monogamous relationship. Mary Battiata, a *Washington Post Book World* contributor believes that Mowat "puts to rest— forever one hopes—the shopworn notion of Fossey as a misanthrope who preferred animals to her own species." But, she goes on to add, "Though Mowat offers an intriguing and credible solution to the mystery of Fossey's unsolved murder, there is little else that is genuinely new here." *Chicago Tribune* contributor Anita Susan Grossman similarly observes that Mowat "limits himself to presenting excerpts from Fossey's own writings, strung together with the barest of factual narration. As a result, the central drama of Fossey's life remains as murky as the circumstances of her death." Although Linden concurs that *Woman in the Mists* does have several problems, including a lack of footnotes, Mowat's "pedestrian" prose, and "interlocutory words [that] add little to our understanding of Fossey or her world," he adds: "Despite these problems, this is a rare, gripping look at the tragically mingled destinies of a heroic, flawed woman and her beloved mountain gorillas amid the high mists of the Parc des Volcans."

Critical appraisal aside, Mowat states that the writing of Fossey's biography had a profound, sobering effect on him and that he will not undertake another biography. "It was a disturbing experience," he told Slopen. "It's almost as though I were possessed. I wasn't the master. I fought for mastery and I didn't win. It really was a transcendental experience and I'm uncomfortable with it."

Although Mowat has spent nearly a lifetime trying to convince humanity that we cannot continue to abuse nature without serious and sometimes irreversible repercussions, he believes that "in the end, my crusades have accomplished nothing." Mowat continues in *People* magazine: "I haven't saved the wolf, the whales, the seals, primitive man or the outpost people. All I've done is to document the suicidal tendencies of modern man. I'm sure I haven't altered the course of human events one iota. Things will change inevitably, but it's strictly a matter of the lottery of fate. It has nothing to do with man's intentions."

BIOGRAPHICAL/CRITICAL SOURCES:

BOOKS

Authors and Artists for Young Adults, Volume 1, Gale, 1988, pp. 175-88.
Children's Literature Review, Volume 20, Gale, 1990.
Contemporary Literary Criticism, Volume 26, Gale, 1983.

Dictionary of Literary Biography, Volume 68: *Canadian Writers, 1920-1959, First Series,* Gale, 1988, pp. 253-58.
Egoff, Sheila, *The Republic of Childhood: A Critical Guide to Canadian Children's Literature in English,* Oxford University Press, 1975.
Lucas, Alex, *Farley Mowat,* McClelland & Stewart, 1976.
Mowat, Farley, *And No Birds Sang,* McClelland & Stewart, 1979, Little, Brown, 1980.
Twentieth-Century Children's Writers, St. James Press, 1989, pp. 702-03.

PERIODICALS

Atlantic Monthly, November, 1963; February, 1993, p. 76.
Audubon, January, 1973.
Best Sellers, February, 1986.
Books in Canada, March, 1985; November, 1985.
Books of the Times, April, 1980.
Book Week, November 24, 1963.
Book World, December 31, 1972.
Canadian Children's Literature, number 5, 1976; number 6, 1976.
Canadian Forum, July, 1974; March, 1976.
Canadian Geographical Journal, June, 1974.
Canadian Literature, spring, 1978.
Chicago Tribune, October 29, 1980; December 23, 1983; May 6, 1985; October 22, 1987.
Chicago Tribune Book World, November 13, 1983.
Christian Science Monitor, May 1, 1952; October 3, 1963; May 15, 1969; May 10, 1970; April 15, 1971; March 6, 1974.
Commonweal, September 6, 1985.
Contemporary Review, February, 1978.
Detroit News, April 21, 1985.
Economist, January 15, 1972.
Globe and Mail (Toronto), November 25, 1989.
Illustrated London News, September 20, 1952.
Los Angeles Times, December 13, 1985.
Los Angeles Times Book Review, March 16, 1980; April 28, 1985.
MacLean's, October 8, 1979; October 11, 1993, p. 76.
Nation, June 10, 1968.
New Republic, March 8, 1980.
Newsweek, February 18, 1980; September 30, 1985.
New Yorker, April 26, 1952; May 11, 1968; March 17, 1980.
New York Times, December 13, 1965; February 19, 1980.
New York Times Book Review, February 11, 1968; June 14, 1970; February 22, 1976; November 6, 1977; February 24, 1980; December 22, 1985; October 25, 1987; August 28, 1994, p. 16.
Observer (London), March 4, 1973.
People, March 31, 1980.

Publishers Weekly, October 2, 1987; February 16, 1990, p. 72.

Quill and Quire, December, 1984.

Saturday Evening Post, July 29, 1950; April 13, 1957.

Saturday Night, October 18, 1952; October 25, 1952; November, 1975.

Saturday Review, June 28, 1952; April 26, 1969; October 21, 1972.

Scientific American, March, 1964.

School Library Journal, October, 1994, p. 162.

Sierra, September, 1978.

Spectator, November 21, 1952.

Time, February 18, 1980; May 6, 1985; October 26, 1987.

Times Literary Supplement, September 12, 1952; March 19, 1971; February 16, 1973.

Washington Post, October 9, 1983; April 25, 1985; October 25, 1985.

Washington Post Book World, February 24, 1980; May 12, 1985; October 25, 1987.

*   *   *

MUNRO, Alice   1931-

PERSONAL: Born July 10, 1931, in Wingham, Ontario, Canada; daughter of Robert Eric (a farmer) and Ann Clarke (Chamney) Laidlaw; married James Armstrong Munro (a bookseller), December 29, 1951 (divorced, 1976); married Gerald Fremlin (a geographer), 1976; children: (first marriage) Sheila, Jenny, Andrea. *Education:* University of Western Ontario, B.A., 1952. *Politics:* New Democratic Party. *Religion:* Unitarian Universalist.

ADDRESSES: Home—Clinton, Ontario, Canada. *Office*—Alfred A. Knopf, Inc., 201 East 50th St., New York, NY 10022.

CAREER: Writer. Artist-in-residence, University of Western Ontario, 1974-75, and University of British Columbia, 1980.

MEMBER: Writers Union of Canada.

AWARDS, HONOURS: Governor General's Literary Award, 1969, for *Dance of the Happy Shades,* 1979, for *The Beggar Maid: Stories of Flo and Rose,* and 1987, for *The Progress of Love;* Canadian Bookseller's Award, 1972, for *Lives of Girls and Women;* D. Litt., University of Western Ontario, 1976; Canada-Australia Literary Prize, 1977; Marian Engel award, 1986; recipient of 1995 Lannan Literary Award.

WRITINGS:

Dance of the Happy Shades (short stories), Ryerson, 1968.

Lives of Girls and Women (novel), McGraw, 1971.

Something I've Been Meaning to Tell You: Thirteen Stories, McGraw, 1974.

Who Do You Think You Are?: Stories, Macmillan (Toronto), 1978, published as *The Beggar Maid: Stories of Flo and Rose,* Knopf, 1979.

The Moons of Jupiter, Macmillan (Toronto), Knopf, 1983.

The Progress of Love (short stories), Knopf 1986.

Friend of My Youth (short stories), Knopf 1990.

Open Secrets (short stories), Knopf, 1994.

TELEVISION SCRIPTS

A Trip to the Coast, To See Ourselves, Canadian Broadcasting Corp. (CBC), 1973.

Thanks for the Ride, To See Ourselves, CBC, 1973.

How I Met My Husband, The Play's the Thing, CBC, 1974, Macmillan (Toronto), 1976.

1847: The Irish, The Newcomers: Inhabiting a New Land, CBC, 1978.

OTHER

Contributor to books, including *Canadian Short Stories,* second series, Oxford University Press, 1968; *Sixteen by Twelve: Short Stories by Canadian Writers,* edited by John Metcalf, Ryerson, 1970; *The Narrative Voice: Stories and Reflections by Canadian Authors,* edited by David Helwig and Joan Harcourt, Oberon, 1974; *Here and Now,* Oberon, 1977; *Personal Fictions,* Oxford University Press, 1977; *Night Light: Stories of Aging,* Oxford University Press, 1986; and *Best American Short Stories, 1989.* Also contributor to periodicals, including *Atlantic, Canadian Forum, Queen's Quarterly, Chatelaine, Grand Street,* and *New Yorker.*

ADAPTATIONS: "Baptising," in *Lives of Girls and Women,* was adapted and filmed for the CBC *Performance* series, 1975.

SIDELIGHTS: Usually concerned with characters living in small towns of southwestern Ontario, the stories of Alice Munro present "ordinary experiences so that they appear extraordinary, invested with a kind of magic," according to Catherine Sheldrick Ross in the *Dictionary of Literary Biography.* "Few people writing today," Beverley Slopen claims in *Publishers Weekly,* "can bring a character, a mood or a scene to life with such economy. And [Munro] has an exhilarating ability to make the readers see the familiar with fresh insight and compassion."

In a review of *Dance of the Happy Shades,* in *New York Times Book Review,* contributor Martin Levin writes that "the short story is alive and well in Canada, where most of the fifteen tales originate like fresh winds from the North. Alice Munro," he continues, "creates a solid habitat for her fiction—southwestern Ontario, a generation or more in the past—and is in sympathetic vibration with the farmers and townspeople who live there." Peter Prince, writing in the *New Statesman,* calls the stories in this collection "beautifully controlled and precise. And always this precision appears unstrained. The proportions so exactly fit the writer's thematic aims that in almost every case it seems that really no other words *could* have been used, certainly no more or less." Ronald Blythe notes in the *Listener* that "the stories are all to do with discovering personal freedom within an accepted curtailment. There is no intentional nostalgia although, strangely enough, one frequently finds oneself rather wistfully caught up in some of the scenes so perfectly evoked; and there is no distortion in the characterisation."

Reviewing *Something I've Been Meaning to Tell You* in *Saturday Night*, Kildare Dobbs writes: "Readers who enjoyed the earlier books because they confirmed the reality of the Canadian small town experience for a certain generation, or because they seemed to reinforce some of the ideology of the women's movement, will find more of the same. But they will find something else, too. There is a hint at hermetic concerns in the first story, ironic suggestions of a quest for the grail. . . . All the stories are told with skill which the author has perfected over the years, narrated with meticulous precision in a voice that is unmistakably Ontarian in its lack of emphasis, its sly humour and willingness to live with a mystery." Reviewing Munro's collection for the *Ontario Review,* writer Joyce Carol Oates finds that the reader will be "most impressed by the feeling behind [Munro's] stories—the evocation of emotions, ranging from bitter hatred to love, from bewilderment and resentment to awe. In all her work . . . there is an effortless, almost conversational tone, and we know we are in the presence of an art that works to conceal itself, in order to celebrate its subject."

Munro "has the ability to isolate the one detail that will evoke the rest of the landscape," writes Urjo Kareda in *Saturday Night,* calling *Who Do You Think You Are,* known in the United States as *The Beggar Maid: Stories of Flo and Rose,* a "remarkable, immensely pleasurable collection." A volume of related short stories, *Who Do You Think You Are?* tells of Rose—a wealthy, middle-aged divorcee who grew up in poverty in Hanratty, Ontario—as she fits the pieces of her life together. According to Oates, writing in the *Ontario Review,* "The most powerful passages are those which evoke, in a single strong image, or in a few fastidiously-chosen lines, Rose's troubled relationship with her step-mother," Flo. Julia O'Faolain, writing in the *New York Times Book Review,* comments: "Alice Munro captures a kaleidoscope of lights and depths. Through the lens of Rose's eye, she manages to reproduce the vibrant prance of life while scrutinizing the working of her own narrative art. This is an exhilarating collection."

"In *The Progress of Love,* the focus has changed," writes Anne Tyler in the *New Republic.* "The characters in these 11 stories are concerned not so much with the journey as

with the journey's hidden meaning—how to view the journey, how to make sense of it. . . . In the most successful of the stories, the end result is a satisfying click as everything settles precisely into place." Munro "is concerned not only with the different configurations of love that occur in the wake of divorces, separations and deaths, but also with the 'progress' of love, the ways in which it endures or changes through time," notes Michiko Kakutani in the *New York Times.* "The results are pictures of life, or relationships, of love, glimpsed from a succession of mirrors and frames—pictures that possess both the pain and immediacy of life and the clear, hard radiance of art." "These stories seem natural and are hugely artful; they seem life-like and are very precisely constructed. They are . . . both real *and* true," writes A.S. Byatt in *Listener.* Oates declares in the *New York Times Book Review* that "Munro writes stories that have the density—moral, emotional, sometimes historical—of other writers' novels"—a claim echoed by Malcom Jones, Jr. writing in *Newsweek* and Ted Solataroff in the *Nation.* Oates continues, "*The Progress of Love* is a volume of unflinching audacious honesty, uncompromisingly downright in its dissection of the ways in which we deceive ourselves in the name of love; the bleakness of its vision is enriched by the author's exquisite eye and ear for detail. Life is heartbreak, but it is also uncharted moments of kindness and reconciliation."

In *Friend of My Youth,* Munro continues to explore the movements of relationships and characters with respect to time. "Movement is central to all Munro's stories," writes Kate Walbert in the *Nation:* "That endings give way to beginnings is the one constant in the lives of these characters." Walbert also asserts that for Munro, "self-identity . . . is a commodity to wage battles for," and for her female protagonists, "self-scrutinization . . . is as habitual as breathing." According to Walbert, the issue for these women is not so much the events of their past—"first marriages, lonely childhoods, severed friendships"—but "who they were in relation to that event." As they trace "their footsteps with . . . How did-I-get-here? wonder" the attempt "to extract the 'I' from a time when who they were was defined *for* them seems a Sisyphean task," since "so many of [their] actions were taken in observance of patriarchal rules."

The success of the stories in *Friend of My Youth* won Munro significant critical acclaim. In *Time,* Stefan Kanfer compares Munro to the great Russian short story writer and dramatist, Anton Chekhov, and the *New York Times Book Review* editors included it among their selections of the "Best Books of 1990." The *New York Times Book Review* contributor calls Munro "hugely gifted, . . . one of the world's great totemic writers" and claims that her writing has "deepened the channels of realism."

Writer and editor Ted Solataroff, too, recognizes Munro's contribution to the development of realism through the short story genre in his review of *Open Secrets* for the *Nation.* He calls her "the mother figure of Canadian fiction" and places her writing in the tradition of "the great stylist of 1920s realism, a Katherine Anne Porter brought up to date." Solataroff also claims that Munro is "as much an architect of the female wing [of realism] as Raymond Carver has been of the male." He notes her "pragmatic experiments in handling time, point of view and new textures of verisimilitude," and explains that the tremendous power of much of her work "comes from her subtle creation of patterns that enable seemingly disparate elements of her story to talk to each other."

Josephine Humphreys, writing in the *New York Times Book Review* also remarks on Munro's stylistic achievements. She notes every story in *Open Secrets* contains "a startling leap"—in time, place, or point of view—which "explod[es]—the fictional context" and allows Munro to reach "toward difficult truths." For, as Humphreys claims, "Ms. Munro's fiction is out to seize—to apprehend—the mystery of existence within time, 'the unforseen intervention,' the unique quality of a person's fate."

But like her previous collections, *Open Secrets* is largely concerned with "sex and its politics" according to Solataroff, who adds that the stories in this collection "develop Munro's master theme from various points in time and from dramatically unexpected angles." Praising "A Wilderness Station"—an epistolary story concerning two brothers, a murder, and a woman's oppression and madness on the Canadian frontier,—as "extraordinary writing," he also proclaims that "there are two great stories in *Open Secrets* which deal with the male shadow on women's lives": "Carried Away," "a beautiful three part variation on the theme of being carried away, in its double meaning of love and death," and "The Albanian Virgin," which first appeared in the *New Yorker,* and which Solataroff proclaims a "masterpiece . . . written with the guts of a burglar." The complicated plot of "The Albanian Virgin" consists of two parallel narrative lines concerning a Canadian tourist, an "esoteric old bohemian named Charlotte" and her Balkan husband, Gjurdhi, and the much younger narrator, "who has taken up . . . a solitary search for her identity."

Humphreys also praises "Carried Away" and "The Albanian Virgin" and claims that Munro's stories have always "dare[d] to teach . . . without giving answers." She adds, "Just when meaning seems almost revealed, the story changes, veers, steps off a cliff." Thus, Munro explores what Solataroff calls the "narrative configuration of life," or what Humphreys terms the way in which the self is made a narrative in order to "guard against despair." The result is, for Humphreys, "a book that dazzles with its faith in language and in life."

"The reader's experience in reading Munro's stories is one of recognition," writes Ross. "We say, yes, that is how life is; we recognize and acknowledge discoveries about our deepest selves. And this recognition is the purpose of the author's journeys in to the past, undertaken with compassion and determination to 'get it right,' to get down the tones, textures, and appearances of things. Instead of plots, Munro's work offers arrangements of materials that shift our perceptions of ordinary events and make us see the ordinary in an extraordinary way." Speaking to Mervyn Rothstein of the *New York Times,* Munro explains: "I never intended to be a short story writer. . . . I started writing them because I didn't have time to write anything else—I had three children. And then I got used to writing stories, so I saw my material that way, and I don't think I'll ever write a novel."

BIOGRAPHICAL/CRITICAL SOURCES:

BOOKS

Authors in the News, Volume 2, Gale, 1976.
Contemporary Literary Criticism, Gale, Volume 6, 1976; Volume 10, 1979; Volume 19, 1981; Volume 50, 1988.
Dahlie, Hallvard, *Alice Munro and Her Works,* ECW Press, 1985.
MacKendrick, Louis K., editor, *Probable Fictions: Alice Munro's Narrative Acts,* ECW Press, 1984.
Martin, W. R., *Alice Munro,* University of Alberta Press, 1987.
Ross, Catherine Sheldrick, "Alice Munro," *Dictionary of Literary Biography,* Volume 53: *Canadian Writers since 1960,* Gale, 1986.

PERIODICALS

Canadian Fiction Magazine, Number 43, 1982, pp. 74-114.
Canadian Forum, February, 1969.
Chatelaine, August, 1975, pp. 42-43; July 1990, p. 10.
Journal of Canadian Studies, spring, 1991, pp. 5-21; summer, 1991, pp. 156-69; summer, 1994, pp. 184-94.
Listener, June 13, 1974; January 29, 1987, pp. 22-23.
Maclean's, September 22, 1986; May 7, 1990, p. 66.
Nation, May 14, 1990, pp. 678-80; November 28, 1994, pp. 665-668.
New Republic, September 15, 1986; pp. 54-55; May 14, 1990, p. 50.
New Statesman, May 3, 1974.
Newsweek, September 26, 1994, p. 63.
New Yorker, December 17, 1990, p. 123.
New York Review of Books, May 17, 1990, p. 38.
New York Times, February 16, 1983; September 3, 1986, p. C22; November 10, 1986; April 17, 1990.

New York Times Book Review, September 23, 1973; September 16, 1979, p. 12; September 14, 1986, pp. 7, 9; March 18, 1990, p. 1; December 2, 1990, p. 3; September 11, 1994, pp. 1, 36-37.

Ontario Review, fall, 1974; fall-winter, 1979-80, pp. 87-90.

Publishers Weekly, August 22, 1986; August 1, 1994, p. 72.

Saturday Night, July 1974, p. 28; January-February, 1979, pp. 62-63.

Time, January 15, 1973; July 2, 1990, p. 66-7.

*   *   *

MUSGRAVE, Susan   1951-

PERSONAL: Born March 12, 1951, in Santa Cruz, CA; daughter of Edward L. and Judith B. (Stevens) Musgrave; married Stephen Douglas Reid, 1986; children: Charlotte Amelia Musgrave Nelson, Sophie Alexandra Musgrave Reid. *Education:* Educated in British Columbia, Canada.

ADDRESSES: Home—Box 2421, Sidney, British Columbia V8L 3Y3, Canada.

CAREER: Writer. University of Waterloo, Ontario, Canada, writer-in-residence, 1983-85.

MEMBER: League of Canadian Poets, National Poetry Secretariat, Writers' Union of Canada.

AWARDS, HONOURS: Canada Council travel grant, 1969-70, arts bursary, 1972-73, and arts grant, 1974-75 and 1976-77; Du Maurier Magazine Award, 1982; R. P. Adams Short Fiction Award, 1989; b. p. nichol Poetry Chapbook Award, 1990.

WRITINGS:

POETRY

Songs of the Sea-Witch, Sono Nis Press (Victoria, British Columbia), 1970.

Entrance of the Celebrant, Macmillan (New York City), 1972.

Grave-Dirt and Selected Strawberries, Macmillan, 1973.

Against (pamphlet), Sceptre Press (Rushden, England), 1974.

Gullband (for children), J. J. Douglas, 1974.

The Impstone, McClelland & Stewart (Toronto, ON), 1976.

Becky Swan's Book, Porcupine's Quill (Erin, ON), 1977.

For Charlie Beaulieu in Yellowknife Who Told Me Go Back to the South and Write Another Poem about Indians (pamphlet), Sceptre Press (Knotting, England), 1977.

(With Sean Virgo) *Kiskatinaw Songs,* illustrated by Douglas Tait, Pharos Press (Victoria, BC), 1977.

Selected Strawberries: Poems, 1969-1973, Sono Nis Press, 1977.

Two Poems for the Blue Moon (pamphlet), Sceptre Press, 1977.

A Man to Marry, A Man to Bury, McClelland & Stewart, 1979.

Conversations during the Omelette Aux Fine Herbes (pamphlet), Sceptre Press, 1979.

Hag-Head, Clarke, Irwin (Toronto, ON), 1980.

Tarts and Muggers: Poems, New and Selected, McClelland & Stewart, 1982.

Cocktails at the Mausoleum, McClelland & Stewart, 1985.

Great Musgrave, Prentice Hall, 1989.

Kestrel and Leonardo (for children), illustrated by Linda Rogers, Studio 123, 1990.

The Embalmer's Art: Poems, 1970-1991, Exile Editions (Toronto, ON), 1991.

NOVELS

The Charcoal Burners, McClelland & Stewart, 1980.

The Dancing Chickens, Methuen (London), 1987.

OTHER

Also author of *Taboo Man,* 1981, and *The Plane Put Down in Sacramento,* 1982. Contributor of poems to numerous publications, including *Canadian Forum, Ellipse, Saturday Night, Toronto Globe & Mail, Poetry Review, New York Times,* and *West Coast Poetry Review.* Poems anthologized in several collections, including *Mindscapes,* 1970; *Aurora: Canadian Writing,* 1978, 1979; *The Poets of Canada,* 1978; *Literature in Canada,* 1978; *Norton Anthology of Modern Poetry.* Poetry has been broadcast on numerous Canadian Broadcasting Corporation (CBC) programs, including *Anthology.* Author of a nationally syndicated bi-weekly column "Writer-in-Residence" for the *Toronto Star.*

ADAPTATIONS: Gullband was adapted for the stage by Toronto's Theatre Passe Muraille, 1976.

WORK IN PROGRESS: The Joy of Sexual Failure; The Crook Book, with Stephen Reid.

SIDELIGHTS: Perhaps the most recognizable trait of Susan Musgrave's poetry is her graphic and often shocking portrayal of sex and violence. The underlying strength of her work, however, has received frequent critical acclaim and has been compared to that of Anne Sexton and Sylvia Plath. Andrew Brooks observes in *Canadian Literature* that Musgrave's poems are effective on many levels: "Infinite, discrete bits of what is familiar blend into a continuum which jolts us with sudden, surprising resonance. Energy crackles in the joints, and the poems are as valuable for what they say implicitly—for their tangential energy—as they are for what they say directly." Rosemary Sullivan similarly contends that what makes Musgrave's poems exceptional "apart from the technical mastery—is the unity of tone and vision which underlies them: a poignant bloodlonging for warmth and relationship which is continually frustrated."

Despite appreciation for Musgrave's honesty and willingness to explore unusual subjects, critics find that some of her images remain unclear or ultimately succeed only in shocking the reader. Sullivan notes that although "Musgrave has honed her language to essentials and made it evocative in combination so that her words have an oracular intensity," she sometimes "asks diction to carry too much, depending heavily on the associative quality of certain favorite words that are rehearsed like ritual. The images are meant to conjure up a nightmare intensity, yet felt meaning sometimes escapes as the words have no sensuous definition." Vivienne Denton writes in *CM* that the poems in Musgrave's collection *Cocktails at the Mausoleum* "seem designed to shock. There is a fair range of subject and tone within the collection, although the poetry is chiefly erotic and the dominant genre is a sort of punk gothicism."

A better understanding of Musgrave's tendency to shock readers may be found in Ed Jewinski's interview for *Cross-Canada Writers' Quarterly*. In the interview, Musgrave explains: "I guess much of my poetry results because things shock me—human relations especially shock me. The way people treat each other shocks me—in love, in war, in prisons, in any thing, even in everyday relationships on the street. I don't know how things work; I don't know how it all stays together. Poetry is the only way I know of trying to make sense of it."

BIOGRAPHICAL/CRITICAL SOURCES:

BOOKS

Contemporary Literary Criticism, Gale, Volume 13, 1980, Volume 54, 1989.

PERIODICALS

Books in Canada, April, 1979, p. 10; December, 1980, p. 30; December, 1982, pp. 22-23; October, 1985, p. 30; December, 1987, pp. 19-20; January, 1990, p. 21; May, 1992, p. 60.
Canadian Forum, August, 1974; October, 1976; June-July, 1979, pp. 42-43.
Canadian Literature, summer, 1972; summer, 1974; autumn, 1983, pp. 62-65; autumn, 1989, p. 184.
CM: A Reviewing Journal of Canadian Materials for Young People, November, 1985, pp. 273-74.
Contemporary Verse II, fall, 1975.
Cross-Canada Writers' Quarterly, Volume 8, number 2, 1986, pp. 3-5.
Maclean's, February 26, 1979, p. 55; September 29, 1980, pp. 58-60; December 15, 1980, p.52.
Quill and Quire, June, 1978, p. 46; December, 1980, p. 29; October, 1987, p. 22.
Saturday Night, January, 1974; November, 1979, p. 60; November, 1980, pp. 72-73.
Times Literary Supplement, January 5, 1973.
Toronto Star, February 3, 1976.*

N

NARRACHE, Jean
See CODERRE, Emile

*   *   *

NEWBOUND, Bernard Slade   1930-
(Bernard Slade)

PERSONAL: Born May 2, 1930, in St. Catharines, Ontario, Canada; came to United States, 1963; son of Fred (a mechanic) and Bessie (maiden name, Walbourne) Newbound; married Jill Foster Hancock (an actress), July 25, 1953; children: Laurel, Christopher. *Education:* Educated in England and Wales. *Religion:* "None." *Avocational interests:* Tennis.

ADDRESSES: Home—1262 Lago Vista Place, Beverly Hills, CA 90210; and Flat 3, 4 Egerton Place, London, S.W.3, England.*Agent*—Jack Hutto, 405 West 23rd St., New York, NY 10011.

CAREER: Writer. Worked as an actor in more than two hundred stage productions in Ontario, 1949-57; television writer for Columbia Pictures, Los Angeles, CA, 1957-74.

MEMBER: Writers Guild of America (West), Dramatists Guild of America, Academy of Motion Picture Arts and Sciences, Society of Authors and Artists (France).

AWARDS, HONOURS: Drama Desk Award, American Academy of Humor Award, and nomination for Antoinette Perry (Tony) Award from American Theatre Wing, all 1975, all for *Same Time, Next Year;* Academy Award nomination for best screenplay, Academy of Motion Picture Arts and Sciences, 1978, for *Same Time, Next Year.*

WRITINGS:

PLAYS; ALL UNDER NAME BERNARD SLADE

Simon Gets Married (three-act comedy), first produced in Toronto, Ontario, at Crest Theatre, December 8, 1960.

A Very Close Family (three-act drama), first produced in Winnipeg, Manitoba, at Manitoba Theatre Centre, May 10, 1963.

Same Time, Next Year (two-act comedy; first produced in Boston at Colonial Theatre, February, 1975; produced in New York City at Brooks Atkinson Theatre, March 13, 1975), Delacorte (New York), 1975.

Tribute (two-act comedy-drama; first produced in Boston at Colonial Theatre, April 6, 1978; produced in New York City at Brooks Atkinson Theatre, June 1, 1978), Samuel French (New York), 1978.

Fling! (two-act comedy), Samuel French, 1979.

Romantic Comedy (three-act comedy; first produced in New York City at Ethel Barrymore Theatre, November 8, 1979), Samuel French, 1980.

Special Occasions (two-act drama; first produced in New York City at Music Box Theatre, February 7, 1982), Samuel French, 1982.

Fatal Attraction (two-act thriller; first produced in Toronto, Ontario, at St. Lawrence Center Theatre, November 8, 1984, Samuel French, 1986.

An Act of the Imagination (two-act mystery; first produced as *Sweet William* in Guildford, England, September 15, 1987), Samuel French, 1988.

Return Engagements (comedy; first produced in Westport, CT, at Westport Summer Theatre, 1988), Samuel French, 1989.

Also author of *Every Time I See You,* 1991.

SCREENPLAYS

Stand Up and Be Counted, Columbia, 1972.
Same Time, Next Year, Universal, 1978.
Tribute, Twentieth Century-Fox, 1980.

Also author of teleplays for Canadian Broadcasting Corp., including *The Prizewinner,* 1957, and *Men Don't Make Passes, Innocent Deception, The Gimmick, Do Jerry Parker, The Most Beautiful Girl in the World, The Big Coin Sound, The Reluctant Angels, A Very Close Family, Blue Is for Boys,* and *The Oddball.* Creator of eight television series and author of more than one hundred television scripts for numerous series, including *Love on a Rooftop, The Flying Nun, The Partridge Family,* and *Bewitched.*

SIDELIGHTS: Bernard Slade Newbound, better known as Bernard Slade, has come a long way since *The Partridge Family.* The popular sitcom's creator (who also originated *Bridget Loves Bernie, Love on a Rooftop,* and *The Flying Nun* and was a writer for *Bewitched*) left television behind for the stage and screen, where he found even greater success. "Ironically," he told Toronto *Globe and Mail* writer Stephen Godfrey, "I went into television to make money, and it was the labor of love [the play] *Same Time Next Year* that made me rich." The Canadian-born playwright's gentle comedy was a critical and commercial hit upon its Broadway debut in 1975. In fact, it was one of Broadway's longest-running comedies. After winning a Drama Desk award and an Antoinette Perry (Tony) Award nomination, the play was made into a popular movie starring Alan Alda and Ellen Burstyn—and Slade's screenplay was nominated for an Academy Award. Slade is also the author of the scripts for the 1981 movie *Tribute* and the 1983 film, *Romantic Comedy,* each adapted from the author's original Broadway plays.

Though *Tribute* is a play about death, and though *Romantic Comedy* and *Same Time, Next Year* explore serious themes, humor is an important element in all three. Slade told *CA:* "I was strongly influenced by the romantic comedies of Philip Barry, John Van Druten, S. N. Behrman, and Noel Coward. I try to write plays that combine comedy with situations and characters that touch the audience emotionally. I deal in the area of comedy because I find listening to two thousand people roaring their heads off enormously satisfying. Besides, nobody has ever convinced me that *life* isn't a comedy."

Same Time, Next Year marked a pinnacle for the author, whose earlier plays (*Simon Gets Married* and *A Very Close Family*) received little attention outside of Canada, and whose succeeding efforts haven't quite matched the critical and popular acclaim earned by this tale of a longterm, once-yearly, extramarital affair. Along with tracing the changes in the lives of the protagonists through the twenty-six years of their relationship, the play traces the

changes America itself undergoes in that same tumultuous time span from the 1950s to the 1970s. For many critics, the combination of these two elements creates a depth that is an important part of the play's appeal. As Chris Johnson explains in the *Dictionary of Literary Biography:* "The slick, sometimes risque comedy offers two human portraits and some pointed comment on the political, social, and economic events which have shaped their lives." Despite its uniquely American backdrop, *Same Time, Next Year* has proved to have a relatively global appeal: the play has been produced in London, Paris, Madrid, Stockholm, Copenhagen, Athens, Rome, Rio de Janeiro, Caracas, Germany, Australia, Mexico, and Japan.

While a critical success in its stage version, the filmed story fared less well in some reviews. In Gene Siskel's opinion, what he terms Slade's "gag writing" works well for the stage, but translates poorly to the screen. In his Chicago *Tribune* review, Siskel concludes that *Same Time, Next Year* is "merely harmless, lightweight entertainment."

Slade's *Tribute,* which opened on Broadway in 1978, "pays homage to all the unknown soldiers of *Variety's* obituary pages," Ronald Bryden writes in *Maclean's* magazine. *Tribute* is the story of the terminally ill Scottie Templeton, an entertaining, witty press agent beloved by nearly everyone in his life—except his son, Jud. Templeton's need to heal his relationship with Jud before he succumbs to leukemia serves as the play's focal point.

Later made into a movie starring Jack Lemmon (who recreated his Broadway role), *Tribute* was a financial success. "The play was so successful during its out-of-town run," Tony Schwartz notes in the *New York Times,* "that its backers had the rare good fortune of having been completely paid off" by *Tribute's* opening night on Broadway. Yet critical acclaim eluded the drama. John Simon in *New York* magazine that "I am not sure about how good a play *Tribute* is; what I know is that it is extremely clever and likable. . . . You have the happy feeling that the many very genuine witticisms in it are not, as usual, made at the expense of other people. . . . Only a nice man could have written [it]." Johnson deems it "More ambitious than [Slade's] earlier plays," but adds that it fails in its "attempts to balance comedy and drama." Others dismiss the play entirely, pronouncing its plot sentimental or contrived, its characters not fully realized.

Slade's *Romantic Comedy* fared similarly. The play traces the long relationship of a man and a woman, both playwrights, whose dramatic collaboration threatens to become romantic despite their untimely meeting on the man's wedding day. "I intended this play as a sort of valentine to those old romantic comedies about the obstacles to consummation," Slade told Schwartz. Theater-goers accepted Slade's valentine, and *Romantic Comedy* was a hit on Broadway.

But the play earned a lukewarm reception from theater critics. John Simon sees *Romantic Comedy* as being only half a success. In a review for *New York* magazine, he writes that it "almost makes up in comedy what it lacks in romance," but asserts that the play suffers in the development of the latter. Like others, Simon attributes some of that failing to characters that have been stereotyped rather than convincingly brought to life. Walter Kerr suggests in the *New York Times* that the characters Slade created belong in two different plays, given the man's "feverishness . . . that does [allow for] climactic outbursts but that tends to make the audience perspire along with him" and the woman who "is—as written—a much milder cup of tea."

In a largely negative review for the Chicago *Tribune* of the play's screen version (starring Dudley Moore and Mary Steenburgen), Siskel points out "one of Slade's dramatic points" with which the critic finds favor: "that some people are destined to be friends and always just miss being more," a point the critic finds "bittersweet." London *Times* columnist Anthony Masters makes a similar claim in his review of the play's London run: "Somewhere in the couple's developing understanding through a dozen hits and flops, and their inability to get it together emotionally, is a genuinely touching play."

Slade's revamping of the format of *Same Time, Next Year* for 1982's *Special Occasions* failed to draw the audiences of his earlier efforts. Though Rosalind Carne termed it an "unusual and, in many ways, endearing comedy" in her *Plays and Players* review, this story of a divorced couple meeting for the shared events of their separate lives closed after a brief run on Broadway. For Masters, the play is an improvement over Slade's previous material, despite what the critic sees as its contrived format and its tendency toward gloss at the expense of depth. For Johnson, it is "in many respects the best of Slade's later plays." Johnson describes Slade's development of the postdivorce relationship between the play's only characters as having been created with "considerable sensitivity and warmth."

Slade turned to darker writing for his next dramatic effort, the murder mystery *Fatal Attraction*. According to Godfrey, the play "is a thriller about a fading Hollywood star who comes back east to Nantucket and becomes involved in a series of murders," and it represents the author's sole attempt at the genre. "No matter what its fate," he explains, "Slade doubts he will write another thriller."

So far, the playwright has remained true to his word. In 1986, however, Slade did return to another genre: along with other well-known playwrights like Beth Henley and Wendy Wasserstein, he contributed a television script to

the Public Broadcasting Service (PBS-TV) comedy series *Trying Times*. But Slade's return to television was only brief. His ensuing efforts include a work entitled *Return Engagements*—a comedy in the genre Slade returns to again and again: the play.

Slade told *CA:* "Each play creates totally different problems. That's what's so fascinating—and so frustrating—about playwriting. Even after you've acquired a certain expertise, there's no formula for the texture, the chemistry, or whatever it is, that makes a play work." According to Schwartz, reviews arguing that a Slade play doesn't work have been known to upset the playwright, but he isn't bothered by suggestions that his dramas lack depth. "I'm an entertainer," Slade told Schwartz. "My plays aren't meant to be life-changing."

BIOGRAPHICAL/CRITICAL SOURCES:

BOOKS

Contemporary Authors Autobiography Series, Volume 9, Gale, 1989.
Contemporary Literary Criticism, Volume 46, Gale, 1988.
Dictionary of Literary Biography, Volume 53: *Canadian Writers since 1960, First Series,* Gale, 1986.

PERIODICALS

Canadian, July 26, 1975.
Chicago Tribune, February 9, 1979, p. 15; October 14, 1980; October 7, 1983.
Esquire, December, 1975.
Globe and Mail (Toronto), November 10, 1984.
Los Angeles Times, April 20, 1975.
McLean's, July 1975; May 15, 1978, p. 80.
Newsday, April 13, 1975.
New York, June 12, 1978; June 19, 1978, p. 74; November 26, 1979, p. 90.
New York Post, April 19, 1975; June 2, 1978.
New York Times, April 13, 1975; May 28, 1978; June 2, 1978; June 3, 1978; June 11, 1978; November 22, 1978; April 13, 1979; October 8, 1979, p. C15; November 4, 1979, p. D23; November 9, 1979, p. C3; May 9, 1980, p. C9; December 14, 1980; February 8, 1982; October 7, 1983; October 7, 1985; December 14, 1986.
Plays and Players, February, 1984, p. 32.
Times (London), February 3, 1983; December 22, 1983; November 1, 1985; November 28, 1985.
Washington Post, February 13, 1981, p. C6; October 12, 1983.*

—Sketch by Heather Aronson

NEWLOVE, John (Herbert) 1938-

PERSONAL: Born June 13, 1938, in Regina, Saskatchewan, Canada; son of Thomas Harold (a lawyer) and Mary Constant (Monteith) Newlove; married Susan Mary Phillips (a teacher), August 9, 1966; stepchildren: Jeremy Charles Gilbert, Tamsin Elizabeth Gilbert. *Education:* Attended school in Saskatchewan, Canada.

ADDRESSES: Home—105 Rochester St., Ottawa, Ontario, Canada K1R 7L9.

CAREER: Poet. McClelland & Stewart, Ltd., Toronto, Ontario, senior editor, 1970-74; Office of the Commissioner of Official Languages, Ottawa, Ontario, English editor, 1986—. Writer-in-residence, Loyola College, Montreal, Quebec, 1974-75, University of Western Ontario, 1975-76, University of Toronto, 1976-77, and Regina Public Library, 1979-80, David Thompson University Center, Nelson, British Columbia, 1982-83.

MEMBER: PEN International, Saskatchewan Writers' Guild, Alcuin Society, Hakluyt Society, Champlain Society.

AWARDS, HONOURS: Koerner Foundation award, 1964; Canada Council grant, 1965, 1967, 1977, 1981; Governor General's award for poetry, 1972; Founder's Award, Saskatchewan Writers' Guild, 1984; Literary Press Group Award, 1986; Deep Springs College Arts Award.

WRITINGS:

Grave Sirs, privately printed by R. Reid and T. Tanabe (Vancouver), 1962.

Elephants, Mothers and Others, Periwinkle Press, 1963.

Moving in Alone, Contact Press (Toronto), 1965, new edition, Oolichan Books, 1977.

Notebook Pages, Charles Pachter (Toronto), 1966.

What They Say, Weed/Flower Press, 1967.

Four Poems, It, 1967.

Black Night Window, McClelland & Stewart, 1968.

The Cave, McClelland & Stewart, 1970.

Lies, McClelland & Stewart, 1972.

(Editor) Joe Rosenblatt, *Dream Craters,* Press Porcepic, 1974.

(Editor) *Canadian Poetry: The Modern Era,* McClelland & Stewart, 1977.

(With John Metcalf) *Dreams Surround Us,* Bastard Press, 1977.

The Fat Man: Selected Poems, 1962-72, McClelland & Stewart, 1977.

(Editor) *The Collected Poems of F. R. Scott,* McClelland & Stewart, 1981.

The Green Plain, Oolichan Books, 1981.

The Night the Dog Smiled, ECW Press, 1986.

Apology for Absence: Selected Poems, 1962-1992, Porcupine's Quill, 1993.

SIDELIGHTS: According to Robin Skelton in *Canadian Literature,* John Newlove's poetry is "enormously well crafted, subtly controlled in tone, and richly various in style, even while remaining consistent to what emerges as an over-all purpose to portray the human tragedy with and economy and elegance." Reviewing *Lies* for *Canadian Forum,* Stephen Scobie saw a similar objective in Newlove's poetry: "*Lies* deals with masks, illusions, self-deception; but in the end the most grotesque masks are true, and the dreams all turn into nightmares."

"Newlove's vision," Skelton asserted, "is indeed dark. His universe is one of solitude, failure, ugliness, and nausea. The only driving forces of life are desire, which is always thwarted, and dreams which are never fulfilled. . . . Newlove has . . . created a place where no other poet has yet had the courage to go without at least a Swiftian irony, a Websterian rhetoric, or a religious conviction as luggage." Scobie found "strange, surrealistic images" in *Lies* which "arrange themselves in shapes which tease meaning towards the reader without ever declaring themselves fully." He also noted "outright pictures of human misery" and a "deep pervading pessimism" throughout the text.

What relieves Newlove's pessimism, Scobie observed, "is Newlove's attitude of acceptance rather than outrage." Skelton characterized Newlove's work as ultimately praising the resilience of man. He called *The Fat Man: Selected Poems, 1962-1972* "a tribute to courage and a statement of the awesome spiritual potential of man." The book, Skelton stated, is "one of the most impressive [poetry collections] to have been published in the English speaking world in the last twenty years." "Newlove," wrote George Bowering in *Canadian Forum,* "is one of our dozen really good poets."

In a *Canadian Literature* article dealing with the rhetoric and role of place in Newlove's poetry, E. F. Dyck claimed that through *The Night the Dog Smiled,* Newlove "grounds his work in a referential space and time: a boyhood in the Verigin, Saskatchewan, home of Doukhobors; growing up in Regina; leaving, endlessly crossing, and finally returning to the plains of Saskatchewan. . . . Newlove and prairie are as inseparable as Newlove and the personae he adopts—the sad-funny-thin-grey man and his double, the fat man." Dyck argues that the prairie is not simply a place for Newlove, but that it "is the locus of the early Newlove's imagination."

While focusing largely on the role of the prairie as metaphor and rhetorical device in Newlove's work, Dyck also praised other aspects of Newlove's poetry: "One of the delights in reading Newlove is his employment of the larger trope of irony." Moreover, he called *The Green Plain* "technically . . . accomplished" and compared it to "that locus of modern poetry, [T. S. Eliot's] *The Wasteland,* whose title it parodies. Whereas Eliot celebrated (in a mournful way) loss, Newlove celebrates (in a mournful way) recovery; whereas *The Waste Land* marked an apogee of poetic despair, *The Green Plain* marks a perigee of muted hope."

Newlove's second edition of his selected poems, *Apology for Absence,* is, according to Bruce Whitman's review in *Canadian Forum,* "a wonderful book." Erin Moure, writing about the volume in *Books in Canada,* claimed that its title "must be apologizing for the whole world outside him because, as for his work, there is no absence," in spite of Newlove's small output between 1986 and 1993. While Whitman observed that "at the centre of [Newlove's] work, and this book, are the poems of an existential loneliness and despair," he pointed out that "its emphasis is on the basic horror of the world, not on one person's horrible experiences of life." He concluded, *Apology for Absence* is "a big and important book" which includes poems that are "amongst the best of [Newlove's] generation."

BIOGRAPHICAL/CRITICAL SOURCES:

BOOKS

Contemporary Literary Criticism, Volume 14, Gale, 1980.

PERIODICALS

Books in Canada, October, 1993, pp. 35-36.
Canadian Forum, May, 1968; November, 1968; November, 1970; March, 1974; November, 1993, pp. 40-41.
Canadian Literature, winter, 1978; autumn-winter, 1989, pp. 69-91.
Fiddlehead, summer, 1968.
Globe and Mail (Toronto), June 21, 1986.
Open Letter, spring, 1973; fall 1974.
Poetry, February, 1970.

*   *   *

NICHOLS, (Joanna) Ruth   1948-

PERSONAL: Born March 4, 1948, in Toronto, Ontario, Canada; daughter of Edward Morris and Ruby (Smith) Nichols; married William Norman Houston, September 21, 1974. *Education:* University of British Columbia, B.A., 1969; McMaster University, M.A., 1974, Ph.D., 1977. *Politics:* None. *Religion:* None.

CAREER: Writer. Carleton University, Ottawa, Ontario, lecturer, 1974.

AWARDS, HONOURS: Shankar's International Literary Contest for Children grand prize, 1962; Woodrow Wilson fellowship, 1969-70; Canada Council fellowship, 1971-74;

Canadian Association of Children's Librarians bronze medal, 1973, for *The Marrow of the World.*

WRITINGS:

JUVENILE

A Walk out of the World, illustrations by Trina Schart Hyman, Harcourt, 1969.
The Marrow of the World, illustrations by Hyman, Atheneum, 1972.
Song of the Pearl, Atheneum, 1976.
The Left-Handed Spirit, Atheneum, 1978.

OTHER

Ceremony of Innocence (novel), Faber, 1969.
A Comparison of Three Group Reading Tests in Surveying the Attainment of First Year Secondary Children (booklet), Centre for the Teaching of Reading, 1975.
The Burning of the Rose (historical novel), Headline, 1990.
What Dangers Deep (historical novel), Headline, 1992.

WORK IN PROGRESS: An autobiography and an historical novel.

SIDELIGHTS: Ruth Nichols, it seems, was always destined to be a writer, for even as a child she enjoyed composing long stories. "My sister was my constant victim and she hasn't quite forgiven me!" Nichols related to Jon Stott in *Canadian Children's Literature.* "We made up vast story cycles about our dolls. I had a doll named Daniel who was a prince and a very mischievous boy. . . . His adventures went on for about five years." Nichols began writing and drawing stories at the age of eight, and at only 14 she won her first literary prize, the Shankar International Literary Contest for children. Her winning entry was a story about Catherine de Medici.

After receiving an honors degree in religious studies from the University of British Columbia, Nichols wrote and had published her first two books, *A Walk out of the World,* for which she wrote the first draft when she was eighteen, and *Ceremony of Innocence. A Walk out of the World* is the story of Judith and Tobit, a sister and brother whom Nichols describes as "slender, silent children who never played with anyone but each other," and who "were not unhappy; they were not anything in particular." Judith and Tobit live in a new city, built quickly to accommodate business and trade, but with no thought of preserving the beauty surrounding the city. From their classroom windows the children can see the lush, remaining forest, which, though it is not dangerous, is off-limits to Judith and Tobit. Their mother has instructed them never to go there.

Their favorite place to go is a seldom-traveled road where season after season they visit to run and play and shout, as though they are set free from their silent, reserved selves. Down their beautiful road a bit begins the woods, not thick like the forest but delicate and beautiful. Tobit and Judith cease playing when they near the woods, captivated by its beauty and its sense of magic.

One day, when Judith is very sad because she has to stay after school and walk home by herself, she asks Tobit to go with her to their favorite place, the road. Despite the rain, he relents, as he loves his sister and wants her to be happy. Nearing the woods, Judith stops, staring into them. Tobit reminds her that it is getting late and they must go home, but Judith sees a light in the woods and begins to enter them, a worried Tobit following. Deep in the woods, the children can no longer see their way out, but because they are fascinated by the changing landscape they make no attempt to go back. The December air becomes so warm that the children remove their heavy winter coats and they come to the edge of a beautiful stream. At this point they soon learn they have become important characters in their ancient ancestor's battle against an evil warrior.

Nichols' first effort was praised by critics, such as Barbara Wersba, writing in the *New York Times Book Review.* Wersba notes Nichols' "impressive" handling of her subject and writes that Nichols succeeds in breaking a fantasy-story rule: "bringing her characters back to the real world in the middle of the story, then swooping them off again."

Published the same year as *A Walk out of the World, Ceremony of Innocence* is the story of Marjorie Baldwin, a young woman whose discovery that her much-respected archaeologist father is having an affair with a student shatters her world. Hurt and betrayed, Marjorie must deal with feelings of guilt when her father dies shortly after she wishes him dead.

During the same year Nichols published her first works, she returned to academic studies at McMaster University, receiving her master's and doctorate degrees in 1972 and 1977, respectively. She never stopped writing, however, producing three more novels.

The Marrow of the World was named children's book of the year by the Canadian Library Association Book for 1973. *The Marrow of the World* chronicles the story of Linda, a woman struggling with an evil power within herself, but also battling externally with her evil half-sister Ygerna, who sends her and her cousin on a search for the sacred marrow. In this other-world fantasy, the evil sister is defeated and Linda realizes her own humanity when she sheds a tear. In her examination of Nichols's work, author Sheila Egoff, in *The Republic of Childhood,* writes, "She comes closer than anyone who has written fantasy in Canada to creating a believable 'sub-world' or 'secondary world' in the great tradition of fantasy."

Nichols's third graduate-school period composition was *The Song of the Pearl.* The pearl in this book is Margaret Redmond, who like many of Nichols's lead characters is a woman in search of herself who is also dealing with a life-altering circumstance. Margaret, harboring bitterness against an abusive uncle, dies and is taken to another world, a mystical island, where she meets an Oriental man who helps her find peace and beauty within herself.

Eventually, Margaret learns that a curse has overshadowed her life through her various incarnations. Able to finally forgive her uncle, Margaret returns to life, whole and renewed. While some critics found the subject matter of *Song of the Pearl* too weighty for young readers, others, such as *Canadian Literature* reviewer Anthony Appenzell, offer praise for Nichols's work, saying "the triumph of *Song of the Pearl* is the sense of concrete experience that is given to the world of death."

Nichols departs from composing purely fantasy works with *The Left-Handed Spirit,* which is more historical and romantic in nature. In it Mariana, a seer in ancient Rome, tells of her kidnapping at the hands of a Chinese ambassador to Rome. He takes her to China, where Mariana develops powers of psychic healing and falls in love with her abductor. As before, some critics questioned Nichols' handling of complex subject matter and description of physical relationships in books for young people. *Books in Canada* reviewer Aeron Rowland wondered if Nichols had a specific audience in mind when she wrote *The Left-Handed Spirit,* writing, "she tends to patronize her adult readers, while writing beyond the scope of most children." A *Commonweal* reviewer, however, deemed the book "superior," and noted it "will appeal to many grownups too."

The Burning of the Rose followed *The Left-Handed Spirit,* with Nichols again trying her hand at historical fiction. Set in the mid-to-late fifteenth century, *The Burning of the Rose* describes the colorful era of Renaissance Europe through the eyes of Claire Tarleton, who is orphaned when her parents succumb to the plague but is later adopted by an aristocratic family. Through Claire's adventures, the reader is given a look at the Hundred Year's War and an introduction to the de Medici family. In a Toronto *Globe & Mail* review of *The Burning of the Rose,* critic Nancy Wigston praises Nichols' work, writing Nichols "lifts the curtain of history so dazzlingly, and so often."

Nichols once remarked: "The meaning of experience is the motivation for writing. In other times this would have been a religious quest. It remains so even after the disintegration of Christianity which I think we are witnessing. . . . In my novels it leads me to ask what sources of hope and self-affirmation can be found in everyday experience."

BIOGRAPHICAL/CRITICAL SOURCES:

BOOKS

Dictionary of Literary Biography: Canadian Writers Since 1960, Second Series, Gale, Volume 60, 1987.
Egoff, Sheila, *The Republic of Childhood,* Oxford University Press, 1975, pp. 76-79.
Nichols, Ruth, *A Walk out of the World,* Harcourt, 1969, pp. 7, 8.

PERIODICALS

Books in Canada, February, 1979.
Canadian Children's Literature, Number 12, 1978, pp. 5-19; Number 15, 1980.
Canadian Literature, spring, 1977.
Canadian Materials, May, 1990, p. 141.
Christian Science Monitor, May 1, 1969.
Commonweal, November 10, 1978, p. 733.
Globe & Mail (Toronto), March 17, 1990.
New York Times Book Review, May 18, 1969.
Observer, November 9, 1969.
Quill & Quire, June, 1982.
Saturday Night, January, 1973.
Times (London), February 14, 1991, p. 24.
Times Literary Supplement, October 23, 1969.
Washington Post Book World, May 4, 1969; November 12, 1978.

*   *   *

NOWLAN, Alden (Albert) 1933-1983

PERSONAL: Born January 25, 1933, near Windsor, Nova Scotia, Canada; son of Freeman and Grace (Reese) Nowlan; married Claudine Orser; children: John Alden.

ADDRESSES: Home—676 Windsor St., Fredericton, New Brunswick, Canada.

CAREER: Newspaper reporter in New Brunswick, 1952-65; *Telegraph-Journal,* Saint John, New Brunswick, night news editor, 1965-67; University of New Brunswick, Fredericton, writer-in-residence, 1968-72, honorary research associate, School of Graduate Studies, 1972—.

AWARDS, HONOURS: Canada Council fellowship, 1961; Canada Council Special Award, 1967; Governor-General's Award for Poetry (Canada), 1967, for *Bread, Wine and Salt*; Guggenheim fellow in poetry, 1967-68; President's Medal, University of Western Ontario, 1970, 1972; D.Litt., University of New Brunswick, 1970; Doctor of Laws, Dalhousie University, 1976; Canadian Authors' Association Silver Medal for Poetry, 1977; Queen's Silver Jubilee Medal, 1978; Evelyn Richardson Award, 1979; National Magazine Association Gold Medal, 1980.

WRITINGS:

Miracle at Indian River (story collection), Clarke, Irwin, 1968.
Various Persons Named Kevin O'Brien (novel), Clarke, Irwin, 1973.
(With Tom Forrestall) *Shaped by This Land,* Brunswick Press, 1974.
Campobello: The Outer Island (history), Clarke, Irwin, 1975.
(With Walter Learning) *Frankenstein: The Man Who Became God* (play; first produced at Theatre New Brunswick, Fredericton, New Brunswick, 1974), Clarke, Irwin, 1975.
(With Learning) *The Dollar Woman,* first produced at Theatre New Brunswick, Fredericton, 1977.
Double Exposure (essays), Brunswick Press, 1978.
(With Learning) *The Incredible Murder of Cardinal Tosca* (play; first produced at Theatre New Brunswick, Fredericton, 1978), Learning Productions, 1979.

POETRY

The Rose and the Puritan, University of New Brunswick Press, 1958.
A Darkness in the Earth, E. V. Griffith, 1959.
Wind in a Rocky Country, Emblem Books, 1960.
Under the Ice, Ryerson Press, 1961.
The Things Which Are, Contact Press, 1962.
Bread, Wine, and Salt, Clarke, Irwin, 1967.
A Black Plastic Button and a Yellow Yoyo, Charles Pachter, 1968.
The Mysterious Naked Man: Poems, Clarke, Irwin, 1969.
Playing the Jesus Game: Selected Poems, New Books, 1971.
Between Tears and Laughter, Clarke, Irwin, 1971.
I'm a Stranger Here Myself, Clarke, Irwin, 1974.
Smoked Glass, Clarke, Irwin, 1977.

Work represented in anthologies including *Poetry: 62,* edited by Eli Mandel, Ryerson, 1962; *Fire and Sleet and Candlelight,* edited by August Derleth, Arkham, 1962; *Love Where the Nights Are Long,* edited by Irving Layton, McClelland & Stewart, 1962; *The First Five Years,* edited by Robert Weaver, Oxford University Press, 1962; *Five New Brunswick Poets,* edited by Fred Cogswell, Fiddlehead Books, 1962; *A Book of Canadian Stories,* edited by Desmond Pacey, Ryerson, 1962; *Modern Canadian Stories,* edited by Giose Rimanelli and Roberto Ruberto, Ryerson, 1966; *Penguin Book of Canadian Verse,* Penguin, 1967; *Oxford Book of Canadian Verse,* Oxford University Press, 1968; and *How Do I Love Thee: Sixty Poets of Canada (and Quebec) Select and Introduce Their Favorite Poems from Their Own Work,* edited by John Robert Colombo, M. G. Hurtig, 1970.

Also author of radio and television scripts for Canadian Broadcasting Corporation. Columnist, *Telegraph Journal* (St. John, New Brunswick) and *Atlantic Advocate* (Fredericton).

WORK IN PROGRESS: A collection of short stories; a play; a book of poems.

SIDELIGHTS: Called by George Woodcock "the most important contemporary poet of the Maritimes, as well as the most prolific," Alden Nowlan writes of the people and places of his native New Brunswick. "Dedicated honestly and humbly to his art [and] equally at home in more than one *genre*," Keath Fraser writes in *Canadian Literature,* "Alden Nowlan furnishes an unhip, thoroughly non-academic world with splashes of exquisite insight."

Nowlan describes his personal background, in an interview with *Fiddlehead,* as "19th Century, a pioneer environment: no electric light or telephones, nothing like that. . . . The soil was too poor for farming. The people there were mostly pulpcutters. A great feeling of insecurity all the time. . . . Those people took religion very seriously but it wasn't something they were preoccupied with. It was an emotional thing. My grandmother believed in Heaven and Hell, in angels and Christ—but in witches and ghosts, too. . . . They weren't concerned really with the moral aspects of religion."

Nowlan said in the interview that he started writing at the age of eleven, partly because of a somewhat Biblical "desire to be a prophet. . . . It would have been more natural for me to become a country and western singer or a boxer. This writing was a very secret thing with me, very private." Although he writes both poetry and short stories, Nowlan prefers writing poetry. "With the poems it's a direct emotional release," he says, "whereas with the stories there's a lot of hard-bone labour involved."

Many reviewers have mentioned the strong regional quality of Nowlan's poetry which shows his continuing interest in the Nova Scotian area. Anne Greer has said: "Irving Layton once asked Alden Nowlan why all Maritime poets were so big; Nowlan replied, half seriously, that the little ones were all killed off before they were twelve. For a Nova Scotian there is a grim satisfaction in the discovery that the Annapolis Valley, in spite of itself, has produced a weed of such strength that it has resisted all the time-proven attempts to eradicate its kind." After meeting Nowlan, Greer wrote: "He is very big. The second thing one notices is his laugh. What one takes away is an impression of great wisdom."

"Mr. Nowlan is, of course, a splendid poet," writes Ernest Buckler in a review of the story collection *Miracle at Indian River.* "And all these stories show the poet's touch. But not in the usual way. . . . No gingerbreads of self-consciously fine phrases, no puffballs of fancy irrelevance. And when he shifts from poetry to prose, the poetic gift does not translate into lint; it is simply that extra eye which sees through things to the core." Louis Dudek classes Nowlan with that group of poets who "seem to write directly from poetic impulse, whatever that is, or from feeling and perception, as though deliberate and conscious complexity was the reverse of poetry, and significance must emerge in the creative process from spontaneity alone." Fred Cogswell, reviewing *Bread, Wine and Salt,* admires "the transparent fluidity of [Nowlan's] presentation. Whether he writes of the inhabitants of Hainesville (Hartland), for whom he feels such ambivalence, his friends, or his own personal feelings and predicament, thought and form merge and change so beautifully and organically that one is not conscious of a seam between them."

BIOGRAPHICAL/CRITICAL SOURCES:

BOOKS

Contemporary Literary Criticism, Volume 15, Gale, 1980.
Dudek, Louis, *Selected Essays and Criticism,* Tecumseh Press, 1978.
Klinck, Carl F., *Literary History of Canada: Canadian Literature in English,* University of Toronto Press, 1965; 2nd edition, 1976.
Oliver, Michael Brian, *Poet's Progress,* Fiddlehead Books, 1978.

PERIODICALS

Canadian Forum, September, 1968; December, 1976; March, 1978.
Canadian Literature, summer, 1970.
Delta, February, 1963.
Fiddlehead, spring, 1968; August-October, 1969.
Saturday Night, February, 1970.

O-P

ONDAATJE, (Philip) Michael 1943-

PERSONAL: Born September 12, 1943, in Colombo, Ceylon (now Sri Lanka); son of Mervyn Ondaatje and Doris Gratiaen. *Education:* Attended St. Thomas' College, Colombo, and Dulwich College, London; attended Bishop's University, Lennoxville, Quebec, 1962-64; University of Toronto, B.A., 1965; Queen's University, Kingston, Ontario, M.A., 1967. *Avocational interests:* Hound breeding, hog breeding.

ADDRESSES: Office—Department of English, Glendon College, York University, 2275 Bayview Ave., Toronto, Ontario M4N 3M6, Canada.*Agent*—c/o Ellen Levine, 15 East 26th Street, Suite 1801, New York, NY 10010.

CAREER: Taught at University of Western Ontario, London, 1967-71; member of Department of English, Glendon College, York University, Toronto, Ontario, 1971—. Visiting professor, University of Hawaii, Honolulu, summer, 1979; Brown University, 1990. Editor, *Mongrel Broadsides.* Director of films, including *Sons of Captain Poetry,* 1970; *Carry on Crime and Punishment,* 1972; *Royal Canadian Hounds,* 1973; and *The Clinton Special,* 1974. Inventor of Dragland Hog Feeder, 1975.

AWARDS, HONOURS: Ralph Gustafson award, 1965; Epstein award, 1966; E. J. Pratt Medal, 1966; President's Medal, University of Western Ontario, 1967; Canadian Governor-General's Award for Literature, 1971, 1980; Canada-Australia prize, 1980; Booker McConnell Prize, British Book Trust, 1992, for *The English Patient.*

WRITINGS:

POETRY

The Dainty Monsters, Coach House Press, 1967.
The Man with Seven Toes, Coach House Press, 1969.

The Collected Works of Billy the Kid: Left Handed Poems (also see below), Anansi, 1970, Norton, 1974.
Rat Jelly, Coach House Press, 1973.
Elimination Dance, Nairn Coldstream (Ontario), 1978, revised, Brick, 1980.
There's a Trick with a Knife I'm Learning To Do: Poems, 1963-1978, Norton, 1979; as *Rat Jelly, and Other Poems, 1963-1978,* Boyars, 1980.
Secular Love, Coach House Press, 1984, Norton, 1985.
All along the Mazinaw: Two Poems (broadside), Woodland Pattern (Wisconsin), 1986.
The Cinnamon Peeler: Selected Poems, Pan, 1989, Knopf, 1991.

NOVELS

Coming Through Slaughter (biographical novel), Anansi, 1976, Norton, 1977.
In the Skin of a Lion (also see below), Knopf, 1987.
The English Patient, Knopf, 1992.

PLAYS

The Collected Works of Billy the Kid (based on his poetry), produced in Stratford, Ontario, 1973, New York City, 1974, and London, 1984.
In the Skin of A Lion (based on his novel), Knopf, 1987.

EDITOR

The Broken Ark (animal verse), Oberon Press, 1971, revised as *A Book of Beasts,* 1979.
Personal Fictions: Stories by Munro, Wiebe, Thomas, and Blaise, Oxford University Press, 1977.
The Long Poem Anthology, Coach House Press, 1979.
(With Russell Banks and David Young) *Brushes with Greatness: An Anthology of Chance Encounters with Greatness,* Coach House Press, 1989.
(With Linda Spalding) *The Brick Anthology,* Coach House Press, 1989.

From Ink Lake: An Anthology of Canadian Short Stories, Viking, 1990.

The Faber Book of Contemporary Canadian Short Stories, Faber, 1990.

OTHER

Leonard Cohen (literary criticism), McClelland & Stewart, 1970.

Claude Glass (literary criticism), Coach House Press, 1979.

Tin Roof, Island (British Columbia), 1982.

Running in the Family (memoir), Norton, 1982.

Author's manuscripts are included in the National Archives, Ottawa, Canada, and the Metropolitan Toronto Library.

SIDELIGHTS: Michael Ondaatje dissolves the lines between prose and poetry through the breadth of his works in both genres. "Moving in and out of imagined landscape, portrait and documentary, anecdote or legend, Ondaatje writes for the eye and the ear simultaneously," notes Diane Wakoski in *Contemporary Poets.* Whether reshaping recollections of friends and family from his childhood in old Ceylon in *Running in the Family,* or retelling an American myth in *The Collected Works of Billy the Kid,* the experiences of many individuals are made vivid, heard, and almost real for his readers. In addition to writing novels, plays, and poetry collections, Ondaatje has edited several books, including *The Faber Book of Contemporary Canadian Short Stories,* praised as a "landmark" by reviewer Christine Bold in the *Times Literary Supplement* for its representation of "Canadian voices accented by native, black, French, Caribbean, Indian, Japanese and Anglo-Saxon origins."

Ondaatje's poetry is seen by critics as continually changing, evolving as the author experiments with the shape and sound of words. Although his poetic forms may differ, his works focus on the myths that root deep in common cultural experience. As a poet, he recreates their intellectual expression in depicting the affinity between the art of legend and the world at large. "He cares more about the relationship between art and nature than any other poet since the Romantics," exclaims Liz Rosenberg in the *New York Times Book Review,* "and more than most contemporary poets care about any ideas at all." Some of Ondaatje's verse has approached the fragmentary, as in *Secular Love,* a collection of poems he published in 1985. In contrast, his most widely-known work, *The Collected Works of Billy the Kid* verges on a prose format while retaining a strong poetic lyricism.

"Concerned always to focus on the human, the private, and the 'real' over the theoretical and the ideological, Ondaatje examines the internal workings of characters who

struggle against and burst through that which renders people passive," notes Diane Watson in *Contemporary Novelists,* "and which renders human experience programmatic and static." *In the Skin of a Lion,* the author's 1987 novel, focuses on a man raised in rural Canada who, at the age of twenty-one, comes to the growing city of Toronto and lives among the immigrants that inhabit its working-class neighborhoods. Physical actions and inner challenges define Ondaatje's characters as individuals, creators within their own lives, and give both purpose to their existence and redemption to their inner reality. In this work, a historical epoch is seen as the struggle of the individual to break free of the confines of his culture rather than simply a collection of social and political goals. As Michael Hulse describes *In the Skin of a Lion* in the *Times Literary Supplement,* it "maps high society and the sub culture of the underprivileged in Toronto in the 1920s and 1930s. . . . But it is also . . . about communication, about men 'utterly alone' who are waiting (in Ondaatje's terms) to break through a chrysalis."

In *Coming Through Slaughter,* a novel well-grounded in the history of early twentieth-century New Orleans, Ondaatje creates a possible life of the late jazz musician Buddy Bolden, remembered as a brilliant coronetist whose performances were never recorded due to a tragic mental collapse at an early age. Mixing interviews with those who remember Bolden, historical fact, and his richly-imagined conception of the musician's inner thoughts on his way to madness, Ondaatje fashions what Wilson terms a "fractured narrative . . . [tracing] the personal anarchy of . . . Bolden and the perspectives on him of those who knew him best."

The English Patient, published in 1992 as Ondaatje's fifth novel, tells the story of a Canadian nurse who stays behind in the bombed remains of a villa near the World War II battlefields of northern Italy to tend to an English soldier who has been severely burned. Joined by two other soldiers, relationships form between these four characters that parallel, as Cressida Connolly notes in the *Spectator,* "those of a small and faded Eden." Ranking the author among such contemporary novelists as Ian McEwan and Martin Amis, Connolly praises the poetic quality of Ondaatje's fiction. "The writing is so heady that you have to keep putting the book down between passages so as not to reel from the sheer force and beauty of it," the reviewer exclaims, adding that "when I finished the book I felt as dazed as if I'd just awoken from a powerful dream."

Running in the Family, a memoir, was published in 1992. In it, Ondaatje blends together family stories—some which attain the stature of myth—with poems, photographs, personal anecdotes, and the like to create a novel that reads more like a poem. As his family history follows a path leading from the genteel innocence of the Ceylonese privileged class as the sun set on the British Empire to the harsh glare of the modern age, so Ondaatje's narrative seeks the inner character of his father, a man of whom the author writes, "my loss was that I never spoke to him as an adult." "In reality, this is a mythology exaggerated and edited by the survivors," writes Anton Mueller in the *Washington Post Book World.* "Seduced by the wealth and luxury of its imaginative reality, Ondaatje enters the myth without disturbing it. With a prose style equal to the voluptuousness of his subject and a sense of humor never too far away, *Running in the Family* is sheer reading pleasure."

BIOGRAPHICAL/CRITICAL SOURCES:

BOOKS

The Annotated Bibliography of Canada's Major Authors 6, ECW Press, 1985.
Contemporary Literary Criticism, Gale, Volume 14, 1980, Volume 29, 1984, Volume 51, 1989, Volume 76, 1993.
Contemporary Novelists, fifth edition, St. James Press, 1991, pp. 710-11.
Contemporary Poets, fifth edition, St. James Press, 1991, pp. 724-25.
Dictionary of Literary Biography, Volume 60: *Canadian Writers since 1960, Second Series,* Gale, 1987.
Solecki, Sam, editor, *Spider Blues: Essays on Michael Ondaatje,* Vehicule Press, 1985.

PERIODICALS

Canadian Forum, January/February, 1993, p. 39.
Fiddlehead, spring, 1968.
Nation, January 4, 1993, p. 22.
National Catholic Reporter, November 19, 1993, p. 30.
New Republic, March 15, 1993, p. 38.
New York Review of Books, January 14, 1993, p. 22.
New York Times Book Review, April 24, 1977; December 22, 1985, pp. 22-23.
People, December 14, 1992, p. 39.
Saturday Night, July, 1968.
Spectator, September 5, 1992, p. 32.
Times Literary Supplement, September 4, 1987, p. 948; November 3, 1989, p. 1217; October 19, 1990, p. 1130: September 22, 1992, p. 23.
Washington Post Book World, January 2, 1983, pp. 9, 13; November 1, 1987, p. 4.

*　　　*　　　*

OSTENSO, Martha   1900-1963

PERSONAL: Born September 17, 1900, in Bergen, Norway; emigrated to United States, 1902; emigrated to Canada, 1915; died November 24, 1963, in Seattle (one source cites Tacoma), WA; daughter of Sigurd Brigt and Lena (Tungeland) Ostenso; married Douglas Durkin (a writer), December 16, 1944 (one source cites 1945). *Education:* Attended University of Manitoba, beginning in 1918; attended Columbia University, 1921-22. *Avocational interests:* Tennis, soccer, badminton, gardening.

CAREER: Lived in Minnesota and South Dakota as a child and began writing as a contributor to the junior page of the *Minneapolis Journal*; later moved to Canada with parents and taught school one semester (1918) in Manitoba; returned to United States as social worker with Bureau of Charities, Brooklyn, NY, 1920-23; novelist and short story writer, beginning 1923; painter.

MEMBER: International PEN, Authors League of America.

AWARDS, HONOURS: National prize, from Pictorial Review, Dodd, Mead & Co., and Famous Players-Lasky, 1925, for *Wild Geese; O River, Remember* was named as a Literary Guild selection, 1943; honorary M.E., Wittenberg University.

WRITINGS:

A Far Land: Poems by Martha Ostenso (verse), Thomas Selzer, 1924.
Wild Geese (also known as *The Passionate Flight*), McClelland & Stewart (Toronto), Dodd, Mead (New York), 1925.
The Dark Dawn, Dodd, Mead, 1926, Hodder & Stoughton (London), 1927.
The Mad Carews, Dodd, Mead, 1927, Heinneman (London), 1928.
The Young May Moon, Dodd, Mead, 1929, Butterworth (London), 1930.
The Waters under the Earth, Dodd, Mead, 1930, Butterworth, 1931.
Prologue to Love, Dodd, Mead, 1932.
There's Always Another Year, McClelland & Stewart (Toronto), Dodd, Mead (New York), 1933.
The White Reef, Dodd, Mead, 1934, McClelland & Stewart (Toronto), Cassell (London), 1935.
The Stone Field, McClelland & Stewart (Toronto), Dodd, Mead (New York), 1937.
The Mandrake Root, Dodd, Mead, 1938.
Love Passed This Way, Dodd, Mead, 1942.
O River, Remember, Dodd, Mead, 1943, Long (London), 1945.
(With Elizabeth Kenny) *And They Shall Walk: The Life Story of Sister Elizabeth Kenny*, Dodd, Mead, 1943.
Milk Route, Dodd, Mead, 1948.
The Sunset Tree, Dodd, Mead, 1949, Long, 1951.
A Man Had Tall Sons, Dodd, Mead, 1958.

Author of serials and short stories to periodicals, including *North American Review, Collier's,* and *Delineator.*

Ostenso's writings have been translated into German, Norwegian, Polish, and other European languages.

ADAPTATIONS: And They Shall Walk was adapted as a motion picture starring Rosalind Russell in 1946.

SIDELIGHTS: Martha Ostenso is best known for *Wild Geese,* a novel about life in rugged, isolated, western Canada. Ostenso was born in 1900 in Norway, and in 1902 her family immigrated to the United States. Ostenso spent much of her childhood in the American midwest. In the mid-1910s, however, her family moved to rural Manitoba. Ostenso entered the university there in 1918 and eventually taught in the region's Interlake area.

In the early 1920s Ostenso lived in New York City and studied at Columbia University. By the middle of the decade she was also devoting herself to writing. In 1924 she published *A Far Land: Poems by Martha Ostenso,* a collection of her verse. This work, though often sentimental in nature, served as evidence that Ostenso was already a writer with an affinity for depicting life in the rural, western farmlands.

By the time that *A Far Land* appeared in print, Ostenso was deeply involved with Douglas Leader Durkin, who, despite estrangement, was still legally married. Durkin would provide considerable assistance to Ostenso in her writing throughout the forthcoming years, and the couple would eventually marry in 1944.

In 1925, with Durkin's assistance, Ostenso completed *Wild Geese,* a novel about a young woman, Judith Gare, who is dominated by her father, Caleb, a zealous farmer. In order to preserve his supply of free farm labor, Caleb resorts to various intimidations to maintain control of his family, which includes three other siblings in addition to Judith. But Judith's desire for love, sexual fulfillment, and a more enriched life eventually compels her to resist her grim, overbearing father, and through the encouragement of her more sophisticated friend, Lind Archer, Judith eventually escapes to the city.

Ostenso submitted *Wild Geese* to a writing contest. It won, topping more than 1300 competing entries and earning Ostenso a first-prize purse of $13,500. Despite this promising start, the novel was consigned to obscurity in Canada until the mid-1940s, when it was championed by Clara Thomas in her study *Canadian Novelists, 1920-1945. Wild Geese* (which has also been published as *The Passionate Flight*) is now widely hailed as a classic depiction of life in the hard Canadian West, and Ostenso thus ranks as an important writer of Canadian—and Canada-related—literature.

Although initially ignored in Canada, *Wild Geese* fared well enough in America to assure Ostenso a literary career. In the ensuing decades she continued to produce novels in collaboration with her husband, who usually provided Ostenso with a rudimentary storyline. Ostenso would then produce a workable manuscript that Durkin shaped and edited into the finished book.

Ostenso followed *Wild Geese* with *The Dark Dawn,* a melodramatic novel about an ambitious, innocent young man, Lucien Dorrit, who succumbs to the charms of a beautiful woman, Hattie Murker, and marries her. In addition to her physical assets, Hattie also owns a considerable parcel of land and a quarry—items that also attract Lucien. As time passes, however, and Lucien devotes himself increasingly to satisfying Hattie's material desires, he begins to feel trapped. He also finds that, due to his lengthy labors, he is unable to maintain his friendship with Mons Torson, a nearby landowner. Lucien's unhappiness increases when he learns that Mons had been Hattie's previous lover. Lucien then withdraws from his wife, who responds by abruptly leaving him. Lucien eventually discovers her wounded in a quarry. While Hattie is recuperating at home, Mons visits her and discloses his undying love. Hattie, her stability already undermined by her husband's sexual withdrawal and her injuries from the quarry, is startled to hear Mons's confession, and she dies of a heart attack.

With *The Young May Moon,* which appeared in 1929, Ostenso returned to *Wild Geese*'s theme of a young woman struggling to realize independence. Marcia Vorse, the heroine of *The Young May Moon,* lives with her husband and his domineering mother in small-town Manitoba. After her husband dies, the pregnant Marcia punishes herself by remaining with her mother-in-law. But Marcia cannot long tolerate small-town life, with its intruders and gossips, and so she flees to an abandoned home outside the village to raise her child alone. As her mental stability begins to degenerate, Marcia is befriended by a kindly doctor, who eventually inspires her to rejoin society, even as it exists in the loathsome small town.

In the ensuing three decades Ostenso continued to publish regularly. Notable among her other works are *The Waters under the Earth,* in which seven siblings attempt to elude their domineering father; 1943's *O River, Remember!,* an epic family drama that spans from the nineteenth to the twentieth century; and *The Mandrake Root,* in which a professor is drawn to the sexually aggressive wife of a pious farmer. Anthony John Harding, writing in the *Dictionary of Literary Biography,* saw *The Mandrake Root* as sharing similar themes of strong womanhood with Ostenso's earlier works. In addition, Harding categorized the depiction of the professor as "one of Ostenso's more successful attempts at the intellectual male."

Ostenso, who eventually settled with her husband in northern Minnesota, died in Seattle, Washington, in 1963. In the years since her death, she continues to be remembered for her compelling depictions of Canadian farm life, particularly as it is delineated in *Wild Geese.* As Harding described Ostenso''s writing in the *Dictionary of Literary Biography:* "In her best work she displays a considerable understanding of the social and economic structure of small western towns, an unusual grasp of the ways in which relationships develop, and a bleak, Ibsen-like vision of human life that is tempered by a real sympathy for children and their imaginative world." Harding concluded that "at the very least Ostenso's strong-willed women . . . deserve to be recognized as honorable precursors of the strong, questing women created by Margaret Laurence, Alice Munro, and Margaret Atwood."

BIOGRAPHICAL/CRITICAL SOURCES:

BOOKS

Dictionary of Literary Biography, Volume 92: *Canadian Writers, 1890-1920,* Gale, 1990, pp. 279-84.
Harrison, Dick, *Unnamed Country: The Struggle for a Canadian Prairie Fiction,* University of Alberta Press, 1977.
Overton, Grant, *The Women Who Make Our Novels,* Dodd, 1931, pp. 245-52.
Stephens, Donald G., editor, *Writers of the Prairies,* University of British Columbia Press, 1973, pp. 39-50.
Thomas, Clara, *Canadian Novelists, 1920-1945,* Longmans, 1946, p. 95.

PERIODICALS

Atlantis, Vol. 4, no. 1, 1978, pp. 2-9.
Canadian Literature, autumn, 1969, pp. 274-76.
Culture, December, 1962, pp. 359-62.
Dalhousie Review, October, 1926, pp. 18-23; summer, 1977, pp. 287-99.
Journal of Canadian Fiction, Vol. 16, 1975, pp. 108-14.
Journal of Popular Culture, Vol. 15, no. 3, 1981, pp. 47-52.
New York Times, November 26, 1963, p. 37.*

*   *   *

PACEY, (William Cyril) Desmond   1917-1975

PERSONAL: Born May 1, 1917, in Dunedin, New Zealand; died of cancer, July 4, 1975; son of William and Mary E. (Hunt) Pacey; married Mary Elizabeth Carson (a painter and sculptor), June 17, 1939; children: Philip, Mary Ann, Patricia, Peter, Margaret, Michael, Penelope. *Education:* University of Toronto, B.A., 1938; Cambridge University, Ph.D., 1941. *Politics:* Independent. *Religion:* United Church of Canada.

CAREER: Brandon College, Brandon, Manitoba, Canada, professor of English, 1940-44; Wartime Information Board, Ottawa, Ontario, Canada, editor, 1943-44; University of New Brunswick, Fredericton, New Brunswick, Canada, professor of English, 1944-75, university professor, 1974, dean of graduate studies, 1960-70, vice president, 1970-75, acting president, 1972-73.

MEMBER: Humanities Research Council of Canada, Association of Canadian University Teachers of English, Canadian Association of University Teachers, Canadian Association of graduate Schools (president, 1966-68), Modern Language Association, Royal Society of Canada (fellow).

AWARDS, HONOURS: Royal Society of Canada fellow, 1955; Canada Council senior research fellowship, 1962-63; Lorne Pierce Medal, Royal Society of Canada, 1972; Doctor of Literature, Mount Allison University, 1973; Doctor of Letters, University of New Brunswick, 1973.

WRITINGS:

(Editor and author of introduction) *Frederick Philip Grove: A Biographical and Critical Study,* Ryerson, 1945.
(Editor, author of introduction and notes) *A Book of Canadian Stories,* Ryerson, 1946, 3rd edition, 1961.
Creative Writing in Canada: A Short History of English-Canadian Literature, Ryerson, 1952, new edition, Greenwood Press, 1976.
Hippity Hobo and the Bee, and Other Verse for Children, Brunswick Press, 1952.
The Cow with the Musical Moo, and Other Verse for Children, Brunswick Press, 1952.
(Editor) *The Selected Poems of Sir Charles G. D. Roberts,* Ryerson, 1956.
(Editor with Earle Birney and others) *New Voices: Canadian University Writing of 1956,* Dent, 1956.
Ten Canadian Poets: A Group of Biographical and Critical Essays, Ryerson, 1958.
The Picnic, and Other Stories, foreword by Roy Daniells, Ryerson, 1958.
(Editor) Mazo de la Roche, *Delight,* McClelland & Stewart, 1960.
(Editor) Ethel Wilson, *Swamp Angel,* McClelland & Stewart, 1962.
(Editor with Carl F. Klinck and others, and contributor) *Literary History of Canada,* University of Toronto Press, 1965, 2nd edition, 1976.
(Editor) *Our Literary Heritage: An Anthology of Literature in English,* Ryerson, 1966.
The Cat, the Cow, and the Kangaroo: The Collected Children's Verse of Desmond Pacey, Brunswick Press, 1967.

(Editor) Theodore G. Roberts, *The Harbour Master*, Mc-Clelland & Stewart, 1968.

Ethel Wilson, Twayne, 1968.

Essays in Canadian Criticism, 1938-1968, Ryerson, 1969.

Tales from the Margin: The Selected Short Stories of Frederick Philip Grove, Ryerson, 1971.

(Editor) *Selections from Major Canadian Writers: Poetry and Creative Prose in English*, McGraw, 1974.

Waken, Lords and Ladies Gay: Selected Stories of Desmond Pacey, University of Ottawa Press, 1974.

(Editor) *Letters of Frederick Philip Grove*, University of Toronto Press, 1976.

Essays: Canadian Literature in English, University of Mysore, 1979.

CONTRIBUTOR

(Author of introduction) *The Selected Poems of Dorothy Livesay*, Ryerson, 1957.

Robert L. McDougall, editor, *Our Living Tradition: Fourth Series*, University of Toronto Press, 1962.

Foster M. Russell, editor, *This Is My Concern*, Northumberland Book Co., 1962.

R. A. Tweedie and others, editors, *The Arts in New Brunswick*, Brunswick Press, 1967.

Louis Dudek and Michael Gnarowski, editors, *The Making of Modern Poetry in Canada*, Ryerson, 1967.

Contributor to periodicals in Canada, the United States, and Europe, including short stories in *Fiddlehead* and *Atlantic Advocate*. Fiction editor, *Fiddlehead*, 1950-66; associate editor, *Canadian Art*, 1960-63.

SIDELIGHTS: Desmond Pacey was a writer and editor best known for his volumes of literary criticism devoted to English-language Canadian writing. Pacey was born in 1917 in Dunedin, New Zealand. After the death of her husband, Pacey's mother moved the family back to her native England. She then married a Canadian farmer, whereupon the family moved to Canada. Pacey studied at the University of Toronto, graduating in 1938, and then taught English at Brandon College (now Brandon University) in Manitoba. In the early 1940s he interrupted his teaching career to attend Trinity College, Cambridge, from which he earned a doctorate in 1941. And during World War II he served as an editor at the Wartime Information Board in Ottawa.

Pacey left Brandon College in 1944 to chair the English department at the University of New Brunswick, where he taught until 1975. At New Brunswick he went against tradition and steered the English department toward the greater study and promotion of Canadian literature, which was then receiving little attention—even at Canadian institutions—in comparison to English and American works.

Along with his contributions as an instructor and administrator, Pacey contributed to education through his writing efforts. Among his important works in the field of literary criticism is the 1952 publication *Creative Writing in Canada: A Short History of English-Canadian Literature.* As Fred Cogswell noted in his *Dictionary of Literary Biography* piece on Pacey, this work "long remained the standard history of anglophone Canadian literature." *Ten Canadian Poets: A Group of Biographical and Critical Essays* ranks as another of Pacey's significant contributions to Canadian literary criticism. In this volume, and in the ensuing collection *Essays in Canadian Criticism, 1938-1968,* Pacey interpreted Canadian literature by assessing it within biographical and cultural considerations.

In addition to producing books and essays devoted to Canadian writing, Pacey also edited numerous volumes. In 1946 he published *A Book of Canadian Stories,* and in 1956 he collaborated on the compilation of *New Voices: Canadian University Writing of 1956* and served as editor of *The Selected Poems of Charles G. D. Roberts.* His subsequent publications as editor include *Our Literary Heritage: An Anthology of Literature in English,* which appeared in 1966, *Selections from Major Canadian Writers: Poetry and Creative Prose in English,* which appeared in 1974.

Although he is most readily recognized for his literary criticism, Pacey also managed to publish short stories. His fiction, essentially the collection *The Picnic, and Other Stories,* was marked by straightforward storytelling and a realism that usually depicted life's difficulties within an ultimately optimistic framework. A frequent element in these narratives is the young man who undergoes an experience, or experiences, that lead him to a greater understanding and appreciation of life. Pacey's stories, though often somber in tone, uphold basic values. Pacey eventually added twelve of *The Picnic's* sixteen tales to two later stories to fashion *Waken, Lords and Ladies Gay: Selected Stories of Desmond Pacey.*

Pacey also produced two volumes of children's verse. In 1952 he completed both *The Cow with the Musical Moo, and Other Verse for Children* and *Hippity Hobo and the Bee, and Other Verse for Children.* The contents of these books were published together in the 1968 volume *The Cat, the Cow, and the Kangaroo: The Collected Children's Verse of Desmond Pacey.*

Throughout his long career as a writer and academic, Pacey received various awards and honors. In 1955 he was named as a fellow to the Royal Society of Canada, and in 1972 he was accorded that organization's Lorne Pierce Medal. He also received honorary degrees from both the University of New Brunswick and Mount Allison University. In 1970 Pacey became academic vice president at the University of New Brunswick. He held that post until his death from cancer in 1975. An annual lectureship continues in his honor at the University.

BIOGRAPHICAL/CRITICAL SOURCES:

BOOKS

Dictionary of Literary Biography, Volume 88: *Canadian Writers, 1920-1959, Second Series,* Gale, 1989, pp. 236-39.

PERIODICALS

International Fiction Review, winter, 1982, pp. 3-16.*

*   *   *

PAGE, P(atricia) K(athleen)   1916-
(Judith Cape, P. K. Irwin)

PERSONAL: Born November 23, 1916, in Swanage, Dorset, England; immigrated to Canada, 1919; daughter of Lionel Frank (a Major General) and Rose Laura (Whitehouse) Page; married William Arthur Irwin (an editor and diplomat), December, 1950; stepchildren: Neal A., Patricia J. Irwin Morley, Shelia A. Irwin Irving. *Education:* Attended Art Students' League, New York City, and Pratt Institute; studied art privately in Brazil and New York.

ADDRESSES: Home—3260 Exeter Rd., Victoria, British Columbia, Canada V8R 6H6.

CAREER: Poet and artist. Has held jobs as sales clerk and radio actress in Saint John, New Brunswick, filing clerk and historical researcher in Montreal, Quebec; script writer for National Film Board, Ottawa, 1946-50. Conductor of workshops at the Writers' Workshop, Toronto, Ontario, 1974-77, and University of Victoria, 1977-78. Member of the Advisory Arts Panel to the Canadian Council, 1976-79. Has had solo exhibitions of paintings (under name P. K. Irwin) at Picture Loan Society, Toronto, 1960, Galeria de Arte Moderna, Mexico City, 1962, and Art Gallery of Greater Victoria, 1965; participant in group exhibitions in Canada and Mexico; work is represented in collections, including National Gallery of Canada, Art Gallery of Ontario, Vancouver Art Gallery, Art Gallery of Greater Victoria, University of Victoria, and private collections in Canada and abroad.

AWARDS, HONOURS: Received by Academia Brazileira de Letras (Rio de Janeiro); Life Member, League of Canadian Poets; Bertram Warr Award from *Contemporary Verse* (Vancouver), 1940; Oscar Blumenthal Award from *Poetry* (Chicago), 1944; Canadian Governor-General's Award in Poetry, 1954, for *The Metal and the Flower;* Officer of the Order of Canada, 1977; National Magazines Award (gold), 1985; D.Litt., University of Victoria, 1985; Canadian Authors' Association Prize for Poetry, 1987;

Hubert Evans Prize, British Columbia Book Awards, 1988, for *A Brazilian Journal;* Banff Centre National Award, 1989; received honorary Doctor of Laws degree, University of Calgary, 1989; honorary Doctor of Letters degree, University of Guelph, 1990; and honorary Doctor of Laws degree, Simon Fraser University, 1990.

WRITINGS:

(Under pseudonym Judith Cape) *The Sun and the Moon* (novel), Macmillan, 1944.
As Ten As Twenty (poems), Ryerson, 1946.
The Metal and the Flower (poems), McClelland & Stewart, 1954.
Cry Ararat! Poems New and Selected, McClelland & Stewart, 1967.
The Sun and the Moon and Other Fictions, Anansi, 1973.
Poems (1942-1973): Selected and New, Anansi, 1974.
(Editor) *To Say the Least: Canadian Poets A-Z,* Press Porcepic, 1979.
Evening Dance of the Grey Flies (poetry and prose), Oxford University Press, 1981.
The Glass Air (poetry, drawings, and essays), Oxford University Press, 1985.
A Brazilian Journal (prose and sketches), Lester & Orpen Dennys, 1987.
A Flask of Sea Water (juvenile), illustrated by Laszlo Gal, Oxford University Press, 1988.
The Traveling Musicians of Bremen (juvenile), illustrated by Kady MacDonald Denton, Kids Can Press and Little, Brown & Company, 1989.
The Glass Air: Poems Selected and New, Oxford, 1991.

Also author of script and commentary for *Teeth Are To Keep,* an animated film; Cannes prizewinner. Author of *Personal Landscape, A Song Cycle,* with music by Bernard Naylor, for Arts National, CBC, and author of the libretto for *The Travelling Musicians,* with music by Murray Adaskin.

Contributor to numerous anthologies, including *Unit of 5,* edited by R. Hambleton, Ryerson, 1944; *Twentieth Century Canadian Poetry,* edited by Earle Birney, Ryerson, 1954; *Canadian Short Stories,* edited by Robert Weaver, Oxford University Press, 1960; *Canadian Poetry: The Modern Era,* edited by John Newlove, McClelland & Stewart, 1977; *The Norton Anthology of Literature by Women,* Norton, 1985. Contributor to periodicals and little magazines, including *Alphabet, Artscanada, Canadian Forum, Canadian Literature, Canadian Poetry, Saturday Night, Contemporary Verse, The White Pelican, Ellipse, Queen's Quarterly, Blackfish, Northern Review, Ontario Review, Poetry, Reading, Tamarack Review, Voices, Ariel, Tuatara, West Coast Review, Poetry Australia, Encounter* and London *Observer.*

Formerly member of the editorial board, *Malahat Review;* coeditor of *Preview* and regional editor for *Northern Review.*

ADAPTATIONS: The Sun and the Moon was dramatized for Canadian Broadcasting Corporation (CBC) radio.

SIDELIGHTS: Canadian poet P. K. Page is an artist in many senses of the word. She is also known as P. K. Irwin, the acclaimed painter, and as Judith Cape, the fiction writer. She was given the Governor General's award for her second book of poems, *The Metal and the Flower* (1953), and was made an Officer of the Order of Canada in 1977. In a *Canadian Literature* review, A. J. M. Smith places Page "among the fine poets of this century" and deems her poem "Arras" "the high point of a school of Canadian symbolist poets." Critics find a unity of vision in all her works. "Page is an almost entirely visual poet," writes *Canadian Literature* essayist Rosemary Sullivan, who believes that Page's line "I suffer shame in all these images" conveys "one of the deepest impulses of her work." Page also reaches out for a reality larger than and beyond the visible world. "Landscapes behind the eyes have appeared in Page's poems since her first collection in 1946. [In *Evening Dance of the Grey Flies*] they shine in the jewelled colouring of her intricately-wrought technique, a technique which has always been dazzling," Ann Mandel notes in a *Canadian Forum* review. Sullivan observes, "The discrepancy between the ideal world of the imagination, the potent world of dream, and the real world of the senses becomes one of her most obsessive subjects."

Sullivan reports that Page "began her poetic career with a reputation as a poet of social commitment and is probably still best known for the poems of the 1940s written while she was a member of the Montreal *Preview* group of poets." During that time, Montreal was the center of Canadian literary activity. The group, which included Page, Patrick Anderson, F. R. Scott, and many other poets, produced *Preview*, the literary magazine in which Page's earliest poems first appeared. According to *Canadian Literature* contributor S. Namjoshi, this group "had leftist leanings, and several of [Page's] poems reveal what may be termed a 'pro-proletarian' consciousness." However, Sullivan maintains that Page's "poetry has more to do with folklore, myth and archetype than with objective time, history and social fact." While the critic finds a "genuine compassion" for society's victims in Page's early poetry, Sullivan notes that "the poet's verbal facility betrays her. The attention she gives to metaphor distracts from the human dilemma that is her theme."

Poet and critic A. J. M. Smith reports in *Canadian Literature* that Page's experiences during the 1950s and early sixties stimulated her attention to detail. During those years, she accompanied her husband, a Canadian editor and diplomat, to Australia, Brazil, and Mexico. Though Page painted more than she published during this time, Smith believes "her painting and her poetry complemented one another: each . . . made the other better, or made it more deeply what it was. . . . And then the immersion in the language, landscape, and the mythology of the strange, intense, and perhaps intensely unCanadian places had a stimulating and enriching influence on all her latest poems." Negative criticism of Page's poetry centers on the abundance of vivid images. "Each of Miss Page's stanzas is so crowded with new and exciting pictures, that . . . [each] seems . . . to require the attention of a whole poem," John Sutherland comments in the *Northern Review.* As Sullivan explains, Page "has such a remarkable verbal gift that the image-making process can become almost too seductive. . . . The poet is trapped by her remarkable responsiveness to nature." Page is so receptive to "sensual detail, to each 'bright glimpse of beauty,' that even the sense of self, of separateness from the world, seems threatened."

This threat is a major element in her novel and first book. The heroine in *The Sun and the Moon* empathizes so thoroughly with inanimate objects that she "becomes a rock, a chair, a tree, experiencing these forms of existence in moments of identity," Sullivan relates. "But there is an alternative rhythm where the self is invaded. . . . Not only her identity, but also the identity of the other is destroyed by her chameleon presence. . . . To control this invasion an extraordinary exertion of will is necessary. For the poet, this means a control through technique, verbal dexterity. But P. K. Page's greatest dilemma is to ensure that this control is not sterile, that language is explored as experience, not evasion."

Page's writings also discuss the danger of becoming trapped in the private world of the imagination. Namjoshi defines the "central persona" of Page's poetry as "the woman caught within the confines of her inner reality, her personal Noah's Ark, seeking some way to reconcile the internal and the external, to make a harmony out of the double landscapes." "That the artist must make the effort to mediate between the internal and the external is central to her poetry," the reviewer states. Namjoshi names the poem "Cry Ararat" Page's "most successful effort at bringing the private world and the external world into alignment. 'Ararat!' is the cry of the isolated individual trapped within the confines of his private ark." Mount Ararat symbolizes a resting place between the "flood" of detail in the physical world, and "the stifling closeness of his own four walls. He need not withdraw into his private world, nor is his individuality submerged in the flood." This poem lends its title to Page's third book of poems, *Cry Ararat!: Poems New and Selected*—a loan that Namjoshi deems "fitting", since the poem "is a definitive and serious investigation of [Page's] theme, and brings the dilemma postulated by her to a final resolution."

In *Evening Dance of the Grey Flies*, the poet's seventh book, *Times Literary Supplement* contributor Fleur Adcock recognizes the characteristic "spiritual quest which expresses itself in highly colorful visionary language." Kevin Lewis, writing in *Quill and Quire*, says of Page, "It is no small feat to write convincing poetry in such a thick, imagistic style. . . . She must stand as one of the premier poets in Canada simply because she has such a beautiful way with words." *Canadian Literature* contributor Tom Marshall concludes, "As poet and calligrapher, [Page] delights in details and images, but has learned . . . to subordinate whimsy to the . . . design or large metaphor that captures a sense of the macrocosm. . . . She is one of our best poets."

BIOGRAPHICAL/CRITICAL SOURCES:

BOOKS

Contemporary Literary Criticism, Gale, Volume 7, 1977; Volume 18, 1981.
Dictionary of Literary Biography, Volume 68: *Canadian Writers, 1920-1959,* Gale, 1988.
Frye, Northrup, *The Bush Garden,* Anansi, 1971.
Lecker, Robert, and Jack David, editors, *The Annotated Bibliography of Canada's Major Authors,* ECW Press, 1985, pp. 207-85.
Ricou, Laurie, *Everyday Magic,* University of British Columbia Press, 1987, pp. 87-102.
Waddington, Miriam, editor, *Essays, Controversies and Poems,* McClelland & Stewart, 1972.
Woodcock, George, editor, *Poets and Critics: Essays from Canadian Literature, 1966-74,* Oxford University Press, 1974.

PERIODICALS

Canadian Forum, May, 1974; May, 1982; March, 1985; March, 1986.
Canadian Literature, autumn, 1970; autumn, 1971, pp. 17-27; spring, 1975; winter, 1976; winter, 1978, pp. 32-42.
Canadian Poetry: Studies, Documents, Reviews, spring/summer, 1979, pp. 65-72.
English Journal, spring-summer, 1979, pp. 1-12.
Globe and Mail (Toronto), June 27, 1987.
Malahat Review, January, 1978, pp. 169-95.
Modern Poetry Studies, autumn, 1974, pp. 175-87.
Northern Review, December/January, 1946-1947, pp. 13-23.
Poetry, October, 1968.
Quill and Quire, January, 1982.

Times Literary Supplement, October 26, 1973; March 18, 1983.
West Coast Review, February, 1979, pp. 8-17.

*   *   *

PANNETON, Philippe   1895-1960
(Ringuet, a pseudonym)

PERSONAL: Born April 30, 1895, in Trois-Rivieres, Quebec, Canada; died December 28, 1960, in Portugal; son of Ephrem-Francois (a doctor) and Eva (Ringuet) Panneton; married France Leriger de Laplante, 1954. *Education:* University of Montreal, M.D., 1920; post-graduate studies in Paris.

CAREER: Practiced medicine in Montreal, Quebec, beginning 1923; Hospital Saint-Eusebe, Joliette, Quebec, consultant, c. 1923-40; University of Montreal, faculty of medicine, beginning 1935; appointed Canadian ambassador to Portugal, 1956-60. Cofounder and twice president of the Academie Canadienne-Francaise.

AWARDS, HONOURS: Prix David, for *Litteratures . . . a la maniere de . . . ,* c. 1924; Prix de la Province de Quebec, Governor General's Award, award from the Academie Francaise, and Prix des Vikings, all c. 1938, all for *Thirty Acres;* Prix de la langue francaise from the Academie Francaise, 1947; Lorne Pierce Medal from the Royal Society of Canada, 1959; numerous other honorary and literary awards.

WRITINGS:

UNDER PSEUDONYM RINGUET

(With Louis Francoeur) *Litteratures . . . a la maniere de . . .* (parodies), Edouard Garand (Montreal, Quebec), 1924.
Je t'aime . . . Je ne t'aime pas (stage play), performed at the Monument National, 1927.
Trente Arpents (novel), Flammarion (Paris), 1938; translated by Felix and Dorothea Walter as *Thirty Acres,* Macmillan (New York), 1940.
Un Monde etait leur empire (nonfiction), Editions Varietes (Montreal, Quebec), 1943.
L'Heritage et autres contes (short stories), Editions Varietes, 1946.
Fausse Monnaie, Editions Varietes, 1947.
Le Poids du jour, Editions Varietes, 1949.
L'Amiral et le facteur ou comment l'Amerique ne fut pas decouverte (nonfiction), Dussault (Montreal), 1954.
Confidences (autobiography), Fides (Montreal and Paris), 1965.

Author of unpublished works, including a verse-play, "Idylle au jardin," and a lengthy diary, including the section "Le Carnet d'un cynique." Contributor of articles, poems, and stories to periodicals, including *Revue Moderne.*

ADAPTATIONS: The story "L'heritage" was made into a short film by the National Film Board of Canada, 1959.

SIDELIGHTS: When Philippe Panneton published his 1938 novel *Trente Arpents* under the pseudonym Ringuet, critics in both Canada and France hailed it as the definitive French-Canadian work of literature. He received prestigious literary prizes for the book from both nations, and it was translated into English as *Thirty Acres* and published in the United States in 1940. Ringuet penned other novels, including *Fausse Monnaie* and *Le Poids du jour;* authored a short story collection, *L'Heritage et autres contes;* and also wrote works of historical nonfiction. Antoine Sirois, discussing Ringuet in the *Dictionary of Literary Biography,* declared him "one of the first major novelists in French Canada" and noted that *Thirty Acres* "is still considered a classic."

Panneton was born in Trois-Rivieres, Quebec, in 1895. Panneton decided to follow in his father's footsteps and become a physician. He obtained his medical degree from the University of Montreal in 1920 and did post-doctoral studies in Paris, France, before returning to Montreal to set up practice in 1923. Though Panneton's soujourn in Paris also included reading French authors who later influenced his literary style, Panneton always put his medical career first. Once, in an interview in *La Revue populaire,* he compared his interest in writing to other people's interest in sports. Panneton eventually joined the medical faculty at the University of Montreal.

In 1924, however, he adopted the pseudonym Ringuet—his mother's maiden name—to collaborate with Louis Francouer on a collection of parodies of French-Canadian authors and political figures entitled *Litteratures . . . a la maniere de . . . .* Though some reviewers criticized the pair's mocking approach to such revered figures as Father Lionel Groulx, the book won the Prix David. A few years later, Ringuet penned a play, *Je t'aime . . . Je ne t'aime pas,* which was produced at the Monument National. This work received little critical attention.

Ringuet's next published effort was *Thirty Acres.* This acclaimed work tells the story of a Quebec family farm and the changes that time and technology wrought upon it. The central characters include the father, Euchariste Moisan, and his sons Etienne and Ephrem. Writing in the *Dictionary of Literary Biography,* Sirois summarized the novel thus: "Moisan manages his farm well and progresses gradually in wealth and reputation in his parish. But, growing old, he becomes careless occasionally and is forced to give the use of his land to Etienne, who has been impatiently coveting the thirty acres and pushing his father aside." At

Etienne's urging, Euchariste goes to live for a time with his more favored son Ephrem, who gave up on farming to work in a New England factory. As Sirois explained, however, "because of the Depression and the unwillingness of the eldest son, Moisan never comes back to his farm but becomes a janitor in a garage." Sirois concluded with this statement of the novel's main theme: "The land, Mother Earth, a hard mistress, remains unchanged, while the aging father has to leave her, giving up the care of his thirty acres to a new generation."

Critical response to *Thirty Acres* in both Canada and in France, where it was first published, was enthusiastic. Reviewers lauded it for breaking with the previous Quebecois tradition of portraying the provincial farmlands as idyllic portions of paradise—Ringuet had been much more realistic than most previous French-Canadian writers in his portrayal of nature. Sirois observed that "critics saw this work as a turning point in the tradition of the French-Canadian novel," and added his own praise, noting that *Thirty Acres* "is better written than most comparable novels of the pre-1938 period."

From his huge novelistic success, Ringuet turned to nonfiction. His 1943 effort, *Un Monde etait leur empire,* is a historic volume concerning pre-Columbian civilizations in Latin America. In it, he discusses the Inca and Maya cultures and their destruction at the hands of European explorers and the soldiers they brought with them. Ringuet also devotes the book's final chapter to criticizing the Europeans' treatment of the natives; however, Sirois labeled *Un Monde etait leur empire* "biased." Ringuet later penned another historical work, *L'Amiral et le facteur ou comment l'Amerique ne fut pas decouverte,* which puts forth his theory that Amerigo Vespucci deserves more credit for the discovery of the New World than does Christopher Columbus.

Directly following *Un Monde etait leur empire,* however, Ringuet published a collection of short stories previously published in magazines, *L'Heritage et autres contes.* The title story, which is similar in theme to *Thirty Acres,* was later adapted as a short motion picture by the National Film Board of Canada.

Ringuet returned to the novel form with 1947's *Fausse Monnaie.* Set in the Laurentian Mountains, it centers on two spoiled young people who disliked each other in childhood but find themselves reunited on a vacation weekend. A passionate but brief affair ensues. Some critics have found the characters to be cliched; none thought *Fausse Monnaie* comparable to *Thirty Acres.* Perhaps Ringuet's second-best received work is his 1949 novel, *Le Poids du jour. Le Poids du jour* is something of a counterpoint to *Thirty Acres;* while Ringuet's masterwork centers on the country, which is almost a character in the novel, the city of Montreal features palpably in the 1949 book. The protagonist of *Le Poids du jour* is Michel Garneau, born in the small Quebec town of Louiseville. Though he has an abusive, alcoholic father, he is for the most part sheltered from the effects of this by his mother and godfather. When Michel goes to Montreal to seek his fortune in the banking business, he learns that this godfather is really his father. Instead of being happy at the news that a man that he has loved all along is his true parent, he is angered at his mother's—and his biological father's—deception. As Sirois described it, Michel "decides vengefully to reject his past, to conquer the city through business, and finally he becomes the owner of a factory." Michel also changes his name to Robert as part of his effort to distance himself from his past, but he is left empty and unfulfilled by his business accomplishments. He eventually returns to the countryside to seek peace, which he finds living with his daughter and his grandson. Though in this ending Ringuet proves that, in Sirois's words, "he was not sure that the urban man would find happiness in his quest," the vivid portrayal of the bustling city of Montreal was more positive than negative. Because of this, Ringuet's *Le Poids du jour* stands among the primary examples of a trend towards more urban subjects that took place in French-Canadian fiction following World War II. Sirois quoted critic Guy Sylvester, a member of the Royal Society of Canada, who proclaimed *Le Poids du jour* "the most important undertaking in French Canada to express the individual and collective drama of migration from the country to the city."

In 1956, two years after his marriage to France Leriger de Laplante, Panneton was appointed as Canada's ambassador to Portugal. He was still serving in this capacity when he died in Portugal in 1960. A collection of talks Ringuet had given on Canadian radio was printed posthumously as *Confidences* in 1965. Ringuet also left a lengthy, unpublished diary. He had considered publishing a section of it, which he called "Le Carnet d'un cynique," but decided against it, fearing his unconventional views on religion, politics, and philosophy would be held against him in both the medical and literary professions.

BIOGRAPHICAL/CRITICAL SOURCES:

BOOKS

Dictionary of Literary Biography, Volume 68: *Canadian Writers, 1920-1959, First Series,* Gale, 1988, pp. 290-94.
Oxford Companion to Canadian Literature, Oxford University Press, 1983, pp. 633-34.
Panneton, Jean, *Ringuet,* Fides, 1970.
Ringuet, *Confidences,* Fides, 1965.

PERIODICALS

Canadian Literature, summer, 1971, pp. 20-27; autumn, 1980, pp. 152-56.
College et Famille, October, 1968, pp. 133-57.
Essays on Canadian Writing, spring, 1980, pp. 102-12.
La Presse, April 3, 1965, p. 10.*

—*Sketch by Elizabeth Wenning*

*   *   *

PEARSON, Kit 1947-

PERSONAL: Born April 30, 1947, in Edmonton, Alberta, Canada; daughter of Hugh and Kay (Hastie) Pearson. *Education:* University of Alberta, B.A., 1969; University of British Columbia, M.L.S., 1976; Simmons College, Center for the Study of Children's Literature, M.A., 1982.

ADDRESSES: Home—3888 West Fifteenth Ave., Vancouver, British Columbia, Canada V6R 2Z9. *Agent*—Lee Davis Creal, c/o Lucinda Vardey Agency, 297 Seaton St., Toronto, Ontario, Canada M5A 2T6.

CAREER: Has worked as a children's librarian, and reviewer and teacher of juvenile literature and writing for children.

AWARDS, HONOURS: Book of the Year for Children award, Canadian Library Association, 1988, for *A Handful of Time;* Book of the Year for Children award, Canadian Library Association, 1990, inaugural Mr. Christie Book award, Geoffrey Bilson Award for historical fiction for young people, and Governor General's Award shortlist citation, all for *The Sky Is Falling;* Governor General's Award shortlist citation, for *Looking at the Moon.*

WRITINGS:

CHILDREN'S NOVELS

The Daring Game, Viking Kestrel, 1986.
A Handful of Time, Viking Kestrel, 1987.
The Sky Is Falling, Viking Kestrel, 1989.
Looking at the Moon, Viking, 1991.
The Lights Go on Again, Viking, 1993.

OTHER

(Reteller) *The Singing Basket,* illustrated by Ann Blades, Firefly Books, 1991.

SIDELIGHTS: Kit Pearson is an award-winning writer of novels about the real-life problems of middle graders. She is often praised for her sensitivity in writing about the pain children feel when they are outsiders. Many of her books are about youngsters separated from their homes and families who are trying to get along in new and unfamiliar settings. Her books for middle graders, each set in Canada, are well regarded for their beautiful writing, attention to detail, and emotional power.

Pearson's life and studies have focused on literature, especially children's literature. She graduated in English at the University of Alberta before going on to get her masters of library science at the University of British Columbia. She also received a master of arts in children's literature at the Center for the Study of Children's Literature, Simmons College, in Boston. Pearson has worked as a children's librarian and has published reviews and articles on the subject. She has also taught courses on juvenile literature. One of the characteristics of her writing is to fill her books with references to classic works of children's fiction.

In an interview with Dave Jenkinson, published in *Emergency Librarian,* Pearson talked about her habit of including titles of children's books in her own works. "I have to watch myself," she said. "I'm a former children's librarian, and I love children's books." She goes on to tell how when she was a child she read the books of Edward Eager. Characters in his books were often reading books by another real-life children's author, E. Nesbit, which would inspire their own magical adventures. Once she finished the Eager books, Pearson "rushed out and got the E. Nesbit books and read those and loved them."

Pearson's first novel, *The Daring Game,* was published in 1986. It takes place in a boarding school for girls in Vancouver in 1964. Eleven-year-old Eliza makes friends with Helen, the school rebel, who suggests the "daring game," in which the dorm mates dare each other to break school rules. Eliza lies to cover for Helen when she leaves campus on a dare and jeopardizes her own standing at the school through her loyalty.

Pearson's interest in boarding schools goes back to her own childhood, when she was sent to Crofton House, a boarding school in Vancouver. As she explained in *Emergency Librarian,* "I find it so intriguing that you can take an assortment of kids and put them in a situation where they're almost like a tribe. The adults have nothing to do with them; they're really on their own."

JoAnna Burns Patton, writing in *CM: Canadian Materials for Schools and Libraries,* praised Pearson's "remarkable insight into the emotional growth of young girls." Lorraine M. York stated in *Canadian Children's Literature* that "the pre-adolescent fear which Pearson has best articulated and which many adults will have forgotten or ignored is the most basic: the fear of becoming an adolescent, a teenager." Pearson explained in *Emergency Librarian:* "Eliza is exactly the way I was. In fact, three friends and I made a pact when we were 12 that we would not grow up, and we really thought we didn't have to." Pearson is definitely *not* advocating staying a child. "What Eliza doesn't want to do," she assessed, "and I don't

blame her, is all the *artificial* stuff about growing up—being a 'feminine' teenager, being an object and all that stuff."

Pearson's next published book was *A Handful of Time,* which uses the fantasy device of a magic watch and traveling backward in time to tell a story about mothers and daughters. Twelve-year-old Patricia is sent by her beautiful but cold mother to her family's lakeside cottage. She is being sent to stay with cousins she's never met while her parents are getting divorced. Patricia, who is shy and unhappy at the cottage, discovers an old watch that transports her back thirty-five years. Made invisible by the powers of the watch, Patricia observes her mother's miserable twelfth summer at the same site. Patricia comes to understand how her mother's difficult childhood affected the woman she has become.

Whereas Patricia's mom had to fight for her freedom growing up, she instead "stifles Patricia by giving her too much freedom," noted Annette Goldsmith in her review in *Books for Young People.* Ultimately, Patricia gains greater strength and self-confidence in the present because of her time travels and the discoveries she has made about her mother.

Yvonne A. Frey, however, writing in *School Library Journal,* faulted the portraits of the two mothers as being "wooden and flat." Nevertheless, she judged that the book can reveal to readers how "relationships in the present are often locked into patterns of the past," and that learning family history "often reveals much about oneself." Similarly, *Bulletin of the Center for Children's Books* reviewer Roger Sutton found the author portrays very well "the tension between family members who are supposed to like each other and don't, and the pain of a child who does not fit in."

Pearson's third book, published in 1989, is *The Sky Is Falling.* Like Pearson's first two books, this one takes place in Canada and focuses on children separated from their families. *The Sky Is Falling,* however, begins in England. It is the summer of 1940, and all of England fears an invasion by Nazi fuhrer Adolph Hitler's army. Many parents are sending their children to safety overseas. This exodus comes to include ten-year-old Norah, who has just started a secret club to watch for German planes and spies and has no desire whatsoever to be sent away. But despite Norah's protests, she and her little brother Gavin are evacuated to be "war guests" of a wealthy widow, Mrs. Ogilvie, in Toronto.

This book, the first of a proposed trilogy, was inspired by storyteller Alice Kane's memory of telling stories to evacuee children in Canada. Pearson explained in *Emergency Librarian* that "I have also heard about the war all my life from my parents. My mother used to tell me how 'adorable' the little English evacuees were. I got the feeling that some of these children were treated almost like little pets." This is not at all the case for Norah, however. Mrs. Ogilvie lavishes all her affection on Gavin, the children at her new school taunt her, and as the news from England becomes worse, she is filled with homesickness. Norah runs away after clashing with Mrs. Ogilvie, but returns to resolve her problems and discovers a surprising responsibility that helps her to accept her new country. Denise Wilms, writing in *Booklist,* calls the book a "compelling, sensitive study of children traumatized by separation. Its strength is in its particularly well realized characterizations."

Similarly, Annette Goldsmith, writing in *Quill and Quire,* points out that it is "Pearson's attention to detail both funny and sad that makes this book so engaging." She feels that readers "will appreciate Norah's feelings of homesickness and isolation in a strange country and be cheered by her hard-won ability to cope." Louise L. Sherman similarly observes in *School Library Journal* that "there is plenty of conflict and action to hold young readers' interest in Norah's struggles with her new family and school." *The Sky Is Falling* won the Canadian Library Association Book of the Year Award for Children, the first Mr. Christie Book Award, and the Geoffrey Bilson Award for historical fiction for young people, which was named after the writer whose nonfiction study of English evacuees in Canada, *The Guest Children,* was published shortly after *The Sky Is Falling.*

Pearson's next book, *Looking at the Moon,* is the second book in her trilogy about "war guests" in Canada. Like *The Sky Is Falling,* this volume continues the story of Norah, who is now thirteen and still living in Toronto with Mrs. Ogilvie. She hasn't seen her parents in three years, and sometimes she isn't even sure if she can remember what they look like. Like Pearson's second book, *A Handful of Time, Looking at the Moon* takes place at a lakeside cottage. When Norah meets nineteen-year-old Andrew, she thinks she may be falling in love for the first time. But Andrew has his own problems: he doesn't want to fight in the war, and yet he knows it's what his family expects. What the two of them learn from each other makes for a gentle and moving story of first loves and growing up.

Until *Looking at the Moon* Pearson had always written about preteen girls. "That was my favorite age and still is," she said in *Emergency Librarian.* "I think about age 11 and 12, just before adolescence, you have a kind of 'power', especially girls for some reason. . . . You have all the freedoms of being a child but you have all the faculties of an adult." Pearson continues, "I have such clear memories of being that age—and of the shock of it all ending at 13."

The story of Norah in *Looking at the Moon* is Pearson's first try at writing about that shocking age. "Norah will be 13 in the second book because I've always wanted to write about the trials of being 13." The last book in the trilogy, *The Lights Go on Again,* is about Norah's younger brother, Gavin, at age ten—Pearson's first book with a boy as the main character. The story is set in 1945, as the war is ending. After the death of his parents, and Aunt Florence's offer to adopt him, Gavin must decide whether to stay with the family and country he loves, or to go back to England with Norah. This is the author's most serious work, with the tragedy of war conflicting with a young boy's innocence.

Pearson's usual writing process begins with a central idea, for example, a girl going back to her mother's past. "I do the whole first draft from beginning to end and *then* I make an outline," she remarked. Then she writes her second draft, straight through. "I always have to do it in order—I can't work on this bit and that bit." She finds that dialogue is the easiest part to write but her descriptions and characters always need more work. She also notes that "characters do take over, and I've never known whether that's good or bad."

For example, Eliza and Helen weren't supposed to become friends until the end of *The Daring Game.* "And lo and behold, they made friends at Christmas, and I didn't know what to do about it," Pearson added. Likewise, Pearson thought *The Sky Is Falling* "would cover the whole war, but when I finished it, it was only Christmas, 1940." This is what ultimately led Pearson to the idea of writing a trilogy covering the entire war.

There is something in the gentleness and warmth of Pearson's characters that makes readers long to reencounter them in new books, to see how they are getting along, how they are changing. A line from Goldsmith's review of *A Handful of Time* encapsulates one of the distinctive qualities of Kit Pearson's writing: "No high dramatics here! This is a subtle and memorable book with a Canadian context and universal appeal."

BIOGRAPHICAL/CRITICAL SOURCES:

BOOKS

Children's Literature Review, Volume 26, Gale, 1992, pp. 172-78.

PERIODICALS

Booklist, May 15, 1990, p. 1805.
Books for Young People, April, 1987, p. 10.
Books in Canada, June-July, 1987, pp. 35-37.
Bulletin of the Center for Children's Books, January, 1987, p. 95; May, 1988, p. 186.

Canadian Children's Literature, number 46, 1987, pp. 79-81; number 49, 1988, pp. 53-55; number 69, 1993, pp. 42-43.
CANSCAIP News, summer, 1990, pp. 1-3.
CM: Canadian Materials for Schools and Libraries, July, 1986, p. 167.
Emergency Librarian, September-October, 1989, pp. 65-69.
Quill and Quire, November, 1989, p. 14.
School Library Journal, May, 1988, p. 100; June, 1990, p. 125.

—*Sketch by Ira Brodsky*

*   *   *

PETER, Laurence J(ohnston)   1919-1990

PERSONAL: Born September 16, 1919, in Vancouver, British Columbia, Canada; died of complications of a stroke, January 12, 1990, in Palos Verdes Estates, CA; son of Victor (an actor) and Vincenta (Steves) Peter; married Nancy Bailey (marriage ended); married Irene Howe, February 25, 1967; children: John, Edward, Alice, Margaret. *Education:*Attended University of British Columbia, 1938-54; Western Washington State College (now Western Washington University), B.A., 1957, M.Ed., 1958; Washington State University, Ed.D., 1963.

CAREER: Teacher of industrial arts in British Columbia, 1941-47; Provincial Prison Department, Burnaby, British Columbia, instructor, 1947-48; Vancouver School Board, Vancouver, British Columbia, mental health coordinator and special counselor, 1948-64; University of British Columbia, Vancouver, assistant professor of education, 1964-66; University of Southern California, Los Angeles, associate professor, 1966-69, professor of education, 1969-70, director of Evelyn Frieden Center for Prescriptive Teaching, 1967-70; John Tracy Clinic, Los Angeles, Calif., professor in residence, 1970-73; University of California, Stanislaus, adjunct professor of education, 1975-79; writer and lecturer. Psychologist, British Columbia Vocational Counselling Service, 1959. Panel member of review board, Department of Health, Education, and Welfare, 1969-70. Consultant to other British Columbia health and service organizations.

MEMBER: National Autistic Association, American Association of University Professors, Canadian Mental Health Association, Canadian Association of University Teachers, PEN, American Federation of Television and Radio Artists, Northwest Writers Conference, Association for Retarded Children, British Columbia Teachers Association, British Columbia Mental Health Association (member of executive committee, 1958-61), Greater Los Angeles Big Brother Association (member of board), Phi Delta Kappa.

AWARDS, HONOURS: The Peter Principle: Why Things Always Go Wrong was named to the bestseller lists of the *New York Times* and *Publishers Weekly,* 1969; Phi Delta Kappa research award, University of Southern California, 1970; alumni awards from Western Washington State College (now Western Washington University) and Washington State University; Canadian University Associated Alumni award; Will Rogers Top Hand award; D.H.L., Heidelberg College, 1982.

WRITINGS:

Prescription Teaching, McGraw, 1965.
(With Raymond Hull) *The Peter Principle: Why Things Always Go Wrong,* Morrow, 1969.
The Peter Prescription and How to Make Things Go Right, Morrow, 1972.
The Peter Plan: A Proposal for Survival, Morrow, 1975.
Competencies for Teaching, four volumes, Wadsworth, 1975.
Peter's Quotations: Ideas for Our Times, Morrow, 1977.
Peter's People and Their Marvelous Ideas, Morrow, 1979.
Peter's Almanac, Morrow, 1982.
(With Bill Dana) *The Laughter Prescription,* Ballantine, 1982.
Why Things Go Wrong, Morrow, 1984.

Contributor to *Education Panorama* (published in five languages) and other education journals; contributor to magazines, including *Psychology Today, Human Behavior,* and *Reader's Digest.*

SIDELIGHTS: In 1969, psychologist and author Laurence J. Peter introduced the world to his Peter Principle: "In a hierarchy individuals tend to rise to their levels of incompetence." As Marshall Berges notes in the *Los Angeles Times,* "Peter's world overflows with incompetents. They have swarmed around him throughout his life. . . . [He] finds incompetents in all shapes and sizes and in practically every field of endeavor. Although they are too numerous to be captured by even the widest lens of a camera, Peter has made copious notes on their activities. At intervals when the stack of notes grows too high, he assembles his findings into a book." To date, Peter has produced several books on his subject, with titles like *The Peter Principle: Why Things Always Go Wrong, The Peter Prescription and How to Make Things Go Right,* and *The Peter Plan: A Proposal for Survival.* More than one critic has suggested, in view of Peter's many similar books, that the author himself has reached his own level of incompetence. But other reviewers find humor in the continuing parade of useless laws, bad ideas, and misleading quotes that Peter chronicles. "No one is immune to Peter's corollaries, not even their lexicographer," declares *Time* critic

Stefan Kanfer. In a passage of his book *Why Things Go Wrong,* the author admits, "It was never my intention to decry the sins, mistakes, vanities and incompetence of my fellow human beings. I am at least as guilty as they." The proof, reports Kanfer, "lies in [Peter's] vain attempts to back a California education center. 'I realized I had reached my level of incompetence as a fund raiser when all my requests from government agencies and private foundations were rejected.' Undismayed, Peter obeyed his own dictum: 'Quit while you're behind.' "

BIOGRAPHICAL/CRITICAL SOURCES:

BOOKS

Peter, Laurence J., *Why Things Go Wrong,* Morrow, 1984.

PERIODICALS

Christian Science Monitor, March 6, 1969.
Los Angeles Times, October 4, 1979, February 16, 1984.
New York Times Book Review, August 13, 1972, February 8, 1976.
Time, November 26, 1984.

OBITUARIES:

BOOKS

Who's Who in U. S. Writers, Editors, and Poets, 1988, December Press, 1988.

PERIODICALS

Chicago Tribune, January 15, 1990.
Los Angeles Times, January 15, 1990.
New York Times, January 15, 1990.
Washington Post, January 17, 1990.

* * *

PINTO, Peter
See BERNE, Eric (Lennard)

* * *

POLLOCK, (Mary) Sharon 1936-

PERSONAL: Born April 19, 1936, in Fredericton, New Brunswick, Canada; daughter of Everett (a physician and politician) Chalmers; married Ross Pollock, 1954 (marriage ended); children: five. *Education:* Attended University of New Brunswick, ending in 1954.

ADDRESSES: Home—319 Manora Dr. N.E., Calgary, Alberta T2A 4R2, Canada.

CAREER: Playwright. University of Alberta, Edmonton, Alberta, Canada, affiliated with the drama department,

1976-77, visiting lecturer, 1976-81; Banff Centre of Fine Arts, Banff, Alberta, head of playwright's colony, 1977-80; Theatre Calgary, Calgary, Alberta, dramaturge and assistant artistic director, 1983-84, artistic director, 1984. Alberta Theatre Projects, playwright-in-residence, 1977-79; National Arts Centre, Ottawa, artist-in-residence, 1981-83. Advisory Arts Panel, Canada Council, member, 1978-80, chair, 1979-80; National Theatre School, member of advisory committee, 1979-80; Playwrights Canada National Exec., vice-chair, 1981-83. Has worked in amateur theatre, including with the theatre group Prairie Players; appeared in *My Name Is Lisabeth,* as Lizzie Borden (title role), produced at Douglas College, New Westminster, British Columbia, Canada, 1976.

AWARDS, HONOURS: Alberta Playwriting Competition winner, 1971, for *A Compulsory Option;* Association of Canadian Television and Radio Artists award for best radio drama, 1980, for *Sweet Land of Liberty;* Governor General's Literary Award for published drama, Canada Council, 1982, for *Blood Relations;* Governor General's Literary Award for English-language drama, Canada Council, 1987, for *Doc.*

WRITINGS:

PLAYS

A Compulsory Option (two-act), produced at New Play Centre, Vancouver, British Columbia, Canada, August, 1972.
Walsh (two-act; produced at Theatre Calgary, Calgary, Alberta, Canada, November 7, 1973; revised version produced at Third State at the Stratford Festival, Stratford, Ontario, Canada, summer, 1974; aired on Canadian Broadcasting Corp. [CBC] Radio, 1974), Talonbooks (Vancouver), 1973, revised edition, 1974.
New Canadians, produced at Playhouse Holiday, Vancouver, 1973.
Superstition Throu' the Ages, produced at Playhouse Holiday, 1973.
Wudjesay?, produced at Playhouse Holiday, 1974.
The Happy Prince, produced at Playhouse Theatre School, Vancouver, 1974.
The Rose and the Nightingale, produced at Playhouse Theatre School, 1974.
Star-child, produced at Playhouse Theatre School, 1974.
The Great Drag Race or Smoked, Choked, and Croaked, commissioned by British Columbia Christmas Seal Society, produced in British Columbia, Canada, secondary schools, 1974.
Lessons in Swizzlery, produced by Caravan Theatre touring ensemble, New Westminster, British Columbia, Canada, 1974.
And Out Goes You (two-act), produced at Vancouver Playhouse, Vancouver, 1975.

The Komagata Maru Incident (one-act; produced at Vancouver Playhouse at the Vancouver East Cultural Center, Vancouver, January 20, 1976), Playwrights Co-op (Toronto), 1978.

My Name Is Lisabeth, produced at Douglas College, New Westminster, 1976.

(With others) *Tracings—The Fraser Story,* produced at Theatre Network, Edmonton, Canada, 1977.

The Wreck of the National Line Car, produced by Alberta Theatre Projects, Calgary, 1978.

Chautaqua Spelt E-N-E-R-G-Y, produced by Alberta Theatre Projects, 1979.

Mail vs. Female, produced at Lunchbox Theatre, Calgary, March, 1979.

One Tiger to a Hill, produced at Citadel Theatre, Edmonton, February, 1980, revised version produced at Festival Lennoxville, Lennoxville, Quebec, Canada, summer, 1980, later produced at Manhattan Theatre Club, New York City, November, 1980; aired on CBC Radio, December 8, 1985.

Blood Relations, produced at Theatre Three, Edmonton, March 12, 1980.

Generations (an adaption of the original radio play *Generation*), produced by Alberta Theatre Projects at Conmore Opera House, Calgary, October 28, 1980.

Blood Relations and Other Plays (contains *Blood Relations, Generations,* and *One Tiger to a Hill*), introduction by Diane Bessai, NeWest Press (Edmonton), 1981.

Whiskey Six, produced at Theatre Calgary, 1983; aired on CBC Radio, October 22, 1983.

Doc (produced at Theatre Calgary, April, 1984; revised version produced at Toronto Free Theatre, Toronto, Ontario, Canada, September, 1984), Playwrights Canada (Toronto), 1986.

Family Trappings (a revised version of *Doc*), produced at Theatre New Brunswick, Fredericton, New Brunswick, Canada, March, 1986.

Also author of plays for children.

FOR TELEVISION

Portrait of a Pig, CBC-Winnipeg, 1973.

The Larsens, CBC-Winnipeg, 1976.

"Ransom", *The Magic Lie* (television series), CBC-Edmonton, 1976.

(With others) *Country Joy,* CBC, 1979-1980.

FOR RADIO

A Split Second in the Life Of, CBC, November 22, 1970.

31 for 2, CBC, February 7, 1971.

We to the Gods, CBC, September 5, 1971.

Generation, CBC, December 10, 1978.

Sweet Land of Liberty, CBC, December 2, 1979.

Intensive Care, CBC, June 5, 1983.

WORK IN PROGRESS: Egg, a play commissioned by Theatre Calgary.

SIDELIGHTS: "Sharon Pollock is one of only a handful of playwrights in Canada who have put together a solid and developing body of work over a number of active years in the theatre," wrote Richard Paul Knowles in *Atlantic Provinces Book Review,* "and of that handful she is one of the best." During Pollack's prolific career—which has established her as one of the "two finest living [Canadian] playwrights," according to *University of Toronto Quarterly* contributor Jerry Wasserman—she has moved from writing plays concerned with historical and political topics to more personal plays with families and individuals as subjects. Her body of work, which also includes writings for television and radio, has brought her wide recognition and led Paul Matthew St. Pierre, writing in the *Dictionary of Literary Biography,* to call her "one of the most innovative and versatile dramatists in [Canada]."

An early play of Pollock's that demonstrates her concern for historical topics is 1976's *The Komagata Maru Incident,* an examination of the real-life plight of a group of Sikh immigrants who, in 1914, attempted to enter Canada but who were illegally turned away. Later in 1976, another of Pollock's plays featuring a factual event opened. Entitled *My Name Is Lisabeth,* the play concerns the life of nineteenth-century American Lizzie Borden, a woman accused of killing her father and stepmother in 1892 but who was acquitted after a now-famous trial.

Lizzie Borden reappears in Pollock's 1980 play *Blood Relations,* in which, ten years after the murder trial, an actor friend of Lizzie's chooses to study Lizzie's character and actions as if she were preparing to perform as Lizzie in a play. Lizzie relives her experiences with her family and of the trial as she tutors her friend in the role. In the play, Pollock "explores the ambivalence of empirical evidence and subjective testimony and of family and especially woman-to-woman relationships," as St. Pierre noted. The critic concluded that Pollock's ability to evoke "dramatic suspense . . . is the source of the play's triumph." *Blood Relations* was the first play recognized with the prestigious Governor General's Literary Award for published drama.

In 1984, Pollock's most autobiographical and most discussed play was produced. *Doc* tells the contemporary story of Catherine, a writer, and her father Ev, a well-known, respected physician. The play follows Catherine as she returns to her childhood home after an absence of years to visit her father, who recently experienced a heart attack. Catherine views her father as a man who forfeited his family life in order to further pursue his career and, by so doing, drove his wife to alcohol and, eventually, suicide. Pollock, however, doesn't trivialize Ev's decision to tend to society's ills and thereby distance himself from his wife and daughter. As Wasserman quoted, Ev explains: "Should I have tended my own little plot when I looked round and there was so damn much to do—so much I could do—I did do! . . . You tell me, was I wrong to do that!" Aside from his wife's suicide, Ev also carries the weight of his mother's apparent suicide, the reasoning of which is purportedly carried in an envelope he holds throughout the play and which he has left unopened for thirty years. Catherine and Ev, at the end of the play, are able to burn the letter, exorcising themselves of their shared, troubled past.

A technical innovation of the play that lends further drama to the situation is the splitting of Catherine's character: not only does she appear as her present self, but another actor plays her as a young girl. This technique allows Catherine to talk to and observe herself through the years and enables Pollock to disregard a traditional, chronological plot in favor of transitions based on the psychological condition of the characters and the emotional responses their memories evoke. The play constantly switches between past and present, a movement Pollock defines with the stage direction "shift."

Aside from winning Pollock her second Governor General's Literary Award, Doc met with a considerable amount of critical acclaim. "Doc's exploration of an unhappy family meets all the criteria of the well-made play while at the same time managing to cast an understanding but unsentimental light on other families as well," noted Alan Stewart in Globe and Mail. Wasserman wrote: "Virtually jettisoning plot for the first time in her career, the better to follow the rhythms of intuition and the unconscious, Pollock takes Catherine on a journey that ends with her able to smile at her father and forgive herself for being human. This is Pollock's most emotionally complex and structurally sure-handed work yet." In Canadian Theatre Review, Cindy Cowan judged that Pollock "compassionately and skillfully [layers] in her thematic concerns regarding the nature of guilt and forgiveness within the realm of the family, where we might find guidance for living with dignity and equality." And Mark Czarnecki commented in Maclean's: "Doc is more ritual than play, a gripping but oppressive exorcism of the demons in Sharon Pollock's past. Coming in the middle of a distinguished career, it stirs curiosity about where the playwright's inspirations will lead her."

BIOGRAPHICAL/CRITICAL SOURCES:

BOOKS

Dictionary of Literary Biography, Volume 60: Canadian Writers since 1960, Second Series, Gale, 1987, pp. 300-06.

Wallace, Robert, and Cynthia Zimmerman, The Work: Conversations with English-Canadian Playwrights, Coach House Press (Toronto), 1982, pp. 114-41.

PERIODICALS

Alberta Report, February 28, 1983, p. 50; April 30, 1984, pp. 54-55; September 10, 1984, pp. 40-41.
Atlantic Advocate, August, 1974, p. 50.
Atlantic Provinces Book Review, February-March, 1987, p. 19.
Books in Canada, April, 1982, p. 8; March, 1987, pp. 17-18.
Canadian Drama, fall, 1979, pp. 104-11.
Canadian Literature, winter, 1984, pp. 51-62.
Canadian Theatre Review, spring, 1982, pp. 34-38; fall, 1987, pp. 95-96.
Cinema Canada, December, 1983, pp. 26-27.
Globe and Mail (Toronto), October 27, 1984.
Maclean's, April 23, 1984, p. 52.
Performing Arts, Volume 22, number 4, 1980, p. 24.
Quill and Quire, April, 1982, p. 29.
Saturday Night, October, 1984, pp. 73-74.
University of Toronto Quarterly, fall, 1987, pp. 67-69.

*   *   *

PRATT, E(dwin) J(ohn) 1883-1964

PERSONAL: Born February 4, 1883, in Western Bay, Newfoundland Canada; died April 26, 1964, in Toronto, Ontario Canada; son of John (a Methodist minister) and Fanny Pitts (Knight) Pratt; married Viola Whitney (an editor), 1918; children: Claire. Education: Attended St. John's Methodist College; Victoria College, University of Toronto, B.A., 1911, M.A., 1913, Ph.D., 1917.

CAREER: Educator and poet. Apprentice to a draper, St. John's, Newfoundland, 1896-98; ordained Methodist minister, 1913; worked briefly as a travelling salesman; Victoria College, University of Toronto, taught in English department, until 1953.

AWARDS, HONOURS: Two Governor-General's awards for poetry, one in 1940 for Brebeuf and His Brethren.

WRITINGS:

VERSE; PUBLISHED BY MACMILLAN OF TORONTO, EXCEPT WHERE NOTED

Rachel: A Sea Story of Newfoundland in Verse, privately printed [New York City], 1917.
Newfoundland Verse, Ryerson, 1923.
The Witches' Brew, Selwyn & Blount, 1925, 1926.
Titans, 1926.
The Iron Door: An Ode, 1927.
The Roosevelt and the Antinoe, Macmillan (New York), 1930.

Verses of the Sea, 1930.

Many Moods, 1932.

The Titanic, 1935.

The Fable of the Goats and Other Poems, 1937.

Brebeuf and His Brethren, 1940, published as *Brebeuf and His Brethren (the North American Martyrs),* Basilian, 1942.

Dunkirk, 1941.

Still Life and Other Verse, 1943.

Collected Poems of E. J. Pratt, 1944, Knopf, 1945, enlarged edition, edited by Northrop Frye, 1958.

They Are Returning, 1945.

Behind the Log, 1947.

Ten Selected Poems, with Notes, 1947.

Towards the Last Spike: A Verse of the Struggle to Build the First Transcontinental from the Time of the Proposed Terms of Union with British Columbia, 1870, to the Hammering of the Last Spike in the Eagle Pass, 1885, 1952.

Here the Tides Flow, edited by D. G. Pitt, 1962.

Selected Poems of E. J. Pratt, edited by Peter Buitenhuis, 1968.

E. J. Pratt: Complete Poems, two volumes, edited by Sandra Djwa and R. G. Moyles, University of Toronto Press, 1989.

OTHER

Studies in Pauline Eschatology and Its Background, Briggs, 1917.

(Editor) *Under the Greenwood Tree* by Thomas Hardy, Macmillan (Toronto), 1937.

(Editor and author of preface and notes) *Heroic Tales in Verse,* Macmillan (Toronto), 1941.

Pionnier de la paix qui vient: William Penn (1644-1718), Editions Gerard de Buren (Geneva), 1945.

(Editor and author of notes and questions) *Poems for Upper School,* Macmillan (Toronto), 1953.

E. J. Pratt: On His Life and Poetry (autobiography), edited by Susan Gingell, University of Toronto Press, 1983.

Contributor of poems to academic journals, including *Acta Victoriana.*

A collection of Pratt's books, manuscripts, lecture notes, clippings, photographs and various memorabilia is housed at the E. J. Pratt Library at Victoria College, University of Toronto.

SIDELIGHTS: E. J. Pratt was described by Michael Darling in the *Dictionary of Literary Biography* (*DLB*) as "a poet whose themes are universal but whose voice is unquestionably unique in Canadian literature." Pratt published his first book of verse, *Rachel: A Sea Story of Newfoundland in Verse,* in 1917 and followed it with the poetry collection *Newfoundland Verse,* which appeared in 1923. These collections established Pratt as an adventur-

ous experimenter in long form narrative verse. In subsequent publications, the poet uses his verse to describe such events as the sinking of an ocean liner in *The Titanic,* the martyrdom of Jesuit missionaries in *Brebeuf and His Brethren,* and the ecological and humanistic aspects of building a cross-continental railway, which he recounts in *Towards the Last Spike.* Pratt's skill with narrative poetry and his concern for Canadian art and life led many to consider him a cornerstone of that country's literature. Darling described Pratt as "Canada's unofficial poet laureate," stating that "few poets can be said to occupy a more secure position in the literary history of their countries."

Pratt was born on February 4, 1882, the son of a Methodist preacher in Western Bay, Newfoundland, Canada. Growing up in a community that revolved around seafaring—Western Bay was predominantly a fishing village—Pratt developed an interest in the ocean, a preoccupation that would later be reflected in his writings. After a religiously influenced education that included studies at St. John's Methodist College, Pratt decided to follow in his father's footsteps and pursue a career with the Methodist ministry. He became a preacher and probationer in Newfoundland. The physical demands of the job proved too strenuous, however, and Pratt sought other means of livelihood. After a brief stint as a travelling salesman, Pratt had raised enough money to attend Victoria College at the University of Toronto. He earned several degrees from the institution, including a Ph.D in 1917, and segued into a faculty position with the college. He retired as a professor emeritus in 1953. It was early in his career as an academic that Pratt began to craft the verse for which he is widely known.

Pratt's *Rachel* was privately published in 1917 and was regarded by both its author and critics as a forgettable, average work. Published in 1923, *Newfoundland Verse* is viewed as the first work to display Pratt's unique literary skills. The collection reflects the poet's early fascination with the sea, chronicling humankind's affinity for vast bodies of water. A majority of the poems are concerned with catastrophes, notably shipwrecks and drownings, that result from seafaring. Pratt impressed critics with his narrative technique and his expansion of form in *Newfoundland Verse.* Dorothy Livesay described the poet's style in *Canadian Literature* as "fresh, muscular, contemporary, and often boisterously amusing." Livesay also praised Pratt for using a meter—a system of word rhythm used in poetry—that was intricate, as well as innovative for Canadian literature at the time.

Pratt's next poetry publication, *The Witches' Brew,* tells the story of three witches who decide to test the effects of alcohol on sea creatures. The concoction awakens hateful racist feelings in certain animals and sparks a spate of destruction and killing. Pratt further explores themes of rac-

ism and warfare in his next volume, *The Titans.* This collection features two poems in the long form style for which Pratt would become very well known: "The Cachalot," which Darling described as "a sympathetic portrayal of the heroic qualities of a great sperm whale," and "The Great Feud," an account of a battle between land dwellers and creatures of the sea. *Dalhousie Review* contributor Harold Horwood characterized the former poem as "Pratt at his technical peak," affirming that it shows "a master of words at work." E. K. Brown wrote in his book *On Canadian Poetry* that "The Cachalot" is "the full, happy, exciting expression of an original temperament." Horwood described "The Great Feud" as "a strange blend of science, humour, allegory, and mythology, always with evocations of racial memories playing like fire-devils above . . . this fantastic Armageddon." While rating the poem as less readable than "The Cachalot," the critic labeled "The Great Feud" as "the most important of Pratt's poems" for its strong arguments against racism and war.

After 1927's *The Iron Door,* an ode inspired by the death of Pratt's mother, he published *The Roosevelt and the Antinoe* in 1930. This book is significant in Pratt's canon, as the protagonists of this narrative about a rescue at sea are all human—a first for the poet. Pratt continued to explore nautical themes with 1932's *Many Moods.* The poems in this collection, including "Sea-Gulls," "The Drag-Irons," and "The Ritual," examine both the splendor and the devastating power of the sea.

The catastrophic consequences of humankind's desire to chart and conquer large bodies of water is examined in Pratt's 1935 narrative poem, *The Titanic,* which relates the events surrounding one of the worst sea disasters in history. The *Titanic* was an ocean liner built to afford its passengers the utmost luxury while crossing great oceanic distances. It was also touted by its owner, the White Star Lines, as an indestructible vessel. On its maiden voyage in April of 1912, however, the *Titanic* collided with an iceberg in the North Atlantic and 1500 people drowned. Pratt's poem approaches the event from two perspectives, that of the ship and that of the iceberg. He chronicles the creation of each entity and follows their progress until their fateful meeting. While numerous songs, stories, and verses were written about the tragedy, Darling contends in *DLB* that "Pratt was the first to see in the story a potential conflict of titans—the irresistible ship and the immovable iceberg—and to fully exploit the cosmic ironies of the event."

Pratt returned to the use of animals as allegorical characters in *The Fable of the Goats and Other Poems* in 1937. The title poem is described by Darling as a "mock-epic" that deals with a racial conflict between two different breeds of goat. Also included in the volume are a number of shorter poems, including "The Prize Cat," "Silences,"

and "The Baritone," which serves as a sharp criticism of dictatorships.

In 1940, Pratt published his longest, and most controversial, poem, *Brebeuf and His Brethren,* for which he received a Governor-General's Award. The narrative recounts the martyrdom of a Jesuit, Jean de Brebeuf, and his fellow missionaries in the British colonies of North America. It was Brebeuf's task to bring Christianity to the Huron Indians, a Native American tribe, in the early 1600s. He was eventually killed by the Iroquois, another tribe, and he was later canonized as a saint in 1930. Pratt's epic examines the determination and moral conviction of both Brebeuf and the Native Americans he seeks to convert. Both parties are headstrong and prideful, willing to die for their beliefs and ways of life. It is this utter devotion to their faith that brings the Jesuits to their death, remaining in a territory that is hostile and unyielding to their evangelical efforts. Critics varyingly argued that the tone of Pratt's poem was proof of his religious beliefs, and numerous debates were initiated by the narrative. Darling interpreted the poem in *DLB* as a tribute to self-sacrifice and heroic discipline that goes beyond organized religion. As he stated: "It is difficult to believe that Pratt feels anything but admiration for the profundity of Brebeuf's faith." Calling Pratt a "storyteller to the end," Livesay remarked in *Canadian Literature* that *Brebeuf and His Brethren* is highlighted by "moments of poetic intensity."

Pratt issued three other narratives in the 1940s, and all three of these poems, *Dunkirk, They Are Returning,* and *Behind the Log,* deal with the overriding social concern of that decade: World War II. *Dunkirk* focuses on England and its status as a seafaring nation. *They Are Returning* is a tribute to the Canadian servicemen that served in the war and discusses the debt that the Canadian people owe to the men who fought for them. In *Behind the Log,* Pratt returns to two of his favorite themes: the sea and the concept of a group working toward a common goal. Much as the Jesuits of *Brebeuf* were united in their task, Pratt details how a convoy of ships in the North Atlantic consolidate to overcome a submarine attack. Northrop Frye wrote in his introduction to *The Collected Poems of E. J. Pratt* that "nothing is truer to the spirit of modern heroism than the story told in *Behind the Log.*"

In addition to the narratives, Pratt published the collection *Still Life and Other Verse* in 1943. This volume is significant for its inclusion of "The Truant," a poem that many consider to be one of the finest examples of Canadian verse. The poem was described by Darling as "Pratt's most forthright assertion of man's ability to survive and triumph in a hostile, mechanistic universe." The story deals with a man, identified as the Truant, who comes to clash with the Panjandrum, a great being who is the embodiment of the capricious power of nature. The Truant is confronted by the Panjandrum and ordered to sublimate himself before the god-like entity, threatening the mortal with great pain if he does not comply. The Truant refuses to acknowledge the entity's superiority, claiming that it was mortal man who defined the inner workings of the universe and thus set the parameters for the Panjandrum's power and lifespan. Pratt closes the poem with an affirmation of resistance in the face of adversity: "We who have learned to clench / Our fists and raise our lightless sockets / To morning skies after the midnight raids, / Yet cocked our ears to bugles on the barricades, / And in cathedral rubble found a way to quench / a dying thirst within a Galilean valley— / No! by the Rood, we will not join your ballet."

Critics praised "The Truant" for its moral on the resilience and strength of the human spirit and for Pratt's technical expertise in crafting the work. Livesay commented in *Canadian Literature* that the poem "represents Pratt at a high technical level, breaking away from the confines of rigid metre." And Frye, writing in his book *The Bush Gardens,* called "The Truant" "the greatest poem in Canadian literature" and labeled it as Pratt's "profoundest poem."

Pratt produced one more narrative poem, *Towards the Last Spike,* in 1952, and many critics consider it to be among his best. The work chronicles the efforts of Sir John A. MacDonald to complete the Pacific Railway across Canada. In addition to facing opposition from groups of people opposed to the conduit's construction, MacDonald and his supporters must also contend with the harsh terrain through which the railway will pass. Pratt describes the landscape as a reptilian creature fighting against those who would tame it: "A hybrid that the myths might have conceived, / But not delivered, as progenitor / Of crawling, gliding things upon the earth." Pratt again used the theme of a group united to illustrate how MacDonald's vision was realized despite the natural and mortal barriers. Glenn Clever, in his book *On E. J. Pratt,* stated that "the poem is a paean to achievers," and Darling noted in *DLB* that in *Toward the Last Spike* "Pratt articulates a political vision of Canadian unity."

Due to the thematic and prominent—though ambiguous—religious nature of Pratt's poetry, more attention was often paid to content than form. An article by John Sutherland in the *Northern Review,* published near the time of *Towards the Last Spike,* did much to change that. According to Darling, Sutherland's article created a new interest in Pratt's innovative use of meter and his other progressive forms. As examinations of Pratt's technique increased, so too did probes into his thematic motivation. Following his death in April of 1964, critics and academics further delved into the content of Pratt's poems. As Darling's 1990 *DLB* entry stated, "recent critics have begun to see Pratt's poetry in its historical and cultural contexts, and to examine the literary and philosophical sources of his ideas." This renewed interest in Pratt's work echoes Frye's summation of the poet in the introduction to *The Collected Poems of E. J. Pratt:* "He had the typical mark of originality: the power to make something poetic out of what everybody had just decided could no longer be poetic material."

BIOGRAPHICAL/CRITICAL SOURCES:

BOOKS

Brown, E. K., *On Canadian Poetry,* Tecumseh Press, 1977, pp. 143-63.

Canadian Writers: A Biographical Dictionary, revised edition, Ryerson, 1966.

Cassell's Encyclopaedia of World Literature, revised edition, Morrow, 1973.

Contemporary Literary Criticism, Volume 19, Gale, 1981, pp. 376-86.

Dictionary of Literary Biography, Volume 92: *Canadian Writers, 1890-1920,* Gale, 1990, pp. 287-97.

Djwa, Sandra, *E. J. Pratt: The Evolutionary Vision,* McGill-Queen's University Press, 1974.

The E. J. Pratt Symposium, edited by Glenn Clever, University of Ottawa Press, 1977.

Frye, Northrop, *Collected Poems of E. J. Pratt,* Macmillan (Canada), 1958.

Frye, *The Bush Garden: Essays on the Canadian Imagination,* House of Anansi Press, 1971, pp. 181-97.

Longman Companion to Twentieth Century Literature, Longman, 1970.

MacPherson, Jay, *Pratt's Romantic Mythology: The Witches' Brew, the Pratt Lecture, 1972,* Memorial University, 1972.

The New Century Handbook of English Literature, revised edition, Appleton, 1967.

The Oxford Companion to Canadian History and Literature, Oxford University Press, 1967.

Pacey, Desmond, *Ten Canadian Poets,* Ryerson, 1958, pp. 165-93.

Pitt, David G., *E. J. Pratt: The Truant Years, 1882-1927,* University of Toronto Press, 1984.

Pitt, *E. J. Pratt: The Master Years, 1927-1964,* University of Toronto Press, 1987.

Pratt, E. J., *Still Life and Other Verse,* Macmillan (Canada), 1943.

Pratt, *Towards the Last Spike: A Verse of the Struggle to Build the First Transcontinental from the Time of the Proposed Terms of Union with British Columbia, 1870, to the Hammering of the Last Spike in the Eagle Pass, 1885,* Macmillan (Canada), 1952.

Pratt, *E. J. Pratt: On His Life and Poetry,* edited by Susan Gingell, University of Toronto Press, 1983.

The Reader's Encyclopedia, 2nd edition, Crowell, 1965.

Sutherland, John, *The Poetry of E. J. Pratt: A New Interpretation,* Ryerson, 1956.

Wells, Henry W. and Carl F. Klinck, *Edwin J. Pratt: The Man and His Poetry,* Ryerson, 1947.

Wilson, Milton, *E. J. Pratt,* McClelland & Stewart, 1969.

PERIODICALS

Canadian Literature, winter, 1964, pp. 13-20, pp. 21-32; summer, 1965, pp. 33-42; winter, 1970, pp. 54-66; winter, 1973, pp. 50-64; autumn, 1976, pp. 32-41; winter, 1980, pp. 6-23; summer, 1983, pp. 48-72.

Dalhousie Review, summer, 1959, pp. 197-207.

Essays on Canadian Writing, winter, 1983-84, pp. 55-69; summer, 1984, pp. 142-51.

Northern Review, Nos. 3 and 4, 1952, pp. 36-64.

Queen's Quarterly, winter, 1978-79, pp. 578-94.

Tamarack Review, winter, 1958, pp. 74-80.

University of Toronto Quarterly, winter, 1984-85, pp. 127-47.

OBITUARIES:

PERIODICALS

New York Times, April 27, 1964.

—*Sketch by David M. Galens*

*   *   *

PURDY, A(lfred) W(ellington) 1918-

PERSONAL: Born December 30, 1918, in Wooler, Ontario, Canada; son of Alfred Wellington (a farmer) and Eleanor Louisa (Ross) Purdy; married Eurithe Mary Jane Parkhurst, November 1, 1941; children: Alfred Alexander. *Education:* Attended Trenton Collegiate Institute and Albert College. *Politics:* New Democratic Party, "i.e., labour or socialist." *Religion:* "Nil."

ADDRESSES: Home and office— R. R. 1, Ameliasburgh, Ontario K0K 1A0, Canada.

CAREER: Writer. Worked in factories until about 1960. Visiting associate professor at Simon Fraser University, Burnaby, British Columbia, 1971; writer-in-residence at Loyola University, Montreal, Quebec, 1973-74, University of Manitoba, Winnipeg, 1975-76, and University of Western Ontario, London, 1977-78. Conducted creative writing classes at Banff Center School of Fine Arts, summers, 1972-74. Has served on the Judging Committee of the Canada Council for junior and senior arts grants and the awards committee for the Governor General's literary awards. *Military service:* Royal Canadian Air Force, six years service during World War II.

MEMBER: League of Canadian Poets.

AWARDS, HONOURS: President's Medal, University of Western Ontario, 1964, for "The Country North of Belleville"; Canada Council fellowships, 1965, 1968-69, 1971; Governor General's Literary award, 1966, for *The Cariboo Horses,* and 1986, for *The Collected Poems of Al Purdy;* Centennial Medal, Canadian Federal Government, 1967, for outstanding service; Senior Literary award, Canada Council, 1973; A. J. M. Smith Award, 1974, for *Sex and Death;* elected to Academy of Canadian Writers, 1977; Jubilee Medal, 1978; Order of Canada, 1987.

WRITINGS:

POETRY

The Enchanted Echo, Clarke & Stuart, 1944.

Pressed on Sand, Ryerson, 1955.

Emu, Remember!, University of New Brunswick Press, 1956.

The Crafte So Longe to Lerne, Ryerson, 1959.

The Old Woman and the Mayflowers, Blue R, 1962.

Poems for All the Annettes, Contact Press, 1962, enlarged edition, Anansi, 1968, enlarged edition, 1973.

The Blur in Between: Poems, 1960-61, Emblem Books, 1962.

The Cariboo Horses, McClelland & Stewart, 1965.

North of Summer: Poems from Baffin Island, McClelland & Stewart, 1967.

The Winemaker's Beat: Etude, Fiddlehead Press, 1968.

Wild Grape Wine, McClelland & Stewart, 1968.

Spring Song, Fiddlehead Press, 1968.

Interruption, Fiddlehead Press, 1968.

Love in a Burning Building, McClelland & Stewart, 1970.

(With others) *Five Modern Canadian Poets,* edited by Eli Mandel, Holt Rinehart, 1970.

The Quest for Ouzo, M. Kerrigan Almey, 1971.

Selected Poems, McClelland & Stewart, 1972.

Hiroshima Poems, Crossing Press, 1972.

On the Bearpaw Sea, Blackfish Press, 1973.

Sex and Death, McClelland & Stewart, 1973.

Scott Hutcheson's Boat, Bailey and McKinnon, 1973.

In Search of Owen Roblin, McClelland & Stewart, 1974.

Sundance at Dusk, McClelland & Stewart, 1976.

The Poems of Al Purdy: A New Canadian Library Selection, McClelland & Stewart, 1976.

A Handful of Earth, Black Moss Press, 1977.

At Marsport Drugstore, Paget Press, 1977.

No Second Spring, Black Moss Press, 1977.

Moths in the Iron Curtain, Black Rabbit Press, 1977.

Being Alive: Poems 1958-78, McClelland & Stewart, 1978.

The Stone Bird, McClelland & Stewart, 1981.

Bursting into Song: An Al Purdy Omnibus, Fiddlehead Press, 1982.

Birdwatching at the Equator: The Galapagos Islands Poems, illustrated by Eurithe Purdy, Paget Press, 1982.

Piling Blood, McClelland & Stewart, 1984.

The Collected Poems of Al Purdy, edited by Russell Brown, McClelland & Stewart, 1986.

Two/Al Purdy, Colophon, 1990.

A Woman on the Shore, McClelland & Stewart, 1990.

EDITOR

The New Romans: Candid Canadian Opinions of the United States, St. Martin's, 1968.

Fifteen Winds: A Selection of Modern Canadian Poems, Ryerson, 1969.

Milton Acorn, *I've Tasted My Blood: Poems 1956-1968,* Ryerson, 1969.

Storm Warning: The New Canadian Poets, McClelland & Stewart, 1971.

Storm Warning II: The New Canadian Poets, McClelland & Stewart, 1976.

Andrew Suknaski, *Wood Mountain Poems,* Macmillan, 1976.

C. H. Gervais, *Into a Blue Morning: Poems Selected and New 1968-1981,* Hounslow Press, 1982.

OTHER

No Other Country (articles and essays), McClelland & Stewart, 1977.

Morning and It's Summer: A Memoir, Quandrant, 1983.

(With Charles Bukowski) *The Bukowski/Purdy Letters: A Decade of Dialogue 1964-1974,* edited by Seamus Cooney, Paget Press, 1983.

(Author of introduction) R. G. Everson, *Everson at Eighty,* Oberon, 1983.

The George Woodcock-Al Purdy Letters: Selected Correspondence 1964-1984, edited by George Galt, ECW Press, 1988.

A Splinter in the Heart (novel), McClelland & Stewart, 1990.

Cougar Hunter (essay), Phoenix Press, 1993.

The Margaret Laurence-Al Purdy Letters, McClelland & Stewart, 1993.

Work also represented in anthologies, including *Five Modern Canadian Poets,* edited by Eli Mandel, Holt, 1970; *The Norton Anthology of Modern Poetry,* edited by Richard Ellman and Robert O'Clair, Norton, 1973; *Twentieth Century Poetry and Poetics,* edited by Gary Geddes, Oxford University Press, 1973; *Canadian Poetry: The Modern Era,* edited by John Newlove, McClelland & Stewart, 1977. Contributor of original and adapted material to Canadian Broadcasting Corporation, both radio and television, 1956—, including *A Gathering of Days,* produced by CBC-Radio, 1954; *Point of Transfer,* produced on CBC-TV's "Shoestring Theatre"; and "Poems for Voices," 1970. Contributor of poems, reviews, articles, and essays to numerous publications, including *Canadian Literature,* *Fiddlehead, Saturday Night, Maclean's Magazine,* and *Canadian Forum.*

Selected poems have been translated into Russian.

Collections of Purdy's papers are housed at the Douglas Library, Queen's University, Kingston, Ontario, and the University of Saskatchewan Library, Saskatoon. The University of British Columbia Library, Vancouver, the Lakehead University Library, Thunder Bay, Ontario, and the Thomas Fisher Rare Book Library, University of Toronto, hold some manuscripts and drafts for Purdy's works.

SIDELIGHTS: Widely recognized as an originator of the modern vernacular poetic style, E. W. Purdy has earned a reputation as one of Canada's finest and most popular contemporary poets. Sometimes elegiac, often humorous, his writing reflects the rural Ontario milieu in which he has spent most of his life. Conveyed in an unaffected colloquial voice with humor and vigor, Purdy's poems typically begin with descriptions of common experiences then move to lyrical themes of transitoriness and transcendence. Purdy is also acknowledged as an influence on younger Canadian poets for being one of the first to employ native Canadian idiom and for his encouragement of others in his role as editor and teacher. Scholars and critics have recognized his contributions to Canadian literature with a variety of awards and prizes including Governor General's awards for his *The Cariboo Horses* (1965) and *The Collected Poems of Al Purdy* (1986).

Purdy was born in Wooler, Ontario, and, after his father's death in 1920, grew up with his mother in nearby Trenton. He attended public schools, including the Trenton Collegiate Institute, where his first published poem appeared in the school magazine, *Spotlight.* As a poet, Purdy is virtually self-taught. Unlike many other prominent Canadian writers such as Margaret Atwood and Irving Layton, he never earned a college degree. Instead he left school at age sixteen to travel aboard trans-Canadian freight trains, supporting his early writing with intermittent employment in fields as various as factory work and bootlegging. Purdy patterned his early poetry after Rudyard Kipling, G. K. Chesterton, Bliss Carman, and other traditional poets. Commentators regard most of Purdy's poetry from this period as conventional apprentice work, and many attribute its weaknesses to his isolation from other young writers. During the early 1950's Purdy began reading such modernist poets as W. H. Auden, Dylan Thomas, and Layton and started experimenting with open forms. By the time *The Crafte So Longe to Lerne* (1959) appeared, Purdy had begun to develop a less formal, more personal style. Purdy himself considers *Poems for All the Annettes* (1962) to be his first fully mature work. He was in his mid-forties when his seventh poetry collection, *The Cariboo*

Horses, established his reputation as a major author; thereafter, Purdy was able to earn his living as a writer and lecturer.

Many critics have lauded the strong sense of geographical location in Purdy's verse. Many of his poems are set in the area near Roblin Lake, Ameliasburg, Ontario, where he has lived for many years. This awareness of his physical surroundings also characterizes the poems that recount his extensive travels in other parts of Canada and in foreign countries, such as "Arctic Rhododendrons" and "Remembering Hiroshima." Critics observe that there is a rough, unfinished quality to much of Purdy's work. Although his poems are deliberately structured, Purdy's relaxed colloquial voice is capable of a wide range of expression. In such poems as "When I Sat Down to Play the Piano" and "Home-Made Beer," he demonstrates a self-deprecatory, earthy sense of humor. While "Love at Roblin Lake" evidences a similar comic sensibility, it also expresses a more serious yearning for mystical transcendence. In "Love at Roblin Lake" and "Archeology of Snow," this spiritual longing is related through sexual imagery. Purdy also evokes a form of transcendence by relating events of the past to the present, creating a feeling of historical continuity. In the poems "The Country North of Belleville" and "The Cariboo Horses" he alludes to the geographical, natural, and social history of rural Canada, connecting it to the present day. Mingled with the recurring themes of past and present is that of mortality, which, reviewers note, has become more pronounced in his later poetry. While Purdy's newest poems show less of his exuberant humor, they convey more powerfully the transcendent emotions common in his work.

For his *Collected Poems,* Purdy chose only those works that he felt merited preservation, including several previously uncollected poems as well as poems from twenty-one of his published volumes, arranged according to the decade in which they were composed. Only one selection in the *Collected Poems,* "Rattlesnake," was written before 1955. More generously represented are his breakthrough works from the 1960s, such as *The Cariboo Horses* and *Wild Grape Wine* (1968), as well as those he produced in the 1970s and 1980s, including *Sex and Death* (1973),

Being Alive (1978), *The Stone Bird* (1981), and *Piling Blood* (1984).

In reviews of *Collected Poems,* critics reaffirmed Purdy's status as one of Canada's most important poets. Although much of the commentary focuses on earlier, established poems, reviewers also commend Purdy's later work. According to critic George Galt, *The Collected Poems of Al Purdy* "is a rare accomplishment, because Purdy's poetry is unique, but also because few poets approaching old age exhibit his fresh imagination and still expanding insights."

BIOGRAPHICAL/CRITICAL SOURCES:

BOOKS

Contemporary Authors Autobiography Series, volume 17, Gale, 1993.

Contemporary Literary Criticism, Gale, Volume 3, 1975, Volume 6, 1976, Volume 14, 1980, Volume 50, 1988.

Contemporary Poets, St. James Press, 1991.

Dictionary of Literary Biography, Volume 88: *Canadian Writers, 1920-1959,* Gale, 1989.

Purdy, Al, *The Collected Poems of Al Purdy,* edited by Russell Brown, McClelland & Stewart, 1986.

PERIODICALS

Books in Canada, January-February, 1987, pp. 16-17.

Canadian Literature, spring, 1966; summer, 1969; winter, 1970; winter, 1972; spring, 1973; winter, 1973; summer, 1974.

Canadian Forum, September, 1965, p. 139; November, 1968; June, 1972, p. 42; January, 1975, p. 47; November, 1984, p. 38; August, 1985, p. 34; April, 1991, p. 30.

Journal of Canadian Studies, May, 1971.

Maclean's Magazine, January, 1971.

Modern Age, summer, 1969.

Poetry, June, 1969, p. 202.

Queen's Quarterly, winter, 1969; summer, 1987, p. 475.

Quill and Quire, May, 1981, p. 31; February, 1985, p. 39; May, 1987, p. 24; November 1990, p. 20.

Saturday Night, August, 1971; July, 1972; September, 1972; December, 1973.

University of Toronto Quarterly, fall, 1987, pp. 33-34.

Q-R

QUARRINGTON, Paul (Lewis) 1953-

PERSONAL: Born July 22, 1953, in Toronto, Ontario, Canada; son of Bruce Joseph (a psychologist) and Mary Ormiston (a psychologist; maiden name, Lewis) Quarrington; married Dorothie Bennie; children: Carson Lara, Flannery. *Education:* Attended University of Toronto, 1970-72. *Politics:* Green party of Canada. *Religion:* Anglican. *Avocational interests:* Fishing, weight lifting, competing in the Toronto Inquisition Pub Trivia League.

*ADDRESSES: Home—*221 Springdale Blvd., Toronto, Ontario, Canada M4C 1Z8. *Agent—*David Johnston, Peter Livingston Associates, 120 Carlton St., Suite 304, Toronto, Ontario, Canada M5A 4K2.

CAREER: Writer, 1975—. Musician with group "Joe Hall and the Continental Drift," 1973-83; The Book Cellar, Yorkville, Toronto, Ontario, salesclerk, 1983-86.

MEMBER: Trout Unlimited, Scarborough Fly & Bait Casting Association, Canadian Sportfishing Club.

AWARDS, HONOURS: Stephen Leacock Award for Humor, 1987, for *King Leary;* Governor's General Literary Award for English Language Fiction in Canda, 1990, for *Whale Music;* Genie Award for best screenplay, for *Perfectly Normal;* Periodical Distributors of Canada Authors Award.

WRITINGS:

The Service (novel), Coach House Press, 1978.
Home Game (novel), Doubleday, 1983.
The Life of Hope (novel), Doubleday, 1985.
King Leary (novel), Doubleday, 1987.
Hometown Heroes: On the Road With Canada's National Hockey Team (nonfiction), Doubleday, 1988.
Logan in Overtime (novel), Doubleday, 1988.
Whale Music (novel), Doubleday, 1989.

Civilization (novel) Random House, 1994.

Also author of screenplays, including *Perfectly Normal* (with Eugene Lipinski), 1990, *Camilla,* 1994, and *Whale Music* (with Richard J. Lewis, an adaptation of Quarrington's novel by the same name), Alliance productions, 1994. Author of two unpublished plays, *The Second,* 1982, and *the Invention of Poetry,* 1987.

SIDELIGHTS: Paul Quarrington's writing has been favourably compared to that of Robertson Davies, Henry David Thoreau, Herman Melville, and Francois Rabelais. Toronto *Globe and Mail* critic William French proclaimed Quarrington "a fresh and zany voice" in Canadian fiction, and his novel *The Life of Hope,* a "first-class farce of the absurd." *The Life of Hope* is narrated by a novelist named Paul who visits a professor friend near the town of Hope. Paul becomes engrossed with the history of the towns, founded by Joseph Benton Hope, a man described by French as a "randy leader of a utopian religious sect that believed in communal living and communal sex." The Perfectionists, as the sect was known, were nudists who later became rich from their fishing gear inventions.

Quarrington followed *The Life of Hope* with his novel *King Leary,* for which he received the Stephen Leacock Medal for Humor in 1987. Protagonist Percival Leary, an aging hockey great, leaves South Grouse Nursing Home to make a ginger ale commercial in Toronto. During the trip he experiences flashbacks of his life. *New York Times Book Review* contributor Ron Carlson observed that "what starts out to be the life story of the King of Ice changes into something more like a mystery." Quarrington begins "tormenting King Leary with memory," wrote Carlson, and "as the layers of memory peel away, Leary is wide-eyed at what he finds his life has been, and he moves toward atonement." Leary remembers his early years learning how to play hockey at the Brothers of St.

Albans Reformatory, where the monks' motto is "To keep a boy out of hot water, put him on ice," and where he met his friend and rival, Manny Oz. Leary repeatedly recalls the household accident that ended his own career, and the uncertain circumstances of Manny's death and funeral fifty years ago. Leary's discoveries—about himself, the death of Manny, and of Leary's son—"make this novel rueful and zany, full of wonder and regret," Carlson concluded.

According to an article in the *New York Times Book Review,* the voice of Leary was inspired by the colorful speech of the late hockey star and vice president of the Toronto Maple Leafs, Francis Michael "King" Clancy. In a phone interview for the *New York Times Book Review,* Quarrington said that the process of writing *King Leary* was similar to that of a character actor learning his role. As he sat down to write each morning, he found himself "a little more like Percival Leary—irritable, cantankerous, more likely to lash out." Quarrington is also the author of *Hometown Heroes,* a nonfiction book about his experiences on the road to the 1988 Olympic Games with the Canadian hockey team.

Quarrington's 1988 novel, *Logan in Overtime,* also takes hockey as its milieu. A one-time NHL goalie, Logan has returned to his home town where he plays for what Doug Bell, writing in *Quill and Quire,* called "a dubious team in a dubious league," and is often drunk. Bell praised the book, asserting that Quarrington's fiction shines when it spotlights "the hilarity and heroism of eccentricity and failure."

Quarrington followed *Logan in Overtime* with *Whale Music,* a novel whose protagonist, Desmond Howell, a reclusive overweight, aging-rock star, bears some resemblance to the Beach Boy's Brian Wilson, according to Justin Smallbridge's *Maclean's* review. The novel won Quarrington a Governor's General Award for fiction, and as Smallbridge reported, it tells the story of the influence on Howell and his "magnum opus, a symphony for sea creatures called *Whale Music*" by Claire, a Toronto runaway with whom he falls in love.

Quarrington adapted the novel for the screen with writer, Richard J. Lewis, during a five-year period that Quarrington spent writing mostly movies. Remarking in *Maclean's* on this period and the difference between writing movies and screenplays, Quarrington stated that for him, screenplays are akin to concertos, rather than symphonies: "Beethoven, Brahms and those other people, they would never say, 'Well I only write symphonies.' But they saved that part of them that was most important for the symphonies. I feel a little bit that way. I can save what's most important for the novels. . . .[Screenplays] are important; they're just not symphonies."

Among Quarrington's screenplay credits is *Camilla,* a movie about a young musician who meets an aging violinist, played by the late Jessica Tandy in her last film role. In his *Maclean's* review, Brian D. Johnson called the screenplay "quirky" and notes that its "whimsical tone—and its concern with the theme of musical ambition—is highly reminiscent of Quarrington's *Whale Music.*"

Fittingly, Quarrington's next published novel concerns the industry he worked in for half a decade. *Civilization* tells the story of Thom Moss, a former western movies star of the 1920s. Moss narrates his rags-to-riches story from his prison cell, where he is imprisoned for a crime not immediately apparent to the reader. The novel, stated Carole Giangrande in *Books in Canada,* is "a wild and woolly look at our confusion of image and reality" which takes "dead aim at . . .our obsessions with media and stardom." Peter Oliva, in his *Quill and Quire* review, called it "a thoroughly engaging novel, full of 1920s vocabulary and Shakespearean street slang" and "a raucous adventure along a tale well told."

Commenting on the author's efforts as a novelist and a screenwriter, Smallbridge stated, "Quarrington tempers a mordant wit with sympathy and affection." He added that his "ability to inhabit the souls of [his] protagonists is what initially attracted film-makers to his work. 'Paul Quarrington has an unparalleled ability with character and voice,' says Steven DeNure, president of production for Alliance. . . . Nobody creates characters like his. They're quirky, they're unique, and there's been some tragedy in their lives.' "

BIOGRAPHICAL/CRITICAL SOURCES:

PERIODICALS

Books in Canada, November, 1994, p. 48.
Globe and Mail (Toronto), September 21, 1985; October 22, 1988.
Maclean's, October 3, 1994, p. 52-53; November 28, 1994, p. 86.
New York Times Book Review, May 1, 1988.
Quill and Quire, Februrary, 1990, p. 24; October, 1994, p. 33.*

*   *   *

REANEY, James (Crerar) 1926-

PERSONAL: Born September 1, 1926, in South Easthope, Ontario, Canada; son of James Nesbitt and Elizabeth (Crerar) Reaney; married Colleen Thibaudeau (a poet), December 29, 1951; children: James Stewart, Susan Alice. *Education:* University of Toronto, B.A., 1948, M.A., 1949, Ph.D., 1958.

ADDRESSES: Office—Department of English, University of Western Ontario, London, Ontario, Canada N6A 2J9. *Agent*—John Miller, Cultural Support Services 206, Gerrard St. East, Toronto, Ontario, Canada M5A 2E6.

CAREER: Playwright, poet, and novelist. University of Manitoba, Winnipeg, Canada, faculty member, 1949-57, assistant professor of English, 1957-60; University of Western Ontario, London, Canada, associate professor, 1960-63, professor of English, 1964—. Founder and editor of *Alphabet,* 1960-71; founder of Listener's Workshop, London, 1966.

MEMBER: Association of Canadian University Teachers of English, Canadian Association of University Teachers, Canadian Theatre Co-op, League of Canadian Poets, Royal Society of Canada (fellow).

AWARDS, HONOURS: Governor General's Award, 1949, for *The Red Heart,* 1958, for *The Suit of Nettles,* 1969, for *The Killdeer and Other Plays,* and for *Twelve Letters to a Small Town;* Massey Award, and Governor General's Award, both 1960, both for *The Killdeer;* Chalmers Outstanding Play Award finalist, 1973, for *Sticks and Stones,* and 1975, for *Handcuffs;* Chalmers Outstanding Play Award, 1974, for *The Saint Nicholas Hotel;* Officer of the Order of Canada, 1975; honorary D.Litt., Carleton University, 1975.

WRITINGS:

POETRY

The Red Heart (also see below), McClellan & Stewart, 1949.
A Suit of Nettles, Macmillan, 1958, 2nd edition, 1975.
Twelve Letters to a Small Town, Ryerson, 1962.
The Dance of Death at London, Ontario, Alphabet Press, 1963.
Poems (includes "The Red Heart" and "Twelve Letters to a Small Town"), edited by Germaine Warkentin, New Press, 1972.
Selected Longer Poems, edited by Warkentin, Porcepic, 1976.
Selected Shorter Poems, edited by Warkentin, Porcepic, 1976.
Performance Poems, Moonstone Press, 1990.

PLAYS

Night-Blooming Cereus (one-act libretto; broadcast as radio play, 1959), produced in Toronto, Canada, 1960.
The Killdeer (three-act), produced in Toronto, 1960, revised version, (two-act), produced in Vancouver, Canada, 1970.
(And director) *One-Man Masque* (one-act), produced in Toronto, 1960.

The Easter Egg (three-act), produced in Hamilton, Ontario, Canada, 1962.
Names and Nicknames (children's; produced in Winnipeg, Canada, 1963), published in *Nobody in the Cast,* edited by Robert Barton and others, Longmans, 1969, published alone, Talonbooks, 1978.
(With Alfred Kunz) *Let's Make a Carol: A Play with Music for Children,* Waterloo Music Co., 1965.
(And director) *Aladdin and the Magic Lamp* (children's with marionettes), produced in London, Ontario, 1965.
(And director) *Apple Butter* (children's with marionettes; produced in London, 1965), Talonbooks, 1978.
(And director) *Little Red Riding Hood* (children's with marionettes), produced in London, 1965.
The Sun and the Moon (three-act), produced in London, 1965.
(And director) *Listen to the Wind* (three-act; produced in London, 1966), Talonbooks, 1972.
Ignoramus (children's; produced in London, 1966), Talonbooks, 1978.
Three Desks (two-act), produced in London, 1967.
The Canada Tree, produced in Morrison Island, Ontario, 1967.
(And director) *Geography Match* (children's; produced in London, 1967), Talonbooks, 1978.
Colours in the Dark (produced in Stratford, Ontario, 1967), Talonbooks-Macmillan (Canada), 1970, revised edition, 1971.
(And director) *Genesis,* produced in London, 1968.
Don't Sell Mr. Aesop, produced in London, 1968.
Sticks and Stones (part one of "The Donnellys" trilogy; produced in Toronto, 1973), published in *Canadian Theatre Review,* spring, 1974.
The Saint Nicholas Hotel (part two of "The Donnellys" trilogy), produced in Toronto, 1974.
Handcuffs (part three of "The Donnellys" trilogy), produced in Toronto, 1975.
(With John Beckwith) *All the Bees and All the Keys,* Porcepic, 1976.
(With Marty Gervais) *Baldoon* (two-act; produced in Toronto, 1976), Porcupine's Quill, 1977.
The Dismissal (produced in Toronto, 1977), Porcepic, 1978.
Wacousta, produced in Toronto, 1977.
At the Big Carwash (puppet play), produced on tour with Caravan Stage Company, 1979.
King Whistle!, produced in Stratford, 1980.
Antler River, produced at the Grand Theatre, London, 1983.
Gyroscope, produced in Toronto, 1983.
I, the Parade, produced at the University of Waterloo, 1983.

The Canadian Brothers, produced at the University of Calgary, 1984.

Imprecations—The Art of Swearing, produced in London, 1984.

Traps, produced in London, 1984.

Also author of the play *Cloud Shadows.* Author of unpublished and unproduced plays, including *The Rules of Joy, The Bacchae,* and *The Shivaree.*

PLAY COLLECTIONS

The Killdeer and Other Plays (contains *Night-Blooming Cereus, The Killdeer, One-Man Masque,* and *The Sun and the Moon,*), Macmillan (Canada), 1962.

Masks of Childhood (contains *The Killdeer* [revised version], *The Easter Egg,* and *Three Desks,*), edited by Brian Parker, New Press, 1972.

Apple Butter and Other Plays for Children (contains *Names and Nicknames, Apple Butter, Ignoramus,* and *Geography Match*), Talonbooks, 1973.

The Donnellys: A Trilogy, Porcepic, Part 1: *Sticks and Stones,* 1975, Part 2: *The Saint Nicholas Hotel,* 1976, Part 3: *Handcuffs,* 1976.

RADIO PLAYS

Poet and City—Winnipeg (broadcast on *Wednesday Night,* Canadian Broadcasting Corporation [CBC], 1960), edited by Eli Mandel and Jean-Guy Pilon, Ryerson Press, 1962.

The Journals and Letters of William Blake, broadcast on *Wednesday Night,* CBC, 1961.

Wednesday's Child, broadcast on *Wednesday Night,* CBC, 1962.

Canada Dash, Canada Dot: Across (Part 1), broadcast on CBC, 1965.

Canada Dash, Canada Dot: The Line Up and Down (Part 2), broadcast on CBC, 1966.

Canada Dot (Part 3), broadcast on CBC, 1967.

OPERA LIBRETTI

(With Beckwith) *Crazy to Kill,* Guelph Spring Festival, 1990.

(With Harry Sanes) *Serinette,* Music at Sharon, 1991.

OTHER

The Boy with an "R" in his Hand (juvenile novel), illustrated by Leo Rampen, Macmillan (Canada), 1965.

Aspects of Nineteenth Century Ontario, edited by F. H. Armstrong, University of Toronto Press, 1974.

Fourteen Barrels from Sea to Sea (travel diary), Porcepic, 1977.

Take the Big Picture (juvenile fiction), illustrated by Barbara Di Lella, Porcupine's Quill, 1986.

Also author of the novel *Afternoon Moon.* Adaptor of *The Revenger's Tragedy.* Collaborator with composer John Beckwith on operas and other musical settings of text. Also contributor of poems, stories, and critical articles to various periodicals, including *Atlantic Monthly, Canadian Forum, Canadian Short Stories, Canadian Theatre Review, Canadian Art, Globe, Contemporary Verse, Black Moss, Canadian Poetry, Queen's Quarterly,* and *Canadian Literature.*

ADAPTATIONS: Reaney's play *One-Man Masque* was adapted by Ron Cameron and published as *Masque* by Simon & Pierre, 1975.

WORK IN PROGRESS: Plays on Emily Bronte and Chatterton; a book on the founding of national theatre; a Donnellys sourcebook; an anthology of material from *Alphabet; Alice Through the Looking Glass,* for Stratford Festival; *Taptoo,* an opera for Toronto Historical Board at Old Fort York.

SIDELIGHTS: English professor James Reaney's long and varied writing career encompasses everything from poetry and plays to children's books. Initially Reaney concentrated on writing poetry, producing four collections of poems between 1949 and 1963. Then, in the early 1960s, he began focussing on play writing, composing over thirty plays since first beginning. Eventually Reaney expanded his writing oeuvre to children's books. "The length of Reaney's career, and the breadth and variety of his achievement mark him as a leading figure in the Canadian theatre," claims John H. Astington in the *Oxford Companion to Canadian Theatre.*

Reaney's interest in theatre began when he was in high school. This interest was fostered by the establishment of the Stratford Festival in his area in 1953. He has written over twenty-five diverse plays, including plays for children, which "liberated Reaney's instinct for fun and energy in the theatre," relates Astington. In 1978 Talonbooks reissued several of Reaney's children's plays, *Apple Butter, Geography Match, Ignoramus,* and *Names and Nicknames,* along with a teacher's guide, to promote the teaching of drama as literature. "As theatre, these plays have been enjoyed by both child and adult audiences. The scope for creativity and imagination on the part of the actors, the emphasis on rhythm, chorus, movement and mime, and the fast-paced, zany action all add up to a lively theatrical experience. . . . It is guaranteed that everyone will enjoy them," comments Anne Bradin in *In Review.*

In addition to writing plays for children, Reaney has also written books for children. His first novel, *The Boy with an "R" in His Hand,* illustrates the divided loyalties and conflicts during the Mackenzie Rebellion of 1837 and the effect of this division on two brothers who align with opposing sides. Commenting on its 1980 reprint, Terence

Scully writes in *Canadian Children's Literature* that *The Boy with an "R" in His Hand* "has already served a generation well with its spirited fantasy, and could very effectively be read aloud to a third generation."

In the fall of 1976, Reaney took a sabbatical from the University of Western Ontario and accompanied a professional Canadian drama group as they toured Canada with his play *The Donnellys: A Trilogy.* The subsequent record of his impressions and of the experiences of the NDWT Company players while on this tour are chronicled in his book *Fourteen Barrels from Sea to Sea.* Dubbing it a "travel book" for lack of a better term, Reaney once remarked that it is actually a commentary on the state of drama in Canada today.

Reaney has said: "Interviewers often ask me if I'm postmodern or do I deconstruct. I'm afraid I'm too naive for that. What I've ended up doing is shamelessly celebrating my love for my portion of the province of Ontario, the same bailiwick as Alice Munro's—Southwestern Ontario. She has all that lies north of Exeter, I've got everything south of that dear prosperous town.

"I'm particularly proud of the opera libretti because our music theatre tradition was incredibly thin when I started in 1944 to write a libretto for my favorite composer, John Beckwith. I've been called the Father of Community Theatre in Canada; I don't know if I want to be a father, but it has been fun going into towns and, at their invitation, livening things up with a play they help me write. In my hometown, Stratford, my proudest achievement along these lines was being asked to write a play—a musical comedy—for the centenary of my high school; *King Whistle.* My other obsession is the Brontes, and Beckwith and I want to do a grand opera on Branwell Bronte and his visionary kingdom of Angria—sort of Tales of Hoffman only it's the Bronte children. Of course, the Brontes lived for years on the moors of Southwestern Ontario."

BIOGRAPHICAL/CRITICAL SOURCES:

BOOKS

Anthony, Geraldine, *Stage Voices: Twelve Canadian Playwrights Talk about Their Lives and Works,* Doubleday, pp. 139-64.
Benson, Eugene, and L. W. Conolly, editors, *Oxford Companion to Canadian Theatre,* Oxford University Press, 1989.
Contemporary Authors Autobiography Series, Volume 15, Gale, 1992.
Contemporary Literary Criticism, Volume 13, Gale, 1980.
Dictionary of Literary Biography, Volume 68: *Canadian Writers, 1920-1959, First Series,* Gale, 1988.
Dragland, Stan, *Approaches to the Work of James Reaney,* ECW Press, 1983.
Lee, Alvin, *James Reaney,* Twayne, 1968.
Reaney, James Stewart, *James Reaney,* Sage, 1977.
Rubin, Don, and Alison Crammer-Byng, editors, *Canada's Playwrights: A Biographical Guide,* Canadian Theatre Review Publications, 1980.
Woodman, Ross, *James Reaney,* McClelland & Stewart (Toronto), 1971.

PERIODICALS

Books for Young People, April 1988, p. 7.
Canadian Children's Literature, Number 23/24, 1981, p. 98.
Canadian Literature, autumn/winter, 1989, pp. 251-53.
In Review, February, 1980, pp. 54-55.

*   *   *

RICCI, Nino   1959-

PERSONAL: Surname is pronounced *"ree*-chee"; born August 23, 1959, in Leamington, Ontario, Canada; son of Virginio (a farmer) and Amelia (a farmer; maiden name, Ingratta) Ricci. *Education:* York University, B.A., 1981; Concordia University, M.A., 1987; attended University of Florence, 1988-89.

ADDRESSES: Home—139 Wolseley St., Toronto, Ontario, Canada M6J 1K3. *Office*—c/o Writers' Union of Canada, 24 Ryerson Ave., Toronto, Ontario, Canada M5P 2P3. *Agent*—Irene Skolnick, Curtis Brown Ltd., 10 Astor Place, New York, NY 10003.

CAREER: Writer. Ogun State Education Board, Nigeria, secondary school teacher, 1981-83; Concordia University, Montreal, Quebec, creative writing, composition, and Canadian literature instructor, 1986-88; Berlitz Language Schools, Montreal, English and Italian instructor, 1987.

MEMBER: PEN, Canadian PEN Center (director, 1990—), Amnesty International (coordinator of human rights education committee, 1987-88).

AWARDS, HONOURS: F. G. Bressani Prize from Italian Cultural Center Society, Governor General's Literary Award from Canada Treasury Board of Canada Secretariat, Winifred Holtby Memorial Prize from Royal Society of Literature, W. H. Smith/*Books in Canada* First Novel Award, and Betty Trask Award from Society of Authors, all 1990, for *Lives of the Saints.*

WRITINGS:

Lives of the Saints, Cormorant Books, 1990, published in the United States as *The Book of Saints,* Knopf, 1991.
In a Glass House, McClelland & Stewart, 1993.

Contributor to books, including *The Moosehead Anthology: A Collection of Contemporary Writing,* DC Books,

1989; *Ricordi: Things Remembered,* edited by C. D. Minni, Guernica Editions, 1989. Contributor to periodicals, including *Saturday Night, Canadian Journal of Political and Social Theory, Fiddlehead,* and *Toronto Life.*

SIDELIGHTS: First-generation Canadian Nino Ricci, author of the award-winning novel *Lives of the Saints,* told Richard E. Nicholls in *New York Times Book Review* that in his writing he wants to portray "the experience of being an immigrant in the modern world." Ricci's parents emigrated from Italy to Canada, but regaled their son with stories of their native village and faithfully observed Italian culture. During his interview with Nicholls, Ricci explained that "being raised in a tight-knit Italian community in Canada, I grew up with a sense of village dynamics." As a secondary school teacher in Nigeria for two years, Ricci found further inspiration for his novel. He told Nicholls that living in this "energetic and flamboyant land" was "like going back to an older Italy. In its strong mix of religion and folk beliefs it gave me a sense of how life might transpire in the small world of a village. My image of life in [the fictional Italian village of] Valle del Sole had at least part of its origins in Africa."

Lives of the Saints, which earned Canada's prestigious Governor General's Literary Award, is set in a small, theistic Italian village in 1960. Seven-year-old narrator Vittorio Innocente and his mother Cristina Innocente live alone in Valle del Sole while Vittorio's father prepares a home for them in Canada. Lonely and unhappy with her marriage, Cristina finds comfort with a non-Italian, but their affair is revealed when she is bitten by a snake during a rendezvous. Outraged by her debauchery, Cristina's fellow villagers believe the snake bite signals her disfavour with God; mother and son become outcasts in the village. Cristina fights the vicious insults in a brazen manner, but naive Vittorio is harassed and beaten by his peers. Because of their neighbors' unforgiving attitudes, they are eventually forced to flee to Canada. *Listener* contributor, Steven Amidon, commented that the novel's "pagan atmosphere adds drama and poignancy both to Cristina's transgression and Vittorio's fall from grace, showing them to be innocents in a world which long ago lost any resemblance to Eden. Their flight from this weedy garden is as fraught and terrifying as expulsion from paradise must be." Barbara Grizzuti Harrison concluded in *New York Times Book Review* that *Lives of the Saints* is "an extraordinary story—brooding and ironic, suffused with yearning, tender and lucid and gritty."

In a Glass House, Ricci's next novel, is the second installment in what Ricci plans will be a trilogy about Vittorio Innocente. The novel begins with Vittorio's arrival in Canada with his baby half-sister—the product of his mother's illicit affair in Italy. His mother has died in childbirth on the passage to Canada, and his father is revealed as a bitter

and angry man, who is part of an immigrant farming community. In an attempt to grow things in the harsh, Canadian climate, he is forever building greenhouses, which become the metaphorical glass houses of the title.

Vittorio struggles to fit in and to love his father and his sister (who is rejected by his father and eventually adopted by a Canadian family). He teaches for a while in Africa, returns to Canada, and, at the end of the novel, confronts his father's death. John Melmoth's review in *Times Literary Supplement* noted that "Vittorio's experience is, in part, representative of the 'subtle' embitterment of the migrant, forever out of place. He is trapped between antithesis: between . . . self-conscious aloofness and the need to belong . . . between Italy and Canada; resistance and acquiescence; dark and light."

Writing in *Maclean's,* Lawrence Scanlan declared "the operative word in the novel is 'humiliation' " and noted that the novel "explores an immigrant's pain as a doctor explores a wound. It is [a] far more personal [novel], even autobiographical than its predecessor." Melmoth claimed that "*In a Glass House* is a novel of great power, but it is almost entirely devoid of any lighter moments."

Yet Scanlan asserted that "Ricci's great gift is to capture, sometimes in exquisite prose, the texture of people and place," and David Prosser, who reviewed the book for *Quill and Quire,* commented: "Vittorio's self-discovery is one in which we all share: it is as if, in focusing a microscope on an unpromising slide, we had caught a glimpse of the human soul." Also praising Ricci's "brilliant descriptive powers," *Spectator* contributor Celestria Noel dubbed Ricci "one of Canada's best novelists to appear for a long time."

BIOGRAPHICAL/CRITICAL SOURCES:

PERIODICALS

Books in Canada, December, 1992, pp. 10-12.
Listener, September 27, 1990, p. 33; October 4, 1993, p. 52.
Maclean's, February 4, 1991, p. 63; October 4, 1993.
New York Times Book Review, June 2, 1991, p. 7.
Quill and Quire, October, 1993, p. 26.
Spectator, July 30, 1994, p. 28.
Studies in Canadian Literature, volume 18, number 2, 1993, pp. 168-84.
Times Literary Supplement, August 12, 1994, p. 22

*   *   *

RICHARDSON, John   1796-1852

PERSONAL: Born October 4, 1796, in Queenston, Ontario, Canada; son of Robert Richardson, a medical officer in the British army, and Madeleine Askin Richardson; died May 12, 1852, in New York, N Y, United States; married Jane Marsh, 1825 (died), married Maria Drayson, 1832 (died, 1845). *Education:* Educated in Detroit and Amherstburg.

CAREER: Reported on rebellions in Upper and Lower Canada for *The Times,* London, 1838. Founded and edited weekly newspapers: *The New Era; or Canadian Chronicle,* in Brockville, Ontario, 1841-1842; *Canadian Loyalist or Spirit of 1812,* in Kingston, Ontario, 1843-44; and *Weekly Expositor,* in Montreal, Quebec, 1846. Superintendent of police on the Welland Canal, 1845. *Military service:* Fought in the War of 1812 as a gentleman volunteer in the British army; prisoner of war in the United States, 1813-14, granted commission in the British army and stationed in the West Indies, 1816-18, returned to England as a half-pay lieutenant, fought in Carlist War, in Spain, 1835-37.

WRITINGS:

(Published anonymously) *Tecumseh; or, The Warrior of the West* (narrative poem), R. Glynn, 1828.

Ecarte; or, The Salons of Paris (novel), H. Colburn, 1829; revised edition published by Dewitt & Davenport, 1851.

Frascati's; or, Scenes in Paris (novel), Colburn & Bentley, 1830.

Kensington Gardens in 1830: A Satirical Trifle (novel), Marsh & Miller, 1830.

Wacousta; or, The Prophecy (novel), T. Cadell, 1832; revised edition published by Dewitt & Davenport, 1851; modern critical edition published as *Wacousta, or The Prophecy: A Tale of the Canadas,* edited by Douglas Cronk, Carleton University Press, 1987.

Journal of the Movements of the British Legion (nonfiction), E. Wilson, 1836; revised edition published as *Journal of the Movements of the British Legion, with Strictures on the Course of Conduct Pursued by Lieutenant-General Evans* (nonfiction), Simpkin, Marshall, 1837.

Personal Memoirs of Major Richardson (memoir), Armour & Ramsay, 1838.

The Canadian Brothers; or, The Prophecy Fulfilled (novel), Armour & Ramsay, 1840; revised edition published as *Matilda Montgomerie; or, The Prophecy Fulfilled,* Dewitt & Davenport, 1851.

War of 1812 (history), [Brockville, Ontario], 1842; enlarged edition, edited by Alexander Clark Casselman, published by Musson, 1902.

Correspondence (Submitted to Parliament) between Major Richardson . . . and the Honorable Dominick Daly (letters), Donoghue & Mantz, 1846.

Eight Years in Canada (autobiography), Cunningham, 1847.

The Guards in Canada; or, The Point of Honor (autobiography), Cunningham, 1848.

A Trip to Walpole Island and Port Sarnia (travel), published in *The Literary Garland,* January, 1849; published as *Tecumseh and Richardson; The Story of a Trip to Walpole Island and Port Sarnia,* edited by A. H. U. Colquhoun, Ontario Book, 1924.

The Monk Knight of St. John (novel), Dewitt & Davenport, 1850.

Hardscrabble; or, The Fall of Chicago (novel), Dewitt & Davenport, 1851.

Wau-Nan-Gee; or, The Massacre at Chicago (novel), Long, 1852.

Westbrook, The Outlaw; or, The Avenging Wolf (novel), Dewitt & Davenport, 1853.

Major John Richardson's Short Stories (short stories), edited by David Beasley, Theytus, 1985.

Contributor to magazines and newspapers including *Copway's American Indian, Graham's Magazine, The Literary Garland, New Era, New Monthly Magazine,* and *Sunday Mercury.*

ADAPTATIONS: Wacousta; or, The Prophecy was adapted for the stage soon after its publication and *Wacousta!,* a melodrama by John Reaney based on Richardson's novel, was published in 1979.

SIDELIGHTS: Largely ignored during his life by critics and the reading public, John Richardson is now regarded as one of Canada's major pre-Confederation novelists. His most successful work, *Wacousta; or, The Prophecy* (1832), is a story of revenge and frontier warfare reminiscent of James Fenimore Cooper.

Born in Queenston, Upper Canada, Richardson spent most of his youth in Amherstburg, Upper Canada, where his father was a medical officer with the British army at Fort Malden. At the age of fifteen, Richardson joined the British army as a gentleman volunteer for service in the War of 1812. Captured after the British defeat at the Battle of Moraviantown in 1813, he spent a year in Kentucky as a prisoner of war. He gained a commission in the British army after his release then spent a short time in England before being posted to the West Indies, where he served two years with the Queen's Regiment, returning to Europe in 1818 as a half-pay officer. In 1828, Richardson anonymously published *Tecumseh; or, The Warrior of the West,* a narrative poem, which was followed by three novels concerning English and French society—*Ecarte; or, The Salons of Paris, Frascati's; or, Scenes in Paris* (1830), and *Kensington Gardens in 1830: A Satirical Trifle* (1830). Following the publication and critical and popular success of *Wacousta* in 1832, Richardson returned to active military service in 1835 and fought in the Carlist War in Spain, an experience about which he wrote several memoirs. In

1838, Richardson returned to Canada to cover political events for the London *Times*. His political opinions, however, conflicted with those of the *Times*'s editors and he was soon released from his contract. Remaining in Canada, Richardson attempted several unsuccessful ventures in newspaper publishing throughout the 1840s and wrote *The Canadian Brothers; or, The Prophecy Fulfilled* (1840), a sequel to *Wacousta* and *War of 1812* (1842), a history of the war. Neither work sparked public interest and Richardson suffered further misfortune in 1845 when his second wife died and he lost his commission as superintendent of police on the Welland Canal. He subsequently published two volumes of autobiography, and then left Canada in 1849 for New York City, where he published his last works—*The Monk Knight of St. John* (1850), a story of the Crusades, and three frontier adventure novels.

Set on the North American frontier, Richardson's major works deal primarily with war and revenge. *Wacousta,* for instance, draws on Chief Pontiac's attacks in 1763 on the English forts at Detroit and Michilimackinac for its historical background; the War of 1812 provides the backdrop for *The Canadian Brothers;* while *Hardscrabble; or, The Fall of Chicago* and *Wau-Nan-Gee; or, The Massacre at Chicago* center on the 1812 massacre at Fort Dearborn. Combining elements from the gothic and romance genres, *Wacousta* centers on the story of Reginald Morton, also known as Wacousta, who—driven by revenge against Colonel de Haldimar, the man who betrayed his trust and stole his lover—disavows his European heritage, allies himself with the Native Americans, and seeks to destroy Haldimar and his family. Though best known for his adventure novels of the North American frontier, Richardson also wrote several works set outside North America. *Ecarte* and *Frascati's,* for instance, depict moral corruption in the gambling halls of Paris, while *The Monk Knight of St. John,* a love story set during the crusades, ranges from the Holy Land to France.

With the exception of *Wacousta,* most critics have derided Richardson's other novels as potboilers. Desmond Pacey, for example, vehemently attacked *The Monk Knight of St. John,* arguing that Richardson's depiction of "sexual aberrations" pushes the novel dangerously close to mere pornography. Critical discussions of *Wacousta* have centered on Richardson's examination of revenge, identity, and the dichotomies between civilization and savagery, reason and passion, and love and hatred. As Leslie Monkman has noted, Richardson died penniless and bitter that his countrymen failed to acknowledge him as a man of letters. "A century later [however] he . . . is now regarded by many as the major anglophone novelist of pre-Confederation Canada." He died in New York City in 1852.

BIOGRAPHICAL/CRITICAL SOURCES:

BOOKS

Ballstady, Carl, *Major John Richardson. A Selection of Reviews and Criticism,* Lawrence M. Lande Foundation, 1972.

Beasley, David, *The Canadian Don Quixote,* Porcupine's Quill, 1977.

Dexter, Gail, editor, *Canadian Literature: Surrender or Revolution,* Steel Rail, 1978, pp. 13-25.

Duffy, Dennis, *John Richardson and His Works,* ECW Press.

Duffy, Dennis, *A Tale of Sad Reality: John Richardson's Wacousta,* ECW Press, 1993.

Duffy, Dennis, *A World under Sentence: John Richardson and the Canadian Frontier,* ECW Press, 1995.

McGregor, Gaile, *The Wacousta Syndrome,* University of Toronto Press, 1985.

Morley, William, *A Bibliographical Study of Major John Richardson,* Bibliographical Society of Canada, 1973.

Moss, John, editor, *The Canadian Novel: Beginnings,* New Canada, 1980, pp. 47-59, 60-9.

Moss, editor, *Future Indicative: Literary Theory and Canadian Literature,* University of Ottawa Press, 1987, pp. 185-94.

Riddell, William Renwick, *John Richardson,* Ryerson Press, 1923.

Richardson, John, *Personal Memoirs of Major Richardson,* Armour & Ramsay, 1838.

Richardson, *Eight Years in Canada,* Cunningham, 1847.

Richardson, *The Guards in Canada; or, The Point of Honor,* Cunningham, 1848.

Ross, Catherine Sheldrick, editor, *Recovering Canada's First Novelist: Proceedings from the John Richardson Conference,* Porcupine's Quill, 1984.

PERIODICALS

American Review of Canadian Studies, autumn, 1992, pp. 363-85.

Black Moss, spring, 1976, pp. 41-74.

Canadian Literature, autumn, 1959, pp. 20-31; winter, 1960, pp. 47-56; No. 81, 1979, pp. 24-36; summer, 1979, pp. 86-94; fall-winter, 1993, pp. 153-55; summer, 1994, pp. 151-52.

Essays on Canadian Writing, winter, 1977/78, pp. 5-11; summer, 1984, pp. 66-84; fall, 1992, pp. 1-25; fall, 1993, pp. 108-13.

Journal of Canadian Fiction, No. 19, 1977, pp. 77-85.

Journal of Canadian Studies, autumn, 1991, pp. 68-79; autumn, 1993, pp. 75-91.

University of Toronto Quarterly, fall, 1993, pp. 211-14.

RICHLER, Mordecai 1931-

PERSONAL: Born January 27, 1931, in Montreal, Quebec, Canada; son of Moses Isaac and Lily (Rosenberg) Richler; married Florence Wood, July 27, 1960; children: Daniel, Noah, Emma, Martha, Jacob. *Education:* Attended Sir George Williams University, 1949-51. *Religion:* Jewish.

ADDRESSES: Home and office—1321 Sherbrooke St. W., Apt. 80C, Montreal, Quebec, Canada H3G 1J4.*Agent*—Lynn Nesbit, International Creative Management, 40 West 57th St., New York, NY 10019; (for films) William Morris Agency, 1350 Avenue of the Americas, New York, NY 10019.

CAREER: Writer. Left Canada in 1951 to become freelance writer in Paris, France, 1952-53, and London, England, 1954-72; returned to Canada, 1972. Sir George Williams University, writer in residence, 1968-69; Carleton University, visiting professor of English, 1972-74. Member of editorial board, Book-of-the-Month Club, 1972—.

AWARDS, HONOURS: President's medal for nonfiction, University of Western Ontario, 1959; Canadian Council junior art fellowships, 1959 and 1960, senior arts fellowship, 1967; Guggenheim Foundation creative writing fellowship, 1961; *Paris Review* humor prize, 1967, for section from *Cocksure* and *Hunting Tigers under Glass;* Governor-General's Literary Award, Canada Council, 1968, for *Cocksure* and *Hunting Tigers under Glass,* and 1971, for *St. Urbain's Horseman; London Jewish Chronicle* literature awards, 1972, for *St. Urbain's Horseman;* Berlin Film Festival Golden Bear, Academy Award nomination, and Screenwriters Guild of America award, all 1974, for the screenplay *The Apprenticeship of Duddy Kravitz;* ACTRA Award for best television writer—drama, Academy of Canadian Cinema and Television, 1975; Book of the Year for Children Award, Canadian Library Association, and Ruth Schwartz Children's Book Award, Ontario Arts Council, both 1976, for *Jacob Two-Two Meets the Hooded Fang; London Jewish Chronicle* H. H. Wingate award for fiction, 1981, for *Joshua Then and Now;* named a Literary Lion, New York Public Library, 1989; Commonwealth Writers Prize, Book Trust, 1990, for *Solomon Gursky Was Here.*

WRITINGS:

NOVELS

The Acrobats, Putnam, 1954, published as *Wicked We Love,* Popular Library, 1955.
Son of a Smaller Hero, Collins (Toronto), 1955, Paperback Library, 1965.
A Choice of Enemies, Collins, 1957.
The Apprenticeship of Duddy Kravitz, Little, Brown, 1959.

The Incompatible Atuk, McClelland & Stewart, published as *Stick Your Neck Out,* Simon & Schuster, 1963.
Cocksure, Simon & Schuster, 1968.
St. Urbain's Horseman (Literary Guild featured alternate), Knopf, 1971.
Joshua Then and Now, Knopf, 1980.
Solomon Gursky Was Here, Viking, 1989.

SCREENPLAYS

(With Nicholas Phipps) *No Love for Johnnie,* Embassy, 1962.
(With Geoffrey Cotterell and Ivan Foxwell) *Tiara Tahiti,* Rank, 1962.
(With Phipps) *The Wild and the Willing,* Rank, 1962, released in United States as *Young and Willing,* Universal, 1965.
Life at the Top, Royal International, 1965.
The Apprenticeship of Duddy Kravitz (adapted from his novel of the same title), Paramount, 1974.
(With David Giler and Jerry Belson) *Fun with Dick and Jane,* Bart/Palevsky, 1977.
Joshua Then and Now (adapted from his novel of the same title), Twentieth Century Fox, 1985.

TELEVISION AND RADIO SCRIPTS

The Acrobats (based on his novel of the same title), Canadian Broadcasting Company (CBC), 1956 (radio), 1957 (television).
Friend of the People, CBC-TV, 1957.
Paid in Full, ATV (England), 1958.
Benny, the War in Europe, and Myerson's Daughter Bella, CBC-Radio, 1958.
The Trouble with Benny (based on a short story), ABC (England), 1959.
The Apprenticeship of Duddy Kravitz (based on his novel of the same title), CBC-TV, 1960.
The Spare Room, CBC-Radio, 1961.
Q for Quest (excerpts from his fiction), CBC-Radio, 1963.
The Fall of Mendel Krick, British Broadcasting Corp. (BBC-TV), 1963.
It's Harder to Be Anybody, CBC-Radio, 1965.
Such Was St. Urbain Street, CBC-Radio, 1966.
The Wordsmith (based on a short story), CBC-Radio, 1979.

OTHER

Hunting Tigers under Glass: Essays and Reports, McClelland & Stewart, 1969.
The Street: Stories, McClelland & Stewart, 1969, New Republic, 1975.
(Editor) *Canadian Writing Today* (anthology), Peter Smith, 1970.
Shoveling Trouble (essays), McClelland & Stewart, 1973.

Notes on an Endangered Species and Others (essays), Knopf, 1974.

Jacob Two-Two Meets the Hooded Fang (juvenile), Knopf, 1975.

The Suit (animated filmstrip), National Film Board of Canada,1976.

Images of Spain, photographs by Peter Christopher, Norton, 1977.

The Great Comic Book Heroes and Other Essays, McClelland & Stewart, 1978.

(Editor) *The Best of Modern Humor,* Knopf, 1984.

Home Sweet Home: My Canadian Album (essays), Knopf, 1984, published as *Home Sweet Home,* Penguin, 1985.

(Author of book) *Duddy* (play; based on his novel *The Apprenticeship of Duddy Kravitz,)* first produced in Edmonton, Alberta, at the Citadel theatre, April, 1984.

Jacob Two-Two and the Dinosaur (juvenile), Knopf, 1987.

(Editor) *Writers on World War II: An Anthology,* Knopf, 1991.

Oh Canada! Oh Quebec!, Knopf, 1992.

The Language of Signs, David McKay Company, Inc., 1992.

This Year in Jerusalem, Knopf, 1994.

Contributor to Canadian, U.S., and British periodicals. Richler's papers are collected at the University of Calgary Library in Alberta.

ADAPTATIONS: Richler's children's book *Jacob Two-Two Meets the Hooded Fang* was filmed by Cinema Shares International and recorded by Christopher Plummer for Caedmon Records, both 1977; film rights have been sold for both *Stick Your Neck Out* and *Cocksure.*

SIDELIGHTS: "To be a Canadian and a Jew," as Mordecai Richler wrote in his book *Hunting Tigers under Glass: Essays and Reports,* "is to emerge from the ghetto twice." He referred to the double pressures of being in both a religious minority and the cultural enigma that is Canada. Yet in his decades as a novelist, screenwriter, and essayist, Richler has established himself as one of the few representatives of Canadian Jewry known outside his native country.

That many of his fictional works feature Jewish-Canadian protagonists in general (most notably in his best-known book, *The Apprenticeship of Duddy Kravitz*), and natives of Montreal in particular, denotes the author's strong attachment to his early years. Richler was born in the Jewish ghetto of Montreal to a religious family of Russian emigres. "In his teens, however, he abandoned Orthodox customs, gradually becoming more interested both in a wider world and in writing," related R. H. Ramsey in a *Dictionary of Literary Biography* article on Richler. After a stint at a university, Richler cashed in an insurance policy and used the money to sail to Liverpool, England. Eventually

he found his way to Paris, where he spent some years emulating such expatriate authors as Ernest Hemingway and Henry Miller, then moved on to London, where he worked as a news correspondent.

During those early years, Richler produced his first novel, *The Acrobats,* a book he later characterized as "more political than anything I've done since, and humorless," as he told Walter Goodman in a *New York Times* interview, adding that the volume, published when he was twenty-three, "was just a very young man's novel. Hopelessly derivative. Like some unfortunate collision of [Jean-Paul] Sartre and Hemingway and [Louis-Ferdinand] Celine, all unabsorbed and undigested. I wasn't writing in my own voice at all. I was imitating people." But Richler found his voice soon after, with novels like *Son of a Smaller Hero, A Choice of Enemies,* and *The Incomparable Atuk.* Ramsey found that from these efforts on, "two tendencies dominate Richler's fiction: realism and satire. [Many of the early stories are] realistic, their plots basically traditional in form, their settings accurately detailed, their characters motivated in psychologically familiar ways." At the other extreme, Ramsey continued, there is "pure satiric fantasy, [with] concessions to realism slight. In [such works] Richler indulges the strong comic vein in his writing as he attacks Canadian provincialism and the spurious gratifications of the entertainment medium."

Richler gained further notice with three of his best-known titles, *The Apprenticeship of Duddy Kravitz, St. Urbain's Horseman,* and *Joshua Then and Now.* These books share a common theme—that of a Jewish-Canadian protagonist at odds with society—and all three novels revolve around the idea of the way greed can taint success. *The Apprenticeship of Duddy Kravitz* presents its eponymous hero as a ghetto-reared youth on a never-ending quest to make a name for himself in business. It is also "the first of Richler's novels to exhibit fully his considerable comic talents, a strain that includes much black humor and a racy, colloquial, ironic idiom that becomes a characteristic feature of Richler's subsequent style," according to Ramsey.

Comparing *The Apprenticeship of Duddy Kravitz* to other such coming-of-age stories as James Joyce's *Portrait of the Artist as a Young Man* and D. H. Lawrence's *Sons and Lovers,* A. R. Bevan, in a new introduction to Richler's novel, found that the book, "in spite of its superficial affinity with the two novels mentioned above, ends with [none of their] affirmation." The character of Duddy, "who has never weighted the consequences of his actions in any but material terms, is less alone in the physical sense than the earlier young men, but he is also much less of a man. . . . He is a modern 'anti-hero' (something like the protagonist in Anthony Burgess's *A Clockwork Orange*) who lives in a largely deterministic world, a world where decisions are not decisions and where choice is not really choice." In

Modern Fiction Studies, John Ower saw *The Apprenticeship of Duddy Kravitz* as "a 'Jewish' novel [with] both a pungent ethnic flavor and the convincingness that arises when a writer deals with a milieu with which he is completely familiar." For the author, Ower continued, "the destructive psychological effects of the ghetto mentality are equalled and to some extent paralleled by those of the Jewish family. Like the society from which it springs, this tends to be close and exclusive, clinging together in spite of its intense quarrels. The best aspect of such clannishness, the feeling of kinship which transcends all personal differences, is exemplified by Duddy. Although he is in varying degrees put down and rejected by all of his relatives except his grandfather, Duddy sticks up for them and protects them."

For all its success, *The Apprenticeship of Duddy Kravitz* was still categorized by most scholars as among Richler's early works. By the time *St. Urbain's Horseman* was published in 1971, the author had all but sealed his reputation as a sharp cultural critic. In this work, a character named Jacob Hersh, a Canadian writer living in London, questions "not only how he rose to prominence but also the very nature and quality of success and why, having made it, [he] is dissatisfied," as Ramsey put it. Hersh's success as a writer "brings with it a guilt, a sense of responsibility, and an overwhelming paranoia, a belief that his good fortune is largely undeserved and that sooner or later he will be called to account," Ramsey added. In his guilt-based fantasies, Hersh dreams that he is a figure of vengeance protecting the downtrodden, a character based on the Horseman, a shadowy figure from Hersh's past. "Richler prefaces *St. Urbain's Horseman* with a quotation from [British poet W. H.] Auden which suggests that he does not wish to be read as a mere entertainer, a fanciful farceur," noted David Myers in *Ariel.* "What is there in the *Horseman* that would justify us as regarding it as such a[n affirming] flame? Certainly the despair that we find there is serious enough; the world around Jake Hersh is sordid and vile." The author accords sympathy "to only two characters in his novel, Jake and his wife Nancy," Myers said. "They are shown to feel a very deep love for one another and the loyalty of this love under duress provides the ethical counterbalance to the sordidness, instability, lack of integrity, injustice, and grasping materialism that Richler is satirizing in this book."

In the opinion of Kerry McSweeney, writing in *Studies in Canadian Literature,* the novel "gives evidence everywhere of technical maturity and full stylistic control, and combines the subjects, themes and modes of Richler's earlier novels in ways that suggest—as does the high seriousness of its epigraph—that Richler was attempting a cumulative fictional statement of his view on the mores and values of contemporary man. But while *St. Urbain's*

Horseman is a solid success on the level of superior fictional entertainment, on the level of serious fiction it must be reckoned a considerable disappointment. It doesn't deliver the goods and simply does not merit the kind of detailed exegesis it has been given by some Canadian critics." Elaborating on this thesis, McSweeney added that everything in the novel "depends on the presentation of Jake, especially of his mental life and the deeper reaches of his character, and on the intensity of the reader's sympathetic involvement with him. Unfortunately, Jake is characterized rather too superficially. One is told, for example, but never shown, that he is charged with contradictions concerning his professional life; and for all the time devoted to what is going on in his head he doesn't really seem to have much of a mental life. Despite the big issues he is said to be struggling with, *St. Urbain's Horseman* can hardly claim serious attention as a novel of ideas."

Robert Fulford offered a different view. In his *Saturday Night* article, Fulford lauded *St. Urbain's Horseman* as "the triumphant and miraculous bringing-together of all those varied Mordecai Richlers who have so densely populated our literary landscape for so many years. From this perspective it becomes clear that all those Richlers have a clear purpose in mind—they've all been waiting out there, working separately, honing their talents, waiting for the moment when they could arrive at the same place and join up in the creation of a magnificent *tour de force,* the best Canadian book in a long time."

The third of Richler's later novels, *Joshua Then and Now,* again explores a Jewish-Canadian's moral crises. Joshua Shapiro, a prominent author married to a Gentile daughter of a senator, veers between religious and social classes and withstands family conflicts, especially as they concern his father Reuben. It is also a novel full of mysteries. Why, asked *Village Voice* critic Barry Yourgrau, "does the book open in the present with this 47-year-old Joshua a rumple of fractures in a hospital bed, his name unfairly linked to a scandalous faggotry, his wife doped groggy in a nuthouse and he himself being watched over by his two elderly fathers?" The reason, Yourgrau continued, "is Time. The cruelest of fathers is committing physical violence on Joshua's dearest friends (and crucial enemies)."

Joshua, sometimes shown in flashback as the son of the ever-on-the-make Reuben and his somewhat exhibitionist mother (she performed a striptease at Joshua's bar mitzvah), "is another one of Richler's Jewish *arrivistes,* like Duddy Kravitz [and] Jacob Hersh," said *New Republic* critic Mark Shechner. After noting Joshua's unrepentant bragging, Shechner called the character "a fairly unpleasant fellow, and indeed, though his exploits are unfailingly vivid and engaging—even fun—they rarely elicit from us much enthusiasm for Joshua himself. He is as callow as he is clever, and, one suspects, Richler means him to be an anti-type, to stand against the more common brands of self-congratulation that are endemic to Jewish fiction. From Sholom Aleichem and his Tevye to [Saul] Bellow and [Bernard] Malamud, . . . Jewish fiction has repeatedly thrown up figures of wisdom and endurance, observance and rectitude. . . . Richler, by contrast, adheres to a tradition of dissent that runs from Isaac Babel's Odessa stories through Daniel Fuchs's *Williamsburg Trilogy* and Budd Schulberg's *What Makes Sammy Run?*, which finds more color, more life, and more fidelity to the facts of Jewish existence in the demimonde of hustlers, heavies, strong-arm types and men on the make than in the heroes of *menschlichkeit* [Yiddish slang for the quality of goodness]."

But whatever message *Joshua Then and Now* might deliver, the lasting appeal of the novel, to John Lahr, is that "Richler writes funny. Laughter, not chicken soup, is the real Jewish penicillin. . . . Richler's characters enter as philosophers and exit as stand-up comics, firing zingers as they go," as Lahr explained in a *New York* article. On the other hand, *New York Times Book Review* writer Thomas R. Edwards, while acknowledging the novel's humor, found it "dangerously similar in theme, situation and personnel to a number of Mordecai Richler's other novels— 'Son of a Smaller Hero,' 'The Apprenticeship of Duddy Kravitz,' 'Cocksure' and 'St. Urbain's Horseman.' It's as if a rich and unusual body of fictional material had become a kind of prison for a writer who is condemned to repeat himself ever more vehemently and inflexibly." *Joshua Then and Now* brought much more critical debate. Mark Harris, on one hand, faulted the novel for its style, "resplendent with every imaginable failure of characterization, relevance, style or grammar," in his *Washington Post Book World* review. An *Atlantic* critic, on the other hand, saw the book as "good enough to last, perhaps Richler's best novel to date."

Nine years passed before Richler published another novel. When he broke the silence in 1989 with *Solomon Gursky Was Here*, several reviewers welcomed the novel as worth the wait, and England's Book Trust honored it with a Commonwealth Writers Prize. The story focuses on Moses Berger, an alcoholic Jewish writer whose life's obsession is to write a biography of the legendary Solomon Gursky. Gursky, of a prominent Jewish-Canadian family of liquor distillers, may have died years ago in a plane crash, but Berger finds numerous clues that suggest he lived on in various guises, a trickster and meddler in international affairs. Jumping forward and backward in time, from events in the Gursky past to its present, Richler "manages to suggest a thousand-page family chronicle in not much more than 400 pages," observed Bruce Cook in Chicago *Tribune Books*. The critic lauded the novel's humor and rich texture, concluding, "Page for page, there

has not been a serious novel for years that can give as much pure pleasure as this one." Acknowledging the inventiveness of Richler's narrative, Francine Prose in the *New York Times Book Review* nonetheless found the book somewhat marred by predictable or flat characters. Other critics suggested that there was too much going on in the novel, and for some its humor seemed a bit too black. *Village Voice* writer Joel Yanofsky affirmed the book despite its weaknesses: "If the structure of Richler's story is too elaborate at times, if the narrative loose ends aren't all pulled together, it's a small price to pay for a book this beguiling and rude, this serious, this fat and funny." Jonathan Kirsch, writing in the *Los Angeles Times Book Review*, called it "a worthy addition" to Richler's canon, the work "of a storyteller at the height of his powers."

Among his nonfiction works, Richler's *Home Sweet Home: My Canadian Album, Oh Canada! Oh Quebec: Requiem for a Divided Country*, and *This Year in Jerusalem* have all drawn attention. While these works focus on Richler's native country and his identity as a Canadian, they have distinctly different styles and purposes. *Home Sweet Home*, for example, focuses on Canadian culture, addressing subjects from nationalism to hockey, while in *Oh Canada! Oh Quebec!* Richler turns his considerable intellect and wit to the problem of Quebec separatism, and *This Year in Jerusalem* focuses more personally on Richler's identity as a Canadian Jew—a theme also present in *Oh Canada! Oh Quebec!*

A Toronto *Globe and Mail* writer called *Home Sweet Home* "a different sort of book, but no less direct and pungent in its observations about what makes a society tick," and in another *Globe and Mail* article, Joy Fielding saw the book as "a cross-country tour like no other, penetrating the Eastern soul, the Western angst, and the French-Canadian spirit." *Home Sweet Home* drew admiring glances from American as well as Canadian critics. Peter Ross, of the *Detroit News*, wrote, "Wit and warmth are constants and though Richler can temper his fondness with bursts of uncompromising acerbity, no reader can fail to perceive the depth of his feelings as well as the complexities of Canada." And *Time*'s Stefan Kanfer observed that "even as he celebrates [Canada's] beauties, the author never loses sight of his country's insularity: when Playboy Films wanted to produce adult erotica in Toronto, he reports, officials wanted to know how much Canadian content there would be in the features. But Richler also knows that the very tugs and pulls of opposing cultures give the country its alternately appealing and discordant character."

It is precisely these tugs and pulls of opposing cultures that Richler sets out to expose in *Oh Canada! Oh Quebec!*, and the resulting book set off a furor among Canadian politicians and press—one Canadian MP even called for a banning of the book (to no avail). Anthony Wilson-Smith summed up the controversy in *Maclean's:* "The objection in each case: that Richler's view of Quebec and its nationalist movement is overly harsh and unfair—particularly his assertion that the province's history reflects a deep strain of anti-Semitism." And in fact, while Richler's earlier works abound with wit and humour, in *Oh Canada! Oh Quebec!,* "his mood . . . hovers much closer to exasperation," wrote Wilson-Smith, and Robin W. Winks, writing in the *New York Times Book Review,* stated more bluntly: "he is, for the most part, simply angry."

Winks declared that in the book Richler is "concerned, above all, with the Condition of Canada," and called the book "an unsystematic but powerful examination of what Mr. Richler regards as the idiocy of the day"—the legislation and organizations which enforce and oversee the exclusive use of the French language on all public signage in the province of Quebec. But even more compelling is Richler's claim that many of Quebec's leading politicians and intellectuals have been anti-Semitic, and, as Winks reported, that this anti-Semitism is linked to the Quebec separatist movement through the figure of Abbe Lionel-Adolphe Groulx. As Wilson-Smith reported, Richler makes the damaging claim that Groulx's paper, *Le Devoir,* " 'more closely resembled *Der Sturmer* [a German nazi newspaper of the same period] than any other newspaper I can think of.' "

Both Wilson-Smith and Winks, who was himself the chairman of the Committee on Canadian Studies at Yale University, question Richler's scholarship and accuracy in *Oh Canada! Oh Quebec!.* Winks claimed the book "is not always as informative as it might be," and questioned Richler's decision not to examine the original sources for his assertions. Wilson-Smith suggested that Richler's assertions are "debatable, largely because dislike and suspicion of Jews was widespread in Canada then among both anglophones and francophones." These problematic assertions led Winks to term the book "very readable" but "something of a missed opportunity."

Still, as Wilson-Smith reported, Richler does evince affection for his native province: " 'There is nowhere else in the country as interesting, or alive.' " And it is this sentiment—love for his native land and all of the contradictory impulses that make for a Canadian Jew—that haunts *This Year in Jerusalem.* Louis Simpson quotes Richler's account of his hybrid identity in his review of the volume for the *New York Times Book Review:* Richler described himself as " 'a Canadian, born and bred, brought up not only on Hillel, Rabbi Akiba and Rashi, but also on blizzards, Andrew Allan's CBC Radio "Stage" series, a crazed Maurice Richard skating in over the blue line . . . the Dieppe raid.' "

This Year in Jerusalem is a nonfiction account of a year Richler spent in Israel and is, for Morton Ritts, writing in *Maclean's,* "less a study of the character of politics than the politics of character." What makes this a book not just about Israel, but about Canada and Richler as well, is that Richler connects his journey to Israel with his own personal history of growing up as a young Zionist in Canada with a grandfather who was both a rabbi and a "celebrated Hasidic scholar," according to Louis Simpson in the *New York Times Book Review:* "*This Year in Jerusalem* is history made personal."

By telling the tale of his own spiritual journey whereby Richler became, in Ritts' words, "more rebel than rebbe (spiritual leader)," by giving his real-life young Zionist companions pseudonyms and tracing their stories over several decades, by talking to Israelis and Palestinians from all walks of life, and by examining, as Ritts also put it, the "trouble between Jew and gentile, French and English, the Orthodox and secular, Arab and Israeli, hawk and dove, Israeli Jew and North American Jew," Richler infuses the book with his novelist's craft. Simpson called the book "lively reporting" and "interesting," but Ritts' praise was higher. In *This Year in Jerusalem,* Ritts claimed, Richler is "at the top of his own game."

"Throughout his career Richler has spanned an intriguing gulf," concluded Ramsey in his *Dictionary of Literary Biography* piece. "While ridiculing popular tastes and never catering to popular appeal, he has nevertheless maintained a wide general audience. Though drawing constantly on his own experience, he rejects the writer as personality, wishing instead to find acceptance not because of some personal characteristic or because of the familiarity of his subject matter to a Canadian reading public but because he has something fresh to say about humanity and says it in a well-crafted form, which even with its comic exuberance, stands firmly in the tradition of moral and intellectual fiction."

BIOGRAPHICAL/CRITICAL SOURCES:

BOOKS

Authors in the News, Volume 1, Gale, 1976.
Children's Literature Review, Volume 1, Gale, 1989.
Contemporary Literary Criticism, Gale, Volume 3, 1975; Volume 5, 1976; Volume 9, 1978; Volume 13, 1980; Volume 18, 1981; Volume 46, 198; Volume 70, 1992.
Dictionary of Literary Biography, Volume 53: *Canadian Writers since 1960, First Series,* Gale, 1986.
Klinck, Carl F., and others, editors, *Literary History of Canada: Canadian Literature in English,* University of Toronto Press, 1965.
New, W. H., *Articulating West,* New Pres, 1972.

Northey, Margot, *The Haunted Wilderness: The Gothic and Grotesque in Canadian Fiction,* University of Toronto Press, 9176.

Ramraj, Victor J., *Mordecai Richler,* Twayne, 1983.

Richler, Mordecai, *The Apprenticeship of Duddy Kravitz,* introduction by A. R. Bevan, McClelland & Stewart, 1969.

Richer, Mordecai, *Hunting Tigers under Glass: Essays and Reports,* McClelland & Stewart, 1969.

Sheps, G. David, editor, *Mordecai Richler,* McGraw-Hill/Ryerson, 1971.

Woodcock, George, *Mordecai Richler,* McClelland & Stewart, 1970.

PERIODICALS

Ariel, January, 1973.

Atlantic, July 1980; May, 1990, p. 132.

Books in Canada, August-September, 1984; January-February 1991, pp. 18-20.

Canadian Literature, spring, 1973; summer, 1973.

Commentary, October, 1980; June 1990.

Detroit News, July 29, 1984.

Esquire, August, 1982.

Globe and Mail (Toronto), May 5, 1984; June 24, 1985; June 13, 1987.

Insight on the News, June 25, 1990, pp. 62-63.

Los Angeles Times Book Review, August 19, 1984; June 17, 1990, p. 4.

Maclean's, May 7, 1984; November 13, 1989, pp. 64-67; December 31, 1990, pp. 18-19; December 30, 1991, p. 26; March 30, 1992, pp. 66-67; April 13, 1992, pp. 28-30; September 12, 1994, pp. 66-7.

Modern Fiction Studies, autumn, 1976.

Nation, July 5, 1980; June 4, 1990, pp. 785-86, 788-91.

New Republic, may 18, 1974; June 14, 1980; December 5, 1983; May 7, 1990, pp. 42-44.

Newsweek, June 16, 1980; February 3, 1986.

New York, June 16, 1980; April 16, 1990, pp. 95-96.

New York Review of Books, July 17, 1980.

New York Times, June 22, 1980.

New York Times Book Review, May 4, 1975; October 5, 1975; June 22, 1980; September 11, 1983; February 5, 1984; June 3, 1984; October 18, 1987; April 8, 1990, p. 7; April 27, 1990, p. 7; May 24, 1992; November 13, 1994, p. 64.

Publishers Weekly, April 27, 1990, pp. 45-46.

Queen's Quarterly, summer, 1990, pp. 325-27.

Saturday Night June 1971; March 1974.

Spectator, August 25, 1981.

Studies in Canadian Literature, summer, 1979.

Time, June 16, 1980; November 7, 1983; April 30, 1984; May 14, 1990, p. 91.

Times Literary Supplement, April 2, 1976; September 26, 1980; August 3, 1984; December 21, 1984; June 15-21, 1990, p. 653.

Tribune Books (Chicago), April 8, 1990, p. 6.

Village Voice, June 2, 1980; May 1, 984; May 1, 1990, p. 86.

Washington Post, November 9, 1983.

Washington Post Book World, June 29, 1980.

World Literature Today, autumn, 1990, pp. 639-40.

* * *

RINGUET
See PANNETON, Philippe

* * *

RINGWOOD, Gwen(dolyn Margaret) Pharis
1910-1984

PERSONAL: Born August 13, 1910, in Anatone, WA, United States; died May 24, 1984; daughter of Leslie (a schoolteacher and farmer) and Mary (a teacher; maiden name, Bowerstock) Pharis; married John Brian Barney Ringwood (a medical doctor), 1939; children: Stephen Michael, Susan Francis Leslie, Carol Blaine, Patrick Brian. *Education:* Attended the University of Montana until 1929; University of Alberta, B.A., 1934; University of North Carolina, M.A., 1939; University of Victoria, D.F.A., 1981.

CAREER: Playwright and novelist. University of Alberta, Edmonton, secretary to Elizabeth Sterling Haynes, 1935; Province of Alberta, department of extension, director of drama, beginning 1939; Banff School of Fine Arts, Alberta, teacher of acting and playwriting, beginning 1939.

MEMBER: Canadian Theatre Centre.

AWARDS, HONOURS: Ronald Holt Cup, 1939, for work in drama; Governor General's Medal, 1941, for outstanding service to Canadian drama; Canadian playwriting prize, Ottawa Little Theatre Workshop, 1959, for *Lament for Harmonica;* named honorary member, Association for Canadian Theatre History, 1979; L.L.D., University of Lethbridge, 1982.

WRITINGS:

PLAYS

The Dragons of Kent (one-act), produced by the Banff School of Fine Arts, Banff, Alberta, 1935.

(With Elsie Park Gowan) *New Lamps for Old* (radio series, includes "Beethoven," "The Man Who Freed Music," "Christopher Columbus," "Florence Nightingale," "Galileo, Father of Science," "Henry, the Navigator," "Nansen of the North," "Oliver Cromwell," "Socrates, Citizen of Athens," "Threat to Planet Earth," and "Valley of Ignorance"), produced for CKUA-Radio, Edmonton, Alberta, 1936-37.

One Man's House (one-act; produced in Chapel Hill, NC, 1937), published in *The Collected Plays of Gwen Pharis Ringwood,* edited by Enid Delgatty Rutland, Borealis (Ottawa), 1982.

Chris Axelson, Blacksmith (one-act; produced in Chapel Hill, 1938), published in *Collected Plays.*

Pasque Flower (one-act; produced in Chapel Hill, 1939), published in *Collected Plays.*

Red Flag at Evening (produced in Edmonton, 1939), published in *Collected Plays.*

Still Stands the House (one-act; produced in Chapel Hill, 1939; adapted for radio, *Prairie Playhouse,* CBC-Radio, 1953), French (Toronto), 1955.

The Courting of Marie Jevrin (produced in Banff, 1941), French, 1951.

The Jack and the Joker, produced in Banff, 1944.

Dark Harvest (three-act; produced in Winnipeg, Manitoba, 1945), Nelson (Toronto), 1945, revised in *Canadian Theatre Review,* winter, 1975.

The Rainmaker (produced in Banff, 1945), Playwrights Co-op (Toronto), 1975.

Stampede (produced in Edmonton, 1946), published in *Collected Plays.*

A Fine Coloured Easter Egg (produced in Banff, 1946; adapted for radio, *Prairie Playhouse,* CBC-Radio, 1953), published in *Collected Plays.*

Widger's Way (produced in Edmonton, 1952), Playwrights Co-op, 1976.

The Wall (radio play), music by Bruce Haak, broadcast on *Prairie Playhouse,* CBC-Radio, 1954.

So Gracious the Time (radio play), CBC-Radio, 1955.

Lament for Harmonica (as *Maya,* produced in Ottawa, 1959, and as part of *Drum Song* in Victoria, BC, 1982; adapted for television, *Shoestring Theatre,* CBC, 1960; adapted for radio, CBC-Radio, 1979), published in *Collected Plays.*

Look behind You, Neighbour, music by Chet Lambertson, produced in Edson, Alberta, 1961.

The Sleeping Beauty (produced in Williams Lake, BC, 1965), published in *The Sleeping Beauty: A New Version of the Old Story, and The Golden Goose: Two Plays for Young People,* Playwrights Co-op, 1979.

The Three Wishes, produced in Williams Lake, 1965.

The Road Runs North, produced in Williams Lake, 1967.

The Deep Has Many Voices (adapted for television, CBC, 1967; produced in Williams Lake, 1971), published in *Collected Plays.*

Jana, produced in Williams Lake, 1971; as *The Stranger,* published in *Collected Plays.*

The Magic Carpets of Antonio Angelini (produced in Winnipeg, 1976), published in *Kids' Plays: Six Canadian Plays for Children,* Playwrights Press, 1980.

Restez, Michelle, Don't Go (radio play), CBC-Radio, 1977.

The Lodge (produced in West Vancouver, BC, 1977), published in *Collected Plays.*

A Remembrance of Miracles (adapted for radio, CBC-Radio, 1979), published in *Collected Plays.*

Mirage (11-act; produced in Saskatoon, Saskatchewan, 1979), published in *Collected Plays.*

Garage Sale (one-act; produced in Vancouver, BC, 1981; adapted for radio, CBC-Radio, 1981), published in *Collected Plays.*

Drum Song (comprises *Maya, The Stranger,* and *The Furies;* produced in Victoria, BC, 1982), *The Stranger* and *The Furies* published separately in *Collected Plays.*

The Collected Plays of Gwen Pharis Ringwood (also includes *The Days May Be Long, Saturday Night, Wail, Wind, Wail,* and *Compensation Will Be Paid*), edited by Rutland, Borealis, 1982.

FICTION

Younger Brother (novel), Longman's, Green (New York City), 1959.

Contributor of short stories to anthologies, including *Wide Open Windows,* edited by Franklin L. Barrett, Copp Clark (Vancouver), 1947; *Canadian Short Stories,* edited by Robert Weaver and Helen James, Oxford University Press (Toronto), 1952; *Stories with John Drainie,* edited by Drainie, Ryerson (Toronto), 1963; and *Stories from across Canada,* edited by Bernard L. McEnvoy, McClelland & Stewart (Toronto), 1966.

OTHER

Contributor of nonfiction to periodicals, including *Atlantis: A Women's Studies Journal/Journal d'Etudes sur la Femme;* contributor to *Transitions I: Short Plays,* edited by Edward Peck, Commcept Press (Vancouver), 1978; and *Canada's Lost Plays,* edited by Anton Wagner, Canadian Theatre Review Publications (Toronto), 1980.

Ringwood's papers are housed in a special collection at the University of Calgary Library, Alberta.

SIDELIGHTS: Dramatist Gwen Pharis Ringwood is noted for her stage depictions of the inhabitants of Canada's western provinces. Born in the United States, Ringwood spent most of her childhood in Alberta; her many plays for stage, radio, and television reflect her love of the area's regional culture, small-town life, and the humanity and everyday foibles of her fellow Canadians. The author of over sixty plays, musicals, comedies, radio dramas, and plays for children, Ringwood's work is considered instrumental in the growth of modern Canadian drama.

Born in Anatone, Washington, in 1910, Ringwood moved to Alberta at age three, and remained there until her family moved south to the state of Montana to start a cattle ranch in 1916. She broke off her college studies at the University of Montana in 1929 when her family moved north once again; she graduated from the University of Alberta in 1934. Her work as secretary to Elizabeth Sterling Haynes, a provincial drama director and a significant force behind the Banff School of Fine Arts, drew Ringwood into the world of community theatre. She began writing stage and radio plays; her first play, *The Dragons of Kent,* was produced by the Banff School of Fine Arts in 1935; between 1936-37, ten of her radio plays were aired on the University of Alberta's radio station.

Three years after graduating from the University of Alberta, Ringwood enrolled at the University of North Carolina, where she became involved with the Carolina Playmakers and received her M.A. in 1939. During this period she wrote and produced several plays, among them *Still Stands the House* and *Dark Harvest,* which are considered by critics to be two of her best works for the stage. Ringwood also received the University's Ronald Holt Cup for her work in drama.

Still Stands the House dramatizes the confrontation between staunch preservation of long-standing tradition and the acceptance of modernization and a changing culture—issues affecting Canada throughout its history. *Dark Harvest,* Ringwood's first full-length play, is a study of excessive pride and obsession within an Alberta farming family. As Chris Johnson noted in the *Dictionary of Literary Biography,* these two plays incorporate "conflict between man and environment, a theme long used by Canadian novelists and poets but one which had for the most part eluded the dramatists."

Her education complete, Ringwood returned to western Canada in 1939 and married John Brian Barney. She took a position as director of drama in Alberta's department of extension and taught at the Banff School of Fine Arts. From 1940-1953, she continued to write plays for community theatre groups. In 1942, Ringwood was commissioned by the Alberta Folklore and History Project to write three plays: *The Jack and the Joker, The Rainmaker,* and *Stampede,* each of which explore a facet of Alberta history. The musical, *Look behind You, Neighbour,* was written to celebrate Edson, Alberta's fiftieth anniversary.

In 1953, Ringwood and her family moved to British Columbia's Williams Lake area. It was a change that would be reflected in Ringwood's writing as an old interest in Canada's native population was rekindled. She wrote several plays about her country's original inhabitants, including *Lament for Harmonica* (also produced as *Maya*), the

story of a Native Canadian girl whose spirit is corrupted by contact with the world of the white settlers. Ringwood also wrote several plays combining Western-themed fairy tales with Native Canadian legends that were produced at Williams Lake's reservation schools. In addition, she was the author of the 1959 young adult novel *Younger Brother,* which tells the story of a young man whose morals are put to the test when a Native Canadian is accused of a crime perpetrated by his best friend. Social concerns continued to be a constant element in Ringwood's later works, which also incorporated more sophisticated dramatic techniques, music, and media. The most ambitious of these plays, *Mirage,* incorporated eleven scenes depicting the history of Saskatchewan through three generations of a farming family in its 1979 production. Ringwood would only live to see two more of her works produced: *Garage Sale,* a one-act, was staged in 1981, and *Drum Song,* a multiple work production featuring *Maya, The Stranger,* and *The Furies,* was presented in 1982. She died May 24, 1984.

BIOGRAPHICAL/CRITICAL SOURCES:

BOOKS

Anthony, Geraldine, *Gwen Pharis Ringwood,* Twayne (Boston), 1981.
Anthony, G., editor, *Stage Voices: Twelve Canadian Playwrights Talk about Their Lives and Work,* Doubleday (Toronto), 1978.
Dictionary of Literary Biography, Volume 88: *Canadian Writers, 1920-1959, Second Series,* Gale, 1989, pp. 260-65.

PERIODICALS

Canadian Children's Literature, Volume 8, 1977, pp. 122-23.
Canadian Drama/L'Art Dramatique Canadien, autumn, 1976, pp. 144-53; autumn, 1977, pp. 183-91; Volume 9, 1985, pp. 514-20; Volume 9, 1985, pp. 216-17, 219-21.
Canadian Theatre Review, winter, 1975, pp. 63-69.
Manitoba Arts Review, spring, 1944, pp. 3-20.*

*   *   *

ROCKWOOD, Roy
See McFARLANE, Leslie (Charles)

*   *   *

ROOKE, Leon 1934-

PERSONAL: Born September 11, 1934, in Roanoke Rapids, NC, United States. *Education:* Attended University of

North Carolina, 1955-58, 1961-62. *Politics:* New Democrat.

ADDRESSES: Home—1019 Terrace Ave., Victoria, British Columbia, Canada V8S 3V2.*Agent*—Liz Darhansoff, 1220 Park Ave., New York, NY 10128.

CAREER: Short story writer, novelist, and dramatist. University of North Carolina at Chapel Hill, writer-in-residence, 1965-66; University of Victoria, Victoria, British Columbia, lecturer in creative writing, 1971-72, visiting professor, 1980-81; Southwest Minnesota State College, Marshall, writer-in-residence, 1975-76; University of Toronto, Toronto, Ontario, writer-in-residence, 1984-85. *Military service:* U.S. Army, Infantry, 1958-60; served in Alaska.

MEMBER: PEN, Writers' Union of Canada.

AWARDS, HONOURS: MacDowell fellowship, 1974; Canada Council theatre and fiction grants, 1974, 1975, 1976, 1979, 1983, and 1985; Yaddo fellowship, 1976; National Endowment for the Arts fellowship, 1978; Best Paperback Novel of the Year, 1981, for *Fat Woman*; Canada/Australia Prize, 1981, for overall body of work; Governor General's Literary Award for fiction, Canada Council, 1984, for *Shakespeare's Dog*; Author's Award for short fiction, Foundation for the Advancement of Canadian Letters, 1986.

WRITINGS:

STORY COLLECTIONS

Last One Home Sleeps in the Yellow Bed, Louisiana State University Press, 1968.
The Love Parlour: Stories, Oberon, 1977.
The Broad Back of the Angel, Fiction Collective, 1977.
Cry Evil, Oberon, 1980.
Death Suite, ECW Press (Toronto), 1981.
The Birth Control King of the Upper Volta, ECW Press, 1982.
Sing Me No Love Songs, I'll Say You No Prayers: Selected Stories, Ecco Press, 1984.
A Bolt of White Cloth, Ecco Press, 1985.

NOVELS

The Magician in Love, Aya Press (Toronto), 1981.
Fat Woman, Knopf, 1981.
Shakespeare's Dog, Knopf, 1983.

PLAYS

Lady Physhie's Cafe, produced in Louisville, Kentucky, at Louisville Art Center, 1960.
Krokodile, Playwrights Co-op (Toronto), 1973.
Ms. America (three-act play), first produced in Toronto, Ontario, 1974.

Sword Play (one-act; first produced in Vancouver, Canada, at New Play Centre, March, 1973; produced Off-Off Broadway, 1975), Playwright's Co-op, 1974.
Of Ice and Men (two-act), produced in Toronto at Theatre Passe Muraille, 1985.
Shakespeare's Dog (one-man show), produced in Toronto at Theatre Passe Muraille, 1985.
The Good Baby (two-act), produced by Caravan Stage Company for British Columbia tour, 1987.

Also author of the play *Evening Meeting of the Club of Suicide,* New Play Centre. Author of radio plays for Canadian Broadcasting Corporation, 1986-87.

Contributor to anthologies, including *Prize Stories of 1965: The O. Henry Awards,* edited by William Abrahams and Richard Poirier, Doubleday, 1965; *Chapel Hill Carousel,* edited by Jessie Rehder, University of North Carolina Press, 1967; *76: New Canadian Stories,* edited by John Metcalf, Oberon, 1977; *Statements,* Fiction Collective, 1977; *The North Carolina Short Story,* edited by Guy Owen, University of North Carolina Press, 1977; *Here and Now,* edited by Metcalf and Clark Blaise, Oberon, 1977; *Transitions II,* edited by Edward Peck, Comancept, 1978; *Stories Plus,* edited by Metcalf, McGraw, 1979; *Best American Short Stories, 1980,* edited by Stanley Elkin and Shannon Ravenel, Houghton, 1980; *Magic Realism,* edited by Geoff Hancock, Aya Press, 1980; *80: Best Canadian Stories,* edited by Metcalf, Oberon, 1980; *Illusions,* edited by Hancock, Aya Press, 1981; *Canadian Short Fiction Anthology,* edited by Paul Belserene, Intermedia Press, 1982; *Rainshadow: Stories from Vancouver Island,* edited by Ron Smith and Stephen Guppy, Oolichon Books/Sono Nis Press, 1982; *West of Fiction,* edited by Leah Flater, Aritha Van Herk, and Ruby Wiebe, NeWest Press, 1982; *Elements of Fiction,* edited by Scholes and Sullivan, Oxford University Press, 1982; *Introduction to Fiction,* edited by Jack David and John Redfern, Holt, 1982; *An Anthology of Canadian Literature in English,* Volume II, edited by Donna Bennett and Russell Brown, Oxford University Press, 1983; *Making It New,* edited by Metcalf, Methuen, 1983; *The Shoe Anthology,* edited by Hancock, Aya Press, 1984; *New: West Coast Fiction,* WCR/Pulp Press, 1984; *Canadian Short Stories,* Oxford University Press, 1985; *Skeleton at Sixty,* edited by Barbara E. Turner, Porcupines Quill, 1986; *The Art of the Tale: An International Anthology of Short Stories, 1945-1985,* edited by Daniel Halpern, Viking, 1986; *The Oxford Book of Canadian Short Stories,* edited by Margaret Atwood and Robert Weaver, Oxford University Press, 1986; *Canadian Short Stories: From Myth to Modern,* edited by W. H. New, Prentice-Hall, 1986; *A Grand Street Reader,* edited by Ben Sonnenberg, Summit Books, 1986; *The Arch of Experience,* edited by Ian W. Mills and Judith H. Mills, Holt, 1986; *Magic Realism and Canadian Literature: Es-*

says and Stories, edited by Peter Hinchcliffe and Ed Jewinski, University of Waterloo Press, 1986; *86: Best Canadian Stories,* edited by David Helwig and Sandra Martin, Oberon, 1987; *Tesseracts 2: Canadian Science Fiction,* Press Porcepic, 1987; and *87: Best Canadian Short Stories,* edited by D. Helwig and Maggie Helwig, Oberon, 1988.

OTHER

Vault, a Story in Three Parts: Conjugal Precepts, Dinner with the Swardians, and Break and Enter, Lillabulero Press, 1973.
(Editor with Metcalf) *81: Best Canadian Stories,* Oberon, 1981.
(Editor with Metcalf) *82: Best Canadian Stories,* Oberon, 1982.
(Editor with Metcalf) *The New Press Anthology: Best Canadian Short Fiction,* General Publishing (Toronto), 1984.
(Editor with Metcalf) *The Macmillan Anthology One,* Macmillan of Canada, 1988.

Contributor of short novels to *Carolina Quarterly, Noble Savage,* and *Descant.* Contributor of about 250 short stories to Canadian and U.S. literary magazines, including *Southern Review, Canadian Fiction Magazine, Antaeus, Yale Review, Mississippi Review,* and *Malahat Review.*

SIDELIGHTS: According to Toronto *Globe and Mail* reviewer William French, "Leon Rooke is unquestionably the most imaginative fiction writer currently practising in Canada. His closest competitor is probably Jacques Ferron, the Montreal fantasist, but Rooke is far more prolific than Ferron." Rooke has authored several volumes of short stories and a growing list of plays, and among his novels are *Fat Woman* and *Shakespeare's Dog.* In the *New York Times Book Review,* Alberto Manguel finds Rooke hard to classify: "[Rooke's] style varies greatly not only from book to book but sometimes from page to page. It is impossible to speak of a typical Leon Rooke paragraph; each one sets out to explore different voices and textures."

Rooke's earliest short story collections, including *Last One Home Sleeps in the Yellow Bed, The Broad Back of the Angel,* and *The Love Parlour,* are noted for their experimental qualities and their intertwining of realism and surrealism. *Sewanee Review* critic George Garrett finds the collection *The Broad Back of the Angel* "mildly surrealist in matter and in manner . . . [like] a French surrealist movie of the late thirties, afflicted with poor subtitles. But Rooke is good at it and knows what he is doing well enough." Lesley Hogan comments in the *Canadian Fiction Magazine* that *The Broad Back of the Angel* and *The Love Parlour* "show masterful control of a variety of techniques. Rooke's concern is with love and the importance of personal relationships in an ever-increasingly impersonal society. . . . He maintains a delicate balance be-

tween the realms of reality and fantasy which gives his stories their double impact of strangeness and familiarity." In this same vein, Stephen Scobie claims in *Books in Canada* that "[one] feature of Rooke's fiction has been the way the ordinary lives of ordinary people coexist with the most extravagant and bizarre events and are presented in exuberantly experimental forms. . . . One key to such an approach is Rooke's insistence on *voice.* . . . Whooping and hollering, cajoling or complaining, Rooke's characters meet the world at an interface of language; their perception *is* their rhetoric."

Although reviewers generally find Rooke's earlier story collections impressive, they are not slow to address the unevenness of these volumes nor the fact that Rooke's avant-garde style, at times, fails. Regarding *The Broad Back of the Angel, Fiddlehead* contributor John Mills notes that although Rooke "writes excellent and sometimes poetic prose," *The Broad Back of the Angel* contains three stories about a magician that "are experimental, and in my opinion they fail—there is a coy air of self-congratulation about them." In turn, Sally Beauman expresses in her *New York Times Book Review* assessment of *Last One Home Sleeps in the Yellow Bed* that "there is a feeling of frustration" about these stories, "as if [Rooke] wanted to write, not short stories at all, but a novel. Not that it's such a bad fault to have themes which are too big for your medium."

With the advent of Rooke's collection entitled *Cry Evil* in 1980, critics detect a change in Rooke's posture. "From the very first words of [*Cry Evil*]," writes Russell M. Brown in the *Canadian Forum,* " . . . it becomes clear that we are dealing with a writer who is now trying out the self-conscious and self-reflexive mode of postmodernism. As we move through this book, we encounter something of the exhaustion, the labyrinths and the narrative games of writers like Barth." In *Canadian Literature,* Jerry Wasserman concurs: "The stories in *Cry Evil* are . . . [baroque and make great] demands on the reader, echoing Barth and Borges, Dostoevsky, Kafka, and Poe. They are not recommended for chronic depressives." Whereas the narrators in Rooke's earlier story collections were conventional, Brown finds that Rooke has informed *Cry Evil* with "a series of ingenious narrative variations that are evidence of the search for renewed creative energy." The story called "The Deacon's Tale," for instance, presents a deacon who has trouble telling his tale, partly due to his wife's incessant harping from the sidelines. Though Brown expresses a degree of distaste for Rooke's drive toward inventive storytelling, he simultaneously maintains that "there is still emotion embedded in these stories, still human compulsions and neuroses," and he believes Rooke's stories contain a valuable depth beyond their wit.

Rooke's succeeding story collections, *Death Suite, The Birth Control King of Upper Volta, Sing Me No Love Songs, I'll Say You No Prayers: Selected Stories,* and *A Bolt of White Cloth,* have also sparked varied critical responses. "Rooke's hyperactive imagination occasionally betrays him, but the general quality of his output remains at an impressively high level," observes French. Of Rooke's 1985 endeavor *A Bolt of White Cloth, Canadian Forum* reviewer Barry Dempster feels Rooke "invents occurrences that are disappointingly unbelievable, endings that stumble and freeze in the unwelcome air," but Paul Steuwe declares in *Books in Canada* that "if for any reason you've been holding back from experiencing the world of Leon Rooke, this is as good a place as any to begin getting acquainted with a master craftsman of Canadian literature."

In the midst of Rooke's additions to his short story collections, he published his first novel, *Fat Woman,* in 1981. *Fat Woman* "is a slim novel with a big heart and a sizable funny bone," according to David Quammen in the *New York Times Book Review.* "Rooke puts us inside the copious body of Ella Mae Hopkins—an obese wife . . .—and we waddle with her through one traumatic day, sharing her secret worries and consolations, . . . her battles of gastronomic will. . . . The small miracle about 'Fat Woman' is that it remains entertaining despite its extreme simplicity of event. One large reason for this is the richness and rhythms and humor of Southern country language, which Rooke has captured wonderfully." Conversely, Timothy Down Adams notes in his *American Book Review* article that Rooke's "tampering with the slapstick humor characteristic of the worst of Southern fiction" almost kept *Fat Woman* from getting off the ground. Adams maintains that the book is redeemed by the development of the tender and humorous love relationship between the leading fat woman and her thin husband. "However," stresses Adams, "like its heroine, *Fat Woman* would have been easier to love if it were reduced by a third and tightened overall." For Tom Marshall in *Canadian Literature, Fat Woman* "is an enjoyable and absorbing read, and . . . has as a central aim an exploration of the dignity and even complexity of the lives of quite ordinary or socially marginal people."

Rooke's award-winning second novel, *Shakespeare's Dog,* is a "real sleeper, a veritable find, a novel to thoroughly delight and amuse the most jaded of readers," praises a *Publishers Weekly* reviewer. As a winner of the Governor General's Literary Award for fiction from the Canada Council in 1984, this highly imaginative tale aims at exposing Shakespeare during his married life with Anne Hathaway before he had ventured to London. The splendor of it all is that Shakespeare's philosophical cur, Mr. Hooker, is narrator. In what *New York Times Book Review* critic Jerome Charyn perceives as Rooke's "sad and

funny novel about the ultimate talking dog[,] Hooker has caught Shakespeare's disease. His head is puffed with language, and the other dogs of Stratford poke fun at him. . . . [*Shakespeare's Dog*] would be a silly novel, imprisoned by its own narrow concerns, were it not for the vitality that . . . Rooke brings to the squabbling household of Hooke, Will Shakespeare and Anne Hathaway. . . . It parodies all the mysteries surrounding Master Will and seems to suggest that the real author of 'Hamlet' and 'Lear' was Hooker himself." Other reviewers proclaim that much of the novel's success stems from Rooke's gambol with language. John Bemrose writes in *Maclean's Magazine* that "*Shakespeare's Dog* is a triumph of Rooke's delight in the language, in how it can be twisted and even reinvented. It is written in pseudo-Elizabethan tongue that effortlessly carries its rich cargo of bawdy epithets and street poetry." And a reviewer in *Vogue* praises Rooke's language as "a breathless, randy mix of Joycean teasers, Elizabethan bawdies, newly-minted Rookisms— even a sprinkling of Shakespeare—that makes for a dark, ferocious lyricism and a whopping good story."

Although there are reviewers who consider *Shakespeare's Dog* short on plot, overall the work is praised as yet another surprise from a writer whose range of talent seemingly knows no confines. S. Schoenbaum declares in the *Washington Post Book World* that "if there is a better novel than Rooke's dealing with Shakespeare's early days I'm not aware of it, although in fairness I'd have to add that his competition isn't that formidable. He has a highly original conception, and his spokespooch is a feisty (as well as intellectual) hound. . . . Through Hooker's eyes, sixteenth-century Stratford lives."

BIOGRAPHICAL/CRITICAL SOURCES:

BOOKS

Contemporary Literary Criticism, Gale, Volume 25, 1983; Volume 34, 1985.

PERIODICALS

American Book Review, March-April, 1982.
Books in Canada, November, 1981; May, 1983; May, 1985.
Canadian Fiction Magazine, Numbers 30-31, 1979.
Canadian Forum, August, 1980; April, 1985.
Canadian Literature, summer, 1981; winter, 1981.
Fiddlehead, spring, 1978.
Globe and Mail (Toronto), January 5, 1985.
Harper's, May, 1983.
Kirkus Reviews, March 1, 1983.
Los Angeles Times, May 4, 1981.
Maclean's, January 11, 1982; May 16, 1983.
New York Times Book Review, March 2, 1969; January 1, 1978; May 17, 1981; May 29, 1983; April 1, 1984.

Publishers Weekly, March 11, 1983.
Quill and Quire, June, 1983.
Sewanee Review, summer, 1978.
Vogue, June, 1983.
Washington Post Book World, June 7, 1981; May 22, 1983;
    August 5, 1984.
WAVES, winter, 1982.

—*Sketch by Cheryl Gottler*

*   *   *

ROSS, (James) Sinclair   1908-

PERSONAL: Born January 22, 1908, in Shellbrook, Saskatchewan, Canada; son of Peter (a farmer) and Catherine (Foster Fraser) Ross. *Education:* Educated in Saskatchewan, Canada. *Religion:* Protestant.

ADDRESSES: Home—Vancouver, British Columbia, Canada. *Agent*—c/o McClelland and Stewart, 481 University Avenue, Toronto, Ontario, Canada M5G 2E9.

CAREER: Royal Bank of Canada, bank clerk in country branches, 1924-31, in Winnipeg, Manitoba, 1931-42, and Montreal, Quebec, 1946-68. Novelist. *Military service:* Canadian Army, 1942-45.

WRITINGS:

NOVELS

As for Me and My House, Reynal and Hitchcock, 1941.
The Well, Macmillan, 1958.
Whir of Gold, McClelland and Stewart, 1970.
Sawbones Memorial, McClelland and Stewart, 1974.

SHORT STORIES

The Lamp at Noon and Other Stories, McClelland and
    Stewart, 1968.
The Race and Other Stories by Sinclair Ross, McClelland
    and Stewart, 1982.

Also contributor of short stories to *Queen's Quarterly, Journal of Canadian Fiction,* and other periodicals.

SIDELIGHTS: Sinclair Ross is best known for his novels and short stories that chronicle life on the Canadian prairies, where his characters struggle with the physical and psychological hardships imposed by the landscape. In his somber, intense works, Ross often explores themes of isolation and alienation, the limits of human communication, and the artistic struggle. Robert D. Chambers, writing in *Sinclair Ross and Ernest Buckler,* commented, "Many of the finest moments in Ross' stories combine these few but simple elements: menacing nature, lonely humans, a tightening claustrophobia. The dominant mood is one of attrition, with a terrible harmony between the working of wind upon soil and snow and the slow undermining of human stamina and strength."

Ross's short stories are featured in two collections, *The Lamp at Noon and Other Stories* and *The Race and Other Stories by Sinclair Ross.* Most of the stories in these volumes are set on the drought-stricken prairie of the 1930s and examine nature's indifference to man's existence. In "The Lamp at Noon," for example, a long-suffering farm wife descends into madness after she is caught in a dust storm, and in "A Field of Wheat," a farmer and his family, after suffering years of failure, see their new crop destroyed by a ferocious hail storm. Other stories, like "Cornet at Night," follow a young narrator as he grapples with the responsibilities of adulthood.

As for Me and My House, Ross's acclaimed first novel, is considered by some critics to be a classic of Canadian literature. *As for Me and My House* focuses on the troubled lives of the Bentleys, a clergyman and his wife engulfed by the repressive atmosphere in the rural Saskatchewan town of Horizon. The story is told through the eyes of Mrs. Bentley, a caring, complex woman who records each day's events in her journal. She watches as her husband Philip—his ministry failing, his own religious beliefs shattered—turns to painting as an outlet for self-expression, only to find that his creative impulses are paralyzed by feelings of frustration and despair. After weathering several threats to their marriage, including an ill-fated adoption and an extramarital affair, the Bentleys leave Horizon to pursue Philip's dream of becoming an artist.

The note of redemption on which the book ends is also found in several of Ross's other works; the author instills his characters with an inner resolve that enables them to transcend their environment. Chambers observed that "despite their entrapment, Ross' characters nonetheless continue to hope, to plan, to dream." He later concluded, "The ultimate value of Ross' writings is his compassion for their plight. As harsh and destructive as the world may be, his characters are seldom touched by the same dark qualities. Our final impression of his world is not of the blackness that surrounds, but rather of the small gleam of beauty and humanity that bravely irradiates—like the after-image of a child's sparkler on the night air."

BIOGRAPHICAL/CRITICAL SOURCES:

BOOKS

Chambers, Robert D., *Sinclair Ross and Ernest Buckler,*
    Copp Clark, 1975.
Contemporary Literary Criticism, Volume 13, Gale, 1980.
Contemporary Novelists, 5th edition, St. James Press,
    1991.
Dictionary of Literary Biography, Volume 88: *Canadian
    Writers, 1920-1959, Second Series,* Gale, 1989.

Mitchell, Ken, *Sinclair Ross: A Reader's Guide,* Thunder Creek, 1981.

Moss, John G., *Patterns of Isolation in English-Canadian Fiction,* McClelland and Stewart, 1974.

Reference Guide to English Literature, 2nd edition, St. James Press, 1991.

Twentieth-Century Western Writers, St. James Press, 1991.

Woodcock, George, editor, *A Choice of Critics,* Oxford University Press, 1966.

PERIODICALS

Canadian Forum, March, 1971, p. 443; November, 1975, p. 37.

Canadian Literature, summer, 1960, pp. 7-20; spring, 1969, pp. 26-32; winter, 1965, pp. 17-24; autumn, 1982, pp. 168-69; winter, 1984, pp. 155-66, 166-74; winter, 1986, pp. 101-13.

Dalhousie Review, winter, 1986, pp. 497-512.

*   *   *

ROUTIER, Simone   1901-1987
(Marie de Villiers)

PERSONAL: Born March 4, 1901, in Quebec, Canada; died November 6, 1987; daughter of Alfred-Charles (a jeweler) and Zelia (La Force) Routier; married J.-Fortunat Drouin, April 8, 1958. *Education:* Attended Convent des Ursulines, Quebec, Universite Laval, and Sorbonne (Universite de Paris). *Religion:* Catholic.

CAREER: Lecturer and poet. Canadian Archives, Paris, France, draftsman, 1930-40; Canadian Archives, Ottawa, Ontario, assistant archivist, 1940-50; Canadian Embassy, Brussels, Belgium, press attache, 1950-54; Canadian consulate, Boston, MA, vice consul, 1954-58.

MEMBER: Academie Canadienne-Francaise, Societe des Poetes (Paris), Societe des Ecrivains Canadiens-Francais, Societe des Poetes de Quebec.

AWARDS, HONOURS: Prix David, 1928, for *L'immortel adolescent,* 1928; Lieutenant Governor's medal, 1934, for *Ceux qui seront aimes;* Diplome aux Jeux Florauz du Languedoc, France, 1931; Medaille Carrel, 1931.

WRITINGS:

L'Immortel Adolescent, Le Soleil (Quebec), 1928, revised and enlarged edition, 1929.

Ceux qui seront aimes, Pierre Roger (Paris), 1931.

Paris-Amour-Deauville, Pierre Roger (Paris), 1932.

Les Tentations, La Caravelle (Paris), 1934.

Adieu, Paris! Journal d'une evacuee canadienne, 10 mai-17 juin 1940, Le Droit (Ottawa), 1940, revised and enlarged edition, Beauchemin (Montreal), 1944.

(Under pseudonym Marie de Villiers) *Reponse a "Desespoir de vielle fille,"* Beauchemin (Montreal), 1943.

Les Psaumes du jardin clos, La Lyre et La Croix/Editions du Levrier (Paris/Montreal), 1947.

Je te fiancerai, La Lyre et La Croix (Paris), 1947, published as *Le Long Voyage,* La Lyre et La Croix (Paris), 1947.

(With Soeur Paul-Emile) *Notre Dame du bel amour,* Le Droit (Ottawa), 1947.

Le Choix de Simone Routier dans l'oeuvre de Simone Routier, Presses Laurentiennes (Notre-Dames-des-Laurentides, Quebec), 1981.

Contributor of poetry to several anthologies, including *The Oxford Book of Canadian Verse,* edited by A. J. M. Smith, Oxford, 1960; *Un siecle de litterature canadienne,* edited by G. Sylvestre, HMH, 1967. Also contributor to *Canadian Poetry, Ecrits du Canada francais,* and *Poesie.* Routier's manuscripts, letters, and other documents are held in the Bibliotheque Nationale du Quebec.

SIDELIGHTS: "Simone Routier's name," writes Louise H. Forsyth in her *Dictionary of Literary Biography* essay, "is usually cited among those of the significant poets of the first half of the twentieth century." Her early work provides a unique perspective on the life and loves of a young French Canadian woman. Her first book, *L'Immortel Adolescent,* may have been based in part on Routier's relationship with her fellow Quebecois poet Alain Grandbois. "A close relationship seems to have developed between the two young poets, which lasted for two years (1920-1922) and then dissolved with some measure of bitterness and misunderstanding," Forsyth explains. A later relationship, with an English-speaking Protestant boy, also ended, because Routier's family disapproved of the match. *L'Immortel Adolescent* traces the transformation of Routier's emotions from those of a disappointed young woman to those of a poet.

L'Immortel Adolescent helped to forge Routier's reputation. On the basis of it, she was admitted to the Societe des Poetes Canadiens-Francais and awarded the Prix David. "By the time she published *Les Tentations*" in 1934, Forsyth declares, "Routier had achieved mastery of her craft." However, her personal romantic life was in turmoil. "The early years of World War II were for her a period of tragedy," the critic explains. "Her fiance, Louis Courty, was killed by an exploding shell two days before their wedding. A short time later she had to leave France, abandoning all her belongings, including her manuscripts, the work of ten years." Routier spent another ten years in her homeland, and her work during this period—among the last of her work published during her lifetime—introduces an interest in a serene life and in religion. "While this represents a new departure in her writing," Forsyth asserts, "Routier's sensitivity remains unchanged:

spiritual fulfillment can come only through full acceptance of experience in the material world."

BIOGRAPHICAL/CRITICAL SOURCES:

BOOKS

Blais, Jacques, *De l'ordre et de l'aventure,* Presses de l'Universite Laval (Quebec), 1975.
Dantin, Louis, *Poetes de l'Amerique francaise,* 2nd series, Albert Levesque (Montreal), 1934.
DesRochers, Alfred, *Paragraphes,* Action Canadienne-Francaise, 1931.
Dictionary of Literary Biography, Volume 88: *Canadian Writers, 1920-1959, Second Series,* Gale, 1989.
Hebert, Maurice, . . . *Et d'un livre a l'autre,* Albert Levesque (Montreal), 1932.
Marcotte, Gilles, *Une litterature qui se fait,* HMH (Montreal), 1962.
Pageau, Rene, *Rencontres avec Simone Routier, suivies des lettres d'Alain Grandbois,* Parabole (Joliette, Quebec), 1978.

PERIODICALS

Ecrits du Canada francais, Volumes 44/45, 1982, pp. 227-74.
Liaison, May, 1947, pp. 268-72.*

*   *   *

ROY, Gabrielle   1909-1983

PERSONAL: Born March 22, 1909, in St. Boniface, Manitoba, Canada; died of cardiac arrest, July 13, 1983, in Quebec City, Quebec, Canada; daughter of Leon (a colonization agent) and Melina (Landry) Roy; married Marcel Carbotte (a physician), August 30, 1947. *Education:* Educated in Canada; attended Winnipeg Normal School, 1927-29. *Religion:* Roman Catholic.

CAREER: Writer. Teacher in a Canadian prairie village school, 1928-29, and in St. Boniface, Manitoba, 1929-37; worked as freelance journalist for *Le Bulletin des agriculteurs, Le Jour,* and *Le Canada.*

MEMBER: Royal Society of Canada (fellow).

AWARDS, HONOURS: Medaille of l'Academie Francaise, 1947; Prixfemina (France), 1947, for *Bonheur d'occasion;* received Canadian Governor General's Award for the following: *Bonheur d'occasion, Rue Deschambault,* and *Ces Enfants de ma vie,;* Duvernay Prix, 1955; Companion of the Order of Canada, 1967; Canadian Council of the Arts Award, 1968; Prix David, 1971; Knight of the Order of Mark Twain.

WRITINGS:

NOVELS

Bonheur d'occasion, Societe des Editions Pascal (Montreal), 1945, translation by Hannah Josephson published as *The Tin Flute* (Literary Guild selection), Reynal, 1947.
La Petite Poule d'eau, Beauchemin (Montreal), 1950, translation by Harry L. Binsse published as *Where Nests the Water Hen: A Novel,* Harcourt, 1951, revised French language edition, Beauchemin, 1970.
Alexandre Chenevert, Caissier, Beauchemin, 1954, translation by Binsse published as *The Cashier,* Harcourt, 1955.
Rue Deschambault, Beauchemin, 1955, translation by Binsse published as *Street of Riches,* Harcourt, 1957.
La Montagne secrete, Beauchemin, 1961, translation by Binsse published as *The Hidden Mountain,* Harcourt, 1962.
La Route d'Altamont, Editions HMH (Montreal), 1966, translation by Joyce Marshall published as *The Road Past Altamont,* Harcourt, 1966.
(With others) *Canada . . .* (includes *La Petite Poule d'eau*), Editions du Burin (St. Cloud, France), 1967.
La Riviere sans repos, Beauchemin, 1970, translation by Marshall published as *Windflower,* McClelland & Stewart, 1970.
Cet ete qui chantait, Editions Francaises, 1972, translation by Marshall published as *Enchanted Summer,* McClelland & Stewart, 1976.
Un Jardin au bout du monde, Beauchemin, 1975, translation by Alan Brown published as *Garden in the Wind,* McClelland & Stewart, 1977.
Ces Enfants de ma vie, Stanke, 1977, translation by Brown published as *Children of My Heart,* McClelland & Stewart, 1979.
Fragiles Lumieres de la terre: Ecrits divers 1942-1970, Quinze, 1978.

Contributor to anthologies, including *Great Short Stories of the World,* Reader's Digest, 1972, and *The Penguin Book of Canadian Short Stories,* Penguin, 1980.

ADAPTATIONS: Bonheur d'Occasion was made into a feature film, 1983.

SIDELIGHTS: Gabrielle Roy, who grew up in rural Manitoba, used Montreal, St. Boniface, and the wilds of northern Canada as settings for her novels. *Saturday Night* critic George Woodcock believed that the complex mixture of cultures in rural Manitoba explains why Roy is "a Canadian writer of truly multi-cultural background and experience." Hugo McPherson, writing in *Canadian Literature,* commented: "Roy's experience has taught her that life offers an endless series of storms and mischances."

Roy filled her novels with people who are underprivileged, people of many origins, and minority people who have difficulty making the transition into the white man's world. "She records their plight with a tolerance and compassion that rests not on patriotism, humanism or religiosity, but on a deep love of mankind," McPherson stated. "Gabrielle Roy *feels* rather than analyzes, and a sense of wonder and of mystery is always with her." Jeannette Urbas, writing in *Journal of Canadian Fiction,* presented a similar view: "Roy immerses us directly in the suffering of her characters: we feel, we think, we live with them. The appeal is directly to the heart."

Canadian Forum critic Paul Socken stated that the link between all of Roy's writings is "people's lifelong struggle to understand the integrity of their own lives, to see their lives as a whole, and their need to create bridges of concern and understanding between themselves and others. . . . It is this very tension, and the success that she has demonstrated in dramatizing it, that makes Gabrielle Roy unique among Canadian writers."

BIOGRAPHICAL/CRITICAL SOURCES:

BOOKS

Amelinckx, Frans C. and Joyce N. Megay, editors, *Travel, Quest, and Pilgrimage as a Literary Theme: Studies in Honor of Reino Virtanen,* Society of Spanish and Spanish-American Studies, 1978, pp. 251-60.

Baby, Ellen R., *The Play of Language and Spectacle: A Structural Reading of Selected Texts by Gabrielle Roy,* ECW Press, 1985.

Chadbourne, Richard, and Hallvard Dahlie, editors, *The New Land: Studies in a Literary Theme,* Wilfrid Laurier University Press, 1978, pp. 92-120.

Contemporary Literary Criticism, Gale, Volume 10, 1979, Volume 14, 1980.

Dictionary of Literary Biography, Volume 68: Canadian Writers, 1920-1959, First Series, Gale, 1988.

Dossiers de Documentation de la litterature canadienne-francaise, Fides, 1967.

Gagne, Marc, *Visages de Gabrielle Roy,* Beauchemin, 1973.

Geniust, Monique, *La Creation romanesque chez Gabrielle Roy,* Cercle du Livre de France, 1966.

Grosskurth, Phyllis, *Gabrielle Roy,* Forum House, 1972.

Hesse, Marta Gudrun, *Gabrielle Roy,* Twayne, 1984.

Hesse, Marta Gudrun, *Gabrielle Roy par elle-meme,* Stanke, 1985.

Hind-Smith, Joan, *The Lives of Margaret Laurence, Gabrielle Roy, Frederick Philip Grove,* Clarke, Irwin, 1975, pp. 62-126.

Hughes, Terrance, *Gabrielle Roy et Margaret Laurence: Deux chemins, une recherche,* Editions du Ble, 1983.

Lecker, Robert, and Jack David, editors, *The Annotated Bibliography of Canada's Major Authors,* volume 1, ECW Press, 1979, pp. 213-63.

Lewis, Paula Gilbert, *The Literary Vision of Gabrielle Roy: An Analysis of Her Works,* Summa Publications, 1984.

Mitcham, Allison, *The Literary Achievement of Gabrielle Roy,* York Press, 1983.

Reisman Babby, Ellen, *The Play of Language and Spectacle: A Structural Reading of Selected Texts by Gabrielle Roy,* ECW Press, 1985.

Ricard, Francois, *Gabrielle Roy,* Fides, 1975.

Shek, Ben-Zion, *Social Realism in the French-Canadian Novel,* Harvest House, 1977, pp. 65-111 and 173-203.

Squier, Susan Merrill, editor, *Women Writers and the City: Essays in Feminist Literary Criticism,* University of Tennessee Press, 1984, pp. 193-209.

Urbas, Jeanette, *From "Thirty Acres" to Modern Times: the Story of French-Canadian Literature,* McGraw-Hill Ryerson, 1976, pp. 45-63.

Warwick, Jack, *The Long Journey: Literary Themes of French Canada,* University of Toronto Press, 1968, pp. 86-100, 140-44.

PERIODICALS

American Review of Canadian Studies, autumn, 1981, pp. 46-66.

Antigonish Review, winter, 1979, pp. 95-9; winter, 1982, pp. 49-55; autumn, 1983, pp. 35-46.

Canadian Children's Literature, Nos. 35-36, 1984, pp. 27-37.

Canadian Forum, February, 1978.

Canadian Literature, summer, 1959, pp. 46-57; autumn, 1969, pp. 6-13; spring, 1981, pp. 161-71; summer, 1984, pp. 183-84.

Canadian Modern Language Review, October, 1964, pp. 20-6; No. 3, 1968, pp. 58-63; No. 2, 1974, pp. 96-100; October, 1983, pp. 105-10.

Canadian Review of Comparative Literature, June, 1984, pp. 205-15.

Essays in French Literature, November, 1981, pp. 86-99.

Essays on Canadian Writing, summer, 1978, pp. 66-71; spring, 1980, pp. 113-26.

Etudes Francaises, June, 1965, pp. 39-65.

Etudes litteraires, winter, 1984, pp. 441-55, 457-79, 481-97, 499-529.

French Review, 1980, pp. 816-25; December, 1981, pp. 207-15.

Humanities Association Bulletin, winter, 1973, pp. 25-31.

Journal of Canadian Fiction, spring, 1972, pp. 69-73; fall, 1972, pp. 51-54.

Journal of Canadian Studies, No. 3, 1968, pp. 3-10.

Journal of Women's Studies in Literature, No. 1, 1979, pp. 133-41 and 243-57.

Maclean's, March 12, 1979.

Malahat Review, October, 1979, pp. 77-85.
Modern Fiction Studies, autumn, 1976, pp. 457-66.
Modern Language Studies, fall, 1981, pp. 44-50; spring, 1982, pp. 22-30.
North Dakota Quarterly, No. 4, 1979, pp. 4-10.
Quebec Studies, spring, 1983, pp. 234-45; No. 2, 1984, pp. 105-17.
Queen's Quarterly, summer, 1962, pp. 177-97; summer, 1965, pp. 334-46.
Revue de L'Universite d'Ottawa, January-March, 1974, pp. 70-77; July-September, 1975, pp. 344-55; July-September, 1976, pp. 309-23; January-March, 1980, pp. 55-61.
Saturday Night, November, 1977.
Studies in Canadian Literature, No. 1, 1982, pp. 90-108.
Tamarack Review, autumn, 1956, pp. 61-70.
Viewpoints, winter, 1969, pp. 29-35.
Voix et Images, No. 3, 1977, pp. 96-115.

OBITUARIES:

PERIODICALS

Chicago Tribune, July 16, 1983.
New York Times, July 15, 1983.
Times (London), July 18, 1983.
Washington Post, July 15, 1983.*

*   *   *

RULE, Jane (Vance) 1931-

PERSONAL: Born March 28, 1931, in Plainfield, NJ; daughter of Arthur Richards (a businessman) and Jane (Packer [one source says "Hink"]) Rule. *Education:* Mills College, B.A., 1952. *Avocational interests:* Civil liberties and international aid programs, gardening, collecting paintings.

ADDRESSES: Home—The Fork, R.R. 1, S-19 C-17, Galiano, British Columbia, Canada V0N 1P0. *Agent*—Georges Borchardt Inc., 136 East 57th St., New York, NY 10022.

CAREER: Writer. Concord Academy, Concord, MA, teacher of English, 1954-56; University of British Columbia, Vancouver, assistant director of International House, 1958-59, periodic lecturer in English, 1959-70, visiting lecturer in creative writing, 1973-74. Has worked variously as typist, teacher of handicapped children, change maker in a gambling house, and store clerk, mostly to obtain background material and information.

MEMBER: P.E.N. International, Writers Union of Canada, Phi Beta Kappa.

AWARDS, HONOURS: Canada Council bursary, 1970-72; Canadian Authors' Association, award for best

novel of 1978, for *The Young in One Another's Arms,* award for best short story of 1978, for "Joy"; Literature Award, American Gay Academic Association, 1978; award of merit, Fund for Human Dignity, 1983; Talking Book of the Year Award, Canadian Institute for the Blind, 1991.

WRITINGS:

The Desert of the Heart (novel), Macmillan (Canada), 1964, World Publishing, 1965, reprinted, Naiad Press (Tallahassee, FL), 1983.
This Is Not for You (novel), McCall Publishing, 1970.
Against the Season (novel), McCall Publishing, 1971.
Theme for Diverse Instruments (short stories), Talon Books (Vancouver), 1975.
Lesbian Images (criticism), Doubleday (Canada), 1975, Crossing Press (Trumansburg, NY), 1982.
The Young in One Another's Arms (novel), Doubleday, 1977.
Contract with the World (novel), Harcourt, 1980.
Outlander (short stories and essays) Naiad Press, 1981.
A Hot-Eyed Moderate, Naiad Press, 1985.
Inland Passage and Other Stories (fiction), Naiad Press, 1985.
Memory Board (fiction), Naiad Press, 1987.
After the Fire (novel), Naiad Press, 1989.

Work is represented in anthologies, including *Best Short Stories of 1972,* Oberon, 1972; *Stories from Pacific and Arctic Canada,* Macmillan, 1975; and *Flaunting It,* edited by Ed Jackson and Stan Persky, Pink Triangle Press, 1982. Author of column "So's Your Grandmother" in *Body Politic.* Contributor of reviews and articles to periodicals, including *Canadian Literature, Redbook, Chatelaine, San Francisco Review, Housewife, Queen's Quarterly,* and *Globe and Mail.*

ADAPTATIONS: The Desert of the Heart was released as the Donna Deitch film *Desert Hearts,* 1985; a film version of *Memory Board* is planned.

WORK IN PROGRESS: Articles and short stories.

SIDELIGHTS: In her writing, Jane Rule explores all facets of women's lives and experiences while generally downplaying or even dismissing the role of men in their lives. Joyce M. Latham asserts in *Library Journal* that Rule's books and stories "reflect the concerns and issues of the lesbian community she most often depicts." When her female characters interact with men, the males are often portrayed as inadequate, useless, and oblivious to the realities of the women. About *The Desert of the Heart,* Rule's first novel, *New York Times Book Review* critic Martin Levin comments, "The men in Miss Rule's novel are faceless types," viewed "with contempt and hostility" by the women in the story. By contrast, the women often share interesting and unconventional relationships. Upon the publication of Rule's 1989 book, Bill Schermbrucker of *Quill and Quire* mentions the author's adherence to her personal intuition throughout her writing history: "By including no major male characters in her new novel, *After the Fire,* Jane Rule puts her own moral vision ahead of conventions that please critics—a stance she has taken throughout her twelve-book career." The reviewer adds, "Rule's career, like her life, has involved a persistent and articulate assertion of herself in the face of the ignorance, bigotry, and denial that surrounds lesbians and books about relationships between women."

Rule had considerable difficulty finding a publisher for *The Desert of the Heart,* a story of two women who meet by chance in Reno, Nevada—one an English teacher visiting the city to obtain a divorce from her husband and the other a casino worker currently dating two losers. The women fall in love and walk away from their respective male relationships. No U.S. publisher would buy the novel, and even after Macmillan of Canada accepted it in 1961, it took another three years until publication. For legal reasons, the publisher required numerous changes in the text. For example, every date had to be omitted to avert any potential libel lawsuits from any casino employees who could document dates, times, and places and sue for the implication of lesbianism. Similarly, *This Is Not For You* languished without a publisher until a new editor at McCall Publishing, who had previously admired the manuscript at another publishing establishment which rejected it, bought and published it.

Theme for Diverse Instruments departs from Rule's earlier fiction, offering a series of short pieces. Elizabeth Fishel writes in the *New York Times Book Review* that the collection "is uneven as well as diverse, presenting brassy, almost snide stories along with sweet and reflective ones, quirky and memorable pieces along with others that strike jarring notes." In *Publishers Weekly,* Penny Kaganoff remarks that Rule's "accomplished" fiction "values individuality; conformity for its own sake is held in low esteem." Latham further declares in *Library Journal,* "This work belongs in all lesbian fiction collections."

In *Lesbian Images,* Rule attempts to trace the evidence and appearance of lesbianism in female writers and their work. As Victoria Glendinning notes in the *Times Literary Supplement,* "*Lesbian Images* is a very personal book: 'a statement of my own attitudes to lesbian experience,' writes Jane Rule, 'as measured against the images made by other women writers in their work and/or lives.'" Glendinning faults the book's overall contributions: "The study of lesbianism in women writers which forms the main part of this book is unrewarding. There is little new that can be said in a few pages about Radclyffe Hall and Gertrude Stein. . . ." Yet a *Publishers Weekly* reviewer

described the book as "nicely balanced, feeling, instructive and altogether very worthwhile."

Returning to the novel form, in *The Young in One Another's Arms* Rule explores the peculiar relationships in a Vancouver boarding house. As the lives of the lodgers intermingle, each person eventually experiences some significant crisis, causing changes in their individual and collective relationships. When the city condemns and sells the boarding house, the group moves to a Gulf island off the Vancouver shore to operate a restaurant. While in *Publishers Weekly* Barbara A. Bannon perceives the characters as "a depressing group of shadowy people, hard to empathize with," a *Kirkus Reviews* critic claims the book "is simply written, . . .and genuinely touching."

Another collection of essays and stories, *Outlander* proposes "that lesbianism is as diverse as the world of heterosexuality," declares Sherrie Tuck in *Library Journal.* The twenty-five pieces were mostly published earlier in periodicals. A *Kirkus Reviews* critic observes that the essays "are short, to the point, admonitory, unabashedly clubby," while the stories "stretch a little further." The reviewer concludes that Rule's *Outlander* compares favorably with other works in the genre.

Rule's next novel, *Memory Board* "explores an unusual situation: the love triangle affected by memory loss, which attracts readers' curiosity . . .and then turns into commentary on our more ordinary lives," explains Eleanor Johnston in *Canadian Literature.* Johnston further comments, "Rule's two central concerns, old age and homosexuality, are described with a precision and respect which compel the reader's involvement with three people who, from the perspective of modern culture, are grotesque old fogeys." About Rule's place in the Canadian literary scene, the critic finds that with *Memory Board,* "Rule has taken up the CanLit tradition of moral exploration while struggling to overcome its reputation of *dullness.*"

After the Fire examines the interactions of five women living on one of British Columbia's Gulf Islands. *Quill and Quire*'s Schermbrucker hails the book as "an engaging, tightly plotted novel about interdependent lives and generations." With connecting threads weaving through the lives of the five protagonists—who range in age from teenaged to elderly and in experience from pregnant to divorced to spinsterly—circumstances compel all the characters to learn about themselves as both individuals and friends. *Publishers Weekly* reviewer Kaganoff remarks that the book's "warmth is not saccharine but realistic." Roz Kaveney writes in the *Times Literary Supplement* that the book "allows the malicious and petty-minded to damn themselves, or come to wisdom at their own speed." She adds, "This is a book which tries for no moments of grandeur or deep passion, but has a wistful dignity entirely its own."

In response to questions about her body of work seeking mainstream endorsement of her lifestyle, Rule, told *Quill and Quire*'s Schermbrucker that she generally ignores public opinion. "I'm *really* not interested in acceptance," Rule says. "I think it's a terrible curse when people are. Self-acceptance is important. But I would hope to be as free as it's possible to be of doing things because I'm expected to. . . ." The reviewer further mentions that Rule consistently answers to her own muse, rejecting outside influences on her writing or her personal choices. Schermbrucker concludes that Rule's is "a world in which voices speak clearly, with humour and great caring, and with tolerance and appreciation of one another's lives."

BIOGRAPHICAL/CRITICAL SOURCES:

BOOKS

Contemporary Literary Criticism, Volume 27, Gale (Detroit), 1984.

PERIODICALS

Canadian Literature, autumn/winter, 1989, pp. 200-02.
Kirkus Reviews, April 15, 1970, p. 482; January 1, 1971, p. 24; January 1, 1977, p. 17; March 1, 1981, p. 340.
Library Journal, June 15, 1981, p. 1324; September 15, 1990, p. 102.
Los Angeles Times Book Review, October 5, 1980.
New York Times Book Review, August 1, 1965, pp. 28-29; September 2, 1990, p. 17.
Observer Review, September 17, 1989, p. 47.
Publishers Weekly, April 6, 1970, p. 54; January 25, 1971, p. 259; May 17, 1976, p. 55; January 3, 1977, p. 59; August 1, 1980, p. 45; February 4, 1983, p. 367; September 15, 1989, p. 113; June 8, 1990, p. 49.
Quill and Quire, September, 1989, p. 69.
Times Literary Supplement, July 23, 1976, p. 904; December 1, 1989, p. 1338.*

—*Sketch by Michaela Swart Wilson*

*   *   *

RYGA, George   1932-1987

PERSONAL: Born July 27, 1932, in Deep Creek, Alberta, Canada; died November 18, 1987, in Summerland, British Columbia, Canada; son of George (a farmer) and Maria (Kolodka) Ryga; married Norma Lois Campbell; children: Lesley, Tanya, Campbell, Sergei, Jamie. *Education:* "Self-educated." *Politics:* Socialist-humanitarian.

CAREER: Worked in farming, construction, and hotel industry; CFRN, Edmonton, Alberta, radio producer, 1950-54; full-time writer, 1962-87. Guest professor at University of British Columbia, Banff School of Fine Arts, and Simon Fraser University.

MEMBER: Association of Canadian Television and Radio Artists, Writers Guild of America—West, British Columbia Civil Liberties Association (honorary member).

AWARDS, HONOURS: Imperial Order Daughters of the Empire Award, 1950 and 1951; Canada Council senior arts grant, 1972; Fringe Frist Award, Edinburgh Festival, 1973; *Ploughmen of the Glacier* won two best play awards in Germany, 1979 and 1980; Governor General's Award nomination, for *A Letter to My Son.*

WRITINGS:

Song of My Hands (poems), National (Edmonton), 1956.
Hungry Hills (novel), Longmans, Green (Toronto), 1963, revised edition, Talonbooks, 1974.
Ballad of a Stone-Picker (novel), Macmillan (Toronto), 1966, revised edition, Talonbooks, 1976.
Night Desk, Talonbooks, 1976.
Beyond the Crimson Morning: Reflections from a Journey through Contemporary China (travel book), Doubleday, 1979.
In the Shadow of the Vulture, Talonbooks, 1985.
Summerland, Talonbooks, 1992.

PLAYS

Nothing But a Man, produced in Edmonton, Alberta, at Walterdale Playhouse, 1966.
Indian (produced in Winnipeg, Manitoba, at Manitoba Theatre Centre, 1974), Book Society of Canada, 1967.
The Ecstasy of Rita Joe (two-act; music by Ann Mortifee and Willy Dunn; produced in Vancouver, British Columbia, at Queen Elizabeth Playhouse, 1967; produced in Washington, DC, 1973), Talonbooks, 1970.
Just an Ordinary Person, produced in Vancouver at Metro Theatre, 1968.
Grass and Wild Strawberries (music by The Collectors), produced in Vancouver at Queen Elizabeth Playhouse, 1969.
(Author of music and lyrics) *Captives of the Faceless Drummer* (produced in Vancouver at Vancouver Art Gallery, 1971), Talonbooks, 1971.
(Author of music) *Sunrise on Sarah* (produced in Banff, Alberta, at Banff School of Fine Arts, 1972), Talonbooks, 1973.
Portrait of Angelica, produced in Banff at Banff School of Fine Arts, 1973.
Paracelsus (published in *Canadian Theatre Review,* fall, 1974), produced in Vancouver at Playhouse Theatre, 1986.

Ploughmen of the Glacier (produced in Vernon, British Columbia, at Vernon Community Centre, 1976), Talonbooks, 1977.

Seven Hours to Sundown (produced in Edmonton at University of Alberta Studio Theatre, 1976), Talonbooks, 1977.

The Last of the Gladiators (adapted from *Night Desk*), produced in Summerland, British Columbia, by Giant's Head Theatre Company, 1976.

Jeremiah's Place (children's play), produced in Victoria, British Columbia, 1978.

A Letter to My Son, produced in North Bay, Ontario, by Kam Theatre Lab, 1981.

One More for the Road, produced in Vancouver at Firehall Theatre, 1985.

RADIO PLAYS

Author of radio plays, including *A Touch of Cruelty,* 1961, *Half-Caste,* 1962, *Masks and Shadows,* 1963, *Bread Route,* 1963, *Departures,* 1963, *Ballad for Bill,* 1963, *The Stone Angel,* 1965, and *Seasons of a Summer Day,* 1975. Also author of scripts for the series, *Miners, Gentlemen, and Other Hard Cases,* 1974-75, and *Advocates of Danger,* 1976.

TELEVISION PLAYS

Author of television plays, including *Indian,* 1962, *The Storm,* 1962, *Bitter Grass,* 1963, *For Want of Something Better to Do,* 1963, *The Tulip Garden,* 1963, *Two Soldiers,* 1963, *The Pear Tree,* 1963, *Man Alive,* 1965, *The Kamloops Incident,* 1965, *A Carpenter by Trade* (documentary), 1967, *Ninth Summer,* 1972, *The Mountains* (documentary), 1973, and *The Ballad of Iwan Lepa* (documentary), 1976. Also author of scripts for the series, *The Manipulators,* 1968, and *The Name of the Game,* 1969.

COLLECTIONS

The Ecstasy of Rita Joe and Other Plays (contains *The Ecstasy of Rita Joe, Indian,* and *Grass and Wild Strawberries*), introduced by Brian Parker, New Press, 1971.

Country and Western (contains *Portrait of Angelica, Ploughmen of the Glacier,* and *Seven Hours to Sundown*), Talonbooks, 1976.

Two Plays (contains *Paracelsus* and *Prometheus Bound*), Turnstone Press, 1982.

Portrait of Angelica [and] *A Letter to My Son,* Turnstone Press, 1984.

The Athabasca Ryga, edited by E. David Gregory, Talonbooks, 1990.

OTHER

A Feast of Thunder (oratorio), music by Morris Surdin, produced in Toronto at Massey Hall, 1973.

Author of other oratorios, including *Twelve Ravens for the Sun,* music by Mikis Theodorakis, 1975. Author of preface, *The Collected Plays of Gwen Pharis Ringwood,* edited by Enid Delgatty Rutland, Borealis, 1982. Also author of short stories, film scripts, and two albums of folk songs. Contributor to periodicals, including *Canadian Theatre Review, Canadian Drama,* and *Canadian Literature.*

A collection of Ryga's papers is housed in the University of Calgary Library.

Ryga's work has been translated into other languages, including Ukrainian.

ADAPTATIONS: The Ecstasy of Rita Joe was adapted for ballet and produced by the Royal Winnipeg Ballet, 1971.

SIDELIGHTS: Canadian playwright and novelist George Ryga was a controversial author who used his work as a voice for social change. He was a champion of the underdog whose plays focus on an individual's struggle within a repressive social structure, battling outside forces and feelings of loneliness and isolation. Usually his heroes and heroines are poor, drawn from the working classes. His early experiences—leaving school at thirteen, taking correspondence courses, and working full-time as a manual laborer—helped to form his identification and sympathy with this group. Ryga also perceived the need for a cultural mythology based on the people themselves, not the "official history" of politicians supported by the government. Jerry Wasserman, writing in the *Dictionary of Literary Biography,* noted that Ryga's dramatic works and fiction are "distinguished by a strong consciousness and the attempt to create a folk art using contemporary themes."

Ryga was perhaps best known for his play *The Ecstasy of Rita Joe,* the story of a Native American woman's attempts to become a part of the white world around her, only to be raped and murdered by a gang of white men. *The Ecstasy of Rita Joe* "established that an English-Canadian play could address serious social issues in vernacular language and nonrealistic style and still be commercially appealing, helping make possible the explosion of Canadian drama that occurred in the late 1960s and early 1970s," commented Wasserman. Neil Carson proclaimed in a 1970 *Canadian Literature* article that *The Ecstasy of Rita Joe* "establishes Ryga as the most exciting talent writing for the stage in Canada today."

Ryga's other plays call up characters similar to Rita Joe—alienated individuals in search of something, such as acceptance. In his first novel, *Hungry Hills,* Ryga creates Snit Mandolin on a quest for his origins and a sense of belonging. What Snit discovers is incest, the barren farmlands of northern Alberta, and his indomitable Aunt. His efforts to reestablish a life there fail in the face of the "cowardly greed of these hungry hills." *Hungry Hills* "shows

Ryga's interest in the lives of the poor and oppressed as well as his preoccupation with problems of structure," declares Carson in the *Journal of Canadian Fiction.*

"Romeo has tales, and no place to tell them except . . . before the night desk," describes W. H. Rockett, writing in *Saturday Night,* of *Night Desk.* The story of Romeo Kuchmir as narrated by his sole listener, the night man or "kid," *Night Desk* tells the tale of one isolated man. His stage is the night desk, but he is the only character in the "play" of this novel. Rockett believes that Kuchmir "has made what Brian Parker had called a Ryga folk ballad. Words trigger words, responses, new anecdotes, old ideas. Everything weaves back on senseless legs to the same loneliness. . . . Romeo is his own best audience."

Ryga's focus on the individual is at the core of his work. His protagonists are isolated, alienated, and rejected by society. "The sense of spiritual homelessness is common in Ryga's work and many of his characters define themselves by their relationship to a country they have lost or one they never find," comments Carson in *Canadian Literature.* He also notes in the *Journal of Canadian Fiction* that "what impresses in [Ryga's] work is not his social criticism, still less his portrayal of the agents of justice and bureaucracy, but his assertion of individual courage and dignity in the face of those most terrible oppressions—loneliness and death."

BIOGRAPHICAL/CRITICAL SOURCES:

BOOKS

Contemporary Literary Criticism, Volume 14, Gale, 1980.
Dictionary of Literary Biography, Volume 60: *Canadian Writers since 1960, Second Series,* Gale, 1987.
Innes, Christopher, *Politics and the Playwright: George Ryga,* Simon & Pierre, 1985.
Moore, Mavor, *Four Canadian Playwrights,* Holt, 1973.
New, William H., editor, *Dramatists in Canada: Selected Essays,* University of British Columbia Press, 1972.
Who's Who in Canadian Literature: 1985-86, Reference Press, 1985.

PERIODICALS

Books and Bookmen, February, 1966.
Canadian Drama, fall, 1979, pp. 139-43; fall, 1982, pp. 160-72.
Canadian Forum, January/February, 1979.
Canadian Literature, summer, 1970, pp. 155-62.
Canadian Theatre Review, summer, 1979, pp. 36-44.
Journal of Canadian Fiction, Volume IV, number 4, 1979, pp. 185-87.
Saturday Night, May, 1966; January/February, 1977, pp. 83-84.
Spectator, January, 1966.

OBITUARIES:

PERIODICALS

Times (London), November 28, 1987.

S

SAFER, Morley 1931-

PERSONAL: Born November 8, 1931, in Toronto, Ontario, Canada; came to the United States in 1964; son of Max (an upholsterer) and Anna (Cohn) Safer; married Jane Fearer (an anthropologist), 1968; children: Sarah. *Education:* Attended University of Western Ontario, 1952. *Avocational interests:* Painting, reading, playing tennis, watching television, baking.

ADDRESSES: Home—Manhattan, NY. *Office*—CBS News, 524 West 57th St., New York, NY 10019.

CAREER: Rueters (news agency), London, England, 1955; Canadian Broadcasting Corporation (CBC-TV), correspondent and producer, 1955-60, writer and London correspondent, 1961-64; British Broadcasting Corporation (BBC-TV), London, correspondent and producer, 1961; Columbia Broadcasting System, Inc. (CBS-TV), New York City, London correspondent, 1964, head of Saigon bureau, 1965-70, chief of London bureau, 1967-70, co-editor and co-host of television news program *Sixty Minutes,* 1970—.

MEMBER: Royal College of Bloviation (fellow; Edinburgh).

AWARDS, HONOURS: Polk Award, Long Island University, 1965; Overseas Press Club of America award, 1965, 1966; Sigma Delta Chi award, 1965; George Foster Peabody Radio and Television Award, 1966, 1983; 7 Emmy Awards, National Academy of Television Arts and Sciences Award, 1981, 1982, and 1985; George Foster Peabody Radio and Television Award, Alfred I. duPont-Columbia University Award, and Emmy Award, 1984, all for *Sixty Minutes* broadcast "Lenell Geter's in Jail."

WRITINGS:

Flashbacks: On Returning to Vietnam (memoir), Random House (New York), 1990.

FILM AND VIDEO SCRIPTS

Thoroughly Modern Millicent (from a *Sixty Minutes* segment), Arthur Mokin Productions, 1981.
The Wrong Stuff: American Architecture (from a *Sixty Minutes* segment), Carousel Films, 1982.
Unknown Genius: The Savant Syndrome (from a *Sixty Minutes* segment), Lawren Productions, 1984.

Writer and editor of numerous other *Sixty Minutes* segments. Also author of news documentary *The Second Battle of Britain,* 1976.

SIDELIGHTS: Sixty Minutes, the CBS weekly television news show, is the only nonfiction program to be ranked consistently in Nielsen's "top ten" rated shows. And Morley Safer helped put it there. He joined the staff in 1970 when the show was experiencing a critical period. Shuffled around from one time slot to another, it never quite mustered a steady following, and with the loss of original correspondent Harry Reasoner to the *ABC News,* the future of *Sixty Minutes* looked dim. The choice of replacement ("We're looking for Reasoner's wit and style, his craggy good looks," explained executive producer Don Hewitt at the time) was crucial, and Morley Safer satisfied the requirements. "It was one of the better fits of all time in television," proclaimed Donovan Moore. "A man of average television conceit, though in a humble way, Safer glided into the '60 Minutes' operation, his essays and softer features balancing [Mike] Wallace's hard stuff. In a medium growing fat on pedestrian entertainment, Safer brought writing—not just reporting, but writing, *good* writing—to the air." Since that time, *Sixty Minutes* has steadily worked its way into the weekly viewing of millions of Americans.

"I think we're popular because you never know how the show is going to end," suggested Safer to Ron Base. "I defy you to name any other regular broadcast where you don't know in the first ten minutes how it's going to end." Another ingredient of its success is the dedication of the staff. Safer and Wallace, co-hosts and co-editors of the show, work six and seven days a week, logging more than 200,000 miles apiece each year as well as writing most of their own material. Dan Rather, until Reasoner's return in 1979 the newest member of the team (he would later depart the show to assume Walter Cronkite's anchor spot for the *CBS Evening News*), denied the existence of regular working hours on the show. "Once in a while," he admitted to Base, "when I'm flying around in the middle of the night, I ask myself why I'm doing this. The answer is that this is what most of us got into journalism for. Hell, I'd pay cash money to do this." Safer agrees: "It's the best job in the world. No question."

Before joining the *Sixty Minutes* team and CBS News, Safer worked for both the Canadian and British Broadcasting Corporations. During that time he reported on a variety of news events, though was best known for his commentary on battle. In his twenty-odd years as a foreign correspondent, Safer "covered nine wars, took a bit of shrapnel, suffered nightmares about Nigeria and made his reputation in Vietnam," observed Mary Vespa.

Safer was sent to southeast Asia in 1965 for a stint as war correspondent in a campaign that was expected to last no longer than six months. In late August of that year, Safer set out for the Marine staging area in Da Nang, where he found them preparing for the next day's mission. When a young lieutenant suggested he accompany them, the newsman considered it an ideal way to delve into the character of the current military action. En route to their destination, Safer queried the officer for details of the operation. He was told that the village of Cam Ne had turned hostile, often firing on U.S. troops; the province chief wanted it stopped. It was supposedly for retribution that the Marines had been called in. Years later, however, it was learned that "the reason Cam Ne was leveled had nothing to do with the Vietcong; rather the Vietnamese province chief was furious that the locals had refused to pay their taxes, and he wanted the village punished; and the Americans, who were to do the punishing, were not aware of that," revealed David Halberstam.

What lay in store at Cam Ne was more than Safer or the American public expected. Instead of a militant populace showering the U.S. forces with artillery, the small community did not fire a single shot in their own defense. The Marines, indiscriminately bombarding and setting fire to

the villager's homes, met with no resistance. The film footage documenting these maneuvers was to shock America into recognizing the harsh realities of the war. President Lyndon Johnson was outraged and accused Safer of being a Communist. He immediately launched an investigation into Safer's past and charged the newsman with bribing or tricking the senior officer into staging the entire "farce." Much to Johnson's dismay, however, none of his accusations could be substantiated.

Because of Morley Safer, Halberstam concluded, the way was cleared for other newsmen and newswomen to seek out the truth and report it fully without self-imposed censorship: "Overnight, one correspondent with one cameraman could have as much effect as ten or fifteen or twenty senators turned dissident."

In his 1990 book, *Flashbacks: On Returning to Vietnam,* Safer revisits the Asian locales where he spent so much time during the conflict. Jeff Danziger writes in the *Los Angeles Times* that "his findings and recollections are well worth reading. His style is spare and sharp. . . . I attribute his manner to his being essentially still a Canadian, despite years at CBS. Like most Canadians, he routinely deducts 90 percent of the ballyhoo of American journalism." In a period of just over a week, Safer toured Hanoi, Saigon, and Ho Chi Minh City, and interviewed several of the important military personages of his wartime journalism. The book contains information about contemporary Vietnam as well as reflections from his past experiences. About the abbreviated visit, Nicholas Lemann comments in the *New York Times Book Review,* "That's a slender reed on which to rest a book, but Mr. Safer has brought it off, thanks in no small part to the richness of his previous association with the country." Lemann further observes: "A trench coat is not mentioned, but the rest of the classic picture is there: the jump-cuts from battlefields to fine restaurants and hotels, the long evenings of male bonding over a diminishing bottle of whisky, the good novel tucked under the arm, the mixture of cynicism about organizations with sentimentality about friends, the air of prefeminist romance (which in this case finds expression in a crush Mr. Safer develops on his straitlaced interpreter, 'the delicious Miss Mai')." Danziger admires Safer's work—"Safer has a gift for vignette"—yet laments the lack of more substantial facts: "Safer is a strong writer and pretty fearless, at least by today's standards, but he should have put more detail in the book." A *Time* reviewer remarks that the book offers "an artful contrast of past and present" as well as a glimpse of how the job of a journalist used to be performed.

BIOGRAPHICAL/CRITICAL SOURCES:

BOOKS

Authors in the News, Volume 2, Gale, 1976.

Safer, Morley, *Flashbacks: On Returning to Vietnam,* Random House (New York), 1990.

PERIODICALS

Atlantic Monthly, February, 1976.
Detroit News Magazine, September 16, 1979.
Los Angeles Times Book Review, April 1, 1990, pp. 2, 8.
Milwaukee Journal, June 1, 1975.
New York Times Book Review, April 15, 1990, pp. 3, 19.
People, January 15, 1979; May 28, 1979.
Rolling Stone, January 12, 1978.
Time, April 30, 1990, p. 104.*

*   *   *

ST. CYR, Cyprian
  See BERNE, Eric (Lennard)

*   *   *

SALVERSON, Laura Goodman   1890-1970

PERSONAL: Born December 9, 1890, in Winnipeg, Manitoba, Canada; died July 13, 1970; daughter of Laurus and Ingiborg (Gudsmundotte) Goodman; married George Salverson (a railway dispatcher), 1913; children: one son. *Education:* Attended public school in Duluth, MN.

CAREER: Novelist and poet.

AWARDS, HONOURS: Governor General's Award for fiction, 1937, for *The Dark Weaver;* Gold Medal for literary merit, Paris Institute of Arts and Letters, 1938; Governor General's Award for nonfiction, 1939, for *Confessions of an Immigrant's Daughter;* Ryerson Fiction Award, 1954, for *Immortal Rock.*

WRITINGS:

The Viking Heart, McClelland & Stewart (Toronto), 1923.
Wayside Gleams (poetry), McClelland & Stewart (Toronto), 1925.
When Sparrows Fall, T. Allen (Toronto), 1925.
Lord of the Silver Dragon: A Romance of Lief the Lucky, McClelland & Stewart (Toronto), 1927.
The Dove, Ryerson (Toronto), 1933.
The Dark Weaver, Ryerson (Toronto), 1937.
Black Lace, Ryerson (Toronto), 1938.
Confessions of an Immigrant's Daughter (autobiography), Ryerson (Toronto), 1939.
Immortal Rock: The Saga of the Kensington Stone, Ryerson (Toronto), 1954.

SIDELIGHTS: Laura Goodman Salverson "was one of the pioneers of Canadian prairie fiction, perhaps Canada's first native prairie novelist," declared Paul Hjartarson in his *Dictionary of Literary Biography* essay. Born in Winnipeg, Manitoba—then the edge of the frontier—to desperately poor Icelandic immigrant parents, Salverson and her family moved often in attempts to escape their poverty. At various points during her youth, Salverson lived in North Dakota, Minnesota, and Mississippi. Partly because of this, and partly because she was sickly as a child, Salverson started school and learned English late. Her education was frequently interrupted by her family's poverty; she worked in a tailor's shop and in a hospital to earn a living. "As a result of her childhood experiences," Hjartarson explained, "[Salverson] developed a sympathy for the poor and an awareness of the plight of women that inform her writing."

Salverson's Icelandic heritage influenced almost all her work, from her first and most famous novel, *The Viking Heart,* to her autobiography, *Confessions of an Immigrant's Daughter.* However, while *The Viking Heart, The Dark Weaver,* and *When Sparrows Fall* are all about immigrants and the ways they adapt to their new land, the rest of her prose draws on history for its inspiration. *Black Lace* is set in the France of the Sun King, Louis XIV, while *Lord of the Silver Dragon, The Dove,* and *The Immortal Rock* are all based on Icelandic or Norse history and legend. *Lord of the Silver Dragon* recounts Leif Ericson's voyages to Greenland and the Atlantic coast of North America. *The Immortal Rock* is a fiction based on the Kensington Stone, a slab of rock discovered in Minnesota in 1898, which supposedly recounts the tale of a fourteenth-century Norse expedition to the Midwest. Salverson's story depicts the last twenty-four hours of the survivors. *The Dove,* on the other hand, tells the fate of an Icelandic woman carried off to slavery in Algiers. "In her books," Hjartarson declared, Salverson "attempts to reconcile the narrative form of the Icelandic saga with that of the popular romance in order to interpret Icelandic life for English-speaking readers."

BIOGRAPHICAL/CRITICAL SOURCES:

BOOKS

Dictionary of Literary Biography, Volume 92: *Canadian Writers, 1890-1920,* Gale, 1990.
Eggleston, Wilfrid, *The Frontier and Canadian Letters,* Ryerson (Toronto), 1957.
Harrison, Dick, *Unnamed Country: The Struggle for a Canadian Prairie Fiction,* University of Alberta Press (Edmonton), 1977.
Ricou, Laurence, *Vertical Man/Horizontal World,* University of British Columbia Press (Vancouver), 1973.
Twentieth Century Romance and Historical Writers, 3rd edition, St. James, 1990.

SAVARD, Felix-Antoine   1896-1982

PERSONAL: Born August 31, 1896, in Quebec City, Quebec, Canada; died August 24, 1982; son of Louis-Joseph and Ida-Genevieve Gosselin. *Education:* Attended the Grand Seminaire in Chicoutimi. *Religion:* Roman Catholic.

CAREER: Grand Seminaire, Chicoutimi, Quebec, instructor in Latin and French, 1919-26; ordained as a Catholic priest, 1922; stayed in a Benedictine monastery, c. 1926; established and administrated rural parishes in the Province of Quebec, c. 1926-1941; Universite Laval, Quebec City, Quebec, professor and folklorist, beginning 1941, dean of the faculty of letters, 1950-57; University of Ottawa, Ottawa, Ontario, research associate, 1970-73; author.

MEMBER: Academie Canadienne-Francaise; Royal Society of Canada.

AWARDS, HONOURS: Medaille de l'Academie Francaise, and Lorne Pierce Medal, both 1945; Prix Duvernay, 1948; Governor General's Award, 1960; Prix du Grand Jury des Lettres, 1961; Prix David, 1968.

WRITINGS:

Menaud, maitre-draveur (novel), Garneau (Quebec City, Quebec), 1937; revised, 1944; translated by Alan Sullivan as *Boss of the River,* Ryerson (Toronto, Ontario), 1947; French version revised twice, Fides (Montreal, Quebec), 1960, 1964; translated by Richard Howard as *Master of the River,* Harvest House (Montreal, Quebec), 1976.
L'Abatis (nonfiction), Fides, 1943, revised edition, 1960.
La Minuit (novel-poem), Fides, 1948.
Le Barachois (stories and poetry), Fides, 1959.
Martin et le pauvre, Fides, 1959.
La Folle (dramatic text), Fides, 1960.
La Dalle-des-Morts (play; produced March 20, 1966, at the Theatre Orpheum, Montreal), Fides, 1965.
Symphonie du Misereor (poem), Editions de l'Universite d'Ottawa (Ottawa, Ontario), 1968.
Le Bouscueil, Fides, 1972.
La Roche Ursule, S. Allard (Quebec City, Quebec), 1972.
Journal et souvenirs I: 1961-1962, Fides, 1973.
Aux Marges du silence, Michel Nantel (Chateauguay, Quebec), 1974.
Journal et souvenirs II: 1963-1964, Fides, 1975.
Discours, Fides, 1975.
Carnet du soir interieur I (memoirs), Fides, 1978.
Carnet du soir interieur II (memoirs), Fides, 1979.

Also contributor of articles to periodicals, including *Lectures, Journal de l'Instruction Publique,* and *Revue de l'Universite Laval.*

ADAPTATIONS: Menaud, maitre-draveur, was adapted as an opera with music by Marc Gagne, Fides, 1987.

SIDELIGHTS: French-Canadian author Felix-Antoine Savard penned works in several genres—creating poetry, novels, plays, and nonfiction pieces. He is best remembered, however, for his poetic 1937 novel, *Menaud, maitre-draveur.* Savard revised *Menaud* several times, and the work was twice translated into English. In 1947 it bore the title *Boss of the River;* in 1976, *Master of the River. Master of the River,* as well as Savard's other creations in print, garnered him several prestigious honors during the course of his career, including the Governor General's Award and the Prix David.

In addition to his writing career, Savard pursued another calling. Born in Quebec City, Quebec, Canada, in 1896, he was ordained as a Catholic priest in 1922. He taught Latin and French at the same school in which he had been a seminarian for four years following his ordination. Then, after a brief sojourn in a Benedictine monastery, Savard became fundamental in the establishment and administration of several rural parishes within the province of Quebec. His experience with one of these, in the Abitibi region of Quebec, later led to his nonfiction book on its inhabitants, *L'Abatis.* Savard eventually became a professor of folklore at the Universite Laval.

Previous to joining that faculty, however, Savard published *Master of the River.* Menaud, the novel's protagonist, is a French-Canadian log-runner who works for English-Canadians. The lifestyle he leads poses many threats to his family's well-being: he loses a son in a river accident, and his daughter is endangered by a bad relationship. These and other pressures lead Menaud to mount a revolt against his English-speaking employers, who he feels are exploiting Quebec's natural resources. As H. R. Runte observed in the *Dictionary of Literary Biography,* "early critics praised [the work's] ideology but were confused as to whether it is a novel, an epic poem, or a drama. . . . Recent criticism has, however, seen [the work] in its masterful unity of form and content." The French-language version of the book was adapted as an opera by Marc Gagne in 1987.

Also among Savard's better-known works is his 1965 play, *La Dalle-des-Morts.* This piece is set in the 1830s, and features a heroine, Delie, who symbolizes what Runte called "mythical feminine forces of stability." She is somewhat in opposition to her fiance, Gildore, who wishes to push further and further into the Quebec wilderness in order to escape the control and influence of English-speaking Canadians.

In addition to his more secular work, Savard wrote poetic explorations of religion, such as *La Folle* and *Symphonie du Misereor.* Both are set in the region of Canada known as Acadia, formerly dominated by French-speaking dwellers. The author-priest also left four volumes of memoirs—two entitled *Journal et souvenirs,* and two entitled *Carnet du soir interieur.* He died in 1982.

BIOGRAPHICAL/CRITICAL SOURCES:

BOOKS

Dictionary of Literary Biography, Volume 68: *Canadian Writers, 1920-1959, First Series,* Gale, 1988, pp. 324-27.

Francois, Ricard, *L'Art de Felix-Antione Savard dans "Menaud, maitre-draveur,"* Fides, 1972.

Major, Andre, *Felix-Antoine Savard,* Fides, 1968.

Samson, Jean-Noel, and Roland M. Charland, *Felix-Antione Savard,* Fides, 1969.

Savard, Felix-Antoine, *Journal et souvenirs I: 1961-1962,* Fides, 1973.

Savard, *Journal et souvenirs II: 1963-1964,* Fides, 1975.

Savard, *Carnet du soir interieur I,* Fides, 1978.

Savard, *Carnet du soir interieur II,* Fides, 1979.

PERIODICALS

Incidences, winter, 1968.*

*   *   *

SCOTT, Duncan Campbell   1862-1947

PERSONAL: Born on August 2, 1862, in Ottawa, Ontario, Canada; died on December 19, 1947, in Ottawa, Ontario, Canada; son of William Scott (a Methodist minister) and Janet Campbell MacCallum; married Belle Warner Botsford (a concert violinest) in 1894 (died, 1929); married Desiree Elise Aylen in 1931; children: (first marriage) Elizabeth Duncan (died at age 12). *Education:* Wesleyan College, Stanstead, Quebec, 1877-79.

CAREER: Indian Branch (later Department of Indian Affairs), Ottawa, Canada: clerk third class, 1879-93, chief clerk, 1893-96, secretary of the department, 1896-1909, superintendent of Indian education, 1909-23, deputy superintendent general, 1923-32. Toronto *Globe,* columnist, 1892-93.

MEMBER: Ottawa Drama League (president), Canadian Authors Association (president, 1931-33).

AWARDS, HONOURS: D. Litt., University of Toronto, 1922; Lorne Pierce Medal, 1927; LL.D., Queens University, 1939; fellow, 1899, honorary secretary, 1911-21, president, 1921-22, Royal Society of Canada; fellow, Royal Society of Literature (United Kingdom); C.M.G. (Companion, Order of St. Michael and St. George), 1934.

WRITINGS:

POETRY

The Magic House, and Other Poems, Durie, 1893.

Labor and the Angel, Copeland & Day, 1898.

New World Lyrics and Ballads, Morang, 1905.

Via Borealis, Tyrrell, 1906.

Lundy's Lane and Other Poems, McClelland, Goodchild & Stewart, 1916.

Beauty and Life, McClelland & Stewart, 1921.

The Poems of Duncan Campbell Scott, McClelland & Stewart, 1926.

The Green Cloister: Later Poems, McClelland & Stewart, 1935.

Selected Poems, edited by E. K. Brown, Ryerson, 1951.

Powassan's Drum: Selected Poems of Duncan Campbell Scott, edited by Raymond Souster and Douglas Lochhead, Tecumseh, 1985.

Also wrote *To the Canadian Mothers and Three Other Poems,* 1916 and *The Poems,* 1926. Poetry also collected in *Powassan's Drum: Poems,* edited by Raymond Souster and Douglas Lochhead, 1985.

FICTION

In the Village of Viger, Copeland & Day, 1896.

The Witching of Elspie: A Book of Stories, McClelland & Stewart, 1923.

Selected Stories of Duncan Campbell Scott, edited by Glenn Clever, University of Ottawa Press, 1972.

Untitled Novel, ca. 1905, University of Toronto Press, 1979.

OTHER

(Editor with Pelham Edgar and W. D. LeSeur) *The Makers of Canada,* 22 volumes, Morang, 1903-08, 1916; revised edition, 12 volumes, edited by W. L. Grant, Oxford University Press, 1926.

John Graves Simcoe (biography), Morang, 1905.

(Contributor) *Canada and Its Provinces,* edited by Adam Shortt and Arthur Doughty, Glasgow, Brook, 1914.

Poetry and Progress (criticism), Royal Society of Canada, 1922.

(Author of foreword) Elise Aylen, *Roses of Shadow,* Macmillan, 1930.

The Administration of Indian Affairs in Canada, Canadian Institute of International Affairs, 1931.

(Author of foreword and editor with E. K. Brown) Archibald Lampman, *At the Long Sault and Other New Poems,* Ryerson, 1943.

The Circle of Affection, and Other Pieces in Prose and Verse, McClelland & Stewart, 1947.

(Editor and contributor) Archibald Lampman, *Selected Poems,* Ryerson, 1947.

Some Letters of Duncan Campbell Scott, Archibald Lampman, & Others, edited by Arthur S. Bourinot, published by the editor in Ottawa, 1959.

More Letters of Duncan Campbell Scott, edited by Bourinot, published by the editor in Ottawa, 1960.

(With William Wilfred Campbell and Archibald Lampman) *At the Mermaid Inn,* University of Toronto Press, 1979.

The Poet and the Critic: A Literary Correspondence Between D. C. Scott and E. K. Brown, edited by Robert L. McDougall, Carleton University Press, 1983.

Also wrote the following plays: *Pierre,* produced 1921, published in *Canadian Plays from Hart House Theatre I,* edited by Vincent Massey, 1926; *Prologue,* produced 1923, published in *The Poems,* 1926; and *Joy! Joy! Joy!,* produced 1927.

SIDELIGHTS: Duncan Campbell Scott is best remembered as one of the leading poets of the "Confederation group." Writing in an era following the formation of the Dominion of Canada, Scott, along with poets Bliss Carman, Archibald Lampman, and Charles G.D. Roberts, helped create and cultivate a sense of national identity. Early cast as a regional writer of the northern wilderness, especially its Indian life, Scott is being reappraised in our time as a writer of great diversity with a complex, though unified, vision and a distinctly Canadian spirit.

Scott's lifelong interest in Native Americans began in his childhood when, with his missionary father, his family spent several years among the Indians. He later entered the civil service in Ottawa's Department of Indian Affairs, spending fifty-two years in a successful administrative career which culminated with his position as Deputy Superintendent General. On his frequent trips in this service, Scott became acquainted with the Canadian wilds and visited many Indian tribes, gaining insight into their customs and life. From these experiences came the material for his narrative poems of Indian life such as "At Gull Lake, 1810" and "The Forsaken." Scott's first poetry writing, however, was prompted by his close friendship with an associate in the civil service, the young poet Archibald Lampman. Together they collaborated with Wilfrid Campbell on a weekly literary column, "At the Mermaid Inn," which appeared in the *Toronto Globe* from 1892-93 and served as a guide to prevailing tastes. A collection of the columns was published as *At the Mermaid Inn* in 1979.

Scott has been alternately praised as a lyric and as a dramatic poet. His best lyric poems are found in the collections *The Magic House, and Other Poems, Beauty and Life,* and *The Green Cloister: Later Poems.* Nature, its moods and seasons, are often the subject of these lyrics, and critics are unfailing in nothing Scott's mastery at painting vivid, colorful descriptions and creating a myste-

rious and compelling atmosphere. Scott's dramatic poems are also highly regarded, especially the narrative pieces on Indian life. Violence emerges as an important theme in many of these narrative studies as well as in Scott's lyric poems. The dialectic of tension and resolution is, in fact, central to Scott's vision—from these conflicts, in nature and between people, issue beauty and peace. An outstanding example of such a dialectic is "The Piper of Arll," called by some Scott's masterpiece, which portrays the role of the artist and the nature of artistic experience. Filled with the tensions of contrasts (secluded bay and wild ocean, rustic shepherd and traveled sailors) and paradoxes (life in death, fulfillment in self-sacrifice), the poem culminates in a transcendent peace.

In the past decade Scott's stories, long neglected by critics, have begun to receive recognition. His two volumes of short stories, *In the Village of Viger* and *The Witching of Elspie: A Book of Stories,* are often contrasted with each other: the first, a prose counterpart to *The Magic House,* is light and pleasurable; the second, wild and bloody stories of the lonely fur-trade areas, is stark and harsh. Recent publication of Scott's only novel, *Untitled Novel, ca. 1905,* sheds new light on his prose, proving Scott an early innovator in the portrayal of the modern antihero. Some critics now conjecture that Scott may be remembered for his prose rather than his poetry.

Despite a long career as a civil servant, Scott received many awards in his lifetime that were a tribute to his literary artistry, including the Lorne Pierce Medal, which honors Canadians for significant achievements in imaginative or critical literature. He was elected a Fellow of the Royal Society of Canada in 1899 and became its President in 1921. Scott is recognized as a commanding poet of distinct Canadian sensibility.

BIOGRAPHICAL/CRITICAL SOURCES:

BOOKS

Brown, E. K., *On Canadian Poetry,* Ryerson, 1944, pp. 118-43.

Dragland, S. L., *Duncan Campbell Scott: A Book of Criticism,* Tecumseh, 1974.

ECW's Biographical Guide to Canadian Poets, ECW Press, 1993, pp. 65-69.

Monkman, Leslie, *A Native Heritage,* University of Toronto Press, 1981.

New, W. H., *Dreams of Speech and Violence,* University of Toronto Press, 1987.

Such, K. P., editor, *The Duncan Campbell Scott Symposium,* University of Ottawa Press, 1979.

Titley, Brian, *A Narrow Vision: Duncan Campbell Scott and the Administration of Indian Affairs in Canada,* University of British Columbia Press, 1986.

Twentieth-Century Literary Criticism, Gale, Volume 6, 1982.

PERIODICALS

Antigonish, fall-winter, 1991-92, pp. 138-45.
Books in Canada, December, 1979, p. 10.
Canadian Literature, summer, 1959, pp. 13-25; autumn, 1962, pp. 43-52; summer, 1968, pp. 15-27; summer, 1979, pp. 142-43; winter, 1986, pp. 10-25, 27-40; autumn, 1990, pp. 176-79; summer, 1994, pp. 86-106.
Canadian Poetry, spring, 1988, pp. 49-67.
Dalhousie Review, April, 1927, pp. 38-46.
Essays on Canadian Writing, fall-winter, 1979-80, pp. 70-77.
Journal of Canadian Fiction, No. 16, 1976, pp. 138-43.

*   *   *

SHATNER, William   1931-

PERSONAL: Born March 22, 1931, in Montreal, Quebec, Canada; son of Joseph and Anne Shatner; married Gloria Rand, August 12, 1956 (divorced, 1969); married Marcy Lafferty (an actress), October 20, 1973; children: (second marriage) three daughters. *Education:* McGill University, B.A., 1952. *Avocational interests:* Breeding American saddle horses.

ADDRESSES: Agent—c/o Larry Thompson Organization, 345 North Maple Dr., Suite 183, Beverly Hills, CA 90210.

CAREER: Film, stage, and television actor. Made stage acting debut in 1952; performed at Montreal Playhouse, summers, 1952-52, Canadian Repertory Theatre, Ottawa, 1952-54, and Stratford Shakespeare Festival, Stratford, Ontario, 1954-56; appeared on Broadway in plays, including *Tamburlaine the Great,* 1956, *The World of Suzie Wong,* 1958, and *A Shot in the Dark,* 1961. Appeared in films, including *The Brothers Karamazov,* 1958, *Judgment at Nuremburg,* 1961, *Dead of Night,* 1974, *The Devil's Rain,* 1975, *Star Trek: The Motion Picture,* 1979, *Star Trek II: The Wrath of Khan,* 1982, *Star Trek III: The Search for Spock,* 1984, *Star Trek IV: The Voyage Home,* 1986, *Star Trek V: The Final Frontier,* 1989, *Bill and Ted's Bogus Journey,* 1991, and *Star Trek VI: The Undiscovered Country,* 1991. Appeared in television series, including *Star Trek,* 1966-69, animated *Star Trek* series, 1973-75, *Barbary Coast,* 1975-76, *T.J. Hooker,* 1982-87, and *Rescue 911,* 1993—. Appeared in television movies, including *Go Ask Alice,* 1972, *Crash,* 1978, and *Secrets of a Married Man,* 1984. Actor, director, and executive producer of *Tekwar* television movies and series based on his novels, USA network, 1994—. Recording artist, albums include *The Transformed Man.*

MEMBER: Actors Equity Association, American Federation of Television and Radio Artists, Screen Actors Guild, Directors Guild.

AWARDS, HONOURS: Tyrone Guthrie Award, 1956; Theatre World Award, 1958, for performance in *The World of Suzie Wong.*

WRITINGS:

"TEK" SERIES OF SCIENCE FICTION NOVELS

TekWar, Putnam (New York), 1989.
TekLab, Putnam, 1991.
TekLords, Putnam, 1991.
Tek Secret, Putnam, 1993.
Tek Vengeance, Putnam, 1993.
Tek Power, Putnam, 1994.

NONFICTION

(With Lisabeth Shatner) *Captain's Log: William Shatner's Personal Account of the Making of Star Trek V: The Final Frontier,* Pocket Books (New York), 1989.
(With Michael Tobias) *Believe,* Berkley Publishing (New York), 1992.
(With Chris Kreski) *Star Trek Memories* (autobiography), HarperCollins (New York), 1993.
(With Kreski) *Star Trek Movie Memories* (autobiography), HarperCollins, 1994.

OTHER

(With Judith and Garfield Reeves-Stevens) *Star Trek: The Ashes of Eden* (novel; part of "Star Trek" series), Pocket Books, 1995.

ADAPTATIONS: Shatner's successful "Tek" novel series has been adapted to a television series titled *Tekwar* on the USA network, 1994.

SIDELIGHTS: William Shatner is an actor who has worked prolifically over four decades in films, television, and on stage. It is for his portrayal of Captain James T. Kirk on the short-lived television series *Star Trek,* however, that he is best known. Shatner's appearances as Kirk in the series, which ran from 1966 to 1969, and the subsequent films elevated him to the role of pop culture hero to millions of viewers. In addition to his acting, Shatner is also the author of the popular "Tek" series of science fiction novels and a number of nonfiction books, including two memoirs dealing with his *Star Trek* experiences.

Nineteen Ninety-three's *Star Trek Memories* was cowritten with Chris Kreski (an editor at MTV and a scriptwriter for *Beavis and Butthead*) and includes interviews with members of the original cast. The book offers a behind-the-scenes portrait of the original series. Shatner tells of *Star Trek* creator Gene Roddenberry's dispute with certain producers who urged him to eliminate from the script the characters of Mr. Spock, the pointy-eared Vulcan portrayed by actor Leonard Nimoy, and Uhura, played by African-American actress Nichelle Nichols. Both characters proved to be cornerstones of the show's popularity. Shatner recalls racial tension on the set and interviews Nichols at length; the actress credits civil rights activist Martin Luther King, Jr., with inspiring her to remain in the cast despite the producers' pressure on her to quit. Learning from Nichols that others in the cast of *Star Trek* often resented him, Shatner also spoke with actors Walter Koenig and George Takei, who remember their indignation at Shatner's attempts to change the scripts by cutting their lines. A reviewer in *Publishers Weekly* described *Star Trek Memories* as "a candid, captivating reminiscence, packed with stellar anecdotes and backstage lore." Rosemary L. Bray, writing in the *New York Times Book Review,* reported that she found "wonderful bits of gossip and a record of happy accidents that led to some of the show's signature moments." In *People,* Michael A. Lipton termed the book a "breezy, entertaining memoir."

Although *Star Trek* aired as a television series for only three seasons, the show produced a legion of devoted fans who refer to themselves as "Trekkers" or "Trekkies." With the advent of his own science fiction creation, the "Tek" series of novels, Shatner has developed another loyal following, the "Tekkies." Despite mixed reviews, such as *Entertainment Weekly*'s Benjamin Svetkey's assessment that Shatner "probably won't win any Pulitzers," the "Tek" series has sold nearly a million copies. Set in the 22nd century, the novels pit Jake Cardigan, former cop turned private investigator, against various killer robots, diabolic computers, and other futuristic evils in the fight to control Tek, an addictive, mind-controlling substance.

The first novel of the series, *TekWar,* received a positive critique by *Locus* reviewer Carolyn Cushman, who considered the novel "an entertaining romp thanks to the author's understanding of plot elements and timing." While London *Times* critic Tom Hutchinson did not believe *TekWar* broke any new ground in the hybrid genre of hard-boiled detective/science fiction, he stated that the story was told "quite entertainingly." By the publication of the fifth "Tek" novel, *Tek Secret,* Shatner's writing style is noticeably "more sober, serious, and realistic," according to Roland Green in *Booklist.* The critic added that the series "is certainly moving in the right direction."

Shatner told *Entertainment Weekly*'s Svetkey that the "Tek" novels came about during a lull in the filming of *Star Trek V: The Final Frontier,* when the actor developed his ideas about Jake Cardigan and his war on Tek. "I'd doodle with a paragraph," he told Svetkey, "and it would grow into two pages. . . . Eventually the book sort of evolved by itself." Apparently surprised by his success as

a novelist, Shatner revealed that he had conceived the "Tek" series "as the sort of books you could read on airplanes and throw away afterwards. . . . But they've become this *phenomenon.*" Also an avid horse breeder and rider, Shatner commented on the creative process, saying it would "be as difficult for me to give up ideas as it would to give up horses. That's why publishing a novel is so wondrous to me. That *I* could have a book in print."

In 1994 Shatner added the volume *Star Trek Movie Memories* to his nonfiction writings, which also includes 1989's *Captain's Log: William Shatner's Personal Account of the Making of Star Trek V: The Final Frontier.* A companion piece to *Star Trek Memories,* the 1994 book recounts Shatner's experiences working on the seven feature films that were inspired by the original series (Shatner's final appearance was in *Star Trek Generations,* which was released just prior to his book). The actor/author, again collaborating with *Beavis and Butthead*'s Kreski, relates the ego and power struggles that were common during filming. As with his first *Star Trek* book, Shatner utilizes interviews with his fellow cast and crew to flesh out the details. In addition to the personal dynamics of the films, the book also contains trivia tidbits about the films themselves (one passage reveals that *Star Trek IV: The Voyage Home* was originally intended as a vehicle for comedian Eddie Murphy). Despite viewing Shatner's discussion of his "efforts to hog the spotlight" as being "frighteningly nonchalant," *Entertainment Weekly* contributor Albert Kim found *Star Trek Movie Memories* to be an "entertaining, well-drawn, and fairly balanced look" at some of the ingredients that have made the *Star Trek* films so phenomenally popular.

BIOGRAPHICAL/CRITICAL SOURCES:

BOOKS

Shatner, William, and Chris Kreski, *Star Trek Memories,* HarperCollins (New York), 1993.
Shatner and Kreski, *Star Trek Movie Memories,* HarperCollins, 1994.

PERIODICALS

Booklist, June 15, 1992, p. 1811; September 1, 1993, p. 6.
Entertainment Weekly, January 15, 1993, pp. 30-33; October 8, 1993, pp. 46-47; November 25, 1994, pp. 64-65.
Library Journal, April 15, 1991, p. 129.
Locus, August, 1989, p. 55.
New York Times Book Review, December 26, 1993, p. 15.
People, November 27, 1989, p. 40; November 1, 1993, p. 27; February 18, 1994, p. 40.
Publishers Weekly, November 8, 1991, pp. 53-54; October 12, 1992, p. 62; October 19, 1992, p. 62; September 13, 1993, pp. 108-109; October 17, 1994, p. 67.
Times (London), March 17, 1990.
USA Today, November 9, 1993, sec. D, p. 3.*

SHIELDS, Carol   1935-

PERSONAL: Born June 2, 1935, in Oak Park, Illinois, United States; daughter of Robert E. and Inez (Selgren) Warner; married Donald Hugh Shields (a professor), July 20, 1957; children: John, Anne, Catherine, Margaret, Sara. *Education:* Hanover College, B.A., 1957; University of Ottawa, M.A., 1975. *Politics:* New Democratic Party. *Religion:* Protestant.

ADDRESSES: Home—582 Driveway, Ottawa, Ontario, Canada K1S 3N5.*Agent*—Virginia Barber Literary Agency, Inc., 44 Greenwich Ave., New York, NY 10011.

CAREER: Canadian Slavonic Papers, Ottawa, Ontario, editorial assistant, 1972-74; freelance writer, 1974—.

AWARDS, HONOURS: Winner of young writers' contest sponsored by Canadian Broadcasting Corp. (CBC), 1965; Canada Council grants, 1972, 1974, 1976; fiction prize from Canadian Authors Association, 1976, for *Small Ceremonies*; CBC Prize for Drama, 1983; National Magazine Award, 1984, 1985; Arthur Ellis Award, 1988; Marian Engel Award, 1990; received Governor General's Award for English-language fiction and National Book Critics Circle Award for fiction, 1994, and Pulitzer Prize for fiction, 1995, all for *The Stone Diaries*.

WRITINGS:

Others, Borealis Press, 1972.
Intersect, Borealis Press, 1974.
Susanna Moodie: Voice and Vision, Borealis Press, 1976.
Small Ceremonies, McGraw, 1976.
The Box Garden, McGraw, 1977.
Happenstance, McGraw, 1980.
A Fairly Conventional Woman, Macmillan, 1982.
Various Miracles, General, 1985.
Swann: A Mystery, General, 1987.
The Orange Fish, Random House, 1989.
Departures and Arrivals, Blizzard, 1990.
A Celibate Season, Coteau, 1991.
(With Blanche Howard) *The Republic of Love*, Random House, 1992.
The Stone Diaries, Random House, 1993.
Coming to Canada, Carleton, 1995.

Author of *The View*, 1982, *Women Waiting*, 1983, and *Face Off*, 1987.

Also author with D. Williamson of *Not Another Anniversary*, 1986.

SIDELIGHTS: Pulitzer Prize-winning author Carol Shields's first few novels were virtually ignored by critics, but when she began to take chances with her work it paid off with critical acclaim. Shields is a popular, award-winning author of novels, short stories, and poetry. Her work is now being published in the United States and her reputation and popularity has followed.

Shields was born on June 2, 1935, in Oak Park, Illinois, to Robert and Inez Warner. Her childhood was typical for a white, middle-class suburban girl, and she gained much of her knowledge and experience through reading. Shields attended Hanover College in Indiana where she received her B.A. in 1957. During her junior year at Hanover, Shields entered an exchange program and studied at Exeter University in England. It was here that she met Donald Shields, a Canadian engineering student whom she married in 1957. She moved with her husband to Canada and took a magazine writing course at the University of Toronto. She sold one of her short stories to a radio program, but did not consider a career as a writer since she was beginning a family. When Shields was 29 years old she entered some of her poetry in a radio contest and won. For the next few years she concentrated on writing poetry and publishing it in magazines. She published two collections of her poetry *Others* (1972) and *Intersect* (1974). Shields entered the University of Ottawa and received her M.A. in 1975. While working on her master's degree, Shields dropped out of school for a year to write her first novel. It was rejected by several publishers, but instead of giving up, Shields set out to write *Small Ceremonies* (1976), her first published novel. Shields has continued to write novels and collections of short stories, and teaches creative writing and literature at the University of Manitoba.

Shields's work is concerned with moments that are experienced by all people, those moments when a person feels that life is meaningless and those moments when a person feels the universe is in harmony. Shields's fiction also explores the relationships between human beings, the way that two people can connect completely and the way that even two people who are close may still be unknowable to each other. Shields has had two distinct phases in her career. Her first four novels *Small Ceremonies*, *The Box Garden* (1977), *Happenstance* (1980), and *A Fairly Conventional Woman* (1982) are portrayals of everyday, middle-class, domestic life. Her heroines are housewives who struggle to define themselves and make human connections in their close relationships. The next phase of Shields's career is marked by risk taking. With her first short story collection *Various Miracles* (1985) Shields began to experiment more with form by using a variety of voices. In *Swann: A Mystery* (1987) Shields continued her experimentation by using four distinct voices to tell the story. In this novel she also developed a theme seen in her other work, that of the mysterious nature of art and creation. In *The Stone Diaries* (1993)—which garnered her the Pulitzer Prize in 1995—Shields returned to the theme of human connection and the search for authenticity. In the novel, the main character is Daisy, a young orphan girl who grows to become the matriarch of a large Canadian family. Her story is told through her own diary entries and, following her death, through the reminiscences of others. During the recollection of Daisy's life, nearly the entire twentieth century passes. In a literary device that blurs the fictional quality of her narrative, Shields includes photographs of people purported to be Daisy's descendants; she also provides a detailed family tree. As critics have noted of her other work, Shields's events and characters need not serve the story—they are in fact often the central attraction themselves. As Jay Parini noted of *The Stone Diaries* in the *New York Times Book Review,* "There is little in the way of conventional plot here, but its absence does nothing to diminish the narrative compulsion of this novel."

Other critics were equally celebratory about *The Stone Diaries.* Explaining that he had previously viewed Shields's writing as good in a craftsman-like manner, *Quill and Quire* reviewer George Woodcock found *The Stone Diaries* to represent "a considerable advance in skill and maturity. Shields has tackled a complex subject on a large scale, for many lives are involved, and she has managed to hold it convincingly together in a long and satisfying novel." Susannah Clapp wrote in the *Times Literary Supplement* that the author's writing is "buoyant and lucid," and opined that "Shield's dexterity with her arguments is impressive." In his *New York Times Book Review* appraisal of the book, Parini admired Shields's mastery of language, stating that "her words ring like stones in a brook, chilled and perfected; the syntax rushes like water, tumbling with the slight forward tilt that makes for narrative." Concluding his review, Parini proclaimed, "*The Stone Diaries* reminds us again why literature matters."

Shields took another risk by attempting the genre of the romance novel in *The Republic of Love* (1992), but she made the form her own by making her main characters wade through the coldness and problems of the twentieth century before reaching the happy ending.

Shields's first four novels were popular but not taken seriously by critics. Some argue that in the early part of her career Shields was underestimated as a stylist and her works were dismissed as being naturalistic. Critics generally praised Shields when she began experimenting more with form. Some of her risks were considered failures, however, as in the case of the last section of *Swann,* in which she attempted to bring all four voices together in a screenplay form. Reviewers argue about whether or not Shields's focus on womanhood represents a feminist viewpoint, but most critics believe that it does not. They assert that Shields presents most revolutionaries as being personally motivated and shallow. An example of this is Shields's portrayal of a young feminist Sarah Maloney in *Swann* who rejects her cause when she becomes pregnant.

BIOGRAPHICAL/CRITICAL SOURCES:

PERIODICALS

Belles Lettres, spring, 1991, p. 56; summer, 1992, p. 20.
Books in Canada, October, 1979, pp. 29-30; May, 1981, pp. 31-32; November, 1982, pp. 18-19; October, 1985, pp. 16-17; October, 1987, pp. 15-16; May, 1989, p. 32; January/February, 1991, pp. 30-31; February, 1993, pp. 51-52; September, 1993, pp. 34-35; October, 1993, pp. 32-33.
The Canadian Forum, July, 1975, pp. 36-38; November, 1993, pp. 44-45; January/February, 1994, pp. 44-45.
Canadian Literature, summer, 1989, pp. 158-60; autumn, 1991, pp. 149-50; spring, 1995.
Christian Science Monitor, December 7, 1990, pp. 10-11.
Journal of Canadian Fiction, Volume 28, number 29, 1980.
Kirkus Reviews, May 1, 1976, p. 559.
London Review of Books, September 27, 1990, pp. 20-21; March 21, 1991, p. 20; May 28, 1992, p. 22.
Los Angeles Times Book Review, August 20, 1989, p. 2; April 17, 1994.
Maclean's, October 11, 1993, p. 74.
New Statesman and Society, August 20, 1993, p. 40.
New York, March 7, 1994.
New York Times, July 17, 1989, p. C15; May 10, 1995.
New York Times Book Review, August 6, 1989, p. 11; August 12, 1990, p. 28; March 14, 1992; March 1, 1992, pp. 14, 16; March 27, 1994, pp. 3, 14.
Publishers Weekly, February 28, 1994.
Quill and Quire, January, 1981, p. 24; September, 1982, p. 59; August, 1985, p. 46; May, 1989, p. 20; August, 1993, p. 31.
Scrivener, spring, 1995.
Spectator, March 21, 1992, pp. 35-36; September 24, 1994, p. 41.
Times Literary Supplement, August 27, 1993, p. 27; February 17, 1995.
West Coast Review, winter, 1988, pp. 38-56, 57-66.
Women's Review of Books, May, 1994, p. 20.

*   *   *

SHIP, Reuben 1915-1975
(Reuben Davis)

PERSONAL: Born October 18, 1915, in Montreal, Quebec, Canada; emigrated to the United States in 1939; deported to Canada, January 12, 1953; emigrated to England in 1956; died August 23, 1975, in England; son of Sam and Bella (Davis) Ship; married Ada Span (a theater actress and director; divorced); married Elaine Grand (a television journalist); children: (first marriage) three daughters. *Education:* McGill University, B.A., 1939.

CAREER: Playwright for stage and radio, lyricist, television scriptwriter, and advertising copywriter. Produced anti-fascist plays with the amateur theatre group, YM-YWHA Little Theatre, 1939; toured northeastern United States and New York with New Theatre Group, 1939-44(?); worked in advertising and writing radio dramas for the Canadian Broadcasting Company (CBC), 1953-56; wrote for British film and Canadian radio in the 1960s.

WRITINGS:

(Lyricist; under pseudonym Reuben Davis) *We Beg to Differ* (play), music by Mel Tolkin, first produced by the New Theatre Group at Victoria Hall, Montreal, Quebec, 1939.

The Life of Riley (radio series), NBC, 1944-51.

"The Man Who Liked Christmas" (radio play), *Stage,* CBC, 1953.

The Night before Christmas (radio play; based on an original play by Laura Perelman and S. J. Perelman), CBC, 1953.

"The Investigator" (radio play), *Stage,* CBC, 1954, produced for BBC radio, 1955, published as *The Investigator: A Narrative in Dialogue,* Sidgwick & Jackson (London), 1956, with illustrations by William Gropper, Oriole Editions (New York), 1969.

"The Greatest Man in the World" (radio play; based on the story by James Thurber), *Stage,* CBC, 1955, revised version televised on *Armchair Theatre,* ABC, 1958.

My Wife's Sister (television series), Grenada-TV, 1956-57.

Try a Little Tenderness (television program), Redifussion, 1968.

"The Taxman Cometh" (radio play), *Stage,* CBC, 1969.

The original radio version of *The Investigator* is included in *All the Bright Company: Radio Drama Produced by Andrew Allan,* edited by Howard Fink and John Jackson, Quarry/CBC Enterprises (Kingston, Ontario, and Toronto), 1987, pp. 235-68. Lyricist for a musical review performed by the New Theatre Group, 1939. Author of scenarios for two films, *There Was a Crooked Man* and *The Girl on the Boat,* in the early 1960s.

ADAPTATIONS: The Investigator was released as an album, with an uncredited cast, on the Discuriosity label, c. 1954.

SIDELIGHTS: Canadian author Reuben Ship is best known for his anti-establishment radio plays and scripts satirizing such powerful targets of the 1950s as U.S. Senator Joseph McCarthy and his House Un-American Activities Committee. Raised in a section of Montreal populated mainly by immigrants, Ship learned to value education, trade unionism, and socialism from his family and surroundings, according to an essay by Gerry Gross in *Dictio-*

nary of Literary Biography. These values, which prompted him to write such works as *The Investigator*—a rambunctious satire of McCarthyism—caused trouble for Ship throughout his career and hindered the success that his talents promised.

A student of English literature at McGill University in the 1930s, Ship was active in the university's Players Club and joined an amateur theatrical troupe called the YM-YWHA Little Theatre after graduating in 1939. The Little Theatre produced antifascist plays, and it was while working with this group that Ship met his first wife, actress and director Ada Span. Ship wrote the lyrics for *We Beg to Differ,* a musical revue performed by the Little Theatre throughout Canada that took political topics of the day as the target for its satire.

Ship and others from the troupe travelled to the United States, playing small venues such as union halls before settling in New York City. It was while in New York, just as his money was running out, that the NBC radio network hired Ship to write scripts for a radio program entitled *The Life of Riley,* about a working-class man and his family. Ship enjoyed brief success with the show, but it was followed by the start of his financial and political problems. When *Riley* went to television in 1950, Ship's contract was not renewed and in 1951 he was interviewed by the United States Immigration and Naturalization Service. He eventually discovered that, at the height of "Red Scare" fears about Communist infiltration of America, he had been denounced as a communist by one of his former colleagues. Ship's defiant appearance before Senator McCarthy's House Un-American Activities Committee (HUAC) in September of 1951 sealed his fate. He was deported to Canada in January, 1953, and settled with his wife and their three daughters near Toronto.

To support his family in Canada, Ship wrote for CBC radio and for an advertising agency. "He still wrote comedies," Gross remarked, "but now they all pointed satirically at hypocrisy in government, business, and other institutions." In addition to *The Investigator* (1954), considered his most important work, Ship wrote *The Night before Christmas* and *The Man Who Liked Christmas* (both 1953) during this period. Adapted from a stage play by Laura and S. J. Perelman, *The Night before Christmas* concerns two bank robbers who pose as furniture salesman who plan to break through a wall in the basement of their store and rob the bank next door on Christmas eve. Their plan is foiled when their own store is robbed on the same night. *The Man Who Liked Christmas* tells the story of a man whose family treats him badly except on Christmas, and who comes to wish every day were Christmas. When he shares his wish with his family and others, they inadvertently reveal their hypocrisy regarding the holiday.

While both plays were well-received, they did not compare to the critical and popular reaction caused by Ship's 1954 radio play. *The Investigator* takes on the perpetrators of the Red Scare directly. In the story the character known as the Investigator dies in a plane crash and ascends to Heaven. In Heaven the Investigator is shocked by the presence of souls that he considers subversive. He sets up a committee with other infamous inquisitors, including the historical figures Torquemada and Cotton Mather, and holds hearings that investigate such famous person-ages as Milton, Socrates, and Voltaire. The investigator's bullying manner and general demeanor in these proceed-ings "unmistakably resembles that of Joseph McCarthy," according to the *Dictionary of Literary Biography*'s Gross. All those examined are sent to hell, where they unionize the other inhabitants and cause such trouble that the devil comes up to heaven to complain. The show caused an up-roar and tapes of the program began circulating in New York almost immediately. An uncredited record was pro-duced on the Discuriosity label, and the BBC aired the program in 1955. In 1956, Ship published *The Investigator* in a narrative form. Despite the underground success, the work did little to better Ship's financial situation, and he continued to work in advertising to support himself and his family.

Ship and his family moved to England in 1956, but his marriage dissolved soon thereafter. He married Elaine Grand, a Canadian television journalist, not long after-wards, and continued to write, often selling scripts, it has been presumed, under pseudonyms in the United States. He also wrote for the British television series *My Wife's Sister.* During this time he revised his radio adaptation of *The Greatest Man in the World* for television and wrote the scenarios for two films, *There Was a Crooked Man* and *The Girl on the Boat,* both satires.

The 1960s saw the production of one of Ship's best plays, according to Gross, and his last for the CBC. *The Taxman Cometh* is a self-reflexive satire about a writer whose trou-ble with the government over his taxes is compounded when he tries to convince a tax officer's secretary to steal his file. The man is simultaneously writing a play about a writer in the identical situation. "Ship's mastery of the form is evident," wrote Gross. Ship died six years later, in 1975, in England. "No doubt his early promise was only partly fulfilled," Gross concluded, "but few Canadians have written dramatic satire for any medium with as much wit and conviction as one finds in Ship's radio drama."

BIOGRAPHICAL/CRITICAL SOURCES:

BOOKS

Dictionary of Literary Biography, Volume 88: *Canadian Writers, 1920-1959,* Gale, 1989, pp. 288-90.

Frick, N. Alice, *Image in the Mind: CBC Radio Drama 1944 to 1954,* Canadian Stage and Arts Publications (Toronto), 1987, pp. 134-43*.

*   *   *

SHULMAN, Morton 1925-

PERSONAL: Born April 2, 1925, in Toronto, Ontario, Canada; son of David (in sales) and Nettie (Wintrope) Shulman; married Gloria Bossin, May 30, 1950; children: Dianne, Geoffrey. *Education:* University of Toronto, M.D., 1948. *Religion:* Jewish. *Avocational interests:* Fine wines, collecting fifteenth-and sixteenth-century watches and clocks.

ADDRESSES: Home—66 Russell Hill Rd., Toronto, On-tario, Canada M4V 2T2. *Office*—378 Roncesvalles Ave., Toronto, Ontario, Canada M6R 2M7.

CAREER: General practitioner of medicine, Toronto, On-tario, 1950—. Chief coroner of Toronto, 1963-67; member of Provincial Parliament of Ontario, 1967-75; Deprenyl Research Ltd., Toronto, Ontario, founder and chief exec-utive officer, 1987-92, co-chair, 1992-93; author. President of Guardian-Morton Shulman Precious Metals, Guardian Investment Management, and FCMI Precious Metals Fund. Host of weekly television show, 1975-83; lecturer on investing.

WRITINGS:

Anyone Can Make a Million, McGraw, 1967, revised edi-tion published as *Anyone Can Still Make a Million,* Stein & Day (New York City), 1973.
The Billion Dollar Windfall, Morrow (New York City), 1969.
Coroner, Fitzhenry & Whiteside, 1975.
Anyone Can Make Big Money Buying Art, Macmillan (New York City), 1977.
Member of the Legislature, Fitzhenry & Whiteside, 1979.
How to Invest Your Money and Profit from Inflation, Hur-tig, 1979, Ballantine (New York City), 1981.

Also author of weekly column for *Toronto Sun*; lead writer for *Moneyletter.*

SIDELIGHTS: Canadian doctor, investor, politician, and best-selling writer Morton Shulman "is somewhat more than the mind-on-the-street can grasp all at once," accord-ing to Edith Hills Coogler in an *Atlanta Journal and Con-stitution* article. "His careers in medicine and the stock market all started . . . when he was an intern. 'I got mar-ried,' " Shulman told Coogler " 'and her cousin advised us to take our $400 and invest it. We lost nearly all of it in penny stocks. . . .' Even now, years afterward, he is somewhat less than enthusiastic about penny stocks.

"But in 1962, he treated his loss like a challenge. 'I started again, and it was a new issue market. And I made mistakes, but it didn't cost me money. In six months I made $25,000. . . . That was exciting. Before long, I could have quit medicine, but I love medicine; it is my way of life. I am still practicing in Toronto every morning, and I am still into the stock market, but that is just a hobby.' "

Another of Shulman's "hobbies" is writing. He has written about his experiences as Toronto's chief coroner in *Coroner*; about his stint as a member of Ontario's Provincial Parliament in *Member of the Legislature*; and about investment strategies in *Anyone Can Make a Million, The Billion Dollar Windfall, Anyone Can Make Big Money Buying Art,* and *How to Invest Your Money and Profit from Inflation.*

In *Member of the Legislature* Shulman tells of his involvement in socialist politics in the late 1960s and early 1970s. Attracted more to the New Democratic Party's "rabble-rousing," as Suzanne McGee states in the *Wall Street Journal,* than to the party's economic positions, Shulman "figured he wouldn't need to worry about them winning power." Shulman applied his talents for publicity to his position as a member of the Ontario parliament, taking photographs of napping colleagues during parliamentary debates, selling copies of the banned book *The Happy Hooker* from his office, and bringing a gun into the legislature to show other members how easy they were to purchase legally.

In what some observers call a striking contrast to his socialist politics, Shulman has written several best-selling investment books. *Anyone Can Make a Million,* a guide to sensible investment for the novice, ironically made Shulman himself a millionaire. In *How to Invest Your Money and Profit from Inflation,* says reviewer James K. Glassman in a *Washington Post Book World* article, "it isn't Shulman's advice that makes this such a good book. It's the way he tells his story. . . . He is relentlessly personal. Shulman has made a fortune, and he shows how he did it. He's so brash, so obnoxious that he's actually endearing. . . . One has to admire Shulman's crass, backslapping, risk-taking style. In an age in which taste counts for so much, he readily admits he doesn't have any—and proves it on any page. As a result, every page is a joy to read."

In 1983 Shulman was diagnosed as having Parkinson's Disease, a debilitating condition in which the victim loses control over his body's movements. Shulman discovered that a European drug, Eldepryl, little-used in North America, relieved his symptoms dramatically. Before using the drug Shulman had needed help climbing out of bed and suffered from severe body tremors. The drug stopped the tremors and other symptoms within a few days. Soon Shulman set up Deprenyl Research Ltd., a Toronto-based company, to market the drug Eldepryl in the United States and Canada. Today some 15,000 Parkinson's patients in Canada are using Eldepryl successfully and Deprenyl enjoys over $5 million in yearly sales. A spin-off drug designed for dogs and cats suffering from Parkinson's is also planned.

Shulman's Deprenyl Research ran into problems in 1992 when the *Wall Street Journal* alleged that another drug Deprenyl was selling, Alzene, was not as effective against Alzheimer's disease as was claimed. Shulman's aggressive sales tactics were also assailed. Deprenyl stock dipped for a time before recovering once more. Shulman retired from Deprenyl in 1993.

David Saks, a stock market analyst with the firm Wedbush Morgan Securities, tells the *Wall Street Journal* that Shulman "doesn't fit the mold of the traditional, conservative investment adviser, medical doctor or banker. But would Deprenyl be where it was today without his flamboyant style, without him behind it and promoting it? Of course not."

BIOGRAPHICAL/CRITICAL SOURCES:

BOOKS

Authors in the News, Volume 1, Gale, 1976.
Dow, Alastair, *Deprenyl: The Inside Story,* Easton Publishing, c.1991.

PERIODICALS

Atlanta Journal and Constitution, September 16, 1973.
Business Week, October 3, 1988, p. 36.
enRoute, February, 1991, pp. 46-48, 55.
Financial Post Magazine, January, 1994, pp. 8-9.
Financial Times of Canada, December 12, 1988, pp. 1, 20-22; September 4, 1989, p. 16.
Investor's Digest, May 1, 1992, p. 114.
Maclean's, April 25, 1988, p. 11; October 5, 1992, pp. S7, S9.
New Republic, June 21, 1980.
New York Times, March 10, 1981.
Wall Street Journal, March 18, 1991, p. C16; September 19, 1991, pp. B1, B12; August 25, 1992, p. A1; September 24, 1992, p. B12; April 20, 1993, p. B5.
Washington Post Book World, April 11, 1980.

*   *   *

SINCLAIR, Bertrand William   1881-1972

PERSONAL: Original name William Brown Sinclair; born January 9, 1881, in Edinburgh, Scotland; emigrated to Canada in 1889; died October 20, 1972; son of George

Bertrand and Robina (maiden name, Williamson) Sinclair; married Bertha M. Brown (a writer; pen name B. M. Bower), in 1905 (divorced, 1911); married Ruth Brown in 1912; children: (first marriage) Della Frances, (second marriage) Cherry Whitaker. *Education:* Attended Stanford University. *Avocational interests:* Angling, hunting, power boats, and sailing.

CAREER: Cowboy, Montana, 1896-1903; freelance writer of stories and novelettes, 1905-40; salmon fisher, 1936-66. Host of the radio program *The Sinclair Hour* in Vancouver, British Columbia.

MEMBER: Royal Vancouver Yacht Club, Marine Drive Golf and Country Club.

WRITINGS:

Raw Gold, illustrations by Clarence H. Rowe, Dillingham (New York), 1908.
The Land of Frozen Suns, Dillingham, 1910.
North of Fifty-Three, Musson (Toronto), 1914, illustrations by Anton Otto Fischer, Little, Brown (Boston), 1914.
Shotgun Jones (screenplay), Selig Polyscope, 1914.
Big Timber: A Story of the Northwest, Copp, Clark (Toronto), 1916.
Burned Bridges, Briggs (Toronto), 1919.
Poor Man's Rock, Ryerson (Toronto), 1920.
The Hidden Places, Ryerson, 1922.
The Inverted Pyramid, Goodchild (Toronto), 1924.
Wild West, Ryerson, 1926.
Pirates of the Plains, Hodder & Stoughton (London), 1928.
Gunpowder Lightning, McClelland & Stewart (Toronto), 1930.
Down the Dark Alley, Hodder & Stoughton, 1935, Little, Brown, 1936.
Both Sides of the Law, Novel Selections (New York), 1951, Wright & Brown (London), 1955.
Room for the Rolling M, Wright & Brown, 1954.

Also published about sixty stories and eleven novelettes in such magazines as *Popular Magazine, Adventure,* and *Short Stories,* from 1905 to 1940.

Sinclair's papers are housed in the Special Collections Division of the University of British Columbia Library in Vancouver.

SIDELIGHTS: Bertrand William Sinclair's adventure novels set in Montana and British Columbia extol the virtues of a hard life lived in the wilderness. Although he forfeited his dream of writing a novel of social commentary, his commercially successful popular westerns are often praised as entertaining, fast-paced adventure stories with realistic details about life on the frontier.

Born in Edinburgh, Scotland, Sinclair came to Canada with his mother in 1889, and spent his boyhood in Saskatchewan. Sinclair ran away to Montana when he was fourteen, and worked as a cowboy for the next six years. According to Laurie Ricou in *Dictionary of Literary Biography,* Sinclair's experiences as a cowboy would provide the inspiration for his first two novels, *Raw Gold* (1908) and *The Land of Frozen Suns* (1910), as well as for his later, more subdued accounts of life as a Montana cowboy, *Wild West* (1926) and *Gunpowder Lightning* (1930). Ricou notes that in a 1902 letter Sinclair wondered why "no cowpuncher ever wrote about his own time and his own people—instead of leaving it to outsiders." Although Sinclair tried to expand the genre of the western to include more realistic depictions of life on the range, Ricou maintains that "none of the Montana fiction offers the texture of locale or culture found in his fiction set in British Columbia."

Sinclair married Bertha M. Brown, a prolific author of westerns under the pseudonym B. M. Bower, in 1905. They had one daughter. Most of their married life was spent in California, where, besides his wife, Ricou counts Upton Sinclair (no relation; author of *The Jungle*) and Jack London (author *Call of the Wild*) among Sinclair's literary influences. Sinclair began publishing short stories and novelettes in popular magazines of the period. "Although he constantly dismissed these as potboilers," Ricou remarks, "they often show a facility for presenting narration by a colloquial raconteur, telling the story from inside, a narrative stance that might have been more productively exploited in some of the often grandiloquently omniscient novels."

Sinclair divorced his first wife in 1911, and married her cousin Ruth in 1912. The couple settled in Vancouver, British Columbia, where Sinclair "found the setting and center for his best fiction," according to Ricou. *North of Fifth-Three* (1914), *Big Timber: A Story of the Northwest* (1916), *Burned Bridges* (1919), *Down the Dark Alley* (1935), and *The Inverted Pyramid* (1924) effectively exploit the setting and history of the Pacific Northwest. *North of Fifty-Three* is an adventure story featuring a young woman from the East who is abducted by a rough westerner. The logging industry provides the background for *Big Timber: A Story of the Northwest* and *The Inverted Pyramid,* the growing automobile industry does the same for *Burned Bridges,* and bootlegging makes an appearance in *Down the Dark Alley.* Although Sinclair used racial epithets and "the rhetoric of affected sentimentality" in many of his works, "what remains of interest," says Ricou, "are his attempts to integrate fiction with precise geographical settings and the economic and cultural structures of emerging societies."

In the 1920s, Sinclair and his wife moved to a seaside community north of Vancouver and bought a salmon troller, which "became an essential part of the couple's love affair with British Columbia," Ricou remarks. Sinclair drew upon his experiences working with a commercial fishing fleet to write *Poor Man's Rock* (1920), which "links tales of love and revenge to a study of the economics of fishing for salmon." This experience also proved useful when the author took up professional salmon fishing on his own in the 1930s, in response to flagging sales of his fiction.

With 1920's *Poor Man's Rock,* Sinclair began receiving positive reviews for what Ricou terms "his most engaging, socially and economically dense novel," but his audience, accustomed to the high adventure of his earlier works, began drifting away. By the 1930s, suffering emotional and economic drain due to his wife's mental illness, Sinclair gave up writing and turned to fishing full-time. It became his primary occupation for the next thirty years. "In many ways the life of Sinclair in the 1940s and 1950s resembles that of the hard-working adventurers portrayed in his fiction," Ricou observes, and his passion for storytelling found its outlet in a daily stint on the radio that he called the "Sinclair Hour," broadcast to the limited audience of the commercial fishing community.

Although Sinclair was a successful novelist and short story writer during his life, he remained dissatisfied with the standard elements of his popular westerns, which he described in a letter quoted by Ricou: "rip-roaring adventure, the utmost conventionality in point of view [and] a liberal garnishing of sentimental slush." Throughout his novels, he struggled to incorporate realistic details about the economics and culture of logging, mining, fishing, and working as a cowboy into adventure stories.

BIOGRAPHICAL/CRITICAL SOURCES:

BOOKS

Dictionary of Literary Biography, Volume 92: *Canadian Writers, 1890-1920,* Gale, 1990, pp. 362-65.
Twigg, Alan, *Vancouver Writers,* Harbour (Madeira Park, B.C.), 1986, pp. 137-39.*

* * *

SINCLAIR, (Allan) Gordon   1900-1984

PERSONAL: Born June 3, 1900, in Toronto, Ontario, Canada; died after a heart attack, May 17, 1984, in Toronto, Ontario, Canada; son of Alexander and Bessie (Eesley) Sinclair; married Gladys Prewett, May 8, 1926; children: Gordon, Jr., Donald, Jean (died, 1943), Jack.

Education: Attended public schools in Toronto, Canada. *Religion:* None. *Avocational interests:* Growing flowers, boating, fishing, bird watching.

CAREER: Writer, journalist, and radio commentator. Worked as clerk at Bank of Nova Scotia, Toronto, Canada; T. Eaton Co. (department store), Toronto, bookkeeper, c. 1917, cashier, 1919; worked at calendar factory, slaughterhouse, and rubber company, 1919-22; *Toronto Star,* Toronto, reporter, 1922-43; CFRB-Radio, Toronto, host of *Let's Be Personal,* beginning in 1942, and news broadcaster, beginning in 1944. Host of traveling radio show, *Ontario Panorama,* 1943; panelist on CBC-TV's *Front Page Challenge,* beginning in 1957; book reviewer and show business critic for CFRB-Radio. Canadian Army, 48th Highlanders Regiment, 1917-19.

AWARDS, HONORS: Gordon Sinclair Award, 1970, for "outspoken opinions and integrity in broadcasting"; named to Canada's News Hall of Fame, 1972; H. Gordon Love News Trophy from Canadian Association of Broadcasters, 1974; distinguished service award from Radio and Television News Directors' Association, 1974, for "challenging and courageous commentary"; appointed officer of Order of Canada, 1979.

WRITINGS:

NONFICTION

Footloose in India, Doubleday, Doran & Gundy, 1932, Farrar & Rinehart, 1933, reprinted, McClelland & Stewart, 1966.
Cannibal Quest, Doubleday, Doran & Gundy, 1933, Farrar & Rinehart, 1934.
Loose among Devils, Farrar & Rinehart, 1935.
Khyber Caravan: Through Kashmir, Waziristan, Afghanistan, Baluchistan, and Northern India, Farrar & Rinehart, 1936, reprinted, Simon & Schuster, 1975.
Signpost to Adventure, McClelland & Stewart, 1947.
Bright Paths to Adventure, McClelland & Stewart, 1952.
Will the Real Gordon Sinclair Please Stand Up (autobiography), McClelland & Stewart, 1966.
The Americans (spoken word recording), Avco Records, 1973.
Will Gordon Sinclair Please Sit Down (memoirs), McClelland & Stewart, 1975.

Contributor of feature articles to magazines.

SIDELIGHTS: Gordon Sinclair has been described as "the unquiet Canadian," a colorful, often "wildly controversial" journalist whom "millions love to cuss." Many Canadians remember him as the reporter who traveled all over the world for the *Toronto Star* in the 1930's, sending back stories about his adventures in faraway lands. He was an institution in Toronto, where his opinion program and daily radio newscasts aired from World War II until his death in 1984, and people across the country knew him as a regular panelist on the weekly quiz show *Front Page Challenge,* the longest continuing program on Canadian television. In the United States, however, he is perhaps best known for a four-minute radio broadcast made in June, 1973, an opinion piece called *The Americans* that praised the country and its people.

Sinclair began his career at the *Toronto Star* in 1922. After what he called four "uneventful years" as a reporter, he was promoted to woman's editor, but found himself unsuited for the job. "Having never had a sister or a wife," he explained, "I knew little or nothing about women, and one day, in desperation, my editor told me to go and write some stories about hoboes." During the assignment he rode a boxcar from Toronto to New York City, signed on as a bootblack aboard the liner *Laurentic,* and sailed in the company of hoboes to England. He was soon after arrested in Germany for smuggling cigarettes.

"All of these adventures made entertaining reading," he wrote, and his editor decided that he should continue his journey, wandering where he pleased with no particular duties or assignments. From 1928 to 1940 Sinclair traveled around the world four times, crossing every continent and all but the Antarctic Ocean. Many of the places he visited became the subjects of books, including the best-selling *Footloose in India* and *Cannibal Quest.*

Among Sinclair's most memorable adventures was a trip to China in 1938. Along with adventurer-author Richard Halliburton, Sinclair was one of the first outsiders to enter the city of Canton after its fall to the Japanese. A few weeks later he was at the center of an international incident when he was stabbed by a Japanese sentry. Evacuated to Hong Kong aboard an American gunboat, he spent the next several weeks with Halliburton, who was building a sea-going junk. Sinclair noted that he was the last living man to have spoken with Halliburton. In March, 1939, Halliburton set out across the Pacific aboard his junk, the *Sea Dragon,* and was never seen again.

By the time Sinclair returned to Toronto in 1940, he was a well-known journalist and the author of four adventure books. A series of dramatic articles about the French penal colony on Devil's Island had been collected for *Loose among Devils,* his third book, and his fourth, *Khyber Caravan,* described his travels along the remote borderland of Afghanistan, Pakistan, Kashmir, and India. According to Sinclair, *Khyber Caravan* was his "first attempt at a serious and literate book," and even though it failed financially, he still considers it his best.

At the outbreak of World War II Sinclair wrote a series of unflattering articles about Canada's military leaders. As a result the Canadian forces branded him a troublemaker and denied him accreditation as a war correspondent. The ban was never lifted, and Sinclair decided to go into radio broadcasting, beginning with a midday personality show, *Let's Be Personal.* When the *Star* compelled him to choose one career or the other, Sinclair resigned from the paper and joined the news department of CFRB-Radio, Canada's largest privately-owned station.

Sinclair gained national exposure in 1957 when he became a charter member of CBC-TV's *Front Page Challenge.* Similar in format to the old *What's My Line?* show on American television, *Front Page* featured a panel of four interviewers who try to guess the identity of a notable person in the news. A round of interviews followed the game, and Sinclair distinguished himself over the years by asking especially blunt or provocative questions. A writer for the *Detroit News* commented, "Sinclair is still one of the best television interviewers in Canada and no subject goes through his probing without facing the question: 'How much do you make?'"

Sinclair's comments often caused public commotions, but he contended that it is "an absolutely natural sort of thing to speak your mind." Listeners protested loudly when he asked an Olympic swimmer how she trained and competed during menstruation, and his publicly-proclaimed agnosticism has upset a number of people, including a group of young evangelists who once prayed for his conversion in the CFRB lobby. In another well-known incident, he complained that a rich man's will had left nothing to charity. His remarks sent lawyers scurrying back to their wealthy clients with a clause that protects them against such criticism, a provision that some lawyers call the Sinclair Clause.

Sinclair didn't hesitate to criticize the United States when it interfered in Canadian affairs, but his popularity with Americans was assured after his radio broadcast of June 5, 1973. At that time the United States was beset with problems, including a shrinking dollar, escalating oil prices, the Watergate investigation, natural disasters, and mounting world criticism. When he heard that the American Red Cross was broke, Sinclair typed out an editorial that extolled the generosity of Americans and attacked the country's critics: "This Canadian thinks it is time to speak up for the Americans as the most generous and possibly the least-appreciated people in all the earth," he wrote. "I'm one Canadian who is damned tried of hearing them kicked around."

Sinclair read his editorial on *Let's Be Personal,* then filed it away. "I didn't expect any reaction at all," he later recounted, but by December his desk was buried under 100,000 pieces of mail, including letters of appreciation from John Wayne and President Richard Nixon. *The Americans* was recorded five times, read into the Congressional Record seven times, and distributed to U.S. Information offices in more than one hundred countries. Sinclair's own recorded version sold 500,000 copies in ten days and brought him hundreds of requests for personal appearances. A version of *The Americans* recorded by newscaster Byron MacGregor found new popularity in the early 1990s with a resurgence of American patriotism following the country's participation in the Persian Gulf War.

The whole affair bemused Sinclair, who preferred not to accept an invitation to read *The Americans* at a Seattle concert with the Mormon Tabernacle Choir singing "The Battle Hymn of the Republic" in the background. Nor did he want to appear on *The Tonight Show* or *The Mike Douglas Show,* or fly with former spy pilot Francis Gary Powers aboard his traffic helicopter in Burbank, California. All the royalties he earned from *The Americans* were to be given to the American Red Cross, he decided, saying that he didn't "want anything for doing something he believes in."

CA INTERVIEW
CA interviewed Gordon Sinclair on May 1, 1980, at his office in Toronto, Ontario.

CA: When did you start making money as a writer?

SINCLAIR: The very first time I ever wrote something for which I was paid was when I was a sales clerk at Eaton's at Christmastime. At that time I was working in the office, but they sent office help down to the sales floor at Christmas for the rush. Well, I sold a necktie one day to Sir John Eaton, and I recognized him and gave him the necktie. I wrote a story about that, which I sold to the *Toronto Star Weekly* for three dollars. That gave me the big idea of getting started as a reporter. That would be about 1920, and I joined the *Toronto Star* about 1922.

CA: I saw that you did a big expose on crime, prostitution, and gambling down in Windsor.

SINCLAIR: Yes, that's right. I guess that would be about 1927. I started on the first foreign assignment (for the *Toronto Star*) in 1928, and I think that was just before that. Yeah, it was kind of a loose-leaf kind of thing. I went to a few whorehouses, stuff like that.

CA: Did the Border Cities *do anything about it?*

SINCLAIR: No, and I was kind of disappointed they didn't. I was a little surprised, but I had the same experience in New Orleans. Huey Long was about to clean up New Orleans. I don't know why, but the papers down

there were ignoring him, so my editor said: "Go down to New Orleans and go around with him. But make sure before you go that he'll see you!" So I phoned, and he said, "Sure, I'll see you." And I went down and spent a week with Long. In fact, the last three days of my week I lived with him in his own house. His wife had walked out on him. And on the very day that I left he was assassinated. The very day.

CA: In those early days at the Star *you met some interesting people—Morley Callaghan and Ernest Hemingway. What were they like?*

SINCLAIR: I disliked Hemingway because I thought he was patronizing. In terms of myself, he was a little older, maybe a year older, but I disliked him. Maybe it was just ego on my part. I was assigned to him on only one story as an assistant, and he made me damn well conscious of the fact that I was his assistant and he was the reporter. As a matter of fact, he didn't get a by-line on that story. The story appeared about a column and a half long, but Hemingway didn't get a by-line.

CA: What is the story about the cinnamon toast?

SINCLAIR: Hemingway corrected the proofs of *The Sun Also Rises* at Child's Restaurant across from the *Star* on King Street while eating cinnamon toast and drinking a lot of coffee. I put that in a book, and a reviewer for *Saturday Night* did a piece that said this couldn't have happened because of the dates. Well, he was wrong, and I was right.

CA: What did you think of Hemingway as a reporter?

SINCLAIR: I think he was a mood guy, he kind of set a mood. The one story I worked on with him was the return to Toronto of some people who had been in a big earthquake in Japan, and his story, if you had a lot of time to write it, was good, because it described how he'd met these people and the costumes they were wearing. They happened to be just unpacking with their Japanese clothes when Hemingway, Mary Lowry, and myself went up there to see this woman. She had just put on her Japanese garments, so it was quite a distinctive meeting. She opened the door, wearing a beautiful scarlet robe. That's what he wrote about. He probably was right to write the story like that, because the earthquake was far behind her.

I remember him writing in that story that when we went into the house, there was water running. It happened to be a bathtub upstairs. We could hear it. I remember him writing this. Looking back on it now, I think my assessment and his editor's assessment were wrong. Maybe that was the right way to write it—the presentation of the women in costumes, the water running, this and that; but anyway, he didn't get a by-line on it.

CA: What about your influences. Today kids go to school to become journalists. In your day, they didn't.

SINCLAIR: There were several influences. I worked personally for Sime Silverman, founder of *Variety,* and I was the *Variety* stringer in Ontario for a time in the mid-1920's. I also worked for Flo Ziegfeld and John Philip Sousa in publicity, and my *Toronto Star* editor, Harry Hindmarsh, was an influence, too. And I was a constant reader of the *New York World*. The *World* was considered at that time to be a very good newspaper, and it had a tremendous influence upon me.

CA: Your background, however, gives you an edge over many journalists today. You wrote in one of your books that you have spoken with every prime minister in Canada from Laurier to the present, and you have even spoken with people who fought in the U.S. Civil War.

SINCLAIR: I've told the anecdote about the Civil War several times, but it doesn't seem to strike a chord, which puzzles me. In 1914 there was not a mile of paved road in North America, but the first paved highway was being built between Toronto and Oakville. I had an uncle who drove from Indiana in his automobile, and he invited me to go back with him. No roads, remember, and he did go back. My mother said to keep a diary of this, and I did. I've kept a diary from that day in 1914 to now. Anyhow, we went first to Indiana to a place called College Corners, a little village, then to Dayton, Ohio. I had a different uncle there who had a house next door to a military hospital, and in that military hospital were maybe eighty men who had fought in the Civil War. This was 1914. The Civil War had ended in 1865, so they didn't have to be all that old. They were very talkative, and I used to go next door to the hospital day after day and talk to these men. I was fourteen.

CA: What was your method of approach in Footloose in India *and your last book,* Will Gordon Sinclair Please Sit Down? *How did you change?*

SINCLAIR: My method of approach with *Footloose in India* was to write it because I had a ready publisher, and I wrote the whole book in nineteen days, largely based on columns that had appeared in the *Star*. That sold well. Mind you, it was a slang book.

CA: But it doesn't sound like columns.

SINCLAIR: No, it doesn't. I went over it quite a bit. I wrote that up in Muskoka in nineteen days. I still get royalty checks from it. They're very small now.

CA: What about the last book?

SINCLAIR: In the last book, *Will Gordon Sinclair Please Sit Down,* or even in *Will the Real Gordon Sinclair*

Please Stand Up, I found my attention span had been acclimated to radio and television. In other words, I could write an item and interest myself in an item up to eight hundred words, and then I'd lose interest. Then I'd start again. So that each of those books, in my view, run downhill. They start out alright, but I think they run downhill because of my own attention span. Also because my radio experience tells me to make it short, make it punchy.

CA: Do you see yourself as a book writer, or do you see yourself as a journalist?

SINCLAIR: As a journalist.

CA: Do you see the books as a kind of higher journalism?

SINCLAIR: I don't, but most people who write books do. They're just journalism, and I think the best-selling books—take Harold Robbins as an example—they're a kind of journalism. Gay Talese is another.

CA: Where do you do most of your book writing?

SINCLAIR: I have written most of them in Muskoka, on Acton Island, four measured miles from Bala. I have a cottage there all my own. That is to say, there is a family cottage, but I had one built for me and me alone. It's not much bigger than this room, and I do my writing there.

CA: In the course of your journalism career you've met some very interesting people, like Gandhi and Adolph Hitler. What was Hitler like? How did you meet him anyway?

SINCLAIR: I met Hitler when he was leader of the Nazi party. He wasn't chancellor yet. I met him by strange circumstances. I was in Munich on a Sunday afternoon. I forget the year. I think it was 1932 or 1933. I was alone in Munich, and I was studying the language. I went to a restaurant that was partly indoors and partly outdoors, like some of them were in Paris. Well, I was seated outside, and it started raining, so I was moved inside. It was crowded, but I had a table for four all to myself.

Some men in brown-shirted uniforms came into the restaurant and put a Nazi flag on my table. They didn't say a word, and I was reading a German newspaper, so they must have thought I was German. Well, this was a signal that I was to get the hell up and out of there. They wanted that table. In a sense they were right. It was a table for four, the place was crowded, and I was alone. When I paid no attention they started to abuse me. Now I could read German, but at their speed of talking I couldn't understand them, and I was a little bewildered. So the proprietor came down and explained to them that I was a foreign journalist. I don't know how he knew I was a journalist, but anyhow they were full of apologies. They lifted the flag, then they got someone who could speak English to me, and they explained how they didn't mean to be nasty to a foreigner, and would I like to meet their leader. They arranged a meeting the following morning, in fact.

They supplied a little girl as an interpreter, and I had no difficulty with Hitler. I do remember the room he was in overlooked a large cemetery. Big high windows and a large cemetery. Then he began to talk, and I could follow him at first, but then I lost him. He began to talk about the terrible injustices his country had suffered, how Germany was in the center of Europe, and how it could move outward in any direction, and people could not keep such a brave and noble people down, and so on. It became his regular speech.

CA: Do you think it was all nonsense?

SINCLAIR: No. I was impressed by him.

CA: Did you think after meeting him that he would become Germany's leader?

SINCLAIR: I thought he would become a very strong force, and I tried to tell my people at home. The interview certainly didn't hit page one—no, it was in the inside. It was used.

CA: What about Gandhi?

SINCLAIR: Gandhi? I met him on various occasions. It was one of the biggest assessments that I ever made badly. I thought in the beginning that Gandhi was a fake, a fraudulent man, and I said so to him. But as I got to meet him afterwards—I met him many, many times—we got to know each other very well. I soon began to realize what a terrible mistake I had made about him.

CA: You seem always to be getting into trouble. I remember when you asked Elaine Tanner, the Olympic swimmer, how she trained and competed when she was menstruating, and how that caused such a furor. Then there was the broadcast in August, 1979, about the boat people (the Vietnamese fleeing to Canada), and you said they could just turn around and go back. Do you do that kind of thing out of conviction?

SINCLAIR: No, I'm a blurter. I sort of blurt these questions out. There's one upcoming that will get me in trouble. There's an astronomer who knows all about the heavens. I asked her, after her four-year examination of the heavens: "Have you ever come across Heaven? Do you believe in God?" She said, "I've never come across Heaven, but I believe in God," and I blurted, "Well, I don't, and I'll tell you why!"

CA: Some of your blurting has made you friends below the border in the United States. I remember the four-and-one-half-minute editorial on the radio which took you only twenty minutes to write.

SINCLAIR: That was in 1973.

CA: With Nixon having been thrown out and the Watergate episode behind us, what do you think of the American people now?

SINCLAIR: It doesn't change my view of the American people at all. They're a generous people, rather native, perhaps, but a very generous people, and that was the idea of my piece. They have helped almost everybody, and who has helped them? That was my theme.

CA: There's a story about how you were one of the first to see the Dionne quintuplets in North Bay. You went up there with Fred Davis, the host of "Front Page Challenge." He was a photographer then with the Toronto Star.

SINCLAIR: I wasn't the first up there. There was another guy called Gordon. He was the first. But I went to see Dionne, and he said, "I'm the kind of man they should kill," or something like that, and then we went into the house. Madame Dionne was in the bed. We picked up the kids and took pictures and everything.

CA: With all the people you have ever met—Gandhi, Hitler, Laurier, and others—what would you ask Nixon if you met him in an interview?

SINCLAIR: That's a tough one. I've never given it a thought. I would have gone somewhere to the Shakespearean idea of "Methinks the Lady dost protest too much!" In other words, he had so often said he was not a thief, not a crook, not a this and that, why was he always on the defensive when he went on the television? The thing with the dog. I would have asked him about that. Why all this protesting of your innocence when you haven't been outwardly accused.

CA: You said in one of your books that your grandmother was one of the greatest storytellers in the world.

SINCLAIR: She told me about the Scot heroes, especially the Black Douglas, and she romanticized Sir Walter Scott's Lochinvar, Bruce, and Wallace. She told them in different ways each time, never accurately. And I'm certainly not one of the most accurate reporters, but I make a good story, and her style did affect me. I think it came as a big surprise to me to be tripped up by accuracy, because I was out to tell a story, and it never occurred to me that newspapers had to have a measure of accuracy. Even now I exaggerate and embellish and add to stories. I don't see anything wrong with that.

That is my major weakness: to make a good story rather than a factual one.

CA: Was there any turning point in your career, something that happened to you that you could peg as the beginning of something exciting for you?

SINCLAIR: The hobo story was the turning point of my career, if anything was. The story came when I was told there was a raid on the Toronto Jungle, as it was called. One hundred twenty-nine hoboes were scooped up, and I was to go with them, because they couldn't put all of them in jail—it was too costly. So I went with them. They were interesting people. Well, I came back. I didn't realize I had a story, and I didn't write one. A couple of days later my editor sent a memo: "Where's your story on the hoboes?" I told him I didn't think there was anything to it, that not much had happened. Well, one of the hoboes had hit me, and I had a black eye, and he said: "That's it! Write it!" So I wrote the story. I figured about nine hundred words. It didn't appear the next day or the next, but on the third day the story was returned to me saying this was very good, but could I break it down into two or three stories, and I did.

CA: It seemed like a big jump to go from that to traveling all over the world, didn't it?

SINCLAIR: It wasn't such a big jump. There's a lot left out. At the end of the four stories on the hoboes, I had said we were near New York City, and these bums I was with were hoping to get on a ship to England, to work their way to England. Whether they did or not, I don't know. But a memo came to me asking, "Why didn't you follow them?" Well, first I had no passport, secondly I had no money, and I had a family at home. "Go anyway!," they said. So I went to Montreal and got a job on the *Laurentic* on the White Star Line as a bookblack. But by the time I reached Quebec City the other guys found out I was a reporter and not a shoe shiner, so they got me tossed out. But I went anyway. I went to England.

CA: Harry Hindmarsh (editor of the Toronto Star) *was such a dynamo of a man. He sent you across the world to write stories. What an assignment. I wonder, are there any people like him today?*

SINCLAIR: No. It's a great regret today. There's no such newspaper and no such editor. It's a terrible thing. I think today there are two spots in the world which need exploring in the old-fashioned way—the Amazon Valley and the socalled Rooftop of the World, the golden road to Samarkand, as it was sometimes called. I was in those countries, and I wrote about them, but very little. Ian Fleming's brother, Peter, has done the best books about them.

CA: So you think it can still be done?

SINCLAIR: Let's put it this way. As I told you, I've kept a diary since I was fourteen, and I often check back to see what I did a year ago, or two years ago, on a certain day. Well, I looked at it this morning, and two years ago—that's usually as far back as I will go—I was asked by the *Toronto Star* to go around the world again, as I did five times. That was 1978, but I'm too old now to do that. I wish there was some young man or some young woman who could do that.

CA: Do you think journalism has become too slick?

SINCLAIR: No, too political! They're interested in politics, not in human interest, not in snake charmers or the old Indian rope trick. They're all interested in who's going to get elected here, what's the political meaning of this and that.

CA: Do you think people read that stuff?

SINCLAIR: I guess they have no alternative. I don't read it myself. I don't use it on the news here.

CA: Well, what are you doing here? What kind of work?

SINCLAIR: I'm doing the worst kind of journalism there is—scalping! That's all I'm doing. I get the stuff off the news ticker machines and write it in my style. But what kind of a life is that?

BOOKS

Authors in the News, Volume I, Gale, 1976.
Biography News, Volume I, Gale, 1974.
Karsh, Yousuf, *Karsh Canadians,* University of Toronto Press, 1978.
Sinclair, Gordon, *Will the Real Gordon Sinclair Please Stand Up,* McClelland & Stewart, 1966.

PERIODICALS

Detroit News, January 6, 1974.
Newsweek, January 7, 1974.
Saturday Night, November, 1975.
Time, January 21, 1974.
Windsor Star, February 15, 1974.*

—*Interview by C. H. Gervais*

* * *

SKELTON, Robin 1925-
(Georges Zuk)

PERSONAL: Born October 12, 1925, in Easington, East Yorkshire, England; son of Frederick William (a schoolmaster) and Eliza (Robins) Skelton; married Margaret Lambert, 1953 (divorced, 1957); married Sylvia Mary Jarrett, February 4, 1957; children: (second marriage) Nicholas John, Alison Jane, Eleanor Brigid. *Education:* Attended Christ's College, Cambridge, 1943-44; University of Leeds, B.A. (first class honors), 1950, M.A., 1951. *Avocational interests:* Book collecting, art collecting, making collages, stone carving, philately.

ADDRESSES: Home—1255 Victoria Ave., Victoria, British Columbia, Canada.*Office*—Department of Creative Writing, University of Victoria, Victoria, British Columbia, Canada V8W 2Y2.

CAREER: University of Manchester, Manchester, England, assistant lecturer, 1951-54, lecturer in English, 1954-63; University of Victoria, Victoria, British Columbia, associate professor, 1963-66, professor of English, 1966—, director of creative writing program, 1967-73, founding chair of department of creative writing, 1973-76. Northern Universities Joint Matriculation Board, examiner, 1954-58, chair of examiners in English O Level, 1958-60; centennial lecturer, University of Massachusetts, 1962-63; visiting professor, University of Michigan, 1967; lecturer, Eastern Washington State Creative Writing Summer School, 1972. Managing director, Lotus Press, 1950-51; founder and director, Pharos Press, 1972—; editor in chief, Sono Nis Press, 1976-83. Founder member, Peterloo Group (artists and poets), 1957-60; founding secretary, Manchester Institute of Contemporary Arts, 1960-62; member of board of directors, Art Gallery of Greater Victoria, 1968-69, 1970-73. Collage-maker, with individual shows in Victoria, 1966, 1968, and 1980. Has appeared on broadcasts for BBC-Radio and other radio and television stations, and given numerous readings and lectures. *Military service:* Royal Air Force, 1944-47; served in India; became sergeant.

MEMBER: Royal Society of Literature (fellow), Writers' Union of Canada (first vice-chair, 1981, chair, 1982-83), PEN.

WRITINGS:

POETRY

Patmos and Other Poems, Routledge & Kegan Paul, 1955.
Third Day Lucky, Oxford University Press, 1958.
Begging the Dialect: Poems and Ballads, Oxford University Press, 1960.
Two Ballads of the Muse, Rampant Lions Press, 1960.
The Dark Window, Oxford University Press, 1962.
A Valedictory Poem, privately printed, 1963.
An Irish Gathering, Dolmen Press, 1964.
A Ballad of Billy Barker, privately printed, 1965.
Inscriptions, privately printed, 1967.

Because of This and Other Poems, Manchester Institute of Contemporary Arts, 1968.
The Hold of Our Hands: Eight Letters to Sylvia, privately printed, 1968.
Selected Poems, 1947-67, McClelland & Stewart, 1968.
Answers, Enitharmon Press, 1969.
(Under pseudonym Georges Zuk) *Selected Verse,* Kayak, 1969.
An Irish Album, Dolmen Press, 1969.
A Different Mountain, Kayak, 1971.
The Hunting Dark, McClelland & Stewart, 1971.
A Private Speech: Messages 1962-1970, Sono Nis Press, 1971.
Remembering Synge: A Poem in Homage for the Centenary of His Birth, 16 April 1971, Dolmen Press, 1971.
A Christmas Poem, privately printed, 1972.
Hypothesis, Dreadnaught Press, 1972.
Musebook, Pharos Press, 1972.
Three for Herself, Sceptre Press, 1972.
Country Songs, Sceptre Press, 1973.
The Hermit Shell, privately printed, 1974.
Timelight, McClelland & Stewart, 1974.
Fifty Syllables for a Fiftieth Birthday, privately printed, 1975.
(Under pseudonym Georges Zuk) *The Underwear of the Unicorn,* Oolichan Books, 1975.
Callsigns, Sono Nis Press, 1976.
Because of Love, McClelland & Stewart, 1977.
Three Poems, Sceptre Press, 1977.
Landmarks, Sono Nis Press, 1979.
Collected Shorter Poems, 1947-1977, Sono Nis Press, 1981.
Limits, Porcupine's Quill, 1981.
De Nihilo, Aloysius Press, 1982.
Zuk, Porcupine's Quill, 1982.
Wordsong, Sono Nis Press, 1983.
Collected Longer Poems, 1947-1977, Sono Nis Press, 1985.
Distances, Porcupine's Quill, 1985.
Openings, Sono Nis Press, 1988.
Popping Fuschias: Poems, 1987-1992, Cacanadadada Press, 1992.
Islands: Poems in the Traditional Forms and Metres of Japan,, Ekstasis Editions, 1993.
I Am Me: Rhymes for Small, illustrated by Arsen Williams, Sono Nis Press, 1994.

Also author of *Words for Witches,,* 1990, and *A Formal Music,,* 1993.

FICTION

The Man Who Sang in His Sleep (short stories), Porcupine's Quill, 1984.
The Parrot Who Could (short stories), Sono Nis Press, 1987.
Telling the Tale (short stories), Porcupine's Quill, 1987.

Fires of the Kindred (novel), Porcepic, 1987.
Hanky Panky and Other Stories, Sono Nis Press, 1990.
Higgledy Piggledy, Pulp Press, 1992.

PLAYS

The Author, first produced in Victoria, BC, 1968.
The Paper Cage, Oolichan Press, 1982.

NONFICTION

John Ruskin: The Final Years, Manchester University Press, 1955.
The Poetic Pattern, University of California Press, 1956.
Painters Talking: Michael Snow and Tony Connor Interviewed, Peterloo Group, 1957.
Cavalier Poets, Longmans, Green, 1960.
Teach Yourself Poetry, English Universities Press, 1963, Dover, 1965.
J. M. Synge and His World, Viking, 1971.
Paintings, Graphics, and Sculpture from the Collection of Robin and Sylvia Skelton, privately printed, 1971.
The Practice of Poetry, Barnes & Noble, 1971.
The Writings of J. M. Synge, Bobbs-Merrill, 1971.
J. M. Synge, Bucknell University Press, 1972.
The Limners, Pharos Press, 1972.
The Poet's Calling, Barnes & Noble, 1975.
Poetic Truth, Barnes & Noble, 1978.
Explorations within a Landscape: New Porcelain by Robin Hopper, Robin Hopper, 1978.
Spellcraft: A Manual of Verbal Magic, McClelland & Stewart, 1978.
Herbert Siebner: A Monograph, Sono Nis Press, 1979.
They Call It the Cariboo, Sono Nis Press, 1980.
House of Dreams: Collages, Porcupine's Quill, 1983.
Talismanic Magic, Samuel Weiser, 1985.
Memoirs of a Literary Blockhead (autobiography), Macmillan, 1988.
The Practice of Witchcraft Today, R. Hale, 1988.
Portrait of My Father (memoir), Sono Nis Press, 1989.
Celtic Contraries, Syracuse University Press, 1990.
(With Jean Kozocari) *A Witches' Book of Ghosts and Exorcism,* State Mutual Book and Periodical Service, 1990.
A Devious Dictionary, collages by Ludwig Zeller, Cacanadadada Press, 1991.
Earth, Air, Fire, Water: Pre-Christian and Pagan Elements in British Songs, Rhymes, and Ballads, Viking, 1991.

Also author of (With Kozocari) *A Gathering of Ghosts,* 1989, and *The Magical Practice of Talismans,* 1991.

EDITOR

Leeds University Poetry 1949, Lotus Press, 1950.
(With D. Metcalfe) *The Acadine Poets, Series I-III,* Lotus Press, 1950.
J. M. Synge, *Translations,* Dolmen Press, 1961.

Synge, *The Collected Poems of J. M. Synge,* Oxford University Press, 1962.
Synge, *Four Plays and "The Aran Islands,"* Oxford University Press, 1962.
Edward Thomas, *Selected Poems,* Hutchinson, 1962.
Six Irish Poets: Austin Clarke, Richard Kell, Thomas Kinsella, John Montague, Richard Murphy, Richard Weber, Oxford University Press, 1962.
Viewpoint: An Anthology of Poetry, Hutchinson, 1962.
(Series editor) *The Collected Works of John Millington Synge,* Volume I: *The Poems,* Volume II: *The Prose,* edited by Alan Price, Volume III: *The Plays, Book 1,* edited by Ann Saddlemyer, Volume IV: *The Plays, Book 2,* edited by Saddlemyer, Oxford University Press, 1962, reprinted, Catholic University Press, 1982.
Five Poets of the Pacific Northwest: Kenneth O. Hanson, Richard Hugo, Carolyn Kizer, William Stafford, and David Wagner, Oxford University Press, 1964.
Poets of the Thirties, Penguin, 1964.
David Gascoyne, *Collected Poems,* Oxford University Press/Deutsch, 1965.
(With David R. Clark) *Irish Renaissance: A Gathering of Essays, Letters, and Memoirs from the "Massachusetts Review,"* Dolmen Press, 1965.
Selected Poems of Byron, Heinemann, 1965, Barnes & Noble, 1966.
(With Saddlemyer) *The World of W. B. Yeats: Essays in Perspective,* Oxford University Press, 1965, University of Washington Press, 1967.
Poetry of the Forties, Penguin, 1968.
Introductions from an Island: A Selection of Student Writing, University of Victoria, annual editions, 1969, 1971, 1973, 1974, 1977.
Synge, *Riders to the Sea,* Dolmen Press, 1969.
(With Alan Clodd) Gascoyne, *Collected Verse Translations,* Oxford University Press, 1970.
Herbert Read: A Memorial Symposium, Methuen, 1970.
The Collected Plays of Jack B. Yeats, Bobbs-Merrill, 1971.
Synge, *Some Sonnets from "Laura in Death" after the Italian of Francesco Petrarch* (bilingual edition), Dolmen Press, 1971.
Six Poets of British Columbia, David Godine, 1973.
Thirteen Irish Writers on Ireland, David Godine, 1973.
(With William David Thomas) *A Gathering in Celebration of the 80th Birthday of Robert Graves,* University of Victoria, 1975.
Ezra Pound, *From Syria: The Worksheets, Proofs, and Text,* Copper Canyon Press, 1981.
The Selected Writings of Jack B. Yeats, Trafalgar Square, 1992.
J. M. Synge, *The Aran Islands,* photographs by Synge, Oxford University Press, 1995.

TRANSLATOR

(And editor) *Two Hundred Poems from "The Greek Anthology,"* McClelland & Stewart, 1971, University of Washington Press, 1972.

(And editor) *George Faludy: Twelve Sonnets,* Pharos Press, 1983.

(With others, and editor) *Selected Poems of George Faludy, 1933-80,* University of Georgia Press, 1985.

(And editor) *George Faludy: Corpses, Brats, and Cricket Music* (bilingual edition), William Hoffer, 1986.

Federico Garcia Lorca, *Selected Poems and Ballads,* Guernica Editions, 1989.

OTHER

Contributor of poems, articles, and reviews to periodicals, including *Observer, Times Literary Supplement, Manchester Guardian, Critical Quarterly, Massachusetts Review, Poetry, Canadian Literature, London Magazine, Poetry Northwest, Listener, New Statesman,* and *Quarterly Review of Literature.* Drama critic, *Union News,* 1950; poetry reviewer, *Books,* 1957; poetry reviewer, 1957-58, and drama reviewer, 1958-60, *Manchester Guardian;* poetry reviewer, *Critical Quarterly,* 1960; art reviewer, Victoria *Daily Times,* 1964-66; mystery book columnist, *Toronto Star,* 1988—. Editor, *The Gryphon,* beginning 1949; co-founder and editor, 1967-71, and sole editor, 1972-83, *Malahat Review.*

Almost all of Skelton's manuscripts, worksheets, proofs, literary correspondence, and unpublished works, as well as a collection of published work, are contained in the Robin Skelton Collection in the Rare Book room of the MacPherson Library at the University of Victoria.

SIDELIGHTS: Among the many publications to his credit, Robin Skelton has over two dozen poetry collections, several critical studies on writers as well as the art of poetry, two plays, three story collections, a social history, and a novel. In addition, Skelton has turned his talents to editing works by other writers, and helped establish and edit the prestigious literary magazine *Malahat Review.* In an interview with Martin Townsend in the *Quill & Quire,* the Canadian author gives three reasons for his "wanton productivity": "I'm compulsive—what else? I feel slightly ill if I'm not writing something—I've got printer's ink in my blood, I think. Also, I'm never satisfied with pigeonholing myself. I find myself frequently daring myself to do something I don't think I can do." Skelton added that for him, writing is the best way to explore something: "If I want to find something out I have to write about it. If I want to read a foreign poet badly, I usually have to attempt translations, which I might or might not publish. My attitude, really, is that if there's a book you want to read and nobody seems to have produced it, produce it yourself."

Skelton has held this self-reliant attitude throughout his career. As a Codes and Cyphers Sergeant for the Royal Air Force, Skelton wrote and produced scripts for All India Radio; while still a student at Leeds University, Skelton edited the University magazine and bought the Lotus Press, a small literary publisher. After graduation the poet joined the staff of Manchester University, and published a volume of poetry as well as several critical studies. Nevertheless, Skelton felt his own work was being stifled, for as he recalls in *Contemporary Authors Autobiography Series,* "my poetry was ignored by most of my colleagues (one of them always left the staff lounge whenever it was mentioned) and I was never invited to meet visiting poets (who sometimes asked after me), or to give readings." It was not until Skelton emigrated to British Columbia, Canada, in 1963, that his poetry began improving: "The escape from English gentility," Skelton recalls in *Quill & Quire,* "was, stylistically, most important. I had to reinvent my language."

Perhaps owing to his varied background and independent outlook, Skelton's poetry is characterized as self-conscious although this self-consciousness manifests itself in an array of forms. Keith Garebian, in a *Dictionary of Literary Biography* essay, calls Skelton "a meditative poet [who] expands his technical freedom while reflecting on profound subjects that often refuse to be fixed in a single form and phrase." Just as his desire for variety has expressed itself in diverse literary forms, Skelton's poetry experiments with many different poetic configurations, this same "technical freedom." "Skelton is a craftsman whose work shows that he has not merely studied but *absorbed* the major traditions of poetry in English, and can write with gracefully assured precision in a variety of tones and rhythmic forms," notes David Jackel in *Canadian Forum.*

In a review of *The Collected Shorter Poems, 1947-1977,* however, a *Choice* writer comments that while Skelton's work traverses many different themes and forms, "nearly all of the poems trace the development of a single personality. . . . The tone is wry, witty, self-mocking, conversational but clearly directed toward statement." "Skelton is a thoroughly self-conscious poet," states D. P. Thomas in the *Fiddlehead,* "capable of standing aside and quizzing his own directions." Nevertheless, Skelton's work is not didactic or overly philosophical; he "is less a philosopher, in most of the commoner sense of the term, than a spokesman for predicaments," comments Thomas. The poet himself echoes this assessment in a *Waves* interview with Dorothy Stott: "In a way, I don't think about what my poems say; my poems are doing the thinking for me. I don't know if that makes sense but the poems tell me, the poems talk to me, I don't necessarily talk through my poems. A lot of the opinions that come out of the poems are not necessarily my own personal opinions and this is something that people don't usually realize. I explain it by saying that a poem is not an affidavit." Although criticism of the author's poetry covers numerous aspects, "in fact all attempts to characterize Skelton's writing centre on confirming his extreme skill and craftsmanship," writes Louise McKinney in the *Quill & Quire.* The critic summarizes: "From the sonorous, internal rhymes of his beautifully baroque early work to the pared-away intensity of the late, Skelton's skill has made him a leading Canadian poet."

After almost thirty years of focusing his creative writing on poetry, Skelton began publishing collections of short stories. "In the stories, I can tell jokes that I can't tell in poetry, and I can point out social oddities, and I can speculate along the lines of 'what if something bizarre happened . . . ,'" the author remarked to Townsend. "There's a whole part of my thinking, feeling, and sense of humour that doesn't get into the verse." *The Man Who Sang in His Sleep,* Skelton's first collection, "contains 10 stories which are sometimes charming, occasionally darker (funny in a Hitchcock sort of way) and always entertaining," remarks Antanas Sileika in the Toronto *Globe and Mail.* Although Skelton is giving voice to a different side of his creativity, these stories contain the same sense of identity found in much of his poetry. Sileika notes that "the voice used in these stories is invariably engaging, the kind that encourages eavesdropping if one overheard it in a bar," while Townsend observes in a review of *The Parrot Who Could* that "the tales nearly always appear richly humorous through their endearingly comical first-person perspective." T. F. Rigelhof similarly praises the stories in *Telling the Tale:* "Skelton casually but craftily honors the conventions that are traditional to [the supernatural] genre," the critic notes in the Toronto *Globe and Mail.* "His narrators speak directly to the reader and frequently seem to be doing little more than passing along stories that they have heard." "Skelton's narrative voice is a rich medium that is a pleasure in itself," remarks Townsend. "Though a few of the story endings may be predictable from the first page and some of the punch lines weak, many among these tales can be read over and over again with pleasure because each paragraph succeeds in its own right with wit and grace."

Despite his varied and vast body of work, Skelton told Townsend that "I find it hard to write fiction and poetry at the same time. At the moment I seem to be emphasizing the writing of fiction, but I know perfectly well that if I tell you now that I am going to concentrate on fiction from now on, I would probably write a poem before the week is out!" When asked about his literary future, Skelton responded that he has at least two books, one fiction and one nonfiction, in the works. The prolific author concluded: "I can't say what's going to happen after that, I'm really not sure. I've got several things I'm interested in doing. At the moment I think it is possible I'll continue writing fiction. But I've been writing so hard these last two or three years that I'm not really contemplating any enormous new task until at least the spring of next year!" Skelton also has his teaching, editing, and exhibiting of collages and stone carving from which to choose; any selection is bound to benefit from his expertise, for as Rigelhof comments, "Skelton, in his more than 20 years in [Canada], has done much to raise standards in numerous areas of our literary life."

BIOGRAPHICAL/CRITICAL SOURCES:

BOOKS

Authors in the News, Gale, 1975.
Contemporary Authors Autobiography Series, Volume 5, Gale, 1987.
Dictionary of Literary Biography, Gale, Volume 27: *Poets of Great Britain and Ireland,* 1984, Volume 53: *Canadian Writers since 1960, First Series,* 1986.
Skeleton, Robin, *Memoirs of a Literary Blockhead,* Macmillan, 1988.
Skeleton, *Portrait of My Father,* Sono Nis Press, 1989.
Turner, Barbara E., editor, *Skelton at Sixty,* Porcupine's Quill, 1987.

PERIODICALS

Books and Bookmen, June, 1971.
Canadian Forum, August, 1977.
Choice, September, 1981, July, 1986.
Fiddlehead, March, 1969.
Globe and Mail (Toronto), September 1, 1984, August 8, 1987, September 5, 1987, April 9, 1988.
Nation, August 30, 1971.
New Statesman, April 30, 1971, August 22, 1975.
Quill & Quire, December, 1975, March, 1986, July, 1987, January, 1988.
Saturday Review, May 1, 1971.
Times Literary Supplement, September 11, 1981.
Waves, Number 1, 1983.

—Sketch by Diane Telgen

*   *   *

SKVORECKY, Josef (Vaclav) 1924-

PERSONAL: Surname pronounced *Shquor*-et-skee; born September 27, 1924, in Nachod, Czechoslovakia; immigrated to Canada, 1969; son of Josef Karel (a bank clerk) and Anna Marie (Kurazova) Skvorecky; married Zdena Salivarova (a writer and publisher), March 31, 1958. *Education:* Charles University, Prague, Ph.D., 1951. *Politics:* Christian democrat. *Religion:* Roman Catholic. *Avoca-*

tional interests: Film, jazz (Skvorecky plays the saxophone), American folklore.

ADDRESSES: Home—487 Sackville St., Toronto, Ontario, Canada M4X 1T6.*Agent*—Louise Dennys, Lester and Orpen Dennys Inc., 78 Sullivan Street, Toronto, Ontario M5T 1C1.*Office*—68 Publishers, 164 Davenport Rd., Toronto, Ontario, Canada M5R 1J2.

CAREER: Odeon Publishers, Prague, Czechoslovakia, editor of Anglo-American department, 1953-56; *World Literature Magazine,* Prague, assistant editor-in-chief, 1956-59; free-lance writer in Prague, 1963-69; University of Toronto, Erindale College, Clarkson, Ontario, special lecturer in English and Slavic drama, 1969-71, writer-in-residence, 1970-71, associate professor, 1971-75, professor of English, 1975-90, professor emeritus, 1990—. 68 Publishers, founder and editor-in-chief, 1972—. *Military service:* Czechoslovak Army, 1951-53.

MEMBER: International PEN, International Association of Crime Writers, Authors Guild, Authors League of America, Mystery Writers of America, Royal Society of Canada (fellow), Crime Writers of Canada, Canadian Writers Union, Czechoslovak Society of Arts and Letters (honorary member).

AWARDS, HONOURS: Literary Award of Czechoslovakian Writers Union, 1968; Neustadt International Prize for Literature, 1980; Guggenheim fellowship, 1980; Silver Award for Best Fiction Publication in Canadian Magazines of 1980, 1981; nominated for the Nobel Prize in literature, 1982; Governor General's Award for Best Fiction, 1985, for *The Engineer of Human Souls*; 1985 City of Toronto Book Award; D.H.L., State University of New York, 1986; Czechoslovak Order of the White Lion, 1990.

WRITINGS:

Zbabelci (novel), Ceskoslovensky spisovatel (Prague), 1958, 4th edition, Nase vojsko (Prague), 1968, translation by Jeanne Nemcova published as *The Cowards,* Grove, 1970.
Legenda Emoke (novel; title means The Legend of Emoke), Ceskoslovensky spisovatel, 1963, 2nd edition, 1965.
Sedmiramenny svicen (stories; title means The Menorah), Nase vojsko, 1964, 2nd edition, 1965.
Napady ctenare detektivek (essays; title means Reading Detective Stories), Ceskoslovensky spisovatel, 1965.
Ze zivota lepsi spolecnosti (stories; title means The Life of Better Society), Mlada fronta (Prague), 1965.
Babylonsky pribeh (stories; title means A Babylonian Story), Svovodne Slovo (Prague), 1965.
Smutek porucika Boruvka (stories), Mlada fronta, 1966, translation published as *The Mournful Demeanor of Lieutenant Boruvka,* Gollancz, 1974.

Konec nylonoveho veku (novel; title means The End of the Nylon Age), Ceskoslovensky spisovatel, 1967.
O nich—o nas (essays; title means About Them—Which Is about Us), Kruh (Hradec Kralove), 1968.
(With Evald Schorm) *Fararuv Konec* (novelization of Skvorecky's filmscript Konec farare; title means End of a Priest; also see below), Kruh, 1969.
Lvice (novel), Ceskoslovensky spisovatel, 1969, translation published as *Miss Silver's Past,* Grove, 1973.
Horkejsvet: Povidky z let, 1946-1967 (title means The Bitter World: Selected Stories, 1947-1967), Odeon (Prague), 1969.
Tankovy prapor (novel; title means The Tank Corps), 68 Publishers (Toronto), 1971.
All the Bright Young Men and Women: A Personal History of the Czech Cinema, translation from the original Czech by Michael Schonberg, Peter Martin Associates, 1971.
Mirakl, 68 Publishers, 1972, translation by Paul Wilson published as *The Miracle Game,* Knopf, 1991.
Hrichy pro patera Knoxe (novel), 68 Publishers, 1973, translation by Kaca Polackova-Henley published as *Sins for Father Knox,* Norton, 1989.
Prima Sezona (novel), 68 Publishers, 1974, translation published as *The Swell Season,* Lester & Orpen Dennys, 1982.
Konec porucika Boruvka (novel), 68 Publishers, 1975, translation published as *The End of Lieutenant Boruvka,* Norton, 1990.
Pribeh inzenyra lidskych dusi (novel), 68 Publishers, 1977, translation published as *The Engineer of Human Souls: An Entertainment of the Old Themes of Life, Women, Fate, Dreams, the Working Class, Secret Agents, Love, and Death,* Knopf, 1984.
The Bass Saxophone, translation from the original Czech by Polackova-Henley, Knopf, 1979.
Navrat porucika Boruvka (novel), 68 Publishers, 1980, translation published as *The Return of Lieutenant Boruvka,* translation by Wilson, Norton, 1991.
Jiri Menzel and the History of the "Closely Watched Trains" (comparative study), University of Colorado Press, 1982.
Scherzo capriccioso (novel), 68 Publishers, 1984, translation published as *Dvorak in Love,* Knopf, 1986.
Talkin' Moscow Blues (essays), Lester & Orpen Dennys, 1988.
Nevesta z Texasu (novel), (title means *A Bride from Texas*), 68 Publishers, 1992.
Republic of Whores: A Fragment from the Time of the Cults, translation by Wilson, Ecco Press, 1994.

EDITOR

Selected Writings of Sinclair Lewis, Odeon, 1964-69.

(With P. L. Doruzka) *Tvar jazzu* (anthology; title means "The Face of Jazz"), Statni hudebni vydavatelstvi (Prague), Part 1, 1964, Part 2, 1966.

Collected Writings of Ernest Hemingway, Odeon, 1965-69.

Three Times Hercule Poirot, Odeon, 1965.

(With Doruzka) *Jazzova inspirace* (poetry anthology; title means "The Jazz Inspiration"), Odeon, 1966.

Nachrichten aus der CSSR (title means "News from Czechoslovakia"), translation from the original Czech by Vera Cerna and others, Suhrkamp Verlag (Frankfurt), 1968.

OTHER

(Author of afterword) Lustig, Arnost, *Indecent Dreams,* Northwestern University Press, 1990.

(Author of introduction) Hrabal, Bohumil, *The Little Town where Time Stood Still,* Pantheon, 1993.

Also author of movie screenplays, including "Zlocin v divci skole" (title means "Crime in a Girl's School"), 1966; "Zlocin v santanu" (title means "Crime in a Night Club"), 1968; "Konec farare" (title means "End of a Priest"), 1969; "Flirt se slecnou Stribrnou" (title means "Flirtations with Miss Silver"), 1969; and "Sest cernych divek" (title means "Six Brunettes"), 1969. Author of scripts for television programs. Author of prefaces and introductions to Czech and Slovak editions of the works of Saul Bellow, Bernard Malamud, Stephen Crane, Rex Stout, Dorothy Sayers, Charles Dickens, Sinclair Lewis, and others. Translator of numerous books from English to Czech, including the works of Ray Bradbury, Henry James, Ernest Hemingway, William Faulkner, Raymond Chandler, and others.

ADAPTATIONS: Tankovy prapor was produced as a feature film by BONTON Co. in Prague, 1991.

SIDELIGHTS: "In his native country, Josef Skvorecky is a household word," fellow Czech author Arnost Lustig tells the *Washington Post.* Skvorecky wrote his first novel, *The Cowards,* in 1948 when he was twenty-four. Not published until 1958, the book caused a flurry of excitement that led to "firings in the publishing house, ragings in the official press, and a general purge that extended eventually throughout the arts," according to Neal Ascherson in the *New York Review of Books.* The book was banned by Czech officials one month after publication, marking "the start of an incredible campaign of vilification against the author," a *Times Literary Supplement* reviewer reports. Skvorecky subsequently included a "cheeky and impenitent Introduction," Ascherson notes, in the novel's 1963 second edition. "In spite of all the suppression," the *Times Literary Supplement* critic explains, "*The Cowards* became a milestone in Czech literature and Joseph Skvorecky one of the country's most popular writers." Formerly a member of the central committees of the Czecho-

slovak Writers' Union and the Czechoslovak Film and Television Artists, Skvorecky chose exile and immigrated to Canada in 1969 following the Soviet invasion of his country.

Ascherson explains why *The Cowards* caused so much controversy: "It is not at all the sort of mirror official Czechoslovakia would wish to glance in. A recurring theme is . . . pity for the Germans, defeated and bewildered. . . . The Russians strike [the main character] as alluring primitives (his use of the word 'Mongolian' about them caused much of the scandal in 1958)." The *Times Literary Supplement* writer adds, "The novel turned out to be anti-Party and anti-God at the same time; everybody felt himself a victim of the author's satire." Set in a provincial Bohemian town, the story's events unfold in May, 1945, as the Nazis retreat and the Russian army takes control of an area populated with "released prisoners of war, British, Italian, French and Russian (Mongolians, these, whom the locals do not find very clean), and Jewish women survivors from a concentration camp," writes Stuart Hood in the *Listener.* The narrator, twenty-year-old Danny Smiricky, and his friends—members of a jazz band—observe the flux of power, human nature, and death around them while devoting their thoughts and energies to women and music. "These are, by definition, no heroes," states Hood. "They find themselves caught up in a farce which turns into horror from one minute to the next." The group may dream of making a bold move for their country, but, as Charles Dollen notes in *Best Sellers,* "they never make anything but music."

Labeled "judeonegroid" (Jewish-Negro) and suppressed by the Nazis, their jazz is, nonetheless, political. To play blues or sing scat is to stand up for "individual freedom and spontaneity," states Terry Winch in *Washington Post Book World.* "In other words, [jazz] stood for everything the Nazis hated and wanted to crush." Skvorecky, like his narrator, was a jazz musician during the Nazi "protectorate." The author wields this music as a "goad, the 'sharp thorn in the sides of the power-hungry men, from Hitler to Brezhnev,'" Saul Maloff declares in the *New York Times Book Review.* Described as a "highly metaphorical writer" by Winch, Skvorecky often employs jazz "in its familiar historical and international role as a symbol (and a breeding-ground) of anti-authoritarian attitudes," according to Russell Davies, writing in the *Times Literary Supplement.*

Skvorecky follows the life of Danny Smiricky in *Tankovy prapor* ("The Tank Corps"), *The Miracle Game, The Bass Saxophone,* and *The Engineer of Human Souls: An Entertainment of the Old Themes of Life, Women, Fate, Dreams, the Working Class, Secret Agents, Love, and Death. The Bass Saxophone* contains a memoir and two novellas first published individually in Czechoslovakia during the 1960s. Like *The Cowards,* the memoir *"Red Music,"* observes Maloff, "evokes the atmosphere of that bleak time [during World War II], the strange career of indigenous American music transplanted abroad to the unlikeliest soil." Although it is only a "brief preface to the stories," Winch maintains that the memoir "in some ways is the more interesting section" of the book. Davies believes that the "short and passionate essay" shows how, "since [the jazz enthusiast in an Iron Curtain country] has sorrows other than his own to contend with, the music must carry for him not just a sense of isolation and longing but a bitterly practical political resentment."

"Emoke," the novella that follows, is "fragile, lyrical, 'romantic'" and, like its title character, "fabulous: precisely the materials of fable," comments Maloff. Davies adds that "in its poetic evocation of Emoke, a hurt and delicate creature with an array of spiritual cravings, . . . the story has a . . . depth of soul and concern." Winch, however, feels the woman "is not a vivid or forceful enough character to bear the burden of all she is asked to represent." The three critics believe that the title story, *"The Bass Saxophone,"* is more successful, "perhaps because music, Skvorecky's real passion, is central to the narrative," Winch explains. Here, writes Davies, "music . . . emerges as a full symbolic and ideological force," whereas in "Emoke" it was "a mere undercurrent." The story of a boy playing music while under Nazi rule, claims Maloff, is "sheer magic, a parable, a fable about art, about politics, about the zone where the two intersect." Writing in the *Atlantic,* Benjamin De Mott calls *The Bass Saxophone* "an exceptionally haunting and restorative volume of fiction, a book in which literally nothing enters except the fully imagined, hence the fully exciting."

Following Danny's travels to Canada as an immigrant, Skvorecky's writing continues to parallel his own life when the main character of *The Engineer of Human Souls* accepts a position at a small University of Toronto college. The main theme, brought out by the author's use of humor in the book, concerns the dangers of dogmatic thinking, the political naivete of Westerners, and the injustices of totalitarianism. *Quill and Quire* critic Mark Czarnecki asserts that as "an exhaustive, insightful document of modern society in both East and West, [*The Engineer of Human Souls*] has no equal." In a *Canadian Forum* review, Sam Solecki notes that *The Engineer of Human Souls* is also a "transitional novel for Skvorecky, in which we see him extending his imagination beyond his Czechoslovak past while still including it." Solecki also writes that this novel, which portrays Smiricky in his sixties, will probably bring "the Smiricky cycle to a close."

However, the theme of music which Skvorecky maintains throughout the Smiricky books is continued in the author's next novel, *Dvorak in Love.* The book is a fictional-

ized account of Skvorecky's compatriot, composer Antonin Dvorak, and his visit to New York City. The life of Dvorak, whose music was influenced by black folk music and jazz, provided the author with the perfect subject for discussing the synthesis "of the two dominant musical cultures of our time—the classical European tradition . . . and the jazzy American tradition," as William French put it in a *Globe and Mail* review. Although some reviewers like Barbara Black have found the narrative structure of the opening chapters of *Dvorak in Love* too complicated to enjoy, the author's characteristic humor later enlivens the story. "Best of all" in this book, remarks Black, "Skvorecky celebrates Dvorak and the musical trail he blazed."

Summarizing the writer's accomplishments in all his works, Hood comments that "Skvorecky is a novelist of real stature, who writes without sentimentality about adolescence, war and death." Yet it is not plot that impresses Winch. He points out that Skvorecky "is a poetic writer whose work depends more on the interplay of words and images than on story-line." Concludes Maloff: "We have had to wait a very long time for the . . . English translation and . . . American publication of [Skvorecky's] superlative, greatly moving works of art. . . . Fortunately, [his] work has lost none of its immediacy or luster, nor is it likely to for a long time to come."

BIOGRAPHICAL/CRITICAL SOURCES:

BOOKS

Contemporary Authors Autobiography Series, Volume 1, Gale, 1984.
Contemporary Literary Criticism, Gale, Volume 15, 1980, Volume 39, 1986, Volume 63, 1991.
Solecki, Sam, editor, *The Achievement of Josef Skvorecky,* University of Toronto Press, 1994.
Solecki, Sam, *Prague Blues: The Fiction of Josef Skvorecky,* ECW Press, 1990.

PERIODICALS

Atlantic, March, 1979.
Best Sellers, November 1, 1970.
Books in Canada, May, 1981, p. 40; February, 1983, pp. 13-4; November, 1986, pp. 17-8; October, 1988, pp. 31-2; December, 1989, p. 9; June-July, 1990, pp. 24-6.
Canadian Forum, November, 1977, pp. 40-1; December-January, 1982-83, p. 40; August-September, 1984.
Canadian Literature, spring, 1992, pp. 166-67 and 212-14.
Chicago Tribune, June 9, 1987.
Chicago Tribune Book World, August 12, 1984; March 1, 1987.
Encounter, July-August, 1985.
Globe and Mail (Toronto), November 25, 1986; November 29, 1986; June 25, 1988; November 24, 1990.
Library Journal, July, 1970.

Listener, October 8, 1970; March 11, 1976; August 17, 1978.

Los Angeles Times Book Review, July 1, 1984; February 15, 1987, pp. 3, 8; August 23, 1987; June 12, 1988; February 26, 1989.

Maclean's, December 31, 1990, p. 47.

Nation, August 4, 1984; March 25, 1991, p. 381.

New Republic, August 27, 1984.

New Statesman, October 2, 1970, p. 426; February 5, 1988, p. 33.

New Statesman & Society, March 1, 1991, p. 37.

Newsweek, August 13, 1984.

New York Review of Books, November 19, 1970, p. 45; April 5, 1973, pp. 34-5; September 27, 1984; April 11, 1991, pp. 45-6.

New York Times, July 23, 1984; August 9, 1984; January 31, 1987, p. 13.

New York Times Book Review, September 21, 1975, p. 38; January 14, 1979, pp. 7, 35; November 25, 1979, p. 46; August 19, 1984; January 12, 1986; February 22, 1987; September 6, 1987, p. 16; February 18, 1990, p. 14; March 10, 1991, p. 21.

Observer, March 3, 1985.

Publishers Weekly, June 22, 1984.

Quill and Quire, May, 1984; November, 1988, p. 18; October, 1989, p. 23; September, 1990, pp. 60-1.

Sewanee Review, winter, 1993, pp. 107-15.

Time, July 30, 1984.

Times Literary Supplement, October 16, 1970; June 23, 1978; August 12, 1983; March 8, 1985; January 23, 1987.

Washington Post, December 4, 1987.

Washington Post Book World, July 29, 1984; March 29, 1987.

World Literature Today, autumn, 1978; summer, 1979, p. 524; autumn, 1985, p. 622; summer, 1986, p. 489; autumn, 1987, pp. 652-53; summer, 1991, pp. 511-12.

*   *   *

SLADE, Bernard
See NEWBOUND, Bernard Slade

*   *   *

SMITH, A(rthur) J(ames) M(arshall)   1902-1980

PERSONAL: Born November 8, 1902, in Montreal, Quebec, Canada; died October, 1980, in East Lansing, Michigan, United States; son of Octavius Arthur and Louise (Whiting) Smith; married Jeannie Dougall Robins, 1927 (deceased); children: Peter G. M. *Education:* McGill University, B.Sc., 1925, M.A., 1926; Edinburgh University, Ph.D., 1931.

CAREER: Ball State Teachers College (now Ball State University), Muncie, IN, assistant professor, 1930-31; Michigan State College (now University), East Lansing, instructor, 1931-33; Doane College, Crete, NE, professor, 1934-35; University of South Dakota, Vermillion, assistant professor, 1935-36; Michigan State University, instructor, 1936-39, assistant professor, 1939-44, associate professor, 1944-46, professor of English, 1946-72, professor emeritus, 1972-80, poet-in-residence, 1961-71, *Centennial Review* Lecturer, 1964. Visiting professor at University of Toronto, fall, 1944, University of Washington, summer, 1949, Queen's University, summers, 1952 and 1960, University of Montana, summer 1956, University of British Columbia, summer, 1956, Dalhousie University, 1966-67, Sir George Williams University, summers, 1967 and 1969, McGill University, 1969-70, and State University of New York at Stony Brook, 1969.

MEMBER: Modern Language Association of America.

AWARDS, HONOURS: Guggenheim fellowship, 1941-43; Harriet Monroe Memorial Prize, 1943, for *Poetry; A Magazine of Verse*; Rockefeller Foundation fellowship, 1944-46; Governor-General's Medal for Poetry, 1944, for *News of the Phoenix and Other Poems*; D.Litt., McGill University, 1958; LL.D., Queen's University, 1966, and Dalhousie University, 1969; Lorne Pierce Gold Medal for Literature, Royal Society of Canada, 1966; D.C.L., Bishop's University, 1967; Centennial Medal, Canadian Government, 1967; Canada Council medal, 1968.

WRITINGS:

POETRY

News of the Phoenix and Other Poems, Coward, 1943.

A Sort of Ecstasy: Poems New and Selected, Michigan State College Press, 1954.

Collected Poems, Oxford University Press (Toronto), 1962.

Poems: New and Collected, Oxford University Press, 1967.

The Classic Shade: Selected Poems, introduction by M. L. Rosenthal, McClelland & Stewart, 1978.

OTHER

(Contributor) A. Preminger, *Encyclopedia of Poetry and Poetics,* Princeton University Press, 1965, enlarged edition, 1974.

(Contributor) O. Williams, *Master Poems of the English Language,* Simon & Schuster, 1966.

Some Poems of E. J. Pratt: Aspects of Imagery and Theme, Memorial University, 1969.

Towards a View of Canadian Letters: Selected Critical Essays, 1928-71, University of British Columbia Press, 1973.

On Poetry and Poets: Selected Essays of A. J. M. Smith with an Introduction by the Author, McClelland & Stewart, 1977.

Contributor to *Encyclopaedia Britannica, Collier's Yearbook,* 1953-55, and to numerous journals and magazines.

EDITOR

(With F. R. Scott) *New Provinces: Poems of Several Authors,* Macmillan (Toronto), 1936.

(And author of introduction and notes) *The Book of Canadian Poetry,* University of Chicago Press, 1943, 3rd edition, Gage, 1957.

Essays for College Writing, St. Martin's, 1965.

Seven Centuries of Verse, Scribner, 1947, 3rd revised edition, 1967.

The Worldly Muse: An Anthology of Serious Light Verse, Abelard, 1951.

(With M. L. Rosenthal) *Exploring Poetry,* Macmillan, 1955, 2nd edition, 1973.

(With Scott) *The Blasted Pine,* Macmillan, 1957, revised edition, 1967.

The Oxford Book of Canadian Verse, Oxford University Press (New York), 1960.

Masks of Fiction: Canadian Critics on Canadian Prose, McClelland & Stewart, 1961.

(With W. H. Mason) *Short Story Study: A Critical Anthology,* Edward Arnold, 1961.

(And author of introduction) *Masks of Poetry: Canadian Critics on Canadian Verse,* McClelland & Stewart, 1962.

(And author of introduction) *100 Poems,* Scribner, 1965.

The Book of Canadian Prose, Gage, Volume I: *Early Beginnings to Confederation,* 1965, published as *The Colonial Century: English-Canadian Writing before Confederation,* 1973, Volume II: *The Canadian Century: English-Canadian Writing since Confederation,* 1973.

Modern Canadian Verse in English and French, Oxford University Press (Toronto), 1967.

The Collected Poems of Anne Wilkinson and a Prose Memoir, Macmillan, 1968.

The Canadian Experience: A Brief Survey of English-Canadian Prose, Gage Educational Pub., 1974.

SIDELIGHTS: As a poet and anthologist of Canadian verse, A.J.M. Smith is credited with bringing recognition to Canadian poetry, written in both French and English. In a review of *Modern Canadian Verse,* a critic for the *Times Literary Supplement* writes: "[Smith's] earlier anthology *The Oxford Book of Canadian Verse* . . . was sensational not so much because it demonstrated the affluence which has come to Canadian poetry in the years be-

tween the wars but more because the editor insisted on recognizing poets of both languages as Canadian poets."

Born in Wesmount, Quebec, in 1902, Smith entered McGill University in 1921 as a science student but later changed to English. Unimpressed with the Maple Leaf School and the late-Victorian, nationalistic poetry popular among Canadian critics during the early 1920s, Smith resolved to promote modernism through his own work and that of others. He published his first poem, "Pagan," in the modernist *Canadian Forum,* and, as editor of the Literary Supplement of the *McGill Daily* and cofounder with F. R. Scott of the *McGill Fortnightly Review,* he favored modernist poetry and published numerous essays on the subject. After receiving an undergraduate degree in 1925 and a Master of Arts in 1926, Smith taught at Montreal High School for a year before entering the University of Edinburgh, where he received his Ph.D. in 1931. On returning to Canada, Smith found academic positions scarce and had to settle for temporary posts in the United States. In 1936, he and Scott published *New Provinces,* an anthology devoted to the work of modernist Canadian poets; and Smith obtained a permanent position at Michigan State University, where he taught until his retirement in 1972. His second anthology, *The Book of Canadian Poetry,* which became a highly influential textbook, and his first collection, *News of the Phoenix and Other Poems,* which recieved a Governor General's Award, appeared in 1943. Throughout his career Smith received numerous honorary degrees and prizes for his work as a poet and critic.

Smith's critical essays and anthologies center on the definition and study of modernist poetry. In such essays as "A Rejected Preface" (1965), which was intended for the 1936 anthology *New Provinces,* Smith derided Canadian poetry at the time for its dreamy romanticism and called for a poetry that was absolute, universal, and timeless. In a subsequent anthology, *The Book of Canadian Poetry,* he divided Canadian verse between native and cosmopolitan traditions and clearly exhibited his preference for the latter, arguing that this strain of poetry "from the beginning, has made a heroic effort to transcend colonialism by entering into the universal, civilizing culture of ideas." Espousing a preference for the cosmopolitan and intellectual, Smith's critical studies usually dealt with the metaphysical poets and such modernists as W. B. Yeats and T. S. Eliot. Smith's own poetry likewise evinces a metaphysical influence in its intellectual approach to such themes as love, nature, death, and faith. Exploring perception and the formulation of the "idea" of a subject, his imagist nature poems celebrate the interconnections through action inherent in the natural world. Such poems as "Sea Cliff" and "The Creek," for instance, focus on the interaction of water and various objects on the shore, producing what Anne Compton describes as an "overall effect . . . of things matted together." As Smith wrote in a discussion of imagist poetry: "The purpose of an Imagist poem is to perceive and to present perceptions, but here we go further in an effort to grasp the idea of the thing and of its place in history."

Reaction to Smith's critical writings and poetry has been mixed. While some scholars have commended his promotion through anthologies and essays of modernist, cosmopolitan verse, others have attacked him, charging that his preferences belittle poetry based on Canadian experiences and reinforce colonialism. In discussing his poetry, critics have praised the universal and timeless qualities of his verse and remarked on his concern with metaphysics, order, and unity. Noting the marked influence of others on his work, some scholars have argued that Smith's poetry is essentially derivative; others, however, have described him as an academic poet who was attempting to create a poetic dialogue. The essential weakness of Smith's verse, commentators have argued, is language, particularly his resort to cliche and his frequent echoing of others, while his major strength derives from his intellectualism—his poetic artifice and passion for the mind.

BIOGRAPHICAL/CRITICAL SOURCES:

BOOKS

Burke, Anne, *A. J. M. Smith: An Annotated Bibliography,* ECW Press, 1983.

Compton, Anne, *A. J. M. Smith: Canadian Metaphysical,* ECW Press, 1994.

Contemporary Literary Criticism, Volume 15, Gale, 1980.

Darling, Michael, *A. J. M. Smith and His Works,* ECW Press.

Darling, Michael, *An Annotated Bibliography,* Vehicule, 1981.

ECW's Biographical Guide to Canadian Poets, ECW Press, 1993, pp. 93-8.

Ferns, John, *Smith,* 1979.

Frye, Northrop, *The Bush Garden: Essays on the Canadian Imagination,* House of Anansi, 1971, pp. 129-43.

Heath, Jeffrey M., editor, *Profiles in Canadian Literature,* Vol. 1, Dundurn, 1980, pp. 73-80.

Klinck, Carl F., *Literary History of Canada,* University of Toronto Press, 1965.

Marshall, Tom, *Harsh and Lovely Land: The Major Canadian Poets and the Making of a Canadian Tradition,* University of British Columbia Press, 1979.

Pacey, Desmond, *Ten Canadian Poets,* 1958, pp. 194-222.

Stevens, Peter, editor, *The McGill Movement: Smith, F. R. Scott, and Leo Kennedy,* 1969.

Waddington, Miriam, editor, *Essays, Controversies and Poems,* 1972, pp. 55-62 and 70-76.

Woodcock, George, *Odysseus Ever Returning,* McClelland & Stewart, 1970.

PERIODICALS

American Review of Canadian Studies, spring, 1990, pp. 31-40.

Canadian Literature, (special A. J. M. Smith issue) winter, 1963; spring, 1975, pp. 83-91; summer, 1975, pp. 42-52.

Canadian Forum, September, 1974.

Canadian Poetry, spring-summer, 1979, pp. 17-28 and 59-64; fall-winter, 1982, pp. 1-48, 86-92.

Essays on Canadian Writing, winter, 1974, pp. 63-64; winter, 1977-78, pp. 55-62; fall-winter, 1979-80, pp. 78-125; winter, 1980-81, pp. 68-76; winter, 1983-84, pp. 81-85.

Modernist Studies, No. 2, 1977, pp. 3-17.

Modern Poetry Studies, spring, 1977, pp. 1-13.

New Statesman, January 26, 1968, pp. 111-12.

Poetry, December, 1944, pp. 157-60; July, 1969.

Queen's Quarterly, summer, 1963, pp. 282-83.

Studies in Canadian Literature, winter, 1978, pp. 17-34.

Times Literary Supplement, February 15, 1968, p. 155.

University of Toronto Quarterly, spring, 1978, pp. 200-13.

T

TEKAHIONWAKE
See JOHNSON, Pauline

*   *   *

THALER, M. N.
See KERNER, Fred

*   *   *

THERIAULT, Yves   1915-

PERSONAL: Born November 28, 1915, in Quebec City, Quebec, Canada; son of Alcide and Aurore (Nadeau) Theriault; married Michelle-Germaine Blanchet (a writer), April 21, 1942; children: Yves-Michel, Marie-Jose. *Education:* Educated in Montreal, Quebec. *Religion:* Roman Catholic.

CAREER: Novelist, playwright, and author of short stories. Worked as a trapper, cheese salesman, truck diver, nightclub host, and tractor salesman in early 1930's; radio announcer in Montreal, New Carlisle, Quebec City, Trois-Rivieres, and Hull, Quebec, 1935-39; director of a newspaper in Toronto, Ontario; publicity manager; National Film Board of Canada, Ottawa, Ontario, script writer and public relations staff member, 1943-45; script writer for Canadian Broadcasting Corp. (CBC-Radio), 1945-50; Department of Indian Affairs, Ottawa, cultural director, 1965-67.

MEMBER: International PEN, Canadian Authors Association (president), Royal Society of Canada (fellow), Societe des Ecrivains Canadiens (president, 1965), Societe des Auteurs Dramatiques, Societe des Gens de Letters, Syndicat National des Ecrivains de France.

AWARDS, HONOURS: First prize for best French radio play, 1952; Quebec Government prize, 1954, for *Aaron,* and first prize, 1958, for *Agaguk*; Canada Council senior arts fellowship and French language prize for fiction from French Academy, both 1961; Governor General's Literary Award from Canada Council, 1961, for *Ashini*; Prix France-Canada, 1961, for *Agaguk* and *Ashini*; Molson Prize from Canada Council, 1971; Prix Mgr Camille Roy for *Le Vendeur d'etoiles et autre contes.*

WRITINGS:

IN ENGLISH TRANSLATION

Agaguk (novel), Grasset, 1958, translation by Miriam Chapin published under same title, Ryerson, 1971.
Ashini (novel), Fides, 1960, translation by Gwendolyn Moore published under same title, Harvest House, 1972.
N'Tsik (novel), Editions de 1'Homme, 1968, translation by Moore published under same title, Harvest House, 1972.
Oeuvre de chair, Stanke, 1975, translation by Jean David published as *Ways of the Flesh,* Gage Publishing, 1977.
Agoak: L'Heritage d'Agaguk, Quinz, 1975, translation by John David Allen published as *Agoak: The Legacy of Agaguk,* McGraw, 1979.

OTHER WRITINGS

Contes pour un homme seul (short stories), Editions de l'Arbre, 1944.
Trois Rivieres: Ville de reflect, Editions de Bien Public, 1954.
Aaron (novel), Grasset, 1957.
Amour au gout de mer (novel), Beauchemin, 1961.
Cul-de-sac (novel), Institut Litteraire du Quebec, 1961.
Le Vendeur d'etoiles et autres contes (short stories), Fides, 1961.

Les Commettants de Caridad (novel), Institut Litteraire du Quebec, 1961.

Sejour a Moscou (nonfiction), Fides, 1961.

La Fille laide (novel), Editions de l'Homme, 1962.

Si la bombe m'etait contee (novel), Editions du Jour, 1962.

Le Grand Roman d'un petit homme (novel), Editions du Jour, 1963.

Le Ru d'Ikoue (prose poem), Fides, 1963, revised edition, 1977.

La Rose de Pierre: Histoires d'amour (short stories), Editions du Jour, 1964.

Les Vendeurs du temple (social satire), Editions de l'Homme, 1964.

Le Dompteur d'ours (social satire), Editions de l'Homme, 1965.

Les Temps du carcajou (novel), Institut Litteraire du Quebec, 1965.

Le Dernier Rayon (novel), Lidec, 1966.

L'Appelante (novel), Editions du Jour, 1967.

Contes erotiques (short stories), Ferron, 1968.

Kesten (novel), Editions du Jour, 1968.

La Mort d'eau (novel), Editions de l'Homme, 1968.

Le Marcheur: Piece en trois actes (three-act play; produced in Montreal, 1950), Lemeac, 1968.

L'Ile introuvable: Nouvelles, Editions du Jour, 1968.

Mahigan: Recit, Lemeac, 1968.

Antoine et sa montagne (novel), Editions du Jour, 1969.

L'Or de la felouque (novel), Jeunesse, 1969.

Tayaout, Fils d'Agaguk, Editions de l'Homme, 1969.

Textes et documents, Lemeac, 1969; *Valerie,* Editions de l'Homme, 1969.

Fredange: Piece en deux actes (two-act play; includes *Les Terres neuves*), Lemeac, 1970.

Le Dernier Havre, L'Actuelle, 1970.

La Passe-au-Crachin (novel), Ferron, 1972.

Le Haut Pays (novel), Ferron, 1973.

Moi, Pierre Huneau: Narration, Hurtubise, 1976.

FOR CHILDREN

Alerte au camp 29, Beauchemin, 1959.

La Revanche du Nascopie, Beauchemin, 1959.

La Loi de l'Apache, Beauchemin, 1960.

L'Homme de la Papinachois, Beauchemin, 1960.

Le Roi de la Cote Nord: La Vie extraordinaire de Napoleon-Alexandre Comeau, Editions de l'Homme, 1960.

La Montagne sacre, Beauchemin, 1962.

Le Rapt du lac cache, Beauchemin, 1962.

Nakika, le petit Algonquin, Lemeac, 1962.

Avea, le petit Tramway, Beauchemin, 1963.

Les Aventures de Ti-Jean, Beauchemin, 1963.

Les Extravagances de Ti-Jean, Beauchemin, 1963.

Maurice le moruceau, Beauchemin, 1963.

Nauya, le petit esquimau, Beauchemin, 1963.

Ti-Jean et le grand geant, Beauchemin, 1963.

Zibou et Coucou, Lemeac, 1964.

La Montagne Creuse, Lidec, 1965.

Le Secret de Muffarti, Lidec, 1965.

Le Chateau des petits hommes verts, Lidec, 1966.

Les Dauphins de Monsieur Yu, Lidec, 1966.

La Bete a 300 tetes, Lidec, 1967.

Les Pieuvres, Lidec, 1967.

Les Vampires de la rue Monsieur-le-Prince, Lidec, 1968.

Also author of plays *Le Samaritain,* 1952, and *Berengere ou la chair en feu,* 1965.

Contributor to periodicals, including *Culture, Maclean's, Saturday Night, Nouveau Journal, Le Jour,* and *Revue de l'Universite Laval.*

SIDELIGHTS: Yves Theriault is considered one of the leading French-Canadian writers of the twentieth century. The book that sealed his reputation was *Agaguk,* published in 1958. It gained him international recognition and has been translated into a number of languages, including German, Italian, Spanish, Japanese, and Portuguese. Theriault explores a number of themes in his writings. Primitivism, exoticism, violence, and eroticism frequent his works, as do characters struggling against basic human passions and instincts or searching for self-identity. Several of his books, including *Les Vendeurs du temple* and *Le Dompteur d'ours,* are social satires. Theriault frequently involves oppressed groups in his works, examining the plights of immigrants, Jews, Eskimos, and Indians.*

* * *

THOMAS, Audrey (Callahan) 1935-

PERSONAL: Born November 17, 1935, in Binghamton, NY; emigrated to Canada; daughter of Donald Earle (a teacher) and Frances (Corbett) Callahan; married Ian Thomas (a sculptor and art teacher), December 6, 1958 (divorced, 1978); children: Sarah, Victoria, Claire. *Education:* Smith College, B.A., 1957; University of British Columbia, M.A., 1963.

ADDRESSES: Home—R.R. #2, Galiano Island, British Columbia, Canada V0N 1P0.

CAREER: Writer. Visiting assistant professor of creative writing, Concordia University, 1978; visiting professor of creative writing, University of Victoria, 1978-79; writer in residence, Simon Fraser University, 1981-82, University of Ottawa, 1987, University of Victoria, University of British Columbia, and David Thompson University Centre; Scottish-Canadian Exchange Fellow in Edinburgh, 1985-86; visiting professor, Concordia University, 1989-90; author.

MEMBER: PEN, Writers Union of Canada, Federation of British Columbia Writers.

AWARDS, HONOURS: Atlantic magazine First award, 1965; Canada Council grant, 1969, 1971, 1972, and 1974; Canada Council senior grant, 1974, 1977, and 1979; CBC Literary Competition, second prize for fiction, 1980, second prize for memoirs, 1981; second prize for fiction, National Magazine Awards, 1980; second prize, *Chatelaine* Fiction Competition, 1981; British Columbia Book prize, 1985, 1990; Ethel Wilson Award, 1985 and 1991; Marian Engle Award, 1987; Canada-Australia Literary Prize, 1989-90.

WRITINGS:

NOVELS

Mrs. Blood, Bobbs-Merrill (Indianapolis), 1970.
Munchmeyer and Prospero on the Island, Bobbs-Merrill, 1972.
Songs My Mother Taught Me, Bobbs-Merrill, 1973.
Blown Figures, Talonbooks (Vancouver), 1974, Knopf, 1975.
Latakia, Talonbooks, 1979.
Intertidal Life, Beaufort Books, 1984.
Graven Images, Viking (Toronto), 1993.

SHORT STORY COLLECTIONS

Ten Green Bottles, Bobbs-Merrill, 1967.
Ladies & Escorts, Oberon (Ottawa), 1977.
Personal Fictions: Stories by Munro, Wiebe, Thomas, and Blaise, edited by Michael Ondaatje, Oxford University Press, 1977.
Two in the Bush and Other Stories, McClelland & Stewart (Toronto), 1979.
Real Mothers, Talonbooks, 1981.
Goodbye Harold, Good Luck, Viking/Penguin, 1986.
The Wild Blue Yonder, Penguin, 1990.

RADIO PLAYS

(With Linda Sorenson and Keith Pepper) *Once Your Submarine Cable Is Gone, What Have You Got?,* first broadcast on Canadian Broadcasting Corp. (CBC-Radio), October 27, 1973.
Mrs. Blood, first broadcast on CBC-Radio, August 16, 1975.
Untouchables, first broadcast on CBC-Radio, December 5, 1981.
The Milky Way, first broadcast on CBC-Radio, November 26, 1983.
The Axe of God, first broadcast as part of *Disasters! Act of God or Acts of Man?,* CBC-Radio, February 24, 1985.
The Woman in Black Velvet, first broadcast on CBC-Radio, May 17, 1985.

In the Groove, first broadcast on CBC-Radio, November 4, 1985.
On the Immediate Level of Events Occurring in Meadows, first broadcast as part of *Sextet,* CBC-Radio, January 26, 1986.

Also author of five other radio plays.

OTHER

Contributor to anthologies, and of short stories to periodicals, including *Atlantic, Maclean's, Saturday Night, Toronto Life, Capilano Review, Fiddlehead, Canadian Literature,* and *Interface.*

SIDELIGHTS: An American-born Canadian author of novels, short stories, and radio plays, Audrey Thomas has won a number of literary prizes, yet, as Urjo Kareda observes in *Saturday Night,* "somehow she has never achieved her rightful place in the hierarchy of Canada's best writers. Her writing tends to be racier, ruder, more raw than that of her contemporaries in the Ontario-centered, female-dominated literary establishment." Thomas's work, as a number of critics have noted, is auto-biographical in nature, and displays an interest in feminism and a love of experimentation, both with language and literary devices.

Employing these techniques in different ways to shed light on her common theme of personal isolation and loneliness, the author has said that her stories are about "the terrible gap between men and women," quotes Margaret Atwood in her *Second Words: Selected Critical Prose.* "Language," Thomas tells Liam Lacey in a *Globe and Mail* interview, "is where men and women get into trouble, I think, . . . they think they mean the same things by the same words when they really don't." The author also sometimes expands the theme of adult relationships to involve children, who are often the casualties of broken marriages. *Saturday Night* contributor Eleanor Wachtel maintains that as a writer who reveals these "politics of the family, . . . Audrey Thomas [is] one of [our] most astute commentators."

A divorced mother of three children, Thomas is well acquainted with the problems of family life about which she writes. Having resided in such places as Ghana, Copenhagen, and Paris, she also "likes to tell her stories of Americans or Canadians set down in an alien culture so that their problems will appear more starkly," writes *Open Letter* critic George Bowering. The author's first novel, *Mrs. Blood,* is about one such character who suffers a miscarriage while living in Africa. It is a stream-of-consciousness novel in which the protagonist, Isobel Cleary, while lying in the hospital, contemplates the problems of her marriage and her painful affair with another man. Critics like Joan Caldwell, a *Canadian Literature* reviewer, have been particularly impressed by the writing skills demonstrated in this first effort. "*Mrs. Blood* is accomplished writing," praised Caldwell; "it does not bear the marks of a first novel and it must surely not be Audrey Thomas's last."

Thomas has written two sequels to *Mrs. Blood*, *Songs My Mother Taught Me* and *Blown Figures*. The first of these takes Isobel back to her childhood, an unhappy time in her life during which she is caught between her parents—an "inadequate man and [a] compulsive angry woman," as *Saturday Night* contributor Anne Montagnes describes them. Longing for love, Isobel does not find happiness until she gets a job at an asylum, where, as Constance Rooke relates in the *Dictionary of Literary Biography*, "she learns something of compassion and something of the madness which has been concealed in her family. Finally, she chooses to be vulnerable." The subject of madness is also a part of *Blown Figures*, which takes up the story of Isobel with her return to Africa to find the body of her miscarried baby. "She is now clearly schizophrenic and addresses many of her remarks to a Miss Miller—an imaginary confidante," remarks Rooke. "Blatantly experimental, *Blown Figures* has numerous nearly blank pages which serve to isolate the fragments (cartoons, one-liners, and so forth) which appear here. The novel depends heavily on Africa as a metaphor for the unconscious." "In hands less skillful than Miss Thomas's," praises Atwood in a *New York Times Book Review* article, "such devices could spell tedious experimentation for its own sake, self-indulgence, or chaos. But she is enormously skillful, and instead of being a defeating pile of confusions 'Blown Figures' is amazingly easy to read."

Three other novels that Thomas has written, *Munchmeyer and Prospero on the Island*, *Latakia*, and *Intertidal Life*, concern male-female relationships and also share in common protagonists who are women writers. These characters, reports Wayne Grady in *Books in Canada*, are "trying to come to terms in their books with the fact that they have been rejected by men who have loved them." Of these books, critics have generally found *Intertidal Life*, the story of a woman named Alice whose husband leaves her after fourteen years of marriage, to be the most significant effort. Grady calls *Intertidal Life* "undoubtedly Thomas's best novel to date." And although Kareda feels that this novel "doesn't rank with Audrey Thomas's finest writing," he asserts that " . . . its desire to reach us, to tell so much, to keep questioning, are the strengths of an exceptional, expressive will."

Thomas, according to Alberto Manguel's *Village Voice* review, also seems to resolve an issue that was raised in her earlier work. *Intertidal Life*, he says, "appears as the culmination of the search for a character that was never quite defined before. Perhaps in the much-neglected *Blown Figures* or in *Songs My Mother Taught Me*, there are sketchier versions of Alice circling the primary question: Who am

I? In *Intertidal Life* the question is answered." Rooke explains further that, in being separated from her husband, Alice is able to assert her independence while overcoming her feelings of isolation by becoming "inextricably involved with others and most particularly with [her] female friends and children."

In *Graven Images* Thomas writes of Charlotte Corbett, a character much like herself: an American-born writer, divorced and living in British Columbia. Charlotte is on a search for her ancestors, traveling to England to trace her heritage and discover who founded the clan in the 11th century. Accompanied by her friend Lydia, a woman who was taken to Canada as a child to avoid the Nazi bombing of World War II and is herself on a quest to locate her own family, the two women arrive in England just as a hurricane hits the island. Writing in *Books in Canada*, Elisabeth Harvor explains that "Thomas is not often a very introspective writer. She instead reserves her love for the surface of life and for the thousands of details that make up the surface. . . . This preference for the surface has a tendency to make *Graven Images* seem somewhat trivial." In contrast, Nancy Wigston in *Quill & Quire* finds that "Charlotte's voice is one of absolute candour; her insights into the multiple phases of women's lives pile up like the gifts she is constantly buying for friends and family. Cluttered and subtle like Charlotte herself, this book is like one of those gifts: special and resonant with meaning."

The themes that Thomas explores in her novels are echoed in her short story writing, which, along with the work she has done for radio, has amounted to a large ouevre since the 1970s. But, laments Atwood in her book, despite this concerted effort and "its ambition, range and quality, she has not yet received the kind of recognition such a body of work merits, perhaps because she is that cultural hybrid, an early-transplanted American. Of course her work has flaws; everyone's does. She can be sentimental, repetitious, and sometimes merely gossipy. But page for page, she is one of [Canada's] best writers." Writing in the *Reference Guide to Short Fiction*, Lorraine M. York claims that "What sets Thomas apart from almost any other writer in Canada is her rich melange of self-conscious fabulation, feminism, and autobiography."

BIOGRAPHICAL/CRITICAL SOURCES:

BOOKS

Atwood, Margaret, *Second Words: Selected Critical Prose*, House of Anansi, 1982.
Authors in the News, Volume 2, Gale, 1976.
Contemporary Literary Criticism, Gale, Volume 7, 1977; Volume 13, 1980; Volume 37, 1986.
Dictionary of Literary Biography, Volume 60: *Canadian Writers since 1960, Second Series*, Gale, 1987.

Reference Guide to Short Fiction, St. James Press (Detroit), 1994.

PERIODICALS

Books in Canada, December, 1979; February, 1982; May, 1985; March, 1993, p. 46.

Canadian Forum, May-June, 1974; June-July, 1980; July-August, 1993, pp. 39-40.

Canadian Literature, autumn, 1971; summer, 1975; winter, 1992, pp. 139-40.

Essays on Canadian Writing, fall, 1992, pp. 43-50.

Fiddlehead, January, 1983.

Globe and Mail (Toronto), April 16, 1977; April 18, 1987; September 22, 1990; November 3, 1990.

Los Angeles Times Book Review, February 10, 1985.

Mosaic, fall, 1993, pp. 69-86.

New York Times Book Review, February 1, 1976.

Open Letter, summer, 1976.

Paragraph Magazine, fall, 1993, p. 39.

Quill & Quire, March, 1993, p. 46.

Room of One's Own, Volume 10, numbers 3-4, 1986.

Saturday Night, July, 1972; May, 1974; April, 1982; January, 1985.

Village Voice, August 6, 1985.

Wascana Review, fall, 1976.

*   *   *

TREMBLAY, Michel   1942-

PERSONAL: Born June 25, 1942, in Montreal, Quebec, Canada; son of Armand (a linotype operator) and Rheauna Tremblay. *Education:* Attended Institut des Arts Graphiques.

ADDRESSES: Agent—Agence Goodwin, 839 Sherbrooke E., Suite 2, Montreal, Quebec H2L 1K6, Canada.

CAREER: Writer. Radio-Canada television, linotype operator, costume department, 1963-66.

MEMBER: Union of Quebec Writers, CEAD, Playwrights Union.

AWARDS, HONOURS: First prize in Radio Canada's Young Author's Competition, 1964, for unpublished play *Le Train;* Meritas Trophy, 1970, 1972; Canada Council Award, 1971; Floyd S. Chalmers Canadian Play awards, Ontario Arts Council, 1972-75, 1978, 1986, and 1989, for *Le Vrai Monde?;* Prix Victor-Morin, Societe Saint-Jean-Baptiste de Montreal, 1974; Canadian Film Festival Award for best scenario, 1975, for *Francoise Durocher, Waitress;* Ontario Lieutenant-Governor's Medal, 1976 and 1977; Prix France-Quebec, Quebec Ministere des Relations Internationales, 1981, for novel *Therese et Pierrette a l'ecole des Saints-Anges,* and 1985, for novel *La Duchesse*

et le Roturier; Premiere Selection, Prix Medicis, 1983; L'Ordre des arts et des lettres (France), Chevalier, 1984, Officier, 1991; *Albertine, en cinq temps* was named best play at Le Festival du theatre des Ameriques, 1985; Montreal's Prix de la Critique, 1986, for *Albertine, en cinq temps;* Athanase-David, 1988; Prix du public au Festival de Bruxelles, 1990, for *Le Coeur decouvert: Roman d'amours;* Grand Prix du Public, 1990; Doctorat Honoris Causa from Concordia University, 1990, McGill University, 1991, Stirling University, Scotland, 1992, and Windsor University, Ontario, 1993; Prix Jacques-Cartier Lyon, 1991; Banff National Center Award, 1993; received six grants from the Canadian Arts Council.

WRITINGS:

PLAYS

Le Train (originally broadcast by Radio Canada, 1964; first produced in Montreal, 1965), Lemeac, 1990.

Cinq (one-act plays; includes *Berthe, Johnny Mangano and His Astonishing Dogs,* and *Gloria Star*), first produced in Montreal, 1966, revised version published as *En pieces detachees* (first produced in Montreal, 1969), Lemeac, 1972, translation by Allan Van Meer published as *Like Death Warmed Over,* (produced in Winnipeg, 1973), Playwrights Co-op (Toronto), 1973, translation published as *Montreal Smoked Meat* (produced in Toronto, 1974), Talon Books, 1975, translation also produced as *Broken Pieces,* Vancouver, 1974.

Les Belles-Soeurs (title means "The Sisters-In-Law"; two-act; first produced in Montreal, 1968), Holt (Montreal), 1968, translation by John Van Burek and Bill Glassco, Talon Books, 1974, published as *The Guid Sisters* (first produced in Toronto and Glasgow, 1987), Exile (Toronto), 1988.

La Duchesse de Langeais (two-act), first produced in Montreal, 1970.

En pieces detachees [and] *La Duchesse de Langeais,* Lemeac, 1970.

Les Paons (one-act fantasy; first produced in Ottawa, 1971), CEAD, 1969.

Trois Petit Tours (television adaptations of *Berthe, Johnny Mangano and His Astonishing Dogs,* and *Gloria Star;* broadcast in 1969), Lemeac, 1971.

A toi, pour toujours, ta Marie-Lou (one-act; first produced in Montreal, 1971), introduction by Michel Belair, Lemeac, 1971, translation by Van Burek and Glassco published as *Forever Yours, Marie-Lou,* Talon Books, 1975.

Demain matin, Montreal m'attend (title means "Tomorrow Morning, Montreal Wait for Me"; first produced in Montreal, 1972), Lemeac, 1972.

Hosanna (two-act; first produced in Montreal, 1973, produced on Broadway, 1981), translation by Van Burek and Glassco, Talon Books, 1974.

Hosanna [and] *La Duchesse de Langeais,* Lemeac, 1973.

Bonjour, la, bonjour (title means "Hello, There, Hello"; first produced in Ottawa, 1974), Lemeac, 1974, translation by Van Burek and Glassco published as *Bonjour, la, bonjour* (produced in 1975), Talon Books, 1975.

Les Heros de mon enfance (musical comedy; title means "My Childhood Heroes"; first produced in Eastman, Quebec, 1975), Lemeac, 1976.

Surprise! Surprise! (one-act), first produced in Montreal, 1975.

Sainte-Carmen de la Main (two-act; first produced in Montreal, 1976), Lemeac, 1976, translation by Van Burek published at *Sainte-Carmen of the Main* (broadcast on BBC-Radio, 1987), Talon Books, 1981.

La Duchesse de Langeais and Other Plays (includes *La Duchesse de Langeais, Trois Petit Tours,* and *Surprise! Surprise!*), translations by Van Burek, Talon Books, 1976.

Damnee Manon, sacree Sandra (one-act; first produced in Montreal, 1977; produced as *Sandra/Manon* in Edinburgh and London, 1984), translation by Van Burek published as *Damnee Manon, sacree Sandra* (produced in United States, 1981), Talon Books, 1981.

Damnee Manon, sacree Sandra [and] *Surprise! Surprise!,* Lemeac, 1977.

L'Impromptu d'Outremont (two-act; first produced in Montreal, 1980), Lemeac, 1980, translation by Van Burek published as *The Impromptu of Outremont* (produced, 1981), Talon Books, 1981.

Les Anciennes Odeurs (first produced in Montreal, 1981), Lemeac, 1981, translation by John Stowe published as *Remember Me,* Talon Books, 1984.

Les Grandes Vacances, first produced in Montreal, 1981.

Albertine, en cinq temps (first produced in Ottawa, 1984), Lemeac, 1984, translation by Van Burek and Glassco published as *Albertine in Five Times* (produced in Toronto, Edinburgh, and London, 1986), Talon Books, 1987.

Le Vrai Monde? (first produced concurrently in Ottawa and Montreal, 1987), Lemeac, 1987, translation published as *The Real World?* (produced in London, 1990), Talon Books, 1988.

La Maison suspendue (first produced in Montreal and Toronto, 1990), Lemeac, 1990, translation by Van Burek, Talonbooks, 1991.

Marcel poursuivi par les chiens (first produced in Montreal, 1992), Lemeac, 1992, translation by Van Burek and Glassco.

Theatre I (includes ten plays), Actes Sud, 1991.

RADIO PLAYS

Six heures au plus tard, Lemeac, 1986.

FICTION

Contes pour buveurs attardes (stories), Editions du Jour, 1966, translation by Michael Bullock published as *Stories for Late Night Drinkers,* Intermedia Press, 1977.

La Cite dans l'oeuf (fantasy novel; title means "The City Inside the Egg"), Editions du Jour, 1969.

C't'a ton tour, Laura Cadieux (title means "It's Your Turn, Laura Cadieux"), Editions du Jour, 1973.

La Grosse Femme d'a cote est enceinte (first novel in "Chroniques du plateau Mont-Royal" tetralogy), Lemeac, 1978, translation by Sheila Fischman published as *The Fat Woman Next Door Is Pregnant,* Talon Books, 1981.

Therese et Pierrette a l'ecole des Saints-Anges (second in tetralogy), Lemeac, 1980, translation by Fischman published as *Therese and Pierrette and the Little Hanging Angel,* McClelland & Stewart, 1984.

La Duchesse et le roturier (third in tetralogy), Lemeac, 1982.

Des Nouvelles d'Edouard (fourth in tetralogy), Lemeac, 1984.

Le Coeur decouvert: Roman d'amours, Lemeac, 1986, translation by Fischman published as *The Heart Laid Bare,* McClelland & Stewart, 1989, published as *Making Room,* Serpent's Tail, 1990.

Le Premier Quartier de la lune, Lemeac, 1989.

Les Vues animees (title means "The Movies"), Lemeac, 1990.

Douze Coups de Theatre, Lemeac, 1992.

Le Coeur Eclate, Lemeac, 1993.

FILMS

(Author of screenplay and dialogue, with Andre Brassard) *Francoise Durocher, Waitress,* National Film Board of Canada, 1972.

(Author of screenplay and dialogue, with Brassard) *Il etait une fois dans l'est* (title means "Once Upon a Time in the East"), Cine Art, 1974.

(Author of scenario and dialogue) *Parlez-nous d'amour* (title means "Speak to Us of Love"), Films 16, 1976.

(Author of scenario and dialogue) *Le Soleil se leve en retard,* Films 16, 1977.

Also author of *Le Coeur decouvert,* 1986, *Le Grand Jour,* 1988, and *Le Vrai Monde?,* 1991.

DRAMATIC ADAPTATIONS

Messe noir (adapted from selected stories in *Contes pour buveurs attardes*), first produced in Montreal, 1965.

(With Andre Brassard) *Lysistrata* (translated and adapted from Aristophanes's play of the same title; first produced in Ottawa, 1969), Lemeac, 1969.

L'Effet des rayons gamma sur les vieux-garcons (translated and adapted from Paul Zindel's *The Effect of Gamma Rays on Man-in-the-Moon Marigolds;* first produced in Montreal, 1970), Lemeac, 1970.

". . . *Et Mademoiselle Roberge boit un peu* . . . " (three-act; translated and adapted from Zindel's *And Miss Reardon Drinks a Little;* first produced in Montreal, 1972), Lemeac, 1971.

Le Pays du Dragon (translated and adapted from four of Tennessee Williams's one-act plays), first produced in Montreal, 1971.

Mistero buffo (translated and adapted from Dario Fo's play of the same name), first produced in Montreal, 1973.

Mademoiselle Marguerite (translated and adapted from Roberto Athayde's *Aparaceu a Margarida;* first produced in Ottawa, 1976), Lemeac, 1975.

(With Kim Yaroshevskaya) *Oncle Vania* (translated and adapted from Anton Chekhov's play of the same name), Lemeac, 1983.

Le Gars de Quebec (adapted from Nikolay Gogol's *Le Revizov;* first produced in Montreal, 1985), Lemeac, 1985.

Six heures au plus tard (adapted from a work by Marc Perrier; first produced in Montreal, 1986), Lemeac, 1986.

Que a peur de Virginia Woolf (translated and adapted from Edward Albee's *Who's Afraid of Virginia Woolf*), first produced in Montreal, 1988.

Les Trompettes de la Mort (adapted from a work by Tilly), first produced in Montreal, 1991.

Premiere de classe (adapted from a work by Casey Kurtti), first produced in Montreal, 1992.

OTHER

(With Claude Paulette and Luc Noppen) *Quebec, trois siecles d'architecture,* Libre Expression, 1979.

Nelligan (opera libretto; produced in Montreal, 1990), Lemeac, 1990.

Also author of *Bonheur d'occasion,* an adaptation of a novel by Gabrielle Roy, 1977. Contributor to anthologies, including *Heroines,* edited by Joyce Doolittle, Players Press, 1992. Also contributor to periodicals, including *La Barre de Jour.* A collection of Tremblay's manuscripts is held at the Bibliotheque National du Canada, Ottawa.

ADAPTATIONS: Sainte-Carmen of the Main was adapted as a two-act opera with music by Sydney Hodkinson, libretto by Lee Devin, and published by Associated Music Publishers, 1986.

SIDELIGHTS: Michel Tremblay is "the most important Quebecois artist of his generation," declared Salem Alaton in a 1986 Toronto *Globe and Mail* review. Beginning his career in the mid-1960s, the French-Canadian playwright, fiction writer, and screenwriter has become best known for dramatic works that challenge traditional myths of French-Canadian life. Indeed, for years critics contended that Tremblay's concentration on the social and cultural problems of Quebec earned him local acclaim at the expense of more universal recognition. In the 1980s, however, Tremblay began to command an international audience. Alaton theorized that it is the "edgy, Quebecois specificity" of Tremblay's work, once considered a liability, that is responsible for the playwright's success. With his work widely translated and produced, Tremblay is now regarded as a world-class dramatist who, in the words of *Quill and Quire* reviewer Mark Czarnecki, provides a persuasive example "of the much-debated cultural proposition that the more local the reference, the more universal the truth."

Tremblay grew up in the east end of Montreal, in the working-class neighborhood of the rue Fabre. The oppressive conditions of life in this impoverished area, along with the glitzy nightlife of the Main district, later provided the backdrop for much of Tremblay's work. Despite the inauspicious environment of his youth, Tremblay began writing when quite young and was a promising student who at thirteen received a scholarship to a classical college. Unable to endure the elitist attitudes fostered at the school, however, Tremblay left after several months to study graphic arts and become a linotype operator. He nevertheless continued to write during those years and by the time he was eighteen had completed his first play, *Le Train.* Several years later, in 1964, it won first prize in Radio Canada's Young Author Competition.

Shortly thereafter, Tremblay made Quebec theater history. Eschewing the classical French typically used in works for the stage, Tremblay wrote a play, *Les Belles-Soeurs,* in *joual,* the language of the people. Though Tremblay had not intended to create a political work, his use of *joual*—regarded by many as a debased form of the French language—signaled to his detractors and supporters alike the desire to supplant the province's traditional French culture with an independent Quebec culture. His critics decried the play while his admirers lauded it as a contribution to what is known in Quebec as the "theatre of liberation."

Written in 1965 but denied production until 1968, *Les Belles-Soeurs* catapulted the young dramatist to fame. The play was not radical, however, for its language alone. *Les Belles-Soeurs* was also controversial for its naturalistic view of French-Canadian life. Its plot is straightforward: after winning one million trading stamps, Gabriel Lauzon, an average east-end Montreal housewife, invites her women friends to a stamp-pasting gathering; by play's end, the women have turned on one another in a battle for the stamps. *Les Belles-Soeurs,* averred John Ripley in a critique for *Canadian Literature,* "explodes two centuries of popular belief, ecclesiastical teaching, and literary myth about Quebecois women. Far from being the traditional guardians of religious and moral values, happy progenitors of large families, and good-humored housekeepers, they stand revealed as malevolent misfits, consumed with hatred of life and of themselves."

Les Belles-Soeurs is the first in what became an eleven-play cycle which, in its entirety, many critics regarded as Tremblay's finest achievement. Ripley suggested that Quebec's "recent past, characterized by a desperate struggle to replace authoritarianism, negative identity, and destructiveness with self-respect, love, and transcendence, is nowhere better encapsulated than in the *Les Belles-Soeurs* cycle." Ripley's sentiments were echoed by critic Renate Usmiani, who in his *Studies in Canadian Literature: Michel Tremblay* stated: "The most general underlying theme of all [Tremblay's] works is the universal desire of the human being to transcend his finite condition." More specifically, Usmiani proposed that the typical Tremblay character is either trying to escape from family life as represented by the rue Fabre, from the false world of the Main, or from the limitations of self into a transcendent ecstasy.

One picture of life along the rue Fabre is offered by *A toi, pour toujours, ta Marie-Lou.* Deemed "a devastating psycho-social analysis of the traditional working-class Quebecois family" by Ripley, the play presents four characters juxtaposed in two different time periods. Marie-Louise is a housewife whose problems manifest themselves as sexual frigidity and religious fanaticism; Leopold, her husband, is a factory worker who becomes an alcoholic. Their marriage, according to Ripley, "is a sado-masochistic battle with no prospect of victory for either side," and thus Leopold ends their lives in a suicidal car crash. The drama progresses as, ten years later, their daughters discuss the tragedy and its impact on their lives. Manon, still living in the family home, has remained loyal to her mother and taken refuge in a similar fanaticism, seemingly unable to save herself. For Carmen, who has managed to make a life for herself as a singer in the Main district, there appears to be some hope. Both characters return in subsequent plays.

Although Leopold and Marie-Louise die to escape the rue Fabre, Tremblay's pen finds others searching for alternatives in the world of the Main. For them, "the Main stands for glamour, freedom, life itself," asserted Usmiani. Typified by prostitutes and transvestites, however, the Main, in Usmiani's opinion, "turns out to be ultimately as inbred, frustrating and limiting, in its own kinky way, as the petty household world around rue Fabre." *La Duchesse de*

Langeais and *Hosanna,* whose title characters seek escape from reality in homosexuality, provide two examples. The former is a dramatic monologue delivered by the Duchess, an aging transvestite prostitute who has been rejected by a younger lover. Ripley theorized that the Duchess has chosen to "escape from male impotence" by "the adoption of a role precisely the opposite of the one normally expected." Cast aside by his young partner, however, the Duchess fails to find satisfaction and remains an essentially pathetic character. More optimistically, *Hosanna* finds lovers Hosanna (Claude), who is forever role-playing, and Cuirette (Raymond) beginning to communicate after a particularly humiliating crisis. They are eventually able to discard their female personas and accept themselves as male homosexuals, freely admitting their love for one another. In so doing, according to Ripley, the two realize that although they are different, they still have a place in the world.

In *Damnee Manon, sacree Sandra,* the final play of the cycle, Tremblay moves away from the nightmare of family life and illusions of the Main to explore the possibility of fulfillment through mysticism. The drama unfolds through the monologues of two characters. Manon, from the earlier *A toi, pour toujours, ta Marie-Lou,* represents an attempt at transcendence through religious mysticism. Sandra, who also appeared previously in Tremblay's work, is a transvestite who seeks transcendence through sex. Both now live on the rue Fabre, as they did in childhood, and during the course of the play each comes to appreciate that the other has chosen a different path toward the same goal. Usmiani described the two characters as "physical incarnations, exteriorizations, of the two paths toward ecstasy conceived by the author," adding that on one level their world "is not a physical reality on the rue Fabre, but the psychological reality of the poet's own mind." The critic concluded that in Tremblay's work "there is no transcendence beyond that which the self can provide."

By the time Tremblay finished the *Belles-Soeurs* cycle in 1977, the political climate in Quebec had improved, and he gave permission, previously withheld, for his plays to be produced in English in Quebec. At this juncture he also switched genres, beginning work on a series of semi-autobiographical novels. The playwright's venture into fiction has been successful, and thus far, at least two of the volumes in his "Chroniques du plateau Mont-Royal" tetralogy have been translated into English. The first volume in the series, *La Grosse Femme d'a cote est enceinte,* was translated as *The Fat Woman Next Door is Pregnant.* Not only are the characters of this novel residents of the rue Fabre, as in so many of Tremblay's dramas, but the fat woman of the title is Tremblay's mother, and the story is based on the author's recollections of life in the apartment of his birth. *Quill and Quire* reviewer Czarnecki contended that *The Fat Woman*'s one-day time frame achieves "a similar effect" to that of James Joyce's famed *Ulysses.* Reviewing for the same publication, Philip Stratford called *The Fat Woman* "a generous, good-natured fresco teeming with life and invention." Regarded as both funny and sentimental, the book became a best-seller in Quebec.

Its sequel, *Therese et Pierrette a l'ecole des Saints-Anges,* translated as *Therese and Pierrette and the Little Hanging Angel,* also fared well, winning the prestigious Prix France-Quebec in 1981. Set during a four-day time period, the volume concentrates on three eleven-year-old students at the Ecole des Saints-Anges, a Roman Catholic girls' school. In this novel censuring the religious education system, Tremblay exhibits "epic gifts," in Czarnecki's opinion, that "extend to capturing life in its smallest details, creating an imaginative world complete in itself, ready to immerse and rebaptize the reader."

Tremblay concluded his tetralogy with *La Duchesse et le Roturier* in 1982 and *Des Nouvelles d'Edouard* in 1984. During the 1980s, however, Tremblay also returned to writing plays. Although some critics regard his dramas of the eighties as unequal to his earlier work, many of them appraise the 1987 *Le Vrai Monde?* as his best.

In this play Tremblay looks back to 1965, to his own beginning as an artist, and questions what right he had to use the lives of family and friends in service to his art. Calling it both "an expression of guilt" and "an eloquent statement about the relationship between art and life," *Globe and Mail* critic Matthew Fraser found *Le Vrai Monde?* "a masterful piece of drama." Another reviewer for the *Globe and Mail,* Ray Conlogue, contended that it is "a formidable play" in which Tremblay tries "to defend his art." In his interview for the Toronto paper with Alaton, Tremblay offered a slightly different perspective, telling the critic: "It is almost a condemnation of what an artist does to real life." And when Alaton asked him why he wrote, the dramatist responded: "Maybe I am an artist because artists give purpose to a thing which has not purpose, which is life. . . . You put [a play] before 500 people every night and you say, 'Sometimes, this is what life might mean.' And people who live the same nonsense life as you understand this."

BIOGRAPHICAL/CRITICAL SOURCES:

BOOKS

Anthony, Geraldine, *Stage Voices: Twelve Canadian Playwrights Talk about Their Lives and Work,* Doubleday, 1978, pp. 275-91.

Belair, Michel, *Michel Tremblay,* Press de L'Universite du Quebec, 1972.

Contemporary Literary Criticism, Volume 29, Gale, 1984.

Contemporary World Writers, 2nd edition, St. James Press, 1993.

Coyle, William, editor, *Aspects of Fantasy,* Greenwood, 1986.

Dictionary of Literary Biography, Volume 60: *Canadian Writers since 1960, Second Series,* Gale, 1987.

Gay and Lesbian Literature, St. James Press, 1994.

Godin, Jean-Cleo, and laurent Mailhot, *Le Theatre quebecois,* HMH, 1970, pp. 191-202.

International Dictionary of Theatre, Volume 2: *Playwrights,* St. James Press, 1994.

Usmiani, Renate, *Michel Tremblay: A Critical Study,* Douglas & McIntyre, 1981.

Usmiani, *Studies in Canadian Literature: Michel Tremblay,* Douglas & McIntyre, 1982.

PERIODICALS

Books in Canada, January/February, 1986; March, 1995, p. 38.

Canadian Drama, Number 2, 1976, pp. 206-18.

Canadian Literature, summer, 1980.

Canadian Theatre Review, fall, 1979, pp. 12-37.

Chicago Tribune, March 8, 1980.

Essays on Canadian Writing, Number 11, 1978.

Globe and Mail (Toronto), November 16, 1986; April 25, 1987; October 3, 1987.

Maclean's, April 30, 1984; April 22, 1985; December 30, 1991, pp. 36-37.

New York Times, December 11, 1983.

Perspectives, February 17, 1973, pp. 6-9.

Quebec Studies, Number 4, 1986.

Quill and Quire, February, 1982; April, 1982; June, 1984.

Studies in Canadian Literature, Volume 14, number 2, 1989.

Washington Post, June 22, 1978.

U-V

URQUHART, Jane 1949-

PERSONAL: Born June 21, 1949, in Geraldton, Ontario, Canada; daughter of W. A. (a professional engineer) and Marianne (a nurse; maiden name, Quinn) Carter; married Paul Brian Keele (an artist), January 1, 1969 (deceased); married Tony Urquhart (a professor and visual artist), May 5, 1976; children: (second marriage) Emily Jane. *Education:* University of Guelph, B.A. (English), 1971, B.A. (art history), 1975.

ADDRESSES: Home—24 Water St., Wellesley, Ontario, Canada N0B 2T0.

CAREER: Canada Manpower Center, Trenton, Ontario, student placement officer, 1971-72; Royal Canadian Navy, Halifax, Nova Scotia, civilian information officer, 1972-73; University of Waterloo, Waterloo, Ontario, tutor/coordinator of art history correspondence program, 1973—. Writer-in-residence, University of Ottawa, 1990.

MEMBER: PEN International, League of Canadian Poets, Writers' Union of Canada.

AWARDS, HONOURS: Grants from Ontario Arts Council, 1980-86, and Canada Council, 1983, 1985, 1990.

WRITINGS:

POETRY

False Shuffles, Press Porcepic, 1982.
I Am Walking in the Garden of His Imaginary Palace, Aya Press, 1982.
The Little Flowers of Madame de Montespan, Porcupine's Quill, 1983.

FICTION

The Whirlpool (novel), David Godine, 1986.
Storm Glass (short stories), Porcupine's Quill, 1987.
Changing Heaven (novel), McClelland and Stewart, 1990.

Away (novel), Viking, 1994.

OTHER

Work represented in anthologies, including *Four Square Garden: A Poetry Anthology,* edited by Burnett, MacKinnon, and Thomas, Pas de Loup Press, 1982; *Illusions,* Aya Press, 1983; *Meta Fictions,* Quadrant Editions, 1983; *Views from the North,* Porcupine's Quill, 1983; *Best Canadian Stories,* Oberon Press, 1986; *Magic Realism and Canadian Literature,* University of Waterloo Press, 1986; and *The Oxford Book of Stories by Canadian Women,* Volume 2, 1988. Also contributor to magazines, including *Canadian Fiction Magazine, Descant, Poetry Canada Review,* and *Antigonish Review.*

SIDELIGHTS: Jane Urquhart is known for her fascination with the Victorian Era and her talented use of language. She has become one of the most popular of Canada's current generation of novelists, with a reputation that transcends her native country.

Urquhart was born on June 21, 1949, in Geraldton, Ontario, Canada, to W. A. and Marianne Carter. Her family lived in a small mining settlement called Little Long Lac until she was five or six years old and then moved to Toronto. As a child she loved to read, and her favorite book was Emily Bronte's *Wuthering Heights.* Despite her interest in literature, she dreamed of becoming a child actress, but she never made it to Broadway as she had hoped. In 1967 she left for Vancouver to attend junior college and then returned to Ontario to attend the University of Guelph, where she received her B.A. in English in 1971. While at the university she met and married visual artist Paul Keele, who later died in a car accident. Urquhart returned to the University of Guelph, this time studying art history and she recieved another B.A. in 1975. She met another visual artist, Tony Urquhart, who she married on May 5, 1976. Together they had a daughter Emily. While caring for Tony's four other children in addition to Emily, Urquhart began to write. She first wrote poetry, publishing several volumes, and then turned her attention to narratives, publishing a collection of short stories and several novels.

Many of Urquhart's stories come from her own family history. The undertaker's widow in *The Whirlpool* (1986) is based on her husband Tony's grandmother, and her novel *Away* (1993) is based on her family's history as Irish Canadians. Her love of *Wuthering Heights* also enters her fiction, especially in *Changing Heaven* (1990), in which the ghost of Emily Bronte appears and discusses her work with the ghost of another character, Arianna Ether. An important element in much of Urquhart's work is its setting in the nineteenth century. *Whirlpool, Changing Heaven,* and *Away,* are all set in the nineteenth century, a favorite era of Urquhart's which allows her to expound upon history and her fascination with the elements. Urquhart's fiction is also filled with mysticism and the supernatural; ghosts are common characters. In *Away* Urquhart explored Celtic myths and the Irish concept of "away," which means being taken by a spirit and returned forever changed. Landscape is an important element as well— Urquhart evokes a strong sense of place through details about the setting of a novel.

Urquhart's novels have received mixed reviews from critics. Most critics praise the language and conception of her fiction, though some complain that she does not follow through with a strong structure. Her short stories, especially, have been criticized for lacking plot. Although many critics praise her poetic language and mystical storylines, some think she pushes the limits too far. Reviewers specifically point out her introduction of the nineteenth-century English poet Robert Browning as a character in *The Whirlpool.* One critic opposed her dramatization of Browning's death as a maudlin romantic addition designed to give the novel the weight of literature. Other critics point to the scene between the ghosts of Emily Bronte and Arianna Ether as problematic and say that Urquhart's attempt to demystify Bronte was a failure.

BIOGRAPHICAL/CRITICAL SOURCES:

PERIODICALS

American Book Review, May/June, 1988, pp. 10, 21.
Belles Lettres, fall, 1993, pp. 23, 43.
The Bloomsbury Review, May/June, 1990, p. 21.
Booklist, March 15, 1993, p. 1296.
Books in Canada, January/February, 1987, p. 26; June/July, 1987, p. 14; October, 1993, p. 44.
Canadian Forum, August/September, 1987, pp. 41-3.
Canadian Literature, spring, 1992, pp. 209-10.
Chicago Tribune, March 21, 1990.
Detroit Free Press, August 17, 1994, p. 3D.

Globe and Mail (Toronto), December 6, 1986; March 17, 1990.
Maclean's, September 21, 1987, p. 54.
New York Times Book Review, March 18, 1990; June 26, 1994, p. 28.
Poetry, August, 1984, p. 305.
Quill and Quire, October, 1982, p. 33; March, 1983, p. 66; May, 1984, p. 35; November, 1986, p. 25.
Saturday Night, March, 1990, p. 55.
Village Voice, October 18, 1988, pp. 52-53, 101.
Village Voice Literary Supplement, June, 1993, pp. 14-6.
World Literature Today, summer, 1991, p. 487; winter, 1995, pp. 143-44.

*   *   *

VALDOMBRE
See GRIGNON, Claude-Henri

*   *   *

VALGARDSON, W(illiam) D(empsey) 1939-

PERSONAL: Born May 7, 1939, in Winnipeg, Manitoba, Canada; son of Dempsey Alfred Herbert (a fisherman) and Rachel Iris (Smith) Valgardson; married Mary Anne Tooth, May 28, 1960 (divorced); children: Nancy-Rae, Val Dempsey. *Education:* University of Manitoba, B.A., 1961, B.Ed., 1966; University of Iowa, M.F.A., 1969. *Religion:* Lutheran. *Avocational interests:* Rock climbing, hiking, folk dancing.

ADDRESSES: Home—1908 Waterloo Rd., Victoria, British Columbia, Canada V8P 1J3.*Office*—Box 1700, Department of Creative Writing, University of Victoria, Victoria, British Columbia, Canada V8W 2Y2.

CAREER: English teacher in Riverton, Manitoba, 1961-62; art teacher in Transcona, Manitoba, 1963-64; English teacher in Snow Lake, Manitoba, 1964-65, Pinawa, Manitoba, 1965-67, and Tuxedo, Manitoba, 1969-70; Cottey College, Nevada, MO, instructor, 1970-72, assistant professor of English, 1972-74, chair of department, 1971-74; University of Victoria, British Columbia, professor, 1974—, chair of creative writing department, 1982-87.

MEMBER: Saanich International Folkdancers, Writers' Union of Canada, Canadian Authors Association (president, 1985-86), American Writers' Program.

AWARDS, HONOURS: First prize, Rochester Festival of Fine Arts, 1968, for poem "Paul Isfeld: Fisherman"; international scholarship to Writer's Workshop, University of Iowa, 1968; Canada Council grant, summer, 1968; honorable mention, Hallmark poetry competition, 1969, for poem "Realization in a Spinning Wheel"; first prize, *Winnipeg Free Press* Nonfiction Contest, 1969, for article "The Hitchhikers"; second prize, Canadian Author's Association, Manitoba branch, 1970, for poem "Raspberries"; President's Medal, University of Western Ontario, 1971, for short story "Bloodflowers"; Star award, *Kansas City Star*-Hallmark competitions, 1972, for poem "Val Playing"; Bread Loaf scholarship, 1972; first prize, Canadian Broadcasting Corporation Annual Short Story Competition, 1980; best first novel, *Books in Canada,* 1981, for *Gentle Sinners;* Con-Pro Gold Award for best commercial television drama of the year, CKNU-TV, 1983, Golden Sheaf award from Yorkton Short Film and Video Festival, Chris Statuette from Columbus International Film Festival, and Ohio State Award from Institute for Education by Radio-Television, all for *The Catch;* drama award, Canadian Authors Association Literary Awards, 1987, for *Granite Point.*

WRITINGS:

Bloodflowers (short stories), Oberon, 1973.
God Is Not a Fish Inspector (short stories), Oberon, 1975.
In the Gutting Shed (poems), Turnstone Press, 1976, revised edition, 1981.
Red Dust (short stories), Oberon, 1978.
Gentle Sinners (novel), Oberon, 1980.
The Carpenter of Dreams: Poems, Skaldhus Press, 1986.
What Can't Be Changed Shouldn't Be Mourned, Douglas & McIntyre, 1990.

RADIO PLAYS

Bloodflowers (adaptation of his short story), first broadcast by Canadian Broadcasting Corporation (CBC), October 30, 1982.
Granite Point, first broadcast by CBC, October 29, 1983.
The Cave, first broadcast by CBC, December 28, 1985.
An Unacceptable Standard of Cockpit Practice, first broadcast by CBC, 1985.
Seiche, first broadcast by CBC, January 10, 1987.

OTHER

The Catch (television screenplay), broadcast by CKND-TV (Canada), December, 1981.

Contributor to anthologies, including *The Best American Short Stories 1971,* edited by Martha Foley and David Burnett, Houghton, 1971; *Stories from Western Canada,* edited by Rudy Wiebe, Macmillan, 1972; *Sunlight and Shadows,* New English Library, 1974; *New Canadian Stories,* Oberon, 1974; *New Canadian Fiction,* Bantam, 1975; and *Moderne Erzaehler der Welt-Kanada,* Erdman, 1976. Contributor of articles, stories, and poems to literary journals, including *Alphabet, Antigonish Review, Atlantic Advocate, Canadian Forum, Dalhousie Review, Fiddlehead,*

Inscape, Jeopardy, Midwest Quarterly, New Student Review, Queen's Quarterly, Reader's Quarterly of Icelandic Literature and Thought, Tamarack Review, and *Windsor Review.*

ADAPTATIONS: Numerous short films have been made of Valgardson's short stories, in addition to a half-hour documentary on Valgardson and the Gimli area, commissioned by the Manitoba government, entitled *Waiting for Morning.* The Canadian Broadcasting Corp. has bought the rights to *Gentle Sinners.*

SIDELIGHTS: W. D. Valgardson's childhood in an Icelandic-Canadian fishing village has provided themes and settings for his stories. He is especially interested in the effects of isolation upon people. Reviewing Valgardson's 1975 short story collections, *God Is Not a Fish Inspector,* Adrian Vale of the *Irish Times* comments that Valgardson's "Manitoba countryside has close affinities with Egdon Heath. There is death and suicide and isolation. These elementals, however, are not dragged in to inflate a final paragraph; they come as hammer-blows, falling inevitably and with complete artistic rightness. Mr. Valgardson is an authoritative writer; he leaves the reader with no inclination to gainsay him or the truth of the events he describes."

Born in Winnipeg, Manitoba, Valgardson grew up in Gimli, a fishing village on Lake Winnipeg. Formerly known as Nya Island (New Iceland), Gimli retains a strong ethnic connection with Iceland and a sense of a collective Icelandic literary heritage. Valgardson says of the Gimli area: "In a sense, [it] was the Appalachia of Canada. The choices people had were incredibly restricted. . . . There was tragedy, poverty, foreignness, displacement and an idealization of the past." Valgardson received his bachelor's of arts degree from the University of Manitoba in 1960. After teaching for a few years he attended the Iowa Writer's Workshop at the University of Iowa, receiving a master's of fine arts degree in 1969. Valgardson later taught English at Cottey College in Missouri, where he was head of the department for three years.

After success in a number of writing contests, Valgardson published *Bloodflowers* (1973), a collection of ten short stories. The title story depicts a young teacher from mainland Canada who comes to teach on an island off the coast of Newfoundland. Once there, he slowly begins to suspect that he is to be made the sacrificial victim in a ritual spring sacrifice. The sinister tone of this story is repeated in the others, which are pessimistic portrayals of life in northern Manitoba; the moments of optimism that exist are brief and qualified. In "The Burning," for instance, a man takes satisfaction in burning his old home down before it can be burned by the local fire department for the purpose of civic renewal.

Valgardson's second collection of short stories, *God Is Not a Fish Inspector,* has been praised for its coherence and attention to the hardships of rural life. Following this volume Valgardson published a collection of poetry, *In The Gutting Shed* (1976), which received mixed reviews but nonetheless went into a second edition during its first year, a rarity in Canadian poetry. Several of the poems deal with personal issues not addressed in Valgardson's short stories, revealing a side of his personality not evident elsewhere. In his third collection of short stories, *Red Dust* (1978), Valgardson continues to examine the poverty and violence that exists in portions of rural Canada. In "Red Dust," for instance, a man permits his niece to be raped in exchange for a hunting dog.

Valgardson's first novel, *Gentle Sinners,* was published in 1980 and won a Books in Canada award as the best first novel of the year. Somewhat different than his other work, *Gentle Sinners* suggests a limited form of redemption and happiness in its account of a boy who flees his authoritative parents and finds a sense of community and ethnic identity with his uncle Sigfus. Despite the guarded optimism of portions of the book, critics note that the themes of tragedy and isolation that are typical of all of Valgardson's works is also apparent in *Gentle Sinners.* Valgardson commented: "I've spent a long time confronting my shadow and I've accepted the fact that I'm capable of any crime. Every writer must take two journeys. The first journey is into the lives of others; the second is the most terrifying. It is the journey into the self. I think that any writer who writes beyond surface entertainment has to make that second journey."

Valgardson accepts comparisons of his work to that of authors such as Anton Chekhov. "My writing has been compared to many Russian writers and I think that's fair. The Interlake area is probably similar to some parts of Russia, with people of a similar background, especially Slavs, facing the cold, the poverty, the isolation, and so on. I speak out of that environment," Valgardson is quoted as saying by David Jackel in the *Dictionary of Literary Biography.*

Writing does not come easily for Valgardson. Multiple rewrites and the use of "every device available," as he told Jackel, are what enable him to continue. One device he avoids, however, is first-person narrative. "I mistrust the first person very much," he told Jackel. "The first person gives the writer the temptation to fall into writing a summary rather than a story that needs to be dramatized. Also my stories are set in a very small locale, which most readers haven't experienced. That requires a very authoritative tone. I also have a strong Lutheran, and conservative,

background that needs to make the statement of belief that the omniscient voice has."

BIOGRAPHICAL/CRITICAL SOURCES:

BOOKS

Dictionary of Literary Biography, Volume 60: *Canadian Writers since 1960, Second Series,* Gale, 1987, pp. 355-58.

PERIODICALS

Books in Canada, November, 1977, pp. 38-39.
Canadian Literature, summer, 1984, pp. 15-34.
Essays on Canadian Writing, fall-winter, 1979-80, pp. 187-90.
Globe and Mail (Toronto), August 30, 1986; July 21, 1990.
Irish Times, July 10, 1976.
University of Toronto Quarterly, summer, 1979, pp. 324-26.

*   *   *

Van VOGT, A(lfred) E(lton) 1912-

PERSONAL: Born April 26, 1912, near Winnipeg, Manitoba, Canada; immigrated to U.S., 1944, naturalized citizen, 1952; son of Henry (an attorney) and Agnes (Buhr) Van Vogt; married Edna Mayne Hull, May 9, 1939 (died January 20, 1975); married Lydia I. Brayman (a linguist and superior court interpreter), October 6, 1979. *Education:* Attended schools in Manitoba; also studied at University of Ottawa and University of California. *Religion:* Rationalist.

ADDRESSES: Agent—c/o Simon & Schuster, 1230 Avenue of the Americas, New York, NY 10020.

CAREER: Professional writer, 1932—, chiefly of science fiction. Census clerk, Ottawa, Ontario, Canada, 1931-32; western representative of trade papers, Maclean Publishing Co., Toronto, Ontario, 1935-39. First managing director of Hubbard Dianetic Research Foundation of California, Los Angeles, 1950-53; co-owner, Hubbard Dianetic Center, Los Angeles, 1953-61. Founder, 200 Language Club, 1974. *Military service:* Served in Department of National Defense, Ottawa, 1939-41.

MEMBER: International Society for General Semantics, International Dianetic Society (president, 1958—), Authors Guild, Authors League of America, Science Fiction Writers of America, California Association of Dianetic Auditors (president, 1959-82).

AWARDS, HONOURS: Guest of honor at 4th World Science Fiction Convention, 1946, European Science Fiction Convention, 1978, and Metz Festival, France, 1985;

Manuscripters Literature award, 1948; Ann Radcliffe Award, Count Dracula Society, 1968; award from Academy of Science Fiction, Fantasy, and Horror Films, 1979; Jules Verne Award, 1983; honorary B.A., Golden Gate College.

WRITINGS:

SCIENCE FICTION NOVELS

Slan (originally serialized in *Astounding Science Fiction,* September-December, 1940), Arkham, 1946, revised edition, Simon & Schuster, 1951, reprinted, Berkley, 1982.

The Book of Ptath (originally serialized in *Unknown,* 1943), Fantasy Press, 1947, published as *Two Hundred Million A.D.,* Paperback Library, 1964, published as *Ptath,* Zebra Books, 1976.

The Voyage of the Space Beagle (based on material, including "Black Destroyer," serialized in *Astounding Science Fiction,* 1939-43, and in *Other Worlds,* 1950), Simon & Schuster, 1950, reprinted, Pocket Books, 1981, published as *Mission: Interplanetary,* New American Library, 1952.

The House That Stood Still, Greenberg, 1950, reprinted, Pocket Books, 1980, published as *The Mating Cry,* Beacon, 1960 (published in England as *The Undercover Aliens,* Panther, 1976).

The Mixed Men (originally serialized in *Astounding Science Fiction,* 1943-45), Gnome Press, 1952, published as *Mission to the Stars,* Berkley, 1955, reprinted, Pocket Books, 1980.

The Universe Maker (originally serialized in *Startling Stories,* 1949, under title "The Shadow Man"), Ace Books, 1953, reprinted, Pocket Books, 1982.

(With wife, E. Mayne Hull) *Planets for Sale* (originally serialized in *Astounding Science Fiction,* 1943-46), Fell, 1954.

The Mind Cage, Simon & Schuster, 1957, reprinted, Pocket Books, 1981.

Siege of the Unseen (originally serialized in *Astounding Science Fiction,* 1946, under title "The Chronicler"; bound with *The World Swappers* by John Brunner), Ace Books, 1959.

The War against the Rull (partially based on material serialized in *Astounding Science Fiction,* 1940-50), Simon & Schuster, 1959, reprinted, Pocket Books, 1982.

(With Hull) *The Winged Man* (originally serialized in *Astounding Science Fiction,* 1944), Doubleday, 1966.

The Silkie, Ace Books, 1969.

Quest for the Future (material originally serialized in *Astounding Science Fiction,* 1943-46), Ace Books, 1970.

Children of Tomorrow, Ace Books, 1970.

The Battle of Forever, Ace Books, 1971.

The Darkness on Diamondia, Ace Books, 1972.

Future Glitter, Ace Books, 1973 (published in England as *Tyranopolis,* Sphere, 1977).

The Secret Galactics, Prentice-Hall, 1974, published as *Earth Factor X,* DAW Books, 1976.

The Man with a Thousand Names, DAW Books, 1974.

Supermind (based on material originally serialized in *If,* 1968, under title "The Proxy Intelligence"), DAW Books, 1977.

The Anarchistic Colossus, Ace Books, 1977.

Renaissance, Pocket Books, 1979.

The Cosmic Encounter, Doubleday, 1980.

Computerworld, DAW Books, 1983, published as *Computer Eye,* Morrison, Raven-Hill, 1985.

"WEAPON SHOP" SERIES; SCIENCE FICTION NOVELS

The Weapon Makers (originally serialized in *Astounding Science Fiction,* 1943), Hadley, 1947, revised edition, Greenberg, 1952, reprinted, Pocket Books, 1979, published as *One against Eternity,* Ace Books, 1955.

The Weapon Shops of Isher (based on material serialized in *Astounding Science Fiction,* 1941-42, and in *Thrilling Wonder Stories,* 1949), Greenberg, 1951, reprinted, Pocket Books, 1981, bound with *Gateway to Elsewhere* by W. P. Jenkins, Ace Books, 1954.

"GOSSEYN" SERIES; SCIENCE FICTION NOVELS

The World of A (originally serialized in *Astounding Science Fiction,* 1945; also see below), Simon & Schuster, 1948, published as *The World of Null-A,* Ace Books, 1953, revised edition, Berkley, 1970, reprinted, 1982.

The Pawns of Null-A (originally serialized in *Astounding Science Fiction,* 1948-49, under title "The Players of A"), Ace Books, 1956, published as *The Players of Null-A,* Berkley, 1966, reprinted, 1982.

Null-A Three, DAW Books, 1985.

"CLANE LINN" SERIES; SCIENCE FICTION NOVELS

Empire of the Atom (partially based on material serialized in *Astounding Science Fiction,* 1946-47), Shasta Publishers, 1957.

The Wizard of Linn (originally serialized in *Astounding Science Fiction,* 1950), Ace Books, 1962.

SHORT STORIES AND NOVELLAS

(With Hull) *Out of the Unknown,* Fantasy Publishing (Los Angeles), 1948, expanded edition, Powell, 1969 (published in England as *The Sea Thing and Other Stories,* Sidgwick & Jackson, 1970).

Masters of Time (includes "Masters of Time" [originally serialized in *Astounding Science Fiction,* 1942, under title "Recruiting Station"] and "The Changeling" [originally serialized in *Astounding Science Fiction,* 1944]), Fantasy Press, 1950, reprinted, McFadden-Bartell, 1967.

Away and Beyond, Pellegrini & Cudahy, 1952.

Destination: Universe!, with an introduction by the author, Pellegrini & Cudahy, 1952.

Earth's Last Fortress (originally published as "Masters of Time"; bound with *Lost in Space* by George O. Smith), Ace Books, 1960.

The Beast (revised and enlarged version of "The Changeling"), Doubleday, 1963 (published in England as *The Moonbeast,* Panther, 1969).

The Twisted Man, (includes material serialized in *Astounding Science Fiction,* 1947, *Super Science Stories,* 1950, and *If,* 1963; bound with *One of Our Planets Is Missing* by Calvin M. Knox), Ace Books, 1964, published as *Rogue Ship,* Doubleday, 1965.

Monsters, edited and with an introduction by Forrest J. Ackerman, Paperback Library, 1965, published as *Science Fiction Monsters,* 1967, published as *The Blal,* Zebra Books, 1976.

The Far-Out Worlds of A. E. Van Vogt, Ace Books, 1968, enlarged edition published as *The Worlds of A. E. Van Vogt,* 1974.

More Than Superhuman, Dell, 1971.

The Proxy Intelligence and Other Mind Benders, Paperback Library, 1971.

M-33 in Andromeda, Paperback Library, 1971.

The Book of Van Vogt, DAW Books, 1972, published as *Lost: Fifty Suns,* 1979.

The Best of A. E. Van Vogt, edited by Angus Wells, Sidgwick & Jackson, 1974.

The Gryb, Zebra Books, 1976.

The Best of A. E. Van Vogt, Pocket Books, 1976.

Pendulum, DAW Books, 1978.

OMNIBUS VOLUMES

Triad (includes *The Voyage of the Space Beagle, Slan,* and *The World of A*), Simon & Schuster, 1959.

A Van Vogt Omnibus, Sidgwick & Jackson, Volume 1: *Planets for Sale, The Beast,* [and] *The Book of Ptath,* 1967, Volume 2: *The Mind Cage, The Winged Man,* [and] *Slan,* 1971.

Two Science Fiction Novels: Three Eyes of Evil and Earth's Last Fortress (*Three Eyes of Evil* originally published as *Siege of the Unseen*), Sidgwick & Jackson, 1973.

The Universe Maker and The Proxy Intelligence, Sidgwick & Jackson, 1976.

OTHER

(Contributor) Lloyd Arthur Esbach, editor, *Of Worlds Beyond,* Fantasy Press, 1947.

(With Charles E. Cooke) *The Hypnotism Handbook* (nonfiction), Borden, 1956.

The Violent Man (novel), Farrar, Straus, 1962, published as *A Report on the Violent Male,* Borgo Press, 1993.

(Author of introduction) William F. Nolan, editor, *The Pseudo-People,* Sherbourne Press, 1965 (published in England as *Almost Human,* Souvenir Press, 1966).

The Money Personality, Parker, 1973, published as *Unlock Your Money Personality,* Morrison, Raven-Hill, 1983.

Reflections of A. E. Van Vogt: The Autobiography of a Science Fiction Giant, with a Complete Bibliography, Fictioneer Books, 1975.

(Contributor) Brian Ash, editor, *Visual Encyclopedia of Science Fiction,* Harmony, 1977.

(Contributor) Rex Malik, editor, *Future Imperfect,* Pinter, 1980.

(Contributor) Martin H. Greenberg, editor, *Fantastic Lives,* Southern Illinois University Press, 1981.

Professional Writer (cassette), J. Norton Publishers, 1984.

The John W. Campbell Letters with Isaac Asimov and A. E. Van Vogt, A.C. Projects, 1991.

Also author of *The Search for Certainty,* 1970, and of play, "The Invalid's Wife." Contributor to periodicals, including *Astounding Science Fiction, Locus, Science Fiction Writers of America Bulletin,* and *Foundation 3.*

SIDELIGHTS: "Along with Robert Heinlein and Isaac Asimov, A. E. Van Vogt must be counted one of the three major SF writers of the Forties," declare Alexei and Cory Panshin of the *Magazine of Fantasy and Science Fiction.* Together they formed the nucleus of a group of writers linked with John W. Campbell, editor of *Astounding Science Fiction.* Their work marked the beginning of what is known as the Golden Age of Science Fiction. Within a year and a half of the publication of Van Vogt's first story, "Black Destroyer," in 1939, records *Dictionary of Literary Biography* contributor Arthur Jean Cox, he "had become an important figure in science fiction, the only writer at that time approximating the stature of Robert A. Heinlein; and, after Heinlein had left for World War II, Van Vogt easily and happily dominated *Astounding Science Fiction,* the most important science-fiction magazine of its day, for some years." Sam Moskowitz reports in *Seekers of Tomorrow: Masters of Modern Science Fiction* that a 1947 poll of science fiction readers "saw Van Vogt edge out such formidable competitors as A. Merritt, H. P. Lovecraft, Robert A. Heinlein, and Henry Kuttner as science fiction's most popular author."

In his stories Van Vogt originated and explored ideas and themes that have since become mainstays of science fiction. As a reviewer for the *Washington Post Book World* states, he "gave permanent form to some of science fiction's most cherished dreams." "From the first," says Donald A. Wolheim in *The Universe Makers,* "his stories have concerned themselves with extraordinary powers, with new concepts in science or in mental gymnastics, and he constantly seems to strive to create new systems of thought and mental order which will permit the creation of supermen."

Slan, for instance, is the story of a young mutant who can read minds, among other powers, fleeing persecution by the society that killed his parents. Although other writers had previously used the superman motif in science fiction stories, declares Moskowitz, "Van Vogt seems to have been the first science-fiction author with the courage to explore the sociological implications of the superhuman race living in and among humans." *Slan* "is still, after forty years, widely regarded as a classic, and continues the mainstay of [Van Vogt's] fame," says Cox. "By any standard," Moskowitz concludes, "it was a milestone in science fiction." Other Van Vogt masterpieces include *The Weapon Shops of Isher* and *The Weapon Makers,* "both grand galactic adventures, omnipotence fantasies laden with dark resonances from incompletely defined elements of mystery," as Charles Platt describes them in *Dream Makers: The Uncommon People Who Write Science Fiction.*

Also famous is Van Vogt's "Null-A" sequence, which relates the adventures of Gilbert Gosseyn, "a developing superman with the ability to transport himself or anything else instantaneously almost anywhere in the galaxy," as Gene DeWeese describes him in the *Science Fiction Review.* Gosseyn "used that power and others to unravel great mysteries and battle great enemies, both seen and unseen. The action was nonstop, and the solution to each mystery only revealed another, more complex mystery," continues DeWeese. But action and mystery were not the focus of the stories; instead, Van Vogt used the science fiction genre to "impress upon the reader something of the [non-Aristotelian] doctrines of . . . the general semantics movement," concludes Cox.

This fascination with a system of thought—in this case, general semantics—is characteristic of Van Vogt's writing. General semantics studies the ways in which the meanings of words and other symbols affect human behavior. The system tries to explain the thought process that goes on in a person's mind when a word is spoken or heard. This system allows Gosseyn "to logically and accurately analyze [his] situation without letting [his] emotions get in the way," according to DeWeese. Van Vogt plots his books using another, dream-related, system, says Platt, that fills "his science-fiction adventures with fantastic images, symbolic figures, a constant sense of discovery and revelation, and a sense of free, flying motion." The author is also an exponent of the Gallishaw method—a technique of writing "in 800-word scenes, the action in each developing through five carefully delineated steps," explains Cox. Van Vogt exhibits as well a "keen interest in such salient concepts as hypnotism, telepathy, semantics, 'similariza-

tion,' and Dianetics," declares Jeffrey M. Elliot in *Science Fiction Voices #2.*

Many critics find Van Vogt's recent work not as good as that which he did for *Astounding* in the 1940s. "Van Vogt thinks they have not properly understood what it is he is trying to do now," declares Cox. The author himself explains to Elliot, "For years, until the 1960s, I consciously wrote pulp-style sentences. They have a certain lush poetry in them. In the late 1960s, I began to concentrate on content and even allowed my protagonist to be neurotic, also. However, these current stories don't seem to win the same approval as when I followed the earlier system." DeWeese, for example, writing about the third volume of Gosseyn's adventures, states, "*Null-A Three* is very close to being a parody of the first two books." Various stylistic oddities tend to detract from the story line, DeWeese continues; he adds, "In the early books, the narrative was so exciting that most readers never noticed such things, but this time there's so little action that they are impossible to overlook." Other critics, however, have enjoyed Van Vogt's current fiction. Gerald Jonas, writing in the *New York Times Book Review* about *Cosmic Encounter,* says, "It is not easy to summarize an A. E. Van Vogt novel, nor to say exactly why one likes it. I liked 'Cosmic Encounter.'"

Despite the diversity of opinion that surrounds Van Vogt's recent efforts, most critics agree with Elliot that "there are few science fiction writers alive today who can boast the singular achievements of A. E. Van Vogt, a long-time talent in the field, who has spent his lifetime giving meaning and import to the shape of things to come." His work taken as a whole, says Cox, shows strengths that outweigh his weaknesses: "The convergence of [the author's] unpredictable restless inventiveness with the violence of feeling with which he charges his characters constitutes a large part of that archetypal power often noted by his admirers; the rest derives from his habit of turning his face ever outward to the Universe, of measuring everything by the Infinite and considering all human matters *sub specie aeternitatis.* He reaches out eagerly to grasp the Cosmos."

BIOGRAPHICAL/CRITICAL SOURCES:

BOOKS

Contemporary Literary Criticism, Volume 1, Gale, 1973.
Dictionary of Literary Biography, Volume 8: *Twentieth-Century American Science Fiction Writers,* Gale, 1981.
Elliot, Jeffrey M., *Science Fiction Voices #2,* Borgo Press, 1979.
Knight, Damon, *In Search of Wonder,* Advent Press, 1956.
Magill, Frank N., editor, *Survey of Science Fiction Literature,* Volume 5, Salem Press, 1979.

Magill, Frank N., editor, *Survey of Modern Fantasy Literature, Volume 1,* Salem Press, 1983.

Moskowitz, Sam, *Seekers of Tomorrow: Masters of Modern Science Fiction,* Hyperion Press, 1966.

Platt, Charles, *Dream Makers: The Uncommon People Who Write Science Fiction,* Berkley, 1980.

Searles, Baird, Martin Last, Beth Meacham, and Michael Franklin, *A Reader's Guide to Science Fiction,* Avon Books, 1979.

Van Vogt, A. E., *Reflections of A. E. Van Vogt: The Autobiography of a Science Fiction Giant, with a Complete Bibliography,* Fictioneer Books, 1975.

Wolheim, Donald A., *The Universe Makers,* Harper, 1971.

PERIODICALS

Algol, spring, 1977.

Amazing Science Fiction, March, 1982.

Analog Science Fact/Science Fiction, July, 1978, December, 1979, February, 1986.

Fantasy Review, September, 1985.

Foundation, March, 1973.

Future, January, 1979.

Magazine of Fantasy and Science Fiction, July, 1976.

New York Herald Tribune Book Review, February 9, 1947, March 21, 1948, August 19, 1951, June 1, 1952, October 26, 1952.

New York Times, June 11, 1950, December 17, 1950, August 5, 1951, August 10, 1952, October 12, 1952, March 17, 1957.

New York Times Book Review, April 14, 1974, October 3, 1976, July 31, 1977, May 11, 1980.

Science Fiction Chronicle, November, 1980.

Science Fiction Review, November, 1977, November, 1985.

Times Literary Supplement, April 4, 1968, April 9, 1970, November 9, 1973, March 15, 1974, August 8, 1975.

Washington Post Book World, March 22, 1981, July 26, 1981, September 29, 1985.

—*Sketch by Kenneth R. Shepherd*

*   *   *

VILLIERS, Marie de
See ROUTIER, Simone

*   *   *

VIZINCZEY, Stephen 1933-

PERSONAL: Born May 12, 1933, in Kaloz, Hungary; immigrated to Canada, 1957, naturalized citizen, 1961; son of Istvan (a school principal and church organist) and Erzsebet (Mohos) Vizinczey; married Gloria Fisher (an editor, researcher, and former Canadian Broadcasting Corporation program organizer), 1963; children: Marianne; stepchildren: Martha, Mary. *Education:* Attended University of Budapest and National College of Theatre and Film Arts in Budapest. *Avocational interests:* Listening to classical music, walking on sandy beaches and in old cities and great galleries, talking with students about great novels.

ADDRESSES: Home—70 Coleherne Ct., Old Brompton Rd., London SW5 0EF, England.

CAREER: Writer. Scriptwriter for National Film Board, Montreal, and writer-producer for Canadian Broadcasting Corporation (CBC), Toronto, 1957-65. Visiting fellow at University of Chicago, spring, 1989.

WRITINGS:

In Praise of Older Women: The Amorous Recollections of Andras Vajda, Contemporary Canada Press (Toronto), 1965, Trident (New York), 1966, revised edition, Seal (Toronto), 1985, Atlantic (New York), 1986, revised edition, University of Chicago Press (Chicago), 1990.

The Rules of Chaos: or, Why Tomorrow Doesn't Work, Macmillan (London), 1969, McCall Publishing, 1970.

An Innocent Millionaire, McClelland & Stewart (Toronto), 1983, Atlantic, 1985, revised edition, University of Chicago Press, 1990.

Truth and Lies in Literature, McClelland & Stewart, 1986, University of Chicago Press, 1988.

El Hombre del Toque Magico (title means "The Man with the Magic Touch"), translation by Ana Maria de la Fuente, Seix Barral, 1995.

Also author of plays, including *The Paszti Family, The Last Word,* and *Mama,* of poems and essays, and of documentaries for the National Film Board of Canada. Work represented in anthologies. Founder and editor of the Canadian literary magazine *Exchange,* c. 1960. Contributor of articles and reviews to periodicals, including the London *Times,* the London *Sunday Telegraph,* and *Harper's.*

ADAPTATIONS: In Praise of Older Women was adapted for film and released, starring Tom Berenger and Karen Black, by Avco Embassy Pictures in 1979.

WORK IN PROGRESS: A novel.

SIDELIGHTS: Stephen Vizinczey gained international attention with his first novel, *In Praise of Older Women: The Amorous Recollections of Andras Vajda,* both for the quality of the work and for the publicity surrounding its publication. Vizinczey, who fought in the Hungarian Revolution of 1956, fled his native land after the revolt was crushed, settling in Canada with only a few words of English at his command. He soon acquired facility in his adopted language by writing scripts for the National Film Board and by later work as a CBC writer-producer. He quit his job in 1965 to publish *In Praise of Older Women* on his own. It became an international best-seller and a modern classic. In the past two and a half decades it has sold more than three million copies worldwide and has gone into forty printings in English alone. In the late 1980s it was reissued in the United Kingdom, United States, Canada, and Germany, and it was published for the first time in Brazil, Israel, Yugoslavia, and Spain, where it sold out six printings in six months. New Portuguese and Swedish translations are in preparation, and it is also being translated into Italian and Hungarian.

In Praise of Older Women, an erotic novel charting the sexual education of a young man growing up in Hungary, Italy, and Canada among women in their thirties and forties, was welcomed by many critics with high praise. "The book is dedicated to older women and is addressed to young men," writes Vizinczey in the book's epigraph. "Vizinczey's *In Praise of Older Women* is . . . driving us reviewers out of our minds," wrote Kildare Dobbs in *Saturday Night.* "Here is this Hungarian rebel who in 1957 could speak scarcely a word of English and who even today speaks it with an impenetrable accent and whose name, moreover, we can't pronounce, and he has the gall to place himself, with his first book and in his thirty-third year, among the masters of plain English prose. . . . We have to go back to Boswell's *London Journal* to find anything that matches Vizinczey's book for freshness, candour and unaffected charm." Similarly, *Hudson Review* contributor Marvin Mudrick found *In Praise of Older Women* "extraordinary in its modesty and buoyancy, its fearlessness and persistent, unemphasized sadness." Mudrick concluded, "It is neither indignant nor compassionate. It is a good novel." "A little masterpiece of impeccable style, verging on the classical, sensitive, graceful and suggestive," raved Maria Dols in the Barcelona *Ajo Blanco.* The book's hero was compared repeatedly to Henry Fielding's Tom Jones, to Stendhal's Julien Sorel, and even to James Joyce's Stephen Dedalus. Much of the American press, however, ignored the book on its first appearance, so much did it scandalize critics who decided the work went too far in the field of sex. Twenty years later, the erotic considerations of the text, fundamental to the narrative and hardly iconoclastic anymore, are viewed as universal experience. In England, where it was widely reviewed and discussed, it became the third best-selling novel of the year. "Cool, comic, elegantly erotic . . . it has the real stuff of immortality," asserted B. A. Young in *Punch.* "A brilliant work," advanced Allan Forrest in the London *Sunday Citizen.* "After reading it, you realise that Vizinczey really *knows* and Henry Miller and the rest— even D. H. Lawrence—only thought they did."

Nor have the passing years dampened enthusiasm for the novel. In 1983 Australia's *National Times* contributor Peter Corris called *In Praise of Older Women* "one of the most charming books of the century" and in 1984 Harry Reid of the *Glasgow Herald* declared: "*In Praise of Older Women* has now the undisputed status of a modern erotic classic." When it was published in Spain in 1988 it was acclaimed in *La Gaceta* "a literary work of the first order" and in *Ajo Blanco* "a little masterpiece in which sex is knowledge and good literature." Quoting the *Sunday Citizen*'s comment "Vizinczey really *knows,*" Clara Janes wrote in *El Pais:* "This knowledge extends to all fields, including the literary one, and is reflected in the absolute efficacy of the narration, whose . . . essential humour is equivalent to the naturalness of the naked body."

Vizinczey's second work, *The Rules of Chaos: or, Why Tomorrow Doesn't Work,* a collection of essays first published in 1969 on such topics as philosophy, politics, and literature, was described in a London *Guardian* editorial as "reflections on the unpredictable incoherence of life" and by *Spectator* contributor Simon Raven as an "elegant and thoughtful book." The essays are linked by Vizinczey's belief that the elemen of chance exerts a great influence on life. Dennis Potter, reviewing *The Rules of Chaos* for the London *Times,* pronounced it "brilliant and challenging," "exhilarating," and "emancipating," and Robert Fulford commented in *Saturday Night:* "The style of Vizinczey the philosopher, like the style of Vizinczey the novelist, is spare and precise; and the content, again, is uniquely a combination of the boyishly naive and the worldly wise. Vizinczey has demonstrated for the second time that his charm is as impressive as his bravado."

Vizinczey's second novel, *An Innocent Millionaire,* which the author spent twelve years writing and rewriting, chronicles the adventures of one Mark Niven, the son of an impoverished American actor in Europe, who becomes obsessed with Spanish treasure ships, in particular one sunk in the Caribbean in the early nineteenth century. Mark abandons school to research the fate of the ship in maritime archives, methodically pinpointing its watery grave. He finds and salvages the ship but, ironically, loses all its treasure to modern pirates: tax officials, terrorists, art dealers, and lawyers. Though succinctly describing *An Innocent Millionaire* as "the story of a young man's obsessive hunt for treasure and the painful consequences of finding it," *Newsday* contributor Leslie Hanscom hastened to add, "But that makes the book sound like an action yarn. It is a far richer invention than that, filled with humane insight, literary poise, high imagination and, best of all, pure comedy."

First published in England and Canada, *An Innocent Millionaire* received rave reviews in both countries— acclaimed by such literary notables as Graham Greene and Anthony Burgess. Beginning his *Punch* review with the statement that Vizinczey could "teach the English how to write English," Burgess announced that "the distinction of the book lies in its calm clean prose style and its sly apophthegms, as well as in the solidity of its characters, good and detestable alike." Burgess ended by saying, "I was entertained but also deeply moved: here is a novel set bang in the middle of our decadent, polluted, corrupt world that, in some curious way, breathes a kind of desperate hope." The London *Observer* described *An Innocent Millionaire* as "a big, plotty, globe-trotting read that straps you into an enthralling roller-coaster of fortunes and emotions," and Terry Coleman, writing in the London *Guardian,* called it "a marvellous story, written by a master."

Helen Hoy, contributor to the *University of Toronto Quarterly,* defined the novel as an "ironic romance" and praised it for its "broad moral vision, exacting and unequivocal but large-spirited, which balances censure with shrewd affirmations . . . and affectionate appreciation for human potential. For all the meanness, unscrupulousness and self-deception mordantly exposed, *An Innocent Millionaire* also provides convincing displays of integrity, selflessness and love." In the Ottawa *Citizen* Burt Heward dubbed *An Innocent Millionaire* "an extraordinary achievement," and in the *Canadian Book Review Annual* Ronald Colman applauded Vizinczey's novel for "its attack on the vices of our society," made "with the finesse of a scalpel but the power of a sledge hammer." *Exeter Express and Echo* reviewer Andrew Mylett described *An Innocent Millionaire* as "on one level . . . an exotic adventure-thriller; on another a unique fable of our corrupt times—but beautifully written, and passionately told, whichever way you read it." *Quill and Quire* contributor Jamie Conklin found the novel "pervaded by an acerbic wit, entertaining and uplifting . . . well worth reading," and Toronto *Financial Post* columnist Arnold Edinborough pronounced Vizinczey "a stylist whose way with words is unique, gripping, and totally enjoyable." Peter Corris, writing in the *National Times* of Australia, could barely contain his enthusiasm. "This is a terrific book," he lauded. "You will love it. You will not wash dishes, neither will you mow lawns but you will sit and read and lament when you have passed the halfway mark."

Reviews from Germany, Spain, and Sweden were also extremely enthusiastic. *Neue Zurcher Zeitung* proposed that Vizinczey "stuns us with a bitter critique of the world in which we live," an achievement made all the more remarkable by the book's "rich, supple, often ironically pointed language, admired by noted English writers and critics, who hailed this novel, rightly, as an event in Anglo-Saxon literary life." *Deutsches Allgemeines Sonntagsblatt* related that "Stephen Vizinczey has written a

great novel, a brilliantly coloured mosaic, as it were, combining with masterly narrative art elements of the crime-story and adventure-story and philosophical reflections, which raise it to the level of universal validity," and Gunter Fischer wrote in *Munchner Stadtzeitung,* "There are books that are so full of life, so filled to bursting with lived experience, that they act like a mirror of reality. Stephen Vizinczey's *An Innocent Millionaire* is such a book. In this novel you discover the world all over again as if it were new." According to Spain's *La Vanguardia,* "*An Innocent Millionaire* leaves the reader with the impression that it is easy to write novels—because it reflects so closely what we think, imagine and dream, what we do and what happens to us."

In spite of this garland of plaudits from abroad, *An Innocent Millionaire* did not find a U.S. publisher until it was a best-seller in the rest of the English-speaking world. An American edition was eventually published by Atlantic Monthly Press in 1985 and was recommended in *Newsweek* by David Lehman for "its strong literary flavor" and "its brilliant fusion of romantic wish-fulfillment and savage moral indignation." Lehman added, "A superb stylist who regularly invokes Stendhal as his master, Vizinczey takes his epic, made-for-the-movies plot and turns it into an angry parable about the deadly sins of avarice and betrayal at the heart of every swindle. . . . With his gift for pungent aphorisms, Vizinczey frequently interrupts his story to comment on it—without ever losing his narrative momentum." In the *New York Times Book Review* Sam Tanenhaus called *An Innocent Millionaire* "a rare accomplishment, a contemporary adventure told with style, wit and wisdom," lauding particularly Vizinczey's "vividly epigrammatic prose." Other critics reviewing *An Innocent Millionaire* for American publications were equally positive in their appraisals. *Memphis Business Journal* contributor Edwin Howard admitted to reading Vizinczey's novel three times, finding it richer each time, and *San Francisco Chronicle* contributor Raymond Mungo judged it "great fun, an action-packed yarn with a real bite."

Reviewers on both sides of the Atlantic compared *An Innocent Millionaire* to nineteenth-century fiction classics. *Best Sellers* contributor William R. Evans, for instance, proclaimed the novel "the most scathing indictment of the legal profession since Dickens' *Bleak House,*" and Christina Monet, writing in the London *Literary Review,* called *An Innocent Millionaire* "a glorious twentieth-century incarnation of the great social novels of the nineteenth century." Monet continued, "After reading *An Innocent Millionaire* one has a sense of having been thoroughly exercised, intellectually and emotionally. Vizinczey has created an authentic social epic which reunites, after an estrangement of nearly a century, intellectual and moral edification with exuberant entertainment." Moreover, she found Vizinczey's "consummate dissection of contemporary society and its institutions, through the sardonic and meticulous presentation of an epic cast of crooks and fools, . . . balanced by a worldly compassion and an expansive humanism worthy of Stendhal" and confessed to having put down the book "with an exhilarated sense of fulfilment at a marvellous journey's end." And Robert Fulford of the *Toronto Star* noted, "It's as if Balzac had come back to life and written a novel about the modern world of jet planes and chemical manufacturers."

In fact, the comparison to Balzac, one of Vizinczey's favorite novelists, was made frequently by reviewers. *Saturday Night* contributor Ronald Bryden viewed the book's denouement as "a savage Balzacian cartoon of the underworlds of North American business, art-dealing and law," while according to Michael Stern of the *San Jose Mercury-News*, "the last third of *An Innocent Millionaire,* the harrowing story of Mark's doomed lawsuit against his tormentors, [is] an anatomy of the ways of the world rivalling Balzac's expose of the publishing business and credit markets in *Lost Illusions.*" "Balzac has come back to earth to continue his *comedie humaine* in contemporary America," wrote Edwin Howard in the *Memphis Press-Scimitar.* "It is extraordinary how many of our modern American concerns the novel deals with—Vietnam and draft avoidance; the Mafia; disposal, or non-disposal, of poisonous wastes; terrorism and, of course, the book's central concern, the eternal search for justice in an unjust world," added Howard.

Those critics who disliked *An Innocent Millionaire* usually objected to what they perceived as cumbersome editorial philosophizing in the second half of the book. *Los Angeles Times Book Review* contributor Ronald Florence, for example, found that in the middle of the novel "the narrative is sidetracked to make way for the bad guys"—burdened with lengthy tirades "on law, publishing and the avarice of anyone who would fleece innocent, deserving millionaires of their just rewards." Similarly, Marghanita Laski commented in *Spectator* that Mark finds his treasure halfway through the book, and the rest "tells how he was cheated out of it, and, at disproportionate length, of the legal processes that ensued." One of Tanenhaus's few reservations about the work was that Vizinczey's "satire of corporate cupidity suffers from overkill." On the other hand, *Neue Zurcher Zeitung* commended *An Innocent Millionaire* for its editorializing, noting that "the second part can teach you what horror is—and here the story, told in a realistic manner with the author's comments on events, becomes almost unbearably exciting—because not for a single day will Mark enjoy his dream come true."

Vizinczey's second book of literary criticism, *Truth and Lies in Literature,* also initially published in England and

Canada, is a collection of essays and reviews that he contributed to various periodicals during a period of twenty years. The articles focus on European literature, particularly the classic past and the world of ideas. An advocate of the great nineteenth-century French and Russian novelists, Vizinczey finds Stendhal, Balzac, Leo Tolstoy, and Fedor Dostoevski infinitely superior to their English counterparts Charles Dickens, William Makepeace Thackeray, and George Eliot. He writes that he abhors the hypocrisy and expediency that mask as truths in literature, and that he despises caution in writers, explaining his point with one of the book's many memorable aphorisms: "Great writers are not those who tell us we shouldn't play with fire, but those who make our fingers burn."

According to Ray Sawhill in *Newsweek,* Vizinczey "doesn't spend much time on analysis and description, or on developing arguments; instead, he scrapes away misconceptions, states why a work does or doesn't matter and then simply stands aside." His intention is to send readers back to the books themselves—a goal accomplished, according to *Books in Canada* contributor I. M. Owen, who lauded Vizinczey for "never los[ing] sight of the primary purpose of a review, the strictly utilitarian one of conveying to his readers a sufficient idea of the book to allow them to judge whether *they* want to read it." In fact, several reviewers remarked that Vizinczey had indeed inspired them to read the novels he wrote about. "Isn't that the measure of the effectiveness of any work of art?" observed *Memphis Commercial Appeal* staff reporter Fredric Koeppel, who also noted that Vizinczey "has no patience with trends in criticism like structuralism or deconstruction." "His concern," Koeppel posited, "lies with the portrayal of human characters in the full range of their passions and attitudes."

As with his novels, *Truth and Lies in Literature* won admiration from critics and fans alike. Koeppel recommended that "all book reviewers should study these essays as models of what reviewing and criticism can be" and bestowed upon Vizinczey's work "classic status." Leon Ferguson, contributor to the Montreal *Gazette,* called *Truth and Lies in Literature* "a great book, a fascinating and invigorating book, a book of extraordinary passion and sense, which cannot be fully extolled in a brief critique." "Few people will read this book without being stung to disagreement or anger; but fewer still will read it without being stimulated, enlightened and elevated," wrote Harry Reid in the *Glasgow Herald. Christian Science Monitor* contributor Thomas D'Evelyn concurred, calling the short literary review "an art form in the hands of Stephen Vizinczey." Mark Le Fanu declared in the London *Times* that Vizinczey's "own knowledge of literature as demonstrated in these essays, is wonderfully wide and relaxed." Le Fanu added, "In fact, what is most impressive about these essays . . . is the way that literature and life are so subtly intertwined with each other. The passion for the one is the passion for the other. As it ought to be in criticism, but seldom is."

"[Vizinczey's] views are as strong as his style, which is swift and vigorous, never sloppy and never, never dull," posited Baltimore *Evening Sun* contributor Jeffrey M. Landaw. *Reason* book review editor Lynn Scarlett proclaimed Vizinczey's essays "stunning," claiming that "he imparts more about man and state than a library of stately tomes." Complimenting the author for "transport[ing] the reader on an intellectual and emotional odyssey," Scarlett added, "Vizinczey does not see the world through rose-colored glasses, yet his world is one of optimism. It is optimistic because his world is peopled with individuals whose intrinsic worth does matter. He shows that even in the most vicious circumstances we do have choices." And Michael Foot, biographer and former leader of Great Britain's Labour Party, concluded his review of *Truth and Lies in Literature* by deeming Vizinczey a "brilliant, incorruptible critic." Bruce Bebb, reviewing Vizinczey's book of essays for the Los Angeles *Reader,* exclaimed, "Every piece in the book is good, and many are so good that, after dipping casually into the middle, I stayed up half the night, reading with growing amazement and admiration."

Norman Snider, in his Toronto *Globe and Mail* review of Vizinczey's book, declared its author "one of the most consistently engaging, eloquent and provocative critics currently writing." His special strength as a critic, according to Snider, is "his belief in the classics as living, breathing texts, his conviction that the great European novelists of the nineteenth century are as alive right now as they were one hundred years ago. Thus he discusses a novel such as Herman Melville's *Billy Budd* not with the reverence usually accorded a dead classic, but as though the book had come out last week and its merits were still a live issue." Conceding that Vizinczey's insistence on the contemporary relevance of some of his favorite books is "occasionally less than conclusively proved" and that his opposition to technology and social progress is "sometimes nothing more than sheer literary reflex," Snider nevertheless maintained that Vizinczey "has gone a long way in *Truth and Lies in Literature* to establish himself as a unique international literary voice."

CA INTERVIEW

Contemporary Authors first interviewed Stephen Vizinczey by telephone on November 14, 1986, at his home in London. A more recent telephone conversation took place March 5, 1989.

CA: You fought in the 1956 Hungarian revolution before going to Canada, where you became a writer-producer for the CBC and then wrote In Praise of Older Women. *You knew almost no English when you arrived in Canada, you told Lauren Long for* Publishers Weekly. *What helped you to learn the language so quickly and so well?*

VIZINCZEY: The terror of starvation.

CA: You were a successful playwright before you went to Canada. How early did you begin writing?

VIZINCZEY: I wrote a Christmas poem when I was five—eight lines with proper rhymes. This made me so happy, I went on writing poems, sometimes two a day, and one of them was actually published when I was twelve. Seeing my name in print gave me such confidence that I wrote a novel—a two-hundred-page story of hopeless love. My literature teacher at the Benedictine Gymnasium spent the better part of an hour discussing my book with me, and he did it during class, ignoring the other kids. Those were the days. Anyway, I published some poetry, went to the University of Budapest when I was sixteen, then went over to the National College of Theatre and Film Arts, and wrote my first play, *The Paszti Family,* for my first year-end exam. The play was taken up by a student director who chose it as his diploma work: this meant a premiere in a provincial theatre.

CA: What was the play about?

VIZINCZEY: It was about a decent communist factory manager who committed suicide. The Ministry of Culture banned it for "anti-socialist tendencies," and my girlfriend, who was already a successful actress, dropped me the same day. I worked myself out of this double shock by writing a kind of black farce about a nymphomaniac Party secretary who punished reluctant or unsatisfactory lovers by denouncing them as enemies of socialism. When I submitted that one to my teachers I was asked to leave the college, but I didn't oblige and they allowed me to stay. Unlike the universities, the College of Theatre and Film Arts was an island of relative freedom.

CA: When was this?

VIZINCZEY: The early fifties. Hungary was an occupied country, a totalitarian state run by quislings appointed by the Kremlin. . . . At that time you were in constant danger of being arrested, imprisoned, tortured, and executed. My next play, *The Last Word,* was about a journalist who tried to expose corruption and was driven to suicide. Since I wasn't ready to kill myself like my heroes, and I wanted to get the play produced, I agreed to move the action from Budapest to a small town, so that the villains were not members of the Central Committee but small-time local functionaries. It got as far as dress rehearsal, the posters were up all over Budapest, I had a new suit for the premiere—and then the security police showed up at the theatre during one of the final run-throughs and took all the copies of the play. The same morning I was told to come to the Ministry for a conference and to bring all my extra copies. They were also seized—the idea was not only to ban the play but to destroy the text. These were the sorts of successes I had—a foretaste of triumph followed by disaster. But they were ego-boosting disasters. I had written something that was important enough to be suppressed by the government. It was a joyride compared with being published and ignored in New York.

CA: What about your play Mama?

VIZINCZEY: Mama is a beautiful young widow with jealous children who destroy her chances with men and then grow up and leave her. That play was banned as well. The son did worse than commit suicide—he escaped to America. But it was 1956: people were getting out of line, the government was losing control of cultural institutions. *Mama* was broadcast by Radio Budapest on October 4, and it was scheduled for production at the National Theatre—the greatest honor a young playwright could conceive. The film rights were sold. I was only twenty-three, I was tasting fame and glory, and I had more money than I knew what to do with. The only thing missing was a free country to write in, so I fought in the revolution. A month later I was a refugee without a country and a writer without a language. I guess this is how I became a readable author. I was lucky enough to be subjected to quite a few traumatic surprises, dramatic reversals of fortune.

CA: In 1957 you went to Canada.

VIZINCZEY: Where I started life all over again and learned to write in English.

CA: What was [Canadian poet and songwriter] Leonard Cohen's connection with Exchange, *the Canadian literary magazine you founded?*

VIZINCZEY: In 1960 Leonard and I were neighbors in Montreal—we used to stay up all night talking about [French authors Albert] Camus and [Jean-Paul] Sartre. One of Leonard's other friends, the son of a rich clothing manufacturer, was bored to distraction working for his father and wanted to finance a literary magazine. He asked Leonard to edit it. Leonard didn't want to do it, but he said he knew a starving writer next door. That was how it started.

CA: What was the magazine's appeal?

VIZINCZEY: Canadian literary life was very fragmented back in 1960. You had a Montreal group of artists—or rather two, French and English—and you had a Toronto group and a West Coast group—isolated circles among hostile hordes of hockey fans. *Exchange* was a kind of unifying mirror in which artists and intellectuals across the continent could see themselves as one community—

including the French of Quebec. We published a Quebec story about a wayward priest which nobody else dared to print. We were the first English magazine to print what the Quebec separatists were thinking and writing. Most Anglos had never heard of them before. We were militantly intellectual. I made a big fuss about poets—[Earle] Birney, [Leonard] Cohen, [Irving] Layton, [A. W.] Purdy. We were critical of received wisdom. The mass media still supported atmospheric nuclear testing; our magazine came out against it. I wrote in defense of Bertrand Russell, a great liberal philosopher, then much abused as a fellow traveler. Incidentally, his books were banned in communist countries, and I felt that one of the great advantages of getting out of Hungary was that I could read Russell. But back to *Exchange:* we brought literature, philosophy, and political discussion together. And we had a great art director and cartoonist, Vittorio Fiorucci.

CA: Why did you stop?

VIZINCZEY: The backer's father kept hearing shocked comments about *Exchange* at his club, and he told his son he would disinherit him if he continued to support us. So the young man took up heroin instead, and a few years later he died of an overdose in a Hong Kong hotel.

CA: It is sad that such a potentially important magazine had to fold.

VIZINCZEY: Well, we had three good issues. And I got the idea for *In Praise of Older Women* while listening to students who came to help me to pack the magazines and address envelopes. They made me realize that I had something to say about growing up.

CA: Did you learn valuable lessons from publishing In Praise of Older Women *yourself the first time around?*

VIZINCZEY: I learned how tough it is to be a book salesman and what it's like to run a small business, with many of your customers never paying their bills. I tend to do crazy things for reasons which make no sense except that they take me out of my bookish life and teach me a lot I didn't know before.

CA: But you made your novel a number one best-seller in Canada, didn't you?

VIZINCZEY: I shouldn't have done it. I published *In Praise of Older Women* because nobody was as enthusiastic about it as I was myself. I didn't see how it could overcome the hostility and ill will generated by its subject, if its own publisher didn't believe in it. So I borrowed money, quit my job to publish the book, telling everybody I had written a masterpiece which was going to be a bestseller. Some writers and critics agreed, others thought I was a conceited idiot. That's where I learned something I put into *An Innocent Millionaire:* "great ambitions numb the pain of ridicule." The biggest joke was that I thought I could compete with big publishing organizations that had coast-to-coast networks of distributors and salesmen. I put in sixteen-hour days for five months, working with the printer, calling on booksellers, doing publicity, packing, shipping, and delivering books, and *In Praise of Older Women* got on top of the best-seller list the second week after publication. But by then I was an exhausted wreck and all I could do was to turn triumph into disaster.

CA: How did you do that?

VIZINCZEY: I turned down Bennett Cerf of Random House—a great publisher, who could have deflected the hostility the novel aroused. It wouldn't have been possible to bury it with silence if he had published it. A few years later everybody was borrowing my title, but at the time *In Praise of Older Women* struck most people as a sick joke which I couldn't possibly mean and which no intelligent reader could possibly entertain. Still, I had made *In Praise of Older Women* a success in Canada, so I decided not to go with the big guy in New York who had a lot of other important books but with the little guy who would devote all his time and energy to launching my controversial novel. I sold it to Ian Ballantine, who immediately resold it and didn't tell me until months later. The next thing I knew *In Praise of Older Women* was being published by Trident Press—the imprint Simon & Schuster had created for Harold Robbins's books, to keep the Simon & Schuster list clean. So *In Praise of Older Women,* already suspect as a first novel by an unknown foreigner, with an unacceptable sexual theme, was paired with the latest Harold Robbins—most review editors wouldn't touch it. This was how I learned that no writer should sign contracts which allow anyone to resell his work without his written consent. Mistakes like that can cost you years of agony and hardship.

CA: But In Praise of Older Women *won many critics and readers in several languages.*

VIZINCZEY: Yes, after bombing in the States it was published in England under a reasonable imprint as a literary work and, as you say, it won many critics and readers. According to the year-end best-seller lists it even outsold Truman Capote's *In Cold Blood.* But I received very little money after the low advance. It was like that everywhere. I contemplated the success of *In Praise of Older Women* living on bank loans.

CA: When In Praise of Older Women *was republished in 1986 by Atlantic Monthly Press, John Podhoretz of the* Washington Times *likened you to James Joyce, saying that you portray sex as "part of a larger education in the ways of the world."*

VIZINCZEY: There must be *some* reason for the new editions that keep appearing. It seems to have continuing validity. And it has also acquired historical interest, I suppose, as a book about life before acquired immune deficiency syndrome (AIDS).

CA: An Innocent Millionaire *was in the making for twelve years, during which time you were distracted by your legal dispute with Ian Ballantine.*

VIZINCZEY: It wasn't a distraction, it was an education. I sued Ballantine and what was then his company for keeping more than their share of my foreign royalties, and other matters. The Supreme Court of the State of New York granted me grounds for action, and we had a seven-year lawsuit. I learned more from that lawsuit than from anything else in my life. I learned how New York attorneys operate, how New York functions—which is how the modern world functions. Also, writing affidavits improved my style—it forced me to be more precise, more concise. So now I'm glad that I did everything wrong with *In Praise of Older Women.* If I had gone with Bennett Cerf and made a couple of million dollars at the age of thirty-two, I'm sure I would be a lesser writer. I certainly wouldn't have been able to write *An Innocent Millionaire.*

CA: Did you go to unusual sources for the research on sunken treasure ships?

VIZINCZEY: You mean apart from the lawsuit? My treasure ship was *In Praise of Older Women,* so the emotional drama of winning and losing a fortune came from personal experience. Apart from that, I spent a couple of years in Florida and the Bahamas, got to know the sea, met some people searching for wrecks, read Latin American history. . . . But one of the main characters in the novel is a chemical magnate, and I did a lot more research on toxic waste than on sunken treasure ships.

CA: What's the story with the movie plans?

VIZINCZEY: United Artists bought the film rights to the novel and signed Tom Cruise to play Mark Niven, the innocent millionaire of the title. Then two years passed while first Ruth Prawer Jhabvala, who wrote the screenplay of *Room With a View,* and then Peter Weir, who wrote that of *Witness,* wrote scripts which were eventually rejected. MGM-UA [Metro-Goldwyn-Mayer and United Artists] still say they are going to make the movie and Tom Cruise is still under contract for it, but as of March, 1989, the studio is up for sale and an actors' strike is looming, so who knows what will happen.

CA: This one should be easier to turn into a movie. In Praise of Older Women *was very subjective, and rather pensive.*

VIZINCZEY: Right. Most of what happens in *In Praise of Older Women* happens inside, but *An Innocent Million-*

aire has a filmable plot—after a great deal of simplification, of course. My only worry is that the studio will insist on a happy ending. It's not a story that can have a happy ending.

CA: You very much believe that literature has a moral function, don't you?

VIZINCZEY: In the sense that it should be truthful. I mean, even in science fiction it has to be clear how the characters, or the robots, treat each other. It has to be clear who hurts whom and how.

CA: It's evident from Truth and Lies in Literature *that you read Stendhal and Balzac and that they are inspirations for your work. Are there current writers whose work you enjoy reading?*

VIZINCZEY: Leaving aside the ones who are too famous to mention, I read everything I come across by Brigid Brophy, Nina Bawden, Richard Ford, Ellen Gilchrist, Paula Fox, Frederic Raphael, Jill Neville, Morris Philipson—it's incredible how many good writers we have, and terrifying how little known some of them are. Alfred Kazin is an eminent literary critic, but is it common knowledge that his *New York Jew* is itself a literary classic? His autobiographical books contain some of the best pages of American prose. The Italian novelist Leonardo Sciascia is a brilliant writer who I think is hardly known in the States, though he's published there. Some of Austin Clark's stories are as good as [Anton] Chekhov's and he would be world-famous if he were a black American, but he is a black Canadian from Barbados, so there are no big groups beating the drums for him. George Jonas is another Canadian who should be better known; his *Final Decree* is an excellent novel which I think hasn't even been published in the States. I still read a lot of poetry—among contemporaries, Earle Birney, Derek Walcott, George Faludy.

CA: How do you feel your writing style may have been affected by coming to English relatively late?

VIZINCZEY: It helped. Because I don't take the language for granted, I write much better in English than I ever wrote in Hungarian. It's a marvelous language, though, and I still miss it. You can say a lot of things in Hungarian that you can't say in English. On the other hand, I think I have a kind of extra perspective on English which I didn't have with Hungarian; in every language you see and feel everything in a slightly different way.

CA: You seem to do a lot of traveling. Does that somehow feed the writing?

VIZINCZEY: After three or four months of sitting at the same desk, looking out of the same window, I get stale. I can't really be away from the city too long, but I can't be away from the sea too long either. I work very well on Anna Maria Island, off the Gulf Coast of Florida, and I work well in London, Rome—and Venice, of course, which is both city and sea. I'm writing a novel that's set in Palermo and I'm going back there soon, but I've got to stop spending so much time in Italy. Italian is too seductive a language, and you can no more live with two languages than you can live with two wives.

CA: There are bits of autobiography in some of your published writing. Will you do more—perhaps a whole book one day?

VIZINCZEY: I don't think so. I use my life as a sculptor uses a quarry. It's where I get the raw material for my novels, so I don't think I'll ever bother with what didn't inspire me to make something out of it. Someday, though, I want to write the story of my father's murder. He was possibly the first man assassinated by the Nazis in Hungary, in 1935, in quite dramatic circumstances. I was only two years old when it happened, but of course I learned about it later—and somehow the older I get, the more I think about him. I'll probably write about him one day.

BIOGRAPHICAL/CRITICAL SOURCES:

BOOKS

Contemporary Literary Criticism, Volume 40, Gale, 1986.
Vizinczey, Stephen, *In Praise of Older Women: The Amorous Recollections of Andras Vajda,* Contemporary Canada Press (Toronto), 1965.
Vizinczey, *Truth and Lies in Literature,* Hamish Hamilton, 1986.

PERIODICALS

Ajo Blanco (Barcelona, Spain), August, 1988.
Australian, July 30, 1983.
Best Sellers, June, 1985.
Books and Bookmen, April, 1983.
Books in Canada, December, 1983; August/September, 1986.
British Book News, September, 1986.
Calgary Herald, November 13, 1983; December 18, 1983; July 13, 1986.
Canadian Book Review Annual, 1983.
Canadian Forum, March, 1970.
Chicago Tribune, July 28, 1985; June 22, 1986.
Christian Science Monitor, July 18, 1985; August 1, 1986.
Citizen (Ottawa), October 8, 1983.
Cleveland Plain Dealer, June 30, 1985.
Corriere della Sera (Milan, Italy), July 12, 1988.
Deutsches Allgemeines Sonntagsblatt (Hamburg, Federal Republic of Germany), October 11, 1987.
Edmonton Journal, November 6, 1983.
Epoca (Segrate, Italy), May 16, 1988.
Evening Herald (Dublin, Ireland), August 3, 1984.
Evening Sun (Baltimore), September 14, 1986.

Exeter Express and Echo, December 20, 1983.

Financial Post (Toronto), November 12, 1983.

Fort Worth Star-Telegram, February 27, 1966; July 7, 1985.

La Gaceta (Seville, Spain), April 22, 1988.

Gazette (Montreal), August 28, 1965; November 19, 1983; September 24, 1984.

Il Giornale (Milan, Italy), July 24, 1988.

Glasgow Herald (Glasgow, Scotland), July 23, 1984; October 25, 1986.

Globe and Mail (Toronto), September 24, 1983; November 5, 1983; April 12, 1986; June 14, 1986.

Guardian (London), August 5, 1966; December 30, 1966; April 21, 1969; May 27, 1969; March 19, 1983.

Ham & High (London), September 19, 1986.

Hilton Head Island Packet, June 23, 1986.

Hudson Review, summer, 1986.

Imprint, February 10, 1984.

Kirkus Reviews, April 15, 1985.

Listener, April 14, 1983.

Literary Review (London), June, 1983; September, 1985.

Los Angeles Daily News, July 13, 1986.

Los Angeles Times Book Review, July 7, 1985.

Maclean's, August 7, 1978; October 3, 1983.

Mail on Sunday (London), March 20, 1983.

Memphis Business Journal, June 24, 1985; September 1, 1986.

Memphis Commercial Appeal, August 24, 1986.

Memphis Press-Scimitar, November 20, 1970; October 27, 1975; October 29, 1983; November 3, 1985.

Miami Herald, June 22, 1986.

Miranda (Aviles, Spain), January 16, 1989.

Munchner Stadtzeitung, November 21, 1987.

National Times (Australia), July 22, 1983.

Neue Zurcher Zeitung (Zurich, Switzerland), June 24, 1984.

Newsday, August 11, 1985.

New Statesman, April 25, 1969; May 2, 1969; March 25, 1983.

Newsweek, June 17, 1985; September, 1986.

New York, June 30, 1986.

New York Daily News, February 28, 1985; June 15, 1985.

New York Times, February 14, 1966; February 9, 1979.

New York Times Book Review, June 16, 1985; May 18, 1986.

Oakland Press, July 20, 1986.

Observer, April 27, 1969; July 29, 1984.

El Pais (Madrid, Spain), May 1, 1988; May 22, 1988.

Province (Vancouver), October 9, 1983; October 30, 1983; July 13, 1986.

Publishers Weekly, June 14, 1985.

Punch, August 24, 1966; March 30, 1983; October 8, 1986.

Quill and Quire, November, 1983; June, 1986.

Reader (Los Angeles), August 22, 1986.

Reason, August/September, 1987.

San Francisco Chronicle, August 11, 1985.

San Jose Mercury-News, June 30, 1985.

Saturday Night, September, 1965; October, 1969; May, 1978; September, 1983.

Spectator, August 12, 1966; May 9, 1969; March 26, 1983.

Spectrum, May 9, 1969.

La Stampa (Turin, Italy), July 6, 1988.

Sunday Citizen (London), October 2, 1966.

Sunday Telegraph (Sydney, Australia), August 14, 1966; January 1, 1967; April 27, 1969; December 14, 1986.

Sunday Times (London), March 20, 1983; July 6, 1986.

Svenska Dagbladet (Stockholm, Sweden), January 20, 1988; October 19, 1988.

Time, April 24, 1978; June 17, 1983.

Time Out (London), August 2, 1984.

Times (London), January 6, 1968; April 26, 1969; December 27, 1969; June 3, 1983; February 14, 1985; August 14, 1986.

Times Literary Supplement, April 15, 1983.

Toronto Star, July 2, 1965; August 9, 1965; April 18, 1982; April 16, 1983; October 23, 1983; November 3, 1983; December 29, 1985; May 25, 1986; December 6, 1986.

Toronto Sun, June 3, 1982; October 25, 1983; November 20, 1983.

University of Toronto Quarterly, summer, 1984.

USA Today, June 14, 1985.

La Vanguardia (Barcelona, Spain), June 9, 1988; December 16, 1988.

Vanity Fair, May, 1985.

Veja (Sao Paulo, Brazil), March 2, 1988.

Vermont Sunday Magazine, May 26, 1985.

Village Voice, June 18, 1985.

Washington Post Book World, July 19, 1970; June 26, 1985.

Washington Times, August 14, 1986.

Die Weltwoche (Hamburg, Federal Republic of Germany), April 9, 1987.

—Sketch by Joanne M. Peters

—Interview by Jean W. Ross

W

WADDINGTON, Miriam 1917-
(E. B. Merritt)

PERSONAL: Born December 23, 1917, in Winnipeg, Manitoba, Canada; daughter of Isidore (a small manufacturer) and Musha (Dobrushin) Dworkin; married Patrick Donald Waddington, July 5, 1939 (divorced, 1965); children: Marcus Frushard, Jonathan John. *Education:* University of Toronto, B.A., 1939, Diploma in Social Work, 1942, M.A., 1968; University of Pennsylvania, M.S.W., 1945.

ADDRESSES: Home—32 Yewfield Crescent, Don Mills, Toronto, Ontario, Canada M3B 2Y6. *Office*—Department of English, York University, Toronto, Ontario, Canada M3J 1P3.

CAREER: Jewish Child Welfare Bureau, Montreal, Quebec, assistant director, 1945-46; McGill University, School of Social Work, Montreal, field instructor, 1946-49; Montreal Children's Hospital, Montreal, staff member, 1952-54; John Howard Society, Montreal, staff member, 1955-57; Jewish Family Bureau, Montreal, caseworker, 1957-60; North York Family Service, Toronto, Ontario, casework supervisor, 1960-62; York University, Toronto, 1964-73, assistant professor, senior scholar and professor of English and Canadian literature, 1973-83, professor emerita, 1983—. Writer in residence, University of Ottawa, 1974, Windsor Public Library, 1983, and Toronto Metropolitan Library, 1986; Canada Council exchange poet to Wales, 1980; has given poetry readings or lectured at International Poetry Evenings, Struga, Yugoslavia, 1980, Yaddo Artists Colony, and most universities across Canada; annual drama awards judge, Association of Canadian Television and Radio Artists.

MEMBER: International PEN, Modern Language Association of America, Otto Rank Association.

AWARDS, HONOURS: Canada Council senior fellowship in creative writing, 1962-63, senior arts fellowship, 1971-72 and 1979-80; Canada Council academic grant, 1968-69; J. I. Segal award, 1972, for *Driving Home: Poems New and Selected,* and 1987, for *Collected Poems;* D.Litt., Lakehead University, 1975, and York University, 1985; Association of Quebec and Canadian Literatures Citation, 1979, for her contribution to Canadian literature.

WRITINGS:

POETRY

Green World, First Statement Press (Montreal), 1945.
The Second Silence, Ryerson (Toronto), 1955.
The Season's Lovers, Ryerson, 1958.
The Glass Trumpet, Oxford University Press (Toronto), 1966.
Call Them Canadians, edited by Lorraine Monk, Duhamel (Ottawa), 1968.
Say Yes, Oxford University Press, 1969.
Driving Home: Poems New and Selected, Oxford University Press, 1972.
The Dream Telescope, Anvil Press (London), 1972.
The Price of Gold, Oxford University Press, 1976.
Mister Never, Turnstone (Winnipeg), 1978.
The Visitants, Oxford University Press, 1981.
Collected Poems, Oxford University Press, 1986.
The Last Landscape, Oxford University Press, 1992.

OTHER

A. M. Klein (criticism), Copp Clark (Toronto), 1970, 2nd edition, 1974.
(Editor) *John Sutherland: Essays, Controversies, and Poems,* McClelland & Stewart (Toronto), 1973.
(Editor and author of introduction) *The Collected Poems of A. M. Klein,* McGraw (Toronto), 1974.

Summer at Lonely Beach and Other Stories, Mosaic Press/
Valley Editions (Oakville, ON), 1982.
Apartment Seven: Essays Selected and New, Oxford University Press, 1989.
(Editor) *Canadian Jewish Short Stories,* Oxford University Press, 1990.

Also author of writings under pseudonym E. B. Merritt.

Writer of radio scripts on Chekhov and Poe. Contributor to *Borestone Mountain Best Poems in English,* 1963, 1966, and 1967, and to many other anthologies. Contributor of translations to anthologies.

Contributor of reviews, stories, and articles to magazines and newspapers, including *Canadian Literature, Tamarack Review, Queen's Quarterly, Canadian Forum,* and *Saturday Night.* Poetry editor, *Poetry Toronto,* 1981-82.

Waddington's work has been translated and published in the Soviet Union, Hungary, Japan, Romania, South America, and China; her poems have been broadcast in Canada, New Zealand, and Australia.

Some of the author's manuscripts and correspondence is housed at the Miriam Waddington Collection at the Public Archives, Ottawa.

ADAPTATIONS: Waddington's poems have been incorporated into a number of works and exhibitions of Canadian artists Helen Duffy, Jo Manning, Tobie Steinhouse, and Sarah Jackson, and about a dozen of her songs have been set to music by various Canadian and American composers.

SIDELIGHTS: Called "one of our durable contemporary forbearers of words," by Phil Hall in *Books in Canada,* Miriam Waddington has published many volumes of poetry, essays and stories. "In all her poems," writes Hilda L. Thomas in *Canadian Literature,* "Waddington strives for a transparency of language, for directness and simplicity in expression."

For many years Waddington was a social services caseworker while publishing poetry in a variety of Canadian magazines. From the beginning her work has been marked by a rejection of the tenets of modernism. The title of her first book, *Green World,* was "deliberately chosen to declare her rejection of the wasteland, the fragmentation, and the grayness in modern poetry," as Laurie Ricou states in the *Dictionary of Literary Biography.* Waddington's poetry is also marked by "careful structure, use of repetition, and sustained metaphor," Ricou explains. At their best, Thomas writes, her poems are "fierce, biblical, uncompromising" and "cry out against injustice, against the hypocrisy and destructiveness of power."

In her collection *Apartment Seven: Essays Selected and New* Waddington examines the nature of poetry as a special form of language. Writing in *Canadian Literature,* Marya Fiamengo explains that "poetry is for Waddington the supreme synthesis, an amalgam of all the resources of language." In this collection she also presents her "preoccupations as a woman writer," Fiamengo writes, including her strong sense of herself as a feminist and a Jew.

Ricou finds that Waddington has "for forty years . . . written intense and subtle lyrics, the equal, certainly, of the much better known poetry of Dorothy Livesay." Dennis Cooley, writing in *Books in Canada,* declares himself to be "one of those who thinks Miriam Waddington has been wrongly overlooked as a poet." Thomas believes that it is time "for a reassessment of Waddington's substantial contribution to Canadian literature—her stories, her critical studies, and her thirteen volumes of poetry."

Waddington once told *CA:* "I began writing poetry when I was ten and never really stopped. I don't know or care what motivates me—maybe it's belief in life itself. To me writing is one aspect of living and being human, of being connected to others. After a lifetime of writing the process is still a mystery to me. I suppose I hope to express the feeling of living in my time and place—not just my own life but in the lives of other people who seem ordinary but never are. It makes me feel less lonesome in the world to believe that I'm part of a huge company of writers—living and dead—who express the continuity of human feeling, making, and learning in a world that is exhausted and violated, but nevertheless inexhaustible.

"The contemporary scene? It is so terrible that it's wonderful that so many authentic writers are still able and willing to write. [George] Gissing's *New Grub Street* was prophetic re the commodification of art and artists in our society. There are too many cookbooks. They tell us how to make and package everything—politics, art, sex, and personality. There is so much individualism in North American art that individuality is (paradoxically) lost. But there are always some authentic artists everywhere at every time, and their work is a refuge, a shelter, and a source of renewal."

BIOGRAPHICAL/CRITICAL SOURCES:

BOOKS

Contemporary Literary Criticism, Volume 28, Gale, 1984.
Dictionary of Literary Biography, Volume 68: *Canadian Writers, 1920-1959,* Gale, 1988.
Heath, Jeffrey M., editor, *Profiles in Canadian Literature 4,* Dundurn Press (Toronto), 1982.
Lecker, Robert and Jack David, editors, *The Annotated Bibliography of Canada's Major Authors,* Volume 6, ECW Press (Downsview, ON), 1985, pp. 237-388.

Lecker, David and Ellen Quigley, editors, *Canadian Writers and Their Works Poetry Series,* Volume 5, ECW Press, 1985, pp. 277-329.

Pearce, John, *Twelve Voices,* Borealis Press, 1980.

PERIODICALS

Books in Canada, May, 1982; May, 1990, pp. 32-33; November, 1990, p. 29; November, 1992, p. 54.

Canadian Forum, May, 1977.

Canadian Literature, spring, 1973; winter, 1991, p. 187; summer, 1994, pp. 166-68.

Canadian Materials, January, 1991, pp. 40-41; October, 1992, p. 280.

Dalhousie Review, summer, 1959, pp. 237-42; winter, 1989, p. 596.

Essays on Canadian Writing, fall, 1978, pp. 144-61.

Maclean's, March, 1974.

Matrix Magazine, spring, 1991, pp. 74-76.

Poetry, February, 1968.

Queen's Quarterly, summer, 1987, p. 474.

*   *   *

WAH, Fred(erick James)   1939-

PERSONAL: Born January 23, 1939, in Swift Current, Saskatchewan, Canada; son of Frederick Clarence and Corrine Marie (Erickson) Wah; married Pauline Butling; children: Jenefer Ann, Erika Robin. *Education:* University of British Columbia, B.A., 1963; attended University of New Mexico; State University of New York at Buffalo, M.A., 1967.

CAREER: Selkirk College, Castlegar, British Columbia, Canada, teacher of creative and applied writing, humanities courses, and computer technology as it applies to writing and publication, 1967-78 and 1984-88; David Thompson University Centre, Nelson, British Columbia, coordinator and instructor in writing program, 1978-84; writer. Writer in residence at Theatre Energy, 1978, Mount Royal College, Calgary, 1979, University of Manitoba, 1982-83, Bemidji State University, 1983, and University of Alberta, 1988-89.

MEMBER: Institute of Further Studies, Writers' Union of Canada.

AWARDS, HONOURS: Macmillan Prize for Poetry, University of British Columbia, 1963; Canada Council Senior Arts Award, 1982-83; Canada Council Governor General's Literary Award for Poetry, 1985, for *Waiting for Saskatchewan.*

WRITINGS:

POEMS, EXCEPT AS NOTED

Lardeau, Island, 1965.

Mountain, Audit Press, 1967.

Among, Coach House Press, 1972.

Tree, Vancouver Community Press, 1972.

(With others) *Pictures and Words,* Cotinneh Books, 1973.

Collection of Poetry and Photographs, Cotinneh Books, 1973.

Earth, Institute of Further Studies, 1974.

Pictograms from the Interior of British Columbia, Talonbooks, 1975.

Selected Poems: Loki Is Buried at Smoky Creek, edited with an introduction by George Bowering, Talonbooks, 1980.

(Editor and author of introduction) Daphne Marlatt, *Selected Writing: Net Work,* Talonbooks, 1980.

Breathin' My Name with a Sigh, Talonbooks, 1981.

Owner's Manual, Island Writing Series, 1981.

Grasp the Sparrow's Tail: A Poetic Diary, Kyoto, 1982.

Waiting for Saskatchewan, Turnstone, 1985.

The SwiftCurrent Anthology, Coach House Press, 1986.

Rooftops, Blackberry Books, 1987.

Music at the Heart of Thinking, Red Deer College Press, 1987.

Limestone Lakes: Utaniki, designed by Peter Bartl, Red Deer College Press, 1989.

So Far, Small Press, 1991.

Alley Alley Home Free, Red Deer College Press, 1993.

Also author of *Seasons Greetings from the Diamond Grill.* Contributor to anthologies, including *New Wave Canada,* Contact Press, 1966; *Place . . . Anyplace and Get Lost,* Cotinneh Books, 1973; *Western Windows,* Comcept Press, 1977; *End Uv th World Speshul,* blewointmentpress, 1977; *New: West Coast,* Intermedia Books, 1977; *To Say the Least,* Press Porcepic, 1979; *The New Oxford Book of Canadian Verse,* Oxford, 1982; *The Contemporary Canadian Poem Anthology,* Coach House Press, 1983; *British Columbia: A Celebration,* Hurtig, 1983; *Vancouver Poetry,* Polestar Books, 1986; *A Mazing Space: Writing Canadian Women Writing,* edited by Smaro Kamboureli and Shirley Neuman, Longspoon, 1987; *Essays on Saskatchewan Writing,* edited by E. F. Dyck, Saskatchewan Writers Guild, 1987. Contributor to journals, including *Open Letter, Magazine of Further Studies,* and *Essays on Canadian Writing.*

Founding associate editor, *Tish,* 1961-63; editor, *Sum,* 1963-66; assistant editor, *Niagara Frontier Review,* 1965-66; associate editor, *Magazine of Further Studies,* 1966-70; editor, *Scree,* 1972-74; founding and contributing associate editor, *Open Letter,* 1970—; coeditor, *SwiftCurrent,* 1985—.

SIDELIGHTS: Although critics frequently use the word "difficult" when describing Fred Wah's poetry, many have praised his award-winning poems as well worth the challenge. Known for eschewing traditional sentence structure, objective or rational discourse, and conventional poetic form, the poet admitted in his 1987 book *Music at the Heart of Thinking* that he is "wary of any attempt to make [his poetry] easy." Wah, heavily influenced by the Black Mountain poets, a group of avant-garde poets affiliated with Black Mountain College in North Carolina, is experimental with the language, content, and particularly the form of his writings, believing that the form of a poem should be dictated by its content. Although his experiments include mixing poetry and prose, reviewers note that his keen ear for rhythms and sounds prevails throughout his work. A number of diverse influences combine in Wah's poems to augment the distinctive and challenging voice for which this Canadian poet has become known. Among these influences are a dual Chinese and European heritage, training as a jazz musician, and a background in linguistics.

In the tradition of the Black Mountain school, Wah grounds his poetry in a highly developed sense of place, but his poetry does not so much describe the physical qualities of his surroundings as it conveys the experience he, as poet, is having in a particular place. "Wah's reader is always aware of his local geographies," Laurie Ricou wrote in the *Dictionary of Literary Biography*, "but aware of them as they are perceived in the mind of the observer, *as he thinks* them, in language, and as the language shapes his thinking." Wah commented in the afterword to his *Selected Poems: Loki Is Buried at Smoky Creek:* "Writing has a lot to do with 'place,' the spiritual and spatial localities of the writer. . . . All of it, out there, is measured from in here. In the particularity of *a* place the writer finds revealed the correspondences of a whole world." Several reviewers have noted the skillful way that Wah's focus on specific locales leads to universal and political themes.

Wah was born in 1939 in Swift Current, Saskatchewan. His father, Frederick Clarence Wah, who was born in Alberta, Canada, to a Chinese-American father and an English mother, was sent at the age of four to China, where he lived until young adulthood. Wah's memory of his father, chronicled in *Waiting for Saskatchewan,* is of a man who suffered pain and anger because he did not feel accepted in either Chinese or Anglo societies in Canada. The elder Wah married a Swedish woman named Corrine Erickson. Four years after their son Fred was born, the family moved to British Columbia, where they lived in the small industrial cities of Trail and Nelson. After high school, the younger Wah went to the University of British Columbia. There he helped found and edit the poetry newsletter, *Tish,* which would serve as Canada's major introduction to the Black Mountain poets. After receiving his bachelor of arts in music and English, Wah studied at the University of New Mexico, where he met the Black Mountain poet Robert Creeley and became an editor of

Sum magazine. He went on to pursue his master's degree at the State University of New York in Buffalo with Creeley and Charles Olson, a principal founder of the Black Mountain school. Wah continued editing several small literary magazines during his graduate studies. In 1967 he began teaching linguistics, humanities, and writing courses at Selkirk College in Castlegar, British Columbia.

Wah's first book of selected poems, *Lardeau,* was published in 1965. These early poems demonstrate the poet's focus on locale—in this case Lardeau, an area in the Kootenay Mountains of British Columbia. Ricou described Wah's approach in this selection as "a crowd of perceptions . . . mediated through the poet's complex personal contact with his world and yet evoking the singular moment of his perceiving." Wah continued to focus on his own—and his readers'—connection to locale and the natural world in his chapbooks, *Mountain, Tree, Among,* and *Earth.* These early works did not reach a large audience, largely, perhaps, because of their difficulty. In his review in *Books in Canada,* Marc Cote summarized: "Immediacy of perception is the most striking aspect of Fred Wah's poetry. This makes, however, for a challenging read. But if one understands the dismissal of standard grammar (replaced by a rhythmical, musical one) and if one reads this poetry more slowly and thoroughly than usual, there are plenty of rewards."

In 1975 Wah published a very different form of poetry in his *Pictograms from the Interior of British Columbia.* The book is, in effect, a reaction to John Corner's 1968 book, *Pictographs in the Interior of British Columbia,* a collection of Indian rock paintings. Wah printed reproductions of the rock paintings with his poetic responses to them, juxtaposing visual and verbal images that compel the reader to work out his or her own meaning from the whole.

Wah published his poem *Breathin' My Name with a Sigh* in 1981, following it the next year with *Grasp the Sparrow's Tail.* Parts of both of these long poems became components of his award-winning book, the four-part *Waiting for Saskatchewan.* In Cote's words, "*Waiting for Saskatchewan* is a search. The poet is searching for himself, his dead father, himself in his dead father, and his dead father in himself. Through this search, Wah creates himself. He becomes the sum of his past and present, his lineage and language." Many reviewers noted the powerful intimacy of the poet's present tense addresses to his father in the first two sections of the poem: "About a year after you died I saw you. You were alone in a car and passed me going the other way. You didn't look at me. Over the past 15 years this has happened maybe once or twice a year. I'll catch a glimpse of you on a street corner, disappearing through a doorway, or gesturing to someone in the booth of a Chinese cafe. What always gives you away is your haircut, your walk or the flash in your eyes. In China your appearances were overwhelming."

Waiting for Saskatchewan is personal and yet supersedes an individual sense of time and place. *Briarpatch* contributor Jean Hillabold noted that river images in the poem represent "time strata and the flow of blood and history." Commenting on one description of a river, the critic remarked that "Wah's river seems to have a distinct ability to flow though several continents and several time-frames at once." The story of the relationship between Wah and his father has universal and historical significance as well. Norbert Ruebsaat commented in *Event* that the poem "brings forward the (usually hidden, usually silent) dialogue between fathers and sons which is the (often unacknowledged) basis of discourse in patriarchies. . . . It mixes 'private' and 'public' utterance, political statement and personal sentiment in ways that are unexpected and hard to control." *Waiting for Saskatchewan* also explores the separateness of the individual in—and in contrast to—the rest of the world, examining at the same time the activity of writing about these things. Judith Fitzgerald summarized in her *Cross-Canada Writers' Quarterly* review: "Not only does Wah embark on a voyage aimed at fixing 'the story' of himself in relation to all not himself . . . he also explores the shape and sound of writing on and beyond the page."

Although *Waiting for Saskatchewan* takes the form of a journal, each of its four parts differs in structure, particularly in the intermingling of prose and poetry. Because it is entirely in verse, *Breathin' My Name with a Sigh* is the most conventional of the four parts. *Grasp the Sparrow's Tail,* a travel journal written when Wah and his wife went to China in 1982, is written in prose and verse. Ruebsaat describes this second section as a series of "beautiful juxtapositions of the 'poetic' and 'prosaic.' Each 'diary' entry is followed by a poetic treatment or working of the material (memory and landscape) to give it music." The third section, *Elite,* in which Wah relates childhood memories of his father and family in his birth place of Swift Current, Saskatchewan, is comprised of prose poems. In the last section of the book, *This Dendrite Map: Father/Mother Haibun,* Wah analyzes present time and his own life. The section is in the form of twenty-one short prose pieces which are, according to Gladys Hindmarch in *Brick: A Journal of Reviews,* "informed by a haiku sensibility and concluded with informal haiku lines."

Waiting for Saskatchewan met with an enthusiastic reception from critics. Hindmarch called it "one of the best books a Canadian has ever written." Ruebsaat, who was concerned at the start of the poem that Wah was "poeticizing" too much, raved that, reading on in the poem, "I realized the form-subject matter tension here worked perfectly." The critic added, "This is a terrific book." Several reviewers remarked that *Waiting for Saskatchewan* is one of Wah's most accessible works, probably because of its theme of searching for his father and heritage. When Wah won the Governor General's Literary Award for *Waiting for Saskatchewan,* he reported that he was happy to receive recognition for his writing after many years of publishing, but indicated that popular acclaim is not what he seeks with his poetry. "I've never considered myself a very popular writer," he is quoted as saying in *Contemporary Literary Criticism.* "I've always considered myself more of an experimental writer. I like to play around and try different forms. But this book is probably more accessible because it has more narrative, and maybe because I'm getting better."

Wah acknowledges that his 1987 book, *Music at the Heart of Thinking,* was not designed to be read easily. The book is a collection of sixty-nine "theoms"—theoretical prose poems about language—in which Wah develops "a critical poetic that sees language as the true practice of thought," according to Margery Fee in *Canadian Literature.* In this "true practice of thought" Wah rejects objectivity and rationality as false notions that separate thought from the rest of the world. Fee explained that Wah sees "language as material, irrevocably in the world, tangled in a web of etymological, intertextual, and social connections, touched by all the forces that move people, including their hates, their loves, their delusions." *Books in Canada* contributor Phil Hall, who compares reading the theoms to fishing with one's body totally submerged in the water, remarked that "the spill of intent is the guide, not the reasoning faculty." The reviewer added that the book "pleases me—as a puzzle guide. Its difficulty is alluring."

BIOGRAPHICAL/CRITICAL SOURCES:

BOOKS

Contemporary Literary Criticism, Volume 44, Gale, 1987, pp. 323-28.
Dictionary of Literary Biography, Volume 60: *Canadian Writers since 1960, Second Series,* Gale, 1987, pp. 369-73.
Wah, Fred, *Music at the Heart of Thinking,* Red Deer College Press, 1987.
Wah, Fred, *Selected Poems: Loki Is Buried at Smoky Creek,* Talonbooks, 1980.
Wah, Fred, *Waiting for Saskatchewan,* Turnstone, 1985.

PERIODICALS

Books in Canada, August-September, 1986, pp. 26-27; November, 1988, pp. 31-32.
Briarpatch, July-August, 1986, p. 28.
Brick: A Journal of Reviews, spring, 1986, pp. 10-12.
Canadian Literature, autumn, 1990, pp. 132-33.

Cross-Canada Writers' Quarterly, Vol. 8, nos. 3 and 4, 1986, pp. 39-40.

Event, summer, 1986, pp. 139-42.

Globe and Mail (Toronto), June 21, 1986.*

—*Sketch by Sonia Benson*

*   *   *

WALKER, George F. 1947-

PERSONAL: Born August 23, 1947, in Toronto, Ontario, Canada; son of Malcolm (a laborer) and Florence (Braybrook) Walker; married c. 1965 (marriage ended); married Susan Purdy (an actor); children: Renata, Courtney.

ADDRESSES: Agent—Great North Artists Management, Inc., 350 Dupont St., Toronto, Ontario M5V 1R5, Canada.

CAREER: Playwright. Factory Theatre Lab, Toronto, Ontario, Canada, dramaturge, 1972-73, resident playwright, 1972-76. Has directed productions of his own work, including *Ramona and the White Slaves,* 1976, and *Rumours of Our Death,* 1980.

AWARDS, HONOURS: Awarded five grants from Canada Council; Chalmers Award for Distinguished Playwriting nominations, 1977, for *Zastrozzi: The Master of Discipline,* and 1981, for *Theatre of the Film Noir;* Dora Award for directing, 1982, for *Rumours of Our Death;* Chalmers Award for Distinguished Playwrighting, 1985, and Governor General's Literary Award for drama, Canada Council, for *Criminals in Love.*

WRITINGS:

PLAYS

Prince of Naples (produced in Toronto, Ontario, Canada, at Factory Theatre Lab, 1971; produced as a radio play by Canadian Broadcasting Corp. [CBC-Radio], 1973), Playwrights Canada (Toronto), 1973.

Ambush at Tether's End (produced at Factory Theatre Lab, 1971; produced as a radio play by CBC-Radio, 1974), Playwrights Canada, 1974.

Sacktown Rag (produced at Factory Theatre Lab, 1972), Playwrights Canada, 1972.

Bagdad Saloon (produced in London, England, at Bush Theatre, 1973, later produced at Factory Theatre Lab, 1973), Playwrights Canada, 1973.

Demerit, produced at Factory Theatre Lab, 1974.

(And director) *Beyond Mozambique* (produced at Factory Theatre Lab, 1974), Playwrights Co-op, 1975.

(And director) *Ramona and the White Slaves,* produced at Factory Theatre Lab, 1976.

Gossip, produced in Toronto at Toronto Free Theatre, 1977.

Zastrozzi: The Master of Discipline (also known as *Zastrozzi: The Master of Discipline: A Melodrama;* produced at Toronto Free Theatre, 1977; later produced in New York at New York Shakespeare Festival, 1981), Playwrights Canada, 1977, second edition, 1991.

Three Plays by George F. Walker (contains *Bagdad Saloon, Beyond Mozambique,* and *Ramona and the White Slaves*), Coach House Press (Toronto), 1978.

Filthy Rich (produced at Toronto Free Theatre, 1979; later produced in New York City at 47th Street Theatre, 1985), Playwrights Canada, 1979.

(And director) *Rumours of Our Death,* produced at Factory Theatre Lab, 1980.

(And director) *Theatre of the Film Noir,* produced by Factory Theatre Lab at Adelaide Court Theatre, 1981.

Science and Madness, produced in Toronto at Tarragon Theatre, 1982.

(And director) *The Art of War* (also known as *The Art of War: An Adventure;* produced by Factory Theatre Lab at Toronto Workshop Productions, 1983), Playwrights Canada, 1982.

Criminals in Love (also known as *George F. Walker's Criminals in Love;* produced at Factory Theatre [formerly Factory Theatre Lab], 1984), Playwrights Canada, 1984.

The Power Plays (contains *Gossip, Filthy Rich,* and *The Art of War*), Coach House Press, 1984.

Better Living, produced in Toronto at CentreStage, 1986.

Beautiful City, produced at Factory Theatre, c. 1987.

Nothing Sacred: Based on "Fathers and Sons" by Ivan Turgenev, Coach House Press, 1988.

Love and Anger, Coach House Press (Ontario), 1990.

Escape from Happiness, InBook, 1992.

Also author of *The East End Plays,* 1988. Works represented in anthologies, including *Now in Paperback: Canadian Playwrights of the 1970s,* edited by Connie Brissenden, Fineglow Plays (Toronto), 1973, and *The Factory Lab Anthology,* edited by Brissenden, Talonbooks (Vancouver), 1974. Contributor to periodicals, including *Descant.*

FOR TELEVISION

Microdrama, Canadian Broadcasting Corp. (CBC-TV), 1976.

Strike, CBC-TV, 1976.

Sam, Grace, Doug, and the Dog, CBC-TV, 1976.

Overlap, CBC-TV, 1977.

Capital Punishment, CBC-TV, 1977.

FOR RADIO

The Private Man, CBC, 1973.

Quiet Days in Limbo, CBC, 1977.

Desert's Revenge, CBC, 1984.

SIDELIGHTS: George F. Walker is a prominent Canadian playwright whose works are characterized by their emphasis on dark comedy and Walker's satirical, contemporary style, which is influenced by popular culture. His long affiliation with the Factory Theatre (formerly the Factory Theatre Lab), which features innovative productions, has brought many of his acclaimed works to the stage, including *Rumours of Our Death, Theatre of the Film Noir,* and *The Art of War.*

Walker's popular 1984 play *Criminals in Love* was awarded the prestigious Governor General's Literary Award; it follows the lives of two young lovers, Junior Dawson, a shipping clerk, and Gail. Junior and Gail are troubled by a cast of characters, mostly Junior's father, a jailed crook whose criminal habits are eventually forced on Junior and Gail by Junior's Aunt Winerva. Walker, according to *Books in Canada* contributor Richard Plant, described the play as one in which "two kids in love have a dilemma, which becomes a crime, then a revolution." In *Canadian Theatre Review,* Paul Walsh wrote that *Criminals in Love* "speaks with an authenticity that renders even the zaniest improbabilities and cliches acutely real. . . . As we try to make sense of a process that constantly eludes us, we want to believe that things will work out for [Walker's characters] because we have come to care for them." James Harrison, writing in *Theatrum,* noted that "George Walker deserves the recognition [*Criminals in Love* has brought him]. His sharp perceptions, his knowledge of dramatic structuring, and his willingness to tackle intelligent themes indicate his voice will continue to be an exciting one in Canadian literature."

BIOGRAPHICAL/CRITICAL SOURCES:

BOOKS

Wallace, Robert, and Cynthia Zimmerman, *The Work: Conversations with English-Canadian Playwrights,* Coach House Press, 1982, pp. 212-25.

PERIODICALS

Books in Canada, April, 1980, p. 5; April, 1982, p. 10; April, 1985, pp. 11-14; April, 1986, pp. 16-18; March, 1989, p. 28; November, 1992, p. 34.
Canadian Drama/L'Art Dramatique Canadien, Volume 10, number 2, 1984, pp. 195-206; Volume 11, number 1, 1985, pp. 141-49 and 221-25.
Canadian Forum, August/September, 1986, pp. 6-11.
Canadian Literature, summer, 1980, pp. 87-103; winter, 1990, pp. 118, 164.
Canadian Theatre Review, winter, 1985, pp. 144-45.
Globe and Mail (Toronto), November 8, 1984, p. E5.
Los Angeles Times, June 14, 1985.
Performing Arts in Canada, fall, 1981, pp. 43-46.
Scene Changes, October, 1975.

Theatrum, April, 1985, pp. 11-14.
Times (London), July 1, 1983.
University of Toronto Quarterly, summer, 1975; fall, 1986, pp. 65-66.
Variety, December 12, 1984, p. 130.
Village Voice, April 2, 1979.*

                    *   *   *

WARWICK, Jarvis
   See GARNER, Hugh

                    *   *   *

WATSON, Sheila   1909-

PERSONAL: Original name, Sheila Martin Doherty; born October 24, 1909, in New Westminster, British Columbia, Canada; daughter of Charles Edward (a doctor and superintendent of the Provincial Mental Hospital) and Elweena (Martin) Doherty; married Wilfred Watson (a poet and playwright), December 25, 1940. *Education:* Attended primary and secondary school at the convent of the Sisters of St. Anne; Attended two years of university at the Convent of the Sacred Heart; University of British Columbia, honors degree in English, 1931, teaching certificate, 1932, M.A., 1933; University of Toronto, Ph.D., 1965. *Religion:* When asked in a 1992 interview if she still embraced the Catholic faith Watson replied, "Like Pascal, groaning."

ADDRESSES: Home—3612 Place Road, Nanaimo, British Columbia V9T 1M8, Canada.

CAREER: St. Louis College, New Westminster, British Columbia, Canada, schools in Dog Creek, Langley Prairie, Duncan, and Mission City, teacher, 1934 until the end of World War II; Moulton College, Toronto, teacher, 1946-48; University of British Columbia, Lecturer, 1948-50; High School in Powell River, British Columbia, 1950-51; University of Alberta, professor, 1961-75; White Pelican, coeditor, 1971-78.

AWARDS, HONOURS: Beta Sigma Phi Canadian Book Award, 1960, for *The Double Hook*; Lorne Pierce Medal, 1984.

WRITINGS:

The Double Hook (novel), McClelland and Stewart, 1959.
Four Stories (short stories), Coach House Press, 1979; republished in *Five Stories,* Coach House Press, 1984.
And the Four Animals (short story), Coach House Press Manuscript Editions, 1980; republished in *Five Stories,* Coach House Press, 1984.
(Editor) *The Collected Poems of Miriam Mandel,* Longspoon/NeWest, 1984.

Five Stories (contains *Four Stories* and *And the Four Animals*), Coach House Press, 1984.

Deep Hollow Creek (novel), McClelland and Stewart, 1992.

SIDELIGHTS: Sheila Watson is best known for her novel *The Double Hook* (1959). Although Watson is not a prolific writer, she has secured a place in the history of Canadian fiction with what many consider the first truly modern Canadian novel.

Watson was born on October 24, 1909, in New Westminster, British Columbia, Canada, to Charles Edward and Elweena (Martin) Doherty. Her father was a doctor and the superintendent of the Provincial Mental Hospital in New Westminster, and the family lived on the grounds of the hospital. Watson received a convent education through primary and secondary school and two years at university. She then went on to the University of British Columbia where she received an honors degree in English in 1931. In 1932 she became a certified teacher, and in 1933 she obtained her M.A. degree, also from the University of British Columbia. Watson then taught in various schools throughout British Columbia, including New Westminster, Dog Creek, Langley Prairie, Duncan, and Mission City. She later used her teaching experiences at Dog Creek in her novels *Deep Creek Hollow* (1992) and *The Double Hook*. In December of 1941 Watson married the poet and playwright Wilfred Watson. After World War II the couple moved to Toronto where Watson taught at Moulton College and began studying part time at the University of Toronto. She also held short-term positions at the University of British Columbia and at a high school in Powell River, British Columbia. From 1951 to 1953 Watson took a break from teaching to complete *The Double Hook*. Shortly after this she published several of her short stories in magazines. In 1957 Watson began her doctoral studies at the University of Toronto where she received her Ph.D. in 1965 after completing a dissertation on Wyndham Lewis. She began teaching at the University of Alberta in 1961 where she continued until her retirement as a full professor in 1975. Since her retirement from teaching, she has published collections of short stories and a novel *Deep Hollow Creek*.

Although *The Double Hook* was published well before *Deep Hollow Creek*, the latter was actually written first. In *Deep Hollow Creek* Watson used a narrator which she abandoned in later writing. Focused on communities that have lost their sense of ritual, the two novels deal with similar themes and draw on Watson's teaching experiences in Dog Creek. Stella is the protagonist and the focus of *Deep Hollow Creek*, while the community is at the center of *The Double Hook*. A search for redemption is a theme common to both, as well as extensive use of allusion and mythology. Although both works are set in the Cari-

boo area of Canada, critics contend that Watson's universal themes extend the novels beyond their regional setting. The characters in both stories are trying to find hope in the midst of their despair. In *The Double Hook,* for example, James Potter attempts to escape his community to free himself, but learns that redemption is to be found in the community itself. *The Double Hook* also addresses the paradox of the human condition that in order for there to be redemption there must be sacrifice, for rebirth there must be death. Watson's short stories incorporate similar imagery and mythology as her novels and focus on a struggle for spirituality.

Most critics agree on Watson's important place in Canadian literature. *The Double Hook,* praised as the first example of Canadian modernism, is considered essential in the study of Canadian literature by scholars and young writers alike. Critics have also lauded the novel's poetic language. *Deep Hollow Creek* was well-received, although critics have lamented that it suffers the flaws common to first novels.

BIOGRAPHICAL/CRITICAL SOURCES:

BOOKS

Bessai, Diane, and David Jackel, editors, *Figures in a Ground: Canadian Essays in Modern Literature Collected in Honor of Sheila Watson,* Western Producer Prairie Books, 1978.

Bowering, Angela, *Figures Cut in Sacred Ground: Illuminati in "The Double Hook,"* NeWest Press, 1989.

Bowering, George, editor, *Sheila Watson and The Double Hook: A Book of Essays,* Golden Dog Press, 1985.

Bowering, George, *The Mask in Place: Essays on Fiction in North America,* Turnstone, 1982, pp. 97-111.

David, Jack, Robert Lecker, and Ellen Quigley, editors, *Canadian Writers and Their Works,* ECW, 1985, pp. 257-312.

Heath, Jeffrey M., editor, *Profiles in Canadian Literature,* Dundurn, 1982, pp. 45-52.

PERIODICALS

Ariel, April, 1987, pp. 65-78.

Antigosh Review, fall, 1992, pp. 31-5.

Books in Canada, February, 1980, p. 8.

Canadian Literature, autumn, 1969, pp. 56-71; spring, 1972, pp. 70-76; autumn, 1984, pp. 7-16; autumn-winter, 1989, pp. 174-75.

Journal of Canadian Fiction, winter, 1973, pp. 63-9.

Studies in Canadian Literature, summer, 1978, pp. 149-65; summer, 1979, pp. 137-46.

WEBB, Phyllis 1927-

PERSONAL: Born April 8, 1927, in Victoria, British Columbia, Canada. *Education:* University of British Columbia, B.A., 1949; attended McGill University, 1953.

ADDRESSES: Home—R.R. 2, Mt. Baker Cr., C-9, Ganges, British Columbia, Canada V0S 1E0.

CAREER: Secretary in Montreal, Quebec, 1956; University of British Columbia, Vancouver, member of staff, 1961-64; Canadian Broadcasting Corporation (CBC), Toronto, Ontario, program organizer, 1964-67, executive producer, 1967-69; freelance writer and broadcaster. Guest lecturer, University of British Columbia, 1976-77. University of Victoria, sessional lecturer, 1977-78 and 1982-84, visiting assistant professor, 1978-79. Writer-in-residence, University of Alberta, 1980-81. Conductor of writing workshops at the Upper Canada Writers Workshop in Kingston, Ontario, and at the Banff Center.

MEMBER: League of Canadian Poets.

AWARDS, HONOURS: Overseas Award from Government of Canada, 1957; Canada Council grant, 1963, senior fellowship, 1969, Senior Canada Council Arts Award, 1981; Governor General's Award for poetry, 1983, for *The Vision Tree.*

WRITINGS:

POEMS

(With Gael Turnbull and Eli Mandel) *Trio,* Contact Press, 1954.
Even Your Right Eye, McClelland & Stewart, 1956.
The Sea Is Also a Garden: Poems, Ryerson Press, 1962.
Naked Poems, Periwinkle Press, 1965.
Selected Poems, 1954-1965, edited and introduced by John Hulcoop, Talonbooks, 1971.
Wilson's Bowl, Coach House Press, 1980.
Sunday Water: Thirteen Anti Ghazals, Island Writing Series, 1982.
The Vision Tree: Selected Poems, edited and introduced by Sharon Thesen, Talonbooks, 1982.
Water and Light: Ghazals and Anti Ghazals, Coach House Press, 1984.
Hanging Fire, Coach House Press, 1990.

Work represented in anthologies, including the *Oxford Book of Canadian Poets, Skookum Wawa,* and *A Garland for Dylan Thomas.*

ESSAYS

Talking, Quadrant Editions, 1982.

Contributor to periodicals, including *Maclean's.*

SIDELIGHTS: "I'm a pressure-cooker writer. I have to let the psychic pressure build up until it is almost unbearable," says Canadian poet Phyllis Webb in a *Books in Canada* interview. The interviewer, Eleanor Wachtel, explains, "[Webb] writes quickly, in bursts, after long silences." Webb's first creative surge carried into print *Trio, Even Your Right Eye, The Sea Is Also a Garden: Poems,* and *Naked Poems.* These poems for the most part were collected in *Selected Poems: 1954-1965* and published by Talonbooks as part of its Canadian poetry series. The next surge began with Webb's decision in 1969 to leave her position as executive producer of the Canadian Broadcasting Corporation's "Ideas" program to devote herself to poetry. Returning to Canada's west coast, Webb settled on Salt Spring Island and discovered the Indian petroglyphs that account for "some of the Indian themes that appear" in the poems, Webb told *CA.* Though she began to write *The Kropotkin Poems,* she "abandoned" that "study of power and anarchism," she related, "as my political commitment shifted away from anarchism to feminism."

The poems that resulted from this second period appeared in 1980 as *Wilson's Bowl.* In 1982, Talonbooks issued a second collection, *The Vision Tree: Selected Poems,* which received the Governor General's Award for poetry. This period also marked a change in critical opinion regarding Webb's importance. As critic John F. Hulcoop comments in the *Dictionary of Literary Biography,* "Before publication of *Wilson's Bowl,* Webb was seen as a major minor poet whose relatively small creative output was perfect in its way, but whose increasing need of self-isolation seemed to be silencing her poetic voice. Since 1980, however, a radical revision of opinion has occurred. She is acknowledged as what it has taken her thirty years to become: a major twentieth-century Canadian poet whose influence is both widespread and seminal."

Poems from *Even Your Right Eye* and *The Sea Is Also a Garden* drew applause for their precision and refinement, but reviewers found the sharpest economy of phrase in *Naked Poems,* which Webb referred to at a 1963 poetry reading as "bone-essential" statements. "This valuable collector's item," Hulcoop notes, is a "slim volume, containing forty-one poems, many of which consist of less than ten words (the last for example, is one word '*OH?*'—a characteristic Webb question), designed and printed by west coast painter Takao Tanabe." Keith Garebian points out in *Books in Canada* that by writing lean poems, Webb "tries to elude 'The Great Iambic Pentameter'"—the traditional rhythm of poetry in English—that she calls "the Hound of Heaven in our stress" in *The Sea Is Also a Garden.*

Garebian's survey of the early books also mentions "a growing pessimism" in the poems—the component that elicited negative responses from John Bentley Mays in *Open Letter* and Frank Davey in *From Here to There.* Robert Weaver explains in a *Saturday Night* article,

"Webb is an intensely, painfully personal writer," one who "causes very personal responses in her readers." Pain is frequently the subject of Webb's poems, which often raise "painful questions," writes Hulcoop. One such inquiry from "Lament" in *Trio* asks "what can love mean in such a world, / and what can we or any lovers hold in this immensity / of hate and broken things?" Gail Fox writes of the despair in such poems and others that treat resignation and suicide, but argues in *Canadian Forum* that detractors who find the poems "neurotic, or self-pitying" have missed the causes for despair catalogued in Webb's canon.

Webb told *CA* that more recent "feminist reinterpretations" of her poems "have led to a more balanced view of the work to date." For example, Sharon Thesen maintains in the introduction to *The Vision Tree* that Webb's "canonization as a sort of priestess of pain hasn't, I think, been warranted. Webb's candour—both in her poetry and in her prose—about the difficulties of her vulnerability, has invited some curious looks into her psyche, some decidedly more competent and respectful than others, but all seeking to explain the sense of loss, futility, and despair that her poems document. The error of such psychologizing, of course, is that it seeks to identify the origins of this sense of loss in terms of a personal grief, whereas more often than not it is anguish's human universality that is expressed." Hulcoop suggests that history and poetics are Webb's other concerns: "What begins to emerge in these poems is an arresting, because unique, combination of politics and lyric form: a tightly controlled but feeling expression of moods/ states of mind/emotions that have to do with rebellion against the political status quo, with socialist ideals, and, eventually, with anarchy."

In 1970, Webb set out to explore Piotr Alekseyevich Kropotkin's vision of anarchist utopia in long-lined pieces to be called *The Kropotkin Poems,* but she later set the project aside for a different frame of reference. Webb told *Books in Canada* interviewer Wachtel: "The Kropotkin utopia enchanted me for a while until I saw that [it] was yet another male-imaginative structure for a new society. It would probably *not* have changed male-female relations."

Webb's increasingly feminist perspective is reflected in *Wilson's Bowl* and subsequent works of the 1980s. The introduction to *Wilson's Bowl* and the prose pieces in *Talking* articulate Webb's perception of the political implications inherent in various poetic forms, particularly the long line, which she sees as a male-imaginative structure. The long line, she says in *Talking,* "comes from assurance (or hysteria), high tide, full moon, open mouth, big-mouthed Whitman, yawp, yawp & Ginsberg—howling. Male."

In *Sunday Water: Thirteen Anti Ghazals* and *Water and Light: Ghazals and Anti Ghazals* Webb employs a poetic form that she finds more conducive to feminine language. The ghazal is an ancient Persian love song usually written in five couplets that are loosely linked by associative leaps rather than by linear logic. Webb discovered the form in John Thompson's *Stilt Jack.* Seeing him adapt the form to his own purposes led her to also play a game of breaking some of the form's traditional rules. According to Hulcoop in *Canadian Literature,* Webb's anti ghazal maintains the intricate rhyme and syllabic schemes of the classical ghazal while it rejects the latter's romantic ideals. Hulcoop sees her adaptations as "an act of liberation: a liberation of self-as-woman from male socio-sexual, political, and poetic conventions. . . . Her autonomy as a woman poet, her growing need to disconnect from a male-dominated tradition, and her profound desire to be disobedient [in an otherwise conventional life] . . . all find expression in the ghazal."

Water and Light, published in 1984, is the last of five books that make up Webb's second "burst" of creativity. Though these works mark some important new directions for Webb, Hulcoop maintains that the books since 1980 further her progress along a path she began to explore in the books of her first efflorescence. The later books show the poet emerging from a protective isolation, symbolized by poems about imprisonment, "*Outwards* . . . into the public world where 'the great dreams pass on / to the common good,'" he writes in *Essays on Canadian Writing,* ending with lines from *Wilson's Bowl.* An awareness of the mythic significance of things in the physical world expressed in spiritual symbols also persists. Wachtel relates that "Christian mysticism and Buddhism provided metaphors for poetic expression" in the early books because "Webb sees parallels between the poetic search and a religious search." Garebian demonstrates how this "iconography" appears in the later books. "Webb envisions a tree akin to the Tree of Life or the shaman's magic sky-ladder" rooted near "Wilson's Bowl, the ancient petroglyph bowl carved into the shoreline rock" of Salt Spring Island, he says. Both represent a link between heaven and earth, and are "eternal centres from which the poet [speaks]."

Webb feels there may be more to discover, and perhaps another "silence," beyond the writing of anti ghazals. She senses the approach of "hard times" that may compel her "to go deeper." Speaking to Wachtel, Webb said, "I think [the ghazals are] a transitional thing for me. A little bit superficial, perhaps. Before I go into the cave again for the big spiritual stuff." But in any case, as Hulcoop maintains in *Essays in Canadian Literature,* "Webb's work stands out like an object in a landscape, a guide to all adventuring critics whose job it is to fathom the depths . . . and explore the farthest reaches of Canadian poetry—a guide also to younger poets whose vocation it is to acknowledge and overcome their great precursors."

BIOGRAPHICAL/CRITICAL SOURCES:

BOOKS

Contemporary Literary Criticism, Volume XVIII, Gale, 1981.

Davey, Frank, and others, *From There to Here: A Guide to English-Canadian Literature since 1960,* Press Porcepic, 1974.

Dictionary of Literary Biography, Volume 53: *Canadian Writers since 1960, First Series,* Gale, 1986.

Lecker, Robert and Jack David, editors, *The Annotated Bibliography of Canada's Major Authors,* Volume VI, ECW, 1985.

Neuman, Shirley and Smaro Kamboureli, editors, *A Mazing Space: Writing Canadian Women Writing,* Longspoon/ Newest, 1986.

Webb, Phyllis, Gael Turnbull, and Eli Mandel, *Trio,* Contact Press, 1954.

Webb, *The Sea Is Also a Garden: Poems,* Ryerson Press, 1962.

Webb, *Selected Poems, 1954-1965,* edited and introduced by John Hulcoop, Talonbooks, 1971.

Webb, *Wilson's Bowl,* Coach House Press, 1980.

Webb, *The Vision Tree: Selected Poems,* edited and introduced by Sharon Thesen, Talonbooks, 1982.

Webb, *Talking,* Quadrant Editions, 1982.

Webb, *Sunday Water: Thirteen Anti Ghazals,* Coach House Press, 1984.

PERIODICALS

Books in Canada, May, 1981; June, 1981; November, 1982; November, 1983; January/February, 1991.

British Columbia Library Quarterly, October-January, 1972-1973.

Canadian Forum, May, 1972; August, 1981.

Canadian Literature, summer, 1961; spring, 1967; spring, 1972; summer, 1986.

Essays on Canadian Writing, summer, 1983; number 30, 1984-1985.

Line, spring, 1984.

Malean's, March 30, 1981.

Open Letter, 1973.

Saturday Night, November, 1971.

Victoria's Monday Magazine, April 15, 1983.

—Sketch by Marilyn K. Basel

WIEBE, Rudy (Henry) 1934-

PERSONAL: Born October 4, 1934, in Fairholme, Saskatchewan, Canada; son of Abram J. (a farmer) and Tena (Knelsen) Wiebe; married Tena F. Isaak, March, 1958; children: Adrienne, Michael, Christopher. *Education:* University of Alberta, B.A., 1956, M.A., 1960; Mennonite Brethren Bible College, B.Th., 1961; additional study at University of Tuebingen, 1957-58; University of Manitoba, 1961, and University of Iowa, 1964. *Religion:* Mennonite. *Avocational interests:* Photography, watching people, travel.

ADDRESSES: Home—5315 143rd St., Edmonton, Alberta, Canada.*Office*—Department of English, University of Alberta, Edmonton, Alberta, Canada T6G 2E5.

CAREER: Glenbow Foundation, Calgary, Alberta, research writer, 1956; Government of Canada, Ottawa, Ontario, foreign service officer, 1960; high school English teacher, Selkirk, Manitoba, 1961; *Mennonite Brethren Herald,* Winnipeg, Manitoba, editor, 1962-63; Goshen College, Goshen, IN, assistant professor of English, 1963-67; University of Alberta, Edmonton, assistant professor, 1967-70, associate professor, 1970-76, then professor of English, 1976—; University of Kiel, Germany, chair of Canadian studies, 1984.

MEMBER: Writers Union of Canada (president, 1985-86), Writers Guild of Alberta (founding president, 1980-81).

AWARDS, HONOURS: Rotary International fellow, 1957-58; Canada council bursary, 1964; senior arts award, 1972; Governor General's Award for Fiction, 1973, for *The Temptations of Big Bear;* honorary D.Litt., University of Winnipeg, 1986; Lorne Pierce Medal, Royal Society of Canada, 1987.

WRITINGS:

NOVELS

Peace Shall Destroy Many, McClelland & Stewart, 1962, Eerdmans, 1964.

First and Vital Candle, Eerdmans, 1966.

The Blue Mountains of China, Eerdmans, 1970.

The Temptations of Big Bear, McClelland & Stewart, 1973.

Riel and Gabriel, McClelland & Stewart, 1973.

The Scorched-Wood People, McClelland & Stewart, 1977.

The Mad Trapper, McClelland & Stewart, 1980.

My Lovely Enemy, McClelland & Stewart, 1983.

SHORT STORIES

Where is the Voice Coming From?, McClelland & Stewart, 1974.

Alberta: A Celebration, photographs by Harry Savage, edited by Tom Radford, Hurtig, 1979.

The Angel of the Tar Sands, and Other Stories, McClelland & Stewart, 1982.

EDITOR

The Story Makers: A Selection of Modern Short Stories, Macmillan, 1970.

Stories from Western Canada, Macmillan (Canada), 1972.

(With Andreas Schroeder) *Stories from Pacific and Arctic Canada,* Macmillan (Canada), 1974.

Double Vision, McClelland & Stewart, 1976.

Getting Here, NeWest Press, 1977.

(With Aritha van Herk) *More Stories from Western Canada,* Macmillan (Canada), 1980.

(With van Herk and Leah Flater) *West of Fiction,* NeWest Press, 1983.

OTHER

(With Theatre Passe Muraille) *As Far As the Eye Can See* (play), NeWest Press, 1977.

(And compiler, with Bob Beal) *War in the West: Voices of the 1885 Rebellion* (history), McClelland & Stewart, 1985.

Playing Dead (essays), McClelland & Stewart, 1989.

Work represented in anthologies, including *Fourteen Stories High,* edited by David Helwig, Oberon Press, 1971; *The Narrative Voice,* edited by John Metcalf, McGraw, 1972; *Modern Stories in English,* edited by W. H. New and H. J. Rosengarten, Crowell, 1975; *Personal Fictions,* edited by Michael Ondaatje, Oxford University Press, 1977; and *Wild Rose Country: Stories from Alberta,* edited by David Carpenter, Oberon Press, 1977.

Contributor of articles, short stories to periodicals, including *Fiddlehead, Tamarack Review, Camrose Review, Canadian Literature, Maclean's, Saturday Night,* and *The Bote.*

ADAPTATIONS: "Someday Soon" was adapted for television by the Canadian Broadcast Corp., January, 1977.

SIDELIGHTS: Canadian novelist Rudy Wiebe explores his personal religious beliefs, modern society, and the traditional values and character of western Canada in his many novels and short stories. His direct and forceful style has earned him the respect of critics and readers alike, and he has been called one of the "most visionary" of Canada's contemporary novelists. In addition, Wiebe has earned two of his country's most prestigious literary awards, the Governor General's Award and the Lorne Pierce medal, for his portrayal of the people who inhabit the prairie lands of western Canada.

Wiebe's first novel, *Peace Shall Destroy Many,* was published in 1962 to mixed critical review. While perceived as a promising first effort, the work caused a great deal of controversy in the Mennonite community due to its exploration of how man's quest for independence conflicts with his relationship with his god. As with his second novel, 1966's *First and Vital Candle,* reviewers found Wiebe's work to be heavily dogmatic. It was not until his third novel, *The Blue Mountains of China,* was published four years later that Wiebe's characters assumed a fully fleshed-out form and evolved from mere symbols used to illustrate a point into complex human beings.

"Rudy Wiebe's first three novels were good, but *Big Bear* represents a quantum jump beyond their achievement," writes Douglas Barbour in a review of *The Temptations of Big Bear* for *Canadian Literature.* "Wiebe's achievement here is to convince us that the white man's view of things is strange and somehow wrong, and that the Indian's perception is the truer one. . . . This is an exciting and arresting narrative, gripping in its violence and passion. . . . I don't think we can ask much more of a novel than that it create for us a world which is so achingly real it becomes our world while we read." Wiebe's sensitive portrayal of the Cree Indians caused Myrna Kostash to note in *Saturday Night:* "I began to understand how it *felt* to grow homeless, to face the buffalo across the border . . . and know they were dying along with you . . . to live cramped and immobile, told to be a farmer on one, small, designated piece of land."

In his later works, Wiebe has stretched the confines of his religious perspective, dealing with other controversial issues. *The Scorched-Wood People* is a history of the nineteenth-century rebellions led by Louis Riel to aid native Canadian Indians in preserving their land. *My Lovely Enemy,* which proved to be confusing in focus to some reviewers, is an exploration of the conflict between physical lust and man's love for his god. While peopled with interesting characters, Lawrence Mathews notes in the *Dictionary of Literary Biography* that the main character "seems to escape his author's control. . . . *My Lovely Enemy* does demonstrate Wiebe's willingness to take risks, to break new ground. . . . but [it] seems destined to represent a false step in an otherwise impressive development."

Through his body of work, Wiebe has filled a gap in the body of Canadian literature. As he wrote in *Canada Writes:* "In my fiction I try to explore the world that I know; the land and people of western Canada, from my particular world view: a radical Jesus-oriented Christianity." Mathews praises Wiebe's effort, noting that Wiebe "has developed from a chronicler of an obscure minority group to a forger of the conscience of the Canadian West and one of the few writers in the country to articulate a Christian vision in literature."

BIOGRAPHICAL/CRITICAL SOURCES:

BOOKS

Cameron, Donald, *Conversations with Canadian Novelists,* Macmillan, 1973, pp. 146-60.

Contemporary Literary Criticism, Gale, Volume 6, 1976; Volume 11, 1979; Volume 14, 1980.

Dictionary of Literary Biography, Volume 60: *Canadian Writers since 1960, Second Series,* Gale, 1987.

Harrison, Dick, *Untamed Country,* University of Alberta Press, 1977.

Keith, W. J., *Epic Fiction: The Art of Rudy Wiebe,* University of Alberta Press, 1981.

Keith, W. J., editor, *A Voice in the Land: Essays by and about Rudy Wiebe,* NeWest, 1981.

Kroetsch, Rupert, and Reingard M. Nischik, editors, *Gaining Ground: European Critics on Canadian Writing,* NeWest, 1985, pp. 53-63.

Morley, Patricia, *The Comedians, Hugh Hood, and Rudy Wiebe,* Clarke, Irwin, 1976.

Moss, John, *Sex and Violence in the Canadian Novel,* McClelland & Stewart, 1977, pp. 256-69.

Moss, John, editor, *The Canadian Novel: Here and Now,* NC Press, 1978.

Twigg, Alan, *For Openers: Conversations with 24 Canadian Writers,* Harbour, 1981, pp. 207-18.

PERIODICALS

Canadian Forum, January, 1968; December, 1977; December, 1980, p. 42; March, 1981, pp. 5-8, 13; May, 1983; p. 29; January, 1990, p. 30.

Canadian Literature, summer, 1974; winter, 1975; summer, 1978, pp. 42-63; spring, 1985, pp. 7-22; spring, 1990, p. 320.

Essays on Canadian Writing, winter, 1980-1981, pp. 134-48; summer, 1983, pp. 70-3.

Rubicon, summer, 1986, pp. 126-59.

Saturday Night, April, 1971, p. 26; February, 1974, p. 33.

*   *   *

WILSON, Ethel Davis (Bryant)   1888(?)-1980

PERSONAL: Born January 20, 1888 (listed in some sources as 1890), in Port Elizabeth, South Africa; immigrated to Canada, 1898; died December 22, 1980, in Vancouver, British Columbia, Canada; daughter of Robert William (a missionary) and Lila (Malkin) Bryant; married Wallace Wilson (a physician), January 4, 1921 (one source cites 1920; died March 12, 1966). *Education:* Educated in England and Canada.

CAREER: Worked as public school teacher in Canada, 1907-1920; writer.

AWARDS, HONOURS: D. Litt., from University of British Columbia, 1955; Canada Council medal, 1961; Royal Society of Canada Lorne Pierce gold medal from Learned Societies, 1964; Order of Canada medal of service, 1970.

WRITINGS:

Hetty Dorval, Macmillan, 1947, reprinted, 1967.
The Innocent Traveller, Macmillan, 1949.
The Equations of Love: Tuesday and Wednesday and Lilly's Story (two novellas), Macmillan, 1952, reprinted, 1974.
Lilly's Story (novella), Harper, 1953.
Swamp Angel (novel), Harper, 1954.
Love and Salt Water (novel), St. Martin's, 1957.
Mrs. Golightly, and Other Stories (short stories), Macmillan, 1961.
Ethel Wilson: Stories, Essays, and Letters, edited by David Stouck, University of British Columbia Press, 1987.

Work represented in anthologies. Editor of *Red Cross,* 1941-45. Contributor of short stories and essays to periodicals, including *New Statesman and Nation, Canadian Forum,* and *Chatelaine.*

SIDELIGHTS: Born in South Africa, Ethel Davis Wilson was taken to England by her grandparents after the death of her mother. They then moved to Canada, where Wilson remained thereafter. During her marriage to Vancouver physician Wallace Wilson she and her husband took trips to the Middle East, the Mediterranean, and Europe.

Wilson came to writing late in life; her first story appeared when she was forty-nine, and her first novel was published ten years later. Thus as Desmond Pacey noted in *Ethel Wilson,* she was a contemporary of James Joyce and T. S. Eliot, though her novels were not written until after World War II. However, she was much less experimental than either Joyce or Eliot. Pacey wrote: "Her stories are almost always told in straightforward chronological order by an omniscient narrator who is not above commenting occasionally, in a very old-fashioned way, on the persons and events he is narrating. . . . Upon everything she writes is the mark of a fastidious and exigent craftsman: her art is quiet, gentle, controlled, exquisitely fashioned and finished."

Wilson strove to imbue her work with "incandescence." She wrote: "There is a moment, I think, within a novelist of any originality, whatever his country or his scope, when some sort of synthesis takes place over which he has only partial control. There is an incandescence, and from it meaning emerges, words appear, they take shape in their order, a fusion occurs. A minor writer, whose gift is small and canvas limited, stands away at last if he can and regards what he has done, without indulgence. This is a counsel of perfection which I myself am not able to take with skill, but I must try to take it. I am sure that the very best writing in our country will result from such an incandescence which takes place in a prepared mind where forces meet."

Wilson has also been compared to Jane Austen and Daniel Defoe. Her sense of reality as well as her devotion to the details of place and social behavior were similar to those earlier writers. And on a psychological level, Wilson has been compared to Marcel Proust and Virginia Woolf, for she enriched her characterizations by portraying the emotional reverberations of phenomena and the subtleties of human relationships.

Many critics have focused on Wilson's style and symbolism. Pacey listed her strengths as "economy, matter-of-fact-statement, limpid style, lack of pretentiousness, and a combination of involvement and detachment." Other reviewers described the quality of her prose in similar terms. Edith James, reviewing Wilson's first novel, *Hetty Dorval,* in the *San Francisco Chronicle,* declared that "Wilson's writing has the precision of Janet Lewis and the singing quality of the early Willa Cather." And V. P. Hass of the *Chicago Tribune* praised the "admirable economy of words" of *Lilly's Story,* a novella first published in 1952.

Beneath the finely crafted simplicity, however, is a complexity of meaning. Reviewing Wilson's 1954 novel, *Swamp Angel,* L. A. G. Strong wrote, "From the quiet but powerful opening to the last Excalibur flight of *Swamp Angel* the story troubles the mind with overtones and reticences, as if each chapter were a moon with a hidden side more important than the one which Mrs. Wilson shows us." Similarly, W. H. New wrote that 1949's *The Innocent Traveller* "has at its base a kind of symbolic structure." Pacey observed that "Wilson's chief themes are loneliness and love, human vulnerability and tenacity, the juxtaposition in the world of innocence and cruelty, beauty and fear, and she treats these themes in a style that is straightforward but also suggestive, realistic but also poetic and symbolic." He added that Wilson "sees human beings as lonely creatures who forever seek, and occasionally find, the comfort and sustaining power of mutual love, and nature as a setting which is at once beautiful and menacing."

BIOGRAPHICAL/CRITICAL SOURCES:

BOOKS

Contemporary Literary Criticism, Volume 13, Gale, 1980.
Dictionary of Literary Biography, Volume 68: *Canadian Writers, 1920-1959, First Series,* Gale, 1988.
Pacey, Desmond, *Ethel Wilson,* Twayne, 1967.

PERIODICALS

British Columbia Library Quarterly, April, 1958.
Canadian Forum, December, 1949.

Canadian Literature, autumn, 1959; autumn, 1965.
Chicago Tribune, May 3, 1953; August 29, 1954.
Christian Science Monitor, October 21, 1949.
Kirkus Review, June 15, 1954.
New York Herald Tribune Book Review, October 19, 1947; January 15, 1950; May 3, 1953; August 29, 1954.
Queen's Quarterly, spring, 1954.
San Francisco Chronicle, August 21, 1947; May 7, 1953.
Saturday Night, July 26, 1952.
Saturday Review of Literature, December 10, 1949; May 16, 1953; September 4, 1954.
Spectator, September 3, 1954.
Times Literary Supplement, July 24, 1948; March 28, 1952.

OBITUARIES:

PERIODICALS

Chicago Tribune, December 24, 1980.*

*   *   *

WRIGHT, L(aurali) R.   1939-

PERSONAL: Born June 5, 1939, in Saskatoon, Saskatchewan, Canada; daughter of Sidney Victor (a teacher) and Evelyn Jane (a teacher; maiden name, Barber) Appleby; married John Wright (a television producer and director), January 6, 1962 (separated, 1986); children: Victoria Kathleen, Johnna Margaret. *Education:* Attended Carleton University, 1958-59; University of British Columbia, 1960 and 1962-63; University of Calgary, 1970-71; and Banff School of Fine Arts, 1976.

ADDRESSES: Home—6695 Hersham Ave., Burnaby, British Columbia V5E 3K7, Canada.*Agent*—Virginia Barber Literary Agency Inc., 353 West 21st St., New York, NY 10011.

CAREER: Saskatoon Star-Phoenix, Saskatoon, Saskatchewan, reporter, 1968-69; *Calgary Albertan,* Calgary, Alberta, reporter, 1969-70; *Calgary Herald,* Calgary, reporter and columnist, 1970-76, assistant city editor, 1976-77; freelance writer, 1977—.

MEMBER: International PEN, Writers Union of Canada, Authors Guild, Authors League of America, Mystery Writers of America, Periodical Writers Association of Canada, Writers Federation of British Columbia.

AWARDS, HONOURS: Winner, New Alberta Novelist Competition, Alberta Culture and Multiculturalism, 1978, for *Neighbours;* Edgar Allan Poe Award for best novel, Mystery Writers of America, 1986, for *The Suspect.*

WRITINGS:

NOVELS

Neighbours: A Novel, Macmillan (Toronto), 1979.
The Favourite, Doubleday (Toronto), 1982.
Among Friends, Doubleday, 1984.
Love in the Temperate Zone, Viking (New York City), 1988.

"KARL ALBERG" MYSTERY SERIES

The Suspect, Viking, 1985.
Sleep While I Sing, Doubleday, 1986.
A Chill Rain in January, Viking, 1989.
Fall from Grace, Viking, 1991.
Prized Possessions, Viking, 1993.
A Touch of Panic, Scribner, 1994.

OTHER

Contributor to anthology *Glass Canyons,* edited by Ian Adam, NeWest Press, 1985.

SIDELIGHTS: Author L. R. Wright lives in British Columbia and uses the town of Sechelt on the Sunshine Coast, a section along the Pacific Ocean accessible only by ferry, as the setting for many of her novels and mysteries. Her character Sergeant Karl Alberg, a member of the Royal Canadian Mounted Police, appears in all of her mysteries, as does Alberg's girlfriend Cassandra Mitchell. The stories concern not only Alberg's efforts to solve local crimes but are also character studies often compared to the works of British mystery writer Ruth Rendell. Writing in *Books in Canada* Robin Skelton claims that Wright's mysteries contain "understanding compassion, . . . real humour, and . . . quick intelligence."

Wright worked as a newspaper journalist for more than a decade before the publication of her first novel, *Neighbours,* in 1979. Set in Calgary, Alberta, the book depicts the lives of three diverse women living next door to one another. Winner of the New Alberta Novelist Competition, the novel examines each characters' struggle to overcome her personal difficulties.

Wright followed *Neighbours* with *The Favorite,* the story of a teenage girl, her terminally ill father, and her mother. The story focuses on the daughter as she copes with the approaching death of the father who has doted on her since she was born. The grief experienced by the girl's mother—a neglected woman who exemplifies the "perfect wife and mother" while disregarding her own desires—is presented in a unique light due to the close relationship between her husband and daughter; she had figuratively lost her husband upon the birth of her daughter many years before. *New York Times* critic Mary Cantwell praises *The Favorite* as "a most agreeable book," adding

that Wright "is a graceful stylist and has a contagious pleasure in the ordinary."

In 1984, Wright published *Among Friends,* telling of the experiences of three women whose lives are intertwined through family and friendship. As the protagonists endure personal crises and loss, they must also battle the demons that have invaded their psyches. Each character's perspective is captured by a narrative from her unique viewpoint. Many reviewers praised Wright's skill in expressing the sense of loneliness felt by her characters. In an interview with Diane Turbide of *Quill & Quire,* Wright commented on the solitude conveyed in *Among Friends*: "I've never lived alone. Maybe I just worry about people who do. A lot of people I know who do live alone said [the depiction of loneliness] as an accurate portrayal."

The Suspect, Wright's first mystery novel, appeared in 1985 and won critical accolades as well as the Edgar Allan Poe Award, the mystery field's highest honor. A departure from Wright's three previous volumes of mainstream fiction, her fourth book evolved into a mystery when, as the author told Turbide, "I inadvertently let a policeman into the story and became very fond of him." Royal Canadian Mounted Police sergeant Karl Alberg developed into one of the central characters of the story set in the seaside town of Sechelt, British Columbia. Commencing with the bizarre murder of eighty-five-year-old Carlyle Burke by his long-time friend George Wilcox, the plot revolves around Wilcox's maneuverings to escape suspicion and prosecution. Tensions mount when Alberg is assigned to the case and begins to question Wilcox. Romantic complications ensue when Alberg's lover learns that Wilcox, a dear friend, is under suspicion and she argues for his innocence. A number of critics praised *The Suspect* for its dramatic structure—the culprit is known from the onset and the mystery for the reader lies in discovering the motive behind the murder. Writing in the *Globe & Mail,* Margaret Cannon calls Wright's "first foray into crime fiction . . . a superb beginning," adding that her "people are fresh and memorable."

Sleep While I Sing carries on several elements of *The Suspect.* Again set in the small coastal town of Sechelt, the story features the characters of Alberg and his girlfriend, Cassandra Mitchell, the town librarian. However, Wright's second mystery is structured around a more traditional "whodunit" plot. A woman's body is found in the woods, brutally murdered. The fact that she is a stranger to the residents of the close-knit town adds an even deeper element of suspense. During the ensuing investigation, Alberg and Mitchell weather a crisis in their love relationship when Mitchell becomes enamored of an actor vacationing in the area; Alberg comes to believe the performer was involved in the slaying. The detective discovers the identity of the murdered woman through an ingenious device, further unravelling the mystery. *Globe & Mail* critic Cannon comments on Wright's "fine writing style and talent for developing characters," but notes that "there aren't quite enough suspects . . . and the pace lags accordingly."

Wright's *Love in the Temperate Zone* marked her return to mainstream fiction. Set in Vancouver, Wright's book tells the story of a woman who suffers a crisis in her marriage that transforms her life in surprising ways. Discovering that her husband of twenty years has been unfaithful, she dissolves the marriage and forms an unexpected bond with a close friend which serves to further complicate her life. After adjusting to her new circumstances, the woman meets a widower with whom she attempts to build a new relationship. Critical reaction to *Love in the Temperate Zone* was mixed. While believing Wright's use of language to be overly "artsy," reviewer Susan Isaacs praises her "talent for pacing and characterization" in the *New York Times Book Review*.

A Chill Rain in January reintroduces Sechelt residents Alberg and Mitchell and once again places the couple in the middle of a series of mysterious occurrences. The suspense centers around the town recluse, an attractive, wealthy woman who is suspected of murdering her brother, a drifter, after he disrupts her idyllic lifestyle. The disappearance of an elderly woman from a nearby nursing home further complicates matters. In the midst of this tumult, Alberg and Mitchell attempt to salvage their damaged relationship. The pair finally reunite in *Fall from Grace,* Wright's subsequent crime novel, and once again find themselves confronting a series of strange goings-on, this time coinciding with the appearance of two strangers in Sechelt: a charismatic ex-convict who is followed by another man harboring a secret about him. The plot accelerates when Alberg and Mitchell witness a body falling from a cliff into the sea. This act of murder is somehow related to the return of both men, and again, the mountie and the town librarian's relationship is the background from which the crime is solved.

Prized Possessions contains three separate strands of plot which come together in the end. The first plot concerns the disappearance of a local husband after six years of supposedly happy marriage. The second follows sergeant Alberg as he attempts to cope with the recent death of his father, his renewed sense of his own mortality, and his worries about his long-time relationship with girlfriend Cassandra. The third plot concerns a mentally-challenged boy who accidently kills a local girl in a car accident and flees to the town of Sechelt. Skelton calls *Prized Possessions* "a fine novel, rich with humour, pathos, and human understanding." Sarah Harvey, writing in *Quill & Quire,* states that "*Prized Possessions* provides the satisfaction mystery lovers dream about: solid character studies neatly integrated with genuine suspense."

In *A Touch of Panic* Alberg and Cassandra begin living together, Alberg deals with the murder of a local drug dealer and a string of local robberies, and Cassandra receives the attentions of a colleague who becomes finally too aggressive. "Wright's mystery-spinning powers are at their height," reports Nancy Wigston in *Quill & Quire.* "She unveils a range of memorable characters who consistently evolve in directions that are unexpected, but true." Diane Turbide, writing in *Maclean's,* finds that "Wright deftly weaves disparate narrative strands into a satisfying whole. With its graceful writing and insight into character, *A Touch of Panic* is another welcome dispatch from Wright's beloved Sunshine Coast."

Viewing Wright's books as a whole, Turbide asserts that she "may be most interested in character," but suggests that the author's "insight into people is complemented by strong descriptive powers."

BIOGRAPHICAL/CRITICAL SOURCES:

BOOKS

Contemporary Literary Criticism, Volume 44, Gale, 1987, pp. 334-35.

PERIODICALS

Belles Lettres, fall, 1994, p. 69.
Books in Canada, August, 1979, p. 38; summer, 1993, p. 36; April, 1994, pp. 36-38.
Entertainment Weekly, October 15, 1993, p. 69.
Globe & Mail (Toronto), September 28, 1985; November 15, 1986.
Kirkus Reviews, July 1, 1993, p. 824.
Maclean's, May 23, 1994, p. 64.
New York Times, August 2, 1982, p. 15.
New York Times Book Review, January 17, 1988, p. 14; September 19, 1993, p. 34; September 18, 1994, p. 34.
Quill & Quire, September, 1986, p. 86; May, 1993, p. 24; February, 1994, p. 24.

Y-Z

YEE, Paul (R.) 1956-

PERSONAL: Born October 1, 1956, in Spalding, Saskatchewan, Canada; son of Gordon and Gim May (Wong) Yee. *Education:* University of British Columbia, B.A., 1978, M.A. 1983. *Avocational interests:* Cycling and swimming.

ADDRESSES: Home—125 Aldwych Ave., Toronto, Ontario, Canada M4J 1X8.

CAREER: City of Vancouver Archives, Vancouver, British Columbia, Assistant City Archivist, 1980-1988; Archives of Ontario, Toronto, Ontario, Portfolio Manager, 1988-91; Ontario Ministry of Citizenship, policy analyst, 1991—. Writer, 1983—. Teacher in British Columbia schools, and at Simon Fraser University, University of Victoria, University of British Columbia, Vancouver Museum, and Chinese Community Library Services Society of Vancouver. *Exhibitions: Saltwater City* exhibition, Chinese Cultural Centre (CCC), Vancouver Centennial, 1986.

AWARDS, HONOURS: Honorable Mention, Canada Council Literature Prizes, 1986, for *The Curses of Third Uncle;* Vancouver Book Prize, 1989, for *Saltwater City;* British Columbia Book Prize for Children's Literature, National I.O.D.E. Book Award, and Parents' Choice Honor, all 1990, all for *Tales from Gold Mountain;* Ruth Schwartz Award, Canadian Booksellers Association, 1992, for *Roses Sing on New Snow.*

WRITINGS:

Teach Me to Fly, Skyfighter! (stories), illustrations by Sky Lee, Lorimer (Toronto), 1983.
The Curses of Third Uncle (novel), Lorimer, 1986.
Saltwater City: An Illustrated History of the Chinese in Vancouver, Douglas & McIntyre (Vancouver), 1988, University of Washington, 1989.

Tales from Gold Mountain: Stories of the Chinese in the New World, illustrations by Simon Ng, Groundwood Books (Toronto), 1989, Macmillan, 1990.
Roses Sing on New Snow: A Delicious Tale, illustrations by Harvey Chan, Macmillan, 1992.
Breakaway (young adult novel), Groundwood, 1994.

WORK IN PROGRESS: Call Me Clark, a juvenile novel, for Groundwood; *The Chinese-Canadians,* nonfiction, for Umbrella Press.

SIDELIGHTS: Born in Spalding, Saskatchewan, in 1956, Paul Yee is a Chinese-Canadian of the third generation. He grew up in the Chinatown area of Vancouver. On the dust jacket of his book, *Saltwater City,* he says he had a "typical Chinese-Canadian childhood, caught between two worlds, and yearning to move away from the neighborhood."

Yee received a Master of Arts degree in history from the University of British Columbia in 1983 after completing his undergraduate work there as well. Although he has taught informally at several institutions in British Columbia, the focus of his career has been on his work as an archivist and policy analyst. He said in an interview for *Junior DISCovering Authors* that "I really don't view myself as a teacher, even though I do classroom visits." An archivist takes care of historical documents that are usually stored in special areas of libraries and cultural or state institutions. These documents or papers are important for historians and other writers to research past events. A policy analyst researches and analyzes options for government decision-making.

In 1988, Yee moved to Toronto, where he became Multicultural Coordinator for the Archives of Ontario. He had been previously employed as an archivist by Vancouver City. In his interview, Yee was asked how, as an archivist, he became a writer of children's literature. "It was a fluke," he replied. "Back in 1983, I was involved in doing work for Chinatown, such as organizing festivals, exhibits, and educational programs. Even though I had written some short stories, I had not done anything in children's literature. A Canadian publishing company, Lorimer, knowing about my work in the Chinese community, asked me to write a children's book that would employ my knowledge of Chinese-Canadian life as a background. *Teach Me to Fly, Skyfighter!* was my first children's book that came out of the request by the publishing company." With his series of four related stories about children living in the immigrant neighborhoods of Vancouver, Yee "has succeeded in portraying the personalities, interests, and dreams of four 11-year-old friends whose voices ring true throughout," according to Frieda Wishinsky in *Quill & Quire.*

Yee very much enjoyed writing his first children's book. "It dovetailed with the work I was doing in building awareness of Chinese-Canadian history and community. I saw my target audience as Canadian children of Chinese ancestry who needed to know more about themselves and their heritage," he said in his interview. Three years later, Lorimer worked with Yee on another book. In 1986, he won honorable mention for his second children's novel, *The Curses of Third Uncle,* from the Canada Council Literature Prizes.

The Curses of Third Uncle is a historical novel that deals with the period of the early twentieth century in which Sun Yat-Sen's revolutionary movement fought against the Chinese Empire. Dr. Sun Yat-Sen, called the "Father of Modern China," had led nine uprisings against the Empire by the time he visited Vancouver in 1910 and 1911, Yee recounts in *Saltwater City.* In *The Curses of Third Uncle,* fourteen-year-old Lillian, living in Vancouver's Chinatown, misses her father, who often travels back to China and throughout the British Columbia frontier—presumably to take care of his clothing business. He is actually a secret agent for Dr. Sun's revolutionary movement.

At one point in his travels, Lillian's father fails to return. His absence is economically hard on the family, but Lillian will not believe that her father has deserted them. Her third uncle, however, threatens to send Lillian's family back to China. In her attempts to locate her father by travelling through British Columbia, Lillian discovers that he has been betrayed by his brother, who has been paid to turn him over to his enemies. Comparing the book in the *Emergency Librarian* to historical epics such as *Shogun* or *Roots,* Christine Dewar states that Yee "has produced a story that is exciting but contrived, with an attractive and reasonably motivated heroine." *Quill & Quire* writer Annette Goldsmith similarly comments that *The Curses of the Third Uncle* is "an exciting, fast-pace, well-written

tale," and praises Yee for his use of legendary Chinese female warriors to reinforce Lillian's story.

Yee's next book, *Saltwater City,* was published in 1988. This book grew out of Yee's work from 1985 to 1986 as chair of the Saltwater City Exhibition Committee of the Chinese Cultural Centre. In the preface to the book, Yee writes: "The book pays tribute to those who went through the hard times, to those who swallowed their pride, to those who were powerless and humiliated, but who still carried on. They all had faith that things would be better for future generations. They have been proven correct."

Saltwater City is a history of Vancouver's Chinatown that covers a long period of time, from its beginnings in 1858 to the present. It has more than 200 photographs, many documents, deals with a large number of political, economic, and social issues, and profiles the lives of many people. Yee remarked in his interview that there were no special problems in assembling all this material: "I had done a lot of research from the Saltwater City Exhibition Committee and then there was all my previous work with Chinatown. I had worked with many people, and they were happy to tell me their stories and show me their photograph albums. Had I been an outsider, it would have been much more difficult."

Yee pointed out that "while *Saltwater City* is not a children's book, it is an extremely accessible book. It can serve as a child's book not in the sense that it is read from cover to cover, but rather as a reference book the child can open at any page and study a photograph or read a profile or sidebar." He also added that *Saltwater City* "is very much localized to the Vancouver scene. It is therefore most important to Chinese in the Vancouver area and to the grandchildren of the people who appear throughout the book," although he noted that "it would be possible to compare some of the history to Chinese experiences in cities of the United States."

Other than commemorating the Saltwater City Exhibition, Yee said in his interview, the book serves another purpose: "The key thing in the Vancouver Chinese community is that a tremendous change is occurring. Since 1967, the arrival of many new Chinese from Hong Kong and other Asian immigrants has overwhelmed the older, established community. I felt it was necessary to recognize the earlier chapters of our history before the new waves of immigrations changed everything. I did chapters on the newer immigrants, and their stories are different from the problems encountered earlier."

Although Yee started his career as a historian, compiling information such as that in *Saltwater City,* he had no particular difficulty in making the switch to fiction. Nevertheless, he remarked, he found that writing fiction was much more "arduous because instead of merely reporting what has happened in non-fiction, fiction requires the creation of a story" that will be believable and enjoyable. "The difference between nonfiction and fiction is the difference between reliable reporting and imaginative creating," he concluded.

Yee also said that his knowledge of folk literature comes partly from his childhood reading of western fairy tales. From those stories he remembered things such as actions happening in groups of three, a principle he makes use of in some of his stories. Other than similar memories, Yee has not relied on the formal study of children's writing to develop his own fiction.

Yee used his familiarity with traditional stories to write *Tales from Gold Mountain,* which was published in 1989. This collection of short stories has won Yee high praise from the critics. Lee Galda and Susan Cox, writing in *Reading Teacher,* believe the book "gives voice to the previously unheard generations of Chinese immigrants whose labor supported the settlement of the west coast of Canada and the United States." The book includes stories about the conflict between the manager of a fish cannery and his greedy boss; a young man who arranges the burial of Chinese railroad workers when he meets his father's ghost; a young woman's gift of ginger root to save her fiance's life; a wealthy merchant who exchanges his twin daughters for sons; and clashes between old traditions and new influences.

Betsy Hearne of the *Bulletin of the Center for Children's Books* notes that "Yee never indulges in stylistic pretensions," yet is able to dramatically blend realism and legend. She explains that Yee moves between lighter tales of love and wit to conflicts between the present and past. The result is that the stories "carry mythical overtones that lend the characters unforgettable dimension—humans achieving supernatural power in defying their fate of physical and cultural oppression." In the afterword, Yee says that he hopes to "carve a place in the North American imagination for the many generations of Chinese who have settled here as Canadians and Americans, and help them stake their claim to be known as pioneers, too."

Yee remarked in his interview that most of *Tales from Gold Mountain* was original material, with only "about five to ten percent of the tales [coming] from the stories I heard when I was growing up." He explained: "The rest comes from my imagination. It's really hard to slice up a book to say which is history and which is imagination. The Chinese stories operate within the particular context of new world history. It's not just a blend of the new with the old but the creation of a new world mythology. Every group that comes to North America leaves an imprint of itself that can be shaped into fiction."

Denise Wilms, writing in *Booklist,* believes that Yee's stories "strikingly reflect traditional Chinese beliefs and customs in new world circumstances," and compares it to Laurence Yep's *Rainbow People. School Library Journal* contributor Margaret A. Chang also compares *Tales* to *Rainbow People* and adds that Yee's stories "will further expand and enhance understanding of the Chinese immigrant experience." The book is "told in richly evocative language," according to a *Horn Book* reviewer, and "the stories skillfully blend the hardships and dangers of frontier life in a new country with the ancient attitudes and traditions brought over from China." The critic concludes that the images of *Tales from the Gold Mountain* "will stay with the reader for a long time."

The heroine of *Roses Sing on New Snow,* Maylin, echoes the idea of the difference between the Old World and the New World when she explains to the governor of South China, who is visiting her father's restaurant in Chinatown to learn the secrets of her delicious recipes, that "this is a dish of the New World. . . . You cannot re-create it in the Old." In this story, the attempt to push Maylin aside so that her father and two brothers can take credit for the excellent cooking that comes from their restaurant, fails when Maylin has to be called to show the governor how the cooking is done. Yee concludes, "From that day on Maylin was renowned in Chinatown as a great cook and a wise person." In *The Bulletin of the Center for Children's Books,* Betsy Hearne notes that "vivid art and clean writing are graced by a neatly feminist ending."

Asked by *Something about the Author* if he felt there may have been a suggestion of a feminist twist in *Roses Sing on New Snow,* Yee replied, "Insofar as the novel shows Maylin asserting herself, I would say yes." He explained: "Children need to see representations of reality in their literature. Chinese immigration to North America has had the unique feature of being predominately male since at first the men were coming by themselves to America. That's a fact about our history. Some of the early communities were almost all male." By portraying positive female characters such as Maylin and Lillian of *Curses of the Third Uncle,* Yee counters the male-dominated history with fictional female role models.

As a historian and observer of Chinese and other immigrant communities in Canada, Yee has noted significant changes in Canadian attitudes and practices toward its racial minority communities. "The change has been for the better in many ways. There are new state initiatives to improve race relations, and even the private sector is learning about managing diversity and employment equity. I am optimistic about the future." In his writing, he concluded, he strives to articulate this philosophy: "From the past, for the future."

BIOGRAPHICAL/CRITICAL SOURCES:

BOOKS

Yee, Paul, *Saltwater City: An Illustrated History of the Chinese in Vancouver,* Douglas & McIntyre (Vancouver), 1988, University of Washington, 1989.

Yee, *Tales from Gold Mountain: Stories of the Chinese in the New World,* Groundwood Books (Toronto), 1989, Macmillan, 1990.

Yee, telephone interview with Jordan Richman for *Junior DISCovering Authors,* August 11, 1993.

PERIODICALS

Booklist, March 1, 1992, p. 1288; March 15, 1990, p. 1464.

Books in Canada, December, 1986; May, 1989; December, 1989, p.19.

Books for Young People, April, 1988.

Bulletin of the Center for Children's Books, January, 1990, p. 178; July, 1992, p. 307.

Canadian Children's Literature, number 70, 1993, pp. 92-94.

Canadian Literature, autumn, 1991, p. 142.

Canadian Materials, September, 1994, p. 139.

Canada Matters, March, 1990, p. 72; May, 1991, p. 156.

Children's Literature Association Quarterly, winter, 1990, p. 198.

Children's Literature in Education, September, 1994, pp. 169-91.

Emergency Librarian, May, 1987, p. 51.

Horn Book, July, 1990, pp. 459-60; March/April, 1992, p. 196.

Journal of Reading, March, 1992, p. 509.

Kirkus Reviews, March 1, 1992, p. 331.

Publishers Weekly, July 21, 1989, p. 49.

Quill and Quire, October, 1983, p. 16; December, 1986, p. 14; October, 1988; December, 1989, p. 23; August, 1991; April, 1994, p. 39.

Reading Teacher, April, 1991, p. 585.

Saturday Night, November, 1988.

School Library Journal, May, 1990, p. 121; May, 1992, p. 95.

*   *   *

YOUNG, Neil 1945-

PERSONAL: Born November 12, 1945, in Toronto, Ontario, Canada; son of Scott (a sports reporter) and Edna (a television celebrity) Young; married second wife, Pegi; children: Zeke, Ben. *Education:* Educated in Canada. *Avocational interests:* Developing toys and hobbies for functionally disabled children, including work with Lionel Trains.

ADDRESSES: Office—c/o Lookout Management, 9120 Sunset Blvd., Los Angeles, CA 90069.

CAREER: Songwriter and performer in rock groups, including the Squires, 1962-64, Rickey James and the Mynah Birds, c. 1965, Buffalo Springfield, 1966-68, Crosby, Stills, Nash, and Young, 1969-71, 1974, and 1989, the Stills-Young Band, 1976, and as solo artist and with accompaniment from Crazy Horse, the Blue Notes, and Pearl Jam. Under pseudonym Bernard Shakey, director of motion pictures, including *Journey through the Past,* Shakey Productions, 1972, and *Rust Never Sleeps,* International Harmony, 1979. Actor in motion pictures, including *Love at Large,* 1986.

AWARDS, HONOURS: Awards for best rock artist, best male vocalist, and for best recording from *Rolling Stone,* 1979, for *Rust Never Sleeps;* numerous other music awards.

WRITINGS:

RECORDINGS AS COMPOSER AND LYRICIST; RELEASED BY REPRISE, UNLESS OTHERWISE NOTED

Neil Young, 1969.
Everybody Knows This Is Nowhere, 1970.
After the Gold Rush, 1971.
Harvest, 1972.
Journey through the Past (motion picture soundtrack), 1972.
Time Fades Away, 1973.
On the Beach, 1974.
Tonight's the Night, 1975.
Zuma, 1975.
(With Stephen Stills, as Stills-Young Band) *Long May You Run,* 1976.
American Stars 'n Bars, 1977.
Decade, 1977.
Comes a Time, 1978.
Rust Never Sleeps, 1979.
Live Rust (live recording of previously released material), 1979.
Hawks & Doves, 1980.
Re-act-or, 1981.
Trans, Geffen, 1982.
Everybody's Rockin', Geffen, 1983.
Old Ways, Geffen, 1985.
Landing on Water, Geffen, 1986.
Life, Geffen, 1987.
This Note's for You, 1988.
Freedom, 1989.
Ragged Glory, 1990.
Arc (noise experiment), 1991.
Weld (live recording of previously released material), 1991.
Arc Weld (combined recording of *Arc* and *Weld*), 1991.

Harvest Moon, 1992.

Unplugged (live recording of acoustic versions of previously released material), 1993.

Lucky Thirteen, Geffen, 1993.

Sleeps with Angels, 1994.

Mirrorball, 1995.

Dead Man (motion picture soundtrack), 1995.

Also author and performer of songs on recordings by Buffalo Springfield, including *Buffalo Springfield,* Atco, 1967, *Buffalo Springfield Again,* Atco, 1967, and *Last Time Around,* Atco, 1968; and by Crosby, Stills, Nash, and Young (CSNY), including *Deja Vu,* Atlantic, 1970, *Four-Way Street* (contains concert versions of previous recordings), Atlantic, 1971, and *American Dream,* Atlantic, 1989.

Performer of songs for soundtracks for motion pictures, including *The Landlord,* United Artists, 1970, *The Strawberry Statement,* Metro-Goldwyn-Mayer, 1970, *Celebration at Big Sur,* Twentieth Century-Fox, 1971, and *Where the Buffalo Roam,* Universal, 1980.

SIDELIGHTS: One of rock music's most eccentric figures, Neil Young has been characterized as a somber folkie, a brooding balladeer, a country rascal, a noise merchant, and a sardonic rocker in his numerous years as a singer/songwriter. Beginning in the mid-1960's with Buffalo Springfield, through the early 1970's with Crosby, Stills, Nash, and Young (CSNY), and into that decade's remainder with his frequent backing band Crazy Horse, Young's career has spanned numerous musical and sociological changes, most of which he has managed to incorporate or epitomize in a canon that most rock critics find comparable to that of Bob Dylan or the Beatles. "Except perhaps for Bob Dylan," *Newsweek's* Tony Schwartz wrote in 1978, "Neil Young . . . is the most consistently compelling figure in American Rock; certainly no one else has covered so much musical ground—folk, country and rock—with such originality."

Young began his career in 1962 when he dropped out of high school to form the Squires. With his enthusiastic mother as manager, Young and the Squires gained notoriety throughout Winnipeg, where Young had moved with his mother after his parents separated. He listened to Elvis Presley, the Beatles, and Bob Dylan, and, inspired by the latter, moved to Toronto to perform in coffee houses. There Young befriended other budding musicians, including Stephen Stills and Joni Mitchell, both of whom proved similarly inspirational. After a brief stint with Rickey James and the Mynah Birds, whose leader later rose to prominence on the strength of the funky tune "Super-freak," (he had by then shortened Rickey to Rick) Young traveled southwest towards Los Angeles. His trip was marred by poor health—Young had earlier been diag-

nosed as both an asthmatic and an epileptic—and an automobile accident, which resulted in his hospitalization in New Mexico. In 1966 Young arrived in Los Angeles and met with Stills and Richie Furay. Soon afterward they formed Buffalo Springfield.

The Springfield quickly developed a following, largely on the strength of "For What It's Worth," Stills's catchy commentary on a repressive America. On tour, however, Young gained notoriety for his stinging guitar solos and brooding renditions of his own compositions such as "Mr. Soul," "Burned," and "Out of My Mind." Unfortunately, creative differences soon disrupted the comraderie among the band members, and within two years they ended the group to embark on other enterprises. Furay formed another band, Stills joined with former Byrd David Crosby and ex-Hollies vocalist Graham Nash and formed one of contemporary music's most acclaimed trios, and Young recorded his first solo album, *Neil Young.* Although many critics considered the record marred by excessive over-dubs—Young lacked confidence in his singing voice, and so insisted on adding the vocals after the instruments were recorded—it received some FM radio attention with "The Loner," a churning portrayal of introspection that many critics deemed blatantly autobiographical.

The following year Young teamed with the band Crazy Horse to produce *Everybody Knows This Is Nowhere.* With favorites such as "Cinnamon Girl" and "Cowgirl in the Sand," the record was enormously popular and helped secure a larger following for Young. In 1969, however, he left Crazy Horse to play with Crosby, Stills, and Nash. Their first performance, at the Woodstock music festival, was an enormous success, with enthusiastic receptions for Stills's "Suite: Judy Blue Eyes" and Young's melancholy "Sea of Madness." The following year they recorded *Deja Vu,* which featured one of Young's most popular tunes, "Helpless," and released at 45 single of "Ohio," Young's commemorization of the Kent State massacre during which students protesting the Vietnam War were shot at (four were killed) by National Guard troops. During the subsequent tour, however, creative differences occurred among the quartet, and soon afterward Young departed to resume his solo career. In subsequent years he would reunite with the trio numerous times for concert appearances. In 1989 they collaborated on the album *American Dream.*

In 1971 Young recorded *After the Gold Rush* for actor Dean Stockwell's prospective film. Although the movie was never made, the album by the same name became a great success, with frequent radio play accorded the songs "Southern Man," "Only Love Can Break Your Heart," and "Don't Let It Bring You Down." Young's performance on the subsequent tour with Crazy Horse was hampered by a back injury that prevented him from playing electric guitar, and his next recording, *Harvest*, was produced despite considerable pain. That album, however, became one of Young's greatest successes, with selections such as "Heart of Gold" and "Old Man" ranked among the most popular songs in America, and it became 1972's biggest seller.

But Young was displeased with all the attention. After devoting several months to directing *Journey through the Past,* a film that ultimately received only limited distribution, the disappointed Young embarked on a tour in which he insisted on performing unfamiliar songs before his inevitably disappointed audience. Selections from the tour comprised *Time Fades Away*, an album which seemed extremely flawed in the wake of *Harvest*, but which nonetheless impressed some listeners with its raw and haphazard style. Young retaliated against his critics the following year with "Walk On," a tune from the album *On the Beach* in which he advises them to "do their thing, and I'll do mine." That album, with its stark accounts of revolutionaries, kidnappings, and general gloom, was also deemed a failure by reviewers comparing it with the more accessible *Harvest*. But Young, despondent over the fatal overdoses of Crazy Horse guitarist Danny Whitten and roadie Bruce Berry, was disinterested in commercial acclaim, and he performed infrequently to promote the work.

The following year Young released his bleakest recording, *Tonight's the Night*, on which he sings about depression, and death. Although the album, like its immediate predecessors, failed to engage the public, it inspired some critics to reappraise Young's recent work, and some rock publications began proclaiming the rather depressing recording as an impressive downer. Then, with the rock media seemingly awaiting another dismal work, Young released *Zuma*, an album of energetic tunes—some country, some electric—that sparked further confusion among his followers. Critics were quick to praise the performances from Young's band, the revived Crazy Horse with Frank Sampedro replacing Whitten, and contended that Young had adapted to yet another style.

After *Zuma*, Young reappeared on tour with Stephen Stills in the Stills-Young Band. The initial concerts enjoyed immense patronage, and the recording, *Long May You Run*, sold reasonably well. But with the tour barely begun, Young fell ill with a throat ailment and was forced to withdraw from performing. The following year he collected some previously recorded material and recent country tunes to create *American Stars 'n Bars*. Although certain selections seemed an extension of the rock elements from *Zuma*, the album's first side is an electrified elaboration of its predecessor's few country aspects. Young described the album as partly about bars and partly about

American heroes, but the album's most popular tune, the wary love song "Like a Hurricane," is about neither.

Young also devoted part of 1977 to a brief tour of small bars around Santa Cruz, California. Playing with the Ducks, Young entertained surprised patrons with rousing renditions of tunes from *Zuma* and *Stars 'n Bars* and selected favorites such as "Cinnamon Girl." As Word of Young's modest tour spread up and down the coast, however, his enthusiasm waned, and he left California for a cross-country tour in a large Van. In Nashville, Young meticulously labored on his next recording, *Comes a Time*, for which he required the services of almost two dozen musicians, including banjo pickers and violinists. The result is his most accessible, and commercial, work since *Harvest*, with tunes such as "Comes a Time" and "Human Highway" receiving attention from pop, rock, and country stations. Another tune, "Lotta Love," became a huge success when rerecorded by Nicolette Larson, a singer whose back-up vocals are heard throughout "Comes a Time."

Despite the popularity of the largely acoustic *Comes a Time*, Young returned to electric music within a year of the album's release. Working once again with Crazy Horse, Young devised a stage show replete with roadies resembling the sand people from the film *Star Wars* and an overall design that suggested an enormous living room, featuring giant amplifiers, a fifteen-foot microphone, and a yard-long harmonica. The concerts began with the playing of guitarist Jimi Hendrix's "Star Spangled Banner" and the Beatles' "A Day in the Life," after which Young was revealed asleep on one of the huge amplifiers. Awakening to the deafening applause, Young would sheepishly don his guitar and began strumming the opening bars of "Sugar Mountain." The entire first half of the show was acoustic. Then, after an intermission in which announcements from the *Woodstock* soundtrack were played over the public address system, Young would return to the stage with Crazy Horse and play extremely loud versions of tunes such as "The Loner" and "Like a Hurricane."

Many of the tour's songs were later featured on Young's next album, *Rust Never Sleeps*, which became an overwhelming success in 1979. The recording received acclaim as one of the year's best releases from several critical quarters, and it earned Young citations for best vocalist and best rock artist from *Rolling Stone*. In addition, Young's film of the tour, also entitled *Rust Never Sleeps* was released to generally complimentary reviews, and another recording, *Live Rust*, offers two records worth of music from the movie.

After the enormous success of *Rust Never Sleeps*, Young once again confounded his fans with *Hawks & Doves*, an album featuring stark, but usually humorous, odes to life in America. The record's first side, with songs such as "The Old Homestead" and "Captain Kennedy," offers somber portraits of life in America, while side two, with tunes such as "Comin' Apart at Every Nail" and "Hawks & Doves," contains lively sing-alongs celebrating America's ability to evolve and endure. Like *Rust Never Sleeps*, the recording was ranked among the best of its year by many critics.

In 1981, Young flip-flopped back to hard rock to record *re-act-or*, considered one of his raunchiest album. Influenced somewhat by more contemporary bands such as the Clash and the Sex Pistols, Young produced tunes full of guitar feedback and a bludgeoning beat. Most notable among the eight songs are "T-Bone," in which Young offered variations on a simple guitar line between chants of "Got mashed potatos, ain't got no t-bone," and "Shots," which punctuated its whining guitars with simulated machine-gun fire. *Rolling Stone's* John Piccarella was particularly impressed with "Young's role as keen-eyed . . . observer and the band's commitment to rock out." He called *re-act-or* a series of "fast-edit intensities."

Young confused his listeners even further the following year when he released *Trans*, an album's worth of primarily computerized rock songs inspired by the robot-like incantations of Devo and Germany's Kraftwerk. For most of the tunes, Young filtered his vocals through a synthesizer device called a vocoder to produce sounds such as a raspy drone and a high-pitched, but melodious, whine. The album was greeted with bewilderment by most critics, some of whom suggested that Young had finally overreached himself in his efforts to defy categorization. Other reviewers, however, received *Trans* as welcome relief from the numerous synthesizer-oriented tunes that dominated radio play in 1982. "Well, Mr. Weird is at it again," a reviewer for *Rolling Stone* reported overhearing as a reaction to *Trans*. But the reviewer added, in an extremely appreciative summary of *Trans*, that "despite his tinkering around with the hardware of the computer age, Neil Young is really still a sweephand clock in a digital world, a solitary quester after truth." He noted that Young "continues to tick for all things enduring: love, humanity, dignity, strength."

Young again shifted musical gears in 1983 with the release of *Everybody's Rockin'*. With *Everybody's Rockin'*, noted David Fricke in a *Rolling Stone* review, "rock's most exasperating quick-change artist bails out of the New Wave and seeks solace in his old roots by cutting ten deeply primitive rockabilly and country-blues tunes with *Sun Sessions* reverence." Young and his vocal backup group, the Shocking Pinks, recaptured the sound and the texture of rock's early recordings on the album, which failed to receive much airplay on radio stations. "But so what if it's commercial suicide?," asked Fricke. "You have to admire

Everybody's Rockin' for its nerve, and eventually you'll come to love it for its frenzied sound and playful humor."

In addition to confounding many of his fans, *Trans* and *Everybody's Rockin'* also earned Young a spot of legal trouble: Geffen Records, the label for which the albums were made, sued the artist for what they termed a deliberate aberration of his trademark style. Young came back with two coolly received albums, 1986's *Landing on Water,* and 1987's *Life,* before regaining critical and popular ground with his 1988 work, *This Note's for You.* Recorded with a backing band dubbed the Bluenotes, the album focuses on rhythm and blues-style rock with an accent on Young's guitar and the Bluenotes horn section. The album's popularity was driven by the song "This Note's for You," whose lyrics deride musicians lured to the big money of corporate sponsorship. The track's accompanying video so riled beer and soft drink manufacturers that they pressured the MTV network into banning the clip (although Young's open mockery of MTV nomenclature in the video probably contributed in some part).

In 1989, following his reunion with Crosby, Stills, and Nash, Young returned to noisy, guitar-driven rock with *Freedom,* another album that received critical plaudits and was driven to popularity by a strong single. On *Freedom* the standout cut is "Rockin' in the Free World," a tongue-in-cheek anthem that, despite its sarcastic tone, was openly embraced by rock fans. Young followed *Freedom* with *Ragged Glory,* a work that finds him delving deeper into distorted guitar experimentation and garage band aesthetics. The 1991 concert tour in support of *Ragged Glory* yielded two live albums: *Weld,* which contains regular songs from *Glory* and previous albums; and *Weld,* which is a thirty-five minute exercise in guitar noise and feedback. The two recordings were also marketed as a single package titled *Arc Weld.*

On the heels of such loud, sonically violent music, Young released *Harvest Moon* in 1992. A sequel of sorts to *Harvest,* the new album was Young's gentlest in years and finds him quietly reflecting on, among smaller issues, love and life. For *Harvest Moon* Young reassembled many of the notable musicians who assisted him in recording of the original *Harvest,* including vocalists Linda Rondstadt and James Taylor. Like its predecessor of twenty years, the new album became one of the major sellers in Young's catalog.

In 1994 Young released another Crazy Horse-backed album, *Sleeps with Angels.* The title track is a eulogy for rock singer Kurt Cobain, who had killed himself earlier that year. In his suicide note, Cobain had quoted lyrics from Young's song "Hey Hey, My My (Into the Black)," writing among his last words, "It's better to burn out than to fade away." While not as popular as *Harvest Moon,* the album was very well-received critically and received a rare five-star rating from *Rolling Stone.* Writing in that periodical, David Fricke praised Young's talents and called the album "among his best." Fricke went on to characterize *Sleeps with Angels* as being "rich with the resonance of Young's . . . long, uncompromised life in music."

As the 1990s progressed, Young simultaneously enjoyed popularity for both his back catalog and his new material—a rare feat for a rock artist. Many younger bands, including Sonic Youth, the Pixies, and Cobain's band Nirvana, cited Young as a primary inspiration for their guitar-based music. Another band who credited a musical debt to the singer/songwriter was Pearl Jam, who began a working relationship with Young in 1993 when they appeared together at an awards show to perform "Rockin' in the Free World." The collaboration proved so fruitful that Pearl Jam served as the opening act for a Young tour in 1994. In 1995 Young recorded the album *Mirrorball* with Pearl Jam as his backing band, with members of the group accompanying him on the tour in support of that album.

Despite a track record that many critics deem erratic and frustrating, Neil Young has had a remarkably enduring career as a musician. He has retained a devoted core audience through his various genre excursions while expanding his appeal to younger fans. He has been honored with tribute albums, deified by a new generation of rock musicians, and seen many of his recordings pass from hit single status to the realm of classic. Rock journalists have speculated, however, that Young's greatest success was reaching these heights by ignoring trends and following his own musical vision.

BIOGRAPHICAL/CRITICAL SOURCES:

BOOKS

Contemporary Literary Criticism, Volume 17, Gale, 1981.
Dufrechou, Carole, *Neil Young,* Quick Fox, 1978.
Einarson, John, *Neil Young: Don't Be Denied, the Canadian Years,* Quarry, 1993.
Fong-Torres, Ben, editor, *Rolling Stone Interviews, 1967-1980,* St. Martin's, 1981.
Miller, Jim, editor, *Rolling Stone Illustrated History of Rock & Roll, 1950-1980,* revised edition, Random House, 1980.

PERIODICALS

Creem, February, 1981.
Los Angeles Times, November 25, 1990, p. 7, 63-65.
Newsweek, November 13, 1978.
Nation, March 11, 1991, pp. 318-20.
New York Times Biographical Service, November 25, 1992, pp. 1532-34.
Rolling Stone, February 8, 1979; January 24, 1980; December 28, 1980; January 8, 1981; January 21, 1982; February 3, 1983; September 15, 1983; May 5, 1988, pp. 73-75; November 26, 1992, pp. 71-72; August 25, 1994, pp. 87-88.
Saturday Review, March 4, 1978.
Stereo Review, April, 1981; March, 1982.*

—*Sketch by Les Stone*

*　　*　　*

ZUK, Georges
See SKELETON, Robin